YOUR Window TO History

Reading
like a Historian

Historians use paintings, like this one from the golden throne of Tutankhamen, to help understand the past. As you study world history, you too will learn how to use different historical sources to **Read like a Historian.**

To find out more about reading like a historian and the historical sources that follow, visit

go.hrw.com
More Online
KEYWORD: HISTORIAN

By Frances Marie Gipson
Secondary Literacy Coordinator
Los Angeles Unified School District, Los Angeles, California

What Does It Mean to Read like a Historian?

In your history class you will be doing a lot of reading, thinking, and problem-solving. Much of your reading and thinking will center on different types of texts or materials. Since you are in a history class reading all sorts of things, a question to consider is, "What does it mean to think, read, and solve problems like a historian?"

Historians work with different types of sources to understand and learn from history. Two categories of sources are **primary** and **secondary** sources.

Primary Sources are historical documents, written accounts by a firsthand witness, or objects that have survived from the past. A study of primary sources might include letters, government documents, diaries, photographs, art objects, stamps, coins, and even clothing.

Secondary Sources are accounts of past events created by people some time after the events happened. This textbook and other books written about historical events are examples of secondary sources.

As you learn more about your work as a historian, you will begin to ask questions and analyze historical materials. You will be working as a detective, digging into history to create a richer understanding of the mysteries of the past.

How to Analyze Art

Art, like these 9,000-year-old rock paintings from Brazil, is another important source for historians. One way to study a piece of art is to write down everything that you think is important about it. Then divide the image into four sections and describe the important elements from each section. As you study art in this textbook, ask questions like the ones below.

- What is the setting for the art?
- When and where in the past was the art created?
- What is the subject of the art?
- What other details can I observe?
- What does the art reveal about its subject?
- How can I describe the artist's point of view?

How to Analyze an Infographic

Rulers of Kush

Like the Egyptians, the people of Kush considered their rulers to be gods. Kush's culture was similar to Egypt's, but there were also important differences.

Like the Egyptians, Kush's rulers built pyramids, but they were much smaller and the style was different.

Kush was ruled by a few different powerful queens. Queens seem to have been more important in Kush than in Egypt.

Stone carvings were made to commemorate important buildings and events, just like in Egypt. Kush's writing system was similar to Egyptian hieroglyphics, but scholars have been unable to understand most of it.

Infographics give you information in a visual format, using captions and call-out boxes to help explain the intent of the drawing. As you study infographics in this textbook, use the helpful tips and questions below.

- List the parts of the drawing and the importance of each part.

- Describe the focus or significance of the drawing.

- Do the captions and call-out boxes clarify the drawing's purpose?

- Does the drawing help me understand the information that I am studying in my textbook better?

The Military in Ancient Egypt

"The pharaohs began . . . leading large armies out of a land that had once known only small police forces and militia. The Egyptians quickly extended their military and commercial influence over an extensive region that included the rich provinces of Syria . . . and the numbers of Egyptian slaves grew swiftly."

–C. Warren Hollister, from *Roots of the Western Tradition*

When reading secondary sources, such as the description of the military in ancient Egypt above, historians ask additional questions to seek understanding. They try to source the text, build evidence, and interpret the message that is being conveyed. For historians, reading is a quest to find evidence to answer or challenge a historical problem. As you study secondary sources, ask questions like the ones below.

- Who is the author? What do I know about this author?
- Did the author have firsthand information? What is the author's relationship to the event?
- What might be the author's motivation in writing this piece?
- What type of evidence did the author look at?
- Are any assumptions or bias present?
- How does this document fit into the larger context of the events I am studying?
- What kind of source is it?
- Is the source an original?
- Is the content probable or reasonable?
- What does the date tell me about the event?
- What do I already know about this topic that will help me understand more of what I am reading?

How to Analyze a Historical Map

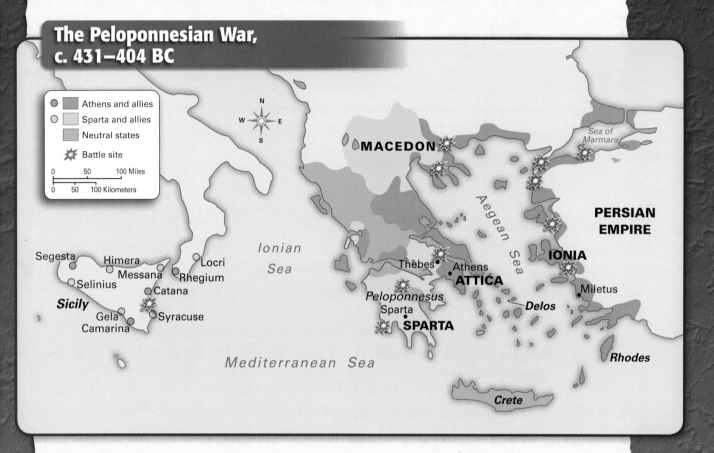

The Peloponnesian War, c. 431–404 BC

Legend:
- Athens and allies
- Sparta and allies
- Neutral states
- Battle site

0   50   100 Miles
0   50   100 Kilometers

MACEDON

Sea of Marmara

PERSIAN EMPIRE

Ionian Sea

Aegean Sea

IONIA

Segesta
Himera
Messana
Locri
Rhegium
Selinius
Catana
Sicily
Gela
Syracuse
Camarina

Thebes
Athens
ATTICA
Peloponnesus
Sparta
SPARTA
Delos
Miletus
Rhodes

Mediterranean Sea

Crete

Maps, such as the one above showing major allies in ancient Greece's Peloponnesian War, are symbolic representations of places shown in relation to one another. All maps necessarily include some details and leave out others. As you study maps in this textbook, ask questions like the ones below.

- What time period does the map show?

- What details has the mapmaker chosen to include (or exclude) on this map?

- Why was the map drawn?

- How can I determine if the map is accurate?

- How are maps used to analyze the past, present, and future?

How to Analyze an Artifact

Artifacts, such as this bronze food vessel from China's Shang dynasty, take many forms. They might be coins, stone tools, pieces of clothing, or even items found in your backpack. As you study artifacts in this textbook, ask yourself questions like the ones below.

- Why was this object created?

- When and where would it have been used?

- Who used the artifact?

- What does the artifact tell me about the technology available at the time it was created?

- What can it tell me about the life and times of the people who used it?

- How does the artifact help to make sense of the time period?

How to Analyze Written Sources

Code of Hammurabi

196. If a man put out the eye of another man, his eye shall be put out.

197. If he break another man's bone, his bone shall be broken.

198. If he put out the eye of a freed man, or break the bone of a freed man, he shall pay one gold mina.

199. If he put out the eye of a man's slave, or break the bone of a man's slave, he shall pay one-half of its value.

222. If he were a freed man he shall pay three shekels.

223. If he were a slave his owner shall pay the physician two shekels.

–Code of Hammurabi, translated by L. W. King

Asking questions can help you determine the relevance and importance of primary sources such as the Code of Hammurabi, the earliest known example of written laws. As you analyze the primary source above and the primary and secondary sources included in this textbook, ask questions like the ones below.

- Who created the source and why?
- Did the writer have firsthand knowledge of the event, or report what others saw or heard?
- Was the writer a neutral party, or did the author have opinions or interests that might have influenced what was recorded?
- Did the writer wish to inform or persuade others?
- Was the information recorded during the event, immediately after the event, or after some lapse of time?

CALIFORNIA SOCIAL STUDIES

HOLT

WORLD HISTORY

Ancient Civilizations

Stanley M. Burstein

Richard Shek

HOLT, RINEHART AND WINSTON

A Harcourt Education Company

Orlando • **Austin** • New York • San Diego • Toronto • London

Authors

Dr. Stanley M. Burstein

Dr. Stanley M. Burstein is Professor Emeritus of Ancient History and former Chair of the Department of History at California State University, Los Angeles. Dr. Burstein received his B.A., M.A., and Ph.D. degrees from the University of California at Los Angeles and is the author of more than 100 books, articles, and chapters on ancient history. His specialties include ancient Greece, Greek and Roman Egypt, and Kush. Dr. Burstein has served as President of the Association of Ancient Historians and as a member of the California History–Social Science Standards/Course Models Project, the California Content Review Panel for History–Social Science, and the Content Review Panel for the California STAR test in history.

Dr. Richard Shek

Dr. Richard Shek is Professor of Humanities and Religious Studies at California State University, Sacramento. A native of China, Dr. Shek did his undergraduate work in Tokyo, Japan, and received his Ph.D. in history from the University of California at Berkeley. His specialties are East Asian cultural and religious history, and he has numerous publications on Confucianism, Daoism, Buddhism, and popular religion in China and Japan. Dr. Shek has served as a member of the California Content Review Panel for History–Social Science and is currently a member of the Content Review Panel for the California STAR test in history.

ISBN 0-03-073462-2

3 4 5 6 7 8 9 032 11 10 09 08 07 06

Program Consultants

Contributing Author

Kylene Beers, Ed.D.
Senior Reading Researcher
School Development Program
Yale University
New Haven, Connecticut

General Editor

Frances Marie Gipson
Secondary Literacy
Los Angeles Unified School
    District
Los Angeles, California

Senior Literature and Writing Specialist

Carol Jago
English Department Chairperson
Santa Monica High School
Santa Monica, California

Consultants

John Ferguson, M.T.S., J.D.
Senior Religion Consultant
Assistant Professor
Political Science/Criminal Justice
Howard Payne University
Brownwood, Texas

Rabbi Gary M. Bretton-Granatoor
Religion Consultant
Director of Interfaith Affairs
Anti-Defamation League
New York, New York

J. Frank Malaret
Senior Consultant
Dean, Downtown and West
    Sacramento Outreach Centers
Sacramento City College
Sacramento, California

Kimberly A. Plummer, M.A.
Senior Consultant
History-Social Science Educator/
    Advisor
Holt, Rinehart and Winston
California Consultant Manager

Andrés Reséndez, Ph.D.
Senior Consultant
Assistant Professor
Department of History
University of California at Davis
Davis, California

California Specialists

Ann Cerny, M.A.
Middle School History Teacher
San Dieguito Union High School
    District
Solana Beach, California

Julie Chan, Ed.D.
Director, Literacy Instruction
Newport-Mesa Unified School
    District
Costa Mesa, California

Gary F. DeiRossi, Ed.D.
Assistant Superintendent
San Joaquin County Office of
    Education
Stockton, California

Fern M. Sheldon, M.Ed.
Curriculum Specialist
Rowland Unified School District
Rowland Heights, California

California Program Advisors

The California program consultants and reviewers included on these pages provided guidance throughout the development of Holt California Social Studies: *World History: Ancient Civilizations.* As the map below demonstrates, their valuable contributions represent the viewpoints of teachers throughout California.

Educational Reviewers

Sally Knudtson Adams
Garden Grove High School
Garden Grove, California

Anne Bjornson
A.P. Giannini Middle School
San Francisco, California

Anthony Braxton
Herbert H. Cruickshank
Middle School
Merced, California

Ann Cerny, M.A.
Middle School History Teacher
San Dieguito Union High
School District
Solana Beach, California

Julie Chan, Ed.D.
Director, Literacy Instruction
Newport-Mesa Unified School
District
Costa Mesa, California

Mary Demetrion
Patrick Henry Middle School
Los Angeles, California

Yolanda Espinoza
Walter Stiern Middle School
Bakersfield, California

Carla Freel
Hoover Middle School
Merced, California

Tim Gearhart
Daniel Lewis Middle School
Paso Robles, California

Frances Marie Gipson
Secondary Literacy
Los Angeles Unified School District
Los Angeles, California

Carol Jago
English Department Chairperson
Santa Monica High School
Santa Monica, California

Noma LeMoine, Ph.D.
Director, Academic English Mastery
Los Angeles Unified School District
Los Angeles, California

J. Frank Malaret
Senior Consultant
Dean, Downtown and West
Sacramento Outreach Centers
Sacramento City College
Sacramento, California

Kimberly A. Plummer, M.A.
Senior Consultant
History-Social Science Educator/
Advisor
Holt, Rinehart and Winston
California Consultant Manager

Andrés Reséndez, Ph.D.
Senior Consultant
Assistant Professor
Department of History
University of California at Davis
Davis, California

Fern M. Sheldon, M.Ed.
Curriculum Specialist
Rowland Unified School District
Rowland Heights, California

Robert Valdez
Pioneer Middle School
Tustin, California

Sheila Weiner
Gasparde Portola Middle School
San Diego, California

Orangevale
Sacramento
Davis Rancho Cordova
San Francisco
Merced
Paso Robles
Bakersfield
Garden Grove
Los Angeles Rowland Heights
Santa Monica Riverside
Lennox Romoland
Tustin Costa Mesa
Oceanside
Solana Beach Lakeside
San Diego

Field Test Teachers

Andy Alexander
Harvest Valley Elementary
Romoland, California

Harriette Bone
Pio Pico Middle School
Los Angeles, California

Christy King
Castle View Elementary
Riverside, California

Nancy Lamott
Tierra Del Sol Middle School
Lakeside, California

Tracy Leathers
Isabelle Jackson Elementary
Sacramento, California

Leigh Mauney
Isabelle Jackson Elementary
Sacramento, California

Susan Mitchell
Jefferson Middle School
Oceanside, California

James Nadler
Lennox Middle School
Lennox, California

Tisha Rugg
Thomas Coleman Middle School
Orangevale, California

JoAnn Wade
Lennox Middle School
Lennox, California

Sheila Weiner
Gasparde Portola Middle School
San Diego, California

Karen York
Mitchell Middle School
Rancho Cordova, California

Academic Reviewers

Jonathan Beecher, Ph.D.
Department of History
University of California, Santa Cruz

Jerry H. Bentley, Ph.D.
Department of History
University of Hawaii

Elizabeth Brumfiel, Ph.D.
Department of Anthropology
Northwestern University
Evanston, Illinois

Eugene Cruz-Uribe, Ph.D.
Department of History
Northern Arizona University

Toyin Falola, Ph.D.
Department of History
University of Texas

Sandy Freitag, Ph.D.
Director, Monterey Bay History and Cultures Project
University of California, Santa Cruz

Yasuhide Kawashima, Ph.D.
Department of History
University of Texas at El Paso

Robert J. Meier, Ph.D.
Department of Anthropology
Indiana University

Marc Van De Mieroop, Ph.D.
Department of History
Columbia University
New York, New York

M. Gwyn Morgan, Ph.D.
Department of History
University of Texas

Robert Schoch, Ph.D.
CGS Division of Natural Science
Boston University

David Shoenbrun, Ph.D.
Department of History
Northwestern University
Evanston, Illinois

Meet the Sikhs is a video that discusses the Sikh community in northern California. Starting with an annual Sikh celebration, the video provides an overview of the Sikh community, including the foundation of its religious beliefs and attire, immigration patterns, and the accomplishments of community members. The video can be downloaded for educational purposes only, and admission cannot be charged for any viewing of the piece. This video is available in QuickTime format at the KVIE Web site at http://www.kvie.org/education/outreachservices/.

California
Teacher's Edition

Contents

Table of Contents.....................T8

California Standards Overview: Grade 6 .... T28

California Standards Overview: Grade 7 .... T32

California Standards Overview: Grade 8 .... T36

Mastering the California Standards............ T42

Professional Development

    **English–Language Arts Standards and the
Social Studies Teacher, by Dr. Carol Jago** T52

    **Standard English Learners: Language
Acquisition as a Scaffold to Social Studies
Curricula, by Dr. Noma LeMoine** T54

    **Making History–Social Science Accessible
to English Learners, by Dr. Julie Chan** T56

Professional Resources and Bibliography....... T58

Contents

Geography and Map Skills H1

Reading Social Studies H12

Academic Words H16

History–Social Science Content Standards H18

Analysis Skills H21

How to Make This Book Work for You H22

Places You Will Study H24

UNIT 1 Early Humans and Societies 1

Planning Guide 1a

CHAPTER 1 Uncovering the Past 2

California Standards

Analysis Skills

HI 5 Recognize that interpretations of history are subject to change as new information is uncovered.

History's Impact Video Series
The Impact of Archaeology

Section 1 Studying History 6

Section 2 Studying Geography 12

Social Studies Skills *Recognizing Personal Conviction and Bias* 20

Standards Review 21

Standards Assessment 23

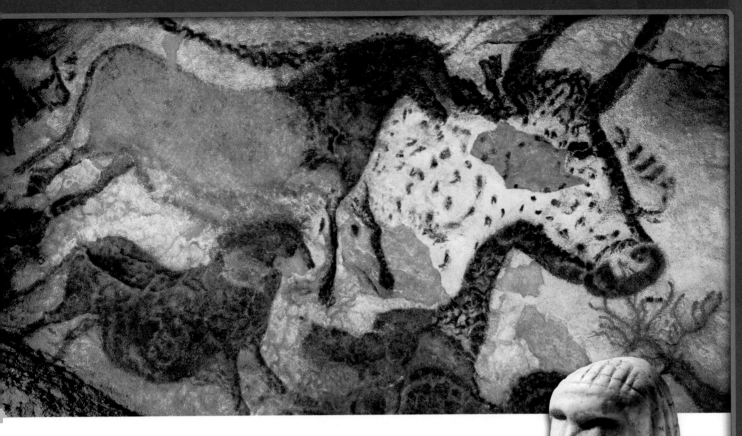

Planning Guide 23a

CHAPTER 2 **The Stone Ages and Early Cultures** 24

 California Standards

History–Social Science

6.1 Students describe what is known through archaeological studies of the early physical and cultural development of humankind from the Paleolithic era to the agricultural revolution.

Analysis Skills

CS 1 Explain how events are related in time.

HI 1 Explain central issues and problems from the past.

 History's Impact Video Series
The Impact of the Early Migrations to North America

Section 1 The First People 28

Section 2 Early Human Migration 36

Section 3 Beginnings of Agriculture 40

Social Studies Skills *Identifying Central Issues* 44

Standards Review 45

Standards Assessment 47

Unit 1 Writing Workshop *Comparing and Contrasting Societies* 48

UNIT 2 Mesopotamia, Egypt, and Kush 50

Planning Guide 51a

CHAPTER 3 Mesopotamia and the Fertile Cresent 52

 California Standards

History–Social Science
6.2 Students analyze the geographic, political, economic, religious, and social structures of the early civilizations of Mesopotamia, Egypt, and Kush.

Analysis Skills
CS 3 Use maps to identify physical features.

 History's Impact Video Series
The Impact of a System of Laws

Section 1 Geography of the Fertile Crescent 56
Section 2 The Rise of Sumer 62
Section 3 Sumerian Achievements 67
Section 4 Later Peoples of the Fertile Crescent 74
Social Studies Skills *Interpreting Physical Maps* 80
Standards Review 81
Standards Assessment 83

Planning Guide 83a

CHAPTER 4 **Ancient Egypt** 84

California Standards

History–Social Science
6.2 Students analyze the geographic, political, economic, religious, and social structures of the early civilizations of Mesopotamia, Egypt, and Kush.

Analysis Skills
HR 4 Assess the credibility of primary and secondary sources.

History's Impact Video Series
The Impact of the Egyptian Pyramids

Section 1 Geography and Early Egypt 88
Section 2 The Old Kingdom 93
Section 3 The Middle and New Kingdoms 101
Section 4 Egyptian Achievements 108
Social Studies Skills *Assessing Primary and Secondary Sources* 114
Standards Review 115
Standards Assessment 117

Planning Guide 117a

CHAPTER 5 **Ancient Kush** 118

California Standards

History–Social Science
6.2 Students analyze the geographic, political, economic, religious, and social structures of the early civilizations of Mesopotamia, Egypt, and Kush.

Analysis Skills
HI 2 Understand and distinguish cause and effect.

History's Impact Video Series
The Impact of the Egyptian Pyramids

Section 1 Kush and Egypt 122
Section 2 Later Kush 127
Social Studies Skills *Participating in Groups* 132
Standards Review 133
Standards Assessment 135

Unit 2 Writing Workshop *A Description of a Historical Place* 136

UNIT 3 Civilization in India and China 138

Planning Guide 139a

CHAPTER 6 Ancient India 140

 California Standards

History–Social Science

6.5 Students analyze the geographic, political, economic, religious, and social structures of the early civilizations of India.

 History's Impact Video Series
The Impact of Buddhism as a World Religion

Section 1 Geography and Early India 144

Section 2 Origins of Hinduism 150

Section 3 Origins of Buddhism 156

Section 4 Indian Empires 162

Section 5 Indian Achievements 167

Social Studies Skills *Interpreting Diagrams* 174
Standards Review 175
Standards Assessment 177

Planning Guide 177a

CHAPTER 7 **Ancient China** 178

 California Standards

History–Social Science

6.6 Students analyze the geographic, political, economic, religious, and social structures of the early civilizations of China.

 History's Impact Video Series
The Impact of Confucius on China Today

Section 1 Geography and Early China 182

Section 2 The Zhou Dynasty and New Ideas 188

Section 3 The Qin Dynasty 194

Section 4 The Han Dynasty 200

Section 5 Han Contacts with Other Cultures 208

Social Studies Skills *Conducting Internet Research* 214

Standards Review. 215

Standards Assessment 217

Unit 3 Writing Workshop *Why Things Happen* 218

UNIT **4** Foundations of Western Ideas 220

Planning Guide 221a

CHAPTER 8 The Hebrews and Judaism 222

 California Standards

History–Social Science
6.3 Students analyze the geographic, political, economic, religious, and social structures of the Ancient Hebrews.

Analysis Skills
HI 2 Understand and distinguish long- and short-term causal relations.
HR 2 Distinguish fact from opinion in historical narratives and stories.

 History's Impact Video Series
The Impact of Judaism throughout the World

Section 1 The Early Hebrews 226
Section 2 Jewish Beliefs and Texts 232
Section 3 Judaism over the Centuries 240
Social Studies Skills *Identifying Short- and Long-Term Effects* 246
Standards Review 247
Standards Assessment 249

Planning Guide 249a

CHAPTER 9 **Ancient Greece** .250

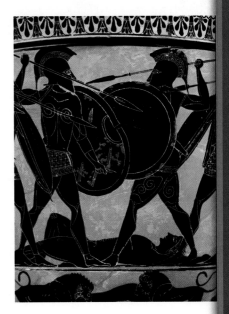

 California Standards

History–Social Science
6.4 Students analyze the geographic, political, economic, religious, and social structures of the early civilizations of ancient Greece.

Analysis Skills
HI 6 Conduct cost-benefit analyses of economic and political issues.

 History's Impact Video Series
The Impact of Democracy

Section 1 Geography and the Early Greeks 254
Section 2 Government in Athens 262
Section 3 Greek Mythology and Literature 268
Social Studies Skills *Analyzing Costs and Benefits* 278
Standards Review 279
Standards Assessment 281

Planning Guide 281a

CHAPTER 10 **The Greek World** 282

 California Standards

History–Social Science
6.4 Students analyze the geographic, political, economic, religious, and social structures of the early civilizations of ancient Greece.

 History's Impact Video Series
The Impact of the Greek Scholars

Section 1 Greece and Persia 286
Section 2 Sparta and Athens 292
Section 3 Alexander the Great 298
Section 4 Greek Achievements 303
Social Studies Skills *Interpreting Charts and Tables* 310
Standards Review 311
Standards Assessment 313

Unit 4 Writing Workshop *A Social Studies Report* 314

UNIT 5 The Roman World

UNIT 5 The Roman World 318

Planning Guide 319a

CHAPTER 11 The Roman Republic 320

 California Standards

History–Social Science
6.7 Students analyze the geographic, political, economic, religious, and social structures during the development of Rome.

Analysis Skills
CS 1 Understand how events are related in time.
CS 2 Construct time lines.

History's Impact Video Series
The Impact of the Roman Republic on American Government Today

Section 1 Geography and the Rise of Rome 324
Section 2 Government and Society 332
Section 3 The Late Republic 338
Social Studies Skills *Interpreting Culture Maps* 344
Standards Review 345
Standards Assessment 347

Planning Guide 347a

CHAPTER 12 **The Roman Empire** 348

California Standards

History–Social Science
6.7 Students analyze the geographic, political, economic, religious, and social structures during the development of Rome.

Analysis Skills
CS 3 Use a variety of maps and documents to identify physical and cultural features.

History's Impact Video Series
The Impact of Ancient Rome on the World Today

Section 1 From Republic to Empire 352
Section 2 A Vast Empire 358
Section 3 Rome's Legacy 366
Social Studies Skills *Interpreting Time Lines* 372
Standards Review 373
Standards Assessment 375

Planning Guide 375a

CHAPTER 13 **Rome and Christianity** 376

California Standards

History–Social Science
6.7 Students analyze the geographic, political, economic, religious, and social structures during the development of Rome.

Analysis Skills
HI 3 Explain the sources of historical continuity and how the combination of ideas and events explains the emergence of new patterns.

History's Impact Video Series
The Impact of Ancient Rome on the World Today

Section 1 Religion in the Roman Empire 380
Section 2 Origins of Christianity 384
Section 3 The Early Christian World 392
Social Studies Skills *Continuity and Change in History* 396
Standards Review 397
Standards Assessment 399

Unit 5 Writing Workshop *Historical Problem and Solution* 400

 **Endings and Beginnings** 402

Planning Guide 403a

CHAPTER 14 **The Fall of Rome** 404

 California Standards

History–Social Science
7.1 Students analyze the (causes and effects) of the vast expansion and ultimate disintegration of the Roman Empire.

Analysis Skills
HI 4 Recognize the role of chance, oversight, and error in history.

 History's Impact Video Series
The Impact of Ancient Rome on the World Today

Section 1 Fall of the Western Roman Empire 408
Section 2 The Byzantine Empire 414
Social Studies Skills *Chance, Error, and Oversight in History* 420
Standards Review 421
Standards Assessment 423

Planning Guide 423a

CHAPTER 15 **The Early Americas** 424

 California Standards

7.7 Students compare and contrast the geographic, political, economic, religious, and social structures of the Meso-American and Andean civilizations.

Analysis Skills
HR 3 Distinguish relevant from irrelevant, essential from incidental, and verifiable from unverifiable information.

 History's Impact Video Series
The Impact of Mayan Achievements on Math and Astronomy

Section 1 Geography and Early Cultures 428

Section 2 The Maya 434

Section 3 Maya Life and Society 439

Social Studies Skills *Accepting Social Responsibility* 446

Standards Review. 447

Standards Assessment 449

Unit 6 Writing Workshop *Persuasion and Historical Issues* 450

References R1

Declaration of Independence R2

U.S. Constitution. R6

Atlas. R26

Gazetteer R38

Facts about the World R42

Biographical Dictionary R48

English and Spanish Glossary R54

Index R66

Credits and Acknowledgments R77

Features

History and Geography

Explore the relationships between history and geography around the world.

Mapping the Past 18
River Valley Civilizations 60
The Silk Road 212
Natural Disaster! 260
Roman Roads 364

Literature in History

Learn about people who lived in other times and places in excerpts from literature.

The Epic of Gilgamesh 72
The Shiji 206
The Epic Poetry of Homer 276
The Aeneid 330
The Popol Vuh 444

Justinian and Theodora

BIOGRAPHIES

Meet the people who have influenced history and learn about their lives.

The Iceman 35
Sargon 63
Queen Hatshepsut 102
Ramses the Great 107
Piankhi 125
Queen Shanakhdakheto 129
Asoka 166
Confucius 191
Laozi 193
Emperor Shi Huangdi 199
Ruth and Naomi 231
Homer 272
Aesop 273
Cyrus the Great 287
Euclid 307
Greek Philosophers—Socrates, Plato,
    and Aristotle 309
Cincinnatus 328
Hannibal 341
Lucius Cornelius Sulla 343
Cleopatra 356
Augustus 357
Constantine 395
Justinian and Theodora 419
Pacal 437

Charts, Graphics, and Time Lines

Analyze information presented visually to learn more about history.

CHARTS

Development of Writing 68
Egyptian Writing 109
Major Beliefs of Hinduism 152
The Eightfold Path 159
Chinese Writing 187
Main Ideas of Confucianism 192
Emperor Shi Huangdi 195
Democracy Then and Now 267
Greek Influence on Language 274
Roman Society 329
Government of the Roman Republic 333
Why Rome Fell 413
The Western Roman and Byzantine
  Empires 418

INFOGRAPHICS

Understanding the World .8
Physical and Human Geography 13
Early Hominids 30
Hunter-Gatherers 32
A Mammoth House 39
An Early Farming Society 42
Irrigation and Civilization 58
The City-State of Ur 64

Mummies and the Afterlife 96
Building the Pyramids 98
Daily Life in Egypt 104
The Temple of Karnak 110
Kush's Trade Network 128
Rulers of Kush 130
Life in Mohenjo-Daro 146
Hindu Gods and Beliefs 152
Indian Science 170
Geography and Living 184
The Warring States Period 190
Han Achievements 204
Hebrew Texts 234
Destruction of the Second Temple 241
Democracy in Action 264
The Parthenon 304
The Roman Forum 336
Rome Battles Carthage 340
Pompeii: A City Preserved 361
A Chariot Race 362
The Roman Arch 367
The Colosseum 368
Glory of Constantinople 416
Palenque 436
A Maya King and His Court 440

TIME LINES

The Stone Ages and Early Cultures 24
Mesopotamia and the Fertile Crescent 52

Heavy mammoth bones were used as a frame for the shelter.

A mammoth house

Ancient Egypt 84
Periods of Egyptian History 101
Ancient Kush 118
Ancient India 140
Ancient China 178
The Zhou Dynasty 188
The Qin Dynasty 194
The Han Dynasty 200
The Hebrews and Judaism 222
Early Hebrew History 228
Ancient Greece 250
The Greek World 282
The Roman Republic 320
The Roman Empire 348
Rome and Christianity 376
Early Christianity 392
The Fall of Rome 404
Key Events in Roman History 412
The Early Americas 424

QUICK FACTS

Examine key facts and concepts quickly and easily with graphics.

Chapter 1 Visual Summary 21
Early Hominids 30
Chapter 2 Visual Summary 45
Hammurabi's Code 75
Chapter 3 Visual Summary 81
Periods of Egyptian History 101
Chapter 4 Visual Summary 115
Chapter 5 Visual Summary 133
The Varnas 151
Major Beliefs of Hinduism 152
The Eightfold Path 159
Chapter 6 Visual Summary 175
Zhou Society 189
Main Ideas of Confucianism 192
Emperor Shi Huangdi 195
Chapter 7 Visual Summary 215
Chapter 8 Visual Summary 247
Government in Athens 262
Democracy Then and Now 267
Chapter 9 Visual Summary 279
Life in Sparta 293
Life in Athens 295
Chapter 10 Visual Summary 311
Legendary Founding of Rome 326
Roman Society 329
Government of the Roman Republic 333
Chapter 11 Visual Summary 345
Chapter 12 Visual Summary 373
Chapter 13 Visual Summary 397
Why Rome Fell 413
The Western Roman and Byzantine
  Empires 418
Chapter 14 Visual Summary 421
Chapter 15 Visual Summary 447

Roman Society

QUICK FACTS

Patricians	Plebeians
■ Wealthy, powerful citizens	■ Common people
■ Nobles	■ Peasants, craftspeople, traders, other workers
■ Small minority of the population	■ Majority of the population
■ Once controlled all aspects of government	■ Gained right to participate in government
■ After 218 BC, not allowed to participate in trade or commerce	■ Only Romans who could be traders, so many became wealthy

History Close-up

See how people lived and how places looked in the past by taking a close-up view of history.

Hunter-Gatherers 32
An Early Farming Society 42
The City-State of Ur 64
Building the Pyramids 98
The Temple of Karnak 110
Rulers of Kush 130
Life in Mohenjo-Daro 146
Destruction of the Second Temple 241
Democracy in Action 264
The Parthenon 304
The Roman Forum 336
Rome Battles Carthage 340
A Chariot Race 362
The Colosseum 368
The Glory of Constantinople 416
Palenque 436

LINKING TO TODAY

Link people and cultures from the past to the world around you today.

Stone Tools 33
The Wheel 69
Nonviolence 154
A Passover Meal 244
Let the Games Begin! 271
Do as the Romans Do 334
Christian Holidays 386

Points of View

See how different people have interpreted historical issues in different ways.

Views of Migration to the Americas 38
Views of Education 294
Views of Caesar 355
Views of Writing 432

Historic Documents

Examine key documents that have shaped world history.

Hammurabi's Code 75
The Analects 192
Law of the Twelve Tables 335
Declaration of Independence R2
U.S. Constitution R6

Social Studies Skills

Learn, practice, and apply the skills you need to study and analyze history.

Recognizing Personal Conviction
  and Bias 20
Identifying Central Issues 44
Interpreting Physical Maps 80
Assessing Primary and Secondary Sources . . . 114
Participating in Groups 132
Interpreting Diagrams 174
Conducting Internet Research 214
Identifying Short- and Long-Term Effects 246
Analyzing Costs and Benefits 278
Interpreting Charts and Tables 310
Interpreting Culture Maps 344
Interpreting Time Lines 372
Continuity and Change in History 396
Chance, Error, and Oversight in History 420
Accepting Social Responsibility 446

Reading Social Studies

Learn and practice skills that will help you read your social studies lessons.

Specialized Vocabulary of History 4

Chronological Order 26

Main Ideas in Social Studies 54

Drawing Conclusions about the Past 86

Causes and Effects in History 120

Inferences about History 142

Summarizing Historical Texts 180

Facts, Opinions, and the Past 224

Greek Word Origins 252

Comparing and Contrasting
Historical Facts 284

Outlining and History 322

Online Research 350

Questioning 378

Stereotypes and Bias in History 406

Analyzing Historical Information 426

Writing Workshop

Learn to write about history.

Comparing and Contrasting Societies 48

A Description of a Historical Place 136

Why Things Happen 218

A Social Studies Report 314

Historical Problem and Solution 400

Persuasion and Historical Issues 450

FOCUS ON WRITING

Use writing to study and reflect on the events and people who made history.

A Job Description 2

A Storyboard 24

A Poster 52

A Riddle 84

A Fictional Narrative 118

An Illustrated Poster 140

A Web Site 222

A Myth 250

A Poem 282

Note Cards for a Screenplay 348

A Magazine Article 376

A Travel Brochure 424

FOCUS ON SPEAKING

Use speaking skills to study and reflect on the events and people who made history.

An Oral Presentation 178

A Legend 320

A Narrative Poem 404

Maps

Interpret maps to see where important events happened and analyze how geography has influenced history.

Mesoamerica	H24
Rome	H25
Greece	H25
China	H25
Mesopotamia, Egypt, and Kush	H25
Eastern Mediterranean	H25
India	H25
California: Physical	14
California: Climates	14
California: Population	15
California: Roads	15
Teotihuacán, c. AD 500	18
Early Hominid Sites	29
Early Human Migration	37
Early Domestication	40
Catal Hüyük	42
Assessment Map	47
The Fertile Crescent	57
River Valley Civilizations	60
Sargon's Empire, c. 2330 BC	63
Babylonian and Assyrian Empires	76
Phoenicia	78
Mesopotamia and the Fertile Crescent	80
Assessment Map	83
Ancient Egypt	89
Egyptian Trade	103
Ancient Kush	123
India: Physical	145
Harappan Civilization	147
Aryan Invasions	149
Early Spread of Buddhism	160
Mauryan Empire, c. 320–185 BC	163
Gupta Empire, c. 400	164
Assessment Map	177
China: Physical	183
Shang Dynasty, c. 1500–1050 BC	186
Zhou Dynasty, c. 1050–400 BC	189
Qin Dynasty, c. 221–206 BC	195
Han Dynasty, c. 206 BC–AD 220	201
The Silk Road	210
The Silk Road	212
Possible Routes of Abraham and Moses	227
Kingdoms of Israel and Judah, c. 920 BC	230

The Dead Sea Scrolls	236
Jewish Migration After AD 70	243
Assessment Map	249
Greece: Physical	255
Minoan and Mycenaean Civilizations	257
Greek City-States and Colonies, c. 600 BC	258
Natural Disaster!	260
The Persian Empire	287
The Persian Wars	290
The Peloponnesian War, c. 431–404 BC	296
Alexander the Great's Empire, c. 323 BC	301
Italy: Physical	325
Italy, 500 BC	328
The Roman Republic, 509–270 BC	339
The Roman Republic, 270 BC–100 BC	342
Languages of Italy	344
Assessment Map	347
Expansion of Rome, 100 BC–AD 117	359
Roman Trade Routes, AD 200	360
Roman Roads	364
Judea	385
Paul's Journeys	388
The Spread of Christianity, 300–400	394
The Eastern and Western Empires	409
Invasions of the Roman Empire	410
The Byzantine Empire, 1025	415
The Americas: Physical	429
Migration to the Americas	430
Early Civilizations in the Americas	433
Maya Civilization	435
Assessment Map	449
World: Political	R26
North America: Physical	R28
North America: Political	R29
South America: Physical	R30
South America: Political	R31
Europe: Physical	R32
Europe: Political	R33
Asia: Physical	R34
Asia: Political	R35
Africa: Physical	R36
Africa: Political	R37

Primary Sources

Relive history through eyewitness accounts, literature, and documents.

CHAPTER 1

Polybius, on history, from *The Histories*,
Book XXXVIII 9

Barbara W. Tuchman, on history, from
Practicing History: Selected Essays 9

Kenneth C. Davis, on geography, from
Don't Know Much About Geography 15

CHAPTER 2

Donald Johanson, on finding Lucy, from
Ancestors: In Search of Human Origins 28

Thomas Canby and James Dixon, views
of migration to the Americas 38

Jared Diamond, on domestication of
plants, from *Guns, Germs, and Steel* 46

CHAPTER 3

Sumerian essay, on the importance of
school, quoted in *History Begins at
Sumer*. 68

From the *Epic of Gilgamesh* 72

Hammurabi, from *The Code of
Hammurabi* 75

CHAPTER 4

Pyramid Text, Utterance 217, on Re, quoted
in *Ancient Egypt* by Lorna Oaks and
Lucia Gahlin. 100

Pen-ta-ur, on Ramses the
Great, from *The Victory of Ramses over
the Khita,* in *The World's Story*, edited
by Eva March Tappan. 107

Hymn to the Nile, on the Nile, from *Library
of Original Sources*, edited by Oliver J.
Thatcher . . . .

C. Warren Hollister, on the New
Kingdom, from *Roots of the Western
Tradition* 114

CHAPTER 5

Strabo, on the Kushites' unique culture,
from *The Geographies* 129

CHAPTER 6

Vedic hymn, on praising the god Indra,
from the *Rigveda*, in *Reading About
the World, Volume I*, edited by Paul
Brians et al. 152

The Buddha, on morality, quoted in
The History of Nations: India 158

On warning listeners to think before they
act, from the *Panchatantra*, translated
by Arthur Wiliam Ryder. 169

From the *Bhagavad Gita* 172

CHAPTER 7

On the Zhou social system, from the
Zhou *Book of Songs*. 189

Confucius, on moral leadership's role
in government, from *The Analects*. 191

Confucius, on knowledge, fairness,
and eagerness, from *The Analects*. 192

Sima Qian, from *The Shiji* 206

CHAPTER 8

Exodus 20:2-14, the Ten Commandments,
from *The Living Torah*, edited by
Rabbi Aryeh Kaplan 228

Psalms 23:1–3, on the Lord, from *The
Book of Tehillim* 235

From the Torah. 238

Flavius Josephus, on the burning of the
Second Temple, from The *Wars of the
Jews* 241

CHAPTER 9

Pericles' Funeral Oration, quoted in
Thucydides, *The History of the
Peloponnesian War* 266

Aesop, on working instead of wasting time, from
"The Ants and the Grasshopper". 273

The Epic Poetry of Homer 276

CHAPTER 10

Herodotus, on Persian transportation routes, from *History of the Persian Wars*...289

Plutarch, on Spartan discipline, from *Life of Lycurgus*.................................293

Plato and Plutarch, views of education 294

Plato, on the death of Socrates, from *Phaedo* 306

CHAPTER 11

Virgil, from *The Aeneid* 330

Polybius, on Roman unity in government, from *The Constitution of the Roman Republic* 335

from Law of the Twelve Tables 335

CHAPTER 12

Julius Caesar, on his victory in battle, from *The Gallic Wars*........................353

Plutarch and Seutonius, views of Caesar.....355

Pliny the Elder, on Rome's splendor, from *Natural History* 362

CHAPTER 13

Paul's Letter to the Romans 389

From the Bible 390

Karen L. King, on women, from *Women in Ancient Christianity: The New Discoveries* 398

CHAPTER 14

Priscus, on the Scythians, from *Fragmenta Historicorum Graecorum* 407

Jordanes, on the terror of Attila the Hun, from *History of the Goths*.................411

Justinian, on the Hagia Sophia, from *The Story of the Building of the Church Of Santa Sophia* 418

Priscus, on Attila, from *Eyewitness to History*, edited by John Carey.............422

CHAPTER 15

David Grove and Mary E. D. Pohl, views of writing 432

Zuni legend, on the importance of maize, quoted in *Kingdoms of Gold, Kingdoms of Jade* by Brian Fagan 433

A Maya Carving 443

From The *Popol Vuh*.......................444

Primary Source

BOOK
The Death of Socrates

In 399 BC Socrates was arrested and charged with corrupting the young people of Athens and ignoring religious traditions. He was sentenced to die by drinking poison. Socrates spent his last hours surrounded by his students. One of them, Plato, later described the event in detail.

Socrates himself does not protest against his sentence but willingly drinks the poison.

The students and friends who have visited Socrates, including the narrator, are much less calm than he is.

" Then raising the cup to his lips, quite readily and cheerfully he drank off the poison. And hitherto most of us had been able to control our sorrow; but now when we saw him drinking . . . my own tears were flowing fast; so that I covered my face and wept . . . Socrates alone retained his calmness: What is this strange outcry? he said . . . I have been told that a man should die in peace. Be quiet then, and have patience.**"**

–Plato, from *Phaedo*

Standards Overview: Grade 6

Standards	Chapters:	1	2	3	4	5	6	7	8	9	10	11	12	13	14	15
6.1 Students describe what is known through archaeological studies of the early physical and cultural development of humankind from the Paleolithic era to the agricultural revolution.																
1. Describe the hunter-gatherer societies, including the development of tools and the use of fire.			●													
2. Identify the locations of human communities that populated the major regions of the world and describe how humans adapted to a variety of environments.			●													
3. Discuss the climatic changes and human modifications of the physical environment that gave rise to the domestication of plants and animals and new sources of clothing and shelter.			●													
6.2 Students analyze the geographic, political, economic, religious, and social structures of the early civilizations of Mesopotamia, Egypt, and Kush.																
1. Locate and describe the major river systems and discuss the physical settings that supported permanent settlement and early civilizations.				●	●											
2. Trace the development of agricultural techniques that permitted the production of economic surplus and the emergence of cities as centers of culture and power.				●	●											
3. Understand the relationship between religion and the social and political order in Mesopotamia and Egypt.				●												
4. Know the significance of Hammurabi's Code.				●												
5. Discuss the main features of Egyptian art and architecture.					●											
6. Describe the role of Egyptian trade in the eastern Mediterranean and Nile valley.					●											
7. Understand the significance of Queen Hatshepsut and Ramses the Great.					●											
8. Identify the location of the Kush civilization and describe its political, commercial, and cultural relations with Egypt.						●										
9. Trace the evolution of language and its written forms.				●	●											
6.3 Students analyze the geographic, political, economic, religious, and social structures of the Ancient Hebrews.																
1. Describe the origins and significance of Judaism as the first monotheistic religion based on the concept of one God who sets down moral laws for humanity.									●							
2. Identify the sources of the ethical teachings and central beliefs of Judaism (the Hebrew Bible, the Commentaries): belief in God, observance of law, practice of the concepts of righteousness and justice, and importance of study; and describe how the ideas of the Hebrew traditions are reflected in the moral and ethical traditions of Western civilization.									●							
3. Explain the significance of Abraham, Moses, Naomi, Ruth, David, and Yohanan ben Zaccai in the development of the Jewish religion.									●							

Standards / Chapters:	1	2	3	4	5	6	7	8	9	10	11	12	13	14	15
4. Discuss the locations of the settlements and movements of Hebrew peoples, including the Exodus and their movement to and from Egypt, and outline the significance of the Exodus to the Jewish and other people.								•							
5. Discuss how Judaism survived and developed despite the continuing dispersion of much of the Jewish population from Jerusalem and the rest of Israel after the destruction of the second Temple in AD 70.								•							
6.4 Students analyze the geographic, political, economic, religious, and social structures of the early civilizations of Ancient Greece.															
1. Discuss the connections between geography and the development of city-states in the region of the Aegean Sea, including patterns of trade and commerce among Greek city-states and within the wider Mediterranean region.									•						
2. Trace the transition from tyranny and oligarchy to early democratic forms of government and back to dictatorship in ancient Greece, including the significance of the invention of the idea of citizenship (e.g., from Pericles' Funeral Oration).									•						
3. State the key differences between Athenian, or direct, democracy and representative democracy.									•						
4. Explain the significance of Greek mythology to the everyday life of people in the region and how Greek literature continues to permeate our literature and language today, drawing from Greek mythology and epics, such as Homer's Iliad and Odyssey, and from Aesop's Fables.									•						
5. Outline the founding, expansion, and political organization of the Persian Empire.										•					
6. Compare and contrast life in Athens and Sparta, with emphasis on their roles in the Persian and Peloponnesian Wars.										•					
7. Trace the rise of Alexander the Great and the spread of Greek culture eastward and into Egypt.										•					
8. Describe the enduring contributions of important Greek figures in the arts and sciences (e.g., Hypatia, Socrates, Plato, Aristotle, Euclid, Thucydides).										•					
6.5 Students analyze the geographic, political, economic, religious, and social structures of the early civilizations of India.															
1. Locate and describe the major river system and discuss the physical setting that supported the rise of this civilization.						•									
2. Discuss the significance of the Aryan invasions.						•									
3. Explain the major beliefs and practices of Brahmanism in India and how they evolved into early Hinduism.						•									
4. Outline the social structure of the caste system.						•									
5. Know the life and moral teachings of Buddha and how Buddhism spread in India, Ceylon, and Central Asia.						•									
6. Describe the growth of the Maurya empire and the political and moral achievements of the emperor Asoka.						•									
7. Discuss important aesthetic and intellectual traditions (e.g., Sanskrit literature, including the Bhagavad Gita; medicine; metallurgy; and mathematics, including Hindu-Arabic numerals and the zero).						•									

Standards	Chapters:	1	2	3	4	5	6	7	8	9	10	11	12	13	14	15
6.6 Students analyze the geographic, political, economic, religious, and social structures of the early civilizations of China.																
1. Locate and describe the origins of Chinese civilization in the Huang-He Valley during the Shang Dynasty.								•								
2. Explain the geographic features of China that made governance and the spread of ideas and goods difficult and served to isolate the country from the rest of the world.								•								
3. Know about the life of Confucius and the fundamental teachings of Confucianism and Taoism.								•								
4. Identify the political and cultural problems prevalent in the time of Confucius and how he sought to solve them.								•								
5. List the policies and achievements of the emperor Shi Huangdi in unifying northern China under the Qin Dynasty.								•								
6. Detail the political contributions of the Han Dynasty to the development of the imperial bureaucratic state and the expansion of the empire.								•								
7. Cite the significance of the trans-Eurasian "silk roads" in the period of the Han Dynasty and Roman Empire and their locations.								•								
8. Describe the diffusion of Buddhism northward to China during the Han Dynasty.								•								
6.7 Students analyze the geographic, political, economic, religious, and social structures during the development of Rome.																
1. Identify the location and describe the rise of the Roman Republic, including the importance of such mythical and historical figures as Aeneas, Romulus and Remus, Cincinnatus, Julius Caesar, and Cicero.												•				
2. Describe the government of the Roman Republic and its significance (e.g., written constitution and tripartite government, checks and balances, civic duty).												•				
3. Identify the location of and the political and geographic reasons for the growth of Roman territories and expansion of the empire, including how the empire fostered economic growth through the use of currency and trade routes.												•	•			
4. Discuss the influence of Julius Caesar and Augustus in Rome's transition from republic to empire.													•			
5. Trace the migration of Jews around the Mediterranean region and the effects of their conflict with the Romans, including the Romans' restrictions on their right to live in Jerusalem.														•		
6. Note the origins of Christianity in the Jewish Messianic prophecies, the life and teachings of Jesus of Nazareth as described in the New Testament, and the contribution of St. Paul the Apostle to the definition and spread of Christian beliefs (e.g., belief in the Trinity, resurrection, salvation).														•		
7. Describe the circumstances that led to the spread of Christianity in Europe and other Roman territories.														•		
8. Discuss the legacies of Roman art and architecture, technology and science, literature, language, and law.													•			

Analysis Skills Standards

Chapters:	1	2	3	4	5	6	7	8	9	10	11	12	13	14	15
Chronological and Spatial Thinking															
1. Students explain how major events are related to one another in time.					•						•				
2. Students construct various time lines of key events, people, and periods of the historical era they are studying													•		
3. Students use a variety of maps and documents to identify physical and cultural features of neighborhoods, cities, states, and countries and to explain the historical migration of people, expansion and disintegration of empires, and the growth of economic systems.			•					•	•		•				
Research, Evidence, and Point of View															
1. Students frame questions that can be answered by historical study and research.	•														
2. Students distinguish fact from opinion in historical narratives and stories.							•								
3. Students distinguish relevant from irrelevant information, essential from incidental information, and verifiable from unverifiable information in historical narratives and stories.															•
4. Students assess the credibility of primary and secondary sources and draw sound conclusions from them.							•								
5. Students detect the different historical points of view on historical events and determine the context in which the historical statements were made (the questions asked, sources used, author's perspectives).												•			
Historical Interpretation															
1. Students explain the central issues and problems from the past, placing people and events in a matrix of time and place.			•												
2. Students understand and distinguish cause, effect, sequence, and correlation in historical events, including the long- and short-term causal relations.				•		•									
3. Students explain the sources of historical continuity and how the combination of ideas and events explains the emergence of new patterns.								•							
4. Students recognize the role of chance, oversight, and error in history.										•			•		
5. Students recognize that interpretations of history are subject to change as new information is uncovered.		•													
6. Students interpret basic indicators of economic performance and conduct cost-benefit analyses of economic and political issues.									•			•			

Standards Overview: Grade 7

Standards	1	2	3	4	5	6	7	8	9	10	11	12	13	14	15	16	17
7.1 Students analyze the causes and effects of the vast expansion and ultimate disintegration of the Roman Empire.																	
1. Study the early strengths and lasting contributions of Rome (e.g., significance of Roman citizenship; rights under Roman law; Roman art, architecture, engineering, and philosophy; preservation and transmission of Christianity) and its ultimate internal weaknesses (e.g., rise of autonomous military powers within the empire, undermining of citizenship by the growth of corruption and slavery, lack of education, and distribution of news).		●															
2. Discuss the geographic borders of the empire at its height and the factors that threatened its territorial cohesion.		●															
3. Describe the establishment by Constantine of the new capital in Constantinople and the development of the Byzantine Empire, with an emphasis on the consequences of the development of two distinct European civilizations, Eastern Orthodox and Roman Catholic, and their two distinct views on church-state relations.		●															
7.2 Students analyze the geographic, political, economic, religious, and social structures of the civilizations of Islam in the Middle Ages.																	
1. Identify the physical features and describe the climate of the Arabian peninsula, its relationship to surrounding bodies of land and water, and nomadic and sedentary ways of life.			●														
2. Trace the origins of Islam and the life and teachings of Muhammad, including Islamic teachings on the connection with Judaism and Christianity.			●														
3. Explain the significance of the Qur'an and the Sunnah as the primary sources of Islamic beliefs, practice, and law, and their influence in Muslims' daily life.			●														
4. Discuss the expansion of Muslim rule through military conquests and treaties, emphasizing the cultural blending within Muslim civilization and the spread and acceptance of Islam and the Arabic language.				●													
5. Describe the growth of cities and the establishment of trade routes among Asia, Africa, and Europe, the products and inventions that traveled along these routes (e.g., spices, textiles, paper, steel, new crops), and the role of merchants in Arab society.				●													
6. Understand the intellectual exchanges among Muslim scholars of Eurasia and Africa and the contributions Muslim scholars made to later civilizations in the areas of science, geography, mathematics, philosophy, medicine, art, and literature.				●													
7.3 Students analyze the geographic, political, economic, religious, and social structures of the civilizations of China in the Middle Ages.																	
1. Describe the reunification of China under the Tang Dynasty and reasons for the spread of Buddhism in Tang China, Korea, and Japan.							●										
2. Describe agricultural, technological, and commercial developments during the Tang and Sung periods.							●										
3. Analyze the influences of Confucianism and changes in Confucian thought during the Sung and Mongol periods.							●										
4. Understand the importance of both overland trade and maritime expeditions between China and other civilizations in the Mongol Ascendancy and Ming Dynasty.							●										
5. Trace the historic influence of such discoveries as tea, the manufacture of paper, woodblock printing, the compass, and gunpowder.							●										
6. Describe the development of the imperial state and the scholar-official class.							●										
7.4 Students analyze the geographic, political, economic, religious, and social structures of the sub-Saharan civilizations of Ghana and Mali in Medieval Africa.																	
1. Study the Niger River and the relationship of vegetation zones of forest, savannah, and desert to trade in gold, salt, food, and slaves; and the growth of the Ghana and Mali empires.					●												
2. Analyze the importance of family, labor specialization, and regional commerce in the development of states and cities in West Africa.					●												

Standards	Chapters:	1	2	3	4	5	6	7	8	9	10	11	12	13	14	15	16	17
3. Describe the role of the trans-Saharan caravan trade in the changing religious and cultural characteristics of West Africa and the influence of Islamic beliefs, ethics, and law.							•											
4. Trace the growth of the Arabic language in government, trade, and Islamic scholarship in West Africa.							•											
5. Describe the importance of written and oral traditions in the transmission of African history and culture.							•											
7.5 Students analyze the geographic, political, economic, religious, and social structures of the civilizations of Medieval Japan.																		
1. Describe the significance of Japan's proximity to China and Korea and the intellectual, linguistic, religious, and philosophical influence of those countries on Japan.										•								
2. Discuss the reign of Prince Shotoku of Japan and the characteristics of Japanese society and family life during his reign.										•								
3. Describe the values, social customs, and traditions prescribed by the lord-vassal system consisting of shogun, daimyo, and samurai and the lasting influence of the warrior code in the twentieth century.										•								
4. Trace the development of distinctive forms of Japanese Buddhism.										•								
5. Study the ninth and tenth centuries' golden age of literature, art, and drama and its lasting effects on culture today, including Murasaki Shikibu's Tale of Genji.										•								
6. Analyze the rise of a military society in the late twelfth century and the role of the samurai in that society.										•								
7.6 Students analyze the geographic, political, economic, religious, and social structures of the civilizations of Medieval Europe.																		
1. Study the geography of the Europe and the Eurasian land mass, including its location, topography, waterways, vegetation, and climate and their relationship to ways of life in Medieval Europe.										•								
2. Describe the spread of Christianity north of the Alps and the roles played by the early church and by monasteries in its diffusion after the fall of the western half of the Roman Empire.										•								
3. Understand the development of feudalism, its role in the medieval European economy, the way in which it was influenced by physical geography (the role of the manor and the growth of towns), and how feudal relationships provided the foundation of political order.										•								
4. Demonstrate an understanding of the conflict and cooperation between the Papacy and European monarchs (e.g., Charlemagne, Gregory VII, Emperor Henry IV).											•							
5. Know the significance of developments in medieval English legal and constitutional practices and their importance in the rise of modern democratic thought and representative institutions (e.g., Magna Carta, parliament, development of habeas corpus, an independent judiciary in England).											•							
6. Discuss the causes and course of the religious Crusades and their effects on the Christian, Muslim, and Jewish populations in Europe, with emphasis on the increasing contact by Europeans with cultures of the Eastern Mediterranean world.											•							
7. Map the spread of the bubonic plague from Central Asia to China, the Middle East, and Europe and describe its impact on global population.											•							
8. Understand the importance of the Catholic church as a political, intellectual, and aesthetic institution (e.g., founding of universities, political and spiritual roles of the clergy, creation of monastic and mendicant religious orders, preservation of the Latin language and religious texts, St. Thomas Aquinas's synthesis of classical philosophy with Christian theology, and the concept of "natural law").											•							
9. Know the history of the decline of Muslim rule in the Iberian Peninsula that culminated in the Reconquista and the rise of Spanish and Portuguese kingdoms.											•							
7.7 Students compare and contrast the geographic, political, economic, religious, and social structures of the Meso-American and Andean civilizations.																		
1. Study the locations, landforms, and climates of Mexico, Central America, and South America and their effects on Mayan, Aztec, and Incan economies, trade, and development of urban societies.															•	•		

Standards	Chapters:	1	2	3	4	5	6	7	8	9	10	11	12	13	14	15	16	17
2. Study the roles of people in each society, including class structures, family life, warfare, religious beliefs and practices, and slavery.															●	●		
3. Explain how and where each empire arose and how the Aztec and Incan empires were defeated by the Spanish.															●	●		
4. Describe the artistic and oral traditions and architecture in the three civilizations.															●	●		
5. Describe the Meso-American achievements in astronomy and mathematics, including the development of the calendar and the Meso-American knowledge of seasonal changes to the civilizations' agricultural systems.															●	●		
7.8 Students analyze the origins, accomplishments, and geographic diffusion of the Renaissance.																		
1. Describe the way in which the revival of classical learning and the arts fostered a new interest in humanism (i.e., a balance between intellect and religious faith).												●						
2. Explain the importance of Florence in the early stages of the Renaissance and the growth of independent trading cities (e.g., Venice), with emphasis on the cities' importance in the spread of Renaissance ideas.												●						
3. Understand the effects of the reopening of the ancient "Silk Road" between Europe and China, including Marco Polo's travels and the location of his routes.												●						
4. Describe the growth and effects of new ways of disseminating information (e.g., the ability to manufacture paper, translation of the Bible into the vernacular, printing).												●						
5. Detail advances made in literature, the arts, science, mathematics, cartography, engineering, and the understanding of human anatomy and astronomy (e.g., by Dante Alighieri, Leonardo da Vinci, Michelangelo di Buonarroti Simoni, Johann Gutenberg, William Shakespeare).												●						
7.9 Students analyze the historical developments of the Reformation.																		
1. List the causes for the internal turmoil in and weakening of the Catholic church (e.g., tax policies, selling of indulgences).													●					
2. Describe the theological, political, and economic ideas of the major figures during the Reformation (e.g., Desiderius Erasmus, Martin Luther, John Calvin, William Tyndale).													●					
3. Explain Protestants' new practices of church self-government and the influence of those practices on the development of democratic practices and ideas of federalism.													●					
4. Identify and locate the European regions that remained Catholic and those that became Protestant and explain how the division affected the distribution of religions in the New World.													●					
5. Analyze how the Counter-Reformation revitalized the Catholic church and the forces that fostered the movement (e.g., St. Ignatius of Loyola and the Jesuits, the Council of Trent).													●					
6. Understand the institution and impact of missionaries on Christianity and the diffusion of Christianity from Europe to other parts of the world in the medieval and early modern periods; locate missions on a world map.													●					
7. Describe the Golden Age of cooperation between Jews and Muslims in medieval Spain that promoted creativity in art, literature, and science, including how that cooperation was terminated by the religious persecution of individuals and groups (e.g., the Spanish Inquisition and the expulsion of Jews and Muslims from Spain in 1492).													●					
7.10 Students analyze the historical developments of the Scientific Revolution and its lasting effect on religious, political, and cultural institutions.																		
1. Discuss the roots of the Scientific Revolution (e.g., Greek rationalism; Jewish, Christian, and Muslim science; Renaissance humanism; new knowledge from global exploration).														●				
2. Understand the significance of the new scientific theories (e.g., those of Copernicus, Galileo, Kepler, Newton) and the significance of new inventions (e.g., the telescope, microscope, thermometer, barometer).														●				
3. Understand the scientific method advanced by Bacon and Descartes, the influence of new scientific rationalism on the growth of democratic ideas, and the coexistence of science with traditional religious beliefs.														●				

Standards

7.11 Students analyze political and economic change in the sixteenth, seventeenth, and eighteenth centuries (the Age of Exploration, the Enlightenment, and the Age of Reason).

Standard	1	2	3	4	5	6	7	8	9	10	11	12	13	14	15	16	17
1. Know the great voyages of discovery, the locations of the routes, and the influence of cartography in the development of a new European worldview.															•		
2. Discuss the exchanges of plants, animals, technology, culture, and ideas among Europe, Africa, Asia, and the Americas in the fifteenth and sixteenth centuries and the major economic and social effects on each continent.															•		
3. Examine the origins of modern capitalism; the influence of mercantilism and cottage industry; the elements and importance of a market economy in seventeenth-century Europe; the changing international trading and marketing patterns, including their locations on a world map; and the influence of explorers and map makers.															•		
4. Explain how the main ideas of the Enlightenment can be traced back to such movements as the Renaissance, the Reformation, and the Scientific Revolution and to the Greeks, Romans, and Christianity.																•	
5. Describe how democratic thought and institutions were influenced by Enlightenment thinkers (e.g., John Locke, Charles-Louis Montesquieu, American founders).																•	
6. Discuss how the principles in the Magna Carta were embodied in such documents as the English Bill of Rights and the American Declaration of Independence.																•	

Analysis Skills Standards

Chronological and Spatial Thinking

Standard	1	2	3	4	5	6	7	8	9	10	11	12	13	14	15	16	17
1. Students explain how major events are related to one another in time.							•										
2. Students construct various time lines of key events, people, and periods of the historical era they are studying.							•										
3. Students use a variety of maps and documents to identify physical and cultural features of neighborhoods, cities, states, and countries and to explain the historical migration of people, expansion and disintegration of empires, and the growth of economic systems.		•	•		•										•	•	

Research, Evidence, and Point of View

Standard	1	2	3	4	5	6	7	8	9	10	11	12	13	14	15	16	17
1. Students frame questions that can be answered by historical study and research..	•																
2. Students construct various time lines of key events, people, and periods of the historical era they are studying.					•												
3. Students distinguish relevant from irrelevant information, essential from incidental information, and verifiable from unverifiable information in historical narratives and stories.										•							
4. Students assess the credibility of primary and secondary sources and draw sound conclusions from them.												•					
5. Students detect the different historical points of view on historical events and determine the context in which the historical statements were made (the questions asked, sources used, author's perspectives).											•						

Historical Interpretation

Standard	1	2	3	4	5	6	7	8	9	10	11	12	13	14	15	16	17
1. Students explain the central issues and problems from the past, placing people and events in a matrix of time and place.								•									
2. Students understand and distinguish cause, effect, sequence, and correlation in historical events, including the long- and short-term causal relations.												•					
3. Students explain the sources of historical continuity and how the combination of ideas and events explains the emergence of new patterns.														•		•	
4. Students recognize the role of chance, oversight, and error in history.								•									
5. Students recognize that interpretations of history are subject to change as new information is uncovered.						•								•			
6. Students interpret basic indicators of economic performance and conduct cost-benefit analyses of economic and political issues.		•													•	•	•

T35

Standards Overview: Grade 8

Standards	1	2	3	4	5	6	7	8	9	10	11	12	13	14	15	16	17	18	19	20
8.1 Students understand the major events preceding the founding of the nation and relate their significance to the development of American constitutional democracy.																				
1. Describe the relationship between the moral and political ideas of the Great Awakening and the development of revolutionary fervor.		•																		
2. Analyze the philosophy of government expressed in the Declaration of Independence, with an emphasis on government as a means of securing individual rights (e.g., key phrases such as "all men are created equal, that they are endowed by their Creator with certain unalienable Rights").			•						•											
3. Analyze how the American Revolution affected other nations, especially France.			•		•															
4. Describe the nation's blend of civic republicanism, classical liberal principles, and English parliamentary traditions.				•																
8.2 Students analyze the political principles underlying the U.S. Constitution and compare the enumerated and implied powers of the federal government.																				
1. Discuss the significance of the Magna Carta, the English Bill of Rights, and the Mayflower Compact.		•																		
2. Analyze the Articles of Confederation and the Constitution and the success of each in implementing the ideals of the Declaration of Independence.				•																
3. Evaluate the major debates that occurred during the development of the Constitution and their ultimate resolutions in such areas as shared power among institutions, divided state-federal power, slavery, the rights of individuals and states (later addressed by the addition of the Bill of Rights), and the status of American Indian nations under the commerce clause.				•																
4. Describe the political philosophy underpinning the Constitution as specified in the Federalist Papers (authored by James Madison, Alexander Hamilton, and John Jay) and the role of such leaders as Madison, George Washington, Roger Sherman, Gouverneur Morris, and James Wilson in the writing and ratification of the Constitution.				•																
5. Understand the significance of Jefferson's Statute for Religious Freedom as a forerunner of the First Amendment and the origins, purpose, and differing views of the founding fathers on the issue of the separation of church and state.					•															
6. Enumerate the powers of government set forth in the Constitution and the fundamental liberties ensured by the Bill of Rights.					•															
7. Describe the principles of federalism, dual sovereignty, separation of powers, checks and balances, the nature and purpose of majority rule, and the ways in which the American idea of constitutionalism preserves individual rights.				•	•															
8.3 Students understand the foundation of the American political system and the ways in which citizens participate in it.																				
1. Analyze the principles and concepts codified in state constitutions between 1777 and 1781 that created the context out of which American political institutions and ideas developed.				•																

Standards / Chapters:	1	2	3	4	5	6	7	8	9	10	11	12	13	14	15	16	17	18	19	20
2. Explain how the ordinances of 1785 and 1787 privatized national resources and transferred federally owned lands into private holdings, townships, and states.				●																
3. Enumerate the advantages of a common market among the states as foreseen in and protected by the Constitution's clauses on interstate commerce, common coinage, and full-faith and credit.					●				●											
4. Understand how the conflicts between Thomas Jefferson and Alexander Hamilton resulted in the emergence of two political parties (e.g., view of foreign policy, Alien and Sedition Acts, economic policy, National Bank, funding and assumption of the revolutionary debt).						●		●												
5. Know the significance of domestic resistance movements and ways in which the central government responded to such movements (e.g., Shays' Rebellion, the Whiskey Rebellion).				●		●														
6. Describe the basic law-making process and how the Constitution provides numerous opportunities for citizens to participate in the political process and to monitor and influence government (e.g., function of elections, political parties, interest groups).					●															
7. Understand the functions and responsibilities of a free press.					●														●	
8.4 Students analyze the aspirations and ideals of the people of the new nation.																				
1. Describe the country's physical landscapes, political divisions, and territorial expansion during the terms of the first four presidents.							●													
2. Explain the policy significance of famous speeches (e.g., Washington's Farewell Address, Jefferson's 1801 Inaugural Address, John Q. Adams's Fourth of July 1821 Address).							●													
3. Analyze the rise of capitalism and the economic problems and conflicts that accompanied it (e.g., Jackson's opposition to the National Bank; early decisions of the U.S. Supreme Court that reinforced the sanctity of contracts and a capitalist economic system of law).								●												
4. Discuss daily life, including traditions in art, music, and literature, of early national America (e.g., through writings by Washington Irving, James Fenimore Cooper).							●													
8.5 Students analyze U.S. foreign policy in the early Republic.																				
1. Understand the political and economic causes and consequences of the War of 1812 and know the major battles, leaders, and events that led to a final peace.							●													
2. Know the changing boundaries of the United States and describe the relationships the country had with its neighbors (current Mexico and Canada) and Europe, including the influence of the Monroe Doctrine, and how those relationships influenced westward expansion and the Mexican-American War.								●												
3. Outline the major treaties with American Indian nations during the administrations of the first four presidents and the varying outcomes of those treaties.						●														
8.6 Students analyze the divergent paths of the American people from 1800 to the mid-1800s and the challenges they faced, with emphasis on the Northeast.																				
1. Discuss the influence of industrialization and technological developments on the region, including human modification of the landscape and how physical geography shaped human actions (e.g., growth of cities, deforestation, farming, mineral extraction).											●		●							

Standards	1	2	3	4	5	6	7	8	9	10	11	12	13	14	15	16	17	18	19	20
2. Outline the physical obstacles to and the economic and political factors involved in building a network of roads, canals, and railroads (e.g., Henry Clay's American System).								•												
3. List the reasons for the wave of immigration from Northern Europe to the United States and describe the growth in the number, size, and spatial arrangements of cities (e.g., Irish immigrants and the Great Irish Famine).													•							
4. Study the lives of black Americans who gained freedom in the North and founded schools and churches to advance their rights and communities.													•							
5. Trace the development of the American education system from its earliest roots, including the roles of religious and private schools and Horace Mann's campaign for free public education and its assimilating role in American culture.													•							
6. Examine the women's suffrage movement (e.g., biographies, writings, and speeches of Elizabeth Cady Stanton, Margaret Fuller, Lucretia Mott, Susan B. Anthony).													•							
7. Identify common themes in American art as well as transcendentalism and individualism (e.g., writings about and by Ralph Waldo Emerson, Henry David Thoreau, Herman Melville, Louisa May Alcott, Nathaniel Hawthorne, Henry Wadsworth Longfellow).													•							
8.7 Students analyze the divergent paths of the American people in the South from 1800 to the mid-1800s and the challenges they faced.																				
1. Describe the development of the agrarian economy in the South, identify the locations of the cotton-producing states, and discuss the significance of cotton and the cotton gin.												•								
2. Trace the origins and development of slavery; its effects on black Americans and on the region's political, social, religious, economic, and cultural development; and identify the strategies that were tried to both overturn and preserve it (e.g., through the writings and historical documents on Nat Turner, Denmark Vesey).												•								
3. Examine the characteristics of white Southern society and how the physical environment influenced events and conditions prior to the Civil War.												•								
4. Compare the lives of and opportunities for free blacks in the North with those of free blacks in the South.												•								
8.8 Students analyze the divergent paths of the American people in the West from 1800 to the mid-1800s and the challenges they faced.																				
1. Discuss the election of Andrew Jackson as president in 1828, the importance of Jacksonian democracy, and his actions as president (e.g., the spoils system, veto of the National Bank, policy of Indian removal, opposition to the Supreme Court).									•											
2. Describe the purpose, challenges, and economic incentives associated with westward expansion, including the concept of Manifest Destiny (e.g., the Lewis and Clark expedition, accounts of the removal of Indians, the Cherokees' "Trail of Tears," settlement of the Great Plains) and the territorial acquisitions that spanned numerous decades.							•		•								•			
3. Describe the role of pioneer women and the new status that western women achieved (e.g., Laura Ingalls Wilder, Annie Bidwell; slave women gaining freedom in the West; Wyoming granting suffrage to women in 1869).										•										

Standards	Chapters:	1	2	3	4	5	6	7	8	9	10	11	12	13	14	15	16	17	18	19	20
4. Examine the importance of the great rivers and the struggle over water rights.											•										
5. Discuss Mexican settlements and their locations, cultural traditions, attitudes toward slavery, land-grant system, and economies.											•										
6. Describe the Texas War for Independence and the Mexican-American War, including territorial settlements, the aftermath of the wars, and the effects the wars had on the lives of Americans, including Mexican Americans today.											•										

8.9 Students analyze the early and steady attempts to abolish slavery and to realize the ideals of the Declaration of Independence.

Standards	Chapters:	1	2	3	4	5	6	7	8	9	10	11	12	13	14	15	16	17	18	19	20
1. Describe the leaders of the movement (e.g., John Quincy Adams and his proposed constitutional amendment, John Brown and the armed resistance, Harriet Tubman and the Underground Railroad, Benjamin Franklin, Theodore Weld, William Lloyd Garrison, Frederick Douglass).															•						
2. Discuss the abolition of slavery in early state constitutions.					•																
3. Describe the significance of the Northwest Ordinance in education and in the banning of slavery in new states north of the Ohio River.					•																
4. Discuss the importance of the slavery issue as raised by the annexation of Texas and California's admission to the union as a free state under the Compromise of 1850.										•					•						
5. Analyze the significance of the States' Rights Doctrine, the Missouri Compromise (1820), the Wilmot Proviso (1846), the Compromise of 1850, Henry Clay's role in the Missouri Compromise and the Compromise of 1850, the Kansas-Nebraska Act (1854), the Dred Scott v. Sandford decision (1857), and the Lincoln-Douglas debates (1858).															•						
6. Describe the lives of free blacks and the laws that limited their freedom and economic opportunities.														•							

8.10 Students analyze the multiple causes, key events, and complex consequences of the Civil War.

Standards	Chapters:	1	2	3	4	5	6	7	8	9	10	11	12	13	14	15	16	17	18	19	20
1. Compare the conflicting interpretations of state and federal authority as emphasized in the speeches and writings of statesmen such as Daniel Webster and John C. Calhoun.															•						
2. Trace the boundaries constituting the North and the South, the geographical differences between the two regions, and the differences between agrarians and industrialists.										•					•						
3. Identify the constitutional issues posed by the doctrine of nullification and secession and the earliest origins of that doctrine.										•					•	•					
4. Discuss Abraham Lincoln's presidency and his significant writings and speeches and their relationship to the Declaration of Independence, such as his "House Divided" speech (1858), Gettysburg Address (1863), Emancipation Proclamation (1863), and inaugural addresses (1861 and 1865).															•	•					
5. Study the views and lives of leaders (e.g., Ulysses S. Grant, Jefferson Davis, Robert E. Lee) and soldiers on both sides of the war, including those of black soldiers and regiments.																•					
6. Describe critical developments and events in the war, including the major battles, geographical advantages and obstacles, technological advances, and General Lee's surrender at Appomattox.																•					

Standards	Chapters:	1	2	3	4	5	6	7	8	9	10	11	12	13	14	15	16	17	18	19	20
7. Explain how the war affected combatants, civilians, the physical environment, and future warfare.																●	●				
8.11 Students analyze the character and lasting consequences of Reconstruction.																					
1. List the original aims of Reconstruction and describe its effects on the political and social structures of different regions.																	●				
2. Identify the push-pull factors in the movement of former slaves to the cities in the North and to the West and their differing experiences in those regions (e.g., the experiences of Buffalo Soldiers).															●						
3. Understand the effects of the Freedmen's Bureau and the restrictions placed on the rights and opportunities of freedmen, including racial segregation and "Jim Crow" laws.																	●				
4. Trace the rise of the Ku Klux Klan and describe the Klan's effects.																	●				
5. Understand the Thirteenth, Fourteenth, and Fifteenth Amendments to the Constitution and analyze their connection to Reconstruction.																	●				
8.12 Students analyze the transformation of the American economy and the changing social and political conditions in the United States in response to the Industrial Revolution.																					
1. Trace patterns of agricultural and industrial development as they relate to climate, use of natural resources, markets, and trade and locate such development on a map.																			●		
2. Identify the reasons for the development of federal Indian policy and the wars with American Indians and their relationship to agricultural development and industrialization.																			●		
3. Explain how states and the federal government encouraged business expansion through t.ariffs, banking, land grants, and subsidies.																					●
4. Discuss entrepreneurs, industrialists, and bankers in politics, commerce, and industry (e.g., Andrew Carnegie, John D. Rockefeller, Leland Stanford).																			●		
5. Examine the location and effects of urbanization, renewed immigration, and industrialization (e.g., the effects on social fabric of cities, wealth and economic opportunity, the conservation movement).																			●	●	
6. Discuss child labor, working conditions, and laissez-faire policies toward big business and examine the labor movement, including its leaders (e.g., Samuel Gompers), its demand for collective bargaining, and its strikes and protests over labor conditions.																			●	●	
7. Identify the new sources of large-scale immigration and the contributions of immigrants to the building of cities and the economy; explain the ways in which new social and economic patterns encouraged assimilation of newcomers into the mainstream amidst growing cultural diversity; and discuss the new wave of nativism.																			●		
8. Identify the characteristics and impact of Grangerism and Populism.																			●		
9. Name the significant inventors and their inventions and identify how they improved the quality of life (e.g., Thomas Edison, Alexander Graham Bell, Orville and Wilbur Wright).																			●		

Analysis Skills Standards

Chapters:	1	2	3	4	5	6	7	8	9	10	11	12	13	14	15	16	17	18	19	20
Chronological and Spatial Thinking																				
CS1 Students explain how major events are related to one another in time.				●																
CS2 Students construct various time lines of key events, people, and periods of the historical era they are studying.		●																		
CS3 Students use a variety of maps and documents to identify physical and cultural features of neighborhoods, cities, states, and countries and to explain the historical migration of people, expansion and disintegration of empires, and the growth of economic systems.																	●			
Research, Evidence, and Point of View																				
HR1 Students frame questions that can be answered by historical study and research.	●														●					
HR2 Students distinguish fact from opinion in historical narratives and stories.																			●	
HR3 Students distinguish relevant from irrelevant information essential from incidental information, and verifiable from unverifiable information in historical narratives and stories.															●					
HR4 Students assess the credibility of primary and secondary sources and draw sound conclusions about them.													●	●						
HR5 Students detect the different historical points of view on historical events and determine the context in which the historical statements were made (the questions asked, sources used, author's perspectives).				●																
Historical Interpretation																				
HI1 Students explain the central issues and problems from the past, placing people and events in a matrix of time and place.								●			●									
HI2 Students understand and distinguish cause, effect, sequence, and correlation in historical events, including the long- and short-term causal relations.					●						●							●		
HI3 Students explain the sources of historical continually and how the combination of ideas and events explains the emergence of new patters.																				●
HI4 Students recognize the role of chance, oversight, and error in history.																●				
HI5 Students recognize the interpretations of history are subject to change as new information is uncovered.			●		●															
HI6 Students interpret basic indicators of economic performance and conduct cost-benefit analyses of economic and political issues.																		●		

HOLT CALIFORNIA SOCIAL STUDIES
provides integrated **practice** and **review** for every California standard

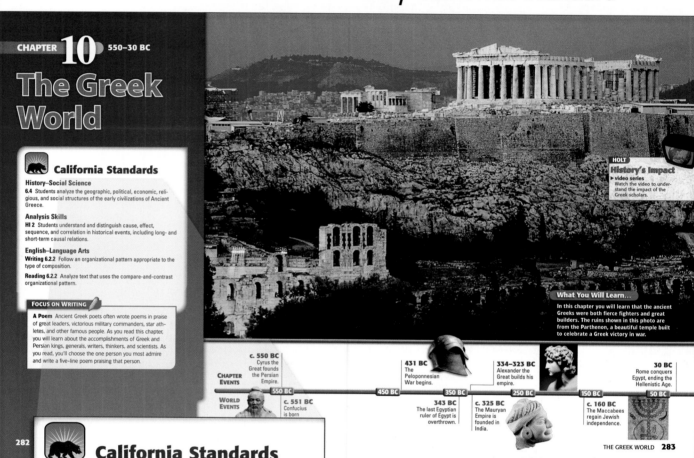

CHAPTER **10** 550–30 BC

The Greek World

California Standards

History–Social Science
6.4 Students analyze the geographic, political, economic, religious, and social structures of the early civilizations of Ancient Greece.

Analysis Skills
HI 2 Students understand and distinguish cause, effect, sequence, and correlation in historical events, including long- and short-term causal relations.

English–Language Arts
Writing 6.2.2 Follow an organizational pattern appropriate to the type of composition.

Reading 6.2.2 Analyze text that uses the compare-and-contrast organizational pattern.

FOCUS ON WRITING

A Poem Ancient Greek poets often wrote poems in praise of great leaders, victorious military commanders, star athletes, and other famous people. As you read this chapter, you will learn about the accomplishments of Greek and Persian kings, generals, writers, thinkers, and scientists. As you read, you'll choose the one person you most admire and write a five-line poem praising that person.

HOLT
History's Impact
▶ video series
Watch the video to understand the impact of the Greek scholars.

What You Will Learn...

In this chapter you will learn that the ancient Greeks were both fierce fighters and great builders. The ruins shown in this photo are from the Parthenon, a beautiful temple built to celebrate a Greek victory in war.

CHAPTER EVENTS

c. 550 BC Cyrus the Great founds the Persian Empire.

431 BC The Peloponnesian War begins.

334–323 BC Alexander the Great builds his empire.

30 BC Rome conquers Egypt, ending the Hellenistic Age.

550 BC   450 BC   350 BC   250 BC   150 BC   50 BC

WORLD EVENTS

c. 551 BC Confucius is born

343 BC The last Egyptian ruler of Egypt is overthrown.

c. 325 BC The Mauryan Empire is founded in India.

c. 160 BC The Maccabees regain Jewish independence.

282

THE GREEK WORLD **283**

California Standards

History–Social Science
6.4 Students analyze the geographic, political, economic, religious, and social structures of the early civilizations of Ancient Greece.

English–Language Arts
Writing 6.2.2 Follow an organizational pattern appropriate to the type of composition.

Reading 6.2.2 Analyze text that uses the compare-and-contrast organizational pattern.

California History-Social Science, Historical Analysis and Social Science Skills, and English-Language Arts Standards are provided at the beginning of every chapter to help prepare students for learning.

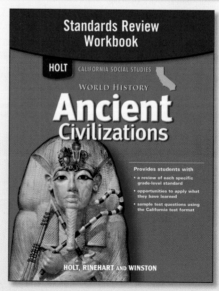

Standards Review Workbook

HOLT CALIFORNIA SOCIAL STUDIES
WORLD HISTORY
Ancient Civilizations

Provides students with
• a review of each specific grade-level standard
• opportunities to apply what they have learned
• sample test questions using the California test format

HOLT, RINEHART AND WINSTON

The *Standards Review Workbook* provides students with a quick review and test preparation for every standard.

SECTION 2

What You Will Learn...

Main Ideas

1. The Spartans built a military society to provide security and protection.
2. The Athenians admired the mind and the arts in addition to physical abilities.
3. Sparta and Athens fought over who should have power and influence in Greece.

The Big Idea

The two most powerful city-states in Greece, Sparta and Athens, had very different

In the *Teacher's Edition,* **Teach the Big Idea: Master the Standards** provides teachers with strategies and activities that help students grasp the big ideas and master the standards for each section.

Teach the Big Idea: Master the Standards   Standards **Proficiency**

Sparta and Athens HSS 6.4.6; HSS **Analysis Skills:** HI 1

1. **Teach** Ask students the Main Idea questions to teach this section.

2. **Apply** As students read this section, have them make an outline of the section using the blue heads (such as "Spartans Build a Military Society") as main ideas and the red heads (such as "Boys and Men in Sparta") as supporting ideas. Have students fill in their outlines. **LS** Verbal/Linguistic

3. **Review** Ask volunteers to share their outlines with the class. Ask the class to

suggest additional information they might add to the outline.

4. **Practice/Homework** Have each student use his or her outline to write a brief, two-paragraph summary comparing and contrasting life in Athens and Sparta. **LS** Verbal/Linguistic

   Alternative Assessment Handbook, Rubric 9: Comparing and Contrasting

---

In the *Teacher's Edition,* **Standards Focus** helps teachers respond to students' questions by telling them what the standard **means** in relation to the section content and why the standard **matters.**

Students also see the **Standards** at the beginning of every section in the *Student Edition.*

HSS **6.4.6** Compare and contrast life in Athens and Sparta, with emphasis on their roles in the Persian and Peloponnesian Wars.

292 CHAPTER 10

Standards Focus

HSS **6.4.6**

Means: Describe the similarities and differences between life in Athens and Sparta and how these similarities and differences influenced each city-state's role in the Persian and Peloponnesian wars.

Matters: The science, literature, and philosophy that form the basis of Western culture were shaped in ancient Athens, not ancient Sparta.

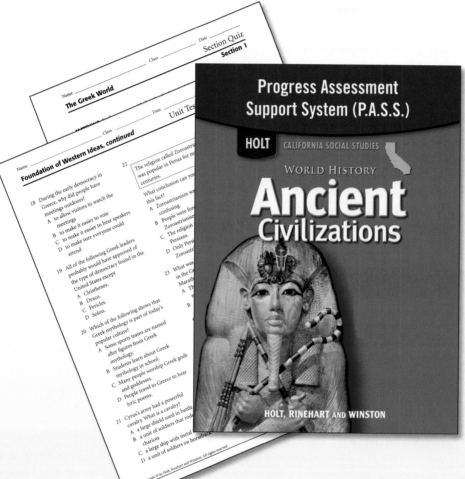

HOLT CALIFORNIA SOCIAL STUDIES

includes **standards assessment** to monitor students' progress effectively

Holt's new *Progress Assessment Support System (P.A.S.S.)* includes all the assessment for every chapter and unit and helps teachers monitor students' progress.

P.A.S.S. includes
- **Section Quizzes**
- **Chapter Tests**
- **Diagnostic Pretest**
- **Benchmark Tests**
- **Summative End-of-the-Year Test**
- **Assessment Rubrics**

ExamView® test generator

Every test on the ExamView® Test Generator, on the *One-Stop Planner® CD-ROM*, is also correlated to the California Standards, making it easy to reteach and offer more support to those students who need it.

A new technology,
Holt Online Assessment,
helps teachers assess students'
mastery of the standards.

Back Forward Stop Refresh Home AutoFill Print Mail

Address: http://HOAP.html

Name: _____ Class: _____ Date: _____

1 Chapter 1 Test

Multiple Choice
Identify the letter of the choice that best completes the statement or answers the question.

_____ 1. A law-making body made up of two houses, or groups, is a
  a. confederation.   c. royal council.
  b. bicameral legislature.   d. consti

_____ 2. The Proclamation of 1763, which banned English settlem
  to prevent further conflicts after
  a. Pontiac's Rebellion.   c. Shay
  b. the Boston Massacre.   d. Baco

_____ 3. In the 1400s Italian city-states had
  a. the power to boycott goods from Chinese merchants.
  b. charters to establish colonies in North America.
  c. a monopoly, or economic control, of trade goods ente
  d. stopped all European trade with Asia.

_____ 4. The purpose of the 1787 Constitutional Convention was t
  a. define the colonists' rights and their complaints again
  b. revise the Articles of Confederation.
  c. petition King George III to repeal the Stamp Act.

▲ **STEP 1**
Create a test

Back Forward Stop Refresh Home AutoFill Print Mail

Address: http://HOAP.html

Holt
Online
Learning

HOLT, RINEHART AND WINSTON

Assignment Manager: Assign a New Test/Activity

Use this screen to search for tests or activities that you would like to assign. Once you've found a test or activity that you wou
click the "Assign" button that you'll find next to it.

You can choose to sort or view resources by your program's Table of Contents or by Resource Type (All Program Resources, H
Assessment, or Test Generator Tests).

View Resources by Table of Contents: View Resourc
Make a Selection   All

Click a Resource to View:	Click to Assign:
Chapter 1 Test	Assign
Chapter 2 Test	Assign
Chapter 3 Test	Assign
Chapter 4 Test	Assign
Chapter 5 Test	Assign
Chapter 6 Test	Assign
	Assign
	Assign

▲ **STEP 2**
Assign a test

Test Score

92%

25% 50% 75% 100%

Legend
Correct   ✔
Incorrect   ✘
Skipped   Ø

Standards Report [View by Question]
Click any question to see part and the correct answer

Standards	Questions
6.1.1	1 ✔
6.1.2	2 ✔ ✘ ✔
6.1.3	3 ✔ ✔

Scores: Green = >90% ; Blue = 70%-90% ; Red = <70% ; **Black** = Incomplete

	Average Score	1st Quarter Benchmark	2nd Quarter Benchmark	3rd Quarter Benchmark
Average	70%	75%	75%	75%
Male	70%	70%	70%	70%
Female	80%	80%	80%	80%
1st Quarter	70%	75%	75%	75%
2nd Quarter	70%	70%	70%	70%
3rd Quarter	80%			
Avg. 1st	70%			
Avg. 2nd	70%			
Avg. 3rd	80%			

Print Export Save A

Scores: Green = >90% ; Blue = 70%-90% ; Red = <70% ; **Black** = Incomplete

	Average Score ▼	1.1.a ▼	1.1.b ▼	1.1.d
Anderson, Kim	100%	100%	100%	100%
Bonilla, Elizabeth	75%	60%	75%	80%
Bretz, Robert	70%	75%	80%	75%
Caldwell, Kelly	70%	80%	90%	80%
Garcia, Anji	60%	45%	40%	65%
Hart, Matthew	60%	70%	90%	80%
Boberts, Hal	70%	75%	80%	75%
Shelton, Thomas	70%	80%	90%	80%
Deleon, John	60%	45%	40%	65%
Carter, Jerry	60%	70%	90%	80%

▲ **STEP 3**
View Reports

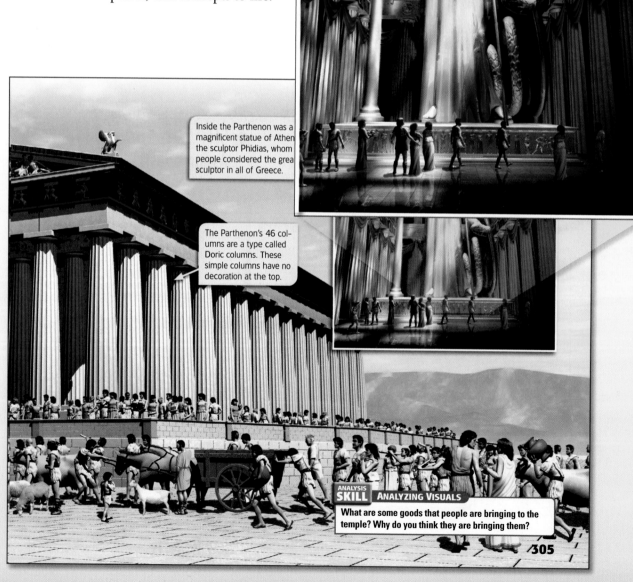
HOLT CALIFORNIA SOCIAL STUDIES
involves students in the study of history and helps them discover **a story well told**

Stunning visuals put students into the context of the time period, bringing people, places, and concepts to life.

Inside the Parthenon was a magnificent statue of Athen the sculptor Phidias, whom people considered the grea sculptor in all of Greece.

The Parthenon's 46 columns are a type called Doric columns. These simple columns have no decoration at the top.

ANALYSIS SKILL ANALYZING VISUALS

What are some goods that people are bringing to the temple? Why do you think they are bringing them?

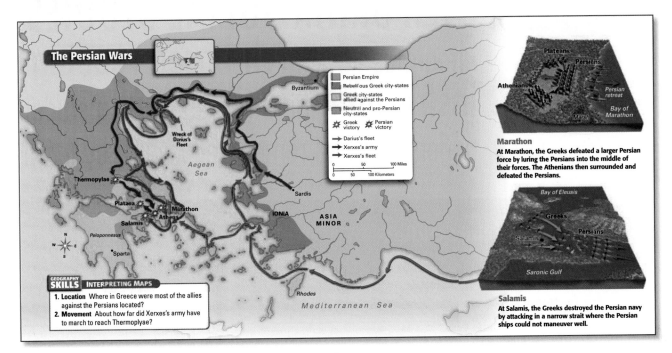

The Persian Wars

Persian Empire
Rebellious Greek city-states
Greek city-states allied against the Persians
Neutral and pro-Persian city-states
☼ Greek victory ☼ Persian victory
→ Darius's fleet
→ Xerxes's army
→ Xerxes's fleet

Byzantium

Wreck of Darius's Fleet

Aegean Sea

Thermopylae

Plataea

Marathon
Athens
Salamis

Peloponnesus

Sparta

Sardis

IONIA

ASIA MINOR

Rhodes

Mediterranean Sea

GEOGRAPHY SKILLS INTERPRETING MAPS

1. **Location** Where in Greece were most of the allies against the Persians located?
2. **Movement** About how far did Xerxes's army have to march to reach Thermoplyae?

Marathon
At Marathon, the Greeks defeated a larger Persian force by luring the Persians into the middle of their forces. The Athenians then surrounded and defeated the Persians.

Plateans
Persians
Athenians
Persian retreat
Bay of Marathon

Salamis
At Salamis, the Greeks destroyed the Persian navy by attacking in a narrow strait where the Persian ships could not maneuver well.

Bay of Eleusis
Greeks
Persians
Salamis
Saronic Gulf

Holt's unique maps offer another way to engage students, showing them the connections between geography and history. **Online Interactive Maps** provide activities that develop map skills.

Sparta and Athens

If **YOU** were there...

Your father, a wandering trader, has decided it is time to settle down. He offers the family a choice between two cities. In one city, everyone wants to be athletic, tough, and strong. They're good at enduring hardships and following orders. The other city is different. There, you'd be admired if you could think deeply and speak persuasively, if you knew a lot about astronomy or history, or if you sang and played beautiful music.

Which city do you choose? Why?

If You Were There, introducing each section, challenges students with a provocative question designed to make the history presented in that section come alive.

HOLT

History's Impact

▶ **video series**
Watch the video to understand the impact of the Greek scholars.

History's Impact Video Program helps students connect history to events in the current world (available on VHS, DVD, and the **Online Textbook**).

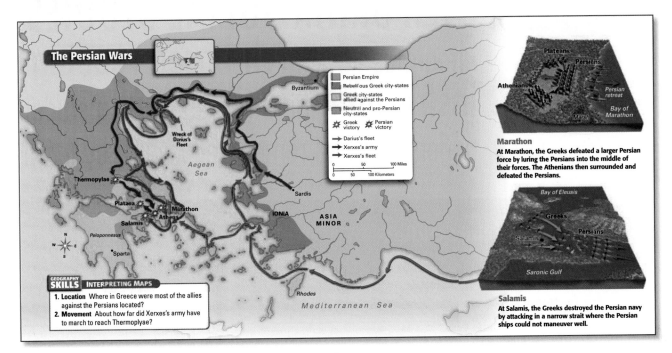

HOLT CALIFORNIA SOCIAL STUDIES

integrates **research-based reading instruction** and offers support so students understand and remember what they learn

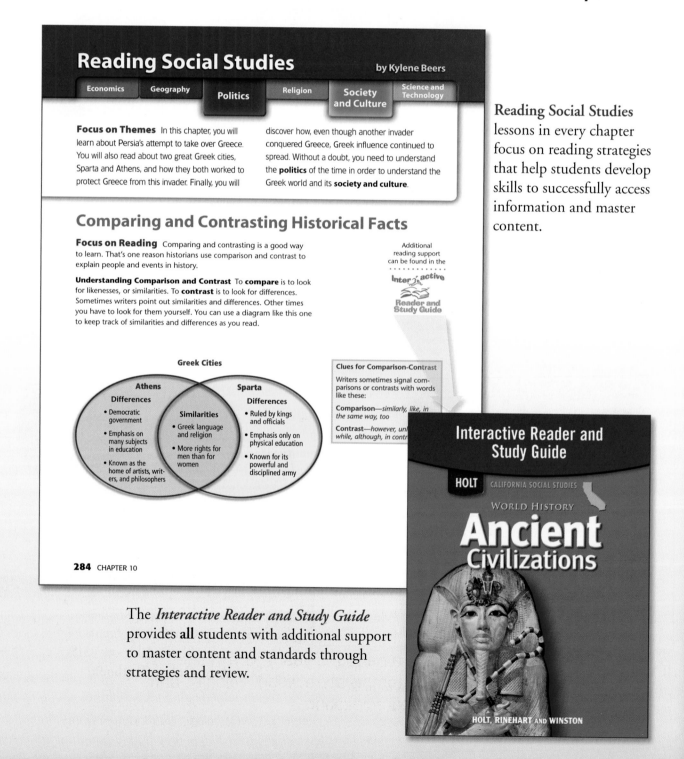

Reading Social Studies lessons in every chapter focus on reading strategies that help students develop skills to successfully access information and master content.

Reading Social Studies

by Kylene Beers

Economics Geography Politics Religion Society and Culture Science and Technology

Focus on Themes In this chapter, you will learn about Persia's attempt to take over Greece. You will also read about two great Greek cities, Sparta and Athens, and how they both worked to protect Greece from this invader. Finally, you will discover how, even though another invader conquered Greece, Greek influence continued to spread. Without a doubt, you need to understand the **politics** of the time in order to understand the Greek world and its **society and culture**.

Comparing and Contrasting Historical Facts

Focus on Reading Comparing and contrasting is a good way to learn. That's one reason historians use comparison and contrast to explain people and events in history.

Understanding Comparison and Contrast To **compare** is to look for likenesses, or similarities. To **contrast** is to look for differences. Sometimes writers point out similarities and differences. Other times you have to look for them yourself. You can use a diagram like this one to keep track of similarities and differences as you read.

Additional reading support can be found in the *Interactive Reader and Study Guide*

Greek Cities

Athens
Differences
• Democratic government
• Emphasis on many subjects in education
• Known as the home of artists, writers, and philosophers

Similarities
• Greek language and religion
• More rights for men than for women

Sparta
Differences
• Ruled by kings and officials
• Emphasis only on physical education
• Known for its powerful and disciplined army

Clues for Comparison-Contrast

Writers sometimes signal comparisons or contrasts with words like these:

Comparison—*similarly, like, in the same way, too*

Contrast—*however, unl... while, although, in contr...*

284 CHAPTER 10

Interactive Reader and Study Guide

HOLT CALIFORNIA SOCIAL STUDIES

WORLD HISTORY

Ancient Civilizations

HOLT, RINEHART AND WINSTON

The *Interactive Reader and Study Guide* provides **all** students with additional support to master content and standards through strategies and review.

live ink®

a new way to read

Live Ink Online Reading Help is an online tool that displays the text of the *Holt California Social Studies Online Editions* in a format that has been proven to improve comprehension and increase test scores.

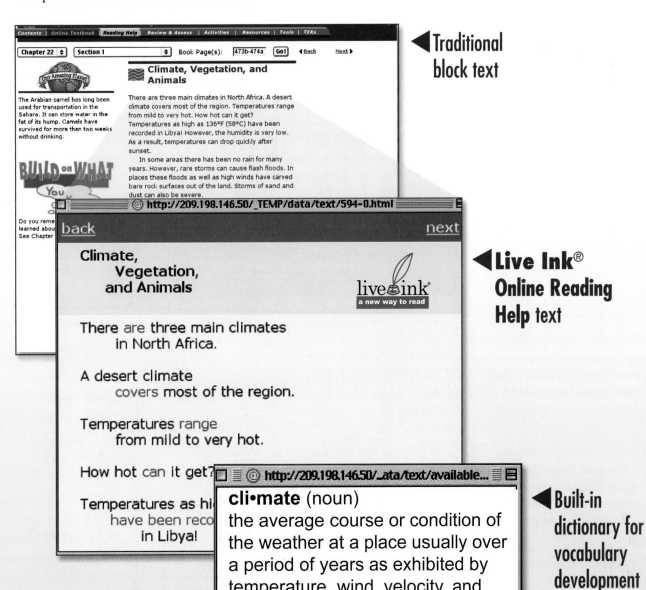

◀ Traditional block text

◀ **Live Ink® Online Reading Help** text

◀ Built-in dictionary for vocabulary development

HOLT CALIFORNIA SOCIAL STUDIES
ensures Universal Access for all students

Holt's award-winning *One-Stop Planner* provides easy-to-use print and technology resources that allow teachers to maximize their effectiveness and save time in planning, teaching, and assessing each lesson.

One-Stop Planner
with Test Generator

One-Stop Planner®
with ExamView® Pro Test Generator

HOLT SOCIAL STUDIES
WORLD HISTORY
Ancient Civilizations

Differentiating Instruction for Universal Access

Learners Having Difficulty   Reaching Standards

1. Organize the class into four groups.

2. Have each group create a mural or posters that depict the lives of men and women in Sparta and Athens. LS Visual/Spatial

3. Ask each group to present its mural or posters to the rest of the class.

4. Have students, using the images on the mural or posters, discuss which parts of both Spartan and Athenian society they like or don't like. LS Verbal/Linguistic

5. **Extend** Refer students back to the carving of Darius meeting with an officer in the previous section. Ask students if any of their images are larger than others. If so, ask if they can explain why.

Alternative Assessment Handbook, Rubrics 3: Artwork; and 28: Posters

HSS 6.4.6; HSS Analysis Skills: HI 1

In the *Teacher's Edition*, **Differentiating Instruction for Universal Access** includes additional strategies for English-Language Learners, Advanced Learners/GATE, and Learners Having Difficulty.

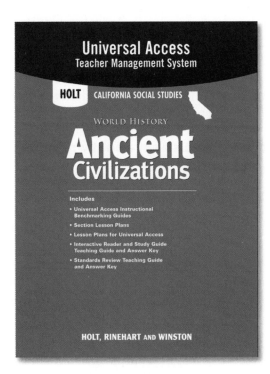

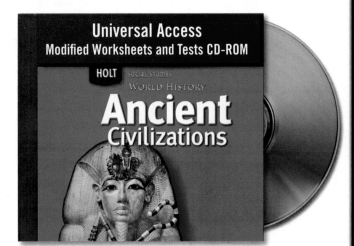

The *Universal Access Modified Worksheets and Tests CD-ROM* provides key resources modified to meet the specifications for students' **Individualized Education Plans (IEPs).**

Holt's *Universal Access Teacher Management System* offers a wide variety of planning and instructional strategies.

The system includes:
- **Section Lesson Plans**
- **Lesson Plans for Universal Access**
- **Instructional Benchmarking Guides**
- **Interactive Reader and Study Guide Teaching Guide**
- **Standards Review Workbook Teaching Guide**

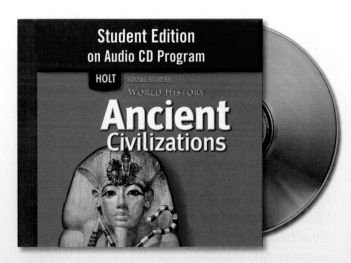

Student Edition on Audio CD Program is a direct read of the *Student Edition,* providing extra support for auditory learners, English-language learners, and reluctant readers. Also available is the *Spanish Chapter Summaries Audio CD Program.*

English–Language Arts Standards and the Social Studies Teacher

by Carol Jago

Carol Jago teaches English at Santa Monica High School and directs the California Reading and Literature Project at UCLA. She is the author of *Cohesive Writing: Why Concept Is Not Enough.*

Q: Why should a social studies teacher have to teach to English–Language Arts Standards?

A: With a full set of standards of their own, many social studies teachers wonder why they should be expected to address English–Language Arts standards as well. In California all students must pass an exit exam in order to graduate. The CAHSEE (California High School Exit Exam) measures student competency in reading, writing, and mathematics. Preparing students to meet this challenge begins long before high school and is the shared responsibility of teachers across the subject areas. The English–Language Arts standards assessed on the CAHSEE are in many cases closely aligned with the social studies curriculum, for example Standard 2.8: "Evaluate the credibility of an author's argument or defense of a claim by critiquing the relationship between generalizations and evidence, the comprehensiveness of evidence, and the way in which the author's intent affects the structure and tone of the text (e.g., in professional journals, editorials, political speeches, primary source materials). Teaching to such standards will not only help students pass the exit exam but also help them learn history.

Q: What does research say about writing in social studies curriculum?

A: The National Commission on Writing in America's Schools and Colleges issued a report titled "The Neglected 'R'" calling for a writing revolution. NAEP research shows that only 50 percent of students meet "basic" levels of performance in writing and only one in five can be called "proficient." One student in five produces completely unsatisfactory prose. The 2003 report recommends that writing be incorporated into all state standards and that writing be required in every curriculum at all grade levels. "Very few things are more important to improving student achievement than restoring writing to its proper place in the classroom," said Commission Vice-Chair Arlene Ackerman, San Francisco superintendent of schools. "Writing is how we can teach students complex skills of synthesis, analysis, and problem solving." Given the controversial nature of so many topics in their curriculum, social studies teachers are uniquely positioned to help students develop these skills through persuasive writing.

Q: But how am I supposed to grade all those papers?

A: It isn't possible for teachers to work any harder. We need to work smarter. One method for assessing student writing effectively is to use rubrics. When the features of each numerical rubric score are laid out alongside a writing task, it is possible to assign a number to each student paper with confidence and, if not ease, efficiency. Social studies teachers needn't feel that they must teach the mechanics of correctness. Language arts teachers recognize that this is their primary responsibility. By assigning writing, social studies teachers reinforce the lessons learned in English–Language Arts.

Sample Scoring Rubric: Persuasive Essays

4 The Writing

- Clearly addresses all parts of the writing task
- Authoritatively defends a position with precise and relevant evidence
- Demonstrates a clear understanding of purpose and audience
- Maintains a consistent point of view, focus, and organizational structure, including the effective use of transitions
- Includes a clearly presented central idea with relevant facts, details, and/or explanations
- Includes a variety of sentence types
- Contains few, if any, errors in the conventions of the English language

2 The Writing

- Addresses only parts of the writing task
- Defends a position with little, if any, evidence and may address the reader's concerns, biases, and expectations
- Demonstrates little understanding of purpose and audience
- Maintains an inconsistent point of view, focus, and organizational structure, which may include ineffective or awkward transitions that do not unify important ideas
- Suggests a central idea with relevant facts, details, and/or explanations
- Includes little variety of sentence types
- Contains several errors in the conventions of the English language

3 The Writing

- Addresses all parts of the writing task
- Generally defends a position with relevant evidence and addresses the reader's concerns, biases, and expectations
- Demonstrates a general understanding of purpose and audience
- Maintains a mostly consistent point of view, focus, and organizational structure, including the effective use of some transitions
- Includes a central idea with relevant facts, details, and/or explanations
- Includes a variety of sentence types
- Contains some errors in the conventions of the English language

1 The Writing

- Addresses only one part of the writing task
- Fails to defend a position with any evidence and fails to address the reader's concerns, biases, and expectations
- Demonstrates no understanding of purpose and audience
- Lacks a point of view, focus, organizational structure, and transitions that unify important ideas
- Lacks a central idea but may contain marginally relevant facts, details, and/or explanations
- Includes no sentence variety
- Contains serious errors in the conventions of the English language

Scoring rubrics help social studies teachers assess student writing efficiently and effectively.

Q: With so much history to read, why are we asking students to read literature?

A: Literature helps bring history to life, animating historical events and allowing students to walk in the shoes of those who have lived long ago in places distant from their own experience. Good literature is also disturbing. It forces readers to examine the lives of others from the inside out, exposing young people to the complexity of the world they live in. Literature doesn't offer simple solutions. While reading fiction is not a vaccine for small-mindedness, it does make it difficult to think only of one's self.

If one purpose of public education is to prepare students for the complex responsibilities of citizenship, I can think of no better preparation for these responsibilities than reading the work of authors such as Stephen Crane, Jack London, Frank Norris, Theodore Dreiser, and Upton Sinclair. Literature creates empathy and without empathy there can be little hope of a civilized society.

Standard English Learners
Language Acquisition as a Scaffold to Social Studies Curricula

by Dr. Noma LeMoine

Dr. Noma LeMoine, Ph.D., is a nationally recognized expert on issues of language variation and learning in African American and other students for whom Standard English is not native. She is Director of Academic English Mastery and Closing the Achievement Gap Branch for the Los Angeles Unified School District. She is a member of the National Citizen's Commission on African American Education, an arm of the Congressional Black Caucus Education Brain Trust. Dr. LeMoine is also the author of *English for Your Success: A Language Development Program for African American Students.*

Who are Standard English Learners?

Standard English Learners (SELs) are students for whom standard English is not native or whose home language—the language acquired between infancy and five years of age—structurally does not match the language of school. Standard English Learners include African American, Hawaiian American, Mexican American, and Native American students that have in common a linguistic history grounded in languages other than English. Prior to coming in contact with English their ancestors spoke African languages, Hawaiian languages, Latin American Spanish, or Native American languages. In each case these "involuntary minorities"—people who were enslaved, colonized, conquered, or otherwise subordinated in the context of America—combined English vocabulary with their native language and fashioned new ways of communicating in their new environments. These language forms, African American Language (often referred to as Black English); Hawaiian American Language (referred

Standard English Learners arrive at school in kindergarten as competent users of the language of their home but demonstrating limited proficiency in the language of school, that is, Standard American English. They are generally classified as English Only on school language surveys even though many of the rules that govern their home language are based in languages other than English. Because of their designation as English Only, these students' need for structured programs that support their acquisition of standard and academic English is often overlooked.

SEL Administrative Support Strategies

- Provide ongoing, comprehensive professional development for teachers and paraeducators including "literature circles" centered around the literature on the culturally and linguistically responsive instruction.

- Support the development of cooperative learning communities at the school site that engage teachers in review of the research, lesson study, peer coaching, and analysis of student work as a condition necessary for effectively educating SELs.

- Infuse information on the origin and historical development of standard and non-standard languages into the instructional curriculum.

to as Hawaiian Pidgin English); Mexican American Language (referred to as Chicano English); and Native American Language (sometimes referred to as Red English) incorporate English vocabulary, but differ in structure and form from standard American English.

Language Variation and Learning in SELs

In order for culturally and linguistically diverse Standard English Learners to succeed academically they must acquire the language, culture, and literacies of school. They must become literate in the forms of English that appear in newspapers, magazines, textbooks, voting materials, and consumer contracts. How best to facilitate this learning in Standard English Learners (SELs) has proven elusive for most American public educational institutions and minimal emphasis has been placed on identifying instructional methodologies that scaffold SELs' access to core curricula. Learning is viewed as a social phenomenon and knowledge is recognized as a social construction that is influenced by the cultural and linguistic experiences, perspectives, and frames or references both students and teachers bring to the learning environment. For Standard English Learners this suggests that an instructional model, which validates and builds on prior knowledge, experiences, language and culture while supporting the acquisition of school language through content learning is an appropriate pedagogy.

The History–Social Science curriculum is perhaps the best vehicle for creating learning opportunities in both content and language acquisition areas. Opportunities to engage in critical thinking and participate in knowledge building abound in the History–Social Science curriculum. As teachers help students develop skills as historians who re-create and share knowledge, students can also be provided opportunities to develop skills as speakers, readers, and writers.

SELs must be provided opportunities to add school language and literacy to their repertoire of skills using instructional approaches that build on the culture and language they bring to the classroom. In order for SELs to experience greater success in accessing core curricula, teachers will need to construct learning environments that are authentic, culturally responsive, support language acquisition, and build upon the experiences, learning styles, and strengths of SELs.

SEL Instructional Support Strategies

- Incorporate contrastive analysis strategies (linguistic, contextual, situational, and elicited) into the daily instruction of SELs to facilitate mastery of academic language.

- Incorporate applicable SDAIE (Specially Designed Academic Instruction in English) strategies into instruction including utilization of visuals, manipulatives, graphic organizers, media and other tools to explain concepts.

- Provide continuous and varied opportunities for students to use language to interact with each other and the content through instructional conversations.

- Provide 30 to 45 minutes per day of Mainstream English Language Development (MELD) instruction that promotes the development of listening, speaking, reading, and writing skills in standard and academic English.

- Establish classroom libraries that include culturally relevant books and provide opportunities for SELs to be read to and to engage in free voluntary reading (FVR) on a daily basis.

- Encourage student/classroom development of a personal thesaurus of conceptually coded words to support the acquisition of academic vocabulary.

- Convey knowledge on ancient Africa, Mexico, Hawaii, and North America; their cultures and history.

- Convey knowledge of the impact of diverse cultures on the modern world with an emphasis on historical and contemporary achievers.

- Make connections to students' prior knowledge, experiences, and cultural funds of knowledge to support learning and retention of learned concepts.

Making History–Social Science Accessible to English Learners

by Dr. Julie Chan

Dr. Julie Chan, Ed.D., is Director of Literacy Instruction in the Newport-Mesa Unified School District, located in Costa Mesa, California. She is a member of the California Reading and Literature Project (CRLP), UCI/Orange County region, and serves on the state level CRLP Secondary Academic Literacy Toolkit (SALT) development team. Dr. Chan also teaches graduate courses on "The Sociocultural Contexts of Literacy and Learning" in the Masters of Reading program at CSU Fullerton and "Linguistics in Action in the Multicultural Classroom" at Concordia University.

As increasing numbers of English Language Learners (ELLs) enter California's secondary schools each year, it is incumbent upon all of us to help each student fully access the History–Social Science curriculum.

History–Social Science instruction relies heavily on language—oral language (listening/speaking) and written language (reading/writing). Because of their limited—but developing—proficiency in the English language, ELLs have a difficult time grasping the information presented orally by the teacher, as well as struggling when reading the printed text in History–Social Science textbooks.

Chamot and O'Malley (1994) identified six areas where teachers can support ELLs: (1) conceptual understanding, (2) vocabulary, (3) language functions and discourse, (4) structures, (5) academic language skills, and (6) study skills and learning strategies. Here are some ways that teachers can make History–Social Science accessible to English Language Learners.

Conceptual Understanding While all students need to develop the concepts of time, chronology, distance, and differing ways of life, some ELLs may have never studied world history or geography and History–Social Science can be one way to learn about the United States. Teachers could approach unfamiliar concepts and content through what the *History–Social Science Framework* calls "a story well told" by reading aloud trade books to build background knowledge and/or to provide a mental model at the beginning of a unit of study.

Vocabulary Students need to learn the specialized and technical terminology of History–Social Science in order to discuss and report on the ideas studied. As students move up through the grades, the academic vocabulary of History–Social Science becomes increasingly difficult because of the complexity of the concepts it represents. Thus, knowing which words and how and when to introduce them is critical.

Language Functions and Discourse According to the California Content Standards, middle school students are expected to analyze, compare, contrast, and make judgments about social studies information. In contrast to the narrative discourse of ELD texts, social studies textbooks feature expository discourse across six text structures. By using graphic organizers that match each of the text structures, teachers can make abstract ideas, concepts, and content visible and concrete for ELLs.

Differentiating Instruction for Universal Access

English-Language Learners | Standards Proficiency |

1. Review with students the key terms from this section: democracy, aristocrats, oligarchy, citizens, and tyrant.

2. Draw a tic-tac-toe diagram (nine-square grid) for students to see. Divide the students into two groups: X's and O's.

3. Determine which group will go first. Then select one student in that group to answer a question. Given one of the vocabulary words, students are to define the term and use it in a sentence. Upon answering correctly, that group puts their mark in the square of their choosing. The first group to get three in a row wins. **LS** **Interpersonal, Verbal/Linguistic**

Alternative Assessment Handbook, Rubric 11: Discussions

CRF: Vocabulary Builder Activity, Section 2

HSS 6.4.2; **HSS** Analysis Skills: CS 1

Lessons designed to support instructions for English-Language Learners can be found throughout the Teacher's Editions.

Structures Oral and written language structures present special challenges to ELLs. When teachers use research-based effective strategies to support oral and written language as well as published text structures, they can nudge their ELLs toward thinking, talking, reading, and writing like historians.

Academic Language Skills Students typically learn History–Social Science through the receptive modes of listening and reading. In contrast, they "show what they know" through the productive modes of class discussion, oral presentations and written products such as projects, reports, and expository/analytical essays. When the academic vocabulary of the content/concept to be studied is explicitly taught, ELLs can be more productive and therefore more successful at showing what they know.

Study Skills and Learning Strategies Chamot and O'Malley (1994) note that study skills, thinking skills, and social skills are also important aspects of the History–Social Science curriculum. ELLs may not have, as yet, developed the learning strategies essential to these three skill areas. Thus, teachers should help ELLs develop these skills so they can be better prepared to cope with the growing amount of new and abstract information found in grade-level History–Social Science classrooms, textbooks, and primary source documents.

Teachers who use research-based best practices in the areas of (1) conceptual understanding, (2) vocabulary, (3) language functions and discourse, (4) structures, (5) academic language skills, and (6) study skills and learning strategies will be better prepared to support growing numbers of ELLs in their History–Social Science classes, regardless of each student's proficiency level in English. Whether a teacher has regular History–Social Science classes or a sheltered section (also known in California as SDAIE, or Specially Designed Academic Instruction in English), the result will be ELLs who have greater access to the History–Social Science curriculum and who will experience greater success as learners moving into the mainstream.

Chamot, Anna Uhl and J. Michael O'Malley (1994). *The CALLA Handbook: Implementing the Cognitive Academic Language Learning Approach.* Reading, MA: Addison-Wesley Publishing Company.

The History-Social Science Framework for California Public Schools, Kindergarten through Grade Twelve (2000). Sacramento, CA: The California Department of Education.

ELL Instructional Support Services

- Use graphic organizers to teach abstract ideas.

- Teach specialized History–Social Science vocabulary and usage.

- Promote development of study skills, thinking skills, and social skills.

- Read aloud content-related materials to help students build background knowledge.

Professional Resources and Bibliography

Professional References

This section provides information about resources that can enrich your World History class. Included are addresses of guest speakers, museum visits, electronic field trips, nonprofit organizations, and many others. Since addresses change frequently, you may want to verify them before you send your requests. You may also want to refer to the HRW Web site at http://www.hrw.com for current information.

GUEST SPEAKERS

K-12 Outreach for International and Area Studies
University of California, Berkeley
2223 Fulton Street Room 338 #2324
Berkeley, CA 94720-2324
orias@berkeley.edu
510-643-0868

Outreach World: A Resource for Teaching Kids about the World
Jonathan Friedlander, project director
jfriedlander@international.ucla.edu
310.206.8631

National Council for History Education
Speakers' Bureau
26915 Westwood Rd., Suite B-2
Westlake, Ohio 44145

MUSEUM VISITS

American Association of Museums
1575 Eye Street NW, Suite 400
Washington, DC 20005

ELECTRONIC FIELD TRIPS

CESA 10 Cooperative Educational Service Agency 10
www.cesa10.k12.wi.us/dl/trips/index.htm

PBS
www.pbs.org/history/history_world.html

GOVERNMENT RESOURCES

U.S. Department of Education
400 Maryland Ave., SW
Washington, D.C. 20202-0498
800-USA-LEARN
www.ed.gov/teachers/landing.jhtml?src=fp

Smithsonian Institution
Smithsonian Information
P.O. Box 37012
SI Building, Room 153, MRC 010
Washington, DC 20013-7012
202-357-2700
www.si.edu/

NONPROFIT ORGANIZATIONS

The World History Association
Sakamaki Hall
A203, 2530 Dole St.
University of Hawai'i at Manoa
Honolulu Hawai'i 96822-2383
808-956-7688

National Middle School Association
4151 Executive Parkway, Suite 300
Westerville, OH 43081
1-800-528-6672
www.nmsa.org

National Council for the Social Studies
8555 Sixteenth Street
Silver Spring, MD 20910
301 588-1800
www.socialstudies.org

PERIODICALS

Calliope: World History for Young People
Cobblestone Publishing, Inc.
30 Grove St.
Peterborough, NH 03458

SUBSCRIPTION SERVICES

Magazines.com Inc.
P.O. Box 682108
Franklin, TX 37068
1-800-929-2691
www.magazines.com

MISCELLANEOUS

Educational Resources Information Center (ERIC)
2277 Research Blvd.
Rockville, MD 20852
800-538-3742

The International Initiatives Program
American Council on Education
One Dupont Circle NW, Washington, DC 20036
(202) 939-9313

K-12 WebSite for Busy Teachers
http://www.ceismc.gatech.edu/busyt/hers.shtml

A Bibliography for the Social Studies Teacher

This bibliography is a select compilation of resources available for professional enrichment.

SELECTED AND ANNOTATED LIST OF READINGS

Social Studies and Language Arts

Burke, Jim. *Writing Reminders: Tools, Tips, and Techniques*
Portsmouth, NH: Heinemann, 2003
Burke offers a collection of strategies for teaching writing, complete with the instructional tools for implementing the strategies.

Jago, Carol. *Cohesive Writing: Why Concept Is Not Enough*
Portsmouth, NH: Heinemann, 2002
This book provides a coherent roadmap for teaching students how to write in each of the writing types required for the STAR assessment: summary, narrative, response to literature, and persuasion.

Social Studies and Standard English Mastery

Adger, C., Christian, D., and Taylor, O., editors. *Making The Connection: Language and Academic Achievement among African American Students*
McHenry, IL: Center for Applied Linguistics, 1999
This collection of essays discusses the complex and often misunderstood issue of language variation in African American Standard English Learners (SELs). The chapters address five domains in which various dimensions of language use affect the education of African American SELs.

Gay, G., *Culturally Responsive Teaching, Theory, Research, and Practice.*
New York and London: Teachers College Press, 2000
This book discusses using culturally responsive teaching to improve the school performance of under-achieving students of color in all content areas.

Harris, J., A. Kamhi, & K. Pollock, Editors. *Literacy in African American Communities*
Mahwah, New Jersey: Lawrence Erlbaum Associates Inc., 2001
These essays acknowledge the importance of language variation as it relates to learning in African American students. It explores the unique sociocultural contexts of literacy development and reveals how social history and cultural values influence learning.

LeMoine, N. and Los Angeles Unified School District. *English for Your Success: A Language Development Program for African American Students.* Handbook of Successful Strategies for Educators.
New Jersey: The Peoples Publishing Group, 1999
English for Your Success provides lessons using proven strategies for facilitating language acquisition and learning in African American Standard English Learners.

Ornstein-Galicia, J. *Form and Function in Chicano English*
Malabar, FL: Krieger Publishing Co., 1988
This text address issues of language and learning in Mexican American Standard English Learners (SELs) who speak mainly Chicano English.

Social Studies and English Learners

Billmeyer, Rachel and Mary Lee Barton. *Teaching Reading in the Content Areas: If Not Me, Then Who?* Second Edition
Aurora, CO: Mid-Continent Regional Educational Laboratory (McREL), 1998
Included are 40 strategies that help students of all ages expand their vocabularies, understand different types of texts, and discuss what they have read.

Buehl, Doug. *Classroom Strategies for Interactive Learning, Second Edition.*
Newark, DE: International Reading Association, 2001
More than 40 literacy skill-building strategies for middle school and high school educators outside the reading field.

Readance, John, Thomas W. Bean and R. Scott Baldwin. *Content Area Literacy: An Integrated Approach. Eighth Edition*
Dubuque, IA: Kendall/Hunt Publishing Company, 2000
The authors provide strategies for helping students read, understand, and enjoy nonfiction. A CD accompanies this widely used text.

Mapping the Earth

A **globe** is a scale model of the earth. It is useful for showing the entire earth or studying large areas of the earth's surface.

A pattern of lines circles the globe in east-west and north-south directions. It is called a **grid**. The intersection of these imaginary lines helps us find places on the earth.

The east-west lines in the grid are lines of **latitude**. Lines of latitude are called **parallels** because they are always parallel to each other. These imaginary lines measure distance north and south of the **equator**. The equator is an imaginary line that circles the globe halfway between the North and South Poles. Parallels measure distance from the equator in **degrees**. The symbol for degrees is °. Degrees are further divided into **minutes**. The symbol for minutes is ´. There are 60 minutes in a degree. Parallels north of the equator are labeled with an N. Those south of the equator are labeled with an S.

The north-south lines are lines of **longitude**. Lines of longitude are called **meridians**. These imaginary lines pass through the Poles. They measure distance east and west of the **prime meridian**. The prime meridian is an imaginary line that runs through Greenwich, England. It represents 0° longitude.

Lines of latitude range from 0°, for locations on the equator, to 90°N or 90°S, for locations at the Poles. Lines of longitude range from 0° on the prime meridian to 180° on a meridian in the mid-Pacific Ocean. Meridians west of the prime meridian to 180° are labeled with a W. Those east of the prime meridian to 180° are labeled with an E.

Lines of Latitude

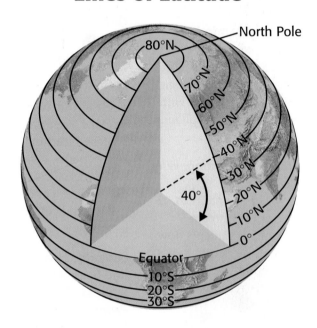

Lines of Longitude

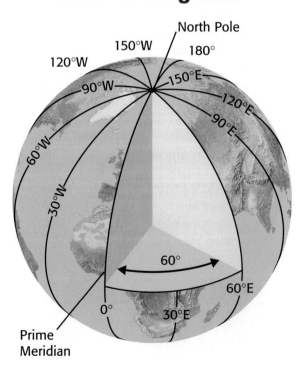

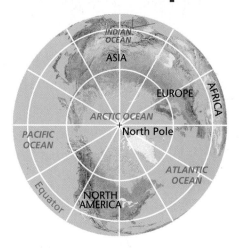

Northern Hemisphere

The equator divides the globe into two halves, called **hemispheres**. The half north of the equator is the Northern Hemisphere. The southern half is the Southern Hemisphere. The prime meridian and the 180° meridian divide the world into the Eastern Hemisphere and the Western Hemisphere. However, the prime meridian runs right through Europe and Africa. To avoid dividing these continents between two hemispheres, some mapmakers divide the Eastern and Western hemispheres at 20°W. This places all of Europe and Africa in the Eastern Hemisphere.

Our planet's land surface is divided into seven large landmasses, called **continents**. They are identified in the maps on this page. Landmasses smaller than continents and completely surrounded by water are called **islands**.

Geographers also organize Earth's water surface into parts. The largest is the world ocean. Geographers divide the world ocean into the Pacific Ocean, the Atlantic Ocean, the Indian Ocean, and the Arctic Ocean. Lakes and seas are smaller bodies of water.

Southern Hemisphere

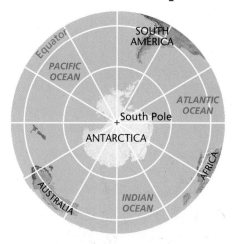

Western Hemisphere

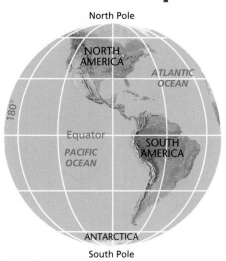

Eastern Hemisphere

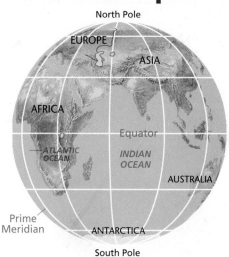

Mapmaking

A **map** is a flat diagram of all or part of the earth's surface. Mapmakers have created different ways of showing our round planet on flat maps. These different ways are called **map projections**. Because the earth is round, there is no way to show it accurately in a flat map. All flat maps are distorted in some way. Mapmakers must choose the type of map projection that is best for their purposes. Many map projections are one of three kinds: cylindrical, conic, or flat-plane.

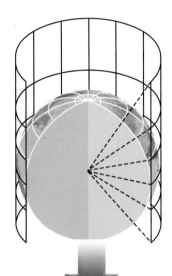

Paper cylinder

Cylindrical Projections

Cylindrical projections are based on a cylinder wrapped around the globe. The cylinder touches the globe only at the equator. The meridians are pulled apart and are parallel to each other instead of meeting at the Poles. This causes landmasses near the Poles to appear larger than they really are. The map below is a Mercator projection, one type of cylindrical projection. The Mercator projection is useful for navigators because it shows true direction and shape. However, it distorts the size of land areas near the Poles.

Mercator projection

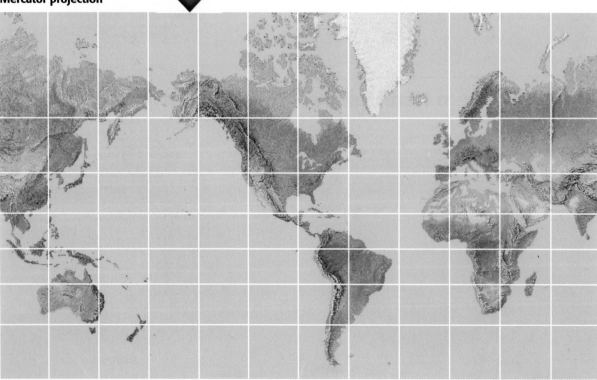

Conic Projections

Conic projections are based on a cone placed over the globe. A conic projection is most accurate along the lines of latitude where it touches the globe. It retains almost true shape and size. Conic projections are most useful for showing areas that have long east-west dimensions, such as the United States.

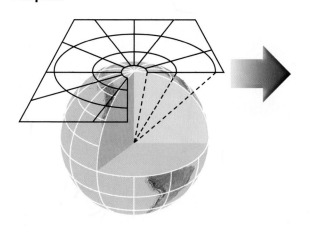

Paper cone

Conic projection

Flat-plane Projections

Flat-plane projections are based on a plane touching the globe at one point, such as at the North Pole or South Pole. A flat-plane projection is useful for showing true direction for airplane pilots and ship navigators. It also shows true area. However, it distorts the true shapes of landmasses.

Flat plane

Flat-plane projection

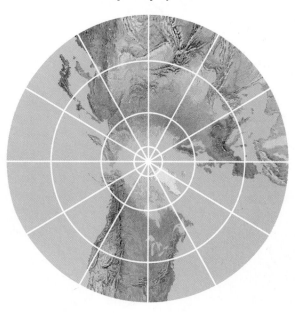

Map Essentials

Maps are like messages sent out in code. Mapmakers provide certain elements that help us translate these codes. These elements help us understand the message they are presenting about a particular part of the world. Of these elements, almost all maps have titles, directional indicators, scales, and legends. The map below has all four of these elements, plus a fifth—a locator map.

❶ Title

A map's **title** shows what the subject of the map is. The map title is usually the first thing you should look at when studying a map, because it tells you what the map is trying to show.

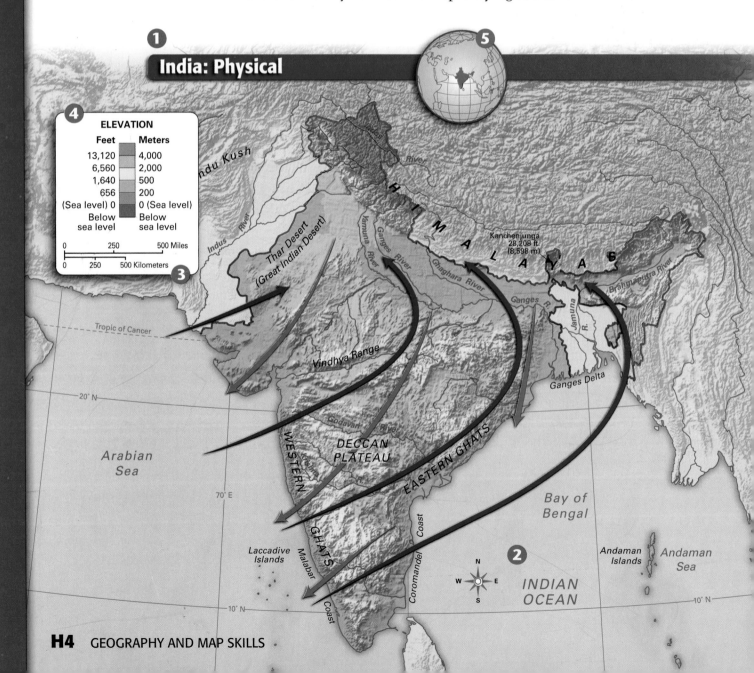

India: Physical

ELEVATION

Feet		Meters
13,120		4,000
6,560		2,000
1,640		500
656		200
(Sea level) 0		0 (Sea level)
Below sea level		Below sea level

0   250   500 Miles

0   250   500 Kilometers

Hindu Kush

Indus River

Thar Desert (Great Indian Desert)

Yamuna River

Ganges River

Ghaghara River

Kanchenjunga 28,208 ft. (8,598 m)

HIMALAYAS

Ganges R.

Jamuna R.

Brahmaputra River

Tropic of Cancer

Vindhya Range

Godavari River

DECCAN PLATEAU

WESTERN GHATS

EASTERN GHATS

Ganges Delta

20° N

Arabian Sea

70° E

Laccadive Islands

Malabar Coast

Coromandel Coast

Bay of Bengal

Andaman Islands

Andaman Sea

N W E S

INDIAN OCEAN

10° N

10° N

❷ Compass Rose

A directional indicator shows which way north, south, east, and west lie on the map. Some mapmakers use a "north arrow," which points toward the North Pole. Remember, "north" is not always at the top of a map. The way a map is drawn and the location of directions on that map depend on the perspective of the mapmaker. Most maps in this textbook indicate direction by using a compass rose. A **compass rose** has arrows that point to all four principal directions, as shown.

❸ Scale

Mapmakers use scales to represent the distances between points on a map. Scales may appear on maps in several different forms. The maps in this textbook provide a bar **scale**. Scales give distances in miles and kilometers.

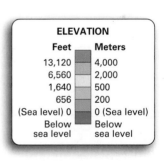

To find the distance between two points on the map, place a piece of paper so that the edge connects the two points. Mark the location of each point on the paper with a line or dot. Then, compare the distance between the two dots with the map's bar scale. The number on the top of the scale gives the distance in miles. The number on the bottom gives the distance in kilometers. Because the distances are given in large intervals, you may have to approximate the actual distance on the scale.

❹ Legend

The **legend**, or key, explains what the symbols on the map represent. Point symbols are used to specify the location of things, such as cities, that do not take up much space on the map. Some legends, such as the one shown here, show colors that represent certain elevations. Other maps might have legends with symbols or colors that represent things such as roads. Legends can also show economic resources, land use, population density, and climate.

❺ Locator Map

A locator map shows where in the world the area on the map is located. The area shown on the main map is shown in red on the locator map. The locator map also shows surrounding areas so the map reader can see how the information on the map relates to neighboring lands.

Working with Maps

The Atlas at the back of this textbook includes both physical and political maps. Physical maps, like the one you just saw, show the major physical features in a region. These features include things like mountain ranges, rivers, oceans, islands, deserts, and plains. Political maps show the major political features of a region, such as countries and their borders, capitals, and other important cities.

Historical Map

In this textbook, most of the maps you will study are historical maps. Historical maps, such as this one, are maps that show information about the past. This information might be which lands an empire controlled, where a certain group of people lived, what large cities were located in a region, or how a place changed over time. Often colors are used to indicate the different things on the map. Be sure to look at the map title and map legend first to see what the map is showing. What does this map show?

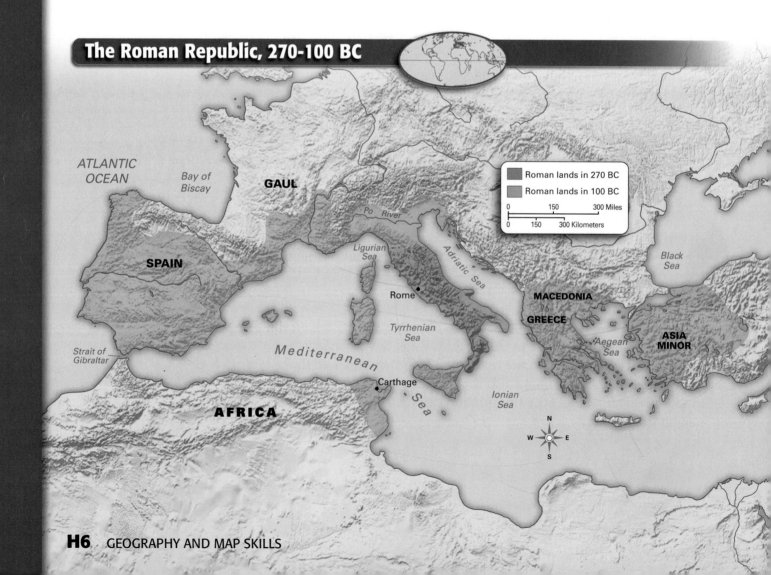

The Roman Republic, 270-100 BC

Roman lands in 270 BC
Roman lands in 100 BC

0   150   300 Miles
0   150   300 Kilometers

ATLANTIC OCEAN
Bay of Biscay
GAUL
Po River
SPAIN
Ligurian Sea
Adriatic Sea
Black Sea
Rome
MACEDONIA
GREECE
Tyrrhenian Sea
ASIA MINOR
Aegean Sea
Strait of Gibraltar
Mediterranean Sea
Carthage
Ionian Sea
AFRICA

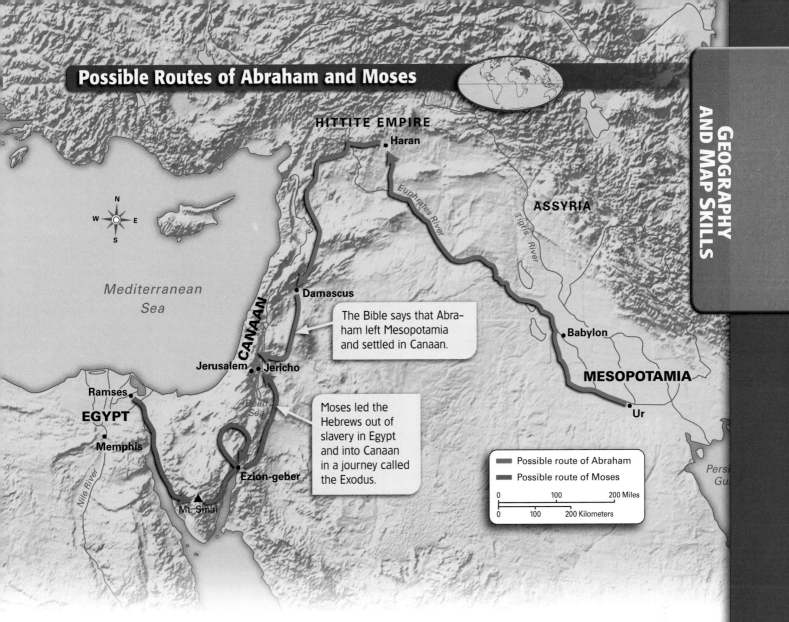

Possible Routes of Abraham and Moses

HITTITE EMPIRE

Haran

Euphrates River

ASSYRIA

Tigris River

Mediterranean Sea

CANAAN

Damascus

The Bible says that Abraham left Mesopotamia and settled in Canaan.

Babylon

MESOPOTAMIA

Jerusalem • Jericho

Dead Sea

Ramses

EGYPT

Moses led the Hebrews out of slavery in Egypt and into Canaan in a journey called the Exodus.

Ur

Memphis

Nile River

Ezion-geber

Mt. Sinai

Pers Gu

Possible route of Abraham

Possible route of Moses

| 0 | 100 | 200 Miles |

| 0 | 100 | 200 Kilometers |

Route Map

One special type of historical map is called a route map. A route map, like the one above, shows the route, or path, that someone or something followed. Route maps can show things like trade routes, invasion routes, or the journeys and travels of people. The routes on the map are usually shown with an arrow. If more than one route is shown, several arrows of different colors may be used. What does this route map show?

The maps in this textbook will help you study and understand history. By working with these maps, you will see where important events happened, where empires rose and fell, and where people moved. In studying these maps, you will learn how geography has influenced history.

Geographic Dictionary

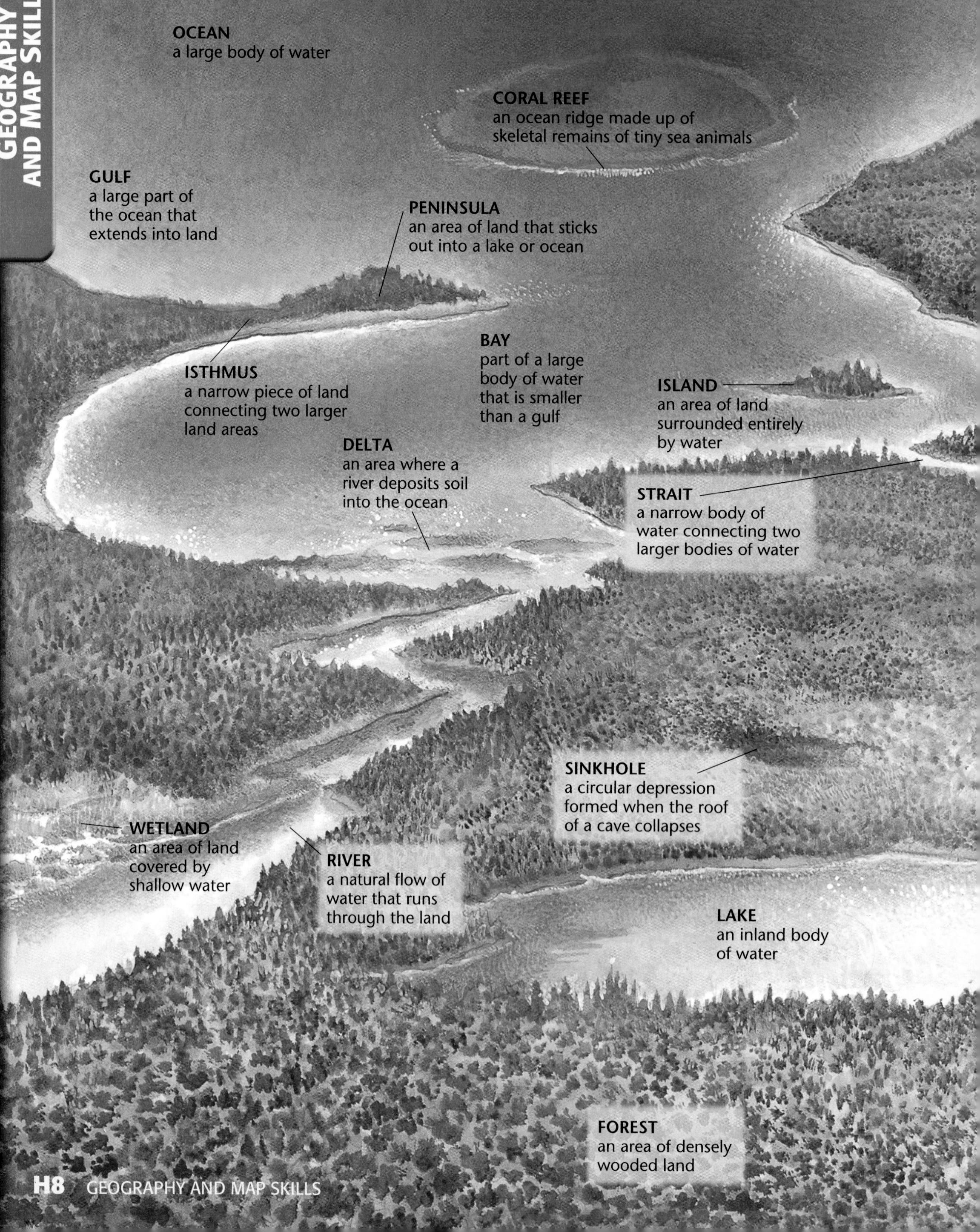

OCEAN
a large body of water

CORAL REEF
an ocean ridge made up of
skeletal remains of tiny sea animals

GULF
a large part of
the ocean that
extends into land

PENINSULA
an area of land that sticks
out into a lake or ocean

ISTHMUS
a narrow piece of land
connecting two larger
land areas

BAY
part of a large
body of water
that is smaller
than a gulf

ISLAND
an area of land
surrounded entirely
by water

DELTA
an area where a
river deposits soil
into the ocean

STRAIT
a narrow body of
water connecting two
larger bodies of water

SINKHOLE
a circular depression
formed when the roof
of a cave collapses

WETLAND
an area of land
covered by
shallow water

RIVER
a natural flow of
water that runs
through the land

LAKE
an inland body
of water

FOREST
an area of densely
wooded land

COAST
an area of land
near the ocean

MOUNTAIN
an area of rugged
land that generally
rises higher than
2,000 feet

VALLEY
an area of low
land between
hills or mountains

GLACIER
a large area of
slow-moving ice

VOLCANO
an opening in Earth's crust
where lava, ash, and gases erupt

CANYON
a deep, narrow valley
with steep walls

HILL
a rounded, elevated
area of land smaller
than a mountain

PLAIN
a nearly
flat area

DUNE
a hill of sand
shaped by wind

OASIS
an area in the
desert with a
water source

DESERT
an extremely dry area with
little water and few plants

PLATEAU
a large, flat,
elevated
area of land

The Five Themes of Geography

Geography is the study of the world's people and places. As you can imagine, studying the entire world is a big job. To make the job easier, geographers have created the Five Themes of Geography. They are: **Location, Place, Human-Environment Interaction, Movement,** and **Region**. You can think of the Five Themes as five windows you can look through to study a place. If you looked at the same place through five different windows, you would have five different perspectives, or viewpoints, of the place. Using the Five Themes in this way will help you better understand the world's people and places.

1 Location The first thing to study about a place is its location. Where is it? Every place has an absolute location—its exact location on Earth. A place also has a relative location—its location in relation to other places. Use the theme of location to ask questions like, "Where is this place located, and how has its location affected it?"

2 Place Every place in the world is unique and has its own personality and character. Some things that can make a place unique include its weather, plants and animals, history, and the people that live there. Use the theme of place to ask questions like, "What are the unique features of this place, and how are they important?"

3 Human-Environment Interaction People interact with their environment in many ways. They use land to grow food and local materials to build houses. At the same time, a place's environment influences how people live. For example, if the weather is cold, people wear warm clothes. Use the theme of human-environment interaction to ask questions like, "What is this place's environment like, and how does it affect the people who live there?"

4 Movement The world is constantly changing, and places are affected by the movement of people, goods, ideas, and physical forces. For example, people come and go, new businesses begin, and rivers change their course. Use the theme of movement to ask questions like, "How is this place changing, and why?"

5 Region A region is an area that has one or more features that make it different from surrounding areas. A desert, a country, and a coastal area are all regions. Geographers use regions to break the world into smaller pieces that are easier to study. Use the theme of region to ask questions like "What common features does this area share, and how is it different from other areas?"

Canada

1

LOCATION
Most of the United States is located in the Western Hemisphere, north of Mexico and south of Canada. This location has good farmland, many resources, and many different natural environments.

4

5

2

United States

3

1

Mexico

2

PLACE
New York City is one of the most powerful cities in the world. The people of New York also make the city one of the most ethnically diverse places in the world.

3

HUMAN-ENVIRONMENT INTERACTION
People near Las Vegas, Nevada, transform the desert landscape by building new neighborhoods. Americans modify their environment in many other ways—by controlling rivers, building roads, and creating farmland.

5

REGION
The United States is a political region with one government. At the same time, smaller regions can be found inside the country, such as the Badlands in South Dakota.

4

MOVEMENT
People, goods, and ideas are constantly moving to and from places such as Seattle, Washington. As some places grow, others get smaller, but every place is always changing.

Become an Active Reader

by Dr. Kylene Beers

Did you ever think you would begin reading your social studies book by reading about reading? Actually, it makes better sense than you might think. You would probably make sure you learned some soccer skills and strategies before playing in a game. Similarly, you need to learn some reading skills and strategies before reading your social studies book. In other words, you need to make sure you know whatever you need to know in order to read this book successfully..

Tip #1
Use the Reading Social Studies Pages

Take advantage of the two pages on reading at the beginning of every chapter. Those pages introduce the chapter themes; explain a reading skill or strategy; and identify key terms, people, and academic vocabulary.

Themes

Why are themes important? They help our minds organize facts and information. For example, when we talk about baseball, we may talk about types of pitches. When we talk about movies, we may discuss animation.

Historians are no different. When they discuss history or social studies, they tend to think about some common themes: Economics, Geography, Religion, Politics, Society and Culture, and Science and Technology.

Reading Skill or Strategy

Good readers use a number of skills and strategies to make sure they understand what they are reading. These lessons will give you the tools you need to read and understand social studies.

Key Terms, People, and Academic Vocabulary

Before you read the chapter, review these words and think about them. Have you heard the word before? What do you already know about the people? Then watch for these words and their meanings as you read the chapter.

Tells which theme or themes are important in the chapter

Explains a skill or strategy good readers use

Gives you practice in the reading skill or strategy.

Identifies the important words in the chapter.

Read like a Skilled Reader

You will never get better at reading your social studies book—or any book for that matter—unless you spend some time thinking about how to be a better reader.

Skilled readers do the following:

- They preview what they are supposed to read before they actually begin reading. They look for vocabulary words, titles of sections, information in the margin, or maps or charts they should study.

- They divide their notebook paper into two columns. They title one column "Notes from the Chapter" and the other column "Questions or Comments I Have."

- They take notes in both columns as they read.

- They read like **active readers**. The Active Reading list below shows you what that means.

- They use clues in the text to help them figure out where the text is going. The best clues are called signal words.

    Chronological Order Signal Words: *first, second, third, before, after, later, next, following that, earlier, finally*

    Cause and Effect Signal Words: *because of, due to, as a result of, the reason for, therefore, consequently*

    Comparison/Contrast Signal Words: *likewise, also, as well as, similarly, on the other hand*

Active Reading

Successful readers are **active readers**. These readers know that it is up to them to figure out what the text means. Here are some steps you can take to become an active, and successful, reader.

Predict what will happen next based on what has already happened. When your predictions don't match what happens in the text, re-read the confusing parts.

Question what is happening as you read. Constantly ask yourself why things have happened, what things mean, and what caused certain events.

Summarize what you are reading frequently. Do not try to summarize the entire chapter! Read a bit and then summarize it. Then read on.

Connect what is happening in the part you're reading to what you have already read.

Clarify your understanding. Stop occasionally to ask yourself whether you are confused by anything. You may need to re-read to clarify, or you may need to read further and collect more information before you can understand.

Visualize what is happening in the text. Try to see the events or places in your mind by drawing maps, making charts, or jotting down notes about what you are reading.

Tip #3
Pay Attention to Vocabulary

It is no fun to read something when you don't know what the words mean, but you can't learn new words if you only use or read the words you already know. In this book, we know we have probably used some words you don't know. But, we have followed a pattern as we have used more difficult words.

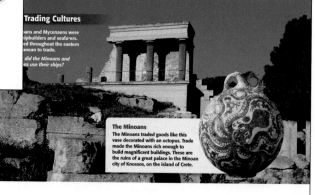

Early Spread of Buddhism

CENTRAL ASIA

PERSIA

CHINA

TIBET

NEPAL

Sarnath

Sanchi • Bodh Gaya

INDIAN OCEAN

INDIA

Bay of Bengal

South China Sea

SOUTHEAST ASIA

Borneo

CEYLON (SRI LANKA)

Sumatra

Early Buddhist area

Spread of Buddhism

0   250   500 Miles
0   250   500 Kilometers

GEOGRAPHY SKILLS | INTERPRETING MAPS

Movement Buddhism spread to what island south of India?

Buddhism Spreads

Buddhism continued to attract followers after the Buddha's death. After spreading through India, the religion began to spread to other areas as well.

Buddhism Spreads in India

According to Buddhist tradition, 500 of the Buddha's followers gathered together shortly after he died. They wanted to make sure that the Buddha's teachings were remembered correctly.

In the years after this council, the Buddha's followers spread his teachings throughout India. The ideas spread very quickly, because Buddhist teachings were popular and easy to understand. Within 200 years of the Buddha's death, his teachings had spread through most of India.

Buddhism Spreads Beyond India

The spread of Buddhism increased after one of the most powerful kings in India, Asoka, became Buddhist in the 200s BC. Once he converted, he built Buddhist temples and schools throughout India. More importantly, though, he worked to spread Buddhism into areas outside of India. You will learn more about Asoka and his accomplishments in the next section.

Asoka sent Buddhist **missionaries**, or people who work to spread their religious beliefs, to other kingdoms in Asia. One group of these missionaries sailed to the island of Sri Lanka around 251 BC. Others followed trade routes east to what is now Myanmar and to other parts of Southeast Asia. Missionaries also went north to areas near the Himalayas.

160 CHAPTER 6

Key Terms and People

At the beginning of each section you will find a list of key terms or people that you will need to know. Be on the lookout for those words as you read through the section.

Asoka sent Buddhist **missionaries**, or people who work to spread their religious beliefs, to other kingdoms in Asia. One ... of these missionaries sailed to the ...

ACADEMIC VOCABULARY

influence
change, or have an effect on

Academic Vocabulary

When we use a word that is important in all classes, not just social studies, we define it in the margin under the heading Academic Vocabulary. You will run into these academic words in other textbooks, so you should learn what they mean while reading this book.

Trading Cultures

...ans and Mycenaens were ...ipbuilders and seafarers. ...ed throughout the eastern ...anean to trade.

...did the Minoans and ...ns use their ships?

The Minoans
The Minoans traded goods like this vase decorated with an octopus. Trade made the Minoans rich enough to build magnificent buildings. These are the ruins of a great palace in the Minoan city of Knossos, on the island of Crete.

It's not surprising that the early Greeks used the sea as a source for food and as a way of trading with other communities.

The Greeks became skilled shipbuilders and sailors. Their ships sailed to Asia Minor, to Egypt, and to the islands of the Mediterranean and Aegean seas. As they traveled around these seas, they found sources of food and other products they needed. They also exchanged ideas with other cultures.

ACADEMIC VOCABULARY
influence
change, or have an effect on

READING CHECK Drawing Conclusions
How did mountains affect the location of Greek settlements?

Trading Cultures Develop

Many cultures settled and developed in Greece. Two of the earliest were the Minoans (muh-NOH-uhnz) and the Mycenaens (my-suh-NEE-uhns). By 2000 BC the

Minoans had built an advanced society on the island of Crete. Crete lay south of the Aegean in the eastern Mediterranean. Later, the Mycenaeans built towns on the Greek mainland. These two civilizations **influenced** the entire Aegean region and helped shape later cultures in Greece.

The Minoans

Because they lived on an island, the Minoans spent much of their time at sea. They were among the best shipbuilders of their time. Minoan ships carried goods such as wood, olive oil, and pottery all around the eastern Mediterranean. They traded these goods for copper, gold, silver, and jewels.

Although Crete's location was excellent for Minoan traders, its geography had its dangers. Sometime in the 1600s BC a huge volcano erupted just north of Crete. This eruption created a giant wave that flooded much of Crete. In addition, the eruption

256 CHAPTER 9

Social Studies Vocabulary

We know that some words are special to this particular topic of social studies, world history. As you read this book, you will be more successful if you know the meaning of the words in the following list.

Social Studies Words to Know

Time

AD	refers to dates after Jesus's birth
BC	refers to dates before the birth of Jesus of Nazareth
BCE	refers to "Before Common Era," dates before the birth of Jesus of Nazareth
CE	refers to "Common Era," dates after Jesus's birth
century	a period of 100 years
decade	a period of 10 years
era	a period of time

The Earth and Its Resources

climate	the weather conditions in a certain area over a long period of time
geography	the study of the earth's physical and cultural features
landforms	the natural features of the land's surface
physical features	the features on the land's surface, such as mountains and rivers
region	an area with one or more features that make it different from surrounding areas
resources	materials found on the earth that people need and value

People and the Way They Live

civilization	the culture of a particular time or place
culture	the knowledge, beliefs, customs, and values of a group of people
custom	a repeated practice; tradition
economy	the system in which people make and exchange goods and services
politics	government
ritual	the regular form for a ceremony or observance
scholar	a person who has completed advanced study
society	a group of people who share common traditions
trade	the exchange of goods or services

Academic Words

If only ...

If only reading in school were like reading a letter from your best friend.

If only reading in History were like reading *Harry Potter.*

It can be . . .if you learn the language!

There is a reason that you might feel uncomfortable with reading academic textbooks. Common words in these books account for less than 2% of the words in your favorite novels. No wonder reading in school seems so different from reading for fun!

Academic vocabulary refers to words that are used in most of your school subjects. The Holt Social Studies program has identified Academic Words that will be highlighted throughout this textbook. The Holt program provides structured practice to help support and improve your knowledge of this specialized vocabulary.

Grade 6 Academic Words

acquire	to get
agreement	a decision reached by two or more people or groups
aspects	parts
authority	power, right to rule
cause	the reason something happens
classical	referring to the cultures of ancient Greece or Rome
contract	a binding legal agreement
development	creation
distribute	to divide among a group of people
effect	the results of an action or decision
establish	to set up or create
ideal	ideas or goals that people try to live up to
impact	effect, result
method	a way of doing something
neutral	unbiased, not favoring either side in a conflict
primary	main, most important
principle	basic belief, rule, or law
process	a series of steps by which a task is accomplished
purpose	the reason something is done
rebel	to fight against authority
role	a part or function
strategy	a plan for fighting a battle or war
vary	to be different

Grade 7 Academic Words

affect	to change or influence
aspects	parts
authority	power, right to rule
classical	referring to the cultures of ancient Greece or Rome
development	the process of growing or improving
efficient/ efficiency	productive and not wasteful
element	part
establish	to set up or create
features	characteristics
impact	effect, result
influence	change, or have an effect on
innovation	a new idea or way of doing something
logical	reasoned, well thought out
policy	rule, course of action
principle	basic belief, rule, or law
procedure	a series of steps taken to accomplish a task
process	a series of steps by which a task is accomplished
rebel	to fight against authority
role	assigned behavior
strategy	a plan for fighting a battle or war
structure	the way something is set up or organized
traditional	customary, time-honored
values	ideas that people hold dear and try to live by
various	of many types

abstract	expressing a quality or idea without reference to an actual thing
acquire	to get
advocate	to plead in favor of
agreement	a decision reached by two or more people or groups
aspects	parts
authority	power, right to rule
circumstances	surrounding situation
complex	difficult, not simple
concrete	specific, real
consequences	the effects of a particular event or events
contemporary	existing at the same time
criteria	rules for defining
develop/ development	the process of growing or improving
distinct	separate
efficient/ efficiency	productive and not wasteful
element	part
establish	to set up or create
execute	to perform, carry out
explicit	fully revealed without vagueness
facilitate	to bring about
factor	cause
function	use or purpose
implement	to put in place
implications	effects of a decision
implicit	understood though not clearly put into words
incentive	something that leads people to follow a certain course of action
influence	change, or have an effect on
innovation	a new idea or way of doing something
method	a way of doing something
motive	a reason for doing something
neutral	unbiased, not favoring either side in a conflict
policy	rule, course of action
primary	main, most important
principle	basic belief, rule, or law
procedure	a series of steps taken to accomplish a task
process	a series of steps by which a task is accomplished
reaction	a response
role	assigned behavior
strategy	a plan for fighting a battle or war
vary/various	of many types

ACADEMIC WORDS

History–Social Science Content Standards

Students in grade six expand their understanding of history by studying the people and events that ushered in the dawn of the major Western and non-Western ancient civilizations. Geography is of special significance in the development of the human story. Continued emphasis is placed on the everyday lives, problems, and accomplishments of people, their role in developing social, economic, and political structures, as well as in establishing and spreading ideas that helped transform the world forever. Students develop higher levels of critical thinking by considering why civilizations developed where and when they did, why they became dominant, and why they declined. Students analyze the interactions among the various cultures, emphasizing their enduring contributions and the link, despite time, between the contemporary and ancient worlds.

6.1 Students describe what is known through archaeological studies of the early physical and cultural development of humankind from the Paleolithic era to the agricultural revolution.

1. Describe the hunter-gatherer societies, including the development of tools and the use of fire.

2. Identify the locations of human communities that populated the major regions of the world and describe how humans adapted to a variety of environments.

3. Discuss the climatic changes and human modifications of the physical environment that gave rise to the domestication of plants and animals and new sources of clothing and shelter.

6.2 Students analyze the geographic, political, economic, religious, and social structures of the early civilizations of Mesopotamia, Egypt, and Kush.

1. Locate and describe the major river systems and discuss the physical settings that supported permanent settlement and early civilizations.

2. Trace the development of agricultural techniques that permitted the production of economic surplus and the emergence of cities as centers of culture and power.

3. Understand the relationship between religion and the social and political order in Mesopotamia and Egypt.

4. Know the significance of Hammurabi's Code.

5. Discuss the main features of Egyptian art and architecture.

6. Describe the role of Egyptian trade in the eastern Mediterranean and Nile valley.

7. Understand the significance of Queen Hatshepsut and Ramses the Great.

8. Identify the location of the Kush civilization and describe its political, commercial, and cultural relations with Egypt.

9. Trace the evolution of language and its written forms.

6.3 Students analyze the geographic, political, economic, religious, and social structures of the Ancient Hebrews.

1. Describe the origins and significance of Judaism as the first monotheistic religion based on the concept of one God who sets down moral laws for humanity.

2. Identify the sources of the ethical teachings and central beliefs of Judaism (the Hebrew Bible, the Commentaries): belief in God, observance of law, practice of the concepts of righteousness and justice, and importance of study; and describe how the ideas of the Hebrew traditions are reflected in the moral and ethical traditions of Western civilization.

3. Explain the significance of Abraham, Moses, Naomi, Ruth, David, and Yohanan ben Zaccai in the development of the Jewish religion.

4. Discuss the locations of the settlements and movements of Hebrew peoples, including the Exodus and their movement to and from Egypt, and outline the significance of the Exodus to the Jewish and other people.

5. Discuss how Judaism survived and developed despite the continuing dispersion of much of the Jewish population from Jerusalem and the rest of Israel after the destruction of the second Temple in AD 70.

6.4 Students analyze the geographic, political, economic, religious, and social structures of the early civilizations of Ancient Greece.

1. Discuss the connections between geography and the development of city-states in the region of the Aegean Sea, including patterns of trade and commerce among Greek city-states and within the wider Mediterranean region.

2. Trace the transition from tyranny and oligarchy to early democratic forms of government and back to dictatorship in ancient Greece, including the significance of the invention of the idea of citizenship (e.g., from *Pericles' Funeral Oration*).

3. State the key differences between Athenian, or direct, democracy and representative democracy.

4. Explain the significance of Greek mythology to the everyday life of people in the region and how Greek literature continues to permeate our literature and language today, drawing from Greek mythology and epics, such as Homer's *Iliad* and *Odyssey*, and from *Aesop's Fables*.

5. Outline the founding, expansion, and political organization of the Persian Empire.

6. Compare and contrast life in Athens and Sparta, with emphasis on their roles in the Persian and Peloponnesian Wars.

7. Trace the rise of Alexander the Great and the spread of Greek culture eastward and into Egypt.

8. Describe the enduring contributions of important Greek figures in the arts and sciences (e.g., Hypatia, Socrates, Plato, Aristotle, Euclid, Thucydides).

6.5 Students analyze the geographic, political, economic, religious, and social structures of the early civilizations of India.

1. Locate and describe the major river system and discuss the physical setting that supported the rise of this civilization.

2. Discuss the significance of the Aryan invasions.

3. Explain the major beliefs and practices of Brahmanism in India and how they evolved into early Hinduism.

4. Outline the social structure of the caste system.

5. Know the life and moral teachings of the Buddha and how Buddhism spread in India, Ceylon, and Central Asia.

6. Describe the growth of the Maurya empire and the political and moral achievements of the emperor Asoka.

7. Discuss important aesthetic and intellectual traditions (e.g., Sanskrit literature, including the *Bhagavad Gita*; medicine; metallurgy; and mathematics, including Hindu-Arabic numerals and the zero).

6.6 Students analyze the geographic, political, economic, religious, and social structures of the early civilizations of China.

1. Locate and describe the origins of Chinese civilization in the Huang-He Valley during the Shang Dynasty.

2. Explain the geographic features of China that made governance and the spread of ideas and goods difficult and served to isolate the country from the rest of the world.

3. Know about the life of Confucius and the fundamental teachings of Confucianism and Daoism.

4. Identify the political and cultural problems prevalent in the time of Confucius and how he sought to solve them.

5. List the policies and achievements of the emperor Shi Huangdi in unifying northern China under the Qin Dynasty.

6. Detail the political contributions of the Han Dynasty to the development of the imperial bureaucratic state and the expansion of the empire.

7. Cite the significance of the trans-Eurasian "silk roads" in the period of the Han Dynasty and Roman Empire and their locations.

8. Describe the diffusion of Buddhism northward to China during the Han Dynasty.

6.7 Students analyze the geographic, political, economic, religious, and social structures during the development of Rome.

1. Identify the location and describe the rise of the Roman Republic, including the importance of such mythical and historical figures as Aeneas, Romulus and Remus, Cincinnatus, Julius Caesar, and Cicero.

2. Describe the government of the Roman Republic and its significance (e.g., written constitution and tripartite government, checks and balances, civic duty).

3. Identify the location of and the political and geographic reasons for the growth of Roman territories and expansion of the empire, including how the empire fostered economic growth through the use of currency and trade routes.

4. Discuss the influence of Julius Caesar and Augustus in Rome's transition from republic to empire.

5. Trace the migration of Jews around the Mediterranean region and the effects of their conflict with the Romans, including the Romans' restrictions on their right to live in Jerusalem.

6. Note the origins of Christianity in the Jewish Messianic prophecies, the life and teachings of Jesus of Nazareth as described in the New Testament, and the contribution of St. Paul the Apostle to the definition and spread of Christian beliefs (e.g., belief in the Trinity, resurrection, salvation).

7. Describe the circumstances that led to the spread of Christianity in Europe and other Roman territories.

8. Discuss the legacies of Roman art and architecture, technology and science, literature, language, and law.

Historical and Social Sciences Analysis Skills

The intellectual skills noted below are to be learned through, and applied to, the content standards for grades six through eight. They are to be assessed *only in conjunction* with the content standards in grades six through eight.

In addition to the standards for grades six through eight, students demonstrate the following intellectual reasoning, reflection, and research skills:

Chronological and Spatial Thinking

1. Students explain how major events are related to one another in time.

2. Students construct various time lines of key events, people, and periods of the historical era they are studying.

3. Students use a variety of maps and documents to identify physical and cultural features of neighborhoods, cities, states, and countries and to explain the historical migration of people, expansion and disintegration of empires, and the growth of economic systems.

Research, Evidence, and Point of View

1. Students frame questions that can be answered by historical study and research.

2. Students distinguish fact from opinion in historical narratives and stories.

3. Students distinguish relevant from irrelevant information, essential from incidental information, and verifiable from unverifiable information in historical narratives and stories.

4. Students assess the credibility of primary and secondary sources and draw sound conclusions from them.

5. Students detect the different historical points of view on historical events and determine the context in which the historical statements were made (the questions asked, sources used, author's perspectives).

Historical Interpretation

1. Students explain the central issues and problems from the past, placing people and events in a matrix of time and place.

2. Students understand and distinguish cause, effect, sequence, and correlation in historical events, including the long- and short-term causal relations.

3. Students explain the sources of historical continuity and how the combination of ideas and events explains the emergence of new patterns.

4. Students recognize the role of chance, oversight, and error in history.

5. Students recognize that interpretations of history are subject to change as new information is uncovered.

6. Students interpret basic indicators of economic performance and conduct cost-benefit analyses of economic and political issues.

ANALYSIS SKILLS

How to Make This Book Work for You

Studying history will be easy for you using this textbook. Take a few minutes to become familiar with the easy-to-use structure and special features of this history book. See how this textbook will make history come alive for you!

Unit

Each chapter of this textbook is part of a Unit of study focusing on a particular time period. Each unit opener provides an illustration showing a young person of the period and gives you an overview of the exciting topics that you will study in the unit.

Chapter

Each Chapter includes a chapter-opener introduction where the California History-Social Science Standards and Analysis Skills are listed out, a Social Studies Skills activity, Standards Review pages, and a Standards Assessment page.

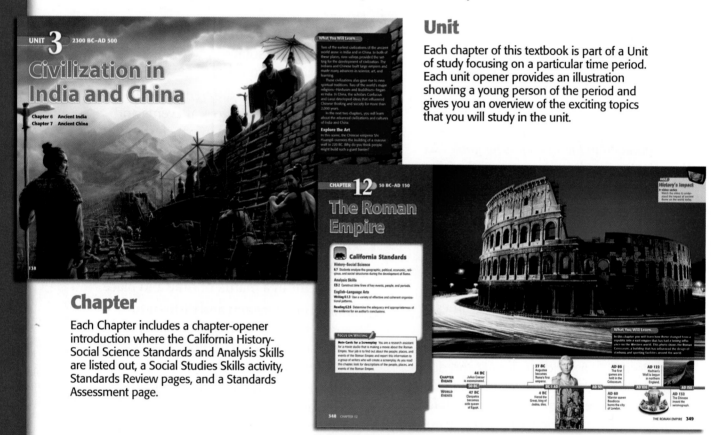

Reading Social Studies These chapter level reading lessons give you skills and practice that you can use to help you read the textbook. Within each chapter there is a Focus on Reading note in the margin on the page where the reading skill is covered. There are also questions in the Standards Review activity to make sure that you understand the reading skill.

Social Studies Skills The Social Studies Skills lessons give you an opportunity to learn and use a skill that you will most likely use again. You will also be given a chance to make sure that you understand each skill by answering related questions in the Standards Review activity.

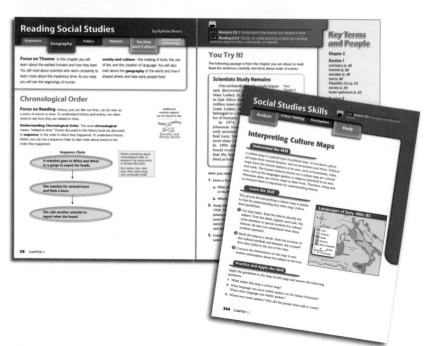

Section

The Section opener pages include Main Idea statements, an overarching big idea statement, and Key Terms and People. In addition, each section includes the following special features.

If You Were There . . . introductions begin each section with a situation for you to respond to, placing you in the time period and in a situation related to the content that you will be studying in the section.

Building Background sections connect what will be covered in this section with what you studied in the previous section.

Short sections of content organize the information in each section into small chunks of text that you shouldn't find too overwhelming.

The California History-Social Science Standards for 6th grade that are covered in each section are listed on the first page of each section of the textbook.

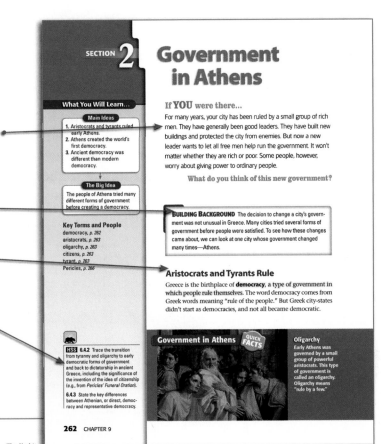

SECTION **2**

Government in Athens

What You Will Learn...

Main Ideas
1. Aristocrats and tyrants ruled early Athens.
2. Athens created the world's first democracy.
3. Ancient democracy was different than modern democracy.

The Big Idea
The people of Athens tried many different forms of government before creating a democracy.

Key Terms and People
democracy, p. 262
aristocrats, p. 263
oligarchy, p. 263
citizens, p. 263
tyrant, p. 263
Pericles, p. 266

HSS **6.4.2** Trace the transition from tyranny and oligarchy to early democratic forms of government and back to dictatorship in ancient Greece, including the significance of the invention of the idea of citizenship (e.g., from Pericles' Funeral Oration).

6.4.3 State the key differences between Athenian, or direct, democracy and representative democracy.

262 CHAPTER 9

If YOU were there...
For many years, your city has been ruled by a small group of rich men. They have generally been good leaders. They have built new buildings and protected the city from enemies. But now a new leader wants to let all free men help run the government. It won't matter whether they are rich or poor. Some people, however, worry about giving power to ordinary people.

What do you think of this new government?

BUILDING BACKGROUND The decision to change a city's government was not unusual in Greece. Many cities tried several forms of government before people were satisfied. To see how these changes came about, we can look at one city whose government changed many times—Athens.

Aristocrats and Tyrants Rule

Greece is the birthplace of **democracy**, a type of government in which people rule themselves. The word democracy comes from Greek words meaning "rule of the people." But Greek city-states didn't start as democracies, and not all became democratic.

Government in Athens QUICK FACTS

Oligarchy
Early Athens was governed by a small group of powerful aristocrats. This type of government is called an oligarchy. Oligarchy means "rule by a few."

When the Assyrians invaded Egypt with their iron weapons, they forced Kush's rulers out of Egypt and south into Nubia.

The Kushite Dynasty
After Piankhi died, his brother Shabaka (SHAB-uh-kuh) took control of the kingdom. Shabaka then declared himself pharaoh. This declaration began the Twenty-fifth, or Kushite, Dynasty in Egypt.

Shabaka and later rulers of his dynasty tried to restore old Egyptian cultural practices. Some of these practices had faded during Egypt's period of weakness. For example, Shabaka was buried in a pyramid. The Egyptians had stopped building pyramids for their rulers centuries before.

The Kushite rulers of Egypt built new temples to Egyptian gods and restored old ones. They also worked to preserve Egyptian writings. As a result, Egyptian culture thrived during the Kushite dynasty.

The End of Kushite Rule in Egypt
The Kushite dynasty remained strong in Egypt for about 40 years. In the 670s BC, however, the powerful army of the Assyrians from Mesopotamia invaded Egypt. The Assyrians' iron weapons were better than the Kushites' bronze weapons, and the Kushites were slowly pushed out of Egypt. In just 10 years the Assyrians had driven the Kushite forces completely out of Egypt.

READING CHECK Identifying Cause and Effect
How did internal problems in Egypt benefit Kush?

SUMMARY AND PREVIEW Kush was conquered by Egypt, but later the Kushites controlled Egypt. In the next section, you will learn how the civilization of Kush developed after the Kushites were forced out of Egypt by the Assyrians.

Reading Check questions end each section of content so that you can test whether or not you understand what you have just studied.

Summary and Preview To connect what you have just studied in the section to what you will study in the next section, we include the Summary and Preview.

Section Assessments The section assessment boxes provide an opportunity for you to make sure that you understand the main ideas of the section. We also provide assessment practice online!

Section 1 Assessment

go.hrw.com
Online Quiz
KEYWORD: SQ6 HP5

Reviewing Ideas, Terms, and People **HSS** 6.2.8
1. a. **Identify** On which river did Kush develop?
   b. **Analyze** How did Nubia's natural resources influence the early history of Kush?
2. a. **Describe** What is ebony?
   b. **Analyze** Why did people in Kush adopt some elements of Egyptian culture?
   c. **Evaluate** Why do you think Thutmose I destroyed the Kushite palace at Kerma?
3. a. **Describe** What territory did **Piankhi** conquer?
   b. **Make Inferences** Why is the Twenty-fifth Dynasty significant in the history of Egypt?
   c. **Predict** What might have happened in Kush and Egypt if Kush had developed iron weapons?

Critical Thinking
4. **Identifying Cause and Effect** Create a chart like the one here. For each cause listed, identify one effect.

Cause	Effect
Villages appear along the Nile.	
Kush trades with Egypt.	
Piankhi conquers Egypt.	
Assyrians use iron weapons.	

FOCUS ON WRITING
5. **Characters and Plot** Make a chart with two columns labeled "Characters" and "Plot." In one column, take notes on the main characters and their interactions. In the other column, note major events and sources of conflict between the characters.

126 CHAPTER 5

Places You Will Study

As you study world history, you will learn about many places around the world. You will discover the places where ancient civilizations began, how geography influenced early cultures, and how early cultures have helped shape the world today.

The maps that you see here show some of the main places you will study in this textbook. These are key places where ancient peoples created the first complex societies, cities, governments, and empires. You will learn much more about these places and the people who lived in them as you begin your study of ancient world history.

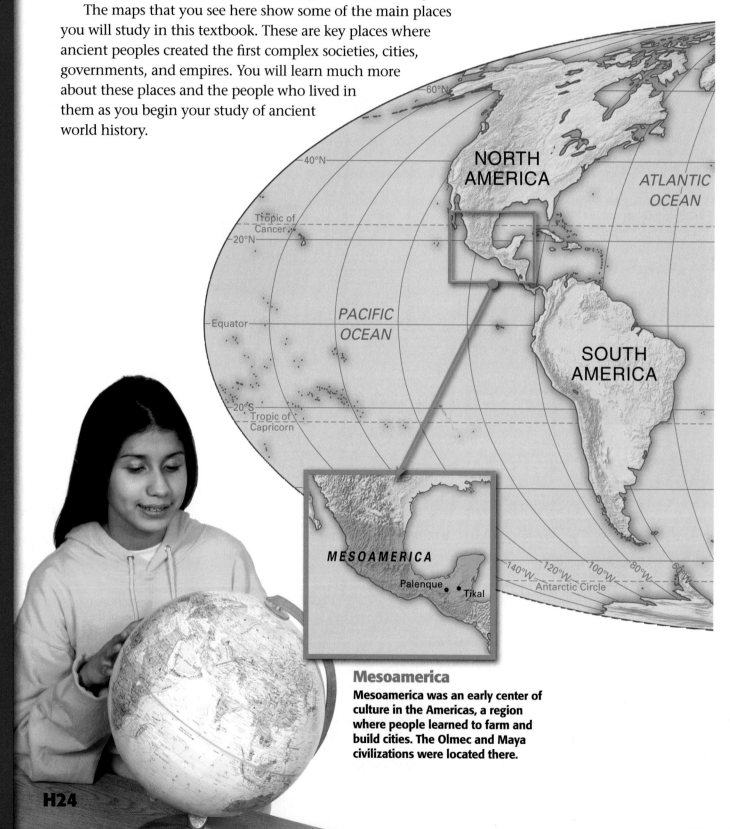

Mesoamerica

Mesoamerica was an early center of culture in the Americas, a region where people learned to farm and build cities. The Olmec and Maya civilizations were located there.

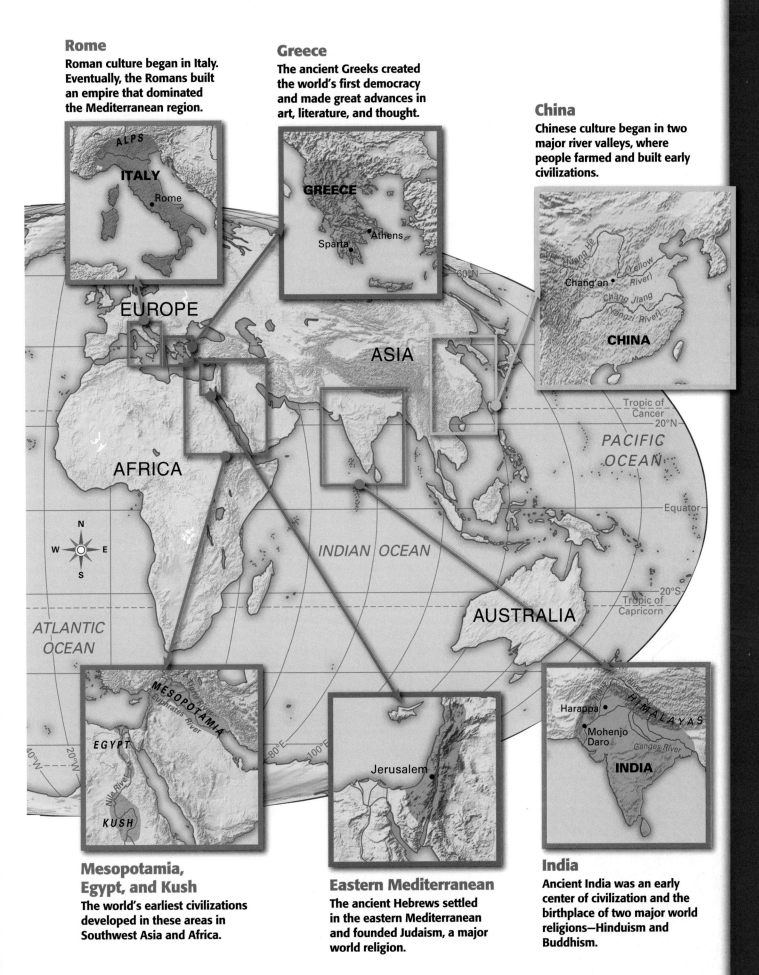

Rome

Roman culture began in Italy. Eventually, the Romans built an empire that dominated the Mediterranean region.

ALPS

ITALY

Rome

Greece

The ancient Greeks created the world's first democracy and made great advances in art, literature, and thought.

GREECE

Sparta

Athens

China

Chinese culture began in two major river valleys, where people farmed and built early civilizations.

Huang He

Yellow River

Chang'an

Chang Jiang

Yangzi River

CHINA

EUROPE

ASIA

60°N

Tropic of Cancer

20°N

PACIFIC OCEAN

AFRICA

N W E S

Equator

INDIAN OCEAN

20°S

Tropic of Capricorn

AUSTRALIA

ATLANTIC OCEAN

40°W

20°W

MESOPOTAMIA

Tigris River

Euphrates River

EGYPT

Nile River

KUSH

80°E

100°E

Jerusalem

HIMALAYAS

Indus River

Harappa

Mohenjo Daro

Ganges River

INDIA

Mesopotamia, Egypt, and Kush

The world's earliest civilizations developed in these areas in Southwest Asia and Africa.

Eastern Mediterranean

The ancient Hebrews settled in the eastern Mediterranean and founded Judaism, a major world religion.

India

Ancient India was an early center of civilization and the birthplace of two major world religions—Hinduism and Buddhism.

H25

Introduce the Unit

Share the information in the chapter overviews with students.

Chapter 1 The text begins by looking at why and how people study the past. Historians and archaeologists, people who study objects of the past, use many tools and methods to learn about history. Learning about geography, the study of the earth's physical and cultural features, contributes to the study of history. Studying geography provides additional clues about where people lived and what the area was like.

Chapter 2 Historians call the time before there was writing prehistory. Scholars study prehistoric peoples by examining the objects they left behind. Prehistoric people learned to make simple tools, to use fire, to use language, and to make art. Scholars believe the earliest people lived in what is now East Africa. Over time, people moved out of Africa as the earth's climates changed. As people moved, they learned to adapt to new environments. In time, people learned how to plant and grow food. The development of agriculture brought great changes to society and helped lead to the development of religion and to the growth of towns.

Standards Focus

For a list of the overarching standards covered in this unit, see the first page of each chapter.

UNIT 1 — BEGINNINGS TO 5,000 YEARS AGO

Early Humans and Societies

Chapter 1   Uncovering the Past
Chapter 2   The Stone Ages and Early Cultures

Unit Resources

Planning

- Universal Access Teacher Management System: Unit Instructional Benchmarking Guides
- One-Stop Planner CD-ROM with Test Generator: Holt Calendar Planner
- Power Presentations with Video CD-ROM
- A Teacher's Guide to Religion in the Public Schools

Standards Mastery

- Standards Review Workbook
- At Home: A Guide to Standards Mastery for World History

Differentiating Instruction

- Universal Access Teacher Management System: Lesson Plans for Universal Access
- Universal Access Modified Worksheets and Tests CD-ROM

Enrichment

- **CRF 1:** Interdisciplinary Project: Studying History: Searching for Roots
- **CRF 2:** Interdisciplinary Project: The First People; Flannel Board Story
- Civic Participation
- Primary Source Library CD-ROM

Assessment

- Progress Assessment Support System: Benchmark Test
- OSP ExamView Test Generator: Benchmark Test
- Holt Online Assessment Program (in the Premier Online Edition)
- Alternative Assessment Handbook

The **Universal Access Teacher Management System** provides a planning and instructional benchmarking guide for this unit.

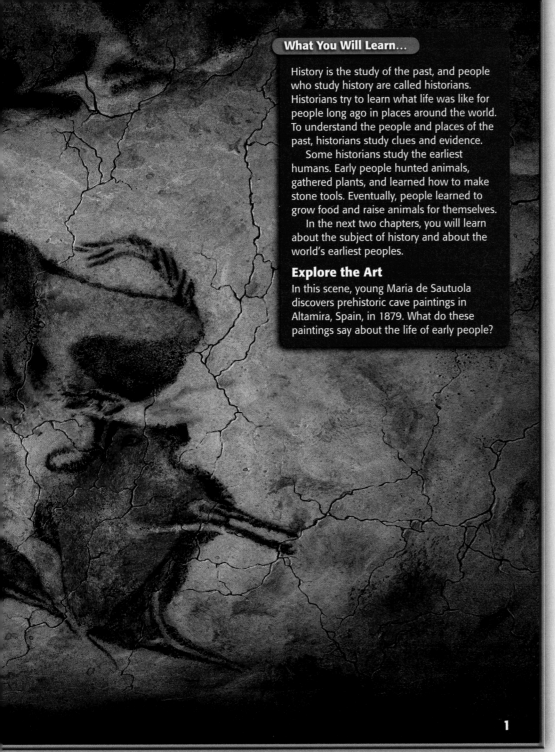

History is the study of the past, and people who study history are called historians. Historians try to learn what life was like for people long ago in places around the world. To understand the people and places of the past, historians study clues and evidence.

Some historians study the earliest humans. Early people hunted animals, gathered plants, and learned how to make stone tools. Eventually, people learned to grow food and raise animals for themselves.

In the next two chapters, you will learn about the subject of history and about the world's earliest peoples.

Explore the Art

In this scene, young Maria de Sautuola discovers prehistoric cave paintings in Altamira, Spain, in 1879. What do these paintings say about the life of early people?

1

Democracy and Civic Education

Standards Proficiency

Responsibility: Finding Information

Research Required

Background For a representative democracy to operate effectively, citizens need to be informed about political issues and history. Knowing where to find different types of information and how to conduct research is an essential skill—and a useful one in studying history.

1. Organize students into small groups. Assign each group a public issue and a historical topic. Contact the school librarian and set up a time to have students learn about library resources and other sources for finding information.

2. Have each group make a list of possible sources of information for each of the group's assigned topics. Have the groups share their findings with the class.

3. Then have the groups combine their findings to create an Information and Research Guide.
LS **Interpersonal, Verbal/Linguistic**

   Alternative Assessment Handbook, Rubrics 1: Acquiring Information; and 14: Group Activity

   Civic Participation

Unit Preview

Connect to the Unit

Activity **History in Popular Culture** Ask students to describe what they know about the Stone Age. Make a list of their answers, and have students explain where they learned the information. Discuss with students how popular depictions of the past often mix accurate and inaccurate information. Then lead a discussion about how historians and archaeologists learn about the past.

During the study of the unit, have students work as a class to create a large collage on butcher paper that shows depictions of prehistory in popular culture. Students might collect comic strips, pictures of famous characters, movie posters or ads, and images from TV shows or books. Use the mural to help students understand the difference between accurate sources of historical information and popular depictions of history. In addition, point out the popularity of history as entertainment.
LS **Interpersonal, Visual/Spatial**

Explore the Art

In 1879, Maria de Sautuola and her father, an amateur archaeologist, were exploring the cave pictured at left. While he looked for fossilized bones, Maria wandered into a side cavern. When she looked up she was amazed to see red, black, and violet paintings of bulls covering the ceiling. Today the images, which are actually bison, remain the earliest known examples of prehistoric cave paintings. The Altamira cave has been named a World Heritage Site.

About the Illustration

This illustration is an artist's conception based on available sources. However, historians are uncertain exactly what this scene looked like.

Answers

Explore the Art *that they had the skill to make tools for drawing, that they were interested in keeping records of animals for reasons we can only speculate about, that they used this cave perhaps as a dwelling or place for holding rituals*

Chapter 1 Planning Guide

Uncovering the Past

Chapter Overview	Reproducible Resources	Technology Resources
Chapter 1 **pp. 2–23** **Overview:** In this chapter, students are introduced to the work of historians and archaeologists. They will also learn about the importance of geography to the study of history.	**Universal Access Teacher Management System:*** • Universal Access Instructional Benchmarking Guides • Lesson Plans for Universal Access **Interactive Reader and Study Guide:** Chapter Graphic Organizer* **Chapter Resource File*** • Chapter Review Activity • Focus on Writing Activity: A Job Description • Social Studies Skills Activity: Recognizing Personal Conviction and Bias	**One-Stop Planner CD-ROM:** Calendar Planner **Student Edition Full-Read Audio CD-ROM** **Universal Access Modified Worksheets and Tests CD-ROM** **Interactive Skills Tutor CD-ROM** **Primary Source Library CD-ROM for World History** **Power Presentations with Video CD-ROM** **History's Impact: World History Video Program (VHS/DVD):** Uncovering the Past* **A Teacher's Guide To Religion in the Public Schools***
Section 1: **Studying History** **The Big Idea:** Historians use many kinds of clues to understand how people lived in the past.	**Universal Access Teacher Management System:*** Section 1 Lesson Plan **Interactive Reader and Study Guide:** Section 1 Summary* **Chapter Resource File*** • Vocabulary Builder Activity, Section 1 • Biography Activity: Howard Carter • Biography Activity: Jean-François Champollion • Interdisciplinary Project: Studying History: Searching for Roots • Literature Activity: "Who Cares About Great Uncle Edgar?" by Lila Perl • Primary Source Activity: *The Discovery of the Tomb of King Tutankhamen,* by Howard Carter • Primary Source Activity: Photographs from King Tutankhamen's Tomb	**Daily Bellringer Transparency:** Section 1* **Internet Activity:** Know Your Sources
Section 2: **Studying Geography** **The Big Idea:** Physical geography and human geography contribute to the study of history.	**Universal Access Teacher Management System:** Section 2 Lesson Plan* **Interactive Reader and Study Guide:** Section 2 Summary* **Chapter Resource File*** • Vocabulary Builder Activity, Section 2 • Economics and History Activity: Economics and History • History and Geography Activity: Human Communities	**Daily Bellringer Transparency:** Section 2* **Map Transparency:** Studying Maps*

Review, Assessment, Intervention

- **Standards Review Workbook***
- **Quick Facts Transparency:** Uncovering the Past Visual Summary*
- **Spanish Chapter Summaries Audio CD Program**
- **Online Chapter Summaries in Six Languages**
- **Quiz Game CD-ROM**
- **Progress Assessment Support System (PASS):** Chapter Test*
- **Universal Access Modified Worksheets and Tests CD-ROM:** Modified Chapter Test
- **One-Stop Planner CD-ROM:** ExamView Test Generator (English/Spanish)
- **Alternative Assessment Handbook**
- **Holt Online Assessment Program (HOAP),** in the Holt Premier Online Student Edition

- **PASS:** Section 1 Quiz*
- **Online Quiz:** Section 1
- **Alternative Assessment Handbook**

- **PASS:** Section 2 Quiz*
- **Online Quiz:** Section 2
- **Alternative Assessment Handbook**

California Resources for Standards Mastery

INSTRUCTIONAL PLANNING AND SUPPORT

- **Universal Access Teacher Management System***
- **One-Stop Planner CD-ROM with Test Generator:** Teacher Management System with Interactive Teacher's Edition

STANDARDS MASTERY

- **Standards Review Workbook***
- **At Home: A Guide to Standards Mastery for World History**

 **Holt Online Learning**

To enhance learning, the following Internet activity is available: **Know Your Sources.**

KEYWORD: SQ6 TEACHER

- Teacher Support Page
- Content Updates
- Rubrics and Writing Models
- Teaching Tips for the Multimedia Classroom

KEYWORD: SQ6 WH1

- Current Events
- Holt Grapher
- Holt Online Atlas
- Holt Researcher
- Interactive Multimedia Activities
- Internet Activities
- Online Chapter Summaries in Six Languages
- Online Section Quizzes
- World History Maps and Charts

HOLT PREMIER ONLINE STUDENT EDITION

Complete online support for interactivity, assessment, and reporting

- Interactive Maps and Notebook
- Standardized Test Prep
- Homework Practice and Research Activities Online

Mastering the Standards: Differentiating Instruction

Reaching Standards	Basic-level activities designed for all students encountering new material
Standards Proficiency	Intermediate-level activities designed for average students
Exceeding Standards	Challenging activities designed for honors and gifted-and-talented students
Standard English Mastery	Activities designed to improve standard English usage

MASTERING THE CALIFORNIA STANDARDS

Frequently Asked Questions

INSTRUCTIONAL PLANNING AND SUPPORT

Where do I find planning aids, pacing guides, lesson plans, and other teaching aids?

Annotated Teacher's Edition:
- Chapter planning guides
- Standards-based instruction and strategies
- Differentiated instruction for universal access
- Point-of-use reminders for integrating program resources

Power Presentations with Video CD-ROM

Universal Access Teacher Management System:
- Year and unit instructional benchmarking guides
- Reproducible lesson plans
- Assessment guides for diagnostic, progress, and summative end-of-the-year tests
- Options for differentiating instruction and intervention
- Teaching guides and answer keys for student workbooks

One-Stop Planner CD-ROM with Test Generator: Teacher Management System with Interactive Teacher's Edition:
- Calendar Planner
- Editable lesson plans
- All reproducible ancillaries in Adobe Acrobat (PDF) format
- ExamView Test Generator (English & Spanish)
- Game Tool for ExamView
- PuzzlePro
- Transparency and video previews

DIFFERENTIATING INSTRUCTION FOR UNIVERSAL ACCESS

What resources are available to ensure that Advanced Learners/GATE students master the standards?

Teacher's Edition Activities:
- History on the Front Page, p. 9

Lesson Plans for Universal Access

Primary Source Library CD-ROM for World History

What resources are available to ensure that English Learners and Standard English Learners master the standards?

Teacher's Edition Activities:
- Mapping Your School, p. 15

Lesson Plans for Universal Access

Chapter Resource File: Vocabulary Builder Activities

Spanish Chapter Summaries Audio CD Program

Online Chapter Summaries in Six Languages

One-Stop Planner CD-ROM:
- PuzzlePro, Spanish Version
- ExamView Test Generator, Spanish Version

What modified materials are available for Special Education?

The *Universal Access Modified Worksheets and Tests CD-ROM* provides editable versions of the following:

Vocabulary Flash Cards

Modified Vocabulary Builder Activities

Modified Chapter Review Activity

Modified Chapter Test

What resources are available to ensure that Learners Having Difficulty master the standards?

Teacher's Edition Activities:
- Back and Forth in Time, p. 7
- Mapping Your School, p. 15
- Geography and History Diagram, p. 16

Interactive Reader and Study Guide

Student Edition Full-Read Audio CD

Quick Facts Transparency: Uncovering the Past Visual Summary

Standards Review Workbook

Social Studies Skills Activity: Developing Personal Participation Skills

Interactive Skills Tutor CD-ROM

How do I intervene for students struggling to master the standards?

Interactive Reader and Study Guide

Quick Facts Transparency: Uncovering the Past Visual Summary

Standards Review Workbook

Social Studies Skills Activity: Developing Personal Participation Skills

Interactive Skills Tutor CD-ROM

PROFESSIONAL DEVELOPMENT

HOLT
Professional Development

What teacher training resources are available to help me grow professionally?

- In-service and staff development as part of your Holt Social Studies product purchase
- Quick Teacher Tutorial Lesson Presentation CD-ROM
- Intensive tuition-based Teacher Development Institute
- Convenient Holt Speaker Bureau face-to-face workshop options

- PRAXIS™ Test Prep (#0089) interactive Web-based content refreshers*
- *Ask A Professional Development Expert* at http://www.hrw.com/prodev/

* PRAXIS is a trademark of Educational Testing Service (ETS). This publication is not endorsed or approved by ETS.

Information Literacy Skills

To learn more about how History–Social Science instruction may be improved by the effective use of library media centers and information literacy skills, go to the Teacher's Resource Materials for Chapter 1 at **go.hrw.com, keyword: SQ6 MEDIA.**

Standards Focus

Teacher's Edition

HSS Analysis Skills: HR 1, HR 4, HI 1, HI 2, HI 4, HI 5

ELA Writing 6.2.2, Reading 6.1.0

Upcoming Standards for Future Learning

Preview the following History–Social Science content standards from upcoming chapters or grade levels to promote learning beyond the current chapter.

HSS **6.1** Students describe what is known through archaeological studies of the early physical and cultural development of humankind from the Paleolithic Era to the agricultural revolution.

6.1.1 Describe the hunter-gatherer societies, including the development of tools and the use of fire.

6.1.2 Identify the locations of human communities that populated the major regions of the world and describe how humans adapted to a variety of environments.

6.1.3 Discuss the climatic changes and human modifications of the physical environment that gave rise to the domestication of plants and animals and new sources of clothing and shelter.

Focus on Writing

The **Chapter Resource File** provides a Focus on Writing worksheet to help students create their job descriptions.

CRF: Focus on Writing Activity: A Job Description

CHAPTER 1

Uncovering the Past

California Standards

Analysis Skills

HI 5 Recognize that interpretations of history are subject to change as new information is uncovered.

English–Language Arts

Writing 6.2.2 Write expository compositions.

Reading 6.1.0 Students use their knowledge of word origins and word relationships, as well as historical and literary context clues, to determine the meaning of specialized vocabulary and to understand the precise meaning of grade-level-appropriate words.

FOCUS ON WRITING

A Job Description What is the job of a historian? an archaeologist? a geographer? In this chapter you will read about the work of people who study the past—its events, its people, and its places. Then you will write a job description to include in a career-planning guide.

2 CHAPTER 1

Introduce the Chapter

Standards Proficiency

History is Happening! **HSS** Analysis Skills: HI 4, HI 5

1. Call on students to suggest a recent event that will probably appear in history books, such as a major scientific advance, a terrorist act, a peaceful change of government, or similar event.

2. Then ask students why people of the future should know about the event. Students may reply, for example, that knowledge of the event could serve as a warning, inspire other people to fight for justice, or help cure diseases. Discuss how understanding the

event cuold help people of the future avoid mistakes. Encourage students to think of specific ways this could work.

3. Point out that history, archaeology, and geography help people learn about the past. Learning about the past then helps us understand the present and predict the future. Students will learn more about the importance of history, archaeology, and geography in this chapter. **LS** Verbal/Linguistic

What You Will Learn...

In this chapter you will learn how historians and geographers study the past. This photo shows clay warriors that were found in China. Finds like these teach us a lot about the history of ancient places.

UNCOVERING THE PAST **3**

● **Chapter Preview** ●

HOLT
History's Impact
► video series
See the Video Teacher's Guide for strategies for using the chapter video **Uncovering the Past: The Impact of Archaeology.**

Chapter Big Ideas

Section 1 Historians use many kinds of clues to understand how people lived in the past.

Section 2 Physical geography and human geography contribute to the study of history.

Explore the Picture

Archaeology Of the three history-related careers you will learn about in this chapter—historian, archaeologist, and geographer—an archaeologist is the person most likely to study these life-size clay warriors. Archaeologists learn about people based on the objects they leave behind.

Analyzing Visuals What might these clay warriors tell you about life in China during the time that they were made? *possible answers—The military was an important segment of society; perhaps warriors were worshipped as gods.* What task may an archaeologist have to perform with broken objects such as these? *repair or reassemble them*

Analyzing Visuals

Asking Historical Questions Because students are just beginning their study of world history, they have more questions than answers. Ask each student to write down at least one question about the clay warriors in the picture. *Examples: How big are they? Who made them? How old are they? Where were they found?* Solicit students' questions. Point out that historians ask similar questions. Challenge students to distinguish between questions that can be answered by examining the statues directly and those that require different kinds of inquiry.

Other People, Other Places

Egyptian Pyramids Explain to students that just as the Chinese honored an emperor with an impressive tomb guarded by these warriors, the Egyptians also built giant structures, the pyramids, to honor their powerful rulers. Tell students they will learn more about these pyramids in a later chapter. Have students imagine that they live in ancient times. Ask them what items might be placed in their own tombs that could be discovered thousands of years later.

Reading Social Studies

Reading Social Studies

by Kylene Beers

| Economics | Geography | Politics | Religion | Society and Culture | Science and Technology |

Focus on Themes This chapter sets the stage for reading the rest of the book. In it you will learn the definitions of many important terms. You will learn how studying history helps you understand the past and the present. You will also read about the study of geography and learn how the world's physical features affected when and where civilization began. Finally, you will begin to think about how **society and culture** and **science and technology** have interacted throughout time.

Specialized Vocabulary of History

Focus on Reading Have you ever done a plié at the barre or sacked the quarterback? You probably haven't if you've never studied ballet or played football. In fact, you may not even have known what those words meant.

Specialized Vocabulary Plié, barre, sack, and quarterback are **specialized vocabulary**, words that are used in only one field. History has its own specialized vocabulary. The charts below list some terms often used in the study of history.

Terms that identify periods of time	
Decade	a period of 10 years
Century	a period of 100 years
Age	a long period of time marked by a single cultural feature
Era	a long period of time marked by great events, developments, or figures
Ancient	very old, or from a long time ago

Terms used with dates	
circa or c.	a word used to show that historians are not sure of an exact date; it means "about"
BC	a term used to identify dates that occurred long ago, before the birth of Jesus Christ, the founder of Christianity; it means "before Christ." As you can see on the time line below, BC dates get smaller as time passes, so the larger the number the earlier the date.
AD	a term used to identify dates that occurred after Jesus's birth; it comes from a Latin phrase that means "in the year of our Lord." Unlike BC dates, AD dates get larger as time passes, so the larger the number the later the date.
BCE	another way to refer to BC dates; it stands for "before the common era"
CE	another way to refer to AD dates; it stands for "common era"

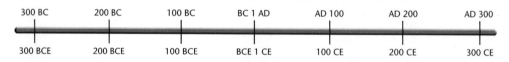

| 300 BC | 200 BC | 100 BC | BC 1 AD | AD 100 | AD 200 | AD 300 |
| 300 BCE | 200 BCE | 100 BCE | BCE 1 CE | 100 CE | 200 CE | 300 CE |

4 CHAPTER 1

You Try It!

As you read this textbook, you will find many examples of specialized vocabulary terms that historians use. Many of these terms will be highlighted in the text and defined for you as key terms. Others may not be highlighted, but they will still be defined. For some examples, read the passage below. Learning these words as you come across them will help you understand what you read later in the book. For your own reference, you may wish to keep a list of important terms in your notebook.

Learning Words through Context

We must rely on a variety of sources to learn history. For information on the very first humans, we have fossil remains. A **fossil** is a part or imprint of something that was once alive. Bones and footprints preserved in rock are examples of fossils.

As human beings learned to make things, by accident they also created more sources of information for us. They made what we call **artifacts**, objects created by and used by humans. Artifacts include coins, arrowheads, tools, toys, and pottery.

From Chapter 1, page 10

Answer the following questions about the specialized vocabulary of history.

1. What is a fossil? What is an artifact? How can you tell?

2. Were you born in a BC year or an AD year?

3. Put the following dates in order: AD 2000, 3100 BC, 15 BCE, AD 476, AD 3, CE 1215

4. If you saw that an event happened c. AD 1000, what would that mean?

Key Terms and People

Chapter 1

Section 1
history *(p. 6)*
culture *(p. 7)*
archaeology *(p. 7)*
fossil *(p. 10)*
artifacts *(p. 10)*
primary source *(p. 10)*
secondary source *(p. 10)*

Section 2
geography *(p. 12)*
landforms *(p. 12)*
climate *(p. 12)*
environment *(p. 13)*
region *(p. 15)*
resources *(p. 16)*

Academic Vocabulary

Success in school is related to knowing academic vocabulary—the words that are frequently used in school assignments and discussions. In this chapter, you will learn the following academic words:

values *(p. 8)*
features *(p. 14)*

As you read Chapter 1, keep a list in your notebook of specialized vocabulary words that you learn.

Reading Social Studies

Key Terms and People

Preteach these words by instructing students to create a Double Door FoldNote. Have students label the two doors *History Terms* and *Geography Terms*. Read the key terms aloud and have students write the term under the appropriate side of the FoldNote. Ask students to discuss the meanings of the words, and define any terms that they do not understand.

LS Verbal/Linguistic, Visual/Spatial

Focus on Reading

See the **Focus on Reading** questions in this chapter for more practice on this reading social studies skill.

Reading Social Studies Assessment

See the **Standards Review** at the end of this chapter for student assessment questions related to this reading skill.

Teaching Tip

Explain to students that specialized vocabulary words can often have double meanings. In other words, the words have a different meaning when applied to a specialized field than they might to someone outside of that field. For instance, the word *check* means something completely different to a person in the banking industry than it does to someone who plays hockey. Have students try to identify other words used in the study of history or geography that have double meanings.

Answers

You Try It! 1. *fossil—part of or imprint of something that was once alive; artifact—object created and used by humans; the words immediately following* artifact *and* fossil *reveal their meaning;* **2.** *AD;* **3.** *3100 BC, 15 BCE, AD 3, AD 476, CE 1215, AD 2000;* **4.** *It happened about 1,000 years after Jesus's birth.*

5

Bellringer

If YOU were there . . . Use the **Daily Bellringer Transparency** to help students answer the question.

📖 Daily Bellringer Transparency, Section 1

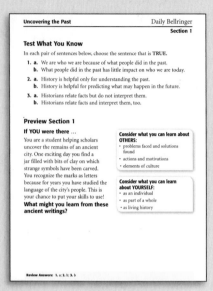

Uncovering the Past   Daily Bellringer
Section 1

Test What You Know
In each pair of sentences below, choose the sentence that is **TRUE.**

1. **a.** We are who we are because of what people did in the past.
   b. What people did in the past has little impact on who we are today.

2. **a.** History is helpful only for understanding the past.
   b. History is helpful for predicting what may happen in the future.

3. **a.** Historians relate facts but do not interpret them.
   b. Historians relate facts and interpret them, too.

Preview Section 1

If YOU were there …
You are a student helping scholars uncover the remains of an ancient city. One exciting day you find a jar filled with bits of clay on which strange symbols have been carved. You recognize the marks as letters because for years you have studied the language of the city's people. This is your chance to put your skills to use!
What might you learn from these ancient writings?

Consider what you can learn about OTHERS:
• problems faced and solutions found
• actions and motivations
• elements of culture

Consider what you can learn about YOURSELF:
• as an individual
• as part of a whole
• as living history

Review Answers: 1. a; **2.** b; **3.** b

Academic Vocabulary

Review with students the high-use academic term in this section.

values ideas that people hold dear and try to live by (p. 8)

Studying History

What You Will Learn...

Main Ideas

1. History is the study of the past.
2. We can improve our understanding of people's actions and beliefs through the study of history.
3. Historians use clues from various sources to learn about the past.

The Big Idea

Historians use many kinds of clues to understand how people lived in the past.

Key Terms

history, *p. 6*
culture, *p. 7*
archaeology, *p. 7*
fossil, *p. 10*
artifacts, *p. 10*
primary source, *p. 10*
secondary source, *p. 10*

If **YOU** were there...

You are a student helping scholars uncover the remains of an ancient city. One exciting day you find a jar filled with bits of clay on which strange symbols have been carved. You recognize the marks as letters because for years you have studied the language of the city's people. This is your chance to put your skills to use!

What might you learn from the ancient writings?

BUILDING BACKGROUND Last year you learned about our country's past. Now you begin a study of world history, which started many centuries before the history of the United States. You will find that we learn about world history in many ways.

The Study of the Past

The people of the ancient world didn't build skyscrapers, invent the automobile, or send spaceships to Mars. But they did remarkable things. Among their amazing feats were building huge temples, inventing writing, and discovering planets. Every step we take—in technology, science, education, literature, and all other fields—builds on what people did long ago. We are who we are because of what people did in the past.

What Is History?

History is the study of the past. A battle that happened 5,000 years ago and an election that happened yesterday are both parts of history.

Historians are people who study history. Their main concern is human activity in the past. They want to know how people lived and why they did the things they did. They try to learn about the problems people faced and how they found solutions.

Teach the Big Idea: Master the Standards   Standards Proficiency

Studying History 🐾 **HSS** Analysis Skills: HI 5

1. **Teach** Ask students the Main Idea questions to teach this section.

2. **Apply** Ask students to imagine that they are historians who are living in the year 2999 writing about the young people of the early 2000s. Call on students to describe how their generation should be remembered. Topics may include music, food, clothing, education, entertainment, and others. Write their comments for students to see.
   LS Verbal/Linguistic

3. **Review** Have students review their comments and list the most important points that a future historian might want to know about this generation.

4. **Practice/Homework** Ask students to use the information to list items for a time capsule for portraying their generation.
   LS Intrapersonal

Historians are interested in how people lived their daily lives. How and where did they work, fight, trade, farm, and worship? What did they do in their free time? What games did they play? In other words, historians study the past to understand people's **culture**—the knowledge, beliefs, customs, and values of a group of people.

What Is Archaeology?

An important field that contributes much information about the past is **archaeology** (ahr-kee-AH-luh-jee). It is the study of the past based on what people left behind.

Archaeologists, or people who practice archaeology, explore places where people once lived, worked, or fought. The things that people left in these places may include jewelry, dishes, or weapons. They range from stone tools to computers.

Archaeologists examine the objects they find to learn what they can tell about the past. In many cases, the objects that people left behind are the only clues we have to how they lived.

READING CHECK **Comparing** How are the fields of history and archaeology similar?

Studying the Past
Historians and archaeologists study the people and places of the past. For example, by studying the remains of an ancient Egyptian temple (right), they can learn about the lives of the ancient Egyptians (left).

7

Collaborative Learning

Reaching Standards

Back and Forth in Time 🐾 **HSS** Analysis Skills: HR 1, HI 5

1. Organize the class into small groups.

2. Have students study the photo on this page to describe and write down the differences between the two sides of the monument. Then ask students to write down possible answers to this question: "How did historians and archaeologists figure out what the temple may have looked like?"

3. As a class, discuss students' responses. Accept all feasible answers. Then invite students to look through this book for other

examples of ancient sites. Ask students to pose questions that historians and archaeologists may ask about those same sites. **LS** **Interpersonal, Visual/Spatial**

　Alternative Assessment Handbook, Rubric 14: Group Activity

Main Idea

❷ Understanding through History

We can improve our understanding of people's actions and beliefs through the study of history.

Identify Name two groups of Americans who might interpret our country's history differently. *Native Americans, European settlers, Asian immigrants, enslaved Africans, and others*

Summarize How does history help citizens around the world know their own countries better? *It teaches people about their past, how their government came into being, their nation's triumphs and tragedies, and the experiences people have been through together.*

Predict What may tomorrow's history books say about today's world? *Answers will vary.*

Activity Holidays and History
Have students select a nonreligious U.S. holiday and write a paragraph about how that holiday helps us to remember our country's history. Examples include Veteran's Day, Thanksgiving, President's Day, or Independence Day

CRF: Literature Activity: Who Cares About Great Uncle Edgar?

Info to Know

The Father of History Herodotus was a Greek author who lived during the 400s BC. He has been called the Father of History for attempting the first real historical narrative. Herodotus's great work is an account of Greece's wars with Persia. Inserted into the history are amusing short stories, dialogue, and speeches. Readers still study the works of Herodotus for insights into the ancient world.

Understanding through History

There are many reasons why people study history. Understanding the past helps us to understand the world today. History can also provide us with a guide to making better decisions in the future.

ACADEMIC VOCABULARY
values ideas that people hold dear and try to live by

Knowing Yourself

History can teach you about yourself. What if you did not know your own past? You would not know which subjects you liked in school or which sports you enjoyed. You would not know what makes you proud or what mistakes not to repeat. Without your own personal history, you would not have an identity.

History is just as important for groups as it is for individuals. What would happen if countries had no record of their past? People would know nothing about how their governments came into being. They would not remember their nation's great triumphs or tragedies. History teaches us about the experiences we have been through as a people. It shapes our identity and teaches us the **values** that we share.

Knowing Others

Like today, the world in the past included many cultures. History teaches about the cultures that were unlike your own. You learn about other peoples, where they lived, and what was important to them. History teaches you how cultures were similar and how they were different.

History also helps you understand why other people think the way they do. You learn about the struggles people have faced. You also learn how these struggles have affected the way people view themselves and others.

[handwritten notes: Why is it important to know about your past? groups/countries to learn; What How can we learn about other cultures]

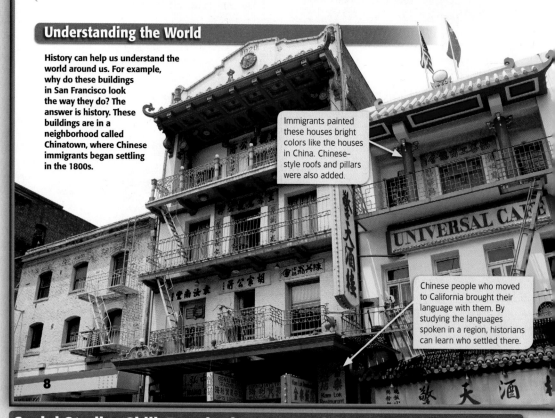

Understanding the World

History can help us understand the world around us. For example, why do these buildings in San Francisco look the way they do? The answer is history. These buildings are in a neighborhood called Chinatown, where Chinese immigrants began settling in the 1800s.

Immigrants painted these houses bright colors like the houses in China. Chinese-style roofs and pillars were also added.

Chinese people who moved to California brought their language with them. By studying the languages spoken in a region, historians can learn who settled there.

Social Studies Skill: Developing Personal Participation Skills

History on TV

Standards Proficiency

1. Ask students to imagine that they are media producers who want to start a new television cable channel. The student "producers" will propose a channel devoted to interesting young people in history.

2. Organize the class into pairs. Have each pair create a proposal for the new cable channel to be presented to financial investors. Students may create any one of a range of products for their proposals—posters, letters, or dialogues,

for example—to discuss the importance of history for young people.

3. Call on volunteers to present their work to the class. Then lead a discussion on how students could apply this imaginary proposal to real-world issues about learning history.

LS Interpersonal

Alternative Assessment Handbook, Rubric 29: Presentations

For example, Native Americans, European settlers, enslaved Africans, and Asian immigrants all played vital roles in our country's history. But the descendants of each group have a different story to tell about their ancestors' contributions.

Learning these stories and others like them that make up history can help you see the viewpoints of other peoples. It can help teach you to respect and understand different opinions. This knowledge helps promote tolerance. History can also help you relate more easily to people of different backgrounds. In other words, knowing about the past can help build social harmony throughout the world today.

Knowing Your World

History can provide you with a better understanding of where you live. You are part of a culture that interacts with the outside world. Even events that happen in other parts of the world affect your culture. History helps you to understand how today's events are shaped by the events of the past. So knowing the past helps you figure out what is happening now.

History is concerned with the entire range of human activities. It is the record of humanity's combined efforts. So while you are studying history, you can also learn more about math, science, religion, government, and many other topics.

Studying the past will also help you develop mental skills. History encourages you to ask important questions. It forces you to analyze the facts you learn. Such analysis teaches you how to recognize which information is important and which is extra. This skill helps you to find the main facts when studying any topic.

History also promotes good decision-making skills. A famous, often repeated saying warns us that those who forget their past are doomed to repeat it. This means

that people who ignore the results of past decisions often make the same mistakes over and over again.

Individuals and countries both benefit from the wisdom that history can teach. Your own history may have taught you that studying for a test results in better grades. In a similar way, world history has taught that providing young people with education makes them more productive when they become adults.

Historians have been talking about the value of history for centuries. More than 2,000 years ago a great Greek historian named Polybius wrote:

FOCUS ON READING
What does the word *century* mean?

❝The purpose of history is not the reader's enjoyment at the moment of perusal [reading it], but the reformation [improvement] of the reader's soul, to save him from stumbling at the same stumbling block many times over.❞

–Polybius, from *The Histories, Book XXXVIII*

READING CHECK **Summarizing** What are some benefits of studying history?

Clues from the Past

This archaeologist is examining ancient pottery in Italy to learn about the past.

❸ Using Clues

Historians use clues from various sources to learn about the past.

Define What is a fossil? *a part or imprint of something that was once alive*

Draw Conclusions How do fossils and artifacts help teach us about the past? *Fossil remains teach us about the first humans, and artifacts teach us about the tools and objects used by humans in the past.*

Predict What are some things that historians of tomorrow may use as primary sources? *possible answers—recordings of televised speeches, digital photographs, a soldier's letters home, and so on*

 CRF: Biography Activity: Howard Carter

CRF: Biography Activity: Jean-Francois Champollion

HSS Analysis Skills: HI 5

go.hrw.com
Online Resources
KEYWORD: SQ6 WH1
ACTIVITY: Know Your
Sources

Connect to Science

Tree-Ring Dating Archaeologists have many methods available to them for determining the age of artifacts. To find the age of wooden objects they may use dendrochronology, or dating by tree-ring growth. Because the growth of annual rings reflects climate conditions, scientists can correlate growth patterns with particular years. In the United States, dendrochronology is particularly useful in the Southwest, because the dry climate there preserves wood well.

Using Clues

We must rely on a variety of sources to learn history. For information on the very first humans, we have fossil remains. A **fossil** is a part or imprint of something that was once alive. Bones and footprints preserved in rock are examples of fossils.

As human beings learned to make things, by accident they also created more sources of information for us. They made what we call **artifacts**, objects created by and used by humans. Artifacts include coins, arrowheads, tools, toys, and pottery. Archaeologists examine artifacts and the places where the artifacts were found to learn about the past.

Sources of Information

 About 5,000 years ago, people invented writing. They wrote laws, poems, speeches, battle plans, letters, contracts, and many other things. In these written sources, historians have found countless clues about how people lived. In addition, people have recorded their messages in many ways over the centuries. Historians have studied writing carved into stone pillars, stamped onto clay tablets, scribbled on turtle shells, typed with typewriters, and sent by computer.

Historical sources are of two types. A **primary source** is an account of an event created by someone who took part in or witnessed the event. Treaties, letters, diaries, laws, court documents, and royal commands are all primary sources. An audio or video recording of an event is also a primary source.

A **secondary source** is information gathered by someone who did not take part in or witness an event. Examples include history textbooks, journal articles, and encyclopedias. The textbook you are reading right now is a secondary source. The historians who wrote it did not take part in the events described. Instead, they gathered information about these events from different sources.

Critical Thinking: Finding Main Ideas
Standards **Proficiency**

Primary and Secondary Sources **HSS** Analysis Skills: HR 4, HI 4
Research Required

1. Ask students to select a newsworthy event in recent history—one that an adult they know has experienced or witnessed. Examples include a severe weather event or an election.

2. Next, have students use primary and secondary sources to learn more about the event. Suggest that they interview a parent or another adult for the primary source and read published accounts for the secondary sources. Point out that a newspaper article can be a primary source if the reporter witnessed the event directly, and that either type of source can be biased.

3. Have each student write a paragraph comparing the information from the two types of sources for similarities and differences.
LS Interpersonal, Verbal/Linguistic

Alternative Assessment Handbook, Rubric 30: Research

Written records, like this writing from a tomb in Egypt, are valuable sources of information about the past.

Sometimes, archaeologists must carefully reconstruct artifacts from hundreds of broken pieces, like they did with this statue of an Aztec bat god from Mexico.

Sources of Change

Writers of secondary sources don't always agree about the past. Historians form different opinions about the primary sources they study. As a result, historians may not interpret past events in the same way.

For example, one writer may say that a king was a brilliant military leader. Another may say that the king's armies only won their battles because they had better weapons than their enemies did. Sometimes new evidence leads to new conclusions. As historians review and reanalyze information, their interpretations can and do change.

READING CHECK **Contrasting** How are primary and secondary sources different?

SUMMARY AND PREVIEW We benefit from studying the past. Scholars use many clues to help them understand past events. In the next section you will learn how geography connects to history.

Section 1 Assessment

Reviewing Ideas, Terms, and People

1. **a. Identify** What is **history**?
   b. Explain What kinds of things do historians try to discover about people who lived in the past?
   c. Predict What kinds of evidence will historians of the future study to learn about your **culture**?
2. **a. Describe** How does knowing its own history provide a group with a sense of unity?
   b. Elaborate Explain the meaning of the phrase, "Those who forget their past are doomed to repeat it."
3. **a. Identify** What is a **primary source**?
   b. Explain How did the invention of writing affect the sources on which historians rely?
   c. Elaborate Could a photograph be considered a primary source? Why or why not?

Critical Thinking

4. **Categorizing** Copy the diagram. In the empty circles, list the types of clues that historians and archaeologists use.

Historians and Archaeologists

FOCUS ON WRITING

5. **Understanding What Historians Do** What is the difference between a historian and an archaeologist? Take notes about the work these people do.

UNCOVERING THE PAST **11**

Section 1 Assessment Answers

1. **a.** the study of the past
   b. how they lived and their knowledge, beliefs, customs, and values
   c. possible answers—television broadcasts, newspapers, books, films, videos, CDs

2. **a.** possible answer—It teaches them about the experiences they have been through as a people and about the values they share.
   b. possible answer—Studying history helps people keep from making the same mistakes that people made in the past.

3. **a.** a firsthand account of an event
   b. It provided them with many more types of records.
   c. possible answer—yes; shows a firsthand account of an event

4. fossils, artifacts, primary sources of information, secondary sources of information

5. Students' answers will vary, but should mention that archaeologists primarily study artifacts whereas historians gather information from sources including writings by witnesses to events.

• Direct Teach •

MISCONCEPTION ALERT

It's Not Over Yet! Some students may think that all the great archaeological discoveries have been made, and nothing remains to be found. It's not true! Point out that the clay warriors in the chapter opener photo were just found in 1974. Although the imperial tomb they guard has been located with some certainty, it has not yet been opened. If ancient written sources are accurate, archaeologists will see amazing things when they finally excavate the tomb.

Every year, archaeologists announce more remarkable finds. New technologies are helping in the search for evidence of past civilizations and peoples.

• Review & Assess •

Close

Briefly review the benefits, the challenges, and the methods of studying history.

Review

Online Quiz, Section 1

Assess

SE Section 1 Assessment
PASS: Section 1 Quiz
Alternative Assessment Handbook

Reteach/Classroom Intervention

California Standards Review Workbook
Interactive Reader and Study Guide, Section 1
Interactive Skills Tutor CD-ROM

Answers

Reading Check *Primary sources provide a firsthand account of an event, while secondary sources include information gathered by someone who did not witness the event.*

11

Bellringer

If YOU were there . . . Use the **Daily Bellringer Transparency** to help students answer the question.

Daily Bellringer Transparency, Section 2

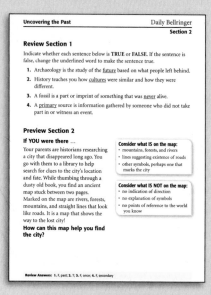

Uncovering the Past | Daily Bellringer
Section 2

Review Section 1

Indicate whether each sentence below is **TRUE** or **FALSE**. If the sentence is false, change the underlined word to make the sentence true.

1. Archaeology is the study of the <u>future</u> based on what people left behind.
2. History teaches you how <u>cultures</u> were similar and how they were different.
3. A fossil is a part or imprint of something that was <u>never</u> alive.
4. A <u>primary</u> source is information gathered by someone who did not take part in or witness an event.

Preview Section 2

If YOU were there ...

Your parents are historians researching a city that disappeared long ago. You go with them to a library to help search for clues to the city's location and fate. While thumbing through a dusty old book, you find an ancient map stuck between two pages. Marked on the map are rivers, forests, mountains, and straight lines that look like roads. It is a map that shows the way to the lost city!

How can this map help you find the city?

Consider what IS on the map:
• mountains, forests, and rivers
• lines suggesting existence of roads
• other symbols, perhaps one that marks the city

Consider what IS NOT on the map:
• no indication of direction
• no explanation of symbols
• no points of reference to the world you know

Review Answers: 1. F, past; **2.** T; **3.** F, once; **4.** F, secondary

Academic Vocabulary

Review with students the high-use academic term in this section.

features characteristics (p. 14)

Studying Geography

What You Will Learn...

Main Ideas

1. Geography is the study of places and people.
2. Studying location is important to both physical and human geography.
3. Geography and history are closely connected.

The Big Idea

Physical geography and human geography contribute to the study of history.

Key Terms

geography, p. 12
landforms, p. 12
climate, p. 12
environment, p. 13
region, p. 15
resources, p. 16

If YOU were there...

Your parents are historians researching a city that disappeared long ago. You go with them to a library to help search for clues to the city's location and fate. While thumbing through a dusty old book, you find an ancient map stuck between two pages. Marked on the map are rivers, forests, mountains, and straight lines that look like roads. It is a map that shows the way to the lost city!

How can this map help you find the city?

BUILDING BACKGROUND You have read how historians and archaeologists help us learn about the past. Another group of scholars—geographers—also contribute to our study of history.

Studying Places and People

When you hear about an event on the news, the first questions you ask may be, "Where did it happen?" and "Who was there?" Historians ask the same questions about events that happened in the past. That is why they need to study geography. **Geography** is the study of the earth's physical and cultural features. These features include mountains, rivers, people, cities, and countries.

Physical Geography

Physical geography is the study of the earth's land and features. People who work in this field are called physical geographers. They study **landforms**, the natural features of the land's surface. Mountains, valleys, plains, and other such places are landforms.

Physical geographers also study **climate**, the pattern of weather conditions in a certain area over a long period of time. Climate is not the same as weather. Weather is the conditions at a specific time and place. If you say that your city has cold winters, you are talking about climate. If you say it is below freezing and snowing today, you are talking about the weather.

[handwritten notes in margin: 1) What are the 2 branches of geography? T or F How is climate diff. from weather?]

12 CHAPTER 1

Teach the Big Idea: Master the Standards   Standards Proficiency

Studying Geography

1. **Teach** Ask students the Main Idea questions to teach this section.

2. **Apply** Write *Physical Geography* and *Human Geography* for students to see, spacing the phrases so that more words and phrases can be added to create a web. Call on students to suggest words and phrases that add details and examples to the two basic terms. For example, *landforms, climate,* and *location* could be added to the

Physical side. Challenge students to add details specific to your state. **LS** Visual/Spatial

3. **Review** Next, ask students to imagine that they are studying your state's history this year. Ask how the details on the web could enhance their study of the state's history.

4. **Practice/Homework** Ask students to create a similar web of the physical and human geography of their neighborhood. **LS** Visual/Spatial

Physical Geography

The study of the earth's physical features and processes, such as mountains, rivers, oceans, rainfall, and climate, including this section of California's coast

Human Geography

The study of the earth's people, including their way of life, homes and cities, beliefs, and travels, such as these members of the Dogon people in the country of Mali

Geography

The study of the earth's physical and cultural features

Climate affects many features of a region. For example, it affects plant life. Tropical rain forests require warm air and heavy rain, while a dry climate can create deserts. Climate also affects landforms. For example, constant wind can wear down mountains into flat plains.

Although climate affects landforms, landforms can also affect climate. For example, the Coast Ranges in northern California are mountains parallel to the Pacific coast. As air presses up against these mountains, it rises and cools. Any moisture that the air was carrying falls as rain. Meanwhile, on the opposite side of the range, the Central Valley stays dry. In this way, a mountain range creates two very different climates.

Landforms and climate are part of a place's environment. The **environment** includes all the living and nonliving things that affect life in an area. This includes the area's climate, land, water, plants, soil, animals, and other features.

Human Geography

The other branch of geography is human geography—the study of people and the places where they live. Specialists in human geography study many different things about people and their cultures. What kind of work do people do? How do they get their food? What are their homes like? What religions do they practice?

Human geography also deals with how the environment affects people. For example, how do people who live near rivers protect themselves from floods? How do people who live in deserts survive? Do different environments affect the size of families? Do people in certain environments live longer? Why do some diseases spread easily in some environments but not in others? As you can see, human geographers study many interesting questions about people and this planet.

READING CHECK **Summarizing** What are the two main branches of geography?

Direct Teach

Main Idea

❶ Studying Places and People

Geography is the study of places and people.

Define What is geography? *the study of the earth's physical and cultural features*

Summarize What are some examples of physical features? *possible answers—mountains, rivers, valleys, plains, oceans*

Contrast What is the difference between climate and weather? *Weather is the conditions at a specific time and place; climate is the weather conditions in a certain area over a longer period of time.*

📄 **CRF:** Economics and History Activity: Economics and History

📄 **CRF:** History and Geography Activity: Human Communities

Info to Know

Global Warming A main component of physical geography seems to be changing: global temperatures are rising. But what is the cause? Many scientists say that human activities are to blame. They say that carbon dioxide in the atmosphere is creating a greenhouse effect, which is raising average temperatures worldwide. Some people say, however, that temperature changes may be caused by natural factors.

Critical Thinking: Finding Main Ideas

Standards Profici

Day in the Life

Research Rec

1. Review with students how physical and human geographers study the earth's features and how environments affect people.

2. Then have each student select a country he or she may like to visit someday. Have students research landforms, climate, and other environmental conditions in their chosen countries. Ask each student to write a short "Day in the Life of . . . " account about what

it may be like to live in that country. H students include information about the physical and human geography.

3. Ask for volunteers to present their essa the class. **LS** **Verbal/Linguistic**

📄 Alternative Assessment Handbook, Rubric Research and 37: Writing Assignments

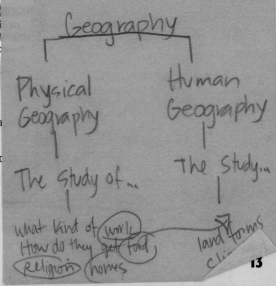

13

Main Idea

❷ Studying Location

Studying location is important to both physical and human geography.

Define What does *location* mean? *the exact description of where something is*

Summarize What are some activities that would use maps? *possible answers—exploring lands, finding one's way in unfamiliar surroundings, planning a new community, and plotting military actions*

Draw Inferences What are some regions within the United States? *possible answers—Southwest, New England, Midwest, Gulf Coast, and so on*

Activity An Original Map Have students create a physical map of a fictional country. Caution students that their maps should describe a possible landscape. For example, rivers must flow from high elevations to lower elevations.

Teaching Tip

California Climates
Have students use Internet sources to check weather reports from the California cities shown on the maps. Point out that only by using many weather reports over a long period of time can one make generalizations about a location's climate.

Answers

Studying Maps 1. *mountains, deserts, rivers, valley; Sierra Nevada;* **2.** *highland, marine, Mediterranean, semiarid, desert; possible answers— highland climate in the highest mountains, marine climate near coast, desert climate in Mojave Desert, semiarid in Central Valley*

ACADEMIC VOCABULARY
features
characteristics

Studying Location

4:33

Both physical and human geographers study location. Location is the exact description of where something is. Every place on Earth has a specific location.

No two places in the world are exactly alike. Even small differences between places can lead to major differences in how people live. That is why geographers try to understand the effects that different locations have on human populations, or groups of people.

By comparing locations, geographers learn more about the factors that affected each of them. For example, they may study why a town grew in one location while a town nearby got smaller.

Learning from Maps

To study various locations, geographers use maps. A map is a drawing of an area. Some maps show physical **features**. Others show cities and the boundaries of states or countries. Most maps have symbols to show different things. For example, large dots often stand for cities. Blue lines show where rivers flow. Most maps also include a guide to show direction.

People have been making maps for more than 4,000 years. Maps help with many activities. Planning battles, looking for new lands, and designing new city parks all require good maps. On the first day of class, you may have used a map of your school to find your classrooms.

Studying Maps

By studying and comparing maps, you can see how a place's physical and human features are related.

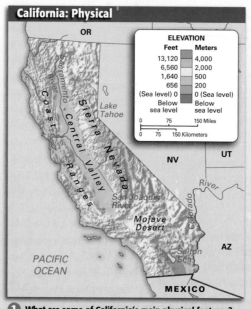

California: Physical

❶ What are some of California's main physical features? Where are the state's highest mountains?

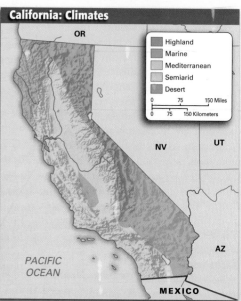

California: Climates

❷ What climates are found in California? How are the climate regions related to California's physical features?

14 CHAPTER 1

Collaborative Learning: Where in the World?

Standards Proficiency

Learning about Regions

Research Required

1. Organize the class into small groups. Ask each group to select a region somewhere in the world and conduct research about the region's physical and human characteristics. Students should concentrate on physical characteristics, however. Next, have each group write five characteristics of its region but not identify the region by name.

2. Have all students open this book to the atlas at the back to help them find the regions.

3. Play a "Where in the World?" game. Have each group read its list of characteristics. Challenge the rest of the class to name or describe the region.

4. Discuss the characteristics of any regions not identified. **LS** Interpersonal, Visual/Spatial

Alternative Assessment Handbook, Rubric 14: Group Activity, and 30: Research

Learning about Regions

Learning about regions is another key part of studying geography. A **region** is an area with one or more features that make it different from surrounding areas. These features may be physical, such as forests or grasslands. There may also be differences in climate. For example, a desert area is a type of region. Physical barriers such as mountains and rivers often form a region's boundaries.

Human features can also define regions. An area with many cities is one type of region. An area with only farms is another type. Some regions are identified by the language that people there speak. Other regions are identified by the religion their people practice.

READING CHECK Categorizing What are some types of features that can identify a region?

Primary Source

BOOK
What Geography Means

Some people think of geography as the ability to read maps or name state capitals. But as geographer Kenneth C. Davis explains, geography is much more. It is related to almost every branch of human knowledge.

❝Geography doesn't simply begin and end with maps showing the location of all the countries of the world. In fact, such maps don't necessarily tell us much. No—geography poses fascinating questions about who we are and how we got to be that way, and then provides clues to the answers. It is impossible to understand history, international politics, the world economy, religions, philosophy, or 'patterns of culture' without taking geography into account.❞

–Kenneth C. Davis, from *Don't Know Much About Geography*

ANALYSIS SKILL **ANALYZING PRIMARY SOURCES**
Why does the writer think that geography is important?

Direct Teach

Main Idea

❷ Studying Location

Studying location is important to both physical and human geography.

Define What is a region? *an area with one or more features that make it different from surrounding areas*

Describe What are some human features that can define a region? *number of cities, an area with many farms, language, religion*

Evaluate Would all people define a region the same way? Why or why not? *possible answer—no, because people interpret both physical and human features differently*
📖 Map Transparency: Studying Maps

Connect to Geography

Ancient Maps People have been making maps for a very long time. The oldest known map is a Babylonian clay tablet that dates from about 2500 BC. People who did not yet have a written language also made diagrams of their world. For example, early Arctic Inuit, Native Americans, and some Pacific Islanders all made maps.

California: Population

- 🔲 One dot represents 25,000 people
- ✹ State capital

0   75   150 Miles
0   75   150 Kilometers

OR · NV · Sacramento · Oakland · San Francisco · San Jose · PACIFIC OCEAN · Los Angeles · Long Beach · San Diego · AZ · MEXICO

❸ Where are California's two main population centers? What kind of climate is found in these areas?

California: Roads

- —— Interstate highways
- —— Other highways
- ✹ State capital

0   75   150 Miles
0   75   150 Kilometers

OR · Eureka · NV · Sacramento · San Francisco · PACIFIC OCEAN · Los Angeles · San Diego · AZ · MEXICO

❹ How are California's roads related to its physical features? How are they related to its population centers?

Critical Thinking Activity: Interpreting Maps

Reaching Standards

Mapping Your School

Standard English Mastery | **Prep Required**

1. On a sheet of butcher paper, draw a rough map of the area surrounding your school. Label the school on the map.

2. Call on students to mark on the map main roads and local landmarks, such as places of worship and favorite restaurants or stores.

3. When all the students have marked information on the map, ask each student to write at least one sentence making a generalization about the map's information.

Example: *The restaurants are located near each other on a main street.*

4. Then have students use the thesaurus or dictionaries to add appropriate adjectives and descriptive phrases to their sentences.
LS Visual/Spatial

📑 Alternative Assessment Handbook, Rubric 20: Map Creation

Answers

Analyzing Primary Sources *because it poses fascinating questions and affects so many other aspects of the world*

Studying Maps 3. *Los Angeles and San Francisco; Mediterranean;* **4.** *fewer major roads in the desert and mountains; more roads in population centers*

Reading Check *physical features such as mountains, forests, and rivers; human features such as religion or language*

❸ Geography and History

Geography and history are closely connected.

Recall What are three aspects of human life that geography affects? *resources, cultures, history*

Draw Conclusions Why can present-day people live in places that lack resources valued by early humans? *possible answers—Irrigation brings water to dry areas; modern transportation brings resources from far away.*

Evaluate How do you think physical geography has affected your community? your state? *Answers will vary but should be logical.*

Activity **Connecting Geography and History** Have students review the maps of fictional countries that they created earlier. Ask each student to imagine how the physical geography of the "country" might affect its development. Instruct students to write brief essays in which they describe those effects.

One way you can see how geography has shaped history is by studying the locations of cities. Certain locations have strategic advantages over others, and as a result, people choose to create cities there. For example, the city of Rio de Janeiro, Brazil, has easy access to the ocean and breathtaking scenery.

Geography and History

Geography gives us important clues about the people and places that came before us. Like detectives, we can piece together a great deal of information about ancient cultures by knowing where people lived and what the area was like.

Geography Affects Resources

An area's geography was critical to early settlements. People could survive only in areas where they could get enough food and water. Early people settled in places that were rich in **resources**, materials found in the earth that people need and value. All through history, people have used a variety of resources to meet their basic needs.

In early times, essential resources included water, animals, fertile land, and stones for tools. Over time, people learned to use other resources, including metals such as copper, gold, and iron.

Geography Shapes Cultures

Geography also influenced the early development of cultures. Early peoples, for example, developed vastly different cultures because of their environments. People who lived along rivers learned to make fishhooks and boats, while those far from rivers did not. People who lived near forests built homes from wood. In other areas, builders had to use mud or stone. Some people developed religious beliefs based on the geography of their area. For example, ancient Egyptians believed that the god Hapi controlled the Nile River.

Geography also played a role in the growth of civilizations. The world's first societies formed along rivers. Crops grown on the fertile land along these rivers fed large populations.

Some geographic features could also protect areas from invasion. A region surrounded by mountains or deserts, for example, was hard for attackers to reach.

16 CHAPTER 1

Differentiating Instruction for Universal Access

Learners Having Difficulty **HSS** Analysis Skills: HI 1 **Reaching Standards**

1. Copy the diagram shown for students to see, omitting the blue answers.

2. Help students fill in the diagram with information from this section that shows how geography relates to history.

3. Then ask students to provide examples for each of the circles shown on the diagram.

4. Review the link between geography and history to conclude the activity.
LS Visual/Spatial

Geography → *Climate and physical features affect human geography.* → *How and where people live varies, depending on geography.* → *Different cultures arise, based on physical geography.* → *Geography affects events—past and future.* → **History**

environments in positive and negative ways. People have planted millions of trees. They have created new lakes in the middle of deserts. But people have also created wastelands where forests once grew and built dams that flooded ancient cities. This interaction between humans and their environment has been a major factor in history. It continues today.

READING CHECK **Describing** What are some ways geography has shaped human history?

SUMMARY AND PREVIEW The field of geography includes physical geography and human geography. Geography has had a major influence on history. In the next chapter you will learn how geography affected the first people.

Geography Influences History

Geography has helped shape history and has affected the growth of societies. People in areas with many natural resources could use their resources to get rich. They could build glorious cities and powerful armies. Features such as rivers also made trade easier. Many societies became rich by trading goods with other peoples.

On the other hand, geography has also caused problems. Floods, for example, have killed millions of people. Lack of rainfall has brought deadly food shortages. Storms have wrecked ships, and with them, the hopes of conquerors. In the 1200s, for example, a people known as the Mongols tried to invade Japan. However, most of the Mongol ships were destroyed by a powerful storm. Japanese history may have been very different if the storm had not occurred.

The relationship between geography and people has not been one-sided. For centuries, people have influenced their

---

go.hrw.com
Online Quiz
KEYWORD: SQ6 HP1

Section 2 Assessment

Reviewing Ideas, Terms, and People

1. **a. Define** What is **geography**?
   b. Summarize What are some of the topics included in human geography?
2. **a. Describe** Identify a **region** near where you live, and explain what sets it apart as a region.
   b. Predict How might a map of a city's **landforms** help an official who is planning a new city park?
3. **a. Recall** Where did early peoples tend to settle?
   b. Compare and Contrast How could a river be both a valuable **resource** and a problem for a region?

Critical Thinking

4. **Categorizing** Draw this chart. Under each heading, list the types of things that are studied in that branch of geography.

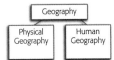

Geography
Physical Geography
Human Geography

FOCUS ON WRITING

5. **Understanding What Geographers Do** In this section you learned how geographers contribute to the study of history. What is the difference between a physical geographer and a human geographer?

UNCOVERING THE PAST **17**

Section 2 Assessment Answers

1. **a.** the study of the Earth's physical and cultural features
   b. what work people do, how they get their food, the homes they live in, religions they practice
2. **a.** Answers will vary but should display an understanding of the concept of a region.
   b. possible answers—A map would show areas that have trees for shade, water for activities, or areas that might not be desirable for building a park, such as steep hills or swamps.

3. **a.** in areas rich in natural resources
   b. Rivers could provide water and access to trade routes; flooding can destroy settlements or leave them open to invasion.
4. Physical—earth's land and features; Human—people and the places where they live
5. Physical geographer—studies earth's land and features; Human geographer—studies people and the places where they live

---

Main Idea

❸ Geography and History

Geography and history are closely connected.

Recall How did a weather event affect Japan's history in the 1200s? *Mongol ships on their way to conquer Japan were destroyed by a deadly storm.*

Summarize How were some societies made richer by the geographic makeup of their region? *more natural resources, access to trade routes*

Close

Call on volunteers to examine the photo on these pages to describe how geography has affected the development of Rio de Janeiro.

Review

Online Quiz, Section 2

Assess

SE Section 2 Assessment
PASS: Section 2 Quiz
Alternative Assessment Handbook

Reteach/Classroom Intervention

California Standards Review Workbook
Interactive Reader and Study Guide, Section 2
Interactive Skills Tutor CD-ROM

Answers

Reading Check *possible answers— Areas rich in resources thrived, access to rivers made trade possible, and events associated with physical geography have changed history.*

History and Geography

Info to Know

Teotihuacán Teotihuacán is located about 30 miles northeast of what is now Mexico City. The city reached its height in the 500s AD. At that time, it was probably the sixth-largest city in the world, with an estimated population of 125,000. The city covered some eight square miles. It contained pyramids, temples, plazas, palaces, and more than 2,000 residential buildings. Many of the people who lived there were farmers or craftspeople. Others were merchants, nobles, or priests. Sometime in the 600s or 700s, a fire destroyed much of Teotihuacán. The event led to the city's swift decline, and it was soon abandoned.

Much of the information in the map at right is based on the Teotihuacán Mapping Project, done in the 1960s and 1970s.

City of the Gods Centuries after the abandonment of Teotihuacán, Aztec travelers came across the ruins. The Aztec believed the place to be holy and the birthplace of the gods. As a result, they named it Teotihuacán, which means "City of the Gods" in the Aztec language. The city's original name and the language its residents spoke remain unknown.

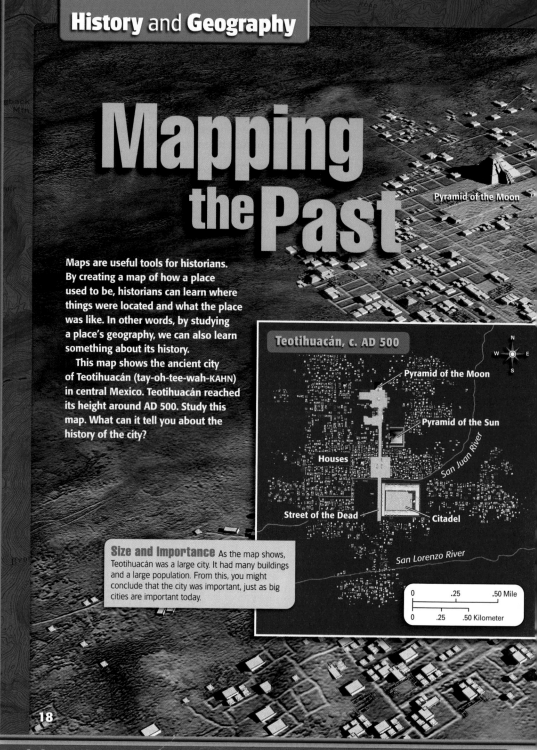

Mapping the Past

Maps are useful tools for historians. By creating a map of how a place used to be, historians can learn where things were located and what the place was like. In other words, by studying a place's geography, we can also learn something about its history.

This map shows the ancient city of Teotihuacán (tay-oh-tee-wah-KAHN) in central Mexico. Teotihuacán reached its height around AD 500. Study this map. What can it tell you about the history of the city?

Teotihuacán, c. AD 500

Pyramid of the Moon

Pyramid of the Sun

San Juan River

Houses

Street of the Dead

Citadel

San Lorenzo River

Size and Importance As the map shows, Teotihuacán was a large city. It had many buildings and a large population. From this, you might conclude that the city was important, just as big cities are important today.

18

Standards Focus

HSS 6.1 Students describe what is known through archaeological studies of the early physical and cultural development of humankind from the Paleolithic era to the agricultural revolution.

6.1.2 Identify the locations of human communities that populated the major regions of the world and describe how humans adapted to a variety of environments.

Social Studies Skill: Interpreting Maps

Standards Proficiency

Detectives in Time 🐻 **HSS** 6.1.2; **HSS** Analysis Skills: CS 3, HR 1

1. Have students examine the map to see what they can learn about the city of Teotihuacán and the people who lived there. Have students consider the following questions:

   • Approximately how big was the area of the city in 500 AD?

   • Why might people have settled there? What natural resources are apparent?

   • How spaced out are the dwellings? Do they appear to have yards or gardens?

   • Why do you think the river's course was changed? How many people and what sort of equipment might such a project have involved?

2. Discuss what the answers reveal about the people and city of Teotihuacán.

3. Then encourage students to ask their own questions about the information on the map. Explain that this process of forming questions based on maps is one way that historians work. **LS Visual/Spatial**

   📖 Alternative Assessment Handbook, Rubric 21: Map Reading

Religion The giant buildings that dominate the heart of the city, such as the Pyramid of the Sun, are religious temples. From this, you can conclude that religion was very important to the people of Teotihuacán.

Pyramid of the Sun

Citadel

Street of the Dead

San Juan River

Technology The map shows that this river turns at right angles, just like the city's streets. The people of Teotihuacán must have changed the course of this river. That tells you that they had advanced engineering skills and technology.

GEOGRAPHY SKILLS INTERPRETING MAPS

1. **Place** How does the map indicate that Teotihuacán was an important place?
2. **Location** What can you conclude from the fact that large religious buildings are located in the heart of the city?

19

Connect to Civics

Early City Planning Teotihuacán was carefully planned. The Street of the Dead, the main axis of the city, runs north-south and points directly at the mountain Cerro Gordo. (The road is slightly off of true north.) On each side of the street, structures are arranged in grids, often in symmetrical layouts. Ask students how a carefully planned city could contribute to civic pride.

Info to Know

Mistaken Interpretations The names of structures in Teotihuacán reveal more about the people who named them than about their original purposes. For example, the Aztec thought the ruined buildings along the city's central road were burial sites. As a result, they named the road the Street of the Dead. Later, Spaniards mistook other ruins for a fortress and named it the Citadel. This large space was more likely used for rituals.

Linking to Today

Pyramids of Teotihuacán Archaeologists continue to dig and discover new finds at Teotihuacán. Recent excavations at the Pyramid of the Moon uncovered the skeletons of three high-ranking priests or officials. The figures were discovered seated cross-legged with their hands clasped in front of them. Their bodies were adorned with collars, ear and nose rings, and possibly headdresses. The archaeologists also found jade stones, figurines, animal remains, and carved seashells in the pyramid.

Draw Conclusions What might this discovery tell us about the culture of Teotihuacán? *possible answers—had a class structure, ceremonies for the deceased, and belief in an afterlife*

Differentiating Instruction for Universal Access

Learners Having Difficulty   Reaching Standards

1. To help students understand how historians learn from maps, draw the following chart for students to see. Complete the chart as you explain each point.

2. Then, encourage students to point out other significant or interesting features in the map and suggest what they might mean.

LS Visual/Spatial

HSS Analysis Skills: CS 3

Alternative Assessment Handbook, Rubrics 7: Charts; and 21: Map Reading

What the Map Shows	What We Can Learn
Size: *large city with many temples, buildings, homes*	*large population; probably important city*
Religion: *pyramids, or religious temples, at key sites in the city*	*religion very important to the people*
Technology: *pyramids, buildings, rerouted river*	*had advanced engineering skills, large labor force*

Answers

Interpreting Maps 1. *It was a large city with many buildings and a large population, and therefore likely an important city.* **2.** *Religion was important to the city's residents.*

Social Studies Skills

Recognizing Personal Conviction and Bias

Activity Bias in the News

Materials: photocopies of newspaper pages

1. Pass out photocopies of the editorial page and the front page from a local newspaper. Have students contrast the articles that appear on each page. Guide students in determining that the front-page news coverage is mainly objective reporting of facts. The editorial page likely contains many opinionated items.

2. Next, have students examine the editorials and letters to the editor. Ask students to identify any biases the writers might hold. How are these biases shaping the writers' viewpoints and opinions? See if students can find examples of stereotyping or prejudice.

3. Then assign students one editorial or letter to the editor. Have each students create a three-column chart listing the verifiable statements, or facts; the unverifiable statements, or opinions; and any examples of bias. Review students' charts as a class.
LS Verbal/Linguistic

📓 Alternative Assessment Handbook, Rubric 7: Charts

💿 Interactive Skills Tutor CD-ROM, Lesson 20: Evaluate Sources of Information for Authenticity, Reliability, and Bias

---

Social Studies Skills

Analysis | Critical Thinking | **Participation** | Study

Recognizing Personal Conviction and Bias

Understand the Skill

Everybody has *convictions*, or things that they strongly believe. However, if we form opinions about people or events based only on our beliefs, we may be showing bias. *Bias* is an idea about someone or something based solely on opinions, not facts.

There are many types of bias. Sometimes people form opinions about others based on the group to which that person belongs. For example, some people might believe that all teenagers are selfish or that all politicians are dishonest. These are examples of a type of bias called *stereotyping*. Holding negative opinions of people based on their race, religion, age, gender, or similar characteristics is known as *prejudice*.

We should always be on guard for the presence of personal biases. Such biases can slant how we view, judge, and provide information. Honest and accurate communication requires people to be as free of bias as possible.

Learn the Skill

As you read or write, watch out for biases. One way to identify a bias is to look for facts that support a statement. If a belief seems unreasonable when compared to the facts, it may be a sign of bias.

Another sign of bias is a person's unwillingness to question his or her belief if it is challenged by evidence. People sometimes cling to views that evidence proves are wrong. This is why bias is defined as a "fixed" idea about something. It also points out a good reason why we should try to avoid being biased. Our biases can keep us from considering new ideas and learning new things.

You will meet many peoples from the past as you study world history. Their beliefs, behaviors, and ways of life may seem different or strange to you. It is important to remain unbiased and to keep an open mind. Recognize that "different" does not mean "not as good."

Understand that early peoples did not have the technology or the accumulation of past knowledge that we have today. Be careful to not look down on them just because they were less advanced or might seem "simpler" than we are today. Remember that their struggles, learning, and achievements helped make us what we are today.

The following guidelines can help you to recognize and reduce your own biases. Keep them in mind as you study world history.

❶ When discussing a topic, try to think of beliefs and experiences in your own background that might affect how you feel about the topic.

❷ Try to not mix statements of fact with statements of opinion. Clearly separate and indicate what you *know* to be true from what you *believe* to be true.

❸ Avoid using emotional, positive, or negative words when communicating factual information.

Practice and Apply the Skill

Professional historians try to be objective about the history they study and report. Being *objective* means not being influenced by personal feelings or opinions. Write a paragraph explaining why you think being objective is important in the study of history.

Social Studies Skills Activity: Recognizing Personal Conviction and Bias

Determining Bias in Primary and Secondary Sources

Standards Proficiency

1. Read the textbook's definitions of primary and secondary sources aloud for students.

   • **primary source:** an account of an event created by someone who took part in or witnessed the event

   • **secondary source:** information gathered by someone who did not take part in or witness an event

2. Ask students to list examples of each type of source (primary—diaries, editorials, letters, newspaper articles, photographs, political cartoons; secondary—biographies, encyclopedias, history textbooks, and monographs). Then discuss with students the bias that might be inherent in each example (e.g., the letters of a military commander and the journal of a soldier will reflect different viewpoints and perspectives on a conflict).
LS Interpersonal, Verbal/Linguistic

📓 Alternative Assessment Handbook, Rubric 11: Discussions

Answers

Practice and Apply the Skill
Answers will vary, but students should note that personal biases will influence the ways in which people interpret events in history. Thus, historians need to remain objective when they interpret events and try to view the events within the context of the period.

Standards Review

Visual Summary

Use the visual summary below to help you review the main ideas of the chapter.

QUICK FACTS

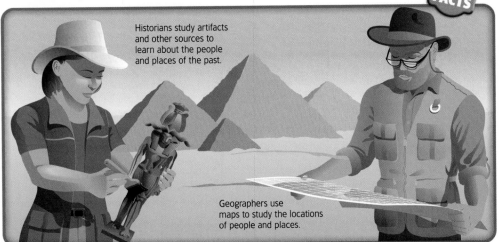

Historians study artifacts and other sources to learn about the people and places of the past.

Geographers use maps to study the locations of people and places.

Reviewing Vocabulary, Terms, and People

*For each statement below, write **T** if it is true or **F** if it is false. If the statement is false, write the correct term that would make the sentence a true statement.*

1. History is the study of the past based on what people left behind.

2. Knowledge, beliefs, customs, and values of a group of people are part of their environment.

3. A handwritten letter from a soldier to his family would be considered a primary source.

4. Geography is the study of the past, whether recent or long ago.

5. Your state probably has many different landforms, such as mountains, plains, and valleys.

6. Weather changes from day to day, but a location's climate does not change as often.

7. Values are ideas that people hold dear and try to live by.

Comprehension and Critical Thinking

SECTION 1 *(Pages 6–11)*

8. **a. Describe** What is history? What is archaeology? How do the two fields work together?

   b. Make Inferences Why may a historian who is still alive disagree with conclusions drawn by a historian who lived a hundred years ago?

   c. Evaluate Do you think primary sources or secondary sources are more valuable to modern historians? Why?

SECTION 2 *(Pages 12–17)*

9. **a. Identify** What are the two main branches of geography, and how does each contribute to our understanding of history?

   b. Analyze If you were asked to divide your state into regions, what features would you use to define those regions? Why?

   c. Predict How might a long period of severe heat or cold affect the history of a city or region?

UNCOVERING THE PAST **21**

Answers

Visual Summary

Review and Inquiry Have students use the visual summary to discuss details related to the professions of historian and geographer.

🖳 Quick Facts Transparency: Uncovering the Past Visual Summary

Reviewing Vocabulary, Terms, and People

1. F; archaeology
2. F; culture
3. T
4. F; history
5. T
6. T
7. T

Comprehension and Critical Thinking

8. **a.** study of the past; study of the past based on what people left behind; possible answer—Each field can help the other fill in the blanks in what they know.

   b. possible answer—New information or new interpretations can lead historians to draw new conclusions.

   c. possible answers—primary, because they are from eyewitnesses; secondary, because they draw from many sources, and even eyewitnesses are not completely reliable

---

Review and Assessment Resources

Review and Reinforce

SE Standards Review

📋 **CRF:** Chapter Review Activity

📋 California Standards Review Workbook

🖳 Quick Facts Transparency: Uncovering the Past Visual Summary

▶ Spanish Chapter Summaries Audio CD Program

💻 Online Chapter Summaries in Six Languages

OSP Holt PuzzlePro; Game Tool for ExamView

⚫ Quiz Game CD-ROM

Assess

SE Standards Assessment

📋 PASS: Chapter Test, Forms A and B

📋 Alternative Assessment Handbook

OSP ExamView Test Generator, Chapter Test

⚫ Universal Access Modified Worksheets and Tests CD-ROM: Chapter Test

💻 Holt Online Assessment Program (in the Premier Online Edition)

Reteach/Intervene

📋 Interactive Reader and Study Guide

📋 Universal Access Teacher Management System: Lesson Plans for Universal Access

⚫ Universal Access Modified Worksheets and Tests CD-ROM

⚫ Interactive Skills Tutor CD-ROM

go.hrw.com

Online Resources

Chapter Resources:
KEYWORD: SQ6 WH1

9. a. physical, human; physical—Landforms, climate, resources, and other aspects of physical geography affect where and how people live; human—Culture affects how people make history.

b. Answers will vary, but students should make logical choices among physical features such as mountains and rivers and human factors such as language or ways of making a living.

c. possible answers—could affect ability to raise food, to transport goods to or from markets, to support a tourist industry, to help vulnerable people survive, and so on

Using the Internet

10. Go to the HRW Web site and enter the keyword shown to access a rubric for this activity.

> KEYWORD: SQ6 TEACHER

Social Studies Skills

11. Students should discuss objects from the room as if they were artifacts from an ancient civilization. Monitor discussions to ensure that students are using personal participation skills.

Reading Skills

12. history, culture, artifacts, values, history or geography

Reviewing Themes

13. possible answer—may reveal how the historian's society or culture viewed war in general or that particular battle, depending on who participated and who won; may also reveal what qualities the historian's society admired in a leader or in warriors

14. possible answer—Technology was important not just for business and basic communication, but also for entertainment.

Using the Internet

go.hrw.com
KEYWORD: SQ6 WH1

10. Activity: Describing Artifacts Archaeologists study the past based on what people have left behind. Enter the activity keyword and explore recent archaeological discoveries. Select one artifact that interests you and write a short article about it. Write your article as if it will be printed in a school magazine. Describe the artifact in detail: What is it? Who made it? Where was it found? What does the artifact tell archaeologists and historians about the society or culture that created it? You may want to create a chart like the one below to organize your information. If possible, include illustrations with your article.

Artifact	
What is it?	
Who made it?	
Where was it found?	
What does it tell us?	

Social Studies Skills

11. Developing Personal Participation Skills Over the course of this year, your teacher will probably organize the class into groups to complete some assignments. Working in groups requires you to have certain skills. Those skills include being sensitive to the opinions of others, expressing your own opinions clearly and calmly, recognizing your personal biases or prejudices, and just being willing to participate.

Practice working in groups by examining objects in the classroom as if they were old artifacts left by an ancient civilization. Discuss with your classmates what these objects could tell later generations about education in the United States in the 2000s. Remember that you should be willing to express your ideas to the other members of your group. At the same time, you must be willing to listen to other people's thoughts, ideas, and opinions.

Reading Skills

12. Understanding the Specialized Language of History Read the following passage in which several words have been left blank. Fill in each of the blanks with the appropriate word that you learned in this chapter.

> " Although _____ is defined as the study of the past, it is much more. It is a key to understanding our _____, the ideas, languages, religions, and other traits that make us who we are. In the _____ left behind by ancient peoples we can see reflections of our own material goods: plates and dishes, toys, jewelry, and work objects. These objects show us that human _____ haven't changed that much. After all, people still hold many of the same ideas dear that they did years and years ago. In other words, studying the past can lead to a new _____ of the present as people re-examine and re-evaluate our lives and change how we view ourselves. "

Reviewing Themes

13. Society and Culture How may a historian's description of a battle reveal information about his or her own society or culture?

14. Science and Technology If hundreds of years from now archaeologists study the things we leave behind, what may they conclude about the role of technology in American society? Explain your answer.

FOCUS ON WRITING

15. Writing Your Job Description Review your notes on the work of historians, archaeologists, and physical and human geographers. Choose one of these jobs and write a description of it. You should begin your description by explaining why the job is important. Then identify the job's tasks and responsibilities. Finally, tell what kind of person would do well in this job. For example, a historian may enjoy reading and an archaeologist may enjoy working outdoors. When you have finished your description, you may be able to add it to a class or school guide for career planning.

Focus on Writing

15. Rubric Students' job descriptions should:

- explain why the job is important.
- describe the tasks and responsibilities of the job.
- end by telling what kind of person would be good for the job.
- use correct grammar, punctuation, spelling, and capitalization.

CRF: Focus on Writing: A Job Description

Standards Assessment

DIRECTIONS: Read each question, and write the letter of the best response.

1

The object with ancient writing that is shown in this photo is a

A primary source and a resource.

B primary source and an artifact.

C secondary source and a resource.

D secondary source and an artifact.

2 Which of the following is the *best* reason for studying history?

A We can learn the dates of important events.

B We can learn interesting facts about famous people.

C We can learn about ourselves and other people.

D We can hear stories about strange things.

3 The study of people and the places where they live is called

A archaeology.

B environmental science.

C human geography.

D history.

4 Which of the following subjects would interest a physical geographer the *least*?

A a place's climate

B a mountain range

C a river system

D a country's highways

5 The type of evidence that an archaeologist would find most useful is a(n)

A artifact.

B primary source.

C secondary source.

D landform.

Connecting with Past Learnings

6 Last year in Grade 5, you learned about American history from several different sources. Which of the following sources you might have studied is a secondary source?

A the Declaration of Independence

B the diary of a classmate's ancestor

C a chapter in your textbook

D a letter written by George Washington

7 Which of the following topics you studied in American History in Grade 5 is an example of a region?

A New England

B the Mayflower Compact

C the Iroquois people

D the slave trade

UNCOVERING THE PAST **23**

Intervention Resources

Reproducible

- Interactive Reader and Study Guide
- Universal Access Teacher Management System: Universal Access Lesson Plans

Technology

- Quick Facts Transparency: Uncovering the Past Visual Summary
- Universal Access Modified Worksheets and Tests CD-ROM
- Interactive Skills Tutor CD-ROM

Tips for Test Taking

Take It All In Encourage students to preview the test to get a mental map of their tasks:

- Know how many questions there are.
- Know where to stop.
- Set time checkpoints.
- Do the easy sections first; easy questions can be worth just as many points as hard ones.

Chapter 2 Planning Guide

The Stone Ages and Early Cultures

Chapter Overview	Reproducible Resources	Technology Resources
Chapter 2 pp. 24–47 **Overview:** In this chapter, students will study our earliest ancestors and the beginnings of agriculture. 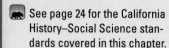 See page 24 for the California History–Social Science standards covered in this chapter.	 **Universal Access Teacher Management System:** * • Universal Access Instructional Benchmarking Guides • Lesson Plans for Universal Access  **Interactive Reader and Study Guide:** Chapter Graphic Organizer* **Chapter Resource File* • Chapter Review Activity • Focus on Writing Activity: A Storyboard • Social Studies Skills Activity: Identifying Central Issues	 **One-Stop Planner CD-ROM:** Calendar Planner **Student Edition Full-Read Audio CD-ROM** **Universal Access Modified Worksheets and Tests CD-ROM** **Interactive Skills Tutor CD-ROM** **Primary Source Library CD-ROM for World History** **Power Presentations with Video CD-ROM** **History's Impact: World History Video Program (VHS/DVD):** The Stone Ages and Early Cultures* **A Teacher's Guide to Religion in the Public Schools***
Section 1: **The First People** **The Big Idea:** Prehistoric people learned to adapt to their environment, to make simple tools, to use fire, and to use language. 6.1.1	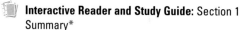 **Universal Access Teacher Management System:** * Section 1 Lesson Plan  **Interactive Reader and Study Guide:** Section 1 Summary* **Chapter Resource File*** • Vocabulary Builder Activity, Section 1 • Biography Activity: Donald Johanson and Tim White • Biography Activity: The Leakey Family • Interdisciplinary Project: The First People: Flannel Board Story • Literature Activity: *Boy of the Painted Cave,* by Justin Denzel • Primary Source Activity: The Discovery of Chauvet Cave	 **Daily Bellringer Transparency:** Section 1* **Map Transparency:** Early Hominid Sites* **Quick Facts Transparency:** Early Hominids* **Internet Activities:** Archaeological Discoveries; In Her Shoes: Mary Leakey
Section 2: **Early Human Migration** **The Big Idea:** As people migrated around the world they learned to adapt to new environments. 6.1.2	**Universal Access Teacher Management System:** * Section 2 Lesson Plan **Interactive Reader and Study Guide:** Section 2 Summary* **Chapter Resource File*** • Vocabulary Builder Activity, Section 2	**Daily Bellringer Transparency:** Section 2* **Map Transparency:** Early Human Migration*
Section 3: **Beginnings of Agriculture** **The Big Idea:** The development of agriculture brought great changes to human society 6.1.3	**Universal Access Teacher Management System:** * Section 3 Lesson Plan **Interactive Reader and Study Guide:** Section 3 Summary* **Chapter Resource File*** • Vocabulary Builder Activity, Section 3 • History and Geography Activity: Agriculture and Animals • Primary Source Activity: Objects from Çatal Hüyük	**Daily Bellringer Transparency:** Section 3* **Map Transparency:** Early Domestication*

Review, Assessment, Intervention

 Standards Review Workbook*

Quick Facts Transparency: The Stone Ages and Early Cultures Visual Summary*

Spanish Chapter Summaries Audio CD Program

Online Chapter Summaries in Six Languages

Quiz Game CD-ROM

Progress Assessment Support System (PASS): Chapter Test*

Universal Access Modified Worksheets and Tests CD-ROM: Modified Chapter Test

One-Stop Planner CD-ROM: ExamView Test Generator (English/Spanish)

Alternative Assessment Handbook

Holt Online Assessment Program (HOAP), in the Holt Premier Online Student Edition

---

PASS: Section 1 Quiz*

Online Quiz: Section 1

Alternative Assessment Handbook

PASS: Section 2 Quiz*

Online Quiz: Section 2

Alternative Assessment Handbook

PASS: Section 3 Quiz*

Online Quiz: Section 3

Alternative Assessment Handbook

 # California Resources for Standards Mastery

INSTRUCTIONAL PLANNING AND SUPPORT

Universal Access Teacher Management System*

One-Stop Planner CD-ROM with Test Generator: Teacher Management System with Interactive Teacher's Edition

STANDARDS MASTERY

Standards Review Workbook*

At Home: A Guide to Standards Mastery for World History

Holt Online Learning

To enhance learning, the following Internet activities are available: **Archaeological Discoveries** and **In Her Shoes: Mary Leakey.**

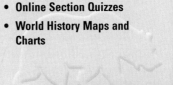

KEYWORD: SQ6 TEACHER

- **Teacher Support Page**
- **Content Updates**
- **Rubrics and Writing Models**

- **Teaching Tips for the Multimedia Classroom**

KEYWORD: SQ6 WH2

- **Current Events**
- **Holt Grapher**
- **Holt Online Atlas**
- **Holt Researcher**
- **Interactive Multimedia Activities**
- **Internet Activities**

- **Online Chapter Summaries in Six Languages**
- **Online Section Quizzes**
- **World History Maps and Charts**

HOLT PREMIER ONLINE STUDENT EDITION

- **Interactive Maps and Notebook**
- **Standardized Test Prep**
- **Homework Practice and Research Activities Online**

Mastering the Standards: Differentiating Instruction

Reaching Standards — Basic-level activities designed for all students encountering new material

Standards Proficiency — Intermediate-level activities designed for average students

Exceeding Standards — Challenging activities designed for honors and gifted-and-talented students

Standard English Mastery — Activities designed to improve standard English usage

MASTERING THE CALIFORNIA STANDARDS

Frequently Asked Questions

INSTRUCTIONAL PLANNING AND SUPPORT

Where do I find planning aids, pacing guides, lesson plans, and other teaching aids?

Annotated Teacher's Edition:
- Chapter planning guides
- Standards-based instruction and strategies
- Differentiated instruction for universal access
- Point-of-use reminders for integrating program resources

Power Presentations with Video CD-ROM

Universal Access Teacher Management System:
- Year and unit instructional benchmarking guides
- Reproducible lesson plans
- Assessment guides for diagnostic, progress, and summative end-of-the-year tests
- Options for differentiating instruction and intervention
- Teaching guides and answer keys for student workbooks

One-Stop Planner CD-ROM with Test Generator: Teacher Management System with Interactive Teacher's Edition:
- Calendar Planner
- Editable lesson plans
- All reproducible ancillaries in Adobe Acrobat (PDF) format
- ExamView Test Generator (English & Spanish)
- Game Tool for ExamView
- PuzzlePro
- Transparency and video previews

DIFFERENTIATING INSTRUCTION FOR UNIVERSAL ACCESS

What resources are available to ensure that Advanced Learners/GATE Students master the standards?

Teacher's Edition Activities:
- Chance and Early People, p. 31
- Presentation on Archaeological Sites, p. 35
- Migration Throughout History, p. 37

Lesson Plans for Universal Access

Primary Source Library CD-ROM for World History

What resources are available to ensure that English Learners and Standard English Learners master the standards?

Teacher's Edition Activities:
- Hominid Sites Map, p. 29
- A Day in the Life, p. 42

Lesson Plans for Universal Access

Chapter Resource File: Vocabulary Builder Activities

Spanish Chapter Summaries Audio CD Program

Online Chapter Summaries in Six Languages

One-Stop Planner CD-ROM:
- PuzzlePro, Spanish Version
- ExamView Test Generator, Spanish Version

What modified materials are available for Special Education?

The *Universal Access Modified Worksheets and Tests CD-ROM* provides editable versions of the following:

Vocabulary Flash Cards

Modified Vocabulary Builder Activities

Modified Chapter Review Activity

Modified Chapter Test

What resources are available to ensure that Learners Having Difficulty master the standards?

Teacher's Edition Activities:
• A Time Capsule, p. 30
• Mural of Ancient Farm Community, p. 41

Interactive Reader and Study Guide

Student Edition Full-Read Audio CD

Quick Facts Transparency: The Stone Ages and Early Cultures Visual Summary

Standards Review Workbook

Social Studies Skills Activity: Identifying Central Issues

Interactive Skills Tutor CD-ROM

How do I intervene for students struggling to master the standards?

Interactive Reader and Study Guide

Quick Facts Transparency: The Stone Ages and Early Cultures Visual Summary

Standards Review Workbook

Social Studies Skills Activity: Identifying Central Issues

Interactive Skills Tutor CD-ROM

PROFESSIONAL DEVELOPMENT

HOLT
**Professional
Development**

What teacher training resources are available to help me grow professionally?

• In-service and staff development as part of your Holt Social Studies product purchase
• Quick Teacher Tutorial Lesson Presentation CD-ROM
• Intensive tuition-based Teacher Development Institute
• Convenient Holt Speaker Bureau face-to-face workshop options

• PRAXIS™ Test Prep (#0089) interactive Web-based content refreshers*
• *Ask A Professional Development Expert* at http://www.hrw.com/prodev/

* PRAXIS is a trademark of Educational Testing Service (ETS). This publication is not endorsed or approved by ETS.

Information Literacy Skills

To learn more about how History–Social Science instruction may be improved by the effective use of library media centers and information literacy skills, go to the Teacher's Resource Materials for Chapter 2 at **go.hrw.com, keyword: SQ6 MEDIA.**

MASTERING THE CALIFORNIA STANDARDS

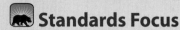

Standards Focus

Standards by Section
Section 1: **HSS** 6.1.1
Section 2: **HSS** 6.1.2
Section 3: **HSS** 6.1.3

Teacher's Edition
HSS Analysis Skills: CS 1, CS 2, CS 3, HR 4, HI 1, HI 2, HI 3, HI 4, HI 5

ELA Writing 6.1.2; Reading 6.2.0

Upcoming Standards for Future Learning
Preview the following History–Social Science content standards from upcoming chapters or grade levels to promote learning beyond the current chapter.

HSS Students compare and contrast the geographic, political, economic, religious and social structures of the Meso-American and Andean civilizations.

7.7.1 Study the locations, landforms, and climates of Mexico, Central America, and South America and their effects on Mayan, Aztec, and Incan economies, trade, and development of urban societies.

Focus on Writing

The **Chapter Resource File** provides a Focus on Writing worksheet to help students organize and create their storyboards.

CRF: Focus on Writing Activity: A Storyboard

CHAPTER 2 5 MILLION YEARS AGO– 5,000 YEARS AGO

The Stone Ages and Early Cultures

California Standards

History–Social Science
6.1 Students describe what is known through archaeological studies of the early physical and cultural development of humankind from the Paleolithic era to the agricultural revolution.

Analysis Skills
CS 1 Understand how events are related in time.

HI 1 Explain central issues and problems from the past.

English–Language Arts
Writing 6.1.2 Conclude with a detailed summary linked to the purpose of the composition.

Reading 6.2.4 Clarify an understanding of texts by creating outlines, logical notes, summaries, or reports.

FOCUS ON WRITING

A Storyboard Prehistoric humans did not write. However, they did carve and paint images on cave walls. In the spirit of these images, you will create a storyboard that uses images to tell the story of prehistoric humans. Remember that a storyboard tells a story with simple sketches and short captions.

4–5 million
Early humanlike creatures called Australopithecus develop in Africa.

5 MILLION YEARS AGO

2.6 million
Hominids make the first stone tools.

Introduce the Chapter

Standards Proficiency

Focus on the Stone Age **HSS** Analysis Skills: HI 1, HI 3

1. Ask students to describe ways in which Stone Age people are shown today in movies, comic strips, television programs, video games, or other media. List students' suggestions for the class to see.

2. Discuss whether these productions show early peoples as stupid or smart, capable or clumsy, aggressive or peaceful.

3. Then challenge students to consider how well they would do if they faced the same challenges that Stone Age peoples faced.

4. Point out that in this chapter, students will learn that early peoples developed remarkable skills in order to survive. **LS** Verbal/Linguistic

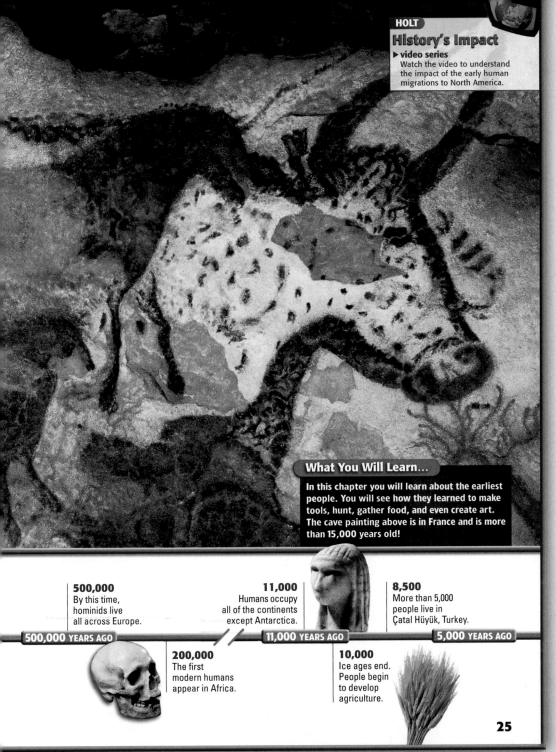

HOLT
History's Impact
► video series
Watch the video to understand
the impact of the early human
migrations to North America.

What You Will Learn...

In this chapter you will learn about the earliest
people. You will see how they learned to make
tools, hunt, gather food, and even create art.
The cave painting above is in France and is more
than 15,000 years old!

500,000
By this time,
hominids live
all across Europe.

500,000 YEARS AGO

200,000
The first
modern humans
appear in Africa.

11,000
Humans occupy
all of the continents
except Antarctica.

11,000 YEARS AGO

10,000
Ice ages end.
People begin
to develop
agriculture.

8,500
More than 5,000
people live in
Çatal Hüyük, Turkey.

5,000 YEARS AGO

25

Explore the Time Line

1. About when did the first modern humans
   appear in Africa? *200,000 years ago*

2. When did the Ice Ages end? *10,000 years ago*

3. About how many years passed between the
   end of the Ice Ages and Çatal Hüyük's growth
   into a large town? *1,500 years*

4. Why does the time line have breaks in it?
   *because it covers such a long period of time
   that it would take up several pages otherwise*

HSS **Analysis Skills:** CS 1

MISCONCEPTION
////**ALERT**\\\\

Multiple Ice Ages Some students may be
under the impression that there was just one
long period when the ice sheets advanced.
Explain to students that there were several ice
ages, however; these periods of glacial action
date back hundreds of millions of years. Some
scientists think that eventually we will enter
another Ice Age.

HOLT
History's Impact
► video series
See the Video Teacher's
Guide for strategies for using the
chapter video **The Stone Ages
and Early Cultures: The Impact
of the Early Migrations to North
America.**

Chapter Big Ideas

Section 1 Prehistoric people learned
to adapt to their environment, to make
simple tools, to use fire, and to use
language. HSS 6.1.1

Section 2 As people migrated around
the world they learned to adapt to new
environments. HSS 6.1.2

Section 3 The development of agriculture brought great changes to human
society. HSS 6.1.3

Explore the Picture

Lascaux Cave Paintings The paintings shown at left are in a cave in
France. They were created 17,000 to
15,000 years ago. Some 600 painted
and drawn animals adorn the walls of
this cave. Four teenage boys discovered
the cave by accident in 1940, and the
site was opened to the public in 1948.
Because they were exposed to artifi-
cial lighting, damp air, and people, the
paintings began to deteriorate. In 1963
the cave was closed to the public. A
partial replica was created and made
available to tourists.

Analyzing Visuals What details can
you identify in the paintings of the
animals? *possible answers—spots on
the cow, horse's mane*

go.hrw.com
Online Resources

Chapter Resources:
KEYWORD: SQ6 WH2
Teacher Resources:
KEYWORD: SQ6 TEACHER

Reading Social Studies

by Kylene Beers

| Economics | Geography | Politics | Religion | Society and Culture | Science and Technology |

Understanding Themes

Introduce the themes of this chapter by asking students to imagine that it is thousands of years ago and they live in a very small group in the wilderness. Their group is responsible for finding its own food, making its own clothing, building its own shelters, and protecting itself. Ask students what kind of geography would best be suited for survival. Have students describe the type of society and culture that might develop in these circumstances.

Chronological Order

Focus on Reading Ask each student to write one or two paragraphs that summarize their typical school day. Have students write their summaries in chronological order, from the time they wake up in the morning until they go to sleep. Ask students to exchange summaries. Have each student circle words or phrases they find that signal chronological order. Then have students use those words to create a sequence chain that tracks the events of a typical day.

Focus on Themes In this chapter you will learn about the earliest humans and how they lived. You will read about scientists who work constantly to learn more about this mysterious time. As you read, you will see the beginnings of human

society and culture—the making of tools, the use of fire, and the creation of language. You will also read about the **geography** of the world and how it shaped where and how early people lived.

Chronological Order

Focus on Reading History, just our like our lives, can be seen as a series of events in time. To understand history and events, we often need to see how they are related in time.

Understanding Chronological Order The word **chronological** means "related to time." Events discussed in this history book are discussed in **sequence**, in the order in which they happened. To understand history better, you can use a sequence chain to take notes about events in the order they happened.

Additional reading support can be found in the

Inter**active**
Reader and Study Guide

Sequence Chain

A scientists goes to Africa and drives to a gorge to search for fossils.

↓

She searches for several hours and finds a bone.

↓

She calls another scientist to report what she found.

> Writers sometimes signal chronological order, or sequence, by using words or phrases like these:
>
> *first, before, then, later, soon, after, before long, next, eventually, finally*

Reading and Skills Resources

Reading Support

- Interactive Reader and Study Guide
- Student Edition on Audio CD
- Spanish Chapter Summaries Audio CD Program

Social Studies Skills Support

- Interactive Skills Tutor CD-ROM

Vocabulary Support

- **CRF:** Vocabulary Builder Activities
- **CRF:** Chapter Review Activity
- Universal Access Modified Worksheets and Tests CD-ROM:
  - Vocabulary Flash Cards
  - Vocabulary Builder Activity
  - Chapter Review Activity

OSP Holt PuzzlePro

Standards Focus

HSS Analysis Skills: CS 1
ELA Reading 6.2.4

HSS Analysis CS 1 Understand how events are related in time.

ELA Reading 6.2.4 Clarify an understanding of texts by creating outlines, logical notes, summaries, or reports.

You Try It!

The following passage is from the chapter you are about to read. Read the sentences carefully and think about order of events.

Scientists Study Remains

One archaeologist who made important discoveries about prehistory was Mary Leakey. In 1959 she found bones in East Africa that were more than 1.5 million years old. She and her husband, Louis Leakey, believed that the bones belonged to a hominid, an early ancestor of humans . . .

In 1974 anthropologist Donald Johanson found bones from another early ancestor . . . Johanson named his find Lucy. Tests showed that she lived more than 3 million years ago . . .

In 1994 anthropologist Tim White found even older remains. He believes that the hominid he found may have lived as long as 4.4 million years ago.

From Chapter 2, pages 28–29

After you read the sentences, answer the following questions.

1. Draw a three-part sequence chain on your own paper.

   a. What are the three dates that tell you the chronological order of the three discoveries?

   b. Where do the discoveries go in your sequence chain?

2. Study the sequence chain you've made. Leakey made her find in 1959. The bones she found were about 1.5 million years old. Johanson found bones in 1974 that were more than 3 million years old. White made his find in 1994 and the bones he found were 4.4 million years old. Why do you think that as time continued anthropologists were able to find older and older bones?

3. Create another sequence chain. Sequence the discoveries in the order of the age of the bones, oldest to youngest.

Key Terms and People

Chapter 2

Section 1
prehistory *(p. 28)*
hominid *(p. 28)*
ancestor *(p. 28)*
tool *(p. 30)*
Paleolithic Era *(p. 31)*
society *(p. 33)*
hunter-gatherers *(p. 33)*

Section 2
migrate *(p. 36)*
ice ages *(p. 36)*
land bridge *(p. 36)*
Mesolithic Era *(p. 38)*

Section 3
Neolithic Era *(p. 41)*
domestication *(p. 41)*
agriculture *(p. 42)*
megaliths *(p. 42)*

Academic Vocabulary

Success in school is related to knowing academic vocabulary—the words that are frequently used in school assignments and discussions. In this chapter, you will learn the following academic words:

distribute *(p. 33)*
development *(p. 42)*

As you read Chapter 2, look for words that indicate the order in which events occurred.

Reading Social Studies

Key Terms and People

Preteach these words by instructing students to create a time line. Have them list on the time line *Paleolithic Era, Mesolithic Era,* and *Neolithic Era.* Write the key terms for the class to see, mixing up the order in which they appear in the chapter. Have students select the terms that they believe represent each era and write these terms under the appropriate era. Discuss the meanings of each term with the students. Then have students correct their time lines, placing the key terms under the appropriate era. **LS Verbal/Linguistic**

Focus on Reading

See the **Focus on Reading** questions in this chapter for more practice on this reading social studies skill.

Reading Social Studies Assessment

See the **Standards Review** at the end of this chapter for student assessment questions related to this reading skill.

THE STONE AGES AND EARLY CULTURES **27**

Teaching Tip

To help students understand the larger context of world history chronology, have them keep a world time line that identifies the various civilizations and cultures and lists what events happened at what time. You might even post a large world time line for students to see. As the class covers different events, add them to the time line.

Answers

You Try It! 1. *1959, Mary Leakey finds bones in East Africa; 1974, Donald Johanson finds Lucy; 1994, Tim White finds hominid remains.* **2.** *possible answer—technology has improved with time, making it possible to judge the age of remains or to locate bones;* **3.** *remains found by Tim White, 4.4 million years old; Lucy, 3 million years old; bones found by Mary Leakey, 1.5 million years old*

The First People

Bellringer

If YOU were there. . . Use the **Daily Bellringer Transparency** to help students answer the question.

📖 Daily Bellringer Transparency, Section 1

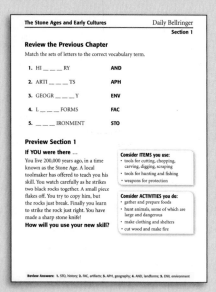

Academic Vocabulary

Review with students the high-use academic term in this section.

distribute to divide among a group of people (p. 33)

📑 **CRF:** Vocabulary Builder Activity, Section 1

🐻 Standards Focus

HSS 6.1.1

Means: Describe how tools and the use of fire helped early human societies.

Matters: Learning to use fire and tools helped hunter-gatherer societies better protect and feed themselves.

28 CHAPTER 2

What You Will Learn...

Main Ideas

1. Scientists study the remains of early humans to learn about prehistory.
2. Hominids and early humans first appeared in East Africa millions of years ago.
3. Stone Age tools grew more complex as time passed.
4. Hunter-gatherer societies developed language, art, and religion.

The Big Idea

Prehistoric people learned to adapt to their environment, to make simple tools, to use fire, and to use language.

Key Terms

prehistory, p. 28
hominid, p. 28
ancestor, p. 28
tool, p. 30
Paleolithic Era, p. 31
society, p. 33
hunter-gatherers, p. 33

🐻

HSS 6.1.1 Describe the hunter-gatherer societies, including the development of tools and the use of fire.

28 CHAPTER 2

If YOU were there...

You live 200,000 years ago, in a time known as the Stone Age. A local toolmaker has offered to teach you his skill. You watch carefully as he strikes two black rocks together. A small piece flakes off. You try to copy him, but the rocks just break. Finally you learn to strike the rock just right. You have made a sharp stone knife!

How will you use your new skill?

> **BUILDING BACKGROUND** Over millions of years early people learned many new things. Making stone tools was one of the earliest and most valuable skills that they developed. Scientists who study early humans learn a lot about them from the tools and other objects that they made.

Scientists Study Remains

Although humans have lived on the earth for more than a million years, writing was not invented until about 5,000 years ago. Historians call the time before there was writing **prehistory**. To study prehistory, historians rely on the work of archaeologists and anthropologists.

One archaeologist who made important discoveries about prehistory was Mary Leakey. In 1959 she found bones in East Africa that were more than 1.5 million years old. She and her husband, Louis Leakey, believed that the bones belonged to an early **hominid** (HAH-muh-nuhd), an early ancestor of humans. An **ancestor** is a relative who lived in the past.

In fact, the bones belonged to an Australopithecus (aw-stray-loh-PI-thuh-kuhs), one of the earliest ancestors of humans. In 1974 anthropologist Donald Johanson (joh-HAN-suhn) found bones from another early ancestor. He described his discovery:

> "We reluctantly headed back toward camp ... I glanced over my right shoulder. Light glinted off a bone. I knelt down for a closer look ... Everywhere we looked on the slope around us we saw more bones lying on the surface."
>
> –Donald Johanson, from *Ancestors: In Search of Human Origins*

Teach the Big Idea: Master the Standards

Standards Proficiency

The First People 🐻 **HSS** 6.1.1; **HSS** Analysis Skills: HI 1, HI 3

1. **Teach** Ask students the Main Idea questions to teach this section.

2. **Apply** Ask each student to choose a time period from the section and to imagine that he or she lived during that time. Have students create drawings to show what daily life was like. Students should include topics such as available tools, food, and activities in their drawings. **LS Visual/Spatial**

3. **Review** Display and discuss the drawings.

4. **Practice/Homework** Ask students to imagine they are archaeologists who have discovered their drawings. Have each student write a paragraph about what an archaeologist might conclude about prehistoric life based on the drawings. Students should base the conclusions on the information in the section. **LS Verbal/Linguistic**

📑 Alternative Assessment Handbook, Rubric 40: Writing to Describe

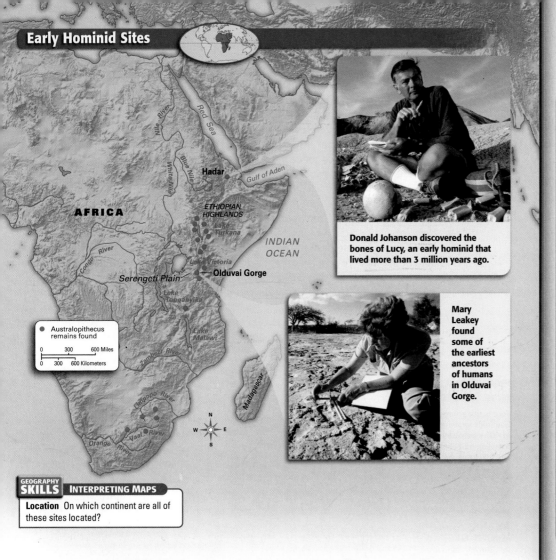

Early Hominid Sites

Hadar

AFRICA

ETHIOPIAN HIGHLANDS

Gulf of Aden

INDIAN OCEAN

Nile River

Red Sea

Blue Nile

White Nile

Congo River

Lake Turkana

Lake Victoria

— Olduvai Gorge

Serengeti Plain

Lake Tanganyika

Lake Malawi

Zambezi River

Limpopo River

Madagascar

Vaal River

Orange River

● Australopithecus remains found

0   300   600 Miles
0   300   600 Kilometers

N W E S

Donald Johanson discovered the bones of Lucy, an early hominid that lived more than 3 million years ago.

Mary Leakey found some of the earliest ancestors of humans in Olduvai Gorge.

GEOGRAPHY SKILLS **INTERPRETING MAPS**
Location On which continent are all of these sites located?

Johanson named his find Lucy. Tests showed that she lived more than 3 million years ago. Johanson could tell from her bones that she was small and had walked on two legs. The ability to walk on two legs was a key step in human development.

In 1994 anthropologist Tim White found even older remains. He believes that the hominid he found may have lived as long as 4.4 million years ago. But some scientists disagree with White's time estimate. Discoveries of ancient bones give us information about early humans and their ancestors, but not all scientists agree on the meaning of these discoveries.

READING CHECK **Drawing Inferences** What can ancient bones tell us about human ancestors?

THE STONE AGES AND EARLY CULTURES **29**

❷ Hominids and Early Humans

Hominids and early humans first appeared in East Africa millions of years ago.

Recall When do many scientists believe the first modern humans appeared? *about 200,000 years ago*

Compare What characteristic did *Homo erectus* have that modern humans also have? *the ability to walk upright*

Make Inferences How did fire help protect *Homo erectus* from wild animals? *Animals were probably afraid of fire, so* Homo erectus *could use fire to keep dangerous animals away.*

Activity **Early Human Time Line**
Have each student construct a time line showing when *Homo habilis*, *Homo erectus*, and *Homo sapiens* most likely first appeared.

📝 Alternative Assessment Handbook, Rubric 36: Time Lines

📝 **CRF:** Biography Activity: The Leakey Family

🖥 Quick Facts Transparency: Early Hominids

🐻 **HSS** 6.1.1; **HSS** Analysis Skills: CS 1, CS 2, HI 1, HI 2, HI 5

go.hrw.com
Online Resources
KEYWORD: SQ6 WH2
ACTIVITY: In Her Shoes: Mary Leakey

Answers

Early Hominids Homo erectus

Reading Check *Unlike* Homo habilis, Homo erectus *walked completely upright and could control fire.*

Hominids and Early Humans

Later groups of hominids appeared about 3 million years ago. As time passed they became more like modern humans.

FOCUS ON READING
Dates in a text can help you keep events in order in your mind.

In the early 1960s Louis Leakey found hominid remains that he called *Homo habilis*, or "handy man." Leakey and his son Richard believed that *Homo habilis* was more closely related to modern humans than Lucy and had a larger brain.

Scientists believe that another group of hominids appeared in Africa about 1.5 million years ago. This group is called *Homo erectus*, or "upright man." Scientists think these people walked completely upright like modern people do.

Scientists believe that *Homo erectus* knew how to control fire. Once fire was started by natural causes, such as lightning, people used it to cook food. Fire also gave them heat and protection against animals.

Eventually hominids developed characteristics of modern humans. Scientists are not sure exactly when or where the first modern humans lived. Many think that they first appeared in Africa about 200,000 years ago. Scientists call these people *Homo sapiens*, or "wise man." Every person alive today belongs to this group.

READING CHECK **Contrasting** How was *Homo erectus* different from *Homo habilis*?

Stone Age Tools

The first humans and their ancestors lived during a long period of time called the Stone Age. To help in their studies, archaeologists divide the Stone Age into three periods based on the kinds of tools used at the time. To archaeologists, a **tool** is any handheld object that has been modified to help a person accomplish a task.

Early Hominids

QUICK FACTS

Four major groups of hominids appeared in Africa between 5 million and about 200,000 years ago. Each group was more advanced than the one before it and could use better tools.

Which early hominid learned to control fire and use the hand ax?

Australopithecus

- Name means "southern ape"
- Appeared in Africa about 4–5 million years ago
- Stood upright and walked on two legs
- Brain was about one-third the size of modern humans

Homo habilis

- Name means "handy man"
- Appeared in Africa about 2.4 million years ago
- Used early stone tools for chopping and scraping
- Brain was about half the size of modern humans

An early Stone Age chopper

Critical Thinking: Drawing Inferences

Reaching Standards

A Time Capsule 🐻 **HSS** 6.1.1; **HSS** Analysis Skills: HI 5

1. Review the definition of the word *tool*. Then discuss with students how discovering tools of our early ancestors helps us understand how early humans lived.

2. Ask students to propose three present-day tools that they would put in a time capsule to teach future generations about today's society. Discuss an example, such as a ballpoint pen, which tells later generations that we used writing.

3. Have students write short descriptions of what their items say about modern society.

4. Ask volunteers to read their lists and descriptions aloud. **LS** **Visual/Spatial**

📝 Alternative Assessment Handbook, Rubric 11: Discussions

The first part of the Stone Age is called the **Paleolithic** (pay-lee-uh-LI-thik) **Era**, or Old Stone Age. It lasted until about 10,000 years ago. During this time people used stone tools.

Describe what the 1st tool was like.

The First Tools

Scientists have found the oldest tools in Tanzania, a country in East Africa. These sharpened stones, about the size of an adult's fist, are about 2.6 million years old. Each stone had been struck with another rock to create a sharp, jagged edge along one side. This process left one unsharpened side that could be used as a handle.

Scientists think that these first tools were mostly used to process food. The sharp edge could be used to cut, chop, or scrape roots, bones, or meat. Tools like these, called choppers, were used for about 2 million years.

Later Tools

Over time people learned to make better tools. For example, they developed the hand ax. They often made this tool out of a mineral called flint. Flint is easy to shape, and tools made from it can be very sharp. People used hand axes to break tree limbs, to dig, and to cut animal hides.

People also learned to attach wooden handles to tools. By attaching a wooden shaft to a stone point, for example, they invented the spear. Because a spear could be thrown, hunters no longer had to stand close to animals they were hunting. As a result, people could hunt larger animals. Among the animals hunted by Stone Age people were deer, horses, bison, and elephantlike creatures called mammoths.

READING CHECK **Summarizing** How did tools improve during the Old Stone Age?

Tree Map

Homo erectus

- Name means "upright man"
- Appeared in Africa about 2–1.5 million years ago
- Used early stone tools like the hand ax
- Learned to control fire
- Migrated out of Africa to Asia and Europe

A hand ax

Homo sapiens

- Name means "wise man"
- Appeared in Africa about 200,000 years ago
- Migrated around the world
- Same species as modern human beings
- Learned to create fire and use a wide variety of tools
- Developed language

A flint knife

History Close-up
Hunter-Gatherers

1. Have students examine the images on this page. Discuss with students what life may have been like for the early hunter-gatherers.

2. Next, have students identify the various activities shown in the illustration. *hunting, painting on cave walls, cooking, gathering food, making tools*

3. Ask students to name some hardships that early hunter-gatherers faced, as suggested by the picture. *possible answers—limited protection from bad weather, limited food supply, had to rely on nearby resources since they only traveled on foot, dangerous animals* **LS** **Visual/Spatial**

🐻 **HSS** 6.1.1; **HSS** Analysis Skills: HI 1

Linking to Today

A New View of Hunter-Gatherers A site in central Texas now shows that some prehistoric people led a fairly settled life. At the 40-acre site, thick layers of earth blackened by cooking fires and countless stone flakes and tools indicate that people had settled there for thousands of years. Other evidence tells archaeologists that a wide range of plants and animals were available in the region. Because there was also a steady water supply along with the food sources, people could stay there for long periods of time instead of moving from place to place.

History Close-up
Hunter-Gatherers

Early people were hunter-gatherers. They hunted animals and gathered wild plants to survive. Life for these hunter-gatherers was difficult and dangerous. Still, people learned how to make tools, use fire, and even create art.

Hunting
Most hunting was done by men. They worked together to bring down large animals.

Art
People painted herds of animals on cave walls.

Gathering
Most gathering was done by women. They gathered food like wild plants, seeds, fruits, and nuts.

Fire
People learned to use fire to cook their food.

Tools
Early people learned to make tools such as this spear for hunting.

ANALYSIS SKILL **ANALYZING VISUALS**
What tools are people using in this picture?

32 CHAPTER 2

Critical Thinking: Comparing and Contrasting
Standards Proficiency

Creating a Venn Diagram 🐻 **HSS** 6.1.1; **HSS** Analysis Skills: HI 1

1. Have students examine the picture on this page, paying close attention to the roles that men and women may have played as hunter-gatherers.

2. Draw an example of a Venn diagram for students to see. Use the following labels: *Men's Chores, Women's Chores, Shared Chores.*

3. Next, have students copy the diagram and complete it by using the information shown in the illustration.

4. Review the answers students listed in their Venn diagrams as a class. **LS** **Visual/Spatial**

📋 Alternative Assessment Handbook, Rubric 13: Graphic Organizers

Answers

Analyzing Visuals *spears*

Hunter-gatherer Societies

As early humans developed tools and new hunting techniques, they formed societies. A **society** is a community of people who share a common culture. These societies developed cultures with languages, religions, and art.

Society

Anthropologists believe that early humans lived in small groups. In bad weather they might have taken shelter in a cave if there was one nearby. When food or water became hard to find, groups of people would have to move to new areas.

The early humans of the Stone Age were **hunter-gatherers**—people who hunt animals and gather wild plants, seeds, fruits, and nuts to survive. Anthropologists believe that most Stone Age hunters were men. They hunted in groups, sometimes chasing entire herds of animals over cliffs. This method was both more productive and safer than hunting alone.

Women in hunter-gatherer societies probably took responsibility for collecting plants to eat. They likely stayed near camps and took care of children.

Language, Art, and Religion

The most important development of early Stone Age culture was language. Scientists have many theories about why language first developed. Some think it was to make hunting in groups easier. Others think it developed as a way for people to form relationships. Still others think language made it easier for people to resolve issues like how to **distribute** food.

Language wasn't the only way early people expressed themselves. They also created art. People carved figures out of stone, ivory, and bone. They painted and carved images of people and animals on cave walls. Scientists still aren't sure why people made art. Perhaps the cave paintings were used to teach people how to hunt, or maybe they had religious meanings.

ACADEMIC VOCABULARY

distribute to divide among a group of people

LINKING TO TODAY

Stone Tools

Did you know that Stone Age people's tools weren't as primitive as we might think? They made knife blades and arrowheads—like the one shown below—out of volcanic glass called obsidian. The obsidian blades were very sharp. In fact, they could be 100 times sharper and smoother than the steel blades used for surgery in modern hospitals.

Today some doctors are going back to using these Stone Age materials. They have found that blades made from obsidian are more precise than modern scalpels. Some doctors use obsidian blades for delicate surgery on the face because the stone tools leave "nicer-looking" scars.

ANALYSIS SKILL ANALYZING INFORMATION
How do you think modern obsidian blades are different from Stone Age ones?

Collaborative Learning

Standards Proficiency

Communicating Without Words HSS 6.1.1; HSS Analysis Skills: HI 1

Materials: index cards

1. Discuss with students why language was so important to human development.

2. Organize students into pairs. Give one member of each pair a card with the sentence "I am thirsty." on it. Give the other student a card with the sentence "The rains washed away our food." Tell the students not to reveal what is written on their cards.

3. Have one member of each pair try to express what is on the card to the other

student without using words. Students can use drawings or body language to make themselves understood. Then have the other student try to express his or her statement.

4. After the activity, ask students to share how successful they were. What frustrations did they experience? Then lead a discussion about the ease or difficulty of communicating without words.

LS **Interpersonal, Kinesthetic, Verbal/Linguistic**

Alternative Assessment Handbook, Rubric 14: Group Activity

Direct Teach

Main Idea

❹ Hunter-gatherer Societies

Hunter-gatherer societies developed language, art, and religion.

Define Who were hunter-gatherers? *early humans who hunted animals and gathered wild plants to survive*

Summarize How did early humans express themselves? *through language and art*

Draw Conclusions Why do you think hunting in groups was safer than hunting alone? *Groups offered protection against dangerous animals.*

CRF: Literature Activity: *Boy of the Painted Cave*, by Justin Denzel

CRF: Primary Source Activity: The Discovery of Chauvet Cave

HSS 6.1.1; HSS Analysis Skills: HI 1, HI 2

Did you know . . .

Early humans used natural dyes from different colors of plants and berries to paint images on cave walls.

Checking for Understanding

True or False Answer each statement *T* if it is true or *F* if it is false. If false, explain why.

1. Historians use the term *prehistory* to refer to the time before there was writing. *T*

2. Scientists think the first tools were developed to use as weapons. *F; think they were developed to process food.*

3. An important development of *Homo erectus* was the ability to control fire. *T*

HSS 6.1.1; HSS Analysis Skills: CS 1, HI 1

Answers

Linking to Today *They are more precise than modern scalpels and leave "nicer-looking" scars.*

Direct Teach

Info to Know

More Than a Pretty Picture Some cave paintings show not just animals that people hunted but also how predator animals hunted their own prey. For example, 32,000-year-old paintings in a Chauvet cave in France show now-extinct lions watching a herd of bison. The way the painter drew the lions with their heads down and their ears back shows that the artist had carefully observed the lions' behavior. In Africa today, lions pose the same way before rushing at their prey.

▢ **CRF:** Primary Source Activity: The Discovery of Chauvet Cave

Review & Assess

Close

Have students summarize the important developments of hunter-gatherer societies covered in this section.

Review

▢ Online Quiz, Section 1

Assess

SE Section 1 Assessment
▢ PASS: Section 1 Quiz
▢ Alternative Assessment Handbook

Reteach/Classroom Intervention

▢ California Standards Review Workbook
▢ Interactive Reader and Study Guide, Section 1
⊙ Interactive Skills Tutor CD-ROM

Cave Paintings
Thousands of years ago, early people decorated cave walls with paintings like this one. No one knows for sure why people created cave paintings, but many historians think they were related to hunting.

Why do you think this cave painting may be connected to hunting?

Scholars know little about the religious beliefs of early people. Archaeologists have found graves that included food and artifacts. Many scientists think these discoveries are proof that the first human religions developed during the Stone Age.

READING CHECK **Analyzing** What was one possible reason for the development of language?

SUMMARY AND PREVIEW Scientists have discovered and studied the remains of hominids and early humans who lived in East Africa millions of years ago. These Stone Age people were hunter-gatherers who used fire, stone tools, and language. In the next section you will learn how early humans moved out of Africa and populated the world.

---

go.hrw.com
Online Quiz
KEYWORD: SQ6 HP2

Section 1 Assessment

Reviewing Ideas, Terms, and People **HSS** 6.1.1

1. **a. Identify** Who found the bones of Lucy?
   b. Explain Why do historians need archaeologists and anthropologists to study **prehistory**?
2. **a. Recall** What is the scientific name for modern humans?
   b. Make Inferences What might have been one advantage of walking completely upright?
3. **a. Recall** What kind of **tools** did people use during the **Paleolithic Era**?
   b. Design Design a stone and wood tool you could use to help you with your chores. Describe your tool in a sentence or two.
4. **a. Define** What is a **hunter-gatherer**?
   b. Rank In your opinion, what was the most important change brought by the development of language?

Critical Thinking

5. **Evaluate** Draw a graphic organizer like the one at right. Use it to rank the three most important advancements, such as the ability to control fire, made in the Paleolithic Era. Next to your organizer, write a sentence explaining why you ranked the advancements in that order.

1. → 2. → 3.

FOCUS ON WRITING

6. **Listing Stone Age Achievements** Look back through this section and make a list of important Stone Age achievements. Which of these will you include on your storyboard? How will you illustrate them?

34 CHAPTER 2

Section 1 Assessment Answers

1. **a.** Donald Johanson
   b. because there are no written records from the earliest times of human development
2. **a.** *Homo sapiens*
   b. possible answers—Humans could use their hands, see farther, and perhaps travel faster.
3. **a.** stone choppers, axes, and spears
   b. Students' tools will vary, but descriptions should be logical.

4. **a.** a person who hunts animals and gathers wild plants, seeds, fruits, and nuts to survive
   b. possible answers—improved hunting; relationships formed; could more easily solve problems, such as how to distribute food
5. Rankings will vary, but students should justify their answers.
6. Lists and storyboards will vary, but students should support their selections.

Answers

Cave Paintings *shows animals that may have provided meat, hides, and other resources*

Reading Check *made it easier to hunt as a group, distribute food, and establish relationships*

The Iceman

Why was a Stone Age traveler in Europe's highest mountains?

The Iceman's dagger and the scabbard, or case, he carried it in

When did he live? about 5,300 years ago

Where did he live? The frozen body of the Iceman was discovered in the snowy Ötztal Alps of Italy in 1991. Scientists nicknamed him Ötzi after this location.

What did he do? That question has been debated ever since Ötzi's body was found. Apparently, he was traveling. At first scientists thought he had frozen to death in a storm. But an arrowhead found in his shoulder suggests that his death was not so peaceful. After he died, his body was covered by glaciers and preserved for thousands of years.

Why is he important? Ötzi is the oldest mummified human ever found in such good condition. His body, clothing, and tools were extremely well preserved, telling us a lot about life during the Stone Ages. His outfit was made of three types of animal skin stitched together. He wore leather shoes padded with grass, a grass cape, a fur hat, and a sort of backpack. He carried an ax with a copper blade as well as a bow and arrows.

Drawing Conclusions Why do you think the Iceman was in the Alps?

Scientists examine the Iceman's body in 1991, before it was removed from the glacier.

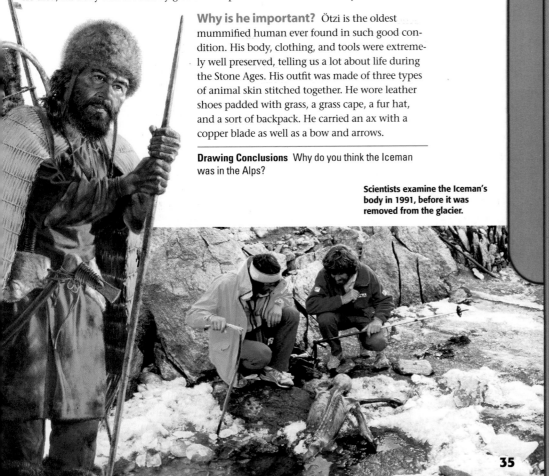

35

Biography

Reading Focus Question

Have students consider the basic needs of a person in the Stone Age, such as needs for food and shelter. Ask: What needs might this man have been trying to fill by climbing in the mountains? *possible answers—hunting, looking for materials to make clothing or shelter*
🐻 HSS 6.1.2

Did You Know . . .

The Iceman may have been hungry when he died. Scientists determined from studying a portion of the Iceman's intestine that he had not eaten within eight hours of his death.

About the Illustration
This illustration of the Iceman is an artist's conception based on available sources. However, historians are uncertain exactly what the Iceman looked like.

Answers

Drawing Conclusions *possible answers—He may have been hunting, escaping from the person or persons who may have killed him, or he could have been exiled from his people.*

Differentiating Instruction for Universal Access

Advanced Learners/GATE 🐻 HSS 6.1.2; HSS Analysis Skills: HI 4 [Exceeding Standards] [Research Required]

1. Remind students that the Iceman's body was undiscovered for thousands of years. Only when surrounding ice had melted did climbers see the body.

2. Point out that archaeological sites both small and large are still being discovered. On the other hand, some sites are being destroyed. Warfare and rising waters from dam construction are two of the most common causes of this destruction.

3. Organize the class into two large groups—one to research recently discovered archaeological sites and the other to research sites that are being destroyed. Then have each group organize into smaller groups to conduct further research on individual sites within the two broad categories.

4. Ask each small group to prepare a presentation on its chosen site. Students should discuss what information the site may provide or has provided and its current condition. Encourage students to use visual aids to enhance their presentations.

📝 Alternative Assessment Handbook, Rubrics 29: Presentations; and 30: Research

Bellringer

If YOU were there. . . Use the **Daily Bellringer Transparency** to help students answer the question.

📖 Daily Bellringer Transparency, Section 2

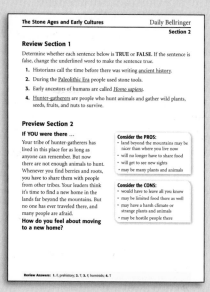

The Stone Ages and Early Cultures — Daily Bellringer — Section 2

Review Section 1

Determine whether each sentence below is **TRUE** or **FALSE**. If the sentence is false, change the underlined word to make the sentence true.

1. Historians call the time before there was writing <u>ancient history</u>.
2. During the <u>Paleolithic Era</u> people used stone tools.
3. Early ancestors of humans are called <u>Homo sapiens</u>.
4. <u>Hunter-gatherers</u> are people who hunt animals and gather wild plants, seeds, fruits, and nuts to survive.

Preview Section 2

If YOU were there …
Your tribe of hunter-gatherers has lived in this place for as long as anyone can remember. But now there are not enough animals to hunt. Whenever you find berries and roots, you have to share with people from other tribes. Your leaders think it's time to find a new home in the lands far beyond the mountains. But no one has ever traveled there, and many people are afraid.
How do you feel about moving to a new home?

Consider the PROS:
• land beyond the mountains may be nicer than where you live now
• will no longer have to share food
• will get to see new sights
• may be many plants and animals

Consider the CONS:
• would have to leave all you know
• may be limited food there as well
• may have a harsh climate or strange plants and animals
• may be hostile people there

Review Answers: 1. f, prehistory; 2. T; 3. f, hominids; 4. T

Building Vocabulary

Preteach or review the following terms:

environment all the living and nonliving things that affect life in an area (p. 38)

pottery dishes and other vessels made from clay (p. 39)

📖 **CRF:** Vocabulary Builder Activity, Section 2

🐻 Standards Focus

HSS 6.1.2
Means: Identify where human communities settled and describe how they adapted to new environments.
Matters: The human race would not have survived if people hadn't learned how to adapt to new situations.

Early Human Migration

What You Will Learn…

Main Ideas

1. People moved out of Africa as the earth's climates changed.
2. People adapted to new environments by making clothing and new types of tools.

The Big Idea

As people migrated around the world they learned to adapt to new environments.

Key Terms

migrate, p. 36
ice ages, p. 36
land bridge, p. 36
Mesolithic Era, p. 38

🌅 **HSS 6.1.2** Identify the locations of human communities that populated the major regions of the world and describe how humans adapted to a variety of environments.

If YOU were there...

Your tribe of hunter-gatherers has lived in this place for as long as anyone can remember. But now there are not enough animals to hunt. Whenever you find berries and roots, you have to share them with people from other tribes. Your leaders think it's time to find a new home in the lands far beyond the mountains. But no one has ever traveled there, and many people are afraid.

How do you feel about moving to a new home?

BUILDING BACKGROUND From their beginnings in East Africa, early humans moved in many directions. Eventually, they lived on almost every continent in the world. People probably had many reasons for moving. One reason was a change in the climate.

People Move Out of Africa

During the Old Stone Age, climate patterns around the world changed, transforming the earth's geography. In response to these changes, people began to **migrate**, or move, to new places.

The Ice Ages

Most scientists believe that about 1.6 million years ago, many places around the world began to experience long periods of freezing weather. These freezing times are called the **ice ages**. The ice ages ended about 10,000 years ago.

During the ice ages huge sheets of ice covered much of the earth's land. These ice sheets were formed from ocean water, leaving ocean levels lower than they are now. Many areas that are now underwater were dry land then. For example, a narrow body of water now separates Asia and North America. But scientists think that during the ice ages, the ocean level dropped and exposed a **land bridge**, a strip of land connecting two continents. Land bridges allowed Stone Age peoples to migrate around the world.

Teach the Big Idea: Master the Standards

Standards Proficiency

Early Human Migration 🐻 HSS 6.1.2; HSS Analysis Skills: HI 1

1. **Teach** Ask students the Main Idea questions to teach this section.

2. **Apply** Organize students into small groups. Ask students to imagine that flooding has forced them to move from dwellings near a river to a colder, mountainous, and rocky environment. Have groups write down ways they could adapt to and survive in this new environment.
   LS Interpersonal, Logical/Mathematical

3. **Review** Have volunteers from each group share their suggestions.

4. **Practice/Homework** Have each student write a short journal entry about this imaginary trek from one environment to another, including how people eventually settled in the new environment.
   LS Verbal/Linguistic

   📄 Alternative Assessment Handbook, Rubric 15: Journals

Early Human Migration

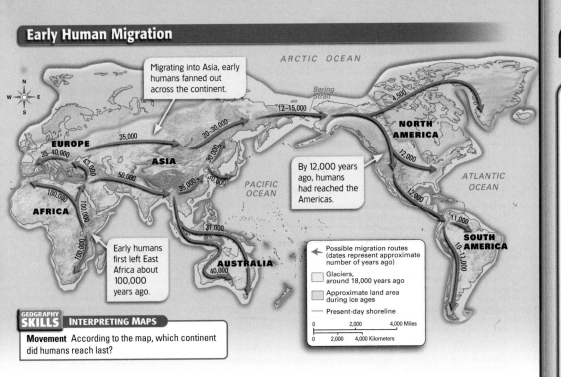

Migrating into Asia, early humans fanned out across the continent.

ARCTIC OCEAN

Bering Strait

4,500

12–15,000

NORTH AMERICA

35,000

20–30,000

30,000

EUROPE

35–40,000

ASIA

43,000

50,000

35,000

30,000

12,000

100,000

100,000

31,000

By 12,000 years ago, humans had reached the Americas.

PACIFIC OCEAN

ATLANTIC OCEAN

AFRICA

12,000

SOUTH AMERICA

100,000

Early humans first left East Africa about 100,000 years ago.

AUSTRALIA

40,000

11,000

10–11,000

Possible migration routes (dates represent approximate number of years ago)

Glaciers, around 18,000 years ago

Approximate land area during ice ages

Present-day shoreline

0   2,000   4,000 Miles
0 2,000 4,000 Kilometers

GEOGRAPHY SKILLS **INTERPRETING MAPS**

Movement According to the map, which continent did humans reach last?

Settling New Lands

Scientists agree that migration around the world took hundreds of thousands of years. Early hominids, the ancestors of modern humans, migrated from Africa to Asia as early as 2 million years ago. From there, they spread to Southeast Asia and Europe.

Later, humans also began to migrate around the world, and earlier hominids died out. Look at the map to see the dates and routes of early human migration.

Humans began to migrate from East Africa to southern Africa and southwestern Asia around 100,000 years ago. From there, people moved east across southern Asia. They could then migrate to Australia. Scientists are not sure exactly how the first people reached Australia. Even though ocean levels were lower then, there was always open sea between Asia and Australia.

From southwestern Asia, humans also migrated north into Europe. Geographic features such as high mountains and cold temperatures delayed migration northward into northern Asia. Eventually, however, people from both Europe and southern Asia moved into that region.

From northern Asia, people moved into North America. Scientists disagree on when and how the first people arrived in North America. Most scholars think people must have crossed a land bridge from Asia to North America. Once in North America, these people moved south, following herds of animals and settling South America. By 9000 BC, humans lived on all continents of the world except Antarctica.

READING CHECK **Analyzing** How did the ice ages influence human migration?

THE STONE AGES AND EARLY CULTURES **37**

Main Idea

❷ People Adapt to New Environments

People adapted to new environments by making clothing and new types of tools.

Explain Why did early humans build shelters? *because they migrated to colder climates*

Recall What types of shelters did early people use? *caves; when no caves available—pit houses, tents, or structures of wood, stone, clay, or other materials*

Elaborate How did new techniques change the daily lives of Middle Stone Age people? *Hooks, fishing spears, bows and arrows, canoes, and pottery enabled people to find new food sources, store various goods, and travel by water. Keeping dogs helped people hunt more efficiently and warned people of dangerous animals or intruders.*

🐻 **HSS** 6.1.2; **HSS** Analysis Skills: HI 1, HI 2

Info to Know

A Third Theory Some archaeologists propose another origin for the first Americans—Europe. This theory says that early Europeans braved the North Atlantic in boats that may have been like those made by modern Arctic Inuit peoples. Similar spear points have been found in Europe and the Americas, which led some archaeologists to develop the new theory.

Answers

Analyzing Primary Sources *possible answer—New discoveries can provide new information and interpretations.*

38

People Adapt to New Environments

As early people moved to new lands, they found environments that differed greatly from those in East Africa. Many places were much colder and had strange plants and animals. Early people had to learn to adapt to their new environments.

Clothing and Shelter

Although fire helped keep people warm in very cold areas, people needed more protection. To keep warm, they learned to sew animal skins together to make clothing.

In addition to clothing, people needed shelter to survive. At first they took shelter in caves. When they moved to areas with no caves, they built their own shelters. The first human-made shelters were called pit houses. They were pits in the ground with roofs of branches and leaves.

Later, people began to build homes above the ground. Some lived in tents made of animal skins. Others built more permanent structures of wood, stone, or clay or other materials. Even bones from large animals such as mammoths were used in building shelters.

New Tools and Technologies

People also adapted to new environments with new types of tools. These tools were smaller and more complex than tools from the Old Stone Age. They defined the **Mesolithic** (me-zuh-LI-thik) **Era**, or the Middle Stone Age. This period began more than 10,000 years ago and lasted to about 5,000 years ago in some places.

During the Middle Stone Age, people found new uses for bone and stone tools. People who lived near water invented hooks and fishing spears. Other groups invented the bow and arrow.

Primary Source

POINTS OF VIEW

Views of Migration to the Americas

For many years scientists were fairly certain that the first Americans came from Asia, following big game through an ice-free path in the glaciers.

"Doubtless it was a formidable [challenging] place . . . an ice-walled valley of frigid winds, fierce snows, and clinging fogs . . . yet grazing animals would have entered, and behind them would have come a rivulet [stream] of human hunters.**"**

—Thomas Canby,
1979, quoted in *Kingdoms of Gold, Kingdoms of Jade* by Brian M. Fagan

New discoveries have challenged beliefs about the first Americans. Some scientists now are not so sure the first Americans came along an ice-free path in the glaciers.

"There's no reason people couldn't have come along the coast, skirting [going around] the glaciers just the way recreational kayakers do today.**"**

—James Dixon,
quoted in *National Geographic,*
December 2000

ANALYSIS SKILL **ANALYZING PRIMARY SOURCES**
Why might a scientist change his or her mind about a long-held belief?

38 CHAPTER 2

Critical Thinking: Drawing Conclusions

Standards Proficiency

Views of Migration 🐻 **HSS** 6.1.2; **HSS** Analysis Skills: HR 4, HI 5

1. Read aloud the quote by Thomas Canby. Ask students whether the journey he describes would have been difficult or easy. Ask students to pick out words or phrases from the quote that support their opinions.

2. Then display a map of the Western Hemisphere. Call on volunteers to point out the routes proposed by the two archaeologists in the feature—across land from northwestern Asia (Canby) and by boat from Asia along the Pacific coast (Dixon).

3. Have students write one to three paragraphs about which theory they think is more logical. Remind students to provide reasons to support their opinions.

LS Logical/Mathematical, Verbal/Linguistic

Alternative Assessment Handbook, Rubric 43: Writing to Persuade

Early people used whatever was available to make shelters. In Central Asia, where wood was scarce, some early people made their homes from mammoth bones.

The frame was probably covered with animal hides to form a solid roof and walls.

Heavy mammoth bones were used as a frame for the shelter.

In addition to tools, people developed new technologies to improve their lives. For example, some learned to make canoes by hollowing out logs. They used the canoes to travel on rivers and lakes. They also began to make pottery. The first pets may also have appeared at this time. People kept dogs to help them hunt and for protection. Developments like these, in addition to clothing and shelter, allowed people to adapt to new environments.

READING CHECK Finding Main Ideas
What were two ways people adapted to new environments?

SUMMARY AND PREVIEW Early people adapted to new environments with new kinds of clothing, shelter, and tools. In Section 3 you will read about how Stone Age peoples developed farming.

Section 2 Assessment

go.hrw.com
Online Quiz
KEYWORD: SQ6 HP2

Reviewing Ideas, Terms, and People HSS 6.1.2
1. **a. Define** What is a **land bridge**?
   b. Analyze Why did it take so long for early people to reach South America?
2. **a. Recall** What did people use to make tools in the **Mesolithic Era**?
   b. Summarize Why did people have to learn to make clothes and build shelters?

Critical Thinking
3. **Sequencing** Draw the graphic organizer below. Complete it to show the order of human migration around the world.

FOCUS ON WRITING
4. **Illustrating** How will you illustrate early migration on your storyboard? Draw some sketches. How does this information relate to your ideas from Section 1?

THE STONE AGES AND EARLY CULTURES **39**

Section 2 Assessment Answers

1. **a.** a strip of land connecting two continents
   b. They had to get across Asia, then across the land bridge into North America, and gradually all the way to South America.
2. **a.** bone and stone
   b. They moved to climates that were colder than those in East Africa.
3. from East Africa to Europe; Southern Asia to Australia and East Asia; North America to South America
4. Sketches will vary. Students' answers should include the development of clothing, shelter, and tools as early humans migrated and adapted to new environments.

Direct Teach

Other People, Other Places

Home on the Range People of many places and times have learned how to build shelters from limited resources. The Inuit who live in Arctic regions build domed shelters called igloos from blocks of snow or ice. Nomads of Mongolia create tent-like structures called yurts. A yurt's basic structure is a frame of wooden poles covered with animal skins, textiles, or felt.

Did you know . . .

The last of the mammoths lived on islands off Russia's Arctic coast. They survived until about 4,000 years ago, when pharaohs ruled Egypt.

Review & Assess

Close
Ask students how the picture of the mammoth-bone shelter on this page contrasts with images of prehistoric people that show them as dull-witted.

Review
go.hrw.com Online Quiz, Section 2

Assess
SE Section 2 Assessment
PASS: Section 2 Quiz
Alternative Assessment Handbook

Reteach/Classroom Intervention
California Standards Review Workbook
Interactive Reader and Study Guide, Section 2
Interactive Skills Tutor CD-ROM

Answers

Reading Check *possible answers—used animal skins for clothing to keep warm; built shelters; developed new hunting tools, such as the bow and arrow and fishing spear*

Bellringer

If YOU were there. . . Use the **Daily Bellringer Transparency** to help students answer the question.

🖥 Daily Bellringer Transparency, Section 3

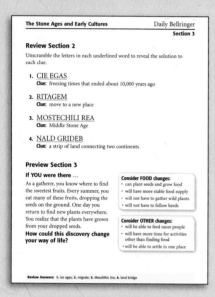

The Stone Ages and Early Cultures — Daily Bellringer Section 3

Review Section 2

Unscramble the letters in each underlined word to reveal the solution to each clue.

1. CIE EGAS
   Clue: freezing times that ended about 10,000 years ago

2. RITAGEM
   Clue: move to a new place

3. MOSTECHILI REA
   Clue: Middle Stone Age

4. NALD GRIDEB
   Clue: a strip of land connecting two continents

Preview Section 3

If YOU were there ...
As a gatherer, you know where to find the sweetest fruits. Every summer, you eat many of these fruits, dropping the seeds on the ground. One day you return to find new plants everywhere. You realize that the plants have grown from your dropped seeds.

How could this discovery change your way of life?

Consider FOOD changes:
- can plant seeds and grow food
- will have more stable food supply
- will not have to gather wild plants
- will not have to follow herds

Consider OTHER changes:
- will be able to feed more people
- will have more time for activities other than finding food
- will be able to settle in one place

Review Answers: 1. ice ages; 2. migrate; 3. Mesolithic Era; 4. land bridge

Academic Vocabulary

Review with students the high-use academic term in this section.

development creation (p. 42)

📄 **CRF:** Vocabulary Builder Activity, Section 3

🐾 Standards Focus

HSS 6.1.3

Means: Discuss how climate change and the human impact on the environment led to the domestication of plants and animals, and from there to changes in clothing and shelter.

Matters: Domestication of plants and animals and the permanent settlements this process made possible are fundamental to modern societies.

SECTION 3

Beginnings of Agriculture

What You Will Learn...

Main Ideas

1. The first farmers learned to grow plants and raise animals in the Stone Age.
2. Farming changed societies and the way people lived.

The Big Idea

The development of agriculture brought great changes to human society.

Key Terms

Neolithic Era, *p. 41*
domestication, *p. 41*
agriculture, *p. 42*
megaliths, *p. 42*

🐾

HSS 6.1.3 Discuss the climatic changes and human modifications of the physical environment that gave rise to the domestication of plants and animals and new sources of clothing and shelter.

If YOU were there...

As a gatherer, you know where to find the sweetest fruits. Every summer, you eat many of these fruits, dropping the seeds on the ground. One day you return to find new plants everywhere. You realize that the plants have grown from your dropped seeds.

How could this discovery change your way of life?

BUILDING BACKGROUND The discovery that plants grew from seeds was one of the major advances of the late Stone Age. Other similar advances led to great changes in the way people lived.

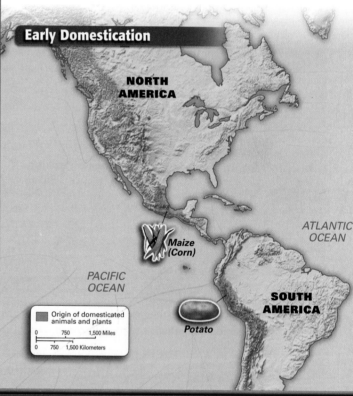

Early Domestication

NORTH AMERICA

ATLANTIC OCEAN

Maize (Corn)

PACIFIC OCEAN

SOUTH AMERICA

Potato

☐ Origin of domesticated animals and plants

0   750   1,500 Miles
0   750   1,500 Kilometers

Teach the Big Idea: Master the Standards

Standards Proficiency

Beginnings of Agriculture 🐾 HSS 6.1.3; HSS Analysis Skills: CS 1, HI 1

1. **Teach** Ask the Main Idea questions to teach this section.

2. **Apply** Draw a circle labeled *Beginnings of Agriculture* for students to see and copy. Call on students to identify basic changes in human societies caused by the development of agriculture. Add these suggestions to create an idea web.

3. **Review** Call on other volunteers to expand the web by suggesting further developments that could have been caused by the basic

changes. For example, building megaliths may have inspired new stonecutting techniques.

4. **Practice/Homework** Have students add to their idea webs by connecting elements already suggested and illustrating the webs.
   LS Visual/Spatial

📄 Alternative Assessment Handbook, Rubric 13: Graphic Organizers

📄 History and Geography Activity: Agriculture and Animals

The First Farmers

After the Middle Stone Age came a period of time that scientists call the **Neolithic** (nee-uh-LI-thik) **Era**, or New Stone Age. It began as early as 10,000 years ago in Southwest Asia. In other places, this era began much later and lasted much longer than it did there.

During the New Stone Age people learned to polish stones to make tools like saws and drills. People also learned how to make fire. Before, they could only use fire that had been started by natural causes such as lightning.

The New Stone Age ended in Egypt and Southwest Asia about 5,000 years ago, when toolmakers began to make tools out of metal. But tools weren't the only major change that occurred during the Neolithic Era. In fact, the biggest changes came in how people produced food.

Plants

After a warming trend brought an end to the ice ages, new plants began to grow in some areas. For example, wild barley and wheat plants started to spread throughout Southwest Asia. Over time, people came to depend on these wild plants for food. They began to settle where grains grew.

People soon learned that they could plant seeds themselves to grow their own crops. Historians call the shift from food gathering to food producing the Neolithic Revolution. Most experts believe that this revolution, or change, first occurred in the societies of Southwest Asia.

Eventually, people learned to change plants to make them more useful. They planted only the largest grains or the sweetest fruits. The process of changing plants or animals to make them more useful to humans is called **domestication**.

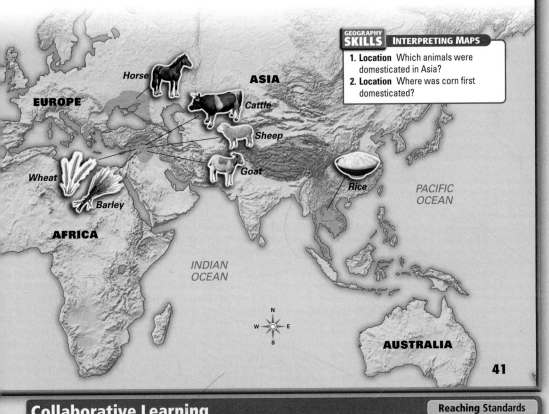

GEOGRAPHY SKILLS INTERPRETING MAPS

1. **Location** Which animals were domesticated in Asia?
2. **Location** Where was corn first domesticated?

41

Direct Teach

Main Idea

❶ The First Farmers

The first farmers learned to grow plants and raise animals in the Stone Age.

Define What was the Neolithic Revolution? *the shift from food gathering to food producing*

Contrast What is the difference between the domestication of plants and simply planting seeds? *Domestication involves changing the plants to make them more useful.*

Rate Which do you think had more significant results—the domestication of plants or of animals? *possible answers—plants, because plants were more important food sources and people could still hunt; animals, because they helped with tasks besides farming, such as pulling loads of building materials.*

- History and Geography Activity: Agriculture and Animals
- Map Transparency: Early Domestication
- HSS 6.1.3; HSS Analysis Skills: CS 1, HI 1, HI 2

Info to Know

Cats and People People domesticated cats not just for catching rats and mice, but also for companionship. In fact, the domestication of cats may have started some 9,500 years ago. This date comes from the earliest known burial of a cat with a human, found in 2004 in Cyprus. Archaeologists have concluded that the cat was the human's pet.

Collaborative Learning

Reaching Standards

Mural of Ancient Farm Community HSS 6.1.3; HSS Analysis Skills: CS 3

Materials: butcher paper, art supplies

1. As a class, review what life was like for early farmers. Then organize the class into small groups and have each group create a mural that depicts early farming communities.

2. Have students use Internet or library resources to find images they can include in their murals, such as images of plants, animals, housing, and religious shrines.

3. Display the groups' murals in the classroom. Call on group volunteers to describe what is illustrated in the murals.

LS Interpersonal, Visual/Spatial

Alternative Assessment Handbook, Rubrics 3: Artwork; and 14: Group Activity

Answers

Interpreting Maps 1. *cattle, sheep, goats* **2.** *southern part of North America*

❷ Farming Changes Societies

Farming changed societies and the way people lived.

Define What are megaliths? *huge stones used as monuments*

Identify What gods did people in the Neolithic Age probably believe in? *those associated with the four elements—air, water, fire, and earth—or with animals*

Draw Conclusions How did a change in the use of fire demonstrate human ingenuity? *People learned how to make fire, not just use fire that had been started by natural causes.*

📋 **CRF:** Primary Source Activity: Objects from Çatal Hüyük

🐻 **HSS** 6.1.3; **HSS** Analysis Skills: HI 1, HI 2

Did you know...

Not all of the changes brought about by agriculture were positive. Although people in farming communities had more food, they did not eat the same variety of foods as hunter-gatherers did. In addition, the presence of animals in or near human communities brought new diseases.

Linking to Today

Major Megaliths A group of huge shaped stones was raised at Stonehenge in southern England starting in about 3100 BC. Neolithic people may have used Stonehenge for predicting the seasons and for religious ceremonies.

Answers

Reading Check *possible answers— People stopped moving around to find food, populations grew with better control of food production, and towns developed in some areas.*

42

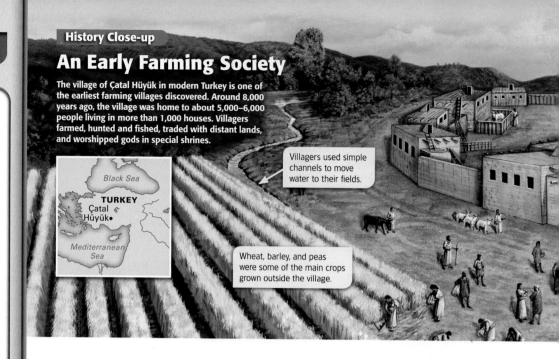

History Close-up

An Early Farming Society

The village of Çatal Hüyük in modern Turkey is one of the earliest farming villages discovered. Around 8,000 years ago, the village was home to about 5,000–6,000 people living in more than 1,000 houses. Villagers farmed, hunted and fished, traded with distant lands, and worshipped gods in special shrines.

Black Sea
TURKEY
Çatal Hüyük●
Mediterranean Sea

Villagers used simple channels to move water to their fields.

Wheat, barley, and peas were some of the main crops grown outside the village.

ACADEMIC VOCABULARY
development
creation

The domestication of plants led to the **development** of **agriculture**, or farming. For the first time, people could produce their own food. This development changed human society forever.

Animals

Learning to produce food was a major accomplishment for early people. But learning how to use animals for their own purposes was almost equally important.

Hunters didn't have to follow wild herds anymore. Instead, farmers could keep sheep or goats for milk, food, and wool. Farmers could also use large animals like cattle to carry loads or to pull large tools used in farming. Using animals to help with farming greatly improved people's chances of surviving.

THE IMPACT TODAY

One famous megalith, Stonehenge in England, attracts millions of curious tourists and scholars each year.

READING CHECK **Identifying Cause and Effect** What was one effect of the switch to farming?

Farming Changes Societies

The Neolithic Revolution brought huge changes to people's lives. With survival more certain, people could focus on activities other than finding food.

✓ Domestication of plants and animals enabled people to use plant fibers to make cloth. The domestication of animals made it possible to use wool from goats and sheep and skins from horses for clothes.

✓ People also began to build permanent settlements. As they started raising crops and animals, they needed to stay in one place. Then, once people were able to control their own food production, the world's population grew. In some areas farming communities developed into towns.

As populations grew, groups of people gathered to perform religious ceremonies. Some put up megaliths. **Megaliths** are huge stones used as monuments or as the sites for religious gatherings.

42 CHAPTER 2

Critical Thinking: Summarizing

Standards Proficiency

A Day in the Life 🐻 **HSS** 6.1.1; **HSS** Analysis Skills: HI 1

Standard English Mastery

1. Discuss with students how domestication of plants and animals changed how Neolithic people lived day-to-day.

2. Have each student write a journal entry describing a day in the life of a Neolithic farm family. Ask students to include such details as the crops and animals on the farm. Remind students to use Standard English in their journal entries. Work with individual students as needed.

3. Ask volunteers to read their journal entries to the class.

4. **Extend** To extend the activity, ask students to add another journal entry in which the farmer reflects on stories he or she has heard about what daily life for the local people used to be like before farming. **LS** Verbal/Linguistic

📋 Alternative Assessment Handbook, Rubric 15: Journals

Houses were made of wood covered with mud. Since they didn't have doors, people entered on ladders through rooftop openings.

Inside their houses, villagers made the earliest known wooden bowls and cups, pottery, and mirrors.

Some houses were built as shrines and had small statues of goddesses and large sculpted bulls' heads.

ANALYSIS SKILL **ANALYZING VISUALS**
How did farmers get water to their fields?

Early people probably believed in gods and goddesses associated with the four elements—air, water, fire, and earth—or with animals. For example, one European group honored a thunder god, while another group worshipped bulls. Some scholars also believe that prehistoric peoples also prayed to their ancestors. People in some societies today still hold many of these same beliefs.

READING CHECK **Analyzing Information** How did farming contribute to the growth of towns?

SUMMARY AND PREVIEW Stone Age peoples adapted to new environments by domesticating plants and animals. These changes led to the development of religion and the growth of towns. In the next chapter you will learn more about early towns.

Section 3 Assessment

Reviewing Ideas, Terms, and People **HSS** 6.1.3
1. **a. Define** What is **domestication** of a plant or animal?
   b. Make Generalizations How did early people use domesticated animals?
2. **a. Describe** What were gods and goddesses probably associated with in prehistoric religion?
   b. Explain How did domestication of plants and animals lead to the development of towns?

Critical Thinking
3. **Identifying Cause and Effect** Copy the graphic organizer at right. Use it to show one cause and three effects of the development of agriculture.

Cause

Development of agriculture

Effects

FOCUS ON WRITING

4. **Beginnings of Agriculture** Now that you've read about the birth of agriculture, you're ready to plan your storyboard. Look back through your notes from previous sections and the text of this one. Make a list of the events and ideas you will include on your storyboard. Then plan how you will arrange these items.

THE STONE AGES AND EARLY CULTURES **43**

Direct Teach

Connect to Art

An Artistic First As people settled in villages and towns, they could pursue other tasks besides finding or growing food. Some people could devote more time to art. In Çatal Hüyük, an artist created the first known landscape painting. This painting, which dates from about 6150 BC, shows the town's houses at the foot of an erupting volcano. In fact, there is a similar volcano, now extinct, within sight of Çatal Hüyük.

Review & Assess

Close
Ask students to compare the farming methods of Neolithic times to food production today.

Review
Online Quiz, Section 3

Assess
SE Section 3 Assessment
PASS: Section 3 Quiz
Alternative Assessment Handbook

Reteach/Classroom Intervention
California Standards Review Workbook
Interactive Reader and Study Guide, Section 3
Interactive Skills Tutor CD-ROM

Section 3 Assessment Answers

1. **a.** changing a plant or animal to make it more useful to humans
   b. for milk, food, and/or wool; for carrying loads or pulling tools used in farming

2. **a.** earth, air, fire, and water or animals
   b. People settled in one place to grow crops and tend animals, and better control of food production enabled populations to grow.

3. cause—Warming trend after ice ages caused new plants to grow; effects—could produce own food, easier to farm, new kinds of clothing, populations grew, settlements became towns, religion more organized

4. Notes should include changes in climate, domestication of plants and animals, growth of populations and settlements, and the emergence of religious ceremonies.

Answers

Analyzing Visuals *Farmers used channels to move water to their fields.*

Reading Check *Because people stayed in one place to control food production, towns developed.*

Identifying Central Issues

Activity **Central Issues in the Community** Write the following statement for students to see: *The school district's budget will be cut $300,000 next year.* Tell students this statement is not true but hypothetical. Ask students to identify the most important questions and concerns that people might have in response to this news. Responses might include the following: What will the schools have to cut to lower their budgets—such as teachers, textbooks, art classes, and so on? Will classes be bigger? Will extracurricular activities be cut? Will free lunches be cut? After a brief period of discussion, ask students to identify what all these concerns have in common. Lead students to realize that the central issue involved is how will budget cuts affect educational quality and school life. To extend the activity, have students practice the skill on an article from their school or local newspaper. **LS** **Logical/Mathematical**

📓 Alternative Assessment Handbook, Rubric 11: Discussions

💿 Interactive Skills Tutor CD-ROM, Lesson 12: Identify Issues and Problems

🐻 **HSS** Analysis Skills: HI 1

Social Studies Skills

| Analysis | Critical Thinking | Participation | Study |

Identifying Central Issues

Understand the Skill

Central issues are the main problems or topics that are related to an event. The issues behind a historical event can be varied and complicated. Central issues in world history usually involve political, social, economic, territorial, moral, or technological matters. The ability to identify the central issue in an event allows you to focus on information that is most important to understanding the event.

Learn the Skill

In this chapter you learned about prehistory. Some of the events you read about may not seem very important. It is hard for people in the computer age to appreciate the accomplishments of the Stone Age. For example, adding wooden handles to stone tools may seem like a simple thing to us. But it was a life-changing advance for people of that time.

This example points out something to remember when looking for central issues. Try not to use only modern-day values and standards to decide what is important about the past. Always think about the times in which people lived. Ask yourself what would have been important to people living then.

The following guidelines will help you to identify central issues. Use them to gain a better understanding of historical events.

❶ Identify the subject of the information. What is the information about?

❷ Determine the source of the information. Is it a primary source or a secondary source?

❸ Determine the purpose of what you are reading. Why has the information been provided?

❹ Find the strongest or most forceful statements in the information. These are often clues to issues or ideas the writer thinks are the most central or important.

❺ Think about values, concerns, ways of life, and events that would have been important to the people of the times. Determine how the information might be connected to those larger issues.

Practice and Apply the Skill

Apply the guidelines to identify the central issue in the following passage. Then answer the questions.

❝What distinguished the Neolithic Era from earlier ages was people's ability to shape stone tools by polishing and grinding. This allowed people to make more specialized tools. Even more important changes took place also. The development of agriculture changed the basic way people lived. Earlier people had been wanderers, who moved from place to place in search of food. Some people began settling in permanent villages. Exactly how they learned that seeds could be planted and made to grow year after year remains a mystery. However, the shift from food gathering to food producing was possibly the most important change ever in history.❞

1. What is the general subject of this passage?

2. What changes distinguished the Neolithic Era from earlier periods?

3. According to this writer, what is the central issue to understand about the Neolithic Era?

4. What statements in the passage help you to determine the central issue?

Social Studies Skills Activity: Identifying Central Issues

Guided and Independent Practice 🐻 **HSS** Analysis Skills: HI 1 **Standards Proficiency**

1. Have volunteers read aloud the Section 1 text in this chapter titled "Scientists Study Remains."

2. Have students work as a class to go through the five guidelines and questions listed above in the bottom of the left-hand column and in the top of the right-hand column.

3. Then assign students the text in Section 2 titled "People Adapt to New Environments."

Have students work independently to answer the same five questions. Review the answers as a class.

4. **Learners Having Difficulty** Have these students practice the skill first on an easier text, such as a selection from a fourth-grade history book or a selection you write. Once students master the skill, have them apply it to grade-level text. **LS** **Verbal/Linguistic**

📓 Alternative Assessment Handbook, Rubric 1: Acquiring Information

Answers

Practice and Apply the Skill **1.** *the changes that distinguish the Neolithic Era from earlier ages;* **2.** *people's ability to shape stone tools by polishing and grinding; the development of agriculture;* **3.** *that advances, such as agriculture, greatly changed the way people lived;* **4.** *first, third, fourth, and last sentences*

Standards Review

Visual Summary

Use the visual summary below to help you review the main ideas of the chapter.

QUICK FACTS

Hominids developed in Africa and learned how to use tools.

Early humans lived as hunter-gatherers.

Humans migrated around the world, adapting to new environments.

Eventually, people learned how to farm and raise animals.

Reviewing Vocabulary, Terms, and People

For each group of terms below, write a sentence that shows how all the terms in the group are related.

1. prehistory
   ancestor
   hominid

   Write a sentence using all 3 words to show understanding.

2. domestication
   Neolithic Era
   agriculture

3. Paleolithic Era
   tool
   hunter-gatherers
   develop

4. land bridge
   ice ages
   migrate

5. society
   megaliths
   Neolithic Era

Comprehension and Critical Thinking

SECTION 1 *(Pages 28–34)* **HSS** 6.1.1

6. **a. Recall** What does *Homo sapiens* mean? When may *Homo sapiens* have first appeared in Africa?

   b. Draw Conclusions If you were an archaeologist and found bead jewelry and stone chopping tools in an ancient woman's grave, what may you conclude?

   c. Elaborate How did stone tools change over time? Why do you think these changes took place so slowly?

SECTION 2 *(Pages 36–39)* **HSS** 6.1.2

7. **a. Describe** What new skills did people develop to help them survive?

   b. Analyze How did global climate change affect the migration of early people?

   c. Evaluate About 15,000 years ago, where do you think life would have been more difficult—in eastern Africa or northern Europe? Why?

THE STONE AGES AND EARLY CULTURES **45**

Answers

Visual Summary

Review and Inquiry Use the visual summary to review the chapter's main ideas. Ask students to provide details about what daily life may have been like for the people shown in the image.

🗃 Quick Facts Transparency: The Stone Ages and Early Cultures Visual Summary

Reviewing Vocabulary, Terms, and People

1. possible answer—Hominids, the ancestors of humans, lived during a time we call prehistory.

2. possible answer—During the Neolithic Era, the domestication of plants and animals led to agriculture.

3. possible answer—Hunter-gatherers developed stone tools during the Paleolithic Era.

4. possible answer—People might have migrated across a land bridge to get to North America during the ice ages.

5. possible answer—A Neolithic Era society might have used megaliths in religious ceremonies.

Comprehension and Critical Thinking

6. **a.** "wise man"; 200,000 years ago

   b. possible answer—that the people who buried her had some form of religion

   c. went from choppers to using flint and having handles; possible answers—because the old tools worked well enough, better materials were not readily

---

Review and Assessment Resources

Review and Reinforce

SE Standards Review

📋 **CRF:** Chapter Review Activity

📋 California Standards Review Workbook

🗃 Quick Facts Transparency: The Stone Ages and Early Cultures Visual Summary

🔊 Spanish Chapter Summaries Audio CD Program

💻 Online Chapter Summaries in Six Languages

OSP Holt PuzzlePro; Game Tool for ExamView

💿 Quiz Game CD-ROM

Assess

SE Standards Assessment

📋 PASS: Chapter Test, Forms A and B

📋 Alternative Assessment Handbook

OSP ExamView Test Generator, Chapter Test

💿 Universal Access Modified Worksheets and Tests CD-ROM: Chapter Test

💻 Holt Online Assessment Program (in the Premier Online Edition)

Reteach/Intervene

📋 Interactive Reader and Study Guide

📋 Universal Access Teacher Management System: Lesson Plans for Universal Access

💿 Universal Access Modified Worksheets and Tests CD-ROM

💿 Interactive Skills Tutor CD-ROM

go.hrw.com
Online Resources

Chapter Resources:
KEYWORD: SQ6 WH2

THE STONE AGES AND EARLY CULTURES **45**

available, or early people couldn't communicate well enough to discuss improvements

7. a. how to make clothing, build shelters, make more complex tools, find new uses for tools, make canoes and pottery, tame dogs

b. created land bridge that allowed people to migrate from northern Asia to the Americas

c. possible answer—northern Europe, because the ice ages would have made survival there difficult

8. a. the shift from food gathering to food producing

b. allowed people to settle down and create towns

c. possible answers—Stone was readily available and long-lasting; large stone structures could be seen from far away; or building with stone required much labor but few tools.

Reviewing Themes

9. possible answers—People had to learn to make clothes and shelter in cold temperatures; warming brought new plants and the development of farming; ice ages caused land bridges, allowing people to migrate around the world.

10. possible answers—Hunting improved because people could communicate; people formed personal relationships; it became easier to solve problems, such as how to distribute food.

Using the Internet

11. Go to the HRW Web site and enter the keyword shown to access a rubric for this activity.

> KEYWORD: SQ6 TEACHER

SECTION 3 (Pages 40–43) **HSS** 6.1.3

8. a. Define What was the Neolithic Revolution?

b. Make Inferences How did domestication of plants and animals change early societies?

c. Predict Why do you think people of the Neolithic Era put up megaliths instead of some other kind of monuments?

Reviewing Themes

9. Geography What were three ways in which the environment affected Stone Age peoples?

10. Society and Culture How did the development of language change hunter-gatherer society?

Using the Internet

11. Activity: Creating a Skit In the beginning of the Paleolithic Era, or the Old Stone Age, early humans used modified stones as tools. As the Stone Age progressed, plants and animals became materials for tools too. Enter the activity keyword and research the development of tools and the use of fire. Then create a skit that tells about an early human society discovering fire, creating a new tool, or developing a new way of doing a task.

Reading and Analysis Skills

Understanding Chronological Order *Below are several lists of events. Arrange the events in each list in chronological order.*

12. Mesolithic Era begins.
Paleolithic Era begins.
Neolithic Era begins.

13. *Homo sapiens* appears.
Homo habilis appears.
Homo erectus appears.

14. People make stone tools.
People make metal tools.
People attach wooden handles to tools.

Social Studies Skills

Identifying Central Issues *Read the primary source passage below and then answer the questions that follow.*

> "Almonds provide a striking example of bitter seeds and their change under domestication. Most wild almond seeds contain an intensely bitter chemical called amygdalin, which (as was already mentioned) breaks down to yield the poison cyanide. A snack of wild almonds can kill a person foolish enough to ignore the warning of the bitter taste. Since the first stage in unconscious domestication involves gathering seeds to eat, how on earth did domestication of wild almonds ever reach that first stage?"
>
> –Jared Diamond, from *Guns, Germs, and Steel*

15. What is the main point of this passage?

16. What does the author suggest is the major issue he will address in the text?

FOCUS ON WRITING

17. Creating Your Storyboard Use the notes you have taken to plan your storyboard. What images will you include in each frame of the storyboard? How many frames will you need to tell the story of prehistoric people? How will you represent your ideas visually?

After you have sketched an outline for your storyboard, begin drawing it. Be sure to include all significant adaptations and developments made by prehistoric people, and don't worry if you can't draw that well. If you like, you might want to draw your storyboard in the simple style of prehistoric cave paintings. As the last frame in your storyboard, write a detailed summary to conclude your story.

Reading and Analysis Skills

12. Paleolithic Era begins.
Mesolithic Era begins.
Neolithic Era begins.

13. *Homo habilis* appears.
Homo erectus appears.
Homo sapiens appears.

14. People make stone tools.
People attach wooden handles to tools. People make metal tools.

Social Studies Skills

15. possible answer—Wild almonds are poisonous, so how people figured out that they could eat them is puzzling.

16. how people figured out that they could change poisonous plants into useful plants

Focus on Writing

17. Rubric Students' storyboards should:

- include numbered panels.
- feature clear but simple sketches.
- end with a clear summary.

CRF: Focus on Writing: A Storyboard

Standards Assessment

DIRECTIONS: *Read each question, and write the letter of the best response.*

1 Use the map to answer the following question.

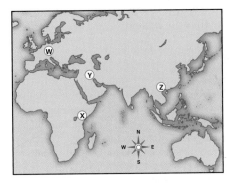

The region in which the first humans lived is shown on the map by the letter

- A W.
- B X.
- C Y.
- D Z.

2 The earliest humans lived

- A by hunting and gathering their food.
- B as herders of sheep and other livestock.
- C alone or in pairs.
- D in farming villages along rivers and streams.

3 The development of farming brought all of the following changes to the lives of early humans *except*

- A the first human-made shelters.
- B a larger supply of food.
- C the construction of permanent settlements.
- D new types of clothing.

4 The region of the world that was likely occupied *last* by early humans was

- A northern Asia.
- B southern Asia.
- C North America.
- D South America.

5 Hunter-gatherer societies in the Old Stone Age possessed all of the following *except*

- A fire.
- B art.
- C bone tools.
- D religious beliefs.

Connecting with Past Learnings

6 You know that history is the study of people and events from the past. To learn about prehistory, historians would likely study all of the following *except*

- A graves.
- B journals.
- C bones.
- D art.

7 Which of the following people that you studied in Grade 5 likely crossed a land bridge to get to the Americas?

- A Pilgrims
- B colonists
- C Native Americans
- D Christopher Columbus

Answers

1. B
Break Down the Question Refer students who missed the question to the map in Section 2.

2. A
Break Down the Question This question requires students to recall the chronology of human development.

3. A
Break Down the Question Remind students that all but one of the answers describe changes to people's lives. Refer students who miss the question to the material titled "Clothing and Shelter" in Section 2.

4. D
Break Down the Question This question requires students to recall information about the land bridge between Asia and the Americas. Refer students who missed the question to the map in Section 2.

5. C
Break Down the Question This question requires that students recall factual information. Refer students who missed the question to the material on the Mesolithic Era in Section 2.

6. B
Break Down the Question This question requires that students recall material covered in the previous chapter about the lack of written information for prehistory.

7. C
Break Down the Question This question requires students to recall information about the chronology of U.S. history from Grade 5.

Intervention Resources

Reproducible
- Interactive Reader and Study Guide
- Universal Access Teacher Management System: Lesson Plans for Universal Access

Technology
- Quick Facts Transparency: The Stone Ages and Early Cultures Visual Summary
- Universal Access Modified Worksheets and Tests CD-ROM
- Interactive Skills Tutor CD-ROM

Tips for Test Taking

Study the Directions In order to follow directions, students have to know what the directions are! Have students read all test directions as if they contain the key to lifetime happiness. Then they should read the directions again and study the answer sheet. How is it laid out? Students should determine if they are arranged

A B

C D   or   A B C D.

Urge students to be sure they know what to do before they make the first mark.

Standards Review
Have students review the following standards in their workbooks.
- California Standards Review Workbook:
HSS 6.1.1, 6.1.2, 6.1.3

48 UNIT 1

Preteach

Bellringer

Motivate Ask volunteers to name a city they have visited and to identify two ways that it is similar to and different from their hometown. Tell students that in this workshop, they will compare and contrast two societies, or show how they are alike and different.

Direct Teach

Points of Comparison

Block Method vs. Point-by-Point Method Provide students with examples of using the block and point-by-point methods by comparing and contrasting apples and oranges. Then help students identify characteristics by which to compare and contrast two societies. For example, students might first compare the societies' social structures, then their governments, economies, religions, and arts. **ELA** Writing 6.2.2.c

Identifying a Big Idea

Main Purpose To help students write their big idea, or thesis, have them first make lists comparing and contrasting the two societies. Then have students consider what they can conclude from the information. Did one society change more quickly? Did one society deal with a problem both societies faced in a better way? **ELA** Writing 6.2.2.a

 Standards Focus
ELA Writing 6.2.2.a, 6.2.2.c, 6.2.3.c

48 UNIT 1

Assignment

Write a paper comparing and contrasting two early human societies.

TIP **Using a Graphic Organizer**
A Venn diagram can help you see ways that the two societies are similar and different.

ELA **Writing 6.2.2.c** Follow an organized pattern appropriate to the type of composition.

Comparing and Contrasting Societies

Comparing means finding likenesses between or among things. Contrasting means finding differences. You often compare and contrast things to understand them better and see how they are related.

1. Prewrite

Getting Started

Unlike most essays, a compare and contrast paper has two subjects. However, it still has only one big idea, or thesis. For example, your idea may be to show how two societies dealt with the same problem or to show how two human societies changed over time.

Begin by choosing two subjects. Then identify specific points of similarities and differences between the two. Support each point with historical facts, examples, and details.

Organizing Your Information

Choose one of these two ways to organize your points of comparison.

- Present all the points about the first subject and then all the points about the second subject: AAABBB, or block style
- Alternate back and forth between the first subject and the second subject: ABABAB, or point-by-point style

2. Write

This framework will help you use your notes to write a first draft.

A Writer's Framework

Introduction	Body	Conclusion
■ Clearly identify your two subjects. ■ Give background information readers will need in order to understand your points of comparison between the societies. ■ State your big idea, or main purpose in comparing and contrasting these two societies.	■ Present your points of comparison in block style or point-by-point style. ■ Compare the two societies in at least two ways, and contrast them in at least two ways. ■ Use specific historical facts, details, and examples to support each of your points.	■ Restate your big idea. ■ Summarize the points you have made in your paper. ■ Expand on your big idea, perhaps by relating it to your own life, to other societies, or to later historical events.

48 UNIT 1

Differentiating Instruction for Universal Access

Advanced Learners/GATE [Exceeding Standards]

1. Advanced learners looking for an additional challenge can conduct research online or at the library to find additional information about the societies to support their thesis.

2. Students should complete a bibliography or works cited list to show the sources they used in their papers. **LS** **Verbal/Linguistic**

 ELA Writing 6.2.2.c, 6.2.3.c

Learners Having Difficulty [Reaching Standards]

1. Have learners having difficulty start by organizing their ideas on note cards. Students should write one similarity or difference on each card and then organize the cards according to the block or point-by-point method.

2. As students write, help them incorporate clue words for similarities and differences. **LS** **Verbal/Linguistic**

 **ELA** Writing 6.2.2.c

3. Evaluate and Revise

Evaluating

Use the following questions to discover ways to improve your paper.

Evaluation Questions for a Comparison/Contrast Paper

- Do you introduce both of your subjects in your first paragraph?
- Do you state your big idea, or thesis, at the end of your introduction?
- Do you present two or more similarities and two or more differences between the two societies?

- Do you use either the block style or point-by-point style of organization?
- Do you support your points of comparison with enough historical facts, details, and examples?
- Does your conclusion restate your big idea and summarize your main points?

TIP   **Help with Punctuation**

Use the correct punctuation marks before and after clue words within sentences. Usually, a comma comes before *and, but, for, nor, or, so,* and *yet,* with no punctuation after the word. When they are in the middle of a sentence, clue words and phrases such as *however, similarly, in addition, in contrast,* and *on the other hand* usually have a comma before and after them.

Revising

When you are revising your paper, you may need to add comparison-contrast clue words. They will help your readers see the connections between ideas.

Clue Words for Similarities	Clue Words for Differences
also, another, both, in addition, just as, like, similarly, too	although, but, however, in contrast, instead, on the other hand, unlike

4. Proofread and Publish

Proofreading

Before sharing your paper, you will want to polish it by correcting any remaining errors. Look closely for mistakes in grammar, spelling, capitalization, and punctuation. To avoid two common grammar errors, make sure that you have used the correct form of *–er* or *more* and *–est* or *most* with adjectives and adverbs when making comparisons.

Publishing

One good way to share your paper is to exchange it with one or more classmates. After reading each other's papers, you can compare and contrast them. How are your papers similar? How do they differ? If possible, share papers with someone whose big idea is similar to yours.

● Practice and Apply

Use the steps and strategies outlined in this workshop to write your compare and contrast paper.

Evaluate and Revise

Evaluate a Partner's Work Before students revise their work, have them evaluate a partner's draft by using the Evaluation Questions listed on this page. Have students use the feedback they receive to revise their work.

Teaching Tip

Proofreading Tell students that when they proofread their papers, they should look for one type of error at a time. For example, they might look first for grammatical errors, then for punctuation errors, next for spelling errors, and last for capitalization errors.

● Practice & Apply ●

Proofread and Publish

Submit to a School Newspaper Have interested students publish their papers by submitting them to a school newspaper, if available. Encourage students to use word-processing software to format the headings and other elements of their paper before submitting it. If a school newspaper is not available, suggest that students publish their papers by displaying them on a bulletin board in a public school area.

🐻 **ELA** Writing 6.1.5

English-Language Learners   [Standards Proficiency]   [Standard English Mastery]

1. English learners may need to review the rules for forming comparative and superlative adjectives and adverbs. Write the words *high, higher,* and *highest* for students to see. Review them with students. Then have students identify the comparative and superlative forms of the following: *good, effective, well, poor,* and *low.*

2. English learners may be more proficient in speaking English than in writing it. To help them organize their ideas, encourage students to discuss their ideas with you or a partner before they start writing. Then review each paragraph that students write to help them correct grammatical and punctuation errors.

LS Verbal/Linguistic

🐻 **ELA** Writing 6.2.2.c

Introduce the Unit

Share the information in the chapter overviews with students.

Chapter 3 The first civilizations grew up in river valleys in Asia and Africa. Such valleys provided water and fertile land for farming. In the region of the Tigris and Euphrates river valley, the Sumerians developed the world's first civilization. The Sumerians' many advances include the wheel and the first system of writing. After the Sumerians, a series of empires rose and fell in the region. These societies also made advances, such as a written code of law, that still influence civilization today.

Chapter 4 Ancient Egypt also developed in a fertile river valley, that of the Nile River. Egyptian government and religion were closely connected, and Egyptians believed their rulers were gods. The Egyptians also had a strong belief in the afterlife. They preserved their rulers' bodies as mummies and buried them in pyramids, huge stone tombs with four triangle-shaped sides. The Egyptians developed a rich culture and made lasting achievements in writing, architecture, and art.

Chapter 5 South of Egypt, the kingdom of Kush developed in a region called Nubia. Kush was the first large kingdom in the interior of Africa. *(continued on p. 51)*

◼ Standards Focus

For a list of the overarching standards covered in this unit, see the first page of each chapter.

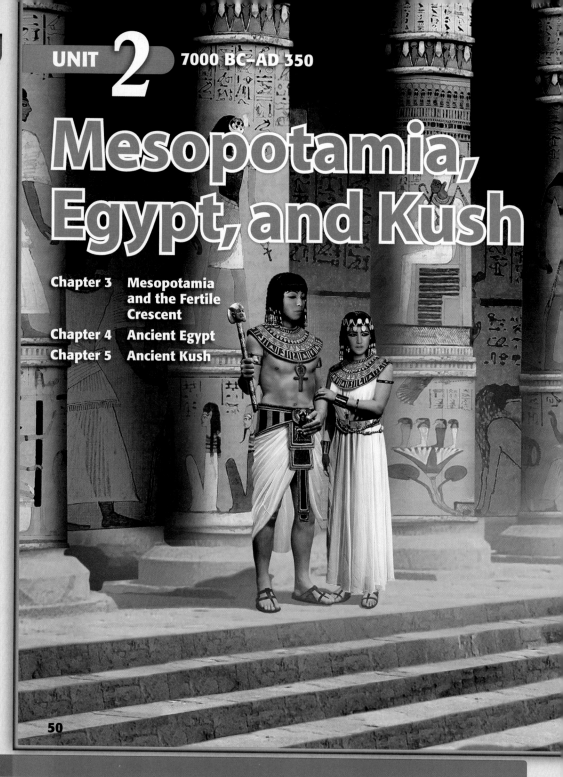

UNIT 2 7000 BC–AD 350

Mesopotamia, Egypt, and Kush

Chapter 3	Mesopotamia and the Fertile Crescent
Chapter 4	Ancient Egypt
Chapter 5	Ancient Kush

50

Unit Resources

Planning

- Universal Access Teacher Management System: Unit Instructional Benchmarking Guides
- One-Stop Planner CD-ROM with Test Generator: Holt Calendar Planner
- Power Presentations with Video CD-ROM
- A Teacher's Guide to Religion in the Public Schools

Standards Mastery

- Standards Review Workbook
- At Home: A Guide to Standards Mastery for World History

Differentiating Instruction

- Universal Access Teacher Management System: Lesson Plans for Universal Access
- Universal Access Modified Worksheets and Tests CD-ROM

Enrichment

- **CRF 3:** Economics and History: The First Coins
- **CRF 3:** Interdisciplinary Project: Mesopotamia: The First Writing
- Civic Participation
- Primary Source Library CD-ROM

Assessment

- Progress Assessment Support System: Benchmark Test
- **OSP** ExamView Test Generator: Benchmark Test
- Holt Online Assessment Program (in the Premier Online Edition)
- Alternative Assessment Handbook

> The **Universal Access Teacher Management System** provides a planning and instructional benchmarking guide for this unit.

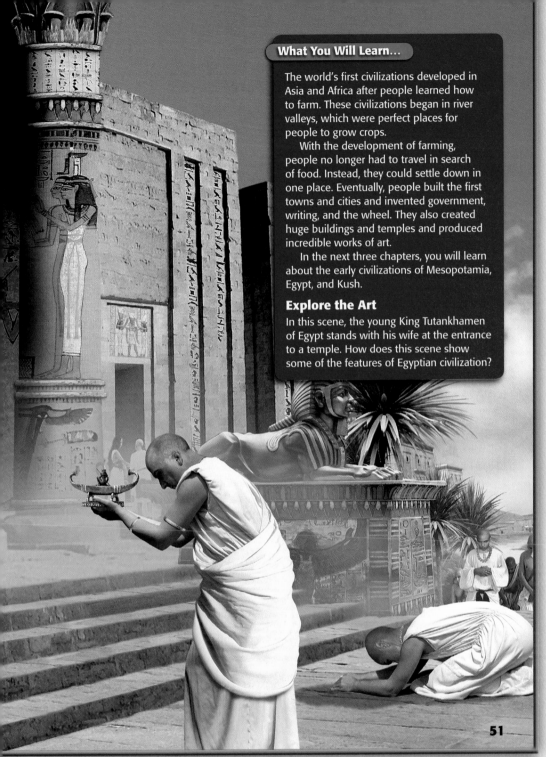

What You Will Learn...

The world's first civilizations developed in Asia and Africa after people learned how to farm. These civilizations began in river valleys, which were perfect places for people to grow crops.

With the development of farming, people no longer had to travel in search of food. Instead, they could settle down in one place. Eventually, people built the first towns and cities and invented government, writing, and the wheel. They also created huge buildings and temples and produced incredible works of art.

In the next three chapters, you will learn about the early civilizations of Mesopotamia, Egypt, and Kush.

Explore the Art

In this scene, the young King Tutankhamen of Egypt stands with his wife at the entrance to a temple. How does this scene show some of the features of Egyptian civilization?

51

Democracy and Civic Education

Standards Proficiency

Justice: Rule of Law and Hammurabi's Code

Background The earliest known written set of laws is Hammurabi's Code. This set of 282 laws established rule of law in the Babylonian Empire.

1. Explain the term *rule of law,* under which all members of a society, including rulers, must follow set laws. Discuss the importance of the rule of law for the protection of individual rights and for promoting the common good.

2. Have students work in small groups to develop standards for evaluating laws. Students should decide what the term *justice* means and how to determine whether a law is just. Have students apply their standards to the excerpt from Hammurabi's Code on p. 75. Are these laws just?

3. Have students work as a class to establish a code of school rules. Students should consider a range of specific situations, from running in the halls to cheating to fighting.
LS Interpersonal

📑 Alternative Assessment Handbook, Rubrics 11: Discussion; and 14: Group Activity

📑 Civic Participation

• Unit Preview •

Unit Overview *continued*

Kush grew wealthy from trade. Then around 1500 BC Egypt conquered Kush and controlled it for about 500 years. During this time, the people of Kush adopted many aspects of Egyptian culture. Kush then regained its independence and later conquered Egypt. In time, however, Kush weakened. In the AD 300s, it fell to a nearby kingdom.

Connect to the Unit

Activity **River Valley Civilizations**
Remind students that the development of farming led to the growth of towns. Explain that in time, towns developed into civilizations, the first of which grew up in river valleys in Asia and Africa. Write the phrase *River Valley* for students to see. Below the phrase, create a two-column chart and label the columns *Advantages* and *Disadvantages*. Ask students to brainstorm why the first civilizations developed in river valleys. Write the responses in the Advantages column. To help students get started, remind them that farming led to population growth and to the development of more complex societies. Then ask students to consider what some of the disadvantages of living in river valleys might be. List the responses in the Disadvantages column. At the end of the unit, have students review the chart and revise it based on what they have learned. **LS Visual/Spatial**

Explore the Art

In 1922, Howard Carter led a team of archaeologists that located the tomb of King Tutankhamen, or King Tut. King Tut was a pharaoh, or ruler, of ancient Egypt. The tomb had been undisturbed and contained many treasures. As a result, King Tut has became one of the most famous of Egypt's pharaohs.

About the Illustration

This illustration is an artist's conception based on available sources. However, historians are uncertain exactly what this scene looked like.

Answers

Explore the Art *shows architecture, clothing styles, jewelry, artifacts, paintings on temple walls, respect shown to king*

51

Chapter 3 Planning Guide

Mesopotamia and the Fertile Crescent

Chapter Overview	Reproducible Resources	Technology Resources
Chapter 3 pp. 52–83 **Overview:** In this chapter, students will learn about the history and achievements of the Sumerians and other peoples of the Fertile Crescent. See page 52 for the California History–Social Science standards covered in this chapter.	**Universal Access Teacher Management System:*** • Universal Access Instructional Benchmarking Guides • Lesson Plans for Universal Access **Interactive Reader and Study Guide:** Chapter Graphic Organizer* **Chapter Resource File*** • Chapter Review Activity • Focus on Writing Activity: A Poster • Social Studies Skills Activity: Interpreting Physical Maps	**One-Stop Planner CD-ROM:** Calendar Planner **Student Edition Full-Read Audio CD-ROM** **Universal Access Modified Worksheets and Tests CD-ROM** **Power Presentations with Video CD-ROM** **History's Impact: World History Video Program (VHS/DVD):** Mesopotamia and the Fertile Crescent*
Section 1: **Geography of the Fertile Crescent** **The Big Idea:** The valleys of the Tigris and Euphrates rivers were the site of the world's first civilizations. 6.2.1, 6.2.2	**Universal Access Teacher Management System:*** Section 1 Lesson Plan **Interactive Reader and Study Guide:** Section 1 Summary* **Chapter Resource File*** • Vocabulary Builder Activity, Section 1 • History and Geography Activity: A Fertile Land	**Daily Bellringer Transparency:** Section 1* **Map Transparency:** The Fertile Crescent*
Section 2: **The Rise of Sumer** **The Big Idea:** The Sumerians developed the first civilization in Mesopotamia. 6.2.3	**Universal Access Teacher Management System:*** Section 2 Lesson Plan **Interactive Reader and Study Guide:** Section 2 Summary* **Chapter Resource File*** • Vocabulary Builder Activity, Section 2 • Biography Activity: Enheduanna • Primary Source Activity: The Sumerian Flood Story	**Daily Bellringer Transparency:** Section 2* **Map Transparency:** Sargon's Empire, c. 2330 BC* **Internet Activities:** City-State Planner; Sumerian Pantheon
Section 3: **Sumerian Achievements** **The Big Idea:** The Sumerians made many advances that helped their society develop. 6.2.9	**Universal Access Teacher Management System:*** Section 3 Lesson Plan **Interactive Reader and Study Guide:** Section 3 Summary* **Chapter Resource File*** • Vocabulary Builder Activity, Section 3 • Interdisciplinary Projects: Mesopotamia • Literature Activity: *The Epic of Gilgamesh*	**Daily Bellringer Transparency:** Section 3*
Section 4: **Later Peoples of the Fertile Crescent** **The Big Idea:** After the Sumerians, many cultures ruled parts of the Fertile Crescent. 6.2.4	**Universal Access Teacher Management System:*** Section 4 Lesson Plan **Interactive Reader and Study Guide:** Section 4 Summary* **Chapter Resource File*** • Vocabulary Builder Activity, Section 4 • Biography Activity: Hammurabi • Biography Activity: King Nebuchadnezzar • Primary Source Activity: The Code of Hammurabi • Primary Source: Descriptions of the Phoenicians	**Daily Bellringer Transparency:** Section 4* **Quick Facts Transparency:** Hammurabi's Code* **Map Transparency:** Babylonian and Assyrian Empires* **Map Transparency:** Phoenicia, c. 800 BC*

MASTERING THE CALIFORNIA STANDARDS

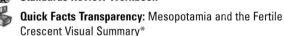

Review, Assessment, Intervention

- **Standards Review Workbook***
- **Quick Facts Transparency:** Mesopotamia and the Fertile Crescent Visual Summary*
- **Spanish Chapter Summaries Audio CD Program**
- **Online Chapter Summaries in Six Languages**
- **Progress Assessment Support System (PASS):** Chapter Test*
- **Universal Access Modified Worksheets and Tests CD-ROM:** Modified Chapter Test
- **One-Stop Planner CD-ROM:** ExamView Test Generator (English/Spanish)

- **PASS:** Section 1 Quiz*
- **Online Quiz:** Section 1
- **Alternative Assessment Handbook**

- **PASS:** Section 2 Quiz*
- **Online Quiz:** Section 2
- **Alternative Assessment Handbook**

- **PASS:** Section 3 Quiz*
- **Online Quiz:** Section 3
- **Alternative Assessment Handbook**

- **PASS:** Section 4 Quiz*
- **Online Quiz:** Section 4
- **Alternative Assessment Handbook**

California Resources for Standards Mastery

INSTRUCTIONAL PLANNING AND SUPPORT

- **Universal Access Teacher Management System***
- **One-Stop Planner CD-ROM with Test Generator:** Teacher Management System with Interactive Teacher's Edition

STANDARDS MASTERY

- **Standards Review Workbook***
- **At Home: A Guide to Standards Mastery for World History**

Holt Online Learning

To enhance learning, the following Internet activities are available: **City-State Planner** and **Sumerian Pantheon.**

> **KEYWORD: SQ6 TEACHER**

- **Teacher Support Page**
- **Content Updates**
- **Rubrics and Writing Models**
- **Teaching Tips for the Multimedia Classroom**

> **KEYWORD: SQ6 WH3**

- **Current Events**
- **Holt Grapher**
- **Holt Online Atlas**
- **Holt Researcher**
- **Interactive Multimedia Activities**
- **Internet Activities**
- **Online Chapter Summaries in Six Languages**
- **Online Section Quizzes**
- **World History Maps and Charts**

HOLT PREMIER ONLINE STUDENT EDITION

- **Interactive Maps and Notebook**
- **Standardized Test Prep**
- **Homework Practice and Research Activities Online**

Mastering the Standards: Differentiating Instruction

Reaching Standards	Basic-level activities designed for all students encountering new material
Standards Proficiency	Intermediate-level activities designed for average students
Exceeding Standards	Challenging activities designed for honors and gifted-and-talented students
Standard English Mastery	Activities designed to improve standard English usage

MASTERING THE CALIFORNIA STANDARDS

Frequently Asked Questions

INSTRUCTIONAL PLANNING AND SUPPORT

Where do I find planning aids, pacing guides, lesson plans, and other teaching aids?

Annotated Teacher's Edition:
- Chapter Planning Guides
- Standards-based instruction and strategies
- Differentiated instruction for universal access
- Point-of-use reminders for integrating program resources

Power Presentations with Video CD-ROM

Universal Access Teacher Management System:
- Year and unit instructional benchmarking guides
- Reproducible lesson plans
- Assessment guides for diagnostic, progress, and summative end-of-the-year tests
- Options for differentiating instruction and intervention
- Teaching guides and answer keys for student workbooks

One-Stop Planner CD-ROM with Test Generator: Teacher Management System with Interactive Teacher's Edition:
- Calendar Planner
- Editable lesson plans
- All reproducible ancillaries in Adobe Acrobat (PDF) format
- ExamView Test Generator (English & Spanish)
- Game Tool for ExamView
- PuzzlePro
- Transparency and video previews

DIFFERENTIATING INSTRUCTION FOR UNIVERSAL ACCESS

What resources are available to ensure that Advanced Learners/GATE Students master the standards?

Teacher's Edition Activities:
- Sumerian Mathematics, p. 69
- Gilgamesh and Enkidu Dialogue, p. 72

- Lawless Land Short Story, p. 75

Lesson Plans for Universal Access

Primary Source Library CD-ROM for World History

What resources are available to ensure that English Learners and Standard English Learners master the standards?

Teacher's Edition Activities:
- Pictograph Activity, p. 68
- Gilgamesh and Humbaba Drawing, p. 72

Lesson Plans for Universal Access

Chapter Resource File: Vocabulary Builder Activities

Spanish Chapter Summaries Audio CD Program

Online Chapter Summaries in Six Languages

One-Stop Planner CD-ROM:
- PuzzlePro, Spanish Version
- ExamView Test Generator, Spanish Version

What modified materials are available for Special Education?

Teacher's Edition Activities:
- Sumerian Inventions Collage, p. 69

The *Universal Access Modified Materials Worksheets and Tests CD-ROM* provides editable versions of the following:

Vocabulary Flash Cards

Modified Vocabulary Builder Activities

Modified Chapter Review Activity

Modified Chapter Test

What resources are available to ensure that Learners Having Difficulty master the standards?

Teacher's Edition Activities:
- Cause-and-Effect Posters, p. 57
- Creating a Farming Community, p. 58
- Rise of Sumer Graphic Organizer, p. 64
- Letter from the Hittite King, p. 76

Interactive Reader and Study Guide

Student Edition Full-Read Audio CD

Quick Facts Transparency: Mesopotamia and the Fertile Crescent Visual Summary

Standards Review Workbook

Social Studies Skills Activity: Interpreting Physical Maps

Interactive Skills Tutor CD-ROM

How do I intervene for students struggling to master the standards?

Interactive Reader and Study Guide

Quick Facts Transparency: Mesopotamia and the Fertile Crescent Visual Summary

Standards Review Workbook

Social Studies Skills Activity: Interpreting Physical Maps

Interactive Skills Tutor CD-ROM

PROFESSIONAL DEVELOPMENT

HOLT Professional Development

What teacher training resources are available to help me grow professionally?

- In-service and staff development as part of your Holt Social Studies product purchase
- Quick Teacher Tutorial Lesson Presentation CD-ROM
- Intensive tuition-based Teacher Development Institute
- Convenient Holt Speaker Bureau face-to-face workshop options

- PRAXIS™ Test Prep (#0089) interactive Web-based content refreshers*
- *Ask A Professional Development Expert* at http://www.hrw.com/prodev/

* PRAXIS is a trademark of Educational Testing Service (ETS). This publication is not endorsed or approved by ETS.

Information Literacy Skills

To learn more about how history–social science instruction may be improved by the effective use of library media centers and information literacy skills, go to the teachers resource materials for Chapter 3 at **go.hrw.com, keyword: SQ6 MEDIA.**

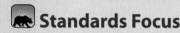

CHAPTER **3** 7000–500 BC

Mesopotamia and the Fertile Crescent

California Standards

History–Social Science
6.2 Students analyze the geographic, political, economic, religious, and social structures of the early civilizations of Mesopotamia, Egypt, and Kush.

Analysis Skills
CS 3 Use maps to identify physical features.

English–Language Arts
Writing 6.1.2a Engage the interest of the reader and state a clear purpose.

Reading 6.2.3 Connect and clarify main ideas by identifying their relationships to other sources and related topics.

FOCUS ON WRITING

A Poster Most elementary school students have not read or heard much about ancient Mesopotamia. As you read this chapter, you can gather information about that land. Then you can create a colorful poster to share some of what you have learned with younger children.

CHAPTER EVENTS

WORLD EVENTS

7000 BC

c. 7000 BC Agriculture first develops in Mesopotamia.

c. 3100 BC Menes becomes the first pharaoh of Egypt.

52 CHAPTER 3

Introduce the Chapter

Standards Proficiency

The Development of Cities

1. Ask students to imagine that they are living in a large farming community in ancient times. Remind students that early farming villages were not technologically advanced. As the communities grew more food, their settlements grew in size. Have students discuss what inventions, technology, or organizations would be needed in the community as it grows. Ask students to explain why each item or idea is needed. What might it take to create these advances?

2. Explain to students that they are going to learn about the world's first civilization, Mesopotamia, and how it grew from small farming communities to a civilization with advanced technology and large cities.

3. Ask students to keep track of the new ideas that were developed in Mesopotamia and the impact those new ideas would have on the world. **LS** Verbal/Linguistic, Interpersonal

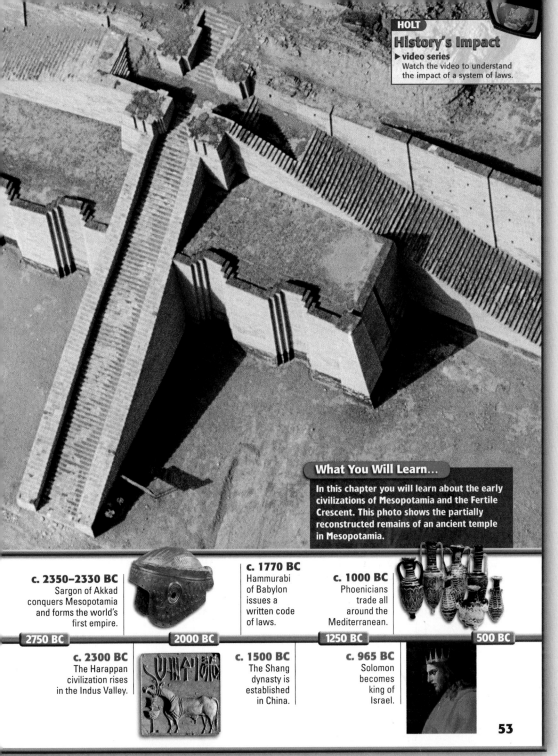

HOLT
History's Impact
▶ video series
Watch the video to understand the impact of a system of laws.

What You Will Learn...

In this chapter you will learn about the early civilizations of Mesopotamia and the Fertile Crescent. This photo shows the partially reconstructed remains of an ancient temple in Mesopotamia.

c. 2350–2330 BC
Sargon of Akkad conquers Mesopotamia and forms the world's first empire.

c. 1770 BC
Hammurabi of Babylon issues a written code of laws.

c. 1000 BC
Phoenicians trade all around the Mediterranean.

2750 BC   **2000 BC**   **1250 BC**   **500 BC**

c. 2300 BC
The Harappan civilization rises in the Indus Valley.

c. 1500 BC
The Shang dynasty is established in China.

c. 965 BC
Solomon becomes king of Israel.

53

Explore the Time Line

1. About how many years passed between the writing of Hammurabi's code of laws and the establishment of the Shang dynasty? *270*

2. When was the world's first empire established? between *2350 and 2330 BC*

3. Which occurred first, the creation of the Harappan civilization in India or the rise of the Shang dynasty in China? *Harappan civilization*

HSS Analysis Skills: CS 1

Info to Know

The Code of Hammurabi One of the oldest known collections of written laws, the Code of Hammurabi contains 282 laws dealing with matters ranging from marriage and divorce to theft and murder. The legal code, engraved on a large stone slab, was discovered in 1901 at the site of the ancient Mesopotamian city of Susa in modern-day Iran. However, historians believe the code of laws originally stood in the temple of Marduk in Babylon.

● **Chapter Preview** ●

HOLT
History's Impact
▶ video series
See the Video Teacher's Guide for strategies for using the chapter video **Mesopotamia and the Fertile Crescent: The Impact of a System of Laws.**

Chapter Big Ideas

Section 1 The valleys of the Tigris and Euphrates rivers were the site of the world's first civilizations. **HSS** 6.2.1, 6.2.2

Section 2 The Sumerians developed the first civilization in Mesopotamia. **HSS** 6.2.3

Section 3 The Sumerians made many advances that helped their society develop. **HSS** 6.2.9

Section 4 After the Sumerians, many cultures ruled parts of the Fertile Crescent. **HSS** 6.2.4

Explore the Picture

Ziggurat at Ur Mesopotamian temples known as ziggurats served as places of worship and were the largest, most important buildings in their cities. The photo here shows one of the most famous Mesopotamian ziggurats, the ziggurat at Ur. The ruins of the ancient Sumerian temple, believed to have been built in about 2100 BC, are located near the present-day city of Nasiriyah, in southeastern Iraq. Attempts at restoring the ziggurat took place in the 1930s, but only the lower level of the temple was restored.

Analyzing Visuals What types of technology or knowledge were probably needed to build this temple? *possible answers—knowledge of architecture, engineering, masonry, surveying*

go.hrw.com
Online Resources
Chapter Resources:
KEYWORD: SQ6 WH3
Teacher Resources:
KEYWORD: SQ6 TEACHER

Reading Social Studies

Understanding Themes

Discuss with students the two key themes of this chapter. Organize the class into small groups. Ask students to imagine that they are members of a culture that has recently adopted a settled, agricultural lifestyle. Have each group discuss what types of technology they might need to function in their villages and cities. Then have students discuss the type of government they might establish in their settlement. Help the class to see that technology and politics were two themes of great importance to early civilizations.

Main Ideas in Social Studies

Focus on Reading Ask students to bring in newspaper or magazine articles that interest them. Have each student read his or her article and select two or three paragraphs to work with. For each paragraph, have students follow the steps listed at right to identify the main idea. Then ask students to find a partner with whom to exchange articles. Have students read the selected paragraphs and identify the main idea for each. When students are finished, have them compare main ideas. Ask students if they each identified the same main idea.

Reading Social Studies

by Kylene Beers

| Economics | Geography | Politics | Religion | Society and Culture | Science and Technology |

Focus on Themes Chapter three introduces you to a region in southwest Asia called Mesopotamia, the home of the world's first civilization. You will read about what made this area one where civilizations could begin and grow. You will learn about one group of people—the Sumerians—and their great **technological** inventions. You will also read about other people who invaded Mesopotamia and brought their own rules of governing and **politics** to the area.

Main Ideas in Social Studies

Focus on Reading Have you ever set up a tent? If you have, you know that one pole provides structure and support for the whole tent. A paragraph has a similar structure. One idea—the **main idea**—provides support and structure for the whole paragraph.

Identifying Main Ideas Most paragraphs written about history include a main idea that is stated clearly in a sentence. At other times, the main idea is suggested, not stated. However, that idea still shapes the paragraph's content and the meaning of all of the facts and details in it.

Identifying Main Ideas

1. Read the paragraph. Ask yourself, "What is this paragraph mostly about, or its topic?"

2. List the important facts and details that relate to that topic.

3. Ask yourself, "What seems to be the most important point the writer is making about the topic?" Or ask, "If the writer could say only one thing about this paragraph, what would it be?" **This is the main idea of the paragraph.**

Having people available to work on different jobs meant that society could accomplish more. Large projects, such as constructing buildings and digging irrigation systems, required specialized workers, managers, and organization. To complete these projects, the Mesopotamians needed structure and rules. Structure and rules could be provided by laws and government.

Topic: The paragraph talks about people, jobs, and structure.

+

Facts and Details:
• People working on different jobs needed structure.
• Laws and government provided this structure.

=

Main Idea: Having people in a society work on many different jobs led to the creation of laws and government.

Additional reading support can be found in the

Inter active
Reader and Study Guide

Reading and Skills Resources

Reading Support

- Interactive Reader and Study Guide
- Student Edition on Audio CD
- Spanish Chapter Summaries Audio CD Program

Social Studies Skills Support

- Interactive Skills Tutor CD-ROM

Vocabulary Support

- **CRF:** Vocabulary Builder Activities
- **CRF:** Chapter Review Activity
- Universal Access Modified Worksheets and Tests CD-ROM:
  - Vocabulary Flash Cards
  - Vocabulary Builder Activity
  - Chapter Review Activity

OSP Holt PuzzlePro

Standards Focus
ELA Reading 6.2.3

ELA Reading 6.2.3 Connect and clarify main ideas by identifying their relationships to other sources and related topics.

You Try It!

The passage below is from the chapter you are about to read. Read it and then answer the questions below.

Technical Advances

From Chapter 3 p. 69

One of the Sumerians' most important developments was the wheel. They were the first people to build wheeled vehicles, including carts and wagons. Using the wheel, Sumerians invented a device that spins clay as a craftsperson shapes it into bowls. This device is called a potter's wheel.

The plow was another important Sumerian invention. Pulled by oxen, plows broke through the hard clay soil of Sumer to prepare it for planting. This technique greatly increased farm production. The Sumerians also invented a clock that used falling water to measure time.

Sumerian advances improved daily life in many ways. Sumerians built sewers under city streets. They learned to use bronze to make stronger tools and weapons. They even produced makeup and glass jewelry.

Answer the following questions about finding main ideas.

1. Reread the first paragraph. What is its main idea?

2. What is the main idea of the third paragraph? Reread the second paragraph. Is there a sentence that expresses the main idea of the paragraph? What is that main idea? Write a sentence to express it.

3. Which of the following best expresses the main idea of the entire passage?

  a. The wheel was an important invention.

  b. The Sumerians invented many helpful devices.

> **As you read Chapter 3,** find the main ideas of the paragraphs you are studying.

Key Terms and People

Chapter 3

Section 1
Fertile Crescent *(p. 57)*
silt *(p. 57)*
irrigation *(p. 58)*
canals *(p. 58)*
surplus *(p. 58)*
division of labor *(p. 58)*

Section 2
rural *(p. 62)*
urban *(p. 62)*
city-state *(p. 62)*
Gilgamesh *(p. 63)*
Sargon *(p. 63)*
empire *(p. 63)*
polytheism *(p. 64)*
priests *(p. 65)*
social hierarchy *(p. 65)*

Section 3
cuneiform *(p. 67)*
pictographs *(p. 68)*
scribe *(p. 68)*
epics *(p. 68)*
architecture *(p. 70)*
ziggurat *(p. 70)*

Section 4
monarch *(p. 74)*
Hammurabi's Code *(p. 75)*
chariot *(p. 76)*
Nebuchadnezzar *(p. 77)*
alphabet *(p. 79)*

Academic Vocabulary

Success in school is related to knowing academic vocabulary—the words that are frequently used in school assignments and discussions. In this chapter, you will learn the following academic words:

role *(p. 64)*
impact *(p. 65)*

Reading Social Studies

Key Terms and People

This chapter has a lengthy list of key terms. Some will be familiar to students, but others will be new. Read the list aloud so that students will know how to pronounce each term or name. After you read each term, ask volunteers to explain what the term might mean. Correct student suggestions if necessary. Then have students copy the words into a two-column chart labeled *People* and *Terms*. As you prepare to study each section, have students define or identify each term or person in their list.
LS Verbal/Linguistic

Focus on Reading

See the **Focus on Reading** questions in this chapter for more practice on this reading social studies skill.

Reading Social Studies Assessment

See the **Standards Review** at the end of this chapter for student assessment questions related to this reading skill.

Teaching Tip

Tell students that in order to get the most out of their studying time, they should make sure they understand the main ideas of what they are reading or studying. One way to do this is to be sure that they understand the main idea of a passage before moving on to the next one. Suggest that while they are reading, they stop after every few paragraphs or after every heading and identify that passage's main idea. This will help students become active readers and retain more of what they have read.

Answers

You Try It! 1. *One of the most important Sumerian developments was the wheel.* **2.** *Sumerian advances improved their daily life; no; possible main idea—Sumerians made other important advances.* **3.** *b*

Bellringer

If YOU were there . . . Use the **Daily Bellringer Transparency** to help students answer the question.

🗓 Daily Bellringer Transparency, Section 1

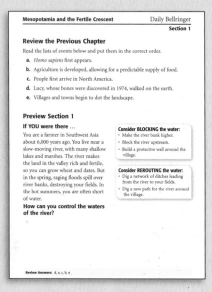

Building Vocabulary

Preteach or review the following terms:

occupations work or ways of making a living (p. 58)

plateau an elevated flatland with a level surface (p. 57)

📋 **CRF:** Vocabulary Builder Activity, Section 1

🐻 Standards Focus

HSS 6.2.1
Means: Identify the major river systems and discuss how they supported human settlements and civilization.
Matters: The earliest civilizations were established along river valleys.

HSS 6.2.2
Means: Trace the advances in agriculture that led to food surpluses and the growth of cities.
Matters: Food surpluses allowed people in early civilizations to build cities with strong governments and lively cultures.

SECTION 1

What You Will Learn...

Main Ideas

1. The rivers of Southwest Asia supported the growth of civilization.
2. New farming techniques led to the growth of cities.

The Big Idea

The valleys of the Tigris and Euphrates rivers were the site of the world's first civilizations.

Key Terms

Fertile Crescent, *p. 57*
silt, *p. 57*
irrigation, *p. 58*
canals, *p. 58*
surplus, *p. 58*
division of labor, *p. 58*

HSS 6.2.1 Locate and describe the major river systems and discuss the physical settings that supported permanent settlement and early civilization.

6.2.2 Trace the development of agricultural techniques that permitted the production of economic surplus and the emergence of cities as centers of culture and power.

Geography of the Fertile Crescent

If YOU were there...

You are a farmer in Southwest Asia about 6,000 years ago. You live near a slow-moving river, with many shallow lakes and marshes. The river makes the land in the valley rich and fertile, so you can grow wheat and dates. But in the spring, raging floods spill over the riverbanks, destroying your fields. In the hot summers, you are often short of water.

How can you control the waters of the river?

BUILDING BACKGROUND In several parts of the world, bands of hunter-gatherers began to settle down in farming settlements. They domesticated plants and animals. Gradually their cultures became more complex. Most early civilizations grew up along rivers, where people learned to work together to control floods.

Rivers Support the Growth of Civilization

Early peoples settled where crops would grow. Crops usually grew well near rivers, where water was available and regular floods made the soil rich. One region in Southwest Asia was especially well suited for farming. It lay between two rivers.

Teach the Big Idea: Master the Standards

Standards Proficiency

Geography of the Fertile Crescent 🐻 **HSS** 6.2.1, 6.2.2; **HSS** Analysis Skills: HI 1, HI 2

1. **Teach** Ask students the Main Idea questions to teach this section.

2. **Apply** Have each student create a proposal to the United Nations requesting a memorial or historical marker for Mesopotamia. Have students explain why they believe there should be a memorial and what significance Mesopotamia has to history. Remind students to cite specific accomplishments from the section and to use persuasive language in their proposal.
LS Verbal/Linguistic

3. **Review** Ask students to exchange their completed proposals with one another as a review of the section.

4. **Practice/Homework** Have students draw sketches of what their proposed memorials or markers might look like and where they could be located. **LS Visual/Spatial**

📋 Alternative Assessment Handbook, Rubrics 3: Artwork; and 43: Writing to Persuade

The Land Between the Rivers

The Tigris and Euphrates rivers are the most important physical features of the region sometimes known as Mesopotamia (mes-uh-puh-TAY-mee-uh). Mesopotamia means "between the rivers" in Greek.

As you can see on the map, the region called Mesopotamia lies between Asia Minor and the Persian Gulf. The region is part of a larger area called the **Fertile Crescent**, a large arc of rich, or fertile, farmland. The Fertile Crescent extends from the Persian Gulf to the Mediterranean Sea.

In ancient times, Mesopotamia was actually made of two parts. Northern Mesopotamia was a plateau bordered on the north and the east by mountains. Southern Mesopotamia was a flat plain. The Tigris and Euphrates rivers flowed down from the hills into this low-lying plain.

The Rise of Civilization

Hunter-gatherer groups first settled in Mesopotamia more than 12,000 years ago. Over time, these people learned how to plant crops to grow their own food. Every year, floods on the Tigris and Euphrates rivers brought **silt**, a mixture of rich soil and tiny rocks, to the land. The fertile silt made the land ideal for farming.

The first farm settlements formed in Mesopotamia as early as 7000 BC. Farmers grew wheat, barley, and other types of grain. Livestock, birds, and fish were also good sources of food. Plentiful food led to population growth, and villages formed. Eventually, these early villages developed into the world's first civilization.

READING CHECK Summarizing What made civilization possible in Mesopotamia?

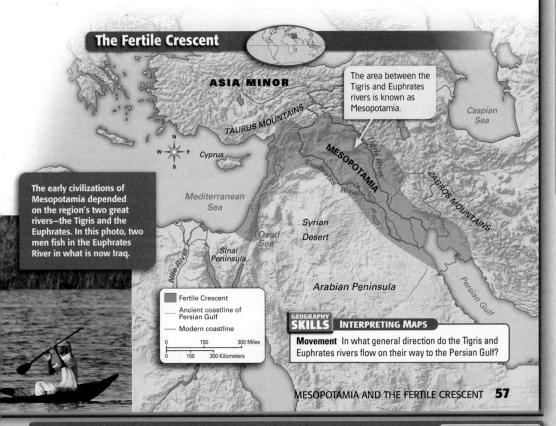

The Fertile Crescent

ASIA MINOR

The area between the Tigris and Euphrates rivers is known as Mesopotamia.

TAURUS MOUNTAINS

Cyprus

MESOPOTAMIA

Tigris River

Euphrates River

ZAGROS MOUNTAINS

Caspian Sea

Mediterranean Sea

Nile River

Dead Sea

Sinai Peninsula

Syrian Desert

Arabian Peninsula

Persian Gulf

The early civilizations of Mesopotamia depended on the region's two great rivers—the Tigris and the Euphrates. In this photo, two men fish in the Euphrates River in what is now Iraq.

☐ Fertile Crescent
⋯ Ancient coastline of Persian Gulf
— Modern coastline

0   150   300 Miles
0   150   300 Kilometers

GEOGRAPHY SKILLS INTERPRETING MAPS

Movement In what general direction do the Tigris and Euphrates rivers flow on their way to the Persian Gulf?

MESOPOTAMIA AND THE FERTILE CRESCENT **57**

Critical Thinking: Understanding Cause and Effect

Reaching Standards

Cause-and-Effect Posters 🐻 HSS 6.2.1; HSS Analysis Skills: HI 1, HI 2

1. Discuss with students the reasons why Mesopotamia was the site of the world's first civilization. Ask students why hunter-gatherers might have decided to settle in the Fertile Crescent. Then, discuss with students what the effects were of settlement in Mesopotamia. Encourage students to take notes about the discussion.

2. Have each student briefly sketch a diagram that depicts the causes of settlement in the Fertile Crescent and the results of this settlement.

Then, have each student create a poster using illustrations to show the causes and effects of settlement in the Fertile Crescent. Remind students that their posters should be easy to understand.

3. Ask volunteers to share their cause-and-effect posters with the class.
   🔲 **Visual/Spatial, Verbal/Linguistic**

📄 Alternative Assessment Handbook, Rubrics 3: Artwork; and 6: Cause and Effect

❷ Farming and Cities

New farming techniques led to the growth of cities.

Explain How did irrigation help farmers? *It provided a way of supplying water to fields and storing water for times of need.*

Analyze What effects did irrigation have on farming settlements? *It made farmers more productive, which led to a food surplus and less need for people to farm, and these in turn led to a division of labor.*

Make Inferences How might big construction projects like the building of canals and large buildings lead to laws and government? *To keep workers organized and following the construction plan, structure and rules were needed, and these would lead to governments and laws.*

🐻 **HSS** 6.2.1, 6.2.2; **HSS** Analysis Skills: HI 1, HI 2

Info to Know

Raw Materials The people of Mesopotamia survived on resources provided by the Tigris and Euphrates rivers and the flat plains along the rivers. Wood, stone, and metal were almost nonexistent in the region. Without wood, buildings had to be made of clay bricks. Without stone, roads were difficult to maintain. However, by carefully using their water resources, people had enough vegetables, grains, fish, and livestock.

Irrigation and Civilization

Early farmers faced the challenge of learning how to control the flow of river water to their fields in both rainy and dry seasons.

❶ Early settlements in Mesopotamia were located near rivers. Water was not controlled, and flooding was a major problem.

❷ Later, people built canals to protect houses from flooding and move water to their fields.

Farming and Cities

Although Mesopotamia had fertile soil, farming wasn't easy there. The region received little rain. This meant that the water levels in the Tigris and Euphrates rivers depended on how much rain fell in eastern Asia Minor where the two rivers began. When a great amount of rain fell there, water levels got very high. Flooding destroyed crops, killed livestock, and washed away homes. When water levels were too low, crops dried up. Farmers knew they needed a way to control the rivers' flow.

Controlling Water

To solve their problems, Mesopotamians used **irrigation**, a way of supplying water to an area of land. To irrigate their land, they dug out large storage basins to hold water supplies. Then they dug **canals**, human-made waterways, that connected these basins to a network of ditches. These ditches brought water to the fields. To protect their fields from flooding, farmers built up the banks of the Tigris and Euphrates. These built-up banks held back floodwaters even when river levels were high.

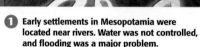

THE IMPACT TODAY
People still build dikes, or earthen walls along rivers or shorelines, to hold back water.

Food Surpluses

Irrigation increased the amount of food farmers were able to grow. In fact, farmers could produce a food **surplus**, or more than they needed. Farmers also used irrigation to water grazing areas for cattle and sheep. As a result, Mesopotamians ate a variety of foods. Fish, meat, wheat, barley, and dates were plentiful.

Because irrigation made farmers more productive, fewer people needed to farm. Some people became free to do other jobs. As a result, new occupations developed. For the first time, people became crafters, religious leaders, and government workers. The type of arrangement in which each worker specializes in a particular task or job is called a **division of labor**.

Having people available to work on different jobs meant that society could accomplish more. Large projects, such as constructing buildings and digging irrigation systems, required specialized workers, managers, and organization. To complete these projects, the Mesopotamians needed structure and rules. Structure and rules could be provided by laws and government.

58 CHAPTER 3

Creating a Farming Community 🐻 **HSS** 6.2.2; **HSS** Analysis Skills: CS 3, HI 1, HI 2

1. Organize the class into small groups. On a sheet of paper, have each group sketch a small farming community in its early stages. Students may use icons for houses, water, and other features.

2. Have groups introduce irrigation to their community. Ask students what adjustments they need to make to their village. Inform students that their village now has a food surplus. Ask groups how the village might change as a result. Have them add the changes to their drawings.

3. Remind students that one result of a food surplus is the division of labor. Have groups decide how their community will develop as a result and revise their drawings.

4. Drawings should gradually get larger, and students should see that their small community is becoming a city. Ask students what features they think are necessary for their city.

LS Visual/Spatial, Logical/Mathematical

📖 Alternative Assessment Handbook, Rubric 14: Group Activity

3 With irrigation, the people of Mesopotamia were able to grow more food.

4 Food surpluses allowed some people to stop farming and concentrate on other jobs, like making clay pots or tools.

Direct Teach

Linking to Today

Irrigation Irrigation is still a necessary part of farming. In fact, over 50 percent of all farmers today use some form of irrigation for their crops. While many farmers still use canals to direct water onto their fields, they use many other methods as well. Sprinkler irrigation and drip irrigation are two forms widely used in the United States.

The Appearance of Cities

Over time, Mesopotamian settlements grew in size and complexity. They gradually developed into cities between 4000 and 3000 BC.

Despite the growth of cities, society in Mesopotamia was still based on agriculture. Most people still worked in farming jobs. However, cities were becoming important places. People traded goods there, and cities provided leaders with power bases.

They were the political, religious, cultural, and economic centers of civilization.

READING CHECK **Analyzing** Why did the Mesopotamians create irrigation systems?

SUMMARY AND PREVIEW Mesopotamia's rich, fertile lands supported productive farming, which led to the development of cities. In Section 2 you will learn about some of the first city builders.

Review & Assess

Close

Discuss with students the role that water, and the control of it, played in the development of Mesopotamian civilizations.

Review

Online Quiz Section 1

Assess

SE Section 1 Assessment

PASS: Section 1 Quiz

Alternative Assessment Handbook

Reteach/Classroom Intervention

California Standards Review Workbook

Interactive Reader and Study Guide, Section 1

Interactive Skills Tutor CD-ROM

Section 1 Assessment

go.hrw.com
Online Quiz
KEYWORD: SQ6 HP3

Reviewing Ideas, Terms, and People **HSS** 6.2.1, 6.2.2

1. a. Identify Where was Mesopotamia?
b. Explain How did the **Fertile Crescent** get its name?
c. Evaluate What was the most important factor in making Mesopotamia's farmland fertile?
2. a. Describe Why did farmers need to develop a system to control their water supply?
b. Explain In what ways did a **division of labor** contribute to the growth of Mesopotamian civilization?
c. Elaborate How might running large projects prepare people for running a government?

Critical Thinking

3. Sequencing Create a flowchart like this one. Use it to explain how farmers used the Tigris and Euphrates to irrigate fields.

Water levels in rivers get too low. → ☐ → ☐ → Mesopotamians enjoy many foods.

FOCUS ON WRITING

4. Understanding Geography Make a list of the words you might use to help young students imagine the land and rivers. Then start to sketch out a picture or map you could use on your poster.

MESOPOTAMIA AND THE FERTILE CRESCENT **59**

Section 1 Assessment Answers

1. a. in Southwest Asia, between the Tigris and Euphrates rivers
b. It came from the arc of fertile land from the Mediterranean Sea to the Persian Gulf.
c. annual flooding of the Tigris and Euphrates
2. a. When the rivers flooded, crops, livestock, and homes were destroyed. Too little water ruined crops. Farmers needed a stable water supply for farming and raising livestock.
b. People developed expertise outside of farming; large-scale projects were com-

pleted, and laws and government needed to carry out such projects were developed.
c. Both require specialized workers, organization, planning, and rules.

3. possible answers—build up riverbanks to hold back floodwaters; dig storage basins to hold excess water; build canals to connect the basins to ditches; dig a network of ditches to bring water to fields; use irrigation to water grazing areas for cattle and sheep

4. possible answers—fertile lands, plentiful crops, beautiful rivers

Answers

Reading Check *to protect against damage from too much or too little water and to ensure a stable supply of water for crops and livestock*

History and Geography

History and Geography

Activity Cause-and-Effect **Chart** Ask students to imagine that they are in a boat floating down either the Tigris or Euphrates River in ancient Mesopotamia. What might be some of the sights and activities they see on their trip? *Students might suggest farming, irrigation, and people in boats fishing or traveling like them.* Then have each student create a chart showing the causes and effects of settlement and farming in river valleys as shown along the river during their voyages. *causes—see the introduction text at right; effects—see the captions at right.*

LS Verbal/Linguistic

Alternative Assessment Handbook, Rubrics 6: Cause and Effect; and 7: Charts

HSS 6.2.1; **HSS** Analysis Skills: CR 3, HI 1, HI 2

Linking to Today

Aswan High Dam Egyptians lived by the flooding cycle of the Nile River for thousands of years. In 1970, however, Egypt built the Aswan High Dam. This dam is 364 feet (111 m.) high and more than two miles (3.2 km.) long at the top. The dam created Lake Nasser. The dam generates large amounts of electricity and provides irrigation to many parts of the Nile River Valley.

Standards Focus

HSS 6.2 Students analyze the geographic, political, economic, religious, and social structures of the early civilizations of Mesopotamia, Egypt, and Kush.

6.2.1 Locate and describe the major river systems and discuss the physical settings that supported permanent settlement and early civilizations.

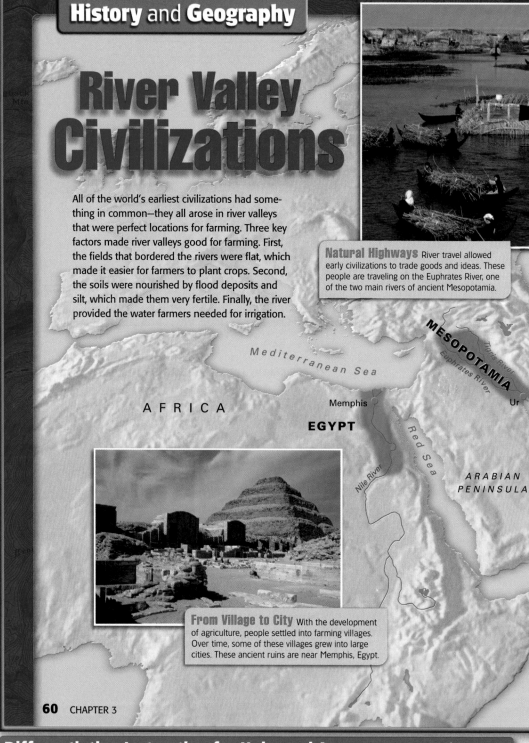

River Valley Civilizations

All of the world's earliest civilizations had something in common—they all arose in river valleys that were perfect locations for farming. Three key factors made river valleys good for farming. First, the fields that bordered the rivers were flat, which made it easier for farmers to plant crops. Second, the soils were nourished by flood deposits and silt, which made them very fertile. Finally, the river provided the water farmers needed for irrigation.

Natural Highways River travel allowed early civilizations to trade goods and ideas. These people are traveling on the Euphrates River, one of the two main rivers of ancient Mesopotamia.

From Village to City With the development of agriculture, people settled into farming villages. Over time, some of these villages grew into large cities. These ancient ruins are near Memphis, Egypt.

Mediterranean Sea

AFRICA

EGYPT

Memphis

MESOPOTAMIA

Euphrates River

Tigris River

Ur

Nile River

Red Sea

ARABIAN PENINSULA

60 CHAPTER 3

Differentiating Instruction for Universal Access

Learners Having Difficulty
Reaching Standards

Learning from Visuals To help struggling readers, have them match the text to the images in the above feature. Read aloud the introduction and each caption. As you do, have students identify images and map elements that correspond to the text, such as cities and river highways. Remind students that this book has many illustrations that can help them learn.

LS Visual-Spatial

HSS 6.2.1; **HSS** Analysis Skills: CS 3, HI 1

Advanced Learners/GATE
Exceeding Standards

Linking to Today Have students discuss how people rely on rivers today. Write students' responses for the class to see. If you have any rivers in your area, ask students if they know how these rivers are used. Then, encourage volunteers to share ways they have seen rivers being used. Remind students that people around the world are dependent on rivers.

LS Verbal/Linguistic

Alternative Assessment Handbook, Rubric 11: Discussions

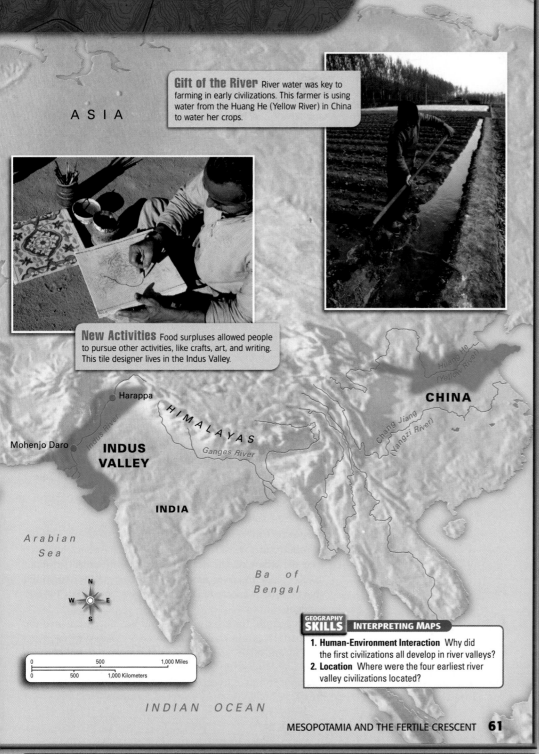

Gift of the River River water was key to farming in early civilizations. This farmer is using water from the Huang He (Yellow River) in China to water her crops.

ASIA

New Activities Food surpluses allowed people to pursue other activities, like crafts, art, and writing. This tile designer lives in the Indus Valley.

Harappa

HIMALAYAS

CHINA

Chang Jiang (Yangzi River)

Huang He (Yellow River)

Mohenjo Daro

INDUS VALLEY

Indus River

Ganges River

INDIA

Arabian Sea

Bay of Bengal

N W E S

0   500   1,000 Miles
0   500   1,000 Kilometers

INDIAN OCEAN

GEOGRAPHY SKILLS   INTERPRETING MAPS

1. **Human-Environment Interaction** Why did the first civilizations all develop in river valleys?
2. **Location** Where were the four earliest river valley civilizations located?

MESOPOTAMIA AND THE FERTILE CRESCENT **61**

History and Geography

Connect to Geography

Human-Environment Interaction If you visit the Indus River Valley today, it will not look like it did 5,000 years ago. Over time, people's presence in the river valley has greatly changed the landscape. One major change has been deforestation, or the widespread cutting down of trees. Few trees grow along the lower Indus River today.

Analyzing Visuals Examine the images on this page. How do they illustrate ways in which people have altered and adapted to river valley environments? *possible answers—altered: built irrigation canals and cities; adapted: used boats for travel*

Activity Researching River Valleys Today Have students create a table with four columns and label the columns *China, Egypt, Indus Valley,* and *Mesopotamia*. In each column have students provide (1) the countries located there today, (2) their capitals, and (3) their populations. A good online source for information is the CIA World Factbook (www.cia.gov/cia/publications/factbook).
LS Verbal/Linguistic

Collaborative Learning

Standards Proficiency

Ranking Geographic Regions HSS 6.2.1; HSS Analysis Skills: HI 1, HI 2, HI 3

1. Draw a chart with four columns and four rows for the class to see. Label the columns *fresh water, flat plain, good soil,* and *transportation*. Label the rows *river valley, seacoast, jungle,* and *desert*.

2. Have the class complete the chart by rating whether each location provides each criteria for settlement and farming. For example, a jungle may provide fresh water and good soil, but it may have poor transportation and does not provide an open flat plain.

3. After students complete the chart, have them discuss how the information relates to the settlement patterns of ancient peoples and why all early civilizations arose in river valleys. **LS** Interpersonal, Visual/Spatial

Alternative Assessment Handbook, Rubric 7: Charts

Answers

Interpreting Maps 1. *because they provided good locations for farming* **2.** *Egypt, Mesopotamia, Indus Valley, and China*

61

Bellringer

If YOU were there . . . Use the **Daily Bellringer Transparency** to help students answer the question.

📁 Daily Bellringer Transparency, Section 2

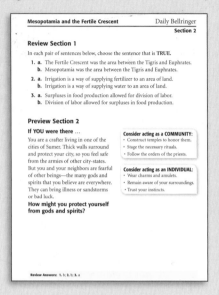

Mesopotamia and the Fertile Crescent — Daily Bellringer, Section 2

Review Section 1

In each pair of sentences below, choose the sentence that is **TRUE.**

1. **a.** The Fertile Crescent was the area between the Tigris and Euphrates.
   b. Mesopotamia was the area between the Tigris and Euphrates.
2. **a.** Irrigation is a way of supplying fertilizer to an area of land.
   b. Irrigation is a way of supplying water to an area of land.
3. **a.** Surpluses in food production allowed for division of labor.
   b. Division of labor allowed for surpluses in food production.

Preview Section 2

If YOU were there . . .

You are a crafter living in one of the cities of Sumer. Thick walls surround and protect your city, so you feel safe from the armies of other city-states. But you and your neighbors are fearful of other beings—the many gods and spirits that you believe are everywhere. They can bring illness or sandstorms or bad luck.

How might you protect yourself from gods and spirits?

Consider acting as a COMMUNITY:
• Construct temples to honor them.
• Stage the necessary rituals.
• Follow the orders of the priests.

Consider acting as an INDIVIDUAL:
• Wear charms and amulets.
• Remain aware of your surroundings.
• Trust your instincts.

Review Answers: 1. b; 2. b; 3. a

Academic Vocabulary

Review with students the high-use academic terms in this section.

impact effect, result (p. 65)

role a part or function (p. 64)

📝 **CRF:** Vocabulary Builder Activity, Section 2

🐻 Standards Focus

HSS 6.2.3

Means: Understand how religion was related to government and society in Mesopotamia and Egypt.

Matters: Religion played a very important role in everyday life in these early civilizations.

The Rise of Sumer

If YOU were there...

You are a crafter living in one of the cities of Sumer. Thick walls surround and protect your city, so you feel safe from the armies of other city-states. But you and your neighbors are fearful of other beings—the many gods and spirits that you believe are everywhere. They can bring illness or sandstorms or bad luck.

How might you protect yourself from gods and spirits?

What You Will Learn...

Main Ideas

1. The Sumerians created the world's first advanced society.
2. Religion played a major role in Sumerian society.

The Big Idea

The Sumerians developed the first civilization in Mesopotamia.

Key Terms and People

rural, *p. 62*
urban, *p. 62*
city-state, *p. 62*
Gilgamesh, *p. 63*
Sargon, *p. 63*
empire, *p. 63*
polytheism, *p. 64*
priests, *p. 65*
social hierarchy, *p. 65*

HSS 6.2.3. Understand the relationship between religion and the social and political order in Mesopotamia and Egypt.

BUILDING BACKGROUND As civilizations developed along rivers, their societies and governments became more advanced. Religion became a main characteristic of these ancient cultures. Kings claimed to rule with the approval of the gods, and ordinary people wore charms and performed rituals to avoid bad luck.

An Advanced Society

In southern Mesopotamia, a people known as the Sumerians (soo-MER-ee-unz) developed the world's first civilization. No one knows where they came from or when they moved into the region. However, by 3000 BC, several hundred thousand Sumerians had settled in Mesopotamia, in a land they called Sumer (SOO-muhr). There they created an advanced society.

The City-States of Sumer

Most people in Sumer were farmers. They lived mainly in **rural**, or countryside, areas. The centers of Sumerian society, however, were the **urban**, or city, areas. The first cities in Sumer had about 10,000 residents. Over time, the cities grew. Historians think that by 2000 BC, some of Sumer's cities had more than 100,000 residents.

As a result, the basic political unit of Sumer combined the two parts. This unit was called a city-state. A **city-state** consisted of a city and all the countryside around it. The amount of countryside controlled by each city-state depended on its military strength. Stronger city-states controlled larger areas.

Teach the Big Idea: Master the Standards

Standards Proficiency

The Rise of Sumer 🐻 **HSS** 6.2.3; **HSS** Analysis Skills: CS 1, HR 1, HI 1

1. **Teach** Ask students the Main Idea questions to teach this section.

2. **Apply** Have students create a three-column chart on their own paper. In the first column ask students to write down any headings, subheadings, or important terms from the section. In the second column, have students create as many questions about each term or heading in the first column as they can. Lastly, have students write the answers to their questions in the third column.
LS Verbal/Linguistic

3. **Review** Have students cover the answer column with a sheet of blank paper as they review the answers to the questions from the section. Students may also quiz a partner.

4. **Practice/Homework** Have students use their charts to create five multiple-choice questions about the section. Remind students to provide an answer key and an explanation of why each answer is correct.
LS Verbal/Linguistic

📝 Alternative Assessment Handbook, Rubric 37: Writing Assignments

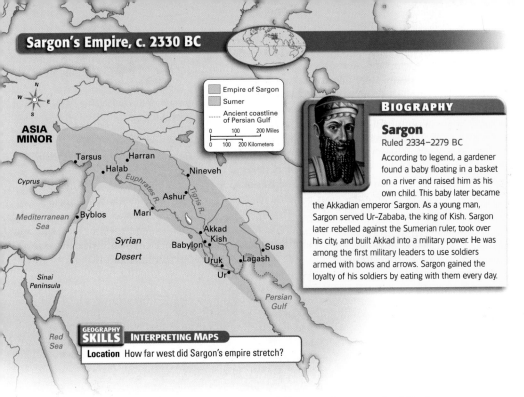

Sargon's Empire, c. 2330 BC

Empire of Sargon

Sumer

Ancient coastline of Persian Gulf

0   100   200 Miles
0 100 200 Kilometers

ASIA MINOR

Tarsus
Harran
Halab
Nineveh
Cyprus
Euphrates R.
Ashur
Tigris R.
Mediterranean Sea
Byblos
Mari
Syrian Desert
Akkad
Babylon
Kish
Uruk
Susa
Lagash
Ur
Sinai Peninsula
Persian Gulf
Red Sea

BIOGRAPHY

Sargon
Ruled 2334–2279 BC

According to legend, a gardener found a baby floating in a basket on a river and raised him as his own child. This baby later became the Akkadian emperor Sargon. As a young man, Sargon served Ur-Zababa, the king of Kish. Sargon later rebelled against the Sumerian ruler, took over his city, and built Akkad into a military power. He was among the first military leaders to use soldiers armed with bows and arrows. Sargon gained the loyalty of his soldiers by eating with them every day.

GEOGRAPHY SKILLS | INTERPRETING MAPS

Location How far west did Sargon's empire stretch?

City-states in Sumer fought each other to gain more farmland. As a result of these conflicts, the city-states built up strong armies. Sumerians also built strong, thick walls around their cities for protection.

Individual city-states gained and lost power over time. By 3500 BC, a city-state known as Kish had become quite powerful. Over the next 1,000 years, the city-states of Uruk and Ur fought for dominance. One of Uruk's kings, known as **Gilgamesh**, became a legendary figure in Sumerian literature.

Rise of the Akkadian Empire

In time, another society developed along the Tigris and Euphrates. It was created by the Akkadians (uh-KAY-dee-uhns). They lived just north of Sumer, but they were not Sumerians. They even spoke a different language than the Sumerians. In spite of their differences, however, the Akkadians and the Sumerians lived in peace for many years.

That peace was broken in the 2300s BC when **Sargon** sought to extend Akkadian territory. He built a new capital, Akkad (A-kad), on the Euphrates River, near what is now the city of Baghdad. Sargon was the first ruler to have a permanent army. He used that army to launch a series of wars against neighboring kingdoms.

Sargon's soldiers defeated all the city-states of Sumer. They also conquered northern Mesopotamia, finally bringing the entire region under his rule. With these conquests, Sargon established the world's first **empire**, or land with different territories and peoples under a single rule. The Akkadian Empire stretched from the Persian Gulf to the Mediterranean Sea.

MESOPOTAMIA AND THE FERTILE CRESCENT **63**

❷ Religion Shapes Society

Religion played a major role in Sumerian society.

Identify What is polytheism? *the worship of many gods*

Explain What kind of powers did Sumerians believe their gods possessed? *power over harvests, floods, illness, health, and wealth*

Make Inferences Why did priests gain high status in Sumer? *because the people believed the priests gained the gods' favor*

📝 **CRF:** Primary Source Activity: Sumerian Flood Story

🐻 **HSS** 6.2.3; **HSS** Analysis Skills: HI 1

go.hrw.com
Online Resources
KEYWORD: SQ6 WH3
ACTIVITY: Sumerian Pantheon

Info to Know

Religion and Government Each city-state in Mesopotamia had a city god and goddess. People built houses for the gods. As the city developed, these houses became large temples, or ziggurats. According to tradition, the ruler of the city, called an *ensi*, was in charge of the temple to the city's god, and the ruler's wife was in charge of the temple to the city's goddess. The people of Mesopotamia believed that the well-being of the city-state depended on the way they treated the gods.

Answers

Reading Check *He was a very capable military leader and used a permanent army to defeat all the city-states of Sumer.*

ACADEMIC VOCABULARY
role a part or function

Sargon was emperor, or ruler of his empire, for more than 50 years. However, the empire lasted only a century after his death. Later rulers could not keep the empire safe from invaders. Hostile tribes from the east raided and captured Akkad. A century of chaos followed.

Eventually, however, the Sumerian city-state of Ur rebuilt its strength and conquered the rest of Mesopotamia. Political stability was restored. The Sumerians once again became the most powerful civilization in the region.

READING CHECK **Summarizing** How did Sargon build an empire?

Religion Shapes Society

Religion was very important in Sumerian society. In fact, it played a **role** in nearly every aspect of public and private life. In many ways, religion was the basis for all of Sumerian society.

Sumerian Religion

The Sumerians practiced **polytheism**, the worship of many gods. Among the gods they worshipped were Enlil, the lord of the air; Enki, god of wisdom; and Inanna, goddess of love and war. The sun and moon were represented by the gods Utu and Nanna. Each city-state considered one god to be its special protector.

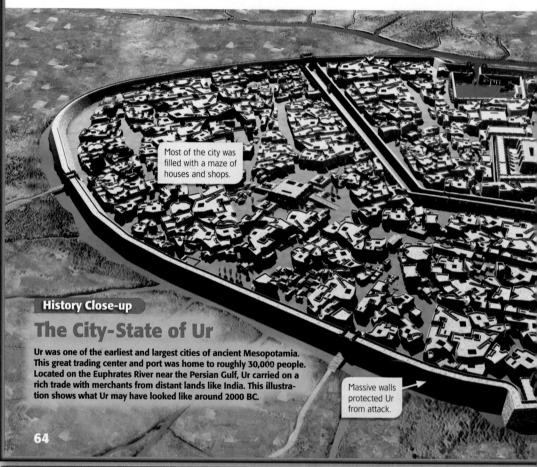

Most of the city was filled with a maze of houses and shops.

History Close-up
The City-State of Ur

Ur was one of the earliest and largest cities of ancient Mesopotamia. This great trading center and port was home to roughly 30,000 people. Located on the Euphrates River near the Persian Gulf, Ur carried on a rich trade with merchants from distant lands like India. This illustration shows what Ur may have looked like around 2000 BC.

Massive walls protected Ur from attack.

64

Differentiating Instruction for Universal Access

Learners Having Difficulty

Reaching Standards

1. To help students learn the major characteristics of Sumer, draw the graphic organizer for students to see. Omit the blue, italicized answers.

2. Have each student copy and complete the graphic organizer. When students are finished, review the answers with the class.

LS Verbal/Linguistic, Visual/Spatial

🐻 **HSS** 6.2.3; **HSS** Analysis Skills: HI 1, HI 2

The Rise of Sumer		
Government	**Religion**	**Society**
• *originally organized into city-states* • *large empire created by Sargon* • *first permanent army*	• *polytheistic* • *each city had a god as protector* • *gods have enormous power* • *priests interpret wishes of gods* • *everyone must serve and worship gods*	• *kings* • *priests* • *skilled crafters, merchants, and traders* • *laborers and farmers* • *slaves*

The Sumerians believed that their gods had enormous powers. Gods could bring a good harvest or a disastrous flood. They could bring illness, or they could bring good health and wealth. The Sumerians believed that success in every area of life depended on pleasing the gods. Every Sumerian had a duty to serve and to worship the gods.

Priests, people who performed religious ceremonies, had great status in Sumer. People relied on them to help gain the gods' favor. Priests interpreted the wishes of the gods and made offerings to them. These offerings were made in temples, special buildings where priests performed their religious ceremonies.

Sumerian Social Order

Because of their status, priests occupied a high level in Sumer's **social hierarchy**, the division of society by rank or class. In fact, priests were just below kings. The kings of Sumer claimed that they had been chosen by the gods to rule.

Below the priests were Sumer's skilled craftspeople, merchants, and traders. Trade had a great **impact** on Sumerian society. Traders traveled to faraway places and exchanged grain for gold, silver, copper, lumber, and precious stones.

Below traders, farmers and laborers made up the large working class. Slaves were at the bottom of the social order.

ACADEMIC VOCABULARY
impact effect, result

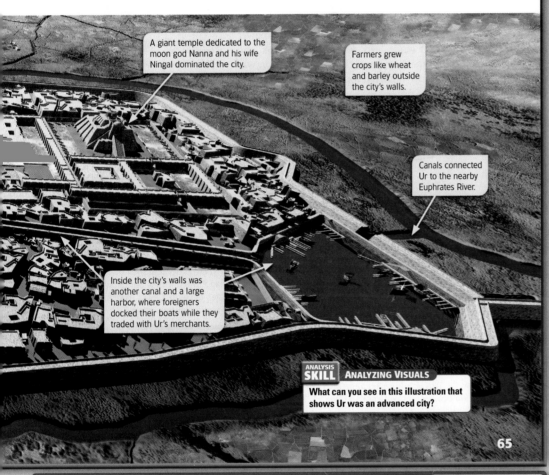

A giant temple dedicated to the moon god Nanna and his wife Ningal dominated the city.

Farmers grew crops like wheat and barley outside the city's walls.

Canals connected Ur to the nearby Euphrates River.

Inside the city's walls was another canal and a large harbor, where foreigners docked their boats while they traded with Ur's merchants.

ANALYSIS SKILL **ANALYZING VISUALS**
What can you see in this illustration that shows Ur was an advanced city?

65

Sumerian society was divided into different groups. This ancient artifact shows Sumerian leaders celebrating a military victory while a musician plays his instrument.

Direct Teach

Main Idea

❷ **Religion Shapes Society**

Religion played a major role in Sumerian society.

Explain Who made up the middle ranks of society? *craftspeople, merchants, and traders*

Make Inferences Why might Enheduanna have had an easier time than other women in becoming a writer? What hurdles might she still have faced? *possible answers—because she was Sargon's daughter and therefore had privileges; still faced ridicule or hostility from men who held powerful positions in society*

📄 **CRF:** Biography Activity: Enheduanna
🐻 **HSS** 6.2.3; **HSS** Analysis Skills: HI 1

Review & Assess

Close

Have students write a short paragraph summarizing the government, religion, and society of Sumer.

Review

📄 Online Quiz Section 2

Assess

SE Section 2 Assessment
📄 PASS: Section 2 Quiz
📄 Alternative Assessment Handbook

Reteach/Classroom Intervention

📄 California Standards Review Workbook
📄 Interactive Reader and Study Guide, Section 2
💿 Interactive Skills Tutor CD-ROM

Answers

Reading Check *It brought important goods like copper and lumber to Sumer and led to greater wealth.*

66

Men and Women in Sumer

Sumerian men and women had different roles. In general, men held political power and made laws, while women took care of the home and children. Education was usually reserved for men, but some upper-class women were educated as well.

Some educated women were priestesses in Sumer's temples. Some priestesses helped shape Sumerian culture. One, Enheduanna, the daughter of Sargon, wrote hymns to the goddess Inanna. She is the first known female writer in history.

READING CHECK **Analyzing** How did trade affect Sumerian society?

SUMMARY AND PREVIEW In this section you learned about Sumerian city-states, religion, and society. In Section 3, you will read about the Sumerians' achievements.

---

go.hrw.com
Online Quiz
KEYWORD: SQ6 HP3

Section 2 Assessment

Reviewing Ideas, Terms, and People **HSS** 6.2.3

1. **a. Recall** What was the basic political unit of Sumer?
   b. Explain What steps did **city-states** take to protect themselves from their rivals?
   c. Elaborate How do you think Sargon's creation of an **empire** changed the history of Mesopotamia? Defend your answer.
2. **a. Identify** What is **polytheism**?
   b. Draw Conclusions Why do you think **priests** were so influential in ancient Sumerian society?
   c. Elaborate Why would rulers benefit if they claimed to be chosen by the gods?

Critical Thinking

3. **Sequencing** Draw a diagram like the one shown. Then place the following events in the order that they occurred: Akkadian Empire forms. Sumerian city-states develop. City of Akkad is built. Farming villages appear.

   [ ]
   [ ]
   [ ]
   [ ]

FOCUS ON WRITING ✐

4. **Gathering Information about Sumer** What aspects of Sumerian society will you include on your poster? What important people, religious beliefs, or social developments do you think the students should learn?

Section 2 Assessment Answers

1. **a.** the city-state
   b. built up strong armies and constructed walls around their cities
   c. possible answers—reduced conflicts between city-states, created better chance for civilization to develop in peacetime

2. **a.** the worship of many gods
   b. because people relied on them to gain the gods' favor
   c. People would do what the rulers said because they did not want to offend the gods by disobeying the rulers.

3. Cities—The Sumerians built the world's first cities. Government—They created the first empire. Religion—Religion influenced every aspect of life. Society—Society was very structured. Summary—The Sumerians developed the world's first advanced civilization.

4. Responses will vary but should be consistent with text content.

Sumerian Achievements

If YOU were there...

You are a student at a school for scribes in Sumer. Learning all the symbols for writing is very hard. Your teacher assigns you lessons to write on your clay tablet, but you can't help making mistakes. Then you have to smooth out the surface and try again. Still, being a scribe can lead to important jobs for the king. You could make your family proud.

Why would you want to be a scribe?

BUILDING BACKGROUND Sumerian society was advanced in terms of religion and government organization. The Sumerians were responsible for many other achievements, which were passed down to later civilizations.

The Invention of Writing

The Sumerians made one of the greatest cultural advances in history. They developed **cuneiform** (kyoo·NEE·uh·fohrm), the world's first system of writing. But Sumerians did not have pencils, pens, or paper. Instead, they used sharp tools called styluses to make wedge-shaped symbols on clay tablets.

Sumerians wrote on clay tablets with a special tool called a stylus.

What You Will Learn...

Main Ideas

1. The Sumerians invented the world's first writing system.
2. Advances and inventions changed Sumerian lives.
3. Many types of art developed in Sumer.

The Big Idea

The Sumerians made many advances that helped their society develop.

Key Terms and People

cuneiform, *p. 67*
pictographs, *p. 68*
scribe, *p. 68*
epics, *p. 68*
architecture, *p. 70*
ziggurat, *p. 70*

HSS 6.2.9 Trace the evolution of language in its written forms.

67

Teach the Big Idea: Master the Standards

Standards Proficiency

Sumerian Achievements **HSS** 6.2.9; **HSS** Analysis Skills: CS 1, HI 3

1. **Teach** Ask students the Main Idea questions to teach this section.

2. **Apply** Tell students to draw a table with two long columns. As they read through the chapter, have them list in one column the different Sumerian achievements, such as those in writing, technology, and art. Once they have finished the section, have them fill in the other column, explaining whether we use each achievement in today's world and, if so, how. **LS Visual/Spatial**

3. **Review** As you review the section's main ideas, have students discuss some of the specific achievements, how they were used at the time, and how they are used today.

4. **Practice/Homework** Have students write down five inventions that have been made in the last 20 years and predict whether or not those inventions might still be used 5,000 years from now. **LS Verbal/Linguistic**

Alternative Assessment Handbook, Rubrics 7: Charts; and 37: Writing Assignments

---

Preteach

Bellringer

If YOU were there . . . Use the **Daily Bellringer Transparency** to help students answer the question.

Daily Bellringer Transparency, Section 3

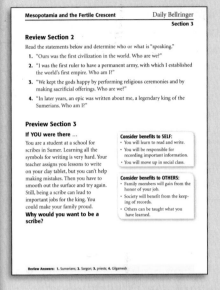

Building Vocabulary

Preteach or review the following terms:

catalogue to make an itemized list of (p. 69)

styluses sharp instruments used for writing (p. 67)

CRF: Vocabulary Builder Activity, Section 3

Standards Focus

HSS 6.2.9

Means: Describe how written language has changed over time.

Matters: Sumerians developed the first known written language.

67

❶ The Invention of Writing

The Sumerians invented the world's first writing system.

Describe How did Sumerians write? *Using a sharp stylus, they made wedge-shaped symbols on clay tablets.*

Explain Why were scribes important? *They kept track of items people traded or records for the government or temples.*

Draw Conclusions How was cuneiform used to express complex ideas? *Cuneiform used symbols to represent syllables and could combine syllables to express complex ideas.*

Activity **Cuneiform Exhibit** Have students create a museum exhibit on cuneiform. Students might create a clay tablet of their own, provide information about cuneiform, or show images of actual cuneiform writing.
LS **Visual/Spatial, Verbal/Linguistic**

📄 **CRF:** Literature Activity: *The Epic of Gilgamesh*

📄 **CRF:** Interdisciplinary Projects: Mesopotamia: The First Writing

🐻 **HSS** 6.2.9; **HSS** Analysis Skills: HI 2

Did you know . . .

Sumerian scribes wrote their symbols on wet clay tablets, which were then dried in the sun or in ovens. Though these clay tablets were the standard writing surface in Mesopotamia, wood, metal, and even stone were used occasionally. The more durable of these materials have lasted thousands of years!

Answers

Reading Check *for keeping business records*

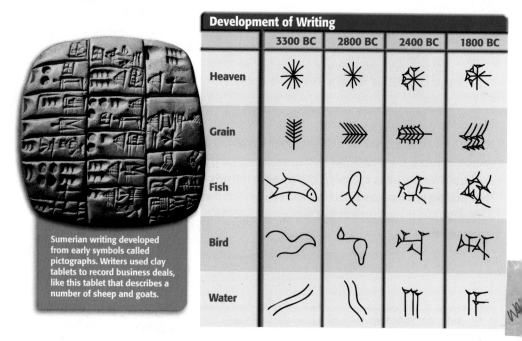

Sumerian writing developed from early symbols called pictographs. Writers used clay tablets to record business deals, like this tablet that describes a number of sheep and goats.

Development of Writing	3300 BC	2800 BC	2400 BC	1800 BC
Heaven				
Grain				
Fish				
Bird				
Water				

Earlier written communication had used **pictographs**, or picture symbols. Each pictograph represented an object, such as a tree or an animal. But in cuneiform, symbols could also represent syllables, or basic parts of words. As a result, Sumerian writers could combine symbols to express more complex ideas such as "joy" or "powerful."

Sumerians first used cuneiform to keep business records. A **scribe**, or writer, would be hired to keep track of the items people traded. Government officials and temples also hired scribes to keep their records. Becoming a scribe was a way to move up in social class.

Sumerian students went to school to learn to read and write. But, like today, some students did not want to study. A Sumerian story tells of a father who urged his son to do his schoolwork:

❝ Go to school, stand before your 'school-father,' recite your assignment, open your schoolbag, write your tablet . . . After you have finished your assignment and reported to your monitor [teacher], come to me, and do not wander about in the street. ❞

–Sumerian essay quoted in *History Begins at Sumer*, by Samuel Noah Kramer

In time, Sumerians put their writing skills to new uses. They wrote works on history, law, grammar, and math. They also created works of literature. Sumerians wrote stories, proverbs, and songs. They wrote poems about the gods and about military victories. Some of these were **epics**, long poems that tell the stories of heroes. Later, people used some of these poems to create *The Epic of Gilgamesh*, the story of a legendary Sumerian king.

READING CHECK **Generalizing** How was cuneiform first used in Sumer?

68 CHAPTER 3

Differentiating Instruction for Universal Access

English-Language Learners   Standards Proficiency

1. Review with students the chart on the development of writing. Discuss with students how pictographs in 3300 BC resembled the objects they expressed. Have students create 10 pictographs for everyday objects or ideas. Ask students to write the English translation next to each pictograph.

2. Remind students that pictographs were only the beginning of the development of writing. Symbols became simpler as people wrote more and more. Have students simplify their pictographs into symbols like those in the chart above.

3. Lastly, have students write only their symbols on a blank sheet of paper. Organize the class into pairs and have students try to guess the meanings of each other's symbols.
LS **Visual/Spatial**

🐻 **HSS** 6.2.9; **HSS** Analysis Skills: HI 1

📄 Alternative Assessment Handbook, Rubric 3: Artwork

Advances and Inventions

Writing was not the only great Sumerian invention. These early people made many other advances and discoveries.

Technical Advances

One of the Sumerians' most important developments was the wheel. They were the first people to build wheeled vehicles, including carts and wagons. Using the wheel, Sumerians invented a device that spins clay as a craftsperson shapes it into bowls. This device is called a potter's wheel.

The plow was another important Sumerian invention. Pulled by oxen, plows broke through the hard clay soil of Sumer to prepare it for planting. This technique greatly increased farm production. The Sumerians also invented a clock that used falling water to measure time.

Sumerian advances improved daily life in many ways. Sumerians built sewers under city streets. They learned to use bronze to make stronger tools and weapons. They even produced makeup and glass jewelry.

Math and Sciences

Another area in which Sumerians excelled was math. In fact, they developed a math system based on the number 60. Based on this system, they divided a circle into 360 degrees. Dividing a year into 12 months—a factor of 60—was another Sumerian idea. Sumerians also calculated the areas of rectangles and triangles.

Sumerian scholars studied science, too. They wrote long lists to record their study of the natural world. These tablets included the names of thousands of animals, plants, and minerals.

The Sumerians also made advances in medicine. They used ingredients from animals, plants, and minerals to produce healing drugs. Items used in these medicines included milk, turtle shells, figs, and salt. The Sumerians even catalogued their medical knowledge, listing treatments according to symptoms and body parts.

READING CHECK **Categorizing** What areas of life were improved by Sumerian inventions?

THE IMPACT TODAY

Like the Sumerians we use a base-60 system when we talk about 60 seconds in a minute and 60 minutes in an hour.

LINKING TO TODAY

The Wheel

Do you realize how much the achievements of ancient Sumer affect your life today—and every day? For instance, try to imagine life without the wheel. How would you get around? Look at the streets outside. The cars, trucks, and buses you see are all modern versions of Sumerian wheeled vehicles. Wheelchairs, bicycles, and in-line skates all depend on wheels as well. Even modern air travel owes a large debt to the Sumerians. As impressive as jets are, they could never get off the ground without their wheels!

ANALYSIS SKILL **ANALYZING INFORMATION**

Generalizing Why is the wheel so important to modern society?

MESOPOTAMIA AND THE FERTILE CRESCENT **69**

69

Main Idea

❸ The Arts of Sumer

Many types of art developed in Sumer.

Recall What was at the center of most Sumerian cities? *the temple, or ziggurat*

Compare and Contrast How were the homes of rich Sumerians similar to and different from those of most Sumerians? *rich—lived in large, two-story homes with many rooms; most Sumerians—smaller, one-story homes, fewer rooms; both—made of mud bricks, built side-by-side on narrow unpaved streets*

Summarize What different types of art did the Sumerians create? *sculpture, pottery, jewelry, cylinder seals, music, and dance*

HSS 6.2.9; HSS Analysis Skills: CS 1, HI 1

Linking to Today

Lost Art Hundreds of thousands of ancient Mesopotamian works of art were housed in the National Museum of Iraq in Baghdad. When the 2003 Iraqi war broke out, museum workers stored many artifacts to protect them from damage. Unfortunately, thousands of pieces were damaged or stolen when thieves looted the museum. In the months following the war, some items were returned, although many priceless items are still missing today.

Sumerian Achievements

The Sumerians' artistic achievements included beautiful works of gold, wood, and stone.

This stringed musical instrument is called a lyre. It features a cow's head and is made of silver decorated with shell and stone.

Cylinder seals like this one were carved into round stones and then rolled over clay to leave their mark.

The Arts of Sumer

The Sumerians' skills in the fields of art, metalwork, and **architecture**—the science of building—are well known to us. The ruins of great buildings and fine works of art have provided us wonderful examples of the Sumerians' creativity.

Architecture

Most Sumerian rulers lived in large palaces. Other rich Sumerians had two-story homes with as many as a dozen rooms. Most people, however, lived in smaller, one-story houses. These homes had six or seven rooms arranged around a small courtyard. Large and small houses stood side by side along the narrow, unpaved streets of the city. Bricks made of mud were the houses' main building blocks.

City centers were dominated by their temples, the largest and most impressive buildings in Sumer. A **ziggurat**, a pyramid-shaped temple tower, rose above each city. Outdoor staircases led to a platform and a shrine at the top. Some architects added columns to make the temples more attractive.

The Arts

Sumerian sculptors produced many fine works. Among them are the statues of gods created for temples. Sumerian artists also sculpted small objects out of ivory and rare woods. Sumerian pottery is known more for its quantity than quality. Potters turned out many items, but few were works of beauty.

Jewelry was a popular item in Sumer. The jewelers of the region made many beautiful works out of imported gold, silver, and gems. Earrings and other items found in the region show that Sumerian jewelers knew advanced methods for putting gold pieces together.

Cylinder seals are perhaps Sumer's most famous works of art. These small objects were stone cylinders engraved with designs. When rolled over clay, the designs would leave behind their imprint. Each seal left its own distinct imprint. As a result, a person could show ownership of a container by rolling a cylinder over the container's wet clay surface. People could also use cylinder seals to "sign" documents or to decorate other clay objects.

Collaborative Learning

Standards Proficiency

Creating a Television Commercial HSS 6.2.9; HSS Analysis Skills: HI 1, HI 2

1. Organize the class into small groups. Then, ask students to imagine that they are the curators of a museum that has a new exhibit titled "Sumerian Achievements."

2. Have each group create a television commercial that promotes the museum exhibit. Commercials should highlight Sumerian achievements discussed in this section and convince people to visit the museum exhibit.

3. Have each group record their commercial or perform it live for the class.

   LS Interpersonal, Visual/Spatial

   Alternative Assessment Handbook, Rubrics 2: Advertisements; and 29: Presentations

The Sumerians were the first people in Mesopotamia to build large temples called ziggurats.

This gold dagger was found in a royal tomb. The bull's head is made of gold and silver.

ANALYSIS SKILL **ANALYZING VISUALS**

What animal is shown in two of these works?

Some seals showed battle scenes. Others displayed worship rituals. Some were highly decorative, with hundreds of carefully cut gems. They required great skill to make.

The Sumerians also enjoyed music. Kings and temples hired musicians to play on special occasions. Sumerian musicians played reed pipes, drums, tambourines, and stringed instruments called lyres. Children learned songs in school. People sang hymns to gods and kings. Music and dance provided entertainment in marketplaces and homes.

READING CHECK **Drawing Inferences** What might historians learn from cylinder seals?

SUMMARY AND PREVIEW The Sumerians greatly enriched their society. Next you will learn about the later peoples who lived in Mesopotamia.

Checking for Understanding

True or False Answer each statement *T* if it is true or *F* if it is false. If false, explain why.

1. The Sumerians based their mathematical system on the number 10. *F: the Sumerian system was based on the number 60.*

2. The Sumerians used rubber stamps to show ownership of objects. *F: They used cylinder seals.*

3. Music was illegal in Sumer. *F: The Sumerians enjoyed music, and kings and temples hired musicians on special occasions.*

Section 3 Assessment

go.hrw.com
Online Quiz
KEYWORD: SQ6 HP3

Reviewing Ideas, Terms, and People **HSS** 6.2.9

1. a. Identify What is **cuneiform**?
b. Analyze Why do you think writing is one of history's most important cultural advances?
c. Elaborate What current leader would you choose to write an **epic** about, and why?
2. a. Recall What were two early uses of the wheel?
b. Explain Why do you think the invention of the plow was so important to the Sumerians?
3. a. Describe What was the basic Sumerian building material?
b. Make Inferences Why do you think cylinder seals developed into works of art?

Critical Thinking

4. Identifying Cause and Effect Draw a diagram like the one at right. List the effect of each invention on Sumerian life.

	Effect
Writing	
Wheel	
Plow	

FOCUS ON WRITING

5. Evaluating Information Review the Sumerian achievements you just read about. Then create a bulleted list of Sumerian achievements for your poster. Would this list replace some of the information you collected in Section 2?

MESOPOTAMIA AND THE FERTILE CRESCENT **71**

Review & Assess

Close
Ask students to name Sumerian achievements and describe why they were important.

Review
Online Quiz, Section 3

Assess
SE Section 3 Assessment
PASS: Section 3 Quiz
Alternative Assessment Handbook

Reteach/Classroom Intervention
California Standards Review Workbook
Interactive Reader and Study Guide, Section 3
Interactive Skills Tutor CD-ROM

Section 3 Assessment Answers

1. a. world's first writing system made up of wedge-shaped symbols on clay tablets
b. Writing makes collecting, storing, and sharing information easier and more accurate.
c. Students should recognize that epics generally deal with heroic people and events.
2. a. wheeled vehicles and the potter's wheel
b. In Sumerian society, farming was the principal activity. Hence, innovations in farming would be extremely valuable.
3. a. mud bricks

b. possible answer—Having a beautiful seal may have been a mark of status or a way of expressing one's identity.
4. writing—improved record keeping; allowed works on law, math, and grammar to be written; made literature possible; wheel—improved transportation; improved pottery-making; plow—increased efficiency and farm production
5. Possible responses might include cuneiform, music, advanced architecture, sculpture, science, mathematics.

Answers

Analyzing Visuals *cattle*
Reading Check *Cylinder seals sometimes show historical events or worship rituals. They also give historians a glimpse of artistic talent and what was valued in the culture.*

71

The Epic of Gilgamesh

As You Read Ask students what qualities they think a king would need to kill a legendary monster. Remind them that Humbaba was large and powerful. As they read, students should make a list of human qualities that Gilgamesh shows, as well as his godly qualities. *human—he sheds tears, has weak arms, cuts cedars; godly—has support of sun-god, has divine father, kills Humbaba*

Info to Know

The Epic of Gilgamesh There is no one author responsible for *The Epic of Gilgamesh.* In fact, there are many versions and tales about the exploits of Gilgamesh. Sumerian priests may have passed along the stories for generations before they were written down on the clay tablets by scribes. Most of the story has been translated from 12 broken clay tablets. These were found in a royal library at Nineveh. Only by piecing together the different parts of the story do we have the entire epic today.

Info to Know

The God Shamash Shamash, the god of the sun, was one of three main gods in ancient Sumer. Sumerians believed Shamash exerted the power of good over evil and served as the god of justice over the whole universe.

Literature in History

from The Epic of Gilgamesh

translated by N. K. Sandars

GUIDED READING

WORD HELP

menacing threatening
succor help
tempest storm
felled cut down

❶ Shamash, the sun-god, supports Gilgamesh.

What human emotion seems to seize Gilgamesh here? How can you tell?

❷ *What stops Humbaba in his tracks?*

❸ Gilgamesh tries to speak and act bravely, but he is terrified by Humbaba's evil glare.

ELA Reading 6.3.2 Analyze the effect of the qualities of the character (e.g., courage or cowardice, ambition or laziness) on the plot and the resolution of the conflict.

About the Reading The Epic of Gilgamesh *is the world's oldest epic, first recorded—carved on stone tablets—in about 2000 BC. The actual Gilgamesh, ruler of the city of Uruk, had lived about 700 years earlier. Over time, stories about this legendary king had grown and changed. In this story, Gilgamesh and his friend Enkidu seek to slay the monster Humbaba, keeper of a distant forest. In addition to his tremendous size and terrible appearance, Humbaba possesses seven splendors, or powers, one of which is fire. Gilgamesh hopes to claim these powers for himself.*

AS YOU READ Notice both the human qualities and the godly qualities of Gilgamesh.

Humbaba came from his strong house of cedar. He nodded his head and shook it, menacing Gilgamesh; and on him he fastened his eye, the eye of death. Then Gilgamesh called to Shamash and his tears were flowing, "O glorious Shamash, I have followed the road you commanded but now if you send no succor how shall I escape?" ❶ Glorious Shamash heard his prayer and he summoned the great wind, the north wind, the whirlwind, the storm and the icy wind, the tempest and the scorching wind; they came like dragons, like a scorching fire, like a serpent that freezes the heart, a destroying flood and the lightning's fork. The eight winds rose up against Humbaba, they beat against his eyes; he was gripped, unable to go forward or back. ❷ Gilgamesh shouted, "By the life of Ninsun my mother and divine Lugulbanda my father . . . my weak arms and my small weapons I have brought to this Land against you, and now I will enter your house." ❸

So he felled the first cedar and they cut the branches and laid them at the foot of the mountain. At the first stroke Humbaba blazed out, but still they advanced. They felled seven cedars and cut and bound the branches and laid them at the foot of the mountain, and seven times Humbaba loosed his glory on them. As the seventh blaze died out they reached his lair. He slapped his thigh in scorn. He approached like a noble wild bull roped on the mountain, a warrior whose elbows

---

Differentiating Instruction for Universal Access

English-Language Learners

Reaching Standards

Have students illustrate the scene on this page. The drawing should contain Gilgamesh and Humbaba approaching each other. Have students re-read the page, noting how the setting contributes to the character's problems. Encourage students to make the illustration as dramatic as the written story.

ELA Reading 6.3.3

Alternative Assessment Handbook, Rubric 3: Artwork

Advanced Learners/GATE

Exceeding Standards

Tell students that a dialogue is a piece of writing that records people talking. When written, the words are placed in quotation marks. Have students write a half-page dialogue between Gilgamesh and Enkidu that takes place just before this battle and describes the two characters planning their attack. Call on volunteers to read their dialogues.

LS Verbal/Linguistic

Alternative Assessment Handbook, Rubric 37: Writing Assignments

ELA Writing 6.2.1c

Answers

Guided Reading 1. *He seems afraid; he is crying.* **2.** *eight winds summoned by Shamash*

were bound together. The tears started to his eyes and he was pale, "Gilgamesh, let me speak. I have never known a mother, no, nor a father who reared me. I was born of the mountain, he reared me, and Enlil made me the keeper of this forest. Let me go free, Gilgamesh, and I will be your servant, you shall be my lord; all the trees of the forest that I tended on the mountain shall be yours. I will cut them down and build you a palace." . . . ❹

Enkidu said, "Do not listen, Gilgamesh: this Humbaba must die. Kill Humbaba first and his servants after." But Gilgamesh said, "If we touch him the blaze and the glory of light will be put out in confusion, the glory and glamour will vanish, its rays will be quenched." Enkidu said to Gilgamesh, "Not so, my friend. First entrap the bird, and where shall the chicks run then? Afterwards we can search out the glory and the glamour, when the chicks run distracted through the grass."

Gilgamesh listened to the word of his companion, he took the ax in his hand, he drew the sword from his belt, and he struck Humbaba with a thrust of the sword to the neck, and Enkidu his comrade struck the second blow. At the third blow Humbaba fell. Then there followed confusion for this was the guardian of the forest whom they had felled to the ground . . .

When he saw the head of Humbaba, Enlil raged at them. "Why did you do this thing? From henceforth may the fire be on your faces, may it eat the bread that you eat, may it drink where you drink." Then Enlil took again the blaze and the seven splendors that had been Humbaba's: he gave the first to the river, and he gave to the lion, to the stone of execration, to the mountain . . . ❺

O Gilgamesh, king and conqueror of the dreadful blaze; wild bull who plunders the mountain, who crosses the sea, glory to him.

GUIDED READING

execration a cursing
plunders takes by force

❹ **What effect does Humbaba hope his words will have on Gilgamesh?**

❺ The angry air-god Enlil curses the heroes for slaying Humbaba. He takes back the monster's powers and gives them to other creatures and elements of nature.

In your opinion, is Gilgamesh more or less heroic for slaying Humbaba and angering Enlil?

CONNECTING LITERATURE TO HISTORY

1. **Analyzing** In Sumerian culture, the gods' powers were thought to be enormous. According to this story, what roles do gods play in people's lives?

2. **Making Inferences** Violence was common in Sumerian society. How does the character of Gilgamesh suggest that Sumerian society could be violent?

73

Literature in History

Info to Know

The God Enlil Enlil was not a god that the Sumerians wanted to anger. Sometimes called the Lord of the Air, Enlil was the god not just of the wind and agriculture but also of all energy and force. According to Mesopotamian myth, Enlil played an important role in the creation of man.

Connect to Art

Stylized Art Point out to students that some design elements of the statue shown are stylized. This means that they are not meant to look real, but have been simplified according to a set of rules. Gilgamesh's beard and the lion cub's fur have been stylized. Challenge students to find other examples of stylized art in this book or books on art history. Egyptian art in particular offers several examples.

Modern creative works also exhibit stylized design elements, however. For example, Japanese anime artists draw human characters with unnaturally big eyes.

Cross-Discipline Activity: Literature

 Standards Proficiency

Writing Alternative Endings 🐘 **ELA** Writing 6.2.1.a

1. Organize the class into pairs. Tell students that Gilgamesh's decision to follow Enkidu's advice and kill Humbaba is a "plot point" in the story. Based on Gilgamesh's actions, the plot changes to reflect his choice. That is why it is an important part of the story.

2. Have students create alternate endings to the story, starting at the point where Enkidu advises Gilgamesh to kill Humbaba.

3. Ask students to imagine what would have happened if Gilgamesh had allowed Humbaba to live, and have them write a new ending to this tale.

4. Ask volunteers to share their stories with the class. **LS Verbal/Linguistic**

📖 Alternative Assessment Handbook, Rubrics 14: Group Activity; and 39: Writing to Create

Answers

Guided Reading 4. *Humbaba hopes to persuade Gilgamesh not to kill him.*
5. *Responses will vary but should be supported with details from the passage.*
Connecting Literature to History
1. *Shamash helps Gilgamesh stop Humbaba by sending powerful winds, and Enlil punishes Gilgamesh for killing Humbaba.* **2.** *Gilgamesh's mindset is one of violence, and this is shown by his actions as he attacks and kills Humbaba.*

Bellringer

If YOU were there . . . Use the **Daily Bellringer Transparency** to help students answer the question.

📖 Daily Bellringer Transparency, Section 4

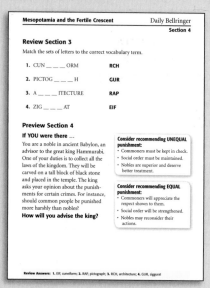

Review Section 3

Match the sets of letters to the correct vocabulary term.

1. CUN _ _ _ ORM   **RCH**
2. PICTOG _ _ _ H   **GUR**
3. A _ _ _ ITECTURE   **RAP**
4. ZIG _ _ _ AT   **EIF**

Preview Section 4

If YOU were there . . .
You are a noble in ancient Babylon, an advisor to the great king Hammurabi. One of your duties is to collect all the laws of the kingdom. They will be carved on a tall block of black stone and placed in the temple. The king asks your opinion about the punishments for certain crimes. For instance, should common people be punished more harshly than nobles?

How will you advise the king?

Consider recommending UNEQUAL punishment:
- Commoners must be kept in check.
- Social order must be maintained.
- Nobles are superior and deserve better treatment.

Consider recommending EQUAL punishment:
- Commoners will appreciate the respect shown to them.
- Social order will be strengthened.
- Nobles may reconsider their actions.

Review Answers: 1. EIF, cuneiform; **2.** RAP, pictograph; **3.** RCH, architecture; **4.** GUR, ziggurat

Building Vocabulary

Preteach or review the following terms:

assassin one who kills an important person (p. 76)

looting seizing goods by force, especially in times of war (p. 77)

penalties punishments for a crime or offense (p. 75)

📄 **CRF:** Vocabulary Builder Activity, Section 4

 Standards Focus

HSS 6.2.4

Means: Know why Hammurabi's Code is important.

Matters: Hammurabi's Code was one of the first written codes of law.

74 CHAPTER 3

What You Will Learn...

Main Ideas

1. The Babylonians conquered Mesopotamia and created a code of law.
2. Invasions of Mesopotamia changed the region's culture.
3. The Phoenicians built a trading society in the eastern Mediterranean region.

The Big Idea

After the Sumerians, many cultures ruled parts of the Fertile Crescent.

Key Terms and People

monarch, *p. 74*
Hammurabi's Code, *p. 75*
chariot, *p. 76*
Nebuchadnezzar, *p. 77*
alphabet, *p. 79*

HSS 6.2.4 Know the significance of Hammurabi's Code.

74 CHAPTER 3

Later Peoples of the Fertile Crescent

If YOU were there...

You are a noble in ancient Babylon, an advisor to the great king Hammurabi. One of your duties is to collect all the laws of the kingdom. They will be carved on a tall block of black stone and placed in the temple. The king asks your opinion about the punishments for certain crimes. For instance, should common people be punished more harshly than nobles?

How will you advise the king?

BUILDING BACKGROUND Many peoples invaded Mesopotamia. A series of kings conquered the lands between the rivers. Each new culture inherited the earlier achievements of the Sumerians. Some of the later invasions of the region also introduced skills and ideas that still influence civilization today, such as a written law code.

The Babylonians Conquer Mesopotamia

Although Ur rose to glory after the death of Sargon, repeated foreign attacks drained its strength. By 2000 BC, Ur lay in ruins. With Ur's power gone, several waves of invaders battled to gain control of Mesopotamia.

The Rise of Babylon

Babylon was home to one such group. That city was located on the Euphrates River near what is today Baghdad, Iraq. Babylon had once been a Sumerian town. By 1800 BC, however, it was home to a powerful government of its own. In 1792 BC, Hammurabi (ham-uh-RAHB-ee) became Babylon's king. He would become the city's greatest **monarch** (MAH-nark), a ruler of a kingdom or empire.

Teach the Big Idea: Master the Standards

Standards Proficiency

Later Peoples of the Fertile Crescent

1. **Teach** Ask students the Main Idea questions to teach this section.

2. **Apply** Have students draw a time line that includes the later empires and kingdoms that developed in Mesopotamia. Students should also include a short note about why each civilization was important. Encourage students to share their time lines with the class. **LS Visual/Spatial**

3. **Review** As a review of the section, have students create seven multiple choice

HSS 6.2.4; **HSS** Analysis Skills: CS 1, CS 2, HI 1

questions. Then have students quiz each other with the questions they have created.

4. **Practice/Homework** Have students use their time lines to help them create at least one illustration for every empire or people mentioned in the section. **LS Visual/Spatial**

📄 Alternative Assessment Handbook, Rubrics 3: Artwork; and 36: Time Lines

Hammurabi's Code

Hammurabi was a brilliant war leader. His armies fought many battles to expand his power. Eventually, he brought all of Mesopotamia into his empire, called the Babylonian Empire, after his capital.

Hammurabi's skills were not limited to the battlefield, though. He was also an able ruler who could govern a huge empire. He oversaw many building and irrigation projects and improved Babylon's tax collection system to help pay for them. He also brought much prosperity through increased trade. Hammurabi, however, is most famous for his code of laws.

Hammurabi's Code was a set of 282 laws that dealt with almost every part of daily life. There were laws on everything from trade, loans, and theft to marriage, injury, and murder. It contained some ideas that are still found in laws today. Specific crimes brought specific penalties. However, social class did matter. For instance, injuring a rich man brought a greater penalty than injuring a poor man.

Hammurabi's Code was important not only for how thorough it was, but also because it was written down for all to see. People all over the empire could read exactly what was against the law.

Hammurabi ruled for 42 years. During his reign, Babylon became the most important city in Mesopotamia. However, after his death, Babylonian power declined. The kings that followed faced invasions from people Hammurabi had conquered. Before long, the Babylonian Empire came to an end.

READING CHECK **Analyzing** What was Hammurabi's most important accomplishment?

Primary Source

QUICK FACTS

HISTORIC DOCUMENT
Hammurabi's Code

The Babylonian ruler Hammurabi is credited with putting together the earliest known written collection of laws. The code set down rules for both criminal and civil law, and informed citizens what was expected of them.

196. If a man put out the eye of another man, his eye shall be put out.

197. If he break another man's bone, his bone shall be broken.

198. If he put out the eye of a freed man, or break the bone of a freed man, he shall pay one gold mina.

199. If he put out the eye of a man's slave, or break the bone of a man's slave, he shall pay one-half of its value.

221. If a physican heal the broken bone or diseased soft part of a man, the patient shall pay the physician five shekels in money.

222. If he were a freed man he shall pay three shekels.

223. If he were a slave his owner shall pay the physician two shekels.

–Hammurabi, from the Code of Hammurabi, translated by L. W. King

ANALYSIS SKILL **ANALYZING PRIMARY SOURCES**

How do you think Hammurabi's code of laws affected citizens of that time?

Direct Teach

Main Idea

❶ **The Babylonians Conquer Mesopotamia**

The Babylonians conquered Mesopotamia and created a code of law.

Recall When did Hammurabi become Babylon's king? *1792 BC*

Explain How did Hammurabi conquer Mesopotamia? *He expanded his power through military victories.*

Draw Conclusions Why would it have been helpful for people to have the law code written down? *Everyone could know what was against the law. Additionally, laws that are written down cannot change as easily as those that are passed down orally.*

📓 CRF: Biography Activity: Hammurabi

📓 CRF: Primary Source Activity: The Code of Hammurabi

🗄 Quick Facts Transparency: Hammurabi's Code

🐻 **HSS** 6.2.4

Primary Source

Reading Like a Historian
Hammurabi's Code Help students practice reading this document like a historian. Ask

- What do these laws indicate about the Babylonian system of justice?
- Why do you think the laws treat freed men differently from slaves?

About the Illustration

This illustration of Hammurabi is an artist's conception based on available sources. However, historians are uncertain exactly what Hammurabi looked like.

Differentiating Instruction for Universal Access

Advanced Learners/GATE   Standards **Proficiency**

1. Ask students to imagine a world in which there are no written laws. Then have each student write a one-page short story in which two characters in such a world come into conflict. Stories may involve topics such as theft, a fight, or an accidental injury.

2. Students shuld include a conflict-resolution or judgment scene that shows how a written code of laws helps resolve the situation.

3. Call on volunteers to read their short stories to the class. Then lead a discussion about how the stories illustrate the importance of Hammurabi's Code. **LS** **Verbal/Linguistic**

🐻 **HSS** 6.2.4; **HSS** **Analysis Skills:** HI 1, HI 3

📄 Alternative Assessment Handbook, Rubric 39: Writing to Create

Answers

Analyzing Primary Sources *possible answer—They may have obeyed the laws, since punishments were often severe.*

Reading Check *his code of laws*

Main Idea

❷ Invasions of Mesopotamia

Invasions of Mesopotamia changed the region's culture.

Recall Why did the Hittite Kingdom come to an end? *Their king was assassinated, and the kingdom was overrun by the Kassites.*

Identify What military advantages did the Assyrians have? *iron weapons, chariots, and good organization*

Draw Conclusions How do you think the use of chariots by Hittites affected the opposing army's foot soldiers? *possible answer—increased their fear and reduced their effectiveness, because they could not predict from where the enemy would appear next, and the chariots were moving targets*

🖳 Map Transparency: Babylonian and Assyrian Empires

🐻 **HSS** 6.2; **HSS** Analysis Skills: CS 1, HI 1

Info to Know

The Assyrian Army The Assyrian military was impressive, even by today's standards. Assyrian field armies consisted of 50,000 men, the equal of five modern U.S. divisions. When taking the field for a battle, the army would stretch about a mile and a half across and 100 yards deep! The Assyrian military was also known for its innovations—cavalry, battering rams, and boots for their soldiers.

Invasions of Mesopotamia

Several other civilizations also developed in and around the Fertile Crescent. As their armies battled each other for fertile land, control of the region passed from one empire to another.

The Hittites and Kassites

A people known as the Hittites built a strong kingdom in Asia Minor, in what is today Turkey. Their success came, in part, from two key military advantages they had over rivals. First, the Hittites were among the first people to master ironworking. This meant that they could make the strongest weapons of the time. Second, the Hittites skillfully used the **chariot**, a wheeled, horse-drawn cart used in battle. The chariots allowed Hittite soldiers to move quickly around a battlefield and fire arrows at their enemy. Using these advantages, Hittite forces captured Babylon around 1595 BC.

Hittite rule did not last long, however. Soon after taking Babylon, the Hittite king was killed by an assassin. The kingdom plunged into chaos. The Kassites, a people who lived north of Babylon, captured the city and ruled for almost 400 years.

The Assyrians

Later, in the 1200s BC, the Assyrians (uh-SIR-ee-unz) from northern Mesopotamia briefly gained control of Babylon. However, their empire was soon overrun by invaders. After this defeat, the Assyrians took about 300 years to recover their strength. Then, starting about 900 BC, they began to conquer all of the Fertile Crescent. They even took over parts of Asia Minor and Egypt.

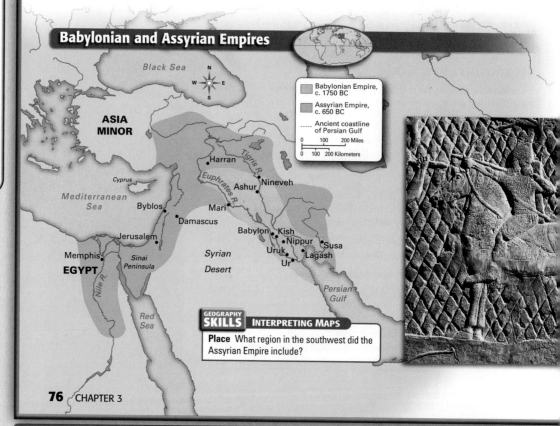

Babylonian and Assyrian Empires

Babylonian Empire, c. 1750 BC
Assyrian Empire, c. 650 BC
Ancient coastline of Persian Gulf

0   100   200 Miles
0   100   200 Kilometers

GEOGRAPHY SKILLS | **INTERPRETING MAPS**

Place What region in the southwest did the Assyrian Empire include?

Differentiating Instruction for Universal Access

Learners Having Difficulty | Reaching Standards

1. Have students work in pairs to write a letter from the Hittite king to the leader of Babylon explaining why the Babylonians should surrender. You may wish to pair a student who has good writing skills with a struggling student to complete this activity.

2. Have students include details about the superiority of the Hittite military and what consequences might result from the Babylonians' refusal to surrender.

3. Ask for volunteers to read their letters to the class. **LS Verbal/Linguistic**

🐻 **HSS** 6.2; **HSS** Analysis Skills: HI 1, HI 2

📝 Alternative Assessment Handbook, Rubric 37: Writing Assignments

Answers

Interpreting Maps *Egypt*

The key to the Assyrians' success was their strong army. Like the Hittites, the Assyrians used iron weapons and chariots. The army was very well organized, and every soldier knew his role.

The Assyrians were fierce in battle. Before attacking, they spread terror by looting villages and burning crops. Anyone who still dared to resist them was killed.

After conquering Mesopotamia, the Assyrians ruled from Nineveh (NI-nuh-vuh). They demanded heavy taxes from across the empire. Areas that resisted these demands were harshly punished.

Assyrian kings ruled their large empire through local leaders. Each governed a small area, collected taxes, enforced laws, and raised troops for the army. Roads were built to link distant parts of the empire. Messengers on horseback were sent to deliver orders to faraway officials.

The Chaldeans

In 652 BC a series of wars broke out in the Assyrian Empire over who should rule. These wars greatly weakened the empire.

Sensing this weakness, the Chaldeans (kal-DEE-uhnz), a group from the Syrian Desert, led other peoples in an attack on the Assyrians. In 612 BC, they destroyed Nineveh and the Assyrian Empire.

In its place, the Chaldeans set up a new empire of their own. **Nebuchadnezzar** (neb-uh-kuhd-NEZ-uhr), the most famous Chaldean king, rebuilt Babylon into a beautiful city. According to legend, his grand palace featured the famous Hanging Gardens. Trees and flowers grew on its terraces and roofs. From the ground the gardens seemed to hang in the air.

The Chaldeans admired Sumerian culture. They studied the Sumerian language and built temples to Sumerian gods.

At the same time, Babylon became a center for astronomy. Chaldeans charted the positions of the stars and kept track of economic, political, and weather events. They also created a calendar and solved complex problems of geometry.

READING CHECK Sequencing List in order the peoples who ruled Mesopotamia.

The Assyrian Army
The Assyrian army was the most powerful fighting force the world had ever seen. It was large and well organized, and it featured iron weapons, war chariots, and giant war machines used to knock down city walls.

What kinds of weapons can you see in this carving?

MESOPOTAMIA AND THE FERTILE CRESCENT **77**

77

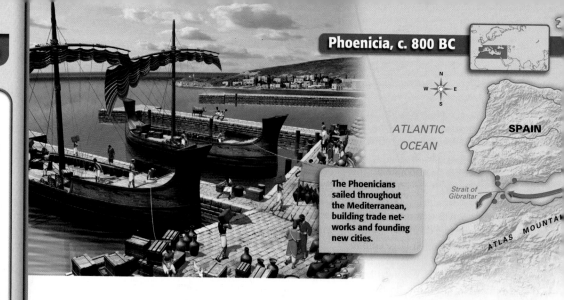

The Phoenicians sailed throughout the Mediterranean, building trade networks and founding new cities.

ATLANTIC OCEAN

SPAIN

Strait of Gibraltar

ATLAS MOUNTAI

Direct Teach

Main Idea

❸ The Phoenicians

The Phoenicians built a trading society in the eastern Mediterranean region.

Identify Where did Phoenician ships sail? *They sailed around the Mediterranean, to Egypt, Greece, Italy, Sicily, and Spain, and through the Straits of Gibraltar into the Atlantic Ocean.*

Explain Why was the Phoenician alphabet an important development? *It made writing much easier and has had a major impact on other languages, including English.*

Draw Conclusions What led the Phoenicians to create a successful sea trade? *Mountains and hostile neighbors blocked overland trade routes, so in order to trade they had to go to sea.*

📓 **CRF:** Primary Source Activity: Descriptions of the Phoenicians

🗺 Map Transparency: Phoenicia, c. 800 BC

🐻 **HSS** 6.2, **HSS** Analysis Skills: HI 1

Connect to Geography

The Cedars of Lebanon The famous trees are so closely tied to the history of Lebanon that a cedar is featured in the middle of the Lebanese flag. However, because people have been cutting down the big trees for centuries, few traces of the old forests remain. Reforestation efforts have begun, though.

The Phoenicians

At the western end of the Fertile Crescent, along the Mediterranean Sea, was a land known as Phoenicia (fi-NI-shuh). It was not home to a great military power and was often ruled by foreign governments. Nevertheless, the Phoenicians created a wealthy trading society.

The Geography of Phoenicia

Today the nation of Lebanon occupies most of what was once Phoenicia. Mountains border the region to the north and east. The western border is the Mediterranean.

THE IMPACT TODAY

Because so many cedar trees have been cut down in Lebanon's forests over the years, very few trees remain.

Phoenicia had few resources. One thing it did have, however, was cedar. Cedar trees were prized for their timber, a valuable trade item. But Phoenicia's overland trade routes were blocked by mountains and hostile neighbors. Phoenicians had to look to the sea for a way to trade.

The Expansion of Trade

Motivated by a desire for trade, the people of Phoenicia became expert sailors. They built one of the world's finest harbors at the city of Tyre. Fleets of fast Phoenician trading ships sailed to ports all around the Mediterranean Sea. Traders traveled to Egypt, Greece, Italy, Sicily, and Spain. They even passed through the Strait of Gibraltar to reach the Atlantic Ocean.

The Phoenicians founded several new colonies along their trade routes. Carthage (KAHR-thij), located on the northern coast of Africa, was the most famous of these. It later became one of the most powerful cities on the Mediterranean.

Phoenicia grew wealthy from its trade. Besides lumber, the Phoenicians traded silverwork, ivory carvings, and slaves. Beautiful glass objects also became valuable trade items after crafters invented glass-blowing—the art of heating and shaping glass. In addition, the Phoenicians made purple dye from a type of shellfish. They then traded cloth dyed with this purple color. Phoenician purple fabric was very popular with rich people.

The Phoenicians' most important achievement, however, wasn't a trade good. To record their activities, Phoenician

78 CHAPTER 3

Critical Thinking: Analyzing

Standards Proficiency

Phoenician Exports 🐻 **HSS** 6.2; **HSS** Analysis Skills: HI 1

1. Tell students that a nation's exports are the goods and products it sells to other nations.

2. To help students identify the exports of the Phoenicians, copy the graphic organizer for students to see. Omit the blue, italicized answers. Have students copy and complete the graphic organizer on their own paper.
LS Visual/Spatial, Verbal/Linguistic

Phoenician Exports

- *lumber*
- *slaves*
- *crafts*
  - *silverwork*
  - *ivory carvings*
  - *glass objects*
- *purple fabric*

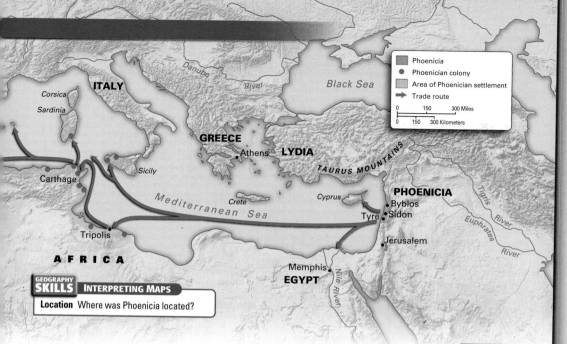

| Phoenicia |
| ● Phoenician colony |
| Area of Phoenician settlement |
| → Trade route |

0   150   300 Miles
0   150   300 Kilometers

GEOGRAPHY SKILLS **INTERPRETING MAPS**

Location Where was Phoenicia located?

traders developed one of the world's first alphabets. An **alphabet** is a set of letters that can be combined to form words. This development made writing much easier. It had a major impact on the ancient world and on our own. In fact, the alphabet we use for the English language is based on the Phoenicians', as modified by later civilizations. Later civilizations, including our own, benefited from the innovations passed along by Phoenician traders.

READING CHECK **Finding Main Ideas** What were the main achievements of the Phoenicians?

SUMMARY AND PREVIEW Many different peoples ruled in the Fertile Crescent after the Sumerians. Some made important contributions that are still valued today. In the next chapter you will learn about another people that created a remarkable civilization—the Egyptians.

Section 4 Assessment

go.hrw.com
Online Quiz
KEYWORD: SQ6 HP3

Reviewing Ideas, Terms, and People   **HSS** 6.2.4

1. **a. Identify** Where was Babylon located?
   b. Analyze What does **Hammurabi's Code** reveal about Babylonian society?
2. **a. Describe** What two advantages did Hittite soldiers have over their opponents?
   b. Rank Which empire discussed in this section do you feel contributed the most to modern-day society? Why?
3. **a. Identify** For what trade goods were the Phoenicians known? For what else were they known?
   b. Analyze How did Phoenicia grow wealthy?

Critical Thinking

4. **Categorizing** Draw a diagram like the one at right. In each circle, list one of the empires of the Fertile Crescent, as well as the empire's most famous leader or major city.

   Fertile Crescent Empires

   Babylon Hittites Assyrians Phoenicians Chaldeans

FOCUS ON WRITING

5. **Gathering Information about Later Peoples** Several different peoples contributed to civilization in the Fertile Crescent after the Sumerians. Which ones, if any, will you mention on your poster? What will you say?

MESOPOTAMIA AND THE FERTILE CRESCENT **79**

Section 4 Assessment Answers

1. **a.** on the Euphrates near what is today Baghdad; Iraq
   b. It was based on social hierarchy and showed the importance of class distinctions. It also reveals the significance of business, trade, and family in the Babylonian Empire.

2. **a.** iron weapons and chariots
   b. possible answers: Babylonians—Hammurabi's laws; Chaldeans—restored Sumerian customs, studies in math and astronomy; Phoenicians—an alphabet

3. **a.** lumber, silverwork, ivory carvings, slaves, beautiful glass objects, and purple cloth; development of an alphabet
   b. Phoenicians were expert sailors with a fast fleet of trading ships and had valuable items to trade.

4. Babylonian—Hammurabi or Babylon; Hittites; Assyrians—Nineveh; Chaldeans—Nebuchadnezzar or Babylon; Phoenicians—Tyre or Carthage

5. Answers will vary but should reflect knowledge of section content.

79

Interpreting Physical Maps

Activity Reading a Local Physical Map Make copies of a physical map of the city, town, or county where your school is located. Have students describe the area's topography by identifying the different natural features and the landscape. Then ask students how the area's topography might affect the people who live in the area. For example, how might the topography affect industry and business in the area? Have students consider an important industry in your area. Then have students discuss how the topography of your area might have affected early settlers there. Last, have students write one to two paragraphs describing how they think the topography might have affected early people in the area.

S Verbal/Linguistic, Visual/Spatial

Alternative Assessment Handbook, Rubric 37: Writing Assignments

Interactive Skills Tutor CD-ROM, Lesson 6: Interpret Maps, Graphs, Charts, Visuals, and Political Cartoons

HSS Analysis Skills: CS 3

Social Studies Skills

| Analysis | Critical Thinking | Participation | Study |

Interpreting Physical Maps

Understand the Skill

A *physical map* is a map that shows the natural features and landscape, or *topography*, of an area. It shows the location and size of such features as rivers and mountain ranges. Physical maps also often show an area's *elevation*, or how high above sea level the land is. Topography and elevation often influence human activities. For example, people will live where they can find water and defend themselves. Therefore, being able to interpret a physical map can help you better understand how the history of an area unfolded.

Learn the Skill

Follow these steps to interpret a physical map.

❶ Read the map's title, distance scale, and legend. These will provide basic information about the map's contents.

❷ Note the colors used to show elevation. Use the legend to connect colors on the map to elevations of specific places.

❸ Note the shapes of the features, such as how high a mountain range is, how far it stretches, and how long a river is. Note where each feature is in relation to others.

❹ Use information from the map to draw conclusions about the effect of the region's topography on settlement and economic activities.

Mesopotamia and the Fertile Crescent

ELEVATION		
Feet		Meters
13,120		4,000
6,560		2,000
1,640		500
656		200
(Sea level) 0		0 (Sea level)
Below sea level		Below sea level

Practice and Apply the Skill

Use the guidelines to answer these questions about the map above.

1. What is the elevation of the western half of the Arabian Peninsula?

2. Describe the topography of Mesopotamia. Why would settlement have occurred here before other places on the map?

3. What feature might have stopped invasions of Mesopotamia?

Social Studies Skills Activity: Interpreting Physical Maps

Special Education Students   **Reaching Standards**

Materials: solid-colored table cloth

Using Visual Aids Lay a table cloth over your desk, a table, or another flat surface in the classroom. Push the table cloth together so that it forms folds and wrinkles similar to those on a physical map. Help students to see how these folds, dips, and flat areas resemble the mountains, valleys, and plains on a physical map. Then show students photographs of mountains and valleys and relate the images to the same features on a physical map.

LS Kinesthetic, Visual/Spatial

English-Language Learners   **Standards Proficiency**

Building Geographic Vocabulary English learners might need help with the vocabulary related to physical maps. Write the following terms for students to see: *elevation, landscape, mountain ranges, plains, sea level, topography,* and *valleys.* Help students write definitions for the terms first in their primary language and then in English. **LS** Verbal/Linguistic

HSS Analysis Skills: CS 3

Alternative Assessment Handbook, Rubric 1: Acquiring Information

---

Answers

Practice and Apply the Skill

1. *between 1,640 (500 m.) and 6,560 (2,000 m.) feet above sea level;* **2.** *fairly flat with two rivers providing good water sources; would be good for agriculture and settlement;* **3.** *possible answers— the desert to the southwest and the mountains to the north and northeast*

Standards Review

Visual Summary

Use the visual summary below to help you review the main ideas of the chapter.

QUICK FACTS

The early Mesopotamians developed irrigation to grow food.

Food production in Mesopotamia led to the world's first civilization.

Sumerian advances included ziggurats, the wheel, and the first writing system.

Later peoples developed the first written laws and the first empires.

Reviewing Vocabulary, Terms, and People

Using your own paper, complete the sentences below by providing the correct term for each blank.

1. Mesopotamian farmers built _____ to irrigate their fields.

2. While city dwellers were urban, farmers lived in _____ areas.

3. The people of Sumer practiced _____, the worship of many gods.

4. Instead of using pictographs, Sumerians developed a type of writing called _____.

5. Horse-drawn _____ gave the Hittites an advantage during battle.

6. The Babylonian king _____ is famous for his code of laws.

7. Another word for effect is _____.

8. Sumerian society was organized in _____, which consisted of a city and the surrounding lands.

Comprehension and Critical Thinking

SECTION 1 *(Pages 56–59)* **HSS** **6.2.1, 6.2.2**

9. **a. Describe** Where was Mesopotamia, and what does the name mean?

b. Analyze How did Mesopotamian irrigation systems allow civilization to develop?

c. Elaborate Do you think a division of labor is necessary for civilization to develop? Why or why not?

SECTION 2 *(Pages 62–66)* **HSS** **6.2.3**

10. **a. Identify** Who built the world's first empire, and what did that empire include?

b. Analyze Politically, how was early Sumerian society organized? How did that organization affect society?

c. Elaborate Why did the Sumerians consider it everyone's responsibility to keep the gods happy?

MESOPOTAMIA AND THE FERTILE CRESCENT **81**

Answers

Visual Summary

Review and Inquiry Have students use the visual summary to write a brief paragraph summarizing the important themes depicted in the illustration.

Quick Facts Transparency: Mesopotamia and the Fertile Crescent Visual Summary

Reviewing Vocabulary, Terms, and People

1. canals
2. rural
3. polytheism
4. cuneiform
5. chariots
6. Hammurabi
7. impact
8. city-states

Comprehension and Critical Thinking

9. **a.** It was located between the Tigris and Euphrates rivers, and the name means " between the rivers" in Greek.

b. They allowed the people to control the flow of the rivers and produce a surplus of food, which freed people to create a civilization.

c. possible answer—yes, because it allows people to focus on building a civilization rather than just surviving

10. **a.** Sargon; the area between the Tigris and Euphrates rivers and much of Mesopotamia

b. Kings and priests made up the upper class, while the middle class was craftspeople, merchants, and traders and the working class

---

Review and Assessment Resources

Review and Reinforce

- Standards Review
- **CRF:** Chapter Review Activity
- California Standards Review Workbook
- Quick Facts Transparency: Mesopotamia and the Fertile Crescent Visual Summary
- Spanish Chapter Summaries Audio CD
- Online Chapter Summaries in Six Languages
- **OSP** Holt PuzzlePro; GameTool for ExamView
- Quiz Game CD-ROM

Assess

- **SE** Standards Assessment
- **PASS:** Chapter Test, Forms A and B
- Alternative Assessment Handbook
- **OSP** ExamView Test Generator
- Universal Access Modified Worksheets and Tests CD-ROM
- Holt Online Assessment Program (in the Premier Online Edition)

Reteach/Intervene

- Interactive Reader and Study Guide
- Universal Access Teacher Management System: Lesson Plans for Universal Access
- Universal Access Modified Worksheets and Tests CD-ROM
- Interactive Skills Tutor CD-ROM

go.hrw.com

Online Resources

Chapter Resources:
KEYWORD: SQ6 WH3

consisted of farmers and laborers. Slaves were at the bottom. Priests and the wealthy ruled society, while the working class supported them.

c. The gods had great powers, and in order for the people to lead happy and prosperous lives, everyone had to do their part in keeping the gods happy.

11. a. cuneiform; significant because it is the world's first system of writing

b. similar—students went to school to learn to read and write, they produced makeup and jewelry, enjoyed music; different—their writing was cuneiform, wrote on clay tablets

c. Answers will vary but should display knowledge of chapter content.

12. a. purple dye, founded Carthage, developed an alphabet

b. possible answer—Separately they stood no chance, but by banding together they were able to make an impact.

c. Answers will vary but should be supported by facts.

Reviewing Themes

13. Answers will vary but should display knowledge of chapter content.

14. possible answer—He was the first to institute such a far-reaching and comprehensive structure of laws, which influenced many future societies.

Reading Skills

15. A

16. B

SECTION 3 *(Pages 67–71)* **HSS** 6.2.9

11. a. Identify What was the Sumerian writing system called, and why is it so significant?

b. Compare and Contrast What were two ways in which Sumerian society was similar to our society today? What were two ways in which it was different?

c. Evaluate Other than writing and the wheel, which Sumerian invention do you think is most important? Why?

SECTION 4 *(Pages 74–79)* **HSS** 6.2.4

12. a. Describe What were two important developments of the Phoenicians?

b. Draw Conclusions Why do you think several peoples banded together to fight the Assyrians?

c. Evaluate Do you think Hammurabi was more effective as a ruler or as a military leader? Why?

Reviewing Themes

13. Science and Technology Which of the ancient Sumerians' technological achievements do you think has been most influential in history? Why?

14. Politics Why do you think Hammurabi is so honored for his code of laws?

Reading Skills

Identifying Main Ideas *For each passage, choose the letter that corresponds to the main idea sentence.*

15. (A) Sumerians believed that their gods had enormous powers. (B) Gods could bring a good harvest or a disastrous flood. (C) They could bring illness or they could bring good health and wealth.

16. (A) The wheel was not the Sumerians' only great development. (B) They developed cuneiform, the world's first system of writing. (C) But Sumerians did not have pencils, pens, or paper. (D) Instead, they used sharp reeds to make wedge-shaped symbols on clay tablets.

Using the Internet

go.hrw.com
KEYWORD: SQ6 WH3

17. Activity: Looking at Writing The Sumerians made one of the greatest cultural advances in history by developing cuneiform. This was the world's first system of writing. Enter the activity keyword and research the evolution of language and its written forms. Look at one of the newest methods of writing: text messaging. Then write a paragraph explaining how and why writing was developed and why it was important using text-messaging abbreviations, words, and symbols.

Social Studies Skills

Using Physical Maps *Could you use a physical map to answer the questions below? For each question, answer yes or no.*

18. Are there mountains or hills in a certain region?

19. What languages do people speak in that region?

20. How many people live in the region?

21. What kinds of water features such as rivers or lakes would you find there?

FOCUS ON WRITING

22. Creating Your Poster Use the notes you have taken to create a plan for your poster. Work it out on a piece of paper before transferring it to poster board. Limit yourself to two or three main points. Remember that you will need to print the words on your poster and use large letters. You won't have room for many words.

Create a title for your poster and center it at the top. Write your main points in one color and your sub-points in another color. Plan where you'll place your map or picture of the Fertile Crescent. It should support the written ideas, not interfere with them. As a last touch for your poster, you might want to add a decorative border or an image that suggests the Fertile Crescent.

Using the Internet

17. Go to the HRW Web site and enter the keyword shown to access a rubric for this activity.

KEYWORD: SQ6 TEACHER

Social Studies Skills

18. yes

19. no

20. no

21. yes

Focus on Writing

22. Rubric Students' posters should
- show main points clearly and accurately.
- use color and illustrations effectively.
- use appropriate vocabulary.

CRF: Focus on Writing: A Poster

Standards Assessment

DIRECTIONS: Read each question, and write the letter of the best response.

1 Use the map to answer the following question.

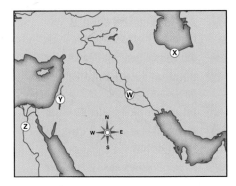

The region known as Mesopotamia is indicated on the map by the letter

- A W.
- B X.
- C Y.
- D Z.

2 All of the following ancient civilizations developed in Mesopotamia *except* the

- A Akkadians.
- B Babylonians.
- C Egyptians.
- D Sumerians.

3 Which of the following is *not* true of the first writing system?

- A It was developed by the Babylonians.
- B It began with the use of pictures to represent syllables and objects.
- C It was recorded on tablets made of clay.
- D It was first used to keep business records.

4 In Sumerian society, people's social class or rank depended on their wealth and their

- A appearance.
- B religion.
- C location.
- D occupation.

5 Hammurabi's Code is important in world history because it was an early

- A form of writing that could be used to record important events.
- B written list of laws that controlled people's daily life and behavior.
- C record-keeping system that enabled the Phoenicians to become great traders.
- D set of symbols that allowed the Sumerians to communicate with other peoples.

6 What was the most important contribution of the Phoenicians to our civilization?

- A purple dye
- B their alphabet
- C founding of Carthage
- D sailing ships

Connecting with Past Learnings

7 In Grade 5 you studied a group of people in American history that placed great importance on religion. Religion was also at the center of Sumerian society. With which American group did the Sumerians share a strong emphasis on religion?

- A the Dutch
- B the Tories
- C the Loyalists
- D the Puritans

Tips for Test Taking

I'm Stuck! Give students these tips for when they get stuck on a standardized test. If you come across a question that stumps you, don't get frustrated. First master the question to make sure you understand what is being asked. Then work through the strategies you have already learned. If you are still stuck, circle the question and go on to others. Come back to it later. What if you still have no idea? Practice the 50/50 strategy and make an educated guess.

Answers

1. A
Break Down the Question Point out that the region labeled Y is part of the Fertile Crescent, but not Mesopotamia. Have students who miss the question review the map in Section 1.

2. C
Break Down the Question Remind students that the word *except* in this question signals that they should identify the false answer choice.

3. A
Break Down the Question Remind students that the word *not* in this question signals that they should identify the false answer choice.

4. D
Break Down the Question This question requires students to recall factual information from Section 2.

5. B
Break Down the Question This question requires students to recall factual information from Section 4.

6. B
Break Down the Question Point out to students that the most lasting contribution from the Phoenicians to our world has been the alphabet.

7. D
Break Down the Question This question requires students to recall factual information about the founding of the English colonies in the Americas.

Standards Review
Have students review the following standards in their workbooks.

California Standards Review Workbook: **HSS** 6.2

Chapter 4 Planning Guide

Ancient Egypt

Chapter Overview	Reproducible Resources	Technology Resources
Chapter 4 pp. 84–117 **Overview:** In this chapter, students learn about the history, culture, and achievements of ancient Egypt. See page 84 for the California History–Social Science standards covered in this chapter.	**Universal Access Teacher Management System:*** • Universal Access Instructional Benchmarking Guides • Lesson Plans for Universal Access **Interactive Reader and Study Guide:** Chapter Graphic Organizer* **Chapter Resource File*** • Chapter Review Activity • Focus on Writing Activity: A Riddle • Social Studies Skills Activity: Assessing Primary and Secondary Sources	**One-Stop Planner CD-ROM:** Calendar Planner **Student Edition Full-Read Audio CD-ROM** **Universal Access Modified Worksheets and Tests CD-ROM** **Interactive Skills Tutor CD-ROM** **Primary Source Library CD-ROM for World History** **Power Presentations with Video CD-ROM** **History's Impact: World History Video Program (VHS/DVD):** Ancient Egypt and Kush*
Section 1: **Geography and Early Egypt** **The Big Idea:** The water and fertile soils of the Nile Valley allowed a great civilization to develop in Egypt. 6.2.1, 6.2.2	**Universal Access Teacher Management System:*** Section 1 Lesson Plan **Interactive Reader and Study Guide:** Section 1 Summary* **Chapter Resource File*** • Vocabulary Builder Activity, Section 1	**Daily Bellringer Transparency:** Section 1* **Map Transparency:** Ancient Egypt*
Section 2: **The Old Kingdom** **The Big Idea:** Egyptian government and religion were closely connected during the Old Kingdom. 6.2.3	**Universal Access Teacher Management System:*** Section 2 Lesson Plan **Interactive Reader and Study Guide:** Section 2 Summary* **Chapter Resource File*** • Vocabulary Builder Activity, Section 2 • Biography Activity: Khufu • History and Geography Activity: Trade on the Nile	**Daily Bellringer Transparency:** Section 2* **Internet Activity:** Explore the Pyramids
Section 3: **The Middle and New Kingdoms** **The Big Idea:** During the Middle and New Kingdoms, order and greatness were restored in Egypt. 6.2.6, 6.2.7	**Universal Access Teacher Management System:*** Section 3 Lesson Plan **Interactive Reader and Study Guide:** Section 3 Summary* **Chapter Resource File*** • Vocabulary Builder Activity, Section 3 • Biography Activity: Akhenaton • Biography Activity: Nefertiti	**Daily Bellringer Transparency:** Section 3* **Quick Facts Transparency:** Time Line: Periods of Egyptian History* **Map Transparency:** Egyptian Trade, c. 1400 BC*
Section 4: **Egyptian Achievements** **The Big Idea:** The Egyptians made lasting achievements in writing, architecture, and art. 6.2.5, 6.2.9	**Universal Access Teacher Management System:*** Section 4 Lesson Plan **Interactive Reader and Study Guide:** Section 4 Summary* **Chapter Resource File*** • Vocabulary Builder Activity, Section 4 • Literature Activity: The Egyptian Cinderella • Primary Source Activity: The Amarna Letters • Primary Source Activity: Tomb Paintings	**Daily Bellringer Transparency:** Section 4* **Internet Activity:** A Hieroglyphic Tale

MASTERING THE CALIFORNIA STANDARDS

Key

SE Student Edition
TE Teacher's Edition
go.hrw.com
OSP One-Stop Planner CD-ROM

Print Resource
Transparency
CA Standards Mastery

Audio CD
CD-ROM
LS Learning Styles

Video
DVD

* also on One-Stop Planner CD

Review, Assessment, Intervention

- Standards Review Workbook*
- Quick Facts Transparency: Ancient Egypt Visual Summary*
- Spanish Chapter Summaries Audio CD Program
- Online Chapter Summaries in Six Languages
- Quiz Game CD-ROM
- Progress Assessment Support System (PASS): Chapter Test*
- Modified Materials for Struggling Students CD: Modified Chapter Test
- One-Stop Planner CD-ROM: ExamView Test Generator (English/Spanish)
- Holt Online Assessment Program (HOAP), in the Holt Premier Online Student Edition

---

- PASS: Section 1 Quiz*
- Online Quiz: Section 1
- Alternative Assessment Handbook

- PASS: Section 2 Quiz*
- Online Quiz: Section 2
- Alternative Assessment Handbook

- PASS: Section 3 Quiz*
- Online Quiz: Section 3
- Alternative Assessment Handbook

- PASS: Section 4 Quiz*
- Online Quiz: Section 4
- Alternative Assessment Handbook

California Resources for Standards Mastery

INSTRUCTIONAL PLANNING AND SUPPORT

- Universal Access Teacher Management System*
- One-Stop Planner CD-ROM with Test Generator: Teacher Management System with Interactive Teacher's Edition

STANDARDS MASTERY

- Standards Review Workbook*
- At Home: A Guide to Standards Mastery for World History

---

go.hrw.com Holt Online Learning

To enhance learning, the following Internet activities are available: Explore the Pyramids and A Hieroglyphic Tale.

KEYWORD: SQ6 TEACHER

- Teacher Support Page
- Content Updates
- Rubrics and Writing Models

- Teaching Tips for the Multimedia Classroom

KEYWORD: SQ6 WH4

- Current Events
- Holt Grapher
- Holt Online Atlas
- Holt Researcher
- Interactive Multimedia Activities
- Internet Activities

- Online Chapter Summaries in Six Languages
- Online Section Quizzes
- World History Maps and Charts

HOLT PREMIER ONLINE STUDENT EDITION

Complete online support for interactivity, assessment, and reporting
- Interactive Maps and Notebook
- Standardized Test Prep
- Homework Practice and Research Activities Online

Mastering the Standards: Differentiating Instruction

Reaching Standards	Basic-level activities designed for all students encountering new material
Standards Proficiency	Intermediate-level activities designed for average students
Exceeding Standards	Challenging activities designed for honors and gifted-and-talented students
Standard English Mastery	Activities designed to improve standard English usage

Frequently Asked Questions

INSTRUCTIONAL PLANNING AND SUPPORT

Where do I find planning aids, pacing guides, lesson plans, and other teaching aids?

Annotated Teacher's Edition:
- Chapter planning guides
- Standards-based instruction and strategies
- Differentiated instruction for universal access
- Point-of-use reminders for integrating program resources

Power Presentations with Video CD-ROM

Universal Access Teacher Management System:
- Year and unit instructional benchmarking guides
- Reproducible lesson plans
- Assessment guides for diagnostic, progress, and summative end-of-the-year tests
- Options for differentiating instruction and intervention
- Teaching guides and answer keys for student workbooks

One-Stop Planner CD-ROM with Test Generator: Teacher Management System with Interactive Teacher's Edition:
- Calendar Planner
- Editable lesson plans
- All reproducible ancillaries in Adobe Acrobat (PDF) format
- ExamView Test Generator (English & Spanish)
- Game Tool for ExamView
- PuzzlePro
- Transparency and video previews

DIFFERENTIATING INSTRUCTION FOR UNIVERSAL ACCESS

What resources are available to ensure that Advanced Learners/GATE Students master the standards?

Teacher's Edition Activities:
- Egyptian Gods Storyboard, p. 95
- The Geometry of Pyramids, p. 98
- Traders' Journals, p. 105
- Saving Abu Simbel, p. 107
- Measuring a Temple, p. 110
- King Tut's Tomb, p. 112

Lesson Plans for Universal Access

Primary Source Library CD-ROM for World History

What resources are available to ensure that English Learners and Standard English Learners master the standards?

Teacher's Edition Activities:
- Growth of Ancient Egypt Graphic Organizer, p. 90
- How the Rosetta Stone Works, p. 109

Lesson Plans for Universal Access

Chapter Resource File: Vocabulary Builder Activities

Spanish Chapter Summaries Audio CD Program

Online Chapter Summaries in Six Languages

One-Stop Planner CD-ROM:
- PuzzlePro, Spanish Version
- ExamView Test Generator, Spanish Version

What modified materials are available for Special Education?

The *Universal Access Modified Worksheets and Tests CD-ROM* provides editable versions of the following:

Vocabulary Flash Cards

Modified Vocabulary Builder Activities

Modified Chapter Review Activity

Modified Chapter Test

What resources are available to ensure that Learners Having Difficulty master the standards?

Teacher's Edition Activities:
- Two New Kingdom Rulers Chart, p. 103
- Egyptian Social Groups Drawing, p. 104

Interactive Reader and Study Guide

Student Edition Full-Read Audio CD

Quick Facts Transparency: Ancient Egypt Visual Summary

Standards Review Workbook

Social Studies Skills Activity: Assessing Primary and Secondary Sources

Interactive Skills Tutor CD-ROM

How do I intervene for students struggling to master the standards?

Interactive Reader and Study Guide

Quick Facts Transparency: Ancient Egypt Visual Summary

Standards Review Workbook

Social Studies Skills Activity: Assessing Primary and Secondary Sources

Interactive Skills Tutor CD-ROM

PROFESSIONAL DEVELOPMENT

HOLT
Professional Development

What teacher training resources are available to help me grow professionally?

- In-service and staff development as part of your Holt Social Studies product purchase
- Quick Teacher Tutorial Lesson Presentation CD-ROM
- Intensive tuition-based Teacher Development Institute
- Convenient Holt Speaker Bureau face-to-face workshop options

- PRAXIS™ Test Prep (#0089) interactive Web-based content refreshers*
- *Ask A Professional Development Expert* at http://www.hrw.com/prodev/

* PRAXIS is a trademark of Educational Testing Service (ETS). This publication is not endorsed or approved by ETS.

Information Literacy Skills

To learn more about how History–Social Science instruction may be improved by the effective use of library media centers and information literacy skills, go to the Teacher's Resource Materials for Chapter 4 at **go.hrw.com, keyword: SQ6 MEDIA.**

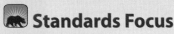 **Standards Focus**

Standards by Section
Section 1: HSS 6.2.1, 6.2.2
Section 2: HSS 6.2.3
Section 3: HSS 6.2.6, 6.2.7
Section 4: HSS 6.2.5, 6.2.9

Teacher's Edition
HSS **Analysis Skills:** CS 1, CS 2, CS 3, HR 1, HI 1, HI 2, HI 3, HI 4, HI 5

Upcoming Standards for Future Learning
Preview the following History–Social Science content standards from upcoming chapters or grade levels to promote learning beyond the current chapter.

HSS **6.3** Students analyze the geographic, political, economic, religious, and social structures of the Ancient Hebrews.

6.3.4 Discuss the locations of the settlements and movements of Hebrew peoples, including the Exodus and their movement to and from Egypt, and outline the significance of the Exodus to the Jewish and other people.

6.4 Students analyze the geographic, political, economic, religious, and social structures of the early civilizations of Ancient Greece.

6.4.7 Trace the rise of Alexander the Great and the spread of Greek culture eastward and into Egypt.

Focus on Writing
The **Chapter Resource File** provides a Focus on Writing worksheet to help students write their riddles.

CRF: Focus on Writing Activity: A Riddle

CHAPTER **4**   c. 4500–500 BC

Ancient Egypt

 California Standards

History–Social Science
6.2 Students analyze the geographic, political, economic, religious, and social structures of the early civilizations of Mesopotamia, Egypt, and Kush.

Analysis Skills
HR 4 Assess the credibility of primary and secondary sources.

English–Language Arts
Writing 6.2.2c Follow an organizational pattern appropriate to the type of content.

Reading 6.2.6 Determine the adequacy and appropriateness of the evidence for an author's conclusions.

FOCUS ON WRITING

A Riddle In this chapter you will read about the fascinating civilization of ancient Egypt. In ancient times a sphinx, an imaginary creature like the one whose sculpture is in Egypt, was supposed to have demanded the answer to a riddle. People died if they didn't answer the riddle correctly. After you read this chapter, you will write a riddle. The answer to your riddle will be "Egypt."

c. 4500 BC
Agricultural communities develop in Egypt.

CHAPTER EVENTS

4500 BC

WORLD EVENTS

c. 4500 BC
People in Europe begin using copper tools.

Introduce the Chapter
Standards Proficiency

Impressions of Egypt HSS **Analysis Skill:** HI 5

1. Ask students what they already know about ancient Egypt. What books or articles have they read? What photos or movies have they seen? Do they have or have they seen any jewelry that has Egyptian designs? Write responses for students to see.

2. Tell students that some things portrayed in popular culture and in the media are true and some are not. For example, workers on the pyramids have often been portrayed as

slaves, but most Egyptologists now think these workers were mostly common people, such as free farmers. Tell students that in their research they may see the term *Egyptologist*, which refers to a person who studies Egyptian antiquities.

3. Tell students that in this chapter they will see how accurately their current knowledge about Egypt reflects ancient Egyptian life.
LS Verbal/Linguistic

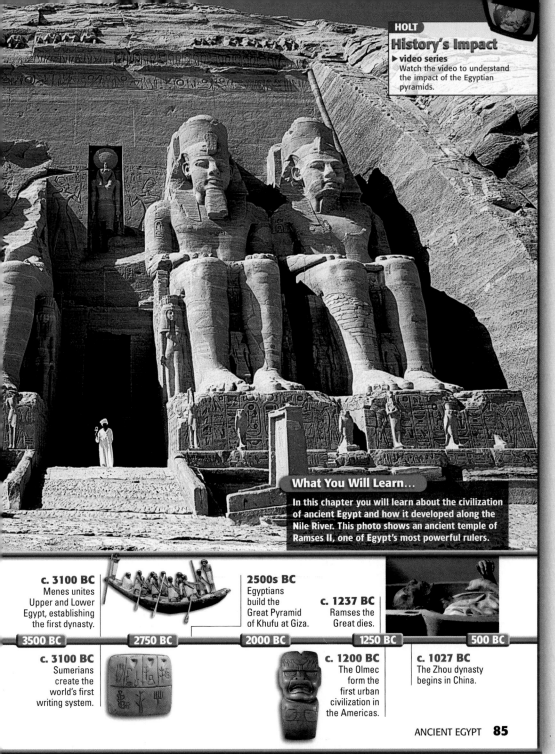

What You Will Learn...

In this chapter you will learn about the civilization of ancient Egypt and how it developed along the Nile River. This photo shows an ancient temple of Ramses II, one of Egypt's most powerful rulers.

Explore the Time Line

c. 3100 BC Menes unites Upper and Lower Egypt, establishing the first dynasty.

2500s BC Egyptians build the Great Pyramid of Khufu at Giza.

c. 1237 BC Ramses the Great dies.

| 3500 BC | 2750 BC | 2000 BC | 1250 BC | 500 BC |

c. 3100 BC Sumerians create the world's first writing system.

c. 1200 BC The Olmec form the first urban civilization in the Americas.

c. 1027 BC The Zhou dynasty begins in China.

ANCIENT EGYPT **85**

Explore the Time Line

1. How many years separate the founding of the first dynasty and the death of Ramses the Great? *1863 years*

2. What culture was developing a writing system while Menes was uniting Upper and Lower Egypt? *Sumerians*

3. What was happening in the Americas at about the same time Ramses died? *The Olmec were forming the first urban civilization in the Americas.*

HSS 6.2.3; HSS Analysis Skills: CS 1, HI 1

Info to Know

Beyond the Time Line Although the time line ends at 500 BC, Egyptian history continued long after that date. However, Egypt was never again as powerful or influential as it had been. One after the other, Assyrians, Persians, and Macedonians conquered Egypt. The Egyptians maintained their own distinct culture, though, until about 30 BC. At that time, Rome took control of Egypt, and Egyptian traditions began to change for all time.

HOLT

History's Impact

► video series
See the Video Teacher's Guide for strategies for using the video **Ancient Egypt and Kush: The Impact of the Egyptian Pyramids.**

Chapter Big Ideas

Section 1 The water and fertile soils of the Nile Valley allowed a great civilization to develop in Egypt. HSS 6.2.1, 6.2.2

Section 2 Egyptian government and religion were closely connected during the Old Kingdom. HSS 6.2.3

Section 3 During the Middle and New Kingdoms, order and greatness were restored in Egypt. HSS 6.2.6, 6.2.7

Section 4 The Egyptians made lasting achievements in writing, architecture, and art. HSS 6.2.5, 6.2.9

Explore the Picture

Ramses the Great This picture shows the entrance to Ramses the Great's temple at Abu Simbel. The entrance is flanked by four 66-foot-high statues of the pharaoh. However, the structure you see in the photo is not in its original location. When dam construction on the Nile River threatened to flood the temple, workers cut the entire structure into blocks and rebuilt it on higher ground.

Analyzing Visuals Why may Ramses have had not just one but four statues of himself placed before the temple? *possible answer—to make the entrance more impressive or to emphasize different roles that he had in Egyptian politics and religion*

Understanding Themes

Introduce the themes of this chapter by asking students to think about what they already know about ancient Egypt. Then write the labels *Geography* and *Religion* for students to see. Ask students to share what they know about Egypt in these two categories. Possible answers might include *in a desert, the Nile River,* and *many gods.*

Drawing Conclusions about the Past

Focus on Reading Have students practice drawing conclusions on their own. Write the following statements for students to see:

All house cats are related to large, wild cats such as the tiger.

My pet, Jimmy, is not related to large, wild cats.

Have students draw a conclusion based on these two facts. *Jimmy is not a house cat.* Then have pairs of students create a list of facts from which a valid conclusion can be drawn. Have students exchange lists and draw conclusions based on the facts.

Reading Social Studies
by Kylene Beers

| Economics | Geography | Politics | Religion | Society and Culture | Science and Technology |

Focus on Themes In this chapter you will read about the development of the fascinating civilization of Egypt. You will learn how the Nile River, nearby deserts, and other **geographic** features shaped early Egyptian society. You will learn about the ancient Egyptians' **religious** beliefs and learn how those beliefs shaped everything from their daily lives to the art they created. Of course, you will also read about the pyramids, mummies, and pharaohs that made Egypt famous.

Drawing Conclusions about the Past

Focus on Reading Have you ever read a mystery story in which a detective puts together various clues to solve a puzzling crime? In other words, he combines various bits of information to reach a conclusion.

Drawing Conclusions A **conclusion** is a judgment someone makes by combining information. When you read, you can put together various bits of information from what you are reading to figure out new information that isn't stated exactly in the text.

Additional reading support can be found in the

Inter active
Reader and Study Guide

Burial Practices

The Egyptians developed a method called embalming to preserve bodies and keep them from decaying. <u>The Egyptians preserved bodies as mummies, specially treated bodies wrapped in cloth.</u> Embalming preserves a dead body for many, many years. <u>A body that was not embalmed would decay quickly in a tomb . . .</u>

Only royalty and other members of Egypt's elite, or people of wealth and power, could afford to have mummies made.

→ The Egyptians preserved dead bodies as mummies.

→ Only mummies could survive for thousands of years in tombs.

→ Embalming was expensive and so it was limited to kings and other rich people.

Conclusion: The mummies that historians have found are the bodies of Egyptian kings and rich people

86 CHAPTER 4

Reading and Skills Resources

Reading Support

- Interactive Reader and Study Guide
- Student Edition on Audio CD
- Spanish Chapter Summaries Audio CD Program

Social Studies Skills Support

- Interactive Skills Tutor CD-ROM

Vocabulary Support

- **CRF:** Vocabulary Builder Activities
- **CRF:** Chapter Review Activity
- Universal Access Modified Worksheets and Tests CD-ROM:
  - Vocabulary Flash Cards
  - Vocabulary Builder Activity
  - Chapter Review Activity

OSP Holt PuzzlePro

Standards Focus
ELA Reading 6.2.6

ELA **Reading 6.2.6** Determine the adequacy and appropriateness of the evidence for an author's conclusions.

You Try It!

The following passage is from the chapter you are getting ready to read. As you read the passage, look for the facts about pyramids.

The Pyramids

The Egyptians believed that burial sites, especially royal tombs, were very important. As a result, they built spectacular monuments in which to bury their rulers. The most spectacular of all were the pyramids—huge, stone tombs with four triangle-shaped sides that met in a point on top.

From Chapter 4 p. 98

The Egyptians first built pyramids during the Old Kingdom. Some of the largest pyramids ever constructed were built during this time. Many of these huge pyramids are still standing. The largest is the Great Pyramid of Khufu near the town of Giza. It covers more than 13 acres at its base and stands 481 feet high. This single pyramid took thousands of workers and more than 2 million limestone blocks to build.

After you have finished the passage, answer the questions below, drawing conclusions about what you have read.

1. Based on their function, do you think pyramids were hollow or solid inside? Why?

2. Considering why the Egyptians built the pyramids, who do you think Khufu was? What makes you think this?

3. Do you think pyramids were first built early in Egypt's history, or late? Why?

4. Think about pictures of the pyramids you have seen. What do you think the landscape near Giza is like?

As you read Chapter 4, think about what you already know about Egypt and draw conclusions to fill gaps in what you are reading.

Key Terms and People

Chapter 4

Section 1
cataracts (p. 89)
delta (p. 89)
Menes (p. 91)
pharaoh (p. 91)
dynasty (p. 91)

Section 2
Old Kingdom (p. 93)
Khufu (p. 94)
nobles (p. 94)
afterlife (p. 96)
mummies (p. 96)
elite (p. 97)
pyramids (p. 98)
engineering (p. 98)

Section 3
Middle Kingdom (p. 102)
New Kingdom (p. 102)
trade routes (p. 102)
Queen Hatshepsut (p. 103)
Ramses the Great (p. 103)

Section 4
hieroglyphics (p. 108)
papyrus (p. 108)
Rosetta Stone (p. 109)
sphinxes (p. 110)
obelisk (p. 110)
King Tutankhamen (p. 113)

Academic Vocabulary

Success in school is related to knowing academic vocabulary—the words that are frequently used in school assignments and discussions. In this chapter, you will learn the following academic words:

acquire (p. 94)
method (p. 96)
contracts (p. 106)

Reading Social Studies

Key Terms and People

Review the chapter key terms and people by instructing students to create a Key-Term FoldNote. Have students fold a sheet of paper in half. Then have students cut along every third line from the right edge of the paper to the center fold to create tabs. Tell students to write a key term or person on each tab. Discuss with the class the meaning of the terms or people with which they are unfamiliar. Have students define or identify each term or person on the inside of the FoldNote. Remind students to study the terms and people regularly.

LS Verbal/Linguistic, Visual/Spatial

Focus on Reading

See the **Focus on Reading** questions in this chapter for more practice on this reading social studies skill.

Reading Social Studies Assessment

See the **Standards Review** at the end of this chapter for student assessment questions related to this reading skill.

Teaching Tip

Explain to students that their background knowledge—what they have read, seen, and heard—can both help and hinder their ability to draw conclusions. Have students discuss what happens when people draw conclusions based on misconceptions or false information. For example, point out that movies often show mummies walking around and attacking people. Would this knowledge provide an accurate conclusion? Point out to students that they should evaluate their background knowledge before using it to draw conclusions.

Answers

You Try It! 1. *some parts must be hollow, because they served as tombs* **2.** *a ruler, because he had his own pyramid;* **3.** *early, because the time is called the Old Kingdom, which sounds like it was probably a long time ago* **4.** *desert-like*

Bellringer

If YOU were there . . . Use the **Daily Bellringer Transparency** to help students answer the question.

📊 Daily Bellringer Transparency, Section 1

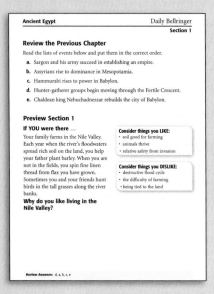

Ancient Egypt   Daily Bellringer
                                                       Section 1

Review the Previous Chapter
Read the lists of events below and put them in the correct order.

a. Sargon and his army succeed in establishing an empire.
b. Assyrians rise to dominance in Mesopotamia.
c. Hammurabi rises to power in Babylon.
d. Hunter-gatherer groups begin moving through the Fertile Crescent.
e. Chaldean king Nebuchadnezzar rebuilds the city of Babylon.

Preview Section 1

If YOU were there …
Your family farms in the Nile Valley. Each year when the river's floodwaters spread rich soil on the land, you help your father plant barley. When you are not in the fields, you spin fine linen thread from flax you have grown. Sometimes you and your friends hunt birds in the tall grasses along the river banks.

Consider things you LIKE:
• soil good for farming
• animals thrive
• relative safety from invasion

Consider things you DISLIKE:
• destructive flood cycle
• the difficulty of farming
• being tied to the land

Why do you like living in the Nile Valley?

Review Answers: d, a, b, c, e

Building Vocabulary

Preteach or review the following terms:

fertile capable of producing plentiful vegetation (p. 88)

silt finely ground soil deposited by flowing water (p. 89)

📝 **CRF:** Vocabulary Builder Activity, Section 1

🐻 Standards Focus

HSS 6.2.1

Means: Locate and describe the Nile River Valley and discuss how it supported early settlements and civilizations.
Matters: Civilization in ancient Egypt flourished because of the fertile soil provided when the Nile flooded. Egypt still depends on the Nile.

HSS 6.2.2

Means: Explain how Egyptian farmers produced surplus food that let cities grow.
Matters: If a civilization has plenty of food, not everyone has to farm; some people can live in cities and pursue other activities.

Geography and Early Egypt

What You Will Learn...

Main Ideas

1. Egypt was called the "gift of the Nile" because the Nile River was so important.
2. Civilization developed after people began farming along the Nile.
3. Strong kings unified all of Egypt.

The Big Idea

The water and fertile soils of the Nile Valley allowed a great civilization to develop in Egypt.

Key Terms and People

cataracts, *p. 89*
delta, *p. 89*
Menes, *p. 91*
pharaoh, *p. 91*
dynasty, *p. 91*

🐻 **HSS 6.2.1** Locate and describe the major river systems and discuss the physical settings that supported permanent settlement and early civilizations.

6.2.2 Trace the development of agricultural techniques that permitted the production of economic surplus and the emergence of cities as centers of culture and power.

If YOU were there...

Your family farms in the Nile Valley. Each year when the river's floodwaters spread rich soil on the land, you help your father plant barley. When you are not in the fields, you spin fine linen thread from flax you have grown. Sometimes you and your friends hunt birds in the tall grasses along the river banks.

Why do you like living in the Nile Valley?

BUILDING BACKGROUND Like the rivers of Mesopotamia, the narrow valley of the Nile River in Egypt also provided fertile land that drew people to live there. The culture that developed in ancient Egypt was more stable and long-lasting than those in Mesopotamia.

The Gift of the Nile

Geography played a key role in the development of Egyptian civilization. The Nile River brought life to Egypt and allowed it to thrive. The river was so important to people in this region that a Greek historian named Herodotus (hi-RAHD-uh-tuhs) called Egypt the gift of the Nile.

Location and Physical Features

The Nile is the longest river in the world. It begins in central Africa and runs north through Egypt to the Mediterranean Sea, a distance of over 4,000 miles. The civilization of ancient Egypt developed along a 750-mile stretch of the Nile.

Ancient Egypt included two regions, a southern region and a northern region. The southern region was called Upper Egypt. It was so named because it was located upriver in relation to the Nile's flow. Lower Egypt, the northern region, was located downriver. The Nile sliced through the desert of Upper Egypt. There, it created a fertile river valley about 13 miles wide. On either side of the Nile lay hundreds of miles of bleak desert sands.

Teach the Big Idea: Master the Standards   Standards Proficiency

Geography and Early Egypt 🐻 **HSS** 6.2.1; **HSS** Analysis Skills: HI 3

1. **Teach** Ask students the Main Idea questions to teach this section.

2. **Apply** Organize the class into pairs. Have each pair write a verse for a national anthem that Menes may have commissioned to celebrate the unification of Upper and Lower Egypt. Verses may focus on any aspect of early Egyptian history as reflected in the section.

3. **Review** Call on volunteers to read their verses. Adventuresome students may want

to sing their verses to the tune of a popular song. Discuss any topics not covered by the verses. **LS Verbal/Linguistic, Auditory/Musical**

4. **Practice/Homework** Have each student write another verse for his or her anthem. **LS Verbal/Linguistic, Auditory/Musical**

📝 Alternative Assessment Handbook, Rubric 26: Poems and Songs

As you can see on the map, the Nile flowed through rocky, hilly land south of Egypt. At several points, this rough terrain caused **cataracts**, or rapids, to form. The first cataract, located 720 miles south of the Mediterranean Sea, marked the southern border of Upper Egypt. Five more cataracts lay farther south. These cataracts made sailing on that portion of the Nile very difficult.

In Lower Egypt, the Nile divided into several branches that fanned out and flowed into the Mediterranean Sea. These branches formed a **delta**, a triangle-shaped area of land made from soil deposited by a river. In ancient times, swamps and marshes covered much of the Nile Delta. Some two-thirds of Egypt's fertile farmland was located in the Nile Delta.

The Floods of the Nile

Because little rain fell in the region, most of Egypt was desert. Each year, however, rainfall far to the south of Egypt in the highlands of East Africa caused the Nile to flood. The Nile's floods were easier to predict than those of the Tigris and Euphrates rivers in Mesopotamia. Almost every year, the Nile flooded Upper Egypt in mid-summer and Lower Egypt in the fall.

The Nile's flooding coated the land around it with a rich silt. As in Mesopotamia, the silt made the soil ideal for farming. The silt also made the land a dark color. That is why Egyptians called their country the black land. They called the dry, lifeless desert beyond the river valley the red land. Each year, Egyptians eagerly awaited the flooding of the Nile. For them, the river's floods were a life-giving miracle. Without the floods, people never could have farmed in Egypt.

READING CHECK Summarizing Why was Egypt called the gift of the Nile?

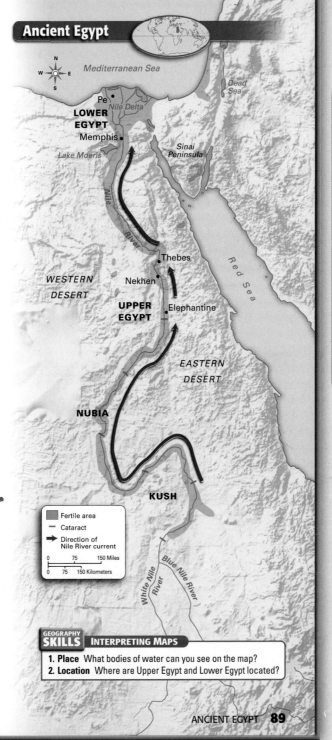

Ancient Egypt

- Fertile area
- — Cataract
- → Direction of Nile River current

0   75   150 Miles
0   75   150 Kilometers

GEOGRAPHY SKILLS INTERPRETING MAPS
1. **Place** What bodies of water can you see on the map?
2. **Location** Where are Upper Egypt and Lower Egypt located?

ANCIENT EGYPT **89**

89

❷ Civilization Develops in Egypt

Civilization developed after people began farming along the Nile.

Recall How did farmers use the Nile to grow their crops? *They built canals to direct the Nile's water to the fields.*

Predict Why might the ruins of early Egyptian settlements lack evidence of protective walls? *because the desert, bodies of water, and cataracts provided natural protection from many enemies*

HSS 6.2.1, 6.2.2; **HSS** Analysis Skills: HI 2

Linking to Today

Damming the Nile The Aswan High Dam on the Nile was completed in 1971. It was built to generate electricity and make water available year-round to farmers. Although the dam fulfilled these goals, it has caused other problems. Because the Nile no longer drops silt on the fields, Egyptian farmers now have to use millions of tons of expensive chemical fertilizers. In addition, because less silt is deposited there, the Mediterranean coastline is eroding more rapidly.

Analyzing Visuals

Ask students what this artwork reveals about farming in ancient Egypt. *possible answers—Farmers did some work by hand and had simple tools; both men and women worked in the fields.*

Civilization Develops in Egypt

The Nile provided both water and fertile soil for farming. Over time, scattered farms grew into villages and then cities. Eventually, an Egyptian civilization developed.

Increased Food Production

Hunter-gatherers first moved into the Nile Valley more than 12,000 years ago. They found plants, wild animals, and fish there to eat. In time, these people learned how to farm, and they settled along the Nile. By 4500 BC, farmers living in small villages grew wheat and barley.

As in Mesopotamia, farmers in Egypt developed an irrigation system. Unlike farmers in Mesopotamia, however, Egyptian farmers did not need to build basins for storing water. The Egyptians simply built a series of canals to direct the river's flow and carry water to their fields.

The Nile provided Egyptian farmers with an abundance of food. In addition to watering their crops, the Nile allowed farmers to raise animals. Farmers in Egypt grew wheat, barley, fruits, and vegetables. They also raised cattle and sheep. The river provided many types of fish, and hunters trapped wild geese and ducks along its banks. Like the Mesopotamians, the Egyptians enjoyed a varied diet.

Two Kingdoms

In addition to a stable food supply, Egypt's location offered another advantage. It had natural barriers that made it hard to invade Egypt. The desert to the west was too big and harsh to cross. To the north, the

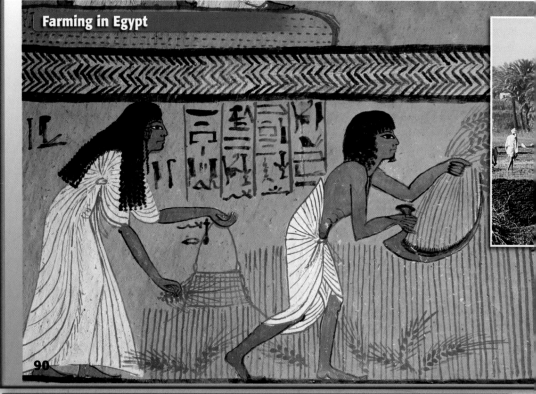

Farming in Egypt

90

Differentiating Instruction for Universal Access

English-Language Learners **Reaching Standards**

1. Draw the diagram shown here for students to see, omitting the answers. Have students copy it.

2. Instruct students to fill in the diagram. Below *The Nile provides life*, they should add at least two ways the Nile helped civilization grow. Below *Natural barriers provide protection*, they should add at least three different types of natural barriers that discouraged invaders.

3. Call on students to discuss their graphic organizers to ensure that they have been completed correctly. **LS Visual/Spatial**

HSS 6.2.1, 6.2.2; **HSS** Analysis Skills: HI 1, HI 2

Alternative Assessment Handbook, Rubric 13: Graphic Organizers

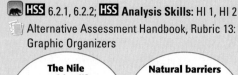

The Nile provides life.
- *fertile soil for crops*
- *water for people, animals, and irrigation*

Natural barriers provide protection.
- *deserts*
- *cataracts along the Nile*
- *bodies of water*

Growth of Ancient Egypt

Mediterranean Sea kept many enemies away. More desert lands and the Red Sea to the east provided protection against invasion as well. In addition, cataracts in the Nile made it difficult for invaders to sail in from the south.

Protected from invaders, the villages of Egypt grew. Wealthy farmers emerged as village leaders, and strong leaders gained control over several villages. By 3200 BC, the villages had grown, banded together, and developed into two kingdoms. One kingdom was called Lower Egypt, and the other was called Upper Egypt.

Each kingdom had its own capital city where its ruler was based. The capital of Lower Egypt was located in the northwest Nile Delta at a town called Pe. There, wearing the red crown that symbolized his authority, the king of Lower Egypt ruled.

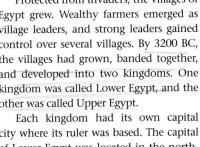

Farmers in ancient Egypt learned how to grow wheat and barley. This tomb painting shows a couple harvesting their crop (left). Farmers in Egypt still use the fertile lands along the Nile River to grow food (above).

The capital city of Upper Egypt was called Nekhen. It was located on the west bank of the Nile. In this southern kingdom, the king wore a cone-shaped white crown. For centuries, Egyptians referred to their country as the two lands.

READING CHECK **Summarizing** What attracted early settlers to the Nile Valley?

Kings Unify Egypt

According to tradition, around 3100 BC **Menes** (MEE-neez) rose to power in Upper Egypt. Some historians think Menes is a myth and that his accomplishments were really those of other ancient kings named Aha, Scorpion, or Narmer.

Menes wanted to unify Upper and Lower Egypt. His armies invaded and took control of Lower Egypt. He then married a princess from Lower Egypt to strengthen his control over the newly unified country. Menes wore both the white crown of Upper Egypt and the red crown of Lower Egypt to symbolize his leadership over the two kingdoms. Later, he combined the two crowns into a double crown.

Many historians consider Menes to be Egypt's first **pharaoh** (FEHR-oh), the title used by the rulers of Egypt. The title *pharaoh* means "great house." Menes also founded Egypt's first **dynasty**, or series of rulers from the same family.

Menes built a new capital city at the southern tip of the Nile Delta. The city was later named Memphis. For centuries, Memphis was the political and cultural center of Egypt. Many government offices were located there, and the city bustled with artistic activity.

The First Dynasty lasted for about 200 years. Rulers who came after Menes also wore the double crown to symbolize their rule over Upper and Lower Egypt.

FOCUS ON READING

What can you conclude about the evidence we have for Menes's accomplishments?

ANCIENT EGYPT **91**

Direct Teach

The pharaoh Menes combined the white crown of Upper Egypt and the red crown of Lower Egypt as a symbol of his rule of Egypt as one kingdom.

Main Idea

❸ Kings Unify Egypt

Strong kings unified all of Egypt.

Define What does the title *pharaoh* mean? *"great house"*

Explain Where did the First Dynasty extend its power? How did the First Dynasty end? *extended Egyptian territory southward along the Nile and into southwest Asia; challengers took over Egypt and established the Second Dynasty*

HSS 6.2.2; **HSS** Analysis Skills CS 1

Analyzing Visuals

Ask students what materials or construction techniques might have been used to make the double crown.

Review & Assess

Close

Call on volunteers to compose additional questions about the illustrations in this section.

Review

Online Quiz, Section 1

Assess

SE Section 1 Assessment

PASS: Section 1 Quiz

Alternative Assessment Handbook

Reteach/Classroom Intervention

California Standards Review Workbook

Interactive Reader and Study Guide, Section 1

Interactive Skills Tutor CD-ROM

Answers

Reading Check *Ruling over both kingdoms brought greater wealth, status, and power.*

92

They extended Egyptian territory southward along the Nile and into Southwest Asia. Eventually, however, rivals arose to challenge the First Dynasty for power. These challengers took over Egypt and established the Second Dynasty.

READING CHECK **Drawing Inferences** Why do you think Menes wanted to rule over both kingdoms?

SUMMARY AND PREVIEW As you have read, ancient Egypt began in the fertile Nile River Valley. Two kingdoms developed. The two kingdoms were later united under one ruler and Egyptian territory grew. In the next section you will learn how Egypt continued to grow and change under later rulers in a period known as the Old Kingdom.

Section 1 Assessment

go.hrw.com
Online Quiz
KEYWORD: SQ6 HP4

Reviewing Ideas, Terms, and People **HSS** 6.2.1, 6.2.2

1. **a. Identify** Where was Lower Egypt located?
   b. Analyze Why was the Nile Delta well suited for settlement?
   c. Predict How might the Nile's **cataracts** have both helped and hurt Egypt?
2. **a. Describe** What foods did the Egyptians eat?
   b. Analyze What role did the Nile play in supplying Egyptians with the foods they ate?
   c. Elaborate How did the desert on both sides of the Nile help ancient Egypt?
3. **a. Identify** Who was the first **pharaoh** of Egypt?
   b. Draw Conclusions Why did the pharaohs of the First Dynasty wear a double crown?

Critical Thinking

4. **Comparing and Contrasting** Draw a diagram like the one here. Use it to show the differences and similarities between the Nile River in Egypt and the Tigris and Euphrates rivers in Mesopotamia.

Egypt   Mesopotamia

FOCUS ON WRITING

5. **Thinking about Geography and Early History** In this section you read about Egypt's geography and early history. What could you put in your riddle about the geography and historical events that would be a clue to the answer?

92 CHAPTER 4

Section 1 Assessment Answers

1. **a.** along the Nile River, in northern Egypt
   b. possible answer—fertile land, abundant wildlife, near the sea
   c. provided protection against invasion but made travel on the river difficult
2. **a.** wheat, barley, fruits, vegetables, beef, lamb, fish, goose, and duck
   b. essential role—provided water for crops and animals, fish, homes for wild geese and ducks
   c. provided strong protection against invasion by enemy forces

3. **a.** Menes
   b. to symbolize the unification of Lower and Upper Egypt.
4. Nile—predictable flooding, gentler flooding pattern; Tigris and Euphrates—destructive, unpredictable flooding; Similarities—provided water, irrigation led to increased crop production, silt enriched the soil, civilizations arose on their banks
5. Answers will vary but should be accurate.

The Old Kingdom

If YOU were there...

You are a farmer in ancient Egypt. To you, the pharaoh is the god Horus as well as your ruler. You depend on his strength and wisdom. For part of the year, you are busy planting crops in your fields. But at other times of the year, you work for the pharaoh. You are helping to build a great tomb so that your pharaoh will be comfortable in the afterlife.

How do you feel about working for the pharaoh?

BUILDING BACKGROUND As in other ancient cultures, Egyptian society was based on a strict order of social classes. A small group of royalty and nobles ruled Egypt. They depended on the rest of the population to supply food, crafts, and labor. Few people questioned this arrangement of society.

Life in the Old Kingdom

The First and Second Dynasties ruled Egypt for about four centuries. Around 2700 BC, though, a new dynasty rose to power in Egypt. Called the Third Dynasty, its rule began a period in Egyptian history known as the Old Kingdom.

Early Pharaohs

The **Old Kingdom** was a period in Egyptian history that lasted for about 500 years, from about 2700 to 2200 BC. During this time, the Egyptians continued to develop their political system. The system they developed was based on the belief that the pharaoh, the ruler of Egypt, was both a king and a god.

The ancient Egyptians believed that Egypt belonged to the gods. They believed that the pharaoh had come to earth in order to manage Egypt for the rest of the gods. As a result, he had absolute power over all land and people in Egypt.

But the pharaoh's status as both king and god came with many responsibilities. People blamed him if crops did not grow well or if disease struck. They also demanded that the pharaoh make trade profitable and prevent wars.

What You Will Learn...

Main Ideas

1. Life in the Old Kingdom was influenced by pharaohs, roles in society, and trade.
2. Religion shaped Egyptian life.
3. The pyramids were built as huge tombs for Egyptian pharaohs.

The Big Idea

Egyptian government and religion were closely connected during the Old Kingdom.

Key Terms and People

Old Kingdom, *p. 93*
Khufu, *p. 94*
nobles, *p. 94*
afterlife, *p. 96*
mummies, *p. 96*
elite, *p. 97*
pyramids, *p. 98*
engineering, *p. 98*

HSS 6.2.3 Understand the relationship between religion and the social and political order in Mesopotamia and Egypt.

Preteach

Bellringer

If YOU were there . . . Use the **Daily Bellringer Transparency** to help students answer the question.

Daily Bellringer Transparency, Section 2

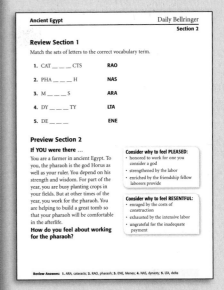

Academic Vocabulary

Review with students the high-use academic terms in this section.

acquire to get (p. 94)

method a way of doing something (p. 96)

CRF: Vocabulary Builder Activity, Section 2

Teach the Big Idea: Master the Standards

Standards Proficiency

The Old Kingdom **HSS** 6.2.3; **HSS** Analysis Skills: CS 1, HI 1

1. **Teach** Ask students the Main Idea questions to teach this section.

2. **Apply** Ask students to imagine that they have been asked by the government of Egypt to design a stamp commemorating the 4,700th anniversary of the Old Kingdom's beginning. Organize the class into three groups—one for each subsection. Then have each student choose a subtopic within that subsection and draw a stamp to illustrate it. **LS** Visual/Spatial

3. **Review** Display the stamps and call on volunteers to describe their illustrations.

4. **Practice/Homework** Have students write summaries of how the topics they illustrated were related to other aspects of the Old Kingdom. **LS** Verbal/Linguistic

   Alternative Assessment Handbook, Rubric 42: Writing to Inform

Standards Focus

HSS 6.2.3

Means: Explain how Egypt's religion and social and political order were related.

Matters: Religion was so important to the ancient Egyptians that it influenced every aspect of their lives.

Main Idea

❶ Life in the Old Kingdom

Life in the Old Kingdom was influenced by pharaohs, roles in society, and trade.

Recall How long did the Old Kingdom last? *about 500 years, from 2700 to 2200 BC*

Draw Conclusions What responsibilities did the pharaoh have that balanced his high status? *according to traditional belief, make crops grow, keep people healthy, make trade profitable, prevent wars*

Make Judgments What may be some advantages and disadvantages of such a large segment of the population being farmers, servants, and slaves? *possible answers—advantages: plenty of food and labor; disadvantages: potential for rebellion*

- 📄 **CRF:** Biography Activity: Khufu
- 📄 **CRF:** History and Geography Activity: Trade on the Nile
- 🐘 **HSS** 6.2.3; **HSS** Analysis Skills: HI 1, HI 5

Primary Source

A Father's Career Advice There is an ancient description of what an Egyptian scribe named Duaf tells his son Khety while taking Khety to be trained as a scribe. Duaf wrote, "I will make you love writing more than your mother, I will show its beauties to you; Now, it is greater than any trade, There is not one like it in the land." Duaf goes on to describe the miseries of the metalworker, carpenter, jeweler, and barber. Ask: Do you think Duaf exaggerated the hardships of the other trades? Why or why not? *yes, to make being a scribe sound better*

Answers

Analyzing Visuals *nobles and priests*
Reading Check *pharaoh at the top; nobles; scribes and craftspeople; farmers, servants, and slaves below*

Egyptian Society

Pharaoh
The pharaoh ruled Egypt as a god.

Nobles
Officials and priests helped run the government and temples.

Scribes and Craftspeople
Scribes and craftspeople wrote and produced goods.

Farmers, Servants, and Slaves
Most Egyptians were farmers, servants, or slaves.

ANALYSIS SKILL ANALYZING VISUALS
Which group helped run the government and temples?

The most famous pharaoh of the Old Kingdom was **Khufu** (KOO-foo), who ruled in the 2500s BC. Even though he is famous, we know relatively little about Khufu's life. Egyptian legend says that he was cruel, but historical records tell us that the people who worked for him were well fed. Khufu is best known for the monuments that were built to him.

Society and Trade

ACADEMIC VOCABULARY
acquire (uh-KWYR) to get

By the end of the Old Kingdom, Egypt had about 2 million people. As the population grew, social classes appeared. The Egyptians believed that a well-ordered society would keep their kingdom strong.

At the top of Egyptian society was the pharaoh. Just below him were the upper classes, which included priests and key government officials. Many of these priests and officials were **nobles**, or people from rich and powerful families.

Next in society was the middle class. It included lesser government officials, scribes, and a few rich craftspeople.

The people in Egypt's lower class, more than 80 percent of the population, were mostly farmers. During flood season, when they could not work in the fields, farmers worked on the pharaoh's building projects. Servants and slaves also worked hard.

As society developed during the Old Kingdom, Egypt traded with some of its neighbors. Traders traveled south along the Nile to Nubia to **acquire** gold, copper, ivory, slaves, and stone for building. Trade with Syria provided Egypt with wood for building and for fire.

Egyptian society grew more complex during this time. It continued to be organized, disciplined, and highly religious.

READING CHECK Generalizing How was society structured in the Old Kingdom?

Critical Thinking: Evaluating

Standards Proficiency

Being Pharaoh 🐘 **HSS** 6.2.3; **HSS** Analysis Skills: HI 1, HI 2

1. Ask students what advantages pharaohs seemed to have in Egyptian society. Write responses for students to see. *possible responses—believed to be a god, wealth and easy life, monuments honored him*

2. Then ask what disadvantages there were to being a pharaoh. Write these next to the advantages. *possible answers—blamed for natural disasters and invasions*

3. Organize students into pairs to discuss with their partners whether or not they would want to be a pharaoh and give specific reasons for their responses.

4. Call on volunteers to share their reasoning with the class.
   📋 **LS** Interpersonal, Logical/Mathematical

📄 Alternative Assessment Handbook, Rubric 11: Discussions

Religion and Egyptian Life

Worshipping the gods was a part of daily life in Egypt. But the Egyptian focus on religion extended beyond people's lives. Many customs focused on what happened after people died.

The Gods of Egypt

The Egyptians practiced polytheism. Before the First Dynasty, each village worshipped its own gods. During the Old Kingdom, however, Egyptian officials expected everyone to worship the same gods, though how they worshipped the gods might differ from place to place.

The Egyptians built temples to the gods all over the kingdom. Temples collected payments from both worshippers and the government. These payments allowed the temples to grow more influential.

Over time, certain cities became centers for the worship of certain gods. In the city of Memphis, for example, people prayed to Ptah, the creator of the world.

The Egyptians worshipped many gods besides Ptah. They had gods for nearly everything, including the sun, the sky, and the earth. Many gods mixed human and animal forms. For example, Anubis, the god of the dead, had a human body but a jackal's head. Other major gods included

- Re, or Amon-Re, the sun god
- Osiris, the god of the underworld
- Isis, the goddess of magic
- Horus, a sky god, god of the pharaohs
- Thoth, the god of wisdom
- Geb, the earth god

Egyptian families also worshipped household gods at shrines in their homes.

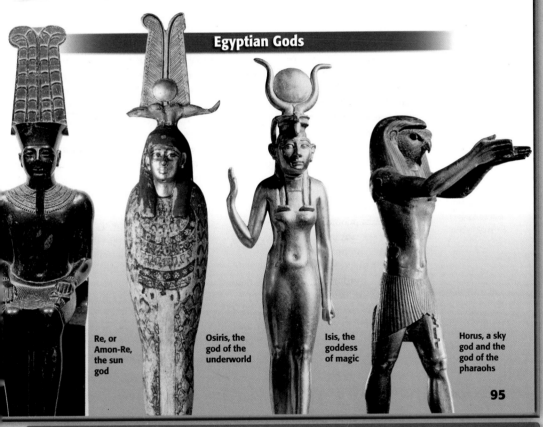

Egyptian Gods

Re, or Amon-Re, the sun god

Osiris, the god of the underworld

Isis, the goddess of magic

Horus, a sky god and the god of the pharaohs

95

❷ Religion and Egyptian Life

Religion shaped Egyptian life.

Describe How did the Egyptians see the afterlife? *as an ideal world where all the people are young and healthy*

Contrast How was the *ka* different from the body? *The ka was not a physical entity, but rather the person's life force. It left the physical body at death.*

Predict How would you expect a pharaoh to be drawn on the walls of his tomb? *possible answer—He would be drawn as young, powerful, happy, and doing the things he enjoyed while alive.*

 HSS 6.2.3

Info to Know

Ancient Absences Builders of pyramids were closely supervised. In Deir el-Medina—a village built especially for tomb builders—records show that scribes kept track of the workers' attendance and their reasons for being absent. Those excuses included an eye ailment, having to embalm the laborer's mother, and having to take a donkey to the veterinarian.

Mummies and the Afterlife

Osiris, god of the underworld, waited to judge the dead person's soul.

The god Anubis weighed the dead person's heart against the feather of truth. If they weighed the same amount, the person was allowed into the underworld.

Emphasis on the Afterlife

Much of Egyptian religion focused on the **afterlife**, or life after death. The Egyptians believed that the afterlife was a happy place. Paintings from Egyptian tombs show the afterlife as an ideal world where all the people are young and healthy.

The Egyptian belief in the afterlife stemmed from their idea of *ka* (KAH), or a person's life force. When a person died, his or her *ka* left the body and became a spirit. The *ka* remained linked to the body and could not leave its burial site. However, it had all the same needs that the person had when he or she was living. It needed to eat, sleep, and be entertained.

To fulfill the *ka*'s needs, people filled tombs with objects for the afterlife. These objects included furniture, clothing, tools, jewelry, and weapons. Relatives of the dead were expected to bring food and beverages to their loved ones' tombs so the *ka* would not be hungry or thirsty.

ACADEMIC VOCABULARY

method a way of doing something

Burial Practices

Egyptian ideas about the afterlife shaped their burial practices. The Egyptians believed that a body had to be prepared for the afterlife before it could be placed in a tomb. This meant the body had to be preserved. If the body decayed, its spirit could not recognize it. That would break the link between the body and spirit. The *ka* would then be unable to receive the food and drink it needed.

To keep the *ka* from suffering, the Egyptians developed a **method** called embalming to preserve bodies and keep them from decaying. The Egyptians preserved bodies as **mummies**, specially treated bodies wrapped in cloth. Embalming preserves a dead body for many, many years. A body that was not embalmed would decay quickly in a tomb.

Embalming was a complex process that took several weeks to complete. In the first step, embalmers cut open the body

96 CHAPTER 4

Collaborative Learning

Standards Proficiency

Egyptian Game Show HSS 6.2.3

Prep and Research Required

1. Prepare a series of 20 to 30 questions on Egyptian gods, beliefs about the afterlife, and burial practices.

2. Organize students into two teams. Each team may want to assign one of the three subtopics to each team member. Provide basic research materials, and challenge students to learn as much as they can about their topics in approximately 30 minutes.

3. Tell students they will now play a game show on the topics they have been reading about.

4. Conduct the game show, awarding a point for each correct answer. Award a prize to the winning team. **LS Interpersonal, Kinesthetic**

Alternative Assessment Handbook, Rubric 14: Group Activity

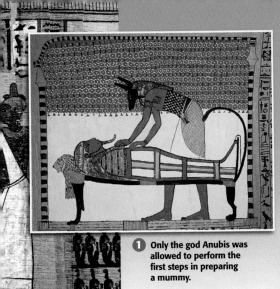

1 Only the god Anubis was allowed to perform the first steps in preparing a mummy.

2 The body's organs were preserved in special jars and kept next to the mummy.

3 The body was preserved as a mummy and kept in a case called a sarcophagus.

and removed all the organs except for the heart. The removed organs were stored in special jars. Next, embalmers used a special substance to dry out the body and later applied some special oils. The embalmers then wrapped the dried-out body with linen cloths and bandages, often placing special charms inside the cloth wrappings. Wrapping the body was the last step in the mummy-making process. Once it was completely wrapped, a mummy was placed in a coffin.

Only royalty and other members of Egypt's **elite** (AY-leet), or people of wealth and power, could afford to have mummies made. Peasant families did not need the process, however. They buried their dead in shallow graves at the edge of the desert. The hot, dry sand of the desert preserved the bodies naturally.

READING CHECK **Analyzing** How did religious beliefs affect Egyptian burial practices?

ANALYSIS SKILL **ANALYZING VISUALS**
How did gods participate in the afterlife?

ANCIENT EGYPT **97**

Direct Teach

Main Idea

❷ Religion and Egyptian Life

Religion shaped Egyptian life.

Define What is a mummy? *a preserved body that is wrapped in cloth*

Analyze Why did the Egyptians believe it was important to preserve the physical body? *If the body decayed, the* ka *would not be able to receive the food and drink it needed.*

Contrast How did burial practices vary among Egypt's social classes? *The elite were mummified, while peasants were buried in shallow graves at the edge of the desert, where the bodies were preserved naturally.*

Activity **Designing a Sarcophagus** Ask students to imagine that they have been hired to design a sarcophagus for a pharaoh's adult son or daughter. How might the sarcophagus be decorated? Have students examine the image of the sarcophagus on this page. Have students prepare their sketches and have volunteers explain their designs to the class.

HSS 6.2.3

Social Studies Skill: Identifying Central Issues   **Standards Proficiency**

Museum Exhibit **HSS** 6.2.3; **HSS** Analysis: HR 1, HI 2   **Prep Required**

Materials: art supplies, photos, or illustrations showing Egyptian burial artifacts and tombs

1. Organize students into small groups.

2. Have students imagine they are museum curators planning an exhibit on Egyptian burial practices. Have them create a list of questions their exhibit will answer.

3. Have each group plan and create its exhibit, making sure the exhibit answers all of the questions. It should contain drawings or photographs of burial artifacts. Encourage the groups to be creative and rely mainly on graphics, keeping text to a minimum.

4. Display the exhibits for the class to view.

LS **Interpersonal, Visual/Spatial**

Alternative Assessment Handbook, Rubrics 3: Artwork; and 14: Group Activity

Answers

Analyzing Visuals *judged souls, allowed persons into the underworld, performed first steps in preparing a mummy*

Reading Check *Believing that the spirit remained linked to the body, Egyptians developed mummification and filled tombs with food and other items the spirit may need in the afterlife.*

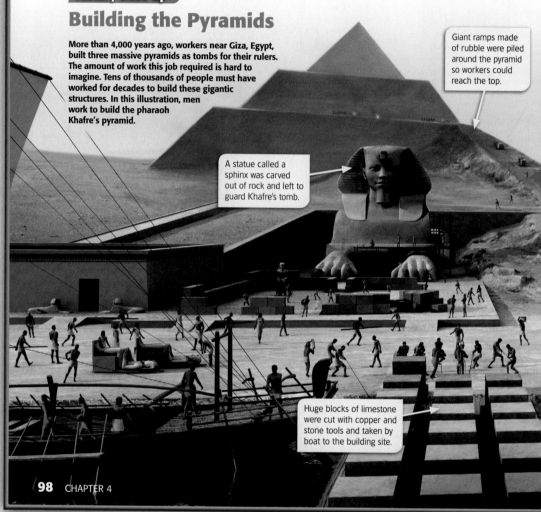

Direct Teach

❸ The Pyramids

The pyramids were built as huge tombs for Egyptian pharaohs.

Recall How many limestone blocks did the Great Pyramid require? *more than 2 million*

Describe What is the shape of a pyramid? *four triangle-shaped walls that meet in a point on top*

Predict How would the invention of large animal-drawn wheeled vehicles have affected pyramid construction? *possible answer—made transporting the blocks of stone much easier, cutting labor needs and construction time considerably*

HSS 6.2.3; **HSS** Analysis Skills: HI 2, HI 4

Did You Know . . .

In 1954, archaeologists made an astonishing discovery. Buried at the base of the Great Pyramid was a 144-foot-long wooden boat. The boat may have carried Khufu's body across the Nile to his tomb. Or, it may have been placed there to symbolically carry Khufu into the afterlife.

Linking to Today

Pyramids and Pollution Even though the pyramids have stood for thousands of years, they are not safe from harm. In fact, the stone shows signs of deterioration. Pollution from nearby Cairo and damage done by tourists may be to blame for the problems.

History Close-up

The Great Sphinx has undergone many restorations, including one by pharaoh Tuthmosis IV in about 1400 BC. The pharaoh dreamed that the Sphinx asked him to clear the sand from around it in return for giving the pharaoh power over both Upper and Lower Egypt.

The Pyramids

The Egyptians believed that burial sites, especially royal tombs, were very important. As a result, they built spectacular monuments in which to bury their rulers. The most spectacular of all were the **pyramids**— huge, stone tombs with four triangle-shaped sides that met in a point on top.

The Egyptians first built pyramids during the Old Kingdom. Some of the largest pyramids ever constructed were built during this time. Many of these huge pyramids are still standing. The largest is the Great Pyramid of Khufu near the town of Giza. It covers more than 13 acres at its base and stands 481 feet high. This single pyramid took thousands of workers and more than 2 million limestone blocks to build. Like all the pyramids, it is an amazing reminder of Egyptian **engineering**, the application of scientific knowledge for practical purposes.

History Close-up

Building the Pyramids

More than 4,000 years ago, workers near Giza, Egypt, built three massive pyramids as tombs for their rulers. The amount of work this job required is hard to imagine. Tens of thousands of people must have worked for decades to build these gigantic structures. In this illustration, men work to build the pharaoh Khafre's pyramid.

Giant ramps made of rubble were piled around the pyramid so workers could reach the top.

A statue called a sphinx was carved out of rock and left to guard Khafre's tomb.

Huge blocks of limestone were cut with copper and stone tools and taken by boat to the building site.

Cross-Discipline Activity: Math

Exceeding Standards

The Geometry of Pyramids

Research Required

Materials: heavy paper or cardboard, glue or tape

1. Explain to students that the Egyptians would not have been able to build the pyramids without a clear understanding of geometry. To construct a pyramid, each side had to slope upward and inward at exactly the same angle. Builders checked their work often, because even a tiny error in the early stages could mean a big error later.

2. Have students use the Internet and other resources to conduct research on the geometry of pyramid building.

3. Have students build and label models to demonstrate their findings.
LS Logical/Mathematical, Verbal/Linguistic
HSS 6.2.3; **HSS** Analysis Skill HI 4
Alternative Assessment Handbook, Rubric 30: Research

Building the Pyramids

The earliest pyramids did not have the smooth sides we usually imagine when we think of pyramids. The Egyptians began building the smooth-sided pyramids we usually see around 2700 BC. The steps of these pyramids were filled and covered with limestone. The burial chamber was deep inside the pyramid. After the pharaoh's burial, workers sealed the passages to this room with large blocks.

Historians are not sure how the Egyptians built the pyramids. What is certain is that such enormous projects required a huge labor force. As many as 100,000 workers may have been needed to build a single pyramid. The government kept records and paid the peasants for their work.

Inside the Great Pyramid, tunnels led to the pharaoh's burial chamber, which was sealed off with rocks.

Teams of workers dragged the stones on wooden sleds to the pyramid.

ANALYSIS SKILL **ANALYZING VISUALS**

How did workers get their stone blocks to the pyramids?

ANCIENT EGYPT **99**

go.hrw.com

Main Idea

❸ The Pyramids

The pyramids were built as huge tombs for Egyptian pharaohs.

Describe How large was the Great Pyramid's base? *more than 13 acres*

Explain How did pyramid design change? *Stepped pyramids evolved into smooth-sided ones when the steps were filled in and the surfaces covered with smooth limestone.*

Analyze Why were the tunnels that led to the pharaoh's burial chamber sealed after his death? *to protect it from invaders or robbers*

CRF: Biography: Khufu

HSS 6.2.3

Online Resources

Online Resources:
KEYWORD: SQ6 WH4
ACTIVITY: Explore the Pyramids

Connect to Economics

Labor Practices Egyptian rulers knew that laborers who were treated humanely were more reliable. For example, records reveal that some laborers worked four-hour shifts separated by a lunch break. After eight days of work, laborers had two days off for holidays and festivals. Workers' graffiti also tell us that the men took pride in their accomplishments, with boasts that a certain group of workers was the best.

Social Studies Skills: Developing Group Interaction Skills

Building a Pyramid

Standards **Proficiency**

1. Ask students to imagine that they are members of a planning committee responsible for building the Great Pyramid.

2. First, have the class elect a lead contractor from a pool of students who campaign for the job. Then, the leader names committee chairpersons for the various components of the task ahead—design, stonecutting, getting provisions for workers, and so on.

3. Ask each committee chair to recruit committee members. Then each committee

meets to brainstorm the tasks, challenges, and possible solutions that lie ahead.

4. Call on each committee chair to report on his or her committee's conclusions. Discuss any problems the group members encountered while working together.

HSS 6.2.3; **HSS** Analysis Skills: HR 1, HI 2, HI 3

Alternative Assessment Handbook, Rubric 14: Group Activity

Answers

Analyzing Visuals *brought to the building site on boats, transported to the pyramids on wooden sleds, hauled up the pyramid on ramps*

Direct Teach

Main Idea

❸ The Pyramids

The pyramids were built as huge tombs for Egyptian pharaohs.

Explain Why did the Egyptians want the pyramids to be spectacular? *because they believed their own fate in the afterlife depended on the pharaoh's afterlife*

Make Judgments Do you think the Egyptians were gloomy and obsessed by death? Why or why not? *possible answer—No, they were more interested in living forever because they loved life.*

HSS 6.2.3 **HSS** Analysis Skills HI 5

Review & Assess

Close

Ask students to imagine what went through the workers' minds as they built the pyramids.

Review

Online Quiz, Section 2

Assess

SE Section 2 Assessment
PASS: Section 2 Quiz
Alternative Assessment Handbook

Reteach/Classroom Intervention

California Standards Review Workbook
Interactive Reader and Study Guide, Section 2
Interactive Skills Tutor CD-ROM

Answers

Reading Check *because the Egyptians believed that their own afterlife was linked to the eternal life of the pharaoh buried in the pyramid*

100

Wages for working on construction projects, however, were paid in goods such as grain instead of money.

For years, scholars have debated how the Egyptians moved the massive stones used to build the pyramids. Some believe that during the Nile's flooding, builders floated the stones downstream directly to the construction site. Most historians believe that workers used brick ramps and strong sleds to drag the stones up the pyramid once they reached the site.

Significance of the Pyramids

Burial in a pyramid demonstrated a pharaoh's importance. The size and shape of the pyramid were symbolic. Pointing to the skies, the pyramid symbolized the pharaoh's journey to the afterlife. The Egyptians wanted the pyramids to be spectacular because they believed that the pharaoh, as their link to the gods, controlled everyone's afterlife. Making the pharaoh's spirit happy was a way of ensuring one's own happy afterlife.

To ensure that pharaohs remained safe after their deaths, the Egyptians sometimes wrote magical spells and hymns on the pharaohs' tombs. Together, these spells and hymns are called Pyramid Texts. The first such text, addressed to Re, was carved into the pyramid of King Unas (OO-nuhs), a pharaoh of the Old Kingdom:

> "Re, this Unas comes to you,
> A spirit indestructible . . .
> Your son comes to you, this Unas . . .
> May you cross the sky united in the dark,
> May you rise in lightland, [where] you shine!"
> *–from Pyramid Text, Utterance 217*

The builders of Unas's pyramid wanted the god to look after their leader's spirit. Even after death, their pharaoh was important to them.

READING CHECK Identifying Points of View
Why were pyramids important to the ancient Egyptians?

SUMMARY AND PREVIEW During the Old Kingdom, new political and social orders were created in Egypt. Religion was important, and many pyramids were built for the pharaohs. In Section 3 you will learn about life in later periods, the Middle and New Kingdoms.

---

go.hrw.com
Online Quiz
KEYWORD: SQ6 HP4

Section 2 Assessment

Reviewing Ideas, Terms, and People **HSS** 6.2.3

1. **a. Define** To what does the phrase **Old Kingdom** refer?
   b. Analyze Why was the pharaoh's authority never questioned?
   c. Elaborate Why do you think pharaohs might have wanted the support of **nobles**?
2. **a. Define** What did Egyptians mean by the **afterlife**?
   b. Analyze Why was embalming important to Egyptians?
3. **a. Describe** What is **engineering**?
   b. Elaborate What does the building of the **pyramids** tell us about Egyptian society?

Critical Thinking

4. **Categorizing** Draw a pyramid like the one here. In each level, write a sentence about the corresponding social class.

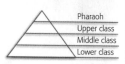
Pharaoh
Upper class
Middle class
Lower class

FOCUS ON WRITING

5. **Noting Characteristics of the Old Kingdom** The Old Kingdom has special characteristics of society and religion. Write down details about any of those characteristics you might want to include in your riddle.

100 CHAPTER 4

Section 2 Assessment Answers

1. **a.** the 500-year period in Egyptian history from 2700 to 2200 BC
   b. The Egyptians thought of him as a god.
   c. possible answer—needed help running the government, may have needed supporters if problems such as disease or invasion occurred
2. **a.** life after death
   b. If a body was allowed to decay, the spirit would not recognize it in the afterlife.

3. **a.** the application of scientific knowledge for practical purposes
   b. possible answer—that Egyptian society was capable of the complex organization and discipline required to build the pyramids
4. Answers will vary but should reflect text information.
5. Answers will vary but should reflect text information.

The Middle and New Kingdoms

If YOU were there...

You are a servant to Hatshepsut, the ruler of Egypt. You admire her, but some people think a woman should not rule. She calls herself king and dresses like a pharaoh—even wearing a fake beard. That was your idea! But you want to help more.

What could Hatshepsut do to show her authority?

BUILDING BACKGROUND The power of the pharaohs expanded during the Old Kingdom. Society was orderly, based on great differences between social classes. But rulers and dynasties changed, and Egypt changed with them. In time, these changes led to new eras in Egyptian history, eras called the Middle and New Kingdoms.

The Middle Kingdom

At the end of the Old Kingdom, the wealth and power of the pharaohs declined. Building and maintaining pyramids cost a lot of money. Pharaohs could not collect enough taxes to keep up with their expenses. At the same time, ambitious nobles used their government positions to take power from pharaohs.

In time, nobles gained enough power to challenge the pharaohs. By about 2200 BC the Old Kingdom had fallen. For the next 160 years, local nobles ruled much of Egypt. The kingdom had no central ruler.

Time Line

QUICK FACTS

Periods of Egyptian History

3000 BC	2000 BC	1000 BC
c. 2700–2200 BC Old Kingdom	c. 2050–1750 BC Middle Kingdom	c. 1550–1050 BC New Kingdom

---

What You Will Learn...

Main Ideas

1. The Middle Kingdom was a period of stable government between periods of disorder.
2. The New Kingdom was the peak of Egyptian trade and military power, but their greatness did not last.
3. Work and daily life were different among Egypt's social classes.

The Big Idea

During the Middle and New Kingdoms, order and greatness were restored in Egypt.

Key Terms and People

Middle Kingdom, p. 102
New Kingdom, p. 102
trade routes, p. 102
Queen Hatshepsut, p. 103
Ramses the Great, p. 103

HSS 6.2.6 Describe the role of Egyptian trade in the eastern Mediterranean and Nile Valley.

6.2.7 Understand the significance of Queen Hatshepsut and Ramses the Great.

ANCIENT EGYPT **101**

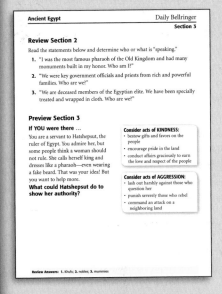

Main Idea

❶ The Middle Kingdom

The Middle Kingdom was a period of stable government between periods of disorder.

Identify Where were the Hyksos from? *southwest Asia*

Analyze What were two reasons the pharaohs' power declined at the end of the Old Kingdom? *They did not collect enough taxes to cover their expenses, and ambitious nobles took power from the pharaohs.*

Evaluate What may the Hyksos conquest indicate about Egypt's level of technological advance? *Although the Egyptians had built pyramids, they may not have had chariots or advanced weapons.*

 Quick Facts Transparency: Time Line: Periods of Egyptian History

About the Illustration

This illustration of Hatshepsut is an artist's conception based on available sources. However, historians are uncertain exactly what Hatshepsut looked like.

Info to Know

A Mysterious Death Thutmose III became pharaoh after Hatshepsut's death. The sources are unclear about how she died. According to some historians, Thutmose had her murdered so he could succeed her as pharaoh.

Answers

Biography *possible answer—to make her role as pharaoh more acceptable to the Egyptian people*

Reading Check *the Hyksos invasion and Ahmose's rise to power*

102

Finally, around 2050 BC, a powerful pharaoh defeated his rivals, and once again all of Egypt was united. His rule began the **Middle Kingdom**, a period of order and stability which lasted to about 1750 BC. Toward the end of the Middle Kingdom, however, Egypt began to fall into disorder once more.

Around 1750 BC, a group from Southwest Asia called the Hyksos (HIK-sohs) invaded. They used horses, chariots, and advanced weapons to conquer Lower Egypt. The Hyksos ruled the region as pharaohs for 200 years.

The Egyptians eventually fought back, however. In the mid-1500s BC, Ahmose (AHM-ohs) of Thebes declared himself king and drove the Hyksos out of Egypt. Ahmose then ruled all of Egypt.

READING CHECK **Summarizing** What caused the end of the Middle Kingdom?

BIOGRAPHY

Queen Hatshepsut
Ruled c. 1503–1482 BC

Hatshepsut was married to the pharaoh Thutmose II, her half-brother. He died young, leaving the throne to Thutmose III, his son by another woman. Because Thutmose III was still very young, Hatshepsut took over power. Many people did not think women should rule, but Hatshepsut dressed as a man and called herself king. After she died, her stepson took back power and vandalized all the monuments she had built.

Identifying Cause and Effect What do you think caused Hatshepsut to dress like a man?

102

The New Kingdom

Ahmose's rise to power marked the beginning of Egypt's eighteenth dynasty. More importantly, it was the beginning of the **New Kingdom**, the period during which Egypt reached the height of its power and glory. During the New Kingdom, which lasted from about 1550 to 1050 BC, conquest and trade brought wealth to the pharaohs.

Building an Empire

After battling the Hyksos, Egypt's leaders feared future invasions. To prevent such invasions from occurring, they decided to take control of all possible invasion routes into the kingdom. In the process, these leaders turned Egypt into an empire.

Egypt's first target was the homeland of the Hyksos. After taking over that area, the army continued north and conquered Syria. As you can see from the map, Egypt took over the entire eastern shore of the Mediterranean and the kingdom of Kush, south of Egypt. By the 1400s BC, Egypt was the leading military power in the region. Its empire extended from the Euphrates River to southern Nubia.

Military conquests made Egypt rich. The kingdoms it conquered regularly sent treasures to their Egyptian conquerors. For example, the kingdom of Kush in Nubia south of Egypt sent annual payments of gold, leopard skins, and precious stones to the pharaohs. In addition, Assyrian, Babylonian, and Hittite kings sent expensive gifts to Egypt in an effort to maintain good relations.

Growth and Effects of Trade

Conquest also brought Egyptian traders into contact with more distant lands. Egypt's trade expanded along with its empire. Profitable **trade routes**, or paths followed by traders, developed. Many of

---

Critical Thinking: Interpreting Maps

Standards Proficiency

Trade Routes of Ancient Egypt HSS 6.2.6; HSS Analysis Skills: HI 1, HI 2

1. Have students examine the map on the opposite page.

2. Lead a class discussion about the following questions: Which of these routes do you think would have been easier to follow? Which would have been more difficult? Why might particular routes have developed? For example, why does the southernmost route loop southward from the Nile and then back north to Elephantine?

3. Ask students to describe the different routes and challenges traders would have faced

along them. Call on volunteers to propose how trade changed both the lives of the Egyptians and the people with whom they traded.

4. Complete the discussion by asking how the Egyptians may have used the products listed in the map legend.

LS Visual/Spatial, Auditory/Musical

Alternative Assessment Handbook, Rubrics 11: Discussions; and 21: Map Reading

the lands that Egypt took over also had valuable resources for trade. The Sinai Peninsula, for example, had large supplies of turquoise and copper.

One ruler who worked to increase Egyptian trade was **Queen Hatshepsut**. She sent Egyptian traders south to trade with the kingdom of Punt on the Red Sea and north to trade with people in Asia Minor and Greece.

Hatshepsut and later pharaohs used the money they gained from trade to support the arts and architecture. Hatshepsut especially is remembered for the many impressive monuments and temples built during her reign. The best known of these structures was a magnificent temple built for her near the city of Thebes.

Invasions of Egypt

Despite its great successes, Egypt's military might did not go unchallenged. In the 1200s BC the pharaoh Ramses (RAM-seez) II, or **Ramses the Great**, fought the Hittites, a group from Asia Minor. The two powers fought fiercely for years, but neither could defeat the other.

Egypt faced threats in other parts of its empire as well. To the west, a people known as the Tehenu invaded the Nile Delta. Ramses fought them off and built a series of forts to strengthen the western frontier. This proved to be a wise decision because the Tehenu invaded again a century later. Faced with Egypt's strengthened defenses, the Tehenu were defeated once again.

Soon after Ramses the Great died, invaders called the Sea Peoples sailed into Southwest Asia. Little is known about these people. Historians are not even sure who they were. All we know is that they were strong warriors who had crushed the Hittites and destroyed cities in Southwest Asia. Only after 50 years of fighting were the Egyptians able to turn them back.

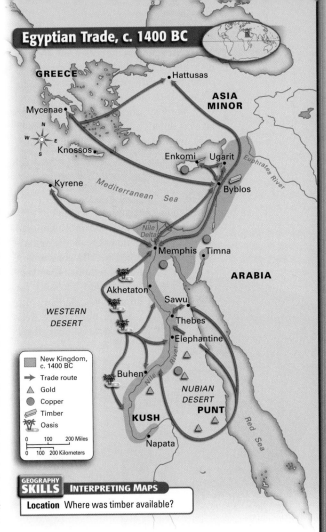

Egyptian Trade, c. 1400 BC

GREECE · Hattusas
ASIA MINOR
Mycenae
Knossos
Enkomi · Ugarit
Kyrene · *Mediterranean Sea* · Byblos
Euphrates River
Nile Delta
Memphis · Timna
ARABIA
Akhetaton
Sawu
WESTERN DESERT
Thebes
Elephantine
Buhen
NUBIAN DESERT · PUNT
Nile River
KUSH
Napata
Red Sea

New Kingdom, c. 1400 BC
→ Trade route
△ Gold
● Copper
Timber
Oasis

0   100   200 Miles
0   100   200 Kilometers

GEOGRAPHY SKILLS | **INTERPRETING MAPS**

Location Where was timber available?

Egypt survived, but its empire in Asia was gone. Shortly after the invasions of the Hittites and the Sea Peoples, the New Kingdom came to an end. Egypt fell into a period of violence and disorder. Egypt would never regain its power.

READING CHECK Identifying Cause and Effect
What caused the growth of trade in the New Kingdom?

ANCIENT EGYPT **103**

Direct Teach

Main Idea

❷ The New Kingdom

The New Kingdom was the peak of Egyptian trade and military power, but their greatness did not last.

Identify Who was Hatshepsut? *a female ruler who expanded trade and built great monuments during the New Kingdom*

Analyze What weakened the New Kingdom? *fighting on several fronts, including invasions of the Hittites and the Sea Peoples*

Make Judgments Why do you think leaders of the New Kingdom wanted to control all of the eastern Mediterranean shore? *possible answers—protection from invasion by peoples beyond the region, had valuable resources*

Map Transparency: Egyptian Trade, c. 1400 BC

HSS 6.2.6, 6.2.7; **HSS** Analysis Skills: HI 1, HI 2, HI 3

Interpreting Maps

Mediterranean Ports Ask students to list the Mediterranean ports visited by Egyptian traders. *Kyrene, Knossos, Mycenae, Ugarit, Enkomi, Byblos*

Critical Thinking: Summarizing

Reaching Standards

Two New Kingdom Rulers **HSS** 6.2.7; **HSS** Analysis Skills: HI 1

1. Draw the following chart for students to see, omitting the blue answers. Explain that both Hatshepsut and Ramses the Great faced challenges during their reigns, yet they also had many accomplishments.

2. Instruct students to complete the table by listing each leader's challenges and accomplishments. Call on volunteers to share their answers with the class.
LS Visual/Spatial, Verbal/Linguistic

	Queen Hatshepsut	**Ramses the Great**
Challenges	*husband died, leaving the throne to his son by another wife; objections to rule by a woman*	*had to fight the Hittites, faced invaders from the west*
Accomplishments	*took over as ruler when her husband died, staying in authority over many objections; increased trade; built many monuments and temples*	*kept the Hittites from conquering Egypt, built forts to strengthen western frontier, built monuments*

Answers

Interpreting Maps *near Byblos*
Reading Check *conquest, efforts by Hatshepsut*

103

Main Idea

❸ Work and Daily Life

Work and daily life were different among Egypt's social classes.

Describe What kinds of writing did scribes do? *kept records and accounts for the state, wrote and copied religious and literary texts*

Analyze Why did the pharaohs value talented architects? *Having well-designed pyramids and temples made the pharaoh powerful and, according to Egyptian religion, ensured a happy afterlife.*

Make Judgments Which of these jobs would you have preferred: scribe, artisan, artist, or architect? Why? *Answers will vary.*

📄 **CRF:** Biography Activity: Nefertiti

📄 **CRF:** Biography Activity: Akhenaton

Did You Know . . .

Some Egyptians slept on their backs, with their heads placed in wooden headrests to keep their hairstyles neat.

Teaching Tip

Ask students to explain the difference between an artist and an artisan. If they are uncertain, ask a student to look up the terms in a dictionary and report to the class.

Connect to Art

Queen Nefertiti The painted limestone statue of Nefertiti shown on this page is one of the most famous works of Egyptian art. Ask: Do you think this is exactly what Queen Nefertiti looked like? *probably not, because few Egyptian portraits are very realistic* Why is the statue usually shown in profile? *because the eye on one side is damaged*

Work and Daily Life

Although Egyptian dynasties rose and fell, daily life for Egyptians did not change very much. But as the population grew, society became even more complex.

A complex society requires people to take on different jobs. In Egypt, these jobs were usually passed on within families. At a young age, boys started to learn their future jobs from their fathers.

Scribes

Other than priests and government officials, no one in Egypt was more honored than scribes. As members of the middle class, scribes worked for the government and the temples. They kept records and accounts for the state. Scribes also wrote and copied religious and literary texts,

including stories and poems. Because they were so respected, scribes did not have to pay taxes, and many became wealthy.

Artisans, Artists, and Architects

Another group in society was made up of artisans whose jobs required advanced skills. Among the artisans who worked in Egypt were sculptors, builders, carpenters, jewelers, metalworkers, and leatherworkers. Most of Egypt's artisans worked for the government or for temples. They made statues, furniture, jewelry, pottery, shoes, and other items. Most artisans were paid fairly well for their work.

Architects and artists were also admired in Egypt. Architects designed the temples and royal tombs for which Egypt is famous. Talented architects could rise to become high government officials. Artists, often employed by the state or the

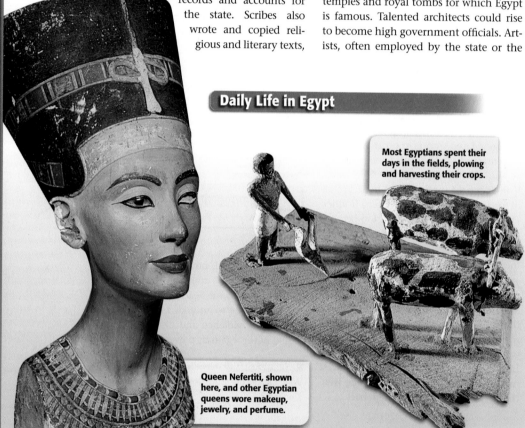

Daily Life in Egypt

Most Egyptians spent their days in the fields, plowing and harvesting their crops.

Queen Nefertiti, shown here, and other Egyptian queens wore makeup, jewelry, and perfume.

104

Differentiating Instruction for Universal Access

Learners Having Difficulty

Reaching Standards

Materials: art supplies

1. Lead a discussion comparing each group in Egyptian society with a similar group of people today. For example, compare the methods used by ancient Egyptian farmers to those used by farmers in the present-day United States.

2. Then have students draw Egyptians at work from at least three of the following groups: government officials, priests, scribes, artists and artisans, architects, merchants and

traders, soldiers, and farmers. Pictures should be as detailed as possible.

3. Have students display and explain their work.
LS Visual/Spatial

🐻 **HSS** 6.2.6, 6.2.7; **HSS** Analysis Skills: HI 1

📄 Alternative Assessment Handbook, Rubric 3, Artwork

temples, produced many different works. Artists often worked in the deep burial chambers of the pharaohs' tombs painting detailed pictures.

Merchants and Traders

Although trade was important to Egypt, only a small group of Egyptians became merchants and traders. Some traveled long distances to buy and sell goods. Merchants were usually accompanied by soldiers, scribes, and laborers on their travels.

Soldiers

After the wars of the Middle Kingdom, Egypt created a professional army. The military offered people a chance to rise in social status. Soldiers received land as payment and could also keep any treasure they captured in war. Those who excelled could be promoted to officer positions.

Farmers and Other Peasants

As in Old Kingdom society, Egyptian farmers and other peasants were toward the bottom of Egypt's social scale. These hardworking people made up the vast majority of Egypt's population.

Farmers grew crops to support their families. Farmers depended on the Nile's regular floods to grow their crops. They used wooden hoes or plows pulled by cows to prepare the land before the flood. After the floodwaters had drained away, farmers planted seeds. They grew crops such as wheat and barley. At the end of the growing season, farmers worked together to gather the harvest.

Farmers had to give crops to the pharaoh as taxes. These taxes were intended to pay the pharaoh for using the land. Under Egyptian law, the pharoah controlled all land in the kingdom.

Servants worked for Egypt's rulers and nobles and did many jobs, like preparing food.

This jar probably held perfume, a valuable trade item.

ANALYSIS SKILL **ANALYZING VISUALS**
What were some luxury goods used by Egypt's queens and rulers?

ANCIENT EGYPT **105**

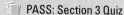
ACADEMIC VOCABULARY
contracts binding legal agreements

All peasants, including farmers, were also subject to special duty. Under Egyptian law, the pharaoh could demand at any time that people work on projects, such as building pyramids, mining gold, or fighting in the army. The government paid the workers in grain.

Slaves

The few slaves in Egyptian society were considered lower than farmers. Many slaves were convicted criminals or prisoners captured in war. They worked on farms, on building projects, in workshops, and in private households. Unlike most slaves in history, however, slaves in Egypt had some legal rights. Also, in some cases, they could earn their freedom.

Family Life in Egypt

Family life was important in Egyptian society. Most Egyptian families lived in their own homes. Sometimes unmarried female relatives lived with them, but men were expected to marry young so that they could start having children.

Most Egyptian women were devoted to their homes and their families. Some, however, had jobs outside the home. A few served as priestesses, and some worked as royal officials, administrators, and artisans. Unlike most ancient women, Egyptian women had a number of legal rights. They could own property, make **contracts**, and divorce their husbands. They could even keep their property after a divorce.

Children's lives were not as structured as adults' lives were. They played with toys such as dolls, tops, and clay animal figurines. Children also played ballgames and hunted. Most children, boys and girls, received some education. At school they learned morals, writing, math, and sports. At age 14 most boys left school to enter their father's profession. At that time, they took their place in Egypt's social structure.

READING CHECK **Categorizing** What types of jobs existed in ancient Egypt?

SUMMARY AND PREVIEW Pharaohs faced many challenges to their rule. After defeating the Hyksos, the kingdom expanded in land and wealth. People in Egypt worked at many different jobs. In the next section you will learn about Egyptian achievements.

Section 3 Assessment

go.hrw.com
Online Quiz
KEYWORD: SQ6 HP4

Reviewing Ideas, Terms, and People **HSS** 6.2.6,

1. **a. Define** What was the **Middle Kingdom**? 6.2.7
   b. Analyze How did Ahmose manage to become king of all Egypt?
2. **a. Identify** For what is **Ramses the Great** best known?
   b. Explain What did **Hatshepsut** do as pharaoh of Egypt?
3. **a. Identify** What job employed the most people in Egypt?
   b. Analyze What rights did Egyptian women have?
   c. Elaborate Why do you think scribes were so honored in Egyptian society?

Critical Thinking

4. **Categorizing** Draw a diagram like this one. Use it to identify two factors in the rise and fall of Egypt's empire during the New Kingdom.

Rise | Fall

FOCUS ON WRITING

5. **Developing Key Ideas from the Middle and New Kingdoms** Your riddle should contain some information about the later pharaohs and daily life in Egypt. Decide which key ideas you should include in your riddle and add them to your list.

106 CHAPTER 4

Section 3 Assessment Answers

1. **a.** a period of order and stability from 2050 to 1750 BC that began after a powerful pharaoh defeated his rivals
   b. by driving the Hyksos out of Egypt
2. **a.** protecting Egypt from the Tehenu
   b. increased trade, built many impressive temples and monuments
3. **a.** farming
   b. the ability to own property, make contracts, and divorce their husbands

c. possible answer—because they were involved in religious procedures, which were very important to the Egyptians, and because they portrayed history to later generations

4. Rise—Ahmose defeats the Hyksos, Egypt becomes an empire through military conquest, trade expands; Fall—invasions by various peoples

5. Students' key ideas will vary.

Ramses the Great

How could a ruler achieve fame that would last 3,000 years?

When did he live? late 1300s and early 1200s BC

Where did he live? As pharaoh, Ramses lived in a city he built on the Nile Delta. The city's name, Pi-Ramesse, means the "house of Ramses."

What did he do? From a young age, Ramses was trained as a ruler and a fighter. Made an army captain at age 10, he began military campaigns even before he became pharaoh. During his reign, Ramses greatly increased the size of his kingdom.

Why is he important? Many people consider Ramses the last great Egyptian pharaoh. He accomplished great things, but the pharaohs who followed could not maintain them. Both a great warrior and a great builder, he is known largely for the massive monuments he built. The temples at Karnak, Luxor, and Abu Simbel stand as 3,000-year-old symbols of the great pharaoh's power.

Drawing Conclusions Why do you think Ramses built monuments all over Egypt?

KEY IDEAS

Ramses had a poem praising him carved into the walls of five temples, including Karnak. One verse of the poem praises Ramses as a great warrior and the defender of Egypt.

" Gracious lord and bravest
　　king, savior–guard
Of Egypt in the battle, be our
　　ward;
Behold we stand alone, in the
　　hostile Hittite ring,
Save for us the breath of life,
Give deliverance from the
　　strife,
Oh! protect us Ramses Miamun!
Oh! save us, mighty king! "

–Pen-ta-ur, quoted in *The World's Story*, edited by Eva March Tappan

This copy of an ancient painting shows Ramses the Great on his chariot in battle against the Hittites.

ANCIENT EGYPT **107**

Reading Focus Question

Point out that Ramses was known not just for wartime accomplishments but also for peacetime achievements. Challenge students to name more recent leaders who have achieved lasting fame in both areas. *possible answers— George Washington, Winston Churchill*

Ramses the Warrior

At one point in a famous battle against the Hittites, Ramses and a few of his charioteers appeared to be doomed when they were completely surrounded by Hittite forces. Fortunately, reinforcements arrived in time to save them. Ramses was extremely proud of his stand against the larger Hittite force. A long poem was written about the battle, and scenes from it were carved into several temple walls.

Ramses the Pharaoh

The reign of Ramses II was the second-longest in Egyptian history. Ramses II was so popular that nine pharaohs of the 20th dynasty used his name.

Analyzing Visuals

Egyptian Warfare What does this painting tell about Egyptian warfare during the time of Ramses the Great? *that the Egyptians used bows and arrows and fought in two-wheeled chariots with spoked wheels drawn by two horses*

About the Illustration

This illustration of Ramses the Great is an artist's conception based on available sources. However, historians are uncertain exactly what Ramses the Great looked like.

Critical Thinking: Solving Problems

Saving Abu Simbel 🐘 **HSS** 6.2.5; **HSS** Analysis Skills: HI 2, HI 4

Exceeding Standards

Research Required

1. Explain to students that in the 1960s Egypt's leaders decided to control the Nile's annual flood by building the Aswan High Dam. Unfortunately, the lake created—Lake Nasser—would flood many Egyptian antiquities, including the temple of Ramses at Abu Simbel. Many organizations worked together to save the Abu Simbel temple.

2. Have students work in pairs to conduct research on this engineering feat and report on their findings.

3. Reports should explain some of the engineering problems that the project presented and how they were solved. Reports may take any form.

4. Challenge students to suggest alternative solutions to the engineering hurdles.
LS Interpersonal, Kinesthetic

📝 Alternative Assessment Handbook, Rubric 30: Research

Answers

Drawing Conclusions *possible answer—to impress possible invaders or rebels with his power, to make sure his fame lasted a long time*

Bellringer

If YOU were there . . . Use the **Daily Bellringer Transparency** to help students answer the question.

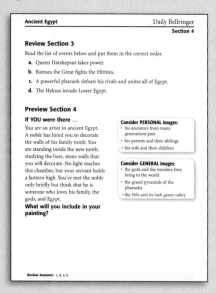

Daily Bellringer Transparency, Section 4

Ancient Egypt | Daily Bellringer
Section 4

Review Section 3

Read the list of events below and put them in the correct order.

a. Queen Hatshepsut takes power.

b. Ramses the Great fights the Hittites.

c. A powerful pharaoh defeats his rivals and unites all of Egypt.

d. The Hyksos invade Lower Egypt.

Preview Section 4

If YOU were there . . .

You are an artist in ancient Egypt. A noble has hired you to decorate the walls of his family tomb. You are standing inside the new tomb, studying the bare, stone walls that you will decorate. No light reaches this chamber, but your servant holds a lantern high. You've met the noble only briefly but think that he is someone who loves his family, the gods, and Egypt.

What will you include in your painting?

Consider PERSONAL images:
• his ancestors from many generations past
• his parents and their siblings
• his wife and their children

Consider GENERAL images:
• the gods and the wonders they bring to the world
• the grand pyramids of the pharaohs
• the Nile and its lush green valley

Review Answers: c, d, a, b

Building Vocabulary

Preteach or review the following term:

lavishly marked by excess or overabundance (p. 110)

CRF: Vocabulary Builder Activity, Section 4

Standards Focus

HSS 6.2.5

Means: Discuss the main features and characteristics of Egyptian art and architecture.

Matters: Egyptian art and architecture tell us about their achievements, how they lived, and what was important to them.

HSS 6.2.9

Means: Explain how the Egyptian writing system evolved.

Matters: Because the Egyptians had a written language, we have been able to learn a great deal about them.

SECTION 4

Egyptian Achievements

What You Will Learn...

Main Ideas

1. Egyptian writing used hieroglyphics.
2. Egypt's great temples were lavishly decorated.
3. Egyptian art filled tombs.

The Big Idea

The Egyptians made lasting achievements in writing, architecture, and art.

Key Terms and People

hieroglyphics, *p. 108*
papyrus, *p. 108*
Rosetta Stone, *p. 109*
sphinxes, *p. 110*
obelisk, *p. 110*
King Tutankhamen, *p. 113*

HSS 6.2.5 Discuss the main features of Egyptian art and architecture.

6.2.9 Trace the evolution of language and its written forms.

If YOU were there...

You are an artist in ancient Egypt. A noble has hired you to decorate the walls of his family tomb. You are standing inside the new tomb, studying the bare, stone walls that you will decorate. No light reaches this chamber, but your servant holds a lantern high. You've met the noble only briefly but think that he is someone who loves his family, the gods, and Egypt.

What will you include in your painting?

BUILDING BACKGROUND The Egyptians had a rich and varied history, but most people today remember them for their cultural achievements, such as their unique writing system. In addition, Egyptian art, including the tomb paintings mentioned above, is admired by millions of tourists in museums around the world.

Egyptian Writing

If you were reading a book and saw pictures of folded cloth, a leg, a star, a bird, and a man holding a stick, would you know what it meant? You would if you were an ancient Egyptian. In the Egyptian writing system, or **hieroglyphics** (hy-ruh-GLIH-fiks), those five symbols together meant "to teach." Egyptian hieroglyphics were one of the world's first writing systems.

Writing in Ancient Egypt

The earliest known examples of Egyptian writing are from around 3300 BC. These early Egyptian writings were carved in stone or on other hard material. Later, the Egyptians learned how to make **papyrus** (puh-PY-ruhs), a long-lasting, paper-like material made from reeds. The Egyptians made papyrus by pressing layers of reeds together and pounding them into sheets. These sheets were tough and durable, yet easy to roll into scrolls. Scribes wrote on papyrus using brushes and ink.

Teach the Big Idea: Master the Standards

Standards Proficiency

Egyptian Achievements **HSS** 6.2.5, 6.2.9; **HSS** Analysis Skills: CS 1, HI 1, HI 2, HI 3

1. **Teach** Ask students the Main Idea questions to teach this section.

2. **Apply** Ask students to imagine that they are Egyptians who contributed to the civilization's achievements. For example, a student may imagine herself as the inventor of papyrus or as a temple painter. Have students create book jackets for autobiographies of their chosen characters. The books' titles should be *My Life as ___* , filling in the chosen role. **LS Visual/Spatial**

3. **Review** Call on students to display and explain their book jackets until all the major achievements have been discussed.

4. **Practice/Homework** Have students write the introductory paragraphs for the blurbs inside their book jackets. **LS Verbal/Linguistic**

Egyptian Writing

Egyptian hieroglyphics used picture symbols to represent sounds.

	Sound	Meaning
	Imn	Amon
	Tut	Image
	Ankh	Living

Translation—"Living image of Amon"

	Heka	Ruler
	Iunu	Heliopolis
	Resy	Southern

Translation—"Ruler of Southern Heliopolis"

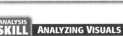

ANALYSIS SKILL **ANALYZING VISUALS**
What does the symbol for ruler look like?

The hieroglyphic writing system used more than 600 symbols, mostly pictures of objects. Each symbol represented one or more sounds in the Egyptian language. For example, a picture of an owl represented the same sound as our letter M.

Hieroglyphics could be written either horizontally or vertically. They could be written from right to left or from left to right. These options made hieroglyphics flexible to write but difficult to read. The only way to tell which way a text is written is to look at individual symbols.

The Rosetta Stone

Historians and archaeologists have known about hieroglyphics for centuries, but for a long time they didn't know how to read it. In fact, it was not until 1799 when a lucky discovery by a French soldier gave historians the key they needed to read ancient Egyptian writing.

That key was the **Rosetta Stone**, a huge, stone slab inscribed with hieroglyphics. In addition to the hieroglyphics, the Rosetta Stone had text in Greek and a later form of Egyptian. Because the text in all three languages was the same, scholars who knew Greek were able to figure out what the hieroglyphics said.

Egyptian Texts

Because papyrus did not decay in Egypt's dry climate, many Egyptian texts still survive. Historians today can read Egyptian government records, historical records, science texts, and medical manuals. In addition, many literary works have survived. Some, such as *The Book of the Dead*, tell about the afterlife. Others tell stories about gods and kings.

THE IMPACT TODAY

An object that helps solve a difficult mystery is sometimes called a Rosetta Stone.

READING CHECK **Comparing** How is our writing system similar to hieroglyphics?

Differentiating Instruction for Universal Access

English-Language Learners   Reaching Standards   Prep Required

1. Locate and display a photo of the Rosetta Stone. Point out the Egyptian hieroglyphics, the other form of Egyptian (called *demotic*), and the Greek text.

2. Then draw an outline of the Rosetta Stone for students to see, and divide it into three bands.

3. Select a sentence from the students' main native language. Print it in one area. Print the English translation in another area. Write the same English phrase in cursive in the third area. Use the drawing to demonstrate how the Rosetta Stone was deciphered.

4. Ask students to write a paragraph summarizing what they have learned.
LS Visual/Spatial, Verbal/Linguistic
HSS 6.2.9; **HSS** Analysis Skills: HI 5

Universal Access Resources
See page 83c for additional resources for differentiating instruction for universal access.

• **Direct Teach** •

Main Idea

1 Egyptian Writing

Egyptian writing used hieroglyphics.

Explain What did each symbol in the hieroglyphic system represent? *one or more sounds in the Egyptian language*

Analyze What were some advantages of using papyrus? *made of readily available materials, tough, durable, could be rolled into scrolls*

Make Judgments What would it have been like to use a language that could be written up or down, right to left, or left to right? *possible answer— It was more flexible than our system, and the Egyptians were used to it, so it probably caused no problems.*

CRF: Literature: The Egyptian Cinderella

CRF: Primary Source: Selections from the Amarna Letters

HSS 6.2.9; **HSS** Analysis Skills: HR 1, HI 1

---

go.hrw.com
Online Resources

KEYWORD: SQ6 WH4
ACTIVITY: A Hieroglyphic Tale

Connect to Math

The Eye of Horus Hieroglyphic symbols also stood for mathematical concepts. For example, the parts of a drawing of an eye, called the Eye of Horus, stand for various fractions. The symbol comes from an Egyptian myth in which the god Horus suffered an injury to his left eye. The god Thoth healed it, and a drawing of the eye became a powerful symbol. Challenge students to research the Eye of Horus as a mathematical symbol and to explain it to the class.

Answers

Analyzing Visuals *possible answer— a shepherd's crook, symbolizing the ruler as a shepherd of his people*

Reading Check *Letters stand for sounds, just as symbols in hieroglyphics stand for sounds.*

109

❷ Egypt's Great Temples

Egypt's great temples were lavishly decorated.

Identify What is a sphinx? *imaginary creature with the body of a lion and the head of another animal or a human*

Recall What are the two types of large structures created by the Egyptian architects? *pyramids and temples*

Analyze Why do you think builders placed obelisks at the gates of temples? *possible answer—because they pointed to the sky, leading the way to the afterlife*

🐻 **HSS** 6.2.5 **HSS** Analysis Skills HI 1, HI 2

Info to Know

Obelisks Most obelisks were carved from red granite. Their pyramid-shaped tops were usually sheathed in electrum, an alloy of gold and silver. Some obelisks weighed more than 100 tons. Because some obelisks have been taken out of Egypt, genuine Egyptian obelisks now stand in London, Rome, and New York City.

Linking to Today

Tourism in Egypt Revenue from tourism accounts for about 25 percent of Egypt's foreign exchange income. The pyramids and temples are major attractions in Egypt. More than 5 million tourists visit Egypt each year.

Answers

Analyzing Visuals *columns covered by paintings and hieroglyphics, high windows*

Reading Check *sphinxes, obelisks, statues, a sanctuary, large hallway filled with stone columns, paintings and hieroglyphic carvings*

110

Egypt's Great Temples

In addition to their writing system, the Egyptians are famous today for their magnificent architecture. You have already read about the Egyptians' most famous structures, the pyramids. But the Egyptians also built massive temples. Those that survive are among the most spectacular sites in Egypt today.

The Egyptians believed that temples were the homes of the gods. People visited the temples to worship, offer the gods gifts, and ask for favors.

Many Egyptian temples shared some similar features. Rows of stone **sphinxes**—imaginary creatures with the bodies of lions and the heads of other animals or humans—lined the path leading to the entrance. That entrance itself was a huge, thick gate. On either side of the gate might stand an **obelisk** (AH-buh-lisk), a tall, four-sided pillar that is pointed on top.

Inside, the temples were lavishly decorated, as you can see in the drawing of the Temple of Karnak. Huge columns supported the temple's roof. In many cases, these columns were covered with paintings and hieroglyphics, as were the temple walls. Statues of gods and pharaohs often stood along the walls as well. The sanctuary, the most sacred part of the building, was at the far end of the temple.

The Temple of Karnak is only one of Egypt's great temples. Others were built by Ramses the Great at Abu Simbel and Luxor. The temple at Abu Simbel is especially known for the huge statues carved out of the sandstone cliffs at the temple's entrance. These 66-foot-tall statues show Ramses as pharaoh. Nearby are some smaller statues of his family.

THE IMPACT TODAY
The Washington Monument, in Washington, DC, is an obelisk.

READING CHECK **Generalizing** What were some features of Egyptian temples?

The Temple of Karnak

The Temple of Karnak was Egypt's largest temple. Built mainly to honor Amon-Re, the sun god, Karnak was one of Egypt's major religious centers for centuries. Over the years, pharaohs added to the temple's many buildings. This illustration shows how Karnak's great hall may have looked during an ancient festival.

Karnak's interior columns and walls were painted brilliant colors.

ANALYSIS SKILL **ANALYZING VISUALS**

What features of Egyptian architecture can you see in this illustration?

Cross-Discipline Activity: Math

Exceeding Standards

Measuring a Temple 🐻 **HSS** 6.2.5; **HSS** Analysis Skills: HR 1

1. Organize students into small groups.

2. Have students calculate various dimensions of the temple's interior. They should use the priests in the foreground as a basic ruler and estimate that the men were about 5'5" tall.

3. To add interest to the activity, challenge groups to race in making their calculations.

4. Lead a discussion about how the Egyptians built and decorated temples with such stupendous dimensions.

LS Interpersonal, Logical/Mathematical

Universal Access Resources
See page 83c for additional resources for differentiating instruction for universal access.

Massive columns, some more than 80 feet high, supported the temple's high roof.

High windows let light and air into the temple.

In the annual Opet festival, priests carried statues of the gods and sacred boats from the temple to the Nile River.

Only the pharaoh and priests were allowed inside the temple, which was considered the home of the gods.

Main Idea

❷ Egypt's Great Temples

Egypt's great temples were lavishly decorated.

Identify What was the most sacred part of a temple? *the sanctuary*

Analyze Why do you think many Egyptian temples had rows of sphinxes leading to the entrance? *possible answer—as symbolic protection for the temple*

Elaborate Why do you suppose the Egyptians drew animals realistically but drew people with their heads and legs from the side and their upper bodies and shoulders straight on? *Answers will vary but should be consistent with text information.*

📄 **CRF:** Primary Source Activity: Ancient Egyptian Tomb Paintings

🐾 **HSS** 6.2.5; **HSS** Analysis Skills: HI 5

History Close-up

Analyzing Visuals Many elements of Egyptian art reflected the Egyptians' close connection to nature. What examples of this do you see in the illustration? *possible answers—tops and bottoms of columns painted like flower buds, bird wings and snake heads over door, animals and birds incorporated into hieroglyphics*

Cross-Discipline Activity: Arts and the Humanities [Standards Proficiency]

The Opet Festival 🐾 **HSS** 6.2.5; **HSS** Analysis Skills: HR1

[Research Required]

Materials: art supplies

1. Have students conduct research on the Opet festival, including its purpose and what kinds of ceremonies took place during that time.

2. Have students paint a picture of an event that might have taken place during Opet. They should not simply copy an existing painting, but create an original one based on what they have learned in their research.

3. Encourage students to include as much detail as possible, showing, for example, the kinds

of garments and jewelry people would have worn. People should be drawn in the Egyptian style.

4. Display students' paintings. **LS Visual/Spatial**

📄 Alternative Assessment Handbook, Rubrics 3: Artwork; and 30: Research

❸ Egyptian Art

Egyptian art filled tombs.

Recall Give examples of two common subjects of Egyptian paintings. *events such as the crowning of kings and founding of temples, religious rituals, and scenes from everyday life*

Analyze Why was the discovery of King Tutankhamen's tomb so important? *It had never been disturbed by tomb robbers.*

HSS 6.2.5 **HSS** Analysis Skill HI 4

Linking to Today

How Did Tut Die? Tutankhamen was a minor ruler, but because his tomb was discovered intact, he is one of the most famous pharaohs. He took the throne when he was about nine years old but ruled briefly before his death at about 18. Because the skull of Tut's mummy displays damage, some Egyptologists think Tutankhamen was murdered. In 2004 archaeologists announced plans to move the mummy for the first time from Luxor to Cairo. There the mummy will undergo CAT X-rays and a radio scan to determine the cause of death.

History Humor

What did the young King Tut say when he got scared? *I want my mummy!*

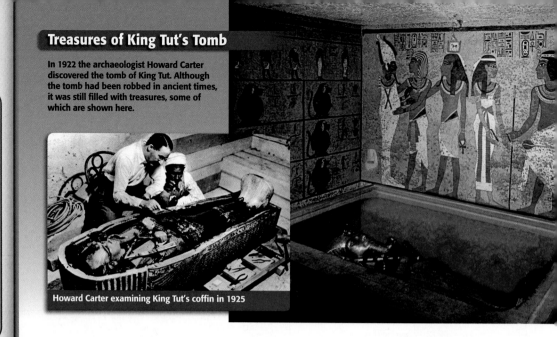

Treasures of King Tut's Tomb

In 1922 the archaeologist Howard Carter discovered the tomb of King Tut. Although the tomb had been robbed in ancient times, it was still filled with treasures, some of which are shown here.

Howard Carter examining King Tut's coffin in 1925

Egyptian Art

One reason Egypt's temples are so popular with tourists is the art they contain. The ancient Egyptians were masterful artists. Many of their greatest works were created to fill the tombs of pharaohs and other nobles. The Egyptians took great care in making these items because they believed the dead could enjoy them in the afterlife.

Paintings

Egyptian art was filled with lively, colorful scenes. Detailed works covered the walls of temples and tombs. Artists also painted on canvas, papyrus, pottery, plaster, and wood. Most Egyptians, however, never saw these paintings. Only kings, priests, and important people could enter temples and tombs, and even they rarely entered the tombs.

The subjects of Egyptian paintings vary widely. Some paintings show important historical events, such as the crowning of kings and the founding of temples. Others illustrate major religious rituals. Still other paintings show scenes from everyday life, such as farming or hunting.

Egyptian painting has a distinctive style. People, for example, are drawn in a certain way. In Egyptian paintings, people's heads and legs are always seen from the side, but their upper bodies and shoulders are shown straight on. In addition, people do not all appear the same size. Important figures such as pharaohs appear huge in comparison to others, especially servants or conquered people. In contrast, Egyptian animals were usually drawn realistically.

Carvings and Jewelry

Painting was not the only art form Egyptians practiced. The Egyptians were also skilled stoneworkers. Many tombs included huge statues and detailed carvings.

The Egyptians also made beautiful objects out of gold and precious stones. They made jewelry for both women and men. This

112 CHAPTER 4

Collaborative Learning

Exceeding Standards

King Tut's Tomb **HSS** 6.2.5; **HSS** Analysis Skills: HR 1, HI 2

Research Required

1. Tell students that many pharaohs were buried not in pyramids but in tombs hidden deep in the Valley of the Kings—the same area where Howard Carter found King Tut's tomb.

2. Organize students in pairs to prepare for an interview of Howard Carter for a television talk show. Have the partners conduct research to compose questions and their replies.

3. Encourage students to use their imaginations to make the interview interesting. For example, the interview might include

information about the conditions under which the team lived and worked.

4. Each pair should decide which student will be Carter and which will be the interviewer. Have students present their interviews to the class. **LS** Interpersonal, Verbal/Linguistic

Alternative Assessment Handbook, Rubrics 30: Research; and 33: Skits and Reader's Theater

The back of King Tut's chair was decorated with this image of the pharaoh and his wife.

Gold mask

ANALYSIS SKILL **ANALYZING VISUALS**

What might archaeologists learn about ancient Egypt from these artifacts?

jewelry included necklaces, collars, and bracelets. The Egyptians also used gold to make burial items for their pharaohs.

Over the years, treasure hunters emptied many pharaohs' tombs. At least one tomb, however, was not disturbed. In 1922 some archaeologists found the tomb of **King Tutankhamen** (too-tang-KAHM-uhn), or King Tut. The tomb was filled with treasures, including boxes of jewelry, robes, a burial mask, and ivory statues. King Tut's treasures have taught us much about Egyptian burial practices and beliefs.

READING CHECK **Summarizing** What types of artwork were contained in Egyptian tombs?

SUMMARY AND PREVIEW Ancient Egyptians developed one of the best-known cultures of the ancient world. Next, you will learn about a culture that developed in the shadow of Egypt—Kush.

Section 4 Assessment

go.hrw.com
Online Quiz
KEYWORD: SQ6 HP4

Reviewing Ideas, Terms, and People HSS 6.2.5, 6.2.9

1. **a. Identify** What are **hieroglyphics**?
   b. Contrast How was hieroglyphic writing different from our writing today?
   c. Evaluate Why was finding the **Rosetta Stone** so important to scholars?
2. **a. Describe** What were two ways the Egyptians decorated their temples?
   b. Evaluate Why do you think pharaohs like Ramses the Great built huge temples?
3. **Recall** Why were tombs filled with art, jewelry, and other treasures?

Critical Thinking

4. **Summarize** Draw a chart like the one below. In each column, list two facts about the achievements of the ancient Egyptians.

Writing	Architecture	Art

FOCUS ON WRITING

5. **Considering Egyptian Achievements** Note some details about Egyptian achievements in writing, architecture, and art that make Egypt different from other places.

ANCIENT EGYPT **113**

Section 4 Assessment Answers

1. **a.** the Egyptian writing system
   b. had 600 symbols, rather than the 26 in our alphabet; could be written horizontally or vertically, left to right, or right to left
   c. allowed scholars to decipher hieroglyphics
2. **a.** possible answers—columns, obelisks, paintings, hieroglyphics, and statues
   b. possible answers—to worship the gods, display the pharaoh's power and wealth
3. The Egyptians believed that the dead enjoyed these items in the afterlife.

4. possible answers—Writing: had over 600 symbols, wrote on papyrus; Architecture: temples covered in hieroglyphics, many buildings were built for religious purposes; Art—people drawn in the same unrealistic way, animals drawn realistically
5. Students' notes will vary but should reflect section content.

113

Assessing Primary and Secondary Sources

Social Studies Skills

Activity **Graphic Organizer** Have students consider the following scenario: They missed the last football game at their school. They asked several of their friends who attended to describe the game. The students then asked other friends who played in the game to discuss it. The students also read a local newspaper article about the game. Have students discuss how each of these accounts of the game might differ. How might some of the accounts be biased or inaccurate? Why might students want to hear or read all of these accounts? How might the accounts combine to form a more complete picture of the game? Encourage student discussion.

Next, have students discuss the importance of primary and secondary sources in the study of history. Then have each student create a graphic organizer of his or her choosing that illustrates what primary and secondary sources are, the problems with each (such as bias), and how they combine to provide a better picture of history.

LS Verbal/Linguistic, Visual/Spatial

📝 Alternative Assessment Handbook, Rubric 13: Graphic Organizers

💿 Interactive Skills Tutor CD-ROM, Lesson 2: Identify Primary and Secondary Sources; Lesson 17: Interpret Primary Sources

🐻 **HSS** Analysis Skills: HR 4

Social Studies Skills

HSS **Analysis HR 4** Assess the credibility of primary and secondary sources and draw sound conclusions from them.

| Analysis | Critical Thinking | Participation | Study |

Assessing Primary and Secondary Sources

Understand the Skill

Primary sources in history are materials created by people who lived during the times they describe. Examples include letters, diaries, and photographs. *Secondary sources* are accounts written later by someone who was not present. They are designed to teach about or discuss a historical topic. This textbook is an example of a secondary source.

Together, primary and secondary sources can present a good picture of a historical period or event. However, they must be used carefully to make sure that the picture they present is accurate.

Learn the Skill

Here are some questions to ask to help you judge the accuracy of primary and secondary sources.

1 **What is it?** Is it a firsthand account or is it based on information provided by others? In other words, is it primary or secondary?

2 **Who wrote it?** For a primary source, what was the author's connection to what he or she was writing about? For a secondary source, what makes the author an authority on this subject?

3 **Who is the audience?** Was the information meant for the public? Was it meant for a friend or for the writer alone? The intended audience can influence what the writer has to say.

4 **What is the purpose?** Authors of either primary or secondary sources can have reasons to exaggerate—or even lie—to suit their own goals or purposes. Look for evidence of emotion, opinion, or bias in the source. These might influence the accuracy of the account.

5 **Does other evidence support the source?** Look for other information that supports the source's account. Compare different sources whenever possible.

Practice and Apply the Skill

Below are two passages about the military in ancient Egypt. Read them both and use the guidelines to answer the questions that follow.

> "The pharaohs began …leading large armies out of a land that had once known only small police forces and militia. The Egyptians quickly extended their military and commercial influence over an extensive region that included the rich provinces of Syria …and the numbers of Egyptian slaves grew swiftly."
>
> –C. Warren Hollister, from *Roots of the Western Tradition*

> "Let me tell you how the soldier fares …how he goes to Syria, and how he marches over the mountains. His bread and water are borne [carried] upon his shoulders like the load of [a donkey]; they make his neck bent as that of [a donkey], and the joints of his back are bowed [bent]. His drink is stinking water …When he reaches the enemy, he is trapped like a bird, and he has no strength in his limbs."
>
> –from *Wings of the Falcon: Life and Thought of Ancient Egypt*, translated by Joseph Kaster

1. Which quote is a primary source, and which is a secondary source?

2. Is there evidence of opinion, emotion, or bias in the second quote? Explain why or why not.

3. Which information is more likely to be accurate on this subject? Explain your answer.

Social Studies Skills Activity: Assessing Primary and Secondary Sources

Applying the Skill 🐻 **HSS** Analysis Skills: HR 4   **Standards Proficiency**

1. Have students look at the Egyptian tomb painting on p. 90, which shows a couple harvesting their crop. Ask students to look closely at the image and write two questions about Egypt that could be answered from the image.

2. Then have students write two questions about Egypt that would best be answered by a secondary source, such as a history book about Egypt.

3. Have volunteers discuss their questions with the class. Continue the exercise by having students suggest other questions about Egypt that could best be answered by a primary source or a secondary source.

4. **Extend** Have students create a poster that lists the five guidelines for assessing primary and secondary sources and provides an image to illustrate each guideline.

LS Logical/Mathematical, Visual Spatial

📝 Alternative Assessment Handbook, Rubrics 11: Discussions; and 28: Posters

Answers

Practice and Apply the Skill

1. *Hollister quote—secondary; Wings of the Falcon quote—primary;* **2.** *yes, emotion and opinion, as the author describes the hardships soldiers face;* **3.** *secondary, to provide an objective overall view of the period, but primary to illustrate how some soldiers of the time thought and felt about events*

Standards Review

Visual Summary

Use the visual summary below to help you review the main ideas of the chapter.

QUICK FACTS

Egyptian civilization developed along the Nile River.

Egypt's kings were considered gods, and people built huge pyramids in their honor.

Egyptians developed a writing system and created beautiful art.

Reviewing Terms and People

Imagine these terms from the chapter are correct answers to items in a crossword puzzle. Write the clues for the answers. Then make the puzzle with some answers written down and some across.

1. cataract
2. Menes
3. pharaoh
4. nobles
5. mummy
6. elite
7. contract
8. Ramses
9. hieroglyphics
10. Tutankhamen

Comprehension and Critical Thinking

SECTION 1 *(Pages 88–92)* HSS 6.2.1, 6.2.2

11. **a. Identify** Where was most of Egypt's fertile land?

b. Make Inferences Why did Memphis become a political and social center of Egypt?

c. Predict How might history have been different if the Nile hadn't flooded every year?

SECTION 2 *(Pages 93–100)* HSS 6.2.3

12. **a. Describe** What responsibilities did pharaohs have?

b. Analyze How were beliefs about the **afterlife** linked to items placed in tombs?

c. Elaborate What challenges, in addition to moving stone blocks, do you think the pyramid builders faced?

SECTION 3 *(Pages 101–106)* HSS 6.2.6, 6.2.7

13. **a. Describe** What did a scribe do?

b. Analyze What two factors contributed to Egypt's wealth during the **New Kingdom**?

c. Evaluate **Ramses the Great** was a powerful pharaoh. Do you think his military successes or his building projects are more important to evaluating his greatness? Why?

Answers

Visual Summary

Review and Inquiry Have students use the visual summary to review the main events, personalities, and achievements of the ancient Egyptians.

Quick Facts Transparency: Ancient Egypt Visual Summary

Reviewing Terms and People

Crossword clues will vary but may include:

1. rapids in a river
2. founder of Egypt's First Dynasty
3. title used by rulers of Egypt
4. people from rich and powerful families
5. specially treated body wrapped in cloth
6. people of wealth and power
7. binding legal agreement
8. a pharaoh who fought off the Tehenu and built a series of forts to strengthen the western frontier
9. the Egyptian writing system
10. a pharaoh whose tomb has taught us a great deal about Egyptian burial practices and beliefs

Comprehension and Critical Thinking

11. **a.** in the Nile Delta
    b. possible answers—because it was the capital city of Egypt's First Dynasty and was near the Nile Delta, a very fertile area
    c. People would not have been able to farm in Egypt, so a civilization would have been less likely to develop.

Review and Assessment Resources

Review and Reinforce

SE Standards Review

CRF: Chapter Review Activity

California Standards Review Workbook

Quick Facts Transparency: Ancient Egypt Visual Summary

Spanish Chapter Summaries Audio CD

Online Chapter Summaries in Six Languages

OSP Holt PuzzlePro; GameTool for ExamView

Quiz Game CD-ROM

Assess

SE Standards Assessment

PASS: Chapter Test, Forms A and B

Alternative Assessment Handbook

OSP ExamView Test Generator, Chapter Test

Universal Access Modified Worksheets and Tests CD-ROM: Chapter Test

Holt Online Assessment Program (in the Premier Online Edition)

Reteach/Intervene

Interactive Reader and Study Guide

Universal Access Teacher Management System: Lesson Plans for Universal Access

Universal Access Modified Worksheets and Tests CD-ROM

Interactive Skills Tutor CD-ROM

go.hrw.com
Online Resources

KEYWORD: SQ6 WH4

12. **a.** The Egyptians believed the pharaoh was responsible for ensuring crops grew, keeping away diseases, making trade profitable, and preventing wars.

b. Items were placed in tombs to fulfill the needs of the buried person's *ka*.

c. possible answers—cutting the stones, organizing and feeding the workers, keeping the dimensions of the pyramids straight

13. **a.** Scribes worked for the government and the temples by keeping records and accounts for the state and writing and copying religious and literary texts.

b. conquest and trade

c. Answers will vary, but students should be familiar with both his military successes and his building projects as mentioned in this section.

14. **a.** as a surface for writing

b. Hieroglyphics had 600 symbols, rather than the 26 in our alphabet. Hieroglyphics could also be written horizontally or vertically, left to right, or right to left. Our writing is horizontal left to right.

c. The size of the pharaohs versus that of the servants reflects the Egyptian social hierarchy.

Social Studies Skills

15. a.

16. b.

17. a.

18. b.

Internet Activity

19. Go to the HRW Web site and enter the keyword shown to access a rubric for this activity.

KEYWORD: SQ6 TEACHER

Reviewing Themes

20. possible answers—yes, if another reliable source of water were found; no, because the Nile and what it provides are unique

21. Because religion was such a large part of their culture, it influenced their government, art, architecture, and almost every aspect of daily life.

SECTION 4 *(Pages 108–113)* **HSS** 6.2.5, 6.2.9

14. **a. Describe** For what was **papyrus** used?

b. Contrast How are the symbols in hieroglyphics different than the symbols used in our writing system?

c. Elaborate How does the Egyptian style of painting people reflect their society?

Social Studies Skills

Judging the Credibility of Sources *Each of the questions below lists two sources that a historian might consult to answer a question about ancient Egypt. For each question, decide which source is likely to be more accurate or believable and why.*

15. What were Egyptian beliefs about the afterlife?

a. tomb inscriptions

b. writings by a priest who visited Egypt in 1934

16. Why did the Nile flood every year?

a. songs of praise to the Nile written by Egyptian priests

b. a book about the rivers of Africa written by a modern geographer

17. What kinds of goods did the Egyptians trade?

a. government records of trade

b. an ancient Egyptian story about a trader

18. What kind of warrior was Ramses the Great?

a. a poem in praise of Ramses

b. a description of a battle written by an impartial observer

Internet Activity

go.hrw.com
KEYWORD: SQ6 WH4

19. **Activity: Creating Egyptian Art** The Egyptians developed an extraordinary artistic civilization. Their architecture included innovative pyramids and temples. Artisans created beautiful paintings, carvings, and jewelry. Enter the activity keyword and research the main features of Egyptian art and architecture. Then imagine you are an Egyptian artisan. Create a piece of art to place inside a pharaoh's tomb. Include hieroglyphics telling the pharaoh about your art.

Reviewing Themes

20. **Geography** Do you think that Egyptian society could have flourished in North Africa if the Nile had not existed? Why or why not?

21. **Religion** How did religious beliefs shape the rest of Egyptian culture?

Reading Skills

Drawing Conclusions from Sources *Read the following passage and answer the questions. If the passage does not provide enough information to answer the question, choose "d. not enough information."*

"Hail to thee, O Nile! Who manifests thyself over this land, and comes to give life to Egypt! Mysterious is thy issuing forth from the darkness, on this day whereon it is celebrated!"

—*Hymn to the Nile,* from *The Library of Original Sources,* edited by Oliver J. Thatcher

22. How do you think the Egyptians felt about the Nile?

a. They admired it.   **c.** They feared it.

b. They ignored it.   **d.** not enough information

23. Where did the Egyptians think the Nile's waters came from?

a. the highlands of Ethiopia

b. the Mediterranean

c. an unknown, mysterious location

d. not enough information

24. What does the name *Nile* mean in Egyptian?

a. inexhaustible   **c.** celebrated

b. mysterious   **d.** not enough information

FOCUS ON WRITING

25. **Writing a Riddle** Choose five details about Egypt. Then write a sentence about each detail. Each sentence of your riddle should be a statement ending with "me." For example, if you were writing about the United States, you might say, "People come from all over the world to join me." After you have written your five sentences, end your riddle with "Who am I?"

Reading Skills

22. a.

23. c.

24. d.

Focus on Writing

25. **Rubric** Students' riddles should:

- end with "me" and be followed by "Who am I?"

- explain something about the civilization of ancient Egypt.

- use correct grammar, punctuation, spelling, and capitalization.

CRF: Focus on Writing Activity: A Riddle

Standards Assessment

DIRECTIONS: Read each question, and write the letter of the best response.

1

> Oh great god and ruler, the gift of Amon-Re,
>   god of the Sun.
> Oh great protector of Egypt and its people.
> Great one who has saved us from the horrible
>   Tehenu.
> You, who have turned back the Hittites.
> You, who have fortified our western border to
>   forever protect us from our enemies.
> We bless you, oh great one.
> We worship and honor you, oh great pharaoh.

A tribute such as the one above would have been written in honor of which Egyptian ruler?

A Khufu

B Ramses the Great

C King Tutankhamen

D Queen Hatshepsut

2 **The Nile helped civilization develop in Egypt in all of the following ways *except* by**

A providing a source of food and water.

B allowing farming to develop.

C enriching the soil along its banks.

D protecting against invasion from the west.

3 **The most fertile soil in Egypt was located in the**

A Nile Delta.

B desert.

C cataracts.

D far south.

4 **The high position priests held in Egyptian society shows that**

A the pharaoh was a descendant of a god.

B government was large and powerful.

C religion was important in Egyptian life.

D the early Egyptians worshipped many gods.

5 **The Egyptians are probably *best* known for building**

A pyramids.

B irrigation canals.

C ziggurats.

D forts.

Connecting with Past Learnings

6 **In this chapter you learned about hieroglyphics, one of the world's first writing systems. In Chapter 3 you read about another ancient writing system called**

A Sumerian.

B Hammurabi.

C ziggurat.

D cuneiform.

7 **In Chapter 3 you read about Sargon I, who first united Mesopotamia under one rule. Which Egyptian ruler's accomplishments were *most* similar to Sargon's?**

A Hyksos

B Khufu

C Menes

D Hatshepsut

ANCIENT EGYPT **117**

Tips for Test Taking

Search for Skips and Smudges Remind students that to avoid losing points on a machine-graded test they should be sure they did not skip any answers, gave only one answer for each question, made the marks dark and within the lines, and erased any smudges. Students should also make sure there are no stray pencil marks, such as from pencil tapping. They should cleanly erase places where they changed their minds.

Answers

1. B
Break Down the Question This question requires students to recall the notable features of four pharaohs' reigns. Refer students who miss it to Section 3.

2. D
Break Down the Question Refer students who miss this question to the map in Section 1 and the fact that desert protected against invasion from the west.

3. A
Break Down the Question This question requires students to recall factual information. Refer students who miss it to Section 1.

4. C
Break Down the Question Although the other choices contain true statements or beliefs, only C fulfills the cause-and-effect requirement.

5. A
Break Down the Question Although the Egyptians built irrigation canals, they were not impressive structures. Likewise, their forts are not well known. Ziggurats were built in Mesopotamia, not Egypt.

6. D
Break Down the Question This question requires students to recall information from the previous chapter on Mesopotamia.

7. C
Break Down the Question Remind students who missed the question that Menes united Egypt, as Sargon I had united Mesopotamia.

Standards Review

Have students review the following standards in their workbooks.

California Standards Review Workbook:
HSS 6.2, 6.2.1, 6.2.2, 6.2.3, 6.2.5, 6.2.6, 6.2.7, 6.2.9

Chapter 5 Planning Guide

Ancient Kush

Chapter Overview	Reproducible Resources	Technology Resources
Chapter 5 pp. 118–135 **Overview:** In this chapter, students will study the kingdom of Kush. See page 118 for the California History–Social Science standards covered in this chapter.	**Universal Access Teacher Management System:*** • Universal Access Instructional Benchmarking Guides • Lesson Plans for Universal Access **Interactive Reader and Study Guide:** Chapter Graphic Organizer* **Chapter Resource File*** • Chapter Review Activity • Focus on Writing Activity: A Fictional Narrative • Social Studies Skills Activity: Participating in Groups	**One-Stop Planner CD-ROM:** Calendar Planner **Student Edition Full-Read Audio CD-ROM** **Universal Access Modified Worksheets and Tests CD-ROM** **Interactive Skills Tutor CD-ROM** **Primary Source Library CD-ROM for World History** **Power Presentations with Video CD-ROM** **History's Impact: World History Video Program (VHS/DVD):** Ancient Egypt and Kush* **A Teacher's Guide to Religion in the Public Schools***
Section 1: **Kush and Egypt** **The Big Idea:** The kingdom of Kush, in the region of Nubia, was first conquered by Egypt but later conquered and ruled Egypt. 6.2.8	**Universal Access Teacher Management System:*** Section 1 Lesson Plan **Interactive Reader and Study Guide:** Section 1 Summary* **Chapter Resource File*** • Vocabulary Builder Activity, Section 1 • Biography Activity: King Taharqa • History and Geography Activity: The Nile	**Daily Bellringer Transparency:** Section 1* **Map Transparency:** Ancient Kush* **Internet Activity:** Destination Ancient Kush
Section 2: **Later Kush** **The Big Idea:** Kush developed an advanced civilization with a large trading network. 6.2.8	**Universal Access Teacher Management System:*** Section 2 Lesson Plan **Interactive Reader and Study Guide:** Section 2 Summary* **Chapter Resource File*** • Vocabulary Builder Activity, Section 2 • Biography Activity: Queen Shanakhdakheto • Literature Activity: The Fall of Meroë • Primary Source Activity: Herodotus, *The Histories*	**Daily Bellringer Transparency:** Section 2*

MASTERING THE CALIFORNIA STANDARDS

Review, Assessment, Intervention

- **Standards Review Workbook***
- **Quick Facts Transparency:** Ancient Kush Visual Summary*
- **Spanish Chapter Summaries Audio CD Program**
- **Online Chapter Summaries in Six Languages**
- **Quiz Game CD-ROM**
- **Progress Assessment Support System (PASS):** Chapter Test*
- **Universal Access Modified Worksheets and Tests CD-ROM:** Modified Chapter Test
- **One-Stop Planner CD-ROM:** ExamView Test Generator (English/Spanish)
- **Alternative Assessment Handbook**
- **Holt Online Assessment Program (HOAP),** in the Holt Premier Online Student Edition

---

- **PASS:** Section 1 Quiz*
- **Online Quiz:** Section 1
- **Alternative Assessment Handbook**

- **PASS:** Section 2 Quiz*
- **Online Quiz:** Section 2
- **Alternative Assessment Handbook**

California Resources for Standards Mastery

INSTRUCTIONAL PLANNING AND SUPPORT

- **Universal Access Teacher Management System***
- **One-Stop Planner CD-ROM with Test Generator:** Teacher Management System with Interactive Teacher's Edition

STANDARDS MASTERY

- **Standards Review Workbook***
- **At Home: A Guide to Standards Mastery for World History**

go.hrw.com Holt Online Learning

To enhance learning, the following Internet activity is available: **Destination: Ancient Kush.**

KEYWORD: SQ6 TEACHER

- **Teacher Support Page**
- **Content Updates**
- **Rubrics and Writing Models**
- **Teaching Tips for the Multimedia Classroom**

KEYWORD: SQ6 WH5

- **Current Events**
- **Holt Grapher**
- **Holt Online Atlas**
- **Holt Researcher**
- **Interactive Multimedia Activities**
- **Internet Activities**
- **Online Chapter Summaries in Six Languages**
- **Online Section Quizzes**
- **World History Maps and Charts**

HOLT PREMIER ONLINE STUDENT EDITION

Complete online support for interactivity, assessment, and reporting

- **Interactive Maps and Notebook**
- **Standardized Test Prep**
- **Homework Practice and Research Activities Online**

Mastering the Standards: Differentiating Instruction

Reaching Standards	Basic-level activities designed for all students encountering new material
Standards Proficiency	Intermediate-level activities designed for average students
Exceeding Standards	Challenging activities designed for honors and gifted-and-talented students
Standard English Mastery	Activities designed to improve standard English usage

Frequently Asked Questions

MASTERING THE CALIFORNIA STANDARDS

INSTRUCTIONAL PLANNING AND SUPPORT

Where do I find planning aids, pacing guides, lesson plans, and other teaching aids?

Annotated Teacher's Edition:
- Chapter planning guides
- Standards-based instruction and strategies
- Differentiated instruction for universal access
- Point-of-use reminders for integrating program resources

Power Presentations with Video CD-ROM

Universal Access Teacher Management System:
- Year and unit instructional benchmarking guides
- Reproducible lesson plans
- Assessment guides for diagnostic, progress, and summative end-of-the-year tests
- Options for differentiating instruction and intervention
- Teaching guides and answer keys for student workbooks

One-Stop Planner CD-ROM with Test Generator: Teacher Management System with Interactive Teacher's Edition:
- Calendar Planner
- Editable lesson plans
- All reproducible ancillaries in Adobe Acrobat (PDF) format
- ExamView Test Generator (English & Spanish)
- Game Tool for ExamView
- PuzzlePro
- Transparency and video previews

DIFFERENTIATING INSTRUCTION FOR UNIVERSAL ACCESS

What resources are available to ensure that Advanced Learners/GATE Students master the standards?

Teacher's Edition Activities:
- Making Iron Skits, p. 128

Lesson Plans for Universal Access

Primary Source Library CD-ROM for World History

What resources are available to ensure that English Learners and Standard English Learners master the standards?

Teacher's Edition Activities:
- Kushite and Egyptian Cultures Venn Diagram, p. 129

Lesson Plans for Universal Access

Chapter Resource File: Vocabulary Builder Activities

Spanish Chapter Summaries Audio CD Program

Online Chapter Summaries in Six Languages

One-Stop Planner CD-ROM:
- PuzzlePro, Spanish Version
- ExamView Test Generator, Spanish Version

What modified materials are available for Special Education?

Teacher's Edition Activities:
- Stone Carving, p. 130

The *Universal Access Modified Worksheets and Tests CD-ROM* provides editable versions of the following:

Vocabulary Flash Cards

Modified Vocabulary Builder Activities

Modified Chapter Review Activity

Modified Chapter Test

What resources are available to ensure that Learners Having Difficulty master the standards?

Teacher's Edition Activities:
• Charting Natural Resources, p. 124

Interactive Reader and Study Guide

Student Edition Full-Read Audio CD

Quick Facts Transparency: Ancient Kush Visual Summary

Standards Review Workbook

Social Studies Skills Activity: Participating in Groups

Interactive Skills Tutor CD-ROM

How do I intervene for students struggling to master the standards?

Interactive Reader and Study Guide

Quick Facts Transparency: Ancient Kush Visual Summary

Standards Review Workbook

Social Studies Skills Activity: Participating in Groups

Interactive Skills Tutor CD-ROM

PROFESSIONAL DEVELOPMENT

HOLT
Professional
Development

What teacher training resources are available to help me grow professionally?

• In-service and staff development as part of your Holt Social Studies product purchase
• Quick Teacher Tutorial Lesson Presentation CD-ROM
• Intensive tuition-based Teacher Development Institute
• Convenient Holt Speaker Bureau face-to-face workshop options

• PRAXIS™ Test Prep (#0089) interactive Web-based content refreshers*
• *Ask A Professional Development Expert* at http://www.hrw.com/prodev/

* PRAXIS is a trademark of Educational Testing Service (ETS). This publication is not endorsed or approved by ETS.

Information Literacy Skills

To learn more about how History–Social Science instruction may be improved by the effective use of library media centers and information literacy skills, go to the Teacher's Resource Materials for Chapter 5 at **go.hrw.com, keyword: SQ6 MEDIA.**

MASTERING THE CALIFORNIA STANDARDS

Standards Focus

Standards by Section
Section 1: **HSS** 6.2.8
Section 2: **HSS** 6.2.8

Teacher's Edition
HSS Analysis Skills: CS 1, CS 3, HR 1, HI 1, HI 2

ELA Writing 6.2.1.b; Reading 6.2.0

Upcoming Standards for Future Learning
Preview the following History–Social Science content standards from upcoming chapters or grade levels to promote learning beyond the current chapter.

HSS 7.4 Students analyze the geographic, political, economic, religious, and social structures of the sub-Saharan civilizations of Ghana and Mali in Medieval Africa.

7.4.5 Describe the importance of written and oral traditions in the transmission of African history and culture.

Focus on Writing

The **Chapter Resource File** provides a Focus on Writing worksheet to help students organize and create their fictional narratives.

CRF: Focus on Writing Activity: A Fictional Narrative

CHAPTER **5** c. 2300 BC–AD 350

Ancient Kush

 California Standards

History–Social Science
6.2 Students analyze the geographic, political, economic, religious, and social structures of the early civilizations of Mesopotamia, Egypt, and Kush.

Analysis Skills
HI 2 Understand and distinguish cause and effect.

English–Language Arts
Writing 6.2.1b Include sensory details and concrete language to develop plot and character.

Reading 6.2.0 Students read and understand grade-level-appropriate material.

FOCUS ON WRITING

A Fictional Narrative In this chapter you will read about events of the rise and fall of Kush. Then you will write a short story about fictional characters who lived through these events. The main character in your story will be from Kush; other main characters could be from Egypt, Assyria, or Aksum.

CHAPTER EVENTS

c. 2000 BC
The kingdom of Kush sets up its capital at Kerma.

2000 BC

WORLD EVENTS

2300 BC
The Harappan civilization rises in the Indus Valley.

Introduce the Chapter

Standards **Proficiency**

Focus on Cultural Influences **HSS** 6.2.8

1. Have students study the illustrations in the chapter. Tell students that Egypt and Kush were neighboring countries that influenced each other.

2. As students examine the chapter photos and other visuals, have them look for examples of Egyptian influence on Kushite culture. (Examples include religion, architecture, art, and clothing.)

3. Based on the images, have students predict ways that Egypt might have influenced Kush,

and why. Write students' predictions for the class to see.

4. After students have finished the chapter, have them review their predictions to see how accurate they were. **LS** Visual/Spatial

What You Will Learn...

In this chapter you will learn about the his-tory and culture of Kush and its connections to Egypt. This photo shows ruins of the royal pyramids in Kush and some pyramids that have been reconstructed.

● Chapter Preview ●

HOLT
History's Impact
▶ video series
See the Video Teacher's Guide for strategies for using the chap-ter video **Ancient Egypt and Kush: The Impact of the Egyptian Pyramids**.

Chapter Big Ideas

Section 1 The kingdom of Kush, in the region of Nubia, was first conquered by Egypt but later conquered and ruled Egypt. **HSS** 6.2.8

Section 2 Kush developed an ad-vanced civilization with a large trading network. **HSS** 6.2.8

Explore the Picture

Pyramids of Kush Pyramids are common to several civilizations, from the ancient Egyptians and the Kushites to the Maya and the Aztec. People have also built pyramid-like structures in India and Thailand and on some Pacific islands. Pyramids in these places vary in design and materials.

Analyzing Visuals What can you assume about Kush just from looking at this picture? *possible answer—It has pyramids similar to those in Egypt, so Kush and Egypt were probably in contact with each other.*

c. 750–700 BC Kush conquers Egypt.

c. 580 BC Meroë becomes capital of Kush.

c. AD 350 Aksum destroys Meroë.

1500 BC

c. 1550 BC The New Kingdom begins in Egypt.

1000 BC

c. 500 BC The Nok culture develops in West Africa.

500 BC

BC 1 AD

AD 330 Constantinople becomes the capital of the Roman Empire.

AD 500

119

Explore the Time Line

1. When did Kush conquer Egypt?
c. 750–700 BC

2. Shortly after Meroë became the capital of Kush, what was happening in West Africa? *The Nok culture was developing.*

3. What happened in Kush about 20 years after Constantinople became the capital of the Roman Empire? *Aksum destroyed Meroë.*

HSS Analysis Skills: CS 1

Other People, Other Places

The Nok Culture The Nok were members of another early African culture. They were named after the village of Nok in Nigeria, where evi-dence of the civilization was found. Historians believe the Nok lived in an area between the Niger and Benue rivers from about 500 BC to AD 200. The Nok were among the first iron-workers in Africa. They left behind iron and stone tools as well as clay figurines representing animals and humans.

Understanding Themes

Two themes, economics and geography, are presented in this chapter. Have students look at a map of Africa and determine where the ancient kingdom of Kush was located. Then have students use the map to draw inferences about the geography of Kush. Finally, ask students how trade might have affected the economy of Kush. Have students use the map to determine with what civilizations Kush might have traded.

Causes and Effects in History

Focus on Reading Ask students to name examples of something in their community or school that has caused a direct effect. For example, lunch lines may have been so long that the school created two lunch periods. In the community, a lack of open land may have been the motivation for the creation of new parks. Have students look for examples of activities, events, or improvements in their own communities that show cause and effect. Have students write their cause-and-effect statements using the signal words on this page.

Reading Social Studies

by Kylene Beers

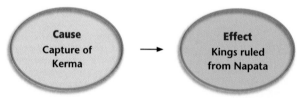

| Economics | Geography | Politics | Religion | Society and Culture | Science and Technology |

Focus on Themes As you read this chapter, you will learn about an ancient kingdom called Kush that developed south of Egypt along the Nile River. You will see that the **geography** of the area helped this kingdom to develop. You will also learn how Egypt conquered and ruled Kush and then how Kush conquered and ruled Egypt. Finally, you will learn how the **economy** of Kush grew as it developed an iron industry and expanded its trade network.

Causes and Effects in History

Focus on Reading Have you heard the saying, "We have to understand the past to avoid repeating it."? That is one reason we look for causes and effects in history.

Identifying Causes and Effects A **cause** is something that makes another thing happen. An **effect** is the result of something else that happened. Most historical events have a number of causes as well as a number of effects. You can understand history better if you look for causes and effects of events.

Additional reading support can be found in the

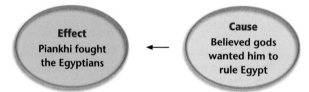

Inter*active*

Reader and Study Guide

1. *Because the Egyptians had captured the city of Kerma, the kings of Kush ruled from the city of Napata.* (p. 125)

Cause
Capture of Kerma

→

Effect
Kings ruled from Napata

> Sometimes writers use words that signal a cause or an effect:
>
> **Cause**—*reason, basis, because, motivated, as*
>
> **Effect**—*therefore, as a result, for that reason, so*

2. *Piankhi fought the Egyptians because he believed that the gods wanted him to rule all of Egypt.* (p. 125)

Effect
Piankhi fought the Egyptians

←

Cause
Believed gods wanted him to rule Egypt

120 CHAPTER 5

Reading and Skills Resources

Reading Support

- Interactive Reader and Study Guide
- Student Edition on Audio CD
- Spanish Chapter Summaries Audio CD Program

Social Studies Skills Support

- Interactive Skills Tutor CD-ROM

Vocabulary Support

- **CRF:** Vocabulary Builder Activities
- **CRF:** Chapter Review Activity
- Universal Access Modified Worksheets and Tests CD-ROM:
  - Vocabulary Flash Cards
  - Vocabulary Builder Activity
  - Chapter Review Activity

OSP Holt PuzzlePro

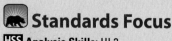 **Standards Focus**

HSS Analysis Skills: HI 2
ELA Reading 6.2.0

HSS Analysis HI 2 Distinguish cause and effect.
ELA Reading 6.2.0 Read and understand grade-level-appropriate material.

You Try It!

The following selections are from the chapter you are about to read. As you read each, identify which phrase or sentence describes a cause and which describes an effect.

Finding Causes and Effects

1. "During the mid-1000s BC the New Kingdom in Egypt was ending. As the power of Egypt's pharaohs declined, Kushite leaders regained control of Kush. Kush once again became independent." (p. 124)

2. "A series of weak pharaohs left Egypt open to attack." (p. 125)

3. 'The Assyrians' iron weapons were better than the Kushites' bronze weapons, and the Kushites were slowly pushed out of Egypt." (p. 126)

4. "Because resources such as iron ore and wood for furnaces were easily available, the industry grew quickly." (p. 128)

5. "When the cows ate all the grass, there was nothing to hold the soil down. As a result, wind blew the soil away. Without this soil, farmers couldn't produce enough food for Kush's people." (p. 131)

After you read the sentences, answer the following questions.

1. In selection 1, is "Kush once again became independent" the cause of the Egyptians growing weaker or the effect?

2. In selection 2, what left Egypt open to attack? Is that the cause of why Egypt was easily attacked or the effect?

3. In selection 3, who is using the iron weapons, the Assyrians or the Kushites? What was the effect of using the weapons?

4. In selection 4, does the word *because* signal a cause or an effect?

5. Read selection 5 again. Decide which sentences identify causes and which identify effects. (Here's a hint: an event can be the effect of one thing and the cause of another.)

Key Terms and People

Chapter 5

Section 1
ebony *(p. 124)*
ivory *(p. 124)*
Piankhi *(p. 125)*

Section 2
trade network *(p. 128)*
merchants *(p. 128)*
exports *(p. 128)*
imports *(p. 128)*
Queen Shanakhdakheto *(p. 129)*
King Ezana *(p. 131)*

Academic Vocabulary

Success in school is related to knowing academic vocabulary— the words that are frequently used in school assignments and discussions. In this chapter, you will learn the following academic word:

authority *(p. 129)*

As you read Chapter 5, look for words that signal causes or effects. Make a chart to keep track of these causes and effects.

Reading Social Studies

Key Terms and People

Preteach these terms and people to the class. Familiarize students with the key terms and people by having students use the terms in sentences about the kingdom of Kush. Then have students rewrite each sentence, leaving a blank where the key term belongs. Have students exchange papers with a partner and fill in the blanks. **LS** Verbal/Linguistic

Focus on Reading

See the **Focus on Reading** questions in this chapter for more practice on this reading social studies skill.

Reading Social Studies Assessment

See the **Standards Review** at the end of this chapter for student assessment questions related to this reading skill.

Teaching Tip

Review the cause-and-effect signal words with students. Ask them to suggest simple sentences that use these signal words. Write the sentences for all students to see, and examine the cause-and-effect relationship. For example, in the sentence *Because it rained last night, baseball practice was cancelled*, the cause is *Because it rained last night*, and the effect is *baseball practice was cancelled*. Have students create sentences that use signal words that indicate cause or effect.

Answers

You Try It! 1. *effect;* **2.** *A series of weak pharaohs was the cause of why Egypt was easily attacked.* **3.** *Assyrians; effect was to drive the Kushites out of Egypt;* **4.** *cause;* **5.** *first sentence— cows eating grass (cause), nothing to hold the soil down (effect); second sentence—nothing to hold the soil down (cause), soil blows away (effect); third sentence—soil being blown away (cause), low food production (effect)*

Bellringer

If YOU were there . . . Use the **Daily Bellringer Transparency** to help students answer the question.

🗄 Daily Bellringer Transparency, Section 1

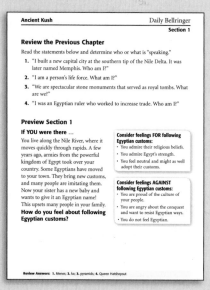

Ancient Kush   Daily Bellringer
                    Section 1

Review the Previous Chapter

Read the statements below and determine who or what is "speaking."

1. "I built a new capital city at the southern tip of the Nile Delta. It was later named Memphis. Who am I?"

2. "I am a person's life force. What am I?"

3. "We are spectacular stone monuments that served as royal tombs. What are we?"

4. "I was an Egyptian ruler who worked to increase trade. Who am I?"

Preview Section 1

If YOU were there ...

You live along the Nile River, where it moves quickly through rapids. A few years ago, armies from the powerful kingdom of Egypt took over your country. Some Egyptians have moved to your town, and many people are imitating them. Now your sister has a new baby and wants to give it an Egyptian name! This upsets many people in your family. **How do you feel about following Egyptian customs?**

Consider feelings FOR following Egyptian customs:
- You admire their religious beliefs.
- You admire Egypt's strength.
- You feel neutral and might as well adopt their customs.

Consider feelings AGAINST following Egyptian customs:
- You are proud of the culture of your people.
- You are angry about the conquest and want to resist Egyptian ways.
- You do not feel Egyptian.

Review Answers: 1. Menes; 2. ka; 3. pyramids; 4. Queen Hatshepsut

Building Vocabulary

Preteach or review the following terms:

pharaoh the title used by the rulers of Egypt (p. 124)

rapids parts of a river where the water is shallow and turbulent (p.123)

📄 **CRF:** Vocabulary Builder Activity, Section 1

Standards Focus

HSS 6.2.8

Means: Discuss where ancient Kush was located and how its politics, trade, and culture affected and were affected by Egypt.

Matters: Kush and Egypt were neighbors and affected each other's history. Kush was important to the trade of the ancient world.

SECTION 1

Kush and Egypt

If YOU were there...

You live along the Nile River, where it moves quickly through rapids. A few years ago, armies from the powerful kingdom of Egypt took over your country. Some Egyptians have moved to your town. They bring new customs, and many people are imitating them. Now your sister has a new baby and wants to give it an Egyptian name! This upsets many people in your family.

How do you feel about following Egyptian customs?

What You Will Learn...

Main Ideas

1. Geography helped early Kush civilization develop in Nubia.
2. Egypt controlled Kush for about 500 years.
3. Kush ruled Egypt after winning its independence and set up a new dynasty there.

The Big Idea

The kingdom of Kush, in the region of Nubia, was first conquered by Egypt but later conquered and ruled Egypt.

Key Terms and People

ebony, *p. 124*
ivory, *p. 124*
Piankhi, *p. 125*

HSS **6.2.8** Identify the location of the Kush civilization and describe its political, commercial, and cultural relations with Egypt.

BUILDING BACKGROUND Egypt dominated the lands along the Nile, but it was not the only ancient culture to develop along the river. Another kingdom, called Kush, arose to the south of Egypt. Through trade, conquest, and political dealings, the histories of Egypt and Kush became closely tied together.

Geography and Early Kush

South of Egypt along the Nile, a group of people settled in the region we now call Nubia. These Africans established the first large kingdom in the interior of Africa. We know this kingdom by the name the ancient Egyptians gave it—Kush. Development of Kushite civilization was greatly influenced by the geography of Nubia.

The Land of Nubia

Nubia is a region in northeast Africa. It lies on the Nile River south of Egypt. Today desert covers much of Nubia, but in ancient times the region was more fertile than it is now. Heavy rainfall south of Nubia flooded the Nile every year. The floods provided a rich layer of fertile soil to nearby lands. The kingdom of Kush developed in this area.

In addition to having fertile soil, ancient Nubia was rich in valuable minerals such as gold, copper, and stone. These natural resources contributed to the region's wealth and played a major role in its history.

Teach the Big Idea: Master the Standards   Standards Proficiency

Kush and Egypt   **HSS** 6.2.8; **HSS** Analysis Skills: CS 3, HI 1

1. **Teach** Ask students the Main Idea questions to teach this section.

2. **Apply** Help students locate and describe ancient Kush and summarize its relations with Egypt. To do so, have each student plan a billboard advertisement with words and pictures for one of the following purposes: to draw new settlers to Kush, to join the Egyptian army in the conquest of Kush, or to join the Kushite army in the fight for independence from Egypt. Organize the class into three groups to ensure all topics are covered.

   LS **Verbal/Linguistic, Visual/Spatial**

3. **Review** As you review the section's main ideas, have students discuss the information contained or implied in their billboard ads.

4. **Practice/Homework** Have each student create an ad for one of the other two topics.

   LS **Verbal/Linguistic, Visual/Spatial**

   📄 Alternative Assessment Handbook, Rubric 2: Advertisements

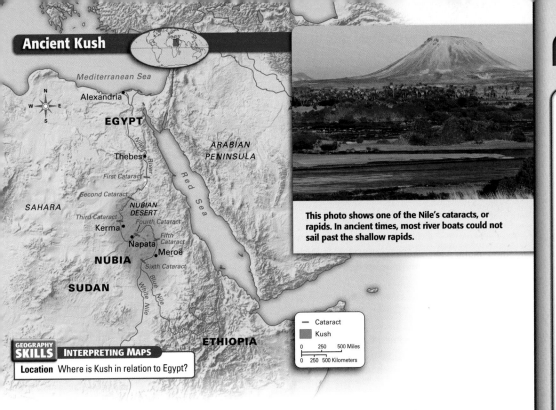

Ancient Kush

Mediterranean Sea

Alexandria

EGYPT

Thebes

First Cataract

Second Cataract

SAHARA

Third Cataract

NUBIAN DESERT

Kerma

Fourth Cataract

Napata

Fifth Cataract

Meroë

NUBIA

Sixth Cataract

SUDAN

ARABIAN PENINSULA

Red Sea

Nile River

White Nile

Blue Nile

ETHIOPIA

— Cataract

▢ Kush

0   250   500 Miles

0   250   500 Kilometers

GEOGRAPHY SKILLS | **INTERPRETING MAPS**

Location Where is Kush in relation to Egypt?

This photo shows one of the Nile's cataracts, or rapids. In ancient times, most river boats could not sail past the shallow rapids.

Early Civilization in Nubia

Like all early civilizations, the people of Nubia depended on agriculture for their food. Fortunately for them, the Nile's floods allowed the Nubians to plant both summer and winter crops. Among the crops they grew were wheat, barley, and other grains. In addition to farmland, the banks of the river provided grazing land for cattle and other livestock. As a result, farming villages thrived all along the Nile by about 3500 BC.

Over time some farmers became richer and more successful than others. These farmers became leaders of their villages. Sometime around 2000 BC, one of these leaders took control of other villages and made himself king of the region. His new kingdom was called Kush.

The kings of Kush ruled from their capital at Kerma (KAR-muh). This city was located on the Nile just south of a cataract, or stretch of rapids. Because the Nile's cataracts made parts of the river hard to pass through, they were natural barriers against invaders. For many years the cataracts kept Kush safe from the more powerful Egyptian kingdom to the north.

As time passed, Kushite society grew more complex. In addition to farmers and herders, some people of Kush became priests or artisans. Early on, Kush was greatly influenced by civilizations to the south. Later, however, Egypt played a greater role in the kingdom's history.

FOCUS ON READING

What words on this page signal causes or effects?

READING CHECK Finding Main Ideas How did geography help civilization grow in Nubia?

ANCIENT KUSH **123**

Cross-Discipline Activity: Geography

Standards Proficiency

Elevation Profiles of Kush 🐻 **HSS** 6.2.8; **HSS** Analysis Skills: CS 3, HI 1

1. Display the Map Transparency map titled "Ancient Kush" for students to see.

2. Using a washable marker, draw three horizontal parallel lines across Nubia—near its northern edge, near its southern edge, and at its center. The lines should be parallel to the top of the page.

3. Instruct students to use these lines to draw elevation profiles. An elevation profile is like a cross-sectional or cutaway view of a region.

4. Have each student use the transparency and the above map to create three elevation profiles of Nubia.

5. After students have drawn their elevation profiles, lead a discussion about how the profiles show mountains to the east, the Nile valley, and the river itself. 🔲 **Visual/Spatial**

📋 Alternative Assessment Handbook, Rubric 21: Map Reading

📦 Map Transparency: Ancient Kush

❷ Egypt Controls Kush

Egypt controlled Kush for about 500 years.

Recall What raw materials did Kush sell to Egypt? *gold, copper, stone, ebony, ivory*

Analyze Why did the Egyptians attack Kush? *They feared Kush was getting too powerful and could even attack Egypt.*

Identify Cause and Effect Egypt ruled Kush for about 450 years. How did Egyptian rule affect the people of Kush? *Egyptian language, styles, and religion became widespread in Kush.*

🐘 **HSS** 6.2.8; **HSS** Analysis Skills: CS 1, HI 1, HI 2

Checking for Understanding

True or False Answer each statement *T* if it is true or *F* if it is false. If false, explain why.

1. After their invasion of Kush, Egyptian leaders respected Kushite buildings and religion. *F; The Egyptians destroyed the Kushite palace at Kerma and built temples in what had been Kushite territory.*

2. Kush remained under Egyptian control for 2,000 years. *F; Kush became independent again after about 500 years.*

🐘 **HSS** 6.2.8; **HSS** Analysis Skills: CS 1, HI 1

Answers

Reading Check *The Kushite people began speaking Egyptian, using Egyptian names, wearing Egyptian-style clothing, and adopting Egyptian religious practices.*

124

Egypt Controls Kush

Kush and Egypt were neighbors. Sometimes the neighbors lived in peace with each other and helped each other prosper. For example, Kush became a supplier of slaves and raw materials to Egypt. The Kushites sent materials such as gold, copper, and stone to Egypt. The Kushites also sent the Egyptians **ebony**, a type of dark, heavy wood, and **ivory**, a white material made from elephant tusks.

Egypt's Conquest of Kush

Relations between Kush and Egypt were not always peaceful. As Kush grew wealthy from trade, its army grew stronger as well. Egypt's rulers soon feared that Kush would grow even more powerful and could even attack Egypt.

To prevent such an attack from occurring, the pharaoh Thutmose I sent an army to take control of Kush around 1500 BC. The pharaoh's army conquered all of Nubia north of the Fifth Cataract. As a result, Kush became part of Egypt.

After his army's victory, the pharaoh destroyed the Kushite palace at Kerma. Later pharaohs—including Ramses the Great—built huge temples in what had been Kushite territory.

Effects of the Conquest

Kush remained an Egyptian territory for about 450 years. During that time, Egypt's influence over Kush grew tremendously. Many Egyptians settled in Kush, and Egyptian became the language of the region. Many Kushites used Egyptian names, and they wore Egyptian-style clothing. They also adopted Egyptian religious practices.

A Change in Power

During the mid-1000s BC the New Kingdom in Egypt was ending. As the power of Egypt's pharaohs declined, Kushite leaders regained control of Kush. Kush once again became independent.

READING CHECK **Identifying Cause and Effect** How did Egyptian rule change Kush?

Kush and Egypt

Early in its history, Egypt dominated Kush, forcing Kushites to give tribute to Egypt.

124 CHAPTER 5

Critical Thinking: Analyzing Information
Reaching Standards

Charting Natural Resources 🐘 **HSS** 6.2.8; **HSS** Analysis Skills: CS 3

1. To promote understanding of Kush's trade in raw materials, copy the chart at right for students to see. Omit the blue, italicized answers.

2. Have students copy the chart and complete it by using what they know, by looking at the section's visuals, and by making predictions. Students should also refer back to the chapter on Egypt for ideas. **LS** **Visual/Spatial**

Kush's Exports	
Natural Resources	How Might Have Been Used
gold	*coins, jewelry*
copper	*coins, pots, tools*
stone	*pyramids, temples, statues*
ebony	*furniture, decorative items*
ivory	*small statues, jewelry, decorative items*

Kush Rules Egypt

We know almost nothing about the history of the Kushites for about 200 years after they regained independence from Egypt. Kush is not mentioned in any historical records until the 700s BC, when armies from Kush swept into Egypt and conquered it.

The Conquest of Egypt

By around 850 BC, Kush had regained its strength. It was once again as strong as it had been before it had been conquered by Egypt. Because the Egyptians had captured the city of Kerma, the kings of Kush ruled from the city of Napata. Napata was located on the Nile, about 100 miles southeast of Kerma.

As Kush was growing stronger, Egypt was losing power. A series of weak pharaohs left Egypt open to attack. In the 700s BC a Kushite king, Kashta, took advantage of Egypt's weakness. Kashta attacked Egypt, and by about 751 BC he had conquered Upper Egypt. He then established relations with Lower Egypt.

After Kashta died, his son **Piankhi** (PYANG-kee) continued to attack Egypt. The armies of Kush captured many cities, including Egypt's ancient capital. Piankhi fought the Egyptians because he believed that the gods wanted him to rule all of Egypt. By the time he died in about 716 BC, Piankhi had accomplished this task. His kingdom extended north from Napata to the Nile Delta.

Later, as Kush's power increased, its warriors invaded and conquered Egypt. This photo shows Kushite and Egyptian warriors.

After conquering Egypt, Kush established a new dynasty. This photo shows one of Kush's pharaohs kneeling before an Egyptian god.

ANALYSIS SKILL **ANALYZING VISUALS**
What did Kushites give to Egypt as tribute?

ANCIENT KUSH **125**

125

Other People, Other Places

Chariots in the Ancient World The use of chariots, such as the one in the photo, probably began in Mesopotamia about 3000 BC. Horses had not been introduced to the region at that time, so the first chariots were drawn by oxen or donkeys. Eventually, chariots contributed to victories not just in Mesopotamia and Egypt but also in Anatolia, India, Greece, China, and western Europe. Each culture developed somewhat different designs. Assyrians were the first warriors to equip the wheels with long blades, which functioned as weapons.

Close

Call on volunteers to pose new questions about the images in this section and for other students to suggest answers.

Review

Online Quiz, Section 1

Assess

SE Section 1 Assessment

PASS: Section 1 Quiz

Alternative Assessment Handbook

Reteach/Classroom Intervention

California Standards Review Workbook

Interactive Reader and Study Guide, Section 1

Interactive Skills Tutor CD-ROM

When the Assyrians invaded Egypt with their iron weapons, they forced Kush's rulers out of Egypt and south into Nubia.

The Kushite Dynasty

After Piankhi died, his brother Shabaka (SHAB-uh-kuh) took control of the kingdom. Shabaka then declared himself pharaoh. This declaration began the Twenty-fifth, or Kushite, Dynasty in Egypt.

Shabaka and later rulers of his dynasty tried to restore old Egyptian cultural practices. Some of these practices had faded during Egypt's period of weakness. For example, Shabaka was buried in a pyramid. The Egyptians had stopped building pyramids for their rulers centuries before.

The Kushite rulers of Egypt built new temples to Egyptian gods and restored old ones. They also worked to preserve Egyptian writings. As a result, Egyptian culture thrived during the Kushite dynasty.

The End of Kushite Rule in Egypt

The Kushite dynasty remained strong in Egypt for about 40 years. In the 670s BC, however, the powerful army of the Assyrians from Mesopotamia invaded Egypt. The Assyrians' iron weapons were better than the Kushites' bronze weapons, and the Kushites were slowly pushed out of Egypt. In just 10 years the Assyrians had driven the Kushite forces completely out of Egypt.

READING CHECK Identifying Cause and Effect How did internal problems in Egypt benefit Kush?

SUMMARY AND PREVIEW Kush was conquered by Egypt, but later the Kushites controlled Egypt. In the next section, you will learn how the civilization of Kush developed after the Kushites were forced out of Egypt by the Assyrians.

Section 1 Assessment

go.hrw.com
Online Quiz
KEYWORD: SQ6 HP5

Reviewing Ideas, Terms, and People **HSS** 6.2.8

1. **a. Identify** On which river did Kush develop?
   b. Analyze How did Nubia's natural resources influence the early history of Kush?
2. **a. Describe** What is **ebony**?
   b. Analyze Why did people in Kush adopt some elements of Egyptian culture?
   c. Evaluate Why do you think Thutmose I destroyed the Kushite palace at Kerma?
3. **a. Describe** What territory did **Piankhi** conquer?
   b. Make Inferences Why is the Twenty-fifth Dynasty significant in the history of Egypt?
   c. Predict What might have happened in Kush and Egypt if Kush had developed iron weapons?

Critical Thinking

4. **Identifying Cause and Effect** Create a chart like the one here. For each cause listed, identify one effect.

Cause	Effect
Villages appear along the Nile.	
Kush trades with Egypt.	
Piankhi conquers Egypt.	
Assyrians use iron weapons.	

FOCUS ON WRITING

5. **Characters and Plot** Make a chart with two columns labeled "Characters" and "Plot." In one column, take notes on the main characters and their interactions. In the other column, note major events and sources of conflict between the characters.

Section 1 Assessment Answers

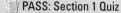

1. **a.** the Nile
   b. Nubia's natural resources were in demand in Egypt, so they helped Kush grow in wealth and power.
2. **a.** a dark wood
   b. For a period, it was the culture of their rulers.
   c. possible answer—to eliminate a symbol of Kushite independence
3. **a.** north from Napata to the Nile Delta
   b. possible answer—because Kushite leaders ruled and restored many ancient Egyptian cultural practices and traditions

c. They might have fought off the Assyrians.

4. possible answers—Villages appear along the Nile: Village leaders become kings, and civilization develops; Kush trades with Egypt: Kush becomes wealthy, and Egypt invades; Piankhi conquers Egypt: Twenty-fifth Dynasty is founded, and old Egyptian cultural practices and traditions are restored; Assyrians use iron weapons: Kushites are defeated and pushed out of Egypt.

5. Students' charts will vary but should reflect section content and mention key people covered.

Answers

Reading Check They made Egypt weak and vulnerable to attack from Kush.

Later Kush

If YOU were there...

You live in Meroë, the capital of Kush, in 250 BC. Your father is a skilled ironworker. From him you've learned to shape iron tools and weapons. Everyone expects that you will carry on his work. If you do become an ironworker, you will likely make a good living. But you are restless. You'd like to travel down the Nile to see Egypt and the great sea beyond it. Now a neighbor who is a trader has asked you to join his next trading voyage.

Will you leave Meroë to travel? Why or why not?

BUILDING BACKGROUND The Assyrians drove the Kushites out of Egypt in the 600s BC, partly through their use of iron weapons. Although the Kushites lost control of Egypt, their kingdom did not disappear. In fact, they built up another empire in the African interior, based on trade and their own iron industry.

Kush's Economy Grows

After they lost control of Egypt, the people of Kush devoted themselves to increasing agriculture and trade, hoping to make their country rich again. Within a few centuries, Kush had indeed become a rich and powerful kingdom once more.

Kushite Metalwork
Kush's craftspeople made iron spearheads and gold jewelry like you see here.

PHOTOGRAPH © 2004
MUSEUM OF FINE ARTS, BOSTON

What You Will Learn...

Main Ideas

1. Kush's economy grew because of its iron industry and trade network.
2. Society and culture in Kush had elements borrowed from other cultures and elements unique to Kush.
3. The decline and defeat of Kush was caused by both internal and external factors.

The Big Idea

Kush developed an advanced civilization with a large trading network.

Key Terms and People

trade network, *p. 128*
merchants, *p. 128*
exports, *p. 128*
imports, *p. 128*
Queen Shanakhdakheto, *p. 129*
King Ezana, *p. 131*

HSS 6.2.8 Identify the location of the Kush civilization and describe its political, commercial, and cultural relations with Egypt.

ANCIENT KUSH **127**

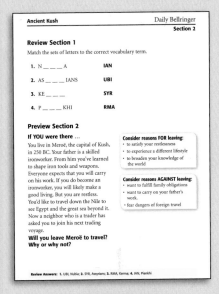

❶ Kush's Economy Grows

Kush's economy grew because of its iron industry and trade network.

Identify What city became the capital and economic center of later Kush? *Meroë*

Recall How did Kush rebuild its economy? *through agriculture and trade*

Make Inferences In what parts of the world might archaeologists find Kushite export items? *Egypt, the Mediterranean and Red seas, southern Africa, possibly India and China*

Activity **Kush's Trade Network**
Photocopy the map on this page and provide a copy for each student. Supply art materials. Have students draw and cut out symbols for the various products that were traded along the network. Ask students to put the symbols in their places of origin and then to move them along the trade route to their destinations.

LS Kinesthetic, Visual/Spatial

📖 Alternative Assessment Handbook, Rubric 21: Map Reading

🐻 **HSS** 6.2.8; **HSS** Analysis Skills: CS 3, HI 1

Kush's Trade Network

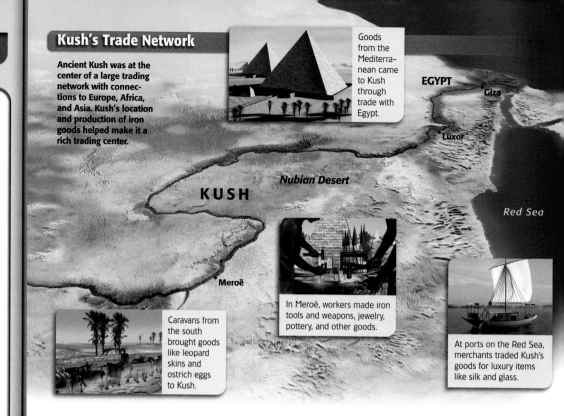

Ancient Kush was at the center of a large trading network with connections to Europe, Africa, and Asia. Kush's location and production of iron goods helped make it a rich trading center.

Goods from the Mediterranean came to Kush through trade with Egypt.

EGYPT

Giza

Luxor

Nubian Desert

KUSH

Red Sea

Meroë

In Meroë, workers made iron tools and weapons, jewelry, pottery, and other goods.

Caravans from the south brought goods like leopard skins and ostrich eggs to Kush.

At ports on the Red Sea, merchants traded Kush's goods for luxury items like silk and glass.

Kush's Iron Industry

The economic center of Kush during this period was Meroë (MER-oh-wee), the kingdom's new capital. Meroë's location on the east bank of the Nile helped Kush's economy. Gold could be found nearby, as could forests of ebony and other wood. More importantly, the area around Meroë was full of iron ore deposits.

In this location the Kushites developed an iron industry. Because resources such as iron ore and wood for furnaces were easily available, the industry grew quickly.

Expansion of Trade

In time, Meroë became the center of a large **trade network**, a system of people in different lands who trade goods back and forth.

The Kushites sent goods down the Nile to Egypt. From there, Egyptian and Greek **merchants**, or traders, carried goods to ports on the Mediterranean and Red seas and to southern Africa. These goods may have eventually reached India and China.

Kush's **exports**—items sent to other regions for trade—included gold, pottery, iron tools, slaves, and ivory. Kushite merchants also exported leopard skins, ostrich feathers, and elephants. In return, the Kushites received **imports**—goods brought in from other regions—such as fine jewelry and luxury items from Egypt, Asia, and lands around the Mediterranean Sea.

READING CHECK **Drawing Inferences** What helped Kush's iron industry grow?

Differentiating Instruction for Universal Access

Advanced Learners/GATE   Exceeding Standards   Research Required

1. Have students conduct research into how ancient peoples made iron. Then organize students into groups of four and have students choose a role from among the following: wood cutter, miner, bellows operator, and blacksmith.

2. Ask each group to write a short skit that explains how iron is made. Skits should be suitable for presentation to elementary school students, as if they were on a field trip to a Kushite iron-making workshop.

3. Have the students perform their skits for the class. Discuss the skits to make sure that students understand the iron-making process.

LS Interpersonal, Kinesthetic

🐻 **HSS** 6.2.8; **HSS** Analysis Skills: HR 1, HI 1

📖 Alternative Assessment Handbook, Rubrics 30: Research; and 33: Skits and Reader's Theater

Answers

Reading Check *the availability of resources such as wood and iron ore*

Society and Culture

As Kushite trade grew, merchants came into contact with people from other cultures. As a result, the people of Kush combined customs from other cultures with their own unique Kushite culture.

Kushite Culture

The most obvious influence on Kushite culture was Egypt. Many buildings in Meroë, especially temples, resembled those in Egypt. Many people in Kush worshipped Egyptian gods and wore Egyptian clothing. Like Egypt's rulers, the rulers of Kush used the title *pharaoh* and were buried in pyramids.

Many elements of Kushite culture were unique and not borrowed from anywhere else. For example, Kushite daily life and houses were different from those in other places. One Greek geographer noted some of these differences.

"The houses in the cities are formed by interweaving split pieces of palm wood or of bricks . . . They hunt elephants, lions, and panthers. There are also serpents, which encounter elephants, and there are many other kinds of wild animals."
– Strabo, from *The Geographies*

In addition to Egyptian gods, people of Kush worshipped their own gods. For example, they prayed to the lion-headed god Apedemek. Also, they developed their own written language, Meroitic. Unfortunately, historians are not able to understand this language.

Women in Kushite Society

Unlike the women of some other early societies, the women of Kush were expected to be active in their society. Like Kushite men, women worked long hours in the fields. They also raised children, cooked, and performed other household tasks. During times of war, many Kushite women fought alongside men.

Some Kushite women rose to positions of great **authority**, especially religious authority. For example, King Piankhi made his sister a powerful priestess. Later rulers followed his example and made other princesses priestesses as well. Other women from royal families led the ceremonies in which new kings were crowned.

Some Kushite women had even more power. These women served as co-rulers with their husbands or sons. A few Kushite women, such as **Queen Shanakhdakheto** (shah-nahk-dah-KEE-toh), even ruled the empire alone. Several other queens ruled Kush later, helping increase the strength and wealth of the kingdom. Throughout most of its history, however, Kush was ruled by kings.

READING CHECK **Contrasting** How was Kushite culture unlike Egyptian culture?

THE IMPACT TODAY

More than 50 ancient Kushite pyramids still stand near the ruins of Meroë.

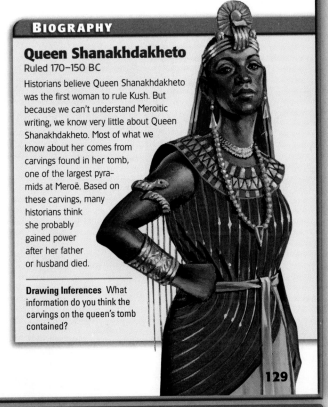

BIOGRAPHY

Queen Shanakhdakheto
Ruled 170–150 BC

Historians believe Queen Shanakhdakheto was the first woman to rule Kush. But because we can't understand Meroitic writing, we know very little about Queen Shanakhdakheto. Most of what we know about her comes from carvings found in her tomb, one of the largest pyramids at Meroë. Based on these carvings, many historians think she probably gained power after her father or husband died.

Drawing Inferences What information do you think the carvings on the queen's tomb contained?

129

129

History Close-up
Rulers of Kush

Activity Ask students these questions to highlight similarities and differences between Kushite and Egyptian culture.

1. Which culture believed their rulers to be gods? *both*

2. How were Kushite pyramids different from Egyptian pyramids? *smaller, different style*

3. How were Kushite queens viewed compared to Egyptian queens? *seem to have been more important*

4. Why did the Kushites and Egyptians carve on stone? *to commemorate important buildings and events*

Linking to Today

Collections of Kushite Artifacts Some of the finest collections of Kushite artifacts are here in the United States. These collections are on display at Boston's Museum of Fine Arts, Philadelphia's University Museum, and Chicago's Oriental Institute Museum. These museums have all participated in archaeological digs in Nubia.

Answers

Analyzing Visuals *pyramids, wigs, clothing and jewelry styles, stone carvings*

130

History Close-up

Rulers of Kush

Like the Egyptians, the people of Kush considered their rulers to be gods. Kush's culture was similar to Egypt's, but there were also important differences.

Like the Egyptians, Kush's rulers built pyramids, but they were much smaller and the style was different.

Kush was ruled by a few different powerful queens. Queens seem to have been more important in Kush than in Egypt.

Stone carvings were made to commemorate important buildings and events, just like in Egypt. Kush's writing system was similar to Egyptian hieroglyphics, but scholars have been unable to understand most of it.

ANALYSIS SKILL **ANALYZING VISUALS**

What can you see in the illustration that is similar to Egyptian culture?

130 CHAPTER 5

Differentiating Instruction for Universal Access

Special Education Students   Reaching Standards

Materials: art supplies

Have students design their own stone carvings to represent information about Kush.

1. Discuss with students what they have learned about ancient Kush and its relations with Egypt.

2. Have each student identify two pieces of information they know about ancient Kush.

3. Have students study the stone carving on this page. Tell students to draw on paper a stone carving that uses pictures to relate their two pieces of information. **LS Visual/Spatial**

HSS 6.2.8; **HSS Analysis Skills:** HI 1

 Alternative Assessment Handbook, Rubric 3: Artwork

Decline and Defeat

The Kushite kingdom centered at Meroë reached its height in the first century BC. Four centuries later, the empire had collapsed. Developments both inside and outside of Kush led to this downfall.

Loss of Resources

A series of problems within Kush weakened its economic power. One possible problem was that farmers allowed their cattle to overgraze the land. When the cows ate all the grass, there was nothing to hold the soil down. As a result, wind blew the soil away. Without this soil, farmers couldn't produce enough food for Kush's people.

In addition, ironmakers probably used up the forests near Meroë. As wood became scarce, furnaces shut down. Kush could no longer produce enough weapons or trade goods. As a result, Kush's military and economic power declined.

Trade Rivals

Kush was also weakened by a loss of trade. Foreign merchants set up new trade routes that went around Kush. For example, a new trade route bypassed Kush in favor of a nearby kingdom, Aksum (AHK-soom).

Rise of Aksum

Aksum was located southeast of Kush on the Red Sea, in present-day Ethiopia and Eritrea. In the first two centuries AD, Aksum grew wealthy from trade. But Aksum's wealth and power came at the expense of Kush. As Kush's power declined, Aksum became the most powerful state in the region.

By the AD 300s, Kush had lost much of its wealth and military might. Seeing that the Kushites were weak, the king of Aksum sent an army to conquer his former trade rival. In about AD 350, the Aksumite army of **King Ezana** (AY-zah-nah) destroyed Meroë and took over the kingdom of Kush.

In the late 300s, the rulers of Aksum became Christian. Their new religion reshaped culture throughout Nubia, and the last influences of Kush disappeared.

THE IMPACT TODAY

Much of the population of Ethiopia, which includes what used to be Aksum, is still Christian.

READING CHECK Summarizing Why did Kush's power decline?

SUMMARY AND PREVIEW From their capital at Meroë, the people of Kush controlled a powerful trading network. Next, you will learn about one of Kush's possible trading partners—India.

---

go.hrw.com
Online Quiz
KEYWORD: SQ6 HP5

Section 2 Assessment

Reviewing Ideas, Terms, and People HSS 6.2.8

1. a. **Recall** What city became Kush's third capital?
   b. **Analyze** Why was this capital in a good location?
2. a. **Identify** Who was **Queen Shanakhdakheto**?
   b. **Compare** How were Kushite and Egyptian cultures similar?
   c. **Elaborate** How does our inability to understand Meroitic affect our knowledge of Kush's culture?
3. a. **Identify** What kingdom conquered Kush in the AD 300s?
   b. **Summarize** What was the impact of new trade routes on Kush?

Critical Thinking

4. **Categorizing** Draw a diagram like this one in your notebook. Use it to list causes of the rise and causes of the fall of the Kushite kingdom centered at Meroë.

Causes of rise	Causes of fall

FOCUS ON WRITING

5. **Adding Details** Add details to your chart. What were your characters' lives like? What events caused Kush to change over time? Note events that your characters might take part in during your story.

ANCIENT KUSH **131**

Section 2 Assessment Answers

1. a. Meroë
   b. nearby gold, ebony and other wood, iron ore deposits
2. a. possibly the first woman to rule Kush
   b. had similar clothing and building styles, used title pharaoh, worshiped some similar gods, had some female rulers
   c. We can read only what non-Meroitic writers have recorded, so many details are missing, and we may have misinterpreted some information.
3. a. Aksum
   b. Kush was weakened by loss of trade.
4. Causes of rise—fertile soil, valuable natural resources, iron industry, trade; Causes of fall—overgrazing that led to loss of fertile soil, forests used up so iron weapons and trade goods no longer produced, new trade routes that bypassed Kush, weakness of Kush
5. Charts will vary, but students should demonstrate knowledge of the key events listed in the previous answer.

Direct Teach

Main Idea

❸ Decline and Defeat

The decline and defeat of Kush was caused by both internal and external factors.

Describe Why did agriculture and ironmaking decline in Kush? *Cows ate the grass, and the soil blew away; ironmakers cut down the forests.*

Analyze How did shifts in trade routes affect Kush? *New trade routes that went around Kush weakened Kush and its economy further.*

CRF: Literature Activity: The Fall of Meroë

HSS 6.2.8; **HSS** Analysis Skills: HI 1

Review & Assess

Close

Review the reasons that a large trading network was important to Kush.

Review

Online Quiz, Section 2

Assess

SE Section 2 Assessment
PASS: Section 2 Quiz
Alternative Assessment Handbook

Reteach/Classroom Intervention

California Standards Review Workbook
Interactive Reader and Study Guide, Section 2
Interactive Skills Tutor CD-ROM

Answers

Reading Check *With the loss of resources such as fertile soil and forests, Kush's military and economic power declined. New trade routes that bypassed Kush furthered its decline.*

131

Participating in Groups

Social Studies Skills

HSS **Participation Skill** Develop group interaction skills.

| Analysis | Critical Thinking | Participation | Study |

Participating in Groups

Understand the Skill

Making decisions can be difficult. It can be even harder if the decision is being made by a group. Organizing tasks and taking actions might be simpler if one person decided what to do, but that approach does not respect the desires and needs of the group's other members. Group participation is an important skill. A successful group depends on its members' ability to work together.

Learn the Skill

To be an effective part of an effective group, you and the other members need to behave in the following ways.

❶ Be an active member of the group. Take part in setting the group's goals, making its decisions, planning, and taking action.

❷ State your views and try to persuade others to accept them. However, be willing to listen to their views too. They have the same rights as you do. You have a duty to listen, even if you disagree.

❸ Be willing to negotiate and compromise to settle differences.

Practice and Apply the Skill

You learned in Chapter 5 that trade caused Egypt to fear Kush's power. Imagine that you are a citizen of Kush. To prevent an invasion by Egypt, the king has named you to a council of merchants, farmers, craftspeople, and soldiers, a council represented by a group of your classmates. The council has been asked to create rules that will govern trade between Egypt and Kush and calm Egypt's fears. When your group has finished, answer the following questions.

1. Did the members of your group have differences of opinion about what to do? Explain. Evaluate your part in this discussion.

2. Did your group work well together to make decisions? Why or why not? Was compromise involved in your final decision? Explain.

Social Studies Skills Activity: Participating In Groups

Planning to Regain Independence from Egypt

Standards Proficiency

1. To extend the "Practice and Apply the Skill" activity, have students stay in their same groups and keep their roles as citizens of Kush. Tell students that it is the mid-100s BC and they are planning how to regain independence from Egypt.

2. Give each group a set amount of time to come up with a plan. Remind the groups to give each member a chance to speak his or her views and to participate.

3. When the groups are finished, have a representative from each group explain the group's plan to the class.

4. Then have each group discuss the activity by answering the two questions listed at the end of the above feature. **LS Interpersonal**

Alternative Assessment Handbook, Rubric 14: Group Activity

Answers

Practice and Apply the Skill
Answers will vary but students should exhibit an understanding of how group members should work together, how to compromise, and what constitutes problems in group interaction and decision-making.

Standards Review

Visual Summary

Use the visual summary below to help you review the main ideas of the chapter.

QUICK FACTS

Egypt dominated early Kush and forced the Kushites to pay tribute.

After Kush conquered Egypt, invaders forced the Kushites to move south to their ancient homeland.

Kush developed an advanced civilization that blended Egyptian culture with cultures from other parts of Africa.

Reviewing Terms and People

Match the words in the columns with the correct definitions listed below.

1. ebony
2. Piankhi
3. authority
4. merchant
5. export
6. import
7. Shanakhdakheto
8. trade network

a. item sent to other regions for trade
b. king who extended the Kushite empire into Egypt
c. a trader
d. dark, heavy wood
e. groups of people in different lands who trade goods back and forth
f. may have been the first woman to rule Kush by herself
g. item brought in for purchase from other regions
h. power or influence

Comprehension and Critical Thinking

SECTION 1 *(Pages 122–126)* **HSS** **6.2.8**

9. **a. Describe** How did Nubia's physical features affect civilization in the region?

   b. Analyze Why did the relationship between Kush and Egypt change more than once over the centuries?

   c. Predict If an archaeologist found an artifact near the Fourth Cataract, why might he or she have difficulty deciding how to display it in a museum?

SECTION 2 *(Pages 127–131)* **HSS** **6.2.8**

10. **a. Identify** Who was Queen Shanakhdakheto? Why don't we know more about her?

    b. Compare and Contrast What are some features that Kushite and Egyptian cultures had in common? How were they different?

    c. Evaluate How did two types of environmental damage contribute to the decline of Kush?

ANCIENT KUSH **133**

Answers

Visual Summary

Review and Inquiry Have students use the visual summary to explain the causes and effects of Kush's rise.

Quick Facts Transparency: Ancient Kush Visual Summary

Reviewing Vocabulary, Terms, and People

1. d
2. b
3. h
4. c
5. a
6. g
7. f
8. e

Comprehension and Critical Thinking

9. **a.** The Nile's annual flooding allowed Nubian farmers to plant both summer and winter crops, which allowed farming villages to thrive. Cataracts on the Nile provided some protection from invasion.

   b. Egypt conquered and ruled Kush and later Kush conquered and ruled Egypt.

   c. because Egypt conquered Kush above the Fifth Cataract, which could make it hard to determine whether the artifact was Kushite or Egyptian; also because Kush and Egypt shared styles

---

10. a. probably the first woman to rule Kush; because historians cannot read Meroitic writing

b. in common—building styles, clothing styles, some gods, use of the title pharaoh, pyramids; in contrast—housing styles, written languages, some unique gods, women had more power in Kush.

c. Farmers allowed their cattle to overgraze the land, which led to soil erosion and a decrease in food production. Also, the destruction of the forest near Meroë caused wood to become scarce and furnaces to shut down. The Kushites could no longer produce enough weapons or trade goods to supply the military or feed the economy.

Using the Internet

11. Go to the HRW Web site and enter the keyword shown to access a rubric for this activity.

> **KEYWORD: SA6 TEACHER**

Reading and Analysis Skills

12. e

13. d

14. a

15. b

16. c

Using the Internet
go.hrw.com
KEYWORD: SQ6 WH5

11. Activity: Researching Life in Ancient Nubia
Would you like to travel back in time to ancient Nubia and explore the wonders of that era? Enter the activity keyword. Then find out about the people, their customs, and their homes. Finally, imagine that you are a person living in ancient Nubia. Take notes about your imagined life and use a chart like the one below to organize your information. Write a journal entry to show what you have learned. In your journal entry, specify which parts of your life have Egyptian influences.

Activities	
Religion	
Homes	

Reading and Analysis Skills

Understanding Cause and Effect *Match each cause in List A with an effect from List B.*

List A

12. The army of Kush conquered Egypt.

13. The Nile flooded every year.

14. Meroë had large deposits of iron ore.

15. Kush and Aksum were trade rivals.

16. The Assyrians' iron weapons were better than the Kushites' bronze weapons.

List B

a. Kush developed an iron industry.

b. Aksum conquered Kush.

c. The Kushites were driven out of Egypt.

d. The soils of Nubia were very fertile.

e. The Kushite dynasty took power.

Reviewing Themes

17. Geography How did Kush's location on the Nile shape its early history?

18. Economics What led to the creation of Africa's first iron industry in Kush?

Social Studies Skills

19. Developing Group Interaction Skills Working with a small group of your classmates, imagine that you are the leaders of a small village located between Egypt and Kush. The rulers of the two countries have demanded that you choose which country you want to belong to. As a group, decide which country you will join. Remember to look at benefits and challenges associated with joining each country before you make your decision. You may want to use a chart like the one below to help your group organize your thoughts and make your decision.

	Benefits	Challenges
Egypt		
Kush		

> **FOCUS ON WRITING**

20. Writing Your Story Use the notes you have taken to write your short story about a character from Kush. First, introduce your characters and describe them to readers. In your next paragraph, develop the plot of your story by telling about the conflicts that arise between the characters. In a final paragraph, describe how these conflicts come to a climax and eventually get resolved. Use as many concrete, descriptive details as possible to make your characters and your story come alive for your readers.

Reviewing Themes

17. The Nile floods allowed agriculture to flourish. The kingdom of Kush grew from farming villages. Also, the cataracts provided some protection from invasion.

18. Kush's new location was rich in iron ore and wood, both of which were necessary for an iron industry.

Social Studies Skills

19. Group responses will vary but should display knowledge of both Kush and Egypt.

Focus on Writing

20. Rubric Students' short stories should:

- include a description of the students' characters.
- offer a well-developed plot.
- contain concrete, descriptive details.

CRF: Focus on Writing: A Short Story

Standards Assessment

DIRECTIONS: Read each question, and write the letter of the best response.

1 Geography greatly influenced the development of Kushite society. Which of the following was *not* a benefit that geography provided for Kush?

A fertile soil for farming

B a port on the Red Sea

C protection against invaders for many years

D valuable gold, copper, and wood for trade

2 The ancient kingdom of Kush arose in what region?

A Egypt

B Nubia

C Aksum

D Mesopotamia

3 Which of the following statements about the relationship of Egypt and Kush is *not* true?

A Egypt ruled Kush for many centuries.

B Kush was an important trading partner of Egypt.

C Egypt sent the first people to colonize Kush.

D Kush ruled Egypt for a period of time.

4 How did Egypt influence Kush?

A Egypt taught Kush how to raise cattle.

B Kush adopted Christianity.

C Egypt taught Kush to make iron products.

D Kush learned about pyramids from Egypt.

5 The fall of the Kushite civilization resulted from all of the following events *except*

A the conquest of Kush by Egypt.

B Kush's exhaustion of its natural resources.

C new trade routes that bypassed Kush.

D the rise of a rival kingdom in the region.

Connecting with Past Learnings

6 You recently learned about the development of civilization in Sumer. Kush and Sumer had all of the following in common *except*

A the importance of farming in their early civilization.

B the rise of manufacturing and crafts.

C involvement in trade.

D the Meroitic writing system.

7 Kush, Egypt, and Sumer all share which of the following characteristics?

A All developed along rivers.

B All worshipped the same gods.

C All used the same money.

D All spoke the same language.

1. B
Break Down the Question Refer students who miss the question to the map on p. 123.

2. B
Break Down the Question This question requires students to recall factual information. Refer students who miss the question to the map on p. 123.

3. C
Break Down the Question This question requires students to recall that connections between Egypt and Kush began later than the establishment of agriculture in Nubia.

4. D
Break Down the Question Refer students who missed the question to the *Society and Culture* material in Section 2.

5. A
Break Down the Question Remind students who missed this question that the conquest of Kush by Egypt had happened long before the fall of Kushite civilization.

6. D
Break Down the Question This question requires students to recall that the Meroitic script was unique to Kush, and that Sumer had its own writing system.

7. A
Break Down the Question Remind students that Egypt also developed along the Nile River, and Sumer developed along the Tigris and Euphrates rivers.

Standards Review

Have students review the following standard in their workbooks.

California Standards Review Workbook:
HSS 6.2.8

Intervention Resources
Reproducible

- Interactive Reader and Study Guide
- Universal Access Teacher Management System: Lesson Plans for Universal Access

Technology

- Quick Facts Transparency: Ancient Kush Visual Summary
- Universal Access Modified Worksheets and Tests CD-ROM
- Interactive Skills Tutor CD-ROM

Tips for Test Taking

Nothing But the Truth Point out to students that it is sometimes easy to get tripped up on true/false questions. To avoid this, students should read the entire question before answering. The entire sentence or statement must be true if the answer is true. If any part of the statement is false, the entire answer is false.

Bellringer

Motivate To help students see the value of sensory descriptions, ask students to think of a favorite place. Then have them use the five senses—touch, taste, sight, sound, and smell—to describe the place. Tell students that good writers use all five senses when writing descriptions. Encourage students to do the same as they write their descriptions of a historical place in ancient Mesopotamia or Africa.

Direct Teach

Vivid Description

Show Me Remind students of the importance of showing versus telling. Give them the following sentences, and have students revise the sentences by adding descriptive details so that they show rather than tell.

1. It rained on the first day of the outdoor market.

2. The stands were full of colorful fruits and vegetables.

3. The gymnasium was brightly decorated for the school dance.

Assignment

Write a description of a place—a city, village, building, or monument—in ancient Mesopotamia or Africa.

TIP **Organizing Details**

Organize the details you gather in one of these ways.

- **Spatial Order** Arrange details according to where they are. You can describe things from right to left, top to bottom, or faraway to close up.

- **Chronological Order** Arrange details in the order they occurred or in the order that you experienced them.

- **Order of Importance** Arrange details from the most to least important or vice versa.

ELA **Writing 6.2.0** Students write descriptive texts.

A Description of a Historical Place

If a picture is worth a thousand words, then a thousand words could add up to a good description. Writers turn to description when they want to explain what a place is like—what you would see if you were there, or what you might hear, smell, or touch.

1. Prewrite

Picking a Subject and a Main Idea

Think about the civilizations of ancient Mesopotamia and Africa. Which civilization seems most interesting to you? What villages, cities, or buildings seem interesting? Select one place and use this textbook, the Internet, or sources in your library to find out more about it.

You also need to decide on your point of view about your subject. For example, was this place scary, exciting, or overwhelming?

Choosing Details

As you conduct your research, look for details to show your readers what it would have been like to actually be in that place.

- **Sensory Details** What color(s) do you associate with your subject? What shape or shapes do you see? What sounds would you hear if you were there? What could you touch—rough walls, dry grass, a smooth, polished stone?

- **Factual Details** How big was this place? Where was it located? When did it exist? If people were there, what were they doing?

When you choose the details to use in your description, think about your point of view on this place. If it was exciting, choose details that will help you show that.

2. Write

This framework will help you use your notes to write a first draft.

A Writer's Framework

Introduction	Body	Conclusion
■ Identify your subject and your point of view on it. ■ Give your readers any background information that they might need.	■ Describe your subject, using sensory and factual details. ■ Follow a consistent and logical order.	■ Briefly summarize the most important details about the place. ■ Reveal your point of view about the place.

136 UNIT 2

Differentiating Instruction for Universal Access

Advanced Learners/GATE   [Exceeding Standards]

Time-Travel Brochure Challenge advanced learners by having them present their descriptions in the form of a time-travel brochure. In addition to description, students should use persuasion to encourage tourists to visit the ancient place of their choice. Have students consider what words and phrases will make the place seem inviting and make people want to go there. **LS** **Verbal/Linguistic**

ELA Writing 6.2.0

Learners Having Difficulty   [Reaching Standards]

Sensory Details Chart English learners may have a limited vocabulary of descriptive words. To help them expand their vocabulary, draw a five-column chart and label the columns *Sight, Sound, Taste, Touch,* and *Smell.* Help students compile a list of lively and rich descriptive words for each sense. Let students refer to the chart as they write. **LS** **Verbal/Linguistic**

ELA Writing 6.2.0

Standards Focus

ELA Writing 6.2.0

3. Evaluate and Revise

Evaluating

Use the following questions to discover ways to improve your paper.

Evaluation Questions for a Description of a Place

- Do you immediately catch the reader's interest?
- Do you use sensory and factual details that work together to create a vivid picture of your subject?
- Do you clearly state your point of view or most important idea?
- Is the information organized clearly?
- Do you end the description by summarizing the most important details?

TIP **Showing Location** When describing the physical appearance of something, make sure you use precise words and phrases to explain where a feature is located. Some useful words and phrases for explaining location are *below, beside, down, on top, over, next to, to the right,* and *to the left.*

Revising

We often help others understand or imagine something by making a comparison. Sometimes we compare two things that are really very much alike. For example, "The city grew like San Diego did. It spread along a protected harbor." At other times we compare two things that are not alike. These comparisons are called figures of speech, and they can help your readers see something in an interesting way.

- Similes compare two unlike things by using words such as *like* or *so.* **EXAMPLE** *The city center curved around the harbor like a crescent moon.*
- Metaphors compare two unlike things by saying one is the other. **EXAMPLE** *The city was the queen of the region.*

When you evaluate and revise your description, look for ways you can make your subject clearer by comparing it to something else.

4. Proofread and Publish

- Make sure you use commas correctly with a list of details. **EXAMPLE** *The temple was 67 feet high, 35 feet wide, and 40 feet deep.*
- Share your paper with students who wrote about a similar place. What details do your descriptions share? How are they different?
- Find or create a picture of the place you have described. Ask a classmate or a family member to read your description and compare it to the picture.

Practice and Apply

Use the steps and strategies outlined in this workshop to write your description of a place in ancient Mesopotamia or Africa.

Learners Having Difficulty | Reaching Standards

1. Some students may benefit from having pictures to look at as they create their descriptions. Help these students find relevant images in books, on the Internet, or in other sources.

2. Pair students and have partners describe aloud to each other what they see in one or more of the pictures they found. As one student describes a picture, have his or her partner take notes and record the sensory details and descriptive words and phrases the student uses.

3. Then have students expand their notes by answering the Sensory Details questions under "Choosing Details" for each picture they found.

4. Have students use the notes as a starting point for writing. Encourage students to refer back to their notes frequently as they write and revise their descriptions.

LS Auditory/Musical, Interpersonal

ELA Writing 6.2.0

Introduce the Unit

Share the information in the chapter overviews with students.

Chapter 6 Indian civilization developed and thrived in the Indus River Valley. The Harappan civilization was followed by the Aryans. As Aryan society became more complex, it divided into strict groups. This class system became a central part of Indian society. Two major religions, Hinduism and Buddhism, developed in India. Two great empires also emerged. The Mauryan Empire and the Gupta Empire in turn united much of India. During these empires, Indians made great advances in the arts and sciences.

Chapter 7 Chinese civilization began in the Huang He and Chang Jiang river valleys. Under the Shang dynasty, people developed a social order and a writing system. The Zhou dynasty succeeded the Shang. This dynasty eventually crumbled, however, and disorder erupted. In response, the new teachings of Confucianism, Daoism, and Legalism emerged. The Qin dynasty unified China with a strong government and a system of standardization. The Han dynasty then created a form of government that valued family, art, and learning. The arts and sciences flourished in China during this period. Trade also expanded, leading to the exchange of products and ideas between China and other cultures. From India, Buddhism came to China and gained many followers.

☀ Standards Focus

For a list of the overarching standards covered in this unit, see the first page of each chapter.

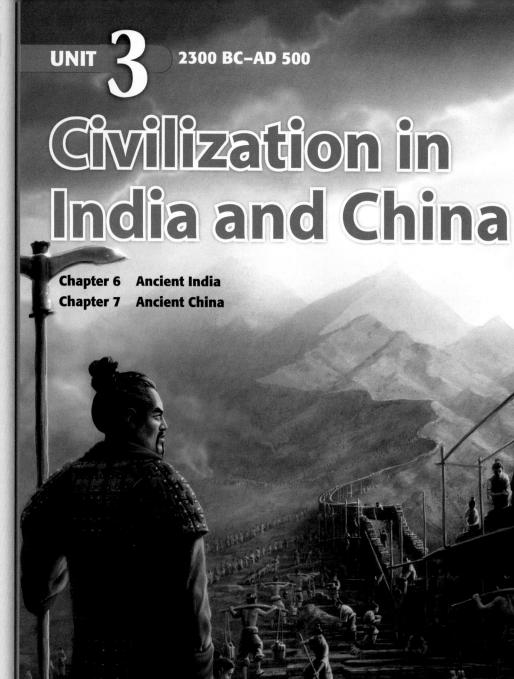

UNIT 3   2300 BC–AD 500

Civilization in India and China

Chapter 6   Ancient India
Chapter 7   Ancient China

138

Unit Resources

Planning

- 📋 Universal Access Teacher Management System: Unit Instructional Benchmarking Guides
- 💿 One-Stop Planner CD-ROM with Test Generator: Holt Calendar Planner
- 💿 Power Presentations with Video CD-ROM
- 📋 A Teacher's Guide to Religion in the Public Schools

Standards Mastery

- 📋 Standards Review Workbook
- 📋 At Home: A Guide to Standards Mastery for World History

Differentiating Instruction

- 📋 Universal Access Teacher Management System: Lesson Plans for Universal Access
- 💿 Universal Access Modified Worksheets and Tests CD-ROM

Enrichment

- 📋 **CRF 6:** Interdisciplinary Project: Ancient India: Aryan Society
- 📋 **CRF 7:** Economics and History: The Chinese Economy
- 📋 Civic Participation
- 💿 Primary Source Library CD-ROM

Assessment

- 📋 Progress Assessment Support System: Benchmark Test
- **OSP** ExamView Test Generator: Benchmark Test
- 🌐 Holt Online Assessment Program (in the Premier Online Edition)
- 📋 Alternative Assessment Handbook

The **Universal Access Teacher Management System** provides a planning and instructional benchmarking guide for this unit.

Two of the earliest civilizations of the ancient world arose in India and in China. In both of these places, river valleys provided the setting for the development of civilization. The Indians and Chinese built large empires and made many advances in science, art, and learning.

These civilizations also gave rise to new spiritual traditions. Two of the world's major religions—Hinduism and Buddhism—began in India. In China, the scholars Confucius and Laozi developed ideas that influenced Chinese thinking and society for more than 2,000 years.

In the next two chapters, you will learn about the advanced civilizations and cultures of India and China.

Explore the Art

In this scene, the Chinese emperor Shi Huangdi oversees the building of a massive wall in 220 BC. Why do you think people might build such a giant barrier?

Connect to the Unit

Activity **Comparing and Contrasting China and India** Draw a two-column table for students to see. Label the columns *Similarities* and *Differences*. Ask students how they think India and China are similar to one another. Then ask students how they think the two countries are different. Write students' responses in the appropriate columns. As students study this unit, encourage them to refer back to this table and to evaluate their responses.
LS **Visual/Spatial**

Explore the Art

Chinese emperor Shi Huangdi unified China. He also supported many building projects, including the massive wall pictured at left. This wall would later become part of what is now the Great Wall of China.

About the Illustration

This illustration is an artist's conception based on available sources. However, historians are uncertain exactly what this scene looked like. Historical records do not show that Emperor Shi Huangdi ever visited the site of the wall himself. He instead sent a trusted commander to supervise the project.

139

Democracy and Civic Education

Standards Proficiency

Justice: Confucianism, Daoism, and Legalism

Research Required

Background The teachings of Confucianism, Daoism, and Legalism emerged in ancient China in response to a period of political disorder. Each teaching provided different views of life, including views about ideal government and justice.

1. Organize students into small groups. Have each group create a three-column chart and label the columns *Confucianism, Daoism,* and *Legalism.* Have group members contrast how the three teachings define ideal government and justice.

2. Have the groups share their responses as you complete a master copy of the chart.

3. Then have the groups conduct research on the court system in their community or state and create charts describing the court system. How does this modern justice system compare to the concept of justice in each Chinese teaching?
LS **Interpersonal, Verbal/Linguistic**

Alternative Assessment Handbook, Rubrics 7: Charts; and 11: Discussion

Civic Participation

Answers

Explore the Art *to define their territory and to protect it from hostile invaders by providing a defensive barrier*

Chapter 6 Planning Guide

Ancient India

Chapter Overview	Reproducible Resources	Technology Resources
Chapter 6 **pp. 140–177** **Overview:** In this chapter, students will study the ancient civilizations of India and the two major religions that developed there. See page 140 for the California History–Social Science standards covered in this chapter.	**Universal Access Teacher Management System:*** • Universal Access Instructional Benchmarking Guides • Lesson Plans for Universal Access **Interactive Reader and Study Guide:** Chapter Graphic Organizer* **Chapter Resource File*** • Chapter Review Activity • Focus on Writing Activity: An Illustrated Poster • Social Studies Skills Activity: Interpreting Diagrams	**One-Stop Planner CD-ROM:** Calendar Planner **Student Edition on Audio CD Program** **Universal Access Modified Worksheets and Tests CD-ROM** **Power Presentations with Video CD-ROM** **History's Impact: World History Video Program (VHS/DVD):** Ancient India* **Music of the World Audio CD Program:** Selections 17 and 18
Section 1: **Geography and Early India** **The Big Idea:** Indian civilization first developed on the Indus River. 6.5.1, 6.5.2	**Universal Access Teacher Management System:*** Section 1 Lesson Plan **Interactive Reader and Study Guide:** Section 1 Summary* **Chapter Resource File*** • Vocabulary Builder Activity, Section 1 • History and Geography Activity: The Indus Valley	**Daily Bellringer Transparency:** Section 1* **Map Transparency:** India: Physical* **Map Transparency:** Aryan Invasions* **Internet Activity:** Travel to Ancient India!
Section 2: **Origins of Hinduism** **The Big Idea:** Hinduism, the largest religion in India today, developed out of ancient Indian beliefs and practices. 6.5.3, 6.5.4	**Universal Access Teacher Management System:*** Section 2 Lesson Plan **Interactive Reader and Study Guide:** Section 2 Summary* **Chapter Resource File*** • Vocabulary Builder Activity, Section 2 • Primary Source Activity: Gandhi's Autobiography	**Daily Bellringer Transparency:** Section 2* **Quick Facts Transparency:** The *Varnas** **Quick Facts Transparency:** Major Beliefs of Hinduism*
Section 3: **Origins of Buddhism** **The Big Idea:** Buddhism began in India and became a major religion. 6.5.5	**Universal Access Teacher Management System:*** Section 3 Lesson Plan **Interactive Reader and Study Guide:** Section 3 Summary* **Chapter Resource File*** • Vocabulary Builder Activity, Section 3	**Daily Bellringer Transparency:** Section 3* **Quick Facts Transparency:** The Eightfold Path* **Map Transparency:** Early Spread of Buddhism*
Section 4: **Indian Empires** **The Big Idea:** The Mauryas and the Guptas built great empires in India. 6.5.6	**Universal Access Teacher Management System:*** Section 4 Lesson Plan **Interactive Reader and Study Guide:** Section 4 Summary* **Chapter Resource File*** • Vocabulary Builder Activity, Section 4 • Biography Activities: Chandragupta Maurya; Kautilya; Mahinda	**Daily Bellringer Transparency:** Section 4* **Map Transparency:** Mauryan Empire, c. 320–185 BC* **Map Transparency:** Gupta Empire, c. 400* **Internet Activity:** Mauryan Leaders
Section 5: **Indian Achievements** **The Big Idea:** The people of ancient India made great contributions to the arts and sciences. 6.5.7	**Universal Access Teacher Management System:*** Section 5 Lesson Plan **Interactive Reader and Study Guide:** Section 5 Summary* **Chapter Resource File*** • Vocabulary Builder Activity, Section 5 • Literature Activity: Comparing Literature • Primary Source Activity: The Story of Savitri	**Daily Bellringer Transparency:** Section 5*

MASTERING THE CALIFORNIA STANDARDS

Key

SE Student Edition		Print Resource		Audio CD		Video
TE Teacher's Edition		Transparency		CD-ROM		DVD
go.hrw.com		CA Standards Mastery	**LS**	Learning Styles		
OSP One-Stop Planner CD-ROM		* also on One-Stop Planner CD				

Review, Assessment, Intervention

- **Standards Review Workbook***
- **Quick Facts Transparency:** Ancient India Visual Summary*
- **Spanish Chapter Summaries Audio CD Program**
- **Online Chapter Summaries in Six Languages**
- **Progress Assessment Support System (PASS):** Chapter Test*
- **Universal Access Modified Worksheets and Tests CD-ROM:** Modified Chapter Test
- **One-Stop Planner CD-ROM:** ExamView Test Generator (English/Spanish)

- **PASS:** Section 1 Quiz*
- **Online Quiz:** Section 1
- **Alternative Assessment Handbook**

- **PASS:** Section 2 Quiz*
- **Online Quiz:** Section 2
- **Alternative Assessment Handbook**

- **PASS:** Section 3 Quiz*
- **Online Quiz:** Section 3
- **Alternative Assessment Handbook**

- **PASS:** Section 4 Quiz*
- **Online Quiz:** Section 4
- **Alternative Assessment Handbook**

- **PASS:** Section 5 Quiz*
- **Online Quiz:** Section 5
- **Alternative Assessment Handbook**

California Resources for Standards Mastery

INSTRUCTIONAL PLANNING AND SUPPORT

- Universal Access Teacher Management System*
- One-Stop Planner CD-ROM with Test Generator: Teacher Management System with Interactive Teacher's Edition

STANDARDS MASTERY

- Standards Review Workbook*
- At Home: A Guide to Standards Mastery for World History

go.hrw.com Holt Online Learning

To enhance learning, the following Internet activities are available: Travel to Ancient India! and Mauryan Leaders.

> **KEYWORD: SQ6 TEACHER**

- Teacher Support Page
- Content Updates
- Rubrics and Writing Models

- Teaching Tips for the Multimedia Classroom

> **KEYWORD: SQ6 WH6**

- Current Events
- Holt Grapher
- Holt Online Atlas
- Holt Researcher
- Interactive Multimedia Activities
- Internet Activities

- Online Chapter Summaries in Six Languages
- Online Section Quizzes
- World History Maps and Charts

HOLT PREMIER ONLINE STUDENT EDITION

Complete online support for interactivity, assessment, and reporting

- Interactive Maps and Notebook
- Standardized Test Prep
- Homework Practice and Research Activities Online

Mastering the Standards: Differentiating Instruction

Reaching Standards	Basic-level activities designed for all students encountering new material
Standards Proficiency	Intermediate-level activities designed for average students
Exceeding Standards	Challenging activities designed for honors and gifted-and-talented students
Standard English Mastery	Activities designed to improve standard English usage

Frequently Asked Questions

INSTRUCTIONAL PLANNING AND SUPPORT

Where do I find planning aids, pacing guides, lesson plans, and other teaching aids?

Annotated Teacher's Edition:
- Chapter planning guides
- Standards-based instruction and strategies
- Differentiated instruction for universal access
- Point-of-use reminders for integrating program resources

Power Presentations with Video CD-ROM

Universal Access Teacher Management System:
- Year and unit instructional benchmarking guides
- Reproducible lesson plans
- Assessment guides for diagnostic, progress, and summative end-of-the-year tests
- Options for differentiating instruction and intervention
- Teaching guides and answer keys for student workbooks

One-Stop Planner CD-ROM with Test Generator: Teacher Management System with Interactive Teacher's Edition:
- Calendar Planner
- Editable lesson plans
- All reproducible ancillaries in Adobe Acrobat (PDF) format
- ExamView Test Generator (English & Spanish)
- Game Tool for ExamView
- PuzzlePro
- Transparency and video previews

DIFFERENTIATING INSTRUCTION FOR UNIVERSAL ACCESS

What resources are available to ensure that Advanced Learners/GATE Students master the standards?

Teacher's Edition Activities:
- Understanding Monsoons, p. 146
- The Caste System, p. 151
- Mohandas Gandhi, p. 154
- Mauryan Time Line, p. 163
- Hindu and Buddhist Beliefs and Practices, p. 173

Lesson Plans for Universal Access

Primary Source Library CD-ROM for World History

What resources are available to ensure that English Learners and Standard English Learners master the standards?

Teacher's Edition Activities:
- Describing an Indian Temple, p. 168
- Building Vocabulary, p. 173

Lesson Plans for Universal Access

Chapter Resource File: Vocabulary Builder Activities

Spanish Chapter Summaries Audio CD Program

Online Chapter Summaries in Six Languages

One-Stop Planner CD-ROM:
- PuzzlePro, Spanish Version
- ExamView Test Generator, Spanish Version

What modified materials are available for Special Education?

Teacher's Edition Activities:
- Map of India, p. 145

The *Universal Access Modified Worksheets and Tests CD-ROM* provides editable versions of the following:

Vocabulary Flash Cards

Modified Vocabulary Builder Activities

Modified Chapter Review Activity

Modified Chapter Test

What resources are available to ensure that Learners Having Difficulty master the standards?

Teacher's Edition Activities:
• Life of the Buddha, p. 157
• Indian Empires Map, p. 164
• A Yellow Pages Ad, p. 170

Interactive Reader and Study Guide

Student Edition on Audio CD Program

Quick Facts Transparency: Ancient India Visual Summary

Standards Review Workbook

Social Studies Skills Activity: Interpreting Diagrams

Interactive Skills Tutor CD-ROM

How do I intervene for students struggling to master the standards?

Interactive Reader and Study Guide

Quick Facts Transparency: Ancient India Visual Summary

Standards Review Workbook

Social Studies Skills Activity: Interpreting Diagrams

Interactive Skills Tutor CD-ROM

PROFESSIONAL DEVELOPMENT

HOLT
Professional
Development

What teacher training resources are available to help me grow professionally?

• In-service and staff development as part of your Holt Social Studies product purchase
• Quick Teacher Tutorial Lesson Presentation CD-ROM
• Intensive tuition-based Teacher Development Institute
• Convenient Holt Speaker Bureau face-to-face workshop options

• PRAXIS™ Test Prep (#0089) interactive Web-based content refreshers*
• *Ask A Professional Development Expert* at http://www.hrw.com/prodev/

* PRAXIS is a trademark of Educational Testing Service (ETS). This publication is not endorsed or approved by ETS.

Information Literacy Skills

To learn more about how History–Social Science instruction may be improved by the effective use of library media centers and information literacy skills, go to the Teacher's Resource Materials for Chapter 6 at **go.hrw.com, keyword: SQ6 MEDIA.**

Standards Focus

Standards by Section
Section 1: **HSS** 6.5.1, 6.5.2
Section 2: **HSS** 6.5.3, 6.5.4
Section 3: **HSS** 6.5.5
Section 4: **HSS** 6.5.6
Section 5: **HSS** 6.5.7

Teacher's Edition
HSS Analysis Skills: CS 1, CS 2, CS 3, HR 1, HR 3, HR 4, HR 5, HI 1, HI 2, HI 3, HI 4, HI 5

ELA Writing 6.1.0, Reading 6.2.0

Upcoming Standards for Future Learning
Preview the following History–Social Science content standards from upcoming chapters or grade levels to promote learning beyond the current chapter.

HSS 6.6 Students analyze the geographic, political, economic, religious, and social structures of the early civilizations of China.

6.6.8 Describe the diffusion of Buddhism northward to China during the Han Dynasty.

Focus on Writing

The **Chapter Resource File** provides a Focus on Writing worksheet to help students organize and create their posters.

CRF: Focus on Writing Activity: An Illustrated Poster

CHAPTER 6   2300 BC–AD 500

Ancient India

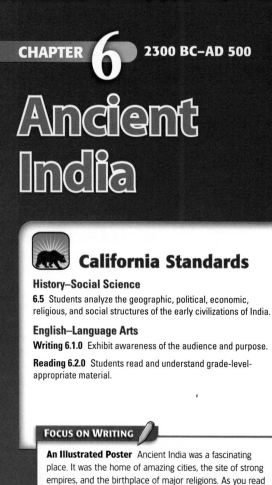

California Standards

History–Social Science

6.5 Students analyze the geographic, political, economic, religious, and social structures of the early civilizations of India.

English–Language Arts

Writing 6.1.0 Exhibit awareness of the audience and purpose.

Reading 6.2.0 Students read and understand grade-level-appropriate material.

FOCUS ON WRITING

An Illustrated Poster Ancient India was a fascinating place. It was the home of amazing cities, the site of strong empires, and the birthplace of major religions. As you read this chapter, think about how you could illustrate one aspect of Indian culture in a poster. When you finish the chapter, you will design such a poster, which will include captions that explain the illustrations you have drawn.

c. 2600 BC
Urban Harappan civilization reaches maturity.

CHAPTER EVENTS

2300 BC

WORLD EVENTS   **2200 BC**
The Old Kingdom ends in Egypt.

140   CHAPTER 6

Introduce the Chapter

Standards Proficiency

Telling Tales in Ancient India   **HSS** 6.5.7

1. Call on a volunteer to answer this question: If you wanted to teach a friend an important lesson about life, which would be more effective—telling him or her what to do or telling a story that makes the point indirectly?

2. Point out that many people respond better to a story. In ancient India, people told stories, also called fables, that taught important lessons. These fables were collected in a work called the *Panchatantra*. Long ago, this collection was translated into other languages. It influenced many works of literature, including *The Thousand and One Nights*, the source of Sinbad the Sailor tales. Ask students if they are familiar with the Sinbad stories.

3. Tell students that ancient India gave birth to more than fun stories; two of the world's most important religions began there. Tell students they will learn about these topics and more in this chapter. **LS** **Verbal/Linguistic**

What You Will Learn...

In this chapter you will learn about the ancient civilization of India, the birthplace of two major world religions—Hinduism and Buddhism. In this photo, crowds of Hindus gather to bathe in the sacred Ganges River.

1500s BC
Aryans begin migrating into India.

c. 1250 BC
Central tenets of Hinduism take shape.

c. 563 BC
Prince Siddhartha Gautama, or the Buddha, is born in northern India.

c. AD 320
Chandragupta founds the Gupta Empire.

| 1500 BC | 1000 BC | 500 BC | BC 1 AD | AD 500 |

c. 1500 BC
The Shang Dynasty is established in China.

334 BC
Alexander the Great begins his conquests.

AD 391 All non-Christian religions are banned in the Roman Empire.

ANCIENT INDIA **141**

Chapter Preview

Chapter Big Ideas

Section 1 Indian civilization first developed on the Indus River. **HSS** 6.5.1, 6.5.2

Section 2 Hinduism, the largest religion in India today, developed out of ancient Indian beliefs and practices. **HSS** 6.5.3, 6.5.4

Section 3 Buddhism began in India and became a major religion. **HSS** 6.5.5

Section 4 The Mauryas and the Guptas built great empires in India. **HSS** 6.5.6

Section 5 The people of ancient India made great contributions to the arts and sciences. **HSS** 6.5.7

Explore the Picture

The Sacred Ganges River Hindus believe that Ganga (also called Ganges) is the daughter of Himalaya, the mountain god. According to Hindu beliefs, the Ganges River is sacred, and bathing in it will wash away one's sins. Many Hindus ask that after death they be cremated on the banks of the Ganges and their ashes sprinkled on the water.

Analyzing Visuals

Besides bathing in the water, how else do the people in the photo seem to be showing their devotion to Ganga, the Hindu goddess of the river? *drinking the water, placing flowers in the water*

go.hrw.com
Online Resources
Chapter Resources:
KEYWORD: SQ6 WH6
Teacher Resources:
KEYWORD: SQ6 TEACHER

Explore the Time Line

1. About when may the Old Kingdom of Egypt and the Harappan civilization of India have overlapped? *from about 2300 to 2200 BC*

2. What was happening in China about the same time that the Aryans began migrating into India? *The Shang dynasty was established.*

3. How many years elapsed from the time Hinduism began to develop in India and Christianity became the official religion of the Roman Empire? *about 1641 years*

HSS Analysis Skills: CS1

Info to Know

The Case of the Missing Art Information on India's distant past is spotty at best. One reason is that for a long span of time in Indian history there are virtually no examples of painting, sculpture, or other forms of the visual arts. Between the end of the Harappan civilization and the beginning of the Mauryan Empire in the 300s BC, the Aryans dominated India. We have remarkable works of literature from that time, but practically no art. Ask students why they think this may be so.

Reading Social Studies

Reading Social Studies

by Kylene Beers

| Economics | Geography | Politics | Religion | Society and Culture | Science and Technology |

Understanding Themes

Like other civilizations students have studied thus far, religion played a major role in people's lives in India. Religion also played an important role in the structure of Indian society and culture. As students read the chapter, ask them to look for relationships between religion and society and culture.

Focus on Themes This chapter outlines and describes the development of India. You will read about India's first civilization, called the Harappan civilization, so advanced that the people had indoor bathrooms and a writing system. You will also learn about the **society and culture** that restricted whom Indian people could talk with or marry. Finally, you will read about the **religions** and empires that united India and about the art and literature that the Indians created.

Inferences about History

Focus on Reading Ask students if they have ever been able to predict the end of a book or a film. Maybe they figured out who the criminal was in a mystery novel. Ask students to discuss what led them to make the correct inference. Did they read or see clues? Point out to students that making inferences often involves paying careful attention to details, and using prior knowledge about a subject. Discuss with students the inference drawn on this page. Explain to students how the information inside and outside the text led to this inference.

Inferences about History

Focus on Reading What's the difference between a good guess and a weak guess? A good guess is an *educated* guess. In other words, the guess is based on some knowledge or information. That's what an inference is, an educated guess.

Making Inferences About What You Read On pages 86 and 87, you practiced drawing conclusions. You use almost the same process to make an inference: combine information from your reading with what you already know, and make an educated guess about what it all means. Once you have made several inferences, you may be able to draw a conclusion that ties them all together.

Additional reading support can be found in the

Inter active

Reader and Study Guide

Question Why did Aryan priests have rules for performing sacrifices?

Inside the Text	Outside the Text
• Sacred texts tell how to perform sacrifices. • Priests sacrificed animals in fire. • Sacrifices were offerings to the gods.	• Other religions have duties only priests can perform. • Many ancient societies believed sacrifices helped keep the gods happy.

Steps for Making Inferences

1. Ask a question.
2. Note information "Inside the Text."
3. Note information "Outside the Text."
4. Use both sets of information to make an educated guess, or inference.

Inference The Aryans believed that performing a sacrifice incorrectly might anger the gods.

142 CHAPTER 6

Reading and Skills Resources

Reading Support

📖 Interactive Reader and Study Guide

🔊 Student Edition on Audio CD

🔊 Spanish Chapter Summaries Audio CD Program

Social Studies Skills Support

💿 Interactive Skills Tutor CD-ROM

Vocabulary Support

📄 **CRF:** Vocabulary Builder Activities

📄 **CRF:** Chapter Review Activity

💿 Universal Access Modified Worksheets and Tests CD-ROM:
  • Vocabulary Flash Cards
  • Vocabulary Builder Activity
  • Chapter Review Activity

OSP Holt PuzzlePro

🐻 **Standards Focus**

ELA Reading 6.2.0

ELA Reading 6.2.0 Read and understand grade-level-appropriate material.

You Try It!

The following passage is from the chapter you are about to read. Read the passage and then answer the questions that follow.

Harappan Achievements

Harappan civilization was very advanced. Most houses had bathrooms with indoor plumbing. Artisans made excellent pottery, jewelry, ivory objects, and cotton clothing. They used high-quality tools and developed a system of weights and measures.

From Chapter 6, p. 148

Harappans also developed India's first known writing system. However, scholars have not yet learned to read this language, so we know very little about Harappan society. Unlike Mesopotamia or Egypt, for example, there are no large religious monuments or palaces, so the relationship between the people and their government is less clear. On the other hand, the remarkable similarity of material culture from widely scattered Harappan sites suggests a high level of social control.

Harappan civilization ended by the early 1700s BC, but no one is sure why.

Answer the following questions to make inferences about Harappan society.

1. Do you think that the Harappan language was closely related to the languages spoken in India today? Consider the information inside the text and things you have learned outside the text to make an inference about the Harappan language.

2. What have you just learned about Harappan achievements? Think back to other civilizations you have studied that made similar achievements. What allowed those civilizations to make their achievements? From this, what can you infer about earlier Harappan society?

As you read Chapter 6, use the information you find in the text to make inferences about Indian society.

Key Terms and People

Chapter 6

Section 1
subcontinent *(p. 144)*
monsoons *(p. 145)*
Sanskrit *(p. 149)*

Section 2
caste system *(p. 151)*
Hinduism *(p. 153)*
reincarnation *(p. 153)*
karma *(p. 154)*
Jainism *(p. 155)*
nonviolence *(p. 155)*

Section 3
fasting *(p. 157)*
meditation *(p. 157)*
the Buddha *(p. 157)*
Buddhism *(p. 158)*
nirvana *(p. 158)*
missionaries *(p. 160)*

Section 4
Chandragupta Maurya *(p. 162)*
Asoka *(p. 163)*
Chandragupta II *(p. 164)*

Section 5
metallurgy *(p. 170)*
alloys *(p. 170)*
Hindu-Arabic numerals *(p. 170)*
inoculation *(p. 170)*
astronomy *(p. 171)*

Academic Vocabulary

Success in school is related to knowing academic vocabulary— the words that are frequently used in school assignments and discussions. In this chapter, you will learn the following academic words:

establish *(p. 164)*
process *(p. 170)*

Reading Social Studies

Key Terms and People

Preteach this chapter's key terms and people by assigning one term or person to each student. Have each student define or identify that term. Then have students teach each other the words they learned. Encourage students to keep a list of key terms and people to study.
LS Interpersonal, Verbal/Linguistic

Focus on Reading

See the **Focus on Reading** questions in this chapter for more practice on this reading social studies skill.

Reading Social Studies Assessment

See the **Standards Review** at the end of this chapter for student assessment questions related to this reading skill.

Teaching Tip

Students may have difficulty learning to make inferences in the activity above. To help students learn how to do this, have students create a T-chart. Ask students to label one column of the chart *Inside the Text*, and the other column *Outside Knowledge*. Then have students pay attention to the details in the reading to complete the first column, and use their own outside knowledge on the subject to complete the second column. Students should then use the information in each column to make an inference.

Answers

You Try It! 1. *No, if Harappan language was similar to modern languages, scientists might have learned how to read it.* **2.** *Harappan achievements— lived in cities, bathrooms, indoor plumbing, pottery, cotton clothing, high-quality tools, system of weights and measures, writing system, had an organized society with artisans, builders, priests, and kings; other civilizations— Education, technology, division of labor, wealth, peace, and stability enabled them to make their achievements; Harappans had many of the same characteristics as other advanced societies.*

Bellringer

If YOU were there . . . Use the **Daily Bellringer Transparency** to help students answer the question.

🗄 Daily Bellringer Transparency, Section 1

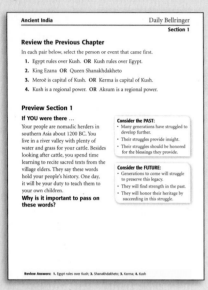

Ancient India   Daily Bellringer
                                       Section 1

Review the Previous Chapter
In each pair below, select the person or event that came first.
1. Egypt rules over Kush. **OR** Kush rules over Egypt.
2. King Ezana **OR** Queen Shanakhdakheto
3. Meroë is capital of Kush. **OR** Kerma is capital of Kush.
4. Kush is a regional power. **OR** Aksum is a regional power.

Preview Section 1
If YOU were there …
Your people are nomadic herders in southern Asia about 1200 BC. You live in a river valley with plenty of water and grass for your cattle. Besides looking after cattle, you spend time learning to recite sacred texts from the village elders. They say these words hold your people's history. One day, it will be your duty to teach them to your own children.
Why is it important to pass on these words?

Consider the PAST:
- Many generations have struggled to develop further.
- Their struggles provide insight.
- Their struggles should be honored for the blessings they provide.

Consider the FUTURE:
- Generations to come will struggle to preserve this legacy.
- They will find strength in the past.
- They will honor their heritage by succeeding in this struggle.

Review Answers: 1. Egypt rules over Kush; **2.** Shanakhdakheto; **3.** Kerma; **4.** Kush

Building Vocabulary

Preteach or review the following terms:
fortress fort (p. 147)
influenced affected (p. 145)

📝 **CRF:** Vocabulary Builder Activity, Section 1

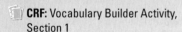 **Standards Focus**

HSS 6.5.1
Means: Locate and describe the Indus River and discuss how it supported early civilization.
Matters: Civilization flourished along the Indus River because the river's flooding provided fertile soil. The area is still densely populated.

HSS 6.5.2
Means: Explain why the Aryan invasion was significant.
Matters: The Aryans brought many cultural changes that still affect India today.

Geography and Early India

What You Will Learn…

Main Ideas
1. The geography of India includes high mountains, great rivers, and heavy seasonal rain.
2. Harappan civilization developed along the Indus River.
3. The Aryan invasion of India changed the region's civilization.

The Big Idea
Indian civilization first developed on the Indus River.

Key Terms
subcontinent, *p. 144*
monsoons, *p. 145*
Sanskrit, *p. 149*

HSS 6.5.1 Locate and describe the major river system and discuss the physical setting that supported the rise of this civilization.

6.5.2 Discuss the significance of the Aryan invasions.

If **YOU** were there…

Your people are nomadic herders in southern Asia about 1200 BC. You live in a river valley with plenty of water and grass for your cattle. Besides looking after cattle, you spend time learning to recite sacred texts from the village elders. They say these words hold your people's history. One day, it will be your duty to teach them to your own children.

Why is it important to pass on these words?

BUILDING BACKGROUND Like Mesopotamia and Egypt, India was home to one of the world's first civilizations. Like other early civilizations, the one in India grew up in a river valley. But the society that eventually developed in India was very different from the ones that developed elsewhere.

Geography of India

Look at a map of Asia in the atlas of this book. Do you see the large, roughly triangular landmass that juts out from the center of the southern part of the continent? That is India. It was the location of one of the world's earliest civilizations.

Landforms and Rivers

India is huge. In fact, it is so big that many geographers call it a subcontinent. A **subcontinent** is a large landmass that is smaller than a continent. Subcontinents are usually separated from the rest of their continents by physical features. If you look at the map on the next page, for example, you can see that mountains largely separate India from the rest of Asia.

Among the mountains of northern India are the Himalayas, the highest mountains in the world. To the west are the Hindu Kush. Though these mountains made it hard to enter India, invaders have historically found a few paths through them.

Teach the Big Idea: Master the Standards   **Standards Proficiency**

Geography and Early India   **HSS** 6.5.1, 6.5.2; **HSS** Analysis Skills: HI 2

1. **Teach** Ask students the Main Idea questions to teach this section.

2. **Apply** Create a Venn diagram for students to see, with Geography and the Harappans and Geography and the Aryans as heads for the circles and Geography and Both Peoples for the overlap. Have students suggest how geography affected early Indian civilizations. For example, Indus River floods made farming possible for the Harappans, but the monsoons would have affected both peoples. Then discuss other details of the two civilizations.
LS Interpersonal, Visual/Spatial

3. **Review** Have students tell what we do know about these civilizations and why we don't know more about the Harappans.

4. **Practice/Homework** Have students create a chart listing the characteristics of the Harappan and Aryan civilizations.
LS Visual/Spatial

📝 Alternative Assessment Handbook, Rubric 7: Charts

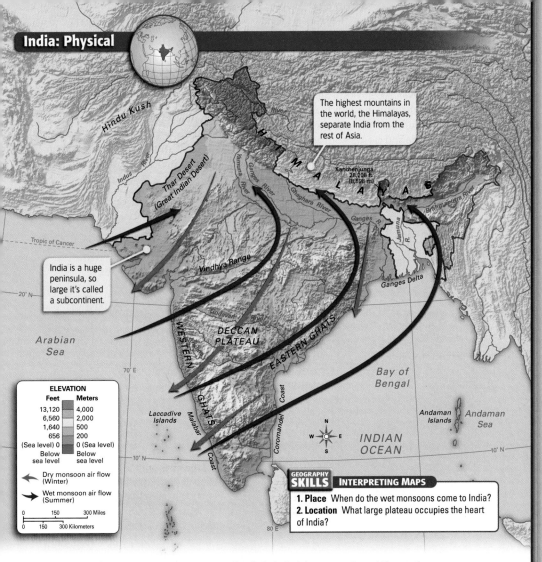

India: Physical

India is a huge peninsula, so large it's called a subcontinent.

The highest mountains in the world, the Himalayas, separate India from the rest of Asia.

Kanchenjunga
28,208 ft.
(8,598 m)

Hindu Kush

Indus River

Thar Desert
(Great Indian Desert)

Tropic of Cancer

20° N

Arabian
Sea

Vindhya Range

DECCAN
PLATEAU

WESTERN GHATS

EASTERN GHATS

Ganges Delta

Jamuna R.

Brahmaputra River

Ganges R.

Bay of
Bengal

Laccadive
Islands

Malabar Coast

Coromandel Coast

70° E

10° N

Andaman
Islands

Andaman
Sea

INDIAN
OCEAN

10° N

80° E

ELEVATION

Feet		Meters
13,120		4,000
6,560		2,000
1,640		500
656		200
(Sea level) 0		0 (Sea level)
Below sea level		Below sea level

◄── Dry monsoon air flow (Winter)

──► Wet monsoon air flow (Summer)

0   150   300 Miles
0   150   300 Kilometers

GEOGRAPHY SKILLS — INTERPRETING MAPS

1. **Place** When do the wet monsoons come to India?
2. **Location** What large plateau occupies the heart of India?

To the west of the Himalayas is a vast desert. Much of the rest of India is covered by fertile plains and rugged plateaus.

Several major rivers flow out of the Himalayas. The valleys and fertile plains of these rivers were the locations of India's early civilizations. The Indus is located in present-day Pakistan, west of India. When heavy snows in the Himalayas melted, the Indus flooded. As in Mesopotamia and Egypt, the flooding left behind a layer of fertile silt. The silt created ideal farmland for early settlers.

Climate

Most of India has a hot and humid climate. This climate is heavily influenced by India's **monsoons**, seasonal wind patterns that cause wet and dry seasons.

ANCIENT INDIA **145**

Main Idea

❷ Harappan Civilization

Harappan civilization developed along the Indus River.

Identify What were the two main cities of the Harappan civilization? Harappa and Mohenjo Daro

Recall When did the Harappan civilization thrive? between 2300 and 1700 BC

Analyze What are some explanations for why Harappa and Mohenjo Daro were very similar? possible answers— People from one of the cities founded the other; communication, travel, and/ or trade made Harappan civilization fairly uniform throughout the region.

🐘 **HSS** 6.5.1; **HSS** Analysis Skills: HI 2

go.hrw.com
Online Resources
KEYWORD: SQ6 WH6
ACTIVITY: Travel to
Ancient India!

History Close-Up

Mohenjo Daro How did the area's physical geography affect the city's defenses? possible answer—The people of Mohenjo Daro had to build a fortress, since the region's flat landscape didn't provide natural barriers.

Linking to Today

Pottery Wheel Much of the Harappan pottery seems to have been made on human-powered potters' wheels. This type of machine is still used around the world today.

Answers

Reading Check *People probably settled where monsoon rains helped farming but tried to avoid places where flooding was common.*

146

In the summer, monsoon winds blow into India from the Indian Ocean, bringing heavy rains that can cause terrible floods. Some parts of India receive as much as 100 or even 200 inches of rain during this time. In the winter, winds blow down from the mountains. This forces moisture out of India and creates warm, dry winters.

READING CHECK **Drawing Conclusions**
How do you think monsoons affected settlement in India?

Harappan Civilization

Historians call the civilization that grew up in the Indus River Valley the Harappan (huh-RA-puhn) civilization. Centered along the Indus, the civilization also controlled large areas on both sides of the river.

Like other ancient societies you have studied, the Harappan civilization grew as irrigation and agriculture improved. As farmers began to produce surpluses of food, towns and cities appeared in India.

History Close-up

Life in Mohenjo Daro

Mohenjo Daro was one of the two major cities of the Harappan civilization. Located next to the Indus River in what is now Pakistan, the city probably covered one square mile. The people who lived in the city enjoyed some of the most advanced comforts of their time, including indoor plumbing.

Harappan merchants used a standard set of weights to measure goods such as precious stones.

146 CHAPTER 6

Cross-Discipline Activity: Science

Exceeding Standards

Understanding Monsoons 🐘 **HSS** 6.5.1; **HSS** Analysis Skills: CS 3, HR 1 | **Research Required**

1. Instruct students to conduct research to learn more about the causes and results of monsoons. Students should use at least two independent, credible sources.

2. Have students prepare presentations on their findings. The presentations should incorporate detailed graphics illustrating wind changes and their effects.

3. Students should give their presentations to the class. **LS** **Verbal/Linguistic**

📋 Alternative Assessment Handbook, Rubrics 29: Presentations; and 30: Research

India's Early Cities

The Harappan civilization was named after the modern city of Harappa (huh-RA-puh), Pakistan. It was near this city that ruins of the civilization were first discovered. From studying these ruins, archaeologists currently estimate that the civilization thrived between 2300 and 1700 BC.

The greatest sources of information we have about Harappan civilization are the ruins of two large cities, Harappa and Mohenjo Daro (mo-HEN-joh DAR-oh). The two cities lay more than 300 miles apart but were remarkably similar. More recent sources include the ruins discovered at Kalibangan, Dholavira, and the port of Lothal, in addition to the 2,600 rural settlements excavated in northwest India.

Both Harappa and Mohenjo Daro were well planned. Each stood near a towering fortress. From these fortresses, defenders could look down on the cities' brick streets, which crossed at right angles and were lined with storehouses, workshops, market stalls, and houses. In addition, both cities had many public wells.

Next to the city was a huge citadel, or fortress, to guard against invasions.

The houses of Mohenjo Daro had flat roofs. Many had staircases that allowed people to climb to the roof from the street.

The city's streets were paved and well drained. They met at right angles, creating a grid pattern.

Harappan Civilization

Harappa

HIMALAYAS

Mohenjo Daro

Indus river

Thar Desert

Arabian Sea

■ Harappan civilization

• Major settlement

0   100   200 Miles
0   100   200 Kilometers

ANALYSIS SKILL   ANALYZING VISUALS

What in this picture suggests that Mohenjo Daro was a well-planned city?

ANCIENT INDIA **147**

147

❸ Aryan Invasion

The Aryan invasion of India changed the region's civilization.

Compare How was the Aryan civilization different from the Harappan? *The Aryans were more warlike, didn't farm at first, didn't build cities, didn't have a single ruling authority, and didn't have a written language.*

Elaborate What skills and tools did the Aryans have that helped them conquer the Indus Valley? *skill as warriors, chariots, advanced weapons*

Evaluate Why are the Vedas so important to us today? *because so much of what we know about the Aryans comes from them*

🐾 **HSS** 6.5.2; **HSS** Analysis Skills: HI 1, HI 2

Other People, Other Places

Indo-European Languages Like English, Sanskrit belongs to the Indo-European language group. Similarities among Indo-European languages show that they are related. For example, look at these words for *mother:* Sanskrit, *matar;* Greek, *meter;* Latin, *mater;* and Old Irish, *mathair.* The languages listed—and many others—developed from a lost language called Proto-Indo-European that may have been spoken between 10,000 and 6,000 years ago.

Info to Know

Debate Over the Aryans In recent years, scholars have begun to question how the Aryans arrived in India. Many no longer believe that the Aryans invaded. Instead, some think the Aryans migrated into India slowly over a period of many decades. Others maintain that the Aryans did not move into India at all but were native to the region.

Answers

Reading Check *because historians cannot read the Harappan language*

148

Harappan Achievements

Harappan civilization was very advanced. Most houses had bathrooms with indoor plumbing. Artisans made excellent pottery, jewelry, ivory objects, and cotton clothing. They used high-quality tools and developed a system of weights and measures.

Harappans also developed India's first known writing system. However, scholars have not yet learned to read this language, so we know very little about Harappan society. Unlike Mesopotamia or Egypt, for example, there are no large religious monuments or palaces, so the relationship between the people and their government is less clear. On the other hand, the remarkable similarity of material culture from widely scattered Harappan sites suggests a high level of social control.

Harappan civilization ended by the early 1700s BC, but no one is sure why. Perhaps invaders destroyed the cities or natural disasters, like floods or earthquakes, caused the civilization to collapse.

READING CHECK **Analyzing** Why don't we know much about Harappan civilization?

Harappan Art

Like other ancient peoples, the Harappans made small seals like the one below that were used to stamp goods. They also used clay pots like the one at right decorated with a goat.

148 CHAPTER 6

Aryan Invasion

Not long after the Harappan civilization crumbled, a new group took power in the Indus Valley. They were called the Aryans (AIR-ee-uhnz). Historians have long debated the origins of the Aryans. Some historians believe they came from Central Asia, but others disagree. Wherever the Aryans came from, some people think they may have helped end the Harappan civilization.

Invaders from the West

The Aryans were skilled warriors. Using chariots and advanced weapons, these invaders took new territory. By 1200 BC Aryan warriors had swept through the Hindu Kush and taken control of the entire Indus Valley. From there they moved east to the Ganges River Valley.

Much of what we know about Aryan society comes from religious writings known as the Vedas (VAY-duhs). These collections of poems, hymns, myths, and rituals were written by Aryan priests. You will read more about the Vedas later in this chapter.

Government and Society

As nomads, the Aryans took along their herds of animals as they moved. But over time, they settled in villages and began to farm. Unlike the Harappans, they did not build big cities.

The Aryan political system was also different from the Harappan system. The Aryans lived in small communities, based mostly on family ties. No single ruling authority existed. Instead, each group had its own leader, often a skilled warrior.

Aryan villages were governed by rajas (RAH-juhz). A raja was a leader who ruled a village and the land around it. Villagers farmed some of this land for the raja. They used other sections as pastures for their cows, horses, sheep, and goats.

Critical Thinking: Making Decisions

A Raja's Choice 🐾 **HSS** 6.5.2; **HSS** Analysis Skills: HI 1, HI 2

1. Ask students to imagine that they are rajas of small villages. Local herders and farmers have come to the raja to tell him they need more land for their crops and animals. The raja has a choice. He can either go to war against the larger, stronger village nearby to take its land, or he can try to find a peaceful solution to his people's growing needs.

2. Have students work in pairs to decide which plan of action they will take.

3. Have each pair write a brief speech in which the raja explains his decision to the people of his village.

4. Have volunteers share their speeches with the class. **LS Verbal/Linguistic**

📃 Alternate Assessment Handbook, Rubric 35: Solving Problems

Although many rajas were related, they didn't always get along. Sometimes rajas joined forces before fighting a common enemy. Other times, however, rajas went to war against each other. In fact, Aryan groups fought each other nearly as often as they fought outsiders.

Language

The first Aryan settlers did not read or write. Because of this, they had to memorize the sacred texts that were important in their culture, such as the Vedas. If people forgot these sacred texts, the works would be lost forever.

The language in which these Aryan sacred texts were composed was **Sanskrit**, the most important language of ancient India. At first, Sanskrit was only a spoken language. Eventually, however, people figured out how to write it down so they could keep records. These Sanskrit records are a major source of information about Aryan society. Sanskrit is no longer widely spoken today, but it is the root of many modern South Asian languages.

READING CHECK Identifying What source provides much of the information we have about the Aryans?

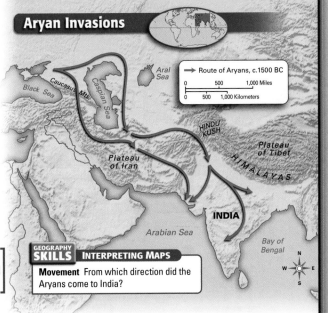

Aryan Invasions

Route of Aryans, c.1500 BC
0   500   1,000 Miles
0   500   1,000 Kilometers

Aral Sea
Black Sea
Caucasus Mts.
Caspian Sea
HINDU KUSH
Plateau of Iran
Plateau of Tibet
HIMALAYAS
INDIA
Arabian Sea
Bay of Bengal

GEOGRAPHY SKILLS | **INTERPRETING MAPS**
Movement From which direction did the Aryans come to India?

SUMMARY AND PREVIEW The earliest civilizations in India were centered on the Indus Valley. First the Harappans and then the Aryans lived in this fertile valley. In the next section, you will learn about a new religion that developed in the Indus Valley after the Aryans settled there—Hinduism.

THE IMPACT TODAY
Hindi, the most widely spoken Indian language, is based on Sanskrit.

Section 1 Assessment

go.hrw.com
Online Quiz
KEYWORD: SQ6 HP6

Reviewing Ideas, Terms, and People **HSS** 6.5.1, 6.5.2

1. **a. Define** What are **monsoons**?
   b. Contrast How does northern India differ from the rest of the region?
   c. Elaborate Why is India called a **subcontinent**?
2. **a. Recall** Where did Harappan civilization develop?
   b. Analyze What is one reason that scholars do not completely understand some important parts of Harappan society?
3. **a. Identify** Who were the Aryans?
   b. Contrast How was Aryan society different from Harappan society?

Critical Thinking

4. **Categorizing** Draw a diagram like this one. Use it to show how Indian society changed after the Aryan invasion.

India before the invasion → India after the invasion

FOCUS ON WRITING

5. **Illustrating Geography and Early Civilizations** This section described two possible topics for your poster: geography and early civilizations. Which of them is more interesting to you? Write down some ideas for a poster about your chosen topic.

ANCIENT INDIA **149**

Bellringer

If YOU were there . . . Use the **Daily Bellringer Transparency** to help students answer the question.

Daily Bellringer Transparency, Section 2

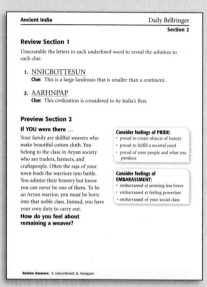

Building Vocabulary

Preteach or review the following term:
rituals ceremonies, rites (p. 152)

CRF: Vocabulary Builder Activity, Section 2

Standards Focus

HSS 6.5.3
Means: Explain the major concepts of Brahmanism and how it developed into early Hinduism.
Matters: Hinduism is India's major religion and affects the daily lives of hundreds of millions of Indians.

HSS 6.5.4
Means: Explain the caste system.
Matters: The caste systems still affects Indians' daily lives.

Origins of Hinduism

What You Will Learn...

Main Ideas

1. Indian society divided into distinct groups under the Aryans.
2. The Aryans practiced a religion known as Brahmanism.
3. Hinduism developed out of Brahmanism and influences from other cultures.
4. The Jains reacted to Hinduism by breaking away to form their own religion.

The Big Idea

Hinduism, the largest religion in India today, developed out of ancient Indian beliefs and practices.

Key Terms

caste system, p. 151
Hinduism, p. 153
reincarnation, p. 153
karma, p. 154
Jainism, p. 155
nonviolence, p. 155

 HSS 6.5.3 Explain the major beliefs and practices of Brahmanism in India and how they evolved into early Hinduism.

6.5.4 Outline the social structure of the caste system.

If YOU were there...

Your family are skillful weavers who make beautiful cotton cloth. You belong to the class in Aryan society who are traders, farmers, and craftspeople. Often the raja of your town leads the warriors into battle. You admire their bravery but know you can never be one of them. To be an Aryan warrior, you must be born into that noble class. Instead, you have your own duty to carry out.

How do you feel about remaining a weaver?

BUILDING BACKGROUND As the Aryans moved into India, they developed a strict system of social classes. As the Aryans' influence spread through India, so did their class system. Before long, this class system was a key part of Indian society.

Indian Society Divides

As Aryan society became more complex, their society became divided into groups. For the most part, these groups were organized by people's occupations. Strict rules developed about how people of different groups could interact. As time passed, these rules became stricter and became central to Indian society.

The *Varnas*

According to the Vedas, there were four main *varnas*, or social divisions, in Aryan society. These *varnas* were:

• Brahmins (BRAH-muhns), or priests,
• Kshatriyas (KSHA-tree-uhs), or rulers and warriors,
• Vaisyas (VYSH-yuhs), or farmers, craftspeople, and traders, and
• Sudras (SOO-drahs), or laborers and non-Aryans.

Teach the Big Idea: Master the Standards
Standards Proficiency

Origins of Hinduism
HSS 6.5.3, 6.5.4; HSS Analysis Skills: HI 3

1. **Teach** Ask students the Main Idea questions to teach this section.

2. **Apply** Ask students to list people and terms associated with Hinduism. Write responses for students to see. *Varnas*, caste system, sacred cow, karma, and reincarnation may be among the terms suggested. Call on volunteers to describe how the terms listed relate to each other.
LS Verbal/Linguistic

3. **Review** Review the major beliefs of Hinduism and ask for volunteers to explain each one.

4. **Practice/Homework** Have students pick one of the major beliefs of Hinduism and, using the information provided in this section, draw a picture or diagram to illustrate the belief. **LS Visual/Spatial**

Alternative Assessment Handbook, Rubric 3: Artwork

The Brahmins were seen as the highest ranking because they performed rituals for the gods. This gave the Brahmins great influence over the other *varnas*.

The Caste System

As the rules of interaction between *varnas* got stricter, the Aryan social order became more complex. In time, each of the four *varnas* in Aryan society was further divided into many castes, or groups. This **caste system** divided Indian society into groups based on a person's birth, wealth, or occupation. At one time, some 3,000 separate castes existed in India.

The caste to which a person belonged determined his or her place in society. However, this ordering was by no means permanent. Over time, individual castes gained or lost favor in society as caste members gained wealth or power. On rare occasions, people could change caste.

Caste Rules

To keep their classes distinct, the Aryans developed sutras, or guides, which listed all the rules for the caste system. For example, people were not allowed to marry anyone from a different class. It was even forbidden for people from one class to eat with people from another. People who broke the caste rules could be banned from their homes and their castes, which would make them untouchables. Because of these rules, people spent almost all of their time with others in their same class.

READING CHECK Drawing Inferences How did a person become a member of a caste?

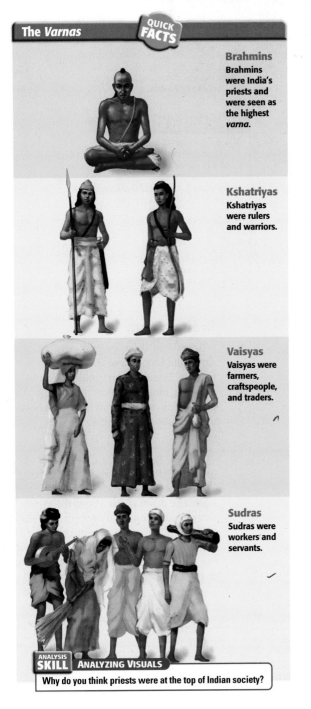

QUICK FACTS

The *Varnas*

Brahmins
Brahmins were India's priests and were seen as the highest *varna*.

Kshatriyas
Kshatriyas were rulers and warriors.

Vaisyas
Vaisyas were farmers, craftspeople, and traders.

Sudras
Sudras were workers and servants.

ANALYSIS SKILL **ANALYZING VISUALS**
Why do you think priests were at the top of Indian society?

ANCIENT INDIA **151**

❷ Brahmanism

The Aryans practiced a religion known as Brahmanism.

Identify What is the *Rigveda? the oldest of the Vedas that contained sacred texts in praise of many deities*

Recall When was the *Rigveda* probably written*? before 1000 BC*

Compare How did the Upanishads differ from other Vedic texts? *The Upanishads were reflections on the Vedas written by religious students and teachers.*

Explain Why did priests place sacrifices into a fire? *They believed the fire would carry the sacrifice to the deities.*

Activity **Standard English Mastery**

Hymn to Indra Read the excerpt from the hymn to Indra. Remind students that an adjective is a word that describes someone or something. Then have students write down adjectives that the Aryans may have used to describe this deity had they spoken English. Encourage students to use a thesaurus or dictionary to find appropriate adjectives. Call on volunteers to share their lists.

📦 Quick Facts Transparency: Major Beliefs of Hinduism

🐘 **HSS** 6.5.3

Did you know . . .
Veda means "knowledge" in Sanskrit.

Hindu Deities and Beliefs

Hindus believe in many deities, but they believe that all the deities are aspects of a single universal spirit called Brahman. Three aspects of Brahman are particularly important in Hinduism—Brahma, Siva, and Vishnu.

Major Beliefs of Hinduism

- A universal spirit called Brahman created the universe and everything in it. Everything in the world is just a part of Brahman.

- Every person has a soul or *atman* that will eventually join with Brahman.

- People's souls are reincarnated many times before they can join with Brahman.

- A person's karma affects how he or she will be reincarnated.

The deity Brahma represents the creator aspect of Brahman. His four faces symbolize the four Vedas.

Brahmanism

Religion had been an important part of Aryan life even before the Aryans moved to India. Eventually, in India, religion took on even more meaning. Because Aryan priests were called Brahmins, their religion is often called Brahmanism.

The Vedas

Aryan religion was based on the Vedas. There are four Vedas, each containing sacred texts. The oldest of the Vedas, the *Rigveda*, was probably compiled in the second millennium BC. It includes hymns of praise to many deities. This passage, for example, is the opening of a hymn praising Indra, a deity of the sky and war.

> "The one who is first and possessed of wisdom when born; the god who strove to protect the gods with strength; the one before whose force the two worlds were afraid because of the greatness of his virility [power]: he, O people, is Indra."
>
> –from the *Rigveda*, in *Reading about the World, Volume I*, edited by Paul Brians, et al

Vedic Texts

Over the centuries, Aryan Brahmins wrote down their thoughts about the Vedas. In time these thoughts were compiled into collections called Vedic texts.

One collection of Vedic texts describes Aryan religious rituals. For example, it describes how sacrifices should be performed. Priests placed animals, food, or drinks to be sacrificed in a fire. The Aryans believed that the fire would carry these offerings to the deities.

A second collection of Vedic texts describes secret rituals that only certain people could perform. In fact, the rituals were so secret that they had to be done in the forest, far from other people.

The final group of Vedic texts are the Upanishads (oo-PAHN-ee-shads), most of which were written by about 600 BC. These writings are reflections on the Vedas by religious students and teachers.

READING CHECK **Finding Main Ideas** What are the Vedic texts?

Cross-Discipline Activity: Literature

Standards Proficiency

The Rigveda 🐘 **HSS** 7.2.4; **HSS** Analysis Skills: CS 1

Prep Required

1. Organize the class into groups. In advance, locate and duplicate examples from the *Rigveda*. Provide each member of a group the same sample, but give each group a different sample.

2. Have each group discuss the meaning of its sample. Provide dictionaries to help students in the task. Ask students also to find examples of descriptive language in the text.

3. Call on volunteers from each group to report their findings.

4. Extend the activity by asking interested students to locate and listen to a modern composition, *Choral Hymns from the Rig Veda*, by Gustav Holst. Ask them to play selections for the class. **LS** Verbal/Linguistic

🐘 **HSS** 6.5.3; **HSS** Analysis Skills: HR 4

📝 Alternative Assessment Handbook, Rubric 14: Group Activity

Siva, the destroyer aspect of Brahman, is usually shown with four arms and three eyes. Here he is shown dancing on the back of a demon he has defeated.

Vishnu is the preserver aspect of Brahman. In his four arms, he carries a conch shell, a mace, and a discus, symbols of his power and greatness.

Hinduism Develops

The Vedas, the Upanishads, and the other Vedic texts remained the basis of Indian religion for centuries. Eventually, however, the ideas of these sacred texts began to blend with ideas from other cultures. People from Persia and other kingdoms in Central Asia, for example, brought their ideas to India. In time, this blending of ideas created a religion called **Hinduism**, the largest religion in India today.

Hindu Beliefs

The Hindus believe in many deities. Among them are three major deities: Brahma the Creator, Siva the Destroyer, and Vishnu the Preserver. At the same time, however, Hindus believe that each deity is part of a single universal spirit called Brahman. They believe that Brahman created the world and preserves it. Deities like Brahma, Siva, and Vishnu represent different aspects of Brahman. In fact, Hindus believe that everything in the world is part of Brahman.

Life and Rebirth

According to Hindu teachings, everyone has a soul, or *atman*, inside them. This soul holds the person's personality, the qualities that make them who they are. Hindus believe that a person's ultimate goal should be to reunite that soul with Brahman, the universal spirit.

Hindus believe that their souls will eventually join Brahman because the world we live in is an illusion. Brahman is the only reality. The Upanishads taught that people must try to see through the illusion of the world. Since it is hard to see through illusions, it can take several lifetimes. That is why Hindus believe that souls are born and reborn many times, each time in a new body. This process of rebirth is called **reincarnation**.

Hinduism and the Caste System

According to the traditional Hindu view of reincarnation, a person who has died is reborn in a new physical form.

THE IMPACT TODAY

More than 800 million people in India practice Hinduism today.

Main Idea

❸ **Hinduism Develops**

Hinduism developed out of Brahmanism and influences from other cultures.

Identify According to Hindu belief, what are the three major forms of Brahman? *Brahma the creator, Siva the destroyer, Vishnu the preserver*

Analyze What led to the development of Hinduism? *the blending of the Vedic texts with ideas from other cultures*

Evaluate How may believing that this world is merely an illusion affect one's behavior? *Answers will vary but should reflect logical thinking.*

HSS 6.5.3; HSS Analysis Skills: HI 1, HI 2

Connect to Art

Lord of the Dance The bronze statue shown portrays Siva as Nataraja, or Lord of the Dance. Stylized flames surround him. Underfoot is the Demon of Ignorance. According to Hindu belief, during his dance Siva destroys the universe, but it is continually reborn. This statue was made in the 1200s.

Collaborative Learning

Standards Proficiency

Collages about Hinduism HSS 6.5.3; HSS Analysis Skills: HR 1

Materials: art supplies

1. First, review the three major forms of Brahman and the main beliefs of Hinduism.

2. Then organize students into small groups. Have some of the groups create collages combining original illustrations and text to describe the Hindu concept of the three aspects of Brahman. Have other groups create collages about the other main Hindu beliefs.

3. Have volunteers present their collages to the class. **LS Visual/Spatial, Interpersonal**

📖 Alternative Assessment Handbook, Rubric 8: Collages

Direct Teach

Main Idea

❸ Hinduism Develops

Hinduism developed out of Brahmanism and influences from other cultures.

Identify What is karma? *the effects that good or bad actions have on a person's soul*

Evaluate Do you think a wealthy Brahmin would want his or her servants to believe in *dharma*? Why or why not? *possible answers—Servants would be more likely to accept their fate in life if they believed in* dharma.

📋 **CRF:** Primary Source Activity: Mohandas Gandhi's Autobiography

🐻 **HSS** 6.5.3

Primary Source

Martin Luther King, Jr. Martin Luther King Jr. described nonviolent resistance as "passive physically but strongly active spiritually; it is nonaggressive physically but dynamically aggressive spiritually." Ask students what they think Dr. King meant by this statement and whether they think Mohandas Gandhi would agree with it. *possible answer—although nonviolent resistance doesn't require physical strength, it does demand a strong spirit; yes, because they both believed in nonviolent protest*

The type of form depends upon his or her **karma**, the effects that good or bad actions have on a person's soul. Evil actions during one's life will build bad karma. A person with bad karma will be born into a lower caste or life form.

In contrast, good actions build good karma. People with good karma are born into a higher caste in their next lives. In time, good karma will bring salvation, or freedom from life's worries and the cycle of rebirth. This salvation is called *moksha*.

Hinduism taught that each person had a duty to accept his or her place in the world without complaint. This is called obeying one's *dharma*. People could build good karma by fulfilling the duties required of their specific caste. Through reincarnation, Hinduism offered rewards to those who lived good lives. Even untouchables could be reborn into a higher caste.

Hinduism was popular at all levels of Hindu society, through all four *varnas*. By teaching people to accept their places in life, Hinduism helped preserve the caste system in India.

READING CHECK **Summarizing** What determined how a person would be reborn?

LINKING TO TODAY

Nonviolence

In modern times, nonviolence has been a powerful tool for social protest. Mohandas Gandhi led a long nonviolent struggle against British rule in India. This movement helped India win its independence in 1947. About 10 years later, Martin Luther King Jr. adopted Gandhi's nonviolent methods in his struggle to win civil rights for African Americans. Then, in the 1960s, César Chávez organized a campaign of nonviolence to protest the treatment of farm workers in California. These three leaders proved that people can bring about social change without using violence. As Chávez once explained, "Nonviolence is not inaction. It is not for the timid or the weak. It is hard work. It is the patience to win."

Mohandas Gandhi (top), Martin Luther King Jr. (above), and César Chávez (right)

ANALYSIS SKILL **ANALYZING INFORMATION**

How did these three leaders prove that nonviolence is a powerful tool for social change?

Differentiating Instruction for Universal Access

Advanced Learners/GATE `Exceeding Standards` `Research Required`

1. Have students research the life of Mohandas Gandhi—particularly how his beliefs affected his nonviolent methods of protest. Point out that some of Gandhi's beliefs contrasted with traditional Hindu beliefs. Students should use library and Internet sources.

2. Students should then write brief reports that tell how Gandhi's religious beliefs affected his actions.

3. To extend the activity, have interested students locate descriptions of Gandhi written by British writers during the 1940s and report on how they portrayed him.

LS Verbal/Linguistic

🐻 **HSS** 6.5.3, 6.5.4; **HSS** Analysis Skills: HI 1, HI 2, HI 3, HI 5

📋 Alternative Assessment Handbook, Rubrics 30: Research; and 42: Writing to Inform

Answers

Analyzing Information *by helping to end British rule in India, winning civil rights for African Americans, improving treatment of farm workers*

Reading Check *their actions during their lifetimes*

154

Jains React to Hinduism

Although Hinduism was widely followed in India, not everyone agreed with its beliefs. Some unsatisfied people and groups looked for new religious ideas. One such group was the Jains (JYNZ), believers in a religion called Jainism (JY-ni-zuhm).

Jainism was based on the teachings of a man named Mahavira. Born into the Kshatriya *varna* around 599 BC, he was unhappy with the control of religion by the Brahmins, whom he thought put too much emphasis on rituals. Mahavira gave up his life of luxury, became a monk, and established the principles of Jainism.

The Jains try to live by four principles: injure no life, tell the truth, do not steal, and own no property. In their efforts not to injure anyone or anything, the Jains practice **nonviolence**, or the avoidance of violent actions. The Sanskrit word for this nonviolence is *ahimsa* (uh-HIM-sah). Many Hindus also practice *ahimsa*.

The Jains' emphasis on nonviolence comes from their belief that everything is alive and part of the cycle of rebirth. Jains are very serious about not injuring or killing any creature—humans, animals, insects, or even plants. They do not believe in animal sacrifice, like the ones the ancient Brahmins performed. Because they don't want to hurt living creatures, Jains are vegetarians. They do not eat any food that comes from animals.

READING CHECK Identifying Points of View
Why do Jains avoid eating meat?

SUMMARY AND PREVIEW You have learned about two religions that developed in India—Hinduism and Jainism. In Section 3, you will learn about another religion that began there—Buddhism.

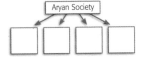
These Jain women are wearing masks to make sure they don't accidentally inhale and kill insects.

Section 2 Assessment

go.hrw.com
Online Quiz
KEYWORD: SQ6 HP6

Reviewing Ideas, Terms, and People HSS 6.5.3, 6.5.4

1. **a. Identify** What is the **caste system**?
   b. Explain Why did strict caste rules develop?
2. **a. Identify** What does the *Rigveda* include?
   b. Analyze What role did sacrifice play in Aryan society?
3. **a. Define** What is **karma**?
   b. Sequence How did Brahmanism develop into **Hinduism**?
   c. Elaborate How does Hinduism reinforce followers' willingness to remain within their castes?
4. **a. Recall** What are the four main teachings of **Jainism**?
   b. Predict How do you think the idea of **nonviolence** affected the daily lives of Jains in ancient India?

Critical Thinking

5. **Categorizing** Draw a graphic organizer like the one shown here. In each box, identify one of the four *varnas* of Aryan society. Below the name, list the people who belonged to that class.

Aryan Society

FOCUS ON WRITING

6. **Illustrating Hinduism** Now you have a new possible topic for your poster. How might you explain a complex religion like Hinduism?

ANCIENT INDIA **155**

Section 2 Assessment Answers

1. **a.** a social system in which people are divided into groups based on a person's birth, wealth or occupation
   b. to keep the classes distinct
2. **a.** sacred texts about many deities
   b. very important to religious ceremonies
3. **a.** the effects that good or bad actions have on a person's soul
   b. from Vedic texts and ideas from other cultures
   c. Hinduism teaches that if a person accepts their dharma, including their caste, they may be reborn into a higher caste.

4. **a.** Injure no life, tell the truth, do not steal, and own no property.
   b. possible answer—could not be soldiers or kill animals for food
5. Brahmins—priests; Kshatriyas—rulers and warriors; Vaisyas—farmers, craftspeople, and traders; Sudras—workers and servants
6. Answers will vary but should be accurate.

Bellringer

If YOU were there . . . Use the **Daily Bellringer Transparency** to help students answer the question.

🎞 Daily Bellringer Transparency, Section 3

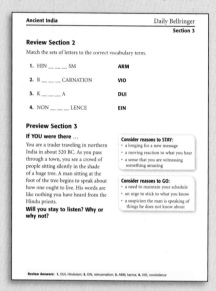

Building Vocabulary

Preteach or review the following term:

enlightenment clarification, understanding (p. 157)

📝 **CRF:** Vocabulary Builder Activity, Section 3

Standards Focus

HSS 6.5.5

Means: Describe Buddha's life and his teachings and how Buddhism spread.

Matters: Buddhism is a major influence on many millions of people around the world.

SECTION 3

Origins of Buddhism

What You Will Learn...

Main Ideas

1. Siddhartha Gautama searched for wisdom in many ways.
2. The teachings of Buddhism deal with finding peace.
3. Buddhism spread far from where it began in India.

The Big Idea

Buddhism began in India and became a major religion.

Key Terms and People

fasting, *p. 157*
meditation, *p. 157*
the Buddha, *p. 157*
Buddhism, *p. 158*
nirvana, *p. 158*
missionaries, *p. 160*

HSS 6.5.5 Know the life and moral teachings of the Buddha and how Buddhism spread in India, Ceylon, and Central Asia.

If YOU were there...

You are a trader traveling in northern India in about 520 BC. As you pass through a town, you see a crowd of people sitting silently in the shade of a huge tree. A man sitting at the foot of the tree begins to speak about how one ought to live. His words are like nothing you have heard from the Hindu priests.

Will you stay to listen? Why or why not?

BUILDING BACKGROUND The Jains were not the only ones to break from Hinduism. In the 500s BC a young Indian prince attracted many people to his teachings about how people should live.

Siddhartha's Search for Wisdom

In the late 500s BC a restless young man, dissatisfied with the teachings of Hinduism, began to ask his own questions about life and religious matters. In time, he found answers. These answers attracted many followers, and the young man's ideas became the foundation of a major new religion in India.

The Quest for Answers

The restless young man was Siddhartha Gautama (si-DAHR-tuh GAU-tuh-muh). Born around 563 BC in northern India, near the Himalayas, Siddhartha was a prince who grew up in luxury. Born a Kshatriya, a member of the warrior class, Siddhartha never had to struggle with the problems that many people of his time faced. However, Siddhartha was not satisfied. He felt that something was missing in his life.

Siddhartha looked around him and saw how hard other people had to work and how much they suffered. He saw people grieving for lost loved ones and wondered why there was so much pain in the world. As a result, Siddhartha began to ask questions about the meaning of human life.

Teach the Big Idea: Master the Standards

Standards Proficiency

Origins of Buddhism   🐾 **HSS 6.5.5;** **HSS** Analysis Skills: HI 1

1. **Teach** Ask students the Main Idea questions to teach this section.

2. **Apply** Organize the class into pairs. Have each pair create a flowchart or another graphic organizer of the students' choosing to show the development of Buddhism from the ideas of Siddhartha Gautama to its influence throughout Asia. Students should add details such as the Four Noble Truths and the steps in the Eightfold Path. **LS Visual/Spatial**

3. **Review** Call on volunteers to present their flowcharts to the class.

4. **Practice/Homework** Have students fill in any missing information on their graphic organizers and write a paragraph describing how the Buddha's teachings differed from Hinduism. **LS Verbal/Linguistic**

   📝 Alternative Assessment Handbook, Rubric 13: Graphic Organizers

The Great Departure

In this painting, Prince Siddhartha leaves his palace to search for the true meaning of life, an event known as the Great Departure. Special helpers called *ganas* hold his horse's hooves so he won't awaken anyone.

Before Siddhartha reached age 30, he left his home and family to look for answers. His journey took him to many regions in India. Wherever he traveled, he had discussions with priests and people known for their wisdom. Yet no one could give convincing answers to Siddhartha's questions.

The Buddha Finds Enlightenment

Siddhartha did not give up. Instead, he became even more determined to find the answers he was seeking. For several years, he wandered in search of answers.

Siddhartha wanted to free his mind from daily concerns. For a while, he did not even wash himself. He also started **fasting**, or going without food. He devoted much of his time to **meditation**, the focusing of the mind on spiritual ideas.

According to legend, Siddhartha spent six years wandering throughout India. He eventually came to a place near the town of Gaya, close to the Ganges River. There, he sat down under a tree and meditated.

After seven weeks of deep meditation, he suddenly had the answers that he had been looking for. He realized that human suffering comes from three things:

- wanting what we like but do not have,
- wanting to keep what we like and already have, and
- not wanting what we dislike but have.

Siddhartha spent seven more weeks meditating under the tree, which his followers later named the Tree of Wisdom. He then described his new ideas to five of his former companions. His followers later called this talk the First Sermon.

Siddhartha Gautama was about 35 years old when he found enlightenment under the tree. From that point on, he would be called **the Buddha** (BOO-duh), or the "Enlightened One." The Buddha spent the rest of his life traveling across northern India and teaching people his ideas.

THE IMPACT TODAY

Buddhists from all over the world still travel to India to visit the Tree of Wisdom and honor the Buddha.

READING CHECK Summarizing What did the Buddha conclude about the cause of suffering?

ANCIENT INDIA **157**

Main Idea

❷ Teachings of Buddhism

The teachings of Buddhism deal with finding peace.

Identify Many of the Buddha's teachings reflect the ideas of which other world religion? *Hinduism*

Recall What are the Four Noble Truths? *See text for answers.*

Analyze What do you think the quote from the Buddha on this page means? *possible answer—People can progress toward enlightenment by responding to bad behavior with good behavior.*

Evaluate What advantage do you think the Buddha saw in following the "middle way"? *possible answer—Extreme behavior of any kind is not helpful or healthy.*

Activity Distinguishing between Hinduism and Buddhism Prepare a list of terms associated with Hinduism and Buddhism. As you read the list to the class, ask with which religion each is associated.

Quick Facts Transparency: The Eightfold Path

🐾 HSS 6.5.5

Linking to Today

The Buddha's Tree at Bodh Gaya The 80-foot statue shown on this page is near the Buddha's Tree of Wisdom. The original tree died long ago. Over the centuries, it has been replaced many times by offshoots of the Buddha's tree. Authorities have placed signs asking visitors not to take leaves from the tree or soil from the ground surrounding it. Near the tree is a golden platform that, according to tradition, marks the exact spot where Siddhartha Gautama sat while waiting for enlightenment.

Teachings of Buddhism

As he traveled, the Buddha gained many followers, especially among India's merchants and artisans. He even taught his views to a few kings. These followers were the first believers in **Buddhism**, a religion based on the teachings of the Buddha.

The Buddha was raised Hindu, and many of his teachings reflected Hindu ideas. Like Hindus, he believed that people should act morally and treat others well. In one of his sermons, he said:

> "Let a man overcome anger by love. Let him overcome the greedy by liberality [giving], the liar by truth. This is called progress in the discipline [training] of the Blessed."
> –The Buddha, quoted in *The History of Nations: India*

Four Noble Truths

At the heart of the Buddha's teachings were four guiding principles. These became known as the Four Noble Truths:

1. Suffering and unhappiness are a part of human life. No one can escape sorrow.

2. Suffering comes from our desires for pleasure and material goods. People cause their own misery because they want things they cannot have.

3. People can overcome desire and ignorance and reach **nirvana** (nir-VAH-nuh), a state of perfect peace. Reaching nirvana frees the soul from suffering and from the need for further reincarnation.

4. People can overcome ignorance and desire by following an eightfold path that leads to wisdom, enlightenment, and salvation.

The chart on the next page shows the steps in the Eightfold Path. The Buddha believed that this path was a middle way between human desires and denying oneself any pleasure. He believed that people should overcome their desire for material goods. They should, however, be reasonable, and not starve their bodies or cause themselves unnecessary pain.

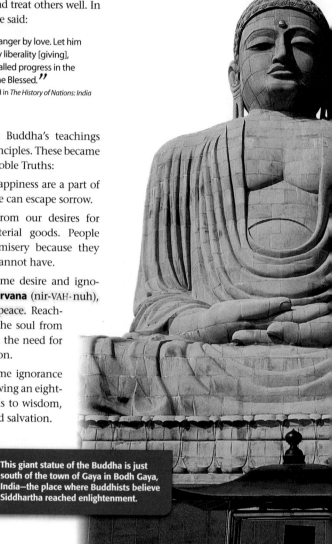

This giant statue of the Buddha is just south of the town of Gaya in Bodh Gaya, India—the place where Buddhists believe Siddhartha reached enlightenment.

Differentiating Instruction for Universal Access:

Advanced Learners /GATE   Exceeding Standards   Research Required

1. Explain to students that some Buddhists become monks and nuns. Read dictionary definitions for both terms.

2. Ask students to imagine that they are newspaper reporters assigned to spend one day with a Buddhist monk or nun and report on their subjects' daily lives.

3. Have students conduct research on Buddhist monks or nuns—either in the present or the past.

4. Then have students write brief newspaper articles describing one day's events in a monk's or nun's life.

5. Encourage students to make their articles as specific as possible. For example, they might discuss the person's chores or the kinds or ceremonies in which he or she participates.

LS Verbal/Linguistic

🐾 HSS 6.5.5; HSS Analysis Skills: HR 1
Alternative Assessment Handbook, Rubric 40: Writing to Describe

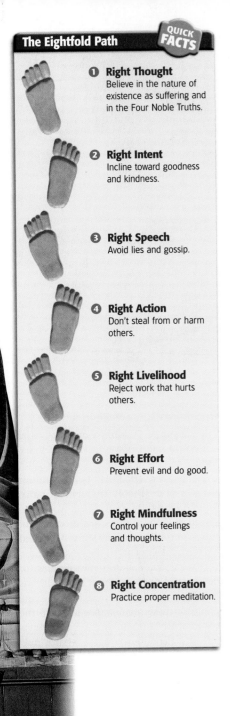

The Eightfold Path

QUICK FACTS

① Right Thought
Believe in the nature of existence as suffering and in the Four Noble Truths.

② Right Intent
Incline toward goodness and kindness.

③ Right Speech
Avoid lies and gossip.

④ Right Action
Don't steal from or harm others.

⑤ Right Livelihood
Reject work that hurts others.

⑥ Right Effort
Prevent evil and do good.

⑦ Right Mindfulness
Control your feelings and thoughts.

⑧ Right Concentration
Practice proper meditation.

Challenging Hindu Ideas

Some of the Buddha's teachings challenged traditional Hindu ideas. For example, the Buddha rejected many of the ideas contained in the Vedas, such as animal sacrifice. He told people that they did not have to follow these texts.

The Buddha challenged the authority of the Hindu priests, the Brahmins. He did not believe that they or their rituals were necessary for enlightenment. Instead, he taught that it was the responsibility of each individual to work for his or her own salvation. Priests could not help them. However, the Buddha did not reject the Hindu teaching of reincarnation. He taught that people who failed to reach nirvana would have to be reborn time and time again until they achieved it.

The Buddha was opposed to the caste system. He didn't think that people should be confined to a particular place in society. Everyone who followed the Eightfold Path properly, he said, would achieve nirvana. It didn't matter what *varna* or caste they had belonged to in life as long as they lived the way they should.

The Buddha's opposition to the caste system won him support from the masses. Many of India's herdsmen, farmers, artisans, and untouchables liked hearing that their low social rank would not be a barrier to enlightenment. Unlike Hinduism, Buddhism made them feel that they had the power to change their lives.

The Buddha also gained followers among the higher classes. Many rich and powerful Indians welcomed his ideas about avoiding extreme behavior while seeking salvation. By the time of his death around 483 BC, the Buddha's influence was spreading rapidly throughout India.

READING CHECK **Comparing** How did Buddha's teachings agree with Hinduism?

Main Idea

❷ Teachings of Buddhism

The teachings of Buddhism deal with finding peace.

Explain What did the Buddha think about the caste system? *He was opposed to it.*

Contrast How is "right thought" different from "right action"? *"Right thought" refers to beliefs, whereas "right action" has to do with how we put beliefs and thoughts into action.*

Evaluate How do you think people reacted to the Buddha's telling them they did not have to accept the Brahmins' authority? *possible answers— The Brahmins would have resented it, while other Hindus may have been relieved.*

Linking to Today

Buddhism in India Many Hindus of India do not see Buddhism as a religion truly separate from Hinduism. Instead, they regard the Buddha as the ninth incarnation of the god Vishnu. As a result, they see Buddhism as a sect within Hinduism.

Checking for Understanding

True or False Answer each statement *T* if it is true or *F* it is false. If false, explain why.

1. Siddhartha Gautama was raised as a Hindu. *T*
2. The Buddha rejected all Hindu ideas. *F; The Buddha believed in reicarnation.*
3. At the heart of the Buddha's teachings were four guiding principles known as the Four Noble Truths. *T*

🐘 **HSS** 6.5.5

Social Studies Skill: Identifying Central Issues   **Standards Proficiency**

Buddhism and Hinduism 🐘 **HSS** 6.5.5

1. Remind students that some of the Buddha's teachings conflicted with Hinduism, while others agreed with Hindu beliefs.

2. Organize students into pairs. Have each pair write a conversation or argument that a traditional Hindu might have had with a Hindu who has adopted the teachings of the Buddha. For traditional Hindus, students may choose a Brahmin or a person from a lower caste.

3. Call on volunteers to read their arguments or conversations.

4. Finally, lead a class discussion about why Buddhism gained followers among all classes.
LS **Interpersonal**

📖 Alternative Assessment Handbook, Rubric 11: Discussions

Answers

Reading Check *Buddha's teachings included reincarnation.*

Main Idea

❸ Buddhism Spreads

Buddhism spread far from where it began in India.

Identify What are some places to which Buddhism spread? *throughout India, Sri Lanka, Myanmar and other parts of Southeast Asia, near the Himalayas, Central Asia, Persia, Syria, Egypt, China, Korea, Japan*

Explain What is one reason why Buddhism spread quickly? *Buddha's teachings were popular and easy to understand.*

Contrast How are the Theravada and Mahayana branches of Buddhism different? *Theravada—follow the Buddha's teachings exactly; Mahayana—can interpret Buddha's teachings to help them reach nirvana*

Map Transparency: Early Spread of Buddhism

HSS 6.5.5

Info to Know

Theravada and Mahayana Theravada and related versions of Buddhism are called Hinayana, or "lesser vehicle" in Sanskrit. Theravada is the older of the two major divisions. Followers trace Theravada traditions all the way back to monks of the first Buddhist community. Theravadins believe that one must become a monk to reach enlightenment. Today, Theravada Buddhism dominates Sri Lanka and Southeast Asia.

Mahayana means "greater vehicle." Mahayanists believe that people who attain enlightenment should stay in the world and help others gain salvation. It is the main form of Buddhism in China, Korea, Japan, and Tibet.

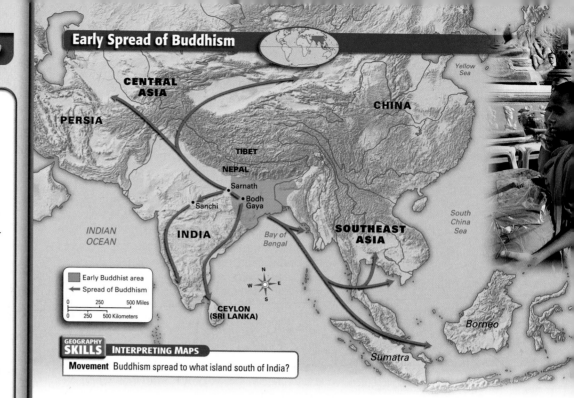

Early Spread of Buddhism

Early Buddhist area

← Spread of Buddhism

0 — 250 — 500 Miles
0 — 250 — 500 Kilometers

GEOGRAPHY SKILLS **INTERPRETING MAPS**

Movement Buddhism spread to what island south of India?

Buddhism Spreads

Buddhism continued to attract followers after the Buddha's death. After spreading through India, the religion began to spread to other areas as well.

Buddhism Spreads in India

According to Buddhist tradition, 500 of the Buddha's followers gathered together shortly after he died. They wanted to make sure that the Buddha's teachings were remembered correctly.

In the years after this council, the Buddha's followers spread his teachings throughout India. The ideas spread very quickly, because Buddhist teachings were popular and easy to understand. Within 200 years of the Buddha's death, his teachings had spread through most of India.

Buddhism Spreads Beyond India

The spread of Buddhism increased after one of the most powerful kings in India, Asoka, became Buddhist in the 200s BC. Once he converted, he built Buddhist temples and schools throughout India. More importantly, though, he worked to spread Buddhism into areas outside of India. You will learn more about Asoka and his accomplishments in the next section.

Asoka sent Buddhist **missionaries**, or people who work to spread their religious beliefs, to other kingdoms in Asia. One group of these missionaries sailed to the island of Sri Lanka around 251 BC. Others followed trade routes east to what is now Myanmar and to other parts of Southeast Asia. Missionaries also went north to areas near the Himalayas.

160 CHAPTER 6

Collaborative Learning

Standards Proficiency

Interviewing a Missionary HSS 6.5.5; Analysis Skills: HR 1, HI 1

1. Ask students to imagine that they lived in Sri Lanka when the first Buddhist missionaries arrived. Then have them imagine what it would have been like had there been television news during that time.

2. Organize students into pairs and instruct each pair to create a skit in which a news commentator interviews a Buddhist missionary.

3. The commentator should create a list of questions for the missionary, such as: Why

have you come to Sri Lanka? What is meant by this word "enlightenment"? How do you think your beliefs can help people?

4. Using the information in this section, the missionary responds to these questions. Ask for volunteers to present their skits to the class. **LS Interpersonal**

Alternative Assessment Handbook, Rubric 33: Skits and Reader's Theater

Answers

Interpreting Maps *Ceylon (Sri Lanka)*

Young Buddhist students carry gifts in Sri Lanka, one of the many places outside of India where Buddhism spread.

Members of the Theravada branch tried to follow the Buddha's teachings exactly as he had stated them. Mahayana Buddhists, though, believed that other people could interpret the Buddha's teachings to help people reach nirvana. Both branches have millions of believers today, but Mahayana is by far the larger branch.

READING CHECK **Sequencing** How did Buddhism spread from India to other parts of Asia?

SUMMARY AND PREVIEW Buddhism, one of India's major religions, grew more popular once it was adopted by rulers of India's great empires. You will learn more about those empires in the next section.

Missionaries also introduced Buddhism to lands west of India. They founded Buddhist communities in Central Asia and Persia. They even taught about Buddhism as far away as Syria and Egypt.

Buddhism continued to grow over the centuries. Eventually it spread via the Silk Road into China, then Korea and Japan. Through their work, missionaries taught Buddhism to millions of people.

A Split within Buddhism

Even as Buddhism spread through Asia, however, it began to change. Not all Buddhists could agree on their beliefs and practices. Eventually disagreements between Buddhists led to a split within the religion. Two major branches of Buddhism were created—Theravada and Mahayana.

Section 3 Assessment

go.hrw.com
Online Quiz
KEYWORD: SQ6 HP6

Reviewing Ideas, Terms, and People **HSS** 6.5.5

1. **a. Identify** Who was **the Buddha**, and what does the term *Buddha* mean?
   b. Summarize How did Siddhartha Gautama free his mind and clarify his thinking as he searched for wisdom?
2. **a. Identify** What is **nirvana**?
   b. Contrast How are Buddhist teachings different from Hindu teachings?
   c. Elaborate Why do Buddhists believe that following the Eightfold Path leads to a better life?
3. **a. Describe** Into what lands did **Buddhism** spread?
   b. Summarize What role did **missionaries** play in spreading Buddhism?

Critical Thinking

4. **Summarizing** Draw a diagram like the one shown here. Use it to identify and describe the Four Noble Truths as taught by the Buddha.

1.	2.
3.	4.

FOCUS ON WRITING

5. **Considering Indian Religions** Look back over what you've just read and the notes you took about Hinduism earlier. Perhaps you will want to focus your poster on ancient India's two major religions. Think about how you could design a poster around this theme.

ANCIENT INDIA **161**

Linking to Today

Zen Buddhism Emphasize that the types of Buddhism practiced today vary around the world. One type of Buddhism commonly practiced in Japan is Zen Buddhism. It teaches that enlightenment can be achieved by breaking through the boundaries of everyday logical thought. This process is best achieved by following the guidance of a master. Zen Buddhism has helped shape not just Japan's religious life, but also its culture. Today almost 10 million Japanese follow Zen Buddhism.

Review & Assess

Close

Have students review the Four Noble Truths and the Eightfold Path.

Review

Online Quiz, Section 3

Assess

SE Section 3 Assessment
PASS: Section 3 Quiz
Alternative Assessment Handbook

Reteach/Classroom Intervention

California Standards Review Workbook
Interactive Reader and Study Guide, Section 3
Interactive Skills Tutor CD-ROM

Section 3 Assessment Answers

1. **a.** Siddhartha Gautama, a prince who found enlightenment; Enlightened One
   b. fasted, didn't bathe, meditated
2. **a.** a state of perfect peace
   b. Buddhists don't believe in sacrifices, the caste system, or that they needed the help of the Brahmins.
   c. It leads them down a path of fulfillment without excess or denial, which then leads to nirvana.
3. **a.** Sri Lanka, Myanmar, other parts of Southeast Asia, Central Asia, Persia, Syria,

Egypt, and eventually to China and then Korea and Japan
   b. important role, because they traveled to distant lands to spread Buddhist teachings
4. See page 158 for answers.
5. Students' ideas will vary, but should display familiarity with text content.

Answers

Reading Check *Missionaries traveled to Sri Lanka, Myanmar, other parts of Southeast Asia, Central Asia, Persia, Syria, Egypt, and eventually to China and then Korea and Japan.*

Bellringer

If YOU were there . . . Use the **Daily Bellringer Transparency** to help students answer the question.

🏛 Daily Bellringer Transparency, Section 4

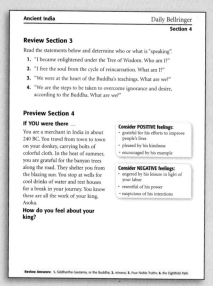

Academic Vocabulary

Review with students the high-use academic term in this section.

establish to set up or create (p. 164)

📄 **CRF:** Vocabulary Builder Activity, Section 4

🐻 Standards Focus

HSS 6.5.6

Means: Describe how the Maurya Empire grew and the achievements of the emperor Asoka.

Matters: The Maurya Empire ruled India for 150 years, and Asoka was its greatest ruler. Asoka's efforts to spread Buddhism have affected the practice of the religion to this day.

Indian Empires

What You Will Learn...

Main Ideas

1. The Mauryan Empire unified most of India.
2. Gupta rulers promoted Hinduism in their empire.

The Big Idea

The Mauryas and the Guptas built great empires in India.

Key People

Chandragupta Maurya, *p. 162*
Asoka, *p. 163*
Chandragupta II, *p. 164*

HSS 6.5.6 Describe the growth of the Maurya Empire and the political and moral achievements of the emperor Asoka.

If YOU were there...

You are a merchant in India in about 240 BC. You travel from town to town on your donkey, carrying bolts of colorful cloth. In the heat of summer, you are grateful for the banyan trees along the road. They shelter you from the blazing sun. You stop at wells for cool drinks of water and rest houses for a break in your journey. You know these are all the work of your king, Asoka.

How do you feel about your king?

BUILDING BACKGROUND For centuries after the Aryan invasion, India was divided into small states. Each state had its own ruler and India had no central government. Then, in the 300s BC, a foreign conqueror, Alexander the Great, took over part of northwestern India. His armies soon left, but his influence continued to affect Indian society. Inspired by Alexander's example, a strong leader soon united India for the first time.

Mauryan Empire Unifies India

In the 320s BC a military leader named **Chandragupta Maurya** (kuhn-druh-GOOP-tuh MOUR-yuh) seized control of the entire northern part of India. By doing so, he founded the Mauryan Empire. Mauryan rule lasted for about 150 years.

The Mauryan Empire

Chandragupta Maurya ruled his empire with the help of a complex government. It included a network of spies and a huge army of some 600,000 soldiers. The army also had thousands of war elephants and thousands of chariots. In return for the army's protection, farmers paid a heavy tax to the government.

In 301 BC Chandragupta decided to become a Jainist monk. To do so, he had to give up his throne. He passed the throne to his son, who continued to expand the empire. Before long, the Mauryas ruled all of northern India and much of central India as well.

Teach the Big Idea: Master the Standards   Standards **Proficiency**

Indian Empires 🐻 **HSS 6.5.6; HSS** Analysis Skills: CS1, CS2, HI 1, HI 2

1. **Teach** Ask students the Main Idea questions to teach this section.

2. **Apply** Have each student place the headings *Mauryan Empire* and *Gupta Empire* at the top of a sheet of paper. Ask half the class to fill in the paper with major events of each empire, along with the dates or approximate dates of those events. The other half of the class should write down details about the empires' societies, cultures, and achievements. **LS** Visual/Spatial

3. **Review** Call on volunteers from the events group to write the main events for all students to see. Have them spread out their entries so that volunteers from the other group can fill in details that they wrote down.

4. **Practice/Homework** Ask each student to write a verse for a national anthem for the Mauryan Empire or the Gupta Empire, using a popular song as the melody. **LS** Verbal/Linguistic, Auditory/Musical

Asoka

Around 270 BC Chandragupta's grandson **Asoka** (uh-SOH-kuh) became king. Asoka was a strong ruler, the strongest of all the Mauryan emperors. He extended Mauryan rule over most of India. In conquering other kingdoms, Asoka made his own empire both stronger and richer.

For many years, Asoka watched his armies fight bloody battles against other peoples. A few years into his rule, however, Asoka converted to Buddhism. When he did, he swore that he would not launch any more wars of conquest.

After converting to Buddhism, Asoka had the time and resources to improve the lives of his people. He had wells dug and roads built throughout the empire. Along these roads, workers planted shade trees

and built rest houses for weary travelers. He also encouraged the spread of Buddhism in India and the rest of Asia. As you read in the previous section, he sent missionaries to lands all over Asia.

Asoka died in 233 BC, and the empire began to fall apart soon afterward. His sons fought each other for power, and invaders threatened the empire. In 184 BC the last Mauryan king was killed by one of his own generals. India divided into smaller states once again.

FOCUS ON READING
What can you infer about the religious beliefs of Asoka's sons?

READING CHECK **Finding Main Ideas** How did the Mauryans gain control of most of India?

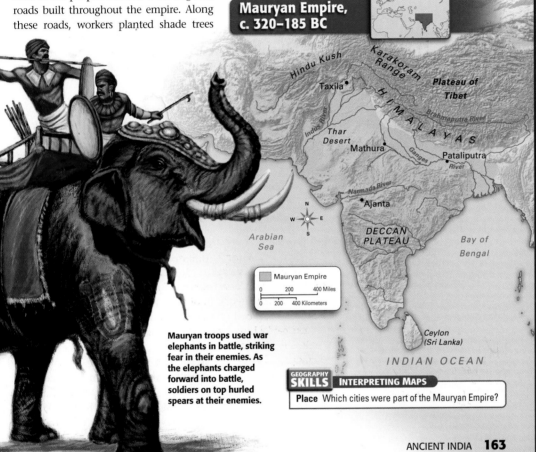

Mauryan Empire, c. 320–185 BC

- Hindu Kush
- Karakoram Range
- Taxila
- Plateau of Tibet
- HIMALAYAS
- Brahmaputra River
- Indus River
- Thar Desert
- Mathura
- Ganges River
- Pataliputra
- Narmada River
- Ajanta
- Arabian Sea
- DECCAN PLATEAU
- Bay of Bengal
- Ceylon (Sri Lanka)
- INDIAN OCEAN

Mauryan Empire

0   200   400 Miles
0   200   400 Kilometers

N W E S

Mauryan troops used war elephants in battle, striking fear in their enemies. As the elephants charged forward into battle, soldiers on top hurled spears at their enemies.

GEOGRAPHY SKILLS | **INTERPRETING MAPS**

Place Which cities were part of the Mauryan Empire?

ANCIENT INDIA **163**

Direct Teach

Main Idea

❶ Mauryan Empire Unifies India

The Mauryan Empire unified most of India.

Identify Who was Chandragupta Maurya? *a military leader who seized control of northern India in the 320s BC, founding the Mauryan Empire*

Describe What was Chandragupta Maurya's government like? *network of spies, army of 600,000 soldiers along with many elephants and chariots, heavy taxes*

Explain How did becoming a Buddhist change Asoka's behavior? *He worked to improve his people's lives and spread Buddhism.*

- **CRF:** Biography Activity: Chandragupta Maurya
- **CRF:** Biography Activity: Kautilya
- **CRF:** Biography Activity: Mahinda
- Map Transparency: Mauryan Empire, c. 320–185 BC
- **HSS** 6.5.6; **HSS** Analysis Skills HI 4

go.hrw.com
Online Resources

KEYWORD: SQ6 WH6
ACTIVITY: Mauryan Leaders

Interpreting Maps

Human/Environment Interaction
How may physical geography have limited the spread of the Mauryan Empire? *Mountains limited the spread to the northeast.*

Answers

Focus on Reading *possible answers—details about battles, Asoka's accomplishments, the end of his empire*

Interpreting Maps *Taxila, Mathura, Pataliputra, Ajanta*

Reading Check *by conquering neighboring kingdoms*

Social Studies Skill: Retrieving and Analyzing Information

Mauryan Time Line   **Exceeding Standards**   **Research Required**

1. Draw a blank time line for students to see. Write 320s BC and 184 BC on the time line. Call on volunteers to tell why those were important years for the Mauryan Empire.

2. Instruct students to create their own time lines titled *History of the Mauryan Empire*. They should start by incorporating information in this section.

3. Then have students conduct additional research on the Mauryan Empire so that they

can include at least two facts not presented in this section in their time lines.

4. Display the time lines for other students to see. Lead a discussion about which events seem to be more significant than others.

LS Visual/Spatial

HSS 6.5.6; **HSS** Analysis Skills: CS 1, CS 2, HI 1, HI 4

Alternative Assessment Handbook, Rubrics 30: Research; and 36: Time Lines

❷ Gupta Rulers Promote Hinduism

Gupta rulers promoted Hinduism in their empire.

Describe What was India like after the fall of the Mauryan Empire? *divided for about 500 years*

Identify Who were Chandragupta I and Chandragupta II? *founder of the Gupta Empire; emperor under whom Gupta society reached its high point*

Predict How do you think India would be different today if the Gupta rulers had not taken over? *possible answer—might be primarily Buddhist*

Activity **Early Indian Empire Tic-Tac-Toe** Have each student write down two questions from this section. Organize the class into two teams: *X*s and *O*s. Have students play a game of tic-tac-toe in which each team member is asked a question and gets to place a mark on the grid when he or she answers correctly. **LS** **Interpersonal**

🗺 Map Transparency: Gupta Empire, c. 400

🐻 **HSS** 6.5.6

Other People, Other Places

Trade with Rome For many years, India and the Roman Empire enjoyed a lively trade relationship. In fact, at one point the Romans had built special warehouses just for pepper imported from India. Although trade between Rome and India was sometimes disrupted, by the 300s and 400s it was again strong. Roman coins found in Sri Lanka are evidence of this trade.

Answers

Interpreting Maps *southern and southwestern*

164

Gupta Rulers Promote Hinduism

After the collapse of the Mauryan Empire, India remained divided for about 500 years. During that time, Buddhism continued to prosper and spread in India, and so the popularity of Hinduism declined.

A New Hindu Empire

ACADEMIC VOCABULARY
establish to set up or create

Eventually, however, a new dynasty was **established** in India. It was the Gupta (GOOP-tuh) Dynasty, which took over India around AD 320. Under the Guptas, India was once again united, and it once again became prosperous.

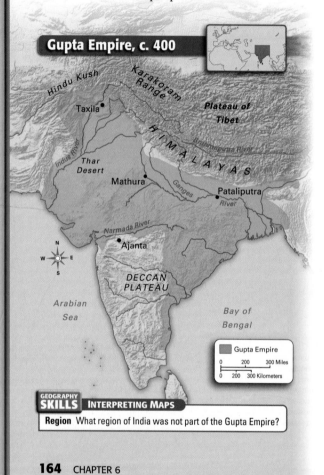

Gupta Empire, c. 400

Hindu Kush · Taxila · Karakoram Range · Plateau of Tibet · Indus River · HIMALAYAS · Brahmaputra River · Thar Desert · Mathura · Ganges River · Pataliputra · Narmada River · Ajanta · DECCAN PLATEAU · Arabian Sea · Bay of Bengal

Gupta Empire

0   200   300 Miles
0   200   300 Kilometers

GEOGRAPHY SKILLS **INTERPRETING MAPS**

Region What region of India was not part of the Gupta Empire?

164 CHAPTER 6

The first Gupta emperor was Chandragupta I. Although their names are similar, he was not related to Chandragupta Maurya. From his base in northern India, Chandragupta's armies invaded and conquered neighboring lands. Eventually he brought much of the northern part of India under his control.

Indian civilization flourished under the Gupta rulers. These rulers were Hindu, so Hinduism became India's major religion. The Gupta kings built many Hindu temples, some of which became models for later Indian architecture. They also promoted a revival of Hindu writings and worship practices.

Although they were Hindus, the Gupta rulers also supported the religious beliefs of Buddhism and Jainism. They promoted Buddhist art and built Buddhist temples. They also established a university at Nalanda that became one of Asia's greatest centers for Buddhist studies.

Gupta Society

In 375 Emperor **Chandragupta II** took the throne in India. Gupta society reached its high point during his rule. Under Chandragupta II, the empire continued to grow, eventually stretching all the way across northern India. At the same time, the empire's economy strengthened, and people prospered. They created fine works of art and literature. Outsiders admired the empire's wealth and beauty.

Gupta kings believed the social order of the Hindu caste system would strengthen their rule. They also thought it would keep the empire stable. As a result, the Guptas considered the caste system an important part of Indian society.

This was not good news for women, whose roles were limited by caste rules. Brahmins taught that a woman's role was to marry and have children. Women couldn't even choose their own husbands.

Differentiating Instruction for Universal Access

Special Education Students

Reaching Standards **Prep Required**

1. Organize students into pairs. Provide each student with an outline map of the Indian subcontinent.

2. One member of the pair should draw the area included in the Mauryan Empire on his or her map. The other student should do the same for the Gupta Empire. Students should label the empires' cities and major geographical features.

3. Then have students exchange maps with their partners and draw the outline of the empire not yet recorded on the map.

4. Call on volunteers to describe how the boundaries of the two empires differed. **LS** **Visual/Spatial**

🐻 **HSS** 6.5.6; **HSS** Analysis Skills: HI 1

📝 Alternative Assessment Handbook, Rubric 20: Map Creation

Gupta Art
This Gupta painting of a palace scene shows some of India's different castes. Gupta rulers supported Hinduism and the caste system.

Parents arranged all marriages. Once married, wives had few rights. They were expected to serve their husbands. Widows had an even lower social status than other women.

Gupta rule remained strong in India until the late 400s. At that time the Huns, a group from Central Asia, invaded India from the northwest. Their fierce attacks drained the Gupta Empire of its power and wealth. As the Hun armies marched farther into India, the Guptas lost hope.

By the middle of the 500s, Gupta rule had ended, and India had divided into small kingdoms yet again.

READING CHECK **Summarizing** What was the Gupta Dynasty's position on religion?

SUMMARY AND PREVIEW The Mauryas and Guptas united much of India in their empires. Next you will learn about their many achievements.

go.hrw.com
Online Quiz
KEYWORD: SQ6 HP6

Section 4 Assessment

Reviewing Ideas, Terms, and People **HSS** 6.5.6

1. **a. Identify** Who created the Mauryan Empire?
   b. Summarize What happened after **Asoka** became a Buddhist?
   c. Elaborate Why do you think many people consider Asoka the greatest of all Mauryan rulers?
2. **a. Recall** What religion did most of the Gupta rulers belong to?
   b. Compare and Contrast How were the rulers **Chandragupta Maurya** and Chandragupta I alike, and how were they different?
   c. Evaluate Do you think the Gupta enforcement of caste rules was a good thing? Why or why not?

Critical Thinking

3. **Categorizing** Draw a chart like this one. Fill it with information about India's rulers.

Ruler	Dynasty	Accomplishments

FOCUS ON WRITING

4. **Comparing Indian Empires** Another possible topic for your poster would be a comparison of the Maurya and Gupta empires. Make a chart in your notebook that shows such a comparison.

ANCIENT INDIA **165**

Section 4 Assessment Answers

1. **a.** Chandragupta Maurya
   b. Asoka focused on improving the lives of the citizens and spreading Buddhism.
   c. He gave up making war and concentrated instead on improving his people's lives.
2. **a.** Hinduism
   b. alike—India flourished under their rule; different—Chandragupta Maurya became a Jainist monk, and Chandragupta I was a Hindu.
   c. Answers will vary but should reflect understanding of caste rules.

3. Chandragupta Maurya—Mauryan; founded the Mauryan empire, gave up his throne to become a Jainist monk; Asoka—Mauryan; extended Mauryan rule, converted to Buddhism, improved people's lives, spread Buddhism; Chandragupta I—Gupta; first Gupta emperor, brought much of the northern part of India under control; Chandragupta II—Gupta; expanded empire, Gupta society at its height
4. Charts will vary but should reflect text content.

Direct Teach

Main Idea

❷ Gupta Rulers Promote Hinduism

Gupta rulers promoted Hinduism in their empire.

Identify What ended the Gupta rule?
the Hun invasion from the northwest

Summarize: What responsibilities and rights did Gupta women have?
to care for husband and family; few rights.

Review & Assess

Close

Refer students to the illustration of the Mauryan war elephants. Ask them to describe what it would be like to face these animals in battle.

Review

Online Quiz, Section 4

Assess

SE Section 4 Assessment
PASS: Section 4 Quiz
Alternative Assessment Handbook

Reteach/Classroom Intervention

California Standards Review Workbook
Interactive Reader and Study Guide, Section 4
Interactive Skills Tutor CD-ROM

Answers

Reading Check *Even though Gupta rulers were Hindus, they supported the beliefs of Buddhism and Jainism.*

165

Asoka

How can one decision change a man's entire life?

When did he live? before 230 BC

Where did he live? Asoka's empire included much of northern and central India.

What did he do? After fighting many bloody wars to expand his empire, Asoka gave up violence and converted to Buddhism.

Why is he important? Asoka is one of the most respected rulers in Indian history and one of the most important figures in the history of Buddhism. As a devout Buddhist, Asoka worked to spread the Buddha's teachings. In addition to sending missionaries around Asia, he built huge columns carved with Buddhist teachings all over India. Largely through his efforts, Buddhism became one of Asia's main religions.

Generalizing How did Asoka's life change after he became Buddhist?

This Buddhist shrine, located in Sanchi, India, was built by Asoka.

166 CHAPTER 6

KEY EVENTS

- **c. 270 BC** Asoka becomes the Mauryan emperor.
- **c. 261 BC** Asoka's empire reaches its greatest size.
- **c. 261 BC** Asoka becomes a Buddhist.
- **c. 251 BC** Asoka begins to send Buddhist missionaries to other parts of Asia.

Reading Focus Question

Lead a discussion about decisions students have made that have affected various aspects of their lives. Or, you may prefer that students discuss decisions made by family members, contemporary world leaders, or other figures in world history. Point out that every day people make decisions that have wide-ranging effects. Use a daily newspaper to spark discussion about decisions and their ramifications.

HSS Analysis Skills: HI 4

Linking to Today

Stupas Originally, Asoka built eight monuments, or *stupas*, at Sanchi, but only three remain today. In 1989, the entire area was added to UNESCO's World Heritage List.

Info to Know

The Great Stupa The hemispherical shape of this monument, called the Great Stupa, has symbolic meaning. Ask students why this shape might have been chosen for the monument. *It symbolizes the dome of the sky as we look at it from the earth.*

About the Illustration

This illustration of Asoka is an artist's conception based on available sources. However, historians are uncertain exactly what Asoka looked like.

Answers

He became a peace-loving ruler dedicated to improving the lives of his people.

Critical Thinking: Solving Problems

Standards Proficiency

Asoka's Plan for Helping His People   **HSS** 6.5.6; **HSS Analysis Skills:** HI 1

1. Organize students into small groups. Ask students to imagine that they are Asoka's advisers.

2. Tell students that Asoka has called the advisers together to announce his conversion to Buddhism. Asoka has asked them to suggest plans for helping his people.

3. Each group should use what members know about Asoka and India to list specific ideas. Students should not limit themselves to those items mentioned in this section.

4. Then have groups add to their lists by suggesting problems or hurdles that may slow the progress of Asoka's plans. Examples include issues related to physical geography, opposition by local rulers, and so on.

5. Challenge students to suggest ways these problems could be overcome.

LS Interpersonal, Logical/Mathematical

Alternative Assessment Handbook, Rubric 14: Group Activity

Indian Achievements

If YOU were there...

You are a traveler in western India in the 300s. You are visiting a cave temple that is carved into a mountain cliff. Inside the cave it is cool and quiet. Huge columns rise all around you. You don't feel you're alone, for the walls and ceilings are covered with paintings. They are filled with lively scenes and figures. In the center is a large statue with calm, peaceful features.

How does this cave make you feel?

> **BUILDING BACKGROUND** The Mauryan and Gupta empires united most of India politically. During these empires, Indian artists, writers, scholars, and scientists made great advances. Some of their works are still studied and admired today.

Religious Art

The Indians of the Maurya and Gupta periods created great works of art, many of them religious. Many of their paintings and sculptures illustrated either Hindu and Buddhist teachings. Magnificent temples—both Hindu and Buddhist—were built all around India. They remain some of the most beautiful buildings in the world today.

Temples

Early Hindu temples were small stone structures. They had flat roofs and contained only one or two rooms. In the Gupta period, though, temple architecture became more complex. Gupta temples were topped by huge towers and were covered with carvings of the god worshipped inside.

Buddhist temples of the Gupta period are also impressive. Some Buddhists carved entire temples out of mountainsides. The most famous such temple is at Ajanta. Its builders filled the caves with beautiful wall paintings and sculpture.

SECTION 5

What You Will Learn...

Main Ideas

1. Indian artists created great works of religious art.
2. Sanskrit literature flourished during the Gupta period.
3. The Indians made scientific advances in metalworking, medicine, and other sciences.

The Big Idea

The people of ancient India made great contributions to the arts and sciences.

Key Terms

metallurgy, *p. 170*
alloys, *p. 170*
Hindu-Arabic numerals, *p. 170*
inoculation, *p. 170*
astronomy, *p. 171*

HSS 6.5.7 Discuss important aesthetic and intellectual traditions (e.g., Sanskrit literature, including the *Bhagavad Gita*; medicine; metallurgy; and mathematics, including Hindu-Arabic numerals and the zero).

ANCIENT INDIA **167**

Teach the Big Idea: Master the Standards

Standards Proficiency

Indian Achievements HSS 6.5.7; HSS Analysis Skills: HI 1

1. **Teach** Ask students the Main Idea questions to teach this section.

2. **Apply** Organize students into three groups. Assign one of the subsections—Religious Art, Sanskrit Literature, or Scientific Advances—to each group. Each group should create a poster or mural to illustrate the main points in its subsection. **LS Visual/Spatial**

3. **Review** As each group presents its illustration to the class, go over the concepts and terms related to that subsection.

4. **Practice/Homework** Instruct students to create a chart listing each of this section's three main ideas. Under each main idea, students should list at least two examples that support the idea. **LS Verbal/Linguistic**

   Alternative Assessment Handbook, Rubric 3: Artwork

Preteach

Bellringer

If YOU were there . . . Use the **Daily Bellringer Transparency** to help students answer the question.

Daily Bellringer Transparency, Section 5

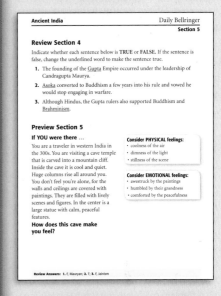

Academic Vocabulary

Review with students the high-use academic term in this section.

process a series of steps by which a task is accomplished (p. 170)

CRF: Vocabulary Builder Activity, Section 5

Standards Focus

HSS 6.5.7

Means: Discuss important artistic, literary, scientific, and mathematical traditions of ancient India.

Matters: Indian intellectual and artistic achievements, including literary works and the concept of zero, have had worldwide impact.

ANCIENT INDIA **167**

❶ Religious Art

Indian artists created great works of religious art.

Describe What is unusual about the temple at Ajanta? *It was carved out of a mountainside.*

Sequence How did Hindu temples change over time? *At first they were small stone structures with flat roofs, but they became complex temples with huge towers.*

 HSS 6.5.7

MISCONCEPTION ALERT

Bindis Some portrayals of women in Indian religious art show them with small colored dots, called *bindis*, on their foreheads. Contrary to popular belief, these marks do not designate a woman's caste. Depending on where the woman lives, the *bindi* may indicate that she is married. Bindis are primarily for decorative purposes, though. Indian women used to apply their bindis in powdered form. Now, however, they can buy peel-and-stick *bindis*.

Connect to Art

Teaching with Art Much of the art of India's great temples tells stories about deities. People who could not read the written language could "read" the stories in the sculpture and paintings and learn more about their religion. The carvings on the temple exteriors were especially important because not everyone was allowed inside the temples.

Answers

Reading Check *Most artists illustrated religious beliefs in their works, many of which can be seen in temples.*

Temple Architecture

This Hindu temple is covered with incredibly detailed carvings and decorations. Many individual sculptures are images of important Hindu deities, like the deity of Vishnu above.

Another type of Buddhist temple was the stupa. Stupas had domed roofs and were built to house sacred items from the life of the Buddha. Many of them were covered with detailed carvings.

Paintings and Sculpture

The Gupta period also saw the creation of great works of art, both paintings and statues. Painting was a greatly respected profession, and India was home to many skilled artists. However, we don't know the names of many artists from this period. Instead, we know the names of many rich and powerful members of Gupta society who paid artists to create works of beauty and significance.

Most Indian paintings from the Gupta period are clear and colorful. Some of them show graceful Indians wearing fine jewelry and stylish clothes. Such paintings offer us a glimpse of the Indians' daily and ceremonial lives.

Artists from both of India's major religions, Hinduism and Buddhism, drew on their beliefs to create their works. As a result, many of the finest paintings of ancient India are found in temples. Hindu painters drew hundreds of deities on temple walls and entrances. Buddhists covered the walls and ceilings of temples with scenes from the life of the Buddha.

Indian sculptors also created great works. Many of their statues were made for Buddhist cave temples. In addition to the temples' intricately carved columns, sculptors carved statues of kings and the Buddha. Some of these statues tower over the cave entrances. Hindu temples also featured impressive statues of their deities. In fact, the walls of some temples, such as the one pictured above, were completely covered with carvings and images.

READING CHECK Summarizing How did religion influence ancient Indian art?

Collaborative Learning

Reaching Standards

Describing an Indian Temple HSS 6.5.7

Standard English Mastery

1. Ask students to imagine that they are Indian farmers who are seeing the temple shown on this page, called Kesava Temple, for the first time. Point out that the temple may have been the most spectacular sight the farmer had ever seen.

2. Have each student write down a completion for either of these prompts: "As I approached Kesava Temple, I felt ___" or "As I approached Kesava Temple, I noticed ___." Encourage students to use the text and

photos to help them write clear, informative sentences using standard English.

3. Provide a thesaurus or dictionary to those students who need assistance.

4. Call on volunteers to read their sentences. Review them as examples of standard English usage. **LS Verbal/Linguistic**

Sanskrit Literature

As you read earlier, Sanskrit was the main language of the ancient Aryans. During the Maurya and Gupta periods, many works of Sanskrit literature were created. These works were later translated into many other languages.

Sacred Texts

The greatest of these Sanskrit writings are two sacred texts, the *Mahabharata* (muh-HAH-BAH-ruh-tuh) and the *Ramayana* (rah-MAH-yuh-nuh). Still popular in India, the *Mahabharata* is one of the world's longest sacred texts. It tells of the struggle between two families for control of a kingdom. Included within it are many long passages about Hindu beliefs. The most famous is called the *Bhagavad Gita* (BUG-uh-vuhd GEE-tah).

The *Ramayana*, according to Hindu tradition written prior to the *Mahabharata*, tells about a prince named Rama. In truth, the prince was the deity Vishnu in human form. He had become human so he could rid the world of demons. He also had to rescue his wife, a princess named Sita. For centuries, the characters of the *Ramayana* have been seen as models for how Indians should behave. For example, Rama is seen as the ideal ruler, and his relationship with Sita as the ideal marriage.

Other Works

Writers in the Gupta period also created plays, poetry, and other types of literature. One famous writer of this time was Kalidasa (kahl-ee-DAHS-uh). His work was so brilliant that Chandragupta II hired him to write plays for the royal court.

Sometime before 500, Indian writers also produced a book of stories called the *Panchatantra* (PUHN-chuh-TAHN-truh). The stories in this collection were intended to teach lessons. They praise people for cleverness and quick thinking. Each story ends with a message about winning friends, losing property, waging war, or some other idea. For example, the message below warns listeners to think about what they are doing before they act.

> " The good and bad of given schemes
> Wise thought must first reveal:
> The stupid heron saw his chicks
> Provide a mongoose meal. "
>
> –from the *Panchatantra*, translated by Arthur William Ryder

Eventually, translations of this collection spread throughout the world. It became popular even as far away as Europe.

READING CHECK **Categorizing** What types of literature did writers of ancient India create?

In this illustration of the *Ramayana*, the monkey king sends the monkey general Hanuman to find Sita. Hanuman helped Rama defeat the demons and win back Sita. Many Indians view him as a model of devotion and loyalty.

ANCIENT INDIA **169**

Main Idea

❸ Scientific Advances

The Indians made scientific advances in metalworking, medicine, and other sciences.

Describe What were some operations that Indian surgeons could perform? *fixing broken bones, treating wounds, removing infected tonsils, reconstructing broken noses, reattaching torn earlobes*

Compare How were metallurgy and alloys connected? *Creating alloys, or mixtures of two or more metals, was a skill within metallurgy that ancient Indians developed.*

Evaluate Why do you think the concept of zero was so important? *Zero acts as a placeholder when using numbers of a specific base such as base 10, allowing mathematicians to make calculations easily.*

⬛ HSS 6.5.7; HSS Analysis Skills: HI 3

Connect to Science

Mystery Solved? Recently, scientists at the Indian Institute of Technology announced that they had figured out why the Iron Pillar has not rusted. They said that phosphorous in the iron had allowed a very thin protective layer of an iron, oxygen, and hydrogen compound to form on the pillar's surface. This film is only one-twentieth of a millimeter thick. Because present-day iron-making processes remove most phosphorous, modern iron rusts more easily.

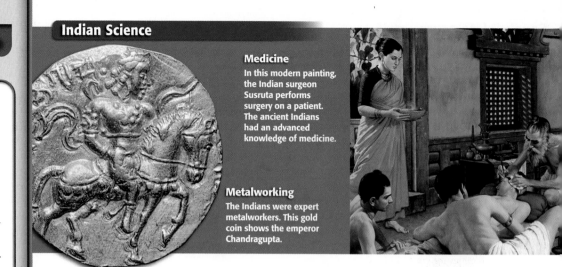

Indian Science

Medicine
In this modern painting, the Indian surgeon Susruta performs surgery on a patient. The ancient Indians had an advanced knowledge of medicine.

Metalworking
The Indians were expert metalworkers. This gold coin shows the emperor Chandragupta.

Scientific Advances

Indian achievements were not limited to art, architecture, and literature. Indian scholars also made important advances in metalworking, math, and the sciences.

Metalworking

ACADEMIC VOCABULARY
process a series of steps by which a task is accomplished

The ancient Indians were pioneers of **metallurgy** (MET-uhl-uhr-jee), the science of working with metals. Their knowledge allowed them to create high-quality tools and weapons. The Indians also knew **processes** for mixing metals to create **alloys**, mixtures of two or more metals. Alloys are sometimes stronger or easier to work with than pure metals.

Metalworkers made their strongest products out of iron. Indian iron was very hard and pure. These features made the iron a valuable trade item.

THE IMPACT TODAY
People still get inoculations against many diseases.

During the Gupta Dynasty, metalworkers built the famous Iron Pillar near Delhi. Unlike most iron, which rusts easily, this pillar is very resistant to rust. The tall column still attracts crowds of visitors. Scholars study this column even today to learn the Indians' secrets.

Mathematics and Other Sciences

Gupta scholars also made advances in math and science. In fact, they were among the most advanced mathematicians of their day. They developed many elements of our modern math system. The very numbers we use today are called **Hindu-Arabic numerals** because they were created by Indian scholars and brought to Europe by Arabs. The Indians were also the first people to create the zero. Although it may seem like a small thing, modern math wouldn't be possible without the zero.

The ancient Indians were also very skilled in the medical sciences. As early as the AD 100s, doctors were writing their knowledge down in textbooks. Among the skills these books describe is making medicines from plants and minerals.

Besides curing people with medicines, Indian doctors knew how to protect people against disease. The Indians practiced **inoculation** (i-nah-kyuh-LAY-shuhn), or injecting a person with a small dose of a virus to help him or her build up defenses to a disease. By fighting off this small dose, the body learns to protect itself.

170 CHAPTER 6

Differentiating Instruction for Universal Access

Learners Having Difficulty
Reaching Standards

Materials: art supplies

1. Discuss with students the wide variety of scientific advances made by the people of ancient India.

2. Ask students to imagine that they are metalworkers, doctors, mathematicians, or scientists of ancient India. Have each student design an advertisement that he or she might have placed in the yellow pages of a phone book of the time, had there been such a thing.

3. Ask students to discuss their yellow pages ads. As they do so, review the accomplishments of ancient Indians.

4. Display the ads in the classroom.
   LS Visual/Spatial

⬛ HSS 6.5.7; HSS Analysis Skills: HI 1

📖 Alternative Assessment Handbook, Rubric 2: Advertisements

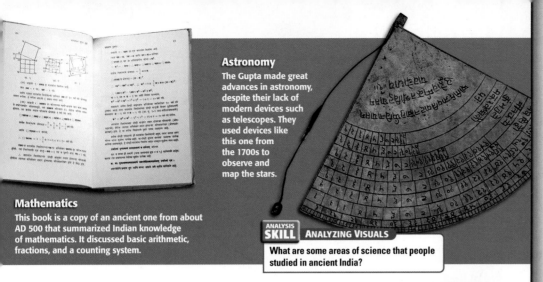

Astronomy
The Gupta made great advances in astronomy, despite their lack of modern devices such as telescopes. They used devices like this one from the 1700s to observe and map the stars.

Mathematics
This book is a copy of an ancient one from about AD 500 that summarized Indian knowledge of mathematics. It discussed basic arithmetic, fractions, and a counting system.

ANALYSIS SKILL **ANALYZING VISUALS**
What are some areas of science that people studied in ancient India?

For people who were injured, Indian doctors could perform surgery. Surgeons repaired broken bones, treated wounds, removed infected tonsils, reconstructed broken noses, and even reattached torn earlobes! If they could find no other cure for an illness, doctors would cast magic spells to help people recover.

Indian interest in **astronomy**, the study of stars and planets, dates back to early times as well. Indian astronomers knew of seven of the nine planets in our solar system. They knew that the sun was a star and that the planets revolved around it. They also knew that the earth was a sphere and that it rotated on its axis. In addition, they could predict eclipses of the sun and the moon.

READING CHECK Finding Main Ideas What were two Indian achievements in mathematics?

SUMMARY AND PREVIEW From a group of cities on the Indus River, India grew into a major empire whose people made great achievements. In the next chapter, you'll read about another civilization that experienced similar growth—China.

Section 5 Assessment

go.hrw.com
Online Quiz
KEYWORD: SQ6 HP6

Reviewing Ideas, Terms, and People HSS 6.5.7

1. **a. Describe** What did Hindu temples of the Gupta period look like?
   b. Analyze How can you tell that Indian artists were well respected?
   c. Evaluate Why do you think Hindu and Buddhist temples contained great works of art?
2. **a. Identify** What is the *Bhagavad Gita*?
   b. Explain Why were the stories of the *Panchatantra* written?
   c. Elaborate Why do you think people are still interested in ancient Sanskrit epics today?
3. **a. Define** What is **metallurgy**?
   b. Explain Why do we call the numbers we use today **Hindu-Arabic numerals**?

Critical Thinking

4. **Categorizing** Draw a chart like the one below. Use it to identify ancient Indian achievements in math and science.

Metallurgy	Math	Medicine	Astronomy

FOCUS ON WRITING

5. **Highlighting Indian Achievements** Make a list of Indian achievements that you could include on a poster. Now look back through your notes from this chapter. Which will you choose as the subject of your poster?

ANCIENT INDIA **171**

171

Sacred Texts

From the Bhagavad Gita

As You Read Point out that, although each verse is one sentence, several of the verses contain compound sentences. Semicolons separate the clauses of those sentences. Students should locate nouns, verbs, and objects within the clauses. Point out also that in many of the verses, the words are not in the order in which we expect to see them. However, the change in word order does not alter the meaning. Help students having difficulty place the words in a more familiar order.

Analyzing Sacred Texts

Plot and Conflict Remind students that even in excerpts such as this one, there is often a conflict—a problem to be solved or a challenge to be overcome. Sometimes the conflict in a story is between characters. Sometimes, however, the conflict is internal. In other words, the character is struggling with himself, trying to find answers to life's questions. In this passage, the conflict is internal. Arjuna is struggling to find inner peace. Remind students that Krishna is speaking. Krishna is giving advice to Arjuna to help him resolve his inner conflict.

Did You Know . . .

The Bhagavad Gita consists of 700 verses divided into 18 chapters. It has been translated into many languages. One can even listen to it in English over the Internet.

GUIDED READING

WORD HELP
lapses breaks
serenity peace
reason thinking
discipline self control

❶ Krishna says that people need to give up the desire for possessions to find peace.

What does Krishna say comes with peace?

HSS **6.5.7** Discuss important aesthetic and intellectual traditions (e.g., Sanskrit literature, including the *Bhagavad Gita*; medicine; metallurgy; and mathematics, including Hindu-Arabic numerals and the zero).

ELA **3.3.4** Define how tone or meaning is conveyed in poetry through word choice, figurative language, sentence structure, line length, punctuation, rhythm, repetition, and rhyme.

172 CHAPTER 6

---

from the
Bhagavad Gita

translated by Barbara Stoler Miller

About the Reading *The Bhagavad Gita, one of Hinduism's most sacred texts, is part of the much longer epic called the* Mahabharata. *The title* Bhagavad Gita *is Sanskrit for "Song of the Lord." The lord to which the title refers is Krishna, who is the deity Vishnu in human form. The Gita, as the poem is sometimes known, is written as a conversation between Krishna and a prince named Arjuna. Faced with a battle in which he will have to fight many of his friends and family members, Arjuna turns to Krishna for advice. As part of his response, Krishna explains to Arjuna how a soul can find peace and eternal happiness.*

AS YOU READ Think about the meaning behind Krishna's advice to Arjuna.

From anger comes confusion;
from confusion memory lapses;
from broken memory understanding is lost;
from loss of understanding, he is ruined.

But a man of inner strength
whose senses experience objects
without attraction and hatred,
in self control, finds serenity. ❶

In serenity, all his sorrows
dissolve;
his reason becomes serene,
his understanding sure.

Critical Thinking: Finding the Main Idea   Standards **Proficiency**

Summarizing a Poem **HSS** 6.5.7 **ELA** Reading 6.2.0

1. To ensure that students understand this excerpt, call on volunteers to re-read each stanza aloud. As each stanza is read, have students write down the main idea of the stanza in a single sentence.

2. Have volunteers read their main idea sentences to the class. Ask students to compare their main idea sentences with those presented. Have students correct their own sentences if needed.

3. When students have revised their 10 main idea sentences, have them write a paragraph that summarizes the main idea of the excerpt.

4. Call on several students to read their paragraphs to the class.
   LS **Verbal/Linguistic, Auditory/Musical**

   Alternative Assessment Handbook, Rubrics 18: Listening; and 37: Writing Assignments

Answers
Guided Reading 1. *serenity*

Without discipline,
he has no understanding or inner power;
without inner power, he has no peace;
and without peace where is joy?

If his mind submits to the play
of the senses,
they drive away insight,
as wind drives a ship on water. ❷

So, Great Warrior, when withdrawal
of the senses
from sense objects is complete,
discernment is firm.

When it is night for all creatures,
a master of restraint is awake;
when they are awake, it is night
for the sage who sees reality. ❸

As the mountainous depths
of the ocean
are unmoved when waters
rush into it,
so the man unmoved
when desires enter into him
attains a peace that eludes
the man of many desires. ❹

When he renounces all desires
and acts without craving,
possessiveness,
or individuality, he finds peace.

This is the place of the infinite spirit;
achieving it, one is freed from delusion;
abiding in it even at the time of death,
one finds the pure calm of infinity.

This painting from the 1700s shows Hindu women entering a forest on their way to meet Krishna.

GUIDED READING

WORD HELP

insight understanding; wisdom

discernment understanding

restraint holding back; self control

sage wise person

eludes escapes

renounces gives up

craving longing, wanting

delusion false belief

❷ Just as the wind pushes a ship along the water, Krishna says, the desire for objects pushes away peace and understanding of the world.

❸ Krishna says that people seeking peace should be more comfortable at night, because the senses are less active then than during the day.

❹ Just as the ocean doesn't change when water rushes into it, people shouldn't be changed by desires.

What does Krishna say will be the reward for people without many desires?

Sacred Texts

Analyzing Sacred Texts

Understanding Figurative Language This excerpt is rich in figurative language and imagery. Remind students that imagery is language that appeals to the senses. Most images are visual. That is, they appeal to the sense of sight. Have students identify the imagery in this passage. For example, in the fifth stanza, the author creates the vision of a ship being pushed by the wind. In the eighth stanza, the author creates the image of waters rushing into the ocean.

The author also uses contrasting images. Have students re-read the seventh stanza where night, the time one should be asleep, is placed in direct contrast with times when one is awake.

🐻 **ELA** 3.3.4

Info to Know

Krishna According to Hindu tradition, the deity Vishnu came to Earth in human form as Krishna to rid the world of a king who was the son of a demon. In the *Bhagavad Gita*, Krishna serves as Arjuna's adviser and charioteer.

CONNECTING SACRED TEXTS TO HISTORY

1. **Analyzing** Hindus believe that the world is an illusion that people must see through to be united with Brahman. How is this idea supported by Krishna's discussion of how to find peace?

2. **Comparing** Krishna says the people who find peace will reach the "place of infinite spirit" and find the "pure calm of infinity." How does this idea compare to the Buddhist concept of nirvana?

173

Differentiating Instruction for Universal Access

English Language Learners
Reaching Standards

Building Vocabulary Write these words for students to see: *confuse, attract, serene, discipline, discern, restrain, sage, elude, renounce, crave, possess, individual, infinite,* and *delude.* Have students work in pairs to look up these words in a dictionary and write at least one synonym for each besides those listed under Word Help in the feature. Then lead a discussion in which students convert the root words to the forms in the excerpt as needed. **LS Visual/Linguistic**

🐻 **HSS** 6.5.7

Advanced Learners/GATE
Exceeding Standards

Remind students that the *Bhagavad Gita* contains concepts essential to Hindu philosophy. One may also see echoes of Buddhist thought in it. Have students review the information about Hindu and Buddhist beliefs and practices in this chapter. Then have students write a brief essay in which they show the relationship between Hindu and Buddhist beliefs and practices and the excerpt presented here. **LS Visual/Linguistic**

🐻 **HSS** 6.5.7

Answers

Guided Reading 4. *peace*
Connecting Sacred Texts to History 1. *Krishna describes desires as illusions; ignoring these illusions is the surest way to find peace.* **2.** *Finding and achieving peace in one's life puts one on the path to finding nirvana.*

Interpreting Diagrams

Activity Guided Practice

Materials: photocopies of sample diagrams

Make photocopies of several diagrams. You might ask the librarian to suggest books that contain some diagrams related to the chapter content. Provide each student with copies of the diagrams and go through the diagrams as a class. Have students identify labeled items and other items. Then have each student select one diagram and write a paragraph describing what the diagram shows. Have volunteers read their paragraphs to the class. Correct any student errors. **LS** Visual/Spatial

📓 Alternative Assessment Handbook, Rubric 37: Writing Assignments

💿 Interactive Skills Tutor CD-ROM, Lesson 6: Interpret Maps, Charts, Visuals, and Political Cartoons

---

Social Studies Skills

| Analysis | Critical Thinking | Participation | **Study** |

Interpreting Diagrams

Understand the Skill

Diagrams are drawings that illustrate or explain objects or ideas. Different types of diagrams have different purposes. The ability to interpret diagrams will help you to better understand historical objects, their functions, and how they worked.

Learn the Skill

Use these guidelines to interpret a diagram:

1 Read the diagram's title or caption to find out what it represents. If a legend is present, study it as well to understand any symbols and colors in the diagram.

2 Most diagrams include labels that identify the object's parts or explain relationships between them. Study these parts and labels carefully.

3 If any written information or explanation accompanies the diagram, compare it to the drawing as you read.

The diagram below is of the Great Stupa at Sanchi in India, which is thought to contain the Buddha's remains. Like most stupas, it was shaped like a dome.

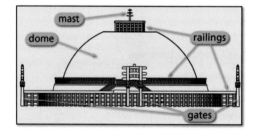

The Sanchi stupa is surrounded by a stone railing with four gates called *torenas*. About halfway up the side of the mound is a second railing next to a walkway. Worshippers move along this walkway in a clockwise direction to honor the Buddha. The stupa is topped by a cube called the *harmika*. Rising from the harmika is a mast or spire. These parts and their shapes all have religious meaning for Buddhists.

Practice and Apply the Skill

Here is another diagram of the Sanchi stupa. Interpret both diagrams on this page to answer the questions that follow.

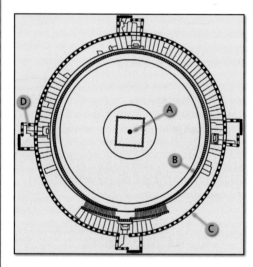

1. Which letter in this diagram labels the *torenas*?
2. What part of the stupa does the letter A label?
3. The walkway and railing are labeled by which letter?

Social Studies Skills Activity: Interpreting Diagrams

Creating Diagrams

Materials: art supplies, poster board

| | Standards Proficiency | Research Required |

1. Have each student conduct research to find a diagram of a historical structure in India.

2. Each student should create a large copy of the diagram on poster board. Below the diagram, students should provide captions explaining the information in the diagram and providing background information about the structure.

3. Ask for volunteers to share their diagrams with the class. Give other students a chance to interpret the diagrams and to ask questions. Then have volunteers explain their diagrams.

4. Display students' diagrams around the classroom. **LS** Visual/Spatial

📓 Alternative Assessment Handbook, Rubrics 3: Artwork; and 30: Research

---

Answers

Practice and Apply the Skill **1.** *D;* **2.** *the mast or spire on the* harmika; **3.** *B*

Standards Review

Visual Summary

Use the visual summary below to help you review the main ideas of the chapter.

QUICK FACTS

The Harappan civilization began in the Indus River Valley.

Hinduism and Buddhism both developed in India.

Indians made great advances in art, literature, science, and other fields.

Reviewing Terms and People

Fill in the blanks with the correct term or name from this chapter.

1. _____ are winds that bring heavy rainfall.

2. A _____ is a division of people into groups based on birth, wealth, or occupation.

3. Hindus believe in _____, the belief that they will be reborn many times after death.

4. _____ founded the Mauryan Empire.

5. The focusing of the mind on spiritual things is called _____.

6. People who work to spread their religious beliefs are called _____.

7. People who practice _____ use only peaceful ways to achieve change.

8. _____ converted to Buddhism while he was ruler of the Mauryan Empire.

9. A mixture of metals is called an _____.

10. The study of the stars and planets is called _____.

Comprehension and Critical Thinking

SECTION 1 *(Pages 144–149)* **HSS** 6.5.1, 6.5.2

11. **a. Describe** What caused floods on the Indus River, and what was the result of those floods?

b. Contrast How was Aryan culture different from Harappan culture?

c. Elaborate Why is the Harappan culture considered a civilization?

SECTION 2 *(Pages 150–155)* **HSS** 6.5.3, 6.5.4

12. **a. Identify** Who were the Brahmins, and what role did they play in Aryan society?

b. Analyze How do Hindus believe karma affects reincarnation?

c. Elaborate Hinduism has been called both a polytheistic religion—one that worships many deities—and a monotheistic religion—one that worships only one. Why do you think this is so?

ANCIENT INDIA **175**

Visual Summary

Review and Inquiry Have students use the visual summary to provide details about the chapter's main ideas.

🎁 Quick Facts Transparency: Ancient India Visual Summary

Reviewing Terms and People

1. monsoons
2. caste system
3. reincarnation
4. Chandragupta Maurya
5. meditation
6. missionaries
7. nonviolence
8. Asoka
9. alloy
10. astronomy

Comprehension and Critical Thinking

11. **a.** melting of heavy snows in the Himalayas; left behind layer of silt, making the land ideal for farming

b. Aryan—nomadic warriors from Central Asia, small settlements based on family ties, kept livestock and later farmed, each village ruled by a raja, no writing system; Harappan—in the Indus River Valley, created fortified and well-planned cities, may have had a strong central government, created India's first writing system

c. had well-planned cities with technical advances, writing system, division of labor as shown by wide range of objects created

12. **a.** priests; highest class in Aryan society

Review & Assessment Resources

Review and Reinforce

SE Standards Review

📋 **CRF:** Chapter Review Activity

📋 California Standards Review Workbook

🎁 Quick Facts Transparency: Ancient India Visual Summary

📢 Spanish Chapter Summaries Audio CD Program

📲 Online Chapter Summaries in Six Languages

OSP Holt PuzzlePro; Game Tool for ExamView

💿 Quiz Game CD-ROM

Assess

SE Standards Assessment

📋 PASS: Chapter Test, Forms A and B

📋 Alternative Assessment Handbook

OSP ExamView Test Generator, Chapter Test

💿 Universal Access Modified Worksheets and Tests CD-ROM: Chapter Test

📲 Holt Online Assessment Program (in the Premier Online Edition)

Reteach/Intervene

📋 Interactive Reader and Study Guide

📋 Universal Access Teacher Management System: Lesson Plans for Universal Access

💿 Universal Access Modified Worksheets and Tests CD-ROM

💿 Interactive Skills Tutor CD-ROM

| KEYWORD: SQ6 WH6 |

b. Karma determines if you are reborn into a higher or lower caste.

c. Hindus believe in three major deities—Brahma, Siva, and Vishnu. However, they also believe these deities are parts of a universal spirit called Brahman.

13. a. wanting what we like but do not have, wanting to keep what we like and already have, not wanting what we dislike but have

b. Missionaries spread Buddhism across Asia; it split into two major branches.

c. possible answers—They were assured that their low social rank was not a barrier to enlightenment and that they had the power to change their lives.

14. a. seized control of northern India and by so doing founded the Mauryan Empire

b. Both unified much of India; Mauryan rulers promoted Buddhism, while Gupta rulers promoted Hinduism.

c. possible answer—Buddhism might not have spread to the rest of Asia, and Hinduism would be even more prevalent in India than it is today.

15. a. Buddhist and Hindu temples, paintings, and sculptures

b. possible answer—Their Hindu beliefs affect how the characters interact.

c. Answers will vary but should display familiarity with the achievements mentioned in this section.

Reviewing Themes

16. Both share belief in reincarnation; Hinduism supported the caste system, while Buddhism did not.

17. defined who one could marry and eat with, along with many other aspects of daily life

Using the Internet

18. Go to the HRW Web site and enter the keyword shown to access a rubric for this activity.

> KEYWORD: SQ6 TEACHER

SECTION 3 *(Pages 156–161)* HSS 6.5.5

13. a. Describe What did the Buddha say caused human suffering?

b. Analyze How did Buddhism grow and change after the Buddha died?

c. Elaborate Why did the Buddha's teachings about nirvana appeal to many people of lower castes?

SECTION 4 *(Pages 162–165)* HSS 6.5.6

14. a. Identify What was Chandragupta Maurya's greatest accomplishment?

b. Compare and Contrast What was one similarity between the Mauryas and the Guptas? What was one difference between them?

c. Predict How might Indian history have been different if Asoka had not become a Buddhist?

SECTION 5 *(Pages 167–171)* HSS 6.5.7

15. a. Describe What kinds of religious art did the ancient Indians create?

b. Make Inferences Why do you think religious discussions are included in the *Mahabharata?*

c. Evaluate Which of the ancient Indians' achievements do you think is most impressive? Why?

Reviewing Themes

16. Religion What is one teaching that Buddhism and Hinduism share? What is one idea about which they differ?

17. Society and Culture How did the caste system affect the lives of most people in India?

Using the Internet

go.hrw.com
KEYWORD: SQ6 WH6

18. Activity: Making a Brochure In this chapter, you learned about India's diverse geographical features and the ways in which geography influenced India's history. Enter the activity keyword. Then research the geography and civilizations of India, taking notes as you go. Finally, use the interactive brochure template to present what you have found.

Reading Skills

19. Drawing Inferences Based on what you learned about the Gupta period, what inference can you draw about religious tolerance in ancient India? Draw a box like the one below to help you organize your thoughts.

Question:	
Inside the Text:	Outside the Text:
Inference:	

Social Studies Skills

20. Understanding Diagrams Look back over the diagram of the Buddhist temple in the skills activity at the end of this chapter. Using this diagram as a guide, draw a simple diagram of your house or school. Be sure to include labels of important features on your diagram. An example has been provided for you below.

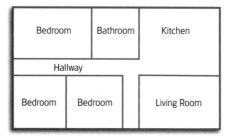

Bedroom	Bathroom	Kitchen
	Hallway	
Bedroom	Bedroom	Living Room

FOCUS ON WRITING

21. Designing Your Poster Now that you have chosen a topic for your poster, it's time to create it. On a large sheet of paper or poster board, write a title that identifies the subject of your poster. Then draw pictures, maps, or diagrams that illustrate your chosen topic.

Next to each picture, write a short caption. Each caption should be two sentences long. The first sentence should identify what the picture, map, or diagram shows. The second sentence should explain why the picture is important to the study of Indian history.

Reading Skills

19. Answers will vary, but students should infer that there was religious tolerance in ancient India.

Social Studies Skills

20. Diagrams will vary but should follow the general format shown.

Focus on Writing

21. Rubric Students' illustrated posters should:
- present the ideas clearly.
- contain appropriate, accurate, and vivid illustrations.
- have proper labels and captions.
- use correct grammar, punctuation, spelling, and capitalization.

CRF: Focus on Writing: An Illustrated Poster

Standards Assessment

DIRECTIONS: Read each question, and write the letter of the best response.

1 Use the map to answer the following question.

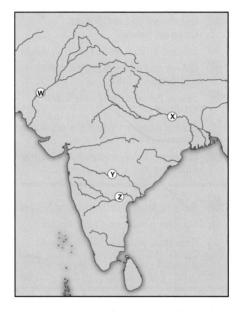

Civilization grew on the Indian subcontinent along the river marked on the map by the letter

A W.

B X.

C Y.

D Z.

2 The people of which *varna* in early India had the hardest lives?

A Brahmins

B Kshatriyas

C Sudras

D Vaisyas

3 What is the *main* goal of people who follow Buddhism as it was taught by the Buddha?

A wealth

B rebirth

C missionary work

D reaching nirvana

4 The Mauryan emperor Asoka is known for all of the following *except*

A expanding the empire across most of India.

B spreading Hinduism.

C working to improve his people's lives.

D practicing nonviolence.

5 Early India's contributions to world civilization included

A developing the world's first calendar.

B creating what is now called algebra.

C inventing the plow and the wheel.

D introducing zero to the number system.

Connecting with Past Learnings

6 In this chapter you learned about two sacred epics, the *Mahabharata* and the *Ramayana*. Which of the following is also an epic poem that you have studied?

A Hammurabi's Code

B the *Book of the Dead*

C *Gilgamesh*

D the Pyramid Texts

7 As you learned earlier in this course, the ancient Egyptians held elaborate religious rituals. Which of these Indian religions also involved many rituals, including sacrifices?

A Buddhism

B Brahmanism

C Jainism

D Mauryanism

Answers

1. A

Break Down the Question This question requires students to recall map information. Refer students who miss it to the maps in Section 1.

2. C

Break Down the Question Refer students who miss this question to the diagram in Section 2 and text information about the caste system.

3. D

Break Down the Question Seeking wealth would be a barrier to reaching nirvana. Rebirth can provide a path to nirvana. Missionary work is not a requirement of Buddhism. Refer students who miss the question to review *Teachings of Buddhism*.

4. B

Break Down the Question This question requires students to recall factual information. Asoka spread Buddhism, not Hinduism. Refer students who miss the question to Section 4.

5. D

Break Down the Question Although ancient India contributed much to world civilization, the only contribution in this list that is mentioned in the chapter is the introduction of zero.

6. C

Break Down the Question This question requires students to recall information from a previous chapter on Mesopotamia.

7. B

Break Down the Question Refer students who miss the question to Section 2. Remind students that Brahmanism involved many rituals, including sacrifices, led by the Brahmins.

Standards Review

Have students review the following standards in their workbooks.

California Standards Review Workbook:
HSS 6.5.1, 6.5.2, 6.5.3, 6.5.4, 6.5.5, 6.5.6, 6.5.7

Intervention Resources

Reproducible

- Interactive Reader and Study Guide
- Universal Access Teacher Management System: Universal Access Lesson Plans Technology

Technology

- Quick Facts Transparency: Ancient India Visual Summary
- Universal Access Modified Worksheets and Tests CD-ROM
- Interactive Skills Tutor CD-ROM

Tips for Test Taking

Getting the Full Picture When a question refers to a table or a chart, students should carefully read all the information in the table or chart, including headings and labels, before answering the question. When a question refers to a graph, encourage students to first carefully study the data plotted on the graph to determine any trends or oddities before answering the question.

ANCIENT INDIA **177**

Chapter 7 Planning Guide

Ancient China

Chapter Overview	Reproducible Resources	Technology Resources
Chapter 7 pp. 178–217 **Overview:** In this chapter, students will learn how Chinese civilization developed and about the contacts between China and other cultures. See page 178 for the California History–Social Science standards covered in this chapter.	**Universal Access Teacher Management System:*** • Universal Access Instructional Benchmarking Guides • Lesson Plans for Universal Access **Interactive Reader and Study Guide:** Chapter Graphic Organizer* **Chapter Resource File*** • Chapter Review Activity • Focus on Speaking Activity: Oral Presentation • Social Studies Skills Activity: Conducting Internet Research	**One-Stop Planner CD-ROM:** Calendar Planner **Student Edition on Audio CD Program** **Universal Access Modified Worksheets and Tests CD-ROM** **Power Presentations with Video CD-ROM** **History's Impact: World History Video Program (VHS/DVD):** Ancient China* **Music of the World Audio CD Program:** Selection 19
Section 1: **Geography and Early China** **The Big Idea:** Chinese civilization began with the Shang dynasty along the Huang He. 6.6.1, 6.6.2	**Universal Access Teacher Management System:*** Section 1 Lesson Plan **Interactive Reader and Study Guide:** Section 1 Summary* **Chapter Resource File*** • Vocabulary Builder Activity, Section 1 • History and Geography Activity: Shang China	**Daily Bellringer Transparency:** Section 1* **Map Transparency:** China: Physical* **Map Transparency:** Shang Dynasty, c. 1500–1050 BC*
Section 2: **The Zhou Dynasty and New Ideas** **The Big Idea:** The Zhou dynasty brought political stability and new ways to deal with political and social problems in ancient China. 6.6.3, 6.6.4	**Universal Access Teacher Management System:*** Section 2 Lesson Plan **Interactive Reader and Study Guide:** Section 2 Summary* **Chapter Resource File*** • Vocabulary Builder Activity, Section 2 • Literature Activity: *The Book of Songs* • Primary Source Activity: The Teachings of Confucius and Laozi	**Daily Bellringer Transparency:** Section 2* **Map Transparency:** Zhou Dynasty, c. 1050–400 BC* **Quick Facts Transparency:** Zhou Society* **Quick Facts Transparency:** Main Ideas of Confucianism* **Internet Activity:** Chinese Philosophers
Section 3: **The Qin Dynasty** **The Big Idea:** The Qin dynasty unified China with a strong government and a system of standardization. 6.6.5	**Universal Access Teacher Management System:*** Section 3 Lesson Plan **Interactive Reader and Study Guide:** Section 3 Summary* **Chapter Resource File*** • Vocabulary Builder Activity, Section 3	**Daily Bellringer Transparency:** Section 3* **Map Transparency:** Qin Dynasty, c. 221–206 BC* **Quick Facts Transparency:** Emperor Shi Huangdi*
Section 4: **The Han Dynasty** **The Big Idea:** The Han dynasty created a new form of government that valued family, art, and learning. 6.6.6	**Universal Access Teacher Management System:*** Section 4 Lesson Plan **Interactive Reader and Study Guide:** Section 4 Summary* **Chapter Resource File*** • Vocabulary Builder Activity, Section 4 • Biography Activities: Liu Bang; Wu-ti	**Daily Bellringer Transparency:** Section 4* **Map Transparency:** Han Dynasty, c. 206 BC–AD 220* **Internet Activity:** Art of Ancient China
Section 5: **Han Contacts With Other Cultures** **The Big Idea:** Trade routes led to the exchange of new products and ideas among China, Rome, and other peoples. 6.6.7, 6.6.8	**Universal Access Teacher Management System:*** Section 5 Lesson Plan **Interactive Reader and Study Guide:** Section 5 Summary* **Chapter Resource File*** • Vocabulary Builder Activity, Section 5 • Economics and History Activity: The Chinese Economy	**Daily Bellringer Transparency:** Section 5* **Map Transparency:** The Silk Road*

MASTERING THE CALIFORNIA STANDARDS

Review, Assessment, Intervention

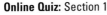

Standards Review Workbook*

Quick Facts Transparency: Ancient China Visual Summary*

Spanish Chapter Summaries Audio CD Program

Online Chapter Summaries in Six Languages

Progress Assessment Support System (PASS): Chapter Test*

Universal Access Modified Worksheets and Tests CD-ROM: Modified Chapter Test

One-Stop Planner CD-ROM: ExamView Test Generator (English/Spanish)

PASS: Section 1 Quiz*

Online Quiz: Section 1

Alternative Assessment Handbook

PASS: Section 2 Quiz*

Online Quiz: Section 2

Alternative Assessment Handbook

PASS: Section 3 Quiz*

Online Quiz: Section 3

Alternative Assessment Handbook

PASS: Section 4 Quiz*

Online Quiz: Section 4

Alternative Assessment Handbook

PASS: Section 5 Quiz*

Online Quiz: Section 5

Alternative Assessment Handbook

California Resources for Standards Mastery

INSTRUCTIONAL PLANNING AND SUPPORT

 Universal Access Teacher Management System*

 One-Stop Planner CD-ROM with Test Generator: Teacher Management System with Interactive Teacher's Edition

STANDARDS MASTERY

Standards Review Workbook*

At Home: A Guide to Standards Mastery for World History

Holt Online Learning

To enhance learning, the following Internet activities are available: **Chinese Philosophers** and **Art of Ancient China.**

KEYWORD: SQ6 TEACHER

- **Teacher Support Page**
- **Content Updates**
- **Rubrics and Writing Models**

- **Teaching Tips for the Multimedia Classroom**

KEYWORD: SQ6 WH7

- **Current Events**
- **Holt Grapher**
- **Holt Online Atlas**
- **Holt Researcher**
- **Interactive Multimedia Activities**
- **Internet Activities**

- **Online Chapter Summaries in Six Languages**
- **Online Section Quizzes**
- **World History Maps and Charts**

HOLT PREMIER ONLINE STUDENT EDITION

Complete online support for interactivity, assessment, and reporting

- **Interactive Maps and Notebook**
- **Standardized Test Prep**
- **Homework Practice and Research Activities Online**

Mastering the Standards: Differentiating Instruction

Reaching Standards	Basic-level activities designed for all students encountering new material
Standards Proficiency	Intermediate-level activities designed for average students
Exceeding Standards	Challenging activities designed for honors and gifted-and-talented students
Standard English Mastery	Activities designed to improve standard English usage

MASTERING THE CALIFORNIA STANDARDS

Frequently Asked Questions

INSTRUCTIONAL PLANNING AND SUPPORT

Where do I find planning aids, pacing guides, lesson plans, and other teaching aids?

Annotated Teacher's Edition:
- Chapter planning guides
- Standards-based instruction and strategies
- Differentiated instruction for universal access
- Point-of-use reminders for integrating program resources

Power Presentations with Video CD-ROM

Universal Access Teacher Management System:
- Year and unit instructional benchmarking guides
- Reproducible lesson plans
- Assessment guides for diagnostic, progress, and summative end-of-the-year tests
- Options for differentiating instruction and intervention
- Teaching guides and answer keys for student workbooks

One-Stop Planner CD-ROM with Test Generator: Teacher Management System with Interactive Teacher's Edition:
- Calendar Planner
- Editable lesson plans
- All reproducible ancillaries in Adobe Acrobat (PDF) format
- ExamView Test Generator (English & Spanish)
- Game Tool for ExamView
- PuzzlePro
- Transparency and video previews

DIFFERENTIATING INSTRUCTION FOR UNIVERSAL ACCESS

What resources are available to ensure that Advanced Learners/GATE Students master the standards?

Teacher's Edition Activities:
- Confucian Sayings, p. 191
- *Fu* and *Shi* Poems, p. 204

- Farming and Manufacturing Advances, p. 209

Lesson Plans for Universal Access

Primary Source Library CD-ROM for World History

What resources are available to ensure that English Learners and Standard English Learners master the standards?

Teacher's Edition Activities:
- *Shiji* Comic Strip, p. 206

Lesson Plans for Universal Access

Chapter Resource File: Vocabulary Builder Activities

Spanish Chapter Summaries Audio CD Program

Online Chapter Summaries in Six Languages

One-Stop Planner CD-ROM:
- PuzzlePro, Spanish Version
- ExamView Test Generator, Spanish Version

What modified materials are available for Special Education?

Teacher's Edition Activities:
- Shang Dynasty Chart, p. 186
- Qin Achievements Poster, p. 197

The *Universal Access Modified Worksheets and Tests CD-ROM* provides editable versions of the following:

Vocabulary Flash Cards

Modified Vocabulary Builder Activities

Modified Chapter Review Activity

Modified Chapter Test

What resources are available to ensure that Learners Having Difficulty master the standards?

Teacher's Edition Activities:

- Travel Poster, p. 183
- The Shang and Zhou Dynasties, p. 189
- Main Ideas and Details, p. 190
- Terra-cotta Army Exhibit, p. 196
- A Eulogy for Shi Huangdi, p. 199
- Han Dynasty Social Structure, p. 202
- Re-creating the Silk Road, p. 210

Interactive Reader and Study Guide

Student Edition on Audio CD Program

Quick Facts Transparency: Ancient China Visual Summary

Standards Review Workbook

Social Studies Skills Activity: Conducting Internet Research

Interactive Skills Tutor CD-ROM

How do I intervene for students struggling to master the standards?

Interactive Reader and Study Guide

Quick Facts Transparency: Ancient China Visual Summary

Standards Review Workbook

Social Studies Skills Activity: Conducting Internet Research

Interactive Skills Tutor CD-ROM

PROFESSIONAL DEVELOPMENT

HOLT
Professional Development

What teacher training resources are available to help me grow professionally?

- In-service and staff development as part of your Holt Social Studies product purchase
- Quick Teacher Tutorial Lesson Presentation CD-ROM
- Intensive tuition-based Teacher Development Institute
- Convenient Holt Speaker Bureau face-to-face workshop options

- PRAXIS™ Test Prep (#0089) interactive Web-based content refreshers*
- *Ask A Professional Development Expert* at http://www.hrw.com/prodev/

* PRAXIS is a trademark of Educational Testing Service (ETS). This publication is not endorsed or approved by ETS.

Information Literacy Skills

To learn more about how History–Social Science instruction may be improved by the effective use of library media centers and information literacy skills, go to the Teacher's Resource Materials for Chapter 7 at **go.hrw.com, keyword: SQ6 MEDIA.**

MASTERING THE CALIFORNIA STANDARDS

Standards Focus

Standards by Section
Section 1: **HSS** 6.6.1, 6.6.2
Section 2: **HSS** 6.6.3, 6.6.4
Section 3: **HSS** 6.6.5
Section 4: **HSS** 6.6.6
Section 5: **HSS** 6.6.7, 6.6.8

Teacher's Edition
HSS Analysis Skills: CS 1, CS 2, CS 3, HR 1, HR 3, HI 1, HI 2, HI 6

Upcoming Standards for Future Learning
Preview the following History–Social Science content standards from upcoming chapters or grade levels to promote learning beyond the current chapter.

HSS **7.3** Students analyze the geographic, political, economic, religious, and social structures of the civilizations of China in the Middle Ages.

7.3.2 Describe agricultural, technological, and commercial developments during the Tang and Sung periods.

7.3.3 Analyze the influences of Confucianism and changes in Confucian thought during the Sung and Mongol periods.

7.3.4 Understand the importance of both overland trade and maritime expeditions between China and other civilizations in the Mongol Ascendancy and Ming Dynasty.

Focus on Speaking

The **Chapter Resource File** provides a Focus on Speaking worksheet to help students organize and create their oral presentations.

CRF: Focus on Speaking Activity: Oral Presentation

CHAPTER 7 1600 BC–AD 1

Ancient China

California Standards

History–Social Science
6.6 Students analyze the geographic, political, economic, religious, and social structures of the early civilizations of China.

English–Language Arts
Speaking 6.2.2 Deliver informative presentations.

Reading 6.2.4 Clarify understanding by summarizing.

FOCUS ON SPEAKING

Oral Presentation In this chapter you will read about China's fascinating early years. Choose one person or event from that history. You will then tell your classmates why the person or event was important to the history of China.

178 CHAPTER 7

CHAPTER EVENTS

c. 1500s BC The Shang dynasty is established in China.

1600 BC

WORLD EVENTS

c. 1480 BC Queen Hatshepsut rules Egypt.

Introduce the Chapter

Standards Proficiency

Focus on China

1. Ask students the following questions: If you were lost in the woods, what could you use to learn which direction is which? On what material is this book printed? What instrument do scientists use to learn about earthquakes that occur far away? What medical procedure uses many tiny needles inserted in a patient's skin?

2. In order, the answers are a compass, paper, seismograph, and acupuncture. Then ask students if they can guess what these questions and answers have in common. *They are all about inventions and innovations created by the Chinese.*

3. Point out that China has one of the world's oldest civilizations and that Chinese civilization has influenced ours in ways that are not always obvious. Tell students they will be introduced to Chinese civilization and its influence in this chapter.
LS Verbal/Linguistic

HOLT

History's Impact

▶ video series

Watch the video to understand the impact of Confucius on China today.

What You Will Learn...

In this chapter you will learn about the geography, history, and culture of ancient China. China was one of the early centers of civilization. China's two major rivers played key roles in Chinese history and the development of Chinese society.

1100s BC
The Zhou dynasty begins.

551 BC
Confucius is born in China.

221 BC
Shi Huangdi unites China under the Qin dynasty.

205 BC
The Han dynasty begins its rule of China.

1200 BC   800 BC   400 BC   BC 1 AD

c. 965 BC
Solomon becomes king of the Israelites.

c. 500 BC
Buddhism begins to emerge in India.

c. 100 BC
The overland Silk Road connects China and Southwest Asia.

ANCIENT CHINA   **179**

Explore the Time Line

1. When did the Shang dynasty begin? *about 1500s BC*

2. How many years passed between Shi Huangdi's unification of China and the beginning of the Han dynasty? *16 years*

3. During which century did both Confucianism and Buddhism emerge? *sixth century BC*

4. Who ruled Egypt while the Shang dynasty ruled China? *Queen Hatshepsut*

5. When did the Silk Road connect China and Southwest Asia? *about 100 BC*

🐻 HSS Analysis Skills: CS 1

Did you know . . .

The dynasties depicted on this time line are only a few of the 10 major dynasties that have ruled over China. The longest-lasting dynasty in Chinese history was the Zhou, which ruled for some 600 years. The shortest major dynasty was the Qin, which ruled for fewer than 20 years. China's imperial age ended with the overthrow of the Qing dynasty in 1912.

• **Chapter Preview** •

HOLT

History's Impact

▶ video series

See the Video Teacher's Guide for strategies for using the chapter video **Ancient China: The Impact of Confucius on China Today.**

Chapter Big Ideas

Section 1 Chinese civilization began with the Shang dynasty along the Huang He. HSS 6.6.1, 6.6.2

Section 2 Confucius and other philosophers taught ways to deal with political and social problems in ancient China. HSS 6.6.3, 6.6.4

Section 3 The Qin dynasty unified China with a strong government and a system of standardization. HSS 6.6.5

Section 4 The Han dynasty created a new form of government that valued family, art, and learning. HSS 6.6.6

Section 5 Trade routes led to the exchange of new products and ideas among China, Rome, and other peoples. HSS 6.6.7, 6.6.8

Explore the Picture

A Chinese Landscape The photo shows unusual formations that have been featured in Chinese paintings for centuries. Point out the odd, steep hills in the background. They are called karst towers and were formed by the erosion of limestone by water. The karst towers attract many tourists.

Analyzing Visuals Ask students what they think the people in the photo are doing. As a hint, point out the bird on the boat in the foreground. Tell students the bird, a cormorant, has been trained to perform a certain task. *The people are fishing. They have trained cormorants to dive into the water for fish. Because a cord is tied around the bird's neck, the cormorant does not swallow the fish but gives it to the fisher.*

go.hrw.com
Online Resources

Chapter Resources:
KEYWORD: SQ6 WH7
Teacher Resources:
KEYWORD: SQ6 TEACHER

Understanding Themes

This chapter focuses on two themes—politics, and society and culture. Ask students to use their knowledge of other civilizations to make predictions about the political structure in ancient China. Write student predictions for everyone to see. Help students to see which of their predictions are correct or incorrect. Then have students discuss what they may already know about Chinese society and culture. Tell students that this chapter will teach them about the development of China, how its governments were formed, and how its society was organized.

Summarizing Historical Texts

Focus on Reading Have students bring newspaper or magazine articles on topics they find interesting. Then have each student write a brief summary of their article. Ask students to exchange their summary with a partner, and have students critique each other's summary. Ask students to discuss what mistakes they saw in the summaries and how they might correct those mistakes.

Reading Social Studies
by Kylene Beers

Economics	Geography		Religion		Science and Technology
		Politics		Society and Culture	

Focus on Themes This chapter will describe the early development of China—how Chinese civilization began and took shape under early dynasties. You will see how these dynasties controlled the government and **politics**. You will also see how the Chinese, influenced by the philosopher Confucius, established traditions such as the importance of families. They also encouraged art and learning, helping to shape the **society and culture** that would last for centuries in China.

Summarizing Historical Texts

Focus on Reading When you are reading a history book, how can you be sure that you understand everything? One way is to briefly restate what you've read in a summary.

Writing a Summary A summary is a short restatement of the most important ideas in a text. The example below shows three steps used in writing a summary. First identify important details. Then write a short summary of each paragraph. Finally, combine these paragraph summaries into a short summary of the whole passage.

Additional reading support can be found in the

Inter active

Reader and Study Guide

> The first dynasty for which we have clear evidence is the Shang, which was firmly established by the 1500s BC. Strongest in the Huang He Valley, the Shang ruled a broad area of northern China. Shang rulers moved their capital several times, probably to avoid floods or attack by enemies.
>
> The king was at the center of Shang political and religious life. Nobles served the king as advisors and helped him rule. Less important officials were also nobles. They performed specific governmental and religious duties.

Summary of Paragraph 1
China's first dynasty, the Shang, took power in northern China in the 1500s BC.

Summary of Paragraph 2
Shang politics and religion were run by the king and nobles.

Combined Summary
The Shang dynasty, which ruled northern China by the 1500s BC, was governed by a king and nobles.

180 CHAPTER 7

Reading and Skills Resources

Reading Support
- Interactive Reader and Study Guide
- Student Edition on Audio CD
- Spanish Chapter Summaries Audio CD Program

Social Studies Skills Support
- Interactive Skills Tutor CD-ROM

Vocabulary Support
- **CRF:** Vocabulary Builder Activities
- **CRF:** Chapter Review Activity
- Universal Access Modified Worksheets and Tests CD-ROM:
  - Vocabulary Flash Cards
  - Vocabulary Builder Activity
  - Chapter Review Activity

OSP Holt PuzzlePro

Standards Focus

ELA Reading 6.2.4

You Try It!

The following passage is from the chapter you are about to read. As you read it, think about what you would include in a summary.

Early Settlements

From Chapter 7 p. 184

Archaeologists have found remains of early Chinese villages. One village site near the Huang He had more than 40 houses. Many of the houses were partly underground and may have had straw-covered roofs. The site also included animal pens, storage pits, and a cemetery.

Some of the villages along the Huang He grew into large towns. Walls surrounded these towns to defend them against floods and hostile neighbors. In towns like these, the Chinese left many artifacts, such as arrowheads, fishhooks, tools, and pottery. Some village sites even contained pieces of cloth.

After you read the passage, answer the following questions.

1. Read the following summaries and decide which one is the better summary statement. Explain your answer.
   a) Archaeologists have found out interesting things about the early settlements of China. For example, they have discovered that the Chinese had homes with straw-covered roofs, pens for their animals, and even cemeteries. Also, they have found that larger villages were surrounded by walls for defense. Finally, they have found tools like arrowheads and fishhooks.
   b) Archaeologists have found remains of early Chinese villages, some of which grew into large walled settlements. Artifacts found there help us understand Chinese culture.

2. What should be included in a good summary?

Key Terms and People

Chapter 7

Section 1
jade *(p. 185)*
oracle *(p. 186)*

Section 2
lords *(p. 189)*
peasants *(p. 189)*
Confucius *(p. 191)*
ethics *(p. 191)*
Confucianism *(p. 191)*
Daoism *(p. 192)*
Laozi *(p. 192)*
Legalism *(p. 192)*

Section 3
Shi Huangdi *(p. 194)*
Great Wall *(p. 197)*

Section 4
sundial *(p. 204)*
seismograph *(p. 204)*
acupuncture *(p. 205)*

Section 5
silk *(p. 209)*
Silk Road *(p. 209)*
diffusion *(p. 211)*

Academic Vocabulary

Success in school is related to knowing academic vocabulary—the words that are frequently used in school assignments and discussions. In this chapter, you will learn the following academic words:

vary *(p. 183)*
structure *(p. 190)*
innovation *(p. 204)*
procedure *(p. 209)*

As you read **Chapter 7**, think about how you would summarize the material you are reading.

Reading Social Studies

Key Terms and People

Preteach the key terms and people from this chapter by asking students what they think each term means or who each person was. Ask the class to identify six of the terms or people about which they know the least. Write the list of six terms for the class to see. Then have each student define or identify the six terms or people. Have students draw an illustration that best represents each term or person.

LS Verbal/Linguistic, Visual/Spatial

Focus on Reading

See the **Focus on Reading** questions in this chapter for more practice on this reading social studies skill.

Reading Social Studies Assessment

See the **Standards Review** at the end of this chapter for student assessment questions related to this reading skill.

Teaching Tip

Students may think that every fact is an important detail to include in a summary. Remind students that not every fact is important. One way to help students keep to the important details is to have them identify the main idea of each paragraph in a few words. Then instruct students to only underline details that support that main idea. Model this strategy for students by summarizing a paragraph or two as a class.

Answers

You Try It! 1. *Summary B, because it briefly covers the main points of the passage, whereas summary A is too long;* **2.** *It should summarize important details from the passage, be brief, and should cover the entire passage.*

Bellringer

If YOU were there . . . Use the **Daily Bellringer Transparency** to help students answer the question.

🎲 Daily Bellringer Transparency, Section 1

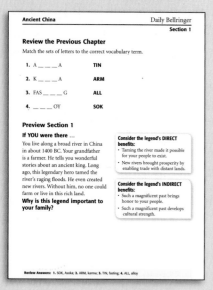

Ancient China   Daily Bellringer
     Section 1

Review the Previous Chapter

Match the sets of letters to the correct vocabulary term.

1. A _ _ _ A   TIN
2. K _ _ _ A   ARM
3. FAS _ _ _ G   ALL
4. _ _ _ OY   SOK

Preview Section 1

If YOU were there …

You live along a broad river in China in about 1400 BC. Your grandfather is a farmer. He tells you wonderful stories about an ancient king. Long ago, this legendary hero tamed the river's raging floods. He even created new rivers. Without him, no one could farm or live in this rich land.

Why is this legend important to your family?

Consider the legend's DIRECT benefits:
• Taming the river made it possible for your people to exist.
• New rivers brought prosperity by enabling trade with distant lands.

Consider the legend's INDIRECT benefits:
• Such a magnificent past brings honor to your people.
• Such a magnificent past develops cultural strength.

Review Answers: 1. SOK, Asoka; 2. ARM, karma; 3. TIN, fasting; 4. ALL, alloy

Academic Vocabulary

Review with students the high-use academic term in this section.

vary to be different (p. 183)

📄 **CRF:** Vocabulary Builder Activity, Section 1

🐻 Standards Focus

HSS 6.6.1

Means: Identify and discuss how Chinese civilization began in the Huang He Valley during the Shang dynasty.

Matters: Chinese civilization originated along the Huang He.

HSS 6.6.2

Means: Explain how China's geography affected its ability to rule the large country and kept China isolated from the rest of the world.

Matters: China is a large country with physical barriers that made it hard to travel and communicate within the country and to connect with other parts of the world.

Geography and Early China

What You Will Learn…

Main Ideas

1. China's physical geography made farming possible but travel and communication difficult.
2. Civilization began in China along the Huang He and Chang Jiang rivers.
3. China's first dynasties helped Chinese society develop and made many other achievements.

The Big Idea

Chinese civilization began with the Shang dynasty along the Huang He.

Key Terms

jade, *p. 185*
oracle, *p. 186*

HSS 6.6.1 Locate and describe the origins of Chinese civilization in the Huang-He Valley during the Shang Dynasty.

6.6.2 Explain the geographic features of China that made governance and the spread of ideas and goods difficult and served to isolate the country from the rest of the world.

If YOU were there…

You live along a broad river in China in about 1400 BC. Your grandfather is a farmer. He tells you wonderful stories about an ancient king. Long ago, this legendary hero tamed the river's raging floods. He even created new rivers. Without him, no one could farm or live in this rich land.

Why is this legend important to your family?

> **BUILDING BACKGROUND** Like other river civilizations, the Chinese people had to learn to control floods and irrigate their fields. China's geographical features divided the country into distinct regions.

China's Physical Geography

Geography played a major role in the development of Chinese civilization. China has many different geographical features. Some features separated groups of people within China. Others separated China from the rest of the world.

A Vast and Varied Land

China covers an area of nearly 4 million square miles, about the same size as the United States. One of the physical barriers that separates China from its neighbors is a harsh desert, the Gobi (GOH-bee). It spreads over much of China's north. East of the Gobi are low-lying plains. These plains, which cover most of eastern China, form one of the world's largest farming regions. The Pacific Ocean forms the country's eastern boundary.

More than 2,000 miles to the west, rugged mountains make up the western frontier. In the southwest the Plateau of Tibet has several mountain peaks that reach more than 26,000 feet. From the plateau, smaller mountain ranges spread eastward. The most important of these ranges is the Qinling Shandi (CHIN-LING shahn-DEE). It separates northern China from southern China.

Teach the Big Idea: Master the Standards   Standards Proficiency

Geography and Early China   🐻 **HSS** 6.6.1, 6.6.2; **HSS** Analysis Skills: CS 3, HI 1, HI 2

1. **Teach** Ask students the Main Idea questions to teach this section.

2. **Apply** Write the following labels for students to see: China's Physical Geography, Civilization Begins, and First Dynasties. Organize the students into three groups, one for each label. Then have each group work together to identify the key points, concepts, and terms that pertain to their topic. Have each group present these main ideas to the class in the form of a skit.
LS Visual/Spatial, Verbal/Linguistic

3. **Review** As each group presents its skit, have students take notes on the main ideas from the presentations. Students can use these notes as a review of the section.

4. **Practice/Homework** Have each student select a skit other than the one on which he or she worked. Have students write reviews of the skit, making sure to state the main ideas presented. **LS** Verbal/Linguistic

📓 Alternative Assessment Handbook, Rubrics 33: Skits and Reader's Theater; and 37: Writing Assignments

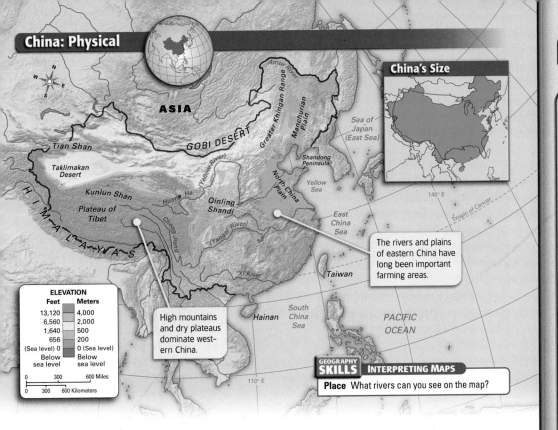

China: Physical

China's Size

ASIA

GOBI DESERT

Tian Shan

Taklimakan Desert

Kunlun Shan

Plateau of Tibet

HIMALAYAS

Huang He (Yellow River)

Qinling Shandi

Chang Jiang (Yangzi River)

Xi River

Amur River

Greater Khingan Range

Manchurian Plain

Shandong Peninsula

North China Plain

Yellow Sea

Sea of Japan (East Sea)

East China Sea

Taiwan

Hainan

South China Sea

PACIFIC OCEAN

Tropic of Cancer

140° E

110° E

ELEVATION

Feet	Meters
13,120	4,000
6,560	2,000
1,640	500
656	200
(Sea level) 0	0 (Sea level)
Below sea level	Below sea level

0   300   600 Miles
0   300   600 Kilometers

High mountains and dry plateaus dominate western China.

The rivers and plains of eastern China have long been important farming areas.

GEOGRAPHY SKILLS INTERPRETING MAPS

Place What rivers can you see on the map?

Weather and temperature patterns **vary** widely across China. In the northeast, the climate is cold and dry. Winter temperatures drop well below 0°F. Rivers there are frozen for more than half of the year. In the northwest, the deserts are very dry. But on the eastern plains of China, heavy rains fall. The tropical southeast is the wettest region. Monsoons can bring 250 inches of rain each year. That's enough water to cover a two-story house!

The Rivers of China

Two great rivers flow from west to east in China. The Huang He, or Yellow River, stretches for nearly 3,000 miles across northern China. The river often floods, and the floods leave behind layers of silt

on the surrounding countryside. Because these floods can be very destructive, the river is sometimes called "China's Sorrow." Over the years, millions of people have died in Huang He floods.

To the south, the Chang Jiang, or Yangzi River, cuts through central China. It flows from the mountains of Tibet to the Pacific Ocean. The Chang Jiang is the longest river in Asia.

In early China, the two rivers helped link people in the eastern part of the country with those in the west. At the same time, the mountains between the rivers limited contact.

READING CHECK **Summarizing** What geographical features limited travel in China?

ACADEMIC VOCABULARY

vary to be different

ANCIENT CHINA **183**

---

❷ Civilization Begins

Civilization began in China along the Huang He and Chang Jiang rivers.

Recall How did the floods along the rivers help the Chinese? *They deposited fertile silt, making the land ideal for growing crops.*

Explain What information have burial sites provided about the culture of early China? *information about works of art, differences in social order, and possibly belief in an afterlife*

Draw Conclusions Why do you think some of the homes of the ancient Chinese were partially underground? *possible answers—to keep them cool; to protect from wind*

🐻 **HSS** 6.6.1; **HSS Analysis Skills:** HI 1

Info to Know

The Mummies of Ürümqi Archaeologists found very interesting burial sites in the Tarim Basin in far western China in the 1970s. They uncovered dozens of mummies whose origins can be traced to about 2000 BC. Many of these incredibly well-preserved mummies are still dressed in the colorful clothing and woolen hats they wore in life. What is truly remarkable is that the mummies have European facial features.

Answers

Geography and Living *river valleys with fertile soil in northern China, to southern China's more tropical climate, to the rugged mountains and deserts of western China*

184

Geography and Living

China is a large country with many different types of environments.

How do these photos show China's diverse geography?

1 In northern China, the Huang He, or Yellow River, has long been the center of civilization. The silt in the river gives it a yellow look.

Civilization Begins

Like other ancient peoples that you have studied, people in China first settled along rivers. There they farmed, built villages, and formed a civilization.

The Development of Farming

Farming in China started along the Huang He and Chang Jiang. The rivers' floods deposited fertile silt. These silt deposits made the land ideal for growing crops.

As early as 7000 BC farmers grew rice in the middle Chang Jiang Valley. North, along the Huang He, the land was better for growing cereals such as millet and wheat.

Along with farming, the early Chinese people increased their diets in other ways. They fished and hunted with bows and arrows. They also domesticated animals such as pigs and sheep. With more sources of food, the population grew.

Early Settlements

Archaeologists have found remains of early Chinese villages. One village site near the Huang He had more than 40 houses. Many of the houses were partly underground and may have had straw-covered roofs. The site also included animal pens, storage pits, and a cemetery.

Some of the villages along the Huang He grew into large towns. Walls surrounded these towns to defend them against floods and hostile neighbors. In towns like these, the Chinese left many artifacts, such as arrowheads, fishhooks, tools, and pottery. Some village sites even contained pieces of cloth.

Separate cultures developed in southern and northeastern China. These included the Sanxingdui (sahn-shing-DWAY) and Hongshan peoples. Little is known about them, however. As the major cultures along the Huang He and Chang Jiang grew, they absorbed these other cultures.

Over time, Chinese culture became more advanced. After 3000 BC people used potter's wheels to make more types of pottery. These people also learned to dig water wells. As populations grew, villages spread out over larger areas in both northern and southeastern China.

184 CHAPTER 7

Critical Thinking: Drawing Conclusions

Standards Proficiency

Early Chinese Settlements 🐻 **HSS** 6.6.1; **HSS Analysis Skills:** HI 1, HI 2

1. Discuss with students the early settlements that developed in China. Ask students how the differing climates and geography of China might have led to differences between cultures of the early settlements.

2. Divide the class into small groups and assign each group one of the regions of China. Have groups discuss how the geography of that region might have affected the culture that developed there. Remind students to consider such things as settlement patterns, housing, crops, and clothing.

3. Then have each group create a scrapbook that highlights the culture of a settlement in their region. Have students use illustrations and captions to explain the influence that geography had on forming the culture in that area.

4. Have groups display their scrapbook pages for the class to see.
LS Verbal/Linguistic, Visual/Spatial

2 Southern China receives more rain than northern China, and farmers can grow several crops of rice a year.

3 Western China's high mountains and wide deserts make travel difficult and isolate China's population centers in the east.

Burial sites have provided information about the culture of this period. Like the Egyptians, the early Chinese filled their tombs with objects. Some tombs included containers of food, suggesting a belief in an afterlife. Some graves contained many more items than others. These differences show that a social order had developed. Often the graves of rich people held beautiful jewelry and other objects made from **jade**, a hard gemstone.

READING CHECK **Generalizing** What were some features of China's earliest settlements?

China's First Dynasties

Societies along the Huang He grew and became more complex. They eventually formed the first Chinese civilization.

The Xia Dynasty

According to ancient stories, a series of kings ruled early China. Around 2200 BC one of them, Yu the Great, is said to have founded the Xia (SHAH) dynasty.

Writers told of terrible floods during Yu's lifetime. According to these accounts, Yu dug channels to drain the water to the ocean. This labor took him more than 10 years and is said to have created the major waterways of north China.

Archaeologists have not yet found evidence that the tales about the Xia are true. However, the stories of Xia rulers were important to the ancient Chinese because they told of kings who helped people solve problems by working together. The stories also explained the geography that had such an impact on people's lives.

The Shang Dynasty

The first dynasty for which we have clear evidence is the Shang, which was firmly established by the 1500s BC. Strongest in the Huang He Valley, the Shang ruled a broad area of northern China. Shang rulers moved their capital several times, probably to avoid floods or attack by enemies.

The king was at the center of Shang political and religious life. Nobles served the king as advisors and helped him rule.

ANCIENT CHINA **185**

❸ China's First Dynasties

China's first dynasties helped Chinese society develop and made many other achievements.

Summarize What advances were made during the Shang dynasty? *the development of China's first writing system, use of oracle bones, war chariots, the use of bronze, and the development of a calendar*

Make Judgments How difficult would daily life have been for farmers during the Shang dynasty? *Answers will vary but should show knowledge of how farmers worked long and hard, had little money, and occupied a low social rank.*

Activity **China's Social Pyramid**
Have students draw a pyramid showing the social structure during the Shang dynasty.

- **CRF:** History and Geography Activity: Shang China
- **Map Transparency:** Shang Dynasty, c. 1500–1050 BC
- **HSS** 6.6.1; **HSS** Analysis Skills: CS 1, HI 1

Info to Know

Offerings to Ancestors During the Shang dynasty, people made offerings of food and drink to the spirits of their ancestors at special religious ceremonies. They prepared food for the dead as though they were preparing a large meal for the living. The food was offered to the ancestors in elaborately decorated cauldrons or dishes.

Answers

Interpreting Maps *Huang He*

186

Less important officials were also nobles. They performed specific governmental and religious duties.

The social order became more organized under the Shang. The royal family and the nobles were at the highest level. Nobles owned much land, and they passed on their wealth and power to their sons. Warrior leaders from the far regions of the empire also had high rank in society. Most people in the Shang ruling classes lived in large homes in cities.

Artisans settled outside the city walls. They lived in groups based on what they made for a living. Some artisans made weapons. Other artisans made pottery, tools, or clothing. Artisans were at a middle level of importance in Shang society.

Farmers ranked below artisans in the social order. Farmers worked long hours but had little money. Taxes claimed much

of what they earned. Slaves, who filled society's lowest rank, were an important source of labor during the Shang period.

The Shang made many advances, including China's first writing system. This system used more than 2,000 symbols to express words or ideas. Although the system has gone through changes over the years, the Chinese symbols used today are based on those of the Shang period.

Shang writing has been found on thousands of cattle bones and turtle shells. Priests had carved questions about the future on bones or shells, which were then heated, causing them to crack. The priests believed they could "read" these cracks to predict the future. The bones were called oracle bones because an **oracle** is a prediction.

In addition to writing, the Shang also made other achievements. Artisans made beautiful bronze containers for cooking and

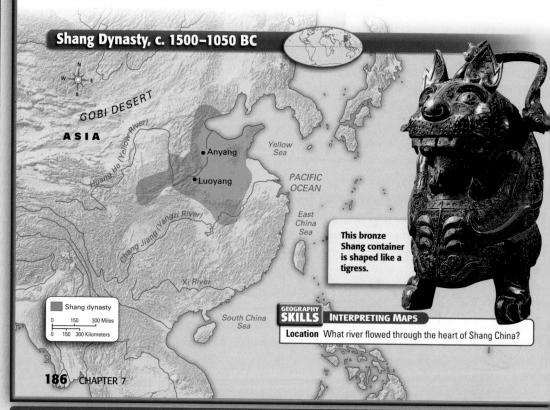

Shang Dynasty, c. 1500–1050 BC

This bronze Shang container is shaped like a tigress.

GEOGRAPHY SKILLS **INTERPRETING MAPS**

Location What river flowed through the heart of Shang China?

186 CHAPTER 7

Differentiating Instruction for Universal Access

Special Education Students   Reaching Standards

1. Help students identify the accomplishments of the Shang dynasty by drawing the chart for students to see. Omit the blue, italicized answers.

2. Divide the class into mixed-ability pairs. Have each student draw the chart on his or her own paper. Then have students work with their partners to complete the chart.
   LS Verbal/Linguistic, Visual/Spatial
   HSS 6.6.1; **HSS** Analysis Skills: HI 1, HI 2

Shang Dynasty	
government	*kings ruled, nobles advised*
religion	*king at center of religion, priests used oracle bones to make predictions*
society	*royal family/nobles at highest level, artisans at middle level, farmers, slaves at lower levels*
achievements	*writing system, use of bronze, calendar, war chariots, and bows*

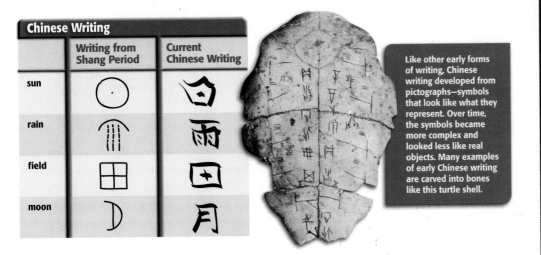

Chinese Writing

	Writing from Shang Period	Current Chinese Writing
sun	◯	日
rain	⋔	雨
field	⊞	田
moon	☽	月

Like other early forms of writing, Chinese writing developed from pictographs—symbols that look like what they represent. Over time, the symbols became more complex and looked less like real objects. Many examples of early Chinese writing are carved into bones like this turtle shell.

religious ceremonies. They also made axes, knives, and ornaments from jade. The military developed war chariots, powerful bows, and bronze body armor. Shang astrologers also made an important contribution. They developed a calendar based on the cycles of the moon.

READING CHECK **Contrasting** What is a major historical difference between the Xia and Shang dynasties?

SUMMARY AND PREVIEW China is a vast land with a diverse geography. Ancient Chinese civilization developed in the fertile valleys of the Huang He and Chang Jiang. Civilization there advanced under Shang rule. People developed a social order, a writing system, and made other achievements. In the next section you will learn about new ideas in China during the rule of the Zhou dynasty.

Section 1 Assessment

go.hrw.com
Online Quiz
KEYWORD: SQ6 HP7

Reviewing Ideas, Terms, and People **HSS** 6.6.1, 6.6.2

1. **a. Identify** Name China's two major rivers.
   b. Analyze How did China's geography affect its development?
2. **a. Identify** In which river valley did China's civilization begin?
   b. Explain What made China's river valleys ideal for farming?
   c. Elaborate What do Chinese artifacts reveal about China's early civilization?
3. **a. Describe** How do historians know about the Xia dynasty?
   b. Draw Conclusions What does the use of **oracle** bones tell us about the early Chinese?

Critical Thinking

4. **Comparing and Contrasting** Copy the diagram shown here. Use it to show similarities and differences in the geography of northern and southern China.

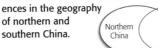

Northern China   Southern China

FOCUS ON SPEAKING

5. **Thinking about Events** Look back over the section to note the important events of China's earliest times. Think about what it is that makes one event more important than another. Write down your ideas in your notebook.

ANCIENT CHINA **187**

Section 1 Assessment Answers

1. **a.** Huang He and Chang Jiang
   b. It made it hard for trade and communication with other civilizations, but Chinese civilizations grew along the rivers, whose fertile soil made farming easier.
2. **a.** Huang He
   b. the fertile soil along the river banks
   c. They hunted, fished, and used pottery for food and water, made cloth, and established settlements.
3. **a.** only through ancient stories
   b. They believed in predicting the future and had a written language.

4. Northern China—climate is cold and dry; Southern China—the wettest region of China; Both—mountain ranges, rivers

5. Possible responses might include that one event had a greater effect than another or that we have evidence about certain events and not about others.

Direct Teach

Did you know . . .

Modern Chinese writing is very complex. While the English alphabet uses 26 letters to spell words, there are more than 1,000 basic characters in the Chinese language. Characters are combined to represent more complex ideas. By some estimates, there are close to 40,000 characters in the Chinese writing system!

Review & Assess

Close

Have students write a short paragraph to summarize the main ideas from this section.

Review

Online Quiz, Section 1

Assess

SE Section 1 Assessment
PASS: Section 1 Quiz
Alternative Assessment Handbook

Reteach/Classroom Intervention

California Standards Review Workbook
Interactive Reader and Study Guide, Section 1
Interactive Skills Tutor CD-ROM

Answers

Reading Check *Archaeologists have not been able to find any evidence of the Xia dynasty but have found artifacts and other evidence from the Shang dynasty.*

187

Bellringer

If YOU were there . . . Use the **Daily Bellringer Transparency** to help students answer the question.

 Daily Bellringer Transparency, Section 2

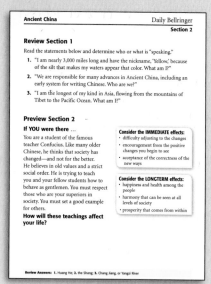

Ancient China   Daily Bellringer
                                       Section 2

Review Section 1

Read the statements below and determine who or what is "speaking."

1. "I am nearly 3,000 miles long and have the nickname, 'Yellow,' because of the silt that makes my waters appear that color. What am I?"

2. "We are responsible for many advances in Ancient China, including an early system for writing Chinese. Who are we?"

3. "I am the longest of my kind in Asia, flowing from the mountains of Tibet to the Pacific Ocean. What am I?"

Preview Section 2

If YOU were there ...

You are a student of the famous teacher Confucius. Like many older Chinese, he thinks that society has changed—and not for the better. He believes in old values and a strict social order. He is trying to teach you and your fellow students how to behave as gentlemen. You must respect those who are your superiors in society. You must set a good example for others.

How will these teachings affect your life?

Consider the IMMEDIATE effects:
• difficulty adjusting to the changes
• encouragement from the positive changes you begin to see
• acceptance of the correctness of the new ways

Consider the LONGTERM effects:
• happiness and health among the people
• harmony that can be seen at all levels of society
• prosperity that comes from within

Review Answers: 1. Huang He; 2. the Shang; 3. Chang Jiang, or Yangzi River

Academic Vocabulary

Review with students the high-use academic term in this section.

structure the way something is set up or organized (p. 190)

CRF: Vocabulary Builder Activity, Section 2

Standards Focus

HSS 6.6.3

Means: Know who Confucius was and why he was important and understand the teachings of Daoism and Confucianism.

Matters: Confucianism and Daoism play a large role in the culture of China today.

HSS 6.6.4

Means: Identify the political and social problems that influenced Confucius, and how his teachings aimed to solve those problems.

Matters: The teachings of Confucius stemmed from the political and social problems he saw in China.

SECTION 2

The Zhou Dynasty and New Ideas

What You Will Learn...

Main Ideas

1. The Zhou dynasty expanded China but then declined.
2. Confucius offered ideas to bring order to Chinese society.
3. Daoism and Legalism also gained followers.

The Big Idea

The Zhou dynasty brought political stability and new ways to deal with political and social problems in ancient China.

Key Terms and People

lords, *p. 189*
peasants, *p. 189*
Confucius, *p. 191*
ethics, *p. 191*
Confucianism, *p. 191*
Daoism, *p. 192*
Laozi, *p. 192*
Legalism, *p. 192*

HSS **6.6.3** Know about the life of Confucius and the fundamental teachings of Confucianism and Daoism.

6.6.4 Identify the political and cultural problems prevalent in the time of Confucius and how he sought to solve them.

If YOU were there...

You are a student of the famous teacher Confucius. Like many older Chinese, he thinks that society has changed—and not for the better. He believes in old values and a strict social order. He is trying to teach you and your fellow students how to behave as gentlemen. You must respect those who are your superiors in society. You must set a good example for others.

How will these teachings affect your life?

BUILDING BACKGROUND The people of the Shang dynasty made many advances, including beautiful metalwork, a writing system, and a calendar. The next dynasty, the Zhou, established other Chinese traditions. Some of these traditions included the importance of family and social order. Later thinkers looked back with admiration to the values of the Zhou period.

The Zhou Dynasty

In the 1100s BC the leaders of a people who came to be known as the Zhou (JOH) ruled over a kingdom in China. They joined with other nearby tribes and attacked and overthrew the Shang dynasty. The Zhou dynasty lasted longer than any other dynasty in Chinese history.

Time Line

The Zhou Dynasty

1100s BC
The Zhou dynasty begins.

551 BC
Confucius is born.

| 1200 BC | 800 BC | 400 BC |

771 BC
Invaders reach the Zhou capital.

481 BC
Civil war spreads across China during the Warring States period.

Teach the Big Idea: Master the Standards

Standards Proficiency

The Zhou Dynasty and New Ideas

HSS 6.6.3, 6.6.4; **HSS** Analysis Skills: CS 2, HI 1

1. **Teach** Ask students the Main Idea questions to teach this section.

2. **Apply** Divide the class into small groups. Then have each group create a brochure that summarizes the period of the Zhou dynasty. Ask students to include an interesting title page, a section on Zhou government, its rise and fall from power, society, and the three main philosophies. Remind students to create illustrations to enliven their brochures. **LS Verbal/Linguistic, Visual/Spatial**

3. **Review** As you review each main idea, have volunteers from different groups read aloud the information they used in their brochures.

4. **Practice/Homework** Have each student create a time line of the Zhou dynasty with at least 10 events. **LS Verbal/Linguistic**

Alternative Assessment Handbook, Rubrics 36: Time Lines; and 37: Writing Assignments

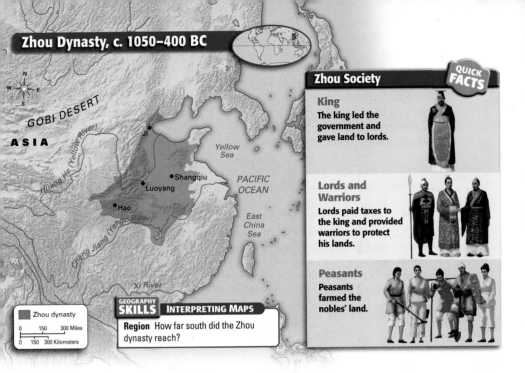

Zhou Dynasty, c. 1050–400 BC

GOBI DESERT

ASIA

Huang He (Yellow River)

Ji

Yellow Sea

•Shangqiu

Luoyang

•Hao

Chang Jiang (Yangzi River)

PACIFIC OCEAN

East China Sea

Xi River

Zhou dynasty

0   150   300 Miles
0   150   300 Kilometers

GEOGRAPHY SKILLS   INTERPRETING MAPS

Region How far south did the Zhou dynasty reach?

Zhou Society

QUICK FACTS

King
The king led the government and gave land to lords.

Lords and Warriors
Lords paid taxes to the king and provided warriors to protect his lands.

Peasants
Peasants farmed the nobles' land.

The Zhou Political System

The Zhou kings claimed to possess the mandate of heaven. According to this idea, heaven gave power to the king or leader, and no one ruled without heaven's permission. If a king was found to be bad, heaven would support another leader.

The Zhou came from an area to the west of the Shang kingdom. Early Zhou rulers used the mandate of heaven to justify their rebellion against the Shang. Later Zhou rulers expanded their territory to the northwest and the east. Zhou soldiers then moved south, eventually expanding their rule to the Chang Jiang.

The Zhou established a new political order. They granted land to others in return for loyalty, military support, and other services. The Zhou king was at the highest level. He granted plots of land to **lords**, or people of high rank. Lords paid

taxes and provided soldiers to the king as needed. **Peasants**, or farmers with small farms, were at the bottom of the order. Each peasant family received a small plot of land and had to farm additional land for the noble. The system was described in the *Book of Songs*:

"Everywhere under vast Heaven
There is no land that is not the king's
Within the borders of those lands
There are none who are not the king's servants."
–from the Zhou *Book of Songs*

The Zhou system brought order to China. Ruling through lords helped the Zhou control distant areas and helped ensure loyalty to the king. Over time, however, the political order broke down. Lords passed their power to their sons, who were less loyal to the king. Local rulers gained power. They began to reject the authority of the Zhou kings.

ANCIENT CHINA **189**

189

❶ The Zhou Dynasty

The Zhou dynasty expanded China but then declined.

Recall Why did the king's armies not rush to help him when invaders reached the capital in 771 BC? *They had been tricked by the king who was lighting the fires to entertain a friend, so they did not take the signal seriously.*

Describe What was the Warring States period? *a time marked by many civil wars and fights for territory among Chinese lords*

Evaluate Why do you think the decline of the Zhou weakened the Chinese family structure? *There was no strong government to stop power struggles within families.*

📄 **CRF:** Literature Activity: The Book of Songs

🐻 **HSS** 6.6.4; **HSS** Analysis Skills: CS 1, HI 1

Connect to Literature

A Guidebook for War *The Art of War* was probably written during the Warring States period. This well-known book offers philosophy, strategy, and logistics of war. It contains military theories such as, "Lure them in with the prospect of gain, take them by confusion," and "Though effective, appear to be ineffective." The book stresses the importance of accurate information, deception, surprise, and flexibility. *The Art of War* has influenced modern military leaders and even business strategists.

Answers

Reading Check *It weakened family structure and caused many civil wars among its citizens.*

Analyzing Visuals *speed, power, height, and maneuverability*

190

The Decline of Zhou Power

As the lords' loyalty to the Zhou king lessened, many refused to fight against invasions. In 771 BC invaders reached the capital. According to legend, the king had been lighting warning fires to entertain a friend. Each time the fires were lit, the king's armies would rush to the capital gates to protect him. When the real attack came, the men thought the fires were just another joke, and no one came. The Zhou lost the battle, but the dynasty survived.

After this defeat the lords began to fight each other. By 481 BC, China had entered an era called the Warring States period, a time of many civil wars. Armies grew. Fighting became brutal and cruel as soldiers fought for territory, not honor.

Internal Problems

ACADEMIC VOCABULARY
structure the way something is set up or organized

The decline of the Zhou took place along with important changes in the Chinese family **structure**. For many centuries the family had been the foundation of life in China. Large families of several generations formed powerful groups. When these families broke apart, they lost their power. Close relatives became rivals.

Bonds of loyalty even weakened within small families, especially among the upper classes. Sons plotted against each other over inheritances. A wealthy father sometimes tried to maintain peace by dividing his land among his sons. But this created new problems. Each son could build up his wealth and then challenge his brothers. Some sons even killed their own fathers. During the Warring States period, China lacked a strong government to stop the power struggles within the ruling-class families. Chinese society fell into a period of disorder.

READING CHECK Identifying Cause and Effect How did the Zhou's decline affect Chinese society?

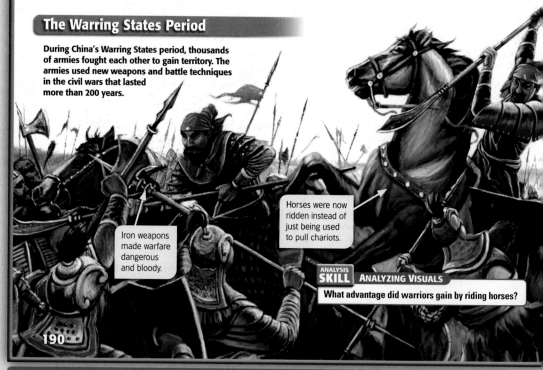

The Warring States Period

During China's Warring States period, thousands of armies fought each other to gain territory. The armies used new weapons and battle techniques in the civil wars that lasted more than 200 years.

Iron weapons made warfare dangerous and bloody.

Horses were now ridden instead of just being used to pull chariots.

ANALYSIS SKILL **ANALYZING VISUALS**
What advantage did warriors gain by riding horses?

190

Differentiating Instruction for Universal Access

Learners Having Difficulty   Reaching Standards

1. Review with students the period of the Warring States. Write the following main idea for students to see: *During the Warring States period, China entered a period of decline.* Help students understand what this statement means.

2. Ask students to write the main idea statement on their own paper. Then have each student re-read the information on the decline of the Zhou dynasty. Ask students to look for details that support the main idea above.

3. Have each student keep a list of the details they found to support the main idea statement. When students have finished, use their suggestions to create a master list for the class to see. **LS** **Verbal/Linguistic**

🐻 **HSS** 6.6.4; **HSS** Analysis Skills: HI 1, HI 2

📄 Alternative Assessment Handbook, Rubric 37: Writing Assignments

Confucius and Society

During the late Zhou period, thinkers came up with ideas about how to restore order to China. One such person, **Confucius**, became the most influential teacher in Chinese history. Confucius is a Western form of the Chinese title of "Master Kong" or "Kongfuzi."

Confucius felt that China was overrun with rude and dishonest people. Upset by the disorder and people's lack of decency, Confucius said that the Chinese needed to return to **ethics**, or moral values. The ideas of Confucius are known as **Confucianism**.

Confucius wanted China to return to ideas and practices from a time when people knew their proper roles in society. These are basic guidelines that Confucius thought would restore family order and social harmony:

- Fathers should display high moral values to inspire their families.
- Children should respect and obey their parents.
- All family members should be loyal to each other.

Confucius's ideas about government were similar to his ideas about family:

- Moral leadership, not laws, brought order to China.
- A king should lead by example, inspiring good behavior in all of his subjects.
- The lower classes would learn by following the example of their superiors.

Confucius expressed this idea when he told kings:

> "Lead the people by means of government policies and regulate them through punishments, and they will be evasive and have no sense of shame. Lead them by means of virtue . . . and they will have a sense of shame and moreover have standards."
>
> –Confucius, from *The Analects*

Confucius
551–479 BC

Confucius, whose Chinese title is Kongfuzi, grew up in extreme poverty. Confucius was a dedicated student into his teenage years. Little is known about how he received his formal education, but he mastered many subjects, including music, mathematics, poetry, and history. He served in minor government positions, then he became a teacher. He never knew his teachings would transform Chinese life and thought.

Drawing Inferences How do you think Confucius's government jobs helped shape his teachings?

As Confucius traveled to many different regions, he earned the reputation of a respected teacher. His ideas were passed down through his students and later compiled into a book called *The Analects*.

Because Confucianism focuses on morality, family, society, and government, people often think of it as a philosophy or way of thinking. But it is much more. Confucianism is a unique teaching that is both philosophical and religious. It has been a guiding force in human behavior and religious understanding in China.

Confucius believed that when people behaved well and acted morally, they were simply carrying out what heaven expected of them. Over the centuries Confucius's ideas about virtue, kindness, and learning became the dominant beliefs in China.

READING CHECK Identifying Points of View
What did Confucius believe about good behavior?

ANCIENT CHINA **191**

191

❸ Daoism and Legalism

Daoism and Legalism also gained followers.

Define What is Daoism? *a philosophy that stresses living in harmony with the Dao, the guiding force of reality*

Identify Who was Laozi? *famous teacher credited with writing the basic text of Daoism*

Summarize What did Legalists believe society needed? *strict laws to keep people in line, punishments that fit the crimes, and holding citizens responsible for the crimes of others*

📋 **CRF:** Primary Source Activity: The Teachings of Confucius and Laozi

🗄 Quick Facts Transparency: Main Ideas of Confucianism

🎞 **HSS** 6.6.3; **HSS** Analysis Skills: HI 1, HI 2

Connect to Art

Yin and Yang The Daoist idea of the balance of opposites often appears in Asian art. This principle is called yin-yang, or literally, the dark side and sunny side of a hill. The symbol of yin-yang is a circle with one dark side and one light side. Within each side is a small circle of the opposite color, which signifies that neither can exist without the other. Traditionally the dark side, yin, represents the feminine, moon, cold, and dark. The light side, or yang, represents the masculine, sun, heat, and light. Modern artists and designers have also embraced the yin-yang symbol.

Answers

Analyzing Primary Sources *honesty, fairness, education*

Primary Source

HISTORIC DOCUMENT
The Analects

The followers of Confucius placed their teacher's sayings together in a work called in Chinese the Lun Yü *and in English* The Analects. *The word* analects *means "writings that have been collected."*

❝Yu, shall I teach you what knowledge is? When you know a thing, say that you know it; when you do not know a thing, admit that you do not know it. That is knowledge.❞

❝Is there any one word that can serve as a principle for . . . life? Perhaps the word is reciprocity [fairness]: Do not do to others what you would not want others to do to you.❞

❝I do not enlighten anyone who is not eager to learn, nor encourage anyone who is not anxious to put his ideas into words.❞

–Confucius, from The Analects

ANALYSIS SKILL **ANALYZING PRIMARY SOURCES**
What are some of the qualities that Confucius valued?

Daoism and Legalism

Other beliefs besides Confucianism influenced China during the Zhou period. Two in particular attracted many followers.

Daoism

Daoism (DOW-ih-zum) takes its name from *Dao,* meaning "the way." **Daoism** stressed living in harmony with the Dao, the guiding force of all reality. In Daoist teachings, the Dao gave birth to the universe and all things in it. Daoism developed in part as a reaction to Confucianism. Daoists didn't agree with the idea that active, involved leaders brought social harmony. Instead, they wanted the government to stay out of people's lives.

Daoists believed that people should avoid interfering with nature or each other. They should be like water and simply let things flow in a natural way. For Daoists,

---

Main Ideas of Confucianism **QUICK FACTS**

- People should be respectful and loyal to their family members.

- Leaders should be kind and lead by example.

- Learning is a process that never ends.

- Heaven expects people to behave well and act morally.

the ideal ruler was a wise man who was in harmony with the Dao. He would govern so effortlessly that his people would not even know they were being governed.

Daoists taught that the universe is a balance of opposites: female and male, light and dark, low and high. In each case, opposing forces should be in harmony.

While Confucianism focused its followers' attention on the human world, Daoists paid more attention to the natural world. Daoists regarded humans as just a part of nature, not better than any other thing. In time the Dao, as represented by nature, became so important to the Daoists that they worshipped it.

Laozi (LOWD-zuh) was the most famous Daoist teacher. He taught that people should not try to gain wealth, nor should they seek power. Laozi is credited with writing the basic text of Daoism, *The Way and Its Power.* Later writers created many legends about Laozi's achievements.

Legalism

Legalism, the belief that people were bad by nature and needed to be controlled, contrasted with both Confucianism and Daoism. Unlike the other two beliefs, Legalism was a political philosophy without religious concerns. Instead, it dealt only with government and social

---

Collaborative Learning   **Standards Proficiency**

Understanding Chinese Philosophies   🐻 **HSS** 6.6.3 **HSS** Analysis Skills HI 1

1. Review with the class the beliefs and teachings of Confucianism, Daoism, and Legalism.

2. Divide the class into small groups and assign each group one of the three belief systems. Have each group work together to create a guide for understanding their assigned belief system. Guides may be in the form of a brochure, a short paper, or a chart.

3. Each group's guide should explain the basic beliefs of their assigned philosophy, include information about the founder, if

available, and present the main guidelines. Students should explain the ideas behind the philosophy in words that are easy to understand. Encourage students to make their guides visually appealing also.

4. Have each group present or display their guide for the class to see.

LS **Verbal/Linguistic, Visual/Spatial**

📋 Alternative Assessment Handbook, Rubric 14: Group Activity

control. Followers of Legalism disagreed with the moral preaching of Confucius. Legalists also rejected Daoism because it didn't stress respect for authority.

Legalists felt that society needed strict laws to keep people in line and that punishments should fit crimes. For example, they believed that citizens should be held responsible for each other's conduct. A guilty person's relatives and neighbors should also be punished. This way, everyone would obey the laws.

Unity and efficiency were also important to Legalists. They wanted appointed officials, not nobles, to run China. Legalists wanted the empire to continue to expand. Therefore, they urged the state to always be prepared for war.

Confucianism, Daoism, and Legalism competed for followers. All three beliefs became popular, but the Legalists were the first to put their ideas into practice throughout China.

READING CHECK **Contrasting** How did Daoism and Legalism differ in their theories about government?

BIOGRAPHY

Laozi
c. 500s or 400s BC

Scholars have found little reliable information about Laozi's life. Some believe that his book on Daoism was actually the work of several different authors. Most ancient sources of information about Laozi are myths. For example, one legend states that when Laozi was born, he was already an old man. In Chinese *Laozi* can mean "Old Baby." Over the years, many Daoists have worshipped Laozi as a supernatural being.

Drawing Inferences What do you think it meant to say Laozi was born "old"?

SUMMARY AND PREVIEW When the Zhou dynasty crumbled, political and social chaos erupted. In response, the new teachings of Confucianism, Daoism, and Legalism emerged. In the next section you will learn how the Qin dynasty applied the teachings of Legalism.

Section 2 Assessment

go.hrw.com
Online Quiz
KEYWORD SQ6 HP7

Reviewing Ideas, Terms, and People HSS 6.6.3, 6.6.4

1. **a. Identify** What is the mandate of heaven?
   b. Explain Describe the political order used by the Zhou kings to rule distant lands.
   c. Elaborate What happened when nobles began to reject the Zhou king's authority?
2. **a. Identify** Who was **Confucius**?
   b. Analyze Why did many of the teachings of Confucius focus on the family?
3. **a. Identify** Who was the most famous Daoist teacher?
   b. Summarize What were the main ideas of **Daoism**?
   c. Elaborate What might be some disadvantages of **Legalism**?

Critical Thinking

4. **Finding Main Ideas** Draw a chart like the one here. Use it to list two main ideas each about Confucianism, Daoism, and Legalism.

Confucianism	
Daoism	
Legalism	

FOCUS ON SPEAKING

5. **Exploring the Importance of Historical Figures** Many important people in history are rulers or conquerors. People who think and teach, however, have also played major roles in history. How did thinkers and teachers shape China's history? Write some ideas in your notebook.

ANCIENT CHINA **193**

Section 2 Assessment Answers

1. **a.** the idea that heaven gave kings the power to rule
   b. granted land to lords for loyalty, military support, and other services
   c. decreased loyalty, civil wars
2. **a.** a teacher and philosopher who wanted to restore family order and social harmony
   b. He believed that moral values needed to be taught by families.
3. **a.** Laozi

b. Let things flow in a natural way; the universe is a balance of opposites; government should stay out of people's lives.
   c. possible answers—too much government power; innocent people punished

4. See information under *Confucius and Society* and *Daoism and Legalism* for possible answers.

5. Students should note the lasting influence of Confucius and other thinkers and teachers.

Bellringer

If YOU were there . . . Use the **Daily Bellringer Transparency** to help students answer the question.

Daily Bellringer Transparency, Section 3

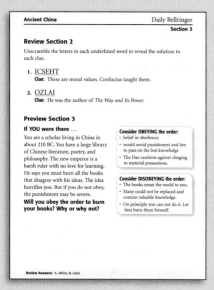

Building Vocabulary

Preteach or review the following terms:

mandate of heaven the idea that kings rule with the permission of heaven (p. 198)

standardized having made things similar (p. 196)

unified joined or combined (p. 198)

CRF: Vocabulary Builder Activity, Section 3

Standards Focus

HSS 6.6.5

Means: List Shi Huangdi's accomplishments that enabled him to unify China under the Qin dynasty.

Matters: Shi Huangdi's rule unified China and established many policies that were used for many years.

The Qin Dynasty

What You Will Learn...

Main Ideas

1. The first Qin emperor created a strong but strict government.
2. A unified China was created through Qin policies and achievements.

The Big Idea

The Qin dynasty unified China with a strong government and a system of standardization.

Key Terms and People

Shi Huangdi, *p. 194*
Great Wall, *p. 197*

HSS **6.6.5** List the policies and achievements of the emperor Shi Huangdi in unifying northern China under the Qin Dynasty.

If YOU were there...

You are a scholar living in China in about 210 BC. You have a large library of Chinese literature, poetry, and philosophy. The new emperor is a harsh ruler with no love for learning. He says you must burn all the books that disagree with his ideas. The idea horrifies you. But if you do not obey, the punishment may be severe.

Will you obey the order to burn your books? Why or why not?

BUILDING BACKGROUND Different dynasties held very different ideas about how to rule. As the Zhou period declined, putting new ideas into effect brought great changes.

The Qin Emperor's Strong Government

The Warring States period marked a time in China when several states battled each other for power. One state, the Qin (CHIN), built a strong army that defeated the armies of the rivaling states. Eventually, the Qin dynasty united the country under one government.

Shi Huangdi Takes the Throne

In 221 BC, the Qin king Ying Zheng succeeded in unifying China. He gave himself the title **Shi Huangdi** (SHEE hwahng-dee), which means "first emperor." Shi Huangdi followed Legalist political beliefs. He created a strong government with strict laws and harsh punishments.

Time Line

The Qin Dynasty

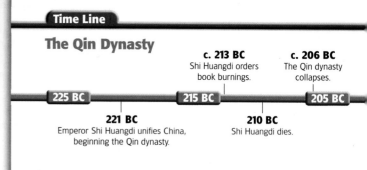

c. 213 BC
Shi Huangdi orders book burnings.

c. 206 BC
The Qin dynasty collapses.

225 BC — 215 BC — 205 BC

221 BC
Emperor Shi Huangdi unifies China, beginning the Qin dynasty.

210 BC
Shi Huangdi dies.

Teach the Big Idea: Master the Standards

Standards Proficiency

The Qin Dynasty **HSS** 6.6.5; **HSS** Analysis Skills: CS 1, CS 2, HI 1

1. **Teach** Ask students the Main Idea questions to teach this section.

2. **Apply** Have students copy the Qin dynasty time line on their own papers. Have students add two or three sentences with supporting details or additional information about the events listed. Have students add other additional events or accomplishments that occurred during the dynasty to their time lines. **LS Verbal/Linguistic, Visual/Spatial**

3. **Review** Have students exchange time lines and study the events and dates as a review.

4. **Practice/Homework** Have students illustrate their time lines by adding images that represent the events on the time line. **LS Visual/Spatial**

Alternative Assessment Handbook, Rubric 36: Time Lines

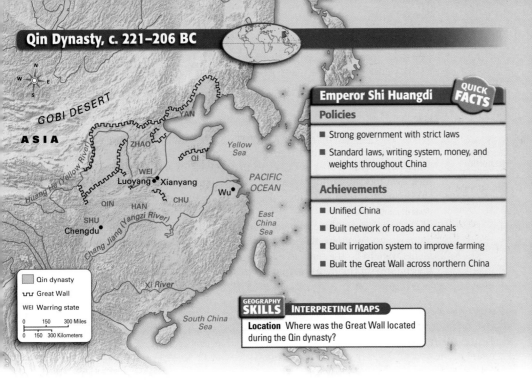

Qin Dynasty, c. 221–206 BC

GOBI DESERT

ASIA

YAN
ZHAO
WEI
QI
Luoyang • Xianyang
Yellow Sea
QIN HAN
Wu •
CHU
SHU
Chengdu •
Chang Jiang (Yangzi River)
Xi River

PACIFIC OCEAN

East China Sea

South China Sea

Legend
Qin dynasty
Great Wall
WEI Warring state

0   150   300 Miles
0   150   300 Kilometers

Emperor Shi Huangdi — QUICK FACTS

Policies
- Strong government with strict laws
- Standard laws, writing system, money, and weights throughout China

Achievements
- Unified China
- Built network of roads and canals
- Built irrigation system to improve farming
- Built the Great Wall across northern China

GEOGRAPHY SKILLS INTERPRETING MAPS
Location Where was the Great Wall located during the Qin dynasty?

Shi Huangdi demanded that everyone follow his policies. He ordered the burning of all writings that did not agree with Legalism. The only other books that were saved dealt with farming, medicine, and predicting the future. Many scholars opposed the book burnings. The emperor responded to the opposition by burying 460 scholars alive.

Shi Huangdi also used his armies to expand the empire. First, they occupied the lands around both of China's major rivers. Then his soldiers turned north and advanced almost to the Gobi Desert. To the south, they invaded more lands and advanced as far as the Xi River.

Shi Huangdi ensured that there would not be any future revolts in his new territories. When his soldiers conquered a city, he had them destroy its walls and take all the weapons.

China under the Qin

Shi Huangdi changed China's old political system. He claimed all the power and did not share it with the lords. He even took land away from them and forced thousands of nobles to move with their families to the capital so he could keep an eye on them. He also forced thousands of commoners to work on government building projects. Workers faced years of hardship, danger, and often, death.

To control China, Shi Huangdi divided it into districts, each with its own governor. Districts were subdivided into counties that were governed by appointed officials. This organization helped the emperor enforce his tax system. It also helped the Qin enforce a strict chain of command.

READING CHECK Summarizing How did Shi Huangdi strengthen the government?

ANCIENT CHINA **195**

---

❷ A Unified China

A unified China was created through Qin policies and achievements.

Recall What steps did Shi Huangdi take to unify China? *He standardized laws, writing, and weights and measures, created a money system, and made trade easier.*

Draw Conclusions Why did Shi Huangdi standardize many elements of Chinese life? *possible answers—to ease trade, communication, and travel and to make the Chinese people feel more like one nation*

Evaluate Which of Shi Huangdi's achievements or policies do you think was most important? Why? *possible answers—building canals and roads, because they linked distant parts of China together; standardizing writing, because it gave the Chinese a common identity*

🐾 HSS 6.6.5; HSS Analysis Skills: HI 1

Info to Know

Shi Huangdi's Tomb In March 1974 farmers near the Chinese city of Xian were digging for a water well. What they uncovered was one of the most famous archaeological discoveries of the twentieth century. Measuring some 20 square miles, the tomb complex of Qin ruler Shi Huangdi is best known for the thousands of life-like terra-cotta soldiers that guard the tomb along with horses and chariots. While the inside of Shi Huangdi's actual tomb has yet to be excavated, historians believe it took some 700,000 workers over 36 years to complete.

A Unified China

Qin rule brought other major changes to China. Under Shi Huangdi, new policies and achievements united the Chinese people.

Qin Policies

FOCUS ON READING
How might you summarize the new Qin policies?

As you read earlier, mountains and rivers divided China into distinct regions. Customs varied, and people in each area had their own money, writing styles, and laws. Shi Huangdi wanted all Chinese people to do things the same way.

Early in his reign, the emperor set up a uniform system of law. Rules and punishments were to be the same in all parts of the empire. Shi Huangdi also standardized the written language. People everywhere were required to write using the same set of symbols. People from different regions could now communicate with each other in writing. This gave them a sense of shared culture and a common identity.

Next, the emperor set up a new money system. Standardized gold and copper coins became the currency used in all of China. Weights and measures were also standardized. Even the axle width of carts had to be the same. With all these changes and the unified writing system, trade between different regions became much easier. The Qin government strictly enforced these new standards. Any citizen who disobeyed the laws would face severe punishment.

Guardians of Shi Huangdi's Tomb

In 1974 archaeologists found the tomb of Emperor Shi Huangdi near Xi'an and made an amazing discovery. Buried close to the emperor was an army of more than 6,000 life-size terra-cotta, or clay, soldiers. They were designed to be with Shi Huangdi in the afterlife. In other nearby chambers of the tomb there were another 1,400 clay figures of cavalry and chariots.

MONGOLIA
Huang He (Yellow River)
Xi'an • Shi Huangdi's Tomb
CHINA
Chang Jiang (Yangzi River)

Collaborative Learning

Reaching Standards

Terra-cotta Army Exhibit 🐾 HSS 6.6.5; HSS Analysis Skills: HR 1, HI 1 — Research Required

1. Discuss with students how Shi Huangdi's tomb was surrounded by an army of weapon-wielding terra-cotta soldiers, each with its own facial features and expression.

2. Organize the class into small groups. Have each group conduct research on the tomb using the library, Internet, or other resources. Ask each group to create a museum exhibit that provides information about the origins and history of the terra-cotta army and of Shi Huangdi's tomb. Encourage students to use images, illustrations, and written information to make an interesting exhibit. They might even want to make small figurines to represent the terra-cotta army.

3. Have each group display their museum exhibit on Shi Huangdi's tomb for the class to see. LS **Visual/Spatial, Verbal/Linguistic**

📝 Alternative Assessment Handbook, Rubrics 14: Group Activity; and 29: Presentations

Qin Achievements

New, massive building projects also helped to unify the country. Under Shi Huangdi's rule, the Chinese built a network of roads that connected the capital to every part of the empire. These roads made travel easier for everyone. Each of these new roads was the same width, 50 paces wide. This design helped the army move quickly and easily to put down revolts in distant areas.

China's water system was also improved. Workers built canals to connect the country's rivers. Like the new roads, the canals improved transportation throughout the country. Using the new canals and rivers together made it easier and faster to ship goods from north to south. In addition, the Qin built an irrigation system to make more land good for farming. Parts of that system are still in use today.

Shi Huangdi also wanted to protect the country from invasion. Nomads from the north were fierce warriors, and they were a real threat to China. Hoping to stop them from invading, the emperor built the **Great Wall**, a barrier that linked earlier walls across China's northern frontier. The first section of the wall had been built in the 600s BC to keep invading groups out of China. The Qin connected earlier pieces of the wall to form a long, unbroken structure. Building the wall required years of labor from hundreds of thousands of workers. Many of them died building the wall.

THE IMPACT TODAY

The Great Wall is a major tourist attraction today.

Each terra-cotta soldier was different, with its own facial features, hairstyle, and unique expression. Here, a computer model shows what a soldier might have looked like when it was created.

Linking to Today

Chinese Currency One of Shi Huangdi's achievements was standardizing China's money. Today, the official currency in China is called the *renminbi*, which means "people's currency." The base unit of the currency is the *yuan*. Images used on different denominations of paper bills include Mao Zedong, the Chairman of the Chinese Communist Party from 1931 until 1976, and pictures of people who represent the various ethnic groups in China.

Did you know . . .

The standardized form of Chinese writing developed during the Qin dynasty is known as *xiaozhuan*, and was created by a government official named Li Si in the 200s BC. The script is no longer in use today, but can be seen occasionally in formal inscriptions.

MISCONCEPTION ALERT

The Great Wall from Space?

Students may have heard that the Great Wall of China is the only manmade object that can be seen from space or even from the moon. It's not true. Despite the fact that the Great Wall of China is thousands of miles long, it is only a few yards wide. Astronauts report that the Great Wall can indeed be seen from low orbit but so can many highways and airport runways.

Differentiating Instruction for Universal Access

Special Education Students   Reaching Standards

1. Review with students the many achievements of the Qin dynasty. Be sure that students understand the importance of each achievement.

2. Ask each student to select one contribution made by the Qin. Have each student create a colorful poster that depicts the achievement.

3. Have each student write a few sentences that explain in his or her own words why the chosen achievement was important.

4. Ask volunteers to share their posters with the class. **LS** Visual/Spatial, Verbal/Linguistic

HSS 6.6.5; **HSS** Analysis Skills: HI 1

Alternative Assessment Handbook, Rubric 28: Posters

Universal Access Resources
See the Chapter Planner for additional resources for differentiating instruction for universal access.

Main Idea

❷ A Unified China

A unified China was created through Qin policies and achievements.

Summarize What happened to China after the death of Shi Huangdi? *The government began to fall apart and the country fell into a civil war.*

Make Judgments Do you think China was better off because of Shi Huangdi? *Answers will vary but should address both his accomplishments and his harsh rule.*

HSS 6.6.5; **HSS** Analysis Skills: HI 1

● Review & Assess ●

Close

Have students create a graphic organizer that includes the policies, achievements, and fall of the Qin dynasty under Shi Huangdi.

Review

Online Quiz, Section 3

Assess

SE Section 3 Assessment

PASS: Section 3 Quiz

Alternative Assessment Handbook

Reteach/Classroom Intervention

California Standards Review Workbook

Interactive Reader and Study Guide, Section 3

Interactive Skills Tutor CD-ROM

The Great Wall has been added to and rebuilt many times since Shi Huangdi ruled China.

The Fall of the Qin

Shi Huangdi's policies unified China. However, his policies also stirred resentment. Many peasants, scholars, and nobles hated his harsh ways.

Still, Shi Huangdi was powerful enough to hold the country together. When he died in 210 BC China was unified, but that didn't last. Within a few years, the government began to fall apart.

Rebel forces formed across the country. Each claimed to have received the mandate of heaven to replace the emperor. One of these groups attacked the Qin capital, and the new emperor surrendered. The palace was burned to the ground. Qin authority had disappeared. With no central government, the country fell into civil war.

READING CHECK **Recall** What massive building projects did Shi Huangdi order to unify China?

SUMMARY AND PREVIEW Qin emperor Shi Huangdi's policies and achievements unified China, but his harsh rule led to resentment. After his death, the dynasty fell apart. In the next section you will learn about the Han dynasty that came to power after the end of the Qin.

Section 3 Assessment

go.hrw.com
Online Quiz
KEYWORD: SQ6 HP7

Reviewing Ideas, Terms, and People **HSS** 6.6.5

1. **a. Identify** What does the title **Shi Huangdi** mean?
   b. Explain After unifying China, why did Shi Huangdi divide the country into military districts?
   c. Rate Which of the following acts do you think best showed how powerful Shi Huangdi was—burning books, forcing nobles to move, or forcing commoners to work on government projects? Explain your answer.
2. **a. Recall** Why was the **Great Wall** built?
   b. Summarize What actions did Shi Huangdi take to unify China and standardize things within the empire?
   c. Evaluate In your opinion, was Shi Huangdi a good ruler? Explain your answer.

Critical Thinking

3. **Analyzing** Draw a chart like the one here. Use it to show how each improvement helped the Qin dynasty.

Improvement	Advantage
1. Road system	
2. Canals	
3. Great Wall	

FOCUS ON SPEAKING

4. **Evaluating Contributions to History** When evaluating a person's contribution to history, it is important to consider both the person's good impact and bad impact. In what ways was Shi Huangdi great? What negative impact did he have on China? Write down your ideas.

198 CHAPTER 7

Section 3 Assessment Answers

1. **a.** "first emperor"
   b. to make governing each area easier and more efficient and to collect taxes
   c. Answers will vary but should be supported by facts.

2. **a.** to stop invaders from the north
   b. He created a uniform system of laws; standardized written language, money, and weights and measures; built uniform roads.
   c. Answers will vary, but should be supported by facts from the text.

3. Road system—connected the capital to all parts of the empire, made travel easier; Canals—taking goods from north to south made easier and faster; Great Wall—kept out invaders

4. Possible responses might include that he unified all of China for the first time, but his policies caused resentment among many Chinese.

Answers

Reading Check *network of roads, improved water system including canals and irrigation, the Great Wall*

198

Emperor Shi Huangdi

If you were a powerful ruler, how would you protect yourself?

When did he live? c. 259–210 BC

Where did he live? Shi Huangdi built a new capital city at Xianyang, now called Xi'an (SHEE-AHN), in eastern China.

What did he do? Shi Huangdi didn't trust people. Several attempts were made on his life, and the emperor lived in fear of more attacks. He was constantly seeking new ways to protect himself and extend his life. By the time Shi Huangdi died, he didn't even trust his own advisors. Even in death, he surrounded himself with protectors: the famous terra-cotta army.

Why is he important? Shi Huangdi was one of the most powerful rulers in Chinese history. The first ruler to unify all of China, he is also remembered for his building programs. He built roads and canals throughout China and expanded what would become the Great Wall.

Drawing Conclusions Why do you think Shi Huangdi feared for his life?

KEY EVENTS

- **246 BC** Shi Huangdi becomes emperor. Because he is still young, a high official rules in his name.
- **238 BC** He exiles the official, whom he suspects of plotting against him, and rules alone.
- **227 BC** An assassination attempt adds fuel to the emperor's paranoia.
- **221 BC** Shi Huangdi unites all of China under his rule.

This painting shows Shi Huangdi's servants burning books and attacking scholars.

199

Bellringer

If YOU were there . . . Use the **Daily Bellringer Transparency** to help students answer the question.

 Daily Bellringer Transparency, Section 4

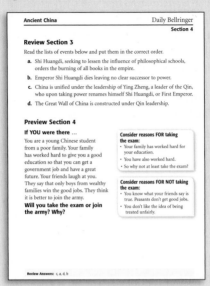

Ancient China | Daily Bellringer
Section 4

Review Section 3
Read the lists of events below and put them in the correct order.

a. Shi Huangdi, seeking to lessen the influence of philosophical schools, orders the burning of all books in the empire.

b. Emperor Shi Huangdi dies leaving no clear successor to power.

c. China is unified under the leadership of Ying Zheng, a leader of the Qin, who upon taking power renames himself Shi Huangdi, or First Emperor.

d. The Great Wall of China is constructed under Qin leadership.

Preview Section 4

If YOU were there …
You are a young Chinese student from a poor family. Your family has worked hard to give you a good education so that you can get a government job and have a great future. Your friends laugh at you. They say that only boys from wealthy families win the good jobs. They think it is better to join the army.
Will you take the exam or join the army? Why?

Consider reasons FOR taking the exam:
• Your family has worked hard for your education.
• You have also worked hard.
• So why not at least take the exam?

Consider reasons FOR NOT taking the exam:
• You know what your friends say is true. Peasants don't get good jobs.
• You don't like the idea of being treated unfairly.

Review Answers: c, a, d, b

Academic Vocabulary

Review with students the high-use academic term in this section.

innovation a new idea, method, or device (p. 204)

Building Vocabulary

Preteach or review the following terms:

artisans a skilled craftsperson (p. 202)

influential having power to affect individuals or events (p. 201)

CRF: Vocabulary Builder Activity, Section 4

Standards Focus

HSS 6.6.6

Means: Discuss how the Han dynasty contributed to the growth of the Chinese empire and its complex government system.

Matters: The Han dynasty created a stronger central government that helped strengthen China.

The Han Dynasty

If **YOU** were there...

You are a young Chinese student from a poor family. Your family has worked hard to give you a good education so that you can get a government job and have a great future. Your friends laugh at you. They say that only boys from wealthy families win the good jobs. They think it is better to join the army.

Will you take the exam or join the army? Why?

> **BUILDING BACKGROUND** Though it was harsh, the rule of the first Qin emperor helped to unify northern China. With the building of the Great Wall, he strengthened defenses on the northern frontier. But his successor could not hold on to power. The Qin gave way to a remarkable new dynasty that would last for 400 years.

Han Dynasty Government

When the Qin dynasty collapsed in 207 BC, several different groups battled for power. After several years of fighting, an army led by Liu Bang (lee-oo bang) won control. Liu Bang became the first emperor of the Han dynasty. This Chinese dynasty lasted for more than 400 years.

The Rise of a New Dynasty

Liu Bang, a peasant, was able to become emperor in large part because of the Chinese belief in the mandate of heaven. He was the first common person to become emperor. He earned people's

What You Will Learn...

Main Ideas

1. Han dynasty government was based on the ideas of Confucius.
2. Family life was supported and strengthened in Han China.
3. The Han made many achievements in art, literature, and learning.

The Big Idea

The Han dynasty created a new form of government that valued family, art, and learning.

Key Terms

sundial, p. 204
seismograph, p. 204
acupuncture, p. 205

 HSS 6.6.6 Detail the political contributions of the Han Dynasty to the development of the imperial bureaucratic state and the expansion of the empire.

Time Line

The Han Dynasty

206 BC
The Han dynasty begins.

200 BC

140 BC
Wudi becomes emperor and tries to strengthen China's government.

BC 1 AD

AD 25
The Han move their capital east to Luoyang.

AD 200

AD 220
The Han dynasty falls.

Teach the Big Idea: Master the Standards

Standards Proficiency

The Han Dynasty HSS 6.6.6; HSS Analysis Skills: HI 1

1. **Teach** Ask students the Main Idea questions to teach this section.

2. **Apply** Have students create an outline of the section. They should list all major heads and subheads that appear in this section. As students read, have them identify two or three supporting details within every head or subhead. Remind students to also include any key terms or people from the section.
LS Verbal/Linguistic

3. **Review** As a review of the section, ask volunteers to share individual parts of their

outlines and record the information for all to see. Have students add missing information and correct inaccurate information.

4. **Practice/Homework** Have each student use his or her outline to write five multiple-choice questions that cover important information from the section.
LS Verbal/Linguistic

Alternative Assessment Handbook, Rubric 1: Acquiring Information

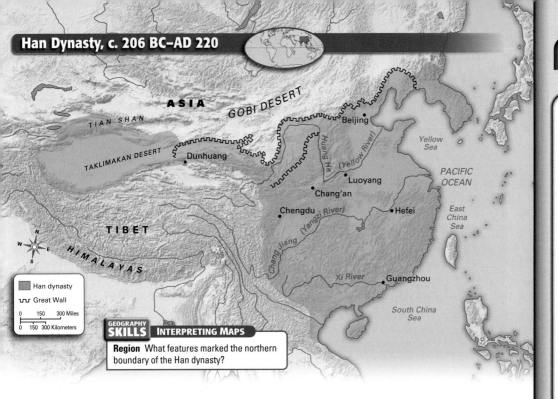

ASIA

TIAN SHAN

GOBI DESERT

TAKLIMAKAN DESERT

Dunhuang

Beijing

Yellow Sea

Huang He (Yellow River)

Luoyang

PACIFIC OCEAN

Chang'an

Chengdu

Chang Jiang (Yangzi River)

Hefei

East China Sea

TIBET

HIMALAYAS

Xi River

Guangzhou

South China Sea

Han dynasty

Great Wall

0   150   300 Miles
0   150   300 Kilometers

GEOGRAPHY SKILLS   INTERPRETING MAPS

Region What features marked the northern boundary of the Han dynasty?

loyalty and trust. In addition, he was well liked by both soldiers and peasants, which helped him to maintain control.

Liu Bang's rule was different from the strict Legalism of the Qin. He wanted to free people from harsh government policies. He lowered taxes for farmers and made punishments less severe. He gave large blocks of land to his supporters.

In addition to setting new policies, Liu Bang changed the way government worked. He set up a government structure that built on the foundation begun by the Qin. He also relied on educated officials to help him rule.

Wudi Creates a New Government

In 140 BC Emperor Wudi (WOO-dee) took the throne. He wanted to create a stronger central government. To do that, he took land from the lords, raised taxes, and placed the supply of grain under the control of the government.

Under Wudi, Confucianism became China's official government philosophy. Government officials were expected to practice Confucianism. Wudi even began a university to teach Confucian ideas.

If a person passed an exam on Confucian teachings, he could get a good position in the government. However, not just anyone could take the test. The exams were only open to people who had been recommended for government service already. As a result, wealthy or influential families continued to control the government.

READING CHECK   Analyzing How was the Han government based on the ideas of Confucius?

ANCIENT CHINA **201**

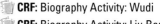 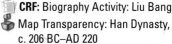

❷ Family Life

Family life was supported and strengthened in Han China.

Describe What were the social classes in Han China? *upper— emperor, royal court, scholars; second class—peasants; third class—artisans; lowest—merchants*

Analyze Why were wealthy merchants in the lowest class? *did not produce anything of their own, only bought and sold goods made by others*

Elaborate How were Han social classes different than most social divisions? *They were not based on wealth or power.*

Activity **A Day in the Life of . . .** Have students write a description of a typical day in the life of a peasant in Han China.

📖 Alternative Assessment Handbook, Rubric 37: Writing Assignments

🐻 **HSS** 6.6.6; **HSS** Analysis Skills: CS 1, HI 1

Info to Know

Dressing the Part Even the clothes the ancient Chinese wore had social distinction. People in the upper classes, such as members of the emperor's court and high-ranking government officials, wore fine robes made of silk, a material that was both luxurious and expensive. The lower classes wore garments made of rough fabrics. Wearing silk was not just a matter of being able to afford the material; the supply of fabrics was regulated by the government. In later dynasties, some merchants who dealt in silk were even punished for wearing silk clothing.

Family Life

The Han period was a time of great social change in China. Class structure became more rigid. The family once again became important within Chinese society.

Social Classes

Based on the Confucian system, people were divided into four classes. The upper class was made up of the emperor, his court, and scholars who held government positions. The second class, the largest, was made up of the peasants. Next were artisans who produced items for daily life and some luxury goods. Merchants occupied the lowest class because they did not produce anything. They only bought and sold what others made. The military was not an official class in the Confucian system. Still, joining the army offered men a chance to rise in social status because the military was considered part of the government.

This Han artifact is an oil lamp held by a servant.

Lives of Rich and Poor

The classes only divided people into social rank. They did not indicate wealth or power. For instance, even though peasants made up the second highest class, they were poor. On the other hand, some merchants were wealthy and powerful despite being in the lowest class.

People's lifestyles varied according to wealth. The emperor and his court lived in a large palace. Less important officials lived in multilevel houses built around courtyards. Many of these wealthy families owned large estates and employed laborers to work the land. Some families even hired private armies to defend their estates.

The wealthy filled their homes with expensive decorations. These included paintings, pottery, bronze lamps, and jade figures. Rich families hired musicians for entertainment. Even the tombs of dead family members were filled with beautiful, expensive objects.

Most people in the Han dynasty, however, didn't live like the wealthy. Nearly 60 million people lived in China during the Han dynasty, and about 90 percent of them were peasants who lived in the countryside. Peasants put in long, tiring days working the land. Whether it was in the millet fields of the north or in the rice paddies of the south, the work was hard. In the winter, peasants were also forced to work on building projects for the government. Heavy taxes and bad weather forced many farmers to sell their land and work for rich landowners. By the last years of the Han dynasty, only a few farmers were independent.

Chinese peasants lived simple lives. They wore plain clothing made of fiber from a native plant. The main foods they ate were cooked grains like barley. Most peasants lived in small villages. Their small, wood-framed houses had walls made of mud or stamped earth.

Differentiating Instruction for Universal Access

Learners Having Difficulty   Reaching Standards

1. Discuss with students the social structure under the Han dynasty. Ask students to identify the various social classes and what people were represented in each class.

2. Have students create a diagram or illustration that shows the social order of Han China. Ask students to include information that clearly shows the occupations of the people in each social class.

3. Then have students compare this social order to the social divisions that existed under the Zhou dynasty. Have students examine the

differences between the two social orders. How did society change in China from the Zhou dynasty to the Han dynasty? Have each student write a short paragraph in which they explain the similarities and differences between the two.

4. Ask volunteers to share their illustrations and explanations with the class.
   LS Visual/Spatial, Verbal/Linguistic

🐻 **HSS** 6.6.6; **HSS** Analysis Skills: CS 1, HI 1, HI 2

📖 Alternative Assessment Handbook, Rubrics 3: Artwork; and 9: Comparing and Contrasting

The Importance of Family
Honoring one's family was an important duty in Han China. In this painting, people give thanks before their family shrine. Only the men participate. The women watch from inside the house.

How are these people giving thanks?

生十雨蒼天濟當年
與後人祭

欽天監五官
鴻臚寺序班

皆世

The Revival of the Family

Since Confucianism was the official government philosophy during Wudi's reign, Confucian teachings about the family were also honored. Children were taught from birth to respect their elders. Disobeying one's parents was a crime. Even emperors had a duty to respect their parents.

Confucius had taught that the father was the head of the family. Within the family, the father had absolute power. The Han taught that it was a woman's duty to obey her husband, and children had to obey their father.

Han officials believed that if the family was strong and people obeyed the father, then people would obey the emperor, too. Since the Han stressed strong family ties and respect for elders, some men even gained government jobs based on the respect they showed their parents.

Children were encouraged to serve their parents. They were also expected to honor dead parents with ceremonies and offerings. All family members were expected to care for family burial sites.

Chinese parents valued boys more highly than girls. This was because sons carried on the family line and took care of their parents when they were old. On the other hand, daughters became part of their husband's family. According to a Chinese proverb, "Raising daughters is like raising children for another family." Some women, however, still gained power. They could actually influence their sons' families. An older widow could even become the head of the family.

READING CHECK Identifying Cause and Effect
Why did the family take on such importance during the Han dynasty?

Main Idea

❸ Han Achievements

The Han made many achievements in art, literature, and learning.

Identify What were some of the cultural and scientific achievements of the Han? *artwork, poetry, history, paper, sundial, acupuncture, and the seismograph*

Contrast How did the *fu* style of poetry differ from the *shi* style? Fu *poetry combined prose and poetry in a long work of literature, while* shi *used short lines of verse that could be sung.*

Evaluate What do you think was the most important invention of the Han dynasty? Why? *possible answers— acupuncture because it improved medicine and is still used today; paper because it is part of our everyday lives.*

HSS 6.6.6; **HSS** Analysis Skills: HI 1

Connect to Science

Seismographs The Chinese seismograph pictured above was a very simple device. It showed when an earthquake occurred and the direction of the earthquake. Modern-day seismographs still serve the same function, but they also record the strength and duration of an earthquake. Scientists use several seismographs in different locations to pinpoint the epicenter of an earthquake. The scale used to measure the strength of an earthquake is known as the Richter scale and was developed by seismologists in 1935.

go.hrw.com
Online Resources

Online Resources:
KEYWORD: SQ6 WH7
ACTIVITY: Art of Ancient China

Han Achievements

During the Han dynasty, the Chinese made many advances in art and learning. Some of these advances are shown here.

Science

This is a model of an ancient Chinese seismograph. When an earthquake struck, a lever inside caused a ball to drop from a dragon's mouth into a toad's mouth, indicating the direction from which the earthquake had come.

Han Achievements

Han rule was a time of great accomplishments. Art and literature thrived, and inventors developed many useful devices.

Art and Literature

The Chinese of the Han period produced many works of art. They became experts at figure painting—a style of painting that includes portraits of people. Portraits often showed religious figures and Confucian scholars. Han artists also painted realistic scenes from everyday life. Their creations covered the walls of palaces and tombs.

In literature, Han China is known for its poetry. Poets developed new styles of verse, including the *fu* style which was the most popular. *Fu* poets combined prose and poetry to create long works of literature. Another style, called *shi*, featured short lines of verse that could be sung. Han rulers hired poets known for the beauty of their verse.

ACADEMIC VOCABULARY

innovation a new idea, method, or device

Han writers also produced important works of history. One historian by the name of Sima Qian wrote a complete history of all the dynasties through the early Han. His format and style became the model for later historical writings.

Inventions and Advances

The Han Chinese invented one item that we use every day—paper. They made it by grinding plant fibers, such as mulberry bark and hemp, into a paste. Then they let it dry in sheets. Chinese scholars produced "books" by pasting several pieces of paper together into a long sheet. Then they rolled the sheet into a scroll.

The Han also made other **innovations** in science. These included the sundial and the seismograph. A **sundial** uses the position of shadows cast by the sun to tell the time of day. The sundial was an early type of clock. A **seismograph** is a device that measures the strength of an earthquake. Han emperors were very interested

204 CHAPTER 7

Cross-Discipline Activity: Literature

Exceeding Standards

Fu and *Shi* Poems **HSS** 6.6.6; **HSS** Analysis Skills: HR 1, HI 1, HI 2

Research Required

1. Review with the class the achievements in literature of the Han dynasty.

2. Organize the class into pairs. Have each pair use the library, Internet, or other sources to research *fu* and *shi* poems. Have each pair select one poem of either type. Tell students that they will create a scroll on which they will copy and illustrate their poems.

3. Check to make sure that students understand the meaning of the poems they selected. Remind students that Han paintings often depicted realistic scenes from everyday life.

4. Have volunteers from each group explain the Chinese poem they selected and then read their poems aloud.

5. Expand the activity by having students write their own *fu* or *shi* poems and illustrate them as well. **LS** Visual/Spatial, Verbal/Linguistic

📓 Alternative Assessment Handbook, Rubrics 3: Artwork; and 26: Poems and Songs

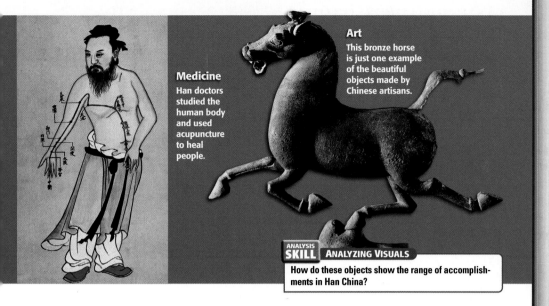

Medicine
Han doctors studied the human body and used acupuncture to heal people.

Art
This bronze horse is just one example of the beautiful objects made by Chinese artisans.

ANALYSIS SKILL **ANALYZING VISUALS**
How do these objects show the range of accomplishments in Han China?

in knowing about the movements of the earth. They believed that earthquakes were signs of future evil events.

Another Han innovation, acupuncture (AK-yoo-punk-cher), improved medicine. **Acupuncture** is the practice of inserting fine needles through the skin at specific points to cure disease or relieve pain. Many Han inventions in science and medicine are still used today.

READING CHECK Categorizing What advances did the Chinese make during the Han period?

SUMMARY AND PREVIEW Han rulers moved away from Legalism and based their government on Confucianism. This strengthened family bonds in Han China. In addition, art and learning thrived under Han rule. In the next section you will learn about China's contact beyond its borders.

go.hrw.com
Online Quiz
KEYWORD: SQ6 HP7

Section 4 Assessment

Reviewing Ideas, Terms, and People **HSS** 6.6.6

1. **a. Identify** Whose teachings were the foundation for government during the Han dynasty?
   b. Summarize How did Emperor Wudi create a strong central government?
   c. Evaluate Do you think that an exam system is the best way to make sure that people are fairly chosen for government jobs? Why or why not?
2. **a. Describe** What was the son's role in the family?
   b. Contrast How did living conditions for the wealthy differ from those of the peasants during the Han dynasty?
3. **Identify** What device did the Chinese invent to measure the strength of earthquakes?

Critical Thinking

4. **Categorizing** Copy the chart below. List the four classes of Chinese society and give at least two facts about each.

Class	Facts
1.	
2.	
3.	
4.	

FOCUS ON SPEAKING

5. **Analyzing Impact on History** Sometimes a ruler has the biggest impact on history. Other times, ideas that develop within a society have a greater impact. Which had a greater impact on Han China? Why?

ANCIENT CHINA **205**

Section 4 Assessment Answers

1. **a.** Confucius
   b. took lands from lords, raised taxes, controlled grain supply
   c. Answers will vary but should display familiarity with the exam system.

2. **a.** to obey his parents, carry on the family line, and take care of his parents
   b. wealthy—in large, richly-furnished homes, had servants, and wore luxurious clothing; peasants—simple houses, ate rice and grains, dressed poorly, and worked hard

3. seismograph

4. upper class—emperor, court, scholars; lived in large homes, many owned estates, had luxury items, wore luxurious clothes; second class—peasant farmers; lived in mud or stamped-earth houses, worked long days, paid heavy taxes, wore plain clothing; third class—artisans; produced items for daily life, produced luxury goods; lowest class—merchants; bought and sold items made by others, could become rich and powerful.

5. Answers will vary but should be supported by text-based facts.

The Shiji

As You Read Have students keep a list of Bu Shi's qualities as they read the passage. After the students have read the passage, ask them to explain what type of person Bu Shi was. Why might a historian be interested in him?

Meet the Writer

Sima Qian Sima Qian was the son of Ssu-ma T'an, the grand historian of the Han court from 140–110 BC. The grand historian was responsible for keeping a daily record of state events and court ceremonies as well as astronomical observations. In his youth, Sima Qian traveled a great deal and even served in the entourage of the emperor. In 110 BC his father died, and Sima Qian was appointed to his father's office of grand historian. He spent many years working on *The Shiji*, fulfilling his father's dream of writing a history of China.

Info to Know

Offending the Emperor Before Sima Qian completed the *Shiji*, he deeply offended Emperor Wudi by defending a general who had fallen out of favor with the emperor. Sima Qian was arraigned for "defaming the Emperor," a crime punishable by death. Sima Qian's life was spared, however, either because the emperor thought he was too valuable or Sima Qian asked that he be allowed to finish his history of China. Later, the emperor lifted his punishment, and Sima Qian again rose in the ranks of the Han dynasty.

Answers

Guided Reading 3. *He showed his loyalty to the government by offering to give them half of his wealth.*

GUIDED READING

WORD HELP

intervals periods of time
dispatched sent
envoy representative

❶ Henan (HUH-NAHN) is a region of eastern China. It is a productive agricultural region.

❷ The Xiongnu were a tribe of nomads. They lived in the north and often raided towns near China's border.

❸ Why do you think the emperor invites Bu Shi to work for the government?

ELA **6.3.0** Students read and respond to historically or culturally significant works of literature that reflect and enhance their studies of history and social science.

Literature in History

from The Shiji

by Sima Qian

Translated by Burton Watson

About the Reading *The Shiji, also called the Records of the Grand Historian, is a history that describes more than two thousand years of Chinese culture. The author, Sima Qian (soo-MAH chee-EN), held the title Grand Historian under the Han emperor Wudi. He spent 18 years of his life writing the Shiji. His hard work paid off, and his history was well received. In fact, the Shiji was so respected that it served as the model for every later official history of China. This passage describes a man named Bu Shi, who attracted the emperor's attention through his generosity and good deeds. Eventually, the emperor invited him to live in the imperial palace.*

AS YOU READ Ask yourself why Sima Qian included Bu Shi in his history.

Bu Shi was a native of Henan, where his family made a living by farming and animal raising. ❶ When his parents died, Bu Shi left home, handing over the house, the lands, and all the family wealth to his younger brother, who by this time was full grown. For his own share, he took only a hundred or so of the sheep they had been raising, which he led off into the mountains to pasture. In the course of ten years or so, Bu Shi's sheep had increased to over a thousand and he had bought his own house and fields. His younger brother in the meantime had failed completely in the management of the farm, but Bu Shi promptly handed over to him a share of his own wealth. This happened several times. Just at that time the Han was sending its generals at frequent intervals to attack the Xiongnu. ❷ Bu Shi journeyed to the capital and submitted a letter to the throne, offering to turn over half of his wealth to the district officials to help in the defense of the border. The emperor dispatched an envoy to ask if Bu Shi wanted a post in the government. ❸

"From the time I was a child," Bu Shi replied, "I have been an animal raiser. I have had no experience in government and would certainly not want such a position" . . .

Differentiating Instruction for Universal Access

English-Language Learners   **Reaching Standards**

1. Review the passage with the class. Then organize students into small groups. Assign each group one paragraph of the story.

2. Have each group draw a cartoon or comic strip that illustrates their portion of the story, writing dialogue and identifying characters just as in an ordinary comic strip. Encourage students to distinguish between relevant and irrelevant information.

3. Have groups post their cartoons or comic strips around the classroom in order for all to see. **LS** **Visual/Spatial, Interpersonal**

HSS Analysis Skills: HR 3

Alternative Assessment Handbook, Rubric 27: Political Cartoons

Universal Access Resources
See p. 177c of the Chapter Planner for additional resources for differentiating instruction for universal access.

"If that is the case," said the envoy, "then what is your objective in making this offer?"

Bu Shi replied, "The Son of Heaven has sent out to punish the Xiongnu. ❹ In my humble opinion, every worthy man should be willing to fight to the death to defend the borders, and every person with wealth ought to contribute to the expense . . ."

The emperor discussed the matter with the chancellor, but the latter said, "The proposal is simply not in accord with human nature! ❺ Such eccentric people are of no use in guiding the populace, but only throw the laws into confusion. I beg Your Majesty not to accept his offer!"

For this reason the emperor put off answering Bu Shi for a long time, and finally after several years had passed, turned down the offer, whereupon Bu Shi went back to his fields and pastures . . .

The following year a number of poor people were transferred to other regions . . . At this point Bu Shi took two hundred thousand cash of his own and turned the sum over to the governor of Henan to assist the people who were emigrating to other regions . . . At this time the rich families were all scrambling to hide their wealth; only Bu Shi, unlike the others, had offered to contribute to the expenses of the government. ❻ The emperor decided that Bu Shi was really a man of exceptional worth after all . . . Because of his simple, unspoiled ways and his deep loyalty, the emperor finally appointed him grand tutor to his son Liu Hong, the king of Qi.

In this painting from the 1600s, government officials deliver a letter.

GUIDED READING

WORD HELP

objective goal
chancellor high official
accord agreement
eccentric someone who acts strangely
populace people
tutor private teacher

❹ The Chinese people believed that their emperor was the "Son of Heaven." They thought he received his power from heavenly ancestors.

❺ The "latter" means the one mentioned last. In this case, the latter is the chancellor.

❻ *What is Bu Shi's attitude toward his wealth? How is it different from the attitude of the rich families?*

CONNECTING LITERATURE TO HISTORY

1. **Drawing Conclusions** Like many Chinese historians, Sima Qian wanted to use history to teach lessons. What lessons could the story of Bu Shi be used to teach?

2. **Analyzing** The Emperor Wudi based his government on the teachings of Confucius. What elements of Confucianism can you see in this story?

207

Literature in History

Teaching Tip

Ask students to point out the elements of Confucianism that are represented in the story of Bu Shi. Remind students that Confucianism is an ethical system that teaches moral values, respect for authority, and treating others as you would want to be treated.

Other People, Other Places

Fables Sima Qian most likely wrote the *Shiji* during the second century BC. Point out to students that fables appear in other cultures as well. Aesop's fables began in sixth-century-BC Greece, and the Indian *Panchatantra* may have come into being in the first century BC.

Critical Thinking: Summarizing

Standards Proficiency

The Story of Bu Shi 🕮 **HSS** Analysis Skills: HR 3, HI 1

1. Read the passage from the *Shiji* aloud with the class, asking for volunteers to read different sections.

2. Then ask students to write a summary of the story of Bu Shi in their own words. Then have students write five multiple-choice questions about the story.

3. Have students work with a partner to quiz each other over the questions each wrote. Students may use their summaries if they cannot answer a question. Award students

that answer each question correctly one point. At the end of the game, ask the pair with the most points to read its summary to the class.

LS Verbal/Linguistic

📝 Alternative Assessment Handbook, Rubric 37: Writing Assignments

Answers

Guided Reading 6. *He believes wealth is to be shared and used his wealth to help the needy and the empire; the rich families wanted to keep their wealth to themselves.*

Connecting Literature to History

1. *possible answers—generosity, goodness towards others, treat others as you would like to be treated;* **2.** *Bu Shi feels it is his duty to help his government and others; the emperor rewards Bu Shi's loyalty and ethics.*

Bellringer

If YOU were there . . . Use the **Daily Bellringer Transparency** to help students answer the question.

🔖 Daily Bellringer Transparency, Section 5

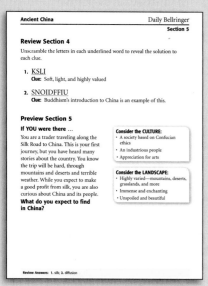

Ancient China   Daily Bellringer
                                      Section 5

Review Section 4
Unscramble the letters in each underlined word to reveal the solution to each clue.

1. KSLI
   Clue: Soft, light, and highly valued

2. SNOIDFFIU
   Clue: Buddhism's introduction to China is an example of this.

Preview Section 5
If YOU were there . . .
You are a trader traveling along the Silk Road to China. This is your first journey, but you have heard many stories about the country. You know the trip will be hard, through mountains and deserts and terrible weather. While you expect to make a good profit from silk, you are also curious about China and its people. **What do you expect to find in China?**

Consider the CULTURE:
• A society based on Confucian ethics
• An industrious people
• Appreciation for arts

Consider the LANDSCAPE:
• Highly varied—mountains, deserts, grasslands, and more
• Immense and enchanting
• Unspoiled and beautiful

Review Answers: 1. silk; 2. diffusion

Academic Vocabulary

Review with students the high-use academic term in this section.

procedure the way a task is accomplished (p. 209)

📄 **CRF:** Vocabulary Builder Activity, Section 5

🐻 Standards Focus

HSS 6.6.7
Means: Understand the routes and importance of the silk roads.
Matters: The silk roads allowed China to exchange products and ideas with other peoples, including the Romans.

HSS 6.6.8
Means: Describe how Buddhism spread to China.
Matters: Buddhism became a major religion in China and still has great influence in Chinese culture.

SECTION 5

What You Will Learn...

Main Ideas

1. Farming and manufacturing grew during the Han dynasty.
2. Trade routes linked China with the Middle East and Rome.
3. Buddhism came to China from India and gained many followers.

The Big Idea

Trade routes led to the exchange of new products and ideas among China, Rome, and other peoples.

Key Terms

silk, *p. 209*
Silk Road, *p. 209*
diffusion, *p. 211*

HSS 6.6.7 Cite the significance of the trans-Eurasian "silk roads" in the period of the Han Dynasty and Roman Empire and their locations.

6.6.8 Describe the diffusion of Buddhism northward to China during the Han Dynasty.

Han Contacts with Other Cultures

If **YOU** were there...

You are a trader traveling along the Silk Road to China. This is your first journey, but you have heard many stories about the country. You know the trip will be hard, through mountains and deserts and terrible weather. While you expect to make a good profit from silk, you are also curious about China and its people.

What do you expect to find in China?

BUILDING BACKGROUND During the Han dynasty Chinese society returned its focus to Confucian ideas, and new inventions were developed. In addition, increased trade allowed other countries to learn about the rich culture of China.

Farming and Manufacturing

Many advances in manufacturing took place during the Han dynasty. As a result, productivity increased and the empire prospered. These changes paved the way for China to make contact with people of other cultures.

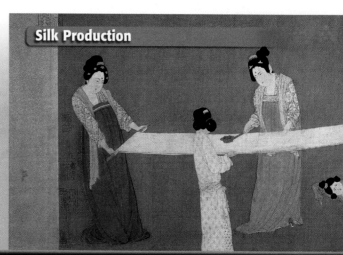

Silk Production

Teach the Big Idea: Master the Standards   Standards Proficiency

Han Contacts with Other Cultures 🐻 HSS 6.6.7, 6.6.8 ; HSS Analysis Skills: CS 1, CS 2

1. **Teach** Ask students the Main Idea questions to teach this section.

2. **Apply** Have students create a chart with three columns labeled *Farming and Manufacturing, Trade Routes,* and *Buddhism Comes to China.* Have students fill in the chart with details about each topic.
   LS Verbal/Linguistic

3. **Review** As you review each of the Main Ideas, ask students to explain how each of these ideas relates to the others.

4. **Practice/Homework** Have each student create an advertisement for products a Chinese trader might try to sell to another country, including how the products will be sent to the buyer and how long it will take for the products to reach the buyer.
   LS Visual/Spatial, Verbal/Linguistic

   📄 Alternative Assessment Handbook, Rubrics 2: Advertisements; and 13: Graphic Organizers

By the Han period, the Chinese had become master ironworkers. They manufactured iron swords and armor that made the army more powerful.

Farmers also gained from advances in iron. The iron plow and the wheelbarrow, a single-wheeled cart, increased farm output. With a wheelbarrow a farmer could haul more than 300 pounds all by himself. With an iron plow, he could till more land and raise more food.

Another item that increased in production during the Han dynasty was **silk**, a soft, light, highly valued fabric. For centuries, Chinese women had known the complicated methods needed to raise silkworms, unwind the silk threads of their cocoons, and then prepare the threads for dyeing and weaving. The Chinese were determined to keep their procedure for making silk a secret. Revealing these secrets was punishable by death.

During the Han period, weavers used foot-powered looms to weave silk threads into beautiful fabric. Garments made from this silk were very expensive.

READING CHECK **Finding Main Ideas** How did advances in technology affect farming and silk production?

Trade Routes

Chinese goods, especially silk and fine pottery, were highly valued by people in other lands. During the Han period, the value of these goods to people outside China helped increase trade.

THE IMPACT TODAY

China still produces about 50 percent of the world's silk.

Expansion of Trade

Trade increased partly because Han armies conquered lands deep in Central Asia. Leaders there told the Han generals that people who lived still farther west wanted silk. At the same time, Emperor Wudi wanted strong, sturdy Central Asian horses for his army. China's leaders saw that they could make a profit by bringing silk to Central Asia and trading the cloth for the horses. The Central Asian peoples would then take the silk west and trade it for other products they wanted.

ACADEMIC VOCABULARY

procedure the way a task is accomplished

The Silk Road

Traders used a series of overland routes to take Chinese goods to distant buyers. The most famous trade route was known as the **Silk Road**. This 4,000-mile-long network of routes stretched westward from China across Asia's deserts and mountain ranges, through the Middle East, until it reached the Mediterranean Sea.

The technique for making silk was a well-kept secret in ancient China, as silk was a valuable trade good in distant lands. Workers made silk from the cocoons of silkworms, just as they do today.

Direct Teach

Main Idea

1 Farming and Manufacturing

Farming and manufacturing grew during the Han dynasty.

Recall What were two inventions that helped farmers become more productive during the Han dynasty? *iron plow and wheelbarrow*

Analyze How did the wheelbarrow aid farmers? *It allowed a single person to carry more than 300 pounds at a time.*

Elaborate Why do you think the Chinese were so determined to keep how they produced silk a secret? *Other countries would have been able to make the silk themselves if they knew the secret, thereby making the Chinese silk trade less valuable.*

CRF: Economic and History Activity: The Chinese Economy

HSS 6.6.7; HSS **Analysis Skills:** HI 1

Teaching Tip

Farming Techniques

The iron plow and the wheelbarrow may seem like very ordinary objects, but they are significant advances. Make sure all students understand how both of them work. Guide students in a discussion of basic farming techniques. Have students compare farming with and without a wheelbarrow or iron plow.

Differentiating Instruction for Universal Access

Advanced Learners/GATE

Exceeding Standards | Research Required

1. Review with the class the advances in farming and manufacturing made in Han China. Ask students to explain how each advance helped the Chinese economy.
2. Have each student select one of the advances mentioned in the section—the iron plow, the wheelbarrow, or silk production. Have students conduct research on the item they selected. Students should identify how the advance aided the Chinese, how it worked, and how that item is used today, if at all.
3. Have each student write a short paper about the past and current uses of the advance they selected and read their papers to the class.

HSS 6.6.7; HSS **Analysis Skills** HI 6

Alternative Assessment Handbook, Rubrics 30: Research; and 42: Writing to Inform

Answers

Reading Check *Technology yielded the wheelbarrow and the iron plow, which greatly increased productivity. Technology also yielded foot-powered looms, which increased silk production.*

Main Idea

❷ Trade Routes

Trade routes linked China with the Middle East and Rome.

Recall For what items did the Chinese trade? *horses, gold, silver, and precious stones*

Summarize What were some of the difficulties traders on the Silk Road faced? *bandits trying to steal cargo and water; harsh weather such as blizzards, heat, and sandstorms*

🔲 Map Transparency: The Silk Road

📖 **HSS** 6.6.7; **HSS** Analysis Skills: HI 1, HI 2

Main Idea

❸ Buddhism Comes to China

Buddhism came to China from India and gained many followers.

Recall From what country did Buddhism come to China? *India*

Draw Conclusions How did the political environment in China lead to the acceptance of Buddhism? *As the government became less stable, hunger and violence became widespread. The Chinese embraced Buddhism because if offered relief from suffering.*

📖 **HSS** 6.6.8; **HSS** Analysis Skills: HI 1

Did you know . . .

The Romans, who valued silk from China, called China *Serica*, which means "Land of Silk."

Answers

Interpreting Maps *the Taklimakan Desert*

Reading Check *Han conquests put the Chinese in contact with more distant peoples who wanted to trade for Chinese goods.*

210

Chinese traders did not travel the entire Silk Road. Upon reaching Central Asia, they sold their goods to local traders who would take them the rest of the way.

Traveling the Silk Road was difficult. Hundreds of men and camels loaded down with valuable goods, including silks and jade, formed groups. They traveled the Silk Road together for protection. Armed guards were hired to protect traders from bandits who stole cargo and water, a precious necessity. Weather presented other dangers. Traders faced icy blizzards, desert heat, and blinding sandstorms.

Named after the most famous item transported along it, the Silk Road was worth its many risks. Silk was so popular in Rome, for example, that China grew wealthy from that trade relationship alone. Traders returned from Rome with silver, gold, precious stones, and horses.

READING CHECK **Summarizing** Why did Chinese trade expand under Han rule?

Buddhism Comes to China

When the Chinese people came into contact with other civilizations, they exchanged ideas along with trade goods. Among these ideas was a new religion. In the first century AD Buddhism spread from India to China along the Silk Road and other trade routes.

Arrival of a New Religion

Over time, the Han government became less stable. People ignored laws, and violence was common. As rebellions flared up, millions of peasants went hungry. Life became violent and uncertain. Many Chinese looked to Daoism or Confucianism to find out why they had to suffer so much, but they didn't find helpful answers.

Buddhism seemed to provide more hope than the traditional Chinese beliefs did. It offered rebirth and relief from suffering. This promise was a major reason the Chinese people embraced Buddhism.

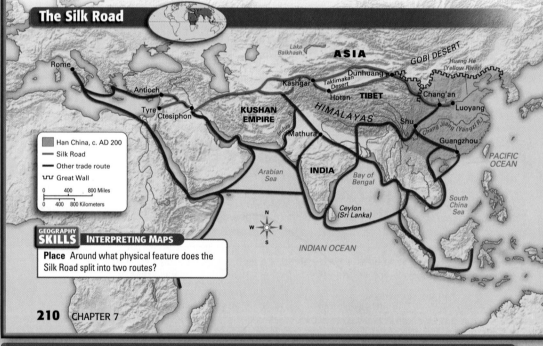

The Silk Road

GEOGRAPHY SKILLS **INTERPRETING MAPS**

Place Around what physical feature does the Silk Road split into two routes?

210 CHAPTER 7

Critical Thinking: Analyzing

Reaching Standards

Re-creating the Silk Road 📖 **HSS** 6.6.8; **HSS** Analysis Skills: CS 3

1. Review with students the map of the Silk Road. Ask students to identify the various regions that benefited from trade along the Silk Road.

2. Have students list the geographical features along the Silk Road.

3. Next, have each student write a letter to a new caravan guide who is going to travel the Silk Road for the first time. In their letters,

students should explain the difficulties of the route, what problems lie ahead, where water can be found, and the length of the journey from Chang'an to Tyre. **LS** **Visual/Spatial, Verbal/Linguistic**

📄 Alternative Assessment Handbook, Rubric 40: Writing to Describe

Impact on China

At first, Indian Buddhists had trouble explaining their religion to the Chinese. Then they used ideas found in Daoism to help describe Buddhist beliefs. Many people grew curious about Buddhism.

Before long, Buddhism caught on in China with both the poor and the upper classes. By AD 200, Buddhist altars stood in the emperor's palace.

Buddhism's introduction to China is an example of **diffusion**, the spread of ideas from one culture to another. Elements of Chinese culture changed in response to the new faith. For example, scholars translated Buddhist texts into Chinese. Many Chinese became Buddhist monks and nuns. Artists carved towering statues of Buddha into mountain walls.

READING CHECK **Finding Main Ideas** How did Chinese people learn of Buddhism?

SUMMARY AND PREVIEW Under the Han, trade brought new goods and ideas, including Buddhism, to China. In the next chapter you'll read about the religion of another people—the Jews.

This giant Buddha statue in China is among the largest in the world. It was carved from a hillside and looks down over the meeting place of three rivers.

Section 5 Assessment

go.hrw.com
Online Quiz
KEYWORD: SQ6 HP7

Reviewing Ideas, Terms, and People **HSS** 6.6.7, 6.6.8

1. **a. Describe** How did wheelbarrows help farmers?
   b. Summarize How was **silk** made in ancient China?
   c. Elaborate Why did the Chinese keep silk-making methods a secret?
2. **a. Identify** Where did the **Silk Road** begin and end?
   b. Elaborate What information would you use to support the argument that the silk trade must have been very valuable?
3. **a. Identify** What is **diffusion**?
   b. Make Generalizations What Buddhist beliefs appealed to millions of Chinese peasants?

Critical Thinking

4. **Categorizing** Copy the chart here. Use it to show the goods and ideas that came into China and the goods that China sent to other countries along the Silk Road.

Goods into China

Trade Along the Silk Road

Goods out of China

FOCUS ON SPEAKING

5. **Evaluating the Importance of Events** Not all the important events in history are wars or invasions. What peaceful events in this section changed Chinese history? Write down some ideas.

ANCIENT CHINA **211**

Section 5 Assessment Answers

1. **a.** They allowed farmers to carry larger loads than before by themselves.
   b. Silkworm cocoons were unwound, the silk thread was prepared for dyeing and weaving, and then woven into fabric.
   c. so they could be the only people who knew how to make the valuable fabric
2. **a.** It began in central China and ended at the Mediterranean Sea.
   b. In exchange for silk, traders returned with gold, silver, horses, and precious stones.

3. **a.** the spread of ideas from one culture to another
   b. the promise that Buddhism offered rebirth and relief from suffering
4. Goods into China—gold, silver, precious stones, horses, and Buddhism; Goods out of China—precious goods, including silk and porcelain
5. technology, trade, and Buddhism

Direct Teach

Main Idea

❸ **Buddhism Comes to China**

Buddhism came to China from India and gained many followers.

Summarize How is Buddhism's spread into China an example of diffusion? *It represents the spread of one idea from one culture to another, and the resulting change in the culture.*

HSS 6.6.8; **HSS** Analysis Skills: CS 1, HI 1

Review & Assess

Close

Challenge students to estimate the height of the statue shown on this page. They should use the human figures at the bottom of the photo as a guide.

Review

Online Quiz, Section 5

Assess

SE Section 5 Assessment
PASS: Section 5 Quiz
Alternative Assessment Handbook

Reteach/Classroom Intervention

California Standards Review Workbook
Interactive Reader and Study Guide, Section 5
Interactive Skills Tutor CD-ROM

Answers

Reading Check *Buddhism offered hope and comfort in a time of political instability and violence.*

211

History and Geography

Activity Remembering Successful Merchants Have students select one of the merchants shown on these pages and write an obituary for him. Obituaries should include information on how the merchants benefited from Silk Road trade. Encourage students to use their imaginations to fill in other details of the merchants' lives, but to stay within historical possibility.

Teaching Tip

Movement Remind your students that movement is one of the five themes of geography. This theme deals not just with the migration of people, but also with the movement of goods and ideas.

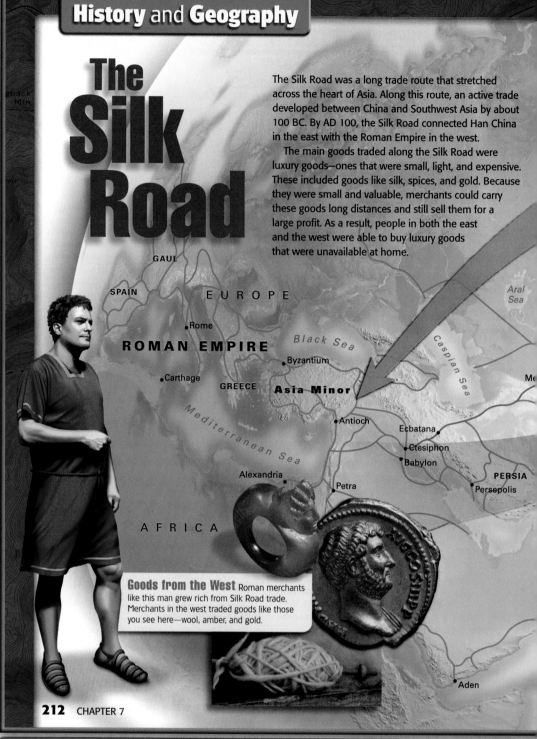

The Silk Road

The Silk Road was a long trade route that stretched across the heart of Asia. Along this route, an active trade developed between China and Southwest Asia by about 100 BC. By AD 100, the Silk Road connected Han China in the east with the Roman Empire in the west.

The main goods traded along the Silk Road were luxury goods—ones that were small, light, and expensive. These included goods like silk, spices, and gold. Because they were small and valuable, merchants could carry these goods long distances and still sell them for a large profit. As a result, people in both the east and the west were able to buy luxury goods that were unavailable at home.

Goods from the West Roman merchants like this man grew rich from Silk Road trade. Merchants in the west traded goods like those you see here—wool, amber, and gold.

Standards Focus

History–Social Science

6.6.7 Cite the significance of the trans-Eurasian "silk roads" in the period of the Han Dynasty and Roman Empire and their locations.

Analysis Skills

CS 3 Students use a variety of maps and documents to identify physical and cultural features of neighborhoods, cities, states, and countries to explain the historical migration of people, expansion and disintegration of empires, and the growth of economic systems.

Cross-Discipline Activity: Economics

Standards Proficiency

Long Road, High Price

HSS 6.6.7; HSS **Analysis Skills:** CS 3

1. Organize students into groups. Have students in each group decide if they want to represent a Roman or Chinese merchant and what items they want to trade on the Silk Road. They should also assign prices that manufacturers charge a trader for the merchandise.
2. Then have each group create a flowchart showing where the merchandise is sold to the next trader and how much that trader pays for it. The goods may change hands several times as they make their way along the Silk Road, and each time the price is slightly higher.
3. Ask groups to report on the original and final prices of their merchandise. They should also calculate how much of the final price had been added along the way to the manufacturer's original price. Point out that some merchant made a profit at each point along the Silk Road. **LS Visual/Spatial, Logical/Mathematical**

Alternative Assessment Handbook, Rubric 13: Graphic Organizers

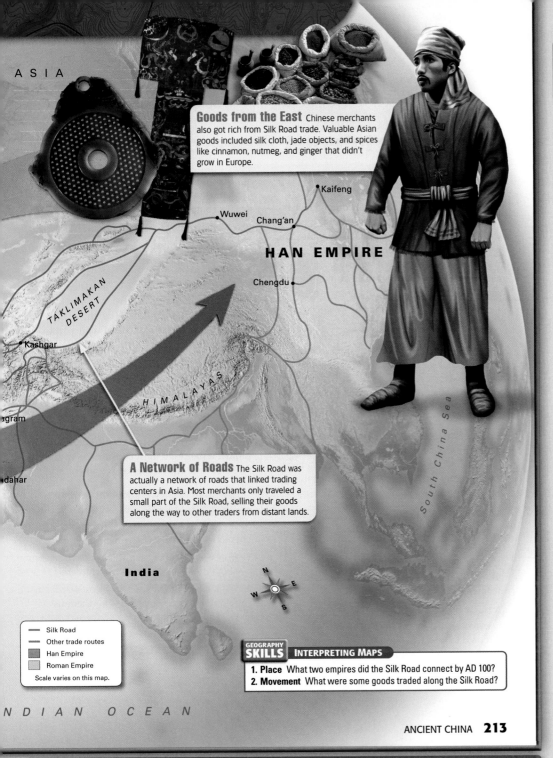

ASIA

Goods from the East Chinese merchants also got rich from Silk Road trade. Valuable Asian goods included silk cloth, jade objects, and spices like cinnamon, nutmeg, and ginger that didn't grow in Europe.

Kaifeng

Wuwei   Chang'an

HAN EMPIRE

Chengdu

TAKLIMAKAN DESERT

Kashgar

HIMALAYAS

agram

dahar

A Network of Roads The Silk Road was actually a network of roads that linked trading centers in Asia. Most merchants only traveled a small part of the Silk Road, selling their goods along the way to other traders from distant lands.

South China Sea

India

— Silk Road
— Other trade routes
▢ Han Empire
▢ Roman Empire
Scale varies on this map.

GEOGRAPHY SKILLS **INTERPRETING MAPS**

1. **Place** What two empires did the Silk Road connect by AD 100?
2. **Movement** What were some goods traded along the Silk Road?

INDIAN OCEAN

ANCIENT CHINA **213**

Info to Know

Traveling the Silk Road Today Fascination with the Silk Road has led to increased tourism. Since China opened its doors to foreign tourism, people have been able to travel along part of the Silk Road. Although travel in the harsh climate of western China is only for the hardy tourist, there are plenty of attractions, even in the deserts. Sites include ruined cities and caves full of Buddhist paintings. One city, Kashgar, has a market where tourists can get some idea of what trade along the old Silk Road was like long ago. At the market, people of many nationalities sell spices, wool, livestock, silver knives, and other items. Have students locate the city of Kashgar on the map on this page.

Connect to Science

From Worm to Wonderful Commercial silk is made by a single species of moth larvae. Each larva, or silkworm, lives on a diet of mulberry leaves before spinning a silk thread that wraps around and around to become a cocoon. This thread can be up to 3,000 feet long. To unwind the cocoon, the manufacturer must first find the end of the thread. Workers wash the silk and treat it with various chemicals to make different types of fabric.

Collaborative Learning

Reaching Standards

Silk Road Collage 🐻 HSS 6.6.7; HSS Analysis Skills: CS 3

Prep Required

Materials: art supplies, butcher paper

1. Organize the class into four groups: Places, People, East to West Goods, and West to East Goods.

2. Have the students in the Places group create a large map that shows the roads themselves and important cities along the Silk Road. Have them draw or find pictures of physical features along the route.

3. Have students in the People group create or find images of the people who traveled the route, the animals that carried their cargo, and the trade caravans.

4. Students from each of the Goods groups should create or find images of goods that were traded along the route.

5. Next, have students create a collage of the Silk Road by placing images on the map created by the Places group. LS **Visual/Spatial**

📖 Alternative Assessment Handbook, Rubric 8: Collages

Answers

Interpreting Maps: 1. *Han China and the Roman Empire;* **2.** *silk, jade objects, spices, wool, amber, gold*

213

Social Studies Skills

Conducting Internet Research

Activity **Web Site for Using the Internet** Explain to students that the Internet offers a wealth of information and sometimes misinformation on many topics. Have students review the Social Studies Skills lesson. Then organize students into small groups and have each group use the information to build a mock Web site explaining how to use the Internet. The page should be the home, or main, page for the site. Remind students to include links and other important features on their page. Students should also include a checklist that people can use to evaluate a Web site. **LS Interpersonal, Visual/Spatial**

📋 Alternative Assessment Handbook, Rubrics 14: Group Activity; and 37: Writing Assignments

💿 Interactive Skills Tutor CD-ROM, Lesson 4: Use a Variety of Sources to Gather Information

Social Studies Skills

| Analysis | Critical Thinking | Participation | Study |

Conducting Internet Research

Understand the Skill

The Internet is a huge network of computers that are linked together. You can connect to this network from a personal computer or from a computer at a public library or school. Once connected, you can go to places called Web sites. Web sites consist of one or more Web pages. Each page contains information that you can view on the computer screen.

Governments, businesses, individuals, and many different types of organizations such as universities, news organizations, and libraries have Web sites. Most library Web sites allow users to search their card catalog electronically. Many libraries also have databases on their Web sites. A database is a large collection of related information that is organized by topic.

The Internet can be a very good reference source. It allows you to gather information on almost any topic without ever having to leave your chair. However, finding the information you need can sometimes be difficult. Having the skill to use the Internet efficiently increases its usefulness.

Learn the Skill

There are millions of Web sites on the Internet. This can make it hard to locate specific information. The following steps will help you in doing research on the Internet.

1 **Use a search engine.** This is a Web site that searches other sites. Type a word or phrase related to your topic into the search engine. It will list Web pages that might contain information on your topic. Clicking on an entry in this list will bring that page to your screen.

2 **Study the Web page.** Read the information to see if it is useful. You can print the page on the computer's printer or take notes. If you take notes, be sure to include the page's URL. This is its location or "address" on the Internet. You need this as the source of the information.

3 **Use hyperlinks.** Many Web pages have connections, called hyperlinks, to related information on the site or on other Web sites. Clicking on these links will take you to those pages. You can follow their links to even more pages, collecting information as you go.

4 **Return to your results list.** If the information or hyperlinks on a Web page are not useful, return to the list of pages that your search engine produced and repeat the process.

The Internet is a useful tool. But remember that information on the Internet is no different than printed resources. It must be evaluated with the same care and critical thinking as other resources.

Practice and Apply the Skill

Answer the following questions to apply the guidelines to Internet research on ancient China.

1. How would you begin if you wanted information about the Qin Dynasty from the Internet?

2. What words might you type into a search engine to find information about Confucianism?

3. Use a school computer to research the Great Wall of China. What kinds of pages did your search produce? Evaluate the usefulness of each type.

Social Studies Skills Activity: Conducting Internet Research

Mock Internet Search

Standards Proficiency   Prep Required

Materials: printouts of a Web search engine, Web search results, and Web sites for evaluation

1. Select one of the following topics or another topic from the chapter: *Laozi, terra-cotta warriors, Shi Huangdi,* or the *Silk Road.*

2. Before class, conduct an Internet search on the topic and print copies of the search engine you use, the search results, and two to three of the Web sites listed. Try to include at least one questionable Web site.

3. Display the printout of the search engine for students to see. Ask what terms they might enter to do a search on the topic you selected. Next, show students the printout of your search results. Have students discuss which of the listed sites look useful. Then show students the sites you printed. Help students to evaluate each site. **LS Visual/Spatial**

📋 Alternative Assessment Handbook, Rubric 16: Judging Information

Answers

Practice and Apply the Skill
1. *possible answers—go to a search engine and type in "Qin dynasty;" go to an online encyclopedia and look up Qin dynasty;* 2. *Confucius, Kongfuzi, Confucianism, Analects, Chinese philosophy;* 3. *Students' results should exhibit an understanding of how to use a search engine and how to evaluate a Web page or site.*

214

Visual Summary

Use the visual summary below to help you review the main ideas of the chapter.

QUICK FACTS

Chinese civilization began along the Huang He (Yellow River).

During the Zhou dynasty, armies fought for power, and the ideas of Confucius spread.

The Qin dynasty unified China with a strong government.

During the Han dynasty, China made advances in learning, and Buddhism spread.

Reviewing Vocabulary, Terms, and People

Match the "I" statement with the person or thing that might have made the statement. Not all of the choices will be used.

a. jade
b. innovation
c. lord
d. oracle
e. peasant
f. Confucius
g. Daoism
h. Shi Huangdi
i. seismograph
j. wheelbarrow
k. Great Wall
l. Legalism

1. "I stressed the importance of living in harmony with nature."
2. "I took a name that means 'first emperor.'"
3. "I stressed that people needed to be controlled with strict laws."
4. "I am a beautiful, hard gemstone that the Chinese made into many objects."
5. "I was built to keep invaders from attacking China."
6. "I can measure the strength of an earthquake."
7. "I am a person of high rank."
8. "I am a new idea, method, or device."
9. "I emphasized the importance of moral values and respect for the family."
10. "I am a farmer who tills a small plot of land."

Comprehension and Critical Thinking

SECTION 1 *(Pages 182–187)* **HSS** 6.6.1, 6.6.2

11. a. Identify In what region did the Shang dynasty develop?

b. Analyze How did China's geography contribute to the country's isolation?

c. Evaluate Considering the evidence, do you think the Xia dynasty was really China's first dynasty or a myth? Explain your answer.

ANCIENT CHINA **215**

Answers

12. **a.** Legalism

b. because Confucius said that the lower classes should learn by following the example of their superiors, which includes the emperor

c. Answers will vary, but students should be familiar with the concepts of both Daoism and Legalism.

13. **a.** Dissention from Shi Huangdi's policies helped stir up rebels after he died, and the government fell apart under the next two emperors.

b. to ensure they would not rise up and revolt against them

c. Answers will vary but should display familiarity with Shi Huangdi's rule.

14. **a.** The first group was the upper class, which included the emperor, his court, and government scholars. The second class was peasants.

b. to put only the people who were wealthy or influential and knew Confucianism into government

c. the seismograph and sundial

15. **a.** the Silk Road, the increased production of silk and the high demand for silk by other countries

b. wealthy people

c. The Chinese would no longer have dominated the silk trade.

Reviewing Themes

16. He was a harsh leader who inflicted many injustices on his people. Although he did many good things for China, his human rights practices were bad for the country.

17. Confucianism stressed moral values, loyalty among family members, good behavior by a king and his subjects, and carrying out what heaven expected of people.

Using the Internet

18. Go to the HRW Web site and enter the keyword shown to access a rubric for this activity.

> KEYWORD: SQ6 TEACHER

---

12. **a. Identify** Which Chinese philosophy encouraged strict laws and severe punishments to keep order?

b. Analyze How would Confucianism benefit Chinese emperors?

c. Evaluate Would you be happier under a government influenced by Legalism or by Daoism? In which type of government would there be more order? Explain your answers.

13. **a. Describe** What were the main reasons for the fall of the Qin dynasty?

b. Make Inferences Why did Shi Huangdi's armies destroy city walls and take weapons from people they conquered?

c. Evaluate Shi Huangdi was a powerful ruler. Was his rule good or bad for China? Why?

14. **a. Identify** During the Han dynasty, who belonged to the first and second social groups?

b. Analyze What was the purpose of the exam system during Wudi's rule?

c. Elaborate What inventions show that the Chinese studied nature?

15. **a. Identify** What factors led to the growth of trade during the Han dynasty?

b. Draw Conclusions Who do you think wore silk garments in China?

c. Predict What might have happened if the Chinese had told foreign visitors how to make silk?

Reviewing Themes

16. **Politics** Why might historians differ in their views of Shi Huangdi's success as a ruler?

17. **Society and Culture** How did Confucianism affect people's roles in their family, in government, and in society?

Using the Internet

go.hrw.com
KEYWORD SQ6 WH7

18. **Activity: Solving Problems** Confucius was one of the most influential teachers in Chinese history. His ideas suggested ways to restore order in Chinese society. Enter the activity keyword and research Confucianism. Take note of the political and cultural problems Confucianism tried to address. Then investigate some of the current political and cultural problems in the United States. Could Confucianism solve problems in the United States? Prepare a persuasive argument to support your answer.

Reading Skills

19. **Summarizing** From the chapter, choose a subsection under a blue headline. For each paragraph within that subsection, write a sentence that summarizes the paragraph's main idea. Continue with the other subsections under the blue heading to create a study guide.

Social Studies Skills

20. **Retrieving and Analyzing Information** Find a topic in the chapter about which you would like to know more. Use the Internet to explore your topic. Compare the sources you find to determine which seem most complete and reliable. Write a short paragraph about your results.

FOCUS ON SPEAKING

21. **Giving Your Oral Presentation** You have chosen a person or event and know why your choice was important to Chinese history. Now you must convince your classmates.

First, write a brief description of what the person did or what happened during the event. Then summarize why your person or event is important to Chinese history.

When you give your oral presentation, use vivid language to create pictures in your listeners' minds. Also, use a clear but lively tone of voice.

Reading Skills

19. Sentences will vary depending on the subsection selected, but should be concise summaries of the text ideas.

Social Studies Skills

20. Students should use sources from governmental, educational, and other reliable organizations.

Focus on Speaking

21. **Rubric** Students' oral presentations should
- include a clear description of the person's or event's importance.
- compare the person or event to others in Chinese history.
- use vivid language.
- be delivered in a clear and lively voice.

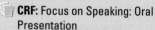 **CRF:** Focus on Speaking: Oral Presentation

Standards Assessment

DIRECTIONS: *Read each question, and write the letter of the best response.*

1

> The connecting link between serving one's father and serving one's mother is love. The connecting link between serving one's father and serving one's prince is reverence [respect]. Thus the mother [brings forth] love, while the prince brings forth reverence. But to the father belong both—love and reverence . . . Likewise, to serve one's elders reverently paves the way for civic obedience.

The observation and advice in this passage *best* express the teachings of

A Buddhism.

B Confucianism.

C Daoism.

D Legalism.

2 Which feature of China's physical geography did *not* separate its early people from the rest of the world?

A the Gobi

B the Huang-He

C the Pacific Ocean

D the Tibetan Plateau

3 How did the Qin emperor Shi Huangdi unify and control China in the 200s BC?

A He created districts and counties that were governed by appointed officials.

B He gave land to China's nobles so that they would be loyal to him.

C He dissolved the army so that it could not be used against him by his enemies.

D He established the Silk Road to get goods from far away.

4 Which of the following developments in China is an example of diffusion?

A the growth of manufacturing and trade

B the building of the Great Wall

C the spread of Buddhism from India

D the use of inventions to improve farming

5 Which dynasty's rulers created a government based on the ideas of Confucius?

A the Shang dynasty

B the Zhou dynasty

C the Qin dynasty

D the Han dynasty

Connecting with Past Learnings

6 In your studies of ancient India, you learned about the Hindu belief in rebirth. Which belief system that influenced early China also emphasized rebirth?

A Buddhism

B Confucianism

C Daoism

D Legalism

7 What characteristic did early civilization in Mesopotamia share with early civilization in China?

A Both developed paper.

B Both were influenced by Buddhism.

C Both built ziggurats.

D Both first developed in river valleys.

Answers

1. B
Break Down the Question Students should recall that Confucianism stressed respect and obedience for family and for authority.

2. B
Break Down the Question Students should recall that the Huang He was a river in the heart of China, and would not have separated China from the rest of the world.

3. A
Break Down the Question This question requires students to recall factual information from Section 3.

4. C
Break Down the Question This question requires students to recall factual information from Section 5.

5. D
Break Down the Question Students should remember that the Han was the first dynasty to use Confucianism as a basis for government policy.

6. A
Break Down the Question This question requires students to recall factual information from Section 5.

7. D
Break Down the Question This question requires students to recall factual information from Chapter 3.

Standards Review

Have students review the following standards in their workbooks.

HSS California Standards Review Workbook: 6.6.1, 6.6.2, 6.6.3, 6.6.4, 6.6.5, 6.6.6, 6.6.7, 6.6.8

Intervention Resources

Reproducible

Interactive Reader and Study Guide

Universal Access Teacher Management System: Universal Access Lesson Plans

Technology

Quick Facts Transparency: Ancient China Visual Summary

Universal Access Modfied Worksheets and Tests CD-ROM

Interactive Skills Tutor CD-ROM

Tips for Test Taking

I'm Done! Offer these test-taking tips to students: You aren't finished with your test until you check it. First, take a look at how much time you have left. Go back and review your answers for any careless mistakes you may have made. Be sure to erase any stray marks, review the hardest questions you answered, and turn the test in at the end of the time period. There is nothing to be gained from finishing first—or last either for that matter!

Why Things Happen

Bellringer

Motivate Explain to students that in some instances there is more than one reason why something happened. Encourage students to give examples of familiar events that often have more than one cause (running late for school, for example, or losing a football game). Tell students that they are going to write an essay that explains all the reasons why an event or situation occurred.

Collecting Information

Using Key Words Tell students that they can make their research simpler by narrowing their search to specific key words. Have students work as a class to develop a list of key words they can use to guide their research on the Internet or in a library card catalogue. Help students create a list of key words for each of the topic choices for their essays.

Evaluating Sources

Check It Out Tell students that they can often determine the validity of an Internet source by skimming a page or two on the site. Students should avoid using Web sites that contain several misspellings, grammatical errors, or unsupported opinions.

Assignment

Write an expository essay explaining one of these topics:

- Why the Aryans developed the caste system
- Why Confucius is considered the most influential teacher in Chinese history

TIP **Organizing Information**

Essays that explain why should be written in a logical order. Consider using one of these:

- **Chronological order,** the order in which things happened
- **Order of importance,** the order of the least important reason to the most important, or vice versa.

ELA **Writing 6.2.2** Write expository compositions (for example, description, explanation, comparison and contrast, problem and solution).

Why do civilizations so often develop in river valleys? Why did early people migrate across continents? You learn about the forces that drive history when you ask why things happened. Then you can share what you learned by writing an expository essay, explaining why events turned out as they did.

1. Prewrite

Considering Topic and Audience

Choose one of the two topics in the assignment, and then start to think about your big idea. Your big-idea statement might start out like this:

- The Aryans developed the caste system to . . .
- Confucius is considered the most influential teacher in Chinese history because he . . .

Collecting and Organizing Information

You will need to collect information that answers the question *Why*. To begin, review the information in this unit of your textbook. You can find more information on your topic in the library or on the Internet.

You should not stop searching for information until you have at least two or three answers to the question *Why*. These answers will form the points to support your big idea. Then take another look at your big idea. You may need to revise it or add to it to reflect the information you have gathered.

2. Write

Here is a framework that can help you write your first draft.

A Writer's Framework

Introduction	Body	Conclusion
- Start with an interesting fact or question. - Identify your big idea. - Include any important background information.	- Include at least one paragraph for each point supporting your big idea. - Include facts and details to explain and illustrate each point. - Use chronological order or order of importance.	- Summarize your main points. - Using different words, restate your big idea.

218 UNIT 3

Differentiating Instruction for Universal Access

Special Education Students   **Reaching Standards**

Guided Writing Have an aide work with students to explain one of the topics. The aide should read aloud the relevant information from the textbook as well as information from other available sources. Students should then create a research question and answer it with the aide's help. **LS** **Auditory/Musical, Verbal/Linguistic**

HSS Analysis Skills: HR 1; **ELA** Writing 6.2.2

Advanced Learners/GATE   **Exceeding Standards**

Precise Writing Have partners exchange essays and review them for any irrelevant, incidental, or unverifiable information. In addition, students should edit the essays to make the writing clear and active by removing wordiness and passive voice, adding transitions, and breaking or combining sentences. **LS** **Interpersonal, Verbal/Linguistic**

HSS Analysis Skills: HR 3; **ELA** Writing 6.1.6

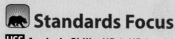

Standards Focus

HSS Analysis Skills: HR 1, HR 3
ELA Writing 6.1.1, 6.1.6, 6.2.2

3. Evaluate and Revise

Evaluating

Effective explanations require clear, straightforward language. Use the following questions to discover ways to improve your draft.

Evaluation Questions for an Expository Essay

- Does your essay begin with an interesting fact or question?
- Does the introduction identify your big idea?
- Have you developed at least one paragraph to explain each point?
- Is each point supported with facts and details?
- Have you organized your points clearly and logically?
- Did you explain any unusual words?
- Does the conclusion summarize your main points?
- Does the conclusion restate your big idea in different words?

Revising

Reread your draft. See whether each point is connected logically to the main idea and the other points you are making. If needed, add transitions—words and phrases that show how ideas fit together.

To connect points and information in time, use words like *after, before, first, later, soon, eventually, over time, as time passed,* and *then.* To show order of importance, use transitional words and phrases like *first, last, mainly, to begin with,* and *more important.*

4. Proofread and Publish

Proofreading

If you create a bulleted or numbered list, be sure to capitalize and punctuate the list correctly.

- **Capitalization:** It is always acceptable to capitalize the first word of each item in the list.
- **Punctuation:** (1) If the items are sentences, put a period at the end of each. (See the list in the tip above.) (2) If the items are not complete sentences, you usually do not need any end punctuation.

Publishing

Share your explanation with students from another class. After they read it, ask them to summarize your explanation. How well did they undertand the points you wanted to make?

Practice and Apply

Use the steps and strategies in this workshop to write your explanation.

TIP **Using Lists** To make an explanation easier to follow, look for information that can be presented in a list.

Sentence/Paragraph Form Confucius gave the Chinese people guidelines for behavior. He felt that fathers should display high moral values, and he thought it was important that women obey their husbands. Children were to be obedient and respectful.

List Form

Confucius gave the Chinese people guidelines for behavior:

- Fathers should display high moral values.
- Wives should obey their husbands.
- Children should obey and respect their parents.

Adding Transitions

Link It Up **Standard English Mastery**

Have students practice using transitions. Have each student write a paragraph explaining why they like something or someone. Tell students to include at least three of the transitions listed at left. Ask volunteers to share their use of transitions. Remind students how to use commas to punctuate their transitions correctly. Explain that transitions are not conjunctions; therefore, different rules of punctuation apply.

Teaching Tip

Learn from the Past Ask students to make a list of common errors that they have made in their past papers. Tell students to refer to this list of "problem" items when they proofread their essays.

Practice & Apply

Rubric

Students' expository essays should

- clearly identify the big idea.
- provide at least one paragraph to explain each supporting point.
- provide facts and details to support and illustrate each point.
- follow chronological order or order of importance.
- conclude with a summary and a restatement of the big idea.
- use correct grammar, punctuation, spelling, and capitalization.

English-Language Learners

Standards Proficiency
Standard English Mastery

Using Compound Sentences Encourage English learners to use compound sentences in their essays. Provide students with guided practice by having them combine the following sentences.

- Fathers should display high values. Children should obey their parents.

If needed, provide additional guided practice.

LS **Verbal/Linguistic**
ELA Writing 6.1.1

Learners Having Difficulty

Reaching Standards

Using Lists Some students might need additional practice making lists. (See Tip above.) Write the bulleted list in the Quick Facts: Main Ideas of Confucianism on p. 192 in narrative form for students to see. Have students work as a class to break the text into a bulleted list. During the activity, give students guidelines to help them identify when to present information in list form to improve clarity. **LS** **Verbal/Linguistic**
ELA Writing 6.1.1

Introduce the Unit

Share the information in the chapter overviews with students.

Chapter 8 The Hebrew people appeared in Southwest Asia sometime between 2000 and 1500 BC. The Hebrews eventually established a kingdom called Israel. The lives of the Hebrews were dominated by their religion, Judaism. In time, the Hebrews became known as Jews. Conquered by different groups, Jews scattered around the world. Their shared beliefs and customs helped them maintain their religion and sense of identity, however.

Chapter 9 The geography of Greece shaped life there. Greece is a mountainous land surrounded by water. Travel across the mountains was difficult. As a result, Greeks turned to the sea for trade. They also developed independent city-states. The city-state became the foundation of Greek civilization. The ancient Greeks made lasting contributions. They created the first democracy as well as myths and works of literature that still influence life today.

Chapter 10 The powerful Greek city-states of Athens and Sparta were very different. They joined forces to defeat a Persian invasion, but later became enemies and went to war. The Spartans defeated the Athenians in 404 BC. Lack of unity among the city-states then *(continued on p. 221)*

Standards Focus

For a list of the overarching standards covered in this unit, see the first page of each chapter.

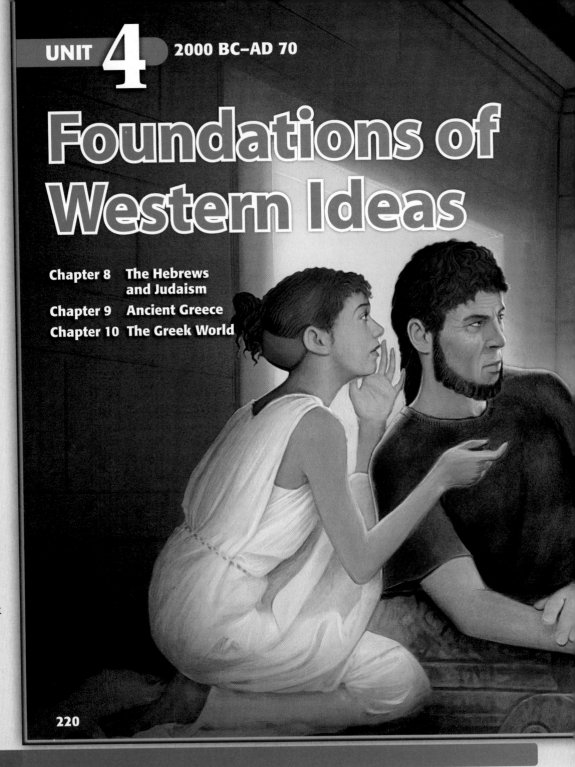

Foundations of Western Ideas

Chapter 8   The Hebrews and Judaism

Chapter 9   Ancient Greece

Chapter 10   The Greek World

220

Unit Resources

Planning

- Universal Access Teacher Management System: Unit Instructional Benchmarking Guides
- One-Stop Planner CD-ROM with Test Generator: Holt Calendar Planner
- Power Presentations with Video CD-ROM
- A Teacher's Guide to Religion in the Public Schools

Standards Mastery

- Standards Review Workbook
- At Home: A Guide to Standards Mastery for World History

Differentiating Instruction

- Universal Access Teacher Management System: Lesson Plans for Universal Access
- Universal Access Modified Worksheets and Tests CD-ROM

Enrichment

- CRF 9: Economics and History: Imports and Exports
- CRF 10: Economics and History: The Importance of Trade
- CRF 10: Interdisciplinary Project: Spartans Versus Athenians Debate; Contributions of Early Greeks
- Civic Participation

Assessment

- Progress Assessment Support System: Benchmark Test
- OSP ExamView Test Generator: Benchmark Test
- Holt Online Assessment Program (in the Premier Online Edition)
- Alternative Assessment Handbook

The **Universal Access Teacher Management System** provides a planning and instructional benchmarking guide for this unit.

The foundations of Western civilization can be traced back more than 2,000 years to the eastern Mediterranean region. There, the ancient Hebrews and Greeks developed many of the ideas and traditions that have shaped the world today.

The Hebrews' religion, Judaism, was based on a belief in one god and basic ideas about right and wrong. The ancient Greeks created the world's first democracy. The Greeks also revolutionized science and mathematics and created some of the world's most famous art and literature.

In the next three chapters, you will learn how the Hebrews and Greeks helped shape the world you live in today.

Explore the Art

In this scene, the daughter of a Greek king warns her father not to trust a general who needs help in a war. What does this scene show about life in ancient Greece?

221

Unit Preview

Unit Overview *continued*

helped Macedonia conquer Greece in the 300s BC. Macedonian Alexander the Great built a large empire across much of Europe, Asia, and Egypt. The ancient Greeks' lasting contributions include achievements in the arts, philosophy, and science.

Connect to the Unit

Activity **Landmarks of the Ancient World** Ask students to identify some of the well-known landmarks they have learned about so far (e.g., the Great Pyramid of Khufu). Ask students if they have heard of the Seven Wonders of the Ancient World. Point out that this list included both the Great Pyramid of Khufu and the Hanging Gardens of Babylon. Explain that the Greeks, whom students will learn about in this unit, built most of the other Seven Wonders of the Ancient World.

Tell students that they are going to create a large mural titled "Landmarks of the Ancient World." Have students conduct research on the Seven Wonders of the Ancient World as well as on other landmarks of the civilizations they have studied so far and the ones in this unit. Have students draw or place images of these landmarks on a large piece of butcher paper. For each landmark, students should provide a caption.
LS Interpersonal, Visual/Spatial

Explore the Art

The scene at left shows the young girl Gorgo offering advice to her father, the Spartan king Cleomenes. The general was trying to bribe her father to convince him to help. Gorgo told her father, "Go away, or the stranger will corrupt you." Cleomenes took her advice.

About the Illustration

This illustration is an artist's conception based on available sources. However, historians are uncertain exactly what this scene looked like.

Democracy and Civic Education

Standards **Proficiency**

Authority: Democracy

Research Required

Background Ancient Greece is the birthplace of democracy. Greek views about democracy have had a major impact on Western political thought.

1. Have students work in small groups to conduct research on Athenian democracy and U.S. representative democracy. Where do officials get their authority to make and enforce laws? In what ways is government in the United States by the people? What power do citizens have to influence lawmakers and the political process?

2. Have each group create a skit that explains what democracy is, the Greek origins of democracy, and the form of democracy that we have in the United States.

3. Groups should assign members specific tasks or roles to share the work and to ensure that everyone participates.
LS Interpersonal, Kinesthetic

📓 Alternative Assessment Handbook, Rubrics 14: Group Activity; and 33: Skits and Reader's Theater
📓 Civic Participation

Answers

Explore the Art *shows clothing styles, architecture, and that there were kings and warfare*

221

The Hebrews and Judaism

MASTERING THE CALIFORNIA STANDARDS

Chapter Overview	Reproducible Resources	Technology Resources

CHAPTER 8
pp. 222–49

Overview: In this chapter, students will learn about the history, religion, and culture of the Jewish people.

 See p. 222 for the California History–Social Science standards covered in this chapter.

 **Universal Access Teacher Management System:***
- Universal Access Instructional Benchmarking Guides
- Lesson Plans for Universal Access

 **Interactive Reader and Study Guide:** Chapter Graphic Organizer*

Chapter Resource File*
- Chapter Review Activity
- Focus on Writing Activity: A Web Site
- Social Studies Skills Activity: Identifying Short- and Long-Term Effects

 One-Stop Planner CD-ROM: Calendar Planner

Student Edition on Audio CD-ROM

Universal Access Modified Worksheets and Tests CD-ROM

Interactive Skills Tutor CD-ROM

Primary Source Library CD-ROM for World History

Power Presentations with Video CD-ROM

History's Impact: World History Video Program (VHS/DVD): The Hebrews and Judaism*

A Teacher's Guide to Religion in the Public Schools*

Section 1:

The Early Hebrews

The Big Idea: Originally desert nomads, the Hebrews established a great kingdom called Israel.

 6.3.3, 6.3.4

 Universal Access Teacher Management System: Section 1 Lesson Plan*

Interactive Reader and Study Guide: Section 1 Summary*

 Chapter Resource File*
- Vocabulary Builder Activity, Section 1
- Biography Activity: Esther
- Biography Activity: Isaac and Ishmael
- Biography Activity: King Solomon

 Daily Bellringer Transparency: Section 1*

Map Transparency: Possible Routes of Abraham and Moses*

Map Transparency: Kingdoms of Israel and Judah, c. 920 BC*

 Internet Activity: Connections to Today

Section 2:

Jewish Beliefs and Texts

The Big Idea: The central ideas and laws of Judaism are contained in sacred texts such as the Torah.

 6.3.1, 6.3.2

 Universal Access Teacher Management System:*
Section 2 Lesson Plan

Interactive Reader and Study Guide: Section 2 Summary*

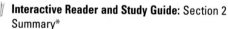 **Chapter Resource File***
- Vocabulary Builder Activity, Section 2
- Literature Activity: "The Creation Story," from the Torah
- Primary Source Activity: Excerpts from the Book of Exodus

 Daily Bellringer Transparency: Section 2*

Section 3:

Judaism over the Centuries

The Big Idea: Although they were forced out of Israel by the Romans, shared beliefs and customs helped Jews maintain their religion.

 6.2.7

 Universal Access Teacher Management System:*
Section 3 Lesson Plan

 Interactive Reader and Study Guide: Section 3 Summary*

 Chapter Resource File*
- Vocabulary Builder Activity, Section 3
- History and Geography Activity: Jewish Migration After AD 70

 Daily Bellringer Transparency: Section 3*

Map Transparency: Jewish Migration after AD 70*

 Internet Activity: Jewish Holy Days

SE Student Edition	Print Resource	Audio CD
TE Teacher's Edition	Transparency	CD-ROM
go.hrw.com	CA Standards Mastery	**LS** Learning Styles
OSP One-Stop Planner CD-ROM	* also on One-Stop Planner CD	

SE Student Edition **Print Resource Audio CD Video**
TE Teacher's Edition Transparency CD-ROM DVD
go.hrw.com CA Standards Mastery **LS** Learning Styles
OSP One-Stop Planner CD-ROM * also on One-Stop Planner CD

Review, Assessment, Intervention

 Standards Review Workbook*

 Quick Facts Transparency: The Hebrews and Judaism Visual Summary

 Spanish Chapter Summaries Audio CD Program

 Online Chapter Summaries in Six Languages

 Quiz Game CD-ROM

 Progress Assessment Support System (PASS): Chapter Test*

 Universal Access Modified Worksheets and Tests CD-ROM: Modified Chapter Test

One-Stop Planner CD-ROM: ExamView Test Generator (English/Spanish)

Alternative Assessment Handbook

Holt Online Assessment Program (HOAP), in the Holt Premier Online Student Edition

---

 PASS: Section 1 Quiz*

 Online Quiz: Section 1

Alternative Assessment Handbook

 PASS: Section 2 Quiz*

 Online Quiz: Section 2

Alternative Assessment Handbook

 PASS: Section 3 Quiz*

 Online Quiz: Section 3

Alternative Assessment Handbook

California Resources for Standards Mastery

INSTRUCTIONAL PLANNING AND SUPPORT

Universal Access Teacher Management System*

One-Stop Planner CD-ROM with Test Generator: Teacher Management System with Interactive Teacher's Edition

STANDARDS MASTERY

Standards Review Workbook*

At Home: A Guide to Standards Mastery for World History

 Holt Online Learning

To enhance learning, the following Internet activities are available: **Connections to Today** and **Jewish Holy Days.**

KEYWORD: SQ6 TEACHER

- Teacher Support Page
- Content Updates
- Rubrics and Writing Models

- Teaching Tips for the Multimedia Classroom

KEYWORD: SQ6 WH8

- Current Events
- Holt Grapher
- Holt Online Atlas
- Holt Researcher
- Interactive Multimedia Activities

- Internet Activities
- Online Chapter Summaries in Six Languages
- Online Section Quizzes
- World History Maps and Charts

HOLT PREMIER ONLINE STUDENT EDITION

Complete online support for interactivity, assessment, and reporting

- Interactive Maps and Notebook
- Standardized Test Prep
- Homework Practice and Research Activities Online

Mastering the Standards: Differentiating Instruction

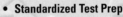

Reaching Standards	Basic-level activities designed for all students encountering new material
Standards Proficiency	Intermediate-level activities designed for average students
Exceeding Standards	Challenging activities designed for honors and gifted-and-talented students
Standard English Mastery	Activities designed to improve standard English usage

MASTERING THE CALIFORNIA STANDARDS

Frequently Asked Questions

INSTRUCTIONAL PLANNING AND SUPPORT

Where do I find planning aids, instructional benchmarking guides, lesson plans, and other teaching aids?

Annotated Teacher's Edition:
- Chapter planning guides
- Standards-based instruction and strategies
- Differentiated instruction for universal access
- Point-of-use reminders for integrating program resources

Power Presentations with Video CD-ROM

Universal Access Teacher Management System:
- Year and unit instructional benchmarking guides
- Reproducible lesson plans
- Assessment guides for diagnostic, progress, and summative end-of-the-year tests
- Options for differentiating instruction and intervention
- Teaching guides and answer keys for student workbooks

One-Stop Planner CD-ROM with Test Generator: Teacher Management System with Interactive Teacher's Edition:
- Calendar Planner
- Editable lesson plans
- All reproducible ancillaries in Adobe Acrobat (PDF) format
- ExamView Test Generator (English & Spanish)
- Game Tool for ExamView
- PuzzlePro
- Transparency and video previews

DIFFERENTIATING INSTRUCTION FOR UNIVERSAL ACCESS

What resources are available to ensure that Advanced Learners/GATE students master the standards?

Teacher's Edition Activities:
- Analyzing the Influence of Sacred Texts: The Torah, p. 238
- "Judaism over Time" Storyboards, p. 244

Lesson Plans for Universal Access

Primary Source Library CD-ROM for World History

What resources are available to ensure that English Learners and Standard English Learners master the standards?

Teacher's Edition Activities:
- Vocabulary for the Ten Commandments, p. 228
- Word Mapping, p. 235

Lesson Plans for Universal Access

Chapter Resource File: Vocabulary Builder Activities

Spanish Chapter Summaries Audio CD Program

Online Chapter Summaries in Six Languages

One-Stop Planner CD-ROM:
- PuzzlePro, Spanish Version
- ExamView Test Generator, Spanish Version

What modified materials are available for Special Education?

The *Universal Access Modified Worksheets and Tests CD-ROM* provides editable versions of the following:

Vocabulary Flash Cards

Modified Vocabulary Builder Activities

Modified Chapter Review Activity

Modified Chapter Test

What resources are available to ensure that Learners Having Difficulty master the standards?

Teacher's Edition Activities:
- Central Beliefs of Judaism Poster, p. 233
- Deciphering and Paraphrasing, p. 238
- Connecting to the Big Idea, p. 244

Interactive Reader and Study Guide

Student Edition on Audio CD Program

Quick Facts Transparency: The Hebrews and Judaism Visual Summary

Standards Review Workbook

Social Studies Skills Activity: Identifying Short- and Long-Term Effects

Interactive Skills Tutor CD-ROM

How do I intervene for students struggling to master the standards?

Interactive Reader and Study Guide

Quick Facts Transparency: The Hebrews and Judaism Visual Summary

Standards Review Workbook

Social Studies Skills Activity: Identifying Short- and Long-Term Effects

Interactive Skills Tutor CD-ROM

HOLT
Professional Development

PROFESSIONAL DEVELOPMENT

What teacher training resources are available to help me grow professionally?

- In-service and staff development as part of your Holt Social Studies product purchase
- Quick Teacher Tutorial Lesson Presentation CD-ROM
- Intensive tuition-based Teacher Development Institute
- Convenient Holt Speaker Bureau face-to-face workshop options

- PRAXIS™ Test Prep (#0089) interactive Web-based content refreshers*
- *Ask A Professional Development Expert* at http://www.hrw.com/prodev/

* PRAXIS is a trademark of Educational Testing Service (ETS). This publication is not endorsed or approved by ETS.

Information Literacy Skills

To learn more about how History–Social Science instruction may be improved by the effective use of library media centers and information literacy skills, go to the Teacher's Resource Materials for Chapter 8 at **go.hrw.com, keyword: SQ6 MEDIA.**

MASTERING THE CALIFORNIA STANDARDS

Standards Focus

Standards by Section
Section 1: **HSS** 6.3.3, 6.3.4
Section 2: **HSS** 6.3.1, 6.3.2
Section 3: **HSS** 6.3.5

Teacher's Edition
HSS Analysis Skills: CS 1, CS 2, CS 3, HR 2, HR 3, HI 1, HI 2

ELA Reading 6.2.7, 6.3.6

Visual Arts Creative Expression 6.2.5

Upcoming Standards for Future Learning
Preview the following History–Social Science content standards from upcoming chapters or grade levels to promote learning beyond the current chapter.

HSS **6.7** Students analyze the geographic, political, economic, religious, and social structures during the development of Rome.

6.7.5 Trace the migration of Jews around the Mediterranean region and the effects of their conflict with the Romans, including the Romans' restrictions on their right to live in Jerusalem.

Focus on Writing

The **Chapter Resource File** provides a Focus on Writing worksheet to help students organize and describe their Web sites.

📝 **CRF:** Focus on Writing Activity: A Web Site

CHAPTER 8   2000 BC–AD 70

The Hebrews and Judaism

 California Standards

History-Social Science
6.3 Students analyze the geographic, political, economic, religious, and social structures of the Ancient Hebrews.

Analysis Skills
HI 2 Students understand and distinguish cause, effect, sequence, and correlation in historical events, including the long- and short-term causal relations.

HR 2 Students distinguish fact from opinion in historical narratives and stories.

English-Language Arts
Writing 6.1.3 Use a variety of effective and coherent organizational patterns.

Reading 6.2.0 Read and understand grade-level-appropriate material.

FOCUS ON WRITING ✎

A Web Site Have you ever designed your own Web site? If not, here's your chance to create one. As you read this chapter, you'll gather information about Hebrew history, beliefs, values, and culture. Then you will write a description of how you would present this same information on a Web site.

CHAPTER EVENTS	**c. 2000 BC** Abraham leaves Mesopotamia.
	2000 BC
WORLD EVENTS	**c. 1750 BC** Hammurabi issues his law code.

Introduce the Chapter

Standards Proficiency

Focus on the Hebrews and Israel

1. Write the following terms for students to see: *Hebrews, Israelites,* and *Jews.* Have students identify what the terms have in common. Help students understand that the terms all refer to the same people but at different times or locations.

2. Have students share anything they already know about the ancient Hebrews, such as the stories of Noah and the Ark; of Abraham, Isaac, and Jacob; or of Moses and the Ten Commandments. Point out any incorrect information. Then identify for students the location of modern-day Israel on a political map of the Middle East.

3. Close by asking students why they think it is important to learn about ancient Hebrew history. Help students understand that the history of the Hebrews and other groups in the Middle East continues to shape the region today. **LS** **Verbal/Linguistic**

What You Will Learn...

In this chapter you will study the history and culture of the Jewish people. In this photo, hundreds of people pray at the Western Wall, the holiest site in the world of Judaism. The wall is about 2,000 years old.

c. 1200 BC
Moses leads the Hebrews out of Egypt during the Exodus.

586 BC
The Jews are enslaved in Babylon.

AD 70
The Romans destroy the Second Temple in Jerusalem.

1475 BC

950 BC

425 BC

AD 100

c. 1240–1224 BC
Ramses the Great rules Egypt.

c. 563 BC
The Buddha is born in India.

27 BC
Augustus becomes the first Roman emperor.

THE HEBREWS AND JUDAISM **223**

● **Chapter Preview** ●

HOLT
History's Impact
► video series
See the Video Teacher's Guide for strategies for using the chapter video **The Hebrews and Judaism: The Impact of Judaism throughout the World.**

Chapter Big Ideas

Section 1 Originally desert nomads, the Hebrews established a great kingdom called Israel. HSS 6.3.3, 6.3.4

Section 2 The central ideas and laws of Judaism are contained in sacred texts such as the Torah. HSS 6.3.1, 6.3.2

Section 3 Although they were forced out of Israel by the Romans, shared beliefs and customs helped Jews maintain their religion. HSS 6.3.5

Explore the Picture

The Western Wall The Western Wall is all that is left of the Second Temple, the holiest site in ancient Israel. Today Jews come from around the world to pray at the Wall. One Jewish custom is to place small written prayers in the cracks between the Wall's stones.

Analyzing Visuals What can you learn about the religion of Judaism from the picture? *possible answers—that Judaism is an old religion, that holy sites and prayer are important parts of the religion, and that some followers of Judaism wear special articles of clothing*

Explore the Time Line

1. When did the Exodus occur? *c. 1200 BC*

2. Who destroyed the Second Temple in Jerusalem, and when? *the Romans; AD 70*

3. How long after the Hebrews were enslaved in Babylon was the Buddha born in India? *about 23 years*

HSS **Analysis Skills:** CS 1

Info to Know

The Second Temple After the Romans destroyed the Second Temple in AD 70, they deliberately did not clear away the ruins of the building. The Romans left the ruins in place as a symbol of the Roman Empire's power.

Reading Social Studies

by Kylene Beers

| Economics | Geography | Politics | **Religion** | Society and Culture | Science and Technology |

Focus on Themes In this chapter, you will read about the Hebrew people and the religion called Judaism. You will learn about Jewish beliefs, texts such as the Torah and the Dead Sea Scrolls, and leaders such as Abraham and Moses.

As you read, pay close attention to how the Hebrews' beliefs affected where and how they lived. In the process, you will discover that the lives of the early Hebrews were dominated by their **religious** beliefs and practices.

Understanding Themes

The theme of this chapter is religion. Tell the students that in this chapter they will learn how the Hebrew people lived under a code of moral laws. Ask students to explain the purpose that laws serve in our society today. Then ask students how a government's laws might differ from moral or religious laws. Tell them that the Hebrews' beliefs have influenced Western cultures and that some of their beliefs are reflected in our laws.

Facts, Opinions, and the Past

Focus on Reading Ask each student to write down two facts and two opinions about activities or clubs at their school or in the community. Collect the papers and share some of these facts and opinions with the class. Ask class members to decide if a particular sentence represents a fact or an opinion. Discuss how to test if a statement is factual by asking: Is there evidence available to prove or disprove this? Remind students that facts can be verified by using reliable sources.

Facts, Opinions, and the Past

Focus on Reading Why is it important to know the difference between a fact and an opinion? Separating facts from opinions about historical events helps you know what really happened.

Identifying Facts and Opinions Something is a **fact** if there is a way to prove it or disprove it. For example, research can prove or disprove the following statement: "The ancient Jews recorded their laws." But research can't prove the following statement because it is just an **opinion**, or someone's belief: "Everyone should read the records of the ancient Jews."

Additional reading support can be found in the

Inter*active

Reader and Study Guide

Use the process below to decide whether a statement is fact or opinion.

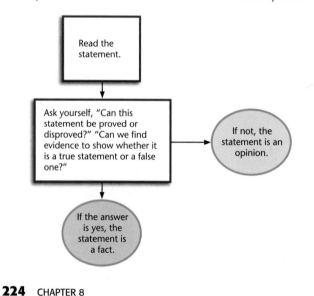

Read the statement.

Ask yourself, "Can this statement be proved or disproved?" "Can we find evidence to show whether it is a true statement or a false one?"

If not, the statement is an opinion.

If the answer is yes, the statement is a fact.

224 CHAPTER 8

Reading and Skills Resources

Reading Support

- Interactive Reader and Study Guide
- Student Edition on Audio CD
- Spanish Chapter Summaries Audio CD Program

Social Studies Skills Support

- Interactive Skills Tutor CD-ROM

Vocabulary Support

- **CRF:** Vocabulary Builder Activities
- **CRF:** Chapter Review Activity
- Universal Access Modified Worksheets and Tests CD-ROM:
  - Vocabulary Flash Cards
  - Vocabulary Builder Activity
  - Chapter Review Activity

OSP Holt PuzzlePro

Standards Focus

HSS Analysis Skills: HR 2
ELA Reading 6.2.0

HSS **Analysis HR 2** Distinguish fact from opinion
ELA **Reading 6.2.0** Read and understand grade-level-appropriate material.

You Try It!

The following passage tells about boys who, years ago, found what came to be called the Dead Sea Scrolls. All the statements in this passage are facts. What makes them facts and not opinions?

Scrolls Reveal Past Beliefs

Until 1947 no one knew about the Dead Sea Scrolls. In that year, young boys looking for a lost goat near the Dead Sea found a small cave. One of the boys went in to explore and found several old jars filled with moldy scrolls.

From Chapter 8, pages 236–237

Scholars were very excited about the boy's find. Eager to find more scrolls, they began to search the desert. Over the next few decades, searchers found several more groups of scrolls.

Careful study revealed that most of the Dead Sea Scrolls were written between 100 BC and AD 50. The scrolls included prayers, commentaries, letters, and passages from the Hebrew Bible. These writings help historians learn about the lives of many Jews during this time.

Identify each of the following as a fact or an opinion and then explain your choice.

1. Boys discovered the Dead Sea Scrolls in 1947.

2. The discovery of the scrolls is one of the most important discoveries ever.

3. All religious leaders should study the Dead Sea Scrolls.

4. The Dead Sea Scrolls were written between 100 BC and AD 50.

Key Terms and People

Chapter 8

Section 1
Abraham *(p. 226)*
Moses *(p. 227)*
Exodus *(p. 227)*
Ten Commandments *(p. 228)*
David *(p. 229)*
Solomon *(p. 229)*
Diaspora *(p. 230)*

Section 2
Judaism *(p. 232)*
monotheism *(p. 232)*
Torah *(p. 234)*
synagogue *(p. 234)*
prophets *(p. 235)*
Talmud *(p. 236)*
Dead Sea Scrolls *(p. 236)*

Section 3
Zealots *(p. 240)*
rabbis *(p. 242)*
Passover *(p. 245)*
High Holy Days *(p. 245)*

Academic Vocabulary

Success in school is related to knowing academic vocabulary—the words that are frequently used in school assignments and discussions. In this chapter, you will learn the following academic word:

principles *(p. 234)*

As you read Chapter 8, look for clues that will help you determine which statements are facts.

Reading Social Studies

Key Terms and People

Read the terms and people to students. Then ask students to choose five terms with which they are unfamiliar. Have students define the terms they selected. Then have each student create a cross-word puzzle using the definitions he or she wrote as clues. If time permits, have students exchange their puzzles with a partner and complete the other person's crossword. Then have students check their answers.

LS Verbal/Linguistic, Visual/Spatial

Focus on Reading

See the **Focus on Reading** questions in this chapter for more practice on this reading social studies skill.

Reading Social Studies Assessment

See the **Standards Review** at the end of this chapter for student assessment questions related to this reading skill.

THE HEBREWS AND JUDAISM **225**

Teaching Tip

Help students who may have difficulty differentiating fact and opinion by instructing them to look for signal words. Oftentimes statements that are facts include phrases like *evidence shows* or gives specific facts or dates. Remind students that opinion statements use phrases like *in my view*, *people believe*, or *should*. Encourage students to circle or underline signal words to determine whether a statement is fact or opinion.

Answers

You Try It! 1. *fact; it is supported in the passage;* **2.** *opinion; that cannot be proved;* **3.** *opinion; there is no evidence to support this;* **4.** *fact; information in the passage supports this*

Bellringer

If YOU were there . . . Use the **Daily Bellringer Transparency** to help students answer the question.

🖱 Daily Bellringer Transparency, Section 1

| The Hebrews and Judaism | Daily Bellringer |
| | Section 1 |

Review the Previous Chapter

Match the sets of letters on the right to the correct vocabulary term on the left.

1. H _ _ _ G HE   CIU
2. _ _ _ U DYNASTY   DHI
3. CONFU _ _ _ S   GDI
4. SHI HUAN _ _ _   UAN
5. BUD _ _ _ SM   ZHO

Preview Section 1

If YOU were there . . .
You are your family are herders, looking after large flocks of sheep. Your grandfather, the leader of your tribe, is very rich, so your life is easy. One day, your grandfather says that your whole family will be moving to a new country. The trip will be very long, and people there may not welcome you.
How do you feel about moving to a faraway land?

Consider the POSITIVES:
• will be a new adventure
• will meet new people and see new sights
• may like your new home better

Consider the NEGATIVES:
• leaving friends and loved ones
• leaving familiar surroundings and places you like
• meeting unfriendly or hostile people

Review Answers: 1. UAN, Huang He; 2. ZHO, Zhou Dynasty; 3. CIU, Confucius; 4. GDI, Shi Huangdi; 5. DHI, Buddhism

---

Building Vocabulary

Preteach or review the following terms:

Hebrews A people who appeared in Southwest Asia sometime between 2000 and 1500 BC (p. 226)

pharaoh ruler of Egypt (p. 227)

plagues disasters (p. 227)

📝 CRF: Vocabulary Builder Activity, Section 1

🐻 Standards Focus

HSS 6.3.3
Means: Identify the importance of Abraham, Moses, Naomi, Ruth, David, and Yohanan ben Zaccai in Jewish religious history.
Matters: These individuals helped shape the Jewish religion, which millions of people follow today.

HSS 6.3.4
Means: Identify where the early Hebrews lived; describe their movements, including the Exodus; and explain the importance of the Exodus for Jews and others.
Matters: The early history of the Hebrews shaped the major religions of Judaism, Christianity, and Islam.

226   CHAPTER 8

The Early Hebrews

What You Will Learn...

Main Ideas

1. Abraham and Moses led the Hebrews to Canaan and to a new religion.
2. Strong kings united the Israelites to fight off invaders.
3. Invaders conquered and ruled the Hebrews after their kingdom broke apart.
4. Some women in Hebrew society made great contributions to their history.

The Big Idea

Originally desert nomads, the Hebrews established a great kingdom called Israel.

Key Terms and People

Abraham, *p. 226*
Moses, *p. 227*
Exodus, *p. 227*
Ten Commandments, *p. 228*
David, *p. 229*
Solomon, *p. 229*
Diaspora, *p. 230*

HSS 6.3.3 Explain the significance of Abraham, Moses, Naomi, Ruth, David, and Yohanan ben Zaccai in the development of the Jewish religion.

6.3.4 Discuss the locations of the settlements and movements of Hebrew peoples, including the Exodus and their movement to and from Egypt, and outline the significance of the Exodus to the Jewish and other people.

226   CHAPTER 8

If YOU were there...

You and your family are herders, looking after large flocks of sheep. Your grandfather, the leader of your tribe, is very rich, so your life is easy. One day, your grandfather says that your whole family will be moving to a new country. The trip will be very long, and people there may not welcome you.

How do you feel about moving to a faraway land?

BUILDING BACKGROUND Like the family described above, the early Hebrews moved to new lands several times. From the beginning, the Hebrews were wanderers. According to Hebrew tradition, their history began with a search for a new home.

Abraham and Moses Lead the Hebrews

Sometime between 2000 and 1500 BC a new people appeared in Southwest Asia. They were the Hebrews (HEE-brooz). The early Hebrews were simple herders, but they developed a culture that became a major influence on later civilizations.

Most of what is known about early Hebrew history comes from the work of archaeologists and from accounts written by Hebrew scribes. These accounts describe the Hebrews' early history and the laws of their religion. In time these accounts became the Hebrew Bible. The Hebrew Bible is also part of the Christian Bible, which includes the New Testament as well.

The Beginnings in Canaan and Egypt

The Hebrew Bible traces the Hebrews back to a man named **Abraham**. One day, the Hebrew Bible says, God told Abraham to leave his home in Mesopotamia. He was to take his family on a long journey to the west. God promised to lead Abraham to a new land and make his descendants into a mighty nation.

Teach the Big Idea: Master the Standards   Standards Proficiency

The Early Hebrews 🐻 HSS 6.3.3, 6.3.4; HSS Analysis Skills: HR 3, HI 1

1. **Teach** Ask students the Main Idea questions to teach this section.

2. **Apply** Have students write each of the blue heads in the section on a piece of paper. Tell students to leave space below each heading. Have students review the material under each heading and then write three to five main ideas under that heading on their papers. 📖 Verbal/Linguistic

3. **Review** To review the section, have volunteers share the main ideas that they wrote with the class. Then have students discuss the section's big idea.

4. **Practice/Homework** Have students write an imaginary interview with one of the key people in the section. The interviews should include at least five questions and answers. Provide students with sample questions. 📖 Verbal/Linguistic

📝 Alternative Assessment Handbook, Rubric 37: Writing Assignments

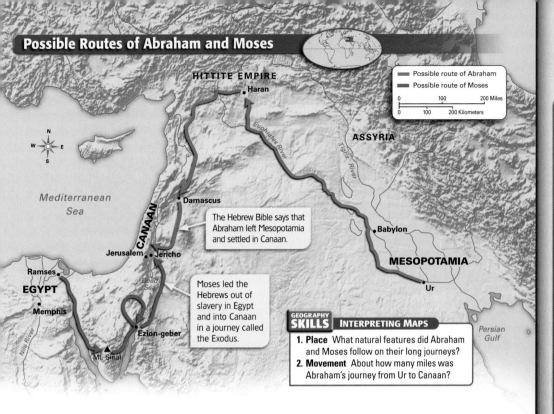

Possible Routes of Abraham and Moses

HITTITE EMPIRE

Haran

ASSYRIA

Euphrates River

Tigris River

Damascus

Babylon

MESOPOTAMIA

Ur

Mediterranean Sea

CANAAN

Jerusalem • Jericho

Dead Sea

Ramses

EGYPT

Memphis

Ezion-geber

Mt. Sinai

Nile River

Persian Gulf

The Hebrew Bible says that Abraham left Mesopotamia and settled in Canaan.

Moses led the Hebrews out of slavery in Egypt and into Canaan in a journey called the Exodus.

Possible route of Abraham
Possible route of Moses

0   100   200 Miles
0   100   200 Kilometers

GEOGRAPHY SKILLS INTERPRETING MAPS
1. **Place** What natural features did Abraham and Moses follow on their long journeys?
2. **Movement** About how many miles was Abraham's journey from Ur to Canaan?

Abraham left Mesopotamia and settled in Canaan (KAY-nuhn), on the Mediterranean Sea. His descendants—the Hebrews—lived in Canaan for many years. Later, however, some Hebrews moved to Egypt, perhaps because of famine in Canaan.

The Hebrews lived well in Egypt, and their population grew. This growth worried Egypt's ruler, the pharaoh. He feared that the Hebrews might soon take over Egypt. To stop this from happening, the pharaoh made the Hebrews slaves.

The Exodus

According to the Hebrew Bible, a leader named **Moses** appeared among the Hebrews in Egypt. In the 1200s BC, God told Moses to lead the Hebrews out of Egypt. Moses went to the pharaoh and demanded that

the Hebrews be freed. The pharaoh refused. Soon afterward a series of terrible plagues, or disasters, struck Egypt.

The plagues frightened the pharaoh so much that he agreed to free the Hebrews. Overjoyed with the news of their release, Moses led his people out of Egypt in a journey called the **Exodus**. To the Hebrews, the release from slavery proved that God was protecting and watching over them. They believed that they had been set free because God loved them.

The Exodus is a major event in Hebrew history, but other people recognize its significance as well. Throughout history, for example, enslaved people have found hope in the story. Before the Civil War, American slaves sang about Moses to keep their hopes of freedom alive.

THE HEBREWS AND JUDAISM **227**

Direct Teach

Main Idea

❶ Abraham and Moses Lead the Hebrews

Abraham and Moses led the Hebrews to Canaan and to a new religion.

Identify According to the Hebrew Bible, who was Abraham, and where did he move? *the man to whom the Hebrew Bible traces the Hebrews; Canaan*

Sequence Briefly trace the events that led to the Exodus. *According to the Hebrew Bible, in the 1200s BC, God told a Hebrew named Moses to demand that the pharaoh free the Hebrews enslaved in Egypt. After a series of plagues struck, the pharaoh agreed. Moses then led the Hebrews out of Egypt in the Exodus.*

📦 Map Transparency: Possible Routes of Abraham and Moses

🐻 **HSS** 6.3.3, 6.3.4; **HSS** Analysis Skills: CS 1, HI 1, HI 2

Interpreting Maps
Possible Routes of Abraham and Moses

Activity **Comparing Maps** Display a current wall map of the region in the map at left. Have students determine the modern countries in which the following cities in the textbook map are located: Babylon, Haran, Jerusalem, and Ur. **LS** Visual/Spatial

📦 Map Transparency: Possible Routes of Abraham and Moses

🐻 **HSS** 6.3.4; **HSS** Analysis Skills: CS 3

Critical Thinking: Comparing and Contrasting   **Standards Proficiency**

Abraham and Moses Venn Diagram 🐻 **HSS** 6.3.3

1. To help students compare and contrast the significance of Abraham and Moses in Jewish history and to the development of Judaism, draw the graphic organizer for students to see. Omit the blue, italicized answers.

2. Have students copy and complete the graphic organizer. Instruct students to refer to the part of the text titled "Abraham and Moses Lead the Hebrews" to complete the activity. **LS** Visual/Spatial

Abraham
• lived in Mesopotamia
• *told by God to move to Canaan*
• *received God's promise that his descendants would become a mighty nation*

• significant person in Hebrew history
• directed and spoken to by God
• led a major migration

Moses
• lived in Egypt
• *told by God to gain freedom of Hebrew slaves and lead them from Egypt*
• *received Ten Commandments from God on Mt. Sinai*

Answers

Interpreting Maps 1. *waterways, such as rivers and seas;* 2. *about 1,200 miles*

227

❶ Abraham and Moses Lead the Hebrews

Abraham and Moses led the Hebrews to Canaan and to a new religion.

Recall According to the Hebrew Bible, what code of moral laws did God give to Moses on Mt. Sinai? *the Ten Commandments*

Explain How did the Ten Commandments shape Hebrew life? *The Hebrews agreed to worship only God and to value human life, self-control, and justice.*

Draw Conclusions Why do you think Moses led the Hebrews to Canaan? *possible answers—Canaan was where Abraham had settled.*

(Activity) Paraphrasing Have students use modern-day language to paraphrase the Ten Commandments.
LS Verbal/Linguistic
HSS 6.3.3, 6.3.4

Reading Time Lines
Early Hebrew History

(Activity) Ask volunteers to use the entries and images in the time line to summarize the key events in the early history of the Hebrews. **LS** Verbal/Linguistic
HSS 6.3.3, 6.3.4; **HSS** Analysis Skills: CS 1

Answers
Reading Check *According to the Hebrew Bible, God told Abraham to leave and move to a new land—Canaan.*

For many years after their release, the Hebrews wandered through the desert, trying to return to Canaan. During their wanderings they reached a mountain called Sinai. On that mountain, the Hebrew Bible says, God gave Moses two stone tablets. On the tablets was written a code of moral laws known as the **Ten Commandments**:

> "I am God your Lord, who brought you out of Egypt, from the place of slavery.
> Do not have any other gods before Me.
> Do not take the name of God your Lord in vain. God will not allow the one who takes his name in vain to go unpunished.
> Remember the Sabbath to keep it holy.
> Honor your father and mother. You will then live long on the land that God your Lord is giving you.
> Do not commit murder.
> Do not commit adultery.
> Do not steal.
> Do not testify as a false witness against your neighbor.
> Do not be envious of your neighbor's house.
> Do not be envious of your neighbor's wife . . . or anything else that is your neighbor's."
>
> —Exodus 20:2–14, from *The Living Torah*

As you can see, by accepting the Ten Commandments, the Hebrews agreed to worship only God. They also agreed to value human life, self-control, and justice. Over time the commandments shaped the development of Hebrew society.

The Return to Canaan

According to the Hebrew Bible, the Hebrews wandered for 40 years before they reached Canaan. Once there, they had to fight to gain control of Canaan before they could settle. After they conquered Canaan and settled down, the Hebrews became known as the Israelites.

In Canaan, the Israelites lived in small, scattered communities. These communities had no central government. Instead, each community selected judges as leaders to enforce laws and settle disputes. Before long, though, a threat arose that called for a new kind of leadership.

READING CHECK Identifying Cause and Effect
Why did Abraham leave Mesopotamia?

Time Line

Early Hebrew History

c. 2000 BC Abraham leaves Mesopotamia and goes to Canaan.

1200s BC Moses leads the Hebrews on the Exodus out of slavery in Egypt.

2100 BC   1300 BC   1200 BC

228 CHAPTER 8

Differentiating Instruction for Universal Access

English-Language Learners   (Standards Proficiency)

Vocabulary for the Ten Commandments
To help English learners with the vocabulary in and associated with the Ten Commandments, preteach the following terms:

- **adultery** sexual relations between a married person and someone to whom he or she is not married
- **envious** wanting what someone else has
- **holy** sacred; set apart; spiritually perfect
- **Sabbath** day of rest and prayer

- **tablet** thick, flat piece of stone for engraving
- **testify** give evidence; tell to a court of law
- **vain** without purpose or meaning
- **witness** onlooker; observer

LS Verbal/Linguistic   **HSS** 6.3.4

Universal Access Resources
See p. 221c of the Chapter Planner for additional resources for differentiating instruction for universal access.

Kings Unite the Israelites

The new threat to the Israelites came from the Philistines (FI-li-steenz), who lived along the Mediterranean coast. In the mid-1000s BC the Philistines invaded the Israelites' lands.

Frightened of these powerful invaders, the Israelites banded together under a single ruler who could lead them in battle. That ruler was a man named Saul, who became the first king of Israel. Saul had some success as a military commander, but he wasn't a strong king. He never won the total support of tribal and religious leaders. They often fought against his decisions.

King David

After Saul died, a man once declared an outlaw became king. That king's name was **David**. As a young man, David had been a shepherd. The Hebrew Bible tells how David slew the Philistine giant Goliath, which brought him to the attention of the king. David was admired for his military skills and as a poet; many of the Psalms are

attributed to him. He established the capital of Israel in Jerusalem. For many years, David lived in the desert, gathering support from local people. When Saul died, David used this support to become king.

Unlike Saul, David was well loved by the Israelites. He won the full support of Israel's tribal leaders. David was admired for his military skills and as a poet; many of the Psalms are attributed to him. He established the capital of Israel in Jerusalem.

King Solomon

David's son **Solomon** (SAHL-uh-muhn) took the throne in about 965 BC. Like his father, Solomon was a strong king. He expanded the kingdom and made nearby kingdoms, including Egypt and Phoenicia, his allies. Trade with these allies made Israel very rich. With these riches, Solomon built a great temple to God in Jerusalem. This temple became the center of the Israelites' religious life and a symbol of their faith.

FOCUS ON READING

Are the sentences in this paragraph facts or opinions? How can you tell?

READING CHECK Finding Main Ideas Why did the Israelites unite under a king?

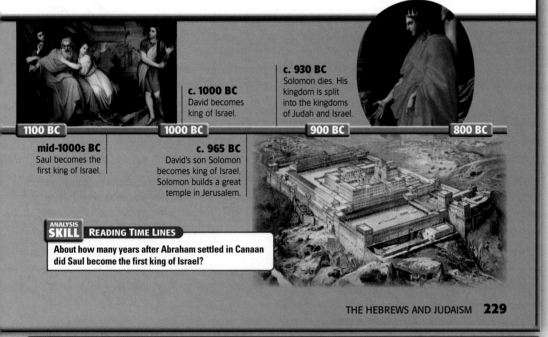

c. 1000 BC
David becomes king of Israel.

c. 930 BC
Solomon dies. His kingdom is split into the kingdoms of Judah and Israel.

1100 BC   1000 BC   900 BC   800 BC

mid-1000s BC
Saul becomes the first king of Israel.

c. 965 BC
David's son Solomon becomes king of Israel. Solomon builds a great temple in Jerusalem.

ANALYSIS SKILL READING TIME LINES

About how many years after Abraham settled in Canaan did Saul become the first king of Israel?

Critical Thinking: Summarizing

Standards Proficiency

Three Kings of Israel Graphic Organizer   HSS 6.3.3; HSS Analysis Skills: HI 1

Materials: gold or yellow construction paper; colored markers or pens

1. Provide each student with a sheet of construction paper. Have each student draw three large crowns on the paper.

2. Tell students to label the crowns *Saul, David,* and *Solomon*. Students should leave enough room in each crown to write four to six lines of additional text.

3. In each crown, have students list the main characteristics and achievements of the named king.

4. Last, have students write a slogan or catch phrase that sums up the importance or significance of each king. **LS** **Verbal/Linguistic, Visual/Spatial**

📝 Alternative Assessment Handbook, Rubric 13: Graphic Organizers

❸ Invaders Conquer and Rule

Invaders conquered and ruled the Hebrews after their kingdom broke apart.

Identify Causes What events led to the Diaspora? *Persians conquered the Chaldeans and let the Jews return to Jerusalem. But many Jews instead moved to other parts of the Persian Empire.*

Analyze Patterns Looking at Jewish history from Abraham to the Roman conquest in 63 BC, what patterns do you see? *patterns of migration, enslavement, and warfare/conquest*

📦 Map Transparency: Kingdoms of Israel and Judah, c. 920 BC

🐻 HSS 6.3.3; HSS Analysis Skills: HI 2

---

go.hrw.com
Online Resources

KEYWORD: SQ6 WH8
ACTIVITY: Connections to Today

About the Illustration

The illustration of Naomi and Ruth on the facing page is an artist's conception based on available sources. However, historians are uncertain exactly what Naomi and Ruth looked like.

Answers

Interpreting Maps *Each was only a small part of Solomon's kingdom.*

Reading Check *Jewish society experienced many great advances, such as in religious education. However, the Jews were still unhappy with Roman rule.*

Invaders Conquer and Rule

After Solomon's death in about 930 BC, revolts broke out over who should be king. Within a year, conflict tore Israel apart. Israel split into two kingdoms called Israel and called Judah (JOO-duh). The people of Judah became known as Jews.

The two new kingdoms lasted for a few centuries. In the end, however, both were conquered. Israel fell to the Assyrians around 722 BC. As a result, the kingdom fell apart and most of its people scattered. Judah lasted longer, but before long it fell to the Chaldeans.

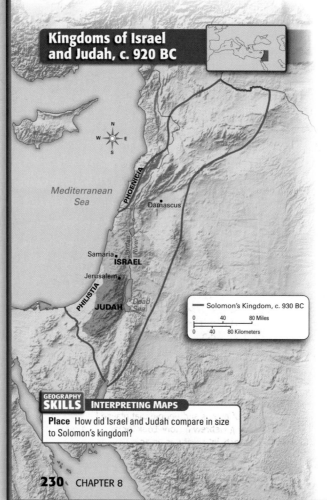

Kingdoms of Israel and Judah, c. 920 BC

Mediterranean Sea

PHOENICIA

Damascus

Samaria
ISRAEL

Jerusalem

PHILISTIA
JUDAH
Dead Sea

Solomon's Kingdom, c. 930 BC

0   40   80 Miles
0   40   80 Kilometers

GEOGRAPHY SKILLS **INTERPRETING MAPS**

Place How did Israel and Judah compare in size to Solomon's kingdom?

The Scattering of the Jews

The Chaldeans captured Jerusalem and destroyed Solomon's Temple in 586 BC. They marched thousands of Jews to their capital, Babylon, to work as slaves. The Jews called this enslavement the Babylonian Captivity. It lasted about 50 years.

In the 530s BC a people called the Persians conquered the Chaldeans and let the Jews return to Jerusalem. Despite this permission, many Jews never returned to Jerusalem. Instead, they moved to other parts of the Persian Empire. Scholars call the scattering of the Jews outside of Israel and Judah the **Diaspora** (dy-AS-pruh).

The rest of the Jews did return home to Jerusalem. There they rebuilt Solomon's Temple, which became known as the Second Temple. The Jews remained Persian subjects until the 330s BC, when the Persians were conquered by invaders.

Independence and Conquest

Tired of foreign rule, a Jewish family called the Maccabees (MA-kuh-beez) led a successful revolt in the 160s BC. For about 100 years, the Jews again ruled their own kingdom. Their independence, however, didn't last. In 63 BC the Jews were conquered again, this time by the Romans.

Although Jewish leaders added to the Second Temple under Roman rule, life was difficult. Heavy taxes burdened the people. The Romans were brutal masters who had no respect for the Jewish religion and way of life.

Some rulers tried to force the Jews to worship the Roman Emperor. The Roman rulers even appointed the high priests, the leaders of the Temple. This was more than the Jews could bear.

READING CHECK **Summarizing** How did Roman rule affect Jewish society?

Social Studies Skills Activity: Using Time Lines
Standards Proficiency

Later Hebrew History Time Line 🐻 HSS 6.3.3, 6.3.4; HSS Analysis Skills: CS 1, CS 2, HR 3

Materials: butcher paper or poster board

1. Have students examine the time line "Early Hebrew History" located on the previous two pages. Point out how the time line includes entries only for key events.

2. Have students work individually or in small groups to create a similar illustrated time line for the events in the material titled "Invaders Conquer and Rule."

3. When students are finished, ask volunteers to indicate some of the events they selected and to explain why they chose them.

4. Have students discuss which events they included were the most significant and why.

LS Visual/Spatial

SE Social Studies Skills: Interpreting Time Lines, p. 372

📝 Alternative Assessment Handbook, Rubric 36: Time Lines

Women in Hebrew Society

Hebrew government and society were dominated by men, as were most ancient societies. Women had few rights. They had to obey their fathers and their husbands. A woman couldn't even choose her own husband. Instead, her husband was chosen by her father. A woman couldn't inherit property either, unless she had no brothers. If she did have a brother, all property went to him.

Some Hebrew women, however, made great contributions to their society. The Hebrew Bible describes them. Some were political and military leaders, such as Queen Esther and the judge Deborah. According to the Hebrew Bible, these women saved the Hebrew people from their enemies. Other women, such as Miriam, the sister of Moses, were spiritual leaders.

Some women in the Hebrew Bible were seen as examples of how Hebrew women should behave. For example, Ruth, who left her people to care for her mother-in-law, was seen as a model of devotion to one's family. The Hebrews told Ruth's story as an example of how people should treat their family members.

READING CHECK **Generalizing** What was life like for most Hebrew women?

BIOGRAPHY

Ruth and Naomi

The story of Ruth and Naomi comes from the Book of Ruth, one of the books of the Hebrew Bible. According to this account, Ruth was not a Hebrew, though her husband was. After he died, Ruth and her mother-in-law, Naomi, resettled in Israel. Inspired by Naomi's faith in God, Ruth joined Naomi's family and adopted her beliefs. She dedicated her life to supporting Naomi.

Drawing Inferences What lessons might the Hebrews have used the story of Ruth and Naomi to teach?

SUMMARY AND PREVIEW The history of the Hebrews and Judaism began some 3,500 to 4,000 years ago. The instructions that Jews believe God gave to the early Hebrews shaped their religion, Judaism. In the next section, you will learn about the main teachings of Judaism.

Section 1 Assessment

go.hrw.com
Online Quiz
KEYWORD: SQ6 HP8

Reviewing Ideas, Terms, and People   HSS 6.3.3, 6.3.4

1. **a. Identify** Who was **Abraham**?
   b. Evaluate Why was the **Exodus** a significant event in Hebrew history?
2. **Summarize** How did **David** and **Solomon** strengthen the kingdom of Israel?
3. **Describe** What happened during the Babylonian Captivity?
4. **a. Describe** Who had more rights in Hebrew society, men or women?
   b. Make Inferences How did Ruth and Naomi set an example for other Hebrews?

Critical Thinking

5. **Summarize** Draw a chart like the one here. In each row, list a key figure from Hebrew history and his or her contributions to Hebrew society. You may add more rows.

Key Figure	Contribution

FOCUS ON WRITING

6. **Taking Notes about Early Hebrew History** Make a list of events and people that played key roles in shaping Hebrew history. Look for ways to group your facts into features on your Web page.

THE HEBREWS AND JUDAISM **231**

Bellringer

If YOU were there . . . Use the **Daily Bellringer Transparency** to help students answer the question.

🖥 Daily Bellringer Transparency, Section 2

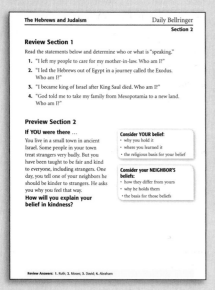

The Hebrews and Judaism   Daily Bellringer
                           Section 2

Review Section 1

Read the statements below and determine who or what is "speaking."

1. "I left my people to care for my mother-in-law. Who am I?"
2. "I led the Hebrews out of Egypt in a journey called the Exodus. Who am I?"
3. "I became king of Israel after King Saul died. Who am I?"
4. "God told me to take my family from Mesopotamia to a new land. Who am I?"

Preview Section 2

If YOU were there …

You live in a small town in ancient Israel. Some people in your town treat strangers very badly. But you have been taught to be fair and kind to everyone, including strangers. One day, you tell one of your neighbors he should be kinder to strangers. He asks you why you feel that way. **How will you explain your belief in kindness?**

Consider YOUR belief:
• why you hold it
• where you learned it
• the religious basis for your belief

Consider your NEIGHBOR'S beliefs:
• how they differ from yours
• why he holds them
• the basis for those beliefs

Review Answers: 1. Ruth; 2. Moses; 3. David; 4. Abraham

Academic Vocabulary

Review with students the high-use academic term in this section.

principles basic beliefs, rules, or laws (p. 234)

📄 **CRF:** Vocabulary Builder Activity, Section 2

🌅 Standards Focus

HSS 6.3.1

Means: Describe how Judaism is based on a belief in one God who defines what is right. Explain why this feature of Judaism is important.

Matters: Judaism may be the first religion in which people worshipped only one god. It is the oldest such religion still widely practiced today.

HSS 6.3.2

Means: Identify the central beliefs and sacred texts of Judaism. Describe how Jewish ideas and beliefs have shaped Western culture.

Matters: Many Jewish beliefs and ideas can be seen in our laws and in our society's rules of behavior.

232   CHAPTER 8

Jewish Beliefs and Texts

What You Will Learn...

Main Ideas

1. Beliefs in God, education, justice, and obedience anchor Jewish society.
2. Jewish beliefs are listed in the Torah, the Hebrew Bible, and the Commentaries.
3. The Dead Sea Scrolls reveal many past Jewish beliefs.
4. The ideas of Judaism have helped shape later cultures.

The Big Idea

The central ideas and laws of Judaism are contained in sacred texts such as the Torah.

Key Terms

Judaism, *p. 232*
monotheism, *p. 232*
Torah, *p. 234*
synagogue, *p. 234*
prophets, *p. 235*
Talmud, *p. 236*
Dead Sea Scrolls, *p. 236*

HSS 6.3.1 Describe the origins and significance of Judaism as the first monotheistic religion based on the concept of one God who sets down moral laws for humanity.

6.3.2 Identify the sources of the ethical teachings and central beliefs of Judaism (the Hebrew Bible, the Commentaries): belief in God, observance of law, practice of the concepts of righteousness and justice, and importance of study; and describe how the ideas of the Hebrew traditions are reflected in the moral and ethical traditions of Western civilization.

232   CHAPTER 8

If YOU were there...

You live in a small town in ancient Israel. Some people in your town treat strangers very badly. But you have been taught to be fair and kind to everyone, including strangers. One day, you tell one of your neighbors he should be kinder to strangers. He asks you why you feel that way.

How will you explain your belief in kindness?

BUILDING BACKGROUND The idea that people should be fair and kind to everyone in the community is an important Jewish teaching. Sometimes, their teachings set the Jews apart from other people in society. But at the same time, their shared beliefs tie all Jews together as a religious community.

Jewish Beliefs Anchor Their Society

Religion is the foundation upon which the Jews base their whole society. In fact, much of Jewish culture is based directly on Jewish beliefs. The central beliefs of **Judaism,** the Jewish religion, are beliefs in God, education, justice, and obedience.

Belief in One God

Most importantly, Jews believe in one God. The Hebrew name for God is YHWH, which is never pronounced by Jews, as it is considered too holy. The belief in only one God is called **monotheism**. Many people believe that Judaism was the world's first monotheistic religion. It is certainly the oldest such religion that is still widely practiced today.

In the ancient world where most people worshipped many gods, the Jews' worship of only God set them apart. This worship also shaped Jewish society. The Jews believed that they were God's chosen people. They believed that God had guided their history through his relationships with Abraham, Moses, and other leaders.

Teach the Big Idea: Master the Standards   Standards Proficiency

Jewish Beliefs and Texts 🌅 HSS 6.3.1, 6.3.2

1. **Teach** Ask students the Main Idea questions to teach this section.

2. **Apply** Draw a four-column chart for students to see. Title the chart *Judaism* and label the columns *Central Beliefs, Sacred Texts, Dead Sea Scrolls*, and *Influence.* Have each student make a copy of the chart and complete it by listing the main ideas and events for each topic based on this section. **LS Verbal/Linguistic**

3. **Review** To review the section's main ideas, have students help you complete a master copy of the chart.

4. **Practice/Homework** For each topic in the chart, have students write one to three sentences summarizing the information in that column. **LS Verbal/Linguistic**

📄 Alternative Assessment Handbook, Rubrics 7: Charts; and 37: Writing Assignments

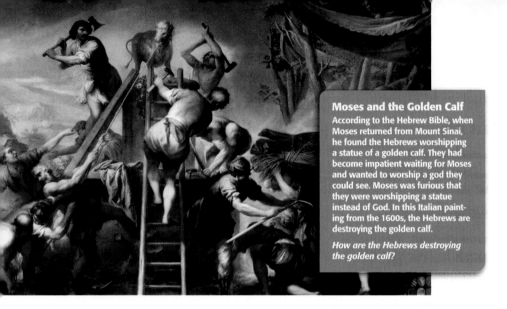

Moses and the Golden Calf
According to the Hebrew Bible, when Moses returned from Mount Sinai, he found the Hebrews worshiping a statue of a golden calf. They had become impatient waiting for Moses and wanted to worship a god they could see. Moses was furious that they were worshipping a statue instead of God. In this Italian painting from the 1600s, the Hebrews are destroying the golden calf.

How are the Hebrews destroying the golden calf?

Main Idea

❶ Jewish Beliefs Anchor Their Society

Beliefs in God, education, justice, and obedience anchor Jewish society.

Recall What is monotheism, and why did this belief set the ancient Hebrews apart? *a belief in only one god; most people in the ancient world worshipped many gods.*

Explain What is the Jewish view of justice and righteousness? *Justice means to treat all people kindly and fairly, and righteousness refers to doing what is proper.*

Draw Conclusions Why do you think that education and study are so important in Judaism? *Jews must learn about their religion and must learn to read and follow the laws.*

 CRF: Primary Source Activity: Mosaic Law and Punishments

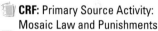 **HSS** 6.3.1, 6.3.2

Belief in Education

Another central element of Judaism is education and study. Teaching children the basics of Judaism has always been important in Jewish society. In ancient Jewish communities, older boys—but not girls—studied with professional teachers to learn their religion. Even today, education and study are central to Jewish life for children and adults.

Belief in Justice and Righteousness

Also central to the Jews' religion are the ideas of justice and righteousness. To Jews, justice means kindness and fairness in dealing with other people. Everyone deserves justice, even strangers and criminals. Jews are expected to give aid to those who need it, including the poor, the sick, and orphans. Jews are also expected to be fair in business dealings.

Righteousness refers to doing what is proper. Jews are supposed to behave properly, even if others around them do not. For the Jews, righteous behavior is more important than rituals, or ceremonies.

Belief in Obedience and Law

Closely related to the ideas of justice and righteousness is obedience to the law. Moral and religious laws have guided Jews through their history and continue to do so today. Jews believe that God gave them these laws to follow.

The most important Jewish laws are the Ten Commandments. The commandments, however, are only part of Jewish law. Jews believe that Moses recorded a whole system of laws that God had set down for them to obey. Named for Moses, this system is called Mosaic law.

Like the Ten Commandments, Mosaic laws guide many areas of Jews' daily lives. For example, Mosaic law governs how people pray and celebrate holy days. The laws prohibit Jews from working on holy days or on the Sabbath, the seventh day of each week. The Sabbath is a day of rest because, in Jewish tradition, God created the world in six days and rested on the seventh. As a result, Jews observe the Sabbath on Saturday, the seventh day of the week.

THE HEBREWS AND JUDAISM **233**

Info to Know

Shabbat The Hebrew word for Sabbath is Shabbat. Shabbat begins at sunset on Friday evening and ends at nightfall on Saturday once three stars are visible in the sky.

Central Beliefs of Judaism Poster 🐻 **HSS** 6.3.2

Materials: poster board, art supplies, markers

1. Have students identify and describe the four central beliefs of Judaism *(beliefs in God, education and study, justice and righteousness, and obedience and law)*. List the beliefs where students can see them.

2. Have each student create a poster identifying and describing the central beliefs of Judaism.

3. Encourage students to illustrate and decorate their posters. In addition, have each student write a paragraph summarizing how the central beliefs of Judaism shape Jewish life.

4. Display students' posters in the classroom.
   LS Visual/Spatial

📋 Alternative Assessment Handbook, Rubric 28: Posters

Answers

Moses and the Golden Calf *They are using axes and sledgehammers to break the calf apart while preparing a fire to melt the pieces.*

❷ Texts List Jewish Beliefs

Jewish beliefs are listed in the Torah, the Hebrew Bible, and the Commentaries.

Define What is the Torah? *most sacred text of Judaism; five books of laws as well as a history of the Jews until the death of Moses*

Recall What are the three parts of the Hebrew Bible? *Torah; eight books of messages of prophets; 11 books of poetry, songs, stories, lessons, and history*

Draw Conclusions Why do Jews consider the Torah the most sacred text of Judaism? *because the Torah contains the laws that Jews believe God set down for them to follow, and because it affirms their participation in the continuity of the Jewish people from ancient times to the present.*

📖 **CRF:** Literature Activity: The Creation Story, from the Torah

🐻 **HSS** 6.3.2

Info to Know

Torah Scrolls The Torah is also known as the Chumash or the Five Books of Moses. Torah scrolls are made from kosher animal parchment. The text of the scriptures are then handwritten on the scroll. When not being read, Torah scrolls are covered with fabric and stored in a special cabinet called an ark.

Answers

Reading Check *beliefs in one God, education and study, justice and righteousness, and obedience and law*

234

Among the Mosaic laws are rules about the foods that Jews can eat and rules that must be followed in preparing them. For example, the laws state that Jews cannot eat pork or shellfish, which are thought to be ritually unclean. Other laws say that meat has to be killed and prepared in a way that makes it acceptable for Jews to eat. Today foods that have been so prepared are called kosher (KOH-shuhr), or fit.

In many Jewish communities today, people still strictly follow Mosaic law. They are called Orthodox Jews. Other Jews choose not to follow many of the ancient laws. They are known as Reform Jews. A third group, the Conservative Jews, falls between the other two groups. These are the three largest groups of Jews in the world today.

READING CHECK **Generalizing** What are the most important beliefs of Judaism?

Texts List Jewish Beliefs

The laws and **principles** of Judaism are described in several sacred texts, or writings. Among the main texts are the Torah, the Hebrew Bible, and the Commentaries.

The Torah

The ancient Jews recorded most of their laws in five books. Together these books are called the **Torah**, the most sacred text of Judaism. In addition to laws, the Torah includes a history of the Jews until the death of Moses.

Readings from the Torah are central to Jewish religious services today. Nearly every **synagogue** (SI-nuh-gawg), or Jewish house of worship, has at least one Torah. Out of respect for the Torah, readers do not touch it. They use special pointers to mark their places in the text.

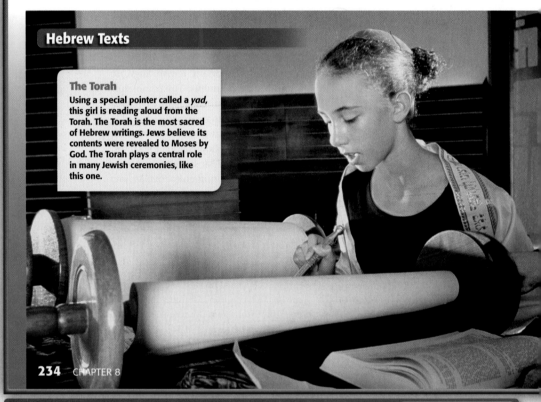

Hebrew Texts

The Torah
Using a special pointer called a *yad*, this girl is reading aloud from the Torah. The Torah is the most sacred of Hebrew writings. Jews believe its contents were revealed to Moses by God. The Torah plays a central role in many Jewish ceremonies, like this one.

234 CHAPTER 8

Collaborative Learning

Standards Proficiency

Prep Required

Jewish Sacred Texts Scrolls 🐻 **HSS** 6.3.2

Materials: butcher paper, wooden rods, art supplies

1. Have students identify and describe the main sacred texts of Judaism (*the Torah, Hebrew Bible, and Commentaries*).

2. Organize students into small groups. Give each group a strip of butcher paper and two wooden rods. Students will use the materials to create scrolls.

3. Have each group create a scroll describing the sacred texts of Judaism. Encourage students to illustrate and decorate their scrolls. If time allows, have students conduct research to include additional information.

4. Display the scrolls around the classroom.
LS **Interpersonal, Kinesthetic**

📋 Alternative Assessment Handbook, Rubrics 3: Artwork; and 14: Group Activity

The Hebrew Bible

The Torah is the first of three parts of a group of writings called the Hebrew Bible, or Tanach (tah-NAHK). The second part is made up of eight books that describe the messages of Hebrew prophets. **Prophets** are people who are said to receive messages from God to be taught to others.

The final part of the Hebrew Bible is 11 books of poetry, songs, stories, lessons, and history. For example, the Book of Daniel tells about a prophet named Daniel, who lived during the Babylonian Captivity. According to the book, Daniel angered the king who held the Hebrews as slaves. As punishment, the king had Daniel thrown into a den of lions. The story tells that Daniel's faith in God kept the lions from killing him, and he was released. Jews tell this story to show the power of faith.

Also in the final part of the Hebrew Bible are the Proverbs, short expressions of Hebrew wisdom. Many of these sayings are attributed to Hebrew leaders, especially King Solomon. For example, Solomon is supposed to have said, "A good name is to be chosen rather than great riches." In other words, it is better to be seen as a good person than to be rich and not respected.

The third part of the Hebrew Bible also includes the Book of Psalms. Psalms are poems or songs of praise to God. Many of these are attributed to King David. One of the most famous psalms is the Twenty-third Psalm. It includes lines often read today during times of difficulty:

> "The Lord is my shepherd, I shall not want [lack anything]. He makes me lie down in green pastures; He leads me beside still waters. He restores my soul [life]; He guides me in the paths of righteousness for His name's sake."
> —Psalms 23:1–3

The Hebrew Bible
These beautifully decorated pages are from a Hebrew Bible. The Hebrew Bible, sometimes called the Tanach, includes the Torah and other ancient writings.

ANALYSIS SKILL **ANALYZING VISUALS**
How does the Torah look different from the Hebrew Bible and the commentaries?

The Commentaries
The Talmud is a collection of laws, commentaries, and discussions about the Torah and the Hebrew Bible. The Talmud is a rich source of information for discussion and debate. Rabbis and religious scholars like these young men study the Talmud to learn about Jewish history and laws.

235

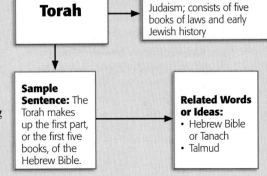
235

Main Idea

❸ Scrolls Reveal Past Beliefs

The Dead Sea Scrolls reveal many past Jewish beliefs.

Recall What are the Dead Sea Scrolls, and when were they first discovered? *writings by Jewish scholars who lived about 2,000 years ago; in 1947*

Analyze How have the Dead Sea Scrolls affected Judaism? *They have provided Jewish scholars with additional insights into the teachings of Judaism and into Jewish history.*

 HSS 6.3.2

Analyzing Visuals

The Dead Sea Scrolls

Based on the image of the cave at right, what challenges might scholars have faced in searching for additional scrolls? *possible answers—having to work in small or dark caves; difficulties bringing scientific equipment into the caves*

Linking to Today

The Shrine of the Book A popular tourist attraction in Israel today is the Shrine of the Book, where visitors can see fragments of the Dead Sea Scrolls. Built specifically to house the scrolls, the building resembles one of the clay jars in which the scrolls were found. The Shrine of the Book is part of the Israel Museum in Jerusalem.

Answers

The Dead Sea Scrolls *difficulty in understanding the language or script; missing text; fragile remains*

Reading Check *Torah, Hebrew Bible, and Commentaries*

The Dead Sea Scrolls

The Dead Sea Scrolls were found in this cave, and in similar caves, near Qumran. The hot, dry desert climate preserved the 2,000-year-old scrolls remarkably well.

Why might historians have had trouble reading the Dead Sea Scrolls?

Commentaries

For centuries scholars have studied the Torah and Jewish laws. Because some laws are hard to understand, the scholars write commentaries to explain them.

Many of these commentaries are found in the **Talmud** (TAHL-moohd), a set of commentaries, stories, and folklore. The writings of the Talmud were produced between AD 200 and 600. Many Jews consider them second only to the Hebrew Bible in their significance to Judaism.

READING CHECK **Analyzing** What texts do Jews consider sacred?

Scrolls Reveal Past Beliefs

Besides the Torah, the Hebrew Bible, and the Commentaries, many other documents also explain ancient Jewish beliefs. Among the most important are the **Dead Sea Scrolls**, writings by Jews who lived about 2,000 years ago.

Until 1947 no one knew about the Dead Sea Scrolls. In that year, young boys looking for a lost goat near the Dead Sea found a small cave. One of the boys went in to explore and found several old jars filled with moldy scrolls.

Scholars were very excited about the boy's find. Eager to find more scrolls, they

---

Critical Thinking: Evaluating Information

Standards Proficiency

Dead Sea Scrolls News Report **HSS** 6.3.2; **HSS** Analysis Skills: HI 1

1. Ask students to imagine that they are reporters working for a newspaper at the time of the discovery of the Dead Sea Scrolls.

2. Have each student write a news report describing the discovery and its significance as both a historical and religious find.

3. Remind students to address the journalistic questions "who, what, when, where, why, and how" in their reports. Have volunteers read their reports aloud. **LS Verbal/Linguistic**

   Alternative Assessment Handbook, Rubric 42: Writing to Inform

began to search the desert. Over the next few decades, searchers found several more groups of scrolls.

Careful study revealed that most of the Dead Sea Scrolls were written between 100 BC and AD 50. The scrolls included prayers, commentaries, letters, and passages from the Hebrew Bible. These writings help historians learn about the lives of many Jews during this time.

READING CHECK Finding Main Ideas What did the Dead Sea Scrolls contain?

Judaism and Later Cultures

For centuries, Jewish ideas have greatly influenced other cultures, especially those in Europe and the Americas. Historians call European and American cultures the Western world to distinguish them from the Asian cultures to the east of Europe.

Because Jews lived all over the Western world, people of many cultures learned of Jewish ideas. In addition, these ideas helped shape the largest religion of Western society today, Christianity. Jesus, whose teachings are the basis of Christianity, was Jewish, and many of his teachings reflected Jewish ideas. These ideas were carried forward into Western civilization by both Jews and Christians. Judaism also influenced the development of another major religion, Islam. The first people to adopt Islam believed that they, like the Hebrews, were descendants of Abraham.

How are Jewish ideas reflected in our society? Many people still look to the Ten Commandments as a guide to how they should live. For example, people are expected not to lie or cheat and to honor their parents, families, and neighbors. Although these ideas were not unique to Judaism, it was through the Jews that they entered Western culture.

Not all of the ideas adopted from Jewish teachings stem from the Ten Commandments. Other Jewish ideas can also be seen in how people live today. For example, many people do not work on weekends in honor of the Sabbath. In addition, people give money or items to charities to help the poor and needy. This concept of charity is based largely on Jewish teachings.

READING CHECK Summarizing How have Jewish ideas helped shape modern laws?

SUMMARY AND PREVIEW Judaism is based on the belief in and obedience to God as described in the Torah and other sacred texts. In the next section you will learn how religion helped unify Jews even when they were forced out of Jerusalem.

Section 2 Assessment

go.hrw.com
Online Quiz
KEYWORD: SQ6 HP8

Reviewing Ideas, Terms, and People HSS 6.3.1, 6.3.2

1. **a. Define** What is **monotheism**?
   b. Explain What is the Jewish view of justice and righteousness?
2. **a. Identify** What are the main sacred texts of Judaism?
   b. Predict Why do you think the commentaries are so significant to many Jews?
3. **Recall** Why do historians study the Dead Sea Scrolls?
4. **Make Generalizations** How are Hebrew teachings reflected in Western society today?

Critical Thinking

5. **Explain** Redraw the diagram shown on a sheet of paper. Use it to identify and explain the basic teachings of Judaism.

Judaism

FOCUS ON WRITING

6. **Thinking about Basic Values and Teachings** While the information in Section 1 was mostly historical, this section has more different kinds of topics. As you write down this information, what links do you see between it and items already on your list?

THE HEBREWS AND JUDAISM **237**

Sacred Texts

Noah's Ark

As You Read As students read the story, have them make a list of the instructions that God gave Noah. As part of the list, students should note who and what Noah is to bring onto the ark. Then ask students to consider and discuss why God gave Noah these particular instructions.

CRF: Literature Activity: The Creation Story, from the Torah

Analyzing Sacred Texts

Theme Remind students that theme is different from a story's subject. The subject is what the story is about. Theme is what the story means. What is the theme of the story of Noah's ark? *God punishes the wicked but protects the righteous.*

HSS 6.3.2; **ELA** Reading 6.3.6

Info to Know

Clean and Unclean Animals Under Mosaic law, clean mammals are those with cloven, or split, hooves and that bring up their cud (partially digested food). All water creatures with fins and scales are clean; those without are unclean. Many insects and birds are also unclean.

---

from The Torah

Noah's Ark   Genesis 7:1–12 The Living Torah

About the Reading *The first book of the Torah is called the Book of Genesis, a Jewish account of the early history of the world. One of the most famous parts of Genesis is the story of Noah's ark.*

According to the Torah, God became angry with people for their wicked behavior. To punish the wicked people, he decided to cause a great flood that would destroy everything. But one man, Noah, was not wicked, and God did not want him to die. He told Noah to build an ark, a great ship, that would carry him and his family safely through the flood. In this passage, God tells Noah to bring animals onto the ark as well, so that they might be spared.

AS YOU READ Note who and what Noah brings onto the ark with him.

God said to Noah, "Come into the ark, you and your family. I have seen that you are righteous before me in this generation. Take seven pairs of every clean animal, each consisting of a male and its mate. Of every animal that is not clean, take two, a male and its mate. ❶ Of the birds of the heaven also take seven pairs, each consisting of a male and its mate. Let them keep seed alive on the face of all the earth, because in another seven days, I will bring rain on the earth for forty days and forty nights. I will obliterate every organism that I have made from the face of the earth."

Noah did all that God had commanded. Noah was 600 years old when the flood occurred; water was on the earth. ❷ Noah, along with his sons, his wife, and his sons' wives, came into the ark ahead of the waters of the flood. The clean animals, the animals which were not clean, the birds, and all that walked the earth came two by two to Noah, to the ark. They were male and female, as God had commanded Noah.

Seven days passed, and the flood waters were on the earth. It was in the 600th year of Noah's life, in the second month, on the 17th of the month. On that day all the wellsprings of the great deep burst forth and the floodgates of the heavens were opened. It would continue to rain on the earth for forty days and forty nights.

GUIDED READING

WORD HELP

righteous proper, free from wrongdoing
obliterate destroy completely
organism a living thing
wellsprings sources of water
floodgates gates that hold back water to prevent floods

❶ Clean animals were those the Hebrews considered ritually clean to eat, such as cows. Unclean animals were those they did not eat, such as pigs, camels, and rabbits.

❷ According to the Torah, Noah lived to be 950 years old.

How old was Noah when he built the ark?

ELA Reading 6.2.7 Make reasonable assertions about a text through accurate, supporting citations.

Differentiating Instruction for Universal Access

Learners Having Difficulty   Reaching Standards

Deciphering and Paraphrasing To help struggling readers and students who find the selections challenging, have the students break down the sentences into smaller phrases. Then have students work together in pairs or as a class to paraphrase each phrase or sentence. Every few sentences, stop and have students review the meaning of what they have read.
LS Verbal/Linguistic

Advanced Learners/GATE   Exceeding Standards

Analyzing the Influence of Sacred Texts: The Torah Have students discuss how the Jewish belief that God punishes the wicked and rewards and protects the righteous is reflected in the story of Noah's ark. Then have students discuss how this same message is reflected in both the Ten Commandments and the laws of the United States today. **LS Verbal/Linguistic**
HSS 6.3.2.; **ELA** Reading 6.2.7

Answers

Guided Reading 2. *Noah was 600 years old.*

The Tower of Babel   Genesis 11:1–9 The Living Torah

About the Reading *The Book of Genesis also tells the story of the Tower of Babel. According to this story, everyone in the world once spoke the same language. In time, however, people became proud and tried to climb to heaven. To punish them for their pride, God scattered people throughout the world and changed their languages so that people could no longer understand one another.*

AS YOU READ Pay attention to the words that people and God speak. What do these words tell you about their moods and actions?

The entire earth had one language with uniform words. When [the people] migrated from the east, they found a valley in the land of Shinar, and they settled there. They said to one another, "Come, let us mold bricks and fire them." Then they had bricks to use as stone, and asphalt for mortar. They said, "Come, let us build ourselves a city, and a tower whose top shall reach the sky. Let us make ourselves a name, so that we will not be scattered all over the face of the earth." ❶

God descended to see the city and the tower that the sons of man had built. God said, "They are a single people, all having one language, and this is the first thing they do! Now nothing they plan to do will be unattainable for them! Come, let us descend and confuse their speech, so that one person will not understand another's speech." ❷

From that place, God scattered them all over the face of the earth, and they stopped building the city. He named it Babel, because this was the place where God confused the world's language. ❸ It was from there that God dispersed [humanity] over all the face of the earth.

The Tower of Babel, by Pieter Brueghel the Elder, 1563

GUIDED READING

WORD HELP

uniform the same
unattainable unreachable
dispersed scattered

❶ What did people do when they first arrived in the land of Shinar?

❷ The ancient Hebrews believed that God sometimes came to Earth to see what people were doing.

What was God's reaction when he saw what the people were building?

❸ In Hebrew, the word *Babel* means "confusion."

CONNECTING SACRED TEXTS TO HISTORY

1. **Analyzing** Jews believe that righteous behavior is very important. How is this belief reflected in the story of Noah's ark?

2. **Finding Main Ideas** Jews also believe that God plays an active role in world history. How does the Torah say God's actions changed the world in the story of the Tower of Babel?

239

Cross-Discipline Activity: Art

Standards Proficiency

Artistic Book Cover 🐾 **Visual Arts** Creative Expression 6.2.5

Materials: art supplies, construction paper, drawing software (optional)

1. Ask students to imagine that they are illustrators hired to create the cover design for a softcover children's book of either the story of Noah's Ark or the Tower of Babel.

2. Students' covers should include the title of the story and an illustration representing either the plot or an essential element of the story.

You might want to approve their cover ideas before students start work.

3. Students might use computer software, pen and ink, watercolors, or other mediums to produce their covers. **LS Visual/Spatial**

4. Display students' book covers in the classroom.

📖 Alternative Assessment Handbook, Rubric 3: Artwork

Sacred Texts

The Tower of Babel

As You Read Have students make a two-column chart and label the columns *People* and *God*. As students read the story, have them list what the people say and what God says in the appropriate columns. When students have finished, ask volunteers to explain what the different phrases indicate about the mood and actions of the people and of God.

Analyzing Sacred Texts

Compare and Contrast Both stories are found in the Hebrew Bible in the Book of Genesis, or *Bereshith* in Hebrew. Ask students the following questions:

1. What do the two stories have in common? *God punishes bad behavior.*

2. How do the themes of the two stories differ? *Noah's Ark emphasizes the importance of righteous behavior, whereas the Tower of Babel explains an aspect of the world's history—in this case, how people came to speak many different languages.*

3. Why might the Book of Genesis contain stories of both types? *possible answer—because both types of stories were important to Jews and their religion*

Answers

Guided Reading 1. *settled and began to mold and fire bricks;* **2.** *He realized that a united people with one language could attain anything, so God scattered the people around the world and made them speak different languages.*

Connecting Sacred Texts to History 1. *God sends a flood to destroy the wicked but saves Noah, a righteous man, and his family.* **2.** *God's actions changed the world from having one language to having many different languages.*

239

Bellringer

If YOU were there . . . Use the **Daily Bellringer Transparency** to help students answer the question.

📖 Daily Bellringer Transparency, Section 3

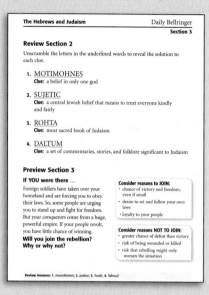

The Hebrews and Judaism | Daily Bellringer
Section 3

Review Section 2

Unscramble the letters in the underlined words to reveal the solution to each clue.

1. MOTIMOHNES
   Clue: a belief in only one god

2. SUJETIC
   Clue: a central Jewish belief that means to treat everyone kindly and fairly

3. ROHTA
   Clue: most sacred book of Judaism

4. DALTUM
   Clue: a set of commentaries, stories, and folklore significant to Judaism

Preview Section 3

If YOU were there ...

Foreign soldiers have taken over your homeland and are forcing you to obey their laws. So, some people are urging you to stand up and fight for freedom. But your conquerors come from a huge, powerful empire. If your people revolt, you have little chance of winning. **Will you join the rebellion? Why or why not?**

Consider reasons to JOIN:
- chance of victory and freedom, even if small
- desire to set and follow your own laws
- loyalty to your people

Consider reasons NOT TO JOIN:
- greater chance of defeat than victory
- risk of being wounded or killed
- risk that rebelling might only worsen the situation

Review Answers: 1. monotheism; 2. justice; 3. Torah; 4. Talmud

Building Vocabulary

Preteach or review the following term:

synagogue Jewish house of worship (p. 242)

📖 **CRF:** Vocabulary Builder Activity, Section 3

🐻 Standards Focus

HSS 6.3.5

Means: Describe how Judaism survived and developed even though many Jews moved to other places after the destruction of the Second Temple in AD 70.

Matters: Judaism is today a major religion practiced by people around the world.

Judaism over the Centuries

What You Will Learn...

Main Ideas

1. Revolt, defeat, and migration led to great changes in Jewish culture.
2. Because Jews settled in different parts of the world, two cultural traditions formed.
3. Jewish traditions and holy days celebrate their history and religion.

The Big Idea

Although they were forced out of Israel by the Romans, shared beliefs and customs helped Jews maintain their religion.

Key Terms

Zealots, *p. 240*
rabbis, *p. 242*
Passover, *p. 245*
High Holy Days, *p. 245*

🐻 **HSS** 6.3.5 Discuss how Judaism survived and developed despite the continuing dispersion of much of the Jewish population from Jerusalem and the rest of Israel after the destruction of the second Temple in AD 70.

If YOU were there...

Foreign soldiers have taken over your homeland and are forcing you to obey their laws. So, some people are urging you to stand up and fight for freedom. But your conquerors come from a huge, powerful empire. If your people revolt, you have little chance of winning.

Will you join the rebellion? Why or why not?

BUILDING BACKGROUND By about AD 60, many Jews in Jerusalem had to decide whether they would join a rebellion against their foreign conquerors. For a little over a century, Jerusalem had been ruled by Rome. The Romans had a strong army, but their disrespect for Jewish traditions angered many Jews.

Revolt, Defeat, and Migration

The teachings of Judaism helped unite the ancient Jews. After the conquest of Israel by the Romans, many events threatened to tear Jewish society apart.

One threat to Jewish society was foreign rule. By the beginning of the first century AD, many Jews in Jerusalem had grown tired of foreign rule. If they could regain their independence, these Jews thought they could re-create the kingdom of Israel.

Revolt against Rome

The most rebellious of these Jews were a group called the **Zealots** (ZE-luhts). This group didn't think that Jews should answer to anyone but God. As a result, they refused to obey Roman officials. The Zealots urged their fellow Jews to rise up against the Romans. Tensions between Jews and Romans increased. Finally, in AD 66, the Jews revolted. Led by the Zealots, they fought fiercely.

Teach the Big Idea: Master the Standards

Standards Proficiency

Judaism over the Centuries 🐻 **HSS** 6.3.5; **HSS** Analysis Skills: HR 3, HI 1

1. **Teach** Ask students the Main Idea questions to teach this section.

2. **Apply** Have each student, working either individually or in pairs, write five main-idea or summary statements for each main part of this section. **LS** Verbal/Linguistic

3. **Review** Have volunteers share their statements with the class to review the section's main ideas.

4. **Practice/Homework** Have each student use the information in this section to write one to three paragraphs expanding upon the section's big idea statement.
   LS Verbal/Linguistic

   📖 Alternative Assessment Handbook, Rubric 37: Writing Assignments

In the end, the Jews' revolt against the Romans was not successful. The revolt lasted four years and caused terrible damage. By the time the fighting ended, Jerusalem lay in ruins. The war had wrecked buildings and cost many lives. Even more devastating to the Jews was the fact that the Romans burned the Second Temple during the last days of fighting in AD 70:

" As the flames went upward, the Jews made a great clamor [shout], such as so mighty an affliction [ordeal] required, and ran together to prevent it; and now they spared not their lives any longer, nor suffered any thing to restrain their force, since that holy house was perishing. "

–Flavius Josephus, *The Wars of the Jews*

After the Temple was destroyed, most Jews lost their will to fight and surrendered. But a few refused to give up their fight. That small group of about 1,000 Zealots locked themselves in a mountain fortress called Masada (muh-SAH-duh).

Intent on smashing the revolt, the Romans sent 15,000 soldiers to capture these Zealots. However, Masada was hard to reach. The Romans had to build a huge ramp of earth and stones to get to it. For two years, the Zealots refused to surrender, as the ramp grew. Finally, as the Romans broke through Masada's walls, the Zealots took their own lives. They refused to become Roman slaves.

THE IMPACT TODAY

The western retaining wall of the Second Temple survived the fire and still stands. Thousands of Jews each year visit the wall.

History Close-up

Destruction of the Second Temple

Frustrated by a century of Roman rule, many Jews rose up in armed rebellion. Led by the Zealots, they fought furiously for four years. But the experienced Roman army crushed the revolt. The Romans even destroyed the Jews' holiest site, the Second Temple in Jerusalem.

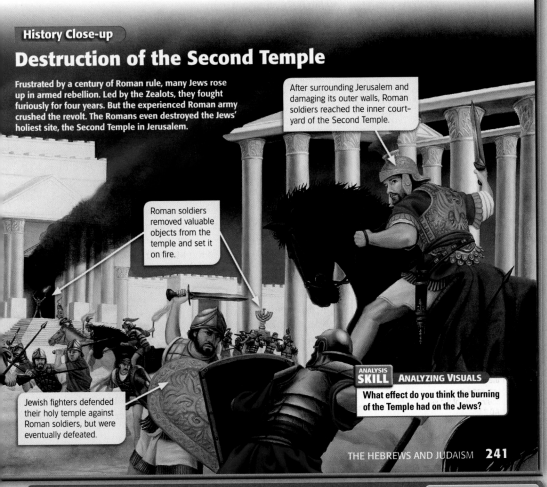

After surrounding Jerusalem and damaging its outer walls, Roman soldiers reached the inner court-yard of the Second Temple.

Roman soldiers removed valuable objects from the temple and set it on fire.

Jewish fighters defended their holy temple against Roman soldiers, but were eventually defeated.

ANALYSIS SKILL **ANALYZING VISUALS**
What effect do you think the burning of the Temple had on the Jews?

THE HEBREWS AND JUDAISM **241**

Main Idea

❶ Revolt, Defeat, and Migration

Revolt, defeat, and migration led to great changes in Jewish culture.

Identify Who were the Zealots? *A group of Jews who refused to obey Roman officials and led their fellow Jews in a revolt.*

Recall Why did the Jews revolt against the Romans? *The Jews were tired of foreign rule and wanted to re-create the kingdom of Israel; Zealots also believed Jews should not answer to anyone but God.*

Make Inferences Why was the Roman destruction of the Second Temple so devastating to the Jews? *The Temple was the center of Jewish religious life and the holiest Jewish site.*

🐻 **HSS** 6.3.5; **HSS** Analysis Skills: HI 1

Linking to Today

Masada The fortress of Masada has become a symbol to modern Jews of their survival as a people and a religious group. Today, Israeli soldiers go to Masada and take the oath, "Masada shall not fall again." The mountain fortress is the second most popular site for Jewish tourists in Israel after the city of Jerusalem.

History Close-up

Destruction of the Second Temple

Analyzing Visuals What valuable items did the Jews lose as part of the destruction of the Second Temple? *sacred Temple objects*

Critical Thinking: Summarizing and Sequencing

Standards Proficiency

Jewish Revolt News Flashes 🐻 **HSS** 6.3.5; **HSS** Analysis Skills: CS 1, HI 1, HI 2

1. Ask students to imagine that television was available in AD 70 and that they are reporters working for the Roman News Network.

2. Have each student write a series of short news flashes covering the main events in the Jewish revolt against Rome.

3. Remind students to address the journalistic questions "who, what, when, where, why, and how" and to be objective in their reporting. In addition, encourage students to make their

news flashes exciting while keeping them historically accurate.

4. Model the activity for students by writing one news flash as an example.

5. Have volunteers deliver their news flashes to the class in the correct order. Then have students summarize the results of the revolt.

LS **Verbal/Linguistic**

Alternative Assessment Handbook, Rubric 42: Writing to Inform

Answers

History Close-up *greatly upset the Jews because the Temple was their holiest site and the center of Jewish religious life*

241

❶ Revolt, Defeat, and Migration

Revolt, defeat, and migration led to great changes in Jewish culture.

Recall How did the nature of Judaism change after the loss of the Second Temple? *Local synagogues became more important in Jewish life, and leaders called rabbis began serving as religious teachers.*

Identify Who was Yohanan ben Zaccai? *A Jewish rabbi who established a school at Yavneh to train rabbis*

Make Inferences Jews have returned to Jerusalem throughout history. Why do you think this is so? *possible answer—because Jerusalem is the most holy place in the world to Jews and is the site of the Western Wall of the Jews' biblical Temple.*

📖 **CRF:** History and Geography Activity: Jewish Migration After AD 70

🗺 **Map Transparency:** Jewish Migration after AD 70

📺 **HSS** 6.3.5; **HSS** Analysis Skills: HI 1, HI 2

Answers

Reading Check *as punishment for Jewish revolts against Roman rule*

Results of the Revolt

With the capture of Masada in AD 73, the Jewish revolt was over. As punishment for the Jews' rebellion, the Romans killed much of Jerusalem's population. They took many of the surviving Jews to Rome as slaves. The Romans dissolved the Jewish power structure and took over the city.

Besides those taken as slaves, thousands of Jews left Jerusalem after the destruction of the Second Temple. With the Temple destroyed, they didn't want to live in Jerusalem anymore. Many moved to Jewish communities in other parts of the Roman Empire. One common destination was Alexandria in Egypt, which had a large Jewish community. The populations of these Jewish communities grew after the Romans destroyed Jerusalem.

A Second Revolt

Some Jews, however, chose not to leave Jerusalem when the Romans conquered it. Some 60 years after the capture of Masada, these Jews, unhappy with Roman rule, began another revolt. Once again, however, the Roman army defeated the Jews. After this rebellion in the 130s the Romans banned all Jews from the city of Jerusalem. Roman officials declared that any Jew caught in or near the city would be killed. As a result, Jewish migration throughout the Mediterranean region increased.

Migration and Discrimination

For Jews not living in Jerusalem, the nature of Judaism changed. Because the Jews no longer had a single temple at which to worship, local synagogues became more important. At the same time, leaders called **rabbis** (RAB-yz), or religious teachers, took on a greater role in guiding Jews in their religious lives. Rabbis were responsible for interpreting the Torah and teaching.

THE IMPACT TODAY
The United States today has a larger Jewish population than any other country in the world.

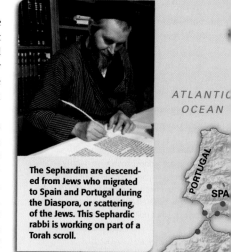

The Sephardim are descended from Jews who migrated to Spain and Portugal during the Diaspora, or scattering, of the Jews. This Sephardic rabbi is working on part of a Torah scroll.

ATLANTIC OCEAN

PORTUGAL

SPA

AFRICA

This change was largely due to the actions of Yohanan ben Zaccai, a rabbi who founded a school at Yavneh, near Jerusalem. In this school, he taught people about Judaism and trained them to be rabbis. Influenced by Yohanan, rabbis' ideas shaped how Judaism was practiced for the next several centuries. Many rabbis also served as leaders of Jewish communities.

Over many centuries, Jews moved out of the Mediterranean region to other parts of the world. In many cases this movement was not voluntary. The Jews were forced to move by other religious groups who discriminated against them. This discrimination forced many Jews to leave their cities and find new places to live. As a result, some Jews settled in Asia, Russia, and much later, the United States.

READING CHECK Identifying Cause and Effect
Why did the Romans force Jews out of Jerusalem?

Social Studies Skills Activity: Understanding Short- and Long-Term Effects [Standards Proficiency]

Charting Short- and Long-Term Effects 📺 **HSS** 6.3.5; **HSS** Analysis Skills: CS 1, HI 2

1. To help students identify short and long-term effects of the Jewish revolt against the Romans, draw the chart here for students to see. Omit the blue, italicized answers.

2. Have students copy the chart and use the section to complete it.

SE Social Studies Skills: Understanding Short- and Long-Term Effects, p. 246

📖 **CRF:** Social Studies Skills Activity: Understanding Short- and Long-Term Effects

Jewish Revolt Against Rome, AD 66–70

Short-Term Effects
- *loss of many lives, particulary Jews*
- *destruction of Jerusalem, Second Temple*
- *Roman enslavement of many surviving Jews*
- *end of Jewish power structure in Jerusalem*
- *migration of many Jews throughout Roman Empire*

Long-Term Effects
- *second unsuccessful revolt against Rome*
- *ban of Jews from Jerusalem*
- *scattering of Jews throughout world*
- *changes in nature of Judaism (synagogues, rabbis)*
- *discrimination against Jews*

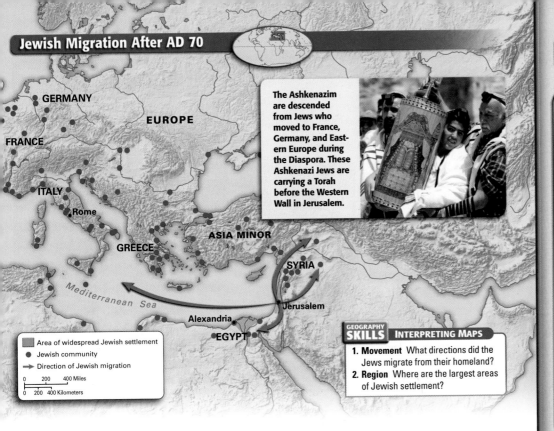

Jewish Migration After AD 70

GERMANY

EUROPE

FRANCE

ITALY
Rome

GREECE

ASIA MINOR

SYRIA

Jerusalem

Mediterranean Sea

Alexandria

EGYPT

The Ashkenazim are descended from Jews who moved to France, Germany, and Eastern Europe during the Diaspora. These Ashkenazi Jews are carrying a Torah before the Western Wall in Jerusalem.

Area of widespread Jewish settlement
● Jewish community
→ Direction of Jewish migration

0   200   400 Miles
0   200   400 Kilometers

GEOGRAPHY SKILLS   INTERPRETING MAPS

1. **Movement** What directions did the Jews migrate from their homeland?
2. **Region** Where are the largest areas of Jewish settlement?

Two Cultural Traditions

As you read earlier, the scattering of Jews around the world is called the Diaspora. It began after the Babylonian Captivity in the 500s BC. After that time, Jewish communities developed all around the world.

Jews everywhere shared the basic beliefs of Judaism. For example, all Jews still believed in one God and tried to obey God's law as set forth in the sacred texts. But communities in various parts of the world had different customs. As a result, the Jewish communities in different parts of the world began to develop their own languages, rituals, and cultures. These differences led to the creation of two main cultural traditions, both of which still exist today.

The Jews in Eastern Europe

One of the two traditions, the Ashkenazim (ahsh-kuh-NAH-zuhm), is made up of descendants of Jews who moved to France, Germany, and eastern Europe during the Diaspora. For the most part, these Jews had communities separate from their non-Jewish neighbors. Therefore, they developed their own customs that were unlike those of their neighbors. As an example, they developed their own language, Yiddish. Yiddish is similar to German but is written in the Hebrew alphabet.

The Jews in Spain and Portugal

Another Jewish cultural tradition developed during the Diaspora in what are now Spain and Portugal in Western Europe.

THE IMPACT TODAY

Some Yiddish words have entered the English language. For example, *schlep* means "to carry."

THE HEBREWS AND JUDAISM **243**

Direct Teach

Main Idea

2 Two Cultural Traditions

Because Jews settled in different parts of the world, two cultural traditions formed.

Recall What language did each Jewish cultural tradition develop? *Ashkenazim—Yiddish; Sephardim—Ladino*

Contrast How do the Ashkenazim and Sephardim differ? *Ashkenazim—settled in France, Germany, and eastern Europe; lived apart from non-Jews and developed a unique culture; spoke Yiddish; Sephardim—settled in Spain and Portugal; mixed with and borrowed from surrounding cultures; spoke Ladino*

HSS 6.3.5

Interpreting Maps

Jewish Migration After AD 70

Location Along what body of water were most Jewish communities located? *the Mediterranean Sea*

Map Transparency: Jewish Migration after AD 70

Info to Know

Yiddish in America Many Yiddish words and expressions have gained common usage in the United States. Share the following with students.

chutzpah	guts; nerve
cockamamie	crazy
futz	to fiddle around
mazel tov	congratulations
mensch	nice gentleman
nosh	to snack
oy	sigh
schlemiel	fool
schmoozing	talking about nothing

Collaborative Learning

Standards Proficiency

Jewish Populations Map and Chart
HSS 6.3.5: **HSS** Analysis Skills: CS 3 [Research Required]

1. Have students conduct research on Jewish populations and communities throughout the world today.

2. Organize students into small groups for the project and assign each group a continent or specific part of the world to research.

3. Have each group create a map and chart to present its findings. Remind the groups to include a title, legend, compass rose, and scale on their maps.

4. Have each group present its work to the class. Have students compare and contrast Jewish populations in the world today to those in the map on this page.
LS Interpersonal, Visual/Spatial

Alternative Assessment Handbook, Rubrics 7: Charts; 20: Map Creation; and 30: Research

Answers

Interpreting Maps 1. *north, west, and southwest;* **2.** *Spain; France; Germany; Italy; Greece; Asia Minor; Syria; and Alexandria, Egypt*

❸ Traditions and Holy Days

Jewish traditions and holy days celebrate their history and religion.

Define What is Hanukkah? *a Jewish holy day remembering an event where enough oil for one day lasted for eight*

Identify What is the most sacred Jewish holy day, and what event does it mark? *Yom Kippur—the day Jews ask God to forgive their sins*

Summarize How do Jewish traditions and holy days unite Jews? *help connect Jews to their long history and help create a strong unifying Jewish identity and culture*

 HSS 6.3.5

Linking to Today
A Passover Meal
Origins of Passover The name "Passover" refers back to an event right before the Exodus. The Hebrew Bible says that in the last plague on Egypt, God came and killed all the firstborn males. But God "passed over" the Jews' firstborn. This event led the pharaoh to free the Jews.

Answers

Linking to Today *Each item and event in the Passover seder tells the story of or symbolizes a part of the Exodus in Hebrew history.*

Reading Check *Ashkenazim, Sephardim*

244

A Passover Meal

Passover honors the Exodus, one of the most important events in Hebrew history. In honor of this event from their past, Jews share a special meal called a seder. Each item in the seder symbolizes a part of the Exodus. For example, bitter herbs represent the Jews' bitter years of slavery in Egypt. Before eating the meal, everyone reads prayers from a book called the Haggadah (huh-GAH-duh). It tells the story of the Exodus and reminds everyone present of the Jews' history. The small picture shows a seder in a copy of the Haggadah from the 1300s.

ANALYSIS SKILL **ANALYZING INFORMATION**
How does the Passover seder reflect the importance of the Exodus in Hebrew history?

The descendants of the Jews there are called the Sephardim (suh-FAHR-duhm). They also have a language of their own—Ladino. It is a mix of Spanish, Hebrew, and Arabic. Unlike the Ashkenazim, the Sephardim mixed with the region's non-Jewish residents. As a result, Sephardic religious and cultural practices borrowed elements from other cultures. Known for their writings and their philosophies, the Sephardim produced a golden age of Jewish culture in the AD 1000s and 1100s. During this period, for example, Jewish poets wrote beautiful works in Hebrew and other languages. Hebrew scholars also made great advances in mathematics, astronomy, medicine, and philosophy.

READING CHECK **Summarizing** What were the two main Jewish cultural traditions?

Traditions and Holy Days

Jewish culture is one of the oldest in the world. Because their roots go back so far, many Jews feel a strong connection with the past. They also feel that understanding their history will help them better follow Jewish teachings. Their traditions and holy days help them understand and celebrate their history.

Hanukkah

One Jewish tradition is celebrated by Hanukkah, which falls in December. It honors the rededication of the Second Temple during the revolt of the Maccabees.

The Maccabees wanted to celebrate a great victory that had convinced their non-Jewish rulers to let them keep their

---

Differentiating Instruction for Universal Access

Learners Having Difficulty
Reaching Standards

Connecting to the Big Idea Students may have difficulty with the section's transition from a chronological to a topical narrative. Explain the connection between the sequence of events at the start of the section and the Jewish cultural traditions discussed next. Last, explain how shared Jewish beliefs and traditions have helped unite Jews and maintain Judaism.

LS **Verbal/Linguistic**

HSS 6.3.5; **HSS** Analysis Skills: CS 1

Advanced Learners/GATE
Exceeding Standards

"Judaism over Time" Storyboards Organize students into small groups. Have each group create a storyboard for a documentary discussing how Judaism has survived and how Jews have maintained a sense of identity and community in spite of the Diaspora.

LS **Interpersonal, Verbal/Linguistic**

HSS 6.3.5; **HSS** Analysis Skills: HI 1

Alternative Assessment Handbook, Rubrics 1: Acquiring Information; and 14: Group Activity.

religion. According to legend, though, the Maccabees didn't have enough lamp oil to perform the rededication ceremony. Miraculously, the oil they had—enough to burn for only one day—burned for eight full days.

Today Jews celebrate this event by lighting candles in a special candleholder called a menorah (muh-NOHR-uh). Its eight branches represent the eight days through which the oil burned. Many Jews also exchange gifts on each of the eight nights.

Passover

More important than Hanukkah to Jews, Passover is celebrated in March or April. **Passover** is a time for Jews to remember the Exodus, the journey of the Hebrews out of slavery in Egypt.

According to Jewish tradition, the Hebrews left Egypt so quickly that bakers didn't have time to let their bread rise. Therefore, during Passover Jews eat only matzo, a flat, unrisen bread. They also celebrate the holy day with ceremonies and a ritual meal called a seder (SAY-duhr). During the seder, participants recall and reflect upon the events of the Exodus.

High Holy Days

Ceremonies and rituals are also part of the **High Holy Days**, the two most sacred of all Jewish holy days. They take place each year in September or October. The first two days of the celebration, Rosh Hashanah (rahsh uh-SHAH-nuh), celebrate the beginning of a new year in the Jewish calendar.

On Yom Kippur (yohm ki-POOHR), which falls soon afterward, Jews ask God to forgive their sins. Jews consider Yom Kippur to be the holiest day of the entire year. Because it is so holy, Jews don't eat or drink anything for the entire day. Many of the ceremonies they perform for Yom Kippur date back to the days of the Second

Temple. These ceremonies help many Jews feel more connected to their long past, to the days of Abraham and Moses.

 READING CHECK Finding Main Ideas What name is given to the two most important Jewish holy days?

SUMMARY AND PREVIEW The Jewish culture is one of the oldest in the world. Over the course of their long history, the Jews' religion and customs have helped them maintain a sense of identity and community. This sense has helped the Jewish people endure many hardships. In the next chapter you will learn about another people who made major contributions to Western culture. These were the Greeks.

Section 3 Assessment

go.hrw.com
Online Quiz
KEYWORD: SQ6 HP8

Reviewing Ideas, Terms, and People HSS 6.3.5

1. **a. Recall** Who won the battle at Masada?
   b. Evaluate How did the defeat by the Romans affect Jewish history?
2. **a. Identify** What language developed in the Jewish communities of eastern Europe?
   b. Contrast How did communities of Ashkenazim differ from communities of Sephardim?
3. **Identify** What event does **Passover** celebrate?

Critical Thinking

4. **Compare and Contrast** Draw a diagram like the one shown here. In the left circle, write facts that describe life for the Jews before the second revolt against the Romans. In the right circle, write facts that describe life after the revolt.

FOCUS ON WRITING

5. **Organizing Your Information** Add notes about what you've just read to the notes you have already collected. Now that you have all your information, organize it into categories that will be windows, links, and other features on your Web page.

THE HEBREWS AND JUDAISM **245**

• **Review & Assess** •

Info to Know

High Holy Days Jews call the period from Rosh Hashanah to Yom Kippur the Days of Awe. During this time, Jews ask God and others for forgiveness of their sins over the past year. Jews believe that on Rosh Hashanah, God writes in books the names of who will have a good or bad year and who will live or die in the coming year. But the books are not sealed until Yom Kippur. So prayer, good deeds, and asking for forgiveness during the Days of Awe can change what is written.

go.hrw.com
Online Resources
KEYWORD: SQ6 WH8
ACTIVITY: Jewish Holy Days

Close

Have students identify three to five details for each section main idea, listed at the start of the section.

Review

Online Quiz, Section 3

Assess

SE Section 3 Assessment
PASS: Section 3 Quiz
Alternative Assessment Handbook

Reteach/Classroom Intervention

California Standards Review Workbook
Interactive Reader and Study Guide, Section 3
Interactive Skills Tutor CD-ROM

Section 3 Assessment Answers

1. **a.** the Romans
   b. The Jews slowly scattered throughout the world, and two Jewish cultural traditions developed in Europe.
2. **a.** Yiddish
   b. Ashkenazim—lived apart from non-Jews and developed a unique culture; spoke Yiddish; Sephardim—mixed with and borrowed from surrounding cultures; spoke Ladino
3. the Exodus

4. Answers will vary but should reflect understanding of Jewish beliefs and customs.

5. Students should add notes that relate to each of the section's main ideas—revolt, defeat, and migration; two cultural traditions; and traditions and holy days.

Answers

Reading Check High Holy Days

Social Studies Skills

HSS **Analysis HI 2** Students understand and distinguish the long- and short-term causal relations.

| Analysis | Critical Thinking | Participation | Study |

Identifying Short- and Long-Term Effects

Understand the Skill

Many events of the past are the result of other events that took place earlier. When something occurs as the result of things that happened earlier, it is an effect of those things.

Some events take place soon after the things that cause them. These events are short-term effects. Long-term effects can occur decades or even hundreds of years after the events that caused them. Recognizing cause-and-effect relationships will help you to better understand the connections between historical events.

Learn the Skill

As you learned in Chapter 5, "clue words" can reveal cause-and-effect connections between events. Often, however, no such words are present. Therefore, you should always be looking for what happened as a result of an action or event.

Short-term effects are usually fairly easy to identify. They are often closely linked to the event that caused them. Take this sentence, for example:

"After Solomon's death around 930 BC, revolts broke out over who should be king."

It is clear from this information that a short-term effect of Solomon's death was political unrest.

Now, consider this other passage:

"Some Hebrews . . . moved to Egypt . . . The Hebrews lived well in Egypt and their population grew. But this growing population worried Egypt's ruler, the pharaoh. He feared that the Hebrews would soon take over Egypt. To prevent this from happening, the pharaoh made the Hebrews slaves."

Look carefully at the information in the passage. No clue words exist. However, it shows that one effect of the Hebrews' move to Egypt was the growth of their population. It takes time for a population to increase, so this was a long-term effect of the Hebrews' move.

Recognizing long-term effects is not always easy, however, because they often occur well after the event that caused them. Therefore, the long-term effects of those events may not be discussed at the time. This is why you should always ask yourself why an event might have happened as you study it.

For example, many of our modern laws are a result of the Ten Commandments of the ancient Hebrews. Religion is a major force in history that makes things happen. Other such forces include economics, science and technology, geography, and the meeting of peoples with different cultures. Ask yourself if one of these forces is a part of the event you are studying. If so, the event may have long-term effects.

Practice and Apply the Skill

Review the information in Chapter 8 and answer the following questions.

1. What were the short-term effects of King Solomon's rule of the Hebrews? What long-term benefit resulted from his rule?

2. What was the short-term effect of the destruction of the temple at Jerusalem in AD 70? What effect has that event had on the world today?

Standards Review

Visual Summary

Use the visual summary below to help you review the main ideas of the chapter.

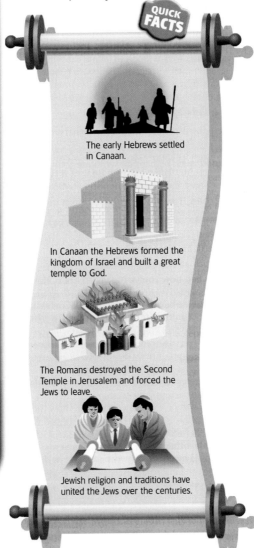

QUICK FACTS

The early Hebrews settled in Canaan.

In Canaan the Hebrews formed the kingdom of Israel and built a great temple to God.

The Romans destroyed the Second Temple in Jerusalem and forced the Jews to leave.

Jewish religion and traditions have united the Jews over the centuries.

Reviewing Vocabulary, Terms, and People

For each group of terms below, write a sentence that shows how the terms in the group are related.

1. Abraham
   Judaism
2. Moses
   Exodus
3. David
   Solomon
4. Torah
   Talmud
5. Passover
   High Holy Days
6. Moses
   Ten Commandments
7. Passover
   Exodus
8. monotheism
   Judaism
9. synagogues
   rabbis
10. principles
   Torah

Comprehension and Critical Thinking

SECTION 1 *(Pages 226–231)* **HSS** 6.3.3, 6.3.4

11. **a. Describe** How did Abraham and Moses shape the history of the Hebrew people?

   b. Compare and Contrast What did Saul, David, and Solomon have in common? How did they differ?

   c. Evaluate Of Esther, Deborah, Miriam, and Ruth, which do you think provided the best example of how people should treat their families? Explain your answer.

SECTION 2 *(Pages 232–237)* **HSS** 6.3.1, 6.3.2

12. **a. Identify** What are the basic beliefs of Judaism?

   b. Analyze What do the various sacred Jewish texts contribute to Judaism?

   c. Elaborate How are Jewish ideas reflected in modern Western society?

Visual Summary

Review and Inquiry Use the visual summary to help students recall and discuss the chapter's main points.

📖 Quick Facts Transparency: The Hebrews and Judaism Visual Summary

Reviewing Vocabulary, Terms, and People

1. Abraham is considered the ancestor of the Hebrews, whose religion is Judaism.

2. Moses led the Hebrews out of slavery in Egypt in the Exodus.

3. Solomon was David's son.

4. The Torah and Talmud are among the sacred texts of Judaism.

5. Passover and the High Holy Days, which includes Rosh Hashanah and Yom Kippur, are important Jewish celebrations.

6. The Hebrew Bible says that God gave Moses the Ten Commandments, a code of moral laws written on two stone tablets, on Mt. Sinai.

7. The Jewish holy day Passover commemorates the freeing of the Hebrews from slavery and their journey out of Egypt in the Exodus.

8. Judaism was the first religion to follow monotheism, the belief in only one God, that is still widely practiced today.

9. At synagogues, Jewish teachers called rabbis interpret the Torah and guide other Jews in Judaism.

10. The Torah describes the laws and principles of Judaism.

Comprehension and Critical Thinking

11. **a.** Abraham—led his family to Canaan and became father of the Hebrew people; Moses—led Hebrews out of Egypt, where the Hebrew people had been enslaved, and received Ten Commandments for the Hebrew people.

   b. all kings of Israel; Saul—military commander, not a strong king, not loved by all the Hebrews; David—military leader, strong king, well loved by the Hebrew people;

Review and Assessment Resources

Review and Reinforce

SE Standards Review

📄 **CRF**: Chapter Review Activity

📄 California Standards Review Workbook

📖 Quick Facts Transparency: The Hebrews and Judaism Visual Summary

🔊 Spanish Chapter Summaries Audio CD Program

💻 Online Chapter Summaries in Six Languages

OSP Holt PuzzlePro; GameTool for ExamView

💿 Quiz Game CD-ROM

Assess

SE Standards Assessment

📄 PASS: Chapter Test, Forms A and B

📄 Alternative Assessment Handbook

OSP ExamView Test Generator, Chapter Test

💿 Universal Access Modified Worksheets and Tests CD-ROM: Chapter Test

💻 Holt Online Assessment Program (in the Premier Online Student Edition)

Solomon—expanded the kingdom with trade and allies, strong king, built the great temple
c. Ruth, because she dedicated her life to supporting her mother-in-law
12. a. monotheism, education, justice and righteousness, obedience and law
b. Torah—laws, history of the Jews until the death of Moses; second and third parts of the Hebrew Bible—messages of Hebrew prophets and poetry songs, stories, lessons, history, Proverbs, Psalms; Talmud—commentaries, stories, folklore; Dead Sea Scrolls—prayers, commentaries, letters, passages from Hebrew Bible
c. possible answer—in the shaping of Christianity and the Ten Commandments as a guide for how to live
13. a. The Jews, led by the Zealots, revolted against Roman rule.
b. the Diaspora
c. Answers will vary but should acknowledge the importance of traditions in Judaism and their survival over many centuries.

Reading Skills

14. fact

15. opinion

16. opinion

17. fact

18. fact

Social Studies Skills

19. the Exodus—short-term: left Egypt, received Ten Commandments, wandered through desert, settled in Canaan; long-term: provided Jews with a significant and culturally binding historical event, which they remember during Passover; the Babylonian Captivity—short-term: Jews enslaved in Babylon for 50 years; long-term: After their release, many Jews did not return and thus began what is called the Diaspora; the expulsion of the Jews from Jerusalem—short-term: Jews slowly scattered throughout Mediterranean region and rest of world; long-term: changed nature of Judaism, led to creation of two Jewish cultural traditions

---

SECTION 3 (Pages 240–245)   **HSS** 6.3.5

13. a. **Describe** What happened as a result of tensions between the Romans and the Jews?

b. **Analyze** What led to the creation of the two main Jewish cultural traditions?

c. **Predict** In the future, what role do you think holy days and other traditions will play in Judaism? Explain your answer.

Reading Skills

Identifying Fact and Opinion *Identify each of the following statements as a fact or an opinion.*

14. Much of what we know about Hebrew history comes from the work of archaeologists.

15. Archaeologists should spend more time studying Hebrew history.

16. The Exodus is one of the most fascinating events in world history.

17. Until 1947, scholars did not know about the Dead Sea Scrolls.

18. Hanukkah is a Jewish holy day that takes place every December.

Social Studies Skills

19. **Identifying Short- and Long-Term Effects** *Identify both the short-term and long-term effects of each of the following events.*

	Short-Term Effects	Long-Term Effects
the Exodus		
the Babylonian Captivity		
the expulsion of the Jews from Jerusalem		

Using the Internet

go.hrw.com KEYWORD: SQ6 WH8

20. **Activity: Interpreting Maps** Migration and conflict were key factors shaping Jewish history and culture. The Exodus, the Babylonian Captivity, and the revolts against Rome forced the Jewish people to adapt their culture and settle in regions outside Israel. Enter the activity keyword. Then create an annotated map showing the birthplace of Judaism and the Jews' movements into other parts of the world. Your map should include a legend as well as labels to identify events and explain their impact on the Jewish people.

Reviewing Themes

21. **Religion** How did monotheism shape the history of the Hebrews?

22. **Religion** Do you agree or disagree with this statement: "The history of Judaism is also the history of the Hebrew people." Why?

23. **Religion** How does Mosaic law affect the daily lives of Jewish people?

FOCUS ON WRITING

24. **Designing Your Web Site** Look back at your notes and how you've organized them. Have you included all important facts and details? Will people be able to find information easily?

Write a description of your Web site. What is its name and Web address? What will you include on the home page? What will appear in menus or as hot links, and elsewhere on the page? What images will you include? Draw a rough diagram or sketch of your page. Be sure to label the parts of your page.

When you're finished, compare how the information is presented in your textbook with how you presented it on your Web site. Most of the information in the book is presented chronologically, by the year or era. How did you present the information?

Using the Internet

20. Go to the HRW Web site and enter the keyword shown to access a rubric for this activity.

KEYWORD: SQ6 TEACHER

Reviewing Themes

21. Monotheism shaped the Hebrews' religion, culture, and history, guiding Hebrew patriarchs and leaders and bringing the Hebrews into conflict with others.

22. possible answers—agree, because Judaism has shaped Jewish history and helped the Jews maintain an identity throughout their history; disagree, because Jewish history includes more than just the history of the Hebrew people

23. Mosaic law governs how Jews pray and celebrate, when Jews should work and worship, and what Jews may eat, among other activities.

Focus on Writing

24. **Rubric** Students' Web sites should:
- have a title and clear labels.
- describe what appears on the home page, menus, and hot links.
- include descriptions of images.
- respect the beliefs and traditions of Judaism.

CRF: Focus on Writing: A Web Site

Standards Assessment

DIRECTIONS: Read each question, and write the letter of the best response.

1 Use the map to answer the following question.

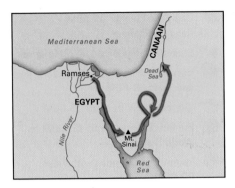

The map above illustrates

A the Babylonian Captivity.

B the Exodus.

C Abraham's migration to Canaan.

D the capture of Jerusalem by the Romans.

2 The Jews believe that the Ten Commandments were given by God to

A Moses.

B Abraham.

C King David.

D King Solomon.

3 The ancient Jews probably were the first people to

A conduct religious ceremonies.

B have a code of laws.

C practice monotheism.

D hold religious beliefs.

4 The basic teachings and laws that guide the Jewish people are found in the

A Talmud.

B Torah.

C Book of the Dead.

D Dead Sea Scrolls.

5 Which group was *most* responsible for the migration of Jews out of Jerusalem to other parts of the Mediterranean region?

A the Israelites

B the Philistines

C the Egyptians

D the Romans

Connecting with Past Learnings

6 In an earlier chapter, you learned about people of Mesopotamia who had a law code. Moses issued a set of laws for the Hebrew people to follow. What other ancient leader is famous for issuing laws?

A Gilgamesh

B Tutankhamen

C Asoka

D Hammurabi

7 Jewish teachings required people to honor and respect their parents. This was an idea also common in China. In his writings, who else encouraged people to respect their parents?

A Chandragupta Maurya

B Shi Huangdi

C Confucius

D Abraham

THE HEBREWS AND JUDAISM **249**

Tips for Test Taking

Read and Re-read If students are taking a reading comprehension test, they should read the selection, master all the questions, and then re-read the selection. The answers will probably pop out the second time around. Students should remember that the test isn't trying to trick them; it's trying to test their knowledge and their ability to think clearly.

Answers

1. B
Break Down the Question Remind students to look at the full routes when reading a map showing movement. Students who answered *C* may have read the map too quickly.

2. A
Break Down the Question This question requires students to recall factual information.

3. C
Break Down the Question Help students see that answers *A*, *B*, and *D* refer to practices common to many ancient religions.

4. B
Break Down the Question Students may confuse the Talmud and the Torah. You might suggest a memory aid to help students distinguish between the two sacred texts.

5. D
Break Down the Question Remind students that italicized words in test questions often significantly affect the question's meaning.

6. D
Break Down the Question This question connects to information in the chapter on Mesopotamia and the Fertile Crescent.

7. C
Break Down the Question This question connects to information in the chapter on China.

Standards Review

Have students review the following standard in their workbooks.

California Standards Review Workbook:
HSS 6.6

Ancient Greece

Chapter Overview	Reproducible Resources	Technology Resources
CHAPTER 9 pp. 250–81 **Overview:** In this chapter, students will begin their study of the history and culture of ancient Geece. See p. 250 for the California History–Social Science standards covered in this chapter.	**Universal Access Teacher Management System:*** • Universal Access Instructional Benchmarking Guides • Lesson Plans for Universal Access **Interactive Reader and Study Guide:** Chapter Graphic Organizer* **Chapter Resource File*** • Chapter Review Activity • Focus on Writing Activity: A Myth • Social Studies Skills Activity: Analyzing Costs and Benefits	 **One-Stop Planner CD-ROM:** Calendar Planner 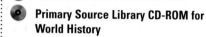 **Student Edition on Audio CD Program** **Universal Access Modified Worksheets and Tests CD-ROM** **Interactive Skills Tutor CD-ROM** **Primary Source Library CD-ROM for World History** **Power Presentations with Video CD-ROM** **History's Impact: World History Video Program (VHS/DVD):** Ancient Greece* **A Teacher's Guide to Religion in the Public Schools***
Section 1: **Geography and the Early Greeks** **The Big Idea:** Greece's geography and its nearness to the sea strongly influenced the development of trade and the growth of city-states. 6.4.1	**Universal Access Teacher Management System:*** Section 1 Lesson Plan **Interactive Reader and Study Guide:** Section 1 Summary* 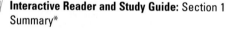 **Chapter Resource File*** • Vocabulary Builder Activity, Section 1 • History and Geography Activity: Greek City-States and Colonization	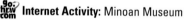 **Daily Bellringer Transparency:** Section 1* **Map Transparency:** Greece: Physical* **Map Transparency:** Minoan and Mycenaean Civilizations* **Map Transparency:** Greek City-States and Colonies, c. 600 BC* **Internet Activity:** Minoan Museum
Section 2: **Government in Athens** **The Big Idea:** The people of Athens tried many different forms of government before creating a democracy. 6.4.2, 6.4.3	**Universal Access Teacher Management System:*** Section 2 Lesson Plan **Interactive Reader and Study Guide:** Section 2 Summary* **Chapter Resource File*** • Vocabulary Builder Activity, Section 2 • Biography Activity: Aspasia • Biography Activity: Pericles • Primary Source Activity: Aristotle's Athenian Constitution	**Daily Bellringer Transparency:** Section 2* **Quick Facts Transparency:** Government in Athens* **Quick Facts Transparency:** Democracy Then and Now*
Section 3: **Greek Mythology and Literature** **The Big Idea:** The ancient Greeks created great myths and works of literature that influence the way we speak and write today. 6.4.4	**Universal Access Teacher Management System:*** Section 3 Lesson Plan **Interactive Reader and Study Guide:** Section 3 Summary* **Chapter Resource File*** • Vocabulary Builder, Section 3 • Biography Activity: Sappho • Literature Activity: "Midas," from *Bulfinch's Mythology* • Primary Source Activity: Sappho's Poetry	**Daily Bellringer Transparency:** Section 3* **Internet Activity:** Olympic Collectibles

SE Student Edition	Print Resource	Audio CD	Video
TE Teacher's Edition	Transparency	CD-ROM	DVD
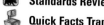 go.hrw.com	CA Standards Mastery	**LS** Learning Styles	
OSP One-Stop Planner CD-ROM	* also on One-Stop Planner CD		

California Resources for Standards Mastery

INSTRUCTIONAL PLANNING AND SUPPORT

 Universal Access Teacher Management System*

 One-Stop Planner CD-ROM with Test Generator: Teacher Management System with Interactive Teacher's Edition

STANDARDS MASTERY

Standards Review Workbook*

At Home: A Guide to Standards Mastery for World History

Review, Assessment, Intervention

- Standards Review Workbook*
- Quick Facts Transparency: Ancient Greece Visual Summary*
- Spanish Chapter Summaries Audio CD Program
- Online Chapter Summaries in Six Languages
- Quiz Game CD-ROM
- Progress Assessment Support System (PASS): Chapter Test*
- Universal Access Modified Worksheets and Tests CD-ROM: Modified Chapter Test
- One-Stop Planner CD-ROM: ExamView Test Generator (English/Spanish)
- Alternative Assessment Handbook
- Holt Online Assessment Program (HOAP), in the Holt Premier Online Student Edition

---

- PASS: Section 1 Quiz*
- Online Quiz: Section 1
- Alternative Assessment Handbook

- PASS: Section 2 Quiz*
- Online Quiz: Section 2
- Alternative Assessment Handbook

- PASS: Section 3 Quiz*
- Online Quiz: Section 3
- Alternative Assessment Handbook

 Holt Online Learning

To enhance learning, the following Internet activities are available: Minoan Museum and Olympic Collectibles.

KEYWORD: SQ6 TEACHER

- Teacher Support Page
- Content Updates
- Rubrics and Writing Models
- Teaching Tips for the Multimedia Classroom

KEYWORD: SQ6 WH9

- Current Events
- Holt Grapher
- Holt Online Atlas
- Holt Researcher
- Interactive Multimedia Activities
- Internet Activities
- Online Chapter Summaries in Six Languages
- Online Section Quizzes
- World History Maps and Charts

HOLT PREMIER ONLINE STUDENT EDITION

Complete online support for interactivity, assessment, and reporting

- Interactive Maps and Notebook
- Standardized Test Prep
- Homework Practice and Research Activities Online

Mastering the Standards: Differentiating Instruction

Reaching Standards	Basic-level activities designed for all students encountering new material
Standards Proficiency	Intermediate-level activities designed for average students
Exceeding Standards	Challenging activities designed for honors and gifted-and-talented students
Standard English Mastery	Activities designed to improve standard English usage

MASTERING THE CALIFORNIA STANDARDS

Frequently Asked Questions

INSTRUCTIONAL PLANNING AND SUPPORT

Where do I find planning aids, instructional benchmarking guides, lesson plans, and other teaching aids?

Annotated Teacher's Edition:
- Chapter planning guides
- Standards-based instruction and strategies
- Differentiated instruction for universal access
- Point-of-use reminders for integrating program resources

Power Presentations with Video CD-ROM

Universal Access Teacher Management System:
- Year and unit instructional benchmarking guides
- Reproducible lesson plans
- Assessment guides for diagnostic, progress, and summative end-of-the-year tests
- Options for differentiating instruction and intervention
- Teaching guides and answer keys for student workbooks

One-Stop Planner CD-ROM with Test Generator: Teacher Management System with Interactive Teacher's Edition:
- Calendar Planner
- Editable lesson plans
- All reproducible ancillaries in Adobe Acrobat (PDF) format
- ExamView Test Generator (English & Spanish)
- Game Tool for ExamView
- PuzzlePro
- Transparency and video previews

DIFFERENTIATING INSTRUCTION FOR UNIVERSAL ACCESS

What resources are available to ensure that Advanced Learners/GATE students master the standards?

Teacher's Edition Activities:
- Greek Assembly Simulation, p. 265
- Biographies of the Gods, p. 269
- Olympic Poetry, p. 271
- The *Iliad* and the *Odyssey*, p. 273
- Greek Word Origins, p. 274
- Using Similes, p. 276

Lesson Plans for Universal Access

Primary Source Library CD-ROM for World History

What resources are available to ensure that English Learners and Standard English Learners master the standards?

Teacher's Edition Activities:
- Greek Terms Tic-Tac-Toe, p. 263
- Greek Literature and Fables, p. 272
- Deciphering Word Meanings, p. 276

Lesson Plans for Universal Access

Chapter Resource File: Vocabulary Builder Activities

Spanish Chapter Summaries Audio CD Program

Online Chapter Summaries in Six Languages

One-Stop Planner CD-ROM:
- PuzzlePro, Spanish Version
- ExamView Test Generator, Spanish Version

What modified materials are available for Special Education?

Teacher's Edition Activities: Geography and the Early Greeks, p. 255

The *Modified Materials for Struggling Students CD-ROM* provides editable versions of the following:

Vocabulary Flash Cards

Modified Vocabulary Builder Activities

Modified Chapter Review Activity

Modified Chapter Test

What resources are available to ensure that Learners Having Difficulty master the standards?

Teacher's Edition Activities:
- Using Time Lines, p. 256
- Evaluating the Athenian Assembly, p. 264
- Illustrated Time Line, p. 266

Interactive Reader and Study Guide

Student Edition on Audio CD Program

Quick Facts Transparency: Ancient Greece Visual Summary

Standards Review Workbook

Social Studies Skills Activity: Analyzing Costs and Benefits

Interactive Skills Tutor CD-ROM

How do I intervene for students struggling to master the standards?

Interactive Reader and Study Guide

Quick Facts Transparency: Ancient Greece Visual Summary

Standards Review Workbook

Social Studies Skills Activity: Analyzing Costs and Benefits

Interactive Skills Tutor CD-ROM

PROFESSIONAL DEVELOPMENT

**HOLT
Professional
Development**

What teacher training resources are available to help me grow professionally?

- In-service and staff development as part of your Holt Social Studies product purchase
- Quick Teacher Tutorial Lesson Presentation CD-ROM
- Intensive tuition-based Teacher Development Institute
- Convenient Holt Speaker Bureau face-to-face workshop options

- PRAXIS™ Test Prep (#0089) interactive Web-based content refreshers*
- *Ask A Professional Development Expert* at http://www.hrw.com/prodev/

* PRAXIS is a trademark of Educational Testing Service (ETS). This publication is not endorsed or approved by ETS.

Information Literacy Skills

To learn more about how History–Social Science instruction may be improved by the effective use of library media centers and information literacy skills, go to the Teacher's Resource Materials for Chapter 9 at **go.hrw.com, keyword: SQ6 MEDIA.**

MASTERING THE CALIFORNIA STANDARDS

Standards Focus

Standards by Section
Section 1: **HSS** 6.4.1
Section 2: **HSS** 6.4.2, 6.4.3
Section 3: **HSS** 6.4.4

Teacher's Edition
HSS Analysis Skills: CS 1, CS 2, CS 3, HR 1, HR 3, HI 1, HI 2, HI 3, HI 6

Upcoming Standards for Future Learning
Preview the following History–Social Science content standards from upcoming chapters or grade levels to promote learning beyond the current chapter.

HSS **6.4** Students analyze the geographic, political, economic, religious, and social structures of the early civilizations of Ancient Greece.

6.4.6 Compare and contrast life in Athens and Sparta, with emphasis on their roles in the Persian and Peloponnesian Wars.

6.4.8 Describe the enduring contributions of important Greek figures in the arts and sciences (e.g., Hypatia, Socrates, Plato, Aristotle, Euclid, Thucydides).

Focus on Writing

The **Chapter Resource File** provides a Focus on Writing worksheet to help students organize and create their myths.

CRF: Focus on Writing Activity: A Myth

CHAPTER 9 ▶ 2000–500 BC

Ancient Greece

California Standards

History–Social Science
6.4 Students analyze the geographic, political, economic, religious, and social structures of the early civilizations of Ancient Greece.

Analysis Skills
HI 6 Conduct cost-benefit analyses of economic and political issues.

English–Language Arts
Writing 6.2.1a Establish and develop a plot and setting and present a point of view that is appropriate to the stories.

Reading 6.2.0 Read and understand grade-level-appropriate material.

FOCUS ON WRITING

A Myth Like most people, the Greeks enjoyed good stories. But they also took their stories seriously. They used stories called myths to explain everything from the creation of the world to details of everyday life. Reading this chapter will provide you with ideas you can use to create your own myth.

CHAPTER EVENTS

c. 2000 BC
The Minoan civilization prospers in Crete.

2000 BC

WORLD EVENTS

c. 2000 BC
The main part o
Stonehenge is
built in England

Introduce the Chapter

Standards Proficiency

Focus on Greek Contributions **HSS** 6.4.8; **HSS** Analysis Skills: HI 1

1. Discuss with students what they already know about ancient Greece. Ask students if they can name any contributions of the Greeks to our modern world. Write students' ideas for the class to see.

2. Give the students several categories to consider if they are having difficulty thinking of ideas. Categories could include government, literature, sports, and culture. Students may require hints to develop ideas

for the list. Students may come up with ideas such as the Olympics, democracy, or Greek mythology.

3. Review with students the list of ideas they developed. Help students to see which ideas are correct and which are incorrect.

4. Have students draw an illustration for one of the contributions from the list. Ask for volunteers to share their illustrations with the class. **LS** Verbal/Linguistic, Visual/Spatial

What You Will Learn...

In this chapter you will study Greece—home to one of the great ancient civilizations. In this photo you see the ruins of the temple at Delphi. It was one of the most sacred places in ancient Greece.

c. 1200 BC
The Greeks and Trojans fight the Trojan War.

c. 750 BC
The Greeks begin to build city-states.

c. 500 BC
Athens becomes the world's first democracy.

1700 BC   1400 BC   1100 BC   800 BC   500 BC

c. 1200 BC
The Olmec civilization develops in the Americas.

c. 900 BC
The Phoenicians dominate trade in the Mediterranean.

753 BC
According to legend, Rome is founded.

ANCIENT GREECE   **251**

• **Chapter Preview** •

HOLT
History's Impact
▶ video series
See the Video Teacher's Guide for strategies for using the chapter video **Ancient Greece: The Impact of Democracy.**

Chapter Big Ideas

Section 1 Greece's geography and its nearness to the sea strongly influenced the development of trade and the growth of city-states. HSS 6.4.1

Section 2 The people of Athens tried many different forms of government before creating a democracy. HSS 6.4.2, 6.4.3

Section 3 The ancient Greeks created great myths and works of literature that influence the way we speak and write today. HSS 6.4.4

Explore the Picture

The Temple at Delphi The Tholos temple at the sanctuary of Athena Pronaia near Delphi was built around 380 BC. The Greeks believed that the oracle of Delphi could foresee the future.

Analyzing Visuals What can you tell about the geography of Greece by looking at this photo? *possible answers—It is very mountainous; Greek cities were built in the mountains; there is considerable vegetation.*

Explore the Time Line

1. What was happening in the Americas at about the time of the Trojan War? *The Olmec civilization was developing.*

2. In about what year did Athens create the world's first democracy? *c. 500 BC*

HSS Analysis Skills: CS 1

Info to Know

Minoan Civilization The image of the dolphins in the time line was one of many frescoes, or wall paintings, discovered in the ruins of the Minoan palace at Knossos on the island of Crete.

Reading Social Studies

by Kylene Beers

| Economics | Geography | Politics | Religion | Society and Culture | Science and Technology |

Focus on Themes In this chapter, you will read about the civilizations of ancient Greece. Whether reading about the Minoans and Mycenaeans or the Spartans and Athenians, you will see that where the people lived affected how they lived.

You will also read how the government of these ancient people changed over the years. By the end of this chapter, you will have learned a great deal about the **geography** and the **politics** of the ancient Greeks.

Greek Word Origins

Focus on Reading Sometimes when you read an unusual word, you can figure out what it means by using the other words around it. Other times you might need to consult a dictionary. But sometimes, if you know what the word's root parts mean, you can figure out its meaning. The chart below shows you several English words that have Greek roots.

In this chapter you'll find...	which means...	and comes from the Greek root
1. geography, p. 254 (jee-AH-gruh-fee)	the study of the earth's surface	*ge-*, which means "earth" *-graphy*, which means "writing about"
2. acropolis, p. 258 (uh-KRAH-puh-luhs)	fortress of a Greek city up on a high hill	*acr-*, which means "top" *polis*, which means "city".
3. democracy, p. 262 (di-MAH-kruh-see)	a form of government in which people hold power	*dem-*, which means "people" *-cracy*, which means "power"
4. tyrant, p. 263 (TY-ruhnt)	a ruler [in modern times, a harsh ruler]	*tyrannos*, which means "master"
5. oligarchy, p. 263 (AH-luh-gahr-kee)	rule by a few people	*olig-*, which means "few" *-archy*, which means "rule"
6. mythology, p. 269 (mi-THAH-luh-jee)	a body of stories about gods and heroes	*mythos*, which means "stories about gods or heroes" *-ology*, which means "study of"

Additional reading support can be found in the

Inter-active Reader and Study Guide

Reading and Skills Resources

Reading Support

📖 Interactive Reader and Study Guide

🔊 Student Edition on Audio CD

🔊 Spanish Chapter Summaries Audio CD Program

Social Studies Skills Support

💿 Interactive Skills Tutor CD-ROM

Vocabulary Support

📖 **CRF:** Vocabulary Builder Activities

📖 **CRF:** Chapter Review Activity

💿 Universal Access Modified Worksheets and Tests CD-ROM:
- Vocabulary Flash Cards
- Vocabulary Builder Activity
- Chapter Review Activity

OSP Holt PuzzlePro

Understanding Themes

Introduce the two main themes in this chapter—geography and politics. Remind students that where people live influences their history. Ask students to suggest ways in which people are affected by where they live. What effects does geography have on trade and culture? Tell students that the geography of Greece led to the establishment of small political units known as city-states. These city-states practiced many different types of government. Tell students that ancient Greeks developed the first democracy. Help students understand the importance of democratic government.

Greek Word Origins

Focus on Reading Review the chart on this page with students. Ask students to examine the Greek roots in the third column. Ask students how they might find out if a word comes from a Greek root. Remind students that word origins are given in dictionary entries. Have students work in pairs to find at least three words that use each of the roots in the chart. Examples for *–graphy* might include *cartography*, *biography*, and *bibliography*. Encourage students to share their lists with the class.

🐻 Standards Focus

ELA Reading 6.2.0

You Try It!

Study each of the words below. Use the chart on the opposite page to find a Greek root or roots for each of them. How do the words' roots relate to their definitions?

Word	Definition
1. geology	a science that deals with the study of the makeup of the earth
2. police	the people who keep order in a city
3. Tyrannosaurus	one of the largest and fiercest dinosaurs
4. architect	the person in charge of designing buildings
5. acrophobia	the fear of heights
6. monarchy	rule by a single person
7. politics	the art or science of governing a city, state, or nation
8. demographer	a scientist who studies the growth of populations

Think about it.

1. How can studying Greek origins help you understand English?

2. Use the chart of roots on the previous page to answer this question. Where do you think a demagogue gets his or her power: the support of the people or a written constitution? Justify your answer.

3. Do you know words in other languages that help you understand English?

Key Terms and People

Chapter 9

Section 1
polis *(p. 258)*
classical *(p. 258)*
acropolis *(p. 258)*

Section 2
democracy *(p. 262)*
aristocrats *(p. 263)*
oligarchy *(p. 263)*
citizens *(p. 263)*
tyrant *(p. 263)*
Pericles *(p. 266)*

Section 3
mythology *(p. 269)*
Homer *(p. 272)*
Sappho *(p. 273)*
Aesop *(p. 273)*
fables *(p. 273)*

Academic Vocabulary

Success in school is related to knowing academic vocabulary—the words that are frequently used in school assignments and discussions. In this chapter, you will learn the following academic word:

influence *(p. 256)*

As you read Chapter 9, pay close attention to the highlighted words. Many of those words are Greek or come from Greek roots. Refer to the chart on the opposite page to help you understand what those words mean.

Reading Social Studies

Key Terms and People

Introduce this chapter's key terms and people by reading the list aloud so that students will know how to pronounce each term or name. Then organize the students into pairs and assign each pair a person or term from the list. Have each pair identify the importance of the person or term. Then have each group draw a picture that represents the significance of that term or person. Have students present their term, description, and illustration to the class. Encourage students to take notes on the presentations.
LS Verbal/Linguistic, Visual/Spatial

Focus on Reading

See the **Focus on Reading** questions in this chapter for more practice on this reading social studies skill.

Reading Social Studies Assessment

See the **Standards Review** at the end of this chapter for student assessment questions related to this reading skill.

Teaching Tip

Have students create a chart that lists roots from commonly used words, as well as their meaning. Remind students to look in a dictionary for word origins. Some possible roots might be *aud-*, hear; *philo-*, loving; *anthro-*, man, and *med-*, middle. Then have students list words in which those roots are used.

Answers

You Try It! 1. *By learning the meaning of Greek root words, we can guess the meaning of some English words that have these roots.* **2.** *The root–dem means* people, *so a demagogue gets his or her power from the support of the people.* **3.** *possible answer—Words with Latin roots might help students who understand Spanish, French, Italian, or Portuguese understand many English words.*

253

Bellringer

If YOU were there . . . Use the **Daily Bellringer Transparency** to help students answer the question.

📖 Daily Bellringer Transparency, Section 1

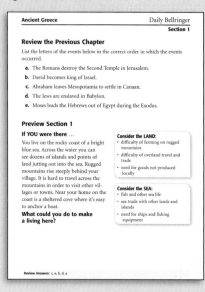

Academic Vocabulary

Review with students the high-use academic term in this section.

influence change, or have an effect on (p. 256)

📄 **CRF:** Vocabulary Builder Activity, Section 1

🐻 Standards Focus

HSS 6.4.1

Means: Discuss how the geography of Greece affected the growth of city-states and trade.

Matters: The geography of Greece led to the creation of independent city-states that relied on trade and the seas.

Geography and the Early Greeks

Main Ideas

1. Geography helped shape early Greek civilization.
2. Trading cultures developed in the Minoan and Mycenaean civilizations.
3. The Greeks created city-states for protection and security.

The Big Idea

Greece's geography and its nearness to the sea strongly influenced the development of trade and the growth of city-states.

Key Terms

polis, *p. 258*
classical, *p. 258*
acropolis, *p. 258*

HSS 6.4.1 Discuss the connections between geography and the development of city-states in the region of the Aegean Sea, including patterns of trade and commerce among Greek city-states and within the wider Mediterranean region.

If YOU were there...

You live on the rocky coast of a bright blue sea. Across the water you can see dozens of islands and points of land jutting out into the sea. Rugged mountains rise steeply behind your village. It is hard to travel across the mountains in order to visit other villages or towns. Near your home on the coast is a sheltered cove where it's easy to anchor a boat.

What could you do to make a living here?

> **BUILDING BACKGROUND** The paragraph you just read could be describing many parts of Greece, a peninsula in southern Europe. Greece's mountain ranges run right up to the coast in many places, making travel and farming difficult. Although it does not seem like the easiest place in the world to live, Greece was home to some of the ancient world's greatest civilizations.

Greece is a land of rugged mountains, rocky coastlines, and beautiful islands. The trees you see are olive trees. Olives were grown by the early Greeks for food and oil.

Teach the Big Idea: Master the Standards   Standards Proficiency

Geography and the Early Greeks 🐻 HSS 6.4.1; HSS Analysis Skills: HI 1, HI 2

1. **Teach** Ask students the Main Idea questions to teach this section.

2. **Apply** Re-create the geography of Greece in your classroom by moving desks to create physical boundaries. Place students into "city-state" groups. Make city-states large, small, isolated, etc. Ask groups to list resources available to their city-states and to solve any issues of scarcity. Ask students to identify the benefits and drawbacks of their cities. **LS Kinesthetic**

3. **Review** As you review the section, have students relate their city-states to those of ancient Greece.

4. **Practice/Homework** Have students write an essay that describes how geography affected the development of city-states.
   LS Verbal/Linguistic

📄 Alternative Assessment Handbook, Rubrics 11: Discussions; and 42: Writing to Inform

Geography Shapes Greek Civilization

The Greeks lived on rocky, mountainous lands surrounded by water. The mainland of Greece is a peninsula, an area of land that is surrounded on three sides by water. But the Greek peninsula is very irregular. It's one big peninsula made up of a series of smaller peninsulas. The land and sea intertwine like your hand and fingers in a bowl of water. In addition, there are many islands. Look at the map of Greece and notice the rugged coastline.

In your mind, picture those peninsulas and islands dominated by mountains that run almost to the sea. Just a few small valleys and coastal plains provide flat land for farming and villages. Now you have an image of Greece, a land where one of the world's greatest civilizations developed.

Mountains and Settlements

Because mountains cover much of Greece, there are few flat areas for farmland. People settled in those flat areas along the coast and in river valleys. They lived in villages and towns separated by mountains and seas.

Travel across the mountains and seas was difficult, so communities were isolated from one another. As a result, the people created their own governments and ways of life. Even though they spoke the same language, Greek communities saw themselves as separate countries.

Seas and Ships

Since travel inland across the rugged mountains was so difficult, the early Greeks turned to the seas. On the south was the huge Mediterranean Sea, to the west was the Ionian (eye-OH-nee-uhn) Sea, and to the east was the Aegean (ee-JEE-uhn) Sea.

Greece: Physical

Black Sea

PINDOS MOUNTAINS

40° N

Ionian Sea

GREECE

Gulf of Corinth

Peloponnesus

Aegean Sea

Mediterranean Sea

ASIA MINOR

Rhodes

Crete

20° E   25° E   30° E

35° N

ELEVATION

Feet	Meters
6,560	2,000
1,640	500
656	200
(Sea level) 0	0 (Sea level)

0   50   100 Miles
0   50   100 Kilometers

GEOGRAPHY SKILLS   INTERPRETING MAPS

Location What bodies of water surround Greece?

ANCIENT GREECE **255**

Differentiating Instruction for Universal Access

Special Education Students   Reaching Standards

1. Review with the class the main features of the geography of Greece.

2. To help students identify the ways in which the Greeks were affected by their geography, draw the graphic organizer for students to see. Omit the blue, italicized answers.

3. Have students copy the graphic organizer and complete it by identifying ways in which mountains and seas affected the ancient Greeks. **LS** Visual/Spatial

🐻 **HSS** 6.4.1; **HSS** Analysis Skills: HI 1

Mountains	**Seas**
Effect on Greeks	**Effect on Greeks**
little farmland	*source of food*
villages and towns separated from each other	*means of trade*
travel difficult	*transportation*
little contact between towns	*helped exchange ideas with other cultures*

255

Main Idea

❷ Trading Cultures Develop

Trading cultures developed in the Minoan and Mycenaean civilizations.

Recall Where was the Minoan civilization located? *on the island of Crete*

Compare How was the decline of the Minoans and Mycenaeans similar? *They both experienced natural disasters.*

Make Inferences Why did the Mycenaeans put such importance on building powerful fortresses? *Answers will vary, but students should indicate that they were used for protection.*

 **HSS** 6.4.1; **HSS** Analysis Skills: HI 1, HI 2

Early Trading Cultures

The Minotaur Greek legend tells of a horrifying half-man, half-bull creature known as the Minotaur that lived in a maze beneath the palace of Knossos.

go.hrw.com
Online Resources

KEYWORD: SQ6 WH9
ACTIVITY: Minoan Museum

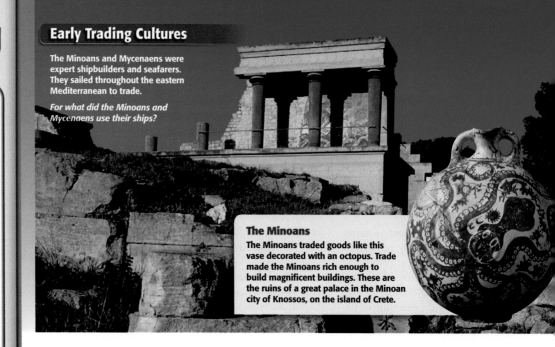

Early Trading Cultures

The Minoans and Mycenaens were expert shipbuilders and seafarers. They sailed throughout the eastern Mediterranean to trade.

For what did the Minoans and Mycenaens use their ships?

The Minoans

The Minoans traded goods like this vase decorated with an octopus. Trade made the Minoans rich enough to build magnificent buildings. These are the ruins of a great palace in the Minoan city of Knossos, on the island of Crete.

It's not surprising that the early Greeks used the sea as a source for food and as a way of trading with other communities.

The Greeks became skilled shipbuilders and sailors. Their ships sailed to Asia Minor, to Egypt, and to the islands of the Mediterranean and Aegean seas. As they traveled around these seas, they found sources of food and other products they needed. They also exchanged ideas with other cultures.

ACADEMIC VOCABULARY
influence
change, or have an effect on

READING CHECK Drawing Conclusions
How did mountains affect the location of Greek settlements?

Trading Cultures Develop

Many cultures settled and developed in Greece. Two of the earliest were the Minoans (muh-NOH-uhnz) and the Mycenaens (my-suh-NEE-uhns). By 2000 BC the

Minoans had built an advanced society on the island of Crete. Crete lay south of the Aegean in the eastern Mediterranean. Later, the Mycenaeans built towns on the Greek mainland. These two civilizations **influenced** the entire Aegean region and helped shape later cultures in Greece.

The Minoans

Because they lived on an island, the Minoans spent much of their time at sea. They were among the best shipbuilders of their time. Minoan ships carried goods such as wood, olive oil, and pottery all around the eastern Mediterranean. They traded these goods for copper, gold, silver, and jewels.

Although Crete's location was excellent for Minoan traders, its geography had its dangers. Sometime in the 1600s BC a huge volcano erupted just north of Crete. This eruption created a giant wave that flooded much of Crete. In addition, the eruption

Social Studies Skills Activity: Using Time Lines
Reaching Standards

Time Line of the Trading Cultures  **HSS** 6.4.1; **HSS** Analysis Skills: CS 2

1. Discuss with students the early trading cultures of the Minoans and Mycenaeans and key events in the history of each society.

2. Next, write the following events on the board for students to copy. Omit dates in italics.

   • Minoan civilization declines *(mid-1400s BC)*

   • Minoans establish society on Crete *(2000 BC)*

   • Invaders enter Greece *(1200s BC)*

   • Volcanic eruption floods Crete *(1600s BC)*

3. Have each student create a time line that includes entries and years(s) for the events listed in the correct chronological order in which each occurred. **LS** Visual/Spatial

📑 Alternative Assessment Handbook, Rubric 36: Time Lines

⦿ Interactive Skills Tutor CD-ROM

Answers

Early Trading Cultures *to trade in the Mediterranean*

Reading Check *Villages and towns were separated by mountains.*

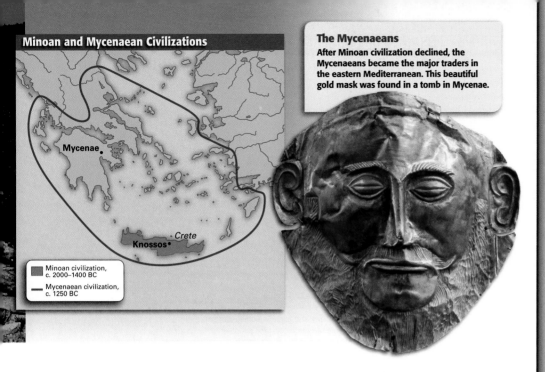

Minoan and Mycenaean Civilizations

Mycenae
Crete
Knossos

Minoan civilization, c. 2000–1400 BC

Mycenaean civilization, c. 1250 BC

The Mycenaeans

After Minoan civilization declined, the Mycenaeans became the major traders in the eastern Mediterranean. This beautiful gold mask was found in a tomb in Mycenae.

threw up huge clouds of ash, ruining crops and burying cities. This eruption may have led to the end of Minoan civilization.

The Mycenaeans

Although they lived in what is now Greece and influenced Greek society, historians don't consider the Minoans to be Greek. This is because the Minoans didn't speak the Greek language. The first people to speak Greek, and therefore the first to be considered Greek, were the Mycenaeans.

While the Minoans were sailing the Mediterranean, the Mycenaeans were building fortresses all over the Greek mainland. The largest and most powerful fortress was Mycenae (my-SEE-nee), after which the Mycenaeans were named.

By the mid-1400s, Minoan society had declined. That decline allowed the Mycenaeans to take over Crete and become the major traders in the eastern Mediterranean.

They set up colonies in northern Greece and Italy from which they shipped goods to markets around the Mediterranean and Black seas.

The Mycenaeans didn't think trade had to be conducted peacefully. They often attacked other kingdoms. Some historians think the Mycenaeans attacked the city of Troy, possibly starting the legendary Trojan War, which is featured in many works of literature.

Mycenaean society began to fall apart in the 1200s BC when invaders from Europe swept into Greece. At the same time, earthquakes destroyed many cities. As Mycenaean civilization crumbled, Greece slid into a period of warfare and disorder, a period called the Dark Age.

READING CHECK Finding Main Ideas

To what regions did Minoan and Mycenaean traders travel?

ANCIENT GREECE **257**

Cross-Discipline Activity: Arts and the Humanities | Standards **Proficiency**

Minoan Frescoes HSS 6.4.1; HSS Analysis Skills: HI 1

Materials: butcher paper, art supplies

1. Have students examine the photo of the palace at Knossos. Point out the mural behind the columns. Explain that these murals are called frescoes.

2. Explain to students that frescoes are a type of painting in which artists paint onto a wall while the wall's plaster is still wet. This technique allows frescoes to survive for very long periods of time.

3. Tell students that Minoan frescoes generally depicted everyday life such as sports, trade, and animals.

4. Organize students into small groups. Have them decide what images of their daily life they would include in a class fresco. Then have students create a fresco on butcher paper. **LS Visual/Spatial**

Alternative Assessment Handbook, Rubric 3: Artwork

Interpreting Maps

Greek City-States and Colonies, c. 600 BC

Activity **Creating a Map** Using an outline map of the Mediterranean, have students label the major Greek colonies and trade routes. Then have students use a current world atlas to identify the modern-day countries where the Greeks had influence.

LS Visual/Spatial

Alternative Assessment Handbook: Rubric 20: Map Creation

HSS 6.4.1; **HSS** Analysis Skills: CS 3

Main Idea

❸ Greeks Create City-States

The Greeks created city-states for protection and security.

Define What is a classical age? *a time marked by great achievements*

Summarize Why did Greeks decide to establish colonies? *They wanted to trade, learn more about their neighbors, and deal with their growing population.*

Draw Conclusions How did city walls and acropolises benefit Greek city-states? *They protected the city-states from attack.*

CRF: History and Geography Activity: Greek City-States and Colonization

Map Transparency: Greek City-States and Colonies, c. 600 BC

HSS 6.4.1; **HSS** Analysis Skills: HI 1, HI 2

Greek City-States and Colonies, c. 600 BC

Legend:
- Area of Greek influence
- Greek city-state or colony
- Trade route

0 — 150 — 300 Miles
0 — 150 — 300 Kilometers

GEOGRAPHY SKILLS **INTERPRETING MAPS**

Location Greek city-states and colonies were spread around the Mediterranean Sea and which other large sea?

Greeks Create City-States

The Greeks of the Dark Age left no written records. All that we know about the period comes from archaeological findings.

About 300 years after the Mycenaean civilization crumbled, the Greeks started to join together in small groups for protection and stability. Over time, these groups set up independent city-states. The Greek word for a city-state is **polis** (PAH-luhs). The creation of city-states marks the beginning of what is known as Greece's classical age. A **classical** age is one that is marked by great achievements.

Life in a City-State

FOCUS ON READING

How do Greek roots give you clues to the meaning of acropolis?

A Greek city was usually built around a strong fortress. This fortress often stood on top of a high hill called the **acropolis** (uh-KRAH-puh-luhs). The town around the acropolis was surrounded by walls for added protection.

Not everyone who lived in the city-state actually lived inside the city walls. Farmers, for example, usually lived near their fields outside the walls. In times of war, however, women, children, and elderly people all gathered inside the city walls for protection. As a result, they remained safe while the men of the polis formed an army to fight off its enemies.

Life in the city often focused on the marketplace, or agora (A-guh-ruh) in Greek. Farmers brought their crops to the market to trade for goods made by craftsmen in the town. Because it was a large open space, the market also served as a meeting place. People held both political and religious assemblies in the market. It often contained shops as well.

The city-state became the foundation of Greek civilization. Besides providing security for its people, the city gave them an identity. People thought of themselves

258 CHAPTER 9

Critical Thinking: Identifying Points of View

Standards Proficiency

Letter Supporting Colonization **HSS** 6.4.1; **HSS** Analysis Skills: HR 5

1. Discuss with students the reasons many Greeks had for establishing colonies in the Mediterranean.

2. Next, have students identify some of the ways in which the Greeks benefited from having colonies. Remind students to consider economic benefits as well as others.

3. Ask students to imagine that they live in a Greek city-state that does not have colonies.

Have each student write a letter to the leaders of their city-state encouraging them to establish colonies in the region.

4. Student letters should be persuasive and should point out the benefits of creating colonies, based on the reasons provided in the section. **LS** Verbal/Linguistic

Alternative Assessment Handbook: Rubric 43: Writing to Persuade

---

Answers

Interpreting Maps *the Black Sea*
Focus on Reading *Polis means city-state, so one can infer that it is some type of city.*

258

as residents of a city, not as Greeks. Because the city-state was so central to their lives, the Greeks expected people to participate in its affairs, especially in its economy and its government.

City-States and Colonization

Life in Greece eventually became more settled. People no longer had to fear raiders swooping down on their cities. As a result, they were free to think about things other than defense. Some Greeks began to dream of becoming rich through trade. Others became curious about neighboring lands around the Mediterranean Sea. Some also worried about how to deal with Greece's growing population. Despite their different reasons, all these people eventually reached the same idea: the Greeks should establish colonies.

Before long, groups from city-states around Greece began to set up colonies in distant lands. After they were set up, Greek colonies became independent. In other words, each colony became a new polis. In fact, some cities that began as colonies began to create colonies of their own. Eventually Greek colonies spread all around the Mediterranean and Black seas. Many big cities around the Mediterranean today began as Greek colonies. Among them are Istanbul (is-tahn-BOOL) in Turkey, Marseille (mahr-SAY) in France, and Naples in Italy.

Patterns of Trade

Although the colonies were independent, they often traded with city-states on the mainland. The colonies sent metals such as copper and iron back to mainland Greece. In return, the Greek city-states sent wine, olive oil, and other products.

Trade made the city-states much richer. Because of their locations, some city-states became great trading centers. By 550 BC

the Greeks had become the greatest traders in the whole Aegean region. Greek ships sailed to Egypt and cities around the Black Sea.

READING CHECK Analyzing Why did the Greeks develop city-states?

SUMMARY AND PREVIEW In this section you learned about the creation of city-states and how they affected Greek society. In the next section you will read about how the government of one city-state changed as people became more interested in how they were ruled.

go.hrw.com
Online Quiz
KEYWORD: SQ6 HP9

Section 1 Assessment

Reviewing Ideas, Terms, and People HSS 6.4.1

1. **a. Identify** What kinds of landforms are found in Greece?
   b. Interpret How did the sea help shape early Greek society?
   c. Predict How might the difficulty of mountain travel have been a benefit to the Greeks?
2. **a. Recall** What was the first major civilization to develop in Greece?
   b. Compare How were the Minoans and Mycenaeans similar?
3. **a. Define** What is a **polis**?
   b. Elaborate Why do you think the Greeks built their cities around a high **acropolis**?

Critical Thinking

4. **Summarize** Draw a diagram like the one here. Use it to identify three functions of the polis in early Greek society.

Polis

FOCUS ON WRITING

5. **Thinking About Geographical Features as Characters** Have you ever thought about physical features as having personalities? For example, you might describe a strong, blustery wind as angry. Think about the physical features of Greece you read about in this section. What kinds of personalities might they have? Write your ideas down in your notebook.

ANCIENT GREECE **259**

History and Geography

Activity **A Bad Day in Crete** Lead a discussion about how the eruption would have affected the buildings and people of Knossos. Then have students work in groups to create storyboards depicting scenes from a movie about the Thera eruption. Or, have students create posters advertising the movie.
LS **Visual/Spatial**

Info to Know

From Reality to Legend The Minoan civilization may have inspired stories about Atlantis, a legendary island kingdom that supposedly disappeared beneath waves caused by earthquakes. The Greek philosopher Plato wrote about Atlantis. He may have gotten the story from ancient Egyptian records that report the Thera eruption.

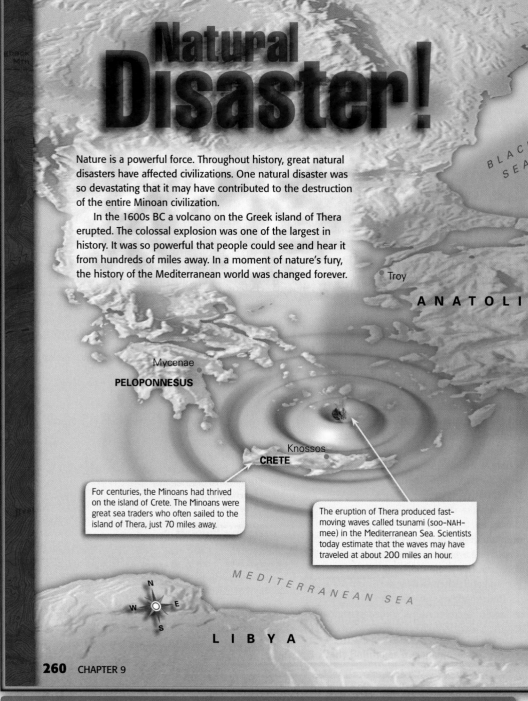

Natural Disaster!

Nature is a powerful force. Throughout history, great natural disasters have affected civilizations. One natural disaster was so devastating that it may have contributed to the destruction of the entire Minoan civilization.

In the 1600s BC a volcano on the Greek island of Thera erupted. The colossal explosion was one of the largest in history. It was so powerful that people could see and hear it from hundreds of miles away. In a moment of nature's fury, the history of the Mediterranean world was changed forever.

BLACK SEA

Troy

ANATOLIA

Mycenae

PELOPONNESUS

Knossos

CRETE

For centuries, the Minoans had thrived on the island of Crete. The Minoans were great sea traders who often sailed to the island of Thera, just 70 miles away.

The eruption of Thera produced fast-moving waves called tsunami (soo-NAH-mee) in the Mediterranean Sea. Scientists today estimate that the waves may have traveled at about 200 miles an hour.

MEDITERRANEAN SEA

LIBYA

260 CHAPTER 9

Social Studies Skills: Recognizing the Role of Chance in History

Changing History **HSS** 6.4.1; **HSS** Analysis Skills: HI 4 **Exceeding Standards**

1. Ask students to skim the remainder of this chapter and the next one. Then ask students to consider these questions. How would the history of the Mediterranean world have proceeded if the Thera volcano had not erupted violently, but instead the lava had flowed slowly into the sea? How may the eruption have affected Greek history? Point out that immediate effects of physical events can have a ripple effect that extends over centuries.

2. Have each student create a booklet in which he or she rewrites key heads and subheads for the rest of this chapter and the next one, basing the rewrites on the assumption that the Thera volcano was not violent.

3. Extend the activity by discussing how even today things could be very different if history had changed that day on Thera.
LS **Interpersonal, Verbal/Linguistic**

Alternative Assessment Handbook, Rubric 11: Discussions

Standards Focus

History–Social Science
HSS **6.4** Students analyze the geographic, political, economic, religious, and social structures of the early civilizations of Ancient Greece.
6.4.1 Discuss the connections between geography and the development of city-states in the region of the Aegean Sea, including patterns of trade and commerce among Greek city-states and within the wider Mediterranean region.

The ancient island of Thera is known as Santorini today. The huge gap on the island's western side and the water in the middle are evidence of the explosion more than 3,500 years ago.

Aleppo

CYPRUS

The explosion produced a massive cloud of ash that smothered crops, cities, and people. For years afterward, the ash dimmed the sunlight, making it difficult for farmers to grow their crops.

GEOGRAPHY SKILLS **INTERPRETING MAPS**

1. **Location** What direction did the ash cloud travel after the island's eruption?
2. **Human-Environment Interaction** How might the effects of the ash cloud have influenced Minoan civilization?

E G Y P T

Jericho

Three Stages of Disaster

Stage 1

Warning Signs Following a series of earthquakes, the volcano begins to shoot ash into the sky. People flee the island in fear.

Stage 2

Explosion Ash and rock are flung into the air and sweep down the volcano's sides, destroying everything in their path. Cracks through the island rock begin to form from the powerful explosions.

Stage 3

Collapse The volcano collapses and falls into the sea, creating massive waves. The powerful waves slam into Crete, flooding coastal areas.

History and Geography

Connect to Science

Stealthy Killer Waves Tsunamis like those that hit Crete in the 1600s BC may be mere ripples way out at sea. A severe earthquake in the middle of the ocean may send out waves more than 100 miles apart. These waves race across the ocean at speeds of up to 450 miles per hour. The tops of the waves are very low, however, so people on board a ship would probably not notice such a wave as it raced by. The trouble comes when the waves near the shore. As the water gets shallower, the waves slow down and grow taller. When they finally crash onto the shore, tsunamis can be 100 feet high.

On December 26, 2004, an underwater earthquake caused tsunamis to hit the coasts of Sri Lanka, Indonesia, India, Thailand, Somalia, and several other countries. The devastation was terrible. A month after the waves struck, the death toll had climbed to more than 212,000. Millions more people were homeless.

MISCONCEPTION ALERT

Name that Wave! Tsunamis are often mistakenly called tidal waves. An alternate and accurate name for a tsunami is seismic sea wave. Tsunamis are not related to tidal action in any way, so the term *tidal wave* is incorrect.

Critical Thinking: Comparing and Contrasting

Standards Proficiency

Natural Disasters and History ⬤ HSS 6.4.1; HSS Analysis Skills: HI 2   Research Required

1. Organize the class into groups. Have each group conduct research on a different major natural disaster. Possibilities may include the eruption of Krakatoa (Indonesia, 1883), the New Madrid earthquakes (North America, 1811), the Tunguska Event (Russia, 1908), or the flood of the Huang He (China, 1887).

2. Ask students to concentrate their research on the short- and long-term effects the disaster had on areas both near and far away.

3. Then have students compare the assigned disaster's effects with the impact that the Thera eruption had on Minoan civilization. Challenge students to compare specific factors, such as the number of people in the area that were affected, communication capabilities, and so on.

4. Ask each group to report to the class in the form of a newscast.
    LS Interpersonal, Kinesthetic
    Alternative Assessment Handbook, Rubric 9: Comparing and Contrasting

Answers

Interpreting Maps: 1. *northeast*
2. *possible answers—caused immediate death and destruction and long-term decline of Minoan civilization due to damage to ships, harbors, and farmland*

261

Bellringer

If YOU were there . . . Use the **Daily Bellringer Transparency** to help students answer the question.

🗄 Daily Bellringer Transparency, Section 2

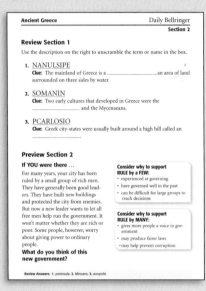

Ancient Greece | Daily Bellringer
Section 2

Review Section 1

Use the description on the right to unscramble the term or name in the box.

1. NANULSIPE
   Clue: The mainland of Greece is a _____, an area of land surrounded on three sides by water.

2. SOMANIN
   Clue: Two early cultures that developed in Greece were the _____ and the Mycenaeans.

3. PCARLOSIO
   Clue: Greek city-states were usually built around a high hill called an

Preview Section 2

If YOU were there ...

For many years, your city has been ruled by a small group of rich men. They have generally been good leaders. They have built new buildings and protected the city from enemies. But now a new leader wants to let all free men help run the government. It won't matter whether they are rich or poor. Some people, however, worry about giving power to ordinary people.

What do you think of this new government?

Consider why to support **RULE by a FEW:**
- experienced at governing
- have governed well in the past
- can be difficult for large groups to reach decisions

Consider why to support **RULE by MANY:**
- gives more people a voice in government
- may produce fairer laws
- may help prevent corruption

Review Answers: 1. peninsula; 2. Minoans; 3. acropolis

Building Vocabulary

Preteach or review the following term:

prosperity the state of being successful (p. 263)

📝 **CRF:** Vocabulary Builder Activity, Section 2

🐻 Standards Focus

HSS 6.4.2

Means: Examine the evolution of government in ancient Greece from oligarchy and tyranny to democracy and dictatorship and understand the importance of the idea of citizenship.

Matters: The Greeks' invention of democracy and the concept of citizenship serve as models for our modern government.

HSS 6.4.3

Means: Explain the difference between direct democracy and representative democracy.

Matters: The Greeks' direct democracy differs from our modern, representative democracy.

Government in Athens

What You Will Learn...

Main Ideas

1. Aristocrats and tyrants ruled early Athens.
2. Athens created the world's first democracy.
3. Ancient democracy was different than modern democracy.

The Big Idea

The people of Athens tried many different forms of government before creating a democracy.

Key Terms and People

democracy, *p. 262*
aristocrats, *p. 263*
oligarchy, *p. 263*
citizens, *p. 263*
tyrant, *p. 263*
Pericles, *p. 266*

HSS 6.4.2 Trace the transition from tyranny and oligarchy to early democratic forms of government and back to dictatorship in ancient Greece, including the significance of the invention of the idea of citizenship (e.g., from *Pericles' Funeral Oration*).

6.4.3 State the key differences between Athenian, or direct, democracy and representative democracy.

If YOU were there...

For many years, your city has been ruled by a small group of rich men. They have generally been good leaders. They have built new buildings and protected the city from enemies. But now a new leader wants to let all free men help run the government. It won't matter whether they are rich or poor. Some people, however, worry about giving power to ordinary people.

What do you think of this new government?

BUILDING BACKGROUND The decision to change a city's government was not unusual in Greece. Many cities tried several forms of government before people were satisfied. To see how these changes came about, we can look at one city whose government changed many times—Athens.

Aristocrats and Tyrants Rule

Greece is the birthplace of **democracy**, a type of government in which people rule themselves. The word democracy comes from Greek words meaning "rule of the people." But Greek city-states didn't start as democracies, and not all became democratic.

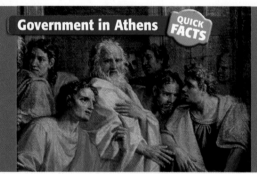

Government in Athens QUICK FACTS

Oligarchy
Early Athens was governed by a small group of powerful aristocrats. This type of government is called an oligarchy. Oligarchy means "rule by a few."

Teach the Big Idea: Master the Standards

Standards Proficiency

Government in Athens 🐻 HSS 6.4.2, 6.4.3; HSS Analysis Skills: HI 2

1. **Teach** Ask students the Main Idea questions to teach this section.

2. **Apply** Write the main ideas from the section for students to see, and discuss each concept with the class. Organize the students into small groups and assign each group one or more main ideas. Ask each group to create a one-to-two minute skit for its main ideas. Ask for groups to volunteer to perform their skits for the class. **LS Interpersonal, Kinesthetic**

3. **Review** After each group performs, review with the class the major concepts from each skit that pertain to the main ideas.

4. **Practice/Homework** Have students select their favorite performance and write a review of the skit, making sure to include the main points that were addressed in the presentation. **LS Verbal/Linguistic**

📝 Alternative Assessment Handbook, Rubrics 33: Skits and Reader's Theater; and 41: Writing to Express

Rule by a Few People

Even Athens, the city where democracy was born, began with a different kind of government. In early Athens, kings ruled the city-state. Later, a group of rich landowners, or **aristocrats** (uh-RIS-tuh-krats), took power. A government in which only a few people have power is called an **oligarchy** (AH-luh-gar-kee).

The aristocrats dominated Athenian society. As the richest men in town, they ran the city's economy. They also served as its generals and judges. Common people had little say in the government.

In the 600s BC a group of rebels tried to overthrow the aristocrats. They failed. Possibly as a result of their attempt, however, a man named Draco (DRAY-koh) created a new set of laws for Athens. These laws were very harsh. For example, Draco's laws made minor crimes such as loitering punishable by death.

The people of Athens thought Draco's laws were too strict. In the 590s BC a man named Solon (SOH-luhn) created a set of laws that were much less harsh and gave more rights to nonaristocrats. Under Solon's laws, all free men living in Athens became **citizens**, people who had the right to participate in government. But his efforts were not enough for the Athenians. They were ready to end the rule of the aristocracy.

The Rise of the Tyrants

Because the Athenians weren't pleased with the rule of the aristocrats, they wanted a new government. In 546 BC a noble named Peisistratus (py-SIS-truht-uhs) overthrew the oligarchy. He became the ruler of Athens. Peisistratus was called a **tyrant**, which meant a leader who held power through the use of force.

Today the word *tyrant* means a ruler who is harsh, but the word had a different meaning in ancient Greece. Athenian tyrants were usually good leaders. Tyrants were able to stay in power because they had strong armies and because the people supported them.

Peisistratus brought peace and prosperity to the city. He began new policies meant to unify the city. He created new festivals and built temples and monuments. During his rule, many improvements were made in Athens.

After Peisistratus died, his son took over as tyrant. Many aristocrats, however, were unhappy because their power was gone. Some of these aristocrats convinced a rival city-state to attack Athens. As a result of this invasion, the tyrants lost power and, for a short time, aristocrats returned to power in Athens.

FOCUS ON READING
How do Greek roots give you clues to the meaning of oligarchy?

Today very harsh laws or rules are called "draconian" after Draco.

READING CHECK Finding the Main Idea
What was a tyrant in ancient Greece?

Tyranny
Peisistratus overthrew the oligarchy in 546 BC, and Athens became a tyranny. Tyranny means "rule by a tyrant"—a strong leader who has power.

Democracy
Around 500 BC Athens became a democracy. Democracy means "rule by the people." For the first time in history, a government was based on the votes of its free citizens.

ANCIENT GREECE **263**

Differentiating Instruction for Universal Access

English-Language Learners   Standards Proficiency

1. Review with students the key terms from this section: democracy, aristocrats, oligarchy, citizens, and tyrant.

2. Draw a tic-tac-toe diagram (nine-square grid) for students to see. Divide the students into two groups: X's and O's.

3. Determine which group will go first. Then select one student in that group to answer a question. Given one of the vocabulary words,

students are to define the term and use it in a sentence. Upon answering correctly, that group puts their mark in the square of their choosing. The first group to get three in a row wins. **LS Interpersonal, Verbal/Linguistic**

📝 Alternative Assessment Handbook, Rubric 11: Discussions

📝 **CRF:** Vocabulary Builder Activity, Section 2

🐻 **HSS** 6.4.2; **HSS** Analysis Skills: CS 1

263

Main Idea

❷ Athens Creates Democracy

Athens created the world's first democracy.

Recall Who was the father of democracy in Athens? *Cleisthenes*

Analyze Why were slaves sent to round up citizens? *because more citizens were needed to vote on a law*

Explain Why was a smaller council of officials necessary? *It was easier to make decisions about which laws the assembly should vote on.*

Activity Democracy Political Cartoon Have each student create an original political cartoon that deals with an element of the democratic process in Athens. Ask for volunteers to share their completed cartoons with the class. **LS** Visual/Spatial

📖 Alternative Assessment Handbook: Rubric 27: Political Cartoons

📄 **CRF:** Primary Source Activity: Aristotle's Athenian Constitution

🐻 **HSS** 6.4.2; **HSS** Analysis Skills: HI 1

Info to Know

Cleisthenes In order to break the power of the aristocrats, Cleisthenes re-organized all Athenians into 10 new tribes. The tribes were an important part of local politics, and many had local assemblies similar to the Athenian assembly.

History Close-up

Democracy in Action

Ancient Athens was the birthplace of democracy—the system of government in which the people rule themselves. Democracy was perhaps the greatest achievement of ancient Athens. In time, it became the Greeks' greatest gift to the world.

Only free male citizens of Athens were members of the assembly with the right to vote. Women, slaves, and foreigners could not participate.

In Athenian democracy, people debated issues in the open air, and these debates were noisy affairs.

Voting was usually done by a show of hands, but sometimes assembly members wrote their votes on broken pieces of pottery. Then officials collected these pottery pieces and counted the votes.

Athens Creates Democracy

Around 500 BC a new leader named Cleisthenes (KLYS-thuh-neez) gained power in Athens. Although he was a member of one of the most powerful families in Athens, Cleisthenes didn't want aristocrats to run the government. He thought they already had too much influence. By calling on the support of the people, Cleisthenes was able to overthrow the aristocracy once and for all. In its place, he established a completely new form of government.

Under Cleisthenes' leadership, Athens developed the world's first democracy. For this reason, he is sometimes called the father of democracy.

Democracy under Cleisthenes

Under Cleisthenes, all citizens in Athens had the right to participate in the assembly, or gathering of citizens, that created the city's laws. The assembly met outdoors on a hillside so that everyone could attend the meetings. During meetings, people stood before the crowd and gave speeches on political issues. Every citizen had the right to speak his opinion. In fact, the Athenians encouraged people to speak. They loved to hear speeches and debates. After the speeches were over, the assembly voted. Voting was usually done by a show of hands, but sometimes the Athenians used secret ballots.

264 CHAPTER 9

Critical Thinking: Evaluating Information

Reaching Standards

Evaluating the Athenian Assembly 🐻 **HSS** 6.4.2; **HSS** Analysis Skills: HI 1

1. Review with students the creation of democracy in Athens as well as the description of the Athenian assembly.

2. Draw the graphic organizer for students to see. Omit the blue, italicized answers. Ask students to identify the benefits and drawbacks of democracy in Athens.

3. Have students evaluate whether democracy in Athens was good or bad. **LS** Visual/Spatial

Athenian Democracy	
Benefits	**Drawbacks**
• *All citizens have a say in government.*	• *Women, slaves, and foreigners have no say.*
• *All citizens can express opinions.*	• *Sometimes forced to attend assembly.*
• *Power of nobles is limited.*	• *Difficult to make decisions with so many people.*

The Athenian assembly met on a hill called the Pnyx (pah-NIKS). Sometimes, more than 6,000 men crowded onto the small hill.

Men spoke before the assembly to support or argue against different issues. Persuasive speakers often convinced others to pass laws they supported.

Men in the crowd often argued with speakers.

ANALYSIS SKILL ANALYZING VISUALS
How did people vote in ancient Athens?

The number of people who voted in the assembly changed from day to day. For major decisions, however, the assembly needed about 6,000 people to vote. But it wasn't always easy to gather that many people together in one place.

According to one Greek writer, the government sent slaves to the market to round up more citizens if necessary. In one of the writer's plays, slaves walked through the market holding a long rope between them. The rope was covered in red dye and would mark the clothing of anyone it touched. Any citizen with red dye on his clothing had to go to the assembly meeting or pay a large fine.

Because the assembly was so large, it was sometimes difficult to make decisions. The Athenians therefore selected citizens to be city officials and to serve on a smaller council. These officials decided which laws the assembly should discuss. This helped the government run more smoothly.

Changes in Athenian Democracy

As time passed, citizens gained more powers. For example, they served on juries to decide court cases. Juries had anywhere from 200 to 6,000 people, although juries of about 500 people were much more common. Most juries had an odd number of members to prevent ties.

THE IMPACT TODAY
Like the ancient Greeks, we use juries to decide court cases. But our modern juries have only 12 people.

ANCIENT GREECE **265**

Primary Source

Pericles' Funeral Oration

Interpret What does Pericles mean when he says that Athens serves as an example to its neighbors? *The government of Athens is so great that it is copied by other city-states.*

📝 **CRF:** Biography Activity: Pericles

🐻 **HSS** 6.4.2; **HSS** Analysis Skills: CS 3

Main Idea

③ **Ancient Democracy Differs from Modern Democracy**

Ancient democracy was different than modern democracy.

Define What is a direct democracy? *a democracy in which each person has a direct vote*

Summarize How does a representative democracy work? *Citizens elect officials to represent them in the government and to make laws.*

Draw Conclusions Why didn't the United States establish a direct democracy? *There are too many people to make voting directly on every law practical.*

📝 **CRF:** Biography Activity: Aspasia

📝 **CRF:** Biography Activity: Pericles

👆 Quick Facts Transparency: Democracy Then and Now

🐻 **HSS** 6.4.3; **HSS** Analysis Skills: CS 1

Answers

Analyzing Primary Sources *that the government of Athens was better than that of other cities*

Reading Check *They participated in the assembly, on juries, and held public offices.*

SPEECH

Pericles' Funeral Oration

In 430 BC Pericles addressed the people of Athens at a funeral for soldiers who had died in battle. In his speech, Pericles tried to comfort the Athenians by reminding them of the greatness of their government.

Pericles is praising the Athenians for creating a democracy.

"Our form of government does not enter into rivalry with the institutions of others. We do not copy our neighbors, but are an example to them. It is true that we are called a democracy, for the administration is in the hands of the many and not of the few . . . There is no exclusiveness [snobbery] in our public life, and . . . we are not suspicious of one another. . . ."

–Pericles, quoted in Thucydides, *The History of the Peloponnesian War*

Athenian government was open to all free men, not just a few.

ANALYSIS SKILL **ANALYZING PRIMARY SOURCES**

How do you think Pericles felt Athenian government compared to other cities' governments?

Athens remained a democracy for about 170 years. It reached its height under a brilliant elected leader named **Pericles** (PER-uh-kleez). He led the government from about 460 BC until his death in 429 BC.

Pericles encouraged the Athenians to take pride in their city. He believed that participating in government was just as important as defending Athens in war. To encourage people to participate in government, Pericles began to pay people who served in public offices or on juries. Pericles also encouraged the people of Athens to introduce democracy into other parts of Greece.

End of Democracy in Athens

Eventually, the great age of Athenian democracy came to an end. In the mid-330s BC Athens was conquered by the Macedonians from north of Greece. After the conquest, Athens fell under strong Macedonian influence.

Even after being conquered by Macedonia, Athens kept its democratic government. But it was a democracy with very limited powers. The Macedonian king ruled his country like a dictator, a ruler who held all the power. No one could make any decisions without his approval.

In Athens, the assembly still met to make laws, but it had to be careful not to upset the king. The Athenians didn't dare make any drastic changes to their laws without the king's consent. They weren't happy with this situation, but they feared the king's powerful army. Before long, though, the Athenians lost even this limited democracy. In the 320s BC a new king took over Greece and ended Athenian democracy forever.

READING CHECK **Summarizing** How were citizens involved in the government of Athens?

Ancient Democracy Differs from Modern Democracy

Like ancient Athens, the United States has a democratic government in which the people hold power. But our modern democracy is very different from the ancient Athenians' democracy.

Direct Democracy

All citizens in Athens could participate directly in the government. We call this form of government a direct democracy. It is called direct democracy because each person's decision directly affects the outcome of a vote. In Athens, citizens gathered

---

Critical Thinking: Sequencing

Reaching Standards

Illustrated Time Line 🐻 **HSS** 6.4.2; **HSS** Analysis Skills: CS 2

1. Review with students the different governments that existed in ancient Athens.

2. Ask students to make a list of the different governments and the order in which each existed. Then ask students to identify the approximate dates of each government.

3. Finally, have students create an illustrated time line of the different governments of Athens. Time lines should list each

government, explain the form of the government, and include an illustration that reflects that style of government (time line answers: *oligarchy—600s BC, tyranny—546 to 500 BC, democracy—500 to 330 BC, monarchy—330 BC)* **⑤ Visual/Spatial**

📝 Alternative Assessment Handbook, Rubrics 3: Artwork; and 36: Time Lines

together to discuss issues and vote on them. Each person's vote counted, and the majority ruled.

The United States is too large for direct democracy to work for the whole country. For example, it would be impossible for all citizens to gather in one place for a debate. Instead, the founders of the United States set up another kind of democracy.

Representative Democracy

The democracy created by the founders of the United States is a representative democracy, or republic. In this system, the citizens elect officials to represent them in the government. These elected officials then meet to make the country's laws and to enforce them. For example, Americans elect senators and representatives to Congress, the body that makes the country's laws. Americans don't vote on each law that Congress passes but trust their chosen representatives to vote for them.

> **READING CHECK** **Contrasting** How are direct democracy and representative democracy different?

Democracy Then and Now

 QUICK FACTS

In Athenian Direct Democracy...	In American Representative Democracy...
■ All citizens met as a group to debate and vote directly on every issue.	■ Citizens elect representatives to debate and vote on issues for them.
■ There was no separation of powers. Citizens created laws, enforced laws, and acted as judges.	■ There is a separation of powers. Citizens elect some people to create laws, others to enforce laws, and others to be judges.
■ Only free male citizens could vote. Women and slaves could not vote.	■ Men and women who are citizens have the right to vote.

SUMMARY AND PREVIEW In this section, you learned about the development and decline of democracy in Athens. You also learned how Athenian democracy influenced the government of the United States. In the next section, you will learn about the beliefs and culture of the ancient Greeks and how they affect our culture and literature today.

Section 2 Assessment

go.hrw.com
Online Quiz
KEYWORD: SQ6 HP9

Reviewing Ideas, Terms, and People HSS 6.4.2, 6.4.3

1. **a. Define** What are **aristocrats**?
   b. Contrast How were **oligarchy** and **tyranny** different?
2. **a. Describe** Describe the **democracy** created by Cleisthenes.
   b. Analyze How did **Pericles** change Athenian democracy?
3. **a. Identify** What type of democracy did Athens have?
   b. Develop In what situations would a representative democracy work better than a direct democracy?

Critical Thinking

4. **Compare and Contrast** Draw a chart like the one to the right. In each column, identify who had power in each type of government. Then write a sentence explaining what role common people had in each government.

Oligarchy	Tyranny	Democracy

FOCUS ON WRITING

5. **Connecting Personalities and Governments** Think back to the personalities you assigned to natural features in Section 1. What if people with these same personalities were working to create a government? What kind would they create? Would they rule as tyrants or build a democracy? Write your thoughts in your notebook.

ANCIENT GREECE **267**

Section 2 Assessment Answers

1. **a.** rich landowners
   b. oligarchy—rule by a few wealthy aristocrats; tyranny—rule by one powerful leader
2. **a.** All citizens could participate in assembly, vote on laws, and debate issues
   b. encouraged people to participate in government and paid public officials
3. **a.** direct democracy
   b. when there are many citizens

4. oligarchy—aristocrats ruled; tyranny—powerful leader ruled; democracy—all citizens ruled; possible sentence—Common people had no role in government under oligarchy and tyranny but were very active in democracy.

5. possible answers—Cruel individuals might create a harsh government, whereas friendly people might tend to create a democratic government.

Direct Teach

QUICK FACTS **Democracy Then and Now**

Review the differences between Athenian and American democracy. Ask the following question: How does the role of a citizen in American democracy differ from that in Athenian democracy? *American—vote to elect officials; Athenian—vote on laws, enforce laws, act as judges*

Quick Facts Transparency: Democracy Then and Now

HSS 6.4.3; HSS Analysis Skills: HI 1, HI 3

Review & Assess

Close

Have students discuss the various governments of ancient Athens and the benefits and drawbacks of each.

Review

Online Quiz, Section 2

Assess

SE Section 2 Assessment
PASS: Section 2 Quiz
Alternative Assessment Handbook

Reteach/Classroom Intervention

California Standards Review Workbook
Interactive Reader and Study Guide, Section 2
Interactive Skills Tutor CD-ROM

Answers

Reading Check *direct democracy—each citizen participates directly in government; representative democracy—elected officials represent citizens in government and make and vote on laws*

267

Bellringer

If YOU were there . . . Use the **Daily Bellringer Transparency** to help students answer the question.

🔲 Daily Bellringer Transparency, Section 3

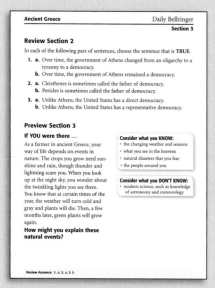

Building Vocabulary

Preteach or review the following term:

oracle a person through whom the gods were believed to speak (p. 270)

🔲 **CRF:** Vocabulary Builder Activity, Section 3

Standards Focus

HSS 6.4.4

Means: Explain the importance of mythol-ogy to everyday Greek life, and explain how Greek mythology influences modern language and literature.

Matters: Greek mythology and literature have greatly influenced modern-day story-telling and culture.

SECTION 3

Greek Mythology and Literature

What You Will Learn...

Main Ideas

1. The Greeks created myths to explain the world.
2. Ancient Greek literature provides some of the world's greatest poems and stories.
3. Greek literature lives in and influences our world even today.

The Big Idea

The ancient Greeks created great myths and works of litera-ture that influence the way we speak and write today.

Key Terms and People

mythology, *p. 269*
Homer, *p. 272*
Sappho, *p. 273*
Aesop, *p. 273*
fables, *p. 273*

 HSS 6.4.4 Explain the significance of Greek mythology to the everyday life of people in the region and how Greek literature continues to perme-ate our literature and language today, drawing from Greek mythology and epics, such as Homer's *Iliad* and *Odyssey*, and from *Aesop's Fables*.

If YOU were there...

As a farmer in ancient Greece, your way of life depends on events in nature. The crops you grow need sunshine and rain, though thunder and lightning scare you. When you look up at the night sky, you wonder about the twinkling lights you see there. You know that at certain times of the year, the weather will turn cold and gray and plants will die. Then, a few months later, green plants will grow again.

How might you explain these natural events?

BUILDING BACKGROUND The Greeks lived in a time long before the development of science. To them, natural events like thunder-storms and changing seasons were mysterious. Today we can explain what causes these events. But to the Greeks, they seemed like the work of powerful gods.

Hephaestus
Hestia
Demeter
Poseidon
Dionysus

Teach the Big Idea: Master the Standards

Standards Proficiency

Greek Mythology and Literature 🐻 HSS 6.4.4; HSS Analysis Skills: CS1, HI1

1. **Teach** Ask students the Main Idea questions to teach this section.

2. **Apply** Organize the class into small groups of three to four students. Assign each group a main idea from this section. Each group will create a poster that uses illustrations to cover the main terms and concepts for its main idea. Groups will present and explain their posters to the class. **LS Visual/Spatial**

3. **Review** As each group presents its poster to the class, review the main idea and concepts with the class.

4. **Practice/Homework** Instruct students to write a letter to a friend in which they summarize all the main ideas from this section that were presented in the group posters. **LS Verbal/Linguistic**

🔲 Alternative Assessment Handbook, Rubrics 25: Personal Letters; and 28: Posters

Myths Explain the World

The ancient Greeks believed in many gods. These gods were at the center of Greek **mythology**—a body of stories about gods and heroes that try to explain how the world works. Each story, or myth, explained natural or historical events.

Greek Gods

People today have scientific explanations for events like thunder, earthquakes, and volcanic eruptions. The ancient Greeks did not. They believed their gods caused these events to happen, and they created myths to explain the gods' actions.

Among the most important Greek gods were the ones in the picture below:

- Zeus, king of the gods
- Hera, queen of the gods
- Poseidon, god of the sea
- Hades, god of the underworld
- Demeter, goddess of agriculture
- Hestia, goddess of the hearth
- Athena, goddess of wisdom
- Apollo, god of the sun
- Artemis, goddess of the moon
- Ares, god of war
- Aphrodite, goddess of love
- Hephaestus, god of metalworking
- Dionysus, god of celebration, and
- Hermes, the messenger god

❶ Myths Explain the World

The Greeks created myths to explain the world.

Recall What was the purpose of telling myths? *to explain natural or historical events, to explain how the world works*

Explain What was often the explanation for natural events such as earthquakes? *The gods had caused the events.*

🐻 **HSS** 6.4.4; **HSS** Analysis Skills; HI 1

Analyzing Visuals
Olympian Gods
Review with students the illustration of the Olympian gods. As you review the various Greek gods described in the text above the illustration, ask students to identify in the illustration what indicates the powers or responsibilities of each god. For example, Demeter, the goddess of agriculture, is holding a bundle of wheat.

Olympian Gods

Zeus

Hermes

Hera

Apollo

Ares

Athena

Aphrodite

Artemis

Hades

ANALYSIS SKILL ANALYZING VISUALS
What can you see that indicates the Olympian gods have superhuman powers?

ANCIENT GREECE **269**

Critical Thinking: Making Generalizations

Exceeding Standards

Biographies of the Gods 🐻 **HSS** 6.4.4; **HSS** Analysis Skills: HI 1

Research Required

1. Review with students the important Greek gods and their powers or responsibilities.

2. Allow students to select one of the Greek gods listed on this page. Students should then research some of the myths relating to that particular god. Good sources are Bulfinch's *Mythology* and Edith Hamilton's *Mythology*.

3. Students will write a brief biography of that god. The biography should explain the god's

relationship to the other gods, summarize major myths related to that god, and explain the importance of that god to the Greeks.

4. Ask for volunteers to share their biographies with the class. **LS Verbal/Linguistic**

📖 Alternative Assessment Handbook, Rubrics 4: Biographies, and 30: Research

Answers

Analyzing Visuals *possible answers—Poseidon is riding a dolphin; Zeus is holding a lightning bolt.*

Main Idea

❶ Myths Explain the World

The Greeks created myths to explain the world.

Summarize What were some events that the Greeks believed their gods were responsible for? *volcanic eruptions and the seasons*

Explain What role did heroes play in Greek myths? *They were featured in adventure stories where they often had special abilities and faced terrible monsters.*

Identify Who are some of the Greek heroes that are featured in myths? *Theseus, Jason, Hercules*

🐾 **HSS** 6.4.4; **HSS Analysis Skills:** HI 1, HI 2

Info to Know

The Labyrinth The Minotaur lived in the Labyrinth, a large chamber with many twisting passageways. Before entering the Labyrinth, Theseus was given a ball of string, which he tied to the door and used to find his way back out of the mazelike chamber after he killed the Minotaur.

Gods and Mythology

The Greeks saw the work of the gods in events all around them. For example, the Greeks lived in an area where volcanic eruptions were common. To explain these eruptions, they told stories about the god Hephaestus (hi-FES-tuhs), who lived underground. The fire and lava that poured out of volcanoes, the Greeks said, came from the huge fires of the god's forge. At this forge he created weapons and armor for the other gods.

The Greeks did not think the gods spent all their time creating disasters, though. They also believed the gods caused daily events. For example, they believed the goddess of agriculture, Demeter (di-MEE-tuhr), created the seasons. According to Greek myth, Demeter had a daughter who was kidnapped by another god. The desperate goddess begged the god to let her daughter go, and eventually he agreed to let her return to her mother for six months every year. During the winter, Demeter is separated from her daughter and misses her. In her grief, she doesn't let plants grow. When her daughter comes home, the goddess is happy, and summer comes to Greece. To the Greeks, this story explained why winter came every year.

To keep the gods happy, the Greeks built great temples to them all around Greece. In return, however, they expected the gods to give them help when they needed it. For example, many Greeks in need of advice traveled to Delphi, a city in central Greece. There they spoke to the oracle, a female priest of Apollo to whom they thought the god gave answers. The oracle at Delphi was so respected that Greek leaders sometimes asked her for advice about how to rule their cities.

Theseus the Hero
According to legend, Athens had to send 14 people to Crete every year to be eaten by the Minotaur, a terrible monster. But Theseus, a hero from Athens, traveled to Crete and killed the Minotaur, freeing the people of Athens from this burden.

270

Collaborative Learning

Standards Proficiency

Mythology Newspaper 🐾 **HSS** 6.4.4; **HSS Analysis Skills:** HR 1

Research Required

1. Organize the class into groups of four to five students. Assign each group several different Greek gods or heroes to research.

2. Students will work together to create a newspaper that reports on the activities of the gods and legendary heroes they have been assigned.

3. Groups should write a news article for each god or hero they have been assigned. Remind students to focus on the "who, what, when, where, and why" of a specific event.

4. Encourage students to create illustrations to coordinate with their news articles and to develop creative and interesting headlines.

5. Ask for groups to volunteer to share their newspapers with the class.

LS Interpersonal, Verbal/Linguistic, Visual/Spatial

📝 Alternative Assessment Handbook, Rubrics 14: Group Activity; and 23: Newspapers

Let the Games Begin!

One way the ancient Greeks honored their gods was by holding sporting contests like the one shown on the vase. The largest took place every four years at Olympia, a city in southern Greece. Held in honor of Zeus, this event was called the Olympic Games. Athletes competed in footraces, chariot races, boxing, wrestling, and throwing events. Only men could compete. The Greeks held these games every four years for more than 1,000 years, until the AD 320s.

In modern times, people began to hold the Olympics again. The first modern Olympics took place in Athens in 1896. Since then, athletes from many nations have assembled in cities around the world to compete. Today the Olympics include 28 sports, and both men and women participate. They are still held every four years. In 2004 the Olympic Games once again returned to their birthplace, Greece.

ANALYSIS SKILL **ANALYZING INFORMATION**

How do you think the modern Olympics are similar to the ancient Games? How do you think they are different?

Heroes and Mythology

Not all Greek myths were about gods. Many told about the adventures of great heroes. Some of these heroes were real people, while others were not. The Greeks loved to tell the stories of heroes who had special abilities and faced terrible monsters. The people of each city had their favorite hero, usually someone from there.

The people of Athens, for example, told stories about the hero Theseus. According to legend, he traveled to Crete and killed the Minotaur, a terrible monster that was half human and half bull. People from northern Greece told myths about Jason and how he sailed across the seas in search of a great treasure, fighting enemies the whole way.

Perhaps the most famous of all Greek heroes was a man called Hercules. The myths explain how Hercules fought many monsters and performed nearly impossible tasks. For example, he fought and killed the hydra, a huge snake with nine heads and poisonous fangs. Every time Hercules cut off one of the monster's heads, two more heads grew in its place. In the end, Hercules had to burn the hydra's neck each time he cut off a head to keep a new head from growing. People from all parts of Greece enjoyed stories about Hercules and his great deeds.

READING CHECK **Finding Main Ideas** How did the Greeks use myths to explain the world around them?

ANCIENT GREECE **271**

Cross-Discipline Activity: English-Language Arts   Exceeding Standards

Olympic Poetry   HSS 6.4.4; HSS Analysis Skills: HI 3

1. Review again the Linking to Today feature, "Let the Games Begin!", on this page.

2. Explain to students that in ancient times, Greek poets would often attend the Olympic Games and write poems in praise of the Olympic athletes. These poems were very popular among the Greeks.

3. Discuss with students the elements of a poem, such as vivid imagery, rhyme, and rhythm.

4. Have students select an athletic event from the modern Olympics with which they are familiar. Students will create an original poem that celebrates an imaginary competitor in that event. Their poems should attempt to "paint a picture" of the athlete and the event. Ask volunteers to share their poems with the class. **LS Intrapersonal, Verbal/Linguistic**

Alternative Assessment Handbook, Rubric 26: Poems and Songs

271

Main Idea

❷ Ancient Greek Literature

Ancient Greek literature provides some of the world's greatest poems and stories.

Explain What purposes did Homer's *Iliad* and *Odyssey* serve for the Greeks? *were used for entertainment and as part of their lessons*

Analyze How have recent writers been influenced by the poems of Homer? *have copied his writing style and borrowed stories from his poems*

Activity **Epic Poem Advertisement** Have students read the descriptions of the *Iliad* and the *Odyssey* on this page. Ask students to select one of the epic poems and create an advertisement encouraging others to read or buy that poem. **LS** Visual/Spatial, **Verbal/Linguistic**

 lternativ ssessment Handbook ubric dvertisements
HSS **HSS** Analysis Skills: H

Answers

Biography *possible answers—There are no records of his life; his poems were never written down.*

Ancient Greek Literature

Because the Greeks loved myths and stories, it is no surprise that they created great works of literature. Early Greek writers produced long epic poems, romantic poetry, and some of the world's most famous stories.

Homer and Epic Poetry

Among the earliest Greek writings are two great epic poems, the *Iliad* and the *Odyssey*, by a poet named **Homer**. Like most epics, both poems describe the deeds of great heroes. The heroes in Homer's poems fought in the Trojan War. In this war, the Mycenaean Greeks fought the Trojans, people of the city called Troy.

The *Iliad* tells the story of the last years of the Trojan War. It focuses on the deeds of the Greeks, especially Achilles (uh-KIL-eez), the greatest of all Greek warriors. It describes in great detail the battles between the Greeks and their Trojan enemies.

The *Odyssey* describes the challenges that the Greek hero Odysseus (oh-DI-see-uhs) faced on his way home from the war. For 10 years after the war ends, Odysseus tries to get home, but many obstacles stand in his way. He has to fight his way past terrible monsters, powerful magicians, and even angry gods.

Both the *Iliad* and the *Odyssey* are great tales of adventure. But to the Greeks Homer's poems were much more than just entertainment. They were central to the ancient Greek education system. People memorized long passages of the poems as part of their lessons. They admired Homer's poems and the heroes described in them as symbols of Greece's great history.

Homer's poems influenced later writers. They copied his writing styles and borrowed some of the stories and ideas he wrote about in his works. Homer's poems are considered some of the greatest literary works ever produced.

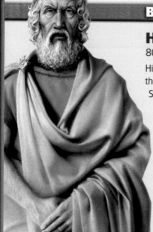

BIOGRAPHY

Homer
800s–700s BC

Historians know nothing about Homer, the greatest poet of the ancient world. Some don't think such a person ever lived. The ancient Greeks believed he had, though, and seven different cities claimed to be his birthplace. According to ancient legend, Homer was blind and recited the *Iliad* and the *Odyssey* aloud. It wasn't until much later that the poems were written down.

Making Predictions Why might scholars not be sure that Homer existed?

In Homer's *Odyssey*, the half woman and half bird Sirens sang sweet songs that made passing sailors forget everything and crash their ships. To trick the Sirens, Odysseus plugged his crew's ears with wax and had himself tied to his ship's mast.

272 CHAPTER 9

Differentiating Instruction for Universal Access

English-Language Learners   Prep Required   Reaching Standards

1. Discuss with students the characteristics of Greek literature and fables. Remind the class that literature often told exciting stories about adventures of Greek heroes, whereas fables attempt to teach the reader some type of lesson.

2. Next, share with students a short story from Greek literature or a fable. Use one discussed in the text above or find your own. Tell the class the entire story or fable.

3. Divide the class into small groups of mixed-ability levels. Instruct each group to draw a series of illustrations that tell the entire story. Each student should participate in illustrating the story or fable.

4. Select one of the illustrated stories and share it with the class. Ask the entire class to develop the text of the story. Write down student suggestions for everyone to see. When the story is complete, ask the students to copy the text of the story on their own paper. Ask for a volunteer to read the story aloud. **LS** Verbal/Linguistic, Visual/Spatial

 lternativ ssessment Handbook ubrics rtwork and ou ctivity
HSS **HSS** Analysis Skills: H

Universal Access Resources

See p. 249c of the Chapter Planner for additional resources for differentiating instruction for universal access.

Lyric Poetry

Other poets wrote poems that were often set to music. During a performance, the poet played a stringed instrument called a lyre while reading a poem. These poets were called lyric poets after their instrument, the lyre. Today, the words of songs are called lyrics after these ancient Greek poets.

Most poets in Greece were men, but the most famous lyric poet was a woman named **Sappho** (SAF-oh). Her poems were beautiful and emotional. Most of her poems were about love and relationships with her friends and family.

Fables

Other Greeks told stories to teach people important lessons. **Aesop** (EE-sahp), for example, is famous for his fables. **Fables** are short stories that teach the reader lessons about life or give advice on how to live.

In most of Aesop's fables, animals are the main characters. The animals talk and act like humans. One of Aesop's most famous stories is the tale of the ants and the grasshopper:

*"*The ants were spending a fine winter's day drying grain collected in the summertime. A Grasshopper, perishing [dying] with famine [hunger], passed by and earnestly [eagerly] begged for a little food. The Ants inquired [asked] of him, "Why did you not treasure up food during the summer?" He replied, "I had not leisure enough. I passed the days in singing." They then said in derision: "If you were foolish enough to sing all the summer, you must dance supperless to bed in the winter.*"*

–Aesop, from "The Ants and the Grasshopper"

The lesson in this fable is that people shouldn't waste time instead of working. Those who do, Aesop says, will be sorry.

Another popular fable by Aesop, "The Tortoise and the Hare," teaches that it is better to work slowly and carefully than to hurry and make mistakes. "The Boy Who Cried Wolf" warns readers not to play pranks on others. Since we still read these fables, you may be familiar with them.

READING CHECK **Summarizing** Why did the Greeks tell fables?

ANCIENT GREECE **273**

Differentiating Instruction for Universal Access

Advanced Learners/GATE [Exceeding Standards]

1. Locate an excerpt from either the *Iliad* or the *Odyssey*. The story of the Trojan horse or the story of Odysseus and the Cyclops would work well.

2. Ask students to read the excerpt and write a review of the story. Reviews should give a brief summary of the story and a reaction to the story itself. Did the student enjoy the story? Why or why not? Would they recommend it to a friend? What might they change about the story? Why?

3. Ask students to share their reviews with the class. **LS** **Verbal/Linguistic**

📝 Alternative Assessment Handbook, Rubric 37: Writing Assignments

HSS 6.4.4; **HSS** Analysis Skills: HR 3

273

❸ Greek Literature Lives

Greek literature lives in and influences our world even today.

Recall Give two examples of terms in our language that have been influenced by Greek stories. *possible answers—odyssey, titanic, Europe, Atlas Mountains, Aegean Sea*

Identify What are some modern references to Greek mythology? *using mythical figures as team mascots or business symbols; borrowing from myths in modern movies and books*

Make Inferences Why have many modern writers and moviemakers borrowed from Greek stories and myths? *possible answers—The stories are interesting; they are heroic examples to live up to.*

📓 **CRF:** Literature Activity: Midas

🌄 **HSS** 6.4.4; **HSS** Analysis Skills: HI 1

Greek Literature Lives

The works of ancient Greek writers such as Homer, Sappho, and Aesop are still alive and popular today. In fact, Greek literature has influenced modern language, literature, and art. Did you know that some of the words you use and some of the stories you hear come from ancient Greece?

Language

Probably the most obvious way we see the influence of the Greeks is in our language. Many English words and expressions come from Greek mythology. For example, we call a long journey an "odyssey" after Odysseus, the wandering hero of Homer's poem. Something very large and powerful is called "titanic." This word comes from the Titans, a group of large and powerful gods in Greek myth.

Many places around the world today are also named after figures from Greek myths. For example, Athens is named for Athena, the goddess of wisdom. Africa's Atlas Mountains were named after a giant from Greek mythology who held up the sky. The name of the Aegean Sea comes from Aegeus, a legendary Greek king. Europe itself was named after a figure from Greek myth, the princess Europa. Even places in space bear names from mythology. For example, Jupiter's moon Io was named after a goddess's daughter.

Literature and the Arts

Greek myths have inspired artists for centuries. Great painters and sculptors have used gods and heroes as the subjects of their works. Writers have retold ancient stories, sometimes set in modern times. Moviemakers have also borrowed stories from ancient myths. Hercules, for example, has been the subject of dozens of films. These films range from early classics to a Walt Disney cartoon.

Mythological references are also common in today's popular culture. Many sports teams have adopted the names of powerful figures from myths, like Titans or

Greek Influence on Language

In Greek Literature and Mythology...	Today...
■ Achilles was a great warrior who was killed when an arrow struck his heel.	■ An "Achilles heel" is a person's weak spot.
■ Hercules was the strongest man on earth who completed 12 almost impossible tasks.	■ When a person has a really hard job to do it is called a "Herculean" task.
■ A fox wanted to eat some grapes but he couldn't reach the branch they were on, so he said, "Those grapes are probably sour anyway."	■ When people pretend they don't want something after they find out they can't have it, they are said to have "sour grapes."
■ King Midas was granted one wish by the god Dionysus, so he wished that everything he touched turned to gold.	■ A person who seems to get rich easily is said to have a "Midas touch."
■ Tantalus was punished for offending the gods. He had to stand up to his chin in water and he was always thirsty, but if he tried to drink the water it went away.	■ Something is "tantalizing" if you want it but it's just out of your reach.

274 CHAPTER 9

Cross Discipline Activity: English–Language Arts

Exceeding Standards

Identifying Greek Word Origins 🌄 HSS 6.4.4; HSS Analysis Skills: HI 3

1. Review the chart "Greek Influence on Language" with the class. Ask the class if they can think of any other examples of Greek stories that are used in our modern language.

2. Divide the class into small groups of three to four students. Write the list of words at right for students to see. Omit answers in italics.

3. Ask the students to look up the following list of words in a dictionary. Students should determine the modern-day meaning of the word as well as the origin of the word in Greek mythology.

- **hypnosis** *modern: a state that resembles sleep; origins: Hypnos, the Greek god of sleep*
- **Pandora's box** *modern: a source of troubles; origins: a box sent by the gods which, when opened, set loose a swarm of troubles*

- **echo** *modern: a repetition of sound; origins: a nymph who suffered from unreturned love until nothing remained but her voice*
- **Trojan horse** *modern: a seemingly harmless computer program that destroys data files; origins: the large wooden horse filled with soldiers that helped the Greeks destroy Troy*

📘 **Verbal/Linguistic**

Greek Names Today

The influence of Greek stories and culture can still be seen in names. Astronomers named one of Jupiter's moons Io (EYE-oh) after a woman from Greek mythology. Sports teams also use Greek names. This college mascot is dressed like a Trojan warrior.

Trojans. Businesses frequently use images or symbols from mythology in their advertising. Although people no longer believe in the Greek gods, mythological ideas can still be seen all around us.

READING CHECK Finding Main Ideas
How did Greek myths influence later language and art?

SUMMARY AND PREVIEW The myths, stories, and poems of ancient Greece have shaped how people today speak, read, and write. Like democracy, these myths, stories, and poems are part of ancient Greece's gift to the world. In the next chapter you will learn more about life and culture in ancient Greece.

Section 3 Assessment

go.hrw.com
Online Quiz
KEYWORD: SQ6 HP9

Reviewing Ideas, Terms, and People **HSS** 6.4.4

1. **a. Define** What is **mythology**?
   b. Summarize Why did the ancient Greeks create myths?
2. **a. Identify** What are **Homer**'s most famous works?
   b. Contrast How are **fables** different from myths?
3. **a. Recall** In what areas have Greek myths influenced our culture?
   b. Analyze Why do you think mythological references are popular with sports teams and businesses today?
   c. Evaluate Why do you think Greek literature has been so influential throughout history?

Critical Thinking

4. **Categorizing** Draw a chart like this one. List two characteristics of each type of Greek literature.

Epic Poetry	Lyric Poetry	Fables

FOCUS ON WRITING

5. **Putting Your Ideas Together** Look at your notes from the previous sections. Think about the personalities you gave physical features and government leaders. Now imagine that those personalities belonged to gods. What stories might be told about these gods? Write some ideas down.

ANCIENT GREECE **275**

Section 3 Assessment Answers

1. **a.** stories about gods and heroes that try to explain how the world works
   b. to explain the gods' actions and how the world works
2. **a.** the *Iliad* and the *Odyssey*
   b. fables—teach some lesson to the reader; myths—are meant to entertain or explain
3. **a.** language, literature, moviemaking, art, team mascots
   b. Answers will vary, but students should indicate an understanding that myths are still very popular and exciting.

   c. Answers will vary, but students should show an understanding that the stories told are timeless and interesting.

4. epic poetry—describe deeds of heroes, tales of adventure; lyric poetry—set to music, emotional; fables—teach a lesson, animals as characters

5. possible answers—The friendly gods would help humans, while the cold god would cause many problems for humans.

275

Literature in History

The *Iliad*

As You Read Ask the students to think about what characteristics they associate with a hero. Make a list of several ideas for students to see. Ask students how they might use imagery to describe some of the traits listed.

Info to Know

Greek Heroes Greek literature often centers around a hero who has special talents and is tested on a quest or adventure. Greek heroes are faced with many challenges and sometimes receive assistance from the gods.

Meet the Writer

Homer While not much is certain about the life of Homer, most historians believe that his poems were not written down until many years after he created them. In fact, the *Iliad* and the *Odyssey* were likely meant to be spoken aloud as entertainment.

Answers

Guided Reading 1. *a racing chariot horse.* **3.** *possible answer—He was intimidated by the sight of Achilles' brilliant armor.*

GUIDED READING

WORD HELP

main strength
resolute determined
imploring begging

❶ **To what is Achilles being compared?**

❷ Priam, Hector's father, knows that the gods have protected and strengthened Achilles.

❸ Achilles' armor was made by the god of metalworking.

Why might the very sight of this armor make Priam afraid?

HSS 6.4.4 Explain the significance of Greek mythology to the everyday life of people in the region and how Greek literature continues to permeate our literature and language today, drawing from Greek mythology and epics, such as Homer's *Iliad* and *Odyssey*, and from *Aesop's Fables*.

ELA Reading 6.3 Students read and respond to historically or culturally significant works of literature that reflect and enhance their studies of history and social science.

The Epic Poetry of Homer

from the *Iliad*

as translated by Robert Fitzgerald

About the Reading *The* Iliad *describes one part of a ten-year war between the Greeks and the city of Troy. As the poem opens, the Greek hero Achilles (uh-KIL-eez) has left the battle to wait for help from the gods. When he learns that his best friend Patroclus is dead, however, Achilles springs back into action. In this passage, the angry Achilles sprints across the plain toward Troy—and Hector, the Trojan warrior who has killed his friend.*

AS YOU READ Look for words and actions that tell you Achilles is a hero.

Then toward the town with might and main
he ran magnificent, like a racing chariot horse
that holds its form at full stretch on the plain. ❶
So light-footed Achilles held the pace.
And aging Priam was the first to see him
sparkling on the plain, bright as that star
in autumn rising, whose unclouded rays
shine out amid a throng of stars at dusk—
the one they call Orion's dog, most brilliant... ❷
So pure and bright
the bronze gear blazed upon him as he ran.
The old man gave a cry. ❸ With both his hands
thrown up on high he struck his head, then
shouted, groaning, appealing to his dear son.
Unmoved, Lord Hector stood in the gateway,
resolute to fight Achilles.

        Stretching out his hands,
old Priam said, imploring him:

        "No, Hector!
... don't try to hold your ground against this man,
or soon you'll meet the shock of doom..."

The painting on this vase shows people fighting in the Trojan War.

Differentiating Instruction for Universal Access

Advanced Learners/ GATE   Exceeding Standards

Point out to students that the comparison of Achilles to a "racing chariot horse" is a simile—a comparison of two seemingly unalike things. Using the characteristics of heroes that the class generated earlier, ask each student to choose one of those characteristics and a hero, real or imagined, who embodies that characteristic. Have students create a simile that compares that hero to another object. Ask each student to explain his or her simile in writing. **LS Verbal/Linguistic**

English- Language Learners   Standards Proficiency

Organize the class into small groups of two to three students of mixed-ability levels. Write the following list of terms for students to see, omitting answers in italics. Ask students to determine the meaning of the words or phrases.

- "with might and main he ran"—*he ran with great strength*
- "light-footed Achilles"—*quick and light on his feet*
- "Orion's dog"—*Sirius, the dog star*

LS Verbal/Linguistic

from the *Odyssey*

About the Reading *The* Odyssey *takes place after the Trojan War has ended. It describes the adventures of another hero, Odysseus (oh-DIS-ee-uhs), as he makes his way home to his kingdom of Ithaca. His voyage is full of obstacles—including the two sea monsters described in this passage. The idea for these monsters probably came from an actual strait in the Mediterranean Sea, where a jagged cliff rose on one side and dangerous whirlpools churned on the other.*

AS YOU READ Try to picture the action in your mind.

> And all this time,
> in travail, sobbing, gaining on the current,
> we rowed into the strait—Scylla to port
> and on our starboard beam Charybdis, dire
> gorge of the salt sea tide. ❶ By heaven! when she
> vomited, all the sea was like a cauldron
> seething over intense fire, when the mixture
> suddenly heaves and rises.
>
>   The shot spume
> soared to the landside heights, and fell like rain.
> But when she swallowed the sea water down
> we saw the funnel of the maelstrom, heard
> the rock bellowing all around, and dark
> sand raged on the bottom far below. ❷
> My men all blanched against the gloom, our eyes
> were fixed upon that yawning mouth in fear
> of being devoured.
>
>   Then Scylla made her strike,
> whisking six of my best men from the ship.
> I happened to glance aft at ship and oarsmen
> and caught sight of their arms and legs, dangling
> high overhead. Voices came down to me
> in anguish, calling my name for the last time . . . ❸
>   We rowed on.
>
> The Rocks were now behind; Charybdis, too,
> and Scylla dropped astern.

GUIDED READING

WORD HELP

travail pain
dire gorge terrible throat
spume foam or froth
maelstrom whirlpool
blanched grew pale
anguish great suffering

❶ Odysseus is the speaker. He is referring to himself and his crew.

Why might the crew be sobbing?

❷ Three times a day, the monster Charybdis (cuh-RIB-duhs) takes in water and then spits it out.

❸ Like many Greek monsters, Scylla (SIL-uh) is part human and part animal. She has the body of a woman, six heads with snake-like necks, and twelve feet.

CONNECTING LITERATURE TO HISTORY

1. **Comparing** Many Greek myths were about heroes who had special abilities. What heroic abilities or traits do Achilles, Hector, and Odysseus share?

2. **Analyzing** The Greeks used myths to explain the natural world. How does the *Odyssey* passage illustrate this?

277

Analyzing Costs and Benefits

Activity Cost-Benefit Analysis in the News Find a newspaper article about a current event in which students might be interested (an election, trial, arrest, environmental concern, and so on). The event and the article's coverage of it should provide students with enough information to determine costs and benefits. Provide each student with a photocopy of the article. Create a costs-benefits chart for students to see. Model the activity by listing one cost and one benefit. Then have students complete the chart independently. Review students' answers as a class. Encourage discussion of any effects that some students see as benefits and other students see as costs.

LS Logical/Mathematical, Visual/Spatial

Alternative Assessment Handbook, Rubric 7: Charts

HSS Analysis Skills: HI 6

Social Studies Skills

HSS Analysis HI 6 Students interpret basic indicators of economic performance and conduct cost-benefit analyses of economic and political issues.

| Analysis | Critical Thinking | Participation | Study |

Analyzing Costs and Benefits

Understand the Skill

Everything you do has both costs and benefits connected to it. *Benefits* are what you gain from something. *Costs* are what you give up to obtain benefits. For example, if you buy a video game, the benefits of your action include the game itself and the enjoyment of playing it. The most obvious cost is what you pay for the game. However, there are also costs that do not involve money. One of these costs is the time you spend playing the game. This is a cost because you give up something else, such as doing your homework or watching a TV show, when you choose to play the game.

The ability to analyze costs and benefits is a valuable life skill as well as a useful tool in the study of history. Weighing an action's benefits against its costs can help you decide whether or not to take it.

Learn the Skill

Analyzing the costs and benefits of historical events will help you to better understand and evaluate them. Follow these guidelines to do a cost-benefit analysis of an action or decision in history.

1 First determine what the action or decision was trying to accomplish. This step is needed in order to determine which of its effects were benefits and which were costs.

2 Then look for the positive or successful results of the action or decision. These are its benefits.

3 Consider the negative or unsuccessful effects of the action or decision. Also think about what positive things would have happened if it had *not* occurred. All these things are its costs.

4 Making a chart of the costs and benefits can be useful. By comparing the list of benefits to the list of costs you can better understand the action or decision and evaluate it.

For example, you learned in Chapter 9 that because of Greece's geography, the early Greeks settled near the sea. A cost-benefit analysis of their dependence on the sea might produce a chart like this one.

Benefits	Costs
Got food from sea	Would have paid more attention to agriculture than they did
Didn't have to depend on Greece's poor soil for food	
Became great shipbuilders and sailors	Had to rely on trade with other peoples for some food and other necessities
Became great traders and grew rich from trade	
Settled colonies throughout the region	

Based on this chart, one might conclude that the Greeks' choice of where to settle was a good one.

Practice and Apply the Skill

In 546 BC a noble named Peisistratus overthrew the oligarchy and ruled Athens as a tyrant. Use information from the chapter and the guidelines above to do a cost-benefit analysis of this action. Then write a paragraph explaining whether or not it was good for the people of Athens.

Answers

Practice and Apply the Skill
benefits—brought peace and prosperity to Athens; began new policies to unify the city, created new festivals, built temples and monuments, oversaw many improvements during his rule; costs—ruled by force; took power from aristocrats, who became unhappy and eventually convinced a rival city-state to attack Athens. Students' paragraphs will vary, but most students will probably say that the rule of Peisistratus was good for the people of Athens.

278

Social Studies Skills Activity: Analyzing Costs and Benefits

Democracy Costs-and-Benefits Chart **HSS Analysis Skills: HI 6 Standards Proficiency**

1. Write the terms *Direct Democracy* and *Representative Democracy* for students to see. Briefly review the meaning of each term.

2. Divide the class. Have the students in one half of the class create costs-and-benefits charts for direct democracy in Athens. Have the students in the other half of the class create costs-and-benefits charts for representative democracy in the United States.

3. Have volunteers share their answers as you complete master charts for the class to see. Then have students compare the two charts to evaluate whether direct democracy or representative democracy is the better system.

LS Logical/Mathematical, Visual/Spatial

Alternative Assessment Handbook, Rubric 7: Charts

Standards Review

Visual Summary

Use the visual summary below to help you review the main ideas of the chapter.

The early Greeks developed trading cultures and independent city-states.

Athens had the world's first direct democracy.

The stories of Greek literature and mythology have influenced language and culture today.

Reviewing Vocabulary, Terms, and People

Unscramble each group of letters below to spell a term that matches the given definition.

1. **olpsi**—a Greek city-state
2. **iciznets**—people who have the right to participate in government
3. **ntaryt**—a person who rules alone, usually through military force
4. **comdeyacr**—rule by the people
5. **bleafs**—stories that teach lessons
6. **tsrarciotas**—rich landowners
7. **coiglhary**—rule by a few people
8. **siclalacs**—referring to a period of great achievements

Comprehension and Critical Thinking

SECTION 1 *(Pages 254–259)* **HSS** 6.4.1

9. **a. Describe** How did geography affect the development of the Greek city-states?

   b. Compare and Contrast What did the Minoans and Mycenaeans have in common? How were the two civilizations different?

   c. Elaborate How did the concept of the polis affect the growth of Greek colonies?

SECTION 2 *(Pages 262–267)* **HSS** 6.4.2, 6.4.3

10. **a. Identify** What roles did Draco, Solon, and Peisistratus play in the history of Greek government?

    b. Contrast The Greeks tried many forms of government before they created a democracy. How did these various forms of government differ?

    c. Evaluate Do you agree or disagree with this statement: "Representative democracy works better than direct democracy in large countries." Defend your answer.

ANCIENT GREECE **279**

Answers

Visual Summary

Review and Inquiry Use the visual summary to review the chapter's main ideas. Have students discuss the significance of each image shown.

Quick Facts Transparency: Ancient Greece Visual Summary

Reviewing Vocabulary, Terms, and People

1. polis
2. citizens
3. tyrant
4. democracy
5. fables
6. aristocrats
7. oligarchy
8. classical

Comprehension and Critical Thinking

9. **a.** Mountains divided the cities, so the city-states developed independently, and each one saw itself as a different state.

   b. in common—traded around Mediterranean, ended partly because of volcanic activity; different—Minoans: lived on Crete, did not speak Greek; Mycenaeans—lived on Greek mainland, built fortresses, spoke Greek, more warlike, established colonies, conquered by invaders from Europe

   c. The polis made people feel safe, so they were free to focus on activites like colonization and trade.

Review and Assessment Resources

Review and Reinforce

SE Standards Review

CRF: Chapter Review Activity

California Standards Review Workbook

Quick Facts Transparency: Ancient Greece Visual Summary

Spanish Chapter Summaries Audio CD Program

Online Chapter Summaries in Six Languages

OSP Holt PuzzlePro; Game Tool for ExamView

Quiz Game CD-ROM

Assess

SE Standards Assessment

PASS: Chapter Test, Forms A and B

Alternative Assessment Handbook

OSP ExamView Test Generator, Chapter Test

Universal Access Modified Worksheets and Tests CD-ROM: Chapter Test

Holt Online Assessment Program (in the Premier Online Edition)

Reteach/Intervene

Interactive Reader and Study Guide

Universal Access Teacher Management System: Lesson Plans for Universal Access

Universal Access Modified Worksheets and Tests CD-ROM

Interactive Skills Tutor CD-ROM

go.hrw.com

Online Resources

Chapter Resources:
KEYWORD: SQ6 WH9

Answers

10. a. Draco—created strict laws to prevent a government overthrow; Solon—created new laws not as strict as Draco's, gave rights to nonaristocrats; Peisistratus—tyrant who unified Athens and made improvements

b. oligarchy—only a few people have power; tyrant—an individual held power through the use of force; democracy—all citizens had right to participate

c. Answers will vary, but students should conclude that direct democracy is hard to achieve in large countries.

11. a. Zeus, Hera, Poseidon, Hades, Demeter, Hestia, Athena, Apollo, Artemis, Ares, Aphrodite, Hephaestus, Dionysus, Hermes; Theseus, Jason, Hercules, Achilles, Odysseus

b. possible answers—adventures, war, heroes, winning despite obstacles, history

c. possible answer—yes, because the English language has many Greek roots and Greek literature appeals to people of many places and times

Reading Skills

12. b

13. a

14. very small

Using the Internet

15. Go to the HRW Web site and enter the keyword shown to access a rubric for this activity.

> KEYWORD: SQ6 TEACHER

Social Studies Skills

16. possible answers—Costs: difficult to make decisions, not everyone represented; Benefits: more rights for all citizens, more pride in Athens, citizens gained power; Sentences will vary but should be supported.

---

11. a. Recall Who were some of the main gods of Greek mythology? Who were some of the main heroes?

b. Analyze What are some of the topics that appear in ancient Greek literature, such as the *Iliad* and the *Odyssey*?

c. Predict Do you think the language and literature of ancient Greece will play roles in Western civilization in years to come? Why or why not?

Reading Skills

Understanding Word Origins *Look at the list of Greek words and their meanings below. Then answer the questions that follow.*

archos (ruler)	*monos* (single)
bios (life)	*oligos* (few)
geo (earth)	*pente* (five)
micros (small)	*treis* (three)

12. Which of the following words means rule by a single person?

a. oligarchy   **c.** pentarchy

b. monarchy   **d.** triarchy

13. Which of the following words means the study of life?

a. biology   **c.** archaeology

b. geology   **d.** pentology

14. Is something that is *microscopic* very small or very large?

Using the Internet

15. Activity: Comparing Greek Governments Greek government had many forms: tyranny, oligarchy, direct democracy, and monarchy. Create a three-dimensional model, a drawing, or a diagram to illustrate what a person's life under each type of government might have looked like. Include information about the type of government you are representing.

Social Studies Skills

16. Analyzing Costs and Benefits Under Cleisthenes' leadership, Athens developed the world's first democracy. Create a chart comparing costs and benefits of this event. Then write a sentence explaining whether or not it was good for the people of Athens.

Cleisthenes' Leadership

Costs	Benefits

Reviewing Themes

17. Geography How do you think Greek society would have been different if Greece were a land-locked country?

18. Geography How did Crete's physical geography both help and hurt the development of Minoan civilization?

19. Politics Why was citizenship so important in Athens?

FOCUS ON WRITING

20. Writing Your Myth First, decide if your main character is going to be a god or if it will be a human who interacts with the gods. Think about the situations and decisions that your character will face, and how he or she will react to them.

Now it's time to write your myth down. Write a paragraph of seven to eight sentences about your character. You may want to include terrible monsters or heroes with great powers. Don't forget that a myth is supposed to explain something about the world.

Reviewing Themes

17. possible answer—The Greek people would have been more unified and would not have developed city-states; they would not have traded by sea or founded colonies.

18. helped—allowed it to trade around the Mediterranean; hurt—may have been destroyed by volcano and wave

19. People who were not citizens could not take part in the government.

Focus on Writing

20. Rubric Students' myths should:
- feature a main character.
- describe that character's actions and personality.
- have a beginning, middle, and end.
- explain something about the world.
- use exact verbs.

CRF: Focus on Writing: A Myth

Standards Assessment

ANCIENT GREECE **281**

DIRECTIONS: *Read each question, and write the letter of the best response.*

1

> ... that multitude of gleaming helms and bossed shields issued from the ships, with plated cuirasses [armor] and ashwood spears. Reflected glintings flashed to heaven, as the plain in all directions shone with glare of bronze and shook with trampling feet of men. Among them Prince Achilles armed. One heard his teeth grind hard together, and his eyes blazed out like licking fire, for unbearable pain had fixed upon his heart. Raging at Trojans, he buckled on the arms Hephaestus forged.

The content of this passage suggests that it was written by

A Homer.

B Zeus.

C Apollo.

D Cleisthenes.

2 What type of ancient Greek literature would *most* likely describe the deeds of a great hero?

A fable

B epic poem

C lyric poem

D oration

3 Which was the main cause for the independence of city-states in ancient Greece?

A the Greeks' location on the sea

B the threat of warlike neighbors to the north

C the geography of mountainous peninsulas

D the spread of Minoan culture

4 Athens was ruled by a single person under the type of government known as

A direct democracy.

B representative democracy.

C oligarchy.

D tyranny.

5 The citizens' assembly in ancient Athens was an example of

A trial by jury.

B rule by aristocrats.

C direct democracy.

D representative democracy.

Connecting with Past Learnings

6 Recently you learned about Hebrew history and beliefs. The ancient Hebrew and Greek civilizations shared all of the following characteristics *except*

A great written works.

B democratic governments.

C strong political leaders.

D influence on later civilizations.

7 You know that early towns in India were controlled by small groups of priests. Like ancient Greek government, this early Indian government was an example of

A oligarchy.

B tyranny.

C monarchy.

D democracy.

ANCIENT GREECE **281**

Answers

1. A
Break Down the Question Students can eliminate Zeus and Apollo, as they are Greek gods. Students can eliminate Cleisthenes, since he was a politician.

2. B
Break Down the Question Students can eliminate a fable, since the passage does not feature animals. They can eliminate lyric poem and oration, as the passage clearly does not represent those styles.

3. C
Break Down the Question Refer students who miss this question to Section 1.

4. D
Break Down the Question Students can eliminate choices *A, B,* and *C* because they involve rule by multiple persons.

5. C
Break Down the Question Direct democracy features input directly from citizens through the assembly.

6. B
Break Down the Question This question connects to information covered in a previous chapter.

7. A
Break Down the Question This question connects to information covered in a previous chapter.

Standards Review

Have students review the following standards in their workbooks.

California Standards Review Workbook:

 HSS 6.4.1, 6.4.2, 6.4.3, 6.4.4

Intervention Resources

Reproducible

Interactive Study Guide

Universal Access Teacher Management System: Lesson Plans for Universal Access

Technology

Quick Facts Transparency: Ancient Greece Visual Summary

Universal Access Modified Worksheets and Tests CD-ROM

Interactive Skills Tutor CD-ROM

Tips for Test Taking

Anticipate the Answers Give students this important tip: Before you read the answer choices, answer the question yourself. Then, read the choices. If the answer you gave is among the choices listed, it is probably correct!

Chapter 10 Planning Guide

The Greek World

Chapter Overview	Reproducible Resources	Technology Resources
CHAPTER 10 pp. 282–313 **Overview:** **In this chapter, students will learn more about the events and accomplishments of ancient Greece.** See p. 282 for the California History–Social Science standards covered in this chapter.	**Universal Access Teacher Management System:*** • Universal Access Instructional Benchmarking Guides • Lesson Plans for Universal Access **Interactive Reader and Study Guide:** Chapter Graphic Organizer* **Chapter Resource File*** • Chapter Review Activity • Focus on Writing Activity: A Poem • Social Studies Skills Activity: Interpreting Charts and Tables	**One-Stop Planner CD-ROM:** Calendar Planner **Student Edition on Audio CD Program** **Universal Access Modified Worksheets and Tests CD-ROM** **Interactive Skills Tutor CD-ROM** **Power Presentations with Video CD-ROM** **History's Impact: World History Video Program (VHS/DVD):** The Greek World*
Section 1: **Greece and Persia** **The Big Idea:** Over time the Persians came to rule a great empire which eventually brought them into conflict with the Greeks. 6.4.5	**Universal Access Teacher Management System:*** Section 1 Lesson Plan **Interactive Reader and Study Guide:** Section 1 Summary* **Chapter Resource File*** • Vocabulary Builder Activity, Section 1 • Biography Activity: Leonidas	**Daily Bellringer Transparency:** Section 1* **Map Transparency:** The Persian Empire* **Map Transparency:** The Persian Wars*
Section 2: **Sparta and Athens** **The Big Idea:** The two most powerful city-states in Greece, Sparta and Athens, had very different cultures and became bitter enemies in the 400s BC. 6.4.6	**Universal Access Teacher Management System:*** Section 2 Lesson Plan **Interactive Reader and Study Guide:** Section 2 Summary* **Chapter Resource File*** • Vocabulary Builder Activity, Section 2 • Economics and History Activity: The Importance of Trade • Interdisciplinary Project: Spartans vs. Athenians	**Daily Bellringer Transparency:** Section 2* **Quick Facts Transparency:** Life in Sparta* **Quick Facts Transparency:** Life in Athens* **Map Transparency:** The Peloponnesian War, c. 431–404 BC* **Internet Activity:** Brains Versus Brawn?
Section 3: **Alexander the Great** **The Big Idea:** Alexander the Great built a huge empire and helped spread Greek culture into Egypt and Asia. 6.4.7	**Universal Access Teacher Management System:*** Section 3 Lesson Plan **Interactive Reader and Study Guide:** Section 3 Summary* **Chapter Resource File*** • Vocabulary Builder Activity, Section 3 • History and Geography Activity: Alexander's Empire • Primary Source Activity: "Alexander" from Plutarch's *Lives*	**Daily Bellringer Transparency:** Section 3* **Map Transparency:** Alexander the Great's Empire*
Section 4: **Greek Achievements** **The Big Idea:** Ancient Greeks made lasting contributions in the arts, philosophy, and science. 6.4.8	**Universal Access Teacher Management System:*** Section 4 Lesson Plan **Interactive Reader and Study Guide:** Section 4 Summary* **Chapter Resource File*** • Vocabulary Builder Activity, Section 4 • Biography Activities: Hipparchia; Hypatia; Thucydides • Interdisciplinary Project: Contributions of Early Greeks • Literature Activity: *Oedipus the King,* by Sophocles • Primary Source Activity: Greek Lyric Poetry	**Daily Bellringer Transparency:** Section 4* **Internet Activity:** The Golden Age of Greece

Review, Assessment, Intervention

- **Standards Review Workbook***
- **Quick Facts Transparency:** The Greek World Visual Summary*
- **Spanish Chapter Summaries Audio CD Program**
- **Online Chapter Summaries in Six Languages**
- **Progress Assessment Support System (PASS):** Chapter Test*
- **Universal Access Modified Worksheets and Tests CD-ROM:** Modified Chapter Test
- **One-Stop Planner CD-ROM:** ExamView Test Generator (English/Spanish)

- **PASS:** Section 1 Quiz*
- **Online Quiz:** Section 1
- **Alternative Assessment Handbook**

- **PASS:** Section 2 Quiz*
- **Online Quiz:** Section 2
- **Alternative Assessment Handbook**

- **PASS:** Section 3 Quiz*
- **Online Quiz:** Section 3
- **Alternative Assessment Handbook**

- **PASS:** Section 4 Quiz*
- **Online Quiz:** Section 4
- **Alternative Assessment Handbook**

California Resources for Standards Mastery

INSTRUCTIONAL PLANNING AND SUPPORT

- **Universal Access Teacher Management System***
- **One-Stop Planner CD-ROM with Test Generator:** Teacher Management System with Interactive Teacher's Edition

STANDARDS MASTERY

- **Standards Review Workbook***
- **At Home: A Guide to Standards Mastery for World History**

 Holt Online Learning

To enhance learning, the following Internet activities are available: **Brains Versus Brawn?** and **The Golden Age of Greece.**

> KEYWORD: SQ6 TEACHER

- **Teacher Support Page**
- **Content Updates**
- **Rubrics and Writing Models**
- **Teaching Tips for the Multimedia Classroom**

> KEYWORD: SQ6 WH10

- **Current Events**
- **Holt Grapher**
- **Holt Online Atlas**
- **Holt Researcher**
- **Interactive Multimedia Activities**
- **Internet Activities**
- **Online Chapter Summaries in Six Languages**
- **Online Section Quizzes**
- **World History Maps and Charts**

HOLT PREMIER ONLINE STUDENT EDITION

Complete online support for interactivity, assessment, and reporting

- **Interactive Maps and Notebook**
- **Standardized Test Prep**
- **Homework Practice and Research Activities Online**

Mastering the Standards: Differentiating Instruction

Reaching Standards	Basic-level activities designed for all students encountering new material
Standards Proficiency	Intermediate-level activities designed for average students
Exceeding Standards	Challenging activities designed for honors and gifted-and-talented students
Standard English Mastery	Activities designed to improve standard English usage

MASTERING THE CALIFORNIA STANDARDS

Frequently Asked Questions

INSTRUCTIONAL PLANNING AND SUPPORT

Where do I find planning aids, instructional benchmarking guides, lesson plans, and other teaching aids?

Annotated Teacher's Edition:
- Chapter planning guides
- Standards-based instruction and strategies
- Differentiated instruction for universal access
- Point-of-use reminders for integrating program resources

Power Presentations with Video CD-ROM

Universal Access Teacher Management System:
- Year and unit instructional benchmarking guides
- Reproducible lesson plans
- Assessment guides for diagnostic, progress, and summative end-of-the-year tests
- Options for differentiating instruction and intervention
- Teaching guides and answer keys for student workbooks

One-Stop Planner CD-ROM with Test Generator: Teacher Management System with Interactive Teacher's Edition:
- Calendar Planner
- Editable lesson plans
- All reproducible ancillaries in Adobe Acrobat (PDF) format
- ExamView Test Generator (English & Spanish)
- Game Tool for ExamView
- PuzzlePro
- Transparency and video previews

DIFFERENTIATING INSTRUCTION FOR UNIVERSAL ACCESS

What resources are available to ensure that Advanced Learners/GATE students master the standards?

Teacher's Edition Activities:
- The Cyrus Cylinder, p. 287
- The Peloponnesian War, p. 296
- Philippics Against Alexander, p. 300
- Greek Architectural Styles, p. 304
- Plays: A New Form of Writing, p. 305
- The Socratic Method, p. 306

Lesson Plans for Universal Access

Primary Source Library CD-ROM for World History

What resources are available to ensure that English Learners and Standard English Learners master the standards?

Teacher's Edition Activities:
- Battle Murals, p. 290

Lesson Plans for Universal Access

Chapter Resource File: Vocabulary Builder Activities

Spanish Chapter Summaries Audio CD Program

Online Chapter Summaries in Six Languages

One-Stop Planner CD-ROM:
- PuzzlePro, Spanish Version
- ExamView Test Generator, Spanish Version

What modified materials are available for Special Education?

The *Universal Access Modified Worksheets and Tests CD-ROM* provides editable versions of the following:

Vocabulary Flash Cards

Modified Vocabulary Builder Activities

Modified Chapter Review Activity

Modified Chapter Test

What resources are available to ensure that Learners Having Difficulty master the standards?

Teacher's Edition Activities:
• Men and Women in Sparta and Athens, p. 294

Interactive Reader and Study Guide

Student Edition on Audio CD Program

Quick Facts Transparency: The Greek World Visual Summary

Standards Review Workbook

Social Studies Skills Activity: Interpreting Charts and Tables

Interactive Skills Tutor CD-ROM

How do I intervene for students struggling to master the standards?

Interactive Reader and Study Guide

Quick Facts Transparency: The Greek World Visual Summary

Standards Review Workbook

Social Studies Skills Activity: Interpreting Charts and Tables

Interactive Skills Tutor CD-ROM

PROFESSIONAL DEVELOPMENT

HOLT
Professional Development

What teacher training resources are available to help me grow professionally?

• In-service and staff development as part of your Holt Social Studies product purchase
• Quick Teacher Tutorial Lesson Presentation CD-ROM
• Intensive tuition-based Teacher Development Institute
• Convenient Holt Speaker Bureau face-to-face workshop options

• PRAXIS™ Test Prep (#0089) interactive Web-based content refreshers*
• *Ask A Professional Development Expert* at http://www.hrw.com/prodev/

* PRAXIS is a trademark of Educational Testing Service (ETS). This publication is not endorsed or approved by ETS.

Information Literacy Skills

To learn more about how History-Social Science instruction may be improved by the effective use of library media centers and information literacy skills, go to the Teacher's Resource Materials for Chapter 10 at **go.hrw.com, keyword: SQ6 MEDIA.**

Standards Focus

Standards by Section
Section 1: **HSS** 6.4.5
Section 2: **HSS** 6.4.6
Section 3: **HSS** 6.4.7
Section 4: **HSS** 6.4.8

Teacher's Edition
HSS Analysis Skills: CS 1, CS 2, CS 3, HR 1, HR 2, HR 4, HI 1, HI 2, HI 4

Upcoming Standards for Future Learning

Preview the following History–Social Science content standards from upcoming chapters or grade levels to promote learning beyond the current chapter.

HSS **6.7** Students analyze the geographic, political economic, religious and social structures during the development of Rome.

6.7.8 Discuss the legacies of Roman art and architecture, technology and science, literature, language, and law.

7.10 Students analyze the historical developments of the Scientific Revolution and its lasting effect on religious, political, and cultural institutions.

7.10.1 Discuss the roots of the Scientific Revolution (eg., Greek rationalism; Jewish, Christian, and Muslim science; Renaissance humanism; new knowledge from global exploration).

7.11 Students analyze political and economic change in the sixteenth, seventeenth, and eighteenth centuries (the Age of Exploration, the Enlightenment, and the Age of Reason).

7.11.4 Explain how the main ideas of the Enlightenment can be traced back to such movements as the Renaissance, the Reformation, and the Scientific Revolution and to the Greeks, Romans, and Christianity.

Focus on Writing

The **Chapter Resource File** provides a Focus on Writing worksheet to help students organize and write their poem.

CRF: Focus on Writing Activity: A Poem

CHAPTER 10 550–30 BC

The Greek World

California Standards

History–Social Science

6.4 Students analyze the geographic, political, economic, religious, and social structures of the early civilizations of Ancient Greece.

Analysis Skills

HI 2 Students understand and distinguish cause, effect, sequence, and correlation in historical events, including long- and short-term causal relations.

English–Language Arts

Writing 6.2.2 Follow an organizational pattern appropriate to the type of composition.

Reading 6.2.2 Analyze text that uses the compare-and-contrast organizational pattern.

FOCUS ON WRITING

A Poem Ancient Greek poets often wrote poems in praise of great leaders, victorious military commanders, star athletes, and other famous people. As you read this chapter, you will learn about the accomplishments of Greek and Persian kings, generals, writers, thinkers, and scientists. As you read, you'll choose the one person you most admire and write a five-line poem praising that person.

282 CHAPTER 10

CHAPTER EVENTS

c. 550 BC Cyrus the Great founds the Persian Empire.

550 BC

WORLD EVENTS

c. 551 BC Confucius is born in China.

Introduce the Chapter

Standards Proficiency

Building on Knowledge of Ancient Greece **HSS** 6.4.5, 6.4.6, 6.4.7, 6.4.8

1. Ask students to list some things they already know about ancient Greece based on their study of the previous chapter. List the responses for the class to see.

2. Have students help you organize their responses into categories, such as government, economy, culture, religion, and so on. In addition, have students identify any categories for which they have not provided any information.

3. Then ask students to create charts organized by the categories they identified and enter the information listed.

4. As students study the chapter, have them add to their charts by listing additional information that they learn in appropriate categories. **LS** Verbal/Linguistic, Visual/Spatial

HOLT

History's Impact

► video series
See the Video Teacher's Guide for strategies for using the chapter video **The Greek World: The Impact of the Greek Scholars.**

HOLT

History's Impact

► video series
Watch the video to understand the impact of the Greek scholars.

Chapter Big Ideas

Section 1 Over time, the Persians came to rule a great empire which eventually brought them into conflict with the Greeks. **HSS** 6.4.5

Section 2 The two most powerful city-states in Greece, Sparta and Athens, had very different cultures and became bitter enemies in the 400s BC. **HSS** 6.4.6

Section 3 Alexander the Great built a huge empire and helped spread Greek culture into Egypt and Asia. **HSS** 6.4.7

Section 4 Ancient Greeks made lasting contributions in the arts, philosophy, and science. **HSS** 6.4.8

Explore the Picture

The Parthenon in Athens The most famous building in ancient Athens—and one of the most famous buildings in the world—is the Parthenon. After the Athenians defeated the Persians nearly 2,500 years ago, the people of Athens built the temple to thank the goddess Athena, the protector of Athens, for the victory.

Analyzing Visuals Based on the photo, how does the Parthenon illustrate the lasting influence of ancient Greece? *possible answers—It still stands; care has been taken to protect the structure, which now sits surrounded by modern buildings.*

What You Will Learn...

In this chapter you will learn that the ancient Greeks were both fierce fighters and great builders. The ruins shown in this photo are from the Parthenon, a beautiful temple built to celebrate a Greek victory in war.

431 BC
The Peloponnesian War begins.

334–323 BC
Alexander the Great builds his empire.

30 BC
Rome conquers Egypt, ending the Hellenistic Age.

450 BC | **350 BC** | **250 BC** | **150 BC** | **50 BC**

343 BC
The last Egyptian ruler of Egypt is overthrown.

c. 325 BC
The Mauryan Empire is founded in India.

c. 160 BC
The Maccabees regain Jewish independence.

THE GREEK WORLD **283**

Explore the Time Line

1. At about the time Alexander the Great was building his empire, where was another empire being founded? What was this empire called? *India; the Mauryan Empire*

2. In what year did the Hellenistic Age end? *30 BC*

HSS Analysis Skills: CS 1

Info to Know

The Acropolis The Parthenon was built on the Acropolis in Athens. *Acropolis* is a Greek term meaning "upper city" and refers to the highest point in the city. From a military point of view, why do you think Athenians (and people in many other cities) built sacred buildings on an acropolis? *possible answer—It is easier to defend a hilltop against invaders, so sacred buildings can be protected better if they are on an acropolis.*

Reading Social Studies

by Kylene Beers

| Economics | Geography | Politics | Religion | Society and Culture | Science and Technology |

Focus on Themes In this chapter, you will learn about Persia's attempt to take over Greece. You will also read about two great Greek cities, Sparta and Athens, and how they both worked to protect Greece from this invader. Finally, you will discover how, even though another invader conquered Greece, Greek influence continued to spread. Without a doubt, you need to understand the **politics** of the time in order to understand the Greek world and its **society and culture**.

Comparing and Contrasting Historical Facts

Focus on Reading Comparing and contrasting is a good way to learn. That's one reason historians use comparison and contrast to explain people and events in history.

Understanding Comparison and Contrast To **compare** is to look for likenesses, or similarities. To **contrast** is to look for differences. Sometimes writers point out similarities and differences. Other times you have to look for them yourself. You can use a diagram like this one to keep track of similarities and differences as you read.

Additional reading support can be found in the

Inter active

Reader and Study Guide

Greek Cities

Athens
Differences
- Democratic government
- Emphasis on many subjects in education
- Known as the home of artists, writers, and philosophers

Similarities
- Greek language and religion
- More rights for men than for women

Sparta
Differences
- Ruled by kings and officials
- Emphasis only on physical education
- Known for its powerful and disciplined army

Clues for Comparison-Contrast

Writers sometimes signal comparisons or contrasts with words like these:

Comparison—*similarly, like, in the same way, too*

Contrast—*however, unlike, but, while, although, in contrast*

Reading and Skills Resources

Reading Support

- Interactive Reader and Study Guide
- Student Edition on Audio CD
- Spanish Chapter Summaries Audio CD Program

Social Studies Skills Support

- Interactive Skills Tutor CD-ROM

Vocabulary Support

- **CRF:** Vocabulary Builder Activities
- **CRF:** Chapter Review Activity
- Universal Access Modified Worksheets and Tests CD-ROM:
  - Vocabulary Flash Cards
  - Vocabulary Builder Activity
  - Chapter Review Activity

OSP Holt PuzzlePro

Reading Social Studies

Understanding Themes

Introduce the key themes of this chapter by writing the labels *Politics* and *Society and Culture* for students to see. Ask students to use what they learned about Greece in the previous chapter to help them make predictions about this chapter. How might the political systems of Greece change? What might be some characteristics of Greece's society and culture during the next phase in their history? Ask students to identify some political and social contributions that the Greeks have made to our world.

Comparing and Contrasting Historical Facts

Focus on Reading Ask students to select two items to compare and contrast—for example, hockey and basketball. Then draw a large Venn diagram for students to see. Ask students to think of similarities and differences between the two items. Add students' suggestions to the Venn diagram. When the class is finished, have students use the diagram to write a paragraph or two in which they compare and contrast these items. Ask students to use signal words to indicate similarities and differences.

Standards Focus

ELA Reading 6.2.2

ELA Reading 6.2.2 Analyze text that uses the compare-and-contrast organizational pattern.

You Try It!

The following passage is from the chapter you are getting ready to read. As you read the passage, look for word clues about similarities and differences.

Boys and Men in Athens

From a young age, Athenian boys from rich families worked to improve both their bodies and their minds. Like Spartan boys, Athenian boys had to learn to run, jump, and fight. But this training was not as harsh or as long as the training in Sparta.

From Chapter 10, pp. 294–295

Unlike Spartan men, Athenian men didn't have to devote their whole lives to the army. All men in Athens joined the army, but only for two years. They helped defend the city between the ages of 18 and 20. Older men only had to serve in the army in times of war.

In addition to their physical training, Athenian students, unlike the Spartans, also learned other skills. They learned to read, write, and count as well as sing and play musical instruments.

After you read the passage, answer the following questions.

1. What does the word *like* (line 3 of the passage) compare or contrast?

2. Which boys had harsher training, Athenian boys or Spartan boys? What comparison or contrast signal word helped you answer this question?

3. What other comparison or contrast words do you find in that passage? How do these words or phrases help you understand the passage?

4. Draw a diagram like the one on the previous page to compare educational opportunities for boys in Athens and Sparta.

Key Terms and People

Chapter 10

Section 1
Cyrus the Great *(p. 287)*
cavalry *(p. 288)*
Darius I *(p. 288)*
Persian Wars *(p. 289)*
Xerxes I *(p. 290)*

Section 2
alliance *(p. 296)*
Peloponnesian War *(p. 297)*

Section 3
Philip II *(p. 298)*
phalanx *(p. 299)*
Alexander the Great *(p. 300)*
Hellenistic *(p. 301)*

Section 4
Socrates *(p. 307)*
Plato *(p. 307)*
Aristotle *(p. 307)*
reason *(p. 307)*
Euclid *(p. 308)*
Hippocrates *(p. 308)*

Academic Vocabulary

Success in school is related to knowing academic vocabulary— the words that are frequently used in school assignments and discussions. In this chapter, you will learn the following academic words:

strategy *(p. 288)*
neutral *(p. 306)*

As you read **Chapter 10**, think about the organization of the ideas. Look for comparison and contrast signal words.

Reading Social Studies

Key Terms and People

Organize the class into small groups. Preteach the key terms and people for this chapter by instructing the groups to write each of the terms and people as a list. Then have groups look up each term in the chapter. For people or events, have students write a date next to each entry. For example, *Cyrus the Great, 550 B.C.* Then have each group construct a time line, adding the significance of the person or event near each entry. Have students write the terms that may not go on the time line on the other side of the paper. Display the time lines for the class to see.

LS Verbal/Linguistic, Visual/Spatial

Focus on Reading

See the **Focus on Reading** questions in this chapter for more practice on this reading social studies skill.

Reading Social Studies Assessment

See the **Standards Review** at the end of this chapter for student assessment questions related to this reading skill.

Teaching Tip

Help students identify comparison and contrast by discussing different ways in which text is organized. Point out to students that sometimes writers will compare and contrast by alternating back and forth between topics. For example, hockey is a game played on ice, while basketball is often played on a wood court. Then tell students that at other times, writers will concentrate on one topic at a time. For example, the writer might describe basketball in one paragraph, and hockey in a separate paragraph. Have students practice comparing and contrasting two items using both styles of organization.

Answers

You Try It! 1. *It compares Athenian boys to Spartan boys.* **2.** *Spartan boys;* but; **3.** *unlike; also; by indicating comparison and contrast;* **4.** *Athenian men—improved minds and bodies, training not harsh or long, did not devote lives to army, served in army for two years, learned to read, write, count, sing; similarities—learned to run, jump and fight, served in army; Spartan men—received long, harsh training, devoted their lives to the army, did not learn to read, write or count*

285

Bellringer

If YOU were there . . . Use the **Daily Bellringer Transparency** to help students answer the question.

🖳 Daily Bellringer Transparency, Section 1

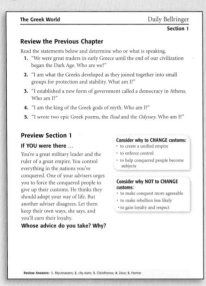

Academic Vocabulary

Review with students the high-use academic term in this section.

strategy plan for fighting a battle or war (p. 288)

Building Vocabulary

Preteach or review the following term:

satraps Persian provincial governors with very wide powers (p. 288)

📄 **CRF:** Vocabulary Builder Activity, Section 1

 Standards Focus

HSS 6.4.5
Means: Describe the beginnings and growth of the Persian Empire, and its political structure.
Matters: The Persian Empire, one of the largest empires in the ancient world, influenced ancient Greece, which influences us today.

286 CHAPTER 10

SECTION 1

Greece and Persia

What You Will Learn...

Main Ideas

1. Persia became an empire under Cyrus the Great.
2. The Persian Empire grew stronger under Darius I.
3. The Persians fought Greece twice in the Persian Wars.

The Big Idea

Over time the Persians came to rule a great empire which eventually brought them into conflict with the Greeks.

Key Terms and People

Cyrus the Great, *p. 287*
cavalry, *p. 288*
Darius I, *p. 288*
Persian Wars, *p. 289*
Xerxes I, *p. 290*

HSS 6.4.5 Outline the founding, expansion, and political organization of the Persian Empire.

286 CHAPTER 10

If YOU were there...

You're a great military leader and the ruler of a great empire. You control everything in the nations you've conquered. One of your advisers urges you to force conquered people to give up their customs. He thinks they should adopt your way of life. But another adviser disagrees. Let them keep their own ways, she says, and you'll earn their loyalty.

Whose advice do you take? Why?

BUILDING BACKGROUND Among the rulers who faced decisions like the one described above were the rulers of the Persian Empire. Created in 550 BC, the empire grew quickly. Within about 30 years, the Persians had conquered many peoples, and Persian rulers had to decide how these people would be treated.

Persia Becomes an Empire

While the Athenians were taking the first steps toward creating a democracy, a new power was rising in the East. This power, the Persian Empire, would one day attack Greece. But early in their history, the Persians were an unorganized nomadic people. It took the skills of leaders like Cyrus the Great and Darius I to change that situation. Under these leaders, the Persians created a huge empire, one of the mightiest of the ancient world.

Cyrus the Great

Early in their history, the Persians often fought other peoples of Southwest Asia. Sometimes they lost. In fact, they lost a fight to a people called the Medes (MEEDZ) and were ruled by them for about 150 years. In 550 BC, however, Cyrus II (SY-ruhs) led a Persian revolt against the Medes. His revolt was successful. Cyrus won independence for Persia and conquered the Medes. His victory marked the beginning of the Persian Empire.

Teach the Big Idea: Master the Standards
Standards Proficiency

Greece and Persia 🐻 **HSS** 6.4.5; **HSS** Analysis Skills: HI 1

1. **Teach** Ask students the Main Idea questions to teach this section.

2. **Apply** Help students list the main people, events, and issues in the section. Write the list for students to see. Then ask students to imagine that they are creating a newspaper story. Have each student write one or two sentences summarizing the information about each of the section's main people, events, and issues. Model the activity for

students by doing the first summary as a class. **LS Verbal/Linguistic**

3. **Review** As you review the section, select students to read their summaries to the class.

4. **Practice/Homework** Have each student use his or her summary to write a one-page newspaper article about the Persian Empire. **LS Verbal/Linguistic**

📄 Alternative Assessment Handbook, Rubrics 23: Newspapers; and 42: Writing to Inform

The Persian Empire

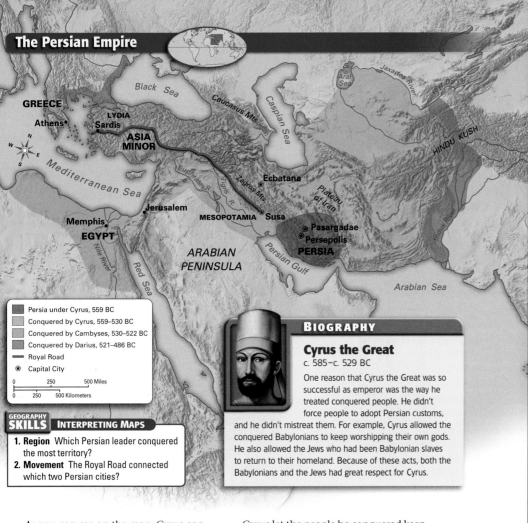

GREECE · Athens · **LYDIA** · Sardis · **ASIA MINOR**

Black Sea · Caspian Sea · Caucasus Mts. · Aral Sea · Jaxartes River · Syr Darya

Mediterranean Sea

Memphis · **EGYPT** · Jerusalem · **MESOPOTAMIA** · Susa · Ecbatana · Zagros Mts. · Plateau of Iran · HINDU KUSH

Nile River · Red Sea · Euphrates R. · Tigris R. · **ARABIAN PENINSULA** · Persian Gulf · Pasargadae · Persepolis · **PERSIA** · Indus River

Arabian Sea

Legend:
- Persia under Cyrus, 559 BC
- Conquered by Cyrus, 559–530 BC
- Conquered by Cambyses, 530–522 BC
- Conquered by Darius, 521–486 BC
- Royal Road
- ⊛ Capital City

0   250   500 Miles
0   250   500 Kilometers

GEOGRAPHY SKILLS   INTERPRETING MAPS

1. **Region** Which Persian leader conquered the most territory?
2. **Movement** The Royal Road connected which two Persian cities?

BIOGRAPHY

Cyrus the Great
c. 585–c. 529 BC

One reason that Cyrus the Great was so successful as emperor was the way he treated conquered people. He didn't force people to adopt Persian customs, and he didn't mistreat them. For example, Cyrus allowed the conquered Babylonians to keep worshipping their own gods. He also allowed the Jews who had been Babylonian slaves to return to their homeland. Because of these acts, both the Babylonians and the Jews had great respect for Cyrus.

As you can see on the map, Cyrus conquered much of Southwest Asia, including nearly all of Asia Minor, during his rule. Included in this region were several Greek cities that Cyrus took over. He then marched south to conquer Mesopotamia.

Cyrus also added land to the east. He led his army into central Asia to the Jaxartes River, which we now call the Syr Darya. When he died around 529 BC, Cyrus ruled the largest empire the world had ever seen.

Cyrus let the people he conquered keep their own customs. He hoped this would make them less likely to rebel. He was right. Few people rebelled against Cyrus, and his empire remained strong. Because of his great successes, historians call him **Cyrus the Great**.

The Persian Army

Cyrus was successful in his conquests because his army was strong. It was strong because it was well organized and loyal.

THE GREEK WORLD **287**

Cross-Discipline Activity: Government

Exceeding Standards

The Cyrus Cylinder 🐾 HSS 6.4.5; HSS Analysis Skills: CS 1

Research Required

1. Have students research Cyrus the Great and the Cyrus Cylinder, which is in the British Museum. (The Cyrus Cylinder is a clay cylinder inscribed by Cyrus reciting his conquest of Babylon and promising reforms that will improve the lives of his subjects.)

2. Ask students to describe the reforms that Cyrus promised in his declaration on the cylinder. Students can write a short report or make a poster or pamphlet to describe their findings.

3. Have students explain how Cyrus the Great and the Cyrus Cylinder are related to human rights documents of today, such as the Declaration of Independence.

4. **Extend** Have students research the tradition among Mesopotamian kings to begin their reigns by declaring reforms.
LS Verbal/Linguistic

📝 Alternative Assessment Handbook, Rubrics 3: Artwork; and 42: Writing to Inform

• Direct Teach •

Interpreting Maps
The Persian Empire

Location Approximately how many miles did Cyrus's Persian Empire stretch from west to east? How many kilometers? *approximately 2,500 miles or 4,000 km* **LS Logical/Mathematical**

🖥 Map Transparency: The Persian Empire
🐾 HSS 6.4.5; HSS Analysis Skills: CS 3

Main Idea

❶ Persia Becomes an Empire

Persia became an empire under Cyrus the Great.

Identify Why do historians call King Cyrus of Persia "Great"? *Cyrus is called "Great" because of his military successes and because of the way he treated conquered peoples.*

Draw Inferences Why was Cyrus able to create and rule the largest empire the world had ever seen? *Cyrus was successful militarily because he led a strong army and politically because he did not disrupt people's daily lives or force them to adopt new customs, so people were less likely to rebel.*

Activity Rules for Rulers Have each student create a guide for new conquerors. The guide should list five rules that the student thinks a conquering ruler should follow to minimize the possibility that the conquered people will rebel. **LS Verbal/Linguistic**

📝 Alternative Assessment Handbook, Rubric 37: Writing Assignments
🐾 HSS 6.4.5; HSS Analysis Skills: HI 1, HI 2

Answers

Interpreting Map 1. *Cyrus the Great;* **2.** *Sardis and Susa*

287

② The Persian Empire Grows Stronger

The Persian Empire grew stronger under Darius I.

Recall How did Darius I organize the Persian Empire politically? *by dividing it into 20 provinces and appointing a satrap to rule each one in his place*

Evaluate What is your opinion about Darius's use of satraps and his system of roads and messengers as ways to govern his empire? *Students' opinions should reflect an understanding of how the combination of political subdivisions, governors, and roads enabled Darius to manage his vast empire.*

🐾 **HSS** 6.4.5; **HSS** Analysis Skills: HI 1

Checking for Understanding

True or False Answer each statement *T* if it is true or *F* if it is false. If false, explain why.

1. The Immortals were a group of 10,000 soldiers mounted on horses. *F; Cavalry are horse-mounted soldiers.*

2. Darius I, Cyrus's son, claimed the throne and killed all his rivals for power. *F; Darius was a young prince not related to Cyrus.*

🐾 **HSS** 6.4.5

Answers

Persia Under Darius *because Darius is the king, and the king is more important and more powerful than any official. The respective size of the images is meant to convey their relative power and importance.*
Reading Check *Cyrus the Great*

Persia Under Darius

Sitting on a throne, the emperor Darius meets with an officer of his empire. Darius restored order to the Persian Empire and then expanded it. His army included royal guards like the two shown here.

Why do you think Darius appears larger than the official he is meeting with?

ACADEMIC VOCABULARY

strategy
(STRA-tuh-jee)
a plan for fighting a battle or war

At the heart of the Persian army were the Immortals, 10,000 soldiers chosen for their bravery and skill. In addition to the Immortals, the army had a powerful cavalry. A **cavalry** is a unit of soldiers who ride horses. Cyrus used his cavalry to charge at and shoot an enemy with arrows. This **strategy** weakened the enemy before the Immortals attacked. Together the cavalry and the Immortals could defeat almost any foe.

READING CHECK Finding Main Ideas
Who created the Persian Empire?

The Persian Empire Grows Stronger

Cyrus's son Cambyses continued to expand the Persian Empire after Cyrus died. For example, he conquered Egypt and added it to the empire. Soon afterward, though, a rebellion broke out in Persia. During this rebellion, Cambyses died. His death left Persia without a clear leader.

Within four years a young prince named **Darius I** (da-RY-uhs) claimed the throne and killed all his rivals for power. Once he was securely in control, Darius worked to restore order in Persia. He also improved Persian society and expanded the empire.

Political Organization

Darius organized the empire by dividing it into 20 provinces. Then he chose governors called satraps (SAY-traps) to rule the provinces for him. The satraps collected taxes for Darius, served as judges, and put down rebellions within their territories. Satraps had great power within their provinces, but Darius remained the empire's real ruler. His officials visited each province to make sure the satraps were loyal to Darius. He called himself king of kings to remind other rulers of his power.

Persian Society

After Darius restored order to the empire, he made many improvements to Persian society. For example, he built many roads.

288 CHAPTER 10

Critical Thinking: Making Decisions

Standards Proficiency

Ruling an Empire 🐾 **HSS** 6.4.5; **HSS** Analysis Skills: HR 1, HI 1

Research Required

1. Ask students to imagine that they are the ruler of the Persian Empire. They have to govern their vast empire and, at the same time, maintain peace and order.

2. Brainstorm with students a list of strategies for holding their empire together and maintaining peace. **LS** **Verbal/Linguistic**

3. Have each student select one strategy from the list and write an explanation about how he or she would use it to rule the empire.

4. Have students conduct research on King Darius and his use of satraps. Then have each student compare his or her strategy with Darius's use of satraps and make a decision about which strategy would be best. Students should indicate and explain their decision in writing.
LS **Verbal/Linguistic, Logical/Mathematical**

📋 Alternative Assessment Handbook, Rubrics 30: Research; and 37: Writing Assignments

Darius had roads built to connect various parts of the empire. Messengers used these roads to travel quickly throughout Persia. One road, called the Royal Road, was more than 1,700 miles long. Even Persia's enemies admired these roads and the Persian messenger system. For example, one Greek historian wrote:

"Nothing mortal travels so fast as these Persian messengers . . . these men will not be hindered from accomplishing at their best speed the distance which they have to go, either by snow, or rain, or heat, or by the darkness of night."

–Herodotus, from *History of the Persian Wars*

Darius also built a new capital for the empire. It was called Persepolis. Darius wanted his capital to reflect the glory of his empire, so he filled the city with beautiful works of art. For example, 3,000 carvings like the ones on the previous page line the city's walls. Statues throughout the city glittered with gold, silver, and precious jewels.

During Darius's rule a new religion arose in the Persian Empire as well. This religion, which was called Zoroastrianism (zawr-uh-WAS-tree-uh-nih-zuhm), taught that there were two forces fighting for control of the universe. One force was good, and the other was evil. Its priests urged people to help the side of good in its struggle. This religion remained popular in Persia for many centuries.

Persian Expansion

Like Cyrus, Darius wanted the Persian Empire to grow. In the east, he conquered the entire Indus Valley. He also tried to expand the empire westward into Europe. However, before Darius could move very far into Europe, he had to deal with a revolt in the empire.

READING CHECK **Summarizing** How did Darius I change Persia's political organization?

The Persians Fight Greece

In 499 BC several Greek cities in Asia Minor rebelled against Persian rule. To help their fellow Greeks, a few city-states in mainland Greece sent soldiers to join the fight against the Persians.

The Persians put down the revolt, but Darius was still angry with the Greeks. Although the cities that had rebelled were in Asia, Darius was enraged that other Greeks had given them aid. He swore to get revenge on the Greeks.

The Battle of Marathon

Nine years after the Greek cities rebelled, Darius invaded Greece. He and his army sailed to the plains of Marathon near Athens. This invasion began a series of wars between Persia and Greece that historians call the **Persian Wars**.

The Athenian army had only about 11,000 soldiers, while the Persians had about 15,000. However, the Greeks won the battle because they had better weapons and clever leaders.

The Persian Wars

This Greek vase shows a Persian soldier (at left) and a Greek soldier in a fight to the death. During the Persian Wars, the Greeks fiercely defended their homeland against massive invasions by the Persians.

With what kinds of weapons are the two soldiers fighting?

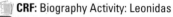

Direct Teach

Main Idea

❸ **The Persians Fight Greece**

The Persians fought Greece twice in the Persian Wars.

Recall Why did Darius swear to get revenge on the Greeks? *Darius was enraged that some mainland Greek city-states had aided Greek cities in Asia Minor that had rebelled against Persia.*

Identify What was the name of the place near Athens where the Persian Wars began? *the plains of Marathon*

📖 **CRF:** Biography Activity: Leonidas

🐻 **HSS** 6.4.6; **HSS** Analysis Skills: CS 1

Linking to Today

The Postal Service Some historians think that the first postal system was created under Cyrus the Great. Cyrus's postal system inspired Herodotus to write of the messengers that they "are stayed neither by snow nor rain nor heat nor darkness from accomplishing their appointed course with all speed." A paraphrase of this quote is today the motto of the United States Postal Service.

Collaborative Learning

Standards Proficiency

Changes in the Persian Empire 🐻 **HSS** 6.4.5; **HSS** Analysis Skills: HI 2   **Research Required**

1. Discuss with students the growth and strengthening of the Persian Empire under Darius I. Make sure that students understand how Darius built upon what Cyrus had begun.

2. Organize the class into groups of three. Assign each group (or let each group select) one of the following topics, related to the reign of Darius: Political Organization, Persian Society, or Persian Expansion.

3. Have each group use the Internet or the library to conduct research on King Darius

and changes in the Persian Empire related to their topic.

4. **Extend** Reorganize the groups so that each new group has at least one member from each of the previous groups. Have each new group prepare a brief presentation on all three topics.

LS Verbal/Linguistic

📄 Alternative Assessment Handbook, Rubrics 1: Acquiring Information; and 29: Presentations

Answers

The Persian Wars *bows and arrows and spears*

Reading Check *Darius organized the empire into 20 provinces, then appointed a governor (satrap) for each province. The satraps had considerable authority to collect taxes, act as judges, and exercise military power in Darius's name.*

Main Idea

❸ The Persians Fight Greece

The Persians fought Greece twice in the Persian Wars.

Identify What were the names of the three battles in Persia's second invasion of Greece? *Thermopylae, Salamis, and Plataea*

Predict After Athens and Sparta joined to defeat Persia, do you think they remained allies? *possible answer— became enemies because each one wanted to be the most influential city-state*

 Map Transparency: The Persian Wars

HSS 6.4.6; **HSS** Analysis Skills: CS 1

Linking to Today

Marathons Although athletes today run marathon races inspired by the legend of the messenger's feat, some historians question whether the legend is true.

Activity Have students conduct research on the legend and write a summary of their findings. Remind students to include their own assessment of the validity of the legend and the latest research. **LS** Verbal/Linguistic

HSS 6.4.6; **HSS** Analysis Skills: CS 1; HR 2, HR 4

Answers

Interpreting Maps 1. *near Sparta and Athens* **2.** *about 700 miles*

Reading Check (p.291) *Darius and Xerxes wanted to invade Greece because parts of Greece were rebelling against the Persian Empire and were trying to break away from Persian rule.*

290

The Persian Wars

Persian Empire
Rebellious Greek city-states
Greek city-states allied against the Persians
Neutral and pro-Persian city-states
⭐ Greek victory
⭐ Persian victory
→ Darius's fleet
→ Xerxes's army
→ Xerxes's fleet

Byzantium
Wreck of Darius's Fleet
Aegean Sea
Thermopylae
Plataea
Marathon
Athens
Salamis
Peloponnesus
Sparta
Sardis
IONIA
ASIA MINOR
Rhodes
Mediterranean Sea

0   50   100 Miles
0   50   100 Kilometers

N W E S

GEOGRAPHY SKILLS **INTERPRETING MAPS**

1. Location Where in Greece were most of the allies against the Persians located?

2. Movement About how far did Xerxes's army have to march to reach Thermoplyae?

THE IMPACT TODAY

Athletes today re-create the Greek messenger's run in 26-mile races called marathons.

According to legend, a messenger ran from Marathón to Athens—a distance of just over 26 miles—to bring news of the great victory. After crying out "Rejoice! We conquer!" the exhausted runner fell to the ground and died.

The Second Invasion of Greece

Ten years after the Battle of Marathon, Darius's son **Xerxes I** (ZUHRK-seez) tried to conquer Greece again. In 480 BC the Persian army set out for Greece. This time they were joined by the Persian navy.

The Greeks prepared to defend their homeland. This time Sparta, a powerful city-state in southern Greece, joined with Athens. The Spartans had the strongest army

in Greece, so they went to fight the Persian army. Meanwhile, the Athenians sent their powerful navy to attack the Persian navy.

To slow the Persian army, the Spartans sent about 1,400 soldiers to Thermopylae (thuhr-MAH-puh-lee), a narrow mountain pass. The Persians had to cross through this pass to attack Greek cities. For three days, the small Greek force held off the Persian army. Then the Persians asked a traitorous Greek soldier to lead them through another pass. A large Persian force attacked the Spartans from behind. Surrounded, the brave Spartans and their allies fought to their deaths. After winning the battle, the Persians swept into Athens, attacking and burning the city.

290 CHAPTER 10

Differentiating Instruction for Universal Access

English-Language Learners   Standards Proficiency   Research Required

Materials: butcher paper; art supplies

1. Discuss with students Persia's two invasions of Greece. Make sure that students understand that the two invasions were at different times and under different rulers.

2. Organize the class into three groups. Assign the first group the battle at Marathon, the second group the battle at Thermopylae, and the third group the battle at Salamis.

3. Have each group conduct research to find out more about its assigned battle.

4. Have each group create a mural depicting its battle. The mural should illustrate the location of the battle, the size and relative positions of each force, and military movements during the battle. **LS** Visual/Spatial

Alternative Assessment Handbook, Rubric 3: Artwork

HSS 6.4.5; **HSS** Analysis Skills: HR 1; HI 1

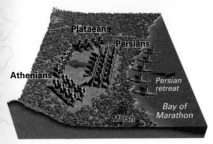

Marathon
At Marathon, the Greeks defeated a larger Persian force by luring the Persians into the middle of their forces. The Athenians then surrounded and defeated the Persians.

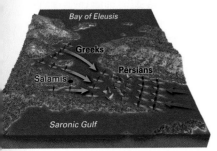

Salamis
At Salamis, the Greeks destroyed the Persian navy by attacking in a narrow strait where the Persian ships could not maneuver well.

Although the Persians won the battle in the pass, the Greeks quickly regained the upper hand. A few days after Athens was burned, the Athenians defeated the Persian navy through a clever plan. They led the larger Persian navy into the narrow straits of Salamis (SAH-luh-muhs). The Persians had so many ships that they couldn't steer well in the narrow strait. As a result, the smaller Athenian boats easily sank many Persian ships. Those ships that were not destroyed soon returned home.

Soon after the Battle of Salamis, an army of soldiers from all over Greece beat the Persians at Plataea (pluh-TEE-uh). This battle ended the Persian Wars. Defeated, the Persians left Greece.

For the Persians, this defeat was humiliating, but it was not a major blow. Their empire remained strong for more than a century after the war. For the Greeks, though, the defeat of the Persians was a triumph. They had saved their homeland.

READING CHECK **Analyzing** Why did Darius and Xerxes want to conquer Greece?

SUMMARY AND PREVIEW Athens and Sparta fought together against Persia. Their friendship didn't last long, though. In the next section, you will learn what happened when they became enemies.

Section 1 Assessment

go.hrw.com
Online Quiz
KEYWORD: SQ6 HP10

Reviewing Ideas, Terms, and People **HSS** 6.4.5
1. **a. Describe** Describe the empire of **Cyrus the Great**.
   b. Make Generalizations Why did peoples conquered by Cyrus the Great seldom rebel?
2. **a. Identify** How did **Darius I** change Persia's political organization?
   b. Make Generalizations How did Persia's roads help improve the empire's organization?
3. **a. Explain** Why did Persia want to invade Greece?
   b. Predict How might the **Persian Wars** have ended if the Spartans had not slowed the Persians at Thermopylae?

Critical Thinking
4. **Categorizing** Draw a chart like the one below. In the first column, list the major battles of the Persian Wars. In the other columns, identify who fought in each battle, who won, and what happened as a result of each battle.

Battle	Armies	Winner	Result

FOCUS ON WRITING

5. **Taking Notes on Persian Leaders** Draw a table with three columns. In the first column, write the names of each leader mentioned in this section. In the second column, list each person's military accomplishments. In the third column, list any other accomplishments.

THE GREEK WORLD **291**

Close
Ask students to discuss why, after the Greeks defeated the Persians, the city-states of Sparta and Athens might have become rivals.

Review
Online Quiz, Section 1

Assess
SE Section 1 Assessment
PASS: Section 1 Quiz
Alternative Assessment Handbook

Reteach/Classroom Intervention
California Standards Review Workbook
Interactive Reader and Study Guide, Section 1
Interactive Skills Tutor CD ROM

292 CHAPTER 10

Preteach

Bellringer

If YOU were there . . . Use the **Daily Bellringer Transparency** to help students answer the question.

📖 Daily Bellringer Transparency, Section 2

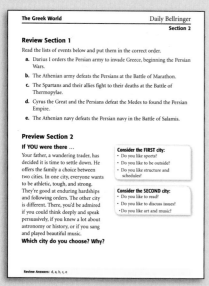

Building Vocabulary

Preteach or review the following term:
league a collection of people, groups, or countries that combine for mutual protection or cooperation (p. 296)

📝 **CRF:** Vocabulary Builder Activity, Section 2

Standards Focus

HSS 6.4.6
Means: Describe the similarities and differences between life in Athens and Sparta and how these similarities and differences influenced each city-state's role in the Persian and Peloponnesian wars.
Matters: The science, literature, and philosophy that form the basis of Western culture were shaped in ancient Athens, not ancient Sparta.

292 CHAPTER 10

Sparta and Athens

What You Will Learn...

Main Ideas

1. The Spartans built a military society to provide security and protection.
2. The Athenians admired the mind and the arts in addition to physical abilities.
3. Sparta and Athens fought over who should have power and influence in Greece.

The Big Idea

The two most powerful city-states in Greece, Sparta and Athens, had very different cultures and became bitter enemies in the 400s BC.

Key Terms and People
alliance, *p. 296*
Peloponnesian War, *p. 297*

HSS 6.4.6 Compare and contrast life in Athens and Sparta, with emphasis on their roles in the Persian and Peloponnesian Wars.

292 CHAPTER 10

If YOU were there...

Your father, a wandering trader, has decided it is time to settle down. He offers the family a choice between two cities. In one city, everyone wants to be athletic, tough, and strong. They're good at enduring hardships and following orders. The other city is different. There, you'd be admired if you could think deeply and speak persuasively, if you knew a lot about astronomy or history, or if you sang and played beautiful music.

Which city do you choose? Why?

BUILDING BACKGROUND Two of the greatest city-states in Greece were Sparta and Athens. Sparta, like the first city mentioned above, had a culture that valued physical strength and military might. The Athenian culture placed more value on the mind. However, both city-states had military strength, and they both played important roles in the defense of ancient Greece.

Spartans Build a Military Society

Spartan society was dominated by the military. According to Spartan tradition, their social system was created between 900 and 600 BC by a man named Lycurgus (ly-KUHR-guhs) after a slave revolt. To keep such a revolt from happening again, he increased the military's role in society. The Spartans believed that military power was the way to provide security and protection for their city. Daily life in Sparta reflected this belief.

Boys and Men in Sparta

Daily life in Sparta was dominated by the army. Even the lives of children reflected this domination. When a boy was born, government officials came to look at him. If he was not healthy, the baby was taken outside of the city and left to die. Healthy boys were trained from an early age to be soldiers.

Teach the Big Idea: Master the Standards

Standards Proficiency

Sparta and Athens 🐻 **HSS** 6.4.6; **HSS** Analysis Skills: HI 1

1. **Teach** Ask students the Main Idea questions to teach this section.

2. **Apply** As students read this section, have them make an outline of the section using the blue heads (such as "Spartans Build a Military Society") as main ideas and the red heads (such as "Boys and Men in Sparta") as supporting ideas. Have students fill in their outlines. **LS** Verbal/Linguistic

3. **Review** Ask volunteers to share their outlines with the class. Ask the class to

suggest additional information they might add to the outline.

4. **Practice/Homework** Have each student use his or her outline to write a brief, two-paragraph summary comparing and contrasting life in Athens and Sparta. **LS** Verbal/Linguistic

📝 Alternative Assessment Handbook, Rubric 9: Comparing and Contrasting

As part of their training, boys ran, jumped, swam, and threw javelins to increase their strength. They also learned to endure the hardships they would face as soldiers. For example, boys weren't given shoes or heavy clothes, even in winter. They also weren't given much food. Boys were allowed to steal food if they could, but if they were caught, they were whipped. At least one boy chose to die rather than admit to his theft:

"One youth, having stolen a fox and hidden it under his coat, allowed it to tear out his very bowels [organs] with its claws and teeth and died rather than betray his theft."

–Plutarch, from *Life of Lycurgus*

To this boy—and to most Spartan soldiers—courage and strength were more important than one's own safety.

Soldiers between the ages of 20 and 30 lived in army barracks and only occasionally visited their families. Spartan men stayed in the army until they turned 60.

The Spartans believed that the most important qualities of good soldiers were self-discipline and obedience. To reinforce self-discipline they required soldiers to live tough lives free from comforts. For example, the Spartans didn't have luxuries like soft furniture and expensive food. They thought such comforts made people weak. Even the Spartans' enemies admired their discipline and obedience.

Girls and Women in Sparta

Because Spartan men were often away at war, Spartan women had more rights than other Greek women. Some women owned land in Sparta and ran their households when their husbands were gone. Unlike women in other Greek cities, Spartan women didn't spend time spinning cloth or weaving. They thought of those tasks as the jobs of slaves, unsuitable for the wives and mothers of soldiers.

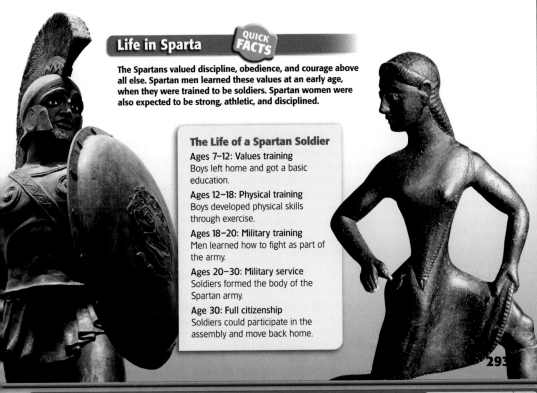

Life in Sparta

QUICK FACTS

The Spartans valued discipline, obedience, and courage above all else. Spartan men learned these values at an early age, when they were trained to be soldiers. Spartan women were also expected to be strong, athletic, and disciplined.

The Life of a Spartan Soldier

Ages 7–12: Values training
Boys left home and got a basic education.

Ages 12–18: Physical training
Boys developed physical skills through exercise.

Ages 18–20: Military training
Men learned how to fight as part of the army.

Ages 20–30: Military service
Soldiers formed the body of the Spartan army.

Age 30: Full citizenship
Soldiers could participate in the assembly and move back home.

293

• **Direct Teach** •

Main Idea

❶ Spartans Build a Military Society

The Spartans built a military society to provide security and protection.

Identify According to legend, who was responsible for the beginnings of the Spartan social system? *Lycurgus, sometime between 900 and 600 BC*

Recall What two qualities did the Spartans think were most important in a good soldier? *self-discipline and obedience*

Analyze In a society organized such as Sparta was, why might women have more rights and responsibilities than in a society organized as Athens was? *While the boys and young men in Sparta were away from home serving as soldiers, women filled the roles, such as property owners and heads of households, that men filled in other societies.*

☝ Quick Facts Transparency: Life in Sparta

🐻 **HSS** 6.4.6; **HSS** Analysis Skills: HI 2

Did you know. . .

Although some modern historians think that Lycurgus was a real person, many other historians think that Lycurgus existed only in legend.

go.hrw.com
Online Resources

KEYWORD: SQ6 WH10
ACTIVITY: Brains Versus Brawn?

Critical Thinking: Evaluating Information   Standards **Proficiency**

Sparta Builds a Military Society 🐻 **HSS** 6.4.6; **HSS** Analysis Skills: CS 1

1. Ask students to describe, in their own words, the structure and organization of Spartan society.

2. Ask students to give their opinion about the following statement: *Sparta's model of a military society is a model that countries should follow today.* Remind students to give reasons for their opinions and to support their opinions with facts. **LS** Verbal/Linguistic

3. **Extend** Have students who hold opposing viewpoints debate the issue. Afterward, have the class vote on which side made the better arguments.

📝 Alternative Assessment Handbook, Rubrics 10: Debates; and 11: Discussions

❶ Spartans Build a Military Society

The Spartans built a military society to provide security and protection.

Recall How many kings officially ruled Sparta? *two*

Draw Conclusions Why did Spartan elected officials have more power than the kings? *Elected officials ran Sparta's day-to-day activities and handled Sparta's dealings with other city-states.*

🐻 **HSS** 6.4.6; **HSS** Analysis Skills: HI 1, HI 2

Linking to Today

Women of Greece Women of Sparta and Athens had different rights. Because Greece is no longer divided into city-states, all Greek women now have the same rights. They have gained some of those rights, however, just in recent decades. In the 1980s the power of Greek fathers over their daughters was limited. At the same time, women received more freedom to divorce. Women can serve in the military and are active in the government.

Answers

Analyzing Points of View
Lycurgus's viewpoint stresses that most of a boy's education should be focused on how to fight and endure pain and how to conquer in battle. This viewpoint is the basis for Sparta's military society. Plato's viewpoint is that both a boy's mind and his body should be trained and educated. This viewpoint reflects the value that Athens placed on both the mind and the body.

Focus on Reading *Like is used to show how two things are similar; unlike is used to show how two things are different. As you read, these words will give you clues about the similarities and differences between Sparta and Athens.*

Reading Check *the military*

294

POINTS OF VIEW
Views of Education

Plato, an Athenian, thought that education for young boys should train both the mind and the body. He wanted students to be prepared for all aspects of life as adults.

❝And what shall be their education? Can we find a better division than the traditional sort?—and this has two divisions, gymnastics for the body, and music for the soul.❞

—Plato
from The Republic

Lycurgus, a Spartan lawgiver, thought education for boys should teach them how to fight. The historian Plutarch described how education was handled in Sparta under Lycurgus:

❝Reading and writing they gave them, just enough to serve their turn; their chief care was to make them good subjects, and to teach them to endure pain and conquer in battle.❞

—Plutarch
from Life of Lycurgus

ANALYSIS SKILL | **ANALYZING POINTS OF VIEW**

How do Plato's and Lycurgus's viewpoints reflect the ideals of Athens and Sparta?

Spartan women also received physical training. Like the men, they learned how to run, jump, wrestle, and throw javelins. The Spartans believed this training would help women bear healthy children.

Government

Sparta was officially ruled by two kings who jointly led the army. But elected officials actually had more power than the kings. These officials ran Sparta's day-to-day activities. They also handled dealings between Sparta and other city-states.

Sparta's government was set up to control the city's helots (HEL-uhts), or slaves. These slaves grew all the city's crops and did many other jobs. Their lives were miserable, and they couldn't leave their land. Although slaves greatly outnumbered Spartan citizens, fear of the Spartan army kept them from rebelling.

FOCUS ON READING
How can the words **like** and **unlike** help you compare and contrast Athens and Sparta?

READING CHECK **Analyzing** What was the most important element of Spartan society?

Athenians Admire the Mind

Sparta's main rival in Greece was Athens. Like Sparta, Athens had been a leader in the Persian Wars and had a powerful army. But life in Athens was very different from life in Sparta. In addition to physical training, the Athenians valued education, clear thinking, and the arts.

Boys and Men in Athens

From a young age, Athenian boys from rich families worked to improve both their bodies and their minds. Like Spartan boys, Athenian boys had to learn to run, jump, and fight. But this training was not as harsh or as long as the training in Sparta.

Unlike Spartan men, Athenian men didn't have to devote their whole lives to the army. All men in Athens joined the army, but for only two years. They helped defend the city between the ages of 18 and 20. Older men only had to serve in the army in times of war.

Differentiating Instruction for Universal Access

Learners Having Difficulty **Reaching Standards**

1. Organize the class into four groups.

2. Have each group create a mural or posters that depict the lives of men and women in Sparta and Athens. **LS** Visual/Spatial

3. Ask each group to present its mural or posters to the rest of the class.

4. Have students, using the images on the mural or posters, discuss which parts of both Spartan and Athenian society they like or don't like. **LS** Verbal/Linguistic

5. **Extend** Refer students back to the carving of Darius meeting with an officer in the previous section. Ask students if any of their images are larger than others. If so, ask if they can explain why.

📖 Alternative Assessment Handbook, Rubrics 3: Artwork; and 28: Posters

🐻 **HSS** 6.4.6; **HSS** Analysis Skills: HI 1

In addition to their physical training, Athenian students, unlike the Spartans, also learned other skills. They learned to read, write, and count as well as sing and play musical instruments. Boys also learned about Greek history and legend. For example, they studied the *Iliad*, the *Odyssey*, and other works of Greek literature.

Boys from very rich families often continued their education with private tutors. These tutors taught their students about philosophy, geometry, astronomy, and other subjects. They also taught the boys how to be good public speakers. This training prepared boys for participation in the Athenian assembly.

Very few boys had the opportunity to receive this much education, however. Boys from poor families usually didn't get any education, although most of them could read and write at least a little. Most of the boys from poor families became farmers and grew food for the city's richer citizens. A few went to work with craftspeople to learn other trades.

Girls and Women in Athens

While many boys in Athens received good educations, girls didn't. In fact, girls got almost no education. Athenian men didn't think girls needed to be educated. A few girls were taught how to read and write at home by private tutors. However, most girls only learned household tasks like weaving and sewing.

Despite Athens's reputation for freedom and democracy, women there had fewer rights than women in many other city-states. Athenian women could not

- serve in any part of the city's government, including the assembly and juries,
- leave their homes, except on special occasions,
- buy anything or own property, or
- disobey their husbands or fathers.

In fact, women in Athens had almost no rights at all.

READING CHECK Identifying Cause and Effect
Why did girls in Athens receive little education?

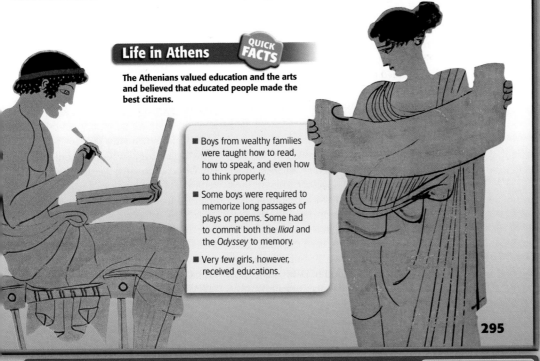

Life in Athens QUICK FACTS

The Athenians valued education and the arts and believed that educated people made the best citizens.

- Boys from wealthy families were taught how to read, how to speak, and even how to think properly.
- Some boys were required to memorize long passages of plays or poems. Some had to commit both the *Iliad* and the *Odyssey* to memory.
- Very few girls, however, received educations.

295

Critical Thinking: Comparing and Constrasting
Standards Proficiency

Understanding Charts and Tables HSS 6.4.6; HSS Analysis Skills: HI 1
Materials: butcher paper, markers

1. Organize the class into small groups.

2. Have each group make a table comparing and contrasting education in ancient Athens with education today. The table should have two main heads (*Education in Ancient Athens* and *Education Today*), and each of those main heads should have two subheads, (*Education for Boys* and *Education for Girls*).

3. Have students complete the table.

4. Have each group present its table to the rest of the class. Have the class discuss similarities and differences between education in ancient Athens and education today. Ask students which education system they would rather have and why. **LS Logical/Mathematical**

Alternative Assessment Handbook, Rubric 9: Comparing and Contrasting

Direct Teach

Main Idea

❷ Athenians Admire the Mind

The Athenians admired the mind and the arts in addition to physical abilities.

Recall What were Athenian girls taught? *to weave and sew, care for the home*

Contrast What was the basic difference between life in Sparta and life in Athens? *Sparta—focused on and organized around the military, so all training and education supported the military; Athens—thought that the mind and the body should be trained, so education, clear thinking, and the arts were valued*

Evaluate Considering only Athens and Sparta, in which city-state would you rather have lived? *possible answer—I would rather have lived in Sparta because I could have owned property, taken care of my house, and been defended by the strong army.*

📑 **CRF:** Interdisciplinary Project: Spartans vs Athenians Debate

📑 **CRF:** Economics and History Activity: The Importance of Trade

📦 Quick Facts Transparency: Life in Athens

🐻 **HSS** 6.4.6; **HSS** Analysis Skills: HI 1

Biography

Anaxagoras of Clazomenae (500–428 BC) Anaxagoras was a Greek philosopher who believed that the sun is a white-hot stone and that the moon is made of material similar to Earth and reflects light from the sun.

🐻 **HSS** 6.4.6

Answers
Reading Check *because men didn't think women needed education*

295

❸ Sparta and Athens Fight

Sparta and Athens fought over who should have power and influence in Greece.

Define In your own words, define the term alliance. *an agreement between parties to work together or to help each other, especially for defense or trade*

Summarize What happened to the Delian League? *Athens increased its influence over the other city-states in the league, began to treat other members unfairly, and used the league's money to benefit Athens. The league became an Athenian empire.*

📋 Map Transparency: The Peloponnesian War, c. 431–404 BC

🐻 **HSS** 6.4.6; **HSS** Analysis Skills: CS 1; HI 1

Interpreting Maps

The Peloponnesian War, c. 431–404 BC

Activity Ask students to imagine that they are generals for either Athens or Greece. Have students analyze the map to see who might have the military advantage in a possible Peloponnesian War. Students should consider the location of Athens and Sparta, the location of their allies, the distance their military would have to travel to fight a battle, and any other things that you as a general might worry about. Who has the advantage? *possible answer—Sparta and its allies, because they control more territory than Athens and its allies; Sparta and its allies can attack Athens from two directions.*

📋 Map Transparency: Peloponnesian War, c. 431–404 BC.

Answers

Interpreting Maps
1. *Athens* **2.** *about 550 miles*

296

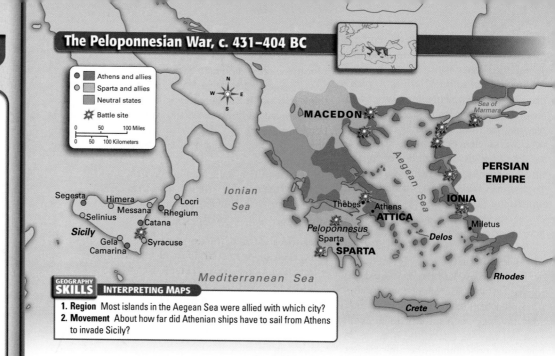

The Peloponnesian War, c. 431–404 BC

- Athens and allies
- Sparta and allies
- Neutral states
- ⭐ Battle site

0   50   100 Miles
0   50   100 Kilometers

MACEDON

Sea of Marmara

PERSIAN EMPIRE

Aegean Sea

IONIA

Thebes • Athens
ATTICA

Ionian Sea

Peloponnesus Sparta
SPARTA

Miletus

Delos

Segesta
Himera
Messana Locri
Selinius Rhegium
Catana
Sicily
Gela Syracuse
Camarina

Rhodes

Mediterranean Sea

Crete

GEOGRAPHY SKILLS **INTERPRETING MAPS**

1. **Region** Most islands in the Aegean Sea were allied with which city?
2. **Movement** About how far did Athenian ships have to sail from Athens to invade Sicily?

Sparta and Athens Fight

As you learned earlier, Sparta and Athens worked together to win the Persian Wars. The Spartans fought most of the battles on land, and the Athenians fought at sea. After the war, the powerful Athenian fleet continued to protect Greece from the Persian navy. As a result, Athens had a great influence over much of Greece.

Athenian Power

After the Persian Wars ended in 480 BC, many city-states formed an **alliance**, or an agreement to work together. They wanted to punish the Persians for attacking Greece. They also agreed to help defend each other and to protect trade in the Aegean Sea. To pay for this defense, each city-state gave money to the alliance. Because the money was kept on the island of Delos, historians call the alliance the Delian League.

With its navy protecting the islands, Athens was the strongest member of the league. As a result, the Athenians began to treat other league members as their subjects. They refused to let members quit the league and forced more cities to join it. The Athenians even used the league's money to pay for buildings in Athens. Without even fighting, the Athenians made the Delian League an Athenian empire.

The Peloponnesian War

The Delian League was not the only alliance in Greece. After the Persian Wars, many cities in southern Greece, including Sparta, banded together as well. This alliance was called the Peloponnesian League after the peninsula on which the cities were located.

The growth of Athenian power worried many cities in the Peloponnesian League. Finally, to stop Athens's growth, Sparta declared war.

296 CHAPTER 10

Critical Thinking: Evaluating Information
Exceeding Standards

The Peloponnesian War 🐻 **HSS** 6.4.6; **HSS** Analysis Skills: CS 1, HR 1, HI 1
Research Required

Materials: butcher paper; art supplies

1. Organize the class into small groups. Assign each group either Sparta's attack on Athens in 431 BC, Athens's attack on Sicily in 415 BC, or Sparta's attack on Athens (and Athens's surrender) in 405–404 BC.

2. Have each group conduct research on its assigned battle. Then ask each group to create a large map or a mural showing the details of its battle and the strategy and tactics used by both sides.

3. Have members of each group prepare a brief presentation explaining its battle to the class.

4. Have the class discuss each battle and evaluate the strategy and tactics used by each side. **LS** **Logical/Mathematical, Visual Spatial**

📝 Alternative Assessment Handbook, Rubrics 1: Acquiring Information; 3: Artwork; and 16: Judging Information

This declaration of war began the **Peloponnesian War**, a war between Athens and Sparta that threatened to tear all of Greece apart. In 431 BC the Spartan army marched north to Athens. They surrounded the city, waiting for the Athenians to come out and fight. But the Athenians stayed in the city, hoping that the Spartans would leave. Instead, the Spartans began to burn the crops in the fields around Athens. They hoped that Athens would run out of food and be forced to surrender.

The Spartans were in for a surprise. The Athenian navy escorted merchant ships to Athens, bringing plenty of food to the city. The navy also attacked Sparta's allies, forcing the Spartans to send troops to defend other Greek cities. At the same time, though, disease swept through Athens, killing thousands. For 10 years neither side could gain an advantage over the other. Eventually, they agreed to a truce. Athens kept its empire, and the Spartans went home.

A few years later, in 415 BC, Athens tried again to expand its empire. It sent its army and navy to conquer the island of Sicily. This effort backfired. The entire Athenian army was defeated by Sicilian allies of Sparta and taken prisoner. Even worse, these Sicilians also destroyed most of the Athenian navy.

Taking advantage of Athens's weakness, Sparta attacked Athens, and the war started up once more. Although the Athenians fought bravely, the Spartans won. They cut off the supply of food to Athens completely. In 404 BC, the people of Athens, starving and surrounded, surrendered. The Peloponnesian War was over, and Sparta was in control.

Fighting Among the City-States

With the defeat of Athens, Sparta became the most powerful city-state in Greece. For about 30 years, the Spartans controlled nearly all of Greece, until other city-states started to resent them. This resentment led to a period of war. Control of Greece shifted from city-state to city-state. The fighting went on for many years, which weakened Greece and left it open to attack from outside.

READING CHECK Identifying Cause and Effect
What happened after the Peloponnesian War?

SUMMARY AND PREVIEW In this section you read about conflicts between city-states for control of Greece. In the next section, you will learn what happened when all of Greece was conquered by a foreign power.

Section 2 Assessment

go.hrw.com
Online Quiz
KEYWORD: SQ6 HP10

Reviewing Ideas, Terms, and People **HSS** 6.4.6

1. **a. Recall** How long did Spartan men stay in the army?
   b. Summarize How did the army affect life in Sparta?
2. **a. Identify** What skills did rich Athenian boys learn in school?
   b. Elaborate How might the government of Athens have influenced the growth of its educational system?
3. **a. Identify** Which city-state won the Peloponnesian War?
   b. Explain Why did many city-states form an **alliance** against Athens?

Critical Thinking

4. **Compare and Contrast** Draw a graphic organizer like the one shown here in your notebook. Use it to compare and contrast life in Sparta and Athens before the Peloponnesian War.

Military
Education
Women

Sparta   Athens

FOCUS ON WRITING

5. **Analyzing Greek Accomplishments** Think about the characteristics you would expect to be admired in Sparta and Athens. Write down some of these characteristics in your notebook. How do they relate to the Persian leaders you listed before?

THE GREEK WORLD **297**

Section 2 Assessment Answers

1. **a.** 40 years
   b. Boys trained for military service from age 18 to 20, and men served in the army from age 20 to 60. Spartan women had more rights than other Greek women.
2. **a.** reading, writing, counting, singing, playing a musical instrument, history, and thinking
   b. It didn't emphasize the military, and it encouraged the arts and sciences.
3. **a.** Sparta
   b. because Athens treated them like subjects

4. Sparta—military: main element in society; education: limited to basics; women: had rights, owned land, trained physically; Athens—military: limited service; education: wealthy boys given education; women: few rights and not educated

5. Students may compare and contrast characteristics, such as the emphasis on military training or on education.

• Review & Assess •

Close
Have students discuss why Spartan society depended so heavily on slaves whereas Athenian society did not. Ask students, "Why might the dependence on slaves be a weakness in the society in Sparta?"

Review
Online Quiz, Section 2

Assess
SE Section 2 Assessment
PASS: Section 2 Quiz
Alternative Assessment Handbook

Reteach/Classroom Intervention
California Standards Review Workbook
Interactive Reader and Study Guide, Section 2
Interactive Skills Tutor CD ROM

Answers

Reading Check *Sparta became the most powerful city-state in Greece.*

297

Bellringer

If YOU were there . . . Use the **Daily Bellringer Transparency** to help students answer the question.

📖 Daily Bellringer Transparency, Section 3

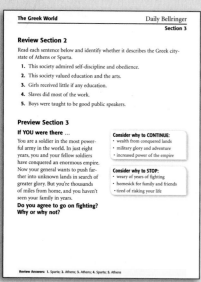

The Greek World Daily Bellringer
Section 3

Review Section 2
Read each sentence below and identify whether it describes the Greek city-state of Athens or Sparta.

1. This society admired self-discipline and obedience.
2. This society valued education and the arts.
3. Girls received little if any education.
4. Slaves did most of the work.
5. Boys were taught to be good public speakers.

Preview Section 3

If YOU were there . . .
You are a soldier in the most powerful army in the world. In just eight years, you and your fellow soldiers have conquered an enormous empire. Now your general wants to push farther into unknown lands in search of greater glory. But you're thousands of miles from home, and you haven't seen your family in years.
Do you agree to go on fighting? Why or why not?

Consider why to CONTINUE:
• wealth from conquered lands
• military glory and adventure
• increased power of the empire

Consider why to STOP:
• weary of years of fighting
• homesick for family and friends
• tired of risking your life

Review Answers: 1. Sparta; 2. Athens; 3. Athens; 4. Sparta; 5. Athens

Vocabulary Builder

Preteach or review the following term:

Hellenic an adjective meaning "Greek"; applied to the cultures of Greek-speaking societies (p. 301)

opponent someone who takes the opposite side in a contest or fight (p. 299)

📝 **CRF:** Vocabulary Builder Activity, Section 3

Standards Focus

HSS 6.4.7
Means: Trace Alexander the Great's life and impact as a conqueror, including the spread of Greek culture into Asia and Egypt.
Matters: Much of our culture is based, directly or indirectly, on the Greek culture that Alexander spread throughout his empire.

SECTION 3

Alexander the Great

If YOU were there...

You are a soldier in the most powerful army in the world. In just eight years, you and your fellow soldiers have conquered an enormous empire. Now your general wants to push farther into unknown lands in search of greater glory. But you're thousands of miles from home, and you haven't seen your family in years.

Do you agree to go on fighting? Why or why not?

What You Will Learn...

Main Ideas

1. Macedonia conquered Greece in the 300s BC.
2. Alexander the Great built an empire that united much of Europe, Asia, and Egypt.
3. The Hellenistic kingdoms formed from Alexander's empire blended Greek and other cultures.

The Big Idea

Alexander the Great built a huge empire and helped spread Greek culture into Egypt and Asia.

Key Terms and People

Philip II, *p. 298*
phalanx, *p. 299*
Alexander the Great, *p. 300*
Hellenistic, *p. 301*

HSS **6.4.7** Trace the rise of Alexander the Great and the spread of Greek culture eastward and into Egypt.

BUILDING BACKGROUND The world's most powerful army in the 300s BC was from Macedonia, a kingdom just north of Greece. The Greeks had long dismissed the Macedonians as unimportant. They thought of the Macedonians as barbarians because they lived in small villages and spoke a strange form of the Greek language. But the Greeks underestimated the Macedonians, barbarians or not.

Macedonia Conquers Greece

In 359 BC **Philip II** became king of Macedonia. Philip spent the first year of his rule fighting off invaders who wanted to take over his kingdom. Once he defeated the invaders, he was ready to launch invasions of his own.

Philip's main target was Greece. The leaders of Athens, knowing they were the target of Philip's powerful army, called for all Greeks to join together. Few people responded.

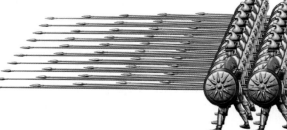

Teach the Big Idea: Master the Standards

Standards Proficiency

Alexander the Great **HSS** 6.4.7; **HSS** Analysis Skills: CS 1, HI 1

1. **Teach** Ask students the Main Idea questions to teach this section.

2. **Apply** Organize the class into four groups. Assign each group one of the following: *Macedonia conquers Greece, Alexander builds an empire, Alexander spreads Greek culture, and Alexander's empire after his death.* Have the groups prepare posters about their topics. Have each group present its findings and discuss them.
LS **Visual/Spatial**

3. **Review** Have the class review Alexander's goals and whether he was successful in attaining them.

4. **Practice/Homework** Have students write a short speech either supporting or opposing Alexander the Great from the point of view of a Greek citizen or a citizen of another conquered area. **LS** **Verbal/Linguistic**

📝 Alternative Assessment Handbook, Rubrics 28: Posters; and 43: Writing to Persuade

As a result, the armies of Athens and its chief ally Thebes were easily defeated by the Macedonians. Having witnessed this defeat, the rest of the Greeks agreed to make Philip their leader.

Philip's Military Strength

Philip defeated the Greeks because he was a brilliant military leader. He borrowed and improved many of the strategies Greek armies used in battle. For example, Philip's soldiers, like the Greeks, fought as a phalanx (FAY-langks). A **phalanx** was a group of warriors who stood close together in a square. Each soldier held a spear pointed outward to fight off enemies. As soldiers in the front lines were killed, others stepped up from behind to fill their spots.

Philip improved upon the Greeks' idea. He gave his soldiers spears that were much longer than those of his opponents. This allowed his army to attack first in any battle. Philip also sent cavalry and archers into battle to support the phalanx.

After conquering Greece, Philip turned his attention to Persia. He planned to march east and conquer the Persian Empire, but he never made it. He was murdered in 336 BC while celebrating his daughter's wedding. When Philip died, his throne—and his plans—passed to his son, Alexander.

READING CHECK Summarizing How was Philip II able to conquer Greece?

Alexander Builds an Empire

When Philip died, the people in the Greek city of Thebes rebelled. They thought that the Macedonians would not have a leader strong enough to keep the kingdom together. They were wrong.

Controlling the Greeks

Although he was only 20 years old, Philip's son Alexander was as strong a leader as his father had been. He immediately went south to end the revolt in Thebes.

The Phalanx
With men holding 16-foot-long spears, a phalanx marches into battle.

Why were the soldiers' spears so long?

THE GREEK WORLD **299**

299

Main Idea

❷ Alexander Builds an Empire

Alexander the Great built an empire that united much of Europe, Asia, and Egypt.

Explain Why is Alexander called "the Great"? *because he took over his father's throne at 20 and then built one of the largest empires the world has ever seen*

Summarize Using the information on this page and in the map of Alexander's empire, summarize Alexander's efforts to conquer the world. *Between 336 and 323 BC, Alexander conquered Greece, Egypt, the Persian Empire, and parts of central Asia and India. He didn't conquer the whole world, but he did create a vast empire.*

📄 **CRF:** Primary Source Activity: "Alexander" from Plutarch's *Lives*

🐻 **HSS** 6.4.7; **HSS** Analysis Skills: CS 1, HI 1, HI 2

Info to Know

Bucephalus Alexander had a favorite horse named Bucephalus. According to Plutarch, Alexander was 12 years old when he won the horse. No one could tame the animal, but Alexander wanted to try. He promised to pay for the horse if he failed. Alexander succeeded by turning the horse toward the sun so it couldn't see its own shadow, which was frightening it. Alexander named his prize Bucephalus. He loved the animal so much that when Bucephalus died, Alexander named a city—Bucephala—after the animal.

Within a year, Alexander had destroyed Thebes and enslaved the Theban people. He used Thebes as an example to other Greeks of what would happen if they turned against him. Then, confident that the Greeks would not rebel again, he set out to build an empire.

Alexander's efforts to build an empire made him one of the greatest conquerors in history. These efforts earned him the name **Alexander the Great**.

Building a New Empire

Like his father, Alexander was a brilliant commander. In 334 BC he attacked the Persians, whose army was much larger than his own. But Alexander's troops were well trained and ready for battle. They defeated the Persians time after time.

According to legend, Alexander visited a town called Gordium in Asia Minor while he was fighting the Persians. There he heard an ancient tale about a knot tied by an ancient king. The tale said that whoever untied the knot would rule all of Asia. According to the legend, Alexander pulled out his sword and cut right through the knot. Taking this as a good sign, he and his army set out again.

THE IMPACT TODAY
We still use the phrase "cutting the Gordian knot" to mean solving a difficult problem easily.

If you look at the map, you can follow the route Alexander took on his conquests. After defeating the Persians near the town of Issus, Alexander went to Egypt, which was part of the Persian Empire. The Persian governor had heard of his skill in battle. He surrendered without a fight in 332 BC and crowned Alexander pharaoh.

After a short stay in Egypt, Alexander set out again. Near the town of Gaugamela (gaw-guh-MEE-luh), he defeated the Persian army for the last time. After the battle, the Persian king fled. The king soon died, killed by one of his nobles. With the king's death, Alexander became the ruler of what had been the Persian Empire.

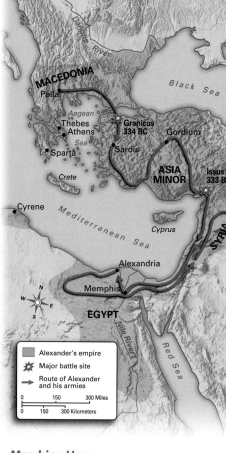

Alexander's empire
⭐ Major battle site
➡ Route of Alexander and his armies

0   150   300 Miles
0   150   300 Kilometers

Marching Home

Still intent on building his empire, Alexander led his army through Central Asia. In 327 BC Alexander crossed the Indus River and wanted to push deeper into India. But his exhausted soldiers refused to go any farther. Disappointed, Alexander began the long march home.

Alexander left India in 325 BC, but he never made it back to Greece. In 323 BC, on his way back, Alexander visited the city of Babylon and got sick. He died a few days later at age 33. After he died, Alexander's body was taken to Egypt and buried in a golden coffin.

300 CHAPTER 10

Cross-Discipline Activity: English–Language Arts   [Exceeding Standards]

Creating a Philippic 🐻 **HSS** 6.4.7; **HSS** Analysis Skills: HI 1   [Prep Required] [Research Required]

1. Discuss with students the Greek belief in using language effectively and persuasively.

2. Have students use the Internet or the library to find information about the orator Demosthenes and his *philippics* (bitter verbal attacks on or denunciations of someone).

3. Read portions of Demosthenes' speeches against Philip. Discuss with students the way Demosthenes used words against Philip in his speeches.

4. Organize the class into small groups. Have each group prepare a philippic against Alexander from the viewpoint of a soldier in the army, a Greek citizen, or a citizen of another country. Ask for volunteers to share their philippics. 🅛🅢 **Verbal/Linguistic**

📄 Alternative Assessment Handbook, Rubrics 1: Acquiring Information; and 14: Group Activity

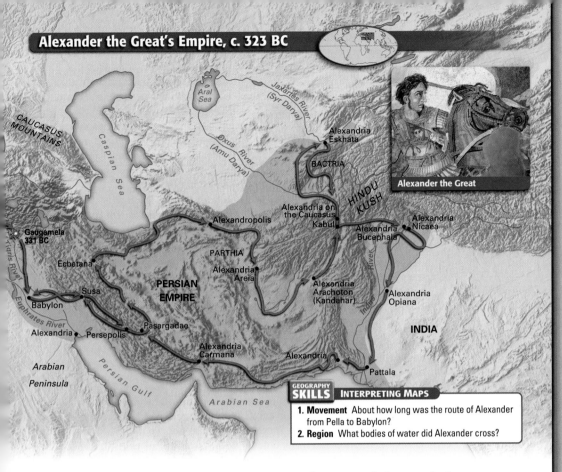

Alexander the Great's Empire, c. 323 BC

Alexander the Great

GEOGRAPHY **SKILLS** | **INTERPRETING MAPS**

1. **Movement** About how long was the route of Alexander from Pella to Babylon?
2. **Region** What bodies of water did Alexander cross?

Spreading Greek Culture

Alexander's empire was the largest the world had ever seen. An admirer of Greek culture, he worked to spread Greek influence throughout his empire by founding cities in the lands he conquered.

Alexander modeled his new cities after the cities of Greece. He named many of them Alexandria, after himself. He built temples and theaters like those in Greece. He then encouraged Greek settlers to move to the new cities. These settlers spoke Greek, which became common throughout the empire. In time, Greek art, literature, and science spread into surrounding lands.

Even as he supported the spread of Greek culture, however, Alexander encouraged conquered people to keep their own customs and traditions. As a result, a new blended culture developed in Alexander's empire. It combined elements of Persian, Egyptian, Syrian, and other cultures with Greek ideas. Because this new culture was not completely Greek, or Hellenic, historians call it **Hellenistic**, or Greek-like. It wasn't purely Greek, but it was heavily influenced by Greek ideas.

READING CHECK Sequencing What steps did Alexander take to create his empire?

THE GREEK WORLD **301**

Critical Thinking: Sequencing

Standards Proficiency

Alexander the Great Time Line HSS 6.4.7; HSS Analysis Skills: CS 1

Materials: butcher paper, markers, art supplies

1. Organize the class into four or five groups.

2. Have each group make an illustrated time line showing the major events in Alexander's life, including his birth and death. Dates for each event should be clearly shown.

3. Have groups decorate and illustrate their time lines. When necessary, groups should also write a brief explanation for an event.

4. Have each group share its time line with the class and describe its illustrations and text notes. **LS** Visual/Spatial

5. **Extend** Ask students to extend their time line to include Philip at one end and Alexander's empire after Alexander's death at the other end.

Alternative Assessment Handbook, Rubric 36: Time Lines

Direct Teach

Main Idea

❸ Hellenistic Kingdoms

The Hellenistic kingdoms formed from Alexander's empire blended Greek and other cultures.

Describe What happened to Alexander's empire after his death? *Three generals divided the empire among themselves. Within 300 years, all of Alexander's empire had been conquered by Rome.*

Evaluate Do you think Alexander was successful as a conqueror? Should he be called "Great"? *possible answer—Alexander was a good conqueror. He built a big empire, and he spread Greek culture everywhere he went. His empire broke up soon after his death, so I'm not sure he was "Great."*

🐻 **HSS** 6.4.7; **HSS** Analysis Skills: CS 1, HI 1

● Review & Assess ●

Close

Ask students to discuss whether blended cultures, such as the Hellenistic cultures, are weaker or stronger than cultures with one source.

Review

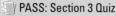 Online Quiz, Section 3

Assess

SE Section 3 Assessment

📄 PASS: Section 3 Quiz

📄 Alternative Assessment Handbook

Reteach/Classroom Intervention

📄 California Standards Review Workbook

📄 Interactive Reader and Study Guide, Section 3

💿 Interactive Skills Tutor CD-ROM

Answers

Reading Check *When Alexander died without an obvious heir, his generals divided the empire.*

Hellenistic Kingdoms

When Alexander died, he didn't have an obvious heir to take over his kingdom, and no one knew who was in power. With no clear direction, Alexander's generals fought for power. In the end, three powerful generals divided the empire among themselves. One became king of Macedonia and Greece, one ruled Syria, and the third claimed Egypt.

Hellenistic Macedonia

As you might expect, the kingdom of Macedonia and Greece was the most Greek of the three. However, it also had the weakest government. The Macedonian kings had to put down many revolts by the Greeks. Damaged by the revolts, Macedonia couldn't defend itself. Armies from Rome, a rising power from the Italian Peninsula, marched in and conquered Macedonia in the mid-100s BC.

Hellenistic Syria

Like the kings of Macedonia, the rulers of Syria faced many challenges. Their kingdom, which included most of the former Persian Empire, was home to many different peoples with many different customs.

Unhappy with Hellenistic rule, many of these people rebelled against their leaders. Weakened by years of fighting, the kingdom slowly broke apart. Finally in the 60s BC the Romans marched in and took over Syria.

Hellenistic Egypt

The rulers of Egypt encouraged the growth of Greek culture. They built the ancient world's largest library in the city of Alexandria. Also in Alexandria, they built the Museum, a place for scholars and artists to meet. Through their efforts, Alexandria became a great center of culture and learning. In the end, the Egyptian kingdom lasted longer than the other Hellenistic kingdoms. However, in 30 BC it too was conquered by Rome.

READING CHECK **Analyzing** Why were three kingdoms created from Alexander's empire?

SUMMARY AND PREVIEW Alexander the Great caused major political changes in Greece and the Hellenistic world. In the next section, you will learn about artistic and scientific advances that affected the lives of people in the same areas.

Section 3 Assessment

go.hrw.com
Online Quiz
KEYWORD: SQ6 HP10

Reviewing Ideas, Terms, and People **HSS** 6.4.7

1. **Identify** What king conquered Greece in the 300s BC?
2. **a. Describe** What territories did **Alexander the Great** conquer?
   b. Interpret Why did Alexander destroy Thebes?
   c. Elaborate Why do you think Alexander named so many cities after himself?
3. **a. Recall** What three kingdoms were created out of Alexander's empire after his death?
   b. Explain Why were these kingdoms called **Hellenistic**?

Critical Thinking

4. **Finding the Main Idea** Draw a diagram like the one here. Use it to identify four major accomplishments of Alexander the Great.

Alexander the Great

FOCUS ON WRITING ✎

5. **Evaluating Alexander** Add Alexander the Great to the table you created earlier. Remember that although Alexander was a military man, not all of his accomplishments were in battle.

302 CHAPTER 10

Section 3 Assessment Answers

1. Philip II of Macedonia
2. **a.** Asia Minor, Egypt, and the Persian Empire
   b. because they rebelled; to make them an example for other Greeks so they would not turn against him
   c. to demonstrate his control and power
3. **a.** Macedonia, Syria, and Egypt
   b. because they were Greek-like

4. successful military leader (conquered Greece and Egypt); conquered the Persian Empire; built new cities; spread Greek culture, and built temples and theatres
5. Alexander—conquered the Persian Empire; spread Greek culture; built cities, temples, theatres

Greek Achievements

If YOU were there...

Everyone in Athens has been talking about a philosopher and teacher named Socrates, so you decide to go and see him for yourself. You find him sitting under a tree, surrounded by his students. "Teach me about life," you say. But instead of answering, he asks you, "What is life?" You struggle to reply. He asks another question, and another. If he's such a great teacher, you wonder, shouldn't he have all the answers? Instead, all he seems to have are questions.

What do you think of Socrates?

> **BUILDING BACKGROUND** Socrates was only one of the brilliant philosophers who lived in Athens in the 400s BC. The city was also home to some of the world's greatest artists and writers. In fact, all over Greece men and women made great advances in the arts and sciences. Their work inspired people for centuries.

The Arts

Among the most notable achievements of the ancient Greeks were those they made in the arts. These arts included sculpture, painting, architecture, and writings.

Statues and Paintings

The ancient Greeks were master artists. Their paintings and statues have been admired for hundreds of years. Examples of these works are still displayed in museums around the world.

Greek sculpture is admired for its realism, natural look, and details.

What You Will Learn...

Main Ideas

1. The Greeks made great contributions to the arts.
2. The teachings of Socrates, Plato, and Aristotle are the basis of modern philosophy.
3. In science, the Greeks made key discoveries in math, medicine, and engineering.

The Big Idea

Ancient Greeks made lasting contributions in the arts, philosophy, and science.

Key Terms and People

Socrates, *p. 307*
Plato, *p. 307*
Aristotle, *p. 307*
reason, *p. 307*
Euclid, *p. 308*
Hippocrates, *p. 308*

 HSS 6.4.8 Describe the enduring contributions of important Greek figures in the arts and sciences (e.g., Hypatia, Socrates, Plato, Aristotle, Euclid, Thucydides).

THE GREEK WORLD **303**

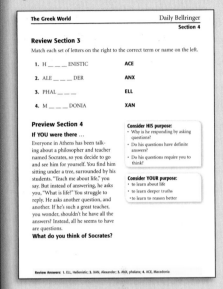
Vocabulary Builder

Preteach or review the following term:

philosopher a person who studies the meaning of life, problems of right and wrong, how we know things, and other related areas (p. 306)

CRF: Vocabulary Builder Activity, Section 4

Teach the Big Idea: Master the Standards

Standards Proficiency

Greek Achievements   **HSS** 6.4.8; **HSS** Analysis Skills: CS 1, HI 1

1. **Teach** Ask students the Main Idea questions to teach this section.

2. **Apply** Organize the class into eight groups. Assign each group one of the following: *Greek statues and painting, Greek architecture, Greek drama, Greek history, Greek philosophy, Greek mathematics, Greek engineering,* and *Greek medicine.* Have each group prepare a presentation on its topic that shows how contributions by the ancient Greeks still affect our ideas and practices.

Have each group make its presentation.
LS Verbal/Linguistic

4. **Review** Discuss with the class how the contributions made by the ancient Greeks have shaped life today.

5. **Practice/Homework** Have students write a paragraph describing Greek contributions to our world and why they are important.
LS Verbal/Linguistic

 Alternative Assessment Handbook, Rubrics 11: Discussions; and 29: Presentations

Standards Focus

HSS 6.4.8
Means: Describe the lasting contributions of ancient Greece in the arts, philosophy, and the sciences.
Matters: Contributions by ancient Greeks still influence us greatly today.

❶ The Arts

The Greeks made great contributions to the arts.

Recall In what four areas of the arts did ancient Greeks make notable achievements and contributions? *sculpture, painting, architecture, and writing*

Explain Why are Greek statues still admired today? *because Greek sculptors wanted to show, with great detail and realism, how beautiful people could be*

🐻 **HSS** 6.4.8; **HSS** Analysis Skills: CS 1

Biography

Phidias (c. 490 to c. 430 BC) Perhaps the greatest Greek sculptor of Greece's Golden Age was Phidias. In 433 BC, Phidias created the gold and ivory statue of Zeus for the temple of Zeus at Olympia. This huge statue stood about 40 feet (12 m) tall. The statue of Zeus was considered one of the Seven Wonders of the World. Phidias also created a similar gold and ivory statue of the goddess Athena for the Parthenon in Athens.

go.hrw.com
Online Resources
KEYWORD: SQ6 WH10
ACTIVITY: The Golden Age of Greece

Greek statues are so admired because the sculptors who made them tried to make them look perfect. They wanted their statues to show how beautiful people could be. To improve their art, these sculptors carefully studied the human body, especially how it looked when it was moving. Then, using what they had learned, they carved stone and marble statues. As a result, many Greek statues look as though they could come to life at any moment.

Greek painting is also admired for its realism and detail. For example, Greek artists painted detailed scenes on vases, pots, and other vessels. These vessels often show scenes from myths or athletic competitions. Many of the scenes were created using only two colors, black and red. Sometimes artists used black glaze to paint scenes on red vases. Other artists covered whole vases with glaze and then scraped parts away to let the red background show through.

Greek Architecture

If you went to Greece today, you would see the ruins of many ancient buildings. Old columns still hold up parts of broken roofs, and ancient carvings decorate fallen walls. These remains give us an idea of the beauty of ancient Greek buildings.

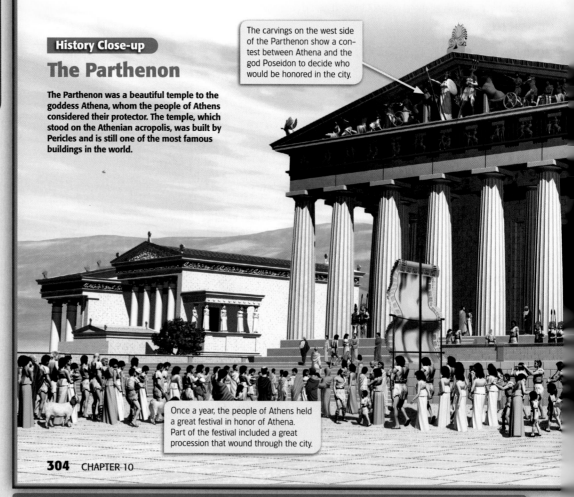

History Close-up
The Parthenon

The Parthenon was a beautiful temple to the goddess Athena, whom the people of Athens considered their protector. The temple, which stood on the Athenian acropolis, was built by Pericles and is still one of the most famous buildings in the world.

The carvings on the west side of the Parthenon show a contest between Athena and the god Poseidon to decide who would be honored in the city.

Once a year, the people of Athens held a great festival in honor of Athena. Part of the festival included a great procession that wound through the city.

304 CHAPTER 10

Differentiating Instruction for Universal Access

Advanced Learners/GATE | Exceeding Standards | Research Required

1. Organize students into groups of three or four.

2. Assign each group one of the following architectural styles to research: Doric, Ionic, or Corinthian.

3. Have each group research its architectural style. Each group should prepare an illustrated report giving the history and design principles of the style. Reports should be two to three pages long. **LS** Verbal/Linguistic

4. Discuss with the class the similarities and differences of the architectural styles. Ask students which style they prefer and why.

5. Have each group make a model of a column or building that demonstrates the principles of its architectural style. **LS** Kinesthetic

📋 Alternative Assessment Handbook, Rubrics 1: Acquiring Information; and 3: Artwork

🐻 **HSS** 6.4.8; **HSS** Analysis Skills: HI 1

The Greeks took great care in designing their buildings, especially their temples. Rows of tall columns surrounded the temples, making the temples look stately and inspiring. Greek designers were very careful when they measured these columns. They knew that columns standing in a long row often looked as though they curved in the middle. To prevent this optical illusion, they made their columns bulge slightly in the middle. As a result, Greek columns look perfectly straight.

Ancient Greek designers took such care because they wanted their buildings to reflect the greatness of their cities. The most impressive of all ancient Greek buildings was the Parthenon (PAHR-thuh-nahn) in Athens, pictured below. This temple to Athena was built in the 400s BC on the Athenian acropolis. It was designed to be magnificent not only outside, but inside as well. As you can see, the interior was decorated with carvings and columns.

New Forms of Writing

Sculpture, painting, and architecture were not the only Greek art forms. The Greeks also excelled at writing. In fact, Greek writers created many new writing forms, including drama and history.

Inside the Parthenon was a magnificent statue of Athena by the sculptor Phidias, whom many people considered the greatest sculptor in all of Greece.

The Parthenon's 46 columns are a type called Doric columns. These simple columns have no decoration at the top.

ANALYSIS SKILL **ANALYZING VISUALS**
Why do you think people are bringing animals and goods with them to the temple?

305

● **Direct Teach**

Main Idea

❶ **The Arts**

The Greeks made great contributions to the arts.

Recall Why did the people of Athens build the Parthenon? *to honor the goddess Athena, whom the people of Athens considered their protector*

Analyze In your opinion, why is the Parthenon considered the most impressive of all ancient Greek buildings? *possible answer—The Parthenon sits on a hilltop above Athens; it was a very large building magnificently decorated inside and out, with a huge statue of Athena inside.*

🐻 **HSS** 6.4.8; **HSS** Analysis Skills: HI 1

Biography

Pericles (495–429 BC) During its Golden Age, Athens was ruled by Pericles, the best orator in a city of great orators. Pericles built the Parthenon, other temples around Athens, the Propylaea (the large gateway or arch at the entrance to the Acropolis), and the long walls to the port city of Piraeus (connecting Athens to its port). While Pericles was building the Parthenon, Socrates and Plato were teaching, and Aeschylus, Sophocles, and Euripides were writing plays.

Cross-Discipline Activity: Drama

Exceeding Standards

Plays: A New Form of Writing 🐻 **HSS** 6.4.8; **HSS** Analysis Skills: CS 2

Research Required

1. Have students use the Internet or library to conduct research on the use of masks in ancient Greek drama. As students do their research, ask them to create a time line of the development of ancient Greek drama from about 625 BC to about 300 BC.

2. Ask students to make a poster showing one or more Greek masks or to make a model of a Greek mask to show to the class. Students should explain what their masks represented, why the masks were important in the play, and whether masks are used the same way in drama today.
LS Verbal/Linguistic, Visual/Spatial

3. **Extend** Have students conduct research on the use of a chorus and the addition of a second and third actor in Greek plays. Students should compare and contrast the results of their research with modern plays.
LS Verbal/Linguistic

📖 Alternative Assessment Handbook, Rubrics 3: Artwork; 30: Research; and 36: Time Lines

Answers

Analyzing Visuals *to trade or for sacrifices to the gods*

305

Main Idea

❶ The Arts

The Greeks made great contributions to the arts.

Identify What were two of the many new forms of writing created by the Greeks? *drama and history*

Analyze How has Thucydides shaped the modern study of history? *His impartial history of the Peloponnesian War influenced later historians to cover history impartially as well.*

📄 **CRF:** Biography Activity: Thucydides

📄 **CRF:** Literature Activity: *Oedipus the King*, by Sophocles

📄 **CRF:** Primary Source Activity: Greek Lyric Poetry

🐻 **HSS** 6.4.8; **HSS** Analysis Skills: HI 1

Biography

Herodotus (c. 484–c. 432 BC) The ancient Greek researcher and storyteller Herodotus is often considered the first historian. His work *The Histories* is not strictly a history text, though. Herodotus wrote about people, places, legends, battles, and heroes—whatever interested him.

Answers

Analyzing Primary Sources
"Be quiet then, and have patience."

Reading Check *The Greeks created sculptures, paintings, and buildings, and wrote drama and history.*

ACADEMIC VOCABULARY

neutral
unbiased, not favoring either side in a conflict

The Greeks created drama, or plays, as part of their religious ceremonies. Actors and singers performed scenes in honor of the gods and heroes. These plays became a popular form of entertainment, especially in Athens.

In the 400s BC Athenian writers created many of the greatest plays of the ancient world. Some writers produced tragedies, which described the hardships faced by Greek heroes. Among the best tragedy writers were Aeschylus (ES-kuh-luhs) and Sophocles (SAHF-uh-kleez). For example, Sophocles wrote about a Greek hero who mistakenly killed his own father. Other Greek dramatists focused on comedies, which made fun of people and ideas. One famous comedy writer was Aristophanes (ar-uh-STAHF-uh-neez). He used his comedy to make serious points about war, courts of law, and famous people.

The Greeks were also among the first people to write about history. They were interested in the lessons history could teach. One of the greatest of the Greek historians was Thucydides (thoo-SID-uh-deez). He wrote a history of the Peloponnesian War based in part on his experiences as an Athenian soldier. Even though he was from Athens, Thucydides tried to be **neutral** in his writing. He studied the war and tried to figure out what had caused it. He may have hoped the Greeks could learn from their mistakes and avoid similar wars in the future. Many later historians modeled their works after his.

READING CHECK **Summarizing** What were some forms of art found in ancient Greece?

Philosophy

The ancient Greeks worshipped gods and goddesses whose actions explained many of the mysteries of the world. But by around 500 BC a few people had begun to think about other explanations. We call these people philosophers. They believed in the power of the human mind to think, explain, and understand life.

Primary Source

BOOK
The Death of Socrates

In 399 BC Socrates was arrested and charged with corrupting the young people of Athens and ignoring religious traditions. He was sentenced to die by drinking poison. Socrates spent his last hours surrounded by his students. One of them, Plato, later described the event in detail.

Socrates himself does not protest against his sentence but willingly drinks the poison.

The students and friends who have visited Socrates, including the narrator, are much less calm than he is.

❝Then raising the cup to his lips, quite readily and cheerfully he drank off the poison. And hitherto most of us had been able to control our sorrow; but now when we saw him drinking . . . my own tears were flowing fast; so that I covered my face and wept . . . Socrates alone retained his calmness: What is this strange outcry? he said . . . I have been told that a man should die in peace. Be quiet then, and have patience.❞

–Plato, from *Phaedo*

ANALYSIS SKILL | **ANALYZING PRIMARY SOURCES**
How does Socrates tell his students to act when he drinks the poison?

Critical Thinking: Analyzing Information

Exceeding Standards

The Socratic Method 🐻 **HSS** 6.4.8

1. Ask students, "What is courage?" or "What is beauty?" (You could also ask what is truth, or honor.) Have students brainstorm answers to your question.

2. Engage the class in a Socratic dialogue. Give the students questions, not answers. Follow answers with more questions. Choose questions that move the discussion along. The table lists some kinds of Socratic questions. Copy the questions for students to see.

3. At the end of the exercise, have students write a brief, one-paragraph response to the original question. Students should indicate if their response is different after the discussion and the reason(s) why they have changed their point of view. **LS** **Verbal/Linguistic**

📄 Alternative Assessment Handbook, Rubric 11: Discussions

Type of Question	Examples
Clarification	What do you mean by . . .? Could you give me an example?
Probe Assumptions	What are you assuming? Is that always the case? Why do you think the assumption holds here?
Probe Reasons and Evidence	Why do you say that? What other information do we need? Is there good evidence for believing that? Is there reason to doubt that evidence?
Viewpoints or Perspectives	How would other groups/types of people respond? Why? Can anyone see this another way? What would someone who disagrees say? How are his and her ideas alike/different?

Socrates

Among the greatest of these thinkers was a man named **Socrates** (SAHK-ruh-teez). He believed that people must never stop looking for knowledge.

Socrates was a teacher as well as a thinker. Today we call his type of teaching the Socratic method. He taught by asking questions. His questions were about human qualities such as love and courage. He would ask, "What is courage?" When people answered, he challenged their answers with more questions.

Socrates wanted to make people think and question their own beliefs. But he made people angry, even frightened. They accused him of questioning the authority of the gods. For these reasons, he was arrested and condemned to death. His friends and students watched him calmly accept his death. He took the poison he was given, drank it, and died.

Plato

Plato (PLAYT-oh) was a student of Socrates. Like Socrates, he was a teacher as well as a philosopher. Plato created a school, the Academy, to which students, philosophers, and scientists could come to discuss ideas.

Although Plato spent much of his time running the Academy, he also wrote many works. The most famous of these works was called *The Republic*. It describes Plato's idea of an ideal society. This society would be based on justice and fairness to everyone. To ensure this fairness, Plato argued, society should be run by philosophers. He thought that only they could understand what was best for everyone.

Aristotle

Perhaps the greatest Greek thinker was **Aristotle** (ar-uh-STAH-tuhl), Plato's student. He taught that people should live lives of moderation, or balance. For example,

people should not be greedy, but neither should they give away everything they own. Instead, people should find a balance between these two extremes.

Aristotle believed that moderation was based on **reason**, or clear and ordered thinking. He thought that people should use reason to govern their lives. In other words, people should think about their actions and how they will affect others.

Aristotle also made great advances in the field of logic, the process of making inferences. He argued that you could use facts you knew to figure out new facts. For example, if you know that Socrates lives in Athens and that Athens is in Greece, you can conclude that Socrates lives in Greece. Aristotle's ideas about logic helped inspire many later Greek scientists.

READING CHECK Generalizing What did ancient Greek philosophers like Socrates, Plato, and Aristotle want to find out?

THE GREEK WORLD **307**

307

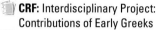

Direct Teach

Main Idea

❸ Science

In science, the Greeks made key discoveries in math, medicine, and engineering.

Explain What did Hippocrates contribute to medicine? *studied diseases to try to figure out how to cure them; gave rules for doctors' behavior.*

Recall Who invented the water screw? *Archimedes*

📑 **CRF:** Interdisciplinary Project: Contributions of Early Greeks

🌐 **HSS** 6.4.8; **HSS** Analysis Skills: HI 1

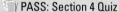

Review & Assess

Close

Ask students to discuss Aristotle's ideas about reason and moderation.

Review

💻 Online Quiz, Section 4

Assess

SE Section 4 Assessment

📑 **PASS:** Section 4 Quiz

📑 Alternative Assessment Handbook

Reteach/Classroom Intervention

📑 California Standards Review Workbook

📑 Interactive Reader and Study Guide, Section 4

💿 Interactive Skills Tutor CD-ROM

Answers

Reading Check *studied human body to see how it worked; causes and treatments of diseases*

308

Science

Aristotle's works inspired many Greek scientists. They began to look closely at the world to see how it worked.

THE IMPACT TODAY
Many doctors recite the Hippocratic Oath, a pledge to behave ethically, when they finish medical school.

Mathematics

Some Greeks spent their lives studying mathematics. One of these people was **Euclid** (YOO-kluhd). He was interested in geometry, the study of lines, angles, and shapes. In fact, many of the geometry rules we learn in school today come straight from Euclid's writings.

Other Greek mathematicians included a geographer who used mathematics to accurately calculate the size of the earth. Years later, in the AD 300s and 400s, a woman named Hypatia (hy-PAY-shuh) taught about mathematics and astronomy.

Medicine and Engineering

Not all Greek scientists studied numbers. Some studied other areas of science, such as medicine and engineering.

Greek doctors studied the human body to understand how it worked. In trying to cure diseases and keep people healthy, Greek doctors made many discoveries.

The greatest Greek doctor was **Hippocrates** (hip-AHK-ruh-teez). He wanted to figure out what caused diseases so he could better treat them. Hippocrates is better known today, though, for his ideas about how doctors should behave.

Greek engineers also made great discoveries. Some of the devices they invented are still used today. For example, farmers in many countries still use water screws to bring water to their fields. This device, which brings water from a lower level to a higher one, was invented by a Greek scientist named Archimedes (ahr-kuh-MEED-eez) in the 200s BC. Greek inventors could be playful as well as serious. For example, one inventor created mechanical toys like birds, puppets, and coin-operated machines.

READING CHECK **Summarizing** What advances did Greek scientists make in medicine?

SUMMARY AND PREVIEW Through their art, philosophy, and science, the Greeks have greatly influenced Western civilization. In the next chapter, you will learn about another group that has helped shape the Western world—the Romans.

Section 4 Assessment

go.hrw.com
Online Quiz
KEYWORD: SQ6 HP110

Reviewing Ideas, Terms, and People **HSS** 6.4.8

1. **a. Identify** What two types of drama did the Greeks invent?
   b. Explain Why did Greek columns bulge in the middle?
   c. Draw Conclusions How did studying the human body help Greek artists make their statues look real?
2. **Describe** How did **Socrates** teach? What is this method of teaching called?
3. **a. Identify** In what fields did **Hippocrates** and **Euclid** make their greatest achievements?
   b. Make Inferences Why do some people call Greece the birthplace of the Western world?

Critical Thinking

4. **Summarizing** Draw a chart like the one here. Use it to list one contribution each person made to the arts and sciences.

Person	Contribution
Thucydides	
Socrates	
Plato	
Aristotle	
Euclid	
Hypatia	

FOCUS ON WRITING

5. **Taking Notes about Artists and Thinkers** Add the artists and thinkers from this section to your chart. Because these people were not military leaders, all of your notes will go in the third column of your chart.

308 CHAPTER 10

Section 4 Assessment Answers

1. **a.** comedies and tragedies
   b. to counter an optical illusion that made straight columns look curved
   c. Sculptors were able to capture movement and create a realistic body carefully, especially while it was moving.

2. by asking questions; the Socratic method

3. **a.** Hippocrates—medicine; Euclid—mathematics
   b. Many of the philosophies, dramas, and scientific ideas upon which our society is based come from ancient Greece.

4. possible answers: Thucydides—wrote history; Socrates—created Socratic method, challenged existing ideas; Plato—founded Academy, proposed a model for a perfect society; Aristotle—taught people to live in moderation, stressed importance of reason; Euclid—created rules of geometry; Hypatia—wrote about mathematics and astronomy

5. See the answer to item 4.

Greek Philosophers—Socrates, Plato, and Aristotle

What would the world be like if no one believed in the importance of knowledge and truth?

When did they live? the 400s and 300s BC

Where did they live? Athens

What did they do? They thought. Socrates, Plato, and Aristotle thought about the world and searched for knowledge, wisdom, and truth. They created the Socratic method of learning, the first political science book, and a method of scientific reasoning.

Why are they important? In most of the ancient world, strong fighters won all the glory. But in Athens, great thinkers and wise men were honored. People listened to them and followed their advice. Even today, people admire the ideas of Socrates, Plato, and Aristotle. Their teachings are at the root of modern philosophy and science.

Making Inferences Do you think these philosophers would have been as influential if they had lived in a different city? Why or why not?

This drawing shows how one artist imagined Plato (left), Aristotle (center), and Socrates (right) to look.

309

Critical Thinking: Analyzing Information

Standards Proficiency

Analyzing the Ideas of the Philosophers   HSS 6.4.8; HSS Analysis Skills: HR 1, HI 1

1. Organize the class into three groups and have each group conduct research on—and represent—the ideas of either Socrates, Plato, or Aristotle.

2. Have students in each group decide how they will present their findings. For example, a group may decide to elect one person to speak for the philosopher, or a group may decide that all members will represent the philosopher.

3. Ask each group about its assigned philosopher's views on topics such as

government, truth, education, or how the world works. Ask each group if its philosopher held a special view about any topic. **LS Verbal/Linguistic**

4. **Extend** Have students discuss the similarities and differences between each of the philosophers. Have each group create a Venn diagram that compares and contrasts their beliefs. **LS Verbal/Linguistic**

📖 Alternative Assessment Handbook, Rubrics 4: Biographies; and 24: Oral Presentations

---

Biography

Reading Focus Question

Write the expressions *Ignorance is bliss* and *Knowledge is power* for students to see. Have students discuss each expression and consider how the Greek philosophers would have felt about them.

Info to Know

Socrates (469–399 BC) Socrates never wrote any philosophical works. Instead, Socrates explored his ideas by holding conversations with almost anyone. Through these conversations, or dialogues, Socrates sought to answer questions such as "What is justice?" and "What is knowledge?" Socrates asked similar questions about piety, truth, courage, art, and love.

Plato (427–347 BC) Plato was a student of Socrates. After Socrates' death, Plato left Athens and traveled to Egypt, Italy, and Sicily. Eventually, Plato returned to Athens and founded his Academy, where he taught philosophy. Many of Plato's writings are in the form of dialogues, a style he learned from Socrates. Plato's best-known work is *The Republic*, a dialogue on the nature of justice. It is often considered the first book about political science.

Aristotle (384–322 BC) At the age of 18, Aristotle went to Athens to study at Plato's Academy. In 343 BC, Aristotle was asked to be the tutor of a young man named Alexander—who later came to be known as Alexander the Great. Aristotle wrote about a wide variety of topics, including logic, politics and ethics, meteorology, learning, anthropology, poetry, and theology.

About the Illustration *This illustration of Socrates, Plato, and Aristotle is an artist's conception based on available sources. However, historians are uncertain exactly what the philosophers looked like.*

Answers

Making Inferences *No, because Athens placed a higher value on knowledge, truth, and trying to understand life than other city-states did. Athens honored philosophers more than other places did.*

Social Studies Skills

Interpreting Charts and Tables

Activity Guided Practice with Charts Photocopy a number of charts from this book as well as other books. If the charts include captions, cover them up. Then display each of the charts in turn for students to see. Have students identify the type of each chart and its purpose. Then select one of the charts and have each student write a caption for the chart. **LS Visual/Spatial**

📋 Alternative Assessment Handbook, Rubric 7: Charts

💿 Interactive Skills Tutor CD-ROM, Lesson 6: Interpret Maps, Graphs, Charts, Visuals, and Political Cartoons

Social Studies Skills

HSS Analysis HI 2 Students understand and distinguish long- and short-term causal relations.

Analysis | Critical Thinking | Participation | Study

Interpreting Charts and Tables

Understand the Skill

Charts present information visually to make it easier to understand. Different kinds of charts have different purposes. *Organizational charts* can show relationships among the parts of something. *Flowcharts* show steps in a process or cause-and-effect relationships. *Classification charts* group information so it can be easily compared. *Tables* are a type of classification chart that organize information into rows and columns for easy comparison. The ability to interpret charts helps you to analyze information and understand relationships.

Learn the Skill

Use these basic steps to interpret a chart:

1 Identify the type of chart and read its title in order to understand its purpose and subject.

2 Note the parts of the chart. Read the headings of rows and columns to determine the categories of information. Note any other labels that accompany the information in the chart. Look for any lines that connect its parts.

3 Study the chart's details. Look for relationships in the information it presents. In classification charts, analyze and compare all content in rows and columns. In flowcharts and organizational charts, read all labels and other information. Follow directional arrows or lines.

Sparta's Government, c. 450 BC

Ephors
- Five adult male citizens
- Elected to one-year terms
- Presided over Assembly and Council
- Ran Sparta's daily affairs

Kings
- Two hereditary rulers
- Commanded armies
- Served as high priests
- Served as judges in minor cases

Assembly
- All male citizens age 30 and above
- Passed or rejected proposals made by Council
- Could not propose actions on its own
- Elected ephors

Council of Elders
- 28 male citizens over age 60
- Elected for life by citizens
- Proposed actions to Assembly
- Served as judges in important cases

Practice and Apply the Skill

Apply the strategies here to interpret the chart above and answer the following questions.

1. What type of chart is this and what is its purpose?

2. In what ways were the ephors and the Assembly connected?

3. How did the roles of the Assembly and the Council of Elders differ?

4. What position in Spartan government had no direct relationship with the Assembly?

Social Studies Skills Activity: Interpreting Charts and Tables

Persia or Alexander the Great Charts   Standards Proficiency

1. Assign students either the Persian Empire or Alexander the Great. Have each student create a chart of his or her own choosing to show information related to the assigned topic. For example, students might create a classification chart giving information about the key battles of the Persian Wars or a flow chart showing the events in the growth of Alexander the Great's empire.

2. Have volunteers display their charts. Have other students identify the type and purpose of each chart. **LS Visual/Spatial**

3. **Extend** Have students select a chart from the textbook that they find interesting. Instruct students to create a five-question quiz that must be answered by looking at the chart. Then have students exchange quizzes and charts, complete the quizzes they receive, and return the quizzes for grading.
LS Interpersonal, Visual/Spatial

📋 Alternative Assessment Handbook, Rubric 7: Charts

Answers

Practice and Apply the Skill
1. *organizational chart; to show the relationships among the different parts of Sparta's government;* **2.** *The Assembly elected the ephors;* **3.** *The Council of Elders served for life and proposed actions; Assembly members voted on the Council's proposals but could not propose actions of their own.* **4.** *kings*

310

Standards Review

Visual Summary

Use the visual summary below to help you review the main ideas of the chapter.

QUICK FACTS

Sparta and Athens fought together to defeat Persia in the Persian Wars.

Spartan culture centered on the military, while Athenian culture emphasized government and the arts.

Alexander the Great built a huge empire and spread Greek culture.

The ancient Greeks made lasting contributions to architecture, philosophy, science, and many other fields.

Reviewing Vocabulary, Terms, and People

Choose one word from each word pair to correctly complete each sentence below.

1. A ruler named _____ created the Persian Empire. **(Cyrus the Great/Xerxes I)**

2. A _____ was a group of soldiers that stood in a square to fight. **(cavalry/phalanx)**

3. _____ built the largest empire the world had ever seen. **(Alexander the Great/Aristotle)**

4. The _____ War(s) pitted two city-states against each other. **(Persian/Peloponnesian)**

5. The philosopher _____ taught people by asking them questions. **(Darius/Socrates)**

6. The greatest medical scholar of ancient Greece was _____. **(Philip II/Hippocrates)**

7. Aristotle taught the importance of _____ in his writings. **(reason/alliance)**

8. _____ was a great mathematician. **(Plato/Euclid)**

Comprehension and Critical Thinking

SECTION 1 *(Pages 286–291)* **HSS** 6.4.5

9. **a. Identify** Who were Cyrus the Great, Darius I, and Xerxes I?

   b. Analyze How did the Greeks use strategy to defeat a larger fighting force?

   c. Elaborate What were some factors that led to the success of the Persian Empire?

SECTION 2 *(Pages 292–297)* **HSS** 6.4.6

10. **a. Describe** What was life like for Spartan women? for Athenian women?

   b. Compare and Contrast How was the education of Spartan boys different from the education of Athenian boys? What did the education of both groups have in common?

   c. Evaluate Do you agree or disagree with this statement: "The Athenians brought the Peloponnesian War on themselves." Defend your argument.

THE GREEK WORLD **311**

Visual Summary

Review and Inquiry Use the visual summary to discuss the chapter's main points.

Quick Facts Transparency: The Greek World Visual Summary

Reviewing Vocabulary, Terms, and People

1. Cyrus the Great
2. phalanx
3. Alexander the Great
4. Peloponnesian
5. Socrates
6. Hippocrates
7. reason
8. Euclid

Comprehension and Critical Thinking

9. **a.** Persian kings

   b. The Greeks led the larger Persian navy into the narrow straits of Salamis, in which the Persian navy could not fit. As a result, the smaller Athenian boats easily sank many Persian ships.

   c. a strong army, efficient political organization under Darius I, good roads

10. **a.** Sparta—Women had rights and responsibilities. They ran households when men were gone, received physical training and competed in sporting events. Athens—Women received no education, could not serve in the government, own property, or even leave their homes.

b. Sparta—trained from an early age to be soldiers and then stayed in the army until they were 60 years old; Athens—only served in the army from ages 18 to 20, learned to read, write and play instruments; in common—had athletic and military training

c. Answers will vary, but students should understand the effect of Athens' treatment of other city-states in the Delian League.

11. a. gave the soldiers longer spears and sent cavalry and archers into battle to support the phalanx

b. They kept some of their own customs and combined others with Greek ideas to create a new culture—Hellenistic.

c. possible answer—Greek rule might have spread throughout India and the rest of Asia, heavily influencing the people there.

12. a. a temple on the acropolis of Athens; Athena

b. All were teachers and philosophers.

c. possible answer—because they still relate to the daily lives of many people

Reviewing Themes

13. The Persians felt humiliated because they had been defeated by a smaller force. The Greeks felt proud for successfully defending their homeland against a larger military force.

14. The kings who led the government also led the army.

15. Women in Sparta had more rights. They could own land, run a household, and get an education. Women in Athens could do none of those things.

Using the Internet

16. Go to the HRW Web site and enter the keyword shown to access a rubric for this activity.

> **KEYWORD: SQ6 TEACHER**

Social Studies Skills

17. Charts will vary but should reflect chapter content.

SECTION 3 *(Pages 298–302)* **HSS** 6.4.7

11. a. Describe How did Philip II improve the phalanx?

b. Analyze How did the cultures that Alexander conquered change after his death?

c. Predict How might history have been different if Alexander had not died so young?

SECTION 4 *(Pages 303–308)* **HSS** 6.4.8

12. a. Identify What is the Parthenon? For which goddess was it built?

b. Compare What did Socrates, Plato, and Aristotle have in common?

c. Evaluate Why do you think Greek accomplishments in the arts and sciences are still admired today?

Reviewing Themes

13. Politics Why did the Persians and the Greeks react differently to the end of the Persian Wars?

14. Politics How were the government and the army related in Sparta?

15. Society and Culture How were the roles of women different in Athens and Sparta?

Using the Internet

go.hrw.com
KEYWORD: SQ6 WH10

16. Activity: Writing a Dialogue While rulers such as Alexander and Cyrus fought to gain land, thinkers like Socrates may have questioned their methods. Enter the keyword activity. Write a dialogue between Socrates and a student on whether it was right to invade another country. Socrates should ask at least 10 questions to his student.

Social Studies Skills

17. Understanding Charts and Tables Create a chart in your notebook that identifies key Greek achievements in architecture, art, writing, philosophy, and science. Complete the chart with details from this chapter.

Reading Skills

18. Comparing and Contrasting Complete the chart below to compare and contrast two powerful leaders you studied in this chapter, Cyrus the Great and Alexander the Great.

Compare

List two characteristics that Cyrus and Alexander shared.
a. _____
b. _____

How did Cyrus's and Alexander's backgrounds differ?	
Cyrus	Alexander
c. _____	d. _____

Contrast

What happened to their empires after they died?	
Cyrus	Alexander
e. _____	f. _____

> **FOCUS ON WRITING**

19. Writing Your Poem Look back over your notes from this chapter. Ask yourself which of the accomplishments you noted are the most significant. Do you admire people for their ideas? their might? their leadership? their brilliance?

Choose one person whose accomplishments you admire. Look back through the chapter for more details about the person's accomplishments. Then write a poem in praise of your chosen figure. Your poem should be five lines long. The first line should identify the subject of the poem. The next three lines should note his or her accomplishments, and the last line should sum up why he or she is respected.

Reading Skills

18. possible answers—
(a) Both had powerful, well-organized armies and created great empires. (b) Both conquered Mesopotamia and Egypt.
(c) Cyrus was a Persian who led a revolt to take power. (d) Alexander was a Macedonian who inherited his throne from his father.
(e) Cyrus passed his empire on to his son.
(f) Alexander's empire fell apart because he had no clear heir.

Focus on Writing

19. Rubric Students' poems should:

- introduce a person that the student admires.
- describe this person's accomplishments.
- contain a summary of why he or she is respected.
- offer precise language to bring the subject to life.

CRF: Focus on Writing: A Poem

Standards Assessment

DIRECTIONS: Read each question and write the letter of the best response.

1

> The freedom which we enjoy in our government extends also to our ordinary life . . . Further, we provide plenty of means for the mind to refresh itself from business. We celebrate games and sacrifices all the year round . . . Where our rivals from their very cradles by a painful discipline seek after manliness . . . we live exactly as we please and yet are just as ready to encounter every legitimate danger.

The information in this passage suggests that the person who wrote it probably lived in

A Athens.

B Persia.

C Sparta.

D Troy.

2 **The Athenians' main rivals were from**

A Sparta.

B Rome.

C Macedonia.

D Persia.

3 **Which people were the chief enemies of the Greeks in the 400s BC?**

A the Romans

B the Persians

C the Egyptians

D the Macedonians

4 **All of the following were Greek philosophers *except***

A Aristotle.

B Plato.

C Socrates.

D Zoroaster.

5 **Hellenistic culture developed as a result of the activities of which person?**

A Darius I

B Philip II

C Cyrus the Great

D Alexander the Great

Connecting with Past Learnings

6 **Cyrus the Great and Alexander the Great both built huge empires. What other leader that you have studied in this course also created an empire?**

A Moses

B Shi Huangdi

C Confucius

D Hatshepsut

7 **In this chapter you have read about many great philosophers and thinkers. Which of the following people you have studied was *not* a philosopher or thinker?**

A Socrates

B Ramses the Great

C Confucius

D Siddhartha Gautama

Intervention Resources

Reproducible

Interactive Reader and Study Guide

Universal Access Teacher Management System: Lesson Plans for Universal Access

Technology

Quick Facts Transparency: The Greek World Visual Summary

Universal Access Modified Worksheets and Tests CD-ROM

Interactive Skills Tutor CD-ROM

Tips for Test Taking

How Much Do I Write? Point out to students that if a writing question contains any of the following terms, they will need to write several sentences for a complete answer: *describe, justify, why, explain,* or *elaborate*. These are not the only words, however, that may indicate several sentences are required.

Preteach

Bellringer

Motivate Have students think of questions they have answered by looking in a reference book, in a newspaper, on the Web, or in another source. Perhaps students wanted to know who won a football game, for example, or when John F. Kennedy was president. Write students' questions for the class to see. Then tell students they will conduct research to answer a question about either the ancient Hebrews or ancient Greeks and present their findings in a report.

Direct Teach

Finding Information

Evaluating Sources Remind students about how to determine reliable sources of information. Point out that students should not trust sources that contain inconsistencies, irrelevant facts, too many extraneous details, and poor organization. Also, explain that tabloids, reality shows, infomercials, and hearsay and gossip are not reliable sources. Reinforce the idea that not everything students read or view is necessarily true.

HSS Analysis Skills: HR 4

Assignment

Collect information and write an informative report on a topic related to the Hebrews or the ancient Greeks.

TIP Narrowing a Topic
Broad: Sparta
Less Broad: Women and Girls in Sparta
Focus Question: What was life like for women and girls in Sparta?

ELA Writing 6.2.3 Write Research Reports:
a. Pose relevant questions.
b. Support the main idea with information from multiple sources.
c. Include a bibliography.

Analysis Skill Students frame questions that can be answered by historical study and research.

314 UNIT 4

A Social Studies Report

The purpose of a social studies report is to share information. Often, this information comes from research. You begin your research by asking questions about a subject.

1. Prewrite

Choosing a Subject

You could ask many questions about the unit you have just studied.

- Why was Ruth an important person in the history of the Jewish religion?
- What was the role of mythology in the lives of the ancient Greeks?
- What were the most important accomplishments of Alexander the Great?

Jot down some topics that interested you. Then, brainstorm a list of questions about one or more of these topics. Make sure your questions are narrow and focused. Choose the question that seems most interesting.

Finding Historical Information

Use at least three sources besides your textbook to find information on your topic. Good sources include

- books, maps, magazines, newspapers
- television programs, movies, videos
- Internet sites, CD-ROMs, DVDs

Keep track of your sources of information by writing them in a notebook or on cards. Give each source a number as shown below.

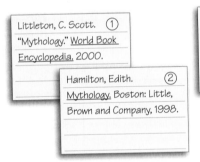

Littleton, C. Scott. ① "Mythology." World Book Encyclopedia. 2000.

Hamilton, Edith. ② Mythology. Boston: Little, Brown and Company, 1998.

Lindemans, Micha F. ③ "Greek Mythology: Persephone." Encyclopedia Mythica. 27 April 2004. http://www.pantheon.org.

Differentiating Instruction for Universal Access

Advanced Learners/GATE
Exceeding Standards

Evaluating Sources Have advanced learners develop a checklist for evaluating sources. Tell students their lists should include how old the sources are, how reliable they are, and how relevant they are. Have students share items from their checklists with the class. Then have students work together to create a class checklist. **LS** Verbal/Linguistic

ELA Writing 6.2.3.b; **HSS** Analysis Skills: HR 4

English-Language Learners
Standards Proficiency
Standard English Mastery

Transition Words Have students review transitions they can use to connect sentences and ideas. Give students this list of transitions to use in their papers: *first, second, then, next, finally, last, however,* and *as a result.* Help students define the meaning of the transitions. Then explain the proper way to punctuate and use them in standard English. **LS** Verbal/Linguistic

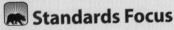

Standards Focus

HSS Analysis Skills: HR 1, HR 3, HR 4
ELA Writing 6.1.5, 6.1.6, 6.2.3.a, 6.2.3.b, 6.2.3.c

Taking Notes

Take notes on important facts and details from your sources. Historical writing needs to be accurate. Carefully record all names, dates, and other information from sources. Copy any direct quotation word for word and enclose the words in quotation marks. Along with each note, include the number of its source and its page number.

Stating the Big Idea of Your Report

You can easily turn your original question into the big idea for your report. If your question changes a bit as you do your research, rewrite it before turning it into a statement. The big idea of a report is often, but not always, stated in the first paragraph.

Organizing Your Ideas and Information

Sort your notes into topics and subtopics. Put them in an order that is logical, that will make sense to your reader. We often use one of these ways to organize information:

- placing events and details in the order they happened
- grouping causes with their effects
- grouping information by category, usually in the order of least to most important

Here is a partial outline for a paper on Greek mythology.

> Big Idea: The ancient Greeks told myths to explain the world.
> I. Purpose of mythology in ancient Greece
>   A. Greeks' questions about the world around them
>   B. Greeks' use of myths for answers
> II. Myths about everyday events in the Greeks' lives
>   A. The myth of Hestia, goddess of the home
>   B. The myth of Hephaestus, god of crafts and fire
> III. Myths about the natural world of the Greeks
>   A. The myth of Apollo, god of the sun
>   B. The myth of Persephone, goddess of the seasons

TIP **Statement or Question** Your big idea statement can be a statement of the point you want to make in your paper.

> The ancient Greeks used mythology to explain nature.

It can also be a question, similar to your original research question.

> How did the ancient Greeks use mythology to explain their lives?

TIP **Making the Most of Your Outline** If you write each of your topics and subtopics as a complete sentence, you can use those sentences to create your first draft.

2. Write

It is good to write a first draft fairly quickly, but it's also helpful to organize it as you go. Use the following framework as a guide.

A Writer's Framework

Introduction	Body	Conclusion
■ Start with a quotation or interesting historical detail.	■ Present your information under at least three main ideas.	■ Restate your main idea, using slightly different words.
■ State the big idea of your report.	■ Write at least one paragraph for each of these main ideas.	■ Close with a general comment about your topic or tell how the historical information in your report relates to later historical events.
■ Provide any historical background readers need in order to understand your big idea.	■ Add supporting details, facts, or examples to each paragraph.	

Taking Notes

Writing an Outline Tell students that each main idea on the model outline shown represents a paragraph. Students should use the same organization in their outlines. For example, if they have three paragraphs in the body of their papers, then number I on their outlines will be the introduction; numbers II, III, and IV will be the three body paragraphs; and number V will be the conclusion.

Writing

Writing the Introduction Ask students how they will grab their audience's attention in the introduction. Have students make a list of ways to grab the audience's attention, such as providing an intriguing fact or an interesting quotation.

Writing the Body Tell students that each detail, fact, or example they include in a paragraph should support the main idea of the paragraph. After students have completed their drafts, have them review each paragraph to check if they have included any irrelevant or incidental details or any unverified information.

HSS Analysis Skills: HR 3

Studying a Model

Here is a model of a social studies report. Study it to see how one student developed a social studies paper. The first and the concluding paragraphs are shown in full. The paragraphs in the body of the paper are summarized.

INTRODUCTORY PARAGRAPH

Attention grabber →

The ancient Greeks faced many mysteries in their lives. How and why did people fall in love? What made rain fall and crops grow? What are the planets and stars, and where did they come from? Through the myths they told about their heroes, gods, and goddesses, the Greeks answered these questions. They used mythology to explain all things, from everyday events to forces of nature to the creation of the universe.

Statement of Big Idea →

Body Paragraphs

The first body paragraph opens with a statement about how the Greeks used myths to explain their daily lives. Then two examples of those kinds of myths are given. The student summarizes myths about Aphrodite, goddess of love, and Hephaestus, god of crafts and fire.

In the next paragraph, the student shows how the Greeks used myths to explain the natural world. The example of such a story is Persephone and her relationship to the seasons.

The last paragraph in the body contains the student's final point, which is about creation myths. The two examples given for these myths are stories about Helios, god of the sun, and Artemis, goddess of the moon.

CONCLUDING PARAGRAPH

First two sentences restate the thesis →

The Greeks had a huge number of myths. They needed that many to explain all of the things that they did and saw. Besides explaining things, myths also gave the Greeks a feeling of power. By praying and sacrificing to the gods, they believed they could affect the world around them. All people want to have some control over their lives, and their mythology gave the Greeks that feeling of control.

Last three sentences make a general comment about the topic, Greek myths. →

Notice that each paragraph is organized in the same way as the entire paper. Each paragraph expresses a main idea and includes information to support that main idea. One big difference is that not every paragraph requires a conclusion. Only the last paragraph needs to end with a concluding statement.

Critical Thinking: Evaluating Information   Reaching Standards

Practice Evaluating Sources **ELA** Writing 6.2.3.c; **HSS** Analysis Skills: HR 4

1. When doing research, students need to learn to evaluate each source quickly to determine its usefulness. As practice, give students the list of fictional sources at right. Have students identify which of the sources they think would be most helpful for an informative report on Alexander the Great.

2. Have students use the following scale to rate each source: 4 = extremely useful; 3 = useful; 2 = might be useful; 1 = not useful.

- *Alexander of Macedon: A Biography* (book)
- "Was Alexander Truly Great?" (editorial)
- "The Life and Times of Alexander the Great" (historical journal article)
- "History of Ancient Greece" (university Web site)
- "My Alexander the Great Page" (personal Web site)

3. Evaluate and Revise

It is important to evaluate your first draft before you begin to revise it. Follow the steps below to evaluate and revise your draft.

Evaluating and Revising an Informative Report

1. Does the introduction grab the readers' interest and state the big idea of your report?
2. Does the body of your report have at least three paragraphs that develop your big idea? Is the main idea in each paragraph clearly stated?
3. Have you included enough information to support each of your main ideas? Are all facts, details, and examples accurate? Are all of them clearly related to the main ideas they support?
4. Is the report clearly organized? Does it use chronological order, order of importance, or cause and effect?
5. Does the conclusion restate the big idea of your report? Does it end with a general comment about your topic?
6. Have you included at least three sources in your bibliography? Have you included all the sources you used and not any you did not use?

4. Proofread and Publish

Proofreading

To correct your report before sharing it, check the following:

- the spelling and capitalization of all proper names for specific people, places, things, and events
- punctuation marks around any direct quotation
- punctuation and capitalization in your bibliography

Publishing

Choose one or more of these ideas to share your report.

- Create a map to accompany your report. Use a specific color to highlight places and routes that are important in your report.
- File a copy of your report in your school's library for other students' reference. Include illustrations to go with the report.
- If your school has a Web site, you might post your report there. See if you can link to other sources on your topic.

> **TIP** Bibliography
>
> - Underline the titles of all books, television programs, and Web sites.
> - Use quotation marks around titles of articles and stories.

● Practice and Apply

Use the steps and strategies outlined in this workshop to research and write an informative report.

Collaborative Learning

Standards Proficiency

Peer Revising and Editing 🐻 **ELA** Writing 6.1.6

1. Have students work in pairs to edit each other's informative reports. Students should evaluate, proofread, and make suggestions for publication.
2. First, have students evaluate their partner's report using the Evaluating and Revising Rubric provided on this page. Suggest that students write their suggestions and comments on a separate piece of paper and attach it to the original. Remind students to comment on parts of the report that they particularly liked as well as problems they found in the report.
3. Have students incorporate their partners' comments. Then have partners exchange papers a second time and proofread each other's work. Finally, editors can make suggestions for publishing the report.

LS Interpersonal, Verbal/Linguistic

Introduce the Unit

Share the information in the chapter overviews with students.

Chapter 11 Rome's location and government helped it to become a major power by about 500 BC. Rome's sophisticated system of laws established many legal traditions we have today. However, many challenges faced the Roman Republic during its latter years.

Chapter 12 The Roman Empire began when the Senate gave Octavian a new name—Augustus, which means "revered one." The empire spread Roman law and technology throughout the region of the Mediterranean Sea.

Chapter 13 Under the Roman Empire, the new religion of Christianity spread throughout the eastern Mediterranean. Eventually Christianity was adopted by the Roman Empire as its official religion.

Standards Focus

For a list of the overarching standards covered in this unit, see the first page of each chapter.

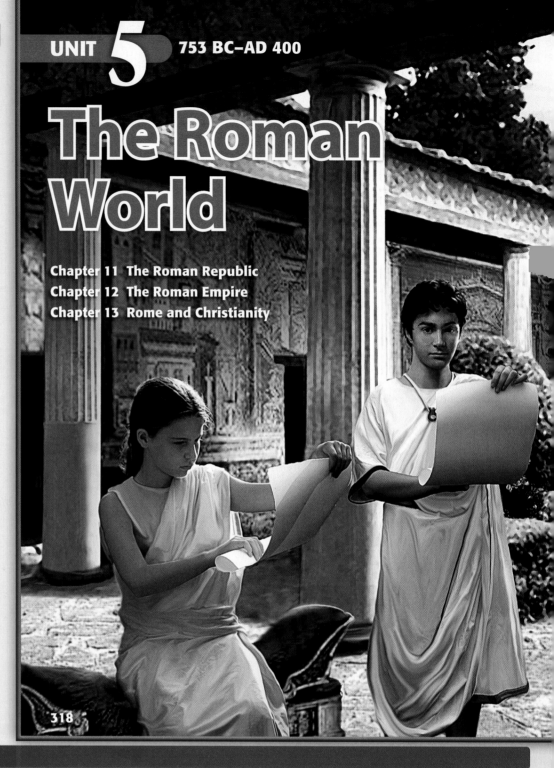

UNIT 5   753 BC–AD 400
The Roman World

Chapter 11 The Roman Republic
Chapter 12 The Roman Empire
Chapter 13 Rome and Christianity

318

Unit Resources

Planning

- Universal Access Teacher Management System: Unit Instructional Benchmarking Guides
- One-Stop Planner CD-ROM with Test Generator: Holt Calendar Planner
- Power Presentations with Video CD-ROM
- A Teacher's Guide to Religion in the Public Schools

Standards Mastery

- Standards Review Workbook
- At Home: A Guide to Standards Mastery for World History

Differentiating Instruction

- Universal Access Teacher Management System: Lesson Plans for Universal Access
- Universal Access Modified Worksheets and Tests CD-ROM

Enrichment

- **CRF 11:** Interdisciplinary Project: The Romans: Response Rally
- **CRF 12:** Economics and History: The Romans and Money
- Civic Participation
- Primary Source Library CD-ROM

Assessment

- Progress Assessment Support System: Benchmark Test
- OSP ExamView Test Generator: Benchmark Test
- Holt Online Assessment Program (in the Premier Online Edition)
- Alternative Assessment Handbook

> The **Universal Access Teacher Management System** provides a planning and instructional benchmarking guide for this unit.

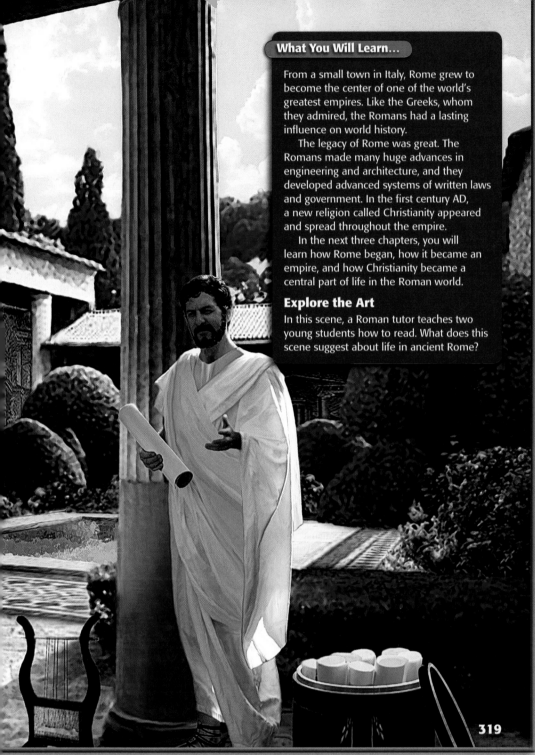

From a small town in Italy, Rome grew to become the center of one of the world's greatest empires. Like the Greeks, whom they admired, the Romans had a lasting influence on world history.

The legacy of Rome was great. The Romans made many huge advances in engineering and architecture, and they developed advanced systems of written laws and government. In the first century AD, a new religion called Christianity appeared and spread throughout the empire.

In the next three chapters, you will learn how Rome began, how it became an empire, and how Christianity became a central part of life in the Roman world.

Explore the Art

In this scene, a Roman tutor teaches two young students how to read. What does this scene suggest about life in ancient Rome?

319

Unit Preview

Connect to the Unit

Activity A Roman Classroom

Ask students: What is the first thing that comes to mind when you think of the Roman world? Tell them that gladiators and togas only make up a small part of Roman history. Rearrange the classroom so that it resembles the layout of the Roman Empire based on maps in the chapter "The Roman Empire." Organize the class into small groups, and instruct those groups to stand around the room in the relative positions of Roman colonies in AD 100. Locations can include Asia Minor, Carthage, Britain, Gaul, Greece, Jerusalem, and Spain. Stand in the middle of the room in the position of Rome and tell the students that you are the emperor. Discuss with students the challenges an emperor and other officials might face in such a vast empire.
LS Interpersonal, Kinesthetic

Explore the Art

Rome was full of sophisticated and beautiful art and architecture. Artists and engineers were respected individuals in Roman society. The Roman world was remarkable for valuing literacy, culture, and a society based on law.

About the Illustration

This illustration is an artist's conception based on available sources. However, historians are uncertain exactly what this scene looked like.

Democracy and Civic Education

Responsibility: Civic Duty and Political Participation

Research Required

Background Explain that the Roman Republic relied on the active participation of the people. Romans participated in their government out of a sense of civic duty, or duty to their city.

1. Discuss with students why it is important in a republic to have a citizenry that actively participates in the political process.

2. Organize students into small groups and have each group conduct research on the responsibilities of citizens and the ways in which they could participate in the political

process in ancient democratic Athens, the Roman Republic, and the United States.

3. Have each group use its research to create a triptych, with one panel for each main topic.

4. Conclude by having students discuss their responsibilities as U.S. citizens and how they can participate in the political process now.
LS Interpersonal, Verbal/Linguistic

📄 Alternative Assessment Handbook, Rubrics 14: Group Activity; and 29: Presentations

📄 Civic Participation

Answers

Explore the Art *People were educated, had a writing system, wrote on scrolls, and wore togas and sandals. The image also shows styles of art and architecture, such as the courtyard, columns, and pond.*

Chapter 11 Planning Guide

The Roman Republic

Chapter Overview	Reproducible Resources	Technology Resources

CHAPTER 11

pp. 320–347

Overview: In this chapter, students will learn about the founding of the Roman Republic, the republic's further development, and the crises the republic faced.

 See page 320 for the California History–Social Science standards covered in this chapter.

 Universal Access Teacher Management System:*
- Universal Access Instructional Benchmarking Guides
- Lesson Plans for Universal Access

 Interactive Reader and Study Guide: Chapter Graphic Organizer*

 Chapter Resource File*
- Chapter Review Activity
- Focus on Speaking Activity: A Legend
- Social Studies Skills Activity: Interpreting Culture Maps

 One-Stop Planner CD-ROM: Calendar Planner

 Student Edition on Audio CD Program

 Universal Access Modified Worksheets and Tests CD-ROM

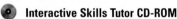 **Interactive Skills Tutor CD-ROM**

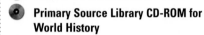 **Primary Source Library CD-ROM for World History**

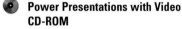 **Power Presentations with Video CD-ROM**

 History's Impact: World History Video Program (VHS/DVD): The Roman Republic*

Section 1:

Geography and the Rise of Rome

The Big Idea: Rome's location and government helped it become a major power in the ancient world.

 6.7.1

 Universal Access Teacher Management System:* Section 1 Lesson Plan

 Interactive Reader and Study Guide: Section 1 Summary*

 Chapter Resource File*
- Vocabulary Builder Activity, Section 1
- Literature Activity: "Romulus and Remus," retold by Robert Hull

Daily Bellringer Transparency: Section 1*

Map Transparency: Italy: Physical*

Map Transparency: Italy, 500 BC*

Quick Facts Transparency: Legendary Founding of Rome*

Quick Facts Transparency: Roman Society*

 Internet Activity: The *Aeneid* Anew

Section 2:

Government and Society

The Big Idea: Rome's tripartite government and written laws helped create a stable society.

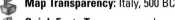 6.7.2

 Universal Access Teacher Management System:* Section 2 Lesson Plan

 Interactive Reader and Study Guide: Section 2 Summary*

 Chapter Resource File*
- Vocabulary Builder Activity, Section 2
- Interdisciplinary Project: The Roman Republic: Unemployment

Daily Bellringer Transparency: Section 2*

Quick Facts Transparency: Government of the Roman Republic*

 Internet Activity: Government Then & Now

Section 3:

The Late Republic

The Big Idea: The later period of the Roman Republic was marked by wars of expansion and political crises.

 6.7.3

 Universal Access Teacher Management System:* Section 3 Lesson Plan

 Interactive Reader and Study Guide: Section 3 Summary*

 Chapter Resource File*
- Vocabulary Builder Activity, Section 3
- Biography Activity: Cornelia
- Biography Activity: Scipio
- Biography Activity: Spartacus
- History and Geography Activity: The Punic Wars
- Primary Source Activity: "The Story of Spartacus," by Plutarch

Daily Bellringer Transparency: Section 3*

Map Transparency: The Roman Republic, 509–270 BC*

Map Transparency: The Roman Republic, 270–100 BC*

SE Student Edition		Print Resource	Audio CD		Video
TE Teacher's Edition		Transparency	CD-ROM		DVD
go.hrw.com		CA Standards Mastery	**LS** Learning Styles		
OSP One-Stop Planner CD-ROM		* also on One-Stop Planner CD			

Review, Assessment, Intervention

 **Standards Review Workbook***

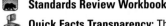 **Quick Facts Transparency:** The Roman Republic Visual Summary*

Spanish Chapter Summaries Audio CD Program

 **Online Chapter Summaries in Six Languages**

Quiz Game CD-ROM

 **Progress Assessment Support System (PASS):** Chapter Test*

 **Universal Access Modified Worksheets and Tests CD-ROM:** Modified Chapter Test

 **One-Stop Planner CD-ROM:** ExamView Test Generator (English/Spanish)

Alternative Assessment Handbook

 **PASS:** Section 1 Quiz*

 **Online Quiz:** Section 1

Alternative Assessment Handbook

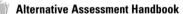 **PASS:** Section 2 Quiz*

 **Online Quiz:** Section 2

Alternative Assessment Handbook

 **PASS:** Section 3 Quiz*

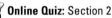 **Online Quiz:** Section 3

Alternative Assessment Handbook

 California Resources for Standards Mastery

INSTRUCTIONAL PLANNING AND SUPPORT

Universal Access Teacher Management System*

One-Stop Planner CD-ROM with Test Generator: Teacher Management System with Interactive Teacher's Edition

STANDARDS MASTERY

Standards Review Workbook*

At Home: A Guide to Standards Mastery for World History

 **Holt Online Learning**

To enhance learning, the following Internet activities are available: The *Aeneid* Anew and Government Then & Now.

 **KEYWORD: SQ6 TEACHER**

- **Teacher Support Page**
- **Content Updates**
- **Rubrics and Writing Models**

- **Teaching Tips for the Multimedia Classroom**

KEYWORD: SQ6 WH11

- **Current Events**
- **Holt Grapher**
- **Holt Online Atlas**
- **Holt Researcher**
- **Interactive Multimedia Activities**

- **Internet Activities**
- **Online Chapter Summaries in Six Languages**
- **Online Section Quizzes**
- **World History Maps and Charts**

HOLT PREMIER ONLINE STUDENT EDITION

Complete online support for interactivity, assessment, and reporting

- **Interactive Maps and Notebook**
- **Standardized Test Prep**
- **Homework Practice and Research Activities Online**

Mastering the Standards: Differentiating Instruction

Reaching Standards	Basic-level activities designed for all students encountering new material
Standards Proficiency	Intermediate-level activities designed for average students
Exceeding Standards	Challenging activities designed for honors and gifted-and-talented students
Standard English Mastery	Activities designed to improve standard English usage

MASTERING THE CALIFORNIA STANDARDS

Frequently Asked Questions

INSTRUCTIONAL PLANNING AND SUPPORT

Where do I find planning aids, pacing guides, lesson plans, and other teaching aids?

Annotated Teacher's Edition:
- Chapter planning guides
- Standards-based instruction and strategies
- Differentiated instruction for universal access
- Point-of-use reminders for integrating program resources

Power Presentations with Video CD-ROM

Universal Access Teacher Management System:
- Year and unit instructional benchmarking guides
- Reproducible lesson plans
- Assessment guides for diagnostic, progress, and summative end-of-the-year tests
- Options for differentiating instruction and intervention
- Teaching guides and answer keys for student workbooks.

One-Stop Planner CD-ROM with Test Generator: Teacher Management System with Interactive Teacher's Edition:
- Calendar Planner
- Editable lesson plans
- All reproducible ancillaries in Adobe Acrobat (PDF) format
- ExamView Test Generator (English & Spanish)
- Game Tool for ExamView
- PuzzlePro
- Transparency and video previews

DIFFERENTIATING INSTRUCTION FOR UNIVERSAL ACCESS

What resources are available to ensure that Advanced Learners/GATE Students master the standards?

Teacher's Edition Activities:
- Etruscan Civilization, p. 327
- Latinus's Diary, p. 330

Lesson Plans for Universal Access

Primary Source Library CD-ROM for World History

What resources are available to ensure that English Learners and Standard English Learners master the standards?

Teacher's Edition Activities:
- Italian Landscape Collage, p. 325
- Roman Forum Video Game, p. 336
- Roman Coin, p. 339

Lesson Plans for Universal Access

Chapter Resource File: Vocabulary Builder Activities

Spanish Chapter Summaries Audio CD Program

Online Chapter Summaries in Six Languages

One-Stop Planner CD-ROM:
- PuzzlePro, Spanish Version
- ExamView Test Generator, Spanish Version

What modified materials are available for Special Education?

The *Universal Access Modified Worksheets and Tests CD-ROM* provides editable versions of the following:

Vocabulary Flash Cards

Modified Vocabulary Builder Activities

Modified Chapter Review Activity

Modified Chapter Test

What resources are available to ensure that Learners Having Difficulty master the standards?

Teacher's Edition Activities:
- Main Ideas on Rome's Beginnings, p. 326
- Basics and Extras, p. 330
- Government Officials, p. 333
- Honoring Heroes, p. 342

Interactive Reader and Study Guide

Student Edition on Audio CD Program

Quick Facts Transparency: The Roman Republic Visual Summary

Standards Review Workbook

Social Studies Skills Activity: Interpreting Culture Maps

Interactive Skills Tutor CD-ROM

How do I intervene for students struggling to master the standards?

Interactive Reader and Study Guide

Quick Facts Transparency: The Roman Republic Visual Summary

Standards Review Workbook

Social Studies Skills Activity: Interpreting Culture Maps

Interactive Skills Tutor CD-ROM

PROFESSIONAL DEVELOPMENT

HOLT
Professional
Development

What teacher training resources are available to help me grow professionally?

- In-service and staff development as part of your Holt Social Studies product purchase
- Quick Teacher Tutorial Lesson Presentation CD-ROM
- Intensive tuition-based Teacher Development Institute
- Convenient Holt Speaker Bureau face-to-face workshop options

- PRAXIS™ Test Prep (#0089) interactive Web-based content refreshers*
- *Ask A Professional Development Expert* at http://www.hrw.com/prodev/

* PRAXIS is a trademark of Educational Testing Service (ETS). This publication is not endorsed or approved by ETS.

Information Literacy Skills

To learn more about how History-Social Science instruction may be improved by the effective use of library media centers and information literacy skills, go to the Teacher's Resource Materials for Chapter 11 at **go.hrw.com, keyword: SQ6 MEDIA.**

MASTERING THE CALIFORNIA STANDARDS

Standards Focus

Standards by Section
Section 1: **HSS** 6.7.1
Section 2: **HSS** 6.7.2
Section 3: **HSS** 6.7.3

Teacher's Edition
HSS Analysis Skills: CS 1, CS 2, CS 3, HI 1, HI 2, HI 3, HI 4, HI 5, HR 1, HR 3, HR 4

ELA Writing 7.2.5a, Reading 6.2.1, Speaking 6.2.1

Upcoming Standards for Future Learning
Preview the following History–Social Science content standards from upcoming chapters or grade levels to promote learning beyond the current chapter.

HSS **6.7** Students analyze the geographic, political, economic, religious, and social structures during the development of Rome.

6.7.4 Discuss the influence of Julius Caesar and Augustus in Rome's transition from republic to empire.

6.7.5 Trace the migration of Jews around the Mediterranean region and the effects of their conflict with the Romans, including the Romans' restrictions on their right to live in Jerusalem.

6.7.6 Note the origins of Christianity in the Jewish Messianic prophecies, the life and teachings of Jesus of Nazareth as described in the New Testament, and the contribution of St. Paul the Apostle to the definition and spread of Christian beliefs (e.g., belief in the Trinity, resurrection, salvation).

Focus on Speaking
The **Chapter Resource File** provides a Focus on Speaking worksheet to help students create and present their legends.

CRF: Focus on Speaking Activity: A Legend

CHAPTER 11 **753–27 BC**

The Roman Republic

California Standards

History–Social Science
6.7 Students analyze the geographic, political, economic, religious, and social structures during the development of Rome.

Analysis Skills
CS 3 Use maps to identify cultural features.

English–Language Arts
Speaking 6.2.1 Deliver narrative presentations.

Reading 6.2.4 Clarify an understanding of texts by creating outlines, logical notes, summaries, or reports.

FOCUS ON SPEAKING

A Legend The ancient Romans created many legends about their early history. They told of heroes and kings who performed great deeds to build and rule their city. As you read this chapter, look for people or events that could be the subjects of legends. When you finish studying this chapter, you will create and present a legend about one of the people or events that you have studied.

CHAPTER EVENTS

753 BC According to legend, Rome is founded.

800 BC

WORLD EVENTS

c. 700 BC The Assyrians conquer Israel.

Introduce the Chapter

Standards Proficiency

Focus on the Impact of the Roman Republic **HSS** 6.7; **HSS** Analysis Skills: HI 1

1. Ask students to imagine that they are establishing a new country. What form of government would they choose? Would a government run by a single person or by an elected group be better? Ask for a show of hands for each type. Call on volunteers to defend their choices.

2. Explain to students that the Romans also struggled with the question about which type of government is best. During the period of the Republic the Romans had a government that involved several people. In fact, elements of the Republic's government can be seen in the U.S. government today.

3. Have students name different parts of the U.S. government. *possible answers—Congress, House of Representatives, Senate, court system, executive branch*

4. Point out that all these elements connect to parts of the government in the Roman Republic. **LS** Verbal/Linguistic

What You Will Learn...

In this chapter you will learn about the history of the Roman Republic. The Roman Forum, the ruins of which are shown above, was a public meeting place at the heart of Rome.

c. 600 BC
The Etruscans take over Rome.

509 BC
The Roman Republic is founded.

264–146 BC
Rome and Carthage fight in the Punic Wars.

27 BC
Augustus becomes Rome's first emperor.

| 600 BC | 400 BC | 200 BC | BC 1 AD |

490 BC
The Persians invade Greece.

334–323 BC
Alexander the Great builds his empire.

c. 221–206 BC
The Qin dynasty rules China.

321

• Chapter Preview •

HOLT

History's Impact

▶ **video series**
See the Video Teacher's Guide for strategies for using the video segment **The Roman Republic: The Impact of the Roman Republic on American Government Today.**

Chapter Big Ideas

Section 1 Rome's location and government helped it become a major power in the ancient world. **HSS** 6.7.1

Section 2 Rome's tripartite government and written laws helped create a stable society. **HSS** 6.7.2

Section 3 The later period of the Roman Republic was marked by wars of expansion and political crises. **HSS** 6.7.3

Explore the Picture

From Marshy to Majestic Point out that just beyond the edges of the picture are two of Rome's famous hills—the Palatine and the Capitoline. Other hills enclose the space on the other sides. Because the land on which the Forum was built lay between these hills, water collected there. Rome's first sewer, the Cloaca Maxima, was built on the site to drain the marshy land.

Analyzing Visuals Ask why the building in the background on the left page is intact, while those in the foreground are in ruins. *It was built hundreds of years after the foreground structures.* Then ask why the Roman buildings are in ruins. *possible answers—damaged by earthquakes, wars, intentional destruction by enemies, or gradual destruction by people taking stones for building material*

go.hrw.com
Online Resources

Chapter Resources:
KEYWORD: SQ6 WH11
Teacher Resources:
KEYWORD: SQ6 Teacher

Explore the Time Line

1. When was the Roman Republic founded? *509 BC*

2. When did a series of wars between Rome and Carthage begin? *264 BC*

3. What did the Persians do in 490 BC? *invaded Greece*

4. What dynasty ruled China during the same time period as the Punic Wars? *Qin dynasty*

5. How long may one infer that the Etruscans ruled Rome? *about 91 years*

HSS Analysis Skills: CS 1

Info to Know

The Temple of Saturn The large eight-columned ruin in the foreground is the Temple of Saturn, an ancient Roman god of harvests. A temple to Saturn was first built on the site in about 498 BC. The temple that still stands, however, dates from the third temple built there in about 42 BC.

Understanding Themes

Introduce the key themes of this chapter—geography and politics—by asking students to find Rome on a map of the world. Point out to students that while Rome today is a city in Italy, the Roman Republic spread throughout Italy and the Mediterranean. Ask students to draw conclusions about the geography of this area. Then have students make predictions about the role the government of Rome might have played during the years of the Republic.

Outlining and History

Focus on Reading Have each student bring in a newspaper article on a topic that interests him or her. Have students work in pairs to create an outline of the story covered in their articles following the format shown here. When their outline is complete, have each pair use scissors to cut the major topics, supporting ideas, and details of their outline into separate strips of paper. Have students cut off the outline numbers and letters. Then have students exchange their outlines with another pair. Ask them to use the article to put the outlines back together in correct form.

Reading Social Studies

by Kylene Beers

| Economics | Geography | Politics | Religion | Society and Culture | Science and Technology |

Focus on Themes In this chapter, you will read about the Roman Republic, about how Rome's location and **geography** helped it become a major power in the ancient world. You will also read about the city's **politics** and discover how its three-pronged government affected all of society. Finally, you will read about the wars the Roman Republic fought as it expanded its boundaries. You will see how this growth led to problems that were difficult to solve.

Outlining and History

Focus on Reading How can you make sense of all the facts and ideas in a chapter? One way is to take notes in the form of an outline.

Outlining a Chapter Here is an example of a partial outline for Section 1 of this chapter. Compare the outline to the information on pages 324–327. Notice how the writer looked at the heads in the chapter to determine the main and supporting ideas.

Additional reading support can be found in the

Inter active
Reader and Study Guide

The writer picked up the first heading in the chapter (page 324) as the first main idea. She identified it with Roman numeral I.

Section 1, Geography and the Rise of Rome

I. The Geography of Italy
  A. Physical features—many types of features
    1. Mountain ranges
    2. Hills
    3. Rivers
  B. Climate—warm summers, mild winters
II. Rome's Legendary Origins
  A. Aeneas
    1. Trojan hero
    2. Sailed to Italy and founded city
  B. Romulus and Remus
    1. Twin brothers
    2. Founded city of Rome
      a. Romulus killed Remus
      b. City named for Romulus
      c. Rome's Early Kings

The writer saw two smaller heads under the bigger head on page 324 and listed them as A and B.

The writer identified two facts that supported II.A (the head on page 326). She listed them as numbers 1 and 2.

The writer decided it was important to note some individual facts under B.2. That's why she added a, b, and c.

Outlining a Few Paragraphs When you need to outline only a few paragraphs, you can use the same outline form. Just look for the main idea of each paragraph and give each one a Roman numeral. Supporting ideas within the paragraph can be listed with A, B, and so forth. You can use Arabic numbers for specific details and facts.

322 CHAPTER 11

Reading and Skills Resources

Reading Support

- Interactive Reader and Study Guide
- Student Edition on Audio CD
- Spanish Chapter Summaries Audio CD Program

Social Studies Skills Support

- Interactive Skills Tutor CD-ROM

Vocabulary Support

- **CRF:** Vocabulary Builder Activities
- **CRF:** Chapter Review Activity
- Universal Access Modified Worksheets and Tests CD-ROM:
  - Vocabulary Flash Cards
  - Vocabulary Builder Activity
  - Chapter Review Activity

OSP Holt PuzzlePro

Standards Focus

ELA Reading 6.2.4

You Try It!

Read the following passage from this chapter. Then fill in the blanks to complete the outline below.

Growth of Territory

Roman territory grew mainly in response to outside threats. In about 387 BC a people called the Gauls attacked Rome and took over the city. The Romans had to give the Gauls a huge amount of gold to leave the city.

Inspired by the Gauls' victory, many of Rome's neighboring cities also decided to attack. With some difficulty, the Romans fought off these attacks. As Rome's attackers were defeated, the Romans took over their lands. As you can see on the map, the Romans soon controlled all of the Italian Peninsula except far northern Italy.

One reason for the Roman success was the organization of the army. Soldiers were organized in legions . . . This organization allowed the army to be very flexible.

From Chapter 11, pages 338–339

Complete this outline based on the passage you just read.

I. Roman territory grew in response to outside threats.

  A. Gauls attacked Rome in 387 BC.

    1. Took over the city

    2. _____

  B. The Gauls' victory inspired other people to attack Rome.

    1. _____

    2. Romans took lands of defeated foes.

    3. _____

II. _____

  A. Soldiers were organized in legions.

  B. _____

Key Terms and People

Chapter 11

Section 1
Aeneas *(p. 326)*
Romulus and Remus *(p. 327)*
republic *(p. 328)*
dictators *(p. 328)*
Cincinnatus *(p. 328)*
plebeians *(p. 329)*
patricians *(p. 329)*

Section 2
magistrates *(p. 333)*
consuls *(p. 333)*
Roman Senate *(p. 333)*
veto *(p. 334)*
Latin *(p. 334)*
checks and balances *(p. 335)*
Forum *(p. 335)*

Section 3
legions *(p. 339)*
Punic Wars *(p. 339)*
Hannibal *(p. 340)*
Gaius Marius *(p. 342)*
Lucius Cornelius Sulla *(p. 343)*
Spartacus *(p. 343)*

Academic Vocabulary

Success in school is related to knowing academic vocabulary— the words that are frequently used in school assignments and discussions. In this chapter, you will learn the following academic words:

primary *(p. 333)*
purpose *(p. 342)*

> **As you read Chapter 11,** identify the main ideas you would use in an outline of this chapter.

Reading Social Studies

Key Terms and People

Preteach the key terms and people for this chapter by hosting a vocabulary game for students. Write the terms and people for students to see. Then organize the class into teams. Read aloud definitions or descriptions, and have teams take turns guessing which term identifies the description you gave. If one team guesses incorrectly, allow the next team an opportunity to guess the answer. Assign points for each correct answer. You might want to have students keep a list of correct descriptions for each term.
LS Interpersonal, Verbal/Linguistic

Focus on Reading

See the **Focus on Reading** questions in this chapter for more practice on this reading social studies skill.

Reading Social Studies Assessment

See the **Standards Review** at the end of this chapter for student assessment questions related to this reading skill.

Teaching Tip

Some students may not be familiar with outlining. Explain to the class that outlines use main ideas to break down information in a way that is easy to understand and simple to write. Point out to students that major topics from a passage are usually noted as Roman numerals (I, II, III). Under each big idea are supporting ideas, noted as capital letters (A, B, C). Supporting details for each idea are identified with Arabic numerals (1, 2, 3). Lastly, information that supports those ideas can be noted by lowercase letters (a, b, c).

Answers

You Try It! I. A. 2. *Romans gave Gauls gold to leave the city.* **I. B. 1.** *Romans fought off attacks.* **I. B. 3.** *Romans gained control of most land except for northern Italy.* **II.** *Romans gained success due to an organized army.* **II. B.** *Organization allowed the army to be flexible.*

Preteach

Bellringer

If YOU were there . . . Use the **Daily Bellringer Transparency** to help students answer the question.

📖 Daily Bellringer Transparency, Section 1

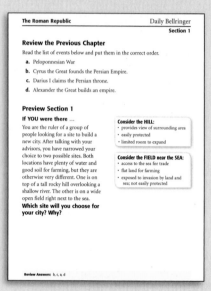

The Roman Republic — Daily Bellringer, Section 1

Review the Previous Chapter

Read the list of events below and put them in the correct order.

a. Peloponnesian War
b. Cyrus the Great founds the Persian Empire.
c. Darius I claims the Persian throne.
d. Alexander the Great builds an empire.

Preview Section 1

If YOU were there ...
You are the ruler of a group of people looking for a site to build a new city. After talking with your advisors, you have narrowed your choice to two possible sites. Both locations have plenty of water and good soil for farming, but they are otherwise very different. One is on top of a tall rocky hill overlooking a shallow river. The other is on a wide open field right next to the sea. **Which site will you choose for your city? Why?**

Consider the HILL:
• provides view of surrounding area
• easily protected
• limited room to expand

Consider the FIELD near the SEA:
• access to the sea for trade
• flat land for farming
• exposed to invasion by land and sea; not easily protected

Review Answers: b, c, a, d

Building Vocabulary

Preteach or review the following terms:

legendary mythical or imaginary (p. 326)

territories regions (p. 324)

📝 **CRF:** Vocabulary Builder Activity, Section 1

🐻 Standards Focus

HSS 6.7.1

Means: Describe the rise of the Roman Republic and some of the people who were important to the republic.

Matters: The Roman Republic arose on the Italian Peninsula and grew out of a rich history of fact and legend.

SECTION 1

What You Will Learn...

Main Ideas

1. The geography of Italy made land travel difficult but helped the Romans prosper.
2. Ancient historians were very interested in Rome's legendary history.
3. Once a monarchy, the Romans created a republic.

The Big Idea

Rome's location and government helped it become a major power in the ancient world.

Key Terms and People

Aeneas, *p. 326*
Romulus and Remus, *p. 327*
republic, *p. 328*
dictators, *p. 328*
Cincinnatus, *p. 328*
plebeians, *p. 329*
patricians, *p. 329*

🐻

HSS 6.7.1 Identify the location and describe the rise of the Roman Republic, including the importance of such mythical and historical figures as Aeneas, Romulus and Remus, Cincinnatus, Julius Caesar, and Cicero.

Geography and the Rise of Rome

If YOU were there...

You are the ruler of a group of people looking for a site to build a new city. After talking with your advisors, you have narrowed your choice to two possible sites. Both locations have plenty of water and good soil for farming, but they are otherwise very different. One is on top of a tall rocky hill overlooking a shallow river. The other is on a wide open field right next to the sea.

Which site will you choose for your city? Why?

BUILDING BACKGROUND From a small town on the Tiber River, Rome grew into a mighty power. Rome's geography—its central location and good climate—were important factors in its success and growth. The city's rise as a military power began when the Romans went to war and conquered neighboring Italian tribes.

The Geography of Italy

Rome eventually became the center of one of the greatest civilizations of the ancient world. In fact, the people of Rome conquered many of the territories you have studied in this book, including Greece, Egypt, and Asia Minor.

Italy, where Rome was built, is a peninsula in southern Europe. If you look at the map, you can see that Italy looks like a high-heeled boot sticking out into the Mediterranean Sea.

Physical Features

Look at the map again to find Italy's two major mountain ranges. In the north are the Alps, Europe's highest mountains. Another range, the Apennines (A-puh-nynz), runs the length of the Italian Peninsula. This rugged land made it hard for ancient people to cross from one side of the peninsula to the other. In addition, some of Italy's mountains, such as Mount Vesuvius, are volcanic. Their eruptions could devastate Roman towns.

Teach the Big Idea: Master the Standards   `Standards Proficiency`

Geography and the Rise of Rome   🐻 HSS 6.7.1; HSS Analysis Skills: CS 1, CS 2

1. **Teach** Ask students the Main Idea questions to teach this section.

2. **Apply** Have students write down the dates—or estimated dates—in this section. Have students work in pairs to create time lines for the history of Rome from its creation to the later years of the Republic. **LS Visual/Spatial**

3. **Review** As you review the section's main ideas, have students check to see if their time lines are accurate. Call on volunteers to

supply details about the events that appear on their time lines.

4. **Practice/Homework** Have each student write a paragraph titled *How Geography May Have Affected the Development and History of the Roman Republic.*

📝 Alternative Assessment Handbook, Rubric 36: Time Lines

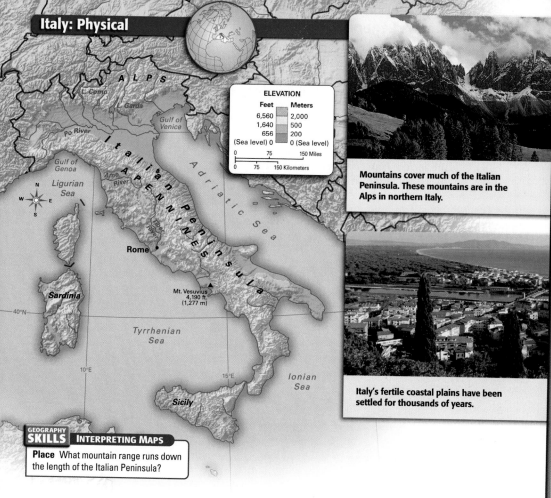

Italy: Physical

ELEVATION

Feet	Meters
6,560	2,000
1,640	500
656	200
(Sea level) 0	0 (Sea level)

0   75   150 Miles
0   75   150 Kilometers

Mountains cover much of the Italian Peninsula. These mountains are in the Alps in northern Italy.

Italy's fertile coastal plains have been settled for thousands of years.

GEOGRAPHY SKILLS **INTERPRETING MAPS**

Place What mountain range runs down the length of the Italian Peninsula?

Not much of Italy is flat. Most of the land that isn't mountainous is covered with hills. Throughout history, people have built cities on these hills for defense. As a result, many of the ancient cities of Italy—including Rome—sat atop hills. Rome was built on seven hills.

Several rivers flow out of Italy's mountains. Because these rivers were a source of fresh water, people also built their cities near them. For example, Rome lies on the Tiber (TY-buhr) River.

Climate

Most of Italy, including the area around Rome, has warm, dry summers and mild, rainy winters. This climate is similar to that of southern California. Italy's mild climate allows people to grow a wide variety of crops. Grains, citrus fruits, grapes, and olives all grow well there. A plentiful food supply was one key factor in Rome's early growth.

READING CHECK **Drawing Conclusions** How did Rome's location affect its early history?

THE ROMAN REPUBLIC **325**

❷ Rome's Legendary Origins

Ancient historians were very interested in Rome's legendary history.

Recall What epic poem tells the story of Aeneas? Who was its author? *the Aeneid; Virgil*

Explain What was remarkable about the childhood of the legendary Romulus and Remus? *The twins were thrown into a river in a basket, rescued and raised by a wolf, and adopted by a shepherd.*

Develop How might a legendary beginning make a country or empire more stable? *possible answer—Belief in the legend could reduce the danger of people trying to destroy the country from within, because they would believe the country was very special.*

📝 **CRF:** Literature Activity: Romulus and Remus

🐻 **HSS** 6.7.1; **HSS** Analysis Skills: HR 3

Other People, Other Places

Another Legendary Beginning Other peoples, too, have created legends about the founding of their countries or empires. For example, Japanese tradition says that a god and goddess came down from heaven to create the Japanese islands. Legend also claims that Japan's royal family is descended directly from Amaterasu, the sun goddess of the Shinto religion.

go.hrw.com
Online Resources

KEYWORD: SQ6 WH11
ACTIVITY: The *Aeneid*
Anew

Rome's Legendary Origins

Rome's early history is wrapped in mystery. No written records exist, and we have little evidence of the city's earliest days. All we have found are ancient ruins that suggest people lived in the area of Rome as early as the 800s BC. However, we know very little about how they lived.

Would it surprise you to think that the ancient Romans were as curious about their early history as we are today? Rome's leaders wanted their city to have a glorious past that would make the Roman people proud. Imagining that glorious past, they told legends, or stories, about great heroes and kings who built the city.

Aeneas

The Romans believed their history could be traced back to a great Trojan hero named **Aeneas** (i-NEE-uhs). When the Greeks destroyed Troy in the Trojan War, Aeneas fled with his followers. After a long and dangerous journey, he reached Italy. The story of this trip is told in the *Aeneid* (i-NEE-id), an epic poem written by a poet named Virgil (VUHR-juhl) around 20 BC.

According to the story, when Aeneas reached Italy, he found several groups of people living there. He formed an

Legendary Founding of Rome QUICK FACTS

Roman historians traced their city's history back to legendary figures such as Aeneas, Romulus, and Remus.

Aeneas

According to the *Aeneid*, Aeneas carried his father from the burning city of Troy and then searched for a new home for the Trojans. After traveling around the Mediterranean, Aeneas finally settled in Italy.

326

Critical Thinking: Finding Main Ideas

Reaching Standards

Main Ideas on Rome's Beginnings 🐻 **HSS** 6.7.1; **HSS** Analysis Skills: CS 2

1. Organize the class into small groups. Call on one student in each group to read the text under *Rome's Legendary Origins* quietly to his or her group, while the other members read silently.

2. Then ask another group member to tell the main idea of the passage. Students should discuss among themselves if the main idea described was correct.

3. Instruct students to take turns reading and naming the main idea in the remaining subheads on these two pages.

4. As a class, review the main ideas for the entire subsection.
   🔲 **Verbal/Linguistic, Auditory/Musical**

alliance with one of these groups, a people called the Latins. Together they fought the other people of Italy. After defeating these opponents, Aeneas married the daughter of the Latin king. Aeneas, his son, and their descendants became prominent rulers in Italy.

Romulus and Remus

Among the descendants of Aeneas were the founders of Rome. According to Roman legends, these founders were twin brothers named **Romulus** (RAHM-yuh-luhs) and **Remus** (REE-muhs). In the story, these boys led exciting lives. When they were babies, they were put in a basket and thrown into the Tiber River. They didn't drown, though, because a wolf rescued them. The wolf cared for the boys for many years. Eventually, a shepherd found the boys and adopted them.

Romulus and Remus
The Romans believed that the twins Romulus and Remus were descendants of Aeneas. In Roman legend, Romulus and Remus were rescued and raised by a wolf. Romulus later killed Remus and built the city of Rome.

After they grew up, Romulus and Remus decided to build a city to mark the spot where the wolf had rescued them. While they were planning the city, Remus mocked one of his brother's ideas. In a fit of anger, Romulus killed Remus. He then built the city and named it Rome after himself.

Rome's Early Kings

According to ancient historians, Romulus was the first king of Rome, taking the throne in 753 BC. Modern historians believe that Rome could have been founded within 50 years before or after that date.

Roman records list seven kings who ruled the city. Not all of them were Roman. Rome's last three kings were Etruscans (i-TRUHS-kuhnz), members of a people who lived north of Rome. The Etruscans, who had been influenced by Greek colonies in Italy, lived in Italy before Rome was founded.

The Etruscan kings made great contributions to Roman society. They built huge temples and Rome's first sewer. Many historians think that the Romans learned their alphabet and numbers from the Etruscans.

The last Roman king was said to have been a cruel man who had many people killed, including his own advisors. Finally, a group of nobles rose up against him. According to tradition, he was overthrown in 509 BC. The nobles, who no longer wanted kings, created a new government.

READING CHECK Drawing Conclusions Why did early Romans want to get rid of the monarchy?

THE ROMAN REPUBLIC **327**

Collaborative Learning

Exceeding Standards

Etruscan Civilization 🐻 HSS 6.7.1; Analysis Skills: HR 4, HI 5

Background: Tell students that historians know less about the Etruscans than about some other ancient peoples because scholars have not been able to decipher Etruscan writing. However, many Etruscan archaeological sites have been explored, and examples of Etruscan painting, sculpture, and jewelry have been found.

1. Organize students into groups and have them compile a portfolio of Etruscan artifacts. Direct students to library or Internet resources for those images. Many museums display

them online. Instruct groups to label the artifacts with basic information.

2. Then lead a class discussion about what we may conclude about the Etruscans by examining their art and how those conclusions may change if Etruscan writing is ever deciphered. **LS** Interpersonal, Visual/Spatial

📄 Alternative Assessment Handbook, Rubric 1: Acquiring Information

---

Connect to Arts and the Humanities

Romulus and Remus Several sculptures of Romulus and Remus can be seen in Italy today. Probably the most famous features an Etruscan sculpture of the wolf, with statues of the infant twins that were added about a thousand years later.

Info to Know

King Tarquin of Rome King Tarquin was one of the first Etruscan kings. He gained power because he served as a tutor for his predecessor's sons. As the former king lay dying, Tarquin sent the sons away so he could be named as the next king. Tarquin's successes continued during his reign. He ordered the construction of the Circus Maximus, Rome's first chariot-racing track. Games at the Circus Maximus were so popular that similar events were held there for another thousand years.

Checking for Understanding

True or False Answer each statement *T* if it is true or *F* if it is false. If false, explain why.

1. According to legend, Remus named the city of Rome after his brother Romulus. *F; Romulus named the city after himself.*

2. Roman records show that Rome's last three kings were not Romans, but Etruscans. *T*

3. The Roman Republic is said to have been founded by Rome's last king, who was known for his visionary leadership and kindness. *F; The last Roman king was said to have been cruel, and a group of nobles rose up against him to create a new government.*

Answers

Reading Check *The last Roman king was said to have been cruel.*

Once a monarchy, the Romans created a republic.

Identify What was the Roman office of dictator? *a ruler with almost absolute power who was in power for only six months*

Explain How is a republic different from a monarchy? *A monarchy is ruled by a king or queen; a republic is governed by elected leaders.*

Make Generalizations What were the first 50 years like for the Roman Republic? *It faced wars and won most of them, but the Romans lost many lives and much property.*

HSS 6.7.1

Activity **Cincinnatus Writes a Letter** Have students imagine they are Cincinnatus after he has returned to his farm. Ask students to write letters to the editor of a Roman newspaper in the voice of Cincinnatus explaining why he wanted to give up his position as dictator. Explain to students that a letter to the editor is often used by people to voice their opinion about a particular issue or current event. **LS Verbal/Linguistic**

The Early Republic

THE IMPACT TODAY
The government of the United States today is a republic.

The government the Romans created in 509 BC was a republic. In a **republic**, people elect leaders to govern them. Each year the Romans elected officials to rule the city. These officials had many powers but only stayed in power for one year. This system was supposed to keep any one person from becoming too powerful in the government.

But Rome was not a democracy. The city's elected officials nearly all came from a small group of wealthy and powerful men. These wealthy and powerful Romans held all the power, and other people had little to no say in how the republic was run.

Italy, 500 BC

Romans
Etruscans
Greeks
Carthaginians

0   30   60 Miles
0   30   60 Kilometers

Ligurian Sea
Adriatic Sea
Rome
Tyrrhenian Sea
Mediterranean Sea
Ionian Sea
Carthage

GEOGRAPHY SKILLS **INTERPRETING MAPS**
Location What group lived mostly north of Rome?

328

Challenges from Outside

Shortly after the Romans created the republic, they found themselves at war. For about 50 years the Romans were at war with other peoples of the region. For the most part the Romans won these wars. But they lost several battles, and the wars destroyed many lives and much property.

During particularly difficult wars, the Romans chose **dictators**—rulers with almost absolute power—to lead the city. To keep them from abusing their power, dictators could only stay in power for six months. When that time was over, the dictator gave up his power.

One of Rome's famous dictators was **Cincinnatus** (sin-suh-NAT-uhs), who gained power in 458 BC. Although he was a farmer, the Romans chose him to defend the city against a powerful enemy that had defeated a large Roman army.

Cincinnatus quickly defeated the city's enemies. Immediately, he resigned as dictator and returned to his farm, long before his six-month term had run out.

The victory by Cincinnatus did not end Rome's troubles. Rome continued to fight its neighbors on and off for many years.

BIOGRAPHY

Cincinnatus
c. 519 BC–?

Cincinnatus is the most famous dictator from the early Roman Republic. Because he wasn't eager to hold on to his power, the Romans considered Cincinnatus an ideal leader. They admired his abilities and his loyalty to the republic. The early citizens of the United States admired the same qualities in their leaders. In fact, some people called George Washington the "American Cincinnatus" when he refused to run for a third term as president. The people of the state of Ohio also honored Cincinnatus by naming one of their major cities, Cincinnati, after him.

Critical Thinking: Comparing

Standards Proficiency

Challenges to the Republic **HSS** 6.7.1; **HSS** Analysis Skills: HI 1, HI 3

1. Copy the graphic organizer for students to see, omitting the italicized answers. Instruct students to copy and complete the graphic organizer.

2. Students should describe the internal and external challenges the Roman Republic faced during its early years.

3. Lead a discussion about which challenges might have been the greater threat to the republic. **LS Visual/Spatial**

Challenges to the Republic	
Challenges from the Outside	Challenges from the Inside
many wars with other peoples of the region	*plebeians calling for change in the government and forming their own council*

Challenges within Rome

Enemy armies weren't the only challenge facing Rome. Within the city, Roman society was divided into two groups. Many of Rome's **plebeians** (pli-BEE-uhnz), or common people, were calling for changes in the government. They wanted more of a say in how the city was run.

Rome was run by powerful nobles called **patricians** (puh-TRI-shuhnz). Only patricians could be elected to office, so they held all political power.

The plebeians were peasants, craftspeople, traders, and other workers. Some of these plebeians, especially traders, were as rich as patricians. Even though the plebeians outnumbered the patricians, they couldn't take part in the government.

In 494 BC the plebeians formed a council and elected their own officials, an act that frightened many patricians. They feared that Rome would fall apart if the two groups couldn't cooperate. The patricians decided that it was time to change the government.

READING CHECK **Contrasting** How were patricians and plebeians different?

Roman Society

QUICK FACTS

Patricians	Plebeians
■ Wealthy, powerful citizens	■ Common people
■ Nobles	■ Peasants, craftspeople, traders, other workers
■ Small minority of the population	■ Majority of the population
■ Once controlled all aspects of government	■ Gained right to participate in government
■ After 218 BC, not allowed to participate in trade or commerce	■ Only Romans who could be traders, so many became wealthy

SUMMARY AND PREVIEW In this section you read about the location and founding of Rome, its early rule by kings, and the creation of the city's republican government. In the next section you'll learn more about that government, its strengths and weaknesses, how it worked, and how it changed over time.

go.hrw.com
Online Quiz
KEYWORD: SQ6 HP11

Section 1 Assessment

Reviewing Ideas, Terms, and People HSS 6.7.1

1. **a. Describe** Where is Italy located?
   b. Explain How did mountains affect life in Italy?
   c. Predict How do you think Rome's location on the Mediterranean affected its history as it began to grow into a world power?
2. **a. Identify** What brothers supposedly founded the city of Rome?
   b. Summarize What role did **Aeneas** play in the founding of Rome?
3. **a. Describe** What type of government did the Romans create in 509 BC?
   b. Contrast How were **patricians** and **plebeians** different?

Critical Thinking

4. **Sequencing** Draw a diagram like the one below. Use it to identify the key events in the legendary history of the founding and growth of Rome.

FOCUS ON SPEAKING

5. **Gathering Background Ideas** In this section you read about several legends the Romans told about their own history. Look back at the text to get some ideas about what you might include in your own legend. Write some ideas in your notebook.

Section 1 Assessment Answers

1. **a.** southern Europe, extending into the Mediterranean Sea
   b. They made inland travel difficult and dictated where people lived.
   c. Its location in the middle of the Mediterranean region made it easy for Rome to control surrounding areas.
2. **a.** Romulus and Remus
   b. He formed an alliance with the Latins, fought other people of Italy, and started a line of prominent rulers in Italy.
3. **a.** a republic
   b. Patricians were nobles who could be elected to office; plebeians were peasants, craftspeople, traders, and other workers who at first were not able to be in government.
4. Aeneas arrives in Italy; Aeneas becomes a ruler in Italy; Romulus and Remus are saved by a wolf and raised by a shepherd; Romulus builds a city and names it Rome.
5. Ideas should be creative and may include a description of the local geography.

Literature in History

The *Aeneid*

As You Read As students read the passage, have them record the goals and desires of Ilioneus and his men and those of Latinus, the king of the Latins. Point out that sometimes people don't reveal their true goals or desires. Ask students to consider if Ilioneus and Latinus seem to be expressing their true feelings in the passage.

Meet the Writer

Virgil Publius Vergilius Maro, later known as Virgil, grew up on a farm in northern Italy. Life on the farm provided much material for the writer's early poetry. Virgil was reportedly encouraged by Augustus to write about the glory of Rome. He spent much of the rest of his life composing the *Aeneid*.

Virgil's poems were so respected and loved that the Romans used them in schools as textbooks. The Romans loved Virgil not just because he was an excellent writer, but also because he fulfilled the role of a national poet. Virgil's popularity has continued for centuries.

Did you know . . .

Notice that Aeneas was supposedly the son of Venus. In many stories from ancient Greece and Rome, heroes are said to be the sons of a human being and a god or goddess. Having such a marvelous parent gave a hero extra strength, wisdom, or talents. In these stories, the supernatural parent could also provide extra protection.

Literature in History

GUIDED READING

WORD HELP

tranquilly calmly
astray off course
broached crossed
moored anchored
constraint force
gale storm

❶ Both "Teucrians" and "sons of Dardanus" are ways of referring to Trojans.

❷ Ilioneus says that the Trojans are not lost. A seamark is similar to a landmark, a feature sailors use to find their way.

How does Ilioneus address the king? Why do you think he does so?

HSS 6.7.1 Identify the location and describe the rise of the Roman Republic, including the importance of such mythical and historical figures as Aeneas, Romulus and Remus, Cincinnatus, Julius Caesar, and Cicero.

ELA Reading 6.3.4 Define how tone or meaning is conveyed in poetry.

---

from the Aeneid

by Virgil

Translated by Robert Fitzgerald

About the Reading *Virgil wrote the* Aeneid *to record the glorious story of Rome's founding and to celebrate the Rome of his present. At the center of the poem stands the hero Aeneas, survivor of the Trojan War and son of the goddess Venus. After wandering for seven years, Aeneas finally reaches southern Italy—then known as Ausonia. Here, Aeneas's friend Ilioneus leads a group of representatives to visit a nearby Latin settlement.*

AS YOU READ Try to identify each group's goals and desires.

> Latinus
> Called the Teucrians before him, saying
> Tranquilly as they entered:
>   "Sons of Dardanus—
> You see, we know your city and your nation,
> As all had heard you laid a westward course—
> Tell me your purpose. ❶ What design or need
> Has brought you through the dark blue sea so far
> To our Ausonian coast? Either astray
> Or driven by rough weather, such as sailors
> Often endure at sea, you've broached the river,
> Moored ship there. Now do not turn away
> From hospitality here. Know that our Latins
> Come of Saturn's race, that we are just—
> Not by constraint or laws, but by our choice
> And habit of our ancient god . . ."
> Latinus then fell silent, and in turn
> Ilioneus began:
>   "Your majesty,
> Most noble son of Faunus, no rough seas
> Or black gale swept us to your coast, no star
> Or clouded seamark put us off our course. ❷

Aeneas, from an Italian painting of the 1700s

Differentiating Instruction for Universal Access

Advanced Learners/GATE
Exceeding Standards

Have students imagine they are Latinus a few hours after he has met Ilioneus. Ask students to write journal entries as Latinus about the meeting. Encourage students to reread the poem closely for tone and meaning to help them make inferences about Latinus' mood. Call on volunteers to read their diary entries aloud. **LS Verbal/Linguistic**

HSS 6.7.1; ELA 6.3.4

Alternative Assessment Handbook, Rubric 14: Journals

Students Having Difficulty
Reaching Standards

Organize the class into small groups. Assign each group a few lines from the passage. Have groups determine which words in their assigned lines are essential subjects and verbs, and which are adjectives and adverbs. Have students read the lines in their basic forms and then add the modifiers back in. Point out that a passage's tone and meaning are often expressed with adjectives and adverbs. **LS Verbal/Linguistic**

HSS 6.7.1; ELA 6.3.4

Alternative Assessment Handbook, Rubric 14: Group Activity

Answers

Guided Reading *Ilioneus addresses the king with respect and honesty; because he needs to ask a favor of him.*

We journey to your city by design
And general consent, driven as we are
From realms in other days greatest by far
The Sun looked down on, passing on his way
From heaven's far eastern height. ❸ Our line's from Jove,
In his paternity the sons of Dardanus
Exult, and highest progeny of Jove
Include our king himself—Trojan Aeneas,
Who sent us to your threshold . . . ❹
So long on the vast waters, now we ask
A modest settlement of the gods of home,
A strip of coast that will bring harm to no one,
Air and water, open and free to all . . .
Our quest was for your country. Dardanus
Had birth here, and Apollo calls us back,
Directing us by solemn oracles
To Tuscan Tiber . . . ❺ Here besides
Aeneus gives you from his richer years
These modest gifts, relics caught up and saved
From burning Troy . . ."
           Latinus heard
Ilioneus out, his countenance averted,
Sitting immobile, all attention, eyes
Downcast but turning here and there. The embroidered
Purple and the scepter of King Priam
Moved him less in his own kingliness
Than long thoughts on the marriage of his daughter,
As he turned over in his inmost mind
Old Faunus' prophecy.
           "This is the man,"
he thought, "foretold as coming from abroad
To be my son-in-law, by fate appointed,
Called to reign here with equal authority—
The man whose heirs will be brilliant in valor
And win the mastery of the world." ❻

GUIDED READING

WORD HELP

progeny offspring
threshold door
oracle person who gives advice
averted turned away
immobile unmoving

❸ Ilioneus explains that the Trojans have come to Italy "by design"—both on purpose and with help from the gods.

❹ Aeneas and Dardanus, the founder of Troy, were both believed to be descendants of Jove, the king of the gods.

❺ The Romans believed that Troy's founder Dardanus was born in Italy.
What does Ilioneus ask the king to give the Trojans?

❻ Virgil included this vision of Rome's great future to point out the city's greatness to his readers.

CONNECTING LITERATURE TO HISTORY

1. **Analyzing** Rome's leaders wanted their city to have a glorious past that would make the Roman people proud. What details in this passage would make Roman readers proud of their past?

2. **Drawing Conclusions** When Aeneas reached Italy, he formed an alliance with the Latins. Think about how Virgil portrays the Latins in this passage. What words or phrases would you use to describe them? Why might such people make good allies?

331

Direct Teach

Did you know . . .

People have written many epic poems throughout history. Although these poems are not entirely factual, they can give us clues about the societies that produced them. They can also tell us how people viewed their own past. Other ancient epic poems and the lands where the events are set include: the *Iliad* (Greece), the *Odyssey* (Greece), the *Epic of Gilgamesh* (Mesopotamia), the *Mahabharata* (India), the *Ramayana* (India), and *Beowulf* (Denmark and Sweden).

Activity **Researching Epic Poems**
Have students conduct research on an epic poem from another culture. Direct students to library or Internet resources to discover an epic poem and to explore its cultural significance. Tell students that some epic poems served as religious texts, while others were primarily for entertainment. Have each student write a one-page report on the epic poem he or she has chosen. Optional: Have students create epic poems of their own based on the culture and time in which they live. **LS** **Verbal/Linguistic**

📖 Alternative Assessment Handbook, Rubrics 30: Research; and 37: Writing Assignments

---

Cross-Discipline Activity: English/Language Arts   **Standards Proficiency**

Understanding Poetry 🐻 **ELA** Reading 6.3.4

1. Work with the English teacher, English textbooks, or dictionaries to define and describe such terms as meter, diction, rhythm, and syntax. Write definitions for the class to see. Tell students that a poet is constantly using these elements to create an effective poem.

2. Once students understand these terms, ask them to find examples of each element of poetry in the excerpt from the *Aeneid*.

3. Then have students write two lines for each term. The two lines should demonstrate an understanding of the term. For example, the two lines should have different rhythm or different diction.

4. Tell students that it might help them if they read the lines aloud. Ask for volunteers to read their lines and demonstrate one of the key terms. **LS** **Verbal/Linguistic**

📖 Alternative Assessment Handbook, Rubric 26: Poems and Songs

Answers

Guided Reading *a piece of land on the coast where the Trojans can settle*

Connecting Literature to History
1. *the heroic trip of Aeneas and his men, the family history of Aeneas and Ilioneus, the story of heroic people working together to found Rome;* 2. *possible answers—noble, respectful, welcoming, kind, generous; because they would treat an ally as an equal*

Bellringer

If YOU were there . . . Use the **Daily Bellringer Transparency** to help students answer the question.

📖 Daily Bellringer Transparency, Section 2

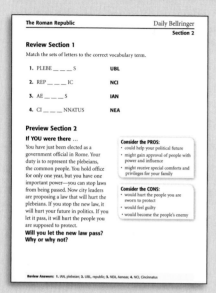

The Roman Republic   Daily Bellringer
                                              Section 2

Review Section 1

Match the sets of letters to the correct vocabulary term.

1. PLEBE _ _ _ S   **UBL**
2. REP _ _ _ IC   **NCI**
3. AE _ _ _ S   **IAN**
4. CI _ _ _ NNATUS   **NEA**

Preview Section 2

If YOU were there ...
You have just been elected as a government official in Rome. Your duty is to represent the plebeians, the common people. You hold office for only one year, but you have one important power—you can stop laws from being passed. Now city leaders are proposing a law that will hurt the plebeians. If you stop the new law, it will hurt your future in politics. If you let it pass, it will hurt the people you are supposed to protect.
Will you let the new law pass? Why or why not?

Consider the PROS:
• could help your political future
• might gain approval of people with power and influence
• might receive special comforts and privileges for your family

Consider the CONS:
• would hurt the people you are sworn to protect
• would feel guilty
• would become the people's enemy

Review Answers: 1. IAN, plebeian; 2. UBL, republic; 3. NEA, Aeneas; 4. NCI, Cincinnatus

Academic Vocabulary

Review with students the high-use academic term in this section.

primary main, most important (p. 333)

📝 **CRF:** Vocabulary Builder Activity, Section 2

🐻 Standards Focus

HSS 6.7.2

Means: Describe the government of the Roman Republic and its importance.

Matters: Elements of the government of the Roman Republic are still apparent today in the U.S. government.

Government and Society

What You Will Learn...

Main Ideas

1. Roman government was made up of three parts that worked together to run the city.
2. Written laws helped keep order in Rome.
3. The Roman Forum was the heart of Roman society.

The Big Idea

Rome's tripartite government and written laws helped create a stable society.

Key Terms

magistrates, *p. 333*
consuls, *p. 333*
Roman Senate, *p. 333*
veto, *p. 334*
Latin, *p. 334*
checks and balances, *p. 335*
Forum, *p. 335*

HSS **6.7.2** Describe the government of the Roman Republic and its significance (e.g. written constitution and tripartite government, checks and balances, civic duty).

If **YOU** were there...

You have just been elected as a government official in Rome. Your duty is to represent the plebeians, the common people. You hold office for only one year, but you have one important power—you can stop laws from being passed. Now city leaders are proposing a law that will hurt the plebeians. If you stop the new law, it will hurt your future in politics. If you let it pass, it will hurt the people you are supposed to protect.

Will you let the new law pass? Why or why not?

BUILDING BACKGROUND Government in Rome was often a balancing act. Like the politician above, leaders had to make compromises and risk the anger of other officials to keep the people happy. To keep anyone from gaining too much power, the Roman government divided power among many different officials.

Roman Government

When the plebeians complained about Rome's government in the 400s BC, the city's leaders knew they had to do something. If the people stayed unhappy, they might rise up and overthrow the whole government.

To calm the angry plebeians, the patricians made some changes to Rome's government. For example, they created new offices that could only be held by plebeians. The people who held these offices protected the plebeians' rights and interests. Gradually, the distinctions between patricians and plebeians began to disappear, but that took a very long time.

As a result of the changes the patricians made, Rome developed a tripartite (try-PAHR-tyt) government, or a government with three parts. Each part had its own responsibilities and duties. To fulfill its duties, each part of the government had its own powers, rights, and privileges.

Teach the Big Idea: Master the Standards   Standards Proficiency

Government and Society 🐻 **HSS** 6.7.2

1. **Teach** Ask students the Main Idea questions to teach this section.

2. **Apply** Have students skim over the section and the Quick Facts information. Then have students pick out the names of key offices, assemblies, and other concepts. Write the names and terms for students to see, but not as a list; space them out randomly across the page to form the basis of an idea web.
LS **Verbal/Linguistic**

3. **Review** As you review the section's main ideas, call on volunteers to add arrows or other symbols to the display of terms to indicate how they were related to each other. Students should also add labels to describe the connections among terms.

4. **Practice/Homework** Have students copy the idea webs and add more connections and/or details.

📝 Alternative Assessment Handbook, Rubric 13: Graphic Organizers

Magistrates

The first part of Rome's government was made up of elected officials, or **magistrates** (MA-juh-strayts). The two most powerful magistrates in Rome were called **consuls** (KAHN-suhlz). The consuls were elected each year to run the city and lead the army. There were two consuls so that no one person would be too powerful.

Below the consuls were other magistrates. Rome had many different types of magistrates. Each was elected for one year and had his own duties and powers. Some were judges. Others managed Rome's finances or organized games and festivals.

Senate

The second part of Rome's government was the Senate. The **Roman Senate** was a council of wealthy and powerful Romans that advised the city's leaders. It was originally created to advise Rome's kings. After the kings were gone, the Senate continued to meet to advise consuls.

Unlike magistrates, senators—members of the Senate—held office for life. By the time the republic was created, the Senate had 300 members. At first most senators were patricians, but as time passed many wealthy plebeians became senators as well. Because magistrates became senators after completing their terms in office, most didn't want to anger the Senate and risk their future jobs.

As time passed the Senate became more powerful. It gained influence over magistrates and took control of the city's finances. By 200 BC the Senate had great influence in Rome's government.

Assemblies and Tribunes

The third part of Rome's government, the part that protected the common people, had two branches. The first branch was made up of assemblies. Both patricians and plebeians took part in these assemblies. Their **primary** job was to elect the magistrates who ran the city of Rome.

FOCUS ON READING

If you were outlining the discussion on this page, what headings would you use?

ACADEMIC VOCABULARY

primary main, most important

Government of the Roman Republic
QUICK FACTS

Magistrates	Senate	Assemblies and Tribunes
■ Consuls led the government and army, judged court cases ■ Served for one year ■ Had power over all citizens, including other officials	■ Advised the consuls ■ Served for life ■ Gained control of financial affairs	■ Represented the common people, approved or rejected laws, declared war, elected magistrates ■ Roman citizens could take part in assemblies all their adult lives, tribunes served for one year ■ Could veto the decisions of consuls and other magistrates

THE ROMAN REPUBLIC **333**

Direct Teach

Main Idea

❶ Roman Government

Roman government was made up of three parts that worked together to run the city.

Define What was a consul? *the most powerful magistrate in Rome*

Explain Why was the Senate so powerful? *because senators held office for life and because magistrates didn't want to anger the Senate*

Draw Conclusions Why were the assemblies and tribunes a necessary part of the government? *They protected the rights of plebeians and had the power to veto actions by other government officials.*

HSS 6.7.2; HSS Analysis Skills: HI 3

go.hrw.com
Online Resources

KEYWORD: SQ6 WH11
ACTIVITY: Government Then & Now

Other People, Other Places

The Qin Dynasty At about the same time that the Romans were developing a republic, a Chinese dynasty was forming a very different sort of government. Emperor Shi Huangdi, the founder of the Qin dynasty, held complete power over the Chinese people. He ruled by very strict laws and made the peasants pay heavy taxes. To prevent criticism and free thought, he ordered all books burned except for those on practical subjects, such as medicine.

Differentiating Instruction for Universal Access

Students Having Difficulty   Reaching Standards

1. Copy the graphic organizer for students to see, omitting the blue, italicized answers. Have students copy it.

2. Remind students that the Roman government had three levels. Tell them the U.S. government also has levels, such as federal, state, and local.

3. Have students use phone books and the Internet to find the names of their government officials at these levels. **LS** Visual/Spatial

HSS 6.7.2; HSS Analysis Skills: HI 3
Alternate Assessment Handbook, Rubric 1: Acquiring Information

Your Elected Officials

Federal	State	Local
President, Senator, Congressperson	*Governor, State Senator, State Representative*	*Mayor, City Council Member, Sheriff*

Answers

Focus on Reading *Magistrates, Senate, Assemblies and Tribunes*

333

Main Idea

❶ Roman Government

Roman government was made up of three parts that worked together to run the city.

Identify What was the veto? Which branch of the Roman government had this authority? *to stop or prohibit actions of other government officials; tribunes*

Explain How did the government keep tribunes from becoming too powerful? *They were limited to serving for only one year.*

Draw Conclusions How was civic duty demonstrated in Rome? *People participated in government by attending meetings and voting; the wealthy felt it was their duty to serve.*

📄 **CRF:** Interdisciplinary Project: The Romans: Response Rally

🐻 **HSS** 6.7.2; **HSS** Analysis Skills: HR 1

Connect to Government

Checks and Balances An elaborate system of checks and balances is written into the U.S. Constitution. This ensures that no one branch obtains too much power. For example, the president has the authority to veto bills from Congress. Only Congress has the authority to declare war, not the president. The Supreme Court has the authority to interpret laws passed by Congress. Every branch of government has some form of check over the other two branches.

Answers

Analyzing Information *possible answers—because it was a government run by many people, not just a few; because it worked well for the Roman Republic*

334

Do as the Romans Do

The government of the Roman Republic was one of its greatest strengths. When the founders of the United States sat down to plan our government, they copied many elements of the Roman system. Like the Romans, we elect our leaders. Our government also has three branches—the president, Congress, and the federal court system. The powers of these branches are set forth in our Constitution, just like the Roman officials' powers were. Our government also has a system of checks and balances to prevent any one branch from becoming too strong. For example, Congress can refuse to give the president money to pay for programs. Like the Romans, Americans have a civic duty to participate in the government to help keep it as strong as it can be.

ANALYSIS SKILL **ANALYZING INFORMATION**

Why do you think the founders of the United States borrowed ideas from Roman government?

THE IMPACT TODAY

Like tribunes, the president of the United States has the power to veto actions by other government officials.

The second branch was made up of a group of elected officials called tribunes. Elected by the plebeians, tribunes had the ability to **veto** (VEE-toh), or prohibit, actions by other officials. Veto means "I forbid" in **Latin**, the Romans' language. This veto power made tribunes very powerful in Rome's government. To keep them from abusing their power, each tribune remained in office only one year.

Civic Duty

Rome's government would not have worked without the participation of the people. People participated in the government because they felt it was their civic duty, or their duty to the city. That civic duty included doing what they could to make sure the city prospered. For example,

they were expected to attend assembly meetings and to vote in elections. Voting in Rome was a complicated process, and not everyone was allowed to do it. Those who could, however, were expected to take part in all elections.

Wealthy and powerful citizens also felt it was their duty to hold public office to help run the city. In return for their time and commitment, these citizens were respected and admired by other Romans.

Checks and Balances

In addition to limiting terms of office, the Romans put other restrictions on their leaders' power. They did this by giving government officials the ability to restrict the powers of other officials. For example, one consul could block the actions of the other.

334 CHAPTER 11

Critical Thinking: Comparing

Standards Proficiency

Civic Duty, Then and Now 🐻 **HSS** 6.7.2; **HSS** Analysis Skills: HI 1, HI 3

1. Discuss with students what they have learned about civic duty in the Roman Republic. Tell them that, just as our government is similar to the Romans' form of government, Americans have similar civic duties.

2. Have students write a brief essay comparing the civic duty of American citizens to the civic duty of a Roman citizen. Tell them to include specific examples of how an American can fulfill his or her civic duty.

Encourage students to consider and discuss in their papers how citizens who are not yet old enough to vote can still perform such duties.

3. Ask for volunteers to read their essays to the class. **LS** Verbal/Linguistic

📄 Alternative Assessment Handbook, Rubric 42: Writing to Inform

Laws proposed by the Senate had to be approved by magistrates and ratified by assemblies. We call these methods to balance power **checks and balances**. Checks and balances keep any one part of a government from becoming stronger or more influential than the others.

Checks and balances made Rome's government very complicated. Sometimes quarrels arose when officials had different ideas or opinions. When officials worked together, however, Rome's government was strong and efficient, as one Roman historian noted:

> "In unison [together] they are a match for any and all emergencies, the result being that it is impossible to find a constitution that is better constructed. For whenever some common external danger should come upon them and should compel [force] them to band together in counsel [thought] and in action, the power of their state becomes so great that nothing that is required is neglected [ignored]."
> –Polybius, from *The Constitution of the Roman Republic*

READING CHECK **Finding Main Ideas** What were the three parts of the Roman government?

Written Laws Keep Order

Rome's officials were responsible for making the city's laws and making sure that people followed them. At first these laws weren't written down. The only people who knew all the laws were the patricians who had made them.

Many people were unhappy with this situation. They did not want to be punished for breaking laws they didn't even know existed. As a result, they began to call for Rome's laws to be written down and made accessible to everybody.

Rome's first written law code was produced in 450 BC on 12 bronze tables, or tablets. These tables were displayed in

the **Forum**, Rome's public meeting place. Because of how it was displayed, this code was called the Law of the Twelve Tables.

Over time, Rome's leaders passed many new laws. Throughout their history, though the Romans looked to the Law of the Twelve Tables as a symbol of Roman law and of their rights as Roman citizens.

READING CHECK **Making Inferences** Why did many people want a written law code?

Primary Source

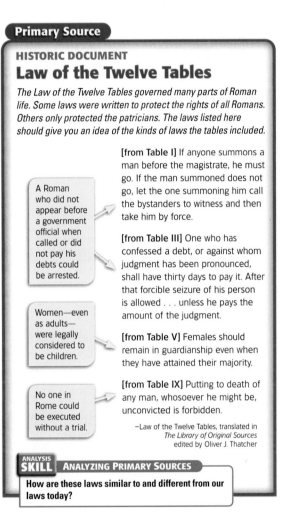

HISTORIC DOCUMENT
Law of the Twelve Tables

The Law of the Twelve Tables governed many parts of Roman life. Some laws were written to protect the rights of all Romans. Others only protected the patricians. The laws listed here should give you an idea of the kinds of laws the tables included.

A Roman who did not appear before a government official when called or did not pay his debts could be arrested.

[from Table I] If anyone summons a man before the magistrate, he must go. If the man summoned does not go, let the one summoning him call the bystanders to witness and then take him by force.

[from Table III] One who has confessed a debt, or against whom judgment has been pronounced, shall have thirty days to pay it. After that forcible seizure of his person is allowed . . . unless he pays the amount of the judgment.

Women—even as adults—were legally considered to be children.

[from Table V] Females should remain in guardianship even when they have attained their majority.

No one in Rome could be executed without a trial.

[from Table IX] Putting to death of any man, whosoever he might be, unconvicted is forbidden.

–Law of the Twelve Tables, translated in *The Library of Original Sources* edited by Oliver J. Thatcher

ANALYSIS SKILL **ANALYZING PRIMARY SOURCES**

How are these laws similar to and different from our laws today?

335

❸ The Roman Forum

The Roman Forum was the heart of Roman society.

Recall Where was the Law of the Twelve Tables kept? *the Forum*

Identify What kind of buildings were in the Forum, and what else drew people there? *important government buildings and temples; shops, fights, public ceremonies*

Predict How do you think an Italian farmer who had never before been to the city of Rome would feel when he first stepped into the Roman Forum? *possible answers—impressed, proud that he was part of so grand a republic*

🐻 **HSS** 6.7.2

Linking to Today

The Basilica Aemilia The building shown to the right of the Senate House, the Basilica Aemilia, was a gathering place for moneylenders and moneychangers. Built in 179 BC, the building was larger than a football field. Today, visitors to the site can still see small round greenish spots on the ruin's pavement stones. These spots may be all that is left of copper coins that melted when fire destroyed the basilica in AD 410. Ask students why the Forum was a good place for money-changers to do business. *possible answers—because people gathered there from all over the republic, and they may have had different kinds of money*

Answers

Analyzing Visuals *possible answers— The buildings are large and impressive, and the square is well maintained; the square is full of citizens.*

336

History Close-up

The Roman Forum

The Forum was the center of life in ancient Rome. The city's most important temples and government buildings were located there, and Romans met there to talk about the issues of the day. The word *forum* means "public place."

The Temple of Jupiter stood atop the Capitoline Hill, overlooking the Forum.

Roman citizens often wore togas, loose-fitting garments wrapped around the body. Togas were symbols of Roman citizenship.

Important government records were stored in the Tabularium.

Public officials often addressed people from this platform.

ANALYSIS SKILL **ANALYZING VISUALS**

What can you see in this illustration that indicates the Forum was an important place?

336 CHAPTER 11

The Roman Forum

The Roman Forum, the place where the Law of the Twelve Tables was kept, was the heart of the city of Rome. It was the site of important government buildings and temples. Government and religion were only part of what made the Forum so important, though. It was also a popular meeting place for Roman citizens. People met there to shop, chat, and gossip.

Collaborative Learning

Reaching Standards

Roman Forum Video Game 🐻 **HSS** 6.7.2; **Analysis Skills:** **HSS** HI 1 | **Standard English Mastery**

1. Organize the class into small groups. Ask students to imagine that they work for a video game company that wants to create a new game called *Roman Forum*.

2. Have students work together to plan some characters and events for their game. For example, they may include government officials and shopkeepers, amazing spectacles, and fiery speeches.

3. Then have students use standard English to write five sentences describing the game's characters and events. Each sentence should have at least 10 words.

4. Call on a volunteer from each group to read the group's sentences. As a class, discuss any necessary corrections to the sentences to align them with standard English usage.

LS Interpersonal, Verbal/Linguistic

The Forum lay in the center of Rome, between two major hills. On one side was the Palatine (PA-luh-tyn) Hill, where Rome's richest people lived. Across the forum was the Capitoline (KA-pet-uhl-yn) Hill, where Rome's grandest temples stood. Because of this location, city leaders could often be found in or near the forum, mingling with the common people. These leaders used the Forum as a speaking area, delivering speeches to the crowds.

But the Forum also had attractions for people not interested in speeches. Various shops lined the open square, and fights between gladiators were sometimes held there. Public ceremonies were commonly held in the Forum as well. As a result, the forum was usually packed with people.

READING CHECK **Making Generalizations** How was the Forum the heart of Roman society?

SUMMARY AND PREVIEW In this section you read about the basic structure of Roman government. In the next section you'll see how that government changed as Rome's territory grew and its influence expanded.

The Senate met here in the curia, or Senate House.

Section 2 Assessment

go.hrw.com
Online Quiz
KEYWORD: SQ6 HP11

Reviewing Ideas, Terms, and People HSS 6.7.2

1. **a. Identify** Who were the **consuls**?
   b. Explain Why did the Romans create a system of **checks and balances**?
   c. Elaborate How do you think the **Roman Senate** gained power?
2. **a. Recall** What was Rome's first written law code called?
   b. Draw Conclusions Why did Romans want their laws written down?
3. **a. Describe** What kinds of activities took place in the Roman **Forum**?

Critical Thinking

4. **Analyzing Information** Draw a diagram like the one at right. In each oval, list the main powers of each part of Rome's government.

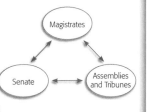

FOCUS ON SPEAKING

5. **Choosing a Topic** You've just read about Roman laws and government. Would anything related to these topics make good subjects for your legend? Write some ideas in your notebook.

THE ROMAN REPUBLIC **337**

Section 2 Assessment Answers

1. **a.** two leaders elected to run the city of Rome
   b. to prevent any one person from gaining too much power
   c. Possible answer—They controlled Rome's finances, which gave them power over magistrates who needed money to do their jobs.

2. **a.** Law of the Twelve Tables
   b. so people wouldn't be accused of breaking laws they didn't know existed

3. religious ceremonies, speeches, social gatherings, shopping, gladiatorial combat

4. Magistrates: elected officials who were judges, managed finances or organized games and festivals; Senate: advised city leaders and later took control of the city finances; Assemblies and Tribunes: assemblies—patricians and plebeians who elected city leaders; tribunes—elected officials who could veto actions of other government officials

5. Ideas should include details about how rulers came into power.

If YOU were there . . . Use the **Daily Bellringer Transparency** to help students answer the question.

 Daily Bellringer Transparency, Section 3

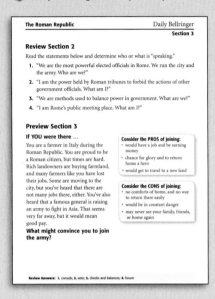

The Roman Republic   Daily Bellringer
                                         Section 3

Review Section 2

Read the statements below and determine who or what is "speaking."

1. "We are the most powerful elected officials in Rome. We run the city and the army. Who are we?"
2. "I am the power held by Roman tribunes to forbid the actions of other government officials. What am I?"
3. "We are methods used to balance power in government. What are we?"
4. "I am Rome's public meeting place. What am I?"

Preview Section 3

If YOU were there ...

You are a farmer in Italy during the Roman Republic. You are proud to be a Roman citizen, but times are hard. Rich landowners are buying farmland, and many farmers like you have lost their jobs. Some are moving to the city, but you've heard that there are not many jobs there, either. You've also heard that a famous general is raising an army to fight in Asia. That seems very far away, but it would mean good pay.

What might convince you to join the army?

Consider the PROS of joining:
• would have a job and be earning money
• chance for glory and to return home a hero
• would get to travel to a new land

Consider the CONS of joining:
• no comforts of home, and no way to return there easily
• would be in constant danger
• may never see your family, friends, or home again

Review Answers: 1. consuls; 2. veto; 3. checks and balances; 4. forum

Academic Vocabulary

Review with students the high-use academic term in this section.

purpose: the reason something is done (p. 342)

 CRF: Vocabulary Builder Activity, Section 3

Standards Focus

HSS 6.7.3

Means: Describe how the Roman Empire spread and gained power through economic growth and trade.

Matters: Economic growth has been key to the expansion of many empires throughout history.

If YOU were there...

You are a farmer in Italy during the Roman Republic. You are proud to be a Roman citizen, but times are hard. Rich landowners are buying farmland, and many farmers like you have lost their jobs. Some are moving to the city, but you've heard that there are not many jobs there, either. You've also heard that a famous general is raising an army to fight in Asia. That seems very far away, but it would mean good pay.

What might convince you to join the army?

What You Will Learn...

Main Ideas

1. The late republic period saw the growth of territory and trade.
2. Through wars, Rome grew beyond Italy.
3. Several crises struck the republic in its later years.

The Big Idea

The later period of the Roman Republic was marked by wars of expansion and political crises.

Key Terms and People

legions, *p. 339*
Punic Wars, *p. 339*
Hannibal, *p. 340*
Gaius Marius, *p. 342*
Lucius Cornelius Sulla, *p. 343*
Spartacus, *p. 343*

HSS **6.7.3** Identify the location of and the political and geographic reasons for the growth of Roman territories and expansion of the empire, including how the empire fostered economic growth through the use of currency and trade routes.

BUILDING BACKGROUND The Roman army played a vital part in the expansion of the republic. Roman soldiers were well trained and defeated many of the city's enemies. As they did so, the Romans took over new lands. As the army conquered these new lands, traders moved in, seeking new products and markets that could make them rich.

Growth of Territory and Trade

After about 400 BC the Roman Republic grew quickly, both geographically and economically. Within 200 years the Roman army had conquered nearly all of Italy. Meanwhile Roman traders had begun to ship goods back and forth around the Mediterranean in search of new products and wealth.

Growth of Territory

Roman territory grew mainly in response to outside threats. In about 387 BC a people called the Gauls attacked Rome and took over the city. The Romans had to give the Gauls a huge amount of gold to leave the city.

Inspired by the Gauls' victory, many of Rome's neighboring cities also decided to attack. With some difficulty, the Romans fought off these attacks. As Rome's attackers were defeated, the Romans took over their lands. As you can see on the map, the Romans soon controlled all of the Italian Peninsula except far northern Italy.

Teach the Big Idea: Master the Standards   Standards Proficiency

The Late Republic   **HSS** 6.7.3; **HSS** Analysis Skills: CS 1, HI 1, HI 3

1. **Teach** Ask students the Main Idea questions to teach this section.

2. **Apply** Have students study the sequencing of this section's events by creating a flowchart that traces the growth of and changes within the late republic. Flowcharts should consist of boxes connected by arrows. The first box should be labeled *Gauls attack Rome.* From there, have students trace the events as the republic faced various crises. **LS** **Visual/Spatial**

3. **Review** As you review the section's main ideas, have students fill in their flowcharts.

4. **Practice/Homework** Have students add relevant facts to the boxes. **LS** **Visual/Spatial**

 Alternative Assessment Handbook, Rubric 7: Charts

One reason for the Roman success was the organization of the army. Soldiers were organized in **legions** (LEE-juhnz), or groups of up to 6,000 soldiers. Each legion was divided into centuries, or groups of 100 soldiers. This organization allowed the army to be very flexible. It could fight as a large group or as several small ones. This flexibility allowed the Romans to defeat most enemies.

Farming and Trade

Before Rome conquered Italy, most Romans were farmers. As the republic grew, many people left their farms for Rome. In place of these small farms, wealthy Romans built large farms in the countryside. These farms were worked by slaves who grew one or two crops. The owners of the farms didn't usually live on them. Instead, they stayed in Rome or other cities and let others run the farms for them.

Roman trade also expanded as the republic grew. Rome's farmers couldn't grow enough food to support the city's increasing population, so merchants brought food from other parts of the Mediterranean. These merchants also brought metal goods and slaves to Rome. To pay for these goods, the Romans made coins out of copper, silver, and other metals. Roman coins began to appear in markets all around the Mediterranean.

READING CHECK **Identifying Cause and Effect** Why did the Romans conquer their neighbors?

Rome Grows Beyond Italy

As Rome's power grew other countries came to see the Romans as a threat to their own power and declared war on them. In the end the Romans defeated their opponents, and Rome gained territory throughout the Mediterranean.

The Roman Republic, 509–270 BC

Roman lands in 509 BC
Roman lands in 270 BC

0   75   150 Miles
0   75   150 Kilometers

Ligurian Sea

Rome

Adriatic Sea

Tyrrhenian Sea

Mediterranean Sea

Ionian Sea

Carthage

GEOGRAPHY SKILLS **INTERPRETING MAPS**
Location What seas bordered Roman lands in 270 BC?

The Punic Wars

The fiercest of the wars Rome fought were the **Punic** (PYOO-nik) **Wars**, a series of wars against Carthage, a city in northern Africa. The word *Punic* means "Phoenician" in Latin. As you learned earlier in this book, the Phoenicians were an ancient civilization that had built the city of Carthage.

Rome and Carthage went to war three times between 264 and 146 BC. The wars began when Carthage sent its armies to Sicily, an island just southwest of Italy. In response, the Romans also sent an army to the island. Before long, war broke out between them. After almost 20 years of fighting, the Romans forced their enemies out and took control of Sicily.

THE ROMAN REPUBLIC **339**

Did you know . . .

Roman coins display various images and words, such as the word *Roma*, the Latin spelling of Rome. Some coins commemorate a victory in battle. These coins were called *victoriates*. When economic times were bad, the crisis was reflected in the coins. Coins made then would contain less of the precious metal. As a result, these coins weighed less than those made during prosperous periods.

339

❷ Rome Grows Beyond Italy

Through wars, Rome grew beyond Italy.

Identify Who did Rome fight in the Punic Wars? *Carthage*

Recall Who was the Carthaginian general who almost defeated Rome? *Hannibal*

Predict How might history have turned out differently if a bad storm at sea had delayed the Romans' crossing to northern Africa? *possible answer— Hannibal might have had time to capture Rome itself, ending the Roman Republic and eliminating Roman power in the region.*

Activity Letters from Spies

Have students write excerpts from mock correspondence between Roman or Carthaginian spies and the generals to whom they reported about the progress of the Punic Wars.

📝 **CRF:** Biography Activity: Scipio

📝 **CRF:** History and Geography Activity: The Punic Wars

💻 **CRF:** Map Transparency: The Roman Republic, 270–100 BC

HSS 6.7.3; **HSS** Analysis Skills: CS 3, HI 2, HI 4

Info to Know

Battle of Zama Scipio had about the same number of troops as Hannibal, but his cavalry was stronger. Despite Hannibal's well-organized defense outside of Carthage, Scipio's troops crushed Hannibal's army. About 20,000 of the Carthaginian soldiers were killed. The city of Carthage quickly accepted Scipio's terms for surrender.

In 218 BC Carthage tried to attack Rome itself. An army led by the brilliant general **Hannibal** set out for Rome. Although he forced the Romans right to the edge of defeat, Hannibal was never able to capture Rome itself. In the meantime, the Romans sent an army to attack Carthage. Hannibal rushed home to defend his city, but his troops were defeated at Zama (ZAY-muh) in the battle illustrated below.

By the 140s BC many senators had grown alarmed that Carthage was growing powerful again. They convinced Rome's consuls to declare war on Carthage, and once again the Romans sent an army to Africa and destroyed Carthage. After this victory, the Romans burned the city, killed most of its people, and sold the rest of the people into slavery. They also took control of northern Africa.

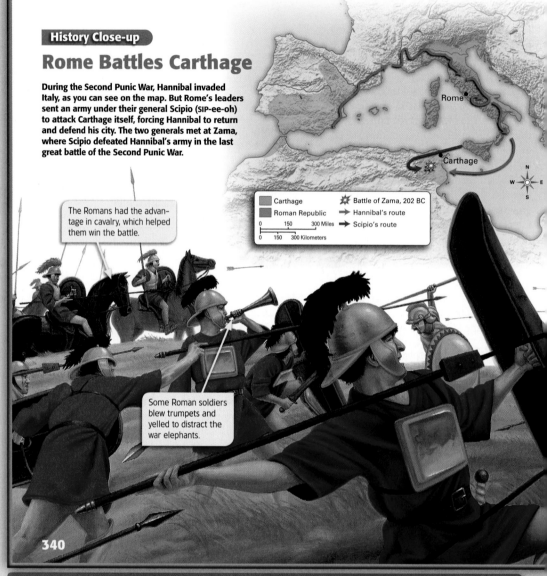

History Close-up

Rome Battles Carthage

During the Second Punic War, Hannibal invaded Italy, as you can see on the map. But Rome's leaders sent an army under their general Scipio (SIP-ee-oh) to attack Carthage itself, forcing Hannibal to return and defend his city. The two generals met at Zama, where Scipio defeated Hannibal's army in the last great battle of the Second Punic War.

The Romans had the advantage in cavalry, which helped them win the battle.

Some Roman soldiers blew trumpets and yelled to distract the war elephants.

	Carthage	☀ Battle of Zama, 202 BC
	Roman Republic	→ Hannibal's route
		➡ Scipio's route

0   150   300 Miles
0   150   300 Kilometers

340

Critical Thinking: Describing

Standards Proficiency

Making News 🐾 **HSS** 6.7.3; **HSS** Analysis Skills: HI 1

1. Tell students that a newsreel was a short film that discussed current events. Tell them that newsreels were often shown before movies in the 1930s and 1940s, often to give news about events that led up to World War II and about the war itself.

2. Have students write the text for a newsreel announcing the defeat of Hannibal at the Battle of Zama. Tell students newsreels were often sensational and dramatic, and they should include similar language.

3. Ask volunteers to read the texts aloud, using dramatic voices. 📢 **Verbal/Linguistic**

📝 Alternative Assessment Handbook, Rubric 42: Writing to Inform

Later Expansion

During the Punic Wars, Rome took control of Sicily, Corsica, Spain, and North Africa. As a result, Rome controlled most of the western Mediterranean region.

In the years that followed, Roman legions marched north and east as well. In the 120s Rome conquered the southern part of Gaul. By that time, Rome had also conquered Greece and parts of Asia.

Although the Romans took over Greece, they were greatly changed by the experience. We would normally expect the victor to change the conquered country. Instead, the Romans adopted ideas about literature, art, philosophy, religion, and education from the Greeks.

READING CHECK **Summarizing** How did the Romans gain territory?

BIOGRAPHY

Hannibal
247–183 BC

Many historians consider Hannibal to be one of the greatest generals of the ancient world. From an early age, he hated Rome. In 218 BC he began the Second Punic War by attacking one of Rome's allies in Spain. After the war he became the leader of Carthage, but later he was forced by the Romans to flee the city. He went to Asia and joined with a king fighting the Romans there. The king was defeated, and Hannibal killed himself so that he wouldn't become a Roman prisoner.

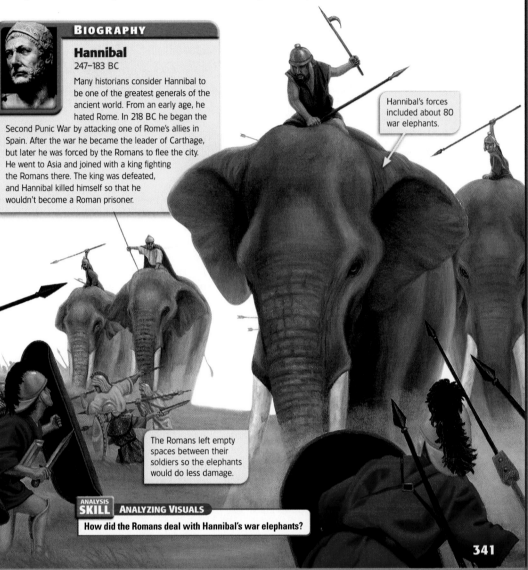

Hannibal's forces included about 80 war elephants.

The Romans left empty spaces between their soldiers so the elephants would do less damage.

ANALYSIS SKILL **ANALYZING VISUALS**

How did the Romans deal with Hannibal's war elephants?

341

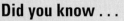

Direct Teach

Did you know . . .

While fighting in Italy, Hannibal found his route blocked by a Roman army. To get past the Romans, Hannibal used a clever tactic. He sent a very odd force out under cover of night—2,000 oxen with lighted torches tied to their horns. The Romans thought they were under attack and moved from their position, clearing the way for Hannibal to march through.

Activity **Hannibal's Journal** Have students imagine they are Hannibal at the time he is about to defeat Rome. Ask them to imagine how he felt when he heard the Romans were attacking Carthage. Instruct students to write a journal entry in the voice of Hannibal expressing his feelings about events that led up to the Battle of Zama. Ask for volunteers to read their entries aloud. **LS** Verbal/Linguistic

Collaborative Learning

Standards Proficiency

Mapping the Elephants' March 🐘 **HSS** 6.7.3; **HSS** Analysis Skills: CS 3   Research Required

Background Hannibal attempted an amazing feat by leading his army, including more than 30 elephants, overland from Spain to Italy. However, all but one of the elephants died along the way.

1. Organize students into small groups to conduct research on Hannibal's trip.

2. Direct students to library or Internet resources where they can find maps of Hannibal's route through Spain and France, through the Alps, and into Italy.

3. Have each group create a map of the Mediterranean that shows Hannibal's route.

4. Tell students to add location names and illustrations to the map. **LS** Interpersonal, Visual/Spatial

   Alternative Assessment Handbook, Rubrics 14: Group Activity; and 20: Map Creation

Answers

Analyzing Visuals *spread out so they would suffer fewer loses; blew trumpets and yelled to distract elephants*

Reading Check *They took control of areas during the Punic Wars. From there, they spread north and east, conquering Gaul, Greece, and parts of Asia.*

❸ Crises Strike the Republic

Several crises struck the republic in its later years.

Describe How did Tiberius and Gaius Gracchus try to help poor Romans? *They tried to create farms for poor Romans and to sell food cheaply to poor citizens.*

Explain Why was violence more common after the Gracchus brothers than before? *People saw that violence could be used as a political weapon.*

Find the Main Idea Why might it be a problem if a nation's army is more loyal to leaders than to the government? *The army could become a political tool, and individuals could take control of the government if they had the army on their side.*

📄 **CRF:** Biography Activity: Cornelia

🐻 **HSS** 6.7.3; **HSS** Analysis Skills: HI 1

Biography

Gaius Gracchus (153–121 BC) In today's political language, Gaius Gracchus would be called a grassroots reformer. He tried to harness the many votes of poor citizens in passing his reforms. These agricultural reforms were similar to the ones for which his brother had been killed. Unfortunately for Gaius, his actions were also unpopular with many senators. He never saw his reforms put into place.

Answers

Interpreting Maps *most of Spain, southern Gaul, northern Italy, islands in the Mediterranean (including Sicily, Corsica, and Sardinia), part of northern Africa, Greece, Macedonia, and Asia Minor*

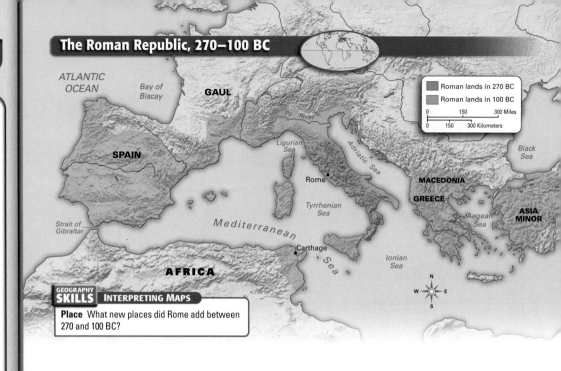

The Roman Republic, 270–100 BC

ATLANTIC OCEAN · Bay of Biscay · GAUL · SPAIN · Po River · Ligurian Sea · Rome · Adriatic Sea · MACEDONIA · GREECE · Black Sea · ASIA MINOR · Aegean Sea · Tyrrhenian Sea · Strait of Gibraltar · Mediterranean Sea · Carthage · Ionian Sea · AFRICA

Roman lands in 270 BC
Roman lands in 100 BC
0 150 300 Miles
0 150 300 Kilometers

GEOGRAPHY SKILLS INTERPRETING MAPS
Place What new places did Rome add between 270 and 100 BC?

Crises Strike the Republic

As the Romans' territory grew, problems arose in the republic. Rich citizens were getting richer, and many leaders feared that violence would erupt between rich and poor.

Tiberius and Gaius Gracchus

Among the first leaders to address Rome's problems were brothers named Tiberius (ty-BIR-ee-uhs) and Gaius Gracchus (GY-uhs GRAK-uhs). Both served as tribunes.

Tiberius, who took office in 133 BC, wanted to create farms for poor Romans. The **purpose** of these farms was to keep the poor citizens happy and prevent rebellions. Tiberius wanted to create his farms on public land that wealthy citizens had illegally taken over. The public supported this idea, but the wealthy citizens opposed it. Conflict over the idea led to riots in the city, during which Tiberius was killed.

ACADEMIC VOCABULARY
purpose the reason something is done

A few years later Gaius also tried to create new farms. He also began to sell food cheaply to Rome's poor citizens. Like his brother, Gaius angered many powerful Romans and was killed for his ideas.

The violent deaths of the Gracchus brothers changed Roman politics. From that time on people saw violence as a political weapon. They often attacked leaders with whom they disagreed.

Marius and Sulla

In the late 100s BC another social change nearly led to the end of the republic. In 107 BC the Roman army desperately needed more troops. In response, a consul named **Gaius Marius** (MER-ee-uhs) encouraged poor people to join the army. Before, only people who owned property had been allowed to join. As a result of this change, thousands of poor and unemployed citizens joined Rome's army.

Cross-Discipline Activity: Arts and the Humanities · Reaching Standards

Honoring Heroes 🐻 **HSS** 6.7.3; **HSS** Analysis Skills: HI 1

1. Have each student design a memorial honoring the Gracchus brothers. Tell students that memorials can take many forms, such as walls, buildings, plaques, or statues.

2. Remind students to remember the causes for which the Gracchus brothers fought, including help for the poor and agricultural reform. The memorials should reflect these causes.

3. Have students sketch their designs from two different angles.

4. Call on volunteers to discuss their designs. Display memorial designs in the classroom.
LS Intrapersonal, Visual/Spatial

📄 Alternative Assessment Handbook, Rubric 3: Artwork

Because Marius was a good general, his troops were more loyal to him than they were to Rome. The army's support gave Marius great political power. Following his example, other ambitious politicians also sought their armies' support.

One such politician, **Lucius Cornelius Sulla** (LOO-shuhs kawr-NEEL-yuhs SUHL-uh), became consul in 88 BC. Sulla soon came into conflict with Marius, a conflict that led to a civil war in Rome. A civil war is a war between citizens of the same country. In the end Sulla defeated Marius. He later named himself dictator and used his power to punish his enemies.

Spartacus

Not long after Sulla died, another crisis arose to challenge Rome's leaders. Thousands of slaves led by a former gladiator, **Spartacus** (SPAHR-tuh-kuhs), rose up and demanded freedom.

Spartacus and his followers defeated an army sent to stop them and took over much of southern Italy. Eventually, though, Spartacus was killed in battle. Without his leadership, the revolt fell apart. Victorious, the Romans executed 6,000 rebellious slaves as an example to others who thought about rebelling. The rebellion was over, but the republic's problems were not.

 **READING CHECK** **Predicting** How do you think Marius and Sulla influenced later leaders?

SUMMARY AND PREVIEW You have read about crises that arose in the late Roman Republic. These crises eventually led to changes in society, as you will see in the next chapter.

Section 3 Assessment

go.hrw.com
Online Quiz
KEYWORD: SQ6 HP11

Reviewing Ideas, Terms, and People HSS 6.7.3

1. **a. Define** What was a Roman **legion**?
   b. Explain Why did the Romans decide to conquer all of Italy?
   c. Elaborate How did the growth of territory help increase Roman trade?
2. **a. Recall** Who fought in the **Punic Wars**?
   b. Summarize What led to the beginning of the Punic Wars?
   c. Elaborate Why do you think the Romans borrowed many ideas from Greek culture?
3. **a. Identify** Who was **Spartacus**?
   b. Explain How did the deaths of the Gracchus brothers change Roman politics?

Critical Thinking

4. **Summarizing** Draw an idea web like the one here. In each of the outer circles, list a crisis that faced Rome during the later period of the republic. Then list two facts about each crisis.

Crises

FOCUS ON SPEAKING

5. **Selecting Characters** In this section you learned about many major figures in Roman history. Choose one of them to be the subject of your legend. Now look back at your notes. How will you make the subject of your legend interesting for your listeners?

THE ROMAN REPUBLIC **343**

Section 3 Assessment Answers

1. **a.** a group of up to 6,000 soldiers
   b. because other groups continually attacked them
   c. Because local farmers couldn't grow enough food to support the city of Rome, merchants brought in food from elsewhere, along with metals and slaves.

2. **a.** Rome and Carthage
   b. Carthage sent armies into Sicily.
   c. possible answer—They admired Greek culture.

3. **a.** a former gladiator who led a slave revolt
   b. After their deaths, people began to see violence as a political tool.

4. possible answers—Crises: Punic Wars, conflicts between the Gracchus brothers and powerful Romans, change in the army under Marius, civil war between Marius and Sulla, slave revolt under Spartacus; Supporting facts will vary but should be consistent with text.

5. possible answers—descriptive words, detailed battle scenes, colorful setting

Social Studies Skills

HSS Analysis CS 3 Use maps to identify cultural features.

| Analysis | Critical Thinking | Participation | Study |

Interpreting Culture Maps

Activity Culture Map Scavenger Hunt Have students go on a culture map scavenger hunt. Give students a set amount of time to find three examples of culture maps in their textbooks. Have students mark the pages of each map. Award the first student to find three maps a prize of some kind. Have the winning student identify the pages on which the maps are located. Then guide students in interpreting each of the three maps. Conclude by having each student write a few sentences describing in his or her own words what a culture map is.

LS Visual/Spatial

Alternative Assessment Handbook, Rubric 21: Map Reading

Interactive Skills Tutor CD-ROM, Lesson 6: Interpret Maps, Graphs, Charts, Visuals, and Political Cartoons

HSS Analysis Skills: CS 3

Interpreting Culture Maps

Understand the Skill

A culture map is a special type of political map. As you know, physical maps show natural features, such as mountains and rivers. Political maps show the human features of an area, such as boundaries, cities, and roads. The human features shown on a culture map are cultural ones, such as the languages spoken or religions practiced in an area. Historians often use culture maps in their work. Therefore, being able to interpret them is important for understanding history.

Learn the Skill

The process for interpreting a culture map is similar to that for understanding any other map. Follow these guidelines.

1. Use map basics. Read the title to identify the subject. Note the labels, legend, and scale. Pay extra attention to special symbols for cultural features. Be sure you understand what these symbols represent.

2. Study the map as a whole. Note the location of the cultural symbols and features. Ask yourself how they relate to the rest of the map.

3. Connect the information on the map to any written information about the subject in the text.

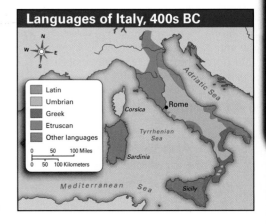

Languages of Italy, 400s BC

Legend:
- Latin
- Umbrian
- Greek
- Etruscan
- Other languages

0 50 100 Miles
0 50 100 Kilometers

Practice and Apply the Skill

Apply the guidelines to the map on this page and answer the following questions.

1. What makes this map a culture map?

2. What language was most widely spoken on the Italian Peninsula? What other language was widely spoken?

3. Where was Greek spoken? Why did the people there talk in Greek?

Social Studies Skills Activity: Interpreting Culture Maps

Comparing and Contrasting Maps   **HSS** Analysis Skills: CS 3   Standards Proficiency

Display the map transparencies "Italy: Physical" and "Italy, 500 BC." Both maps are in Section 1 of this chapter. Have students compare and contrast the two maps. Then ask the following questions:

- How are the two maps similar? *They both show the region of the Italian Peninsula.*

- How are the two maps different? *One is a physical map showing elevations; one is a political map showing culture regions.*

- Based on the maps, how did the topography of Italy affect settlement there? *The culture map shows less settlement in the highly mountainous regions, such as the Apennines.*

- What groups lived on the Italian Peninsula in 500 BC? *Etruscans, Greeks, Romans*

LS Visual/Spatial

Alternative Assessment Handbook, Rubric 21: Map Reading

Map Transparencies: Italy: Physical; Italy, 500 BC

Answers

Practice and Apply the Skill

1. *It shows where different languages were spoken in Italy in the 400s BC.*
2. *Umbrian, Etruscan;* 3. *along parts of the coast on the Italian Peninsula; because the Greeks had founded colonies and traded there*

Standards Review

Visual Summary

Use the visual summary below to help you review the main ideas of the chapter.

QUICK FACTS

The Romans created many legends about their city's glorious history.

The early Romans set up a type of government called a republic.

The Roman Republic conquered lands in Italy and around the Mediterranean.

Reviewing Vocabulary, Terms, and People

Match each numbered definition with the correct lettered vocabulary term.

a. republic   g. Forum
b. plebeians   h. dictator
c. Spartacus   i. veto
d. legions   j. Roman Senate
e. Aeneas   k. patricians
f. consuls   l. primary

1. Rome's public meeting place
2. groups of about 6,000 soldiers
3. the legendary Trojan founder of Rome
4. main, most important
5. a government in which people elect leaders
6. a council that advised Rome's leaders
7. a leader with absolute power for six months
8. the common people of Rome
9. the two most powerful officials in Rome
10. leader of a slave rebellion
11. prohibit
12. noble, powerful Romans

Comprehension and Critical Thinking

SECTION 1 *(Pages 324–329)* **HSS** 6.7.1

13. **a. Describe** What are two legends that describe Rome's founding? How are the two legends connected?

b. Compare and Contrast What roles did the plebeians and the patricians take in the early Roman government? In what other ways were the two groups different?

c. Predict How do you think Italy's geography and Rome's location would affect the spread of Rome's influence?

THE ROMAN REPUBLIC **345**

Visual Summary

Review and Inquiry Use the visual summary to review the chapter's main ideas. Call on students to provide as many key concepts related to the three images as they can.

🖐 Quick Facts Transparency: The Roman Republic Visual Summary

Reviewing Vocabulary, Terms, and People

1. g
2. d
3. e
4. l
5. a
6. j
7. h
8. b
9. f
10. c
11. i
12. k

Comprehension and Critical Thinking

13. **a.** the legend of Aeneas and his search for a home that ends in Italy; the legend of Romulus and Remus and their desire to build a city to mark the spot where a wolf had rescued and cared for them; Romulus and Remus believed to have been descendants of Aeneas

b. plebeians—couldn't take part in government; patricians—could be elected to office, so they held all political power; Plebeians were the majority and were common people;

Review & Assessment Resources

Review and Reinforce

SE Standards Review

📋 **CRF:** Chapter Review Activity

📋 California Standards Review Workbook

🖐 Quick Facts Transparency: The Roman Republic Visual Summary

📢 Spanish Chapter Summaries Audio CD Program

💻 Online Chapter Summaries in Six Languages

OSP Holt Puzzle Pro; Game Tool for ExamView

💿 Quiz Game CD-ROM

Assess

SE Standards Assessment

📋 PASS: Chapter Test, Forms A and B

📋 Alternative Assessment Handbook

OSP ExamView Test Generator, Chapter Test

💿 Universal Access Modified Worksheets and Tests CD-ROM: Chapter Test

💻 Holt Online Assessment Program (in the Premier Online Edition)

Reteach/Intervene

📋 Interactive Reader and Study Guide

📋 Universal Access Teacher Management System: Lesson Plans for Universal Access

💿 Universal Access Modified Worksheets and Tests CD-ROM

💿 Interactive Skills Tutor CD-ROM

go.hrw.com
Online Resources

Chapter Resources:
KEYWORD: SQ6 WH11

Answers

Patricians were the minority, and were wealthy, powerful citizens.

c. possible answer—Italy had a mild climate, so people there could raise plenty of food. Its location in the middle of the Mediterranean would allow the people of Italy to spread control in all directions. Rome's inland location protected it somewhat from invasion by sea.

14. a. magistrates, the senate, assemblies and tribunes

b. Checks and balances keep one part of the government from being stronger than others; written laws protect people from being punished for breaking laws they did not know existed.

c. possible answers—shopping malls, courthouse squares, college campuses, recreation/activity centers, downtown plazas

15. a. Hannibal—invaded Italy, fought Rome; Sulla—started a conflict with Marius, which incited a civil war in Rome; Spartacus—incited a slave riot

b. occupations—fewer small farmers; economics—expanded trade; society—increased violence, civil war

c. Both were commercial powers in the central Mediterranean region, and both wanted to expand.

Reviewing Themes

16. to keep them from becoming too powerful

17. Italy was in the center of the Mediterranean, which meant that the Romans did not have to travel too far to face any opponents.

Using the Internet

18. Go to the HRW Web site and enter the keyword shown to access a rubric for this activity.

KEYWORD: SQ6 TEACHER

SECTION 2 *(Pages 332–337)* **HSS** 6.7.2

14. a. Describe What were the three parts of Rome's government?

b. Analyze How do checks and balances protect the rights of the people? How do written laws do the same thing?

c. Elaborate What are some places in modern society that serve purposes similar to those of the Roman Forum?

SECTION 3 *(Pages 338–343)* **HSS** 6.7.3

15. a. Identify What difficulties did Hannibal, Lucius Cornelius Sulla, and Spartacus cause for Rome?

b. Analyze How did Roman occupations, economics, and society change during the Late Republic?

c. Evaluate Some historians say that Rome and Carthage were destined to fight each other. Why do you think they say this?

Reviewing Themes

16. Politics Why did Roman magistrates only hold office for one year?

17. Geography How do you think Rome's location helped the Romans in their quest to conquer the entire Mediterranean region?

Using the Internet

18. Activity: Explaining Roman Society A key reason the Roman Republic fell was because the Roman people gave up on it. The army, once Rome's protector, let itself be turned against the Roman people. The Senate gave up on debate and compromise when it turned to political violence. Enter the keyword. Research the fall of the Roman Republic and create an exhibit for a local history museum. Make sure your exhibit contains information about key figures in the Roman military and government. Use words and pictures to explain the political, religious, and social structures that made Rome an empire and what caused its eventual downfall.

Reading Skills

19. Creating Outlines Look back at the discussion "Crises Strike the Republic" in the last section of this chapter. Prepare an outline that will help clarify the people, events, and ideas of this discussion. Before you prepare your outline, decide what your major headings will be. Then choose the details that will appear below each heading. Remember that most outlines follow this basic format:

> I. Main Idea
>   A. Supporting Idea
>   B. Supporting Idea
>   1. Detail
>   2. Detail
> II. Main Idea
>   A. Supporting Idea

Social Studies Skills

Using Culture Maps *Look back at the map of Italy in 500 BC that appears in Section 1 of this chapter. Use the map to answer the following questions.*

20. Which people controlled the most land on the Italian Peninsula?

21. Which peoples on this map had learned to sail across the sea? How can you tell?

22. What evidence on this map suggests that the Romans and the Etruscans had contact with each other?

FOCUS ON SPEAKING

23. Presenting Your Legend Now that you've chosen the subject for your legend, it's time to write and present it. As you write your legend, focus on exciting details that will bring the subject to life in your listeners' minds. Once you've finished writing, share your legend with the class. Try to make your legend exciting as you present it. Remember to alter the tone and volume of your voice to convey the appropriate mood.

Reading Skills

19. Outlines will vary, but the main heads should coincide with red heads in text.

Social Studies Skills

20. Etruscans

21. Greeks, because the areas they settled were far from Greece and on the coast; and Carthaginians, because areas they settled are across the sea from Carthage

22. Their territories lie next to each other.

Focus on Speaking

23. Rubric Students' legends should:
- include at least one major figure from Roman history.
- introduce characters, a setting, and an event in the first paragraph.
- tell about an event from history.
- include a conflict that is resolved in the final paragraph.

CRF: Focus on Writing: A Legend

Standards Assessment

DIRECTIONS: Read each question, and write the letter of the best response.

1 Use the map to answer the following question.

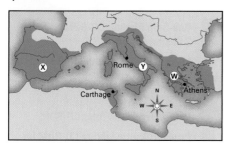

The order in which Rome expanded its control in the Mediterranean region is shown by which of the following sequences of letters?

A Y–W–X

B X–W–Y

C Y–X–W

D W–X–Y

2 Which was the *least* important reason for the growth of Rome's power and influence in the Mediterranean region?

A religion

B trade

C military organization

D wars and conquests

3 According to Roman legend, the city of Rome was founded by

A Latin peoples who moved to Italy from ancient Egypt.

B two men named Romulus and Remus who were raised by a wolf.

C the gods of Greece, who were looking for a new home.

D a Greek warrior named Achilles who had fled from the destruction of Troy.

4 Roman nobles were called

A patricians.

B plebeians.

C tribunes.

D magistrates.

5 Which of the following characteristics did *not* apply to Roman government?

A system of checks and balances

B sense of civic duty

C written code of laws

D equality of all people

Connecting with Past Learnings

6 You learned earlier in this course about other ancient peoples who, like the Romans, founded their civilizations along rivers. These peoples include all of the following *except* the

A Chinese.

B Egyptians.

C Sumerians.

D Hebrews.

7 Virgil's *Aeneid* is similar to what other piece of ancient literature that you've learned about in this course?

A the *Shiji*

B the *Book of the Dead*

C *The Odyssey*

D the *Bhagavad Gita*

Tips for Test Taking

Rely on 50/50 Ask students if they have ever said "I have no clue" while taking a test. That is the time to make an educated guess. They should read every choice carefully. Give students these pointers:

- Watch out for distracters—choices that may be true, but are too broad, too narrow, or not relevant to the question.

- Eliminate the least likely choice. Eliminate the next, until you find the best one.

- If two choices seem equally correct, look to see if "All of the above" is an option.

Chapter 12 Planning Guide

The Roman Empire

Chapter Overview	Reproducible Resources	Technology Resources

CHAPTER 12

pp. 348–375

Overview: In this chapter, students will analyze the history and lasting contributions of the Roman Empire.

 See p. 348 for the California History–Social Science standards covered in this chapter.

 Universal Access Teacher Management System:*
- Universal Access Instructional Benchmarking Guides
- Lesson Plans for Universal Access

 Interactive Reader and Study Guide: Chapter Graphic Organizer*

 Chapter Resource File*
- Chapter Review Activity
- Focus on Writing Activity: Note Cards for a Screenplay
- Social Studies Skills Activity: Interpreting Time Lines

 One-Stop Planner CD-ROM: Calendar Planner

 **Student Edition on Audio CD Program**

Universal Access Modified Worksheets and Tests CD-ROM

Interactive Skills Tutor CD-ROM

Primary Source Library CD-ROM for World History

Power Presentations with Video CD-ROM

 **History's Impact: World History Video Program (VHS/DVD):** The Roman Empire and Christianity*

A Teacher's Guide To Religion in the Public Schools*

Section 1:

From Republic to Empire

The Big Idea: Julius Caesar and Augustus led Rome's transition from a republic to an empire.

 6.7.4

 **Universal Access Teacher Management System:*** Section 1 Lesson Plan

Interactive Reader and Study Guide: Section 1 Summary*

Chapter Resource File*
- Vocabulary Builder Activity, Section 1
- Biography Activity: Cicero
- Biography Activity: Marc Antony
- Interdisciplinary Project: The Romans: Response Rally
- Primary Source Activity: The Death of Caesar
- Primary Source Activity: Plutarch's Cleopatra
- Primary Source Activity: Statue of Augustus

 Daily Bellringer Transparency: Section 1*

Internet Activity: Caesar vs. Augustus

Section 2:

A Vast Empire

The Big Idea: After Augustus became emperor, the Roman Empire grew politically and economically, and life improved for the Roman people.

6.7.3

 **Universal Access Teacher Management System:*** Section 2 Lesson Plan

 **Interactive Reader and Study Guide:** Section 2 Summary*

Chapter Resource File*
- Vocabulary Builder Activity, Section 2
- Economics and History Activity: The Romans and Money
- History and Geography Activity: Roman Trade

 Daily Bellringer Transparency: Section 2*

 Map Transparency: Expansion of Rome, 100 BC–AD 117*

Map Transparency: Roman Trade Routes, AD 200*

Section 3:

Rome's Legacy

The Big Idea: Many features of Roman culture were copied by later civilizations and continue to influence our lives today.

 6.7.8

 Universal Access Teacher Management System:* Section 3 Lesson Plan

Interactive Reader and Study Guide: Section 3 Summary*

Chapter Resource File*
- Vocabulary Builder Activity, Section 3
- Biography Activity: Marcus Aurelius
- Literature Activity: Tales from Ovid
- Primary Source Activity: The Meditations

 Daily Bellringer Transparency: Section 3*

Internet Activity: Roman Style

MASTERING THE CALIFORNIA STANDARDS

Review, Assessment, Intervention

🐻 **Standards Review Workbook***

🖨 **Quick Facts Transparency:** The Roman Empire Visual Summary*

🔊 **Spanish Chapter Summaries Audio CD Program**

🐻 **Online Chapter Summaries in Six Languages**

💿 **Quiz Game CD-ROM**

🐻 **Progress Assessment Support System (PASS):** Chapter Test*

💿 **Universal Access Modified Worksheets and Tests CD-ROM:** Modified Chapter Test

💿 **One-Stop Planner CD-ROM:** ExamView Test Generator (English/Spanish)

🖨 **Alternative Assessment Handbook**

🐻 **Holt Online Assessment Program (HOAP),** in the Holt Premier Online Student Edition

---

🖨 **PASS:** Section 1 Quiz*

🐻 **Online Quiz:** Section 1

🖨 **Alternative Assessment Handbook**

🖨 **PASS:** Section 2 Quiz*

🐻 **Online Quiz:** Section 2

🖨 **Alternative Assessment Handbook**

🖨 **PASS:** Section 3 Quiz*

🐻 **Online Quiz:** Section 3

🖨 **Alternative Assessment Handbook**

California Resources for Standards Mastery

INSTRUCTIONAL PLANNING AND SUPPORT

🖨 **Universal Access Teacher Management System***

💿 **One-Stop Planner CD-ROM with Test Generator:** Teacher Management System with Interactive Teacher's Edition

STANDARDS MASTERY

🖨 **Standards Review Workbook***

🖨 **At Home: A Guide to Standards Mastery for World History**

🐻 **Holt Online Learning**

To enhance learning, the following Internet activities are available: Caesar vs. Augustus and Roman Style.

KEYWORD: SQ6 TEACHER

- **Teacher Support Page**
- **Content Updates**
- **Rubrics and Writing Models**
- **Teaching Tips for the Multimedia Classroom**

KEYWORD: SQ6 WH12

- **Current Events**
- **Holt Grapher**
- **Holt Online Atlas**
- **Holt Researcher**
- **Interactive Multimedia Activities**
- **Internet Activities**
- **Online Chapter Summaries in Six Languages**
- **Online Section Quizzes**
- **World History Maps and Charts**

HOLT PREMIER ONLINE STUDENT EDITION

Complete online support for interactivity, assessment, and reporting

- **Interactive Maps and Notebook**
- **Standardized Test Prep**
- **Homework Practice and Research Activities Online**

Mastering the Standards: Differentiating Instruction

Reaching Standards	Basic-level activities designed for all students encountering new material
Standards Proficiency	Intermediate-level activities designed for average students
Exceeding Standards	Challenging activities designed for honors and gifted-and-talented students
Standard English Mastery	Activities designed to improve standard English usage

MASTERING THE CALIFORNIA STANDARDS

Frequently Asked Questions

INSTRUCTIONAL PLANNING AND SUPPORT

Where do I find planning aids, pacing guides, lesson plans, and other teaching aids?

Annotated Teacher's Edition:
- Chapter planning guides
- Standards-based instruction and strategies
- Differentiated instruction for universal access
- Point-of-use reminders for integrating program resources

Power Presentations with Video CD-ROM

Universal Access Teacher Management System:
- Year and unit instructional benchmarking guides
- Reproducible lesson plans
- Assessment guides for diagnostic, progress, and summative end-of-the-year tests
- Options for differentiating instruction and intervention
- Teaching guides and answer keys for student workbooks

One-Stop Planner CD-ROM with Test Generator: Teacher Management System with Interactive Teacher's Edition:
- Calendar Planner
- Editable lesson plans
- All reproducible ancillaries in Adobe Acrobat (PDF) format
- ExamView Test Generator (English & Spanish)
- Game Tool for ExamView
- PuzzlePro
- Transparency and video previews

DIFFERENTIATING INSTRUCTION FOR UNIVERSAL ACCESS

What resources are available to ensure that Advanced Learners/GATE Students master the standards?

Lesson Plans for Universal Access

Primary Source Library CD-ROM for World History

What resources are available to ensure that English Learners and Standard English Learners master the standards?

Teacher's Edition Activities:
- Hadrian's Memo, p. 359

Lesson Plans for Universal Access

Chapter Resource File: Vocabulary Builder Activities

Spanish Chapter Summaries Audio CD Program

Online Chapter Summaries in Six Languages

One-Stop Planner CD-ROM:
- PuzzlePro, Spanish Version
- ExamView Test Generator, Spanish Version

What modified materials are available for Special Education?

Teacher's Edition Activities:
- Gumdrop Arches, p. 367

The *Universal Access Modified Worksheets and Tests CD-ROM* provides editable versions of the following:

Vocabulary Flash Cards

Modified Vocabulary Builder Activities

Modified Chapter Review Activity

Modified Chapter Test

What resources are available to ensure that Learners Having Difficulty master the standards?

Teacher's Edition Activities:
- Qualities of Julius Caesar, p. 353
- Marc Antony's Funeral Speech, p. 355
- Roman City Life, p. 361

Interactive Reader and Study Guide

Student Edition on Audio CD Program

Quick Facts Transparency: The Roman Empire Visual Summary

Standards Review Workbook

Social Studies Skills Activity: Interpreting Time Lines

Interactive Skills Tutor CD-ROM

How do I intervene for students struggling to master the standards?

Interactive Reader and Study Guide

Quick Facts Transparency: The Roman Empire Visual Summary

Standards Review Workbook

Social Studies Skills Activity: Interpreting Time Lines

Interactive Skills Tutor CD-ROM

PROFESSIONAL DEVELOPMENT

HOLT Professional Development

What teacher training resources are available to help me grow professionally?

- In-service and staff development as part of your Holt Social Studies product purchase
- Quick Teacher Tutorial Lesson Presentation CD-ROM
- Intensive tuition-based Teacher Development Institute
- Convenient Holt Speaker Bureau face-to-face workshop options

- PRAXIS™ Test Prep (#0089) interactive Web-based content refreshers*
- *Ask A Professional Development Expert* at http://www.hrw.com/prodev/

* PRAXIS is a trademark of Educational Testing Service (ETS). This publication is not endorsed or approved by ETS.

Information Literacy Skills

To learn more about how History–Social Science instruction may be improved by the effective use of library media centers and information literacy skills, go to the Teacher's Resource Materials for Chapter 12 at **go.hrw.com, keyword: SQ6 MEDIA.**

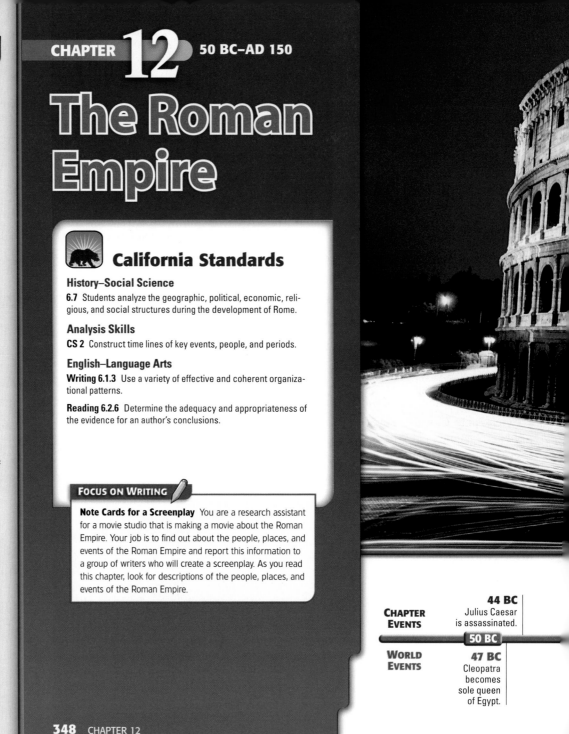

CHAPTER 12 50 BC–AD 150

The Roman Empire

California Standards

History–Social Science
6.7 Students analyze the geographic, political, economic, religious, and social structures during the development of Rome.

Analysis Skills
CS 2 Construct time lines of key events, people, and periods.

English–Language Arts
Writing 6.1.3 Use a variety of effective and coherent organizational patterns.

Reading 6.2.6 Determine the adequacy and appropriateness of the evidence for an author's conclusions.

FOCUS ON WRITING

Note Cards for a Screenplay You are a research assistant for a movie studio that is making a movie about the Roman Empire. Your job is to find out about the people, places, and events of the Roman Empire and report this information to a group of writers who will create a screenplay. As you read this chapter, look for descriptions of the people, places, and events of the Roman Empire.

CHAPTER EVENTS	**44 BC** Julius Caesar is assassinated.
	50 BC
WORLD EVENTS	**47 BC** Cleopatra becomes sole queen of Egypt.

348 CHAPTER 12

Introduce the Chapter

Standards **Proficiency**

Images of the Roman Empire **HSS** Analysis Skills: HR 3

1. Create a two-column chart titled *The Roman Empire* for students to see with these heads: *From textbooks* and *From other sources*. Ask students to tell the impressions they have of the Roman Empire from schoolwork for the first column and from TV shows, movies, video games, comic books, cartoons, and similar sources for the second column.

2. Ask students which impressions they feel are probably accurate and which are false

or exaggerations. Point out that some of the facts of the Roman Empire's history are so amazing that they may seem to be exaggerations but are not.

3. Have students copy the completed chart. Encourage students to refer to the chart as they study the chapter to check which impressions are factual. **LS** Verbal/Linguistic

What You Will Learn...

In this chapter you will learn how Rome changed from a republic into a vast empire that has had a lasting influence on the Western world. This photo shows the Roman Colosseum, a building that has influenced the design of stadiums and sporting facilities around the world.

27 BC
Augustus becomes Rome's first emperor.

4 BC
Herod the Great, king of Judea, dies.

BC 1 AD

AD 50

AD 60
Warrior queen Boudicca burns the city of London.

AD 100

AD 80
The first games are held in the Colosseum.

AD 122
Hadrian's Wall is begun in northern England.

AD 150

AD 132
The Chinese invent the seismograph.

THE ROMAN EMPIRE   **349**

Explore the Time Line

1. Who was Rome's first emperor, and when did he come to power? *Augustus; 27 BC*

2. When did construction of Hadrian's Wall begin? *AD 122*

3. What did the Chinese invent in AD 132? *the seismograph*

4. How many years separated the events associated with two queens? *107 years*

HSS Analysis Skills: CS 1

Info to Know

Naval Battles in the Colosseum? Roman writers tell that the Colosseum was sometimes flooded with water so that ships could fight mock naval battles there. However, for years scholars have argued over whether such a feat was possible. Recently, some archaeologists and computer experts said that the Colosseum could indeed have been flooded to a depth of five feet. Filling the arena floor would have required 4 million gallons of water. Research and discussions on this topic will probably continue.

• Chapter Preview •

HOLT
History's Impact
▶ video series
See the Video Teacher's Guide for strategies for using the chapter video **The Roman Empire and Christianity: The Impact of Ancient Rome on the World Today.**

Chapter Big Ideas

Section 1 Julius Caesar and Augustus led Rome's transition from a republic to an empire. HSS 6.7.4

Section 2 After Augustus became emperor, the Roman Empire grew politically and economically, and life improved for the Roman people. HSS 6.7.3

Section 3 Many features of Roman culture were copied by later civilizations and continue to influence our lives today. HSS 6.7.8

Explore the Picture

The Colosseum While the Colosseum's original decoration has been stripped away, the massive scale of the structure remains. The Colosseum's outside dimensions are 620 feet by 513 feet. In length it's about twice the size of a football field! Some 50,000 spectators could sit in the stands.

Analyzing Visuals The wall on the left side of the picture is taller than that on the right. What can you conclude about the original structure? *The wall on the right was an inner wall. The outer wall of that section, which would have continued from the diagonal walls, no longer stands.*

go.hrw.com
Online Resources
Chapter 12 Resources:
KEYWORD: SQ6 WH12
Teacher Resources:
KEYWORD: SQ6 TEACHER

Reading Social Studies

Understanding Themes

Introduce the key themes of this chapter—geography and technology—by explaining to students that the Roman Empire was very large and diverse. Show students the extent of the Roman Empire on a map. Ask students what benefits and drawbacks Rome's geography might have had on the empire. Ask students to imagine what it might have been like to live in the faraway provinces of the empire. Then ask students what types of science and technology might have aided such a large empire. Point out to students that ruling such a large empire was difficult, but the Romans developed many advances to help them improve the empire.

Online Research

Focus on Reading Organize the class into small groups. Have students in each group discuss their Internet use and Web sites that they find useful for conducting research. Ask groups to list what elements they find most valuable about those sites—for example, quality of information, layout, or ease of use. Remind students that not all sites contain verifiable information. Ask students to list how they determine the quality of information when they are using the Internet. Have each group report its opinions to the class. Discuss the most important qualities of a Web site.

Reading Social Studies

by Kylene Beers

| Economics | Geography | Politics | Religion | Society and Culture | Science and Technology |

Focus on Themes This chapter will describe the development of Rome as it grew from a republic into a strong and vast empire. First, you will learn about the **geographic** expansion of the empire under such powerful leaders as Julius Caesar, Marc Antony, and Augustus. You will also learn about how the Romans' many contributions to literature, language, law, and **science and technology** have shaped how people have lived since the days of Rome some 2,000 years ago.

Online Research

Focus on Reading Finding information on the World Wide Web can be easy. Just enter a word or two into a search engine and you will instantly find dozens—or hundreds—of sites full of information.

Evaluating Web Sites However, not all web sites have good or accurate information. How do you know which sites are the ones you want? You have to evaluate, or judge, the sites. You can use an evaluation form like the one below to evaluate a Web site.

Additional reading support can be found in the

Inter*active

Reader and Study Guide

Evaluating Web-Based Resources

Name of site: _____ URL: _____ Date of access: _____

I. Evaluating the author of the site
   A. Who is the author? What are his or her qualifications?
   B. Is there a way to contact the author?

II. Evaluating the content of the site
   A. Is the site's topic related to the topic you are studying?
   B. Is there enough information at this site to help you?
   C. Is there too much information for you to read or understand?
   D. Does the site include pictures or illustrations to help you understand the information?
   E. Does the site discuss more than one point of view about the topic?
   F. Does the site express the author's opinions rather than facts?
   G. Does the site provide references for its information, including quotes?
   H. Are there links to other sites that have valuable information?

III. Evaluating the overall design and quality
   A. Is the site easy to navigate or to find information on?
   B. When was the site last updated?

IV. My overall impression
   Does this site have good information that will help me with my research?

---

350 CHAPTER 12

Reading and Skills Resources

Reading Support

- Interactive Reader and Study Guide
- Student Edition on Audio CD
- Spanish Chapter Summaries Audio CD Program

Social Studies Skills Support

- Interactive Skills Tutor CD-ROM

Vocabulary Support

- **CRF:** Vocabulary Builder Activities
- **CRF:** Chapter Review Activity
- Universal Access Modified Worksheets and Tests CD-ROM:
  - Vocabulary Flash Cards
  - Vocabulary Builder Activity
  - Chapter Review Activity

OSP Holt PuzzlePro

Standards Focus

ELA Reading 6.2.6

You Try It!

Below is an example of an evaluation of a fictional Web site on Julius Caesar. Review the student's answers to the questions on the previous page and then answer the questions at the bottom of the page.

Web Site Evaluation

I. Evaluating the author
 A. Author is listed as Klee O. Patra. She has read many books about Julius Caesar.
 B. No information is listed for contacting the author.

II. Evaluating content of the site
 A. Yes. It is about Julius Caesar.
 B. There appears to be a lot of information about Julius Caesar.
 C. No, it looks easy to understand.
 D. There are some pictures, but most are from movies. There are no historical images.
 E. No.
 F. Yes, it is all about how she loves Caesar.
 G. I can't find any references.
 H. There are two links, but they are both dead.

III. Evaluating Overall Design and quality
 A. No. It takes a long time to find any specific information. Also, the layout of the page is confusing.
 B. It was last updated in July 1998.

Study the evaluation then answer the following questions.

1. What do you know about the author of this site? Based on the evaluation information, do you think she is qualified to write about Caesar?

2. Does the content of the site seem valuable and reliable? Why?

3. The site has not been updated for many years, but that may not be a major problem for a site about Julius Caesar. Why? When might recent updates be more important?

4. Overall, would you say this site would be helpful? Why or why not?

Key Terms and People

Chapter 12

Section 1
Cicero *(p. 352)*
orator *(p. 352)*
Julius Caesar *(p. 353)*
Pompey *(p. 353)*
Brutus *(p. 355)*
Marc Antony *(p. 355)*
Augustus *(p. 355)*
Cleopatra *(p. 356)*

Section 2
Hadrian *(p. 359)*
provinces *(p. 360)*
currency *(p. 360)*
Pax Romana *(p. 361)*
villas *(p. 362)*

Section 3
Galen *(p. 366)*
aqueduct *(p. 367)*
vault *(p. 367)*
Virgil *(p. 370)*
Ovid *(p. 370)*
satire *(p. 370)*
Romance languages *(p. 371)*
civil law *(p. 371)*

Academic Vocabulary

Success in school is related to knowing academic vocabulary— the words that are frequently used in school assignments and discussions. In this chapter, you will learn the following academic words:

agreement *(p. 353)*
effect *(p. 361)*

As you read **Chapter 12,** think about what topics would be interesting to research on the Web. If you do any research on the Web, remember to evaluate the site and its contents.

Reading Social Studies

Key Terms and People

Introduce the key terms and people from this chapter by briefly reviewing each term and person with the class. Instruct students to look in the chapter for more information on each term or person. Then have students write a statement for each term or person that provides a description of the item, and then asks, "Who am I?" For example, "I am a structure that carries water from mountains into the city. Who am I?" Collect the statements from students and read some of them to the class.
LS Verbal/Linguistic

Focus on Reading

See the **Focus on Reading** questions in this chapter for more practice on this reading social studies skill.

Reading Social Studies Assessment

See the **Standards Review** at the end of this chapter for student assessment questions related to this reading skill.

Teaching Tip

Tell students that many of the things they read or hear may be biased, whether it is on Web sites, television and radio, or in newspapers, magazines, and books. Remind students that asking some of the questions listed in this feature will help them evaluate not just Web sites, but all sources of information. Remind students that by asking questions and thinking critically they can avoid getting fooled by incorrect information. They can also become responsible, informed citizens.

Answers

You Try It! 1. *that she has read many books about Julius Caesar; she may not be a reliable source or have validated any of her information.* **2.** *no, because it seems to be a personal Web site on a topic the author finds interesting but for which she does not provide sources;* **3.** *because Julius Caesar lived long ago, information about him has changed very little; Recent topics or topics about which new information is being added require updated information.* **4.** *not very helpful; the information cannot be verified; lack of historical information; biased*

Bellringer

If YOU were there . . . Use the **Daily Bellringer Transparency** to help students answer the question.

📖 Daily Bellringer Transparency, Section 1

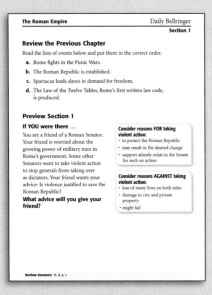

The Roman Empire — Daily Bellringer, Section 1

Review the Previous Chapter
Read the lists of events below and put them in the correct order.
a. Rome fights in the Punic Wars.
b. The Roman Republic is established.
c. Spartacus leads slaves in demand for freedom.
d. The Law of the Twelve Tables, Rome's first written law code, is produced.

Preview Section 1
If YOU were there . . .
You are a friend of a Roman Senator. Your friend is worried about the growing power of military men in Rome's government. Some other Senators want to take violent action to stop generals from taking over as dictators. Your friend wants your advice: Is violence justified to save the Roman Republic?
What advice will you give your friend?

Consider reasons FOR taking violent action:
• to protect the Roman Republic
• may result in the desired change
• support already exists in the Senate for such an action

Consider reasons AGAINST taking violent action:
• loss of many lives on both sides
• damage to city and private property
• might fail

Review Answers: b, d, a, c

Academic Vocabulary

Review with students the high-use academic term in this section:

agreement a decision reached by two or more people or groups (p. 353)

📝 **CRF:** Vocabulary Builder Activity, Section 1

🐻 Standards Focus

HSS 6.7.4
Means: Discuss how Julius Caesar and Augustus helped turn Rome's republic into an empire.
Matters: Two men were primarily responsible for changing Rome from a republic into an empire. Many times over the centuries, individuals with strong personalities have changed history.

Answers

Reading Check *to work together to make Rome a better place, limit the power of generals, give more support to the Senate, and restore checks and balances*

352

From Republic to Empire

What You Will Learn...

Main Ideas
1. Romans called for change in their government.
2. Julius Caesar rose to power and became the sole ruler of Rome.
3. Augustus became Rome's first emperor after defeating Caesar's killers and his own former allies.

The Big Idea
Julius Caesar and Augustus led Rome's transition from a republic to an empire.

Key Terms and People
Cicero, *p. 352*
orator, *p. 352*
Julius Caesar, *p. 353*
Pompey, *p. 353*
Brutus, *p. 355*
Marc Antony, *p. 355*
Augustus, *p. 355*
Cleopatra, *p. 356*

🐻 **HSS** 6.7.4 Discuss the influence of Julius Caesar and Augustus in Rome's transition from republic to empire.

352 CHAPTER 12

If YOU were there...

You are a friend of a Roman Senator. Your friend is worried about the growing power of military men in Rome's government. Some other Senators want to take violent action to stop generals from taking over as dictators. Your friend wants your advice: Is violence justified to save the Roman Republic?

What advice will you give your friend?

BUILDING BACKGROUND By the first century BC, the government of the Roman Republic was in trouble. Politicians looked for ways to solve the problems. Philosophers offered ideas, too. In the end, however, the republic could not survive the great changes that were taking place in Rome.

The Call for Change

Rome in the 70s BC was a dangerous place. Politicians and generals went to war to increase their power even as political order broke down in Rome. Unemployed Romans rioted in the streets because they couldn't get enough food. All the while more and more people from all around the republic flooded into the city, further adding to the confusion.

Some Romans tried to stop the chaos in Rome's government. One such person was **Cicero** (SIS-uh-roh), a gifted philosopher and **orator**, or public speaker. In his speeches Cicero called on Romans to make Rome a better place. One way to do this, he argued, was to limit the power of generals. Cicero wanted the Romans to give more support to the Senate and to restore the checks and balances on government.

But Cicero was unsuccessful. Many Romans didn't agree with him. Others were too caught up in their own affairs to pay any attention. Rome's government did not change.

READING CHECK **Summarizing** What did Cicero want Romans to do?

Teach the Big Idea: Master the Standards
Standards Proficiency

From Republic to Empire 🐻 **HSS** 6.7.4; **HSS** Analysis Skills: CS 1, CS 2, HI 1, HI 2

1. **Teach** Ask students the Main Idea questions to teach this section.

2. **Apply** Draw a chart with two columns for students to see. Label the columns *Julius Caesar* and *Octavian (Augustus)*. Have each student copy the chart and enter five or more facts about each man. **LS** Visual/Spatial

3. **Review** Have volunteers share the information they listed. Write the facts on the chart. Then add columns titled *Before* and *After* to the left and right of the chart.

Call on volunteers to add information on the events that led to Julius Caesar's rise and on the events that followed Augustus' rise to power. Add the information to the *Before* and *After* columns in the chart.

4. **Practice/Homework** Have each student write a paragraph contending which man had the greater influence on Rome. **LS** Verbal/Linguistic

 Alternative Assessment Handbook, Rubrics 7: Charts; and 40: Writing to Describe

Caesar's Rise to Power

As Cicero was calling on the Romans to take power away from the generals, a new group of generals was working to take over the government. The most powerful of these generals was **Julius Caesar** (JOOL-yuhs SEE-zuhr).

Caesar the General

Caesar was probably the greatest general in Roman history. Other Romans admired him for his bravery and skill in battle. At the same time, his soldiers respected him because he treated them well.

Between 58 and 50 BC Caesar conquered nearly all of Gaul—a region that included much of modern France, Germany, and northern Italy—and part of Britain. He wrote a description of this conquest, describing in great detail how he defeated each of the tribes he faced.

Here he describes how he defeated a group called the Menapii. Notice how he refers to himself as Caesar:

> " Caesar, having divided his forces . . . and having hastily [quickly] constructed some bridges, enters their country in three divisions, burns their houses and villages, and gets possession of a large number of cattle and men. Constrained [forced] by these circumstances the Menapii send ambassadors to him for the purpose of suing [asking] for peace. "
>
> –Julius Caesar, from *The Gallic Wars*

Caesar's military successes made him a major figure in Roman politics. In addition to being a good leader, Caesar was an excellent speaker. He won many people to his side with his speeches in the forum.

Caesar also had powerful friends. Before he went to Gaul he made an **agreement** with two of the most powerful men in Rome, **Pompey** and Crassus. The three agreed to work together to fight against the Senate. Together, Caesar and his allies changed the course of Roman history.

ACADEMIC VOCABULARY
agreement a decision reached by two or more people or groups

Julius Caesar conquered Gaul and added it to the empire. This painting from the late 1800s shows a Frankish leader surrendering to Caesar by dropping his weapons at Caesar's feet.

353

Main Idea

❷ Caesar's Rise to Power

Julius Caesar rose to power and became the sole ruler of Rome.

Recall What did Caesar do to Pompey? *pursued him for a year until Pompey was killed in Egypt*

Make Generalizations Why was Caesar killed? *Romans, especially Senators, feared that Caesar was trying to make himself king.*

📋 **CRF:** Primary Source Activity: The Death of Julius Caesar according to Suetonius

🐾 **HSS** 6.7.4; **HSS** Analysis Skills: CS 1, HI 1, HI 2

go.hrw.com

Online Resources

KEYWORD: SQ6 WH12
ACTIVITY: Caesar vs. Augustus

Connect to Literature

Julius Caesar Many people know of Julius Caesar primarily as the title character in a 400-year-old play. William Shakespeare wrote *Julius Caesar* in 1599, more than 1,600 years after the events described in the play took place.

Conflict with an Ally

At the end of the fighting in Gaul, Caesar was one of the most powerful men in the Roman Republic. He was so powerful that even his friends were jealous and afraid of him. This jealousy and fear changed Caesar's relationship with Pompey.

In 50 BC Pompey's allies in the Senate ordered Caesar to give up command of his armies and return to Rome. Caesar refused. He knew that Pompey was trying to take power away from him and would arrest him if he gave up his command. As a result, Caesar led his army into Italy. In 49 BC Caesar and his troops crossed the Rubicon River, the boundary between Gaul and Italy.

Because Roman law said that no general could enter Italy with his army, Pompey and the Senate considered Caesar's return to Italy a sign of war. Afraid that Caesar would attack him, Pompey and his allies fled Italy. They didn't think they had enough troops to defeat Caesar.

Caesar and his army chased Pompey's forces around the Mediterranean for a year. Eventually they drove Pompey into Egypt, where he was killed. There Caesar met Cleopatra, whom he made queen. As queen, Cleopatra became his new ally.

Conflict with the Senate

Finally, Caesar returned to Rome. When he got there, he forced the Senate to name him dictator for 10 years. Later this term was extended and Caesar became dictator for life.

Although Caesar wanted to improve Roman society, some people resented the way he had gained power. They feared that Caesar was trying to make himself the king of Rome. The Romans certainly didn't want a king.

Some Senators were especially angry with Caesar. On March 15—a date the Romans called the Ides of March—in 44 BC, a group of Senators attacked Caesar in the Senate house and stabbed him to death.

The Death of Julius Caesar

Caesar was stabbed to death on March 15, 44 BC. To the Romans, March 15 was called the Ides of March, and before Caesar was killed he was warned to "beware the Ides of March."

354

Cross-Discipline Activity: Literature
Standards Proficiency

Reader's Theater 🐾 **HSS** 6.7.4; **HSS** Analysis Skills: HR 4

Materials: copies of scenes from Shakespeare's *Julius Caesar*

1. Organize the class into small groups and give each group a scene from *Julius Caesar* to read. Tell students that they will read scenes from a historical play.

2. Have each group practice its scene by having each member take turns reading different characters' lines.

3. Call on groups to read their scenes to the class. Encourage students to act out the scenes as much as possible and to read with expression.

4. Discuss each scene and help students interpret the meaning of Shakespeare's language.

🔲 **Interpersonal, Verbal/Linguistic**

📋 Alternative Assessment Handbook, Rubric 23: Skits and Reader's Theater

Among the attackers was a young Senator named **Brutus** (BROOT-uhs), who had been a friend and ally of Caesar's. Some Romans even believed that Brutus may have been Caesar's son but didn't know it. According to Roman historians, Caesar was shocked by Brutus's betrayal and stopped fighting against his attackers when he recognized him.

Rather than becoming heroes, Caesar's murderers were forced to flee for their lives. Rome was shocked by Caesar's murder, and many people were furious about it. He had been loved by many common people, and many of these people rioted after his death. From the chaos that followed Caesar's assassination, the Senate had to act quickly to restore order.

READING CHECK **Sequencing** What were the events that led to Caesar's gaining power in Rome?

Augustus the Emperor

Two leaders emerged to take control of Roman politics. One was Caesar's former assistant, **Marc Antony**. The other was Caesar's adopted son Octavian (ahk-TAY-vee-uhn), later called **Augustus** (aw-GUHS-tuhs).

Antony and Octavian

Antony and Octavian worked to punish the people who had killed Caesar. At Caesar's funeral, Antony delivered a famous speech that turned even more Romans against the killers. Shortly afterward, he and Octavian set out with an army to try to avenge Caesar's death.

Their army caught up to the killers near Philippi (FI-luh-py) in northern Greece. In 42 BC Antony and Octavian soundly defeated their opponents. After the battle the leaders of the plot to kill Caesar, including Brutus, killed themselves.

THE IMPACT TODAY

Some people today still use the name Brutus to refer to people who betray them.

Primary Source

POINTS OF VIEW

Views of Caesar

Some Senators admired Caesar and were horrified by his murder. The biographer Plutarch (PLOO-tahrk) described their reactions to the event.

❝So the affair began, and those who were not privy to the plot were filled with consternation [dismay] and horror at what was going on; they dared not fly, nor go to Caesar's help, nay, nor even utter a word.❞

–Plutarch
from *Life of Caesar*

The historian Suetonius (swe-TOH-nee-uhs) explained that other Senators thought Caesar deserved to be killed because his actions were threatening the republic.

❝He abused his power and was justly slain. For not only did he accept excessive honors, such as an uninterrupted consulship, the dictatorship for life, and the censorship of public morals . . . but he also allowed honors to be bestowed on him which were too great for mortal man.❞

–Suetonius
from *The Lives of the Caesars, The Deified Julius*

ANALYSIS SKILL **ANALYZING PRIMARY SOURCES**

How does Plutarch say people reacted to Caesar's death?

THE ROMAN EMPIRE **355**

Differentiating Instruction for Universal Access

Learners | Reaching Standards | Prep Required | Standard English Mastery

Having Difficulty

Materials: copies of Marc Antony's speech from William Shakespeare's *Julius Caesar*

1. Tell students that great speeches often have dramatic consequences, but they may contain language that is difficult to understand.

2. Give each student a copy of Marc Antony's funeral speech from Shakespeare's *Julius Caesar.*

3. Have students work in pairs to rewrite the speech, or excerpts from it, in modern

standard English. Ask students to leave blanks for words or sentences they don't understand.

4. Call on volunteers to read parts of the speech and their rewritten version. As you go, discuss words and phrases that caused difficulties. For students to see, write down any sentences that still need to be put in standard English form.

LS **Interpersonal, Verbal/Linguistic**

HSS 6.7.4; **Analysis Skills:** HR 5, HI 1

• **Direct Teach** •

Main Idea

❸ Augustus the Emperor

Augustus became Rome's first emperor after defeating Caesar's killers and his own former allies.

Identify How did most Romans feel about the death of Caesar? *They were angered by it.*

Recall What happened to Caesar's killers after the assassination? *Marc Antony and Octavian defeated them, and the leaders killed themselves.*

Draw Conclusions Why did Octavian turn against Mark Antony? *Antony divorced his wife, who was Octavian's sister, in order to marry Cleopatra. Octavian saw this as an insult to his sister and to himself.*

📋 **CRF:** Biography Activity: Marc Antony
📋 **CRF:** Primary Source Activity: Plutarch's Story of Cleopatra
📋 **CRF:** Primary Source Activity: Statue of the Emperor Augustus
HSS 6.7.4; **HSS** **Analysis Skills:** CS 1, HR 5, HI 1

Primary Source

Reading Like a Historian

Views of Caesar Help students practice reading the document like historians. Ask the following:

• Which of the authors quoted would probably have agreed with Cicero's ideas for improving Rome? *Suetonius*

• Which statements appear to be facts, and which appear to be opinions? *facts—accepted uninterrupted consulship, dictatorship for life; opinions—filled with consternation and horror; abused his power and was justly slain; honors . . . too great for mortal man*

HSS 6.7.4; **HSS** **Analysis Skills:** HR 2, HR 4

Answers

Analyzing Primary Sources *He says they were filled with dismay and horror.*

Reading Check *He returned to Rome with his army and forced the Senate to name him dictator.*

355

The Egyptian Queen? Cleopatra was the queen of Egypt, but she had no Egyptian blood. Her ancestors were Macedonians who had come to Egypt during the time of Alexander the Great.

Teaching Tip

Refer students back to Section 3 of the chapter in this book titled *The Greek World* to review information on Alexander the Great and his conquests in the Mediterranean world.

Review & Assess

Close
Ask students how both Caesar and Octavian undermined, or took the power away from, the Roman Senate.

Review
Online Quiz Section 1

Assess
SE Section 1 Assessment
PASS: Section 1 Quiz
Alternative Assessment Handbook

Reteach/Classroom Intervention
California Standards Review Workbook
Interactive Reader and Study Guide, Section 1
Interactive Skills Tutor CD-ROM

Answers

Biography *She did not like him and had allied with his enemies.*

Reading Check *After Marc Antony's death, the Senate gave Octavian nearly limitless powers and named him Augustus, meaning "revered one."*

356

BIOGRAPHY

Cleopatra
69–30 BC

Cleopatra was a devoted ally of Julius Caesar and Marc Antony, but she didn't like Octavian. After the Battle of Actium, she feared that Octavian would arrest her and take over Egypt. Rather than see Octavian running her kingdom, Cleopatra chose to commit suicide. According to tradition, she poisoned herself with the venom of a deadly snake.

Drawing Conclusions Why do you think Cleopatra feared that Octavian would take over Egypt?

Octavian Becomes Emperor
After the Battle of Philippi, Octavian returned to Italy while Antony went east to fight Rome's enemies. In Turkey, Antony met **Cleopatra**, the queen of Egypt, and the two fell in love. Antony divorced his wife, Octavian's sister, to be with Cleopatra. Octavian saw this divorce as an insult to his sister and to himself.

Antony's behavior led to civil war in Rome. In 31 BC Octavian sent a fleet to attack Antony. Antony sailed out to meet it, and the two forces met just west of Greece in the Battle of Actium (AK-shee-uhm). Antony's fleet was defeated, but he escaped back to Egypt with Cleopatra. There the two committed suicide so they wouldn't be taken prisoner by Octavian.

With Antony's death, Octavian became Rome's sole ruler. Over the next few years he gained power. In 27 BC Octavian announced that he was giving up all his power to the Senate, but, in reality, he kept much power. He took the title *princeps* (PRIN-seps), or first citizen. The Senate gave him a new name—Augustus, which means "revered one." Modern historians consider the naming of Augustus to mark the end of the Roman Republic and the beginning of the Roman Empire.

READING CHECK **Summarizing** How did the Roman Republic become an empire?

SUMMARY AND PREVIEW In this section, you learned how Augustus gained power and made the Roman Republic into an empire. In the next section you'll learn what he and his successors did as the heads of that empire.

Section 1 Assessment

go.hrw.com
Online Quiz
KEYWORD: SQ6 HP12

Reviewing Ideas, Terms, and People HSS 6.7.4
1. a. Recall Whom did **Cicero** want Romans to give power to?
   b. Explain Why did some Romans call for change in their government?
2. a. Identify Who killed **Julius Caesar**?
   b. Explain Why did many Senators consider Caesar a threat?
   c. Elaborate Why do you think Caesar wanted the title of dictator for life?
3. a. Identify Who took over Rome after Caesar's death?
   b. Summarize How did Octavian take power from **Marc Antony**?

Critical Thinking
4. Sequencing Draw a time line like the one shown here. Use it to identify key events in Rome's change from a republic to an empire.

|—|—|—|—|—|—|—|—|—|

FOCUS ON WRITING
5. Taking Notes for a Screenplay Create a chart with columns labeled "Characters," "Setting," and "Plot." In appropriate columns, write notes about people, events, and locations in this section that should appear in the movie.

356 CHAPTER 12

Section 1 Assessment Answers

1. a. the Senate
b. because the political order was breaking down, and politicians and generals were fighting each other

2. a. a group of Senators
b. The Senators thought he was trying to make himself king, and they did not want a king.
c. possible answers—He didn't want anyone to take power from him; he wanted to rule his whole life.

3. a. Octavian

b. Octavian defeated him in battle, so Antony committed suicide.

4. 58–50 BC: Caesar conquers Gaul; 50 BC: Pompey's allies order Caesar to return to Rome; 49 BC: Caesar goes to Italy to defeat Pompey's forces; 44 BC: Senators stab Caesar; 42 BC: Antony and Octavian defeat Caesar's murderers; 31 BC: Octavian's fleet defeats Antony's fleet; 27 BC: Octavian says he is giving up all his power to the Senate.

5. Charts will vary, but students should include several major details from the section.

Augustus

What would you do if you had great power?

When did he live? 63 BC–AD 14

Where did he live? Rome

What did he do? As the leader of Rome, Augustus made many improvements in the city. He created a fire department and a police force to protect the city's people. He built new aqueducts and repaired old ones to increase Rome's water supply. Augustus also worked on improving and expanding Rome's road network.

Why is he important? As Rome's first emperor, Augustus is one of the most significant figures in Roman history. Almost singlehandedly, he changed the nature of Roman government forever. But Augustus is also known for the great monuments he had built around Rome. He built a new forum that held statues, monuments, and a great temple to the god Mars. In writing about his life, Augustus wrote, "I found Rome a city of brick and left it a city of marble."

Identifying Points of View Why do you think many Romans greatly admired Augustus?

This drawing shows how the Roman Forum appeared at the time of Augustus.

357

KEY EVENTS

- **45 BC** Julius Caesar adopts Octavian as his son and heir.
- **44 BC** Octavian moves to Rome when Caesar dies.
- **42 BC** Octavian and Antony defeat Brutus.
- **31 BC** Octavian defeats Antony.
- **27 BC** Octavian takes the name Augustus and becomes emperor of Rome.

Critical Thinking: Analyzing Information

Standards **Proficiency**

Augustus the Candidate HSS 6.7.4; HSS Analysis Skills: HI 1

1. Ask students to imagine that, in contrast to what was really the situation, Augustus had to be elected to a second term as emperor.

2. Ask students to further imagine that they are workers in Augustus's political campaign.

3. Have students compose bumper stickers and banners for Augustus's campaign. Call on volunteers to read, display, and explain their slogans or banners. **LS Verbal/Linguistic**

 Alternative Assessment Handbook, Rubric 34: Slogans and Banners

---

Biography

Reading Focus Question

Ask students to think about what they would do if they ruled their households as absolute leaders. What rules would they change? What improvements would they make? Would they declare any special holidays? How would they keep family members happy so that they wouldn't rebel?

Did You Know . . .

When you are the ruler of the largest empire in the world, your name shows up in many places. For example, Augustus had a month named after him. (Students should know which one.) August was originally called Sextilis, but was renamed in 8 BC.

Connect to Economics

Activity Designing a Coin for Augustus Augustus had his own name printed on coins. Some of the coins contained symbols that glorified the emperor. For example, he could add the name *Caesar* to Augustus to remind everyone that the popular Julius Caesar was his great uncle and adoptive father.

Have students design coins to commemorate the life or achievements of Augustus. Display the coins in the classroom.

 Alternative Assessment Handbook, Rubric 3: Artwork

Analyzing Visuals

Roman Architecture Have students look at the drawing of the Roman Forum. Ask them to describe features of Roman architecture shown. *arches, columns* Ask them to name a building in this country that has one of these features. *Possible answer: The White House (columns)*

Answers

Biography *He made many improvements to Rome.*

357

Bellringer

If YOU were there . . . Use the **Daily Bellringer Transparency** to help students answer the question.

Daily Bellringer Transparency, Section 2

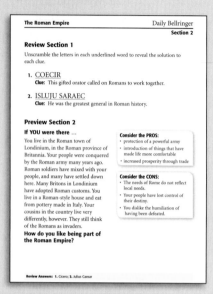

The Roman Empire — Daily Bellringer Section 2

Review Section 1

Unscramble the letters in each underlined word to reveal the solution to each clue.

1. COECIR
   Clue: This gifted orator called on Romans to work together.

2. ISLUJU SARAEC
   Clue: He was the greatest general in Roman history.

Preview Section 2

If YOU were there . . .
You live in the Roman town of Londinium, in the Roman province of Britannia. Your people were conquered by the Roman army many years ago. Roman soldiers have mixed with your people, and many have settled down here. Many Britons in Londinium have adopted Roman customs. You live in a Roman-style house and eat from pottery made in Italy. Your cousins in the country live very differently, however. They still think of the Romans as invaders.
How do you like being part of the Roman Empire?

Consider the PROS:
- protection of a powerful army
- introduction of things that have made life more comfortable
- increased prosperity through trade

Consider the CONS:
- The needs of Rome do not reflect local needs.
- Your people have lost control of their destiny.
- You dislike the humiliation of having been defeated.

Review Answers: 1. Cicero; **2.** Julius Caesar

Academic Vocabulary

Review with students the high-use academic term in this section:

effect the result of an action or decision (p. 361)

CRF: Vocabulary Builder Activity, Section 2

Standards Focus

HSS 6.7.3

Means: Explain how political and economic factors contributed to the growth of the Roman Empire.

Matters: Conquest and economic growth have been key to the expansion of empires throughout history.

A Vast Empire

What You Will Learn...

Main Ideas

1. The Roman Empire expanded to control the entire Mediterranean world.
2. Trade increased in Rome, both within the empire and with other people.
3. The Pax Romana was a period of peace and prosperity in the cities and the country.

The Big Idea

After Augustus became emperor, the Roman Empire grew politically and economically, and life improved for the Roman people.

Key Terms and People

Hadrian, *p. 359*
provinces, *p. 360*
currency, *p. 360*
Pax Romana, *p. 361*
villas, *p. 362*

HSS 6.7.3 Identify the location of and the political and geographic reasons for the growth of Roman territories and expansion of the empire, including how the empire fostered economic growth through the use of currency and trade routes.

If YOU were there...

You live in the Roman town of Londinium, in the Roman province of Britannia. Your people were conquered by the Roman army many years ago. Roman soldiers have mixed with your people, and many have settled down here. Many Britons in Londinium have adopted Roman customs. You live in a Roman-style house and eat from pottery made in Italy. Your cousins in the country live very differently, however. They still think of the Romans as invaders.

How do you like being part of the Roman Empire?

BUILDING BACKGROUND Since the days of the republic, Rome had grown steadily. The conquests of generals such as Julius Caesar and Pompey added more territory. Once Rome became an empire, its rulers continued to expand its power. Soldiers and settlers carried Roman culture to distant provinces such as Britannia, or Britain.

The Empire Expands

When Rome became an empire, it already controlled most of the Mediterranean world. Within about 150 years, though, the empire had grown even bigger. Augustus and the emperors who followed him pushed the boundaries of their empire, taking over huge chunks of Europe, Africa, and Asia. At its height Rome ruled one of the largest empires in all of world history.

Reasons for Expansion

Why did emperors add so much land to the empire? They had many reasons. One of these reasons was to control hostile neighbors. Some countries that shared borders with Rome were threatening Rome. To keep these countries from attacking the empire or its citizens, the Romans conquered them.

Not all of the territories the Romans conquered were political threats. Some were conquered for economic reasons. Many of these territories had vast supplies of gold, good farmlands, or other resources the Romans wanted. Other areas were conquered for another reason: Some emperors liked a good fight.

Teach the Big Idea: Master the Standards
Standards Proficiency

A Vast Empire HSS 6.7.3; HSS Analysis Skills: HI 1

1. **Teach** Ask students the Main Idea questions to teach this section.

2. **Apply** Ask students to imagine that they were residents of the Roman Republic who fell into a magical sleep in about 200 BC. They awaken 200 years later and find themselves citizens of the Roman Empire. Have each student write a paragraph that starts with "When I awoke after my long sleep, I was amazed to find that . . ." **LS Verbal/Linguistic**

3. **Review** Call on volunteers to read their paragraphs. If any major events or characteristics of the empire were not covered, discuss those as a class.

4. **Practice/Homework** Have each student write a second paragraph in which they describe the change they like or dislike the most. **LS Verbal/Linguistic**

   Alternative Assessment Handbook, Rubric 37: Writing Assignments

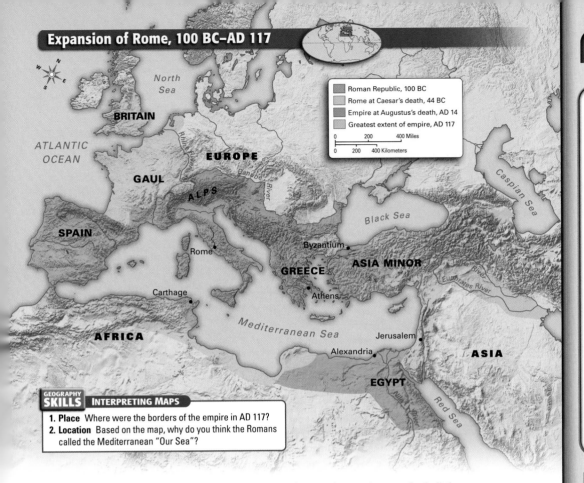

Expansion of Rome, 100 BC–AD 117

North Sea

BRITAIN

ATLANTIC OCEAN

EUROPE

GAUL

ALPS

Rhine River

Danube River

SPAIN

Rome

Carthage

GREECE

Athens

Byzantium

Black Sea

ASIA MINOR

Caspian Sea

AFRICA

Mediterranean Sea

Jerusalem

Alexandria

ASIA

EGYPT

Nile River

Red Sea

Euphrates River

Roman Republic, 100 BC
Rome at Caesar's death, 44 BC
Empire at Augustus's death, AD 14
Greatest extent of empire, AD 117

0   200   400 Miles
0   200   400 Kilometers

GEOGRAPHY SKILLS | **INTERPRETING MAPS**

1. **Place** Where were the borders of the empire in AD 117?
2. **Location** Based on the map, why do you think the Romans called the Mediterranean "Our Sea"?

Directions of Expansion

As the map above shows, the Roman Empire grew after Augustus died. By the early 100s the Romans had taken over Gaul and much of central Europe.

By the time of the emperor **Hadrian**, the Romans had also conquered most of the island of Britain. The people of Britain, the Celts (KELTZ), had fought fiercely against the Roman army. Fearing attacks by barbarian invaders in the north, Hadrian built a huge wall across northern Britain. Hadrian's Wall marked the border between Roman and non-Roman territory.

In the east the empire stretched all the way into Mesopotamia. Other Asian territories the Romans ruled included Asia Minor and the eastern coast of the Mediterranean. All of the north African coast belonged to Rome as well, so the Romans controlled everything that bordered the Mediterranean. In fact, Roman control of the Mediterranean was so great that they called it *Mare Nostrum*, or "Our Sea."

READING CHECK **Drawing Conclusions** Why did Roman emperors want to expand the empire?

THE ROMAN EMPIRE **359**

Main Idea

② Trade Increases

Trade increased in Rome, both within the empire and with other people.

Identify What are the territories that Rome conquered called? *provinces*

Recall What did Rome ship out of its ports? *goods made by artisans, including jewelry, glass, and clothing*

Drawing Conclusions What trade routes were probably faster—overland on the Silk Road or by sea? *possible answer—depends on the distance, but sea routes are usually faster*

- **CRF:** Economics and History Activity: The Romans and Money
- **CRF:** History and Geography Activity: Roman Trade
- Map Transparency: Roman Trade Routes, AD 200
- **HSS** 6.7.3; **HSS** Analysis Skills: CS 3, HI 1

Linking to Today

The New Silk Road The old Silk Road connected the east to the west. A new Silk Road is being built and will be called the Asian Highway Network. It will connect at least 26 Asian countries with a standardized highway system. Supporters of this plan claim that the new highway will reach remote parts of Asia and allow people there to trade with their neighbors and the rest of the world.

Answers

Interpreting Maps *grains, olives and olive oil, grapes and wine, silk, spices, gold, and iron*

Reading Check *Roman currency was accepted everywhere, so trade was easier; Romans could trade even if they did not have any items other people wanted.*

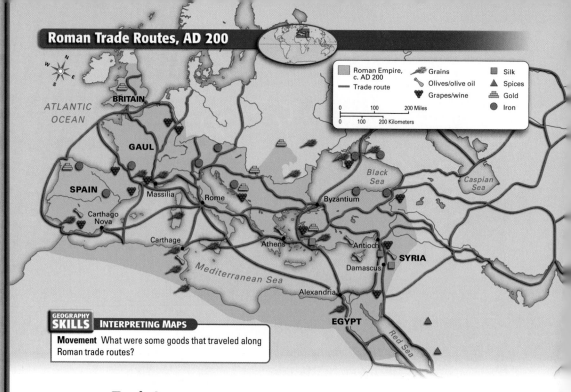

Roman Trade Routes, AD 200

GEOGRAPHY **SKILLS** | INTERPRETING MAPS

Movement What were some goods that traveled along Roman trade routes?

Trade Increases

As the empire grew, the Romans met many different peoples. In many cases these peoples had goods that the Romans wanted. Thinking that there would be a market for these products in Rome, merchants began to travel all over the empire, as you can see on the map.

People in the city of Rome needed raw materials that they couldn't produce themselves. Many of the materials could be found, though, in Rome's **provinces**, the areas outside of Italy that the Romans controlled. Traders brought metals, cloth, and food from the provinces to the city. They also brought more exotic goods, like spices from Asia and animals from Africa. In return the Romans sent goods made by artisans to the provinces. These goods included jewelry, glass, and clothing.

Some Roman traders also traveled beyond the empire's borders. They sailed as far as eastern Africa, India, and what is now Vietnam to find goods they couldn't get in the empire. Others traveled overland into Asia to meet merchants bringing goods from China on the Silk Road. Silk was especially popular in Rome. Wealthy Romans were willing to pay high prices for it.

To pay for their trade goods, Romans used **currency**, or money. They traded coins made of gold and silver for the items they wanted. These coins allowed the Romans to trade with people even if they had no items their trade partners wanted. Nearly everyone accepted Roman coins, which helped trade grow even more.

READING CHECK **Identifying Cause and Effect** How did currency help Roman trade grow?

360 CHAPTER 12

Critical Thinking: Interpreting Maps

Standards Proficiency

HSS 6.7.3; **HSS** Analysis Skills: CS 3, HI 1

1. Have students examine the map on this page.

2. Ask students which routes they think were more difficult to travel than others. Remind students to consider geographic obstacles such as mountains and rough seas. Also, remind them that physical maps of the world are provided in the atlas in the back of this textbook.

3. Have each student create a picture postcard from a location along one of the trade routes. Students should illustrate one side of the card and write a brief message on the other.

LS Visual/Spatial

- Alternative Assessment Handbook, Rubrics 3: Artwork; and 21: Map Reading

The Pax Romana

The first 200 years of the Roman Empire were a time of general peace and prosperity. Several characteristics, such as a stable government and an organized military, helped the empire to thrive and maintain peace during these years. There were no major wars or rebellions in the empire. We call this peaceful period the **Pax Romana**, or Roman Peace. It lasted until about AD 180.

During the Pax Romana the empire's population grew. Trade continued to increase, and many Romans became wealthy through this trade. One **effect** of these changes was an improvement in the quality of life for people living in Rome and in its provinces.

Life in Cities

During the Pax Romana many Romans lived in cities scattered throughout the empire. Some of these cities, like Alexandria in Egypt, were major centers of trade and had huge populations. Other cities, like Pompeii (pom-PAY) in Italy, had much smaller populations.

By far the largest city in the empire was, of course, Rome. Some historians think that Rome may have had more than a million residents at its height. Although many were wealthy, many were not, and that large population led to difficulties for many poorer residents. Many poor Romans lived in crowded, sometimes dangerous, apartment buildings.

ACADEMIC VOCABULARY

effect the result of an action or decision

Pompeii: A City Preserved

Pompeii was located at the foot of a volcano called Mount Vesuvius. In AD 79 Vesuvius suddenly erupted, and ash buried Pompeii. The well-preserved remains of Pompeii have taught us a great deal about life in the Roman Empire.

This famous painting shows a young couple that lived in Pompeii.

ANALYSIS SKILL **ANALYZING VISUALS**

What do the ruins tell us about the kind of entertainment people in Pompeii might have enjoyed?

361

Direct Teach

Main Idea

❸ The Pax Romana

The Pax Romana was a period of peace and prosperity in the cities and the country.

Describe What was the Pax Romana, and how long did it last? *a peaceful period during which there were no major wars or rebellions in the Roman Empire; about 200 years*

Identify What was the largest city in the Roman Empire? What is an example of one of the small cities? *Rome; Pompeii*

Predict How might a poor city-dweller have felt about the label *Pax Romana?* *possible answer—might have felt it was not a good label, because living in the city could be dangerous and therefore not very peaceful*

HSS 6.7.4; HSS Analysis Skills: CS 1, HR 5, HI 1

Connect to Science

Mount Vesuvius On August 24, AD 79, Mount Vesuvius erupted. The eruption happened in two stages. First, a tall column of material shot from the volcano into the air. Scientists estimate that the column may have towered more than 12 miles into the atmosphere. The column then collapsed, raining rock on the town. The next day, a fast-moving cloud of poisonous gas and dust poured down the volcano's sides. This type of cloud is called pyroclastic flow. After only 24 hours, Pompeii lay buried under almost 20 feet of rock and ash.

Differentiating Instruction for Universal Access

Learners Having Difficulty   Reaching Standards

1. Discuss with students how daily life in the city would vary from life in the country.

2. Have students imagine that they are living in the city of Rome. Tell them to write letters to a cousin who lives in the country. The letter should describe life in the city. Encourage students to include details. You may need to teach or review the format for a personal letter.

3. Tell students to attach a drawing of their house or apartment building.

4. Ask for volunteers to read their letters and share their drawings.
   LS Verbal/Linguistic, Visual/Spatial

HSS 6.7.3; HSS Analysis Skills: HI 1

Alternative Assessment Handbook, Rubrics 3: Artwork; and 25: Personal Letters

Answers

Analyzing Visuals *The remains of stadiums and open-air theatres tell us that the people in Pompeii may have enjoyed sporting events, drama, and gladiatorial combat.*

361

❸ The Pax Romana

The Pax Romana was a period of peace and prosperity in the cities and the country.

Identify Who worked the villa owner's fields? *slaves*

Explain Why did rich Romans want villas? *to visit when they wanted a break from their responsibilities or the city's crowds*

Make Generalizations Where did the majority of people in the Roman Empire live? How did they make a living? *on small farms; growing only enough food for themselves*

🐻 **HSS** 6.7.4; **HSS** Analysis Skills: HI 1, HI 2

Linking to Today

Bathing in Bath We know Romans enjoyed their baths, so it is no wonder they built a settlement at what is now Bath, England. The hot mineral springs located there provided the Romans with water for luxurious soaking. The site has been occupied ever since. In the 1700s, the hot springs made the city a fashionable resort. Today the city is still a popular tourist destination rich in Roman and English history.

History Close-up
A Chariot Race

Chariot racing was the most popular sport in ancient Rome. Slaves, soldiers, Senators, and emperors all loved to go to the track and watch the thrilling competitions. Devoted fans cheered for their favorite teams and drivers.

The *spina* ran down the middle of the circus, and chariots raced around it seven times.

Chariots were organized into teams, in this case the red team and the white team.

ANALYSIS SKILL **ANALYZING VISUALS**
How can you tell from this illustration that chariot racing was popular?

Despite their poor living conditions, the people of Rome enjoyed many types of entertainment. They could go to comic plays, thrilling chariot races, or fierce gladiator fights. Those who wanted more peace and quiet could head for one of Rome's public baths. The huge bath complexes in Rome were more like spas or health clubs than bathtubs. At the bath people could swim, soak in a hot pool, or mingle with other Romans.

Romans looking for fun could also just tour the city. Rome was filled with beautiful temples and monuments built by city leaders. The Romans were proud of their city and took great pride in how it looked:

❝In great buildings as well as in other things the rest of the world has been outdone by us Romans. If, indeed, all the buildings in our City are considered . . . together in one vast mass, the united grandeur of them would lead one to imagine that we were describing another world, accumulated in a single spot.❞
–Pliny the Elder, from *Natural History*

Life in the Country

When we think of life in the Roman Empire, we often think of a city. In truth, though, more people lived in the country than in the empire's cities. People outside of the cities had a very different way of life than city dwellers did.

In rural areas most people farmed. On their small farms they grew just enough food for themselves and their families. Many of these farmers spoke languages other than Latin. In fact, many people in the country didn't seem Roman at all. These people had kept many of their own customs and traditions when they were conquered by the Romans.

Scattered among the groups of farmers, though, were large farms and **villas**, or country homes belonging to rich Romans. Many people from the cities liked to have a house outside the city. They visited these homes when they wanted a break from the city crowds.

362 CHAPTER 12

Collaborative Learning

Standards Proficiency

The Roman Villa 🐻 **HSS** 6.7.3; Analysis Skills: HR 1, HI 1

Research Required

1. Organize the class into small groups. Tell students that they will conduct research on different styles of Roman villas and try to design a villa of their own.

2. Direct students to library or Internet resources for information.

3. After students have studied examples of the classic Roman villa, have them design their own. Instruct students to use photos and

information in this chapter to help them come up with a design.

4. Ask for volunteers to display their villa designs and explain to the class their villas' features and the function or purpose of those features. **LS** Interpersonal, Visual/Spatial

📖 Alternative Assessment Handbook, Rubrics 3: Artwork, and 30: Research

Answers

Analyzing Visuals *The stands are full, and people are watching and cheering.*

The lively crowd included men and women from all classes of society.

The hardest part of the race was the turn. Chariots often crashed while making this difficult maneuver.

At their villas, these wealthy Romans lived much like they did at home. They hosted huge, elaborate dinner parties where they served exotic foods. Some of the foods served at these parties sound very unusual to modern people. For example, Romans cooked and served peacocks, ostriches, jellyfish, and even mice!

These meals were often served by slaves who worked in the villas. Other slaves worked in the villa owners' fields. The sale of crops grown in these fields helped pay for the villa owners' extravagant expenses.

READING CHECK **Contrasting** How was life different in the country than in the city?

SUMMARY AND PREVIEW The Roman Empire grew and changed during its first 200 years. In the next section you will learn about the great advances made in art, engineering, and other fields.

Section 2 Assessment

go.hrw.com
Online Quiz
KEYWORD: SQ6 HP12

Reviewing Ideas, Terms, and People **HSS** 6.7.3

1. **a. Identify** What areas of the world did the Romans take over?
   b. Explain Why did **Hadrian** build a wall in northern Britain?
2. **a. Define** What were **provinces**?
   b. Summarize Why did trade increase as the Roman Empire expanded?
3. **a. Explain** Why is the period before AD 180 called the **Pax Romana**?
   b. Evaluate Would you have preferred to live in a Roman city or the country? Why?

Critical Thinking

4. **Contrasting** Draw two houses like these. In the house on the left, write two facts about life in a Roman city. In the house on the right, write two facts about life in the country.

City   Country

FOCUS ON WRITING

5. **Adding Details** Add information about additional characters to your chart. Under the "Setting" column, add information about life during the Pax Romana.

THE ROMAN EMPIRE **363**

History and Geography

Activity Ask students to imagine that they are road builders in the Roman Empire. What geographical, political, or logistical challenges and dangers might they face as they build roads through newly conquered provinces? Lead a class discussion about these challenges.

Info to Know

The Appian Way Of all the roads leading to Rome, the most famous is the *Via Appia Antica*, or Old Appian Way. Begun in 312 BC, the Appian Way was the first major Roman road built. It eventually stretched more than 350 miles (563 km.) from Rome to Brindisi, a seaport in southern Italy on the Adriatic Sea. The road served as the main highway to Greece and points east. Large monuments and tombs lined the first few miles of the road as it left Rome. The road's solid construction has passed the test of time, and the Appian Way remains. The initial stretch of the road from Rome is now protected and a popular tourist attraction.

The Postal Service One of the most important uses of the Roman road system was the *cursus publicus*, or postal service. Although average citizens were not allowed to use the postal service, it allowed the Roman government to send information and instructions across the empire.

Roman Roads

The Romans are famous for their roads. They built a road network so large and well constructed that parts of it remain today, roughly 2,000 years later. Roads helped the Romans run their empire. Armies, travelers, messengers, and merchants all used the roads to get around. They stretched to every corner of the empire in a network so vast that people even today say that "all roads lead to Rome."

Roman roads stretched as far north as Scotland.

The Romans built about 50,000 miles of roads. That's enough to circle the earth—twice!

In the west, roads crisscrossed Spain.

Roman roads in the south connected different parts of northern Africa.

EUROPE

PYRENEES

ITALY

Rome

AFRICA

Standards Focus

HSS 6.7 Students analyze the geographic, political, economic, religious, and social structures during the development of Rome.

6.7.3 Identify the location of and the political and geographic reasons for the growth of Roman territories and expansion of the empire, including how the empire fostered economic growth through the use of currency and trade routes.

Differentiating Instruction for Universal Access

Learners Having Difficulty
Reaching Standards

Comparing Maps To help students understand the full extent of the Roman road network, have them compare the map on this page with the map in Section 2 titled "Expansion of Rome" and to a current world map. Have students identify the regions through which the Roman roads passed and the countries located there today.

LS Visual/Spatial

HSS 6.7.3; HSS Analysis Skills: CS 3

Alternative Assessment Handbook, Rubric 21: Map Reading

Advanced Learners/GATE
Exceeding Standards

Calculating Distances Organize the class into small groups. Assign each group a present-day country that lay partially or completely within the Roman Empire. Have each group use modern maps of the Mediterranean world to calculate about how many miles of roads the Romans built within its assigned country. **LS Logical/Mathematical**

HSS 6.7.3; HSS Analysis Skills: CS 3

Alternative Assessment Handbook, Rubrics 14: Group Activity; and 21: Map Reading

Paving stones

Drainage ditch

Curbstones

Sand, clay, and gravel

Stone chips

Gravel concrete

Roman roads were built to last. They were constructed of layers of sand, concrete, rock, and stone. Drainage ditches let water drain off, preventing water damage.

The roads were built by and for the military. The main purpose of the roads was to allow Rome's armies to travel quickly throughout the empire.

In the east, Roman roads stretched into Southwest Asia.

The Romans built tall "milestones" along their roads to mark distances. Just like modern highway signs, the markers told travelers how far it was to the next town.

GEOGRAPHY SKILLS INTERPRETING MAPS

1. **Movement** Why did the Romans build their roads?
2. **Location** How does the map show that "all roads lead to Rome"?

THE ROMAN EMPIRE **365**

Info to Know

Travel along Roman Roads The most common vehicle on Roman roads was the two-wheeled chariot, pulled by either two or four horses. Four-wheeled versions provided transportation for passengers. Goods were hauled in carts pulled by 8 to 10 horses. Average distance traveled along Roman roads ranged from 15 to 75 miles per day.

Did you know . . .

The thickness of a completed Roman road was from three to six feet.

Connect to Science and Technology

The First Roads The first roads were animal paths that people then improved. Records refer to such paths being used as roads around Jericho in about 6000 BC. The earliest known constructed roads date to about 4000 BC. Roads from this period have been found at Ur, in what is now Iraq, and at Glastonbury, England.

Social Studies Skills: Interpreting Maps

Standards Proficiency

Roman Road Maps HSS 6.7.3; HSS Analysis Skills: CS 3

Prep Required

Materials: colored markers; photocopies of above map

1. Provide each student with a photocopy of the above map and colored markers.

2. Have students use the maps in this chapter to add the major Roman cities and the borders of the Roman Empire at its peak to their map.

3. Then, have students refer to their maps as you lead a discussion about transportation in the Roman Empire. **LS** Visual/Spatial

Alternative Assessment Handbook, Rubric 21: Map Reading

Bellringer

If YOU were there . . . Use the **Daily Bellringer Transparency** to help students answer the question.

🖳 Daily Bellringer Transparency, Section 3

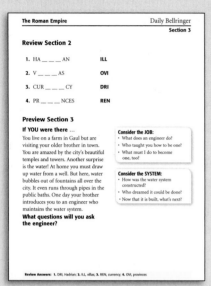

Building Vocabulary

Preteach or review the following terms:

majestic grand, magnificent (p. 368)

masterpiece a work done with extraordinary skill (p. 370)

📝 **CRF:** Vocabulary Builder Activity, Section 3

 Standards Focus

HSS 6.7.8

Means: Discuss how Roman achievements in art, architecture, technology, science, literature, and law have influenced world history.

Matters: The Romans made important contributions to civilization that have endured for more than 2,000 years.

Rome's Legacy

What You Will Learn...

Main Ideas

1. The Romans looked for ways to use science and engineering to improve their lives.
2. Roman architecture and art were largely based on Greek ideas.
3. Roman literature and language have influenced how people write and speak.
4. Roman law serves as a model for modern law codes around the world.

The Big Idea

Many features of Roman culture were copied by later civilizations and continue to influence our lives today.

Key Terms and People

Galen, *p. 366*
aqueduct, *p. 367*
vault, *p. 367*
Virgil, *p. 370*
Ovid, *p. 370*
satire, *p. 370*
Romance languages, *p. 371*
civil law, *p. 371*

HSS 6.7.8 Discuss the legacies of Roman art and architecture, technology and science, literature, language, and law.

If YOU were there...

You live on a farm in Gaul but are visiting your older brother in town. You are amazed by the city's beautiful temples and towers. Another surprise is the water! At home you must draw up water from a well. But here, water bubbles out of fountains all over the city. It even runs through pipes in the public baths. One day your brother introduces you to the engineer who maintains the water system.

What questions will you ask the engineer?

BUILDING BACKGROUND Ideas of law and government spread widely. But those were not the Romans' only accomplishments. Roman scientists, engineers, artists, and writers also made contributions to life in Rome. Many of the ideas the Romans developed 2,000 years ago are still influential today.

Roman Science and Engineering

The Romans took a practical approach to their study of science and engineering. Unlike the Greeks, who studied the world just to know about it, the Romans were more concerned with finding knowledge that they could use to improve their lives.

Science

Roman scientists wanted to produce results that could benefit their society. For example, they studied the stars not just to know about them but to produce a calendar. They studied plants and animals to learn how to produce better crops and meat.

The practical Roman approach to science can also be seen in medicine. Most of the greatest doctors in the Roman Empire were Greek. One doctor in the empire was **Galen**, who lived in the AD 100s. He was a Greek surgeon who made many discoveries about the body. For example, Galen described the valves of the heart and noted differences between arteries and veins. For centuries, doctors based their ideas on Galen's teachings and writings.

Teach the Big Idea: Master the Standards

Standards Proficiency

Rome's Legacy 🐻 **HSS** 6.7.8; **HSS** Analysis Skills: HI 1, HI 3

1. **Teach** Ask students the Main Idea questions to teach this section.

2. **Apply** Organize the class into small groups. Assign each group one of Rome's contributions to civilization, such as engineering or architecture. Tell each group to take notes on its assigned contribution. **LS** **Interpersonal, Verbal/Linguistic**

3. **Review** As you review the section's main ideas, have each group share information about its topic.

4. **Practice/Homework** Have students draw or describe in writing an example of their topic. Have volunteers share their work with the class. **LS** **Visual/Spatial**

📝 Alternative Assessment Handbook, Rubrics 3: Artwork; and 42: Writing to Inform

Engineering

The Romans' practical use of science can also be seen in their engineering. The Romans were great builders. Even today people walk along Roman roads and drive over Roman bridges built almost 2,000 years ago. How have these structures survived for so long?

The Romans developed some new building materials to help their structures last. The most important of these materials was cement. They made cement by mixing a mineral called lime with volcanic rock and ash. The resulting material dried to be very hard and watertight.

More important than the materials they used, though, were the designs the Romans had for their structures. For example, they built their roads in layers. Each layer was made of a different material. This layered construction made the road durable. Many Roman roads have not worn down even after centuries of traffic and exposure to wind and rain.

Another way the Romans created structures to last was by using arches. Because of its rounded shape, an arch can support much heavier weights than other shapes can. This strength has allowed arched structures such as Roman bridges to last until the present.

The Romans also used arches in their aqueducts (A-kwuh-duhkts). An **aqueduct** was a channel used to carry water from mountains into cities. When they crossed deep valleys, aqueducts were supported by rows of arches. The Romans' aqueducts were so well built that many still stand.

Roman builders also learned how to combine arches to create vaults. A **vault** is a set of arches that supports the roof of a building. The Romans used vaults to create huge, open areas within buildings. As a result, Roman buildings were much larger than anything that had come before.

THE IMPACT TODAY
People still build aqueducts today. One of the largest carries water from northern to southern California.

READING CHECK Summarizing What were two ways the Romans built strong structures?

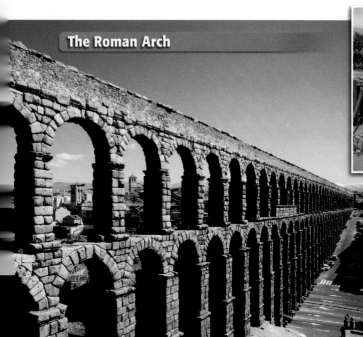

The Roman Arch

The Romans were the first people to make wide use of the arch. The photograph at left shows a Roman aqueduct supported by hundreds of arches. Above is a drawing showing how Roman engineers built their tall and strong arches.

How did the Romans support arches during their construction?

THE ROMAN EMPIRE **367**

Direct Teach

Main Idea

❶ **Roman Science and Engineering**

The Romans looked for ways to use science and engineering to improve their lives.

Identify What is an example of an important medical discovery during the Roman Empire? *Galen's description of the valves of the heart and the differences between arteries and veins*

Explain Why was cement such a useful material? *It was very hard and watertight when it dried.*

Draw Conclusions How were Romans able to increase the size of their buildings? *by using combinations of vaults and arches*

HSS 6.7.8; **HSS** Analysis Skills: CS 1, HI 1

Linking to Today

The Segovia Aqueduct Residents of Segovia, Spain, still benefit from Roman engineering. In about AD 100, Romans built a huge aqueduct there that required some 24,000 stone blocks. One section of the aqueduct, shown in the photo at left, still stands. The part that is above ground stands 30 feet high in most places. Where the ground level dips very low, the aqueduct is 93.5 feet tall. The aqueduct continues to carry water to Segovia.

Differentiating Instruction for Universal Access

Special Education Students   Reaching Standards

Materials: blocks or small boxes of various sizes and shapes, including half-circles; large gumdrops; toothpicks

1. Organize the class into small groups. Provide each group with the listed materials.

2. Use blocks or boxes to demonstrate how the Romans built forms for their arches, referring to the drawing above. Help students build similar structures.

3. Then point out that the gumdrops have a narrow end and a wide end, like the stone blocks that made the arches. Help students build arches from the gumdrops, resting the arches on the block forms and holding them together with toothpicks.

4. Students should be able to remove the forms when finished and the gumdrop arches should remain intact. **LS** Interpersonal, Kinesthetic

HSS 6.7.8; **HSS** Analysis Skills: CS 3, HI 1

Alternative Assessment Handbook, Rubric 14: Group Activity

Answers

The Roman Arch *with a wooden form that supported the arch's weight*

Reading Check *new materials such as concrete and new building methods such as the arch and vault*

② Architecture and Art

Roman architecture and art were largely based on Greek ideas.

Identify What architectural features were used more on Roman buildings than Greek ones? *vaults, domes*

Recall What are four types of art at which the Romans excelled? *possible answers—mosaics, paintings, frescoes, portraits, sculpture*

Make Inferences Why might a historian say that the Romans' talent for building large structures is directly related to aspects of Roman society? *possible answer—Romans gathered in large groups for various purposes, such as participating in government and recreation. These activities required large buildings to house the large crowds. Arches, vaults, and domes enabled the construction of these big buildings.*

HSS 6.7.8; **HSS** Analysis Skills: HI 1

Did you know . . .

An immense, retractable fabric canopy over the Colosseum shaded spectators from the sun. To this day, engineers are not certain how it was rigged.

Architecture and Art

The Romans weren't only interested in practicality, though. They also admired beauty. Roman appreciation for beauty can be seen in their architecture and art. People still admire their magnificent buildings, statues, and paintings.

Architecture

Roman architecture was largely based on older Greek designs. Like the ancient Greeks, the Romans used columns to make their public buildings look stately and impressive. Also like the Greeks, the Romans covered many of their buildings with marble to make them more majestic.

But Roman engineering techniques allowed them to take architecture beyond what the Greeks had done. For example, the Roman vault let them build huge structures, much larger than anything the Greeks could build. One such Roman structure that used vaults was the Colosseum pictured below. It was built to hold fights between gladiators.

The Colosseum

The Colosseum was a huge arena in ancient Rome. The giant building was more than 150 feet tall and could seat about 50,000 people, who came to watch events like gladiator fights. The building's design was based on many arches and vaults, hallmarks of Roman engineering.

This modern sports stadium in Oakland, California, is known as the Coliseum after the building in ancient Rome.

The arches on the outside of the building were decorated with statues of Roman gods.

People entered the Colosseum through 80 arched entrances, each with its own number.

368 CHAPTER 12

Collaborative Learning

Standards Proficiency

Gladiator Playbill **HSS** 6.7.8; **HSS** Analysis Skills: HI 1

Materials: poster board, colored pencils, and markers

1. Tell students that a playbill is a poster that advertises a play or other event. It is similar to a movie poster.

2. Organize the class into small groups. Have each group design a playbill advertising an event at the Colosseum. The playbill should describe the event and when it will occur. Encourage students to use dramatic and sensational language and drawings. Events

may include gladiator fights, animal fights, or mock naval battles.

3. Tell students to divide the tasks between the groups and to assign each member specific tasks. Some students may do lettering while others may draw or conduct research.

4. Display completed playbills in a classroom exhibit. **LS** Interpersonal, Visual/Spatial

Alternative Assessment Handbook, Rubrics 2: Advertisements; and 3: Artwork

The Romans also used more domes in their architecture than the Greeks had. Domes were difficult to build and required a great deal of support. Once the Romans developed cement, they could provide that support. Many Roman structures are topped with huge domes, some of the largest ever built.

Art

The artists of the Roman Empire were known for their beautiful mosaics, paintings, and statues. Mosaics and paintings were used to decorate Roman buildings. Many Roman homes and businesses had elaborate mosaics built into their floors. The walls of these buildings were often covered with paintings. Most Roman paintings were frescoes. A fresco is a type of painting done on wet plaster.

Many Roman artists were particularly skilled at creating portraits, or pictures of people. When they made a portrait, artists tried to show their subject's personality. We can guess a great deal about individual Romans by studying their portraits.

Many public buildings in the United States are modeled after Roman designs.

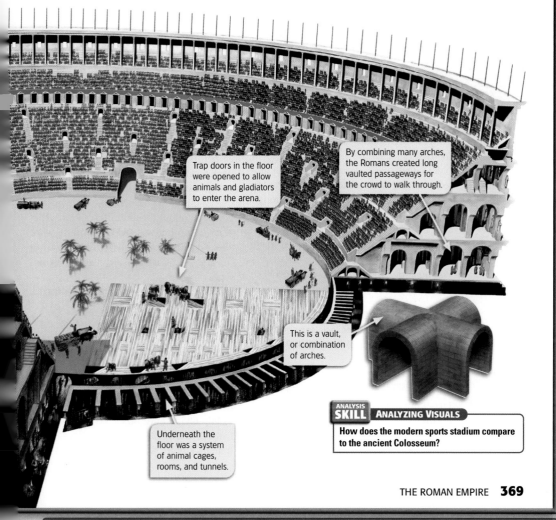

Trap doors in the floor were opened to allow animals and gladiators to enter the arena.

By combining many arches, the Romans created long vaulted passageways for the crowd to walk through.

This is a vault, or combination of arches.

Underneath the floor was a system of animal cages, rooms, and tunnels.

ANALYSIS SKILL **ANALYZING VISUALS**

How does the modern sports stadium compare to the ancient Colosseum?

THE ROMAN EMPIRE **369**

Critical Thinking: Describing

Standards Proficiency

Local Architecture HSS 6.7.8; Analysis Skills: HI 3

Prep Required

1. Ask students to list examples of Roman architecture, such as courthouses or other government buildings, in or near your community. Roman influence is apparent in details such as columns, arches, and domes.

2. If your community lacks such buildings, provide books on American architecture to familiarize students with the style.

3. Have each student write a short description of how the community buildings or buildings in the books have been influenced by Roman architecture. **LS Verbal/Linguistic, Visual/Spatial**

Alternative Assessment Handbook, Rubric 40: Writing to Describe

❸ Literature and Language

Roman literature and language have influenced how people write and speak.

Identify Who were two great Roman writers? *Ovid, Virgil*

Explain Why did the Roman Empire have two official languages? *It was huge, and people in the east spoke a different language than people in the west.*

Find the Main Idea How has Latin influenced present-day European and American languages? *Latin developed into the Romance languages, was used widely throughout Europe, and influenced English.*

📄 **CRF:** Biography Acitvity: Marcus Aurelius

📄 **CRF:** Literature Activity: Tales from Ovid

📄 **CRF:** Primary Source Activity: The Meditations of Marcus Aurelius

🐻 **HSS** 6.7.8; **HSS** Analysis Skills: HI 1, HI 3

Connect to English–Language Arts

Metamorphosis Ovid's most famous work is titled *Metamorphoses*. It is a collection of myths. Point out that the word *metamorphosis* means "change" or "transition". The myths that Ovid tells have to do with transformations, such as humans being turned into animals as punishment from the gods.

A Roman Fresco
A fresco is a type of painting in which paint is applied to wet plaster and then left to dry. Roman artists painted many beautiful frescoes like this one.

What activities can you see in this fresco?

Roman sculptors were also talented. They created some original works, but many Roman statues are actually copies of older Greek works. Roman sculptors studied what the Greeks had done and tried to re-create it in their own statues. Although their works are not original, we owe a great deal to these Roman artists. Many of the original Greek works they copied have been destroyed over time. Without the Roman copies, the world would know little about many Greek masterpieces.

READING CHECK Drawing Conclusions
Why did many Roman architects and artists base their work on earlier Greek works?

Literature and Language

Like Roman artists, Roman authors are greatly admired. In addition, the works they created and the language they used have shaped our language today.

Literature

The Romans admired good writers. Many emperors encouraged authors to write. As a result, Rome was home to many of the greatest authors of the ancient world. One such author was **Virgil**, who wrote a great epic about the founding of Rome, the *Aeneid*. Another was **Ovid** (AHV-uhd), who wrote poems about Roman mythology.

The Romans also excelled in other types of writing:

• **satire**, a style of writing that pokes fun at people or society
• history and speeches
• drama, both tragedies and comedies

Many of these works have served as models for hundreds of years and are still enjoyed today.

Language

Virgil, Ovid, and other poets wrote in Latin, the language of ancient Rome. The Roman Empire was huge, and it had two

---

Cross-Discipline Activity: Arts and Humanities   Standards Proficiency

Roman Art 🐻 **HSS** 6.7.8; **HSS** Analysis Skills: HI 1   Research Required

1. Direct students to library or Internet resources about Roman art.

2. Copy the graphic organizer here for students to see. Have them copy the organizer and fill in the empty boxes by describing each type of art and locating one example for each type.

LS Visual/Spatial

📄 Alternative Assessment Handbook, Rubrics 1: Acquiring Information; and 13: Graphic Organizers

A Guide to Roman Art		
mosaics	frescoes	sculpture

Answers

A Roman Fresco *possible answers—reading, tending children, looking at cloth, serving food*

Focus on Reading *possible answers—sites provided by art museums, universities, professional architects' associations*

Reading Check *because they greatly respected the Greeks and admired their art and architecture*

official languages. In the east, some people spoke Greek. People throughout the western Roman world wrote, conducted business, and kept records in Latin. This wide use of Latin helped tie people in various parts of the empire together.

After the Roman Empire ended, Latin developed into many different languages. Together, the languages that developed from Latin are called **Romance languages**. The main Romance languages are Italian, French, Spanish, Portuguese, and Romanian. They share many elements with each other and with Latin.

Over time, Latin also influenced other languages. For example, many Latin words entered non-Romance languages, including English. Words like *et cetera, circus,* and *veto* were all originally Latin terms. Latin words are also common in scientific terms and mottoes. For example, the motto of the United States is the Latin phrase *e pluribus unum* (ee PLOOHR-uh-buhs OO-nuhm), which means "out of many, one." Many legal terms also come from Latin.

READING CHECK Finding the Main Idea How did Roman literature and language influence later societies?

Law

Perhaps even more influential than Rome's artistic and literary traditions was its system of law. Roman law was enforced across much of Europe. After the empire fell apart, Roman laws continued to exist.

Over time, Roman law inspired a system called civil law. **Civil law** is a legal system based on a written code of laws, like the one created by the Romans.

Most countries in Europe today have civil law traditions. In the 1500s and 1600s, European explorers and colonists carried civil law around the world. As a result, some countries in Africa, Asia, and the Americas developed law codes as well.

READING CHECK Summarizing How are Roman legal ideas reflected in the modern world?

SUMMARY AND PREVIEW In this section you learned about many of Rome's contributions to the world and how they have influenced our society. In the next chapter you will learn about an even more influential development that changed life in Rome—Christianity.

● **Direct Teach** ●

Main Idea

❹ **Law**

Roman law serves as a model for modern law codes around the world.

Identify What is the term for a legal system that is based on a written code of laws? *civil law*

Find the Main Idea What happened to Roman law after the empire ended? *continued to exist and influenced present-day law codes around the world*

 HSS 6.7.8; **HSS** Analysis Skills: CS 1, HI 1, HI 3

● **Review & Assess** ●

Close
Ask students what influences from the Roman Empire they experience in their daily lives.

Review
 Online Quiz, Section 3

Assess
SE Section 3 Assessment
 PASS: Section 3 Quiz
 Alternative Assessment Handbook

Reteach/Classroom Intervention
 California Standards Review Workbook
 Interactive Reader and Study Guide, Section 3
 Interactive Skills Tutor CD-ROM

Section 3 Assessment

go.hrw.com
Online Quiz
KEYWORD: SQ6 HP12

Reviewing Ideas, Terms, and People **HSS** 6.7.8
1. **a. Identify** What were **aqueducts** used for?
   b. Contrast How was the Romans' attitude toward science different from the Greeks'?
2. **a. Define** What is a **fresco**?
   b. Explain What influence did Greek art have on Roman art?
3. **a. Recall** What were three forms of writing in which the Romans excelled?
   b. Elaborate Why did Latin develop into different languages after the fall of the Roman Empire?
4. **Identify** What type of law is based on the Roman law code?

Critical Thinking
5. **Comparing and Contrasting** Draw a chart like this one. In the first column, list two ways Greek and Roman architecture were similar. In the other, list two ways they were different.

Similar	Different

FOCUS ON WRITING ✎
6. **Completing Your Notes** Add some information on Roman achievements to your chart. For example, you might add a description of architecture under "Setting." Decide what details you will give to the movie studio.

THE ROMAN EMPIRE **371**

Section 3 Assessment Answers

1. **a.** to carry water from the mountains into the cities
   b. The Romans wanted new knowledge to improve their lives, not just to know more.
2. **a.** type of painting in which paint is applied to wet plaster
   b. Roman artists often copied Greek works.
3. **a.** possible answers—epics, poetry, satire, history and speeches, drama
   b. possible answer—Local languages blended with Latin to create different languages.

4. civil law
5. Science and engineering—We use vaults and arches; Architecture and art—Columns, domes, and sports stadiums are modeled after Roman works; Literature and language—Latin words entered the English language; Law—We have a system of civil law.
6. Students' responses will vary, but they should display familiarity with the Roman achievements listed in this section.

Answers

Reading Check (left): *Roman forms of writing were used for hundreds of years; Latin evolved into the Romance languages and influenced other languages as well.*

Reading Check (right): *Many European countries have civil law traditions. Civil law was also spread to other continents.*

Interpreting Time Lines

Activity Life Events Time Lines
Ask two volunteers to identify at least five important events in their lives since they were born. Create a time line for students to see that shows the events for one student on one side and the events for the other student on the other side. Then ask students questions to have them compare and contrast the events in the two students' lives. To extend the activity, have students find important world events that happened at about the same time as one of the student's life events. Have volunteers add these world events to the time line. **LS Visual/Spatial**

- Alternative Assessment Handbook, Rubric 36: Time Lines
- Interactive Skills Tutor CD-ROM, Lesson 3: Interpret and Create a Time Line and Sequence Events
- **HSS Analysis Skills: CS 2**

Social Studies Skills

HSS Analysis CS 2 Construct time lines of key events, people, and periods.

| Analysis | Critical Thinking | Participation | Study |

Interpreting Time Lines

Understand the Skill

A time line is a visual summary of important events that occurred during a period of history. It displays the events in the order in which they happened. It also shows how long after one event another event took place. In this way time lines allow you to see at a glance what happened and when. You can better see relationships between events and remember important dates when they are displayed on a time line.

Learn the Skill

Some time lines cover huge spans of time—sometimes even many centuries. Other time lines, such as the one on this page, cover much shorter periods of time.

Time lines can be arranged either vertically or horizontally. This time line is vertical. Its dates are read from top to bottom. Horizontal time lines are read from left to right.

Follow these steps to interpret a time line.

1. Read the time line's title. Note the range of years covered and the intervals of time into which it is divided.

2. Study the order of events on the time line. Note the length of time between events.

3. Note relationships. Ask yourself how an event relates to others on the time line. Look for cause-and-effect relationships and long-term developments.

Practice and Apply the Skill

Interpret the time line to answer the following questions.

1. What is the subject of this time line? What years does it cover?

2. How long did Octavian and Antony rule Rome together?

3. How long after dividing the empire did Antony ally with Cleopatra?

4. What steps did Octavian take to end his alliance with Antony and become emperor? When did he take them? How long did it take?

AUGUSTUS BECOMES EMPEROR

50 BC

44 BC Caesar becomes dictator and is murdered.

43 BC Octavian and Antony decide to rule Rome together.

42 BC Octavian and Antony divide Rome and rule separately.

40 BC

37 BC Antony allies with Cleopatra, queen of Egypt.

31 BC Octavian defeats Antony and Cleopatra in a naval battle near Greece.

30 BC Octavian conquers Egypt. Antony and Cleopatra avoid capture by killing themselves.

30 BC

27 BC Octavian becomes emperor and is renamed Augustus.

23 BC Augustus becomes ruler for life.

Social Studies Skills Activity: Interpreting Time Lines

Roman Empire Time Line **HSS** Analysis Skills: CS 2   **Standards Proficiency**

Materials: art supplies, butcher paper, colored markers

1. Have students work as a class to create a large time line on butcher paper of the events covered in this chapter.

2. Organize students into groups and assign each group a specific part of the time line to complete. Start by having students copy the events from the time line that appears at the beginning of the chapter. Either tell students to leave off the other world events or to keep the chapter events and other world events separate, as on the chapter time line.

3. Have groups complete the time line by adding events from the chapter. Each group should also add photos, images, drawings, and quotes to illustrate its part of the time line. **LS Interpersonal, Visual/Spatial**

- Alternative Assessment Handbook, Rubric 36: Time Lines

Answers

Practice and Apply the Skill
1. *events leading to Augustus becoming emperor; 44 BC–23 BC;* 2. *one year;*
3. *five years;* 4. *31 BC: defeated Antony and Cleopatra in a naval battle, 30 BC: conquered Egypt, 27 BC: became emperor; took four years*

Visual Summary

Use the visual summary below to help you review the main ideas of the chapter.

QUICK FACTS

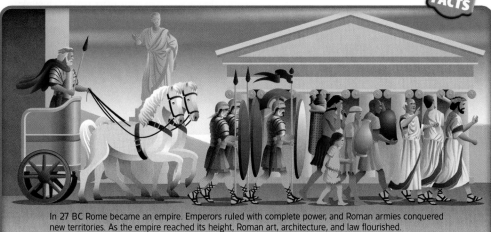

In 27 BC Rome became an empire. Emperors ruled with complete power, and Roman armies conquered new territories. As the empire reached its height, Roman art, architecture, and law flourished.

Reviewing Vocabulary, Terms, and People

Choose the letter of the answer that best completes each statement below.

1. The first emperor of Rome was
   a. Galen.   c. Augustus.
   b. Julius Caesar. d. Marc Antony.

2. A region that lay outside the city of Rome but was controlled by the Romans was called a(n)
   a. aqueduct.   c. orator.
   b. province.   d. villa.

3. Another word for money is
   a. currency.   c. vault.
   b. province.   d. octavian.

4. The time of peace and prosperity that lasted for the first 200 years of the Roman Empire was the
   a. Ovid.   c. civil law.
   b. Romance language. d. Pax Romana.

Comprehension and Critical Thinking

SECTION 1 *(Pages 352–356)* **HSS** **6.7.4**

5. **a. Describe** What action did Cicero recommend? How were the goals of Julius Caesar, Pompey, and Crassus different from Cicero's?

   b. Analyze What were the most important events in the life of Julius Caesar? Which event best qualifies as a turning point in Caesar's life? Defend your choice.

   c. Elaborate How did personal relationships—between Marc Antony and Octavian, and between Marc Antony and Cleopatra—affect the history of the Roman Empire?

SECTION 2 *(Pages 358–363)* **HSS** **6.7.3**

6. **a. Identify** What natural disaster has allowed us to learn more about Roman cities? What is the name of the main city affected by that disaster?

THE ROMAN EMPIRE **373**

THE ROMAN EMPIRE **373**

allies, making Octavian angry; all these relationships led to Octavian's rise to power

6. a. eruption of Mt. Vesuvius; Pompeii

b. made the currency more popular because people didn't have to change money as they traded across the empire

c. Answers will vary, but students should be familiar with the dangerous, crowded conditions that people endured in the city, along with the entertainment available.

7. a. architecture—Colosseum, use of domes, arches, and vaults; literature—satire, history and speeches, drama; language—Latin, which later developed into the Romance languages and influenced non-Romance languages

b. The Romans were concerned with using knowledge to improve their lives, whereas the Greeks studied the world just to know about it; Galen made many discoveries about the body, which aided doctors in helping people.

c. Answers will vary, but students should have a good working knowledge of the achievements listed in this section.

Reviewing Themes

8. Europe, Africa and Asia

9. Answers will vary but should display knowledge of the Roman achievements.

Reading Skills

10. b

11. b

SECTION 2 (continued)

b. Make Inferences How do you think the size of the Roman Empire affected the popularity of Roman currency?

c. Evaluate For a poor resident of Rome, do you think the benefits of living in the city would have outweighed the problems? Why or why not?

SECTION 3 (Pages 366–371) **HSS** 6.7.8

7. a. Describe What were the main Roman achievements in architecture? in literature and language?

b. Contrast How did the Roman attitude toward science compare to the traditional Greek attitude? What is an example of the Roman attitude?

c. Evaluate Of all the Romans' achievements, which do you think has affected the most people? Defend your answer.

Reviewing Themes

8. Geography Into what main areas did the Roman Empire expand during its early years?

9. Technology What Roman achievement in science or engineering do you think is most impressive? Why?

Reading Skills

Evaluating Web Sites *Each question below lists two types of Web sites you could use to answer the question. Decide which Web site is likely to be a more valuable and reliable source of information.*

10. What was Roman sculpture like?
   a. a site describing someone's trip to Rome
   b. a site by a university's art history department

11. What happened after Antony met Cleopatra?
   a. a movie studio site for a movie about Cleopatra
   b. an online encyclopedia

Social Studies Skills

12. Creating Time Lines Create a time line that shows the key events in the creation and expansion of the Roman Empire. First, look back through this chapter for key dates and events. Decide which of these dates you will include. Once you have completed your time line, compare it to those of your classmates to see if you have included different information.

70 BC ———————— AD 180

Using the Internet

13. Activity: Researching Culture By studying art and culture, you can see into the thoughts and values of the people making up the society. Enter the keyword. Study the background on the Roman legal code and the artifacts provided. Then present an oral report with visual aids that explains what we learn about Rome by studying its art and legal institutions.

FOCUS ON WRITING

14. Creating Note Cards Now you're ready to prepare note cards for studio executives. Choose the most intriguing details from your chart to present on note cards labeled "Characters," "Setting," and "Plot." On each card write a one- to two-sentence description of a person, place, or event that could be featured in the screenplay. Then write another sentence that tells why you think the person, place, or event might be a good one to feature. Prepare six cards that you could give to a screenwriter to use.

Social Studies Skills

12. possible answers—58–50 BC: Caesar conquers Gaul; 50 BC: Caesar ordered back to Rome; 49 BC: Caesar crosses Rubicon into Italy; 44 BC: Julius Caesar assassinated; 42 BC: Antony and Octavian defeat their opponents; 31 BC: Battle of Actium; 27 BC: Octavian becomes emperor; early AD 100s: Romans have Gaul and much of central Europe; 117: Roman Empire at its greatest extent; 180: end of Pax Romana

Using the Internet

13. Go to the HRW Web site and enter the keyword shown to access a rubric for this activity.

   KEYWORD: SQ6 TEACHER

Focus on Writing

14. Rubric Students' note cards for a screenplay should:
   • contain intriguing details.
   • include all necessary information about the people, places, or events described.
   • offer a compelling reason why the person, place, or event should be featured.

CRF: Focus on Writing: Note Cards for a Screenplay

Standards Assessment

DIRECTIONS: Read each question, and write the letter of the best response.

1 Use the time line to answer the following question.

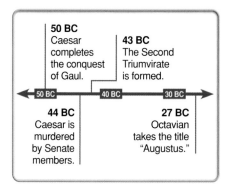

50 BC
Caesar completes the conquest of Gaul.

43 BC
The Second Triumvirate is formed.

50 BC — 40 BC — 30 BC

44 BC
Caesar is murdered by Senate members.

27 BC
Octavian takes the title "Augustus."

Most historians mark the end of the Roman Republic and the beginning of the Roman Empire as taking place in the year

A 50 BC.
B 44 BC.
C 43 BC.
D 27 BC.

2 Roman emperors conquered new lands for all of the following reasons *except*

A to end threats to Rome.
B because they enjoyed fighting.
C to gain resources.
D to defeat people of different religions.

3 Which Roman leader seized power from the Senate and became the dictator of the entire Roman Republic?

A Julius Caesar
B Hadrian
C Brutus
D Marc Antony

4 Roman traders

A refused to trade with people outside of the empire.
B tried to overthrow the emperor.
C carried goods between Rome and its provinces.
D made very little money.

5 Rome's contributions to the world include all of the following *except*

A techniques used to build strong bridges and other structures.
B the building of pyramids.
C the idea of civil law.
D the creation of great works of literature.

Connecting with Past Learnings

6 In Grade 5 you learned about George Washington's contributions as a military leader during the Revolution and as the nation's first president. Which person's contributions to Rome were *most* like those Washington made to the United States?

A Cicero
B Cleopatra
C Augustus
D Galen

7 Earlier in this course you learned about Homer, the poet who told about Greek myths and heroes. Which Roman's writing was *most* like Homer's poetry?

A Virgil
B Cicero
C Horace
D Pompey

Answers

1. D
Break Down the Question Remind students who missed the question that Octavian became the first emperor of Rome, and an emperor rules an empire.

2. D
Break Down the Question Refer students who missed the question to the first page of Section 2.

3. A
Break Down the Question This question requires students to recall factual information. If students missed the question, review the identities of the men with students.

4. C
Break Down the Question This question requires students to recall information on Roman trade. Refer students who missed it to Section 2.

5. B
Break Down the Question This question requires students to recall that, although the Romans had many achievements, building pyramids was not among them.

6. C
Break Down the Question This question requires that students recall that Augustus was both a military leader and the first Roman emperor, just as Washington was both a military leader and the first president.

7. A
Break Down the Question This question requires that students recall that Virgil was the author of *The Aeneid*, which was a long poem similar to Homer's poem, *The Odyssey*.

Standards Review
Have students review the following standards in their workbooks.
California Standards Review Workbook:
HSS 6.7.1, 6.7.3, 6.7.4

Intervention Resources

Reproducible
- Interactive Reader and Study Guide
- Universal Access Teacher Management System: Lesson Plans for Universal Access

Technology
- Quick Facts Transparency: The Roman Empire Visual Summary
- Universal Access Modified Worksheets and Tests CD-ROM
- Interactive Skills Tutor CD-ROM

Tips for Test Taking

Look All Around If the test item asks for vocabulary knowledge, encourage students to look at the surrounding sentences, or context, to see which definition fits. To identify the best definition of the word as it is used in the context, students should consider the surrounding words and phrases.

Chapter 13 Planning Guide

Rome and Christianity

MASTERING THE CALIFORNIA STANDARDS

Chapter 13
pp. 376–399

Overview: In this chapter, students will learn about the development of the Christian faith and its influence on the Roman Empire.

See p. 376 for the California History–Social Science standards covered in this chapter.

Universal Access Teacher Management System:*
- Universal Access Instructional Benchmarking Guides
- Lesson Plans for Universal Access

Interactive Reader and Study Guide: Chapter Graphic Organizer*

Chapter Resource File*
- Chapter Review Activity
- Focus on Writing Activity: A Magazine Article
- Social Studies Skills Activity: Continuity and Change in History

One-Stop Planner CD-ROM: Calendar Planner

Student Edition on Audio CD Program

Universal Access Modified Worksheets and Tests CD-ROM

Interactive Skills Tutor CD-ROM

Primary Source Library CD-ROM for World History

Power Presentations with Video CD-ROM

History's Impact: World History Video Program (VHS/DVD): The Roman Empire and Christianity*

A Teacher's Guide To Religion in the Public Schools*

Section 1:
Religion in the Roman Empire

The Big Idea: The Roman Empire accepted many religions, but it came into conflict with Judaism.

6.7.5

Universal Access Teacher Management System:* Section 1 Lesson Plan

Interactive Reader and Study Guide: Section 1 Summary*

Chapter Resource File*
- Vocabulary Builder Activity, Section 1

Daily Bellringer Transparency: Section 1*

Section 2:
Origins of Christianity

The Big Idea: Christianity, based on the teachings of Jesus of Nazareth, spread quickly after his death.

6.7.6

Universal Access Teacher Management System:* Section 2 Lesson Plan

Interactive Reader and Study Guide: Section 2 Summary*

Chapter Resource File*
- Vocabulary Builder Activity, Section 2
- Biography Activity: Saint Peter
- Literature Activity: The Parable of the Prodigal Son

Daily Bellringer Transparency: Section 2*

Map Transparency: Paul's Journeys*

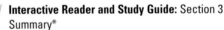 **Internet Activity:** Inspired Art

---

Section 3:
The Early Christian World

The Big Idea: Within 300 years after Jesus' death, Christianity had spread through the empire and become Rome's official religion.

6.7.7

Universal Access Teacher Management System:* Section 3 Lesson Plan

Interactive Reader and Study Guide: Section 3 Summary*

Chapter Resource File*
- Vocabulary Builder Activity, Section 3
- Biography Activity: Theodosius
- Biography Activity: Saint Perpetua
- History and Geography Activity: Spread of Christianity
- Primary Source Activity: The Diary of Perpetua
- Primary Source Activity: The Letters of Pliny and Trajan
- Primary Source Activity: "The Life of Constantine," by Eusebius

Daily Bellringer Transparency: Section 3*

Map Transparency: The Spread of Christianity, 300–400*

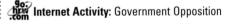 **Internet Activity:** Government Opposition

---

Review, Assessment, Intervention

Standards Review Workbook*

Quick Facts Transparency: Rome and Christianity Visual Summary*

Spanish Chapter Summaries Audio CD Program

Online Chapter Summaries in Six Languages

Quiz Game CD-ROM

Progress Assessment Support System (PASS): Chapter Test*

Universal Access Modified Worksheets and Tests CD-ROM: Modified Chapter Test

One-Stop Planner CD-ROM: ExamView Test Generator (English/Spanish)

Alternative Assessment Handbook

Holt Online Assessment Program (HOAP), in the Holt Premier Online Student Edition

---

PASS: Section 1 Quiz*

Online Quiz: Section 1

Alternative Assessment Handbook

PASS: Section 2 Quiz*

Online Quiz: Section 2

Alternative Assessment Handbook

PASS: Section 3 Quiz*

Online Quiz: Section 3

Alternative Assessment Handbook

 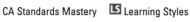

California Resources for Standards Mastery

INSTRUCTIONAL PLANNING AND SUPPORT

Universal Access Teacher Management System*

One-Stop Planner CD-ROM with Test Generator: Teacher Management System with Interactive Teacher's Edition

STANDARDS MASTERY

Standards Review Workbook*

At Home: A Guide to Standards Mastery for World History

Holt Online Learning

To enhance learning, the following Internet activities are available: Inspired Art and Government Opposition.

> KEYWORD: SQ6 TEACHER

- **Teacher Support Page**
- **Content Updates**
- **Rubrics and Writing Models**

- **Teaching Tips for the Multimedia Classroom**

> KEYWORD: SQ6 WH13

- **Current Events**
- **Holt Grapher**
- **Holt Online Atlas**
- **Holt Researcher**
- **Interactive Multimedia Activities**

- **Internet Activities**
- **Online Chapter Summaries in Six Languages**
- **Online Section Quizzes**
- **World History Maps and Charts**

HOLT PREMIER ONLINE STUDENT EDITION

Complete online support for interactivity, assessment, and reporting

- **Interactive Maps and Notebook**
- **Standardized Test Prep**
- **Homework Practice and Research Activities Online**

Mastering the Standards: Differentiating Instruction

Reaching Standards	Basic-level activities designed for all students encountering new material
Standards Proficiency	Intermediate-level activities designed for average students
Exceeding Standards	Challenging activities designed for honors and gifted-and-talented students
Standard English Mastery	Activities designed to improve standard English usage

ROME AND CHRISTIANITY

Frequently Asked Questions

INSTRUCTIONAL PLANNING AND SUPPORT

Where do I find planning aids, pacing guides, lesson plans, and other teaching aids?

Annotated Teacher's Edition:
- Chapter planning guides
- Standards-based instruction and strategies
- Differentiated instruction for universal access
- Point-of-use reminders for integrating program resources

Power Presentations with Video CD-ROM

Universal Access Teacher Management System:
- Year and unit instructional benchmarking guides
- Reproducible lesson plans
- Assessment guides for diagnostic, progress, and summative end-of-the-year tests
- Options for differentiating instruction and intervention
- Teaching guides and answer keys for student workbooks

One-Stop Planner CD-ROM with Test Generator: Teacher Management System with Interactive Teacher's Edition:
- Calendar Planner
- Editable lesson plans
- All reproducible ancillaries in Adobe Acrobat (PDF) format
- ExamView Test Generator (English & S panish)
- Game Tool for ExamView
- PuzzlePro
- Transparency and video previews

DIFFERENTIATING INSTRUCTION FOR UNIVERSAL ACCESS

What resources are available to ensure that Advanced Learners/GATE Students master the standards?

Teacher's Edition Activities:
- Writing a Parable, p. 386
- Martyrs and Persecution, p. 393

Lesson Plans for Universal Access

Primary Source Library CD-ROM for World History

What resources are available to ensure that English Learners and Standard English Learners master the standards?

Lesson Plans for Universal Access

Chapter Resource File: Vocabulary Builder Activities

Spanish Chapter Summaries Audio CD Program

Online Chapter Summaries in Six Languages

One-Stop Planner CD-ROM:
- PuzzlePro, Spanish Version
- ExamView Test Generator, Spanish Version

What modified materials are available for Special Education?

The *Universal Access Modified Worksheets and Tests CD-ROM* provides editable versions of the following:

Vocabulary Flash Cards

Modified Vocabulary Builder Activities

Modified Chapter Review Activity

Modified Chapter Test

What resources are available to ensure that Learners Having Difficulty master the standards?

Teacher's Edition Activities:
- Jewish Rebellion Causes and Effects, p. 382
- Life of Jesus, p. 385
- Writing Interview Questions, p. 387
- Sermon on the Mount Chart, p. 390

Interactive Reader and Study Guide

Student Edition on Audio CD Program

Quick Facts Transparency: Rome and Christianity Visual Summary

Standards Review Workbook

Social Studies Skills Activity: Continuity and Change in History

Interactive Skills Tutor CD-ROM

How do I intervene for students struggling to master the standards?

Interactive Reader and Study Guide

Quick Facts Transparency: Rome and Christianity Visual Summary

Standards Review Workbook

Social Studies Skills Activity: Continuity and Change in History

Interactive Skills Tutor CD-ROM

PROFESSIONAL DEVELOPMENT

HOLT
Professional
Development

What teacher training resources are available to help me grow professionally?

- In-service and staff development as part of your Holt Social Studies product purchase
- Quick Teacher Tutorial Lesson Presentation CD-ROM
- Intensive tuition-based Teacher Development Institute
- Convenient Holt Speaker Bureau face-to-face workshop options

- PRAXIS™ Test Prep (#0089) interactive Web-based content refreshers*
- *Ask A Professional Development Expert* at http://www.hrw.com/prodev/

* PRAXIS is a trademark of Educational Testing Service (ETS). This publication is not endorsed or approved by ETS.

Information Literacy Skills

To learn more about how History–Social Science instruction may be improved by the effective use of library media centers and information literacy skills, go to the Teacher's Resource Materials for Chapter 13 at **go.hrw.com, keyword: SQ6 MEDIA.**

Standards Focus

Standards by Section

Section 1: HSS 6.7.5
Section 2: HSS 6.7.6
Section 3: HSS 6.7.7

Teacher's Edition

HSS **Analysis Skills:** CS 1, CS 2, HR 1, HR 2, HR 4, HR 5, HI 1, HI 2, HI 3

ELA Reading 6.1.2, 6.2.3, 6.3.6

Upcoming Standards for Future Learning

Preview the following History–Social Science content standards from upcoming chapters or grade levels to promote learning beyond the current chapter.

HSS **6.7.8** Discuss the legacies of Roman art and architecture, technology and science, literature, language, and law.

7.1 Students analyze the causes and effects of the vast expansion and ultimate disintegration of the Roman Empire.

7.1.1 Study the early strengths and lasting contributions of Rome (e.g., significance of Roman citizenship; rights under Roman law; Roman art, architecture, engineering, and philosophy; preservation and transmission of Christianity) and its ultimate internal weaknesses (e.g., rise of autonomous military powers within the empire, undermining of citizenship by the growth of corruption and slavery; lack of education, and distribution of news).

Focus on Writing

The **Chapter Resource File** provides a Focus on Writing worksheet to help students organize and write their magazine articles.

CRF: Focus on Writing Activity: Magazine Article

CHAPTER 13 AD 1–400

Rome and Christianity

California Standards

History–Social Science

6.7 Students analyze the geographic, political, economic, religious, and social structures during the development of Rome.

Analysis Skills

HI 3 Explain the sources of historical continuity and how the combination of ideas and events explains the emergence of new patterns.

English–Language Arts

Writing 6.1.2a Engage the interest of the reader and state a clear purpose.

Reading 6.2.0 Read and understand grade-level-appropriate material.

FOCUS ON WRITING

Magazine Article You're a freelance writer who has been assigned to write a short magazine article about religion and early Christianity in the Roman Empire. As you read this chapter, identify main ideas and interesting details that you can use in your article.

CHAPTER EVENTS

c. 30 Jesus is crucified.

BC 1 AD

WORLD EVENTS

43 London is built as a Roman city.

376 CHAPTER 13

Introduce the Chapter

Standards Proficiency

The Spread of Christianity HSS 6.7; HSS Analysis Skills: CS 1, HI 1

1. Ask students what different factors might lead to the beginning of a new religion. What might affect how a new religion spreads? Write the labels *Support for New Religion* and *Opposition to New Religion* for students to see. Ask the class for ideas for each category that might affect the spread of a new religion.

2. Next, show the class a map of the Roman Empire. Ask students how fast a new religion could have spread across the Roman Empire. Remind students to consider such factors

as language, transportation, and existing religions.

3. Explain to students that they are going to learn about the early years of Christianity. Tell students they will be able to track the religion over time and location, as it spread across the Mediterranean region.

4. Have students track the growth of Christianity using maps and time lines in this chapter.
LS Visual/Spatial, Verbal/Linguistic

HOLT
History's Impact
► video series
Watch the video to under-
stand the impact of ancient
Rome on the world today.

What You Will Learn...

In this chapter you will learn about the beginnings of Christianity in the Roman Empire. In this photo, members of one Christian church, the Roman Catholic Church, gather in Vatican City in Rome.

100s–200s
From time to time, Christians are per-secuted in Rome.

309
Emperor Constantine ends the persecution of Christians.

381
Emperor Theodosius bans all non-Christian religions in Rome.

| 100 | 200 | 300 | 400 |

c. 65 According to tradition, Buddhism is introduced into China.

c. 250
The Maya Classical Age begins in Mexico.

320
The Gupta dynasty takes charge in India.

ROME AND CHRISTIANITY **377**

• Chapter Preview •

Chapter Big Ideas

Section 1 The Roman Empire ac-cepted many religions, but it came into conflict with Judaism. HSS 6.7.5

Section 2 Christianity, based on the teachings of Jesus of Nazareth, spread quickly after his death. HSS 6.7.6

Section 3 Within three centuries after Jesus's death, Christianity had spread through the empire and become Rome's official religion. HSS 6.7.7

Explore the Picture

Saint Peter's Square No picture better illustrates the connection between Rome and Christianity than this image of the famous Saint Peter's Square. One of the central sites in Vatican City, the plaza still serves as a gathering place for Christians today. The large domed building is Saint Peter's Basilica, which according to tradition is built over the tomb of Saint Peter. The pope still holds public masses both in Saint Peter's Square and Saint Peter's Basilica.

Analyzing Visuals Why might there be a large gathering of people in Saint Peter's Square? *possible answers—to see the pope, to attend mass, to see the headquarters of the Roman Catholic Church*

Explore the Time Line

1. In what year was Jesus crucified? *AD 30*
2. What did Emperor Theodosius do in 381? *banned all non-Christian religions in Rome*
3. What religious event occurred in China in AD 65? *Buddhism was introduced.*
4. Which occurred first—the founding of London by the Romans or the crucifixion of Jesus? *crucifixion of Jesus*
5. When did the Maya Classical Age begin? *about AD 250*

HSS **Analysis Skills:** CS 1

Info to Know

Persecution of Christians During the time of the Roman Empire, there were several large-scale persecutions of Christians. The first was ordered by Emperor Nero about AD 64. He tried to blame Christians for the fire that destroyed much of Rome. Several other emperors called for new persecutions of Christians because the Christians refused to take part in the worship of Roman gods and rituals to the emperor. Persecu-tion of Christians came to an end when Emperor Constantine passed the Edict of Milan in 313.

Understanding Themes

This chapter focuses on two themes—religion, and society and culture. Guide students in a discussion of how these themes are related. Ask students how a religion or philosophy might spread throughout a country. Then ask students how religion could have influenced a government or society as big and diverse as the Roman Empire. Remind students of the relationship between other religions they have already studied, such as Hinduism and Confucianism, and their relationship to society and culture.

Questioning

Focus on Reading Organize the class into pairs. Give each pair a short article from a newspaper or magazine, or ask students to bring in one of their own. Have each group apply the W questions (who, what, where, and when) to their article. After students have had some time to work on their article, ask them how questioning the article might affect what they think about the information in it and how they might remember it. Remind students that when they ask themselves questions while they read, they will remember more information.

Reading Social Studies

by Kylene Beers

| Economics | Geography | Politics | Religion | Society and Culture | Science and Technology |

Focus on Themes In this chapter, you will learn about the early beginnings of Christianity. You will read about the life and teachings of Jesus of Nazareth and about the Apostles who spread Jesus's teachings after his death. Later in the chapter, you will see how Christianity spread through the Roman Empire and became its official religion. Throughout the chapter, you will see how the Christian **religion** has shaped the **society and culture** of many people throughout history.

Questioning

Focus on Reading If you don't understand something your teacher says in class, how do you get an explanation? You ask a question. You can use the same method to improve your understanding while reading.

The W Questions The most basic questions you can ask about a historical text are who, what, when, and where—the W questions. Answering these questions will help you get to the very basics of what you need to learn from a passage.

Additional reading support can be found in the

Inter active

Reader and Study Guide

Who?
Augustine of Hippo, a Christian writer

What?
read works of classical philosophers

Growth of Territory

As Christianity spread through the Roman world, Christian writers read the works of classical philosophers. One such writer was Augustine of Hippo. He lived in Hippo, a town in northern Africa, in the late 300s and early 400s.

Where?
Hippo, a town in northern Africa

When?
the late 300s and early 400s

Reading and Skills Resources

Reading Support

- Interactive Reader and Study Guide
- Student Edition on Audio CD
- Spanish Chapter Summaries Audio CD Program

Social Studies Skills Support

- Interactive Skills Tutor CD-ROM

Vocabulary Support

- **CRF:** Vocabulary Builder Activities
- **CRF:** Chapter Review Activity
- Universal Access Modified Worksheets and Tests CD-ROM:
  - Vocabulary Flash Cards
  - Vocabulary Builder Activity
  - Chapter Review Activity

OSP Holt PuzzlePro

Standards Focus

ELA Reading 6.2.0

You Try It!

Read the following passage, and then answer the questions below.

Christianity Spreads Quickly in Rome

From Chapter 13, Pages 392–393

Early Christians like Paul wanted to share their message about Jesus with the world. Because of their efforts, Christianity spread quickly in many Roman communities. But as it grew more popular, Christianity began to concern some Roman leaders. They looked for ways to put an end to this new religion.

Early Growth

The first Christians worked to spread Jesus's teachings only among Jews. But some early Christians, including Paul, wanted to introduce Christianity to non-Jews as well. As a result, Christianity began to spread in the Roman Empire. Within a hundred years after Jesus's death, historians estimate that thousands of Christians lived in the Roman Empire.

Answer the following questions about the passage above.

1. Who is this passage about?

2. What did they do?

3. When did they live?

4. Where did they live and work?

5. How can knowing the answers to these questions help you better understand what you've read?

Key Terms and People

Chapter 13

Section 1
Christianity (p. 382)
Jesus of Nazareth (p. 382)
Messiah (p. 383)
John the Baptist (p. 383)

Section 2
Bible (p. 384)
crucifixion (p. 385)
Resurrection (p. 385)
disciples (p. 385)
Apostles (p. 387)
Paul (p. 387)
saint (p. 388)

Section 3
martyrs (p. 393)
persecution (p. 393)
bishops (p. 393)
Eucharist (p. 393)
pope (p. 394)
Augustine of Hippo (p. 394)
Constantine (p. 395)

Academic Vocabulary

Success in school is related to knowing academic vocabulary—the words that are frequently used in school assignments and discussions. In this chapter, you will learn the following academic words:

ideals (p. 388)
classical (p. 394)

> **As you read Chapter 13,** use the W questions as guides to help you clarify your understanding of the text.

Reading Social Studies

Key Terms and People

Preteach the key terms and people from this chapter by having students create a three-panel flip chart like the one below. Have students fold a piece of paper in half from top to bottom. Then fold the paper into thirds from side to side. Have students cut along each of the vertical fold lines to the fold in the middle of the paper. Have students label the flaps *Section 1*, *2*, and *3*, then have them write the key terms or people for that section on the outside of the flap. On the inside of the chart, have students write a definition or description of each term.

LS Verbal/Linguistic

Focus on Reading

See the **Focus on Reading** questions in this chapter for more practice on this reading social studies skill.

Reading Social Studies Assessment

See the **Standards Review** at the end of this chapter for student assessment questions related to this reading skill.

Teaching Tip

One way to help students use questions to understand texts is to have students take notes over a reading assignment. Ask students to read a section from the chapter and apply the W questions to the section. First have students write the main headings and subheadings on their paper. Under each subheading, have students write the W questions and then answer each question. When students have finished, ask them to exchange papers. Ask students to see if they have the same questions and answers. If not, have them determine why they are different.

Answers

You Try It! 1. *early Christians;* **2.** *They spread Christianity.* **3.** *within a hundred years of Jesus's death;* **4.** *in the Roman Empire;* **5.** *It helps to understand the basic details of the passage.*

Preteach

Bellringer

If YOU were there . . . Use the **Daily Bellringer Transparency** to help students answer the question.

📦 Daily Bellringer Transparency, Section 1

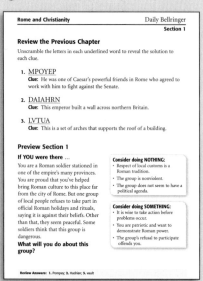

Building Vocabulary

Preteach or review the following terms:

banned outlawed (p. 382)

Olympian gods the gods of ancient Greece, who lived on Mount Olympus (p. 381)

prophecies predictions of things to come (p. 383)

📝 **CRF:** Vocabulary Builder Activity, Section 1

🐻 Standards Focus

HSS 6.7.5

Means: Identify the movement of Jews throughout the Roman Empire that resulted from their conflict with the Romans.

Matters: Conflict between Rome and the Jews led to the removal of most Jews from Jerusalem and their settlement in other parts of the world.

Religion in the Roman Empire

What You Will Learn...

Main Ideas

1. The Romans allowed many religions to be practiced in their empire.
2. Jews and Romans clashed over religious and political ideas.
3. The roots of Christianity had appeared in Judea by the end of the first century BC.

The Big Idea

The Roman Empire accepted many religions, but it came into conflict with Judaism.

Key Terms and People

Christianity, *p. 382*
Jesus of Nazareth, *p. 382*
Messiah, *p. 383*
John the Baptist, *p. 383*

🐻 **HSS 6.7.5** Trace the migration of Jews around the Mediterranean region and the effects of their conflict with the Romans, including the Romans' restrictions on their right to live in Jerusalem.

If YOU were there...

You are a Roman soldier stationed in one of the empire's many provinces. You are proud that you've helped bring Roman culture to this place far from the city of Rome. But one group of local people refuses to take part in official Roman holidays and rituals, saying it is against their beliefs. Other than that, they seem peaceful. Some soldiers think that this group is dangerous.

What will you do about this group?

BUILDING BACKGROUND As the Roman Empire expanded, it came to include people who spoke many different languages and followed many different religions. While Roman officials were generally tolerant of local religions and cultures, they did not allow anything—like the religion noted above—that might threaten their authority.

Romans Allow Many Religions

The Romans were a very religious people. To celebrate their religious beliefs, the Romans held many festivals in honor of their gods. Because of the empire's huge size and diverse population, the nature of these festivals varied widely from place to place.

As you have read, the Romans were a very practical people. This practicality also extended into their religious lives. The Romans didn't think that they could be sure which gods did or did not exist. To avoid offending any gods who did exist, the Romans prayed to a wide range of gods and goddesses. Many of the most popular gods in the Roman Empire were adopted from people the Romans had conquered.

Because of their ideas about religion, the Romans allowed people they conquered to keep their beliefs. In many cases these beliefs also spread among nearby Romans. As time passed the Romans built temples to the gods of these new religions, and knowledge of them spread throughout the empire.

Religion in the Roman Empire 🐻 HSS 6.7.5; HSS Analysis Skills: CS 1, CS 2, HI 1, HI 2

1. **Teach** Ask students the Main Idea questions to teach this section.

2. **Apply** Have students construct an illustrated time line that depicts the history presented in this section. Where dates do not appear in the text, have students write out the sequenced events on the time line. Ask students to include a simple illustration or symbol to signify each event on the time line. 🔲 **Visual/Spatial**

3. **Review** As you review the section's main ideas, have students discuss why conflict existed between Jews and Romans.

4. **Practice/Homework** Have students share their time lines, filling in anything they missed. Tell them to use this time line when reviewing the chapter later.
   🔲 **Visual/Spatial, Interpersonal**

   📝 Alternative Assessment Handbook, Rubric 36: Time Lines

For example, many Romans worshipped the Olympian gods of Greece. When the Romans conquered Greece they learned about Greek mythology. Before long, the Greek gods became the main gods of Rome as well. In the same way, many Romans also adopted gods from the Egyptians, Gauls, or Persians.

The only time the Romans banned a religion was when the rulers of Rome considered it a political problem. In these cases, government officials took steps to prevent problems. Sometimes they placed restrictions on when and where members of a religion could meet. One religion that some Roman leaders came to consider a political problem was Judaism.

READING CHECK Finding Main Ideas Why did the Romans forbid certain religions?

Jews and Romans Clash

Roman leaders considered Judaism to be a potential problem for two reasons. One reason was religious, the other political. Both reasons led to conflict between the Romans and the Jews of the empire.

Religious Conflict

Unlike the Romans, the Jews did not worship many gods. They believed that their God was the only god. Some Romans, though, thought the Jews were insulting Rome's gods by not praying to them.

Still, the Romans did not attempt to ban Judaism in the empire. They allowed the Jews to keep their religion and practice it as they pleased. It was not until later when political conflict arose with the Jews that the Romans decided to take action.

FOCUS ON READING
Before you read this discussion, look at the heads and subheads. Who is this paragraph about? What did they do?

The Romans built many temples to honor their many gods. Temples built to honor all the gods were called pantheons, and the most famous of these is the Pantheon in Rome, first built in the 20s BC. Its huge dome awes visitors even today.

381

Direct Teach

Main Idea

❷ Jews and Romans Clash

Jews and Romans clashed over religious and political ideas.

Recall When did Rome conquer Judea? *63 BC*

Contrast How was Hadrian's policy different from previous Roman policies? *Hadrian banned the practice of some Jewish rituals and eventually destroyed Jerusalem.*

Analyze Despite some tolerance from the Romans, why did the Jews continue to rebel? *They wanted to be ruled only by Jews and did not want to worship Roman gods and violate their religious beliefs.*

🐾 **HSS** 6.7.5; **HSS** Analysis Skills: CS 1, HI 1, HI 3

Info to Know

Resistance to Rome Jewish rebels known as Zealots fled Jerusalem to hide in the Masada fortress, located atop a huge cliff overlooking the Dead Sea. The fortress, originally built by King Herod of Judea, included a synagogue, bathhouses, an armory, and several storerooms. During the four-year siege, the Roman Tenth Legion tried many times to attack the fortress. They used battering rams, catapults, and even built a large ramp to the top of the fortress to defeat the Zealots holding out within Masada.

Answers

Reading Check *because Jews continued to rebel and demand independence*

382

Resistance to Rome

Unhappy with Roman rule, many Jews rebelled in the AD 60s but were defeated. Refusing to accept defeat, about 1,000 Jews locked themselves in a mountain fortress called Masada and held off the Romans for four years. In the end, these rebels killed themselves to avoid surrendering to the Romans.

The Roman general Titus captured Jerusalem in AD 70. To celebrate this victory, the Romans built this arch that shows Roman soldiers carrying a stolen menorah from Jerusalem's holy Second Temple.

Political Conflict

Political conflict arose because the Jews rebelled against Roman rule. Judea, the territory in which most Jews lived, had been conquered by Rome in 63 BC. Since then, many Jews had been unhappy with Roman rule. They wanted to be ruled only by Jews, not by outsiders. As a result, the Jews rebelled in the AD 60s. The rebellion was defeated, however, and the Jews were punished for their actions.

In the early 100s the Jews rebelled once more against the Romans. Tired of putting down Jewish revolts, the emperor Hadrian banned the practice of certain Jewish rituals. He thought this ban would cause people to give up Judaism and end their desire for independence.

Hadrian was wrong. His actions made the Jews even more upset with Roman rule. Once again they rebelled. This time Hadrian decided to end the rebellions in Jerusalem once and for all.

The Roman army crushed the Jews' revolt, destroyed the Jewish capital of Jerusalem, and forced all Jews to leave the city. Then the Romans built a new city on the ruins of Jerusalem and brought settlers from other parts of the empire to live there. Jews were forbidden to enter this new city more than once a year. Forced out of their ancient city, many Jews moved into other parts of the Roman world.

READING CHECK **Summarizing** Why did the Romans come to consider Judaism a threat?

The Roots of Christianity

Early in the first century AD, before the Jews' first rebellion against the Romans, what would become a new religion appeared in Judea. This religion began as one of the many Jewish sects, and later developed into **Christianity.** It was based on the life and teachings of the Jew **Jesus of Nazareth.** Christianity was rooted in Jewish ideas and traditions.

382 CHAPTER 13

Differentiating Instruction for Universal Access

Learners Having Difficulty   Reaching Standards

1. To help students understand the reasons why Jews rebelled against the Roman Empire and what the results of that rebellion were, draw the graphic organizer here for students to see. Omit the blue, italicized answers.

2. Have students copy and complete the graphic organizer. Then review the answers as a class.
   LS Visual/Spatial

🐾 **HSS** 6.7.5; **HSS** Analysis Skills CS 1, HI 1, HI 2

Causes	Event	Effects
• *Romans conquer Judea.*	**Jews rebel against Rome.**	• *Hadrian bans certain Jewish rituals.*
• *Jews oppose Roman rule.*		• *Revolts are crushed.*
• *Differing religious views*		• *Jerusalem is destroyed.*
		• *Jews forced to leave Jerusalem.*

When the Romans took over Judea in 63 BC, many Jews thought the Messiah would soon appear. Prophets wandered throughout Judea, announcing that the Messiah was coming. The most famous of these prophets was **John the Baptist**. Inspired by the prophets' teachings, many Jews anxiously awaited the Messiah.

READING CHECK **Summarizing** Why were Jews waiting for the Messiah to arrive?

SUMMARY AND PREVIEW You just read about Jewish prophecies that foretold the coming of a Messiah. In the next section you'll learn what happened when a man many people believed to be that Messiah—Jesus—was born.

At the time that Jesus was born, there were several groups of Jews in Judea. The largest of these groups was very strict in how it practiced Judaism. Members of this group were particularly strict in obeying the laws of Moses. Jews believed that Moses had given them these laws to follow.

Many Jews followed the laws closely because Jewish prophets had said that a new leader would appear among the Jews. Many people thought this leader was more likely to appear if they were strict in their religious behavior.

According to the prophecies, the Jews' new leader would be a descendent of King David. When he came, he would restore the greatness of David's ancient kingdom, Israel. The prophets called this leader the **Messiah** (muh-SY-uh), which means "anointed" in Hebrew. In other words, the Jews believed that the Messiah would be chosen by God to lead them. However, no one knew when the Messiah would come.

Section 1 Assessment

go.hrw.com
Online Quiz
KEYWORD: SQ6 HP13

Reviewing Ideas, Terms, and People HSS 6.7.5

1. **a. Describe** What was the Roman attitude toward religion?
   b. Explain Why did the Romans ban some religions?
2. **a. Recall** What was a major religious difference between the Romans and the Jews?
   b. Analyze Why did the Romans destroy Jerusalem?
   c. Elaborate How do you think the spreading of Jews through the Roman world affected Jewish culture?
3. **a. Define** Who did Jews believe the **Messiah** was?
   b. Make Inferences How did the anticipation of the Messiah's arrival lead many Jews to follow laws strictly?

Critical Thinking

4. **Categorizing** Draw a graphic organizer like the one here. Use it to identify reasons the Romans might accept or forbid a religion.

FOCUS ON WRITING

5. **Taking Notes** Create a chart with columns labeled Main Ideas and Supporting Details. Then write two main ideas in your chart: "Romans allowed many religions" and "Jews and Romans differed over religion." Take notes about these ideas in the Supporting Details column.

ROME AND CHRISTIANITY **383**

383

Bellringer

If YOU were there . . . Use the **Daily Bellringer Transparency** to help students answer the question.

🗄 Daily Bellringer Transparency, Section 2

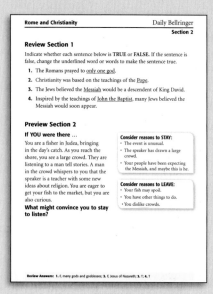

Rome and Christianity — Daily Bellringer, Section 2

Review Section 1

Indicate whether each sentence below is TRUE or FALSE. If the sentence is false, change the underlined word or words to make the sentence true.

1. The Romans prayed to only one god.
2. Christianity was based on the teachings of the Pope.
3. The Jews believed the Messiah would be a descendent of King David.
4. Inspired by the teachings of John the Baptist, many Jews believed the Messiah would soon appear.

Preview Section 2

If YOU were there . . .

You are a fisher in Judea, bringing in the day's catch. As you reach the shore, you see a large crowd. They are listening to a man tell stories. A man in the crowd whispers to you that the speaker is a teacher with some new ideas about religion. You are eager to get your fish to the market, but you are also curious.

What might convince you to stay to listen?

Consider reasons to STAY:
• The event is unusual.
• The speaker has drawn a large crowd.
• Your people have been expecting the Messiah, and maybe this is he.

Consider reasons to LEAVE:
• Your fish may spoil.
• You have other things to do.
• You dislike crowds.

Review Answers: 1. F, many gods and goddesses; 2. F, Jesus of Nazareth; 3. T; 4. T

Academic Vocabulary

Review with students the high-use academic term in this section.

ideals ideas or goals that people try to live up to (p. 388)

Building Vocabulary

Preteach or review the following terms:

denomination a group that holds the same set of beliefs (p. 387)

parable a story that teaches a moral or religious lesson (p. 386)

📝 CRF: Vocabulary Builder Activity, Section 2

🐻 Standards Focus

HSS 6.7.6

Means: Discuss the life and teachings of Jesus, the main beliefs of Christianity, and the contributions of Paul in founding Christianity.

Matters: The teachings of Jesus and the efforts of Paul were essential to the creation of the Christian religion.

SECTION 2

Origins of Christianity

What You Will Learn...

Main Ideas

1. In Christian belief, Jesus was the Messiah and the son of God.
2. Jesus taught about salvation, love for God, and kindness.
3. Jesus's followers, especially Paul, spread his teachings after his death.

The Big Idea

Christianity, based on the teachings of Jesus of Nazareth, spread quickly after his death.

Key Terms and People

Bible, *p. 384*
crucifixion, *p. 385*
Resurrection, *p. 385*
disciples, *p. 385*
Apostles, *p. 387*
Paul, *p. 387*
saint, *p. 388*

🐻 **HSS 6.7.6** Note the origins of Christianity in the Jewish Messianic prophecies, the life and teachings of Jesus of Nazareth as described in the New Testament, and the contributions of St. Paul the Apostle to the definition and spread of Christian beliefs (e.g., belief in the Trinity, resurrection, salvation).

If YOU were there...

You are a fisher in Judea, bringing in the day's catch. As you reach the shore, you see a large crowd. They are listening to a man tell stories. A man in the crowd whispers to you that the speaker is a teacher with some new ideas about religion. You are eager to get your fish to the market, but you are also curious.

What might convince you to stay to listen?

BUILDING BACKGROUND In the first century AD, Judea was a province of the Roman Empire. Roman soldiers occupied the country, but the Jews living there held firmly to their own beliefs and customs. During that time, religious teachers could attract large followings among the people of Judea. One such teacher was Jesus of Nazareth.

The Life and Death of Jesus of Nazareth

Jesus of Nazareth, the man whom many people believe was the Jewish Messiah, lived at the beginning of the first century AD. Although Jesus was one of the most influential figures in world history, we know relatively little about his life. Most of what we know about Jesus is contained in the New Testament of the Christian **Bible**, the holy book of Christianity.

The Christian Bible is made up of two parts. The first part, the Old Testament, is largely the same as the Hebrew Bible. It tells the history and ideas of the Hebrew people. The second part, the New Testament, is an account of the life and teachings of Jesus and of the early history of Christianity.

The Birth of Jesus

According to the Bible, Jesus was born in a small town called Bethlehem (BETH-li-hem) at the end of the first century BC. In fact, in our dating system his birth marks the shift from BC to AD. Jesus's mother, Mary, was married to a carpenter named Joseph. But Christians believe God, not Joseph, was Jesus's father.

Teach the Big Idea: Master the Standards

Standards Proficiency

Origins of Christianity 🐻 HSS 6.7.6; HSS Analysis Skills: CS 1, HI 1

1. **Teach** Ask students the Main Idea questions to teach this section.

2. **Apply** Guide students in a discussion of this section. Write the labels *Life of Jesus, Acts and Teachings,* and *Jesus's Followers* for students to see. Discuss with students the important details from each topic. Then have each student create a three-column chart that uses the three labels as headings. **LS Verbal/Linguistic**

3. **Review** Have students exchange charts as a review of the section.

4. **Practice/Homework** Have students create a glossary for their chart that includes the key terms and people from the section and the definition or description of each term or person. **LS Verbal/Linguistic**

📝 Alternative Assessment Handbook, Rubrics 7: Charts; and 42: Writing to Inform

As a young man Jesus lived in the town of Nazareth and probably studied with Joseph to become a carpenter. Like many young Jewish men of the time, he also studied the laws and teachings of Judaism. By the time he was about 30, Jesus had begun to travel and teach. Stories of his teachings and actions from this time make up the beginning of the New Testament.

The Crucifixion

As a teacher, Jesus drew many followers with his ideas. But at the same time, his teachings challenged the authority of political and religious leaders. According to the Christian Bible, Roman authorities arrested Jesus while he was in Jerusalem in or around AD 30.

Shortly after his arrest, Jesus was tried and executed. He was killed by **crucifixion** (kroo-suh-FIK-shuhn), a type of execution in which a person was nailed to a cross. In fact, the word *crucifixion* comes from the Latin word for "cross." After he died Jesus's followers buried him.

The Resurrection

According to Christian beliefs, Jesus rose from the dead and vanished from his tomb three days after he was crucified. Christians refer to Jesus's rise from the dead as the **Resurrection** (re-suh-REK-shuhn).

Christians further believe that after the Resurrection, Jesus appeared to several groups of his **disciples** (di-SY-puhls), or followers. Jesus stayed with these disciples for the next 40 days, teaching them and giving them instructions about how to pass on his teachings. Then Jesus rose up into heaven.

Early Christians believed that the Resurrection was a sign that Jesus was the Messiah and the son of God. Some people began to call him Jesus Christ, from the Greek word for Messiah, *Christos*. It is from this word that the words *Christian* and *Christianity* eventually developed.

THE IMPACT TODAY

Because Jesus was crucified, the cross is an important symbol of Christianity today.

READING CHECK **Summarizing** What do Christians believe happened after Jesus died?

Jesus of Nazareth

The Bible says that Jesus was born in Bethlehem but grew up in Nazareth. This painting from about 1300 shows Jesus with his followers.

385

385

Main Idea

❷ Acts and Teachings

Jesus taught about salvation, love for God, and kindness.

Explain What effect did stories of Jesus's miracles have on his followers? *They convinced people to follow Jesus.*

Compare What two teachings of Jesus were rooted in Jewish traditions? *love for God and love for others*

Analyze Why did different denominations of Christianity develop over time? *because different people interpreted the teachings of Jesus in different ways*

📝 **CRF:** Literature Activity: The Parable of the Prodigal Son

🐻 **HSS** 6.7.6; **HSS** Analysis Skills: CS 1, HI 1

Linking to Today

Christian Holidays Some people celebrate Christmas with a Christmas tree. But why? In the 700s, the monk Saint Boniface said that the triangular shape of an evergreen tree resembled the Trinity—the Father, the Son, and the Holy Ghost. Several hundred years later, evergreen trees were set up inside homes during Christmas. A thousand years later, millions of Christians still set up and decorate Christmas trees as part of their celebration of the birth of Jesus.

Answers

Analyzing Information *Possible answer—A celebration of his life is a celebration of his beliefs and teachings.*

Christian Holidays

For centuries, Christians have honored key events in Jesus's life. Some of these events inspired holidays that Christians celebrate today.

The most sacred holiday for Christians is Easter, which is celebrated each spring. The exact date changes from year to year. Easter is a celebration of the Resurrection. Christians usually celebrate Easter by attending church services. Many people also celebrate by dyeing eggs because eggs are seen as a symbol of new life.

Another major Christian holiday is Christmas. It honors Jesus's birth and is celebrated every December 25. Although no one knows on what date Jesus was actually born, Christians have placed Christmas in December since the 200s. Today, people celebrate with church services and the exchange of gifts. Some, like people in this picture, reenact scenes of Jesus's birth.

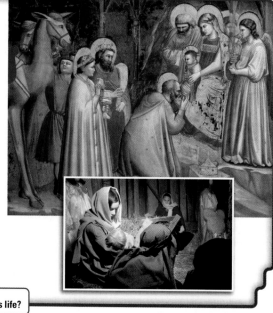

ANALYSIS SKILL **ANALYZING INFORMATION**
Why do you think people celebrate events in Jesus's life?

Acts and Teachings

During his lifetime, Jesus traveled from village to village spreading his message among the Jewish people. As he traveled, he attracted many followers. These early followers later became the first Christians.

Miracles

According to the New Testament, many people became Jesus's followers after they saw him perform miracles. A miracle is an event that cannot normally be performed by a human. For example, the books of the New Testament tell how Jesus healed people who were sick or injured. One passage also describes how Jesus once fed an entire crowd with just a few loaves of bread and a few fish. Although there should not have been enough food for everyone, people ate their fill and had food to spare.

Parables

The Bible says that miracles drew followers to Jesus and convinced them that he was the son of God. Once Jesus had attracted followers, he began to teach them. One way he taught was through parables, stories that teach lessons about how to live. Parables are similar to fables, but they usually teach religious lessons. The New Testament includes many of Jesus's parables.

Through his parables, Jesus linked his teachings to people's everyday lives. The parables explained complicated ideas in ways that people could understand. For example, Jesus compared people who lived sinfully to a son who had left his home and family. Just as the son's father would joyfully welcome him home, Jesus said, God would forgive sinners who turned away from sin.

Differentiating Instruction for Universal Access

Advanced Learners/GATE   [Exceeding Standards]

1. Remind students that Jesus often attracted large crowds of followers who gathered to hear his teachings. Discuss with the class how Jesus often taught his followers by telling parables that linked his message to events in everyday life with which the people might be familiar. His famous parables include "The Parable of the Prodigal Son" and "The Parable of the Tares [Weeds] and the Wheat."

2. Encourage students to read the "Parable of the Good Samaritan" at the end of this section in order to become familiar with the style and the way in which a moral lesson is delivered.

3. Have students write a parable or short story that teaches a lesson. If they have difficulty thinking of a moral, suggest "be nice to your neighbor" or "don't be greedy."

4. Ask volunteers to share their parables with the class. **LS Verbal/Linguistic**

🐻 **HSS** 6.7.6; **HSS** Analysis Skills: CS 1, HI 3

📝 Alternative Assessment Handbook, Rubric 37: Writing Assignments

Jesus's Message

Much of Jesus's message was rooted in older Jewish traditions. For example, he emphasized two rules that were also in the Torah: love God and love other people.

Jesus expected his followers to love all people, not just friends or family. He encouraged his followers to be generous to the poor and the sick. He told people that they should even love their enemies. The way people treated others, Jesus said, showed how much they loved God.

Another important theme in Jesus's teachings was salvation, or the rescue of people from sin. Jesus taught that people who were saved from sin would enter the Kingdom of God when they died. Many of his teachings dealt with how people could reach the kingdom.

Over the many centuries since Jesus lived, people have interpreted his teachings in different ways. As a result, many different denominations of Christians have been developed. A denomination is a group of people who hold the same beliefs. Still, despite their differences, Christians around the world share some basic beliefs about Jesus and his importance to the world.

READING CHECK Summarizing Why did Jesus tell parables?

Jesus's Followers

Shortly after the Resurrection, the Bible says, Jesus's followers traveled throughout the Roman world telling about Jesus and his teachings. Among the people to pass on Jesus's teachings were 12 chosen disciples called **Apostles** (uh-PAHS-uhls), the writers of the Gospels (GAHS-puhlz), and a man named **Paul**.

The Apostles

The Apostles were 12 men whom Jesus chose to receive special teaching. During Jesus's lifetime they were among his closest followers and knew him very well. Jesus frequently sent the Apostles to spread his teachings. After the Resurrection, the Apostles continued this task.

One of the Apostles, Peter, became the leader of the group after Jesus died. Peter traveled to a few Roman cities and taught about Jesus in the Jewish communities there. Eventually he went to live in Rome, where he had much authority among Jesus's followers. In later years after the Christian Church was more organized, many people looked back to Peter as its first leader.

The Last Supper
This famous painting by Italian artist Leonardo da Vinci shows Jesus and his Apostles at the Last Supper. The Last Supper was the last meal they shared before Jesus was arrested. Later, the Apostles would spread Jesus's teachings.

387

Critical Thinking: Drawing Inferences

Reaching Standards

Writing Interview Questions 🐻 **HSS** 6.7.6; **HSS** Analysis Skills: HR 1, HI 1, HI 2

1. Review with the class the teachings of Jesus and his followers. Write the main rules and teachings for students to see. Ask students to infer what people's reactions might have been to the teachings of Jesus. Why might people have become followers of Jesus?

2. Ask students to imagine that they are newspaper reporters covering an event where Jesus is speaking to a large crowd. Have students create 10 interview questions a reporter might ask a person in the crowd who has just heard Jesus speak.

3. Remind students to keep their interview questions objective. Questions could cover such topics as the roots of Jesus's message, key ideas and beliefs of his teachings, Jesus's parables, or reactions to his message.

4. Ask volunteers to share their questions with the class. **LS** Verbal/Linguistic

📖 Alternative Assessment Handbook, Rubric 37: Writing Assignments

387

Paul's Journeys

First journey
Second journey
Third journey
Fourth journey

GEOGRAPHY SKILLS | INTERPRETING MAPS

Movement Where did Paul go on his fourth journey?

Direct Teach

Main Idea

❸ Jesus's Followers

Jesus's followers, especially Paul, spread his teachings after his death.

Recall How did Paul describe the Trinity? *It is the idea that God is made up of three persons—God the Father, Jesus the Son, and the Holy Spirit.*

Explain Why did Paul become a Christian? *According to Christian beliefs, he had an experience in which he saw a light and heard the voice of Jesus calling to him.*

Map Transparency: Paul's Journeys

HSS 6.7.6; HSS Analysis Skills: CS 1, HI 1

Other People, Other Places

Buddhism At about the same time that Jesus's followers were spreading Christianity throughout the Roman Empire, Buddhism was first being introduced to China. According to tradition, in about AD 65 the Han emperor Ming Ti had a vision that led him to send scholars to India to learn about their religion. However, it is more likely that Buddhism came to China gradually, thanks to the efforts of traders traveling along the Silk Roads between India and China.

The Gospels

Some of Jesus's disciples wrote accounts of his life and teachings. These accounts are called the Gospels. Four Gospels are found in the New Testament of the Bible. They were written by men known as Matthew, Mark, Luke, and John. Both historians and religious scholars depend on the Gospels for information about Jesus's life.

Paul

ACADEMIC VOCABULARY

ideals ideas or goals that people try to live up to

Probably the most important figure in the spread of Christianity after Jesus's death was named Paul of Tarsus. He had never met Jesus, but Paul did more to spread Christian **ideals** than anyone else did. He was so influential that many people consider him an additional Apostle. After he died, Paul was named a **saint**, a person known and admired for his or her holiness.

Like most of Jesus's early followers, Paul was born Jewish. At first he didn't like Jesus's ideas, which he considered a threat to Judaism. For a time, Paul even worked to prevent the followers of Jesus from spreading their message.

According to the Bible, though, one day while Paul was traveling to Damascus he saw a blinding light and heard the voice of Jesus calling out to him. Soon afterward, Paul became a Christian.

After his conversion Paul traveled widely, spreading Christian teachings. As you can see on the map, he visited many of the major cities along the eastern coast of the Mediterranean on his journeys. In addition, he wrote long letters that he sent to communities throughout the Roman world. These letters helped explain and elaborate on Jesus's teachings.

388 CHAPTER 13

Collaborative Learning

Standards Proficiency

Writing a Travelogue HSS 6.7.6; HSS Analysis Skills: CS 1, HI 1

Research Required

1. Review with students the contributions of Paul of Tarsus. Remind students that Paul is best known for his efforts to spread Christianity. Ask students to examine the map of Paul's Journeys.

2. Organize students into small groups. Have each group use the library, internet, or other resources to find information about the areas in which Paul traveled on his four journeys. What cities did he visit? How did he travel from place to place?

3. Next, explain to students that a travelogue is a description of a person's travels. Have each group create a travelogue that describes where and how Paul traveled on each of his journeys. Encourage students to create illustrations and maps to enhance their travelogues.

4. Ask groups to share their travelogues with the class. **LS Verbal/Linguistic, Visual/Spatial**

Alternative Assessment Handbook, Rubric 42: Writing to Inform

Answers

Interpreting Maps *Malta, Crete, and Rome*

388

LETTER

Paul's Letter to the Romans

In the late AD 50s Paul traveled to Corinth, a city in Greece. While there he wrote a letter to the people of Rome. In this letter he told the Romans that he planned to come to their city to deliver God's message. In the meantime, he told them, they should learn to live together peacefully.

"Let love be genuine; hate what is evil, hold fast to what is good; love one another with mutual affection; outdo one another in showing honor. Do not lag in zeal, be ardent [strong] in spirit, serve the Lord. Rejoice in hope, be patient in suffering, persevere in prayer. Contribute to the needs of the saints; extend hospitality to strangers.

Bless those who persecute you; bless and do not curse them. Rejoice with those who rejoice, weep with those who weep. Live in harmony with one another; do not be haughty, but associate with the lowly; do not claim to be wiser than you are. Do not repay anyone evil for evil, but take thought for what is noble in the sight of all. If it is possible, so far as it depends on you, live peaceably with all."

—Romans 12:9–18 NRSV

ANALYSIS SKILL | **ANALYZING PRIMARY SOURCES**

How did Paul's letter express Jesus's teachings?

In his letters Paul wrote at length about the Resurrection and about salvation. He also mentioned ideas of the Trinity. The Trinity is a central Christian belief that God is made up of three persons—God the Father, Jesus the Son, and the Holy Spirit. But even though there are three persons, there is still only one God.

Both Jews and non-Jews were attracted to Christianity by Paul's teachings. In time, this helped the Christian Church break away from its Jewish roots.

READING CHECK **Drawing Conclusions** Why was Paul important to early Christianity?

SUMMARY AND PREVIEW By AD 100, Christianity had spread beyond Judea into many parts of the Roman world. As you will learn, the Christian Church would come to have a huge influence on Roman society.

Section 2 Assessment

go.hrw.com
Online Quiz
KEYWORD: SQ6 HP13

Reviewing Ideas, Terms, and People HSS 6.7.6

1. **a. Define** In Christian teachings, what was the **Resurrection**?
   b. Elaborate Why do you think Christians use the cross as a symbol of their religion?
2. **a. Identify** What did Jesus mean by salvation?
   b. Explain How have differing interpretations of Jesus's teachings affected Christianity?
3. **a. Recall** Who were the **Apostles**?
   b. Summarize How did **Saint Paul** influence early Christianity?

Critical Thinking

4. **Finding the Main Idea** Draw a graphic organizer like the one shown here. Use it to identify and describe some of Jesus's acts and teachings.

   Acts and Teachings of Jesus of Nazareth

Miracles	Parables	Message

FOCUS ON WRITING

5. **Adding to Your Notes** Add two main ideas about the origins of Christianity to your notebook. What details support these main ideas?

ROME AND CHRISTIANITY **389**

Section 2 Assessment Answers

1. **a.** Jesus's rising from the dead
   b. to honor Jesus, who died on a cross
2. **a.** the rescuing of people from evil and punishment after they died
   b. They have led to the creation of different denominations of Christianity.
3. **a.** 12 chosen followers of Jesus who worked to spread Jesus's teachings after he died
   b. He spread Christianity through the Roman Empire and explained Jesus's teachings.

4. Miracles—healed the sick, fed a large crowd with little food; Parables—a father forgives his son like God forgives sinners; Message—love all people, be generous, salvation, love God.
5. main idea 1—the life and death of Jesus; supporting details—the New Testament tells his life story; he was crucified; and according to the Christian faith, he was resurrected; main idea 2—Jesus's teachings; supporting details—be kind, love God, help the needy

---

Primary Source

Reading Like a Historian

Paul's Letter to the Romans Help students practice reading the document like historians. Ask:

- What was Paul's purpose in writing this letter to the Romans?
- Why might Paul's message have appealed to the Romans?

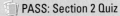 **HSS** 6.7.6; **HSS** Analysis Skill: HR 4, HR 5, HI 1

● **Review & Assess** ●

Close

Ask students to write a short paragraph that describes the basic teachings of Christianity.

Review

Online Quiz, Section 2

Assess

SE Section 2 Assessment
PASS: Section 2 Quiz
Alternative Assessment Handbook

Reteach/Classroom Intervention

California Standards Review Workbook
Interactive Reader and Study Guide, Section 2
Interactive Skills Tutor CD-ROM

Answers

Analyzing Primary Sources *It tells the reader to love one's neighbor and to commit one's life to serving God.*

Reading Check *He spread Jesus's teachings throughout the Roman Empire and further developed the religion.*

The Sermon on the Mount

As You Read As students read the Beatitudes, have them make a list of the people who Jesus says are blessed. Then ask students what it means to be "meek," "merciful," and the other words that Jesus uses to describe the blessed. Use a dictionary if necessary to clarify the meanings of words in the passage. **ELA** Reading 6.1.2

Analyzing Sacred Texts

Identify Main Ideas Have students read the sermon again and identify the main idea. What is the point that Jesus is attempting to make? *Those who are needy or have good qualities will be rewarded.* Then ask students to cite specific passages in the reading that support that main idea. *possible answers— Those who mourn . . . will be comforted.*

HSS 6.7.6 **ELA** Reading 6.2.3

Info to Know

The New Testament The Sermon on the Mount is found in the Gospel of Matthew, the first book of the New Testament of the Bible. A similar version of this sermon is told in the Gospel of Luke, the third book of the New Testament.

Answers

Guided Reading *Christians should not be afraid to show their faith in God or their goodness.*

390

GUIDED READING

WORD HELP

meek enduring hardships without complaining
righteousness good living
persecute to punish someone for their beliefs
revile hate
trampled stepped on

❶ The poor in spirit are those people who give up material goods out of love for God.

❷ Here Jesus is saying that people who are punished or killed for their beliefs will be honored in heaven.

❸ Jesus compares his ideals with light.

What do you think Jesus means when he says "let your light shine before others"?

ELA Reading 6.1.2 Identify and interpret figurative language and words with multiple meanings.

390 CHAPTER 13

---

from
The Bible

The Sermon on the Mount
Matthew 5:1–16 New Revised Standard Version

About the Reading *The Bible says that Jesus attracted many followers. One day he led his followers onto a mountainside to preach a sermon, or religious speech, called the Sermon on the Mount. Jesus taught that people who love God will be blessed when they die. The sayings that Jesus used to express this message are called the Beatitudes (bee-A-tuh-toodz), because in Latin they all begin with the word* beati, *or blessed.*

AS YOU READ Note who Jesus says are blessed.

When Jesus saw the crowds, he went up the mountain; and after he sat down, his disciples came to him. Then he began to speak, and taught them, saying:

"Blessed are the poor in spirit, for theirs is the kingdom of heaven. ❶

"Blessed are those who mourn, for they will be comforted.

"Blessed are the meek, for they will inherit the earth.

"Blessed are those who hunger and thirst for righteousness, for they will be filled.

"Blessed are the merciful, for they will receive mercy.

"Blessed are the pure in heart, for they will see God.

"Blessed are the peacemakers, for they will be called children of God.

"Blessed are those who are persecuted for righteousness' sake, for theirs is the kingdom of heaven. ❷

"Blessed are you when people revile you and persecute you and utter all kinds of evil against you falsely on my account. Rejoice and be glad, for your reward is great in heaven, for in the same way they persecuted the prophets who were before you.

"You are the salt of the earth; but if salt has lost its taste, how can its saltiness be restored? It is no longer good for anything, but is thrown out and trampled under foot.

"You are the light of the world. A city built on a hill cannot be hid. No one after lighting a lamp puts it under the bushel basket, but on the lampstand, and it gives light to all in the house. In the same way, let your light shine before others, so that they may see your good works and give glory to your Father in heaven." ❸

Differentiating Instruction for Universal Access

Learners Having Difficulty   Reaching Standards

1. Review with students the Sermon on the Mount. Help students understand terms with which they may not be familiar.

2. Then have students create a three-column chart on their own paper. Have students list in the first column the different people that Jesus says are blessed or the different instances in which people are blessed.

3. Next, have students identify in the second column the prediction that Jesus makes for each of the people listed.

4. In the third column, students should interpret what they think each prediction means. For example, *the pure in heart . . . will see God* might mean that true believers will come to understand God.

5. As a class, review the meanings that students wrote.

LS Verbal/Linguistic, Logical/Mathematical

HSS 6.7.5; **HSS** Analysis Skills: HI 1

Alternative Assessment Handbook, Rubric 11: Discussions

The Parable of the Good Samaritan

Luke 10:29–37 New Revised Standard Version

About the Reading *In his teaching, Jesus used many parables, or stories intended to teach lessons about how people should live. One of his most famous parables is the story of the Good Samaritan. The Samaritans were a minority group living in what is now northern Israel. The parable of the Good Samaritan is Jesus's response to someone who asks what Jesus means when he says to love your neighbor.*

AS YOU READ Think about the lesson Jesus is trying to teach.

But wanting to justify himself, he asked Jesus, "And who is my neighbor?" Jesus replied, "A man was going down from Jerusalem to Jericho, and fell into the hands of robbers, who stripped him, beat him, and went away, leaving him half dead. Now by chance a priest was going down that road; and when he saw him, he passed by on the other side. So likewise a Levite, when he came to the place and saw him, passed by on the other side. But a Samaritan while traveling came near him; and when he saw him, he was moved with pity. He went to him and bandaged his wounds, having poured oil and wine on them. ❶ Then he put him on his own animal, brought him to an inn, and took care of him. The next day he took out two denarii, gave them to the innkeeper, and said, 'Take care of him; and when I come back, I will repay you whatever you spend.' Which of these three, do you think, was a neighbor to the man who fell into the hands of the robbers?" He said, "The one who showed him mercy." Jesus said to him, "Go and do likewise." ❷

GUIDED READING

WORD HELP

Levite (LEE-vyt) a member of the Hebrew priest class

denarii (di-NAR-ee-eye) Roman coins

❶ Oil and wine were used to clean cuts and wounds.

What does the Samaritan do after he cleans the traveler's wounds?

❷ *Which person did the man say was the traveler's neighbor?*

The Samaritans lived in the northern part of what is now Israel.

CONNECTING SACRED TEXTS TO HISTORY

1. **Analyzing** Jesus taught that people who loved God and lived good lives would achieve salvation. How do the Beatitudes support this teaching?

2. **Supporting a Point of View** Jesus also told people that they should be kind to everyone, even their enemies. How is the parable of the Good Samaritan an example of this?

391

Sacred Texts

The Parable of the Good Samaritan

As You Read Ask students why a parable might be more effective in teaching a lesson than a sermon. Ask them how an audience might respond to a parable as compared to a sermon. Remind students that people often don't like to be told what to do. Discuss with them the benefits of putting a lesson into a story, such as in this parable.

Analyzing Sacred Texts

Identifying Themes Remind students that the theme of a work is the unspoken message. Ask students what the theme of this parable is. Then have students discuss how effective this parable is in conveying that message.
ELA Reading 6.3.6

Did you know . . .

This parable is so well-known that the term *Good Samaritan* is commonly used to refer to people who go out of their way to help people in need.

Cross-Discipline Activity: Civics

Standards Proficiency

Responsibility: Good Samaritan Laws

Research Required

1. Have students think of good deeds that they have heard about, or perhaps have performed themselves. Good deeds may be small, such as picking up litter, or extreme, such as saving someone's life.

2. Explain to students that laws have been named after the Good Samaritan in the parable. Have students use the library, internet, or other resources to research Good Samaritan laws, which provide protection to people who try to render aid in an emergency. Have students find information on how the law applies in their state and in other states.

3. Have students write a paragraph on how the laws might be used, and what their thoughts are about the laws. **LS** Verbal/Linguistic

HSS 6.7.6; **HSS** Analysis Skills: CS 1, HR 1, HI 3

Alternative Assessment Handbook, Rubrics 30: Research; and 37: Writing Assignments

Answers

Guided Reading 1. *bandages his wounds, takes him to an inn, and tells the innkeeper to care for him;* **2.** *the Samaritan*

Connecting Sacred Texts to History 1. *They describe different behaviors that can result in salvation;* **2.** *It tells of someone who does a very good and loving thing for a person.*

Bellringer

If YOU were there . . . Use the **Daily Bellringer Transparency** to help students answer the question.

🞐 Daily Bellringer Transparency, Section 3

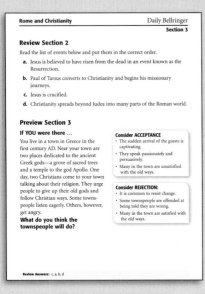

Rome and Christianity   Daily Bellringer
                                              Section 3

Review Section 2

Read the list of events below and put them in the correct order.

a. Jesus is believed to have risen from the dead in an event known as the Resurrection.

b. Paul of Tarsus converts to Christianity and begins his missionary journeys.

c. Jesus is crucified.

d. Christianity spreads beyond Judea into many parts of the Roman world.

Preview Section 3

If YOU were there . . .

You live in a town in Greece in the first century AD. Near your town are two places dedicated to the ancient Greek gods—a grove of sacred trees and a temple to the god Apollo. One day, two Christians come to your town talking about their religion. They urge people to give up their old gods and follow Christian ways. Some townspeople listen eagerly. Others, however, get angry.

What do you think the townspeople will do?

Consider ACCEPTANCE
· The sudden arrival of the guests is captivating.
· They speak passionately and persuasively.
· Many in the town are unsatisfied with the old ways.

Consider REJECTION:
· It is common to resist change.
· Some townspeople are offended at being told they are wrong.
· Many in the town are satisfied with the old ways.

Review Answers: c, a, b, d

Academic Vocabulary

Review with students the high-use academic term in this section.

classical referring to the cultures of ancient Greece or Rome (p. 394)

Building Vocabulary

Preteach or review the following term:

successors people who follow another in an office or position (p. 394)

📝 **CRF:** Vocabulary Builder Activity, Section 3

Standards Focus

HSS 6.7.7
Means: Describe how Christianity spread throughout the Roman Empire and into Europe.
Matters: Christianity spread throughout the Roman Empire and eventually became its official religion.

The Early Christian World

What You Will Learn...

Main Ideas

1. Christianity spread quickly in Rome, but its growing strength worried some emperors.
2. As the church grew, new leaders and ideas appeared and Christianity's status in the empire changed.

The Big Idea

Within three centuries after Jesus's death, Christianity had spread through the empire and become Rome's official religion.

Key Terms and People

martyrs, *p. 393*
persecution, *p. 393*
bishops, *p. 393*
Eucharist, *p. 393*
pope, *p. 394*
Augustine of Hippo, *p. 394*
Constantine, *p. 395*

HSS **6.7.7** Describe the circumstances that led to the spread of Christianity in Europe and other Roman territories.

If YOU were there...

You live in a town in Greece in the first century AD. Near your town are two places dedicated to the ancient Greek gods—a grove of sacred trees and a temple to the god Apollo. One day, two Christians come to your town talking about their religion. They urge people to give up their old gods and follow Christian ways. Some townspeople listen eagerly. Others, however, get angry.

What do you think the townspeople will do?

BUILDING BACKGROUND From its origins in Judea, Christianity began to spread quickly. Apostles such as Peter and Paul traveled throughout the eastern Mediterranean world, preaching and writing letters to local churches. They were welcomed in some places but met anger and hostility in others.

Christianity Spreads Quickly in Rome

Early Christians like Paul wanted to share their message about Jesus with the world. Because of their efforts, Christianity spread quickly in many Roman communities. But as it grew more popular, Christianity began to concern some Roman leaders. They looked for ways to put an end to this new religion.

Time Line

Early Christianity

BC 1 AD

c. 30
Jesus is crucified.

Teach the Big Idea: Master the Standards

Standards Proficiency

The Early Christian World 🐻 **HSS** 6.7.7

1. **Teach** Ask students the Main Idea questions to teach this section.
2. **Apply** Discuss the main events in this section with the class. Have students re-read the section to see what events they might include on a time line. Then have each student create an annotated time line that includes dates from this section, as well as other important events in the spread of early Christianity.
   LS Verbal/Linguistic, Visual/Spatial

3. **Review** As you review the section, have students check their time lines to see if they have accurately traced the main events described in the section.
4. **Practice/Homework** Have students take the time lines they created and copy it onto a larger piece of paper and then add drawings to the time line in order to illustrate the events on the time line. **LS Visual/Spatial**

   📝 Alternative Assessment Handbook, Rubric 36: Time Lines

Early Growth

The first Christians worked to spread Jesus's teachings only among Jews. But some early Christians, including Paul, wanted to introduce Christianity to non-Jews as well. As a result, Christianity began to spread in the Roman Empire. Within a hundred years after Jesus's death, historians estimate that thousands of Christians lived in the Roman Empire.

As Christianity spread, Christians began to write down parts of Jesus's message, including the Gospels. They distributed copies of the Gospels and other writings to strengthen people's faith.

Persecution

From time to time, Christians trying to spread their beliefs faced challenges from local officials. Some of these officials even arrested and killed Christians who refused to worship Rome's gods. We call such people who suffer death for their religious beliefs **martyrs** (MAHR-tuhrz). Many leaders of the early Christians—including Peter and Paul—were killed for spreading Christian teachings. Even today, Christians honor them as martyrs and saints.

Most of Rome's emperors let Christians worship as they pleased. A few emperors in the 200s and 300s, though, feared that the Christians could cause unrest in the empire. To prevent such unrest, these emperors banned Christianity. This ban led to several periods of persecution (puhr-si-KYOO-shuhn) against Christians. **Persecution** means punishing a group because of its beliefs or differences.

Because their religion had been banned, Christians were often forced to meet in secret. To arrange their meetings, they used secret symbols to identify people who shared their beliefs. One of the most common symbols they used was a fish. The fish became a Christian symbol because the Greek word for fish begins with the same letters as the Greek words for *Jesus* and *Christ*.

THE IMPACT TODAY
The fish is still commonly used as a symbol of Christianity.

READING CHECK Identifying Cause and Effect Why did the Romans begin persecuting Christians?

The Church Grows

Because the early church largely had to meet in secret, it didn't have any single leader to govern it. Instead, **bishops**, or local Christian leaders, led each Christian community. Most bishops lived in cities. They helped people understand and live by Christian teachings.

One of the bishops' most important duties was leading Christians in celebrating the Eucharist (YOO-kuh-ruhst). The **Eucharist** was the central ceremony of the Christian Church. It was created to honor the last supper Jesus shared with his Apostles. During the Eucharist, Christians ate bread and drank wine in memory of Jesus's death.

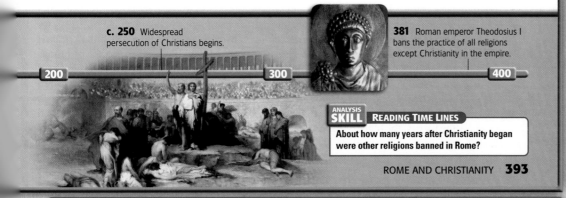

c. 250 Widespread persecution of Christians begins.

381 Roman emperor Theodosius I bans the practice of all religions except Christianity in the empire.

200 — 300 — 400

ANALYSIS SKILL READING TIME LINES
About how many years after Christianity began were other religions banned in Rome?

ROME AND CHRISTIANITY **393**

393

❷ The Church Grows

As the church grew, new leaders and ideas appeared, and Christianity's status in the empire changed.

Explain How did the bishop of Rome become the head of the Christian Church? *Peter had been bishop of Rome and he was a leader in the church; people came to see that office as the head of the church.*

Analyze How did Saint Augustine help shape Christian beliefs? *His writings influenced Christian ideas, like shifting focus from worldly goods to God's plan for the world.*

Summarize How did the actions of Roman emperors affect the development of Christianity? *Constantine removed bans against Christian practice; Theodosius banned all non-Christian religions; both called councils to clarify church teachings.*

📰 **CRF:** Biography Activity: Theodosius I

🐢 **HSS** 6.7.7; **HSS** Analysis Skills: CS 1, HI 1, HI 3

Teaching Tip

Explain to students that Rome is still a major center of the Christian world. The Catholic Church is centered in Vatican City, home to the pope and headquarters of the Catholic Church. The Basilica of St. Peter's, located at the Vatican, is the largest Christian church in the world and is believed to be built over the tomb of Peter, the original bishop of Rome.

Answers

Interpreting Maps *Africa, Europe, and Asia*

394

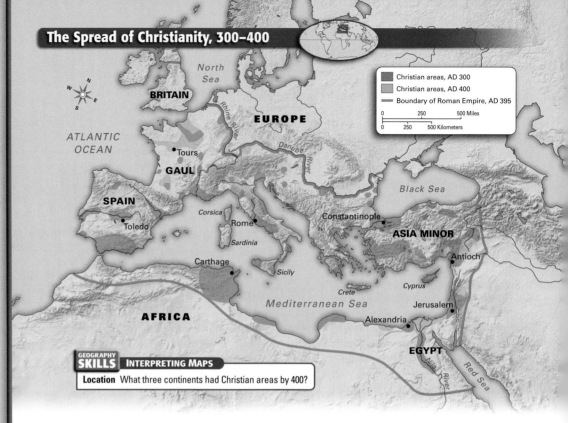

The Spread of Christianity, 300–400

Christian areas, AD 300
Christian areas, AD 400
Boundary of Roman Empire, AD 395

0   250   500 Miles
0   250   500 Kilometers

North Sea
BRITAIN
EUROPE
ATLANTIC OCEAN
Tours
GAUL
Rhine River
Danube River
SPAIN
Corsica
Rome
Toledo
Sardinia
Carthage
Sicily
Crete
Black Sea
Constantinople
ASIA MINOR
Antioch
Cyprus
Mediterranean Sea
AFRICA
Jerusalem
Alexandria
EGYPT
Nile River
Red Sea

GEOGRAPHY SKILLS | **INTERPRETING MAPS**

Location What three continents had Christian areas by 400?

Growth of the Papacy

By the late 100s Christians were looking to the bishops of large cities for guidance. These bishops had great influence, even over other bishops. The most honored of all the empire's bishops was the bishop of Rome, or the **pope**. The word *pope* comes from the Greek word for father. The pope was so honored in the Christian world largely because Peter, the leader of the Apostles and a key figure in the early church, had been the first bishop of Rome. Later popes were seen as his spiritual successors.

Gradually, the pope's influence grew and many people in the West came to see him as the head of the whole Christian Church. As the church grew, so did the influence of the papacy, the office of the pope.

New Teachings and Emperors

As Christianity spread through the Roman world, Christian writers read the works of **classical** philosophers. One such writer was **Augustine** (AW-guhs-teen) **of Hippo**. He lived in Hippo, a town in northern Africa, in the late 300s and early 400s. As a young man, Augustine studied the works of Plato. When he became a Christian, he applied Plato's ideas to Christian beliefs. Augustine taught that Christians should focus not on worldly goods but on God's plan for the world. His ideas helped shape Christian beliefs for hundreds of years.

At about the same time that Saint Augustine was writing, an event changed the standing of Christians in Rome. The emperor himself became a Christian.

394 CHAPTER 13

Collaborative Learning

Standards Proficiency

Spread of Christianity Posters 🐢 **HSS** 6.7.7; **HSS** Analysis Skills: CS 1, HI 1, HI 2

1. Review with students the role that certain individuals played in the spread of the Christian church throughout the Roman Empire.

2. Organize the class into small groups. Then have each group select one of the following individuals who played an important role in the growth of Christianity: Peter, Augustine, Constantine, or Theodosius.

3. Have each group work together to create a poster that explains the contributions of

the person they chose. Remind students to concentrate on how each individual helped to influence the growth of the Christian church.

4. Ask groups to volunteer to present their posters to the class. 🔲 **Interpersonal, Verbal/Linguistic**

📝 Alternative Assessment Handbook, Rubric 28: Posters

The emperor who became a Christian was **Constantine** (KAHN-stuhn-teen). He came to power in 306 after fighting and defeating many rivals. According to legend, Constantine was preparing for battle against one of these rivals when he saw a cross in the sky. He thought that this vision meant he would win the battle if he converted to Christianity. Constantine did convert, and he won the battle. As a result of his victory he became the emperor of Rome.

As emperor, Constantine removed bans against the practice of Christianity. He also called together a council of Christian leaders from around the empire to clarify Christian teaching.

Almost 60 years after Constantine died, another emperor, Theodosius I (thee-uh-DOH-shuhs), banned all non-Christian religious practices in the Empire. Like Constantine, Theodosius was a Christian. As emperor, he called together Christian leaders to clarify church teachings. He wanted to be sure that all Christians believed the same things he did.

READING CHECK **Sequencing** How did Constantine and Theodosius influence Christianity?

BIOGRAPHY

Constantine

c. 280–337

Constantine grew up in the court of the Roman emperor. As a young man he became a general and led his army in many successful campaigns. After he converted to Christianity, Constantine came to believe that he had been successful all his life because he had God's favor. He built several great churches in the empire, including one in Jerusalem at the spot where Jesus was believed to have been buried. Throughout history Christians have considered him one of Rome's greatest emperors.

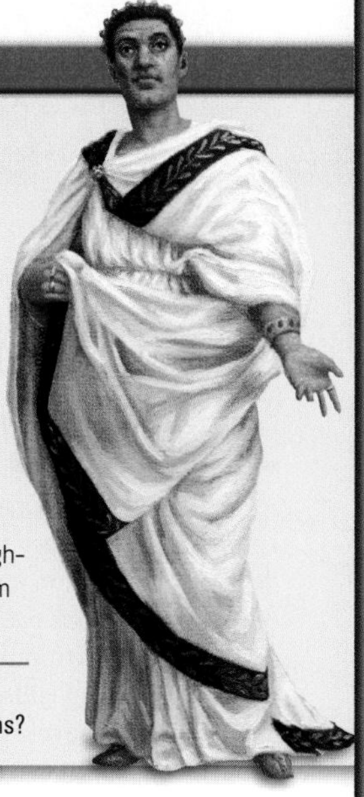

Drawing Conclusions Why do you think Constantine was so popular with Christians?

SUMMARY AND PREVIEW By the late 300s Christianity had become one of the most influential forces in the Roman world. Its influence provided security and stability for many people when the once mighty Roman Empire began to fall apart in the 400s.

Section 3 Assessment

go.hrw.com
Online Quiz
KEYWORD: SQ6 HP13

Reviewing Ideas, Terms, and People HSS 6.7.7

1. a. **Define** What is **persecution**?
   b. **Summarize** How did Paul change the way people spread Christianity?
   c. **Elaborate** Why do you think **martyrs** are admired?
2. a. **Identify** Who was Rome's first Christian emperor?
   b. **Contrast** How did **Constantine**'s policies toward Christianity differ from Theodosius's?
3. a. **Recall** What was the role of **bishops** in the early church?
   b. **Explain** Why did the **pope** have influence over many other bishops?

Critical Thinking

4. **Sequencing** Draw a diagram like the one below. In each box identify one step in the relationship between Christianity and the Roman Empire.

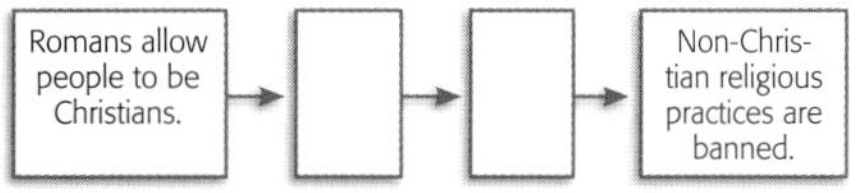

FOCUS ON WRITING

5. **Completing Your Chart** Finish your chart by adding two more main ideas and details that support them.

Direct Teach

Biography

Constantine

Activity **Journal Entries** Ask students to imagine that they are Roman citizens during the reign of Emperor Constantine. Have students write journal entries that describe changes that occurred in Rome as a result of the emperor's conversion to Christianity and their reaction to the changes. Ask volunteers to share their entries with the class.

HSS 6.7.7; HSS **Analysis Skills:** CS 1, HI 1

Review & Assess

Close

Have students discuss how Christianity spread throughout the Roman Empire, and what changes took place within the church.

Review

Online Quiz, Section 3

Assess

SE Section 3 Assessment

PASS: Section 3 Quiz

Alternative Assessment Handbook

Reteach/Classroom Intervention

California Standards Review Workbook

Interactive Reader and Study Guide, Section 3

Interactive Skills Tutor CD-ROM

Section 3 Assessment Answers

1. **a.** the punishment of people because of their beliefs or differences
   b. He encouraged people to spread Christian ideas to Jews and non-Jews.
   c. Possible answer—People admire them for the courage they displayed in dying for their faith.
2. **a.** Constantine
   b. Constantine allowed people to practice other religions, but Theodosius did not.
3. **a.** were leaders in their individual communities
   b. Peter had been bishop of Rome, and people carried their respect for him over to his successors, known as popes.
4. Romans persecute Christians; Constantine allows Christianity
5. Some possible responses might include: main idea 1—Christianity spreads in Roman Empire; supporting details—Gospels written; Paul spreads teachings; main idea 2—church grows; supporting details—bishops become local leaders; pope becomes church leader

Answers

Biography *He supported Christians and converted to Christianity.*

Reading Check *Constantine removed bans on Christianity, and Theodosius banned non-Christian religious practices.*

Social Studies Skills

Analysis | Critical Thinking | Participation | Study

Continuity and Change in History

Understand the Skill

A well-known saying claims that "the more things change, the more they stay the same." Nowhere does this observation apply more than to the study of history. Any look back over the past will show many changes—nations expanding or shrinking, empires rising and falling, changes in leadership, and people on the move, to name just a few.

The reasons for change have not changed, however. The same general forces have driven the actions of people and nations across time. These forces are the "threads" that run through history and give it continuity, or connectedness. They are the "sameness" in a world of constant change.

Learn the Skill

You can find the causes of all events of the past in one or more of these major forces or themes that run throughout history.

1 Cooperation and Conflict: Throughout time, people and groups have worked together to achieve goals. They have also opposed others who stood in the way of their goals.

2 Cultural Invention and Interaction: The values and ideas expressed in peoples' art, literature, customs, and religion have enriched the world. But the spread of cultures and their contact with other cultures has also sometimes produced conflict.

3 Geography and Environment: Physical environment and natural resources have shaped how people live. Efforts to gain or protect land and resources have been a major cause of cooperation and conflict in history.

4 Science and Technology: Technology, or the development and use of tools, has helped people make better use of their environment. Science has always changed people's lives also.

5 Economic Opportunity: From hunting and gathering to farming, manufacturing, and trade, people have tried to make the most of their resources. Hope for a better life is a main reason people have moved from one place to another.

6 The Impact of Individuals: Political, religious, military, business, and other leaders have been a major influence in history. The actions of many ordinary people have also shaped history.

7 Nationalism and Imperialism: Nationalism is the desire of a people to have their own country. Imperialism is the wish to control other peoples. Both have existed through history.

8 Political and Social Systems: People have always been part of groups—families, villages, nations, or religious groups, for example. The groups to which people belong affect how they relate to people around them. History is mostly the study of past interactions of people.

Practice and Apply the Skill

Check your understanding of the sources of continuity and change in history by answering the following questions.

1. How did relations between the Romans and the Jews show cultural interaction and conflict in history?

2. Identify three forces of history that are illustrated by the rise and spread of Christianity.

Social Studies Skills Activity: Continuity and Change in History

Continuity and Change Mural **HSS** Analysis Skills: HI 3 | Standards Proficiency

1. Organize students into eight small groups or pairs. Assign each group or pair one of the eight themes listed in the "Learn the Skill" section above.

2. Have each group or pair use butcher paper to create a mural illustrating its theme. Students should incorporate events from the chapters they have studied in their textbook as well as modern examples. Students might include drawings, photographs, slogans, quotes, maps, and charts in their murals.

3. Display all the murals and have students try to identify which theme each one represents. Then have each group or pair explain the images in its mural to the class.
LS Interpersonal, Visual/Spatial

4. **Extend** As homework, have each student write an essay analyzing how the theme of cooperation and conflict applies to the Roman Empire. **LS** Verbal/Linguistic

- Alternative Assessment Handbook, Rubrics 3: Artwork; and 37: Writing Assignments

Visual Summary

Use the visual summary below to help you review the main ideas of the chapter.

QUICK FACTS

In the Roman Empire, people practiced many religions and worshipped many gods.

The teachings of Jesus of Nazareth inspired a new religion called Christianity.

After Jesus died, his followers spread Christianity throughout the Roman Empire.

Reviewing Vocabulary, Terms, and People

Match the "I" statement with the person or thing that might have made the statement.

a. Messiah   **f.** martyr
b. Constantine   **g.** pope
c. Apostle   **h.** Paul
d. Jesus of Nazareth   **i.** Augustine of Hippo
e. Bible   **j.** ideal

1. "I helped spread Christian teachings through the Mediterranean world through my journeys and letters."
2. "I died for my religious beliefs."
3. "My teachings became the foundations for Christianity."
4. "I was the first Christian emperor of Rome."
5. "I was a Christian writer who combined Plato's ideas with Christian teachings."
6. "I am an idea or goal that people try to live up to."
7. "I am the holy book of Christianity."
8. "I was the bishop of Rome who became the head of the Christian Church."
9. "I was a promised leader who was to appear among the Jews."
10. "I was one of Jesus's 12 chosen followers."

Comprehension and Critical Thinking

SECTION 1 *(Pages 380–383)* **HSS** 6.7.5

11. **a. Identify** Who were Jesus of Nazareth and John the Baptist?

    b. Contrast How did the Romans' attitude toward religion differ from the Jews' attitude?

    c. Evaluate Why might a historian say that one ancient religion, Judaism, set the scene for a new religion, Christianity?

Visual Summary

Review and Inquiry Have students use the visual summary to describe major people and events related to the growth and spread of Christianity in Rome.

🖘 Quick Facts Transparency: Rome and Christianity Visual Summary

Reviewing Vocabulary, Terms, and People

1. h
2. f
3. d
4. b
5. i
6. j
7. e
8. g
9. a
10. c

Comprehension and Critical Thinking

11. **a.** Jesus—a man whose teachings inspired Christianity; John the Baptist—prophet who announced the arrival of the Messiah

    b. Romans worshipped many gods; Jews worshipped one God and refused to worship the Roman gods.

    c. possible answer—because Christianity was rooted in Jewish ideas and traditions

12. **a.** the elements that comprised the death and rebirth of Jesus; that Jesus is the Messiah and the son of God

Review and Assessment Resources

Review and Reinforce

SE Standards Review
📋 **CRF:** Chapter Review Activity
📋 California Standards Review Workbook
🖘 Quick Facts Transparency: Rome and Christianity Visual Summary
🔊 Spanish Chapter Summaries Audio CD Program
Online Chapter Summaries in Six Languages
OSP Holt PuzzlePro; GameTool for ExamView
💿 Quiz Game CD-ROM

Assess

SE Standards Assessment
📋 PASS: Chapter Test, Forms A and B
📖 Alternative Assessment Handbook
OSP ExamView Test Generator, Chapter Test
💿 Universal Access Modified Worksheets and Tests CD-ROM: Chapter Test
Holt Online Assessment Program (in the Premier Online Edition)

Reteach/Intervene

📋 Interactive Reader and Study Guide
📋 Universal Access Teacher Management System: Lesson Plans for Universal Access
💿 Universal Access Modified Worksheets and Tests CD-ROM
💿 Interactive Skills Tutor CD-ROM

go.hrw.com

Online Resources

Chapter Resources:
KEYWORD: SQ6 WH13

b. Many people were uneducated, and Jesus linked his teachings to people's everyday lives by putting his complicated ideas in ways that people could understand. In addition, Jesus promised salvation and heaven to people whose lives were hard.

c. because he helped spread Christian teachings throughout the empire and preached Christianity to non-Jews

13. a. Peter was the first bishop of Rome, and later popes were seen as his spiritual successors.

b. in common—both called together Christian leaders to clarify church teachings; different—Constantine allowed the practice of other religions, Theodosius I only allowed the practice of Christianity

c. possible answer—because it offered salvation, and because people were inspired by the martyrs' courage

Reviewing Themes

14. They spread Christian ideas among non-Jews.

15. possible answer—It might not have spread outside of Judea and throughout the Roman Empire.

Social Studies Skills

16. Answers should explain how one factor has played a role in the long-lasting influence of Christianity. Refer students to the skills activity earlier in the chapter for more information.

SECTION 2 *(Pages 384–389)* **HSS** **6.7.6**

12. a. Describe According to the Bible, what were the crucifixion and Resurrection? What do Christians believe the Resurrection means?

b. Analyze Why do you think Jesus's teachings appealed to many people within the Roman Empire?

c. Evaluate Why is Saint Paul considered one of the most important people in the history of Christianity?

SECTION 3 *(Pages 392–395)* **HSS** **6.7.7**

13. a. Describe What was the connection between the Apostle Peter and the papacy?

b. Compare and Contrast What did Roman emperors Constantine and Theodosius I have in common? How did their actions differ?

c. Predict Why do you think Christianity spread despite the fact that early Christians were often persecuted?

Reviewing Themes

14. Society and Culture How did early Christian leaders such as Paul help separate Christianity from Judaism?

15. Religion How do you think the early Christian Church would have been different if Paul had not converted to Christianity?

Social Studies Skills

16. Understanding Historical Continuity Christianity has been one of the forces that has most influenced the course of world history. Why has its influence been so great? Choose one of the following factors that help promote historical continuity. Then write a sentence explaining how that factor is related to Christianity's influence.

Cooperation and conflict	Economic opportunity
Cultural interaction	Impact of individuals
Geography and environment	Nationalism and imperialism
Science and technology	Political and social systems

398 CHAPTER 13

Using the Internet

go.hrw.com
KEYWORD: SQ6 WH13

17. Activity: Creating Maps Within 400 years of Jesus's death, Christianity had grown from a small group of Jesus's disciples into the only religion practiced in the entire Roman Empire. Although 400 years sounds like a long time, to a historian it's practically the blink of an eye. What explains the rapid growth of Christianity? Enter the activity keyword. Then research the key figures, events, and factors in the spread of Christianity. Use what you learn to create an illustrated and annotated map of the spread of Christianity.

Reading Skills

Using Questions *Read the following passage and answer the questions that follow.*

> "Women were among Jesus's earliest followers. From the beginning, Jewish women disciples, including Mary Magdalene, Joanna, and Susanna, had accompanied Jesus during his ministry and supported him out of their private means (Luke: 8:1–3). After the death of Jesus, women continued to play prominent roles in the early movement. Some scholars have even suggested that the majority of Christians in the first century may have been women."
>
> –Karen L. King, from *Women in Ancient Christianity: The New Discoveries*

18. Who is this passage about?

19. When did they live?

20. What did they do that made them important?

FOCUS ON WRITING

21. Writing Your Article Now that you've taken notes on the main ideas and supporting details about early Christianity in the Roman Empire, you have the information you'll need to write your two- to three-paragraph magazine article. Write the article in chronological order and include a catchy title that describes the article. You might begin the article with a question or an intriguing fact to get your audience's attention.

Using the Internet

17. Go to the HRW Web site and enter the keyword shown to access a rubric for this activity.

KEYWORD: SQ6 TEACHER

Reading Skills

18. women disciples of Jesus

19. during and after the life of Jesus; first century AD

20. They accompanied Jesus during his ministry and provided support; they played prominent roles in the early years of the Christian movement.

Focus on Writing

21. Rubric Students' magazine articles should:
- have a title that grabs the reader's attention.
- begin with a question or an intriguing fact.
- include paragraphs that are in chronological order, discuss a main idea, and contain interesting and factually correct details.

CRF: Focus on Writing: Magazine Article

Standards Assessment

DIRECTIONS: *Read each question, and write the letter of the best response.*

1

> The practice of any other religion but Christianity shall be against the law.
>
> All temples to the ancient gods shall be closed and become property of the Roman government.
>
> All festivals and other celebrations and gatherings in honor of the ancient gods shall be banned.

Which person would have been *most* likely to have issued a document like this one?

- **A** Jesus of Nazareth
- **B** Emperor Constantine
- **C** Emperor Theodosius I
- **D** Paul

2 Early Christianity grew out of the beliefs, practices, and values of which early people?

- **A** Jews
- **B** Greeks
- **C** Chinese
- **D** Egyptians

3 Which persons were *most* active in and responsible for spreading the Christian faith immediately after the death of Jesus?

- **A** Constantine and Theodosius I
- **B** Peter and Augustine
- **C** Paul and Constantine
- **D** Peter and Paul

4 Which statement about Jesus is *not* true?

- **A** Some people believed Jesus was the Messiah that Jewish prophets had predicted.
- **B** Some Roman leaders viewed Jesus as a threat to their power.
- **C** Jesus led a rebellion of the Jews against the Romans.
- **D** Jesus taught people to love God and to be kind to each other.

Connecting with Past Learnings

5 In Grade 5, you learned about religious leaders who explained Puritan beliefs through their writings, teaching, and preaching. All of the following made the same contribution to Christianity during Roman times *except*

- **A** Augustine.
- **B** Constantine.
- **C** the Gospel writers.
- **D** Paul.

6 The role of Jesus in Christianity is *most* like the role in earlier times of

- **A** Moses among the ancient Hebrews.
- **B** Hammurabi among the ancient Babylonians.
- **C** Pericles among the ancient Greeks.
- **D** Ramses among the ancient Egyptians.

Answers

1. C
Break Down the Question Students should recall that Emperor Theodosius I banned all religions except Christianity.

2. A
Break Down the Question This question requires students to recall factual information from Section 1.

3. D
Break Down the Question Students should eliminate the choices that include names of Roman emperors, who reacted to the earlier spread of Christianity.

4. C
Break Down the Question Point out to students that the word *not* indicates that the answer is the *false* statement.

5. B
Break Down the Question Students should recall that of the people or groups listed—except Constantine— each wrote, preached, and taught about Christianity.

6. A
Break Down the Question This question requires students to recall information from the chapter on the Hebrews and Judaism.

Standards Review

Have students review the following standards in their workbooks.

California Standards Review Workbook:
HSS 6.7.5, 6.7.6, 6.7.7

Intervention Resources

Reproducible

- Interactive Reader and Study Guide
- Universal Access Teacher Management System: Universal Access Lesson Plans

Technology

- Quick Facts Transparency: Rome and Christianity Visual Summary
- Universal Access Modified Worksheets and Tests CD-ROM
- Interactive Skills Tutor CD-ROM

Tips for Test Taking

Negative Does Not Fit Give students this test-taking tip: Be sure to watch for negative words in test questions. Words such as *never*, *unless*, *not*, and *except* are negative words to look for. When a question contains one of these negative words, look for the answer that **does not fit** with the other answers.

Bellringer

Motivate Write the following problem for students to see: "You and your sibling share a bedroom, and you have little privacy and time to yourself." Ask students to offer possible solutions to this problem. List students' solutions and have the class discuss them. Help students to see that there are often multiple solutions to a problem. Tell them that in this workshop, they will write about a problem and a possible solution.

Identifying a Problem

Problems-Solutions Chart To help students select a problem for their papers, have them create a two-column chart and label the columns *Problems* and *Solutions*. Next, tell students to skim the chapters on the Romans and to list each major problem and solution in their charts. Then have students share the information they found. Use it to create a class Problems-Solutions chart for students to use.

Identifying a Solution

Analyzing Causes and Effects To help students develop solutions, have them analyze the causes and effects of the problems they selected. Students might create a chart or linear cause-and-effect chain to list contributing factors and effects. Then have students test possible solutions by seeing how well they address the causes and effects listed.

HSS Analysis Skills: HI 2

Assignment

Write about a problem the Romans faced and what their solution was or what you think would be a better solution.

ELA Writing 6.2.2d Offer persuasive evidence to validate arguments and conclusions as needed.

Historical Problem and Solution

History is the story of how individuals have solved political, economic, and social problems. Learning to write an effective problem-solution paper will be useful in school and in many other situations.

1. Prewrite

Identifying a Problem

Think of a problem the Romans faced. Look at the problem closely. What caused it? What were its effects? Here is an example.

Problem: The Gauls overran Rome.

Solution A: Pay the Gauls a huge ransom to leave Rome. [caused other cities to attack in the hope of getting similar ransoms]

Solution B: Attack other cities. [caused other cities to stop attacking Rome; let Rome gain power and wealth]

Finding a Solution and Proof

Compare the Roman solution to the problem to one they didn't try. Choose either the Roman solution or your own solution to write about. Your explanation should answer these questions.

- How does the solution address the cause of the problem?
- How does the solution fix the effects of the problem?

Use historical evidence to support what you say about the problem:
- facts, examples, or quotations
- comparisons with similar problems your readers know about

2. Write

This framework can help you clearly explain the problem and its solution.

A Writer's Framework

Introduction	Body	Conclusion
■ Tell your reader what problem the Romans faced. ■ Explain the causes and effects of the problem. ■ State your purpose in presenting this problem and its solution.	■ Explain the solution. ■ Connect the solution directly to the problem. ■ Give supporting historical evidence and details that show how the solution deals with the problem.	■ Summarize the problem and the solution. ■ Discuss how well the solution deals with the problem.

400 UNIT 5

Differentiating Instruction for Universal Access

Advanced Learners/GATE
Exceeding Standards

1. Encourage advanced learners to develop multiple solutions to their problems. Then organize students into small groups. Have each student present his or her problem and possible solutions to the group. Have the other group members analyze and evaluate each solution.

2. Tell students to use the feedback to select the best solution for their papers. **LS Interpersonal**

Learners Having Difficulty
Reaching Standards

1. Some students may have difficulty selecting problems and solutions on their own. To help these students, create a list of problems and solutions from the text and provide page references for each one. Give students copies of the list to choose from.

2. Then have students use the text to create outlines of their problems and solutions. **LS Verbal/Linguistic**

Standards Focus

HSS Analysis Skills: HI 1, HI 2
ELA Writing 6.2.2.d

3. Evaluate and Revise

Evaluating

Now you'll want to evaluate your draft to see where you can improve your paper. Try using the following questions to decide what to revise.

Evaluation Questions for a Historical Problem and Solution

- Does your introduction state the problem clearly and describe it fully?
- Does the introduction give causes and effects of the problem?
- Do you clearly explain how the solution relates to the problem?

- Do you give supporting historical evidence showing how the solution deals with the problem?
- Do you conclude by summarizing the problem and the solution?

TIP **Problem-Solution Clue Words.** It's not enough simply to tell your reader what the problem and solution are. You need to show how they are related. Here is a list of words and phrases that will help you do so.

as a result	therefore
consequently	this led to
nevertheless	thus

Revising

Revise your draft to make what you say clear and convincing. You may need to

- Add historical facts, examples, quotations and other evidence to give your readers all the information they need to understand the problem and solution
- Reorganize paragraphs to present information in a clear, logical order
- Insert words like *thus, therefore,* and *as a result* to show how causes link to effects and how the solution deals with the problem

4. Proofread and Publish

Proofreading

To improve your paper before sharing it, check the following:

- spelling of all names, places, and other historical information, especially Latin words, because they can be tricky
- punctuation around linking words such as *so, thus,* and *in addition* that you use to connect causes with effects and solutions with problems

Publishing

Choose one or more of these ideas to share your report.

- Create a poster that Roman leaders might put up to announce how they will solve the problem.
- Hold a debate between teams of classmates who have chosen similar problems but different solutions. Have the rest of the class vote on whose solutions are best.

TIP **Seeing Your Paper as Others See It.** To you, your paper makes perfect sense. To others, it may not. Whenever possible, ask someone else to read your paper. Others can see flaws and errors that you never will see. Listen closely to questions and suggestions. Do your best to see the other person's point before defending what you have written.

● Practice and Apply

Use the steps and strategies outlined in this workshop to write a problem-solution paper.

English-Language Learners [Standards Proficiency] [Standard English Mastery]

1. English learners might benefit from hearing their papers read aloud. Pair students and have partners take turns reading each other's paper aloud. Tell students to listen for problems with tone, grammar, organization, and transitions. Students should also listen for slang, informal writing, and other incorrect uses of standard English.

2. Instruct students to ask their partners to stop frequently so that they have time to take notes about items that need attention. Students should look for places where they can add transition words to their essays or make cause-and-effect or other organizational problems clearer.
LS **Interpersonal, Verbal/Linguistic**

Reteach

Evaluate and Revise

Using Standard English Students should use standard English for their papers. As practice, have students revise the underlined words in these sentences to make them standard English.

1. The solution <u>would of</u> worked if there had been more support for it. *(would have)*

2. The people did not agree with <u>none</u> of the solutions. *(any)*

3. The leaders felt <u>bummed</u> about the proposed solution. *(bad)*

4. They had <u>all ready</u> proposed that solution. *(already)*

Standard English Mastery

Teaching Tip

Proofreading Allow students in-class time for proofreading and revising. Have them evaluate a classmate's work first and then take a fresh look at their own work. Tell students that it is helpful to set work aside for a time before evaluating it so they can see it with a fresh eye.

● Practice & Apply ●

Proofread and Publish

Creating a Poster Remind students who choose to create a poster that they should include a minimal amount of text—just enough to explain the central elements of the problem and its solution. Students should then select one to two powerful images to illustrate and support their posters.

Introduce the Unit

Share the information in the chapter overviews with students.

Chapter 14 The Roman Empire made lasting contributions to government, law, and culture, but internal weaknesses and Germanic invasions caused the collapse of the empire in the West in 476. The eastern empire continued as the Byzantine Empire and lasted for hundreds of years more. This empire was centered in its capital, Constantinople. The Orthodox Church, which flourished in this empire, experienced a split from the Roman Catholic Church.

Chapter 15 Most scholars think humans probably migrated to the Americas across a land bridge from Asia during the last Ice Age. As they spread throughout the Americas, humans developed varied cultural groups and in time formed civilizations. In Mesoamerica—the southern part of North America and the northern part of Central America—the Maya developed an advanced culture by about AD 200. Maya civilization was characterized by great cities, trade, and warfare, but it disappeared for reasons that are still unclear. While the Maya Empire flourished, the Maya made great achievements in art, science, math, and writing.

Standards Focus

For a list of the overarching standards covered in this unit, see the first page of each chapter.

UNIT 6
12,000 BC–AD 1453

Endings and Beginnings

Chapter 14 The Fall of Rome
Chapter 15 The Early Americas

402

Unit Resources

Planning

- Universal Access Teacher Management System: Unit Instructional Benchmarking Guides
- One-Stop Planner CD-ROM with Test Generator: Holt Calendar Planner
- Power Presentations with Video CD-ROM
- A Teacher's Guide to Religion in the Public Schools

Standards Mastery

- Standards Review Workbook
- At Home: A Guide to Standards Mastery for World History

Differentiating Instruction

- Universal Access Teacher Management System: Lesson Plans for Universal Access
- Universal Access Modified Worksheets and Tests CD-ROM

Enrichment

- **CRF 14:** Economics and History: Inflation and the Fall of the Roman Empire
- **CRF 14:** Interdisciplinary Project: The Fall of Rome
- **CRF 15:** Interdisciplinary Project: The Maya: Web It
- Civic Participation
- Primary Source Library CD-ROM

Assessment

- Progress Assessment Support System: Benchmark Test
- **OSP** ExamView Test Generator: Benchmark Test
- Holt Online Assessment Program (in the Premier Online Edition)
- Alternative Assessment Handbook

The **Universal Access Teacher Management System** provides a planning and instructional benchmarking guide for this unit.

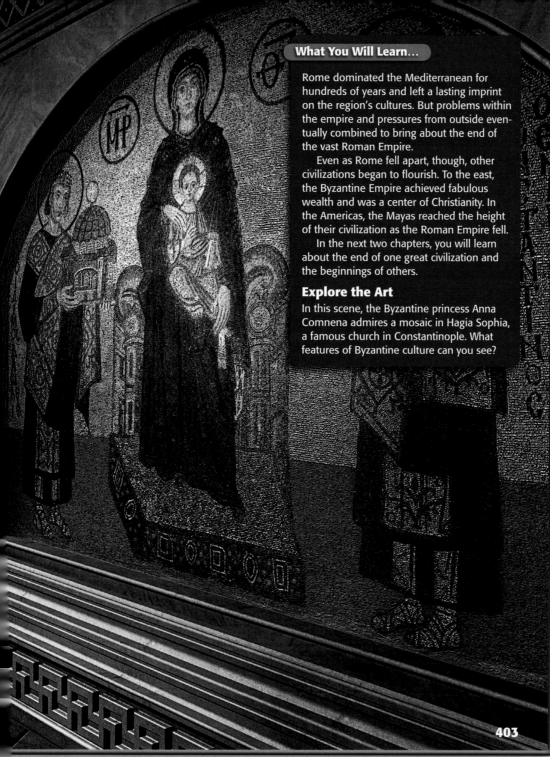

Rome dominated the Mediterranean for hundreds of years and left a lasting imprint on the region's cultures. But problems within the empire and pressures from outside eventually combined to bring about the end of the vast Roman Empire.

Even as Rome fell apart, though, other civilizations began to flourish. To the east, the Byzantine Empire achieved fabulous wealth and was a center of Christianity. In the Americas, the Mayas reached the height of their civilization as the Roman Empire fell.

In the next two chapters, you will learn about the end of one great civilization and the beginnings of others.

Explore the Art

In this scene, the Byzantine princess Anna Comnena admires a mosaic in Hagia Sophia, a famous church in Constantinople. What features of Byzantine culture can you see?

403

Unit Preview

Connect to the Unit

Activity **Graphing an Empire** Tell students that empires often go through similar cycles of rise and decline. Have students work together to draw a large line graph entitled *The Rise and Fall of Empires*. The x-axis should be labeled *Time*, and the y-axis should be labeled *Power*. Discuss how empires often grow in power and expand in size over time and some of the reasons for which they often decline. Draw a line on the graph that rises and then falls. Have students label places along the graph with common achievements of empires, such as government, expansion, trade, and cultural developments. Next, have students label common problems that empires face, such as internal strife or invasion. During the unit, have students create a second graph specific to the rise and fall of the Roman Empire.

LS **Mathematical/Logical, Visual/Spatial**

Explore the Art

The church of Hagia Sophia is considered one of the finest examples of Byzantine architecture. Located in what is now Istanbul, Turkey (once Constantinople), the church was completed in AD 537. When Turkish Muslims conquered Constantinople in 1453, they converted Hagia Sophia to a mosque and covered the interior mosaics with plaster. The plaster has since been removed, and today visitors can tour the church and see mosaics like the one shown at left.

About the Illustration

This illustration is an artist's conception based on available sources. However, historians are uncertain exactly what this scene looked like.

Democracy and Civic Education

Authority: Law Enforcement and Order

Standards Proficiency

Research Required

Background Explain that as the Roman Empire declined, it began to experience chaos as order and authority weakened.

1. Discuss with students the need for law enforcement to maintain order in society.

2. Organize students into groups and assign each group a different aspect of local law enforcement to research.

3. Have each group create a display or software presentation providing information about its assigned topic.

4. If possible, during the project have a member of local law enforcement speak to the class about ways in which students can help and support law enforcement. Students should prepare questions in advance for the speaker.
LS **Interpersonal, Verbal/Linguistic**

📋 Alternative Assessment Handbook, Rubrics 14: Group Activity; and 29: Presentations

📋 Civic Participation

Answers

Explore the Art *that they had impressive art and churches, that religion was important, the style of clothing for the rich and powerful*

Chapter 14 Planning Guide

The Fall of Rome

Chapter Overview	Reproducible Resources	Technology Resources

CHAPTER 14
pp. 404–23

Overview: In this chapter, students will analyze the decline of the Roman Empire and learn about the Byzantine Empire, which survived for several centuries in the east.

 See p. 404 for the California History–Social Science standards covered in this chapter.

 Universal Access Teacher Management System: *
- Universal Access Instructional Benchmarking Guides
- Lesson Plans for Universal Access

Interactive Reader and Study Guide: Chapter Graphic Organizer*

Chapter Resource File *
- Chapter Review Activity
- Focus on Writing Activity: A Narrative Poem
- Social Studies Skills Activity: Chance, Error, and Oversight in History

 One-Stop Planner CD-ROM: Calendar Planner

Student Edition on Audio CD Program

 **Universal Access Modified Worksheets and Tests CD-ROM**

 **Interactive Skills Tutor CD-ROM**

Primary Source Library CD-ROM for World History

Power Presentations with Video CD-ROM

History's Impact: World History Video Program (VHS/DVD): The Roman Empire and Christianity*

A Teacher's Guide To Religion in the Public Schools *

Section 1:

Fall of the Western Empire

The Big Idea: Problems from both inside and outside caused the Roman Empire to split and the western half to collapse.

 7.1.2

 Universal Access Teacher Management System: *
Section 1 Lesson Plan

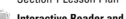 **Interactive Reader and Study Guide:** Section 1 Summary*

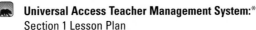 **Chapter Resource File** *
- Vocabulary Builder Activity, Section 1
- Biography Activity: Attila the Hun
- Biography Activity: Diocletian
- Economics and History Activity: Inflation and the Fall of the Roman Empire
- History and Geography Activity: Constantinople
- Interdisciplinary Project: The Fall of Rome
- Primary Source Activity: Jerome's Letter about Attacks against Rome
- Primary Source Activity: "Attila the Hun" by Priscus

 Daily Bellringer Transparency: Section 1*

Map Transparency: Eastern and Western Empires*

Map Transparency: Invasions of the Roman Empire, 340–500*

Quick Facts Transparency: Why Rome Fell*

Internet Activity: Barbarian Invasions

Section 2:

The Byzantine Empire

The Big Idea: The Roman Empire split into two parts, and the eastern Roman Empire prospered for hundreds of years after the western empire fell.

 7.1.3

 Universal Access Teacher Management System: *
Section 2 Lesson Plan

 Interactive Reader and Study Guide: Section 2 Summary*

 Chapter Resource File *
- Vocabulary Builder Activity, Section 2
- Biography Activity: Belisarius
- Literature Activity: Byzantine Poetry
- Primary Source Activity: "The Body of Civil Law" by Justinian

 Daily Bellringer Transparency: Section 2*

Map Transparency: The Byzantine Empire, 1025*

 Quick Facts Transparency: The Western Roman and Byzantine Empires*

 Internet Activity: Military Might

Review, Assessment, Intervention

🐻 **Standards Review Workbook***

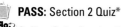 **Quick Facts Transparency:** The Fall of Rome*

🔊 **Spanish Chapter Summaries Audio CD Program**

Online Chapter Summaries in Six Languages

💿 **Quiz Game CD-ROM**

🐻 **Progress Assessment Support System (PASS):** Chapter Test*

💿 **Universal Access Modified Worksheets and Tests CD-ROM:** Modified Chapter Test

🐻 **One-Stop Planner CD-ROM:** ExamView Test Generator (English/Spanish)

Alternative Assessment Handbook

Holt Online Assessment Program (HOAP), in the Holt Premier Online Student Edition

PASS: Section 1 Quiz*

Online Quiz: Section 1

Alternative Assessment Handbook

PASS: Section 2 Quiz*

Online Quiz: Section 2

Alternative Assessment Handbook

California Resources for Standards Mastery

INSTRUCTIONAL PLANNING AND SUPPORT

Universal Access Teacher Management System*

One-Stop Planner CD-ROM with Test Generator: Teacher Management System with Interactive Teacher's Edition

STANDARDS MASTERY

Standards Review Workbook*

At Home: A Guide to Standards Mastery for World History

Holt Online Learning

To enhance learning, the following Internet activities are available: Barbarian Invasions and Military Might.

> **KEYWORD: SQ6 TEACHER**

- **Teacher Support Page**
- **Content Updates**
- **Rubrics and Writing Models**
- **Teaching Tips for the Multimedia Classroom**

> **KEYWORD: SQ6 WH14**

- **Current Events**
- **Holt Grapher**
- **Holt Online Atlas**
- **Holt Researcher**
- **Interactive Multimedia Activities**
- **Internet Activities**
- **Online Chapter Summaries in Six Languages**
- **Online Section Quizzes**
- **World History Maps and Charts**

HOLT PREMIER ONLINE STUDENT EDITION

Complete online support for interactivity, assessment, and reporting

- **Interactive Maps and Notebook**
- **Standardized Test Prep**
- **Homework Practice and Research Activities Online**

Mastering the Standards: Differentiating Instruction

Reaching Standards	Basic-level activities designed for all students encountering new material
Standards Proficiency	Intermediate-level activities designed for average students
Exceeding Standards	Challenging activities designed for honors and gifted-and-talented students
Standard English Mastery	Activities designed to improve standard English usage

THE FALL OF ROME   **403b**

MASTERING THE CALIFORNIA STANDARDS

Frequently Asked Questions

INSTRUCTIONAL PLANNING AND SUPPORT

Where do I find planning aids, pacing guides, lesson plans, and other teaching aids?

Annotated Teacher's Edition:
- Chapter planning guides
- Standards-based instruction and strategies
- Differentiated instruction for universal access
- Point-of-use reminders for integrating program resources

Power Presentations with Video CD-ROM

Universal Access Teacher Management System:
- Year and unit instructional benchmarking guides
- Reproducible lesson plans
- Assessment guides for diagnostic, progress, and summative end-of-the-year tests
- Options for differentiating instruction and intervention
- Teaching guides and answer keys for student workbooks

One-Stop Planner CD-ROM with Test Generator: Teacher Management System with Interactive Teacher's Edition:
- Calendar Planner
- Editable lesson plans
- All reproducible ancillaries in Adobe Acrobat (PDF) format
- ExamView Test Generator (English & Spanish)
- Game Tool for ExamView
- PuzzlePro
- Transparency and video previews

DIFFERENTIATING INSTRUCTION FOR UNIVERSAL ACCESS

What resources are available to ensure that Advanced Learners/GATE Students master the standards?

Lesson Plans for Universal Access

Primary Source Library CD-ROM for World History

What resources are available to ensure that English Learners and Standard English Learners master the standards?

Teacher's Edition Activities:
- Constantinople and Trade, p. 416

Lesson Plans for Universal Access

Chapter Resource File: Vocabulary Builder Activities

Spanish Chapter Summaries Audio CD Program

Online Chapter Summaries in Six Languages

One-Stop Planner CD-ROM:
- PuzzlePro, Spanish Version
- ExamView Test Generator, Spanish Version

What modified materials are available for Special Education?

Teacher's Edition Activities:
- The Sack of Rome, p. 410

The *Universal Access Modified Worksheets and Tests CD-ROM* provides editable versions of the following:

Vocabulary Flash Cards

Modified Vocabulary Builder Activities

Modified Chapter Review Activity

Modified Chapter Test

What resources are available to ensure that Learners Having Difficulty master the standards?

Teacher's Edition Activities:
• Causes of Rome's Collapse, p. 412
Interactive Reader and Study Guide
Student Edition on Audio CD Program
Quick Facts Transparency: The Fall of Rome
Visual Summary

Standards Review Workbook
Social Studies Skills Activity: Chance, Error, and
Oversight in History
Interactive Skills Tutor CD-ROM

How do I intervene for students struggling to master the standards?

Interactive Reader and Study Guide
Quick Facts Transparency: The Fall of Rome
Visual Summary
Standards Review Workbook

Social Studies Skills Activity: Chance, Error, and
Oversight in History
Interactive Skills Tutor CD-ROM

PROFESSIONAL DEVELOPMENT

HOLT
**Professional
Development**

What teacher training resources are available to help me grow professionally?

• In-service and staff development as part of your Holt
  Social Studies product purchase
• Quick Teacher Tutorial Lesson Presentation CD-ROM
• Intensive tuition-based Teacher Development Institute
• Convenient Holt Speaker Bureau face-to-face workshop
  options

• PRAXIS™ Test Prep (#0089) interactive Web-based
  content refreshers*
• *Ask A Professional Development Expert* at
  http://www.hrw.com/prodev/

* PRAXIS is a trademark of Educational Testing Service (ETS). This publication is
  not endorsed or approved by ETS.

Information Literacy Skills

To learn more about how History–Social
Science instruction may be improved by the
effective use of library media centers and
information literacy skills, go to the Teacher's
Resource Materials for Chapter 14
at **go.hrw.com, keyword: SQ6 MEDIA.**

Standards Focus

Standards by Section
Section 1: **HSS** 7.1.2
Section 2: **HSS** 7.1.3

Teacher's Edition
HSS Analysis Skills: CS 1, CS 2, CS 3, HR 1, HI 1, HI 2, HI 3

ELA Speaking 7.1.6; Reading 6.2.8

Upcoming Standards for Future Learning
Preview the following History–Social Science content standards from upcoming chapters or grade levels to promote learning beyond the current chapter.

HSS 7.2 Students analyze the geographic, political, economic, religious, and social structures of the civilizations of Islam in the Middle Ages.

7.2.6 Understand the intellectual exchanges among Muslim scholars of Eurasia and Africa and the contributions Muslim scholars made to later civilizations in the areas of science, geography, mathematics, philosophy, medicine, art, and literature.

7.6 Students analyze the geographic, political, economic, religious, and social structures of the civilizations of Medieval Europe.

7.6.2 Describe the spread of Christianity north of the Alps and the roles played by the early church and by monasteries in its diffusion after the fall of the western half of the Roman Empire.

Focus on Writing

The **Chapter Resource File** provides a Focus on Writing worksheet to help students organize and write their narrative poems.

CRF: Focus on Writing Activity: A Narrative Poem

CHAPTER **14** 200–1453

The Fall of Rome

California Standards

History–Social Science
7.1 Students analyze the causes and effects of the vast expansion and ultimate disintegration of the Roman Empire.

Analysis Skills
HI 4 Recognize the role of chance, oversight, and error in history.

English–Language Arts
Speaking 7.1.6 Use speaking techniques, including voice modulation, inflection, tempo, enunciation, and eye contact, for effective presentations.

Reading 6.2.8 Note instances of unsupported inferences, fallacious reasoning, persuasion, and propaganda in text.

FOCUS ON SPEAKING

A Narrative Poem How do people remember great historical events like the fall of Rome? Sometimes it's because a poet created a poem to tell the story. As you read this chapter, you'll learn what happened to Rome as it became weak and lost its power. Then you'll write and present a short poem—8 to 10 lines—about this fascinating story.

CHAPTER EVENTS

200

WORLD EVENTS

220
The Han dynasty ends in China.

Introduce the Chapter

Standards Proficiency

Focus on the Fall of Empires

1. Ask students to think of all the civilizations or empires they can. Make a list for students to see. Ask students which of the civilizations or empires no longer exist today. Erase the existing civilizations, leaving only the ones that have ended.

2. Have students discuss why these civilizations are no longer around today. Encourage discussion of reasons why an empire or civilization might collapse. Remind students to consider conditions that might lead to either a gradual or a sudden collapse of a

civilization. Make a list of reasons for the fall of empires for students to see.

3. Ask students if empires completely disappear, or if some part of them might continue. Have students think of the Greek city-states or the Persian Empire, if they need examples.

4. Explain to students that in this chapter they will be learning about the collapse of the great Roman Empire, and about its successor, the Byzantine Empire.
LS Interpersonal, Verbal/Linguistic

What You Will Learn...

In this chapter you will learn about the fall of the Roman Empire in the west and the growth of a new empire in the east. This photo shows Roman ruins in what is now Syria.

293
Diocletian divides the Roman Empire.

410
The Goths sack the city of Rome.

476
The last western Roman emperor is overthrown.

527
Justinian and Theodora come to power in Constantinople.

1453 The Byzantine Empire is defeated.

| 300 | 400 | 500 | 600 | 1450 |

c. 320
The Gupta Empire is founded in India.

570
Muhammad, the founder of Islam, is born in Mecca.

587
The first Buddhist monastery in Japan is established.

THE FALL OF ROME **405**

Explore the Time Line

1. When was the last western Roman emperor overthrown? *476*

2. What important religious leader was born about 50 years after Justinian and Theodora come to power in Constantinople? *Muhammad, the founder of Islam*

3. How many years passed between the sack of Rome by the Visigoths and the overthrow of the last western emperor of Rome? *about 66 years*

HSS **Analysis Skills:** HI 1

Connecting to Past Learning

Global Trade Many of the empires on this time line were linked to each other through a global trade network that developed in ancient times. The Roman Empire, the Han dynasty in China, and the Gupta dynasty in India were connected in many ways by the Silk Road. Along this trans-Asian caravan route, goods and ideas were exchanged between many cultures. Other trade routes connected these empires to Arabia and other empires. In fact, Mecca and Constantinople were two crucial trade centers between Europe and Asia.

• **Chapter Preview** •

HOLT
History's Impact
▶ **video series:**
See the Video Teacher's Guide for strategies for using the chapter video **The Roman Empire and Christianity: The Impact of Ancient Rome on the World Today.**

Chapter Big Ideas

Section 1 Problems from both inside and outside caused the Roman Empire to split and the western half to collapse. HSS 7.1.2

Section 2 The Roman Empire split into two parts, and the eastern Roman Empire prospered for hundreds of years after the western empire fell. HSS 7.1.3

Explore the Picture

Palmyra One ancient Syrian city is Palmyra, which was named by the Greeks and Romans and means "city of palm trees." The city was a prosperous trading center, located on an east-west caravan route. The city's main street was once lined with 1,500 Corinthian columns and numerous grand arches, stretching for nearly a mile. Today in Palmyra's ruins, you can still see the city's agora, Senate House, theatre, inn for caravans, and temples.

Analyzing Visuals What clues does the picture show about how the Romans constructed their columns? *Students should note that the columns are built in sections (called drums) rather than in one continuous piece.*

go.hrw.com
Online Resources
Chapter Resources:
KEYWORD: SQ6 WH14
Teacher Resources:
KEYWORD: SQ6 TEACHER

Reading Social Studies

Understanding Themes

Introduce the two key themes of this chapter—politics and religion—by asking students to discuss what might lead to the collapse of a once-great empire. Ask students what political causes might have led to the fall of the Roman Empire. Point out to students that the Roman Empire in the west collapsed, but in the east it continued as the Byzantine Empire. Ask students to speculate how these two empires might have been different in terms of religion.

Stereotypes and Bias in History

Focus on Reading Review with students the examples of stereotypes and bias discussed at right. Then have students think of sources that might use stereotype or bias. For example, a sports announcer might favor one team over another, or an advertisement for a product or service might stereotype all its competitors as inferior. Ask the class why it is important to be able to identify bias and stereotype. What are the dangers of not being able to identify them?

Reading Social Studies
by Kylene Beers

Economics · Geography · **Politics** · **Religion** · Society and Culture · Science and Technology

Focus on Themes In this chapter, you will read about the fall of one of the great ancient civilizations—the Roman Empire. You will learn about problems that arose in its cities and about the invaders who attacked the weakened empire. You will read about the division of the empire into the western empire and the eastern empire and about the reasons for that division. You will see how **political** and **religious** practices differed in the two parts of the empire and learn what those differences meant.

Stereotypes and Bias in History

Focus on Reading Historians today try to be impartial in their writing. They don't let their personal feelings affect what they write.

Roman writers, however, didn't always feel the need to be impartial. Their writings were often colored by their pride in their city and their attitudes about other people, places, and ideas.

Identifying Stereotypes and Bias Two ways in which writing can be colored by the author's ideas are stereotypes and bias. A **stereotype** is a generalization about a whole group of people. **Bias** is an attitude that one group is superior to another. The examples below can help you identify stereotypes and bias in the things you read.

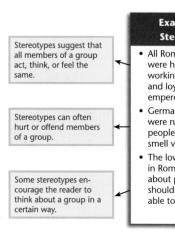

Stereotypes suggest that all members of a group act, think, or feel the same.

Stereotypes can often hurt or offend members of a group.

Some stereotypes encourage the reader to think about a group in a certain way.

Examples of Stereotypes

- All Roman citizens were honest, hard-working, trustworthy, and loyal to their emperors.
- German barbarians were rude, disgusting people who didn't smell very good.
- The lower classes in Rome didn't care about politics and shouldn't have been able to vote.

Examples of Bias

- On the whole, the people who lived in Roman cities were better citizens than those in the country.
- In my opinion, the early Roman Empire was the greatest time in the whole of human history.
- The Romans had an advanced society, unlike the Goths, who were barbaric and backward.

A biased statement obviously favors one person or group over another.

Bias is based on the author's opinions, not facts.

Bias is often the result of an author's dislike of a particular group.

Additional reading support can be found in the

Inter*active
Reader and
Study Guide

Reading and Skills Resources

Reading Support

- Interactive Reader and Study Guide
- Student Edition on Audio CD
- Spanish Chapter Summaries Audio CD Program

Social Studies Skills Support

- Interactive Skills Tutor CD-ROM

Vocabulary Support

- **CRF:** Vocabulary Builder Activity
- **CRF:** Chapter Review Activity
- Universal Access Modified Worksheets and Tests CD-ROM:
  - Vocabulary Flash Cards
  - Vocabulary Builder Activity
  - Chapter Review Activity

OSP Holt PuzzlePro

Standards Focus

ELA Reading 6.2.8

You Try It!

The following passage is from a Roman history. It describes a former Roman citizen that has chosen to live among the Scythians, a group the Romans considered barbarians. As you read the passage, look for examples of stereotypes and bias.

Romans and Scythians

He considered his new life among the Scythians better than his old life among the Romans, and the reasons he gave were as follows: "After war the Scythians live in inactivity, enjoying what they have got, and not at all, or very little, harassed. The Romans, on the other hand, are in the first place very liable to perish in war . . . But the condition of the subjects in time of peace is far more grievous than the evils of war, for the exaction of taxes is very severe, and unprincipled men inflict injuries on others, because the laws are practically not valid against all classes . . .

In reply to this attack on the Empire . . . I said . . . The Romans treat their servants better than the king of the Scythians treats his subjects. They deal with them as fathers or teachers . . . They are not allowed, like the Scythians, to inflict death upon them.

—Priscus, from Fragmenta Historicorum Graecorum, translated by J. B. Bury

Answer the following questions about the passage you just read.

1. Is the man whom the author describes biased in favor of Roman or Scythian society? How can you tell?

2. Is the author himself biased in favor of one society? How can you tell?

3. What stereotypes about Rome and Roman citizens does the former Roman citizen express?

4. What stereotypes about the Scythians does the author express? What stereotypes about the Romans does he express? Are these stereotypes positive or negative?

Key Terms and People

Chapter 14

Section 1
Diocletian *(p. 409)*
Clovis *(p. 411)*
Attila *(p. 411)*
corruption *(p. 412)*

Section 2
Justinian *(p. 414)*
Theodora *(p. 415)*
Byzantine Empire *(p. 416)*
mosaics *(p. 417)*

Academic Vocabulary

Success in school is related to knowing academic vocabulary— the words that are frequently used in school assignments and discussions. In this chapter, you will learn the following academic word:

cause *(p. 412)*

As you read **Chapter 14**, notice examples of Roman bias against other groups and peoples.

Reading Social Studies

Key Terms and People

Preteach the key terms and people from this chapter by reviewing each term or person with the class. Then have each student create a set of flashcards for the key terms and people. Have students write the term or name on one side of the card and the definition or description of that term on the other side of the card. Encourage students to review their flashcards regularly. **LS** Verbal/Linguistic

Focus on Reading

See the **Focus on Reading** questions in this chapter for more practice on this reading social studies skill.

Reading Social Studies Assessment

See the **Standards Review** at the end of this chapter for student assessment questions related to this reading skill.

Teaching Tip

Point out to students that they should be on the lookout for stereotype and bias whenever they read a text or document. Looking for stereotype and bias are two important skills of a critical reader. Bring in political cartoons, primary source documents, and editorials for students to examine for stereotype and bias. Ask students questions about each item to help them identify stereotype and bias.

Answers

You Try It! 1. *Scythian; He describes Scythians' life as better than that of the Romans.* **2.** *yes; He argues with the man that the Romans are superior to Scythians.* **3.** *He says the condition of Roman citizens in times of peace is very poor and that "unprincipled men inflict injury on others."* **4.** *Scythians—he implies that the Scythians are uncivilized; the king mistreats his people, negative stereotypes; Romans—he implies that they are superior to Scythians, they treat their servants better than Scythians treat each other; positive stereotype*

407

If YOU were there . . . Use the **Daily Bellringer Transparency** for this section to help students answer the question.

🖐 Daily Bellringer Transparency, Section 1

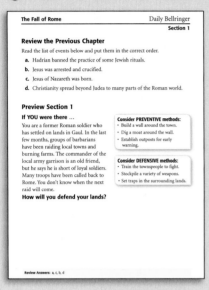

The Fall of Rome   Daily Bellringer
                                    Section 1

Review the Previous Chapter

Read the list of events below and put them in the correct order.

  a. Hadrian banned the practice of some Jewish rituals.

  b. Jesus was arrested and crucified.

  c. Jesus of Nazareth was born.

  d. Christianity spread beyond Judea to many parts of the Roman world.

Preview Section 1

If YOU were there ...

You are a former Roman soldier who has settled on lands in Gaul. In the last few months, groups of barbarians have been raiding local towns and burning farms. The commander of the local army garrison is an old friend, but he says he is short of loyal soldiers. Many troops have been called back to Rome. You don't know when the next raid will come.

How will you defend your lands?

Consider PREVENTIVE methods:
• Build a wall around the town.
• Dig a moat around the wall.
• Establish outposts for early warning.

Consider DEFENSIVE methods:
• Train the townspeople to fight.
• Stockpile a variety of weapons.
• Set traps in the surrounding lands.

Review Answers: a, c, b, d

Academic Vocabulary

Review with students the high-use academic term in this section.

cause the reason something happens (p. 412)

Building Vocabulary

Preteach or review the following term:

barbarians people the Romans considered uncivilized (p. 408)

📝 **CRF:** Vocabulary Builder Activity, Section 1

🐻 Standards Focus

HSS 7.1.2

Means: Identify the regions of the world that were ruled by the Roman Empire at its height, and discuss the problems of ruling such a far-flung empire.

Matters: Questions still exist today about how to best govern large numbers of people spread over great distances.

SECTION 1

Fall of the Western Roman Empire

What You Will Learn...

Main Ideas

1. Many problems threatened the Roman Empire, leading one emperor to divide it in half.
2. Barbarians invaded Rome in the 300s and 400s.
3. Many factors contributed to Rome's fall.

The Big Idea

Problems from both inside and outside caused the Roman Empire to split and the western half to collapse.

Key Terms and People

Diocletian, *p. 409*
Clovis, *p. 411*
Attila, *p. 411*
corruption, *p. 412*

🐻 **HSS 7.1.2** Discuss the geographic borders of the empire at its height and the factors that threatened its territorial cohesion.

If YOU were there...

You are a former Roman soldier who has settled on lands in Gaul. In the last few months, groups of barbarians have been raiding local towns and burning farms. The commander of the local army garrison is an old friend, but he says he is short of loyal soldiers. Many troops have been called back to Rome. You don't know when the next raid will come.

How will you defend your lands?

BUILDING BACKGROUND Though the Roman Empire remained large and powerful, it faced serious threats from both outside and inside. Beyond the borders of the empire, many different groups of people were on the move. They threatened the peace in Rome's provinces—and eventually attacked the heart of the empire itself.

Problems Threaten the Empire

At its height the Roman Empire included all the land around the Mediterranean Sea. The empire in the early 100s stretched from Britain south to Egypt, and from the Atlantic Ocean all the way to the Persian Gulf.

But the empire did not stay that large for long. By the end of the 100s emperors had given up some of the land the Roman army had conquered. These emperors feared that the empire had become too large to defend or govern efficiently. As later rulers discovered, these emperors were right.

Problems in the Empire

Even as emperors were giving up territory, new threats to the empire were appearing. Tribes of Germanic warriors, whom the Romans called barbarians, attacked Rome's northern borders. At the same time, Persian armies invaded in the east. The Romans defended themselves for 200 years, but only at great cost.

Teach the Big Idea: Master the Standards   Standards Proficiency

Fall of the Western Roman Empire   🐻 HSS 7.1.2; HSS Analysis Skills: CS 1, HI 1, HI 2

1. **Teach** Ask students the Main Idea questions to teach this section.

2. **Apply** Write the labels *Internal Problems, External Problems,* and *Invasions* for students to see. Have each student create a three-column chart on his or her own paper that uses the labels as column headings. Then have each student identify problems mentioned in the section and determine under which category each problem falls. **Visual/Spatial**

3. **Review** Have students discuss the problems they identified on their charts and agree upon a class list of problems that led to the fall of Rome.

4. **Practice/Homework** Have each student write a short paragraph identifying the problem the student feels played the largest role in the fall of the western Roman empire. Students should provide reasons to support their choices. **LS Verbal/Linguistic**

   📝 Alternative Assessment Handbook, Rubric 13: Graphic Organizers; and 37: Writing Assignments

The Romans struggled with problems within the empire as well. As frontier areas were abandoned because they were too dangerous, Germanic tribes moved in. To help produce more food, the Romans even invited Germanic farmers to grow crops on Roman lands. These farmers often came from the same tribes that threatened Rome's borders. Over time, whole German communities had moved into the empire. They chose their own leaders and largely ignored the emperors, which caused problems for the Romans.

Other internal problems also threatened Rome's survival. Disease swept through the empire, killing many people. The government increased taxes to pay for the defense of the empire. Desperate, the Romans looked for a strong emperor to solve their problems.

Division of the Empire

The emperor the Romans were looking for was **Diocletian** (dy-uh-KLEE-shuhn), who took power in the late 200s. Convinced that the empire was too big for one person to rule, Diocletian divided the empire. He ruled the eastern half of the empire and named a co-emperor to rule the west.

Not long after Diocletian left power, Emperor Constantine (KAHN-stuhn-teen) reunited the two halves of the Roman Empire for a short time. Constantine also moved the empire's capital to the east into what is now Turkey. He built a grand new capital city there. It was called Constantinople (KAHN-stant-uhn-oh-puhl), which means "the city of Constantine." Although the empire was still called the Roman Empire, Rome was no longer the real seat of power. Power had moved to the east.

READING CHECK Identifying Cause and Effect Why did Diocletian divide the Roman Empire in two?

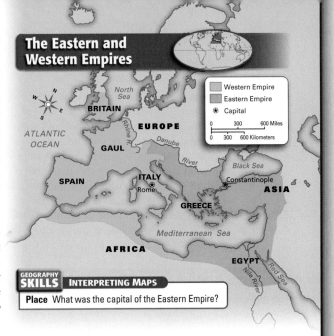

The Eastern and Western Empires

- Western Empire
- Eastern Empire
- ✳ Capital

0   300   600 Miles
0   300   600 Kilometers

NORTH SEA
BRITAIN
EUROPE
ATLANTIC OCEAN
GAUL
Danube River
SPAIN
ITALY
Rome
GREECE
Black Sea
Constantinople
ASIA
Mediterranean Sea
AFRICA
EGYPT
Nile River
Red Sea

GEOGRAPHY SKILLS INTERPRETING MAPS
Place What was the capital of the Eastern Empire?

Barbarians Invade Rome

Not long after Constantine moved Rome's capital, German barbarians—people the Romans considered uncivilized—from the north began to raid the Roman Empire. As you have already read, barbarian tribes had settled along the empire's northern border in the 200s. For more than 100 years these tribes mostly stayed out of Roman territory. Late in the 300s, though, the barbarians began raiding deep into the heart of the empire.

Early Invasions

The source of these raids was a new group of people who moved into Europe. Called the Huns, they were fierce warriors from Central Asia.

As you can see on the map on the next page, the Huns invaded southeastern Europe. From there they launched raids on nearby kingdoms. Among the victims of these raids were several groups of people called the Goths.

FOCUS ON READING
How is the Roman attitude toward the Germans both a bias and a stereotype?

THE IMPACT TODAY
Constantinople is now called Istanbul. It is Turkey's largest city and a thriving economic center.

THE FALL OF ROME **409**

Main Idea

❷ Barbarians Invade Rome

Barbarians invaded Rome in the 300s and 400s.

Recall How did the Romans deal with Goth invaders? *They sent armies against the invaders and even paid some invaders not to attack.*

Sequence What sequence of events led to the sack of Rome in 410? *The Huns pushed the Goths into Roman territory; the Goths raised an army and were paid to withhold their attacks on Rome; when payments from Rome stopped, the Goths destroyed Rome.*

 Map Transparency: Invasions of the Roman Empire, 340–500

📖 HSS 7.1.2; HSS Analysis Skills CS 1, HI 1, HI 2

Linking to Today

The Vandals Among the threats posed by the many groups that troubled Rome, one of the most serious came from the Vandals. A Germanic tribe from Northern Europe, the Vandals attacked Gaul, Spain, and North Africa before setting their sights on the heart of the western empire. In 455 they launched an attack on Rome. Today's use of the word *Vandal* comes from the damage and destruction raids had on the Roman Empire.

go.hrw.com
Online Resources
KEYWORD: SQ6 WH14
ACTIVITY: Barbarian Invasions

Answers

Interpreting Maps *Visigoths*

410

The Goths could not defeat the Huns in battle. As the Huns continued to raid their territories, the Goths fled. Trapped between the Huns and Rome, they had nowhere to go but into Roman territory.

Rome's leaders were afraid that the Goths would destroy Roman land and property. To stop this destruction, the emperors fought to keep the Goths out of Roman lands. In the east the armies were largely successful. They forced the Goths to move farther west. As a result, however, the western armies were defeated by the Goths, who moved into Roman territory.

The Sack of Rome

The Romans fought desperately to keep the Goths away from Rome. They also paid the Goths not to attack them. For many years this strategy worked. In 408, however, the Romans stopped making payments. This made the Goths furious. Despite the Romans' best efforts to defend their city, the Goths sacked, or destroyed, Rome in 410.

The destruction of Rome absolutely devastated the Romans. No one had attacked their city in nearly 800 years. For the first time, many Romans began to feel afraid for the safety of their empire.

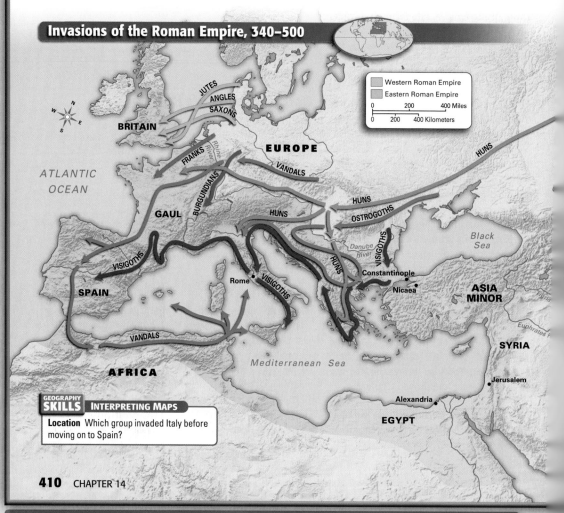

Invasions of the Roman Empire, 340–500

GEOGRAPHY SKILLS   INTERPRETING MAPS

Location Which group invaded Italy before moving on to Spain?

410 CHAPTER 14

Differentiating Instruction for Universal Access

Special Education Students   [Reaching Standards]

1. To help students understand the events leading up to the sack of Rome, write the following list of events in random order for students to see. *Huns invade southeastern Europe; Huns launch raids on Goths; Goths flee to Roman territory; Romans try to fight off Goths; Rome is sacked in 410.*

2. Organize students into mixed-ability level pairs. Have each pair work together to place the events in their proper sequence. Remind students to work together.

3. Once students have properly sequenced the events, have each group use a blank outline map of Europe to depict the events on their list. **LS** **Logical/Mathematical, Visual/Spatial**

📖 HSS 7.1.2; HSS Analysis Skills: CS 1, CS 2, CS 3, HI 2

📄 Alternative Assessment Handbook, Rubrics 14: Group Activity; and 20: Map Creation

The Empire in Chaos

Unfortunately for Rome, the city's fall to the Goths in 410 wasn't the end of the invasions. The Gothic victory served as an example for other barbarian groups to invade the western half of the empire.

In the early 400s the Vandals invaded Spain. Then they crossed into northern Africa and destroyed Roman settlements there. As they passed through Roman areas, the Vandals destroyed nearly everything in their path. At about the same time, the Angles, Saxons, and Jutes invaded Britain, and the Franks invaded Gaul.

By the 480s a Frankish king named **Clovis** had built a huge kingdom in Gaul. Clovis, a Christian, was one of the most powerful of all the German kings.

Meanwhile, the Huns, under a new leader named **Attila** (AT-uhl-uh), raided Roman territory in the east. Attila was a brilliant leader and a very scary enemy. Here is one description that shows why he was so terrifying.

" He was a man born into the world to shake the nations, the scourge of all lands, who in some way terrified all mankind by the dreadful rumors noised abroad concerning him. "
–Jordanes, from *History of the Goths*

THE IMPACT TODAY

We still use the word *vandal* today to describe someone who destroys property.

The Goths and Huns were just two of the groups that invaded the Roman Empire. In this illustration, a Goth warrior is shown on the right, and a Hun is shown on the left. These invaders also battled each other, as Huns attacked Goths and fought for territory and riches.

THE FALL OF ROME **411**

Direct Teach

Main Idea

❷ Barbarians Invade Rome

Barbarians invaded Rome in the 300s and 400s.

Identify What different groups invaded the Roman Empire? *barbarian tribes such as the Huns, Goths, Vandals, Angles, Saxons, Jutes, and Franks*

Analyze What caused the final collapse of the western empire? *Weak emperors and fighting among military leaders enabled barbarians to invade and overthrow the last emperor of Rome.*

📄 **CRF:** Biography Activity: Attila the Hun
📄 **CRF:** Primary Source Activity: Jerome's Letter about Attacks Against Rome
📄 **CRF:** Primary Source Activity: Atilla the Hun
🐻 **HSS** 7.1.2; **HSS** Analysis Skills: HI 1, HI 2

Other People, Other Places

Nomadic Invasions At about the time of the barbarian invasions of Rome, two other powerful empires experienced invasions by nomadic groups. The Han dynasty in China struggled with nomadic invaders from Central Asia, known as the Xiongnu, for hundreds of years. Xiongnu barbarians even established several small kingdoms in northern China in the 300s. In India, the Gupta dynasty collapsed in the early 500s in part due to the invasions of the Huns.

Critical Thinking: Drawing Conclusions

Standards Proficiency

Studying Invasion Routes 🐻 **HSS** 7.1.2; **HSS** Analysis Skills: CS 3, HR 5, HI 1

1. Review with students the invasions that troubled the Roman Empire in the 300s and 400s.

2. Have students examine the map, "Invasions of the Roman Empire, 340–500." Then have students create a chart in which they list the groups of invaders and identify what parts of the Roman Empire each invaded.

3. As you review the answers with the class, ask the following questions: Which invaders would have needed ships or boats to reach their target? *Saxon, Angles, Jutes, Vandals;* Which parts of the empire had the least problems with invaders? *Asia Minor, Syria, and Egypt;* Looking at the map, why do you think the Huns did not invade Asia Minor? *possible answer—Mountains might have prevented easy access into Asia Minor.*

4. After analyzing the map, ask each student to select one of the groups of invaders. Have students write a series of short journal entries as if he or she was a member of the invading tribe. Have students describe what part of the Roman Empire they were located in and what sights they might have seen there. Have volunteers share their journal entries with the class.
LS Verbal/Linguistic, Visual/Spatial

📝 Alternative Assessment Handbook, Rubrics 15: Journals; and 21: Map Reading

Main Idea

❸ Factors in Rome's Fall

Many factors contributed to Rome's fall.

Identify What factors weakened Roman government? *Empire was too large to govern efficiently, corrupt officials ignored needs of citizens.*

Identify Cause and Effect What were the effects of wealthy citizens leaving Rome? *population of Rome decreased, taxes and prices soared, schools closed, and wealthy citizens set up estates in the countryside with their own private armies, which weakened the emperors*

Elaborate Which factor do you think played the biggest part in the downfall of Rome? Why? *Answers will vary, but students should indicate a rationale for their choice.*

📋 **CRF:** Economics and History Activity: Inflation and the Fall of the Roman Empire

🗂 **Quick Facts Transparency:** Why Rome Fell

📖 **HSS** 7.1.2; **HSS Analysis Skills:** CS 1, HI 1, HI 2

Info to Know

The Last Western Emperor As Roman emperors became weaker, they were often subject to replacement by military commanders. One of these commanders, Orestes, placed his teenage son on the throne. His son, Romulus Augustulus, would be the last western Roman emperor. His overthrow in 476 by the German warrior Odoacer signaled the end of the western Roman Empire.

Answers

Reading Check *because the emperors were weak and military leaders were busy fighting among themselves, which allowed a barbarian general to overthrow the last emperor in Rome and name himself king of Italy*

412

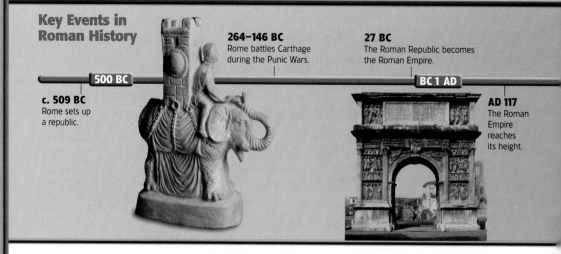

Key Events in Roman History

264–146 BC
Rome battles Carthage during the Punic Wars.

27 BC
The Roman Republic becomes the Roman Empire.

500 BC

BC 1 AD

c. 509 BC
Rome sets up a republic.

AD 117
The Roman Empire reaches its height.

ACADEMIC VOCABULARY
cause the reason something happens

Attila led the Huns in raids against Constantinople, Greece, Gaul, and parts of northern Italy. But because he was told that diseases ran wild in southern Italy, he decided not to go south to Rome.

The End of the Western Empire

Rome needed strong leaders to survive these constant attacks, but the emperors of the 400s were weak. As attacks on Rome's borders increased, military leaders took power away from the emperors. By the 450s military leaders ruled Rome.

Unfortunately for Rome, most of these military leaders were too busy fighting among themselves to protect the empire. Barbarian leaders took advantage of this situation and invaded Rome. In 476 a barbarian general overthrew the last emperor in Rome and named himself king of Italy. Many historians consider this event the end of the western Roman Empire.

READING CHECK **Analyzing** Why did Rome fall to barbarians in the 400s?

412 CHAPTER 14

Factors in Rome's Fall

Barbarian invasions are often considered the **cause** of Rome's decline. In truth, they were only one of several causes.

One cause of Rome's decline was the vast size of the empire. In some ways, Rome had simply grown too big to govern. Communication among various parts of the empire was difficult, even in peaceful times. During times of conflict it became even more difficult.

Political crises also contributed to the decline. By the 400s **corruption**, the decay of people's values, had become widespread in Rome's government. Corrupt officials used threats and bribery to achieve their goals, often ignoring the needs of Roman citizens. Because of officials like these, Rome's government was no longer as efficient as it had been in the past.

In the face of this corruption, many wealthy citizens fled the city of Rome to their country estates. This action created a series of causes and effects that further weakened the empire.

Critical Thinking: Identifying Cause and Effect
Reaching Standards

Causes of Rome's Collapse 📖 **HSS** 7.1.2; **Analysis Skills:** CS 1, HI 2

1. Discuss with students the factors involved in the decline of the western Roman Empire.

2. To help students understand the cause and effect of factors that led to the fall of Rome, draw the chart for students to see. Omit the blue, italicized answers.

3. Have students copy and complete the chart. Then review the answers as a class.
LS Verbal/Linguistic, Visual/Spatial

📋 Alternative Assessment Handbook, Rubric 7: Charts

Causes	Events	Effects
weak emperors; growing power of military	**Military Leaders Take Power**	*leaders fight among themselves; Rome falls*
corrupt government ignores citizens	**Wealthy Citizens Flee Rome**	*taxes and prices rise, rich create private armies*

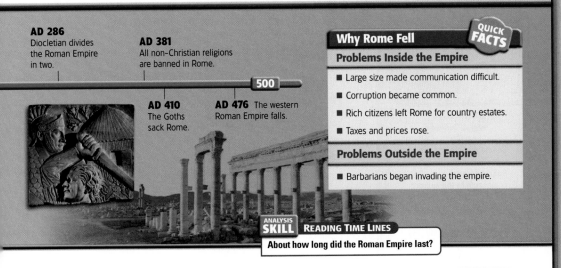

AD 286 Diocletian divides the Roman Empire in two.

AD 381 All non-Christian religions are banned in Rome.

500

AD 410 The Goths sack Rome.

AD 476 The western Roman Empire falls.

Why Rome Fell **QUICK FACTS**

Problems Inside the Empire

■ Large size made communication difficult.
■ Corruption became common.
■ Rich citizens left Rome for country estates.
■ Taxes and prices rose.

Problems Outside the Empire

■ Barbarians began invading the empire.

ANALYSIS SKILL **READING TIME LINES**
About how long did the Roman Empire last?

Outside Rome, many landowners used slaves or serfs to work on their lands. To protect their estates and their wealth, many landowners created their own armies. Ambitious landowners used these personal armies to overthrow emperors and take power for themselves.

As wealthy citizens abandoned Rome and other cities, city life became more difficult for those who remained. Rome's population decreased, and schools closed. At the same time taxes and prices soared, leaving more and more Romans poor. By the end of the 400s Rome was no longer the city it had once been. As it changed, the empire slowly collapsed around it.

READING CHECK **Finding Main Ideas** How did corruption alter Roman society in the 400s?

SUMMARY AND PREVIEW By the early 500s Rome no longer ruled western Europe. But as you will read in the next section, the empire in the east continued to prosper for several hundred years.

Section 1 Assessment

go.hrw.com
Online Quiz
KEYWORD: SQ6 HP14

Reviewing Ideas, Terms, and People **HSS** 7.1.2

1. **a. Recall** Where did Constantine move Rome's capital?
   b. Explain Why did **Diocletian** divide the empire in two?
2. **a. Identify** Who was **Attila**?
   b. Summarize Why did the Goths move into the Roman Empire in the 300s?
   c. Elaborate Why do you think the sack of Rome was so devastating?
3. **a. Describe** What kinds of problems did Rome's size cause for its emperors?
   b. Make Generalizations How did **corruption** weaken Rome in the 400s?

Critical Thinking

4. **Drawing Conclusions** Draw a word web like the one shown on the right. In each of the outer circles, list a factor that helped lead to the fall of the western Roman Empire. You may add more circles if needed.

Fall of the Western Roman Empire

FOCUS ON SPEAKING

5. **Adding Details** Make a list of the most important events that led to the fall of the western Roman Empire. Then circle the events you will mention in your poem.

THE FALL OF ROME **413**

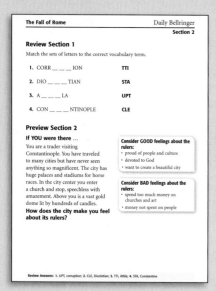
Bellringer

If YOU were there . . . Use the **Daily Bellringer Transparency** to help students answer the question.

🔖 Daily Bellringer Transparency, Section 2

The Fall of Rome   Daily Bellringer
                                           Section 2

Review Section 1

Match the sets of letters to the correct vocabulary term.

1. CORR _ _ _ ION   TTI
2. DIO _ _ _ TIAN   STA
3. A _ _ _ LA   UPT
4. CON _ _ _ NTINOPLE   CLE

Preview Section 2

If YOU were there . . .
You are a trader visiting Constantinople. You have traveled to many cities but have never seen anything so magnificent. The city has huge palaces and stadiums for horse races. In the city center you enter a church and stop, speechless with amazement. Above you is a vast gold dome lit by hundreds of candles.
How does the city make you feel about its rulers?

Consider GOOD feelings about the rulers:
• proud of people and culture
• devoted to God
• want to create a beautiful city

Consider BAD feelings about the rulers:
• spend too much money on churches and art
• money not spent on people

Review Answers: 1. UPT, corruption; 2. CLE, Diocletian; 3. TTI, Attila; 4. STA, Constantine

---

Building Vocabulary

Preteach or review the following terms:

devotion dedication and loyalty (p. 417)

guarantee promise (p. 415)

influences factors that have an effect on an event or person (p. 416)

🔖 **CRF:** Vocabulary Builder Activity, Section 2

Standards Focus

HSS 7.1.3

Means: Trace the development of Constantinople and the Byzantine Empire, including the rise of the Eastern Orthodox Church and its effect on the empire.

Matters: The Byzantine Empire preserved much of the information about the Roman Empire that we know today.

The Byzantine Empire

What You Will Learn...

Main Ideas

1. Eastern emperors ruled from Constantinople and tried but failed to reunite the whole Roman Empire.
2. The people of the eastern empire created a new society that was very different from society in the west.
3. Byzantine Christianity was different from religion in the west.

The Big Idea

The Roman Empire split into two parts, and the eastern Roman Empire prospered for hundreds of years after the western empire fell.

Key Terms and People

Justinian, *p. 414*
Theodora, *p. 415*
Byzantine Empire, *p. 416*
mosaics, *p. 417*

 HSS 7.1.3 Describe the establishment by Constantine of the new capital in Constantinople and the development of the Byzantine Empire, with an emphasis on the consequences of the development of two distinct European civilizations, Eastern Orthodox and Roman Catholic, and their two distinct views on church-state relations.

If YOU were there...

You are a trader visiting Constantinople. You have traveled to many cities but have never seen anything so magnificent. The city has huge palaces and stadiums for horse races. In the city center you enter a church and stop, speechless with amazement. Above you is a vast, gold dome lit by hundreds of candles.

How does the city make you feel about its rulers?

BUILDING BACKGROUND Even before the western empire fell to the Goths, power had begun to shift to the richer, more stable east. The people of the eastern empire considered themselves Romans, but their culture was very different from that of Rome itself.

Emperors Rule from Constantinople

Constantinople was built on the site of an ancient Greek trading city called Byzantium (buh-ZAN-shuhm). It lay near both the Black Sea and the Mediterranean Sea. This location between two seas protected the city from attack and let the city control trade between Europe and Asia. Constantinople was in an ideal place to grow in wealth and power.

Justinian

After Rome fell in 476, the emperors of the eastern Roman Empire dreamed of taking it back and reuniting the old Roman Empire. For **Justinian** (juh-STIN-ee-uhn), an emperor who ruled from 527 to 565, reuniting the empire was a passion. He couldn't live with a Roman Empire that didn't include the city of Rome, so he sent his army to retake Italy. In the end this army conquered not only Italy but also much land around the Mediterranean.

Justinian's other passions were the law and the church. He ordered officials to examine all of Rome's laws and remove any out-of-date or unchristian laws. He then organized all the laws

---

Teach the Big Idea: Master the Standards   Standards Proficiency

The Byzantine Empire   HSS 7.1.3; HSS Analysis Skills: HI 1

1. **Teach** Ask students the Main Idea questions to teach this section.

2. **Apply** Help students list the main people, events, and issues in the section. Write the list for all to see. Then ask students to imagine they are news reporters. Have each student write one news headline for each of the section's main events and issues. Model the activity by doing the first headline as a class. **LS Verbal/Linguistic**

3. **Review** As you review the section's main ideas, have students share their related headlines with the class.

4. **Practice/Homework** Select one headline and have each student write a news article to accompany the headline. Have them answer the five Ws (who, what, where, when, and why) when creating their article. **LS Verbal/Linguistic**

🔖 Alternative Assessment Handbook, Rubric 42: Writing to Inform

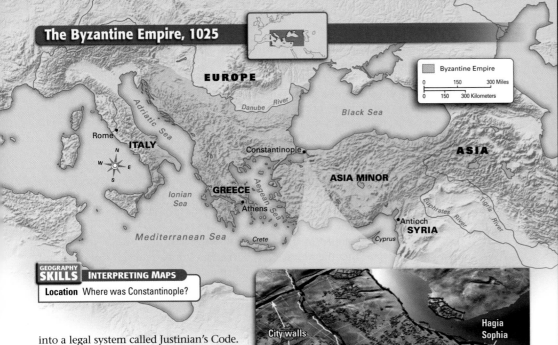

The Byzantine Empire, 1025

EUROPE

Rome
ITALY

Adriatic Sea

Danube River

Black Sea

Constantinople

ASIA

ASIA MINOR

GREECE

Ionian Sea

Aegean Sea

Athens

Antioch
SYRIA

Euphrates River

Tigris River

Mediterranean Sea

Crete

Cyprus

Byzantine Empire

0   150   300 Miles
0   150   300 Kilometers

GEOGRAPHY SKILLS **INTERPRETING MAPS**

Location Where was Constantinople?

into a legal system called Justinian's Code. By simplifying Roman law, this code helped guarantee fair treatment for all.

Despite his achievements, Justinian made many enemies. Two groups of these enemies joined together and tried to overthrow him in 532. These groups led riots in the streets and set fire to buildings. Scared for his life, Justinian prepared to leave Constantinople.

Justinian was stopped from leaving by his wife, **Theodora** (thee-uh-DOHR-uh). She convinced Justinian to stay in the city. Smart and powerful, Theodora helped her husband rule effectively. With her advice, he found a way to end the riots. Justinian's soldiers killed all the rioters—some 30,000 people—and saved the emperor's throne.

The Empire after Justinian

After the death of Justinian in 565, the eastern empire began to decline. Faced with invasions by barbarians, Persians, and Muslims, later emperors lost all the

City walls

Forum

Harbor

Hippodrome

Hagia Sophia

Imperial Palace

Constantinople was strategically located where Europe and Asia meet. As a result, the city was in a perfect location to control trade routes between the two continents.

land Justinian had gained. The eastern empire remained a major power for several hundred years, but it never regained its former strength.

The eastern empire's struggles finally ended nearly 900 years after the death of Justinian. In 1453 a group called the Ottoman Turks captured Constantinople. With this defeat the 1,000-year history of the eastern Roman Empire came to an end.

READING CHECK **Drawing Conclusions** Why did Justinian reorganize Roman law?

Cross-Discipline Activity: Civics

Standards Proficiency

Responsibility: Making Laws **HSS** 7.1.3; **HSS** Analysis Skills: HI 1

1. Discuss with students Justinian's Code and why it was necessary to update and reorganize the laws of the empire. Tell students they will be creating a code of laws.

2. Organize the class into small groups. Have each group discuss what laws they would like to see enacted in the classroom. Remind students that, like Justinian's Code, their laws should guarantee fair treatment for all.

3. Have a representative from each group write the group's list for the class to see.

4. Discuss with the class how to combine the individual lists into one master list. After agreeing to a class list, have volunteers write the laws on butcher paper.

5. Lastly, discuss with students the importance of updating laws. Have students consider the need to create an organized code of laws and some of the problems involved in creating one. **LS** Interpersonal, Verbal/Linguistic

Alternative Assessment Handbook, Rubrics 11: Discussions; and 14: Group Activity

---

Direct Teach

Main Idea

❶ Emperors Rule from Constantinople

Eastern emperors ruled from Constantinople and tried but failed to reunite the whole Roman Empire.

Recall What were Justinian's passions as emperor? *reuniting the old Roman Empire, organizing Roman law, and the church*

Identify Who was Theodora, and what role did she play in the Byzantine Empire? *She was the wife of Emperor Justinian; she helped him rule effectively.*

Draw Conclusions Why did the empire decline after the rule of the emperor Justinian? *Invasions by barbarians, Persians, and Muslims reduced the size of the empire and thereby its power.*

📑 **CRF:** Biography Activity: Belisarius

🗺 Map Transparency: The Byzantine Empire, 1025

📑 **CRF:** Primary Source Activity: "The Body of Civil Law" by Justinian

HSS 7.1.3; **HSS** Analysis Skills: CS 1, HI 1, HI 2

---

go.hrw.com

Online Resources

KEYWORD: SQ6 WH14
ACTIVITY: Military Might

Linking to Today

Constantinople, Now Istanbul First known as Byzantium, and later as Constantinople, the city located at the junction of Europe and Asia is today known as Istanbul. The largest city in Turkey, Istanbul is a popular site for tourists.

Answers

Interpreting Maps *on a peninsula where Europe and Asia meet*

Reading Check *to help guarantee fair treatment for all*

415

Main Idea

❷ A New Society

The people of the eastern empire created a new society that was very different from society in the west.

Recall In what ways did the eastern empire change from the western empire? *People began to speak Greek rather than Latin and study Greek philosophy, and a new society developed.*

Analyze Why were eastern emperors more powerful than those in the West? *They had more power, and people believed they were chosen by God to rule the empire and the church.*

🐻 **HSS** 7.1.3; **HSS** Analysis Skills: HI 1

Primary Source

Primary Sources

An Impression of Byzantine Emperors In the 900s an Italian bishop, Liudprand of Cremona, visited Constantinople. In this passage, he describes the elaborate lengths to which emperors went to impress visitors.
"The throne itself was so marvellously fashioned that at one moment it seemed a low structure, and at another it rose high into the air. It was of immense size and was guarded by lions, made either of bronze or of wood covered over with gold . . . After I had three times made obeisance [bowed] to the emperor with my face upon the ground, I lifted my head, and behold! the man whom just before I had seen sitting on a moderately elevated seat had now changed his raiment [clothing] and was sitting on the level of the ceiling."

A New Society

In many ways Justinian was the last Roman emperor of the eastern empire. After he died, non-Roman influences took hold throughout the empire. People began to speak Greek, the language of the eastern empire, rather than Latin. Scholars studied Greek, not Roman, philosophy. Gradually, the empire lost its ties to the old Roman Empire, and a new society developed.

The people who lived in this society never stopped thinking of themselves as Romans. But modern historians have given their society a new name. They call the society that developed in the eastern Roman Empire after the west fell the **Byzantine** (BI-zuhn-teen) **Empire**, named after the Greek town of Byzantium.

Outside Influence

One reason eastern and western Roman society was different was the Byzantines' interaction with other groups. This interaction was largely a result of trade. Because Constantinople's location was ideal for trading between Europe and Asia, it became the greatest trading city in Europe.

Merchants from all around Europe, Asia, and Africa traveled to Constantinople to trade. Over time Byzantine society began to reflect these outside influences as well as its Roman and Greek roots.

Government

The forms of government that developed in the eastern and western empires also created differences. Byzantine emperors had

History Close-up

The Glory of Constantinople

Constantinople was a crossroads for traders, a center of Christianity, and the capital of an empire. It was a magnificent city filled with great buildings, palaces, and churches. The city's rulers led processions, or ceremonial walks, to show their wealth and power.

This procession went from the church to the royal palace. The procession showed the power and importance of the emperor as head of the church.

416

Differentiating Instruction for Universal Access

English-Language Learners   Standards Proficiency   Standard English Mastery

1. Review with students the location of Constantinople and the effects of trade on the city and its people.

2. Ask students to imagine that they are merchants in Constantinople who trade with faraway places, either importing or exporting goods.

3. Ask each student to write a business letter to someone in another empire, convincing him or her to do business in Constantinople.

4. Suggest that students write the letter in their first or primary languages. Then help students

to translate their letters into English. Work with students to help them identify words and phrases to make their letters descriptive and persuasive, and to ensure their use of standard English.

5. Ask volunteers to share their letters with the class. **LS** Verbal/Linguistic

🐻 **HSS** 7.1.3; **HSS** Analysis Skills: HI 1, HI 2

📓 Alternative Assessment Handbook, Rubric 5: Business Letters

more power than western emperors did. They liked to show off their great power. For example, people could not stand while they were in the presence of the eastern emperor. They had to crawl on their hands and knees to talk to him.

The power of an eastern emperor was greater, in part, because the emperor was considered the head of the church as well as the political ruler. The Byzantines thought the emperor had been chosen by God to lead both the empire and the church. In the west the emperor was limited to political power. Popes and bishops were the leaders of the church.

READING CHECK Contrasting What were two ways in which eastern and western Roman society were different?

Byzantine Christianity

Just as it was in the west, Christianity was central to the Byzantines' lives. From the beginning, nearly everyone who lived in the Byzantine Empire was Christian.

To show their devotion to God and the Christian church Byzantine artists created beautiful works of religious art. Among the grandest works were **mosaics**, pictures made with pieces of colored stone or glass. Some mosaics sparkled with gold, silver, and jewels.

The procession began at Hagia Sophia, the Byzantines' famous church.

Citizens and visitors crowded the square to see the royal rulers pass by.

ANALYSIS SKILL **ANALYZING VISUALS**
Where did the procession begin and end?

417

Critical Thinking: Supporting Points of View

Standards **Proficiency**

Making Procession Fliers HSS 7.1.3; HSS Analysis Skills: HR 5, HI 1,

1. Have students examine the illustration above. Point out to students that one purpose of the procession was to show the power of the emperor as head of state as well as the head of the church.

2. Ask students to imagine what responses the people of the Byzantine Empire likely had to these processions. Did people support or oppose the power of the emperor? Why? Ask students why emperors took part in processions. What did they hope to achieve?

3. Ask students to imagine that they work for the emperor of the Byzantine Empire. Have students create flyers to advertise an upcoming procession. Remind them that their flyers should support the emperor and use language that would encourage people to attend the procession.

4. Ask volunteers to post their flyers around the classroom for others to see.
LS **Verbal/Linguistic**

Alternative Assessment Handbook, Rubric 2: Advertisements

417

Direct Teach

Main Idea

❸ Byzantine Christianity

Byzantine Christianity was different from religion in the West.

Contrast How did Christianity in the eastern empire differ from that of the western empire? *East—services in Greek, emperor was head of church, priests could marry; West—services in Latin, popes and bishops led the church, priests could not marry.*

Analyze What caused Christians in the East to break with the Roman Catholic Church? *Differences in ideas and practices between the two groups grew too large.*

📋 CRF: Literature Activity: Byzantine Poetry

🗄 Quick Facts Transparency: The Western Roman and Byzantine Empires

HSS 7.1.3; HSS Analysis Skills: HI 2, HI 3

Review & Assess

Close

Have students work in pairs to write a short summary of the history of the Byzantine Empire.

Review

🖥 Online Quiz, Section 2

Assess

SE Section 2 Assessment

📋 PASS: Section 2 Quiz

📋 Alternative Assessment Handbook

Reteach/Classroom Intervention

📋 California Standards Review Workbook

📋 Interactive Reader and Study Guide, Section 2

💿 Interactive Skills Tutor CD-ROM

Answers

Reading Check *differences in the practice of Christianity between the East and the West*

418

The Western Roman and Byzantine Empires

In the Western Roman Empire . . .

- Popes and bishops led the church, and the emperor led the government.
- Latin was the main language.

In the Byzantine Empire . . .

- Emperors led the church and the government.
- Greek was the main language.

THE IMPACT TODAY

The Orthodox Church is still the main religion in Russia, Greece, and other parts of eastern Europe.

Even more magnificent than their mosaics were Byzantine churches, especially Hagia Sophia (HAH-juh soh-FEE-uh). Built by Justinian in the 530s, its huge domes rose high above Constantinople. According to legend, when Justinian saw the church he exclaimed in delight

"Glory to God who has judged me worthy of accomplishing such a work as this! O Solomon, I have outdone you!"

–Justinian, quoted in *The Story of the Building of the Church of Santa Sophia*

As time passed, people in the east and west began to interpret and practice some elements of Christianity differently. For

example, eastern priests could get married, while priests in the west could not. Religious services were performed in Greek in the east. In the west they were held in Latin.

For hundreds of years, church leaders from the east and west worked together peacefully despite their differences. However, the differences between their ideas continued to grow. In time the differences led to divisions within the Christian Church. In the 1000s the split between east and west became official. Eastern Christians formed what became known as the Orthodox Church. As a result, eastern and western Europe were divided by religion.

READING CHECK **Contrasting** What led to a split in the Christian Church?

SUMMARY AND PREVIEW The Roman Empire and the Christian Church both divided into two parts. As Christianity became a major force in the Byzantine Empire, a civilization across the world was reaching its height. You will read about this civilization—the Maya—in the next chapter.

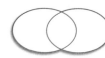

Section 2 Assessment

go.hrw.com
Online Quiz
KEYWORD: SQ6 HP14

Reviewing Ideas, Terms, and People HSS 7.1.3

1. **a. Describe** Where was Constantinople located?
   b. Summarize What were two of **Justinian**'s major accomplishments?
   c. Elaborate What do you think **Theodora**'s role in the government says about women in the eastern empire?
2. **a. Identify** What was one major difference between the powers of emperors in the east and the west?
   b. Explain How did contact with other cultures help change the **Byzantine Empire**?
3. **a. Define** What is a **mosaic**?
   b. Make Generalizations What led to the creation of two different Christian societies in Europe?

Critical Thinking

4. **Comparing and Contrasting** Draw a Venn diagram like the one shown here. In the left oval describe the western Roman Empire. In the right oval describe the eastern empire. Where the ovals overlap, list features the two had in common.

FOCUS ON SPEAKING

5. **Organizing Dates** Add key events from Byzantine history to the list you made in the last section. Once you have your list complete, arrange the events on your list in the order they happened.

418 CHAPTER 14

Section 2 Assessment Answers

1. **a.** on a peninsula where Europe and Asia meet
   b. possible answers—He reconquered parts of the former Roman Empire, simplified Roman law, put down a rebellion, and had the Hagia Sophia built.
   c. possible answer—Women in the East were allowed to participate in politics more than women in many other societies of the time.
2. **a.** Emperors in the East had both political and religious power.
   b. People from other cultures introduced new ideas to the Byzantines.

3. **a.** image made from bits of glass or stone
   b. differences in the ways people practiced Christianity in the East and West
4. possible answers: West—popes and bishops led the church, emperor led the government, Latin was main language, priests couldn't marry; East—emperors led church and government, Greek was main language, priests could marry; Both—practiced Christianity, followed Roman laws
5. possible answers—476: Rome falls; 527–565: Justinian rules; 1453: Ottoman Turks capture Constantinople; 1000s: Christian Church splits

Justinian and Theodora

How would you rebuild a fallen empire?

When did they live? Justinian, 483–565; Theodora, c. 500–548

Where did they live? Constantinople

What did they do? As Byzantine emperor, Justinian reconquered parts of the fallen western empire and simplified Roman laws. He also ordered the building of many beautiful public buildings and churches, including Hagia Sophia.

KEY EVENTS

- **525** Justinian and Theodora are married.
- **527** Justinian becomes emperor and names Theodora empress.
- **532** Theodora persuades Justinian not to flee Constantinople during riots.
- **534** Justinian's Code is produced.
- **534–565** Justinian's armies reconquer parts of the Roman Empire, from North Africa to Italy to Spain.

Why are they important?

Justinian and Theodora worked together to restore the power, beauty, and strength of the Roman Empire. They made Constantinople into a grand capital city and the center of a strong empire. While Justinian tried to reconquer the west, Theodora helped create laws to aid women and children and to end government corruption.

Evaluating Which of Justinian and Theodora's accomplishments do you find most impressive? Why?

Hagia Sophia rises high above Istanbul, Turkey, the city once called Constantinople.

419

Biography

Reading Focus Question

The damage that occurs after an empire has fallen may be similar to damage caused by a hurricane or tornado. Ask students to think about how they would rebuild a town hit by a natural disaster and restore its buildings and works of art. Remind students that Justinian and Theodora helped to rebuild the glory of the Roman Empire.

Info to Know

Justinian and the Law Justinian's interest in legal studies seems to have stemmed from his desire to get rid of corruption in government and to provide justice for his subjects. One of his most important reforms was to prohibit the sale of provincial governorships. Before this reform, many governors who paid for their offices would cover their costs by extorting money from the population.

Did you know . . .

Before Theodora met and married Justinian, she worked as an actress in Constantinople. Justinian is said to have fallen in love with not only her great beauty but also her keen intelligence.

About the Illustration

This illustration of Justinian and Theodora is an artist's conception based on available sources. However, historians are uncertain exactly what Justinian and Theodora looked like.

Critical Thinking: Supporting a Point of View

Standards Proficiency

Letters to the Editor 🐻 **HSS** 7.1.3; **HSS** Analysis Skills: CS 1, HI 1, HI 2

Research Required

1. Review the biography above with the class. Tell students that Theodora's name is mentioned in almost every law passed during Justinian's reign. Some historians take this as a sign of how important she was and of the great influence she had in government. Ask students if the wives of emperors or kings typically had such influence. Tell students that Theodora's influence with her husband attracted many supporters and critics.

2. Ask students to imagine that they are living during the time of Justinian's rule. Have each student write a letter to the editor of the local newspaper expressing their point of view about the power and influence of Empress Theodora. Remind students that their letters should politely express their opinions.

3. Ask volunteers to share their letters with the class. 🅛🅢 **Verbal/Linguistic**

📄 Alternative Assessment Handbook, Rubric 17: Letters to Editors

Answers

Evaluating *possible answers— reuniting the Roman Empire, because it brought order to the West; simplifying Roman laws, because they promoted fairness for all people*

Social Studies Skills

Chance, Error, and Oversight in History

Activity **Real-Life Examples** Ask students if they think differently about chance, error, and oversight after learning the critical ways in which it can shape history. After a brief discussion, ask volunteers to share examples of when chance, error, or oversight shaped events in their own lives. Then challenge students to identify examples of chance, error, or oversight shaping recent national or world events. Correct students' interpretations where necessary. Use the discussion to make certain that students understand the differences among error, chance, and oversight and how they can affect historical events.

LS **Intrapersonal, Verbal/Linguistic**

Alternative Assessment Handbook, Rubric 11: Discussions

HSS Analysis Skills: HI 4

Social Studies Skills

HSS **Analysis HI 4** Students recognize the role of chance, oversight, and error in history.

| Analysis | Critical Thinking | Participation | Study |

Chance, Error, and Oversight in History

Understand the Skill

History is nothing more than what people thought and did in the past, and the people of the past were just as human as people today. Like us, they occasionally forgot or overlooked things. They made mistakes in their decisions or judgments. Unexpected things happened that they couldn't control. Sometimes, these oversights, errors, and just plain luck shaped history.

Learn the Skill

This chapter notes several examples of the role of error, chance, and oversight in history.

1 **Error:** The Gothic chief Alaric offered peace with Rome in return for land and supplies for his people. Rome's leaders paid for many years, but then they stopped. Stopping the payments was a mistake, because Alaric attacked and looted Rome in 410. For the first time in 800 years, Rome fell to an outside invader.

2 **Chance:** In 452 Attila the Hun attacked northern Italy. After several victories, however, he halted his invasion and turned back. Southern Italy was suffering from a plague, and Attila did not want to risk weakening his army by entering the region. If not for this chance occurrence, Rome might have been conquered again.

3 **Oversight:** Emperor Justinian's subjects failed to appreciate his wife's importance. Theodora was a commoner, so they gave her little respect. When they launched a revolt in 532, Justinian was ready to flee. However, Theodora gave a powerful speech about the rewards of risking one's life for a great cause. Her speech inspired Justinian's supporters to attack and defeat the rebels.

Practice and Apply the Skill

As you read in the chapter, military leaders ruled the western empire by the 450s. Analyze the reasons for this development. Write a paragraph to explain how chance, error, or oversight influenced this shift in power in Rome.

420 CHAPTER 14

Social Studies Skills Activity: Chance, Error, and Oversight in History

Analyzing the Byzantine Empire   **HSS** Analysis Skills: HI 4   **Standards Proficiency**

1. Have each student review Section 2 about the growth of the Byzantine Empire.

2. Instruct students to list all the key events in the empire's development. Students should list the events horizontally or vertically. Then have students indicate which events occurred because of chance, oversight, or error.

3. When students have completed the activity, have them help you create a master list of the events. Write the list for students to see. Then have volunteers indicate the events shaped by

chance, error, or oversight. Students should explain their reasoning. *(Examples include Justinian's luck at having such a smart and powerful wife, and the mistake the rioters made who rose up against Justinian only to lose their lives.)*

LS **Logical/Mathematical, Verbal Linguistic**

Alternative Assessment Handbook, Rubric 16: Judging Information

---

Answers

Practice and Apply the Skill
Students' paragraphs will vary but should reflect an understanding of chance, oversight, and error in the events, such as shown in the first two examples given in the feature.

420

Visual Summary

Use the visual summary below to help you review the main ideas of the chapter.

QUICK FACTS

Western Roman Empire
Eastern Roman Empire

The eastern Byzantine Empire remained after the Roman Empire fell and was an important center of Christianity and trade.

Barbarian invasions and internal problems caused the split and collapse of the Roman Empire.

Reviewing Vocabulary, Terms, and People

Unscramble each group of letters below to spell a term that matches the given definition.

1. **anzbtinye**—name given to the eastern half of the Roman Empire

2. **latcodeiin**—emperor who divided the Roman Empire into two parts

3. **zticeins**—people who had the right to participate in Rome's government

4. **ohtradoe**—empress of the Byzantine Empire

5. **rcotponiur**—the decay of people's values

6. **smiacso**—pictures made from pieces of colorful glass or stone

7. **vlsioc**—powerful Frankish king

8. **tatali**—leader of the Huns who invaded Rome in the 400s

9. **njiasunti**—Byzantine emperor who tried to reunite the entire Roman Empire

Comprehension and Critical Thinking

SECTION 1 *(Pages 408–413)* **HSS** 7.1.2

10. **a. Identify** Who were the Huns? Who were the Goths?

b. Compare and Contrast What did Diocletian and Constantine have in common? How did their actions differ?

c. Evaluate Of all the causes for the fall of the western Roman Empire, which, if any, could have been prevented? Explain your answer.

SECTION 2 *(Pages 414–418)* **HSS** 7.1.3

11. **a. Identify** Who were Justinian and Theodora, and what did they accomplish?

b. Contrast In what ways was the Byzantine Empire different from the western Roman Empire?

c. Elaborate Would Constantinople have been an exciting place to visit in the 500s? Why or why not?

THE FALL OF ROME **421**

---

11. a. Justinian—emperor who reunited parts of the Roman Empire; Theodora—Justinian's wife who helped him rule effectively; Together they saved the emperor's throne and helped restore the power, beauty, and strength of the Roman Empire.

b. possible answers—Western Roman Empire: popes and bishops led the church, emperor led government, Latin was main language, priests couldn't get married; Byzantine Empire: emperors led church and government, Greek was main language, priests could marry; both—Christian, based on Roman laws.

c. possible answer—yes, because it was the greatest trading city in Europe and people from all over the world visited there

Social Studies Skills

12. Answers will vary, but students should understand that the decision was a factor in the invasion.

13. Answers will vary, but students should indicate that the Huns would likely have continued their raids.

14. Answers will vary, but students should provide examples of mistakes that rulers could make and how a ruler could prevent a revolt.

Using the Internet

15. Go to the HRW Web site and enter the keyword shown to access a rubric for this activity.

> KEYWORD: SQ6 TEACHER

Reviewing Themes

16. possible answer—Military leaders took power in the government, but fought among themselves instead of defending the empire.

17. possible answer—The two societies spoke different languages, interpreted Christian ideas differently, and expressed their faith in different artistic forms.

Social Studies Skills

Recognizing Chance, Oversight, and Error in History *Answer the following questions about the role of chance, oversight, or error in history.*

12. Would you consider the decision by Rome's leaders to stop paying Alaric and the Goths an error in judgment? Why or why not?

13. Attila planned to lead the Huns in an attack on the eastern Roman Empire in 453, but he died of a nosebleed the night of his wedding that year. How might history have been different if Attila had not happened to die?

14. How might the revolt against Justinian in 532 have been caused by an oversight on his part? What might he have done to prevent the revolt?

Using the Internet
KEYWORD: SQ6 WH14

15. Activity: Summarizing Most law students are required to learn about Justinian's Code because it had such a strong influence on modern law. Enter the keyword. Then create a chart like the one below that summarizes the ways in which Justinian's Code influences modern issues such as the rights and responsibilities of individuals. Explain how values such as an individual's right to equality before the law influenced the world. You may be asked to present your summaries to the class.

Justinian's Code	Modern Issues

Reviewing Themes

16. Politics How did weak government and ineffective leaders help lead to the end of the western Roman Empire?

17. Religion Do you agree or disagree with this statement: By the 1000s, Europe was divided into two distinct Christian societies. Why or why not?

Reading Skills

Understanding Bias and Stereotypes *The passage below is taken from a Roman historian's description of Attila, the leader of the Huns. Read the passage and then answer the questions that follow.*

> "A lavish meal, served on silver trenchers, was prepared for us and the other barbarians, but Attila just had some meat on a wooden platter, for this was one aspect of his self-discipline. For instance, gold or silver cups were presented to the other diners, but his own goblet was made of wood. His clothes, too, were simple, and no trouble was taken except to have them clean. The sword that hung by his side, the clasps of his barbarian shoes and the bridle of his horse were all free from gold, precious stones or other valuable decorations affected by the other Scythians … As twilight came on torches were lit, and two barbarians entered before Attila to sing some songs they had composed, telling of his victories and valour in war. The guests paid close attention to them, and some were delighted with the songs, others excited at being reminded of the wars, but others broke down and wept if their bodies were weakened by age and their warrior spirits forced to remain inactive."
>
> –Priscus, quoted in *Eyewitness to History*, edited by John Carey

18. What does the word *barbarian* suggest that Priscus thought of Attila and his allies? What do you think he expected the Huns to be like?

19. How does Priscus think the Huns view war? How can you tell?

20. Does Priscus appear to have let his opinions color his description of Attila? Why or why not?

FOCUS ON SPEAKING

21. Presenting a Narrative Poem Look back over the details and events you listed while reading this chapter. Choose five or six of these events to include in your poem. Write your poem. In the first one or two lines, introduce the subject. Write five or six more lines, each about one event that occurred during Rome's decline. Then write one or two lines about the importance of the fall of Rome. Once you have finished writing, present your poem. Practice altering your voice and the rhythm of your words to make your poem more interesting to listeners.

Reading Skills

18. possible answers—that they were uncivilized; that they would all have bad manners, eat bad food, and wear rough clothing

19. that it was very important and exciting to them; they wept if they could no longer fight, they told stories of victories and valor

20. possible answers—he portrays Attila as different from the other barbarians in terms of dress and self-discipline

Focus on Speaking

21. Rubric Students' narrative poems should:
- offer an introduction that clearly tells the topic of the poem.
- tell five or six important events that occurred during Rome's decline.
- include enough detail to give a clear picture of the fall of Rome.
- contain alliteration, rhyme, or a refrain.

CRF: Focus on Writing: Narrative Poem

Standards Assessment

DIRECTIONS: Read each question, and write the letter of the best response.

1

- Empire is ruled by all-powerful emperors.
- Emperors are both religious leaders and political leaders.
- Women have significant roles in government.
- Greek, Egyptian, and Muslim cultural influences shape society.
- People practice the Orthodox Christian religion.
- People identify themselves as Romans.

The six characteristics listed above describe

A the eastern Roman Empire.
B the western Roman Empire.
C both the eastern and western empires.
D neither the eastern nor the western empire.

2 Byzantine artists were known *especially* for creating colorful

A statues.
B mosaics.
C frescoes.
D pottery.

3 Which of the following was *not* a reason for the fall of the Roman Empire?

A the empire's vast size
B corruption in Roman government
C pressure on the Goths from the Huns
D the influence of Greek government

4 The eastern Roman Empire is also known as the

A Holy Roman Empire.
B Eastern Orthodox Empire.
C Ottoman Empire.
D Byzantine Empire.

5 In 410 the city of Rome was destroyed for the first time in 800 years by the army of a foreign people called the

A Huns.
B Vandals.
C Goths.
D Franks.

Connecting with Past Learnings

6 Constantine unified the entire Roman Empire and introduced a new religion into the Roman government. Which leader that you learned about earlier in this course is known for his similar accomplishments?

A Asoka
B Hammurabi
C Alexander
D Piankhi

7 Earlier in this course you learned that the Persians threatened Greek civilization for a time. All of the following peoples played a similar role in Roman history *except* the

A Byzantines.
B Goths.
C Vandals.
D Huns.

Answers

1. A
Break Down the Question Students should recall that the eastern Roman Empire practiced Orthodox Christianity, and was strongly influenced by Greek culture.

2. B
Break Down the Question This question requires students to recall factual information from Section 2.

3. D
Break Down the Question Remind students that the word *not* in the question indicates that they should identify the *false* statement.

4. D
Break Down the Question This question requires students to recall factual information from Section 2.

5. C
Break Down the Question This question requires students to recall factual information. Refer students who missed this question to Section 1.

6. A
Break Down the Question This question requires students to recall information from a previous chapter.

7. A
Break Down the Question Point out to students that the word *except* indicates that they should identify which people did *not* threaten the Romans.

Standards Review

Have students review the following standards in their workbooks.

California Standards Review Workbook:
HSS 7.1.1, 7.1.2, 7.1.3

Intervention Resources

Reproducible

- Interactive Reader and Study Guide
- Universal Access Teacher Management System: Universal Access Lesson Plans

Technology

- Quick Facts Transparency: The Fall of Rome Visual Summary
- Universal Access Modified Worksheets and Tests CD-ROM
- Intertactive Skills Tutor CD-ROM

Tips for Test Taking

Master the Question Ask students this question and offer these tips: Have you ever said, "I knew the answer, but I thought the question asked something else"? Be very sure that you **know what a question is asking.** Read the question at least twice before reading the answer choices. Watch especially for words like *not* and *except*—they tell you to look for the choice that is false or different from the other choices or opposite in some way.

Chapter 15 Planning Guide

The Early Americas

Chapter Overview	Reproducible Resources	Technology Resources
Chapter 15 pp. 424–49 **Overview: In this chapter, students will learn about early peoples of the Americas and the Maya Empire.** See p. 424 for the California History–Social Science standards covered in this chapter.	**Universal Access Teacher Management System:*** • Universal Access Instructional Benchmarking Guides • Lesson Plans for Universal Access **Interactive Reader and Study Guide:** Chapter Graphic Organizer* **Chapter Resource File*** • Chapter Review Activity • Focus on Writing Activity: A Travel Brochure • Social Studies Skills Activity: Accepting Social Responsibility	**One-Stop Planner CD-ROM:** Calendar Planner **Student Edition on Audio CD Program** **Universal Access Modified Worksheets and Tests CD-ROM** **Interactive Skills Tutor CD-ROM** **Primary Source Library CD-ROM for World History** **Multimedia Presentation CD-ROM** **History's Impact: World History Video Program (VHS/DVD):** The Early Civilizations of the Americas* **A Teacher's Guide To Religion in the Public Schools***
Section 1: **Geography and Early Cultures** **The Big Idea:** The landforms and climate of the Americas affected farming and the development of early cultures 7.7.1	**Universal Access Teacher Management System:*** Section 1 Lesson Plan **Interactive Reader and Study Guide:** Section 1 Summary* **Chapter Resource File*** • Vocabulary Builder Activity, Section 1	**Daily Bellringer Transparency:** Section 1* **Map Transparency:** The Americas: Physical* **Map Transparency:** Migration to the Americas* **Map Transparency:** Early Civilizations in the Americas* **Internet Activity:** Discovering Olmec Culture
Section 2: **The Maya** **The Big Idea:** Maya civilization was characterized by great cities, trade, and warfare, but it disappeared for reasons that are still unclear. 7.7.1	**Universal Access Teacher Management System:*** Section 2 Lesson Plan **Interactive Reader and Study Guide:** Section 2 Summary* **Chapter Resource File*** • Vocabulary Builder Activity, Section 2 • History and Geography Activity: Maya Trade	**Daily Bellringer Transparency:** Section 2* **Map Transparency:** Maya Civilization*
Section 3: **Maya Life and Society** **The Big Idea:** People played different roles in Maya society, but together they made great achievements in art, science, math, and writing. 7.7.2, 7.7.4, 7.7.5	**Universal Access Teacher Management System:*** Section 3 Lesson Plan **Interactive Reader and Study Guide:** Section 3 Summary* **Chapter Resource File*** • Vocabulary Builder Activity, Section 3 • Biography Activity: Ah Cacao • Biography Activity: Bishop Diego de Landa • Interdisciplinary Project: The Maya: Web It • Literature Activity: *Popol Vuh:* The Hero Twins • Primary Source Activity: Maya Ceramics of the Classic Age	**Daily Bellringer Transparency:** Section 3* **Internet Activity:** Adding the Maya Way

Review, Assessment, Intervention

- **Standards Review Workbook***
- **Quick Facts Transparency:** The Early Americas Visual Summary*
- **Spanish Chapter Summaries Audio CD Program**
- **Online Chapter Summaries in Six Languages**
- **Quiz Game CD-ROM**
- **Progress Assessment Support System (PASS):** Chapter Test*
- **Universal Access Modified Worksheets and Tests CD-ROM:** Modified Chapter Test
- **One-Stop Planner CD-ROM:** ExamView Test Generator (English/Spanish)
- **Alternative Assessment Handbook**
- **Holt Online Assessment Program (HOAP),** in the Holt Premier Online Student Edition

---

- **PASS:** Section 1 Quiz*
- **Online Quiz:** Section 1
- **Alternative Assessment Handbook**

- **PASS:** Section 2 Quiz*
- **Online Quiz:** Section 2
- **Alternative Assessment Handbook**

- **PASS:** Section 3 Quiz*
- **Online Quiz:** Section 3
- **Alternative Assessment Handbook**

California Resources for Standards Mastery

INSTRUCTIONAL PLANNING AND SUPPORT

- Universal Access Teacher Management System*
- One-Stop Planner CD-ROM with Test Generator: Teacher Management System with Interactive Teacher's Edition

STANDARDS MASTERY

- Standards Review Workbook*
- At Home: A Guide to Standards Mastery for World History

Holt Online Learning

To enhance learning, the following Internet activities are available: Discovering Olmec Culture and Adding the Maya Way.

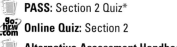 KEYWORD: SQ6 TEACHER

- Teacher Support Page
- Content Updates
- Rubrics and Writing Models
- Teaching Tips for the Multimedia Classroom

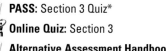 KEYWORD: SQ6 WH15

- Current Events
- Holt Grapher
- Holt Online Atlas
- Holt Researcher
- Interactive Multimedia Activities
- Internet Activities
- Online Chapter Summaries in Six Languages
- Online Section Quizzes
- World History Maps and Charts

HOLT PREMIER ONLINE STUDENT EDITION

Complete online support for interactivity, assessment, and reporting

- Interactive Maps and Notebook
- Standardized Test Prep
- Homework Practice and Research Activities Online

Mastering the Standards: Differentiating Instruction

Reaching Standards	Basic-level activities designed for all students encountering new material
Standards Proficiency	Intermediate-level activities designed for average students
Exceeding Standards	Challenging activities designed for honors and gifted-and-talented students
Standard English Mastery	Activities designed to improve standard English usage

THE EARLY AMERICAS **423b**

Frequently Asked Questions

INSTRUCTIONAL PLANNING AND SUPPORT

Where do I find planning aids, pacing guides, lesson plans, and other teaching aids?

Annotated Teacher's Edition:
- Chapter planning guides
- Standards-based instruction and strategies
- Differentiated instruction for universal access
- Point-of-use reminders for integrating program resources

Power Presentations with Video CD-ROM

Universal Access Teacher Management System:
- Year and unit instructional benchmarking guides
- Reproducible lesson plans
- Assessment guides for diagnostic, progress, and summative end-of-the-year tests
- Options for differentiating instruction and intervention
- Teaching guides and answer keys for student workbooks

One-Stop Planner CD-ROM with Test Generator: Teacher Management System with Interactive Teacher's Edition:
- Calendar Planner
- Editable lesson plans
- All reproducible ancillaries in Adobe Acrobat (PDF) format
- ExamView Test Generator (English & Spanish)
- Game Tool for ExamView
- PuzzlePro
- Transparency and video previews

DIFFERENTIATING INSTRUCTION FOR UNIVERSAL ACCESS

What resources are available to ensure that Advanced Learners/GATE Students master the standards?

Teacher's Edition Activities:
- Migration Theories Table, p. 430
- Maya Classic Age Recipe, p. 436
- Step Into the Picture, p. 437

Lesson Plans for Universal Access

Primary Source Library CD-ROM for World History

What resources are available to ensure that English Learners and Standard English Learners master the standards?

Teacher's Edition Activities:
- Hunter-Gatherer Cave Drawings, p. 430
- Use Visual Aids, p. 437
- Maya Achievements Mural, p. 442

Lesson Plans for Universal Access

Chapter Resource File: Vocabulary Builder Activities

Spanish Chapter Summaries Audio CD Program

Online Chapter Summaries in Six Languages

One-Stop Planner CD-ROM:
- PuzzlePro, Spanish Version
- ExamView Test Generator, Spanish Version

What modified materials are available for Special Education?

The *Universal Access Modified Worksheets and Tests CD-ROM* provides editable versions of the following:

Vocabulary Flash Cards

Modified Vocabulary Builder Activities

Modified Chapter Review Activity

Modified Chapter Test

What resources are available to ensure that Learners Having Difficulty master the standards?

Teacher's Edition Activities:
• Chart Characteristics, p. 437
• Maya Life and Society Graphic Organizer, p. 441

Interactive Reader and Study Guide

Student Edition on Audio CD Program

Quick Facts Transparency: The Early Americas Visual Summary

Standards Review Workbook

Social Studies Skills Activity: Accepting Social Responsibility

Interactive Skills Tutor CD-ROM

How do I intervene for students struggling to master the standards?

Interactive Reader and Study Guide

Quick Facts Transparency: The Early Americas Visual Summary

Standards Review Workbook

Social Studies Skills Activity: Accepting Social Responsibility

Interactive Skills Tutor CD-ROM

PROFESSIONAL DEVELOPMENT

HOLT
Professional
Development

What teacher training resources are available to help me grow professionally?

• In-service and staff development as part of your Holt Social Studies product purchase
• Quick Teacher Tutorial Lesson Presentation CD-ROM
• Intensive tuition-based Teacher Development Institute
• Convenient Holt Speaker Bureau face-to-face workshop options

• PRAXIS™ Test Prep (#0089) interactive Web-based content refreshers*
• *Ask A Professional Development Expert* at http://www.hrw.com/prodev/

* PRAXIS is a trademark of Educational Testing Service (ETS). This publication is not endorsed or approved by ETS.

Information Literacy Skills

To learn more about how History–Social Science instruction may be improved by the effective use of library media centers and information literacy skills, go to the Teacher's Resource Materials for Chapter 15 at **go.hrw.com, keyword: SQ6 MEDIA.**

Standards Focus

Standards by Section
Section 1: **HSS** 7.7.1
Section 2: **HSS** 7.7.1, 7.7.3
Section 3: **HSS** 7.7.2, 7.7.4, 7.7.5

Teacher Edition
HSS Analysis Skills: CS 1, CS 3, HR 3, HI 1, HI 2, HI 5

ELA Writing 7.2.5a

Upcoming Standards for Future Learning

Preview the following History–Social Science content standards from upcoming chapters or grade levels to promote learning beyond the current chapter.

HSS 7.11 Students analyze political and economic change in the sixteenth, seventeenth, and eighteenth centuries (the Age of Exploration, the Enlightenment, and the Age of Reason).

HSS 7.11.1 Know the great voyages of discovery, the locations of the routes, and the influence of cartography in the development of a new European worldview.

HSS 7.11.2 Discuss the exchanges of plants, animals, technology, culture, and ideas among Europe, Africa, Asia, and the Americas in the fifteenth and sixteenth centuries and the major economic and social effects on each continent.

Focus on Writing

The **Chapter Resource File** provides a Focus on Writing worksheet to help students organize and write their travel brochures.

CRF: Focus on Writing Activity: A Travel Brochure

CHAPTER 15   12,000 BC–AD 1000

The Early Americas

California Standards

History–Social Science

7.7 Students compare and contrast the geographic, political, economic, religious, and social structures of the Meso-American and Andean civilizations.

Analysis Skill

HR 3 Distinguish relevant from irrelevant, essential from incidental, and verifiable from unverifiable information.

English–Language Arts

Writing 7.1.2 Support all statements and claims with anecdotes, descriptions, facts and statistics, and specific examples.

Reading 7.2.6 Assess the adequacy, accuracy, and appropriateness of the author's evidence.

FOCUS ON WRITING

A Travel Brochure Each year, millions of people visit the places you'll read about in this chapter. Try your hand at writing part of a brochure for a historical tour of the early Americas. As you read, you'll discover spots you won't want to miss.

CHAPTER EVENTS

WORLD EVENTS

12,000 BC

c. 12,000–10,000 BC
The first people arrive in the Americas.

c. 5000 BC
Irrigation is used in Mesopotamia and Egypt.

424   CHAPTER 15

Introduce the Chapter

Standards Proficiency

Lost Cities in the Jungle

1. Ask students to imagine that they are on an archaeological expedition in the jungles of Central America. They hack their way through the growth and, suddenly, there before them is a large, elaborately carved stone. Beyond are other ruins of an ancient lost city.

2. Have students discuss what they might feel at the sight of the ancient ruins. Encourage discussion.

3. Then ask students what they and other scientists might do to find out more about the people who lived in this ancient city. What questions might they ask? What objects might they study?

4. Explain to students that in this chapter they will be learning about the first people who came to the Americas and some of the early civilizations that developed.
   LS Intrapersonal, Verbal/Linguistic

What You Will Learn...

In this chapter you will learn about the development of civilization in the Americas. This photo shows the ruins of a great Maya temple in Tikal, Guatemala. More than 1,500 years ago the Maya built large cities in their American homeland.

c. 3500 BC Maize is domesticated in Mesoamerica.

c. 1200 BC The Olmec civilization begins in Mesoamerica.

c. AD 200 The Maya begin building large cities in the Americas.

c. AD 900 The Maya Classic Age ends.

3000 BC | 2000 BC | 1000 BC | BC 1 AD | AD 1000

c. 3000 BC Egyptians begin to write using hieroglyphics.

c. 500 BC Athens develops the world's first democracy.

AD 476 The Roman Empire falls.

THE EARLY AMERICAS **425**

Explore the Time Line

1. Did the Olmec or the Maya civilization develop first in Mesoamerica? *Olmec*

2. About how long after people migrated to the Americas did they begin growing maize? *c. 8,500 to 6,500 years*

3. What empire declined not too long before the Maya Classic Age ended? *Roman Empire*

🐻 **HSS** Analysis Skills: CS 1

Info to Know

Tikal The Maya city of Tikal is located in what is now northern Guatemala. At its peak, the city covered an area of about 75 square miles (120 km²) and was home to some 60,000 people. Some 30,000 more people may have lived in the surrounding areas. In the Itzá Maya language, *Tikal* means "Place of Voices."

Perhaps the first European to see Tikal was a Spanish friar, Andres de Avendaño, in 1696. He wrote about passing through an impressive ancient city full of buildings and houses.

● **Chapter Preview** ●

HOLT
History's Impact
▶ video series
See the Video Teacher's Guide for strategies for using the chapter video **The Early Civilizations of the Americas: The Impact of Mayan Achievements on Math and Astronomy**.

Chapter Big Ideas

Section 1 The landforms and climate of the Americas affected farming and the development of early cultures. **HSS** 7.7.1

Section 2 Maya civilization was characterized by great cities, trade, and warfare, but it disappeared for reasons that are still unclear. **HSS** 7.7.1, 7.7.3

Section 3 People played different roles in Maya society, but together they made great achievements in art, science, math, and writing. **HSS** 7.7.2, 7.7.4, 7.7.5

Explore the Picture

Maya Temples Maya kings went to a temple, such as the one in Tikal pictured at left, to communicate with the gods. The king would cut himself to shed blood. He then went into a trance, or dreamlike state. As smoke from incense rose and coiled around the king, the Maya believed he formed a path between the earth and the world of the gods.

Analyzing Visuals What can you predict about the Maya people, based on the temple shown here? *possible answers—They had the skill to build great structures, and they likely had an advanced civilization and religion.*

go.hrw.com
Online Resources

Chapter Resources:
KEYWORD: SQ6 WH15
Teacher Resources:
KEYWORD: SQ6 TEACHER

Reading Social Studies
by Kylene Beers

| Economics | Geography | Politics | Religion | Society and Culture | Science and Technology |

Reading Social Studies

Understanding Themes

Introduce the key themes of this chapter to the class by asking them what they know about the geography of Central and South America. Responses might include that it is isolated and has tropical jungles. Point out to students that the geography of Mesoamerica had a great effect on the way of life that developed there. Ask students to predict how geography affected life there. Then lead a discussion of how the people of Mesoamerica might have developed science and technology in response to their lifestyle.

Analyzing Historical Information

Focus on Reading Explain to students that sometimes writers include details and descriptions that add interest but are not completely necessary to understand the main idea. Have students examine a magazine article or primary source document. Ask students to look for a paragraph that includes information that is incidental or irrelevant to the main idea or purpose. Ask each student to re-write the paragraph without the incidental information.

Focus on Themes In this chapter, you will read about the development of civilizations in Mesoamerica, which is in the southern part of North America, and in the Andes, which is in South America. As you read about the Olmec and Maya in Mesoamerica and Chavín in South America, you will see how the **geography** of the areas affected their way of life. You will learn that these ancient civilizations made interesting advancements in **science and technology**.

Analyzing Historical Information

Focus on Reading History books are full of information. As you read, you are confronted with names, dates, places, terms, and descriptions on every page. Because you're faced with so much information, you don't want to have to deal with unimportant or untrue material in a history book.

Identifying Relevant and Essential Information Information in a history book should be relevant, or related to the topic you're studying. It should also be essential, or necessary, to understanding that topic. Anything that is not relevant or essential distracts from the important material you are studying.

The passage below comes from an encyclopedia, but some irrelevant and nonessential information has been added so that you can learn to identify it.

The Maya

The first sentence of the paragraph expresses the main idea. Anything that does not support this idea is nonessential.

Who They Were Maya were an American Indian people who developed a magnificent civilization in Mesoamerica, which is the southern part of North America. They built their largest cities between AD 250 and 900. Today, many people travel to Central America to see Maya ruins.

The last sentence does not support the main idea and is nonessential.

This paragraph discusses Maya communication. Any other topics are irrelevant.

Communication The Maya developed an advanced form of writing that used many symbols. Our writing system uses 26 letters. They recorded information on large stone monuments. Some early civilizations drew pictures on cave walls. The Maya also made books of paper made from the fig tree bark. Fig trees need a lot of light.

The needs of fig trees have nothing to do with Maya communication. This sentence is irrelevant.

Portions of this text and the one on the next page were taken from the 2004 World Book Online Reference Center.

Additional reading support can be found in the

Inter_active Reader and Study Guide

Reading and Skills Resources

Reading Support

📖 Interactive Reader and Study Guide

🔊 Student Edition on Audio CD

🔊 Spanish Chapter Summaries Audio CD Program

Social Studies Skills Support

💿 Interactive Skills Tutor CD-ROM

Vocabulary Support

📄 **CRF:** Vocabulary Builder Activities

📄 **CRF:** Chapter Review Activity

💿 Universal Access Modified Worksheets and Tests CD-ROM:
  - Vocabulary Flash Cards
  - Vocabulary Builder Activity
  - Chapter Review Activity

OSP Holt PuzzlePro

🐻 Standards Focus

HSS Analysis Skills: HR 3
ELA Reading 7.2.6

HSS Analysis HR 3 Distinguish relevant from irrelevant information.
ELA 7.2.6 Assess the adequacy, accuracy, and appropriateness of the author's evidence.

You Try It!

The following passage has some sentences that aren't important, necessary, or relevant. Read the passage and identify those sentences.

The Maya Way of Life

Religion The Maya believed in many gods and goddesses. More than 160 gods and goddesses are named in a single Maya manuscript. Among the gods they worshipped were a corn god, a rain god, a sun god, and a moon goddess. The early Greeks also worshipped many gods and goddesses.

Family and Social Structure Whole families of Maya—including parents, children, and grandparents—lived together. Not many houses today could hold all those people. Each family member had tasks to do. Men and boys, for example, worked in the fields. Very few people are farmers today. Women and older girls made clothes and meals for the rest of the family. Now most people buy their clothes.

After you read the passage, answer the following questions.

1. Which sentence in the first paragraph is irrelevant to the topic? How can you tell?

2. Which three sentences in the second paragraph are not essential to learning about the Maya? Do those sentences belong in this passage?

Key Terms and People

Chapter 15

Section 1
Mesoamerica (p. 428)
maize (p. 431)

Section 2
obsidian (p. 434)
Pacal (p. 436)

Section 3
observatories (p. 442)
Popol Vuh (p. 443)

Academic Vocabulary

Success in school is related to knowing academic vocabulary—the words that are frequently used in school assignments and discussions. In this chapter, you will learn the following academic words:

rebel (p. 438)
aspects (p. 441)

As you read **Chapter 15**, notice how the writers have left out information that is not essential or relevant to what you are reading.

Reading Social Studies

Key Terms and People

Preteach the key terms and people from this chapter by first reviewing each term with the class. Then have students use the page numbers listed to locate each term or person in the chapter. Have each student write the word and the definition as it appears in the text on their own sheet of paper. Then have each student write a paragraph in which they use each key term or person. Remind students to use each term correctly.
LS Verbal/Linguistic

Focus on Reading

See the **Focus on Reading** questions in this chapter for more practice on this reading social studies skill.

Reading Social Studies Assessment

See the **Standards Review** at the end of this chapter for student assessment questions related to this reading skill.

Teaching Tip

Remind students that the easiest way to identify irrelevant and incidental information is to first identify the main idea of the paragraph. The main idea will be supported by specific facts and details. However, there will often be incidental details as well. Have students identify which details specifically support the main idea and which are not important to the main idea. Those that do not support the main idea are considered irrelevant or non-essential information.

Answers

You Try It! 1. *the last sentence; it discusses the Greeks rather than the Maya.* **2.** *the second, fifth, and last sentences; no, because they discuss modern-day examples*

427

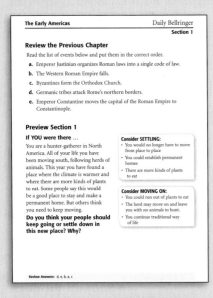
Building Vocabulary

Preteach or review the following terms:

domesticate to change plants or animals to make them more useful to humans (p. 432)

hunter-gatherers People who hunt animals and gather wild plants, seeds, fruits, and nuts to survive (p. 430)

irrigate to supply water to an area of land (p. 432)

land bridge strip of land connecting two continents (p. 430)

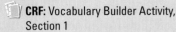 **CRF:** Vocabulary Builder Activity, Section 1

Standards Focus

HSS 7.7.1

Means: Describe the geography of Mexico, Central America, and South America and its effect on early peoples in the Americas.

Matters: The geography of the Americas played an important role in the development of early societies there and continues to do so today.

Geography and Early Cultures

What You Will Learn...

Main Ideas

1. The geography of the Americas is varied with a wide range of landforms.
2. The first people to arrive in the Americas were hunter-gatherers.
3. The development of farming led to early settlements in the Americas.

The Big Idea

The landforms and climate of the Americas affected farming and the development of early cultures.

Key Terms

Mesoamerica, *p. 428*
maize, *p. 431*

 HSS **7.7.1** Study the locations, landforms, and climates of Mexico, Central America, and South America and their effects on Mayan, Aztec, and Incan economies, trade, and development of urban societies.

If YOU were there...

You are a hunter-gatherer in North America. All of your life you have been moving south, following herds of animals. This year you have found a place where the climate is warmer and there are more kinds of plants to eat. Some people say this would be a good place to stay and make a permanent home. But others think you need to keep moving.

Do you think your people should keep going or settle down in this new place? Why?

BUILDING BACKGROUND The first people to arrive in the Americas were hunter-gatherers. Their ability to find food greatly depended on the geography of this new land.

Geography of the Americas

Two continents—North America and South America—make up the region we call the Americas. These two continents have a wide range of landforms and climates.

The northern continent, North America, has high mountains, desert plateaus, grassy plains, and forests. Look at the map to find the location of some of these physical features. In the northern part of the continent, the climate is cold and icy. Temperatures get warmer toward the south.

In the southern part of North America lies Mesoamerica. **Mesoamerica** is a region that includes the southern part of what is now Mexico and parts of the northern countries of Central America. Steamy rain forests cover some of this region. In some places, volcanoes rise above the forest. Their activity over the years has made the surrounding soil very fertile. Fertile mountain valleys, rivers, and a warm climate make Mesoamerica good for farming. In fact, the first farmers in the Americas domesticated plants in Mesoamerica.

Teach the Big Idea: Master the Standards
                             Standards Proficiency

Geography and Early Cultures 🐻 **HSS** 7.7.1; **HSS** Analysis Skills: HR 3, HI 1

1. **Teach** Ask students the Main Idea questions to teach this section.

2. **Apply** Have students turn a piece of paper sideways and fold it vertically into thirds to create a trifold. Have students label the trifold sections *Geography of the Americas, First People Arrive,* and *Farming and Settlement.* As students read the section, have them list the main ideas for each topic in the trifold. **LS Verbal/Linguistic**

3. **Review** As you review the section, have students share the main ideas that they listed in their trifolds.

4. **Practice/Homework** Have students create a series of cave drawings illustrating the main ideas that they listed on their trifolds. **LS Visual/Spatial**

📎 Alternative Assessment Handbook, Rubrics 3: Artwork; and 13: Graphic Organizers

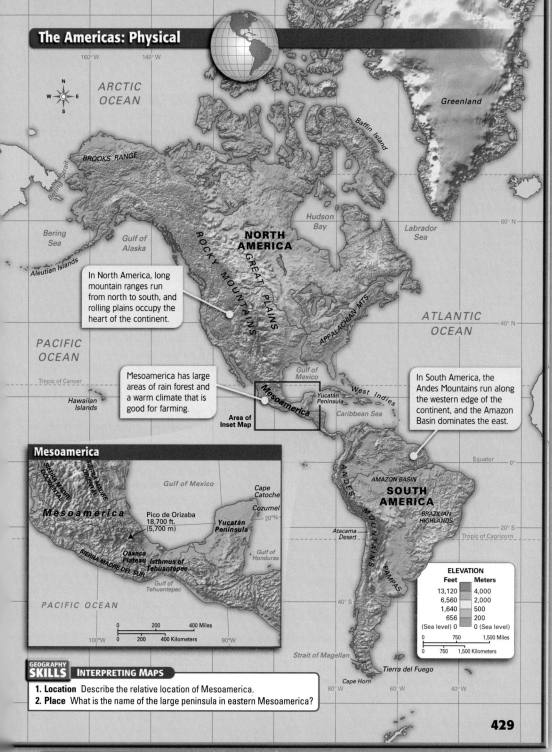

The Americas: Physical

ARCTIC OCEAN

Greenland

Baffin Island

BROOKS RANGE

Bering Strait

Bering Sea

Gulf of Alaska

Aleutian Islands

Hudson Bay

Labrador Sea

NORTH AMERICA

ROCKY MOUNTAINS

GREAT PLAINS

APPALACHIAN MTS.

60° N

In North America, long mountain ranges run from north to south, and rolling plains occupy the heart of the continent.

PACIFIC OCEAN

Tropic of Cancer

Hawaiian Islands

40° N

ATLANTIC OCEAN

Gulf of Mexico

Mesoamerica has large areas of rain forest and a warm climate that is good for farming.

Mesoamerica

Yucatán Peninsula

West Indies

Caribbean Sea

Area of Inset Map

In South America, the Andes Mountains run along the western edge of the continent, and the Amazon Basin dominates the east.

Equator 0°

AMAZON BASIN

SOUTH AMERICA

ANDES MOUNTAINS

BRAZILIAN HIGHLANDS

20° S

Atacama Desert

Tropic of Capricorn

PAMPAS

40° S

Strait of Magellan

Tierra del Fuego

Cape Horn

80° W   60° W   40° W

Mesoamerica

SIERRA MADRE OCCIDENTAL

SIERRA MADRE ORIENTAL

Gulf of Mexico

Cape Catoche

Cozumel

Mesoamerica

Pico de Orizaba 18,700 ft. (5,700 m)

Yucatán Peninsula

20°N

SIERRA MADRE DEL SUR

Oaxaca Plateau

Isthmus of Tehuantepec

Gulf of Honduras

Gulf of Tehuantepec

PACIFIC OCEAN

0   200   400 Miles
0   200   400 Kilometers

100°W   90°W

ELEVATION

Feet		Meters
13,120		4,000
6,560		2,000
1,640		500
656		200
(Sea level) 0		0 (Sea level)

0   750   1,500 Miles
0   750   1,500 Kilometers

GEOGRAPHY SKILLS   INTERPRETING MAPS

1. **Location** Describe the relative location of Mesoamerica.
2. **Place** What is the name of the large peninsula in eastern Mesoamerica?

429

Cross-Discipline Activity: Geography

Standards Proficiency

Geography of Early Migration to the Americas   HSS 7.7.1; HSS Analysis Skills: CS 3, HI 1

1. Ask students to describe the landforms and climate of their area. List the information for students to see.

2. Have students discuss how the local geography affects life in their community. Encourage students to consider the history of their community as well as the present.

3. Have students examine the maps above and on the next page. In the Migration to the

Americas map, point out the routes early people took.

4. Have students discuss the following question: *How do you think geography shaped the migration routes of the first people to the Americas?* **LS** Visual/Spatial

Alternative Assessment Handbook, Rubric 21: Map Reading

Map Transparencies: The Americas: Physical; Migration to the Americas

❷ The First People Arrive

The first people to arrive in the Americas were hunter-gatherers.

Explain What part do most scientists think climate change played in early migration to the Americas? *An ice age lowered ocean levels, exposing a land bridge to the Americas.*

Make Generalizations In what ways is migration today similar to early migration to the Americas? *People migrate for some similar reasons, such as to escape shortages or to find a better place to live.*

Map Transparency: Migration to the Americas

HSS 7.7.1; **HSS** Analysis Skills: HI 1, HI 2, HI 3

Linking to Today

New Theories on Migration to the Americas Scientists have determined that Monte Verde, an archaeological site in Chile, is at least 12,500 years old. Another part of the site may be more than 30,000 years old. Monte Verde is located some 10,000 miles south of the Bering Strait. As a result, some scientists think the first Americans may have come from Asia by boat and sailed south along the coast.

Answers

Interpreting Maps 1. *Asia;* **2.** *west*

Reading Check (top) *Both have mountains, deserts, and forests.*

Reading Check (bottom) *determined the types of plants and animals available for food*

Like North America, South America has many different kinds of landforms. The towering Andes Mountains run along the western shore of the continent. There, a narrow desert sits on the edge of rich fishing waters in the Pacific Ocean. East of the Andes lies the Amazon region—a huge, hot, and wet rain forest. The mighty Amazon River drains this region. As you will see, the geography of the Americas played an important role in the development of early societies there.

READING CHECK **Comparing** What kinds of landforms and climates do North and South America have in common?

The First People Arrive

No one is sure how the first people got to the Americas or when they arrived. Most historians think they came to North America from Asia by 12,000 BC. They probably walked across a land bridge that crossed the Bering Strait. A land bridge may have formed there during the ice ages when ocean levels dropped and exposed land.

Most scientists accept the theory of the land bridge to explain how the first people came to the Americas. But some scientists today are challenging that theory. They think the first Americans may have arrived even earlier—perhaps by sea.

Regardless of how they arrived, the first people to arrive in the Americas were hunter-gatherers. They hunted herds of large animals that wandered the land. These animals, including bison and huge woolly mammoths, provided their main food source. Early people also gathered fruits, nuts, and wild grains to eat. Early people didn't settle in one place very long, because they were always looking for food.

Eventually, some early people began to settle down. They formed small settlements on the coasts of North and South America, where they fished and gathered food. As populations grew, people started to experiment with seeds.

READING CHECK **Drawing Inferences** How do you think the geography of the Americas affected early peoples' search for food?

Migration to the Americas

ASIA

ARCTIC OCEAN

BERINGIA · Bering Strait

NORTH AMERICA

ATLANTIC OCEAN

Gulf of Mexico

PACIFIC OCEAN

SOUTH AMERICA

— Possible land route
— Possible sea route
▨ Glacier
▨ Sea ice

0   750   1,500 Miles
0   750   1,500 Kilometers

GEOGRAPHY SKILLS **INTERPRETING MAPS**

1. **Place** According to the map, from which continent did the first Americans come?
2. **Movement** The coastal route runs along which American coast—east or west?

430 CHAPTER 15

Differentiating Instruction for Universal Access

English-Language Learners

Standards Proficiency

1. Ask students to imagine that they are hunter-gatherers who have migrated to the Americas.
2. Have each student create a series of four to five cave drawings illustrating things he or she might have seen and done during the journey.

LS Visual/Spatial

HSS Analysis Skills: HI 1

Alternative Assessment Handbook, Rubric 3: Artwork

Advanced Learners/GATE

Exceeding Standards

Research Required

1. Have students conduct research on theories about how the first people came to the Americas.
2. Tell students to create a table briefly describing the main theories and the support for each one.
3. Then have students discuss how interpretations of history can change.

LS Verbal/Linguistic, Visual/Spatial

HSS Analysis Skills: HI 1, HI 5

Alternative Assessment Handbook, Rubric 30: Research

Farming and Settlement

From their experiments with seeds, people eventually learned to farm. Farming allowed people to stop following animal herds and settle permanently in one place.

First Farming Settlements

The first permanent farming settlements in the Americas appeared in Mesoamerica. This region had rich soils, warm temperatures, and plenty of rain. By 3500 BC people in Mesoamerica were growing **maize** (MAYZ), or corn. Later they learned to grow beans and squash. By growing these foods, settlements could support larger populations. More advanced societies grew, and people began to focus on activities such as building, trade, art, and organized religion. Eventually, settlements developed into towns and cities.

The Olmec

The Olmec (OHL-mek) formed the first urban civilization in Mesoamerica around 1200 BC. Most Olmec lived in small villages, but some lived in larger towns. These towns were religious and government centers with temples and plazas. Impressive sculptures and buildings mark the Olmec as the first complex civilization in the Americas. They built the first pyramids in the Americas. They also made sculptures of huge stone heads. Each head probably represented a different Olmec ruler. Other sculptures, such as jaguars, probably represented Olmec gods.

Other factors that may mark the Olmec as a complex civilization are writing and scientific study. Some researchers think the Olmec may have developed the first writing system in the Americas. Scientists recently found an Olmec artifact with symbols that might be an early form of writing. The Olmec may have also had a calendar.

Maize
A man sits on a stack of maize, or corn, in Mexico City. In the early Americas, maize was most widely grown among large urban populations.

Why do you think large urban populations grew maize?

The Olmec civilization also had a large trading network. Villages traded with each other and with other peoples farther away. The Olmec may have even established a string of trading colonies along the Pacific coast. Through trade the Olmec got valuable goods such as the stones they used for building and sculpture.

Olmec civilization ended around 400 BC. By then trade had spread Olmec influence around Mesoamerica. Later peoples were able to build on their achievements. Some later peoples in Mesoamerica also followed some Olmec traditions.

Direct Teach

Main Idea

❸ Farming and Settlement

The development of farming led to early settlements in the Americas.

Recall Where and when did farming first develop in the Americas? *in Mesoamerica about 3500 BC*

Identify Effects How did farming affect life in the Americas? *See the cause-and-effect chart in the activity on the bottom of this page.*

Evaluate Why are the Olmec important in the history of the Americas? *influenced later groups throughout Mesoamerica, who then built on Olmec achievements*

HSS 7.7.1; HSS Analysis Skills: HI 1, HI 2

Did you know . . .
The Olmec society has been called the mother culture because it highly influenced most later civilizations in Mesoamerica.

go.hrw.com
Online Resources
KEYWORD: SQ6 WH15
ACTIVITY: Discovering Olmec Culture

Critical Thinking: Understanding Cause and Effect | Standards Proficiency

Agriculture in the Americas HSS 7.7.1; HSS Analysis Skills: HI 1, HI 2, HI 3

1. To help students explain the causes and effects of the development of agriculture in the Americas, draw the chart here for students to see. Omit the blue, italicized answers.

2. Have students copy the chart and refer to the text under the heading "Farming and Settlement" to complete it. **LS Visual/Spatial**

Alternative Assessment Handbook, Rubric 13: Graphic Organizers

CAUSE
People in the Americas tried planting seeds.

↓

Development of Agriculture in the Americas
Where: *Mesoamerica* **When:** *about 3500 BC*
Why: *rich soils, warm temperature, plenty of rain*
What: *maize, beans, squash*

↓

EFFECTS
• *enabled people to settle in one place*
• *led to steady food supply; population growth*
• *led to more advanced societies; towns and cities*
• *enabled people to focus on activities such as building, trade, art, and organized religion*

Answers

Maize *By growing maize, settlements could support larger populations.*

431

❸ Farming and Settlement

The development of farming led to early settlements in the Americas.

Recall Where did farming first develop in South America, and what crop did people grow? *in the Andes Mountains; potatoes*

Summarize How did early people in the southwestern United States adapt farming to the region? *learned to choose fertile soils and use river water for irrigation to grow crops in the dry climate*

⬛ Map Transparency: Early Civilizations in the Americas

🐻 **HSS** 7.7.1; **HSS** Analysis Skills: HI 1

Primary Source

Views of Writing

Discussing Points of View Have students discuss which point of view in the feature at right they agree with and why. Use the discussion to help students understand why experts may disagree about some interpretations of history.

🐻 **HSS** 7.7.1; **HSS** Analysis Skills: HR 5, HI 1

Answers

Analyzing Points of View *because people disagree about whether written language is written communication or visual symbols representing oral communication*

Focus on Reading *states the theme of the topic discussed in this part of the text; no*

432

POINTS OF VIEW
Views of Writing

Scientists have discovered an Olmec roller used for printing symbols. It may be evidence of the earliest writing system in the Americas. Some people don't believe the Olmec had a written language. Scientists disagree on what defines a written language. Some scientists think written language must include symbols that stand for sounds—not just for images.

❝Even if you have symbols—like a light bulb in a cartoon—that's not writing.❞

—David Grove,
Professor Emeritus of Anthropology,
University of Illinois Urbana–Champaign

Other scientists think a system of symbols is a form of written communication. The symbols do not have to represent sound or spoken language. These scientists think written communication is the same thing as written language.

❝We're not arguing that we have phonetics (sounds). But we say we do have logographs (symbols representing words), and we're arguing the Maya copied this. We have a system here that goes back to the Olmec.❞

—Mary E. D. Pohl,
Professor of Anthropology, Florida State University

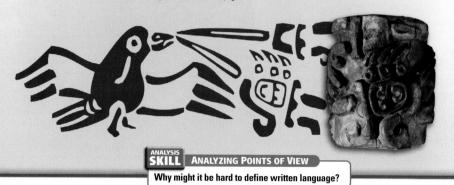

ANALYSIS SKILL **ANALYZING POINTS OF VIEW**
Why might it be hard to define written language?

Farming and the Growth of Other Civilizations

Early civilizations also developed in other parts of the Americas. As in Mesoamerica, people in North and South America formed civilizations after they domesticated plants and learned how to farm.

FOCUS ON READING
What is the purpose of this paragraph? Are any sentences irrelevant?

About the time Mesoamericans started growing maize, South Americans in the Andes started growing potatoes. Later, maize farming spread south into the Andes from Mesoamerica. By about 2000 BC, South Americans were growing maize and beans as well as potatoes.

A number of small civilizations developed in South America, but the first major civilization began in the Andes. It is known as the Chavín (chah-VEEN) culture, and it lasted from about 900 to 200 BC. Its city was a major religious and trading center. The Chavín culture is known for its woven textiles, carved stone monuments, and pottery shaped like animals and humans.

Several hundred years after farming began in South America, maize farming also spread north from Mesoamerica. People began growing maize in what is now the southwestern United States. The dry climate made farming difficult there, so people learned to choose fertile soils and use river water to irrigate their crops. Eventually maize became an important crop to people in the region. It was the main food of people in hundreds of small villages.

Collaborative Learning
Standards Proficiency

Farming in the Americas Map 🐻 **HSS** 7.7.1; **HSS** Analysis Skills: CS 1, CS 3, HI 1

Materials: butcher paper, colored markers, blank outline map of the Americas (optional)

1. Organize students into small groups. Give each group a piece of butcher paper and a set of colored markers. If available, display a blank outline map of the Americas for students to see.

2. Have each group create a map of the Americas showing the spread of farming from Mesoamerica to the Andes, in South America, and then north to what is now the southwestern United States.

3. In addition, have students include on their maps the locations of the Olmec and Chavín cultures. Then have students illustrate their maps with symbols that represent aspects of each culture and the crops grown in each area.

LS Interpersonal, Visual/Spatial

📝 Alternative Assessment Handbook, Rubric 20: Map Creation

This Native American legend reveals the importance of maize, or corn:

"The breaths of the corn maidens blew rain-clouds from their homes in the Summer-land, and when the rains had passed away green corn plants grew everywhere the grains had been planted."

—Zuni legend, quoted in *Kingdoms of Gold, Kingdoms of Jade* by Brian Fagan

The development of farming was important in the growth of civilizations all over the Americas. As with other peoples you have studied, a steady food supply led to population growth. Farming also encouraged people to establish permanent villages and cities.

READING CHECK **Finding Main Ideas** How did farming influence settlement patterns in the Americas?

SUMMARY AND PREVIEW You have learned that geography affected settlement and farming in the Americas. Early civilizations, such as the Olmec and Chavín, developed there. In Section 2 you will learn about a later civilization influenced by the Olmec—the Maya.

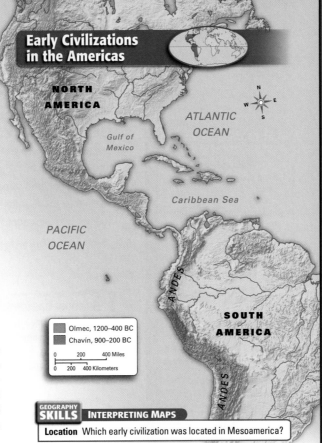

Early Civilizations in the Americas

NORTH AMERICA

ATLANTIC OCEAN

Gulf of Mexico

Caribbean Sea

PACIFIC OCEAN

SOUTH AMERICA

ANDES

Olmec, 1200–400 BC
Chavín, 900–200 BC

0   200   400 Miles
0   200   400 Kilometers

GEOGRAPHY SKILLS **INTERPRETING MAPS**

Location Which early civilization was located in Mesoamerica?

Section 1 Assessment

go.hrw.com
Online Quiz
KEYWORD: SQ6 HP15

Reviewing Ideas, Terms, and People **HSS** 7.7.1

1. **a. Recall** Where is **Mesoamerica**?
   b. Explain In what ways is the geography of Mesoamerica good for agriculture?
2. **a. Identify** What landform do most scientists think the first people crossed to reach America?
   b. Make Inferences Why do you think scientists aren't sure how the first people came to the Americas?
3. **a. Identify** What was the first crop domesticated in Mesoamerica?
   b. Predict How might the Olmec civilization have influenced later civilizations in Mesoamerica?

Critical Thinking

4. **Sequencing** Draw the graphic organizer below. Use it to show how the development of maize farming laid the foundation for cultural advances.

Maize Farming → ☐ → ☐ → ☐

FOCUS ON WRITING

5. **Taking Notes about Early Settlements in the Americas** Note where people first settled in the Americas. What sites would show how early hunter-gatherers and farmers lived? What geographical features are important to mention?

THE EARLY AMERICAS **433**

Section 1 Assessment Answers

1. **a.** southern part of what is now Mexico and the northern part of Central America
   b. rich soils, warm temperatures, plenty of rain
2. **a.** a land bridge across the Bering Strait
   b. because the events took place long ago, and scientists have only a few artifacts and findings upon which to base their ideas
3. **a.** maize
   b. Through trade, Olmec ideas about architecture, art, science, and religion probably spread and influenced later groups.

4. second box—Maize farming enabled people to settle in one place and promoted population growth; third box—People could focus on activities other than finding food, such as building, trade, and art; fourth box—Settlements developed into towns and cities.

5. first settled—along the coasts of North and South America and in parts of Central America; sites—caves and coastal and river regions; Olmec and Chavín sites; features—rivers, caves, areas where land provided access to game or fertile soil

---

Answers

Interpreting Maps *Olmec*
Reading Check *Farming enabled people to stop following animal herds and to settle in one place.*

433

434 CHAPTER 15

Preteach

Bellringer

If YOU were there . . . Use the **Daily Bellringer Transparency** to help students answer the question.

🖰 Daily Bellringer Transparency, Section 2

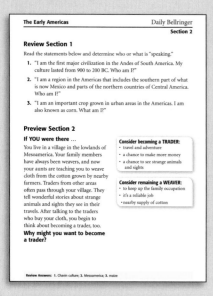

The Early Americas   Daily Bellringer
                                          Section 2

Review Section 1

Read the statements below and determine who or what is "speaking."

1. "I am the first major civilization in the Andes of South America. My culture lasted from 900 to 200 BC. Who am I?"

2. "I am a region in the Americas that includes the southern part of what is now Mexico and parts of the northern countries of Central America. Who am I?"

3. "I am an important crop grown in urban areas in the Americas. I am also known as corn. What am I?"

Preview Section 2

If YOU were there ...

You live in a village in the lowlands of Mesoamerica. Your family members have always been weavers, and now your aunts are teaching you to weave cloth from the cotton grown by nearby farmers. Traders from other areas often pass through your village. They tell wonderful stories about strange animals and sights they see in their travels. After talking to the traders who buy your cloth, you begin to think about becoming a trader, too.

Why might you want to become a trader?

Consider becoming a TRADER:
• travel and adventure
• a chance to make more money
• a chance to see strange animals and sights

Consider remaining a WEAVER:
• to keep up the family occupation
• it's a reliable job
• nearby supply of cotton

Review Answers: 1. Chavin culture; **2.** Mesoamerica; **3.** maize

Academic Vocabulary

Review with students the high-use academic term in this section.

rebel to fight against authority (p. 438)

📝 **CRF:** Vocabulary Builder Activity, Section 2

🐻 Standards Focus

HSS 7.7.1

Means: Describe the geography of Mexico, Central America, and South America and its effect on the Maya civilization.

Matters: The geography of Mesoamerica played an important role in the development of the Maya civilization and continues to do so today.

HSS 7.7.3

Means: Explain how and where the Maya civilization arose.

Matters: Many Maya still live in villages throughout Mesoamerica.

The Maya

What You Will Learn...

Main Ideas

1. Geography affected early Maya civilization.
2. The Maya Classic Age was characterized by great cities, trade, and warfare.
3. Maya civilization declined, and historians have several theories as to why.

The Big Idea

Maya civilization was characterized by great cities, trade, and warfare, but it disappeared for reasons that are still unclear.

Key Terms and People

obsidian, p. 434
Pacal, p. 436

HSS 7.7.1 Study the locations, landforms, and climates of Mexico, Central America, and South America and their effects on Mayan, Aztec, and Incan economies, trade, and development of urban societies.

7.7.3 Explain how and where each empire arose and how the Aztec and Incan empires were defeated by the Spanish.

If YOU were there...

You live in a village in the lowlands of Mesoamerica. Your family members have always been weavers, and now your aunts are teaching you to weave cloth from the cotton grown by nearby farmers. Traders from other areas often pass through your village. They tell wonderful stories about strange animals and sights they see in their travels. After talking to the traders who buy your cloth, you begin to think about becoming a trader, too.

Why might you want to become a trader?

BUILDING BACKGROUND Through trade, people get resources unavailable in their own natural environment. The natural environment, or geography, of Mesoamerica affected how a people called the Maya lived.

Geography Affects Early Maya

The Maya (MY-uh) civilization developed in Mesoamerica. Early Maya lived in the lowlands of this region beginning around 1000 BC. Thick forests covered most of the land, so the Maya had to clear wooded areas for farmland. Like earlier Mesoamericans, the Maya grew maize and other crops.

Although the thick forests made farming hard, they provided valuable resources. Forest animals such as deer and monkeys were a source of food. In addition, trees and other plants made good building materials. For example, the Maya used wood poles and vines, along with mud, to build their houses.

The early Maya lived in small villages. Eventually these villages started trading with one another. They traded goods such as cloth and **obsidian**, a sharp, glasslike volcanic rock, that came from different parts of Mesoamerica. As trade helped support larger populations, villages grew. By about AD 200 the Maya were building large cities in the Americas.

READING CHECK Finding Main Ideas What were two ways in which the early Maya relied on their physical environment?

Teach the Big Idea: Master the Standards   Standards Proficiency

The Maya 🐻 **HSS** 7.7.1, 7.7.3; **HSS** Analysis Skills: HR 3, HI 1

Materials: colored paper, colored markers, scissors, string, tape

1. **Teach** Ask students the Main Idea questions to teach this section.

2. **Apply** Have students create Maya mobiles. The parts of the mobile should illustrate aspects of the Maya civilization and Classic Age. For example, students might include a map of the main Maya cities and trade routes. Provide students with instructions and materials for creating their mobiles.
   LS Kinesthetic, Visual/Spatial

Prep Required

3. **Review** As you review the section, have students share how they represented different aspects of Maya civilization in their mobiles.

4. **Practice/Homework** Have each student write a fictional obituary for the "death" of the Maya civilization. Encourage students to look at some real obituaries for models.
   LS Verbal/Linguistic

   📝 Alternative Assessment Handbook, Rubrics 3: Artwork; and 37: Writing Assignments

Maya Classic Age

The Maya civilization reached its height between about AD 250 and 900. Historians call this period of Maya history the Classic Age. During the Classic Age, Maya civilization spread to the Yucatán Peninsula and grew to include more than 40 cities of 5,000 to 50,000 people each.

Trade

Maya cities in the highlands traded with those in the lowlands. In this way people all over Maya territory got things that they didn't have nearby.

Look at the trade routes on the map to see the goods that were available in different areas of Mesoamerica. For example, the warm lowlands were good for growing cotton, rubber trees, and cacao (kuh-KOW) beans, the source of chocolate. Cacao beans had great value. Chocolate was known as the food of rulers and of the gods. The Maya even used cacao beans as money.

Lowland crops didn't grow well in the cool highlands. Instead, the highlands had valuable stones such as jade and obsidian. People carried these and other products along Maya trade routes.

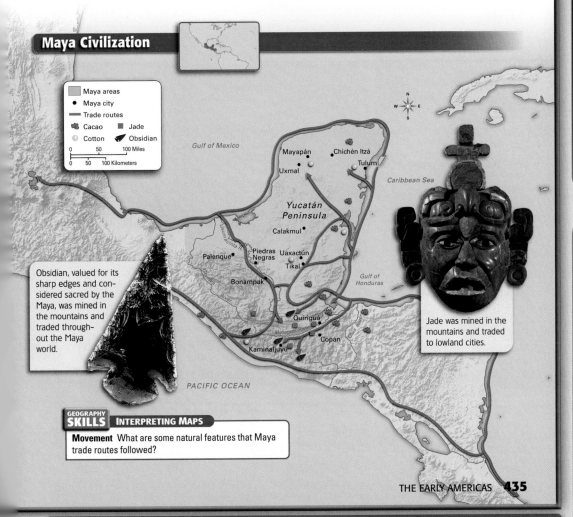

Maya Civilization

Maya areas
• Maya city
— Trade routes
◆ Cacao ▪ Jade
○ Cotton ◆ Obsidian

0   50   100 Miles
0   50   100 Kilometers

Gulf of Mexico

Mayapán
Uxmal
Chichén Itzá
Tulum

Caribbean Sea

Yucatán Peninsula

Calakmul

Palenque
Piedras Negras
Uaxactún
Tikal

Bonampak

Gulf of Honduras

Quiriguá
Copán
Kaminaljuyú

PACIFIC OCEAN

Obsidian, valued for its sharp edges and considered sacred by the Maya, was mined in the mountains and traded throughout the Maya world.

Jade was mined in the mountains and traded to lowland cities.

GEOGRAPHY SKILLS INTERPRETING MAPS
Movement What are some natural features that Maya trade routes followed?

THE EARLY AMERICAS **435**

Main Idea

❷ Maya Classic Age

The Maya Classic Age was characterized by great cities, trade, and warfare.

Describe List some nouns and adjectives that describe Maya cities. *Nouns might include temples, palaces, plazas, canals, ball courts, city-states, warfare; adjectives might include grand, regal, decorative, warlike, terraced, and paved.*

Summarize How did the Maya change their environment to improve city life? *built large buildings, terraced land for farming, paved areas for gatherings, built canals to control water flow*

HSS 7.7.1 **HSS** Analysis Skills: HI 1

Biography

John Lloyd Stephens (1805–1852) In the 1830s John Lloyd Stephens, an American lawyer, was advised to travel for his health. He went to the Middle East and eastern Europe, where he toured ruins and archaeological sites. Having developed a passion for exploration, in 1839 Stephens went to Honduras. He was in search of ancient ruins said to exist deep in the Yucatán jungle. After struggling through dense tropical rain forest, Stephens came upon a magnificent carved stone. He had found the ruins of the ancient Maya city of Palenque. News of the find sparked interest in the Maya and led to modern historical study of Maya civilization. Today scientists and explorers continue to find Maya ruins hidden in the jungle.

Cities

Maya cities had many grand buildings, including large stone pyramids, temples, and palaces. Some of these buildings honored local Maya kings. For example, in the city of Palenque (pah-LENG-kay), a temple honored the king **Pacal** (puh-KAHL). Pacal had the temple built to record his achievements as a ruler. Maya artists decorated temples and palaces with carvings and colorful paintings.

In addition to temples and palaces, the Maya also built structures to improve life in their cities. For example, builders paved large plazas for public gatherings, and they built canals to control the flow of water through their cities. Farmers shaped nearby hillsides into flat terraces so they could grow crops on them.

Most Maya cities also had a special ball court. People played or watched a type of ball game in these large stone arenas. Using only their heads, shoulders, or hips, players tried to bounce a heavy, hard rubber ball through a stone ring above their heads. Players weren't allowed to use their hands or feet. The winners were awarded jewels and clothing. The losers were sometimes killed. This ball game was one that the Maya had picked up from Olmec traditions.

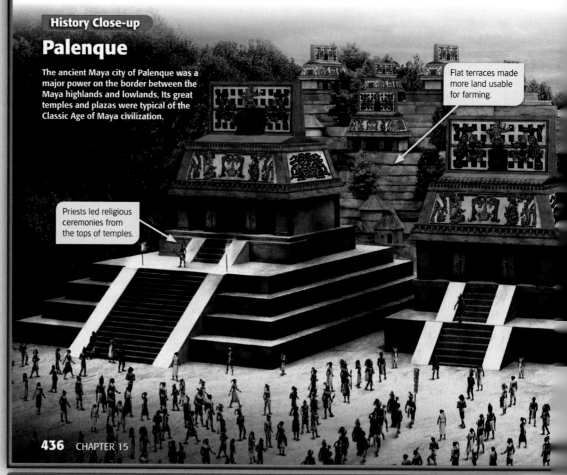

History Close-up

Palenque

The ancient Maya city of Palenque was a major power on the border between the Maya highlands and lowlands. Its great temples and plazas were typical of the Classic Age of Maya civilization.

Flat terraces made more land usable for farming.

Priests led religious ceremonies from the tops of temples.

436 CHAPTER 15

Critical Thinking: Synthesizing

Exceeding Standards

Maya Classic Age Recipe **HSS** 7.7.1, 7.7.3; **HSS** Analysis Skills: HI 1, HI 2

1. Have students create an imaginary recipe for the Maya Classic Age. The recipe should include a list of ingredients and preparation steps. Students will specify the "dish" they want to make.

2. Explain that the recipe's ingredients should be the defining characteristics of the Maya Classic Age. Ingredient amounts should reflect the importance of each characteristic. Preparation or cooking instructions should be creative or symbolize aspects of the Maya Classic Age. For example, preparation might require actively beating two ingredients together to symbolize the warfare common to the Maya Classic Age. Or the recipe might include a warning not to overcook the dish to symbolize theories about the decline of the Maya civilization.

3. Encourage students to illustrate or decorate their recipes. **LS** **Verbal/Linguistic**

Alternative Assessment Handbook, Rubric 37: Writing Assignments

The Maya cities were really city-states. Each had its own government and its own king. No single ruler united the many cities into one empire.

Warfare

Conflicts between cities often led to fighting. Maya cities usually battled each other to gain power and land. For example, the city of Tikal (tee-KAHL) fought many battles with its rival Calakmul (kah-lahk-MOOL). Both cities wanted to control a smaller city that lay between them. Power shifted back and forth between the two larger cities for years.

Maya warfare was bloody. Warriors fought hand-to-hand using spears, flint knives, and wooden clubs. The Maya often captured enemy prisoners and killed them in religious ceremonies as a sacrifice to their gods. They burned enemy towns and villages. Warfare probably tore up the land and destroyed crops. Maya warfare was so destructive that some scholars think it may have contributed to the end of the Maya civilization.

READING CHECK **Summarizing** What were two ways Maya cities interacted with each other?

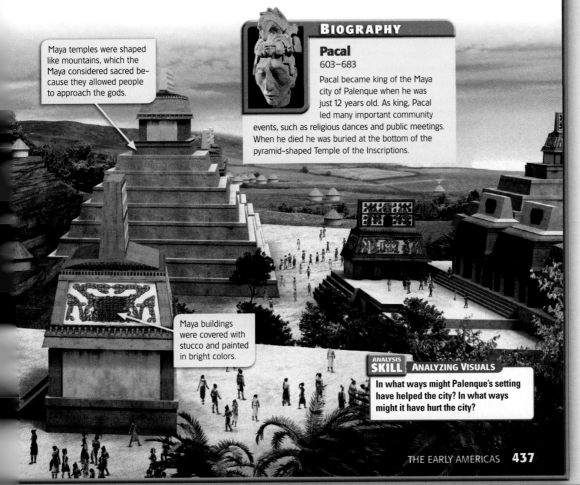

Maya temples were shaped like mountains, which the Maya considered sacred because they allowed people to approach the gods.

Maya buildings were covered with stucco and painted in bright colors.

BIOGRAPHY

Pacal
603–683
Pacal became king of the Maya city of Palenque when he was just 12 years old. As king, Pacal led many important community events, such as religious dances and public meetings. When he died he was buried at the bottom of the pyramid-shaped Temple of the Inscriptions.

ANALYSIS SKILL **ANALYZING VISUALS**
In what ways might Palenque's setting have helped the city? In what ways might it have hurt the city?

THE EARLY AMERICAS **437**

Differentiating Instruction for Universal Access

Advanced Learners/GATE   **Exceeding Standards**

Step Into the Picture Ask students to imagine that they are one of the people in the "History Close-up" image above. Have students use the information in this section and their historical imaginations to write a short narrative based on the picture.
LS Verbal/Linguistic, Visual/Spatial
HSS 7.7.1, 7.7.3
Alternative Assessment Handbook, Rubric 37: Writing Assignments

English-Language Learners   **Standards Proficiency**

Use Visual Aids Have students use the map and other visuals in this section to describe the Maya civilization. Focus students by asking questions, such as "Where did the Maya live?" "What were their cities like?" As students read through the section, have them relate what they are reading to the visuals.
LS Visual/Spatial
HSS 7.7.1, 7.7.3; **HSS** Analysis Skills: HI 1

Learners Having Difficulty   **Reaching Standards**

Chart Characteristics To help students focus on the characteristics of the Maya Classic Age, make a three-column chart for students to see. Label the columns *Trade, Cities,* and *Warfare.* Point out that these titles match the three red titles in the text under "Maya Classic Age." Have students copy and fill in the chart as they read. **LS** Verbal/Linguistic
HSS 7.7.1, 7.7.3; **HSS** Analysis Skills: HI 1

❸ **Maya Civilization Declines**

Maya civilization declined, and historians have several theories as to why.

Recall When did the Maya civilization decline, and what resulted? *In the 900s, the Maya stopped building temples and other structures and left their cities.*

Evaluate Which theory do you think best explains why the Maya civilization collapsed, and why? *Answers will vary, but students should accurately describe the theory they choose.*

🐻 **HSS** 7.7.1, 7.7.3; **HSS** Analysis Skills: CS 1, HI 1

Close

Have students summarize and discuss the different theories for the decline of the Classic Age in Maya civilization.

Review

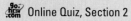 Online Quiz, Section 2

Assess

SE Section 2 Assessment

📄 PASS: Section 2 Quiz

📄 Alternative Assessment Handbook

Reteach/Classroom Intervention

📄 California Standards Review Workbook

📄 Interactive Reader and Study Guide, Section 2

💿 Interactive Skills Tutor CD-ROM

Answers

Reading Check *because they have to speculate about what happened based on the surviving artifacts*

438

Maya Civilization Declines

THE IMPACT TODAY
Many Maya still live in villages throughout Mesoamerica. Others have moved to big cities.

Maya civilization began to collapse in the 900s. People stopped building temples and other structures. They left the cities and moved back to the countryside. What caused this collapse? Historians aren't sure, but they do have some theories.

One theory says that increased warfare brought about the end of the Maya Classic Age. A related theory is that, as cities grew, perhaps the Maya could not grow enough food to feed everyone. Growing the same crops year after year might have left the soil too weak for farming. As a result, competition between cities for land may have increased. This competition could have led to even more warfare than before. Increased warfare would have destroyed more crops and made farming more difficult.

ACADEMIC VOCABULARY
rebel to fight against authority

Another possible cause of the decline of Maya civilization is the demands Maya kings made on their people. Kings forced people to build huge temples or farm for them. Maybe people didn't want to work for the kings. They might have **rebelled** or left the cities because of these demands.

Some historians also think climate might have played a role in the collapse of Maya civilization. Scientists have learned that the region suffered from a long dry period and droughts for about 150 years. This dry period took place about the time the Maya moved away from their cities. A drier climate and droughts would have made it hard to grow enough food to feed everyone in the cities.

Most researchers agree that there was probably no single event that caused the end of the Classic Age. More likely, a mix of several factors led to the decline of the Maya civilization.

READING CHECK **Drawing Inferences** Why do you think scientists aren't sure what caused the end of Maya civilization?

SUMMARY AND PREVIEW You have learned that the Maya built a great civilization, but it collapsed for what were probably several reasons. In Section 3 you will learn more about what Maya life and society was like at its height.

Section 2 Assessment

go.hrw.com
Online Quiz
KEYWORD: SQ6 HP15

Reviewing Ideas, Terms, and People **HSS** 7.7.1, 7.7.3

1. **a. Recall** What resources did the Maya get from the forest?
   b. Make Inferences How might the Maya have used **obsidian**?
2. **a. Identify** Who was an important king of Palenque?
   b. Make Generalizations Why did Maya cities fight each other?
3. **a. Describe** What happened to Maya civilization in the 900s?
   b. Analyze In what way did growth of cities, warfare, and drought possibly affect Maya civilization?
   c. Elaborate What might scientists study to find out about the end of Maya civilization?

Critical Thinking

4. **Identifying Cause and Effect** Draw a diagram like the one to the right. Use it to show four possible causes for the decline of the Classic Age in Maya civilization.

FOCUS ON WRITING

5. **Gathering Information about the Maya** Much of the tour would likely be devoted to the Maya. Use the maps and pictures in this chapter to help you choose which places to write about. What areas and features of each site would you point out? What would you say about the history of these different places?

438 CHAPTER 15

Section 2 Assessment Answers

1. **a.** deer and monkeys for food; wood poles, vines, and mud for building materials
   b. as a tool for uses such as cutting, carving, or scraping items
2. **a.** Pacal
   b. to gain power and land
3. **a.** The Maya stopped building temples and other large structures, left the cities, and went to live in the countryside.
   b. These factors likely made it too hard to produce enough food to support large populations.

   c. possible answers—Maya artifacts such as carvings, writing, artwork, ruins; soil; historical weather and climate patterns
4. increased warfare; city growth and decline of soil fertility, leading to increased warfare; rebellion against heavy demands of kings; drought
5. Students should list some of the cities on the Maya Civilization map and describe some features of Maya cities that they want to include on their tour.

Maya Life and Society

If YOU were there...

You are a Maya farmer, growing corn on a farm near the city. Often you enter the city to join the crowd at a religious ceremony. You watch the king and his priests, standing at the top of a tall pyramid. They wear capes of brightly colored feathers and many heavy gold ornaments that glitter like the sun. As the king offers a sacrifice to the gods, a ray of sun strikes the pyramid.

How do these ceremonies make you feel about your king?

> **BUILDING BACKGROUND** Fancy clothes and important responsibilities showed the role kings and priests played in Maya society. The roles people played determined what their daily life was like.

Roles in Maya Society

Maya society had a complex class structure. As you might expect, life for the upper social classes differed greatly from life for the lower classes.

Upper Class

The upper class of Maya society included different groups of people. The king held the highest position in society. Priests, warriors, and merchants were also part of the upper class.

> Maya society had a rigid class structure.

An attendant brings gifts to two Maya rulers.

What You Will Learn...

Main Ideas

1. Roles in Maya society were based on a complex class structure.
2. Religion in Maya society was often bloody.
3. The Maya made achievements in art, science, math, and writing.

The Big Idea

People played different roles in Maya society, but together they made great achievements in art, science, math, and writing.

Key Terms

observatories, p. 442
Popol Vuh, p. 443

HSS **7.7.2** Study the roles of people in each society, including class structures, family life, warfare, religious beliefs and practices, and slavery.

7.7.4 Describe the artistic and oral traditions and architecture in the three civilizations.

7.7.5 Describe the Meso-American achievements in astronomy and mathematics, including the development of the calendar and the Meso-American knowledge of seasonal changes to the civilizations' agricultural systems.

THE EARLY AMERICAS **439**

Teach the Big Idea: Master the Standards

Standards Proficiency

Maya Life and Society **HSS** 7.7.2, 7.7.4, 7.7.5; **HSS** Analysis Skills: HR 3, HI 1

1. **Teach** Ask students the Main Idea questions to teach this section.

2. **Apply** Organize students into groups and have each group brainstorm a list of 10 items for a museum exhibit about Maya society, religion, and achievements. The items should represent significant aspects of each topic. **LS** Interpersonal

3. **Review** As you review the section, have each group share and explain some of the items on its list. Encourage other groups to give feedback.

4. **Practice/Homework** Have students write captions explaining why each item their group listed is representative of some aspect of Maya life and society. To extend the activity, have students complete the Maya Interdisciplinary Project listed below.
   LS Interpersonal, Verbal/Linguistic

   Alternative Assessment Handbook, Rubrics 14: Group Activity; and 37: Writing Assignments

---

• Preteach •

Bellringer

If YOU were there . . . Use the **Daily Bellringer Transparency** to help students answer the question.

Daily Bellringer Transparency, Section 3

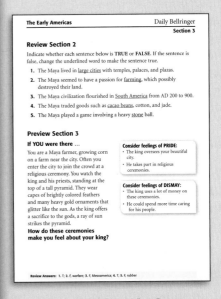

The Early Americas — Daily Bellringer, Section 3

Review Section 2
Indicate whether each sentence below is **TRUE** or **FALSE**. If the sentence is false, change the underlined word to make the sentence true.
1. The Maya lived in large cities with temples, palaces, and plazas.
2. The Maya seemed to have a passion for farming, which possibly destroyed their land.
3. The Maya civilization flourished in South America from AD 200 to 900.
4. The Maya traded goods such as cacao beans, cotton, and jade.
5. The Maya played a game involving a heavy stone ball.

Preview Section 3
If YOU were there . . .
You are a Maya farmer, growing corn on a farm near the city. Often you enter the city to join the crowd at a religious ceremony. You watch the king and his priests, standing at the top of a tall pyramid. They wear capes of brightly colored feathers and many heavy gold ornaments that glitter like the sun. As the king offers a sacrifice to the gods, a ray of sun strikes the pyramid.
How do these ceremonies make you feel about your king?

Consider feelings of PRIDE:
• The king oversees your beautiful city.
• He takes part in religious ceremonies.

Consider feelings of DISMAY:
• The king uses a lot of money on these ceremonies.
• He could spend more time caring for his people.

Review Answers: 1. T; 2. F, warfare; 3. F, Mesoamerica; 4. T; 5. F, rubber

Academic Vocabulary

Review with students the high-use academic term in this section.

aspects parts (p. 441)

CRF: Vocabulary Builder Activity, Section 3

Standards Focus

HSS 7.7.2
Means: Study the different roles in Maya society, including social classes, family life, warfare, religious roles, and slavery.
Matters: Maya society had a complex class structure, and people's roles determined what their lives were like.

HSS 7.7.4
Means: Describe Maya art, architecture, and oral traditions.
Matters: The Maya made great achievements in art and writing.

HSS 7.7.5
Means: Describe the Maya's achievements in astronomy and mathematics, including the development of calendars and a knowledge of the seasons.
Matters: The Maya made discoveries in the fields of astronomy, math, and science.

439

❶ Roles in Maya Society

Roles in Maya society were based on a complex class structure.

Identify Besides the king, who else made up the Maya upper classes? *priests, warriors, merchants*

Contrast How did the roles of men and women differ in Maya society? *Men crafted tools, hunted, farmed; women cared for children, cooked, made yarn, wove cloth.*

Summarize In general, what was life like for members of the Maya lower classes? *They farmed, hunted, and served the upper classes.*

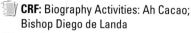 **CRF:** Biography Activities: Ah Cacao; Bishop Diego de Landa

HSS 7.7.2; **HSS** Analysis Skills: HI 1

Analyzing Visuals
A Maya King and His Court

Making Inferences In the image at right, a bodyguard stands behind the king. Why do you think Maya kings needed bodyguards? *Because of kings' power and control, other people may have wanted to hurt them out of anger or a desire to take their power.*

Linking to Today

A Mexican Minority People descended from the ancient Maya today form a minority in Mexico. Like many indigenous Mexicans, the Maya receive less health care, education, and other services from the government. The Maya and other indigenous peoples have tried to become more independent. A law passed in 2001 fell short of the goal, however.

Answers

Reading Check *by being captured in battle, in debt, orphaned, or born to a slave*

440

The Maya believed their rulers were related to the gods. For this reason, rulers were often involved in religious ceremonies. They also led battles. As the richest people in Maya society, rulers had beautiful clothing and jewelry. Kings wore huge feather headdresses and capes of cotton, jaguar skins, and feathers.

Priests were usually born into their role in Maya society. They led religious ceremonies. They were also the most educated people. Priests used their knowledge of astronomy and math to plan the best times for religious ceremonies.

Professional warriors fought battles against other Maya cities. In battle, these warriors wore animal headdresses, jade jewelry, and jaguar-skin capes. They painted their bodies red and black.

Merchants directed trade among the cities. They organized the transportation and distribution of goods. They also supervised the people who carried goods between cities. Together, the members of the upper class controlled the politics, religion, and economy in Maya society.

Lower Classes

Although the upper classes had the most power, most Maya belonged to the lower classes as farming families. These Maya lived in small houses outside the cities. Girls learned from their mothers how to cook, make yarn, and weave. Women cared for children. Men crafted household tools such as knives. They had to provide food for their family, so they also spent a lot of time hunting and farming. They kept small gardens next to their houses and worked together to farm larger fields.

Farmers had to give some of their crops to their rulers. Lower-class Maya also had to "pay" their rulers with goods such as cloth and salt. They had to work on building temples, palaces, and other buildings.

440 CHAPTER 15

They also had to serve in the army during times of war. If captured in battle, a lower-class man usually became a slave.

Slaves held the lowest position in society. Orphans, slaves' children, and people who owed money also became slaves. Slaves had to carry trade goods between cities. They also served upper-class Maya by working as farmers or household servants.

The lower class supported the upper class with food and labor, but the upper class also helped the lower class. For example, upper-class Maya led the religious ceremonies that were vital to daily life for all classes of society.

READING CHECK Identifying Cause and Effect How might one become a slave in Maya society?

A Maya King and His Court
The king and his court were the center of Maya government and religious life. This vase painting shows a Maya king relaxing with some of his servants. Kings enjoyed all the luxuries of Maya life, such as music, fine clothing and food, and even chocolate.

Critical Thinking: Categorizing

Standards Proficiency

Maya Social Class Pyramid **HSS** 7.7.2; **HSS** Analysis Skills: HI 1

1. Review the information on the ancient Maya class structure with the class. Have students identify the different roles in Maya society.

2. Remind students of the class structures in other civilizations they have studied, particularly the Egyptians. Ask students how the Egyptian class structure was similar to the Maya social class structure. Remind students that the Egyptian social class structure resembled a pyramid.

3. Have students draw an Egyptian-style pyramid that shows the ancient Maya class structure. Before students begin, make sure they understand that the king should be at the top of the pyramid and the slaves at the bottom of the pyramid.

4. When students have finished, ask volunteers to share their pyramids and to explain why they put certain groups in certain places on the pyramid. **LS** Visual/Spatial

Alternative Assessment Handbook, Rubric 13: Graphic Organizers

Religion

The Maya worshipped many gods related to different **aspects** of their daily life. The most important god was the creator. This god would take many different forms. Others included a sun god, moon goddess, and maize god. The Maya believed their kings communicated with the gods.

According to Maya beliefs, the gods could be helpful or harmful, so people tried to please the gods to get their help. The Maya believed their gods needed blood to prevent disasters or the end of the world. Every person offered blood to the gods by piercing their tongue or skin. The Maya sometimes held special ceremonies to give blood at events such as births, weddings, and funerals.

On special occasions the Maya believed they needed extra amounts of blood. On these occasions they made human sacrifices to their gods. They usually used prisoners captured in battle for this ritual. A priest would offer human hearts to stone carvings of gods. These sacrifices usually took place at a temple.

ACADEMIC VOCABULARY
aspects parts

READING CHECK **Generalizing** Why did the Maya want to please their gods?

Achievements

The Maya's many artistic and architectural skills are reflected in their sculpture and in their temples. Maya achievements also included discoveries in science and math, as well as developments in writing.

The king is gazing at this mirror, which the Maya believed held magical powers.

A bodyguard stands behind the king.

These vases held a chocolate drink, a favorite of Maya nobles.

The fly whisk in the king's hand is a symbol of authority.

ANALYSIS SKILL **ANALYZING VISUALS**
What about the king indicates he is an important person?

441

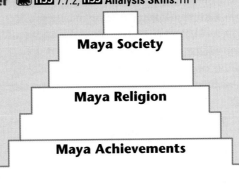

❸ Achievements

The Maya made achievements in art, science, math, and writing.

Summarize What advances did the Maya make in astronomy? *built observatories; developed calendars; determined length of year, cycles of moon and seasons, and how to predict eclipses.*

Make Generalizations Why might builders today be impressed with Maya building methods? *The Maya built great cities without metal tools or wheeled vehicles.*

📄 **CRF:** Literature Activity: *Popol Vuh: The Hero Twins*

📄 **CRF:** Primary Source Activity: Maya Ceramics

🐻 **HSS** 7.7.4, 7.7.5; **HSS** Analysis Skills: HI 1

Connect to Science

Maya Astronomy The Maya considered stars and planets to be gods. They watched the stars to predict events on Earth that they believed the gods controlled. The planet Venus was one of the Maya's most important "stars." The Maya determined that Venus took about 584 days to reappear at the same point on the horizon.

go.hrw.com
Online Resources

Chapter 15 Resources:
KEYWORD: SQ6 WH15
ACTIVITY: Adding the Maya Way

Art and Architecture

Some of the best-known Maya art is their sculpture and their jade and gold jewelry. They carved stone sculptures of kings or gods for their cities.

Maya cities showed the talent of their architects and builders. The Maya built cities without using metal tools. They didn't even have wheeled vehicles to carry supplies. Instead, workers used obsidian tools to cut limestone into blocks. Then, to move the giant blocks, workers rolled them over logs and lifted them with ropes. It took many workers to build Maya cities, perhaps the most recognizable Maya achievement.

Science and Math

Maya achievements in science and math were just as important as their achievements in art and architecture. The Maya built **observatories**, or buildings to study astronomy, so their priests could study the stars. Maya astronomers figured out that a year is about 365 days long. They also learned about the cycles of the moon and how to predict eclipses.

Partly based on their discoveries in astronomy, the Maya developed calendars. They had a religious calendar to plan religious events. The Maya used a different calendar for agriculture. It had symbols for different months tied to farming activities such as planting or harvesting. These activities matched changes in the seasons. The Maya calendar was more accurate than the calendar used in Europe at that time.

To go along with their calendars, the Maya created a number system that included some new concepts in math. For example, the Maya were among the first people with a symbol for zero. The Maya used their number system to record important dates in their history.

Writing and Oral Traditions

The Maya also developed a writing system. It was similar to Egyptian hieroglyphics. Symbols represented both objects and sounds. The Maya created records, especially about achievements of their kings, by carving symbols into large stone tablets. They also wrote in bark-paper books.

Maya Astronomy and Calendars

This photo shows the observatory at the Maya city of Chichén Itzá. The diagram shows the Maya religious and farming calendars. The Maya used these two calendars together to coordinate planting, harvesting, and important religious events.

365-day farming calendar

260-day religious calendar

442 CHAPTER 15

Differentiating Instruction for Universal Access

English-Language Learners [Reaching Standards] [Prep Required]

Materials: butcher paper, art supplies

1. Ask students to imagine that they are Maya artists during the Classic Age and that the king has asked them to create a mural showing Maya achievements in art, science, math, and writing.

2. Organize students into small groups. If possible, place students who are proficient in English in the same groups with English learners.

3. Have students examine the examples of Maya artwork in this section and use the artwork as a model.

4. Then have each group create and display its mural. 🔲 **Interpersonal, Visual/Spatial**

🐻 **HSS** 7.7.4, 7.7.5; **HSS** Analysis Skills: HI 1

📄 Alternative Assessment Handbook, Rubrics 3: Artwork; and 14: Group Activity

ART
A Maya Carving

This carving comes from the palace at Yaxchilán (yahsh-chee-LAHN). The Maya recorded historical events on carvings like this one. Historians can now translate most Maya writing. They study the pictures and writings to learn about events in Maya history.

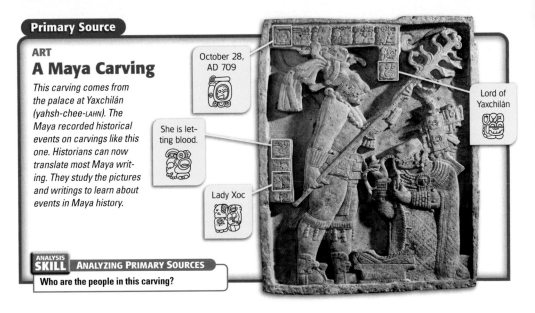

October 28, AD 709

She is letting blood.

Lady Xoc

Lord of Yaxchilán

ANALYSIS SKILL **ANALYZING PRIMARY SOURCES**
Who are the people in this carving?

Stories and poetry got passed down orally from one generation to the next. After the Spanish arrived, Maya legends and history were written in a book called the **Popol Vuh** (poh-pohl VOO). This book provides valuable information about the Maya.

READING CHECK Analyzing What activities did the Maya calendar regulate?

SUMMARY The Maya had a complex social structure. They also made great achievements in art and learning. The Maya left behind many records of their culture, society, and history. By studying these records, archaeologists and historians may be able to learn more about the achievements of the Maya.

Section 3 Assessment

go.hrw.com
Online Quiz
KEYWORD:SQ6 HP15

Reviewing Ideas and Terms **HSS** 7.7.2, 7.7.4, 7.7.5

1. **a.** Identify Who were members of the upper class in Maya society?
   b. Explain In what ways did lower-class Maya support upper-class Maya?
2. **a.** Describe What did the Maya do to try to please their gods?
   b. Explain Why did the Maya practice human sacrifice?
3. **a.** Recall What did the Maya study from **observatories**?
   b. Rank What do you think was the most impressive Maya achievement?

Critical Thinking

4. **Analyzing Information** Draw a diagram like the one to the right. Use it to identify some major achievements of the Maya.

Writing system
Achievements

FOCUS ON WRITING

5. **Identifying Key Details about Maya Culture** Some sites might have displays of Maya art and tools. There could even be scenes and live performances of how the Maya lived. Make a list of what the people on the tour might see of Maya culture.

THE EARLY AMERICAS **443**

Section 3 Assessment Answers

1. **a.** kings, priests, professional warriors, merchants
   b. paid their rulers with crops, cloth, or other goods; worked on public building projects; served in the army during times of war
2. **a.** offered blood to the gods by piercing themselves or offering human sacrifices
   b. to provide extra amounts of blood, which the Maya believed they needed to offer to the gods on special occasions
3. **a.** astronomy, the stars
   b. Answers will vary, but students should

exhibit an understanding of Maya contributions in art, mathematics, science, and writing and provide reasons to support their opinions.

4. Answers may include Maya sculpture, jewelry, architecture, observatories, calendars, math and number system, writing system, and oral traditions.

5. Students should include some of the main Maya achievements, listed in the previous answer, and some of the Maya sites mentioned in this section.

Direct Teach

Primary Source
A Maya Carving

Reading Maya Glyphs Scientists struggled for years to decipher Maya glyphs, or symbols, such as those highlighted in the carving at left. Then in the 1970s a small group of scholars combined their theories. The group determined that Maya glyphs did not represent just historical events but an actual spoken language. The interpretations of Maya glyphs has met with controversy, but historians now know that Maya writing was used for much more than just to record events.

HSS Analysis Skills: HI 5

Review & Assess

Close

Ask students what they think is the most significant achievement of the Maya. Remind students to provide reasons to support their opinions.

Review

Online Quiz, Section 3

Assess

SE Section 3 Assessment
PASS: Section 3 Quiz
Alternative Assessment Handbook

Reteach/Classroom Intervention

California Standards Review Workbook
Interactive Reader and Study Guide, Section 3
Interactive Skills Tutor CD-ROM

Answers

Analyzing Primary Sources *Lady Xoc and Lord of Yaxchilán*

Reading Check *religious events and farming activities*

443

Literature in History

Popol Vuh

As You Read Tell students as they read to make a list of the different types of behaviors that the creator-gods exhibit during the myth. Then have students conclude what they think the Maya creator-gods were like, based on their behaviors. Encourage student discussion and feedback.

CRF: Literature Activity: *Popol Vuh: The Hero Twins*

Literary Focus

Plot Review the parts of a plot with students—basic situation (conflict, external conflict, and internal conflict), series of events or complications, climax, and resolution. Have students identify these elements in the excerpts here.

ELA Reading 7.3.2

GUIDED READING

WORD HELP

disintegrating breaking apart
mason one who works with stone or brick
dismantled took apart

❶ **Why do the gods wish to make human beings?**

❷ **What do the gods use to make the body? What happens to it?**

ELA Reading 7.3.2 Identify events that advance the plot and determine how each event explains past or present action(s) or foreshadows future action(s).

444 CHAPTER 15

---

from the
Popol Vuh

translated by Dennis Tedlock

About the Reading *In the language of the Maya,* Popol Vuh *means "Council Book." This work contains both the myths and the history of a group of Maya. It was first used by Maya kings and lords to help them govern their people. Today, the* Popol Vuh *helps modern readers understand how the Maya lived and what they believed. The following myth, for example, tells us how the gods tried to create people several times before they eventually succeeded.*

AS YOU READ Pay close attention to the behavior of the creator-gods.

Again there comes an experiment with the human work, the human design, by the Maker, Modeler, Bearer, Begetter:

"It must simply be tried again. The time for the planting and dawning is nearing. For this we must make a provider and nurturer. ❶ How else can we be invoked and remembered on the face of the earth? We have already made our first try at our work and design, but it turned out that they didn't keep our days, nor did they glorify us."

"So now let's try to make a giver of praise, giver of respect, provider, nurturer," they said.

So then comes the building and working with earth and mud. They made a body, but it didn't look good to them. It was just separating, just crumbling, just loosening, just softening, just disintegrating, and just dissolving. ❷ Its head wouldn't turn, either. Its face was just lopsided, its face was just twisted. It couldn't look around. It talked at first, but senselessly. It was quickly dissolving in the water.

"It won't last," the mason and sculptor said then. "It seems to be dwindling away, so let it just dwindle. It can't walk and it can't multiply, so let it be merely a thought," they said.

So then they dismantled, again they brought down their work and design. Again they talked:

"What is there for us to make that would turn out well, that would succeed in keeping our days and praying to us?" they said. Then they planned again . . .

Cross-Discipline Activity: Art

Standards Proficiency

Illustrating the Plot **ELA** Reading 7.3.2 **Prep Required**

Materials: art supplies, colored markers and pens, paper or poster board

1. Have students reread the story. Go through the reading with students to ensure that the class understands the two passages.

2. Next, have students fold a piece of notebook paper so that there are five horizontal sections, or have students divide poster boards into five sections.

3. Have students use the sections to illustrate five main events in the story that advanced the plot.

4. Below each illustration, have students paraphrase the event or write a caption explaining the drawing.

5. Have volunteers share their drawings with the class. As they do, review the parts of the story's plot and how events are connected.
   LS Verbal/Linguistic, Visual/Spatial

   Alternative Assessment Handbook, Rubric 3: Artwork

Answers

Guided Reading 1. *wanted to create providers and nurturers to take care of the planting and to invoke, remember, and glorify the creator-gods;* **2.** *earth and mud; separates, crumbles, softens, disintegrates, dissolves, dwindles away*

The creator-gods try again. This time, they produce a group of wooden creatures called "manikins."
They came into being, they multiplied, they had daughters, they had sons, these manikins, woodcarvings. But there was nothing in their hearts and nothing in their minds, no memory of their mason and builder. They just went and walked wherever they wanted. They did not remember the Heart of Sky. ❸

And so they fell, just an experiment and just a cutout for humankind.

They were not competent, nor did they speak before the builder and sculptor who made them and brought them forth, and so they were killed, done in by a flood:

There came a rain of resin from the sky.

There came the one named Gouger of Faces: he gouged out their eyeballs.

There came Sudden Bloodletter: he snapped off their heads.

There came Crunching Jaguar: he ate their flesh.

There came Tearing Jaguar: he tore them open.

They were pounded down to the bones and tendons, smashed and pulverized even to the bones . . . ❹

Such was the scattering of the human work, the human design. The people were ground down, overthrown. The mouths and faces of all of them were destroyed and crushed. And it used to be said that the monkeys in the forests today are a sign of this. They were left as a sign because wood alone was used for their flesh by the builder and sculptor.

❺ And so this is why monkeys look like people: they are a sign of a previous human work, human design—mere manikins, mere woodcarvings.

Monkeys were common subjects in Maya carvings.

GUIDED READING

WORD HELP

competent capable; fit
resin a gooey substance that comes from trees
pulverized crushed

❸ The Heart of Sky is the father-god of the Maya.

❹ *In your own words, explain what happened to the creatures.*

❺ *This myth explains the origin, or beginning, of what animal?*

CONNECTING LITERATURE TO HISTORY

1. **Evaluating** According to Maya beliefs, the gods could be helpful or harmful, so people tried to please the gods to get their help. Are the gods in this myth helpful or harmful? Explain your answer.

2. **Analyzing** By studying Maya records, archaeologists are learning about the achievements of the Maya. What have you learned about the Maya by reading this "record" of their life and society?

445

Literature in History

Reading Skills

Making Predictions Remind students that to make a prediction, they use their own knowledge to connect clues in the story. Then have students predict what they think the creator-gods did next in the story here. Have students explain the clues that they used as the basis for their predictions. *Students might predict that the gods will use a different material to create humans again, because the gods still need someone to serve as Earth's providers and nurturers.*

Info to Know

Maya Creation Beliefs The Maya believed that the gods had created several worlds before the current one and then destroyed each of these worlds in turn with a flood.

Following the creator-gods' attempts to make people of earth and wood, the Maya believed that the gods made people of corn gruel, or a thin corn soup. According to the Maya, these people survived and were their ancestors.

Differentiating Instruction for Universal Access

Advanced Learners/GATE   Exceeding Standards

1. Ask students to imagine that they are going to make a movie of this story. What major plot elements would their movie include? Would their movie be a horror film, a comedy, a drama, or something else? Would the movie be animated or performed by a real cast? Have students discuss their movie ideas.

2. Organize students into small groups. Have each group outline its movie idea. Outlines should list the main parts of the movie's plot.

3. Each group should predict how the story ends

and include this ending in their movie outline.

4. Have each group present its movie concept to the class.

5. Close by having students relate the plot of this story to what they know about the Maya. What can students infer about the Maya based on the events in this story?

🅛🅢 **Interpersonal, Verbal/Linguistic**
🅔🅛🅐 Reading 7.3.2

📝 Alternative Assessment Handbook, Rubric 14: Group Activity

Answers

Guided Reading 4. *The creator-gods sent a resin flood to destroy them, and several gods also came and attacked the manikins.* **5.** *monkeys*

Connecting Literature to History
1. *Answers will vary, but students might respond that the gods were helpful when they made people to tend to the world but harmful when they decided to destroy people.* **2.** *They believed in gods and had developed writing and literature, including creation myths.*

Accepting Social Responsibility

Activity **Getting Involved** Lead students in a discussion about the need for all members of society to behave in socially responsible ways. Ask students to identify the type of socially responsible behavior listed in the lesson (*obligation to not do anything that harms society, duty to participate in society by fulfilling the responsibilities of citizenship such as voting, keeping informed about important issues, and serving on juries; and becoming involved in change to benefit society*). Write the list for students to see.

Then have students discuss ways in which they can get involved to benefit society. Help students consider means of protest as well as other means. Then give students 15 minutes to free-write about why Americans should get involved and take action to improve society. Have volunteers read their responses to the class. Encourage discussion and feedback. **LS** **Verbal/Linguistic**

Alternative Assessment Handbook, Rubric 37: Writing Assignments

Answers

Practice and Apply the Skill
1. *possible answer—more peace might bring population growth, economic prosperity, increase in food production;*
2. *because they think warfare is a necessary part of life and defense;*
3. *might be seen as a traitor and executed;* **4.** *Answers will vary, but students should clearly state and explain their choice of action.*

446

Social Studies Skills

Analysis	Critical Thinking		Study
		Participation	

Accepting Social Responsibility

Understand the Skill

"No man is an island entire of itself; every man is a piece of the continent, a part of the main." The great English poet John Donne made this observation almost 400 years ago. It is a famous quotation that remains as true today as when Donne wrote it. It means that no one exists alone. We are all members of society—"a part of the main."

Donne's poem continues, "If a clod be washed away by the sea, Europe is the less." This was Donne's way of saying that a society's strength depends on the contributions of its members. They must be willing to fulfill their roles in that society and to do what is best for it.

Learn the Skill

As a member of society, you have obligations to the people around you. The most obvious obligation is to do nothing that might harm society. This duty can range from small things, such as not littering, to large things, such as not committing a crime.

In addition, you have a duty to participate in society. At the very least, this means using the rights and responsibilities of citizenship. These responsibilities include being informed about important issues in your school, community, and country. Later, when you are older, they will also include serving on juries and voting in elections.

Another level of social responsibility and participation is becoming involved in change to benefit society. It goes beyond just being informed about issues to trying to do something about them. Before you take this important step, however, here are some points to consider.

1 Few changes that benefit society will have everyone's support. Some people always want things to stay the same. They may get upset or treat you badly if you work for change. You must be prepared for this possibility if you decide to take action.

2 Sometimes efforts to improve things involve opposing laws or rules that you believe need to be changed. No matter how just your cause is, if you break laws or rules, you must be willing to accept the consequences of your behavior.

3 Remember that violence is *never* an acceptable method for change. People who use force in seeking change are not behaving in a socially responsible manner, even if their cause is good.

Practice and Apply the Skill

Review the "If You Were There" scene in Section 3. Imagine yourself as that Maya farmer. You respect your king as the leader of your city and its army. War is very important in your culture. Your city is at war nearly all the time, and you feel this fighting is hurting your society. Farming is difficult because farmers must spend so much time in the army. In addition, enemy attacks destroy the crops farmers are able to grow. Food shortages are common.

1. If you did something to try to end the warfare, in what ways might that benefit your society?

2. Why might some people oppose your efforts?

3. What might the consequences be for you if you refuse to fight?

4. If you were this Maya farmer, what would you do? Explain your answer.

Social Studies Skills Activity: Accepting Social Responsibility

Posters Promoting Social Responsibility

Standards Proficiency

Materials: art supplies, colored markers, poster board

1. Have students create posters urging their fellow students to get involved in change to benefit society. Students might focus the theme of their posters on a specific type of involvement or cause, or instead focus on social action and involvement in general.

2. Students' posters should include a slogan and one or more images. Students might also include additional text to explain the meaning of their message. Remind students that one or two large, emotionally charged images often are more powerful than many smaller images.

3. Display students' posters in public areas of the school. **LS** **Visual/Spatial**

Alternative Assessment Handbook, Rubric 28: Posters

Visual Summary

Use the visual summary below to help you review the main ideas of the chapter.

QUICK FACTS

People arrived in the Americas sometime before 10,000 BC.

By 2500 BC people in Mesoamerica had domesticated maize.

The Maya built cities in the Americas during their Classic Age.

The Maya civilization eventually collapsed, but no one knows why.

Reviewing Vocabulary, Terms, and People

Imagine that these terms from the chapter are correct answers to six items in a crossword puzzle. Write the six clues for the answers. Then make the puzzle with some answers written down and some across.

1. Mesoamerica
2. Pacal
3. obsidian
4. observatories
5. maize
6. Popol Vuh

Comprehension and Critical Thinking

SECTION 1 *(Pages 428–433)* **HSS** 7.7.1

7. a. Identify What plants did early farmers in Mesoamerica grow for food? What plants did farmers grow in South America?

b. Make Inferences What do Olmec towns, sculptures, and other items tell us about Olmec society?

c. Evaluate Evaluate this statement: "Global temperature change had a big impact on the history of the Americas."

SECTION 2 *(Pages 434–438)* **HSS** 7.7.1, 7.7.3

8. a. Recall What were two important trade goods for the early Maya?

b. Analyze Why did the Maya civilization decline?

c. Elaborate For which people in Maya society was life probably pleasant and secure? For which people was life less pleasant or secure?

SECTION 3 *(Pages 439–443)* **HSS** 7.7.2, 7.7.4, 7.7.5

9. a. Describe What are some things that happened during Maya religious ceremonies?

b. Contrast How did daily life for the upper and lower classes of Maya society differ?

c. Evaluate Of the Maya's many achievements, which do you think is the most important? Why?

THE EARLY AMERICAS **447**

Answers

8. **a.** cloth and obsidian

   b. increased warfare; a population increase, which left a food shortage, weak soil, and competition for land; harsh demands of Maya kings, which may have led people to rebel; climate issues, such as drought

   c. possible answer—Life was probably pleasant for kings and the upper classes, but less pleasant for the lower classes, who farmed and were forced to work on building projects and to fight in wars.

9. **a.** blood-lettings, human sacrifices

   b. Members of the lower classes worked all day to support themselves and to serve the upper classes; members of the upper classes lived very comfortably.

   c. Answers will vary, but students should exhibit an understanding of Maya achievements and how these achievements contributed to Maya society.

Reviewing Themes

10. possible answers: agree—because they accomplished great things with limited resources; disagree—because they didn't think of inventions that would make work easier

11. People traded natural resources found locally throughout the region of the Maya civilization.

Using the Internet

12. Go to the HRW Web site and enter the keyword shown to access a rubric for this activity.

Reviewing Themes

10. **Science and Technology** Do you agree or disagree with this statement: "The Maya were clever and talented because they built their cities without the help of metal tools or wheeled vehicles." Why?

11. **Geography** How did geography play a role in the Maya economy?

Using the Internet

go.hrw.com KEYWORD: SQ6 WH15

12. **Activity: Understanding Maya Math** The ancient Maya invented a number system that helped them construct buildings and keep track of their agriculture and commerce. Number glyphs are mostly simple dots and lines. The Maya also used head glyphs, which are more intricate drawings for numbers. Enter the activity keyword. Then visit the Web sites and complete some math problems using Maya numbers.

Reading and Analysis Skills

Analyzing Information In each of the following passages, one underlined selection is irrelevant or nonessential to the meaning of the sentence, or it cannot be verified as true. Identify the irrelevant, nonessential, or unverifiable selection in each sentence.

13. Pacal was greatly honored by the Maya. He was very tall. The Maya built a great temple to record his achievements.

14. Ball games were popular in Maya cities. Players could not use their hands or feet to touch the ball. The Maya would not enjoy modern basketball very much.

15. Chocolate was valuable in Maya society. Only rulers and gods could have chocolate. Today, many people enjoy chocolate every day.

16. The Maya developed an accurate calendar system. They knew that a year had 365 days. The ancient Romans also had a calendar. The Maya calendar used symbols to represent months.

17. Mesoamerica is largely covered by rain forests. Many kinds of plants and animals live in rain forests. The people of Mesoamerica probably liked to watch monkeys playing in the trees.

Social Studies Skills

18. **Accepting Responsibility and Consequences** Organize your class into groups. Choose one member of your group to represent the ruler of a Maya city. The rest of the group will be his or her advisers. As a group, decide how you will behave toward other cities. Will you go to war, or will you trade? Once you have made your decisions, declare your intentions to other cities. Ask the representatives of those cities how they will respond to your action. As a class, discuss the consequences of the actions you have chosen to take.

FOCUS ON WRITING

19. **Writing Your Brochure** Travel brochures often feature exciting descriptions of tours. Use your notes to help you write such a description for a historical tour of the ancient Americas.

   Choose sites from the most ancient ones to the Maya cities. For each site, write several sentences about the people who lived there. You might tell how they came to live there or how an object there played a part in their lives.

   Most travel brochures show lots of pictures. What pictures would you choose to go with what you've written?

Reading and Analysis Skills

13. was very tall

14. would not enjoy modern basketball very much

15. enjoy chocolate every day

16. The ancient Romans also had a calendar.

17. probably liked to watch monkeys playing in trees

Social Studies Skills

18. Discussions will vary, but students should conclude that both positive and negative actions have consequences and that one must take responsibility for those consequences.

Focus on Writing

19. **Rubric** Students' travel brochures should:
   - contain a catchy title and interesting art.
   - highlight the attractions that people can expect to see on the tour.
   - offer interesting historical information about each attraction.
   - use easy-to-see subheads to introduce each culture.

   CRF: Focus on Writing: Travel Brochure

Standards Assessment

DIRECTIONS: Read each question, and write the letter of the best response.

1 Use the map to answer the following question.

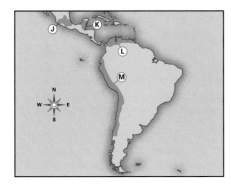

Which of the areas on the map shows the location of the Maya civilization?

A J
B K
C L
D M

2 Mesoamerica contains all of the following geographic features *except*

A mountains.
B rain forests.
C deserts.
D rivers.

3 Which word *best* describes the Maya civilization during its Classic Age?

A peaceful
B religious
C united
D democratic

4 Despite their accomplishments, the Maya did *not* have

A a reliable calendar.
B wheeled vehicles.
C a writing system.
D knowledge of mathematics.

5 Which class of people held the lowest position in Maya society?

A priests
B farmers
C slaves
D merchants

Connecting with Past Learnings

6 In this chapter you read that Maya civilization during the Classic Age included independent city-states. What other civilization that you have studied was organized into city-states?

A ancient Greece
B ancient Persia
C Han China
D the Roman Empire

7 The Maya believed their rulers were related to the gods. What other ancient civilization believed the same thing?

A Jews
B Indians
C Phoenicians
D Egyptians

1. B
Break Down the Question Refer students who miss the question to the "Maya Civilization" map in Section 2 of this chapter. Explain that the map on this page shows a larger area than the map in Section 2, which might be confusing to some students.

2. C
Break Down the Question Point out to students that the word *not* in the question indicates that they should select the statement that is *not* true.

3. B
Break Down the Question Remind students that italicized words in test questions often significantly affect the question's meaning.

4. B
Break Down the Question This question requires students to recall factual information. Refer students who miss the question to the list of Maya achievements in Section 3.

5. C
Break Down the Question This question requires students to recall factual information. Refer students to the material on "Roles in Maya Society" in Section 3.

6. A
Break Down the Question This question connects to information in a previous chapter.

7. D
Break Down the Question This question connects to information in a previous chapter.

Intervention

Reproducible

Interactive Reader and Study Guide, Ch. 15

Universal Access Teacher Management System: Lesson Plans for ELL, Special Education, and Advanced Learners

Technology

Quick Facts Transparency: The Early Americas Visual Summary

Modified Material for Struggling Students CD-ROM

Interactive Skills Tutor CD-ROM

Tips for Test Taking

I'm Stuck! If students come across a question that stumps them, tell them not to get frustrated or worried. Remind them first to master the question to make sure they understand what is being asked. Then they should go through the list of test-taking strategies they have learned. If still stuck, they should practice the 50/50 strategy or make their best educated guess.

Standards Review

Have students review the following standards in their workbooks.

California Standards Review Workbook:
HSS 7.7.1, 7.7.2, 7.7.3, 7.7.4, 7.7.5

Bellringer

Motivate Have students think of a time they were successful in persuading someone to do something (for example, persuading their parents to let them stay out past their curfew). Ask students how they did so. What arguments did they present? What methods of persuasion did they use? Explain that providing a list of well-thought-out reasons and evidence is the most effective method of persuasion—and a highly useful skill in life. Tell students that they will hone their persuasive skills in this essay.

Choosing Evidence

Just the Facts Remind students to examine their evidence carefully to eliminate opinions other than expert opinions. Provide students with practice by having them identify whether each of the following is a fact or an opinion.

1. Few leaders are as successful as Caesar was. *(opinion)*

2. Julius Caesar was a Roman dictator. *(fact)*

3. Italians should be proud of their rich history. *(opinion)*

🔵 Interactive Skills Tutor CD-ROM: Lesson 10: Distinguish between Fact, Opinion, and Reasoned Judgment

🐻 **HSS** Analysis Skills: HR 3

Assignment

Write an essay stating your opinion on this topic or another historical topic of your choice: All great empires are likely to end in the same way the Roman and Maya empires did.

TIP **Fact vs. Opinion** A fact is a statement that can be proved true. Facts include
- measurements
- dates
- locations
- definitions

An opinion is a statement of a personal belief. Opinions often include judgmental words and phrases such as *better, should,* and *think.*

ELA **Writing 6.2.5** Write persuasive compositions.

Persuasion and Historical Issues

The study of history raises questions, or issues, that can be argued from both sides. Effective persuasive writing supports a point of view with evidence.

1. Prewrite

Taking a Position

Do you think all great empires will follow the same course as the Romans and Maya, or could an empire take a different course? Write a sentence that states your position, or opinion about, this topic or another topic.

Supporting Your Position

To convince your audience to agree with your position, you will need reasons and evidence. **Reasons** tell *why* a writer has a particular point of view. **Evidence** backs up, or helps prove, the reasons. Evidence includes facts, examples, and opinions of experts, like historians. You can find this evidence in this textbook or other books recommended by your teacher.

Organizing Reasons and Evidence

Try to present your reasons and evidence in order of importance, so that you can end with your most convincing points. Use transitions such as *mainly, last,* and *most important* to emphasize ideas.

2. Write

This framework can help you state your position clearly and present convincing reasons and evidence.

A Writer's Framework

Introduction	Body	Conclusion
■ Introduce the topic by using a surprising fact, quotation, or comparison to get your reader's attention. ■ Identify at least two differing positions on this topic. ■ State your own position on the topic.	■ Present at least two reasons to support your position. ■ Support each reason with evidence (facts, examples, expert opinions). ■ Organize your reasons and evidence in order of importance with your most convincing reason last.	■ Restate your position. ■ Summarize your supporting reasons and evidence. ■ Project your position into history by using it to predict the course of current and future events.

450 UNIT 6

Differentiating Instruction for Universal Access

Special Education Students [Reaching Standards]

1. In persuasive writing, some students may benefit from visual-motor processing. Use the following dialogue and listing technique.

2. Ask the student to choose the position he or she wants to support in the essay. Have an aide or assistant take the opposing stand. Then have the student and aide discuss the two positions.

3. As the aide and the student discuss the two sides, the aide should assist the student in listing the opposing viewpoints in a two-column chart.

4. Then have the aide help the student use the chart to provide reasons and evidence for the student's essay. **LS** **Verbal/Linguistic**

🐻 **ELA** Writing 6.2.5.b

Standards Focus

🐻 **HSS** Analysis Skills: HR 3
ELA Writing 6.2.5

3. Evaluate and Revise

Evaluating

Use the following questions to evaluate your draft and find ways to make your paper more convincing.

Evaluation Questions for a Persuasive Essay

- Does your introduction include an opinion statement that clearly states your position?
- Have you given at least two reasons to support your position?
- Do you provide convincing evidence to back up your reasons?

- Are your reasons and evidence organized by order of importance, ending with the most important?
- Does your conclusion restate your position and summarize your reasons and evidence? Do you apply your opinion to future history?

Revising

Strengthen your argument with loaded words. Loaded words are words with strong positive or negative connotations.

- Positive—leader
- Negative—tyrant, despot
- Neutral—ruler, emperor

Loaded words can add powerful emotional appeals to your reader's feelings and help convince them to agree with your opinion.

4. Proofread and Publish

Proofreading

Keep the following guidelines in mind as you reread your paper.

- Wherever you have added, deleted, or changed anything, make sure your revision fits in smoothly and does not introduce any errors.
- Double-check names, dates, and other factual information.

Publishing

Team up with one of your classmates who has taken the same position you have. Combine your evidence to create the most powerful argument you can. Challenge a team that has taken an opposing view to a debate. Ask the rest of the class for feedback: Which argument was more convincing? What were the strengths and weaknesses of each position?

● Practice and Apply

Use the steps and strategies outlined in this workshop to write a persuasive composition.

> **TIP** **Using a Computer to Check Spelling in History Papers** Whenever you can, use a spell-checker program to help you catch careless errors. However, keep in mind that it will not solve all your spelling problems.
>
> - It will not catch misspellings that correctly spell other words, such as *their*, *they're*, and *there*, or *an* instead of *and*.
> - It will highlight but not give the preferred spelling for many proper names.
> - It cannot be relied upon for correct capitalization.

ENDINGS AND BEGINNINGS **451**

References

Declaration of Independence R2

U.S. Constitution R6

Atlas R26

Gazetteer R38

Facts about the World R42

Biographical Dictionary R48

English and Spanish Glossary R54

Index R66

Credits and Acknowledgments R77

The Declaration of Independence

In Congress, July 4, 1776
The unanimous Declaration of the thirteen united States of America,

When in the Course of human events, it becomes necessary for one people to dissolve the political bands which have connected them with another, and to assume among the Powers of the earth, the separate and equal station to which the Laws of Nature and of Nature's God entitle them, a decent respect to the opinions of mankind requires that they should declare the causes which **impel** them to the separation.

We hold these truths to be self-evident, that all men are created equal, that they are **endowed** by their Creator with certain unalienable Rights, that among these are Life, Liberty, and the pursuit of Happiness. That to secure these rights, Governments are instituted among Men, deriving their just powers from the consent of the governed, That whenever any Form of Government becomes destructive of these ends, it is the Right of the People to alter or to abolish it, and to institute new Government, laying its foundation on such principles and organizing its powers in such form, as to them shall seem most likely to effect their Safety and Happiness. Prudence, indeed, will dictate that Governments long established should not be changed for light and transient causes; and accordingly all experience hath shown, that mankind are more disposed to suffer, while evils are sufferable, than to right themselves by abolishing the forms to which they are accustomed. But when a long train of abuses and **usurpations**, pursuing invariably the same Object **evinces** a design to reduce them under absolute **Despotism**, it is their right, it is their duty, to throw off such Government, and to provide new Guards for their future security.—Such has been the patient sufferance of these Colonies; and such is now the necessity which constrains them to alter their former Systems of Government. The history of the present King of Great Britain is a history of repeated injuries and usurpations, all having in direct object the establishment of an absolute **Tyranny** over these States. To prove this, let Facts be submitted to a **candid** world.

He has refused his Assent to Laws, the most wholesome and necessary for the public good.

He has forbidden his Governors to pass Laws of immediate and pressing importance, unless suspended in their operation till his Assent should be obtained; and when so suspended, he has utterly neglected to attend to them.

Vocabulary

impel force

endowed provided

usurpations wrongful seizures of power

evinces clearly displays

despotism unlimited power

tyranny oppressive power exerted by a government or ruler

candid fair

He has refused to pass other Laws for the accommodation of large districts of people, unless those people would **relinquish** the right of Representation in the Legislature, a right **inestimable** to them and **formidable** to tyrants only.

He has called together legislative bodies at places unusual, uncomfortable, and distant from the depository of their Public Records, for the sole purpose of fatiguing them into compliance with his measures.

He has dissolved Representative Houses repeatedly, for opposing with manly firmness his invasions on the rights of the people.

He has refused for a long time, after such dissolutions, to cause others to be elected; whereby the Legislative Powers, incapable of **Annihilation**, have returned to the People at large for their exercise; the State remaining in the mean time exposed to all the dangers of invasion from without, and **convulsions** within.

He has endeavored to prevent the population of these States; for that purpose obstructing the Laws of **Naturalization of Foreigners**; refusing to pass others to encourage their migration hither, and raising the conditions of new **Appropriations of Lands**.

He has obstructed the Administration of Justice, by refusing his Assent to Laws for establishing Judiciary Powers.

He has made Judges dependent on his Will alone, for the **tenure** of their offices, and the amount and payment of their salaries.

He has erected **a multitude of** New Offices, and sent hither swarms of Officers to harass our people, and eat out their substance.

He has kept among us, in times of peace, Standing Armies without the Consent of our legislature.

He has affected to render the Military independent of and superior to the Civil Power.

He has combined with others to subject us to a jurisdiction foreign to our constitution, and unacknowledged by our laws; giving his Assent to their Acts of pretended legislation:

For **quartering** large bodies of armed troops among us:

For protecting them, by a mock Trial, from Punishment for any Murders which they should commit on the Inhabitants of these States:

For cutting off our Trade with all parts of the world:

For imposing taxes on us without our Consent:

For depriving us in many cases, of the benefits of Trial by Jury:

Vocabulary

relinquish release, yield

inestimable priceless

formidable causing dread

annihilation destruction

convulsions violent disturbances

naturalization of foreigners the process by which foreign-born persons become citizens

appropriations of lands setting aside land for settlement

tenure term

a multitude of many

quartering lodging, housing

Vocabulary

arbitrary not based on law

render make

abdicated given up

foreign mercenaries soldiers hired to fight for a country not their own

perfidy violation of trust

insurrections rebellions

petitioned for redress asked formally for a correction of wrongs

unwarrantable jurisdiction unjustified authority

magnanimity generous spirit

conjured urgently called upon

consanguinity common ancestry

acquiesce consent to

For transporting us beyond Seas to be tried for pretended offences:

For abolishing the free System of English Laws in a neighboring Province, establishing therein an **Arbitrary** government, and enlarging its Boundaries so as to **render** it at once an example and fit instrument for introducing the same absolute rule into these Colonies:

For taking away our Charters, abolishing our most valuable Laws, and altering fundamentally the Forms of our Governments:

For suspending our own Legislature, and declaring themselves invested with Power to legislate for us in all cases whatsoever.

He has **abdicated** Government here, by declaring us out of his Protection and waging War against us.

He has plundered our seas, ravaged our Coasts, burnt our towns, and destroyed the lives of our people.

He is at this time transporting large armies of **foreign mercenaries** to complete the works of death, desolation and tyranny, already begun with circumstances of Cruelty & **perfidy** scarcely paralleled in the most barbarous ages, and totally unworthy the Head of a civilized nation.

He has constrained our fellow Citizens taken Captive on the high Seas to bear Arms against their Country, to become the executioners of their friends and Brethren, or to fall themselves by their Hands.

He has excited domestic **insurrections** amongst us, and has endeavored to bring on the inhabitants of our frontiers, the merciless Indian Savages, whose known rule of warfare, is an undistinguished destruction of all ages, sexes and conditions.

In every stage of these Oppressions We have **Petitioned for Redress** in the most humble terms: Our repeated Petitions have been answered only by repeated injury. A Prince, whose character is thus marked by every act which may define a Tyrant, is unfit to be the ruler of a free People.

Nor have We been wanting in attention to our British brethren. We have warned them from time to time of attempts by their legislature to extend an **unwarrantable jurisdiction** over us. We have reminded them of the circumstances of our emigration and settlement here. We have appealed to their native justice and **magnanimity**, and we have **conjured** them by the ties of our common kindred to disavow these usurpations, which, would inevitably interrupt our connections and correspondence. They too have been deaf to the voice of justice and of **consanguinity**. We must, therefore, **acquiesce** in the necessity, which denounces our Separation, and hold them, as we hold the rest of mankind, Enemies in War, in Peace Friends.

We, therefore, the Representatives of the united States of America, in General Congress, Assembled, appealing to the Supreme Judge of the world for the **rectitude** of our intentions, do, in the Name, and by Authority of the good People of these Colonies, solemnly publish and declare, That these United Colonies are, and of Right ought to be Free and Independent States; that they are Absolved from all Allegiance to the British Crown, and that all political connection between them and the State of Great Britain, is and ought to be totally dissolved; and that as Free and Independent States, they have full Power to levy War, conclude Peace, contract Alliances, establish Commerce, and to do all other Acts and Things which Independent States may of right do. And for the support of this Declaration, with a firm reliance on the Protection of Divine Providence, we mutually pledge to each other our Lives, our Fortunes and our sacred Honor.

Vocabulary

rectitude rightness

John Hancock	Benjamin Harrison	Lewis Morris
Button Gwinnett	Thomas Nelson, Jr.	Richard Stockton
Lyman Hall	Francis Lightfoot Lee	John Witherspoon
George Walton	Carter Braxton	Francis Hopkinson
William Hooper	Robert Morris	John Hart
Joseph Hewes	Benjamin Rush	Abraham Clark
John Penn	Benjamin Franklin	Josiah Bartlett
Edward Rutledge	John Morton	William Whipple
Thomas Heyward, Jr.	George Clymer	Samuel Adams
Thomas Lynch, Jr.	James Smith	John Adams
Arthur Middleton	George Taylor	Robert Treat Paine
Samuel Chase	James Wilson	Elbridge Gerry
William Paca	George Ross	Stephen Hopkins
Thomas Stone	Caesar Rodney	William Ellery
Charles Carroll of Carrollton	George Read	Roger Sherman
George Wythe	Thomas McKean	Samuel Huntington
Richard Henry Lee	William Floyd	William Williams
Thomas Jefferson	Philip Livingston	Oliver Wolcott
	Francis Lewis	Matthew Thornton

The Constitution of the United States

Preamble

We the People of the United States, in Order to form a more perfect Union, establish Justice, insure domestic Tranquility, provide for the common defense, promote the general Welfare, and secure the Blessings of Liberty to ourselves and our Posterity, do ordain and establish this Constitution for the United States of America.

Article I The Legislature

Section 1. Congress

All legislative Powers herein granted shall be vested in a Congress of the United States, which shall consist of a Senate and House of Representatives.

Section 2. The House of Representatives

1. Elections The House of Representatives shall be composed of Members chosen every second Year by the People of the several States, and the Electors in each State shall have the Qualifications requisite for Electors of the most numerous Branch of the State Legislature.

2. Qualifications No Person shall be a Representative who shall not have attained to the Age of twenty five Years, and been seven Years a Citizen of the United States, and who shall not, when elected, be an Inhabitant of that State in which he shall be chosen.

3. Number of Representatives Representatives and direct Taxes shall be apportioned among the several States which may be included within this Union, according to their respective Numbers, which shall be determined by adding to the whole Number of free Persons, including **those bound to Service**[1] for a Term of Years, and excluding Indians not taxed, three fifths of **all other Persons**.[2] The actual **Enumeration**[3] shall be made within three Years after the first Meeting of the Congress of the United States, and within every subsequent Term of ten Years, in such Manner as they shall by Law direct. The Number of Representatives shall not exceed one for every

Note: The parts of the Constitution that have been lined through are no longer in force or no longer apply because of later amendments. The titles of the sections and articles are added for easier reference.

Legislative Branch

Article I explains how the legislative branch, called Congress, is organized. The chief purpose of the legislative branch is to make laws. Congress is made up of the Senate and the House of Representatives.

The House of Representatives

The number of members each state has in the House is based on the population of the individual state. In 1929 Congress permanently fixed the size of the House at 435 members.

Vocabulary

[1] **those bound to Service** indentured servants

[2] **all other Persons** slaves

[3] **Enumeration** census or official population count

thirty Thousand, but each State shall have at Least one Representative; and until such enumeration shall be made, the State of New Hampshire shall be entitled to choose three, Massachoosetts eight, Rhode-Island and Providence Plantations one, Connecticut five, New-York six, New Jersey four, Pennsylvania eight, Delaware one, Maryland six, Virginia ten, North Carolina five, South Carolina five, and Georgia three.

4. Vacancies When vacancies happen in the Representation from any State, the Executive Authority thereof shall issue Writs of Election to fill such Vacancies.

5. Officers and Impeachment The House of Representatives shall choose their Speaker and other Officers; and shall have the sole Power of impeachment.

Section 3. The Senate

1. Number of Senators The Senate of the United States shall be composed of two Senators from each State, chosen by the Legislature thereof, for six Years; and each Senator shall have one Vote.

2. Classifying Terms Immediately after they shall be assembled in Consequence of the first Election, they shall be divided as equally as may be into three Classes. The Seats of the Senators of the first Class shall be vacated at the Expiration of the second Year, of the second Class at the Expiration of the fourth Year, and of the third Class at the Expiration of the sixth Year, so that one third may be chosen every second Year; and if Vacancies happen by Resignation, or otherwise, during the Recess of the Legislature of any State, the Executive thereof may make temporary Appointments until the next Meeting of the Legislature, which shall then fill such Vacancies.

3. Qualifications No Person shall be a Senator who shall not have attained to the Age of thirty Years, and been nine Years a Citizen of the United States, and who shall not, when elected, be an Inhabitant of that State for which he shall be chosen.

4. Role of Vice-President The Vice President of the United States shall be President of the Senate, but shall have no Vote, unless they be equally divided.

5. Officers The Senate shall choose their other Officers, and also a President **pro tempore**,[4] in the Absence of the Vice President, or when he shall exercise the Office of President of the United States.

6. Impeachment Trials The Senate shall have the sole Power to try all **Impeachments**.[5] When sitting for that Purpose, they shall be on Oath or Affirmation. When the President of the United States is tried, the Chief Justice shall preside: And no Person shall be convicted without the Concurrence of two thirds of the Members present.

7. Punishment for Impeachment Judgment in Cases of Impeachment shall not extend further than to removal from Office, and disqualification to hold

The Vice President

The only duty that the Constitution assigns to the vice president is to preside over meetings of the Senate. Modern presidents have usually given their vice presidents more responsibilities.

Vocabulary

[4] **pro tempore** temporarily

[5] **Impeachments** official accusations of federal wrongdoing

and enjoy any Office of honor, Trust or Profit under the United States: but the Party convicted shall nevertheless be liable and subject to Indictment, Trial, Judgment and Punishment, according to Law.

Section 4. Congressional Elections

1. Regulations The Times, Places and Manner of holding Elections for Senators and Representatives, shall be prescribed in each State by the Legislature thereof; but the Congress may at any time by Law make or alter such Regulations, except as to the Places of choosing Senators.

2. Sessions ~~The Congress shall assemble at least once in every Year, and such Meeting shall be on the first Monday in December, unless they shall by Law appoint a different Day.~~

Section 5. Rules/Procedures

1. Quorum Each House shall be the Judge of the Elections, Returns and Qualifications of its own Members, and a Majority of each shall constitute a **Quorum**[6] to do Business; but a smaller Number may **adjourn**[7] from day to day, and may be authorized to compel the Attendance of absent Members, in such Manner, and under such Penalties as each House may provide.

2. Rules and Conduct Each House may determine the Rules of its Proceedings, punish its Members for disorderly Behaviour, and, with the Concurrence of two thirds, expel a Member.

3. Records Each House shall keep a Journal of its Proceedings, and from time to time publish the same, excepting such Parts as may in their Judgment require Secrecy; and the Yeas and Nays of the Members of either House on any question shall, at the Desire of one fifth of those Present, be entered on the Journal.

4. Adjournment Neither House, during the Session of Congress, shall, without the Consent of the other, adjourn for more than three days, nor to any other Place than that in which the two Houses shall be sitting.

Section 6. Payment

1. Salary The Senators and Representatives shall receive a Compensation for their Services, to be ascertained by Law, and paid out of the Treasury of the United States. They shall in all Cases, except Treason, Felony and Breach of the Peace, be privileged from Arrest during their Attendance at the Session of their respective Houses, and in going to and returning from the same; and for any Speech or Debate in either House, they shall not be questioned in any other Place.

2. Restrictions No Senator or Representative shall, during the Time for which he was elected, be appointed to any civil Office under the Authority of the United States, which shall have been created, or the **Emoluments**[8]

Vocabulary

[6] **Quorum** the minimum number of people needed to conduct business

[7] **adjourn** to stop indefinitely

[8] **Emoluments** salary

whereof shall have been increased during such time; and no Person holding any Office under the United States, shall be a Member of either House during his **Continuance**[9] in Office.

Section 7. How a Bill Becomes a Law

1. Tax Bills All **Bills**[10] for raising Revenue shall originate in the House of Representatives; but the Senate may propose or concur with Amendments as on other Bills.

2. Lawmaking Every Bill which shall have passed the House of Representatives and the Senate, shall, before it become a Law, be presented to the President of the United States: If he approve he shall sign it, but if not he shall return it, with his Objections to that House in which it shall have originated, who shall enter the Objections at large on their Journal, and proceed to reconsider it. If after such Reconsideration two thirds of that House shall agree to pass the Bill, it shall be sent, together with the Objections, to the other House, by which it shall likewise be reconsidered, and if approved by two thirds of that House, it shall become a Law. But in all such Cases the Votes of both Houses shall be determined by yeas and Nays, and the Names of the Persons voting for and against the Bill shall be entered on the Journal of each House respectively. If any Bill shall not be returned by the President within ten Days (Sundays excepted) after it shall have been presented to him, the Same shall be a Law, in like Manner as if he had signed it, unless the Congress by their Adjournment prevent its Return, in which Case it shall not be a Law.

3. Role of the President Every Order, Resolution, or Vote to which the Concurrence of the Senate and House of Representatives may be necessary (except on a question of Adjournment) shall be presented to the President of the United States; and before the Same shall take Effect, shall be approved by him, or being disapproved by him, shall be repassed by two thirds of the Senate and House of Representatives, according to the Rules and Limitations prescribed in the Case of a Bill.

Section 8. Powers Granted to Congress

1. Taxation The Congress shall have Power To lay and collect Taxes, **Duties**,[11] **Imposts**[12] and **Excises**,[13] to pay the Debts and provide for the common Defense and general Welfare of the United States; but all Duties, Imposts and Excises shall be uniform throughout the United States;

2. Credit To borrow Money on the credit of the United States;

3. Commerce To regulate Commerce with foreign Nations, and among the several States, and with the Indian Tribes;

4. Naturalization and Bankruptcy To establish an uniform **Rule of Naturalization**,[14] and uniform Laws on the subject of Bankruptcies throughout the United States;

Vocabulary

[9] **Continuance** term

[10] **Bills** proposed laws

[11] **Duties** tariffs

[12] **Imposts** taxes

[13] **Excises** internal taxes on the manufacture, sale, or consumption of a commodity

[14] **Rule of Naturalization** a law by which a foreign-born person becomes a citizen

THE CONSTITUTION

Vocabulary

[15] **Securities** bonds

[16] **Letters of Marque and Reprisal** documents issued by governments allowing merchant ships to arm themselves and attack ships of an enemy nation

5. Money To coin Money, regulate the Value thereof, and of foreign Coin, and fix the Standard of Weights and Measures;

6. Counterfeiting To provide for the Punishment of counterfeiting the **Securities**[15] and current Coin of the United States;

7. Post Office To establish Post Offices and post Roads;

8. Patents and Copyrights To promote the Progress of Science and useful Arts, by securing for limited Times to Authors and Inventors the exclusive Right to their respective Writings and Discoveries;

9. Courts To constitute Tribunals inferior to the supreme Court;

10. International Law To define and punish Piracies and Felonies committed on the high Seas, and Offences against the Law of Nations;

11. War To declare War, grant **Letters of Marque and Reprisal,**[16] and make Rules concerning Captures on Land and Water;

12. Army To raise and support Armies, but no Appropriation of Money to that Use shall be for a longer Term than two Years;

13. Navy To provide and maintain a Navy;

14. Regulation of the Military To make Rules for the Government and Regulation of the land and naval Forces;

15. Militia To provide for calling forth the Militia to execute the Laws of the Union, suppress Insurrections and repel Invasions;

16. Regulation of the Militia To provide for organizing, arming, and disciplining, the Militia, and for governing such Part of them as may be employed in the Service of the United States, reserving to the States respectively, the Appointment of the Officers, and the Authority of training the Militia according to the discipline prescribed by Congress;

17. District of Columbia To exercise exclusive Legislation in all Cases whatsoever, over such District (not exceeding ten Miles square) as may, by Cession of particular States, and the Acceptance of Congress, become the Seat of the Government of the United States, and to exercise like Authority over all Places purchased by the Consent of the Legislature of the State in which the Same shall be, for the Erection of Forts, Magazines, Arsenals, dock-Yards, and other needful Buildings;—And

18. Necessary and Proper Clause To make all Laws which shall be necessary and proper for carrying into Execution the foregoing Powers, and all other Powers vested by this Constitution in the Government of the United States, or in any Department or Officer thereof.

The Elastic Clause

The framers of the Constitution wanted a national government that was strong enough to be effective. This section lists the powers given to Congress. The last portion of Section 8 contains the so-called elastic clause.

Section 9. Powers Denied Congress

1. Slave Trade ~~The Migration or Importation of such Persons as any of the States now existing shall think proper to admit, shall not be prohibited~~

~~by the Congress prior to the Year one thousand eight hundred and eight, but a Tax or duty may be imposed on such Importation, not exceeding ten dollars for each Person.~~

2. Habeas Corpus The Privilege of the **Writ of Habeas Corpus**[17] shall not be suspended, unless when in Cases of Rebellion or Invasion the public Safety may require it.

3. Illegal Punishment No **Bill of Attainder**[18] or **ex post facto Law**[19] shall be passed.

4. Direct Taxes No **Capitation**,[20] or other direct, Tax shall be laid, unless in Proportion to the Census or enumeration herein before directed to be taken.

5. Export Taxes No Tax or Duty shall be laid on Articles exported from any State.

6. No Favorites No Preference shall be given by any Regulation of Commerce or Revenue to the Ports of one State over those of another; nor shall Vessels bound to, or from, one State, be obliged to enter, clear, or pay Duties in another.

7. Public Money No Money shall be drawn from the Treasury, but in Consequence of Appropriations made by Law; and a regular Statement and Account of the Receipts and Expenditures of all public Money shall be published from time to time.

8. Titles of Nobility No Title of Nobility shall be granted by the United States: And no Person holding any Office of Profit or Trust under them, shall, without the Consent of the Congress, accept of any present, Emolument, Office, or Title, of any kind whatever, from any King, Prince, or foreign State.

Section 10. Powers Denied the States

1. Restrictions No State shall enter into any Treaty, Alliance, or Confederation; grant Letters of Marque and Reprisal; coin Money; emit Bills of Credit; make any Thing but gold and silver Coin a Tender in Payment of Debts; pass any Bill of Attainder, ex post facto Law, or Law impairing the Obligation of Contracts, or grant any Title of Nobility.

2. Import and Export Taxes No State shall, without the Consent of the Congress, lay any Imposts or Duties on Imports or Exports, except what may be absolutely necessary for executing it's inspection Laws: and the net Produce of all Duties and Imposts, laid by any State on Imports or Exports, shall be for the Use of the Treasury of the United States; and all such Laws shall be subject to the Revision and Control of the Congress.

3. Peacetime and War Restraints No State shall, without the Consent of Congress, lay any Duty of Tonnage, keep Troops, or Ships of War in time of Peace, enter into any Agreement or Compact with another State, or with a foreign Power, or engage in War, unless actually invaded, or in such imminent Danger as will not admit of delay.

Vocabulary

[17] **Writ of Habeas Corpus** a court order that requires the government to bring a prisoner to court and explain why he or she is being held

[18] **Bill of Attainder** a law declaring that a person is guilty of a particular crime

[19] **ex post facto Law** a law that is made effective prior to the date that it was passed and therefore punishes people for acts that were not illegal at the time

[20] **Capitation** a direct uniform tax imposed on each head, or person

Article II | The Executive

Section 1. | The Presidency

1. Terms of Office The executive Power shall be vested in a President of the United States of America. He shall hold his Office during the Term of four Years, and, together with the Vice President, chosen for the same Term, be elected, as follows:

2. Electoral College Each State shall appoint, in such Manner as the Legislature thereof may direct, a Number of Electors, equal to the whole Number of Senators and Representatives to which the State may be entitled in the Congress: but no Senator or Representative, or Person holding an Office of Trust or Profit under the United States, shall be appointed an Elector.

3. Former Method of Electing President ~~The Electors shall meet in their respective States, and vote by Ballot for two Persons, of whom one at least shall not be an Inhabitant of the same State with themselves. And they shall make a List of all the Persons voted for, and of the Number of Votes for each; which List they shall sign and certify, and transmit sealed to the Seat of the Government of the United States, directed to the President of the Senate. The President of the Senate shall, in the Presence of the Senate and House of Representatives, open all the Certificates, and the Votes shall then be counted. The Person having the greatest Number of Votes shall be the President, if such Number be a Majority of the whole Number of Electors appointed; and if there be more than one who have such Majority, and have an equal Number of Votes, then the House of Representatives shall immediately choose by Ballot one of them for President; and if no Person have a Majority, then from the five highest on the List the said House shall in like Manner choose the President. But in choosing the President, the Votes shall be taken by States, the Representation from each State having one Vote; A quorum for this purpose shall consist of a Member or Members from two thirds of the States, and a Majority of all the States shall be necessary to a Choice. In every Case, after the Choice of the President, the Person having the greatest Number of Votes of the Electors shall be the Vice President. But if there should remain two or more who have equal Votes, the Senate shall choose from them by Ballot the Vice President.~~

4. Election Day The Congress may determine the Time of choosing the Electors, and the Day on which they shall give their Votes; which Day shall be the same throughout the United States.

5. Qualifications No Person except a natural born Citizen ~~, or a Citizen of the United States, at the time of the Adoption of this Constitution,~~ shall be eligible to the Office of President; neither shall any Person be eligible to

Executive Branch

The president is the chief of the executive branch. It is the job of the president to enforce the laws. The framers wanted the president's and vice president's terms of office and manner of selection to be different from those of members of Congress. They decided on four-year terms, but they had a difficult time agreeing on how to select the president and vice president. The framers finally set up an electoral system, which varies greatly from our electoral process today.

Presidential Elections

In 1845 Congress set the Tuesday following the first Monday in November of every fourth year as the general election date for selecting presidential electors.

that Office who shall not have attained to the Age of thirty five Years, and been fourteen Years a Resident within the United States.

6. Succession In Case of the Removal of the President from Office, or of his Death, Resignation, or Inability to discharge the Powers and Duties of the said Office, the Same shall devolve on the Vice President, and the Congress may by Law provide for the Case of Removal, Death, Resignation or Inability, both of the President and Vice President, declaring what Officer shall then act as President, and such Officer shall act accordingly, until the Disability be removed, or a President shall be elected.

7. Salary The President shall, at stated Times, receive for his Services, a Compensation, which shall neither be increased nor diminished during the Period for which he shall have been elected, and he shall not receive within that Period any other Emolument from the United States, or any of them.

8. Oath of Office Before he enter on the Execution of his Office, he shall take the following Oath or Affirmation:—"I do solemnly swear (or affirm) that I will faithfully execute the Office of President of the United States, and will to the best of my Ability, preserve, protect and defend the Constitution of the United States."

Section 2. Powers of Presidency

1. Military Powers The President shall be Commander in Chief of the Army and Navy of the United States, and of the Militia of the several States, when called into the actual Service of the United States; he may require the Opinion, in writing, of the principal Officer in each of the executive Departments, upon any Subject relating to the Duties of their respective Offices, and he shall have Power to grant **Reprieves**[21] and **Pardons**[22] for Offences against the United States, except in Cases of Impeachment.

2. Treaties and Appointments He shall have Power, by and with the Advice and Consent of the Senate, to make Treaties, provided two thirds of the Senators present concur; and he shall nominate, and by and with the Advice and Consent of the Senate, shall appoint Ambassadors, other public Ministers and Consuls, Judges of the supreme Court, and all other Officers of the United States, whose Appointments are not herein otherwise provided for, and which shall be established by Law: but the Congress may by Law vest the Appointment of such inferior Officers, as they think proper, in the President alone, in the Courts of Law, or in the Heads of Departments.

3. Vacancies The President shall have Power to fill up all Vacancies that may happen during the Recess of the Senate, by granting Commissions which shall expire at the End of their next Session.

Presidential Salary

In 1999 Congress voted to set future presidents' salaries at $400,000 per year. The president also receives an annual expense account. The president must pay taxes only on the salary.

Commander in Chief

Today the president is in charge of the army, navy, air force, marines, and coast guard. Only Congress, however, can decide if the United States will declare war.

Appointments

Most of the president's appointments to office must be approved by the Senate.

Vocabulary

[21] **Reprieves** delays of punishment

[22] **Pardons** releases from the legal penalties associated with a crime

Section 3. | Presidential Duties |

He shall from time to time give to the Congress Information of the State of the Union, and recommend to their Consideration such Measures as he shall judge necessary and expedient; he may, on extraordinary Occasions, convene both Houses, or either of them, and in Case of Disagreement between them, with Respect to the Time of Adjournment, he may adjourn them to such Time as he shall think proper; he shall receive Ambassadors and other public Ministers; he shall take Care that the Laws be faithfully executed, and shall Commission all the Officers of the United States.

Section 4. | Impeachment |

The President, Vice President and all civil Officers of the United States, shall be removed from Office on Impeachment for, and Conviction of, Treason, Bribery, or other high Crimes and Misdemeanors.

Article III | The Judiciary |

Section 1. | Federal Courts and Judges |

The judicial Power of the United States shall be vested in one supreme Court, and in such inferior Courts as the Congress may from time to time ordain and establish. The Judges, both of the supreme and inferior Courts, shall hold their Offices during good Behavior, and shall, at stated Times, receive for their Services a Compensation, which shall not be diminished during their Continuance in Office.

Section 2. | Authority of the Courts |

1. General Authority The judicial Power shall extend to all Cases, in Law and Equity, arising under this Constitution, the Laws of the United States, and Treaties made, or which shall be made, under their Authority;—to all Cases affecting Ambassadors, other public Ministers and Consuls;—to all Cases of admiralty and maritime Jurisdiction;—to Controversies to which the United States shall be a Party;—to Controversies between two or more States —between a State and Citizens of another State; —between Citizens of different States;—between Citizens of the same State claiming Lands under Grants of different States, and between a State, or the Citizens thereof, and foreign States, Citizens or Subjects.

2. Supreme Authority In all Cases affecting Ambassadors, other public Ministers and Consuls, and those in which a State shall be Party, the supreme Court shall have original Jurisdiction. In all the other Cases before mentioned, the supreme Court shall have appellate Jurisdiction, both as to Law and Fact, with such Exceptions, and under such Regulations as the Congress shall make.

3. Trial by Jury The Trial of all Crimes, except in Cases of Impeachment, shall be by Jury; and such Trial shall be held in the State where the said Crimes shall have been committed; but when not committed within any State, the Trial shall be at such Place or Places as the Congress may by Law have directed.

Section 3. Treason

1. Definition Treason against the United States, shall consist only in levying War against them, or in adhering to their Enemies, giving them Aid and Comfort. No Person shall be convicted of Treason unless on the Testimony of two Witnesses to the same overt Act, or on Confession in open Court.

2. Punishment The Congress shall have Power to declare the Punishment of Treason, but no Attainder of Treason shall work **Corruption of Blood**,[23] or Forfeiture except during the Life of the Person attainted.

Article IV Relations among States

Section 1. State Acts and Records

Full Faith and Credit shall be given in each State to the public Acts, Records, and judicial Proceedings of every other State. And the Congress may by general Laws prescribe the Manner in which such Acts, Records and Proceedings shall be proved, and the Effect thereof.

Section 2. Rights of Citizens

1. Citizenship The Citizens of each State shall be entitled to all Privileges and Immunities of Citizens in the several States.

2. Extradition A Person charged in any State with Treason, Felony, or other Crime, who shall flee from Justice, and be found in another State, shall on Demand of the executive Authority of the State from which he fled, be delivered up, to be removed to the State having Jurisdiction of the Crime.

3. Fugitive Slaves ~~No Person held to Service or Labour in one State, under the Laws thereof, escaping into another, shall, in Consequence of any Law or Regulation therein, be discharged from such Service or Labour, but shall be delivered up on Claim of the Party to whom such Service or Labour may be due.~~

Section 3. New States

1. Admission New States may be admitted by the Congress into this Union; but no new State shall be formed or erected within the Jurisdiction of any other State; nor any State be formed by the Junction of two or more States, or Parts of States, without the Consent of the Legislatures of the States concerned as well as of the Congress.

The States

States must honor the laws, records, and court decisions of other states. A person cannot escape a legal obligation by moving from one state to another.

2. Congressional Authority The Congress shall have Power to dispose of and make all needful Rules and Regulations respecting the Territory or other Property belonging to the United States; and nothing in this Constitution shall be so construed as to Prejudice any Claims of the United States, or of any particular State.

Section 4. Guarantees to the States

The United States shall guarantee to every State in this Union a Republican Form of Government, and shall protect each of them against Invasion; and on Application of the Legislature, or of the Executive (when the Legislature cannot be convened), against domestic Violence.

Article V Amending the Constitution

The Congress, whenever two thirds of both Houses shall deem it necessary, shall propose Amendments to this Constitution, or, on the Application of the Legislatures of two thirds of the several States, shall call a Convention for proposing Amendments, which, in either Case, shall be valid to all Intents and Purposes, as Part of this Constitution, when ratified by the Legislatures of three fourths of the several States, or by Conventions in three fourths thereof, as the one or the other Mode of Ratification may be proposed by the Congress; Provided that no Amendment which may be made prior to the Year One thousand eight hundred and eight shall in any Manner affect the first and fourth Clauses in the Ninth Section of the first Article; and that no State, without its Consent, shall be deprived of its equal Suffrage in the Senate.

Article VI Supremacy of National Government

All Debts contracted and Engagements entered into, before the Adoption of this Constitution, shall be as valid against the United States under this Constitution, as under the Confederation.

This Constitution, and the Laws of the United States which shall be made in Pursuance thereof; and all Treaties made, or which shall be made, under the Authority of the United States, shall be the supreme Law of the Land; and the Judges in every State shall be bound thereby, any Thing in the Constitution or Laws of any State to the Contrary notwithstanding.

The Senators and Representatives before mentioned, and the Members of the several State Legislatures, and all executive and judicial Officers, both of the United States and of the several States, shall be bound by Oath or Affirmation, to support this Constitution; but no religious Test shall ever be required as a Qualification to any Office or public Trust under the United States.

National Supremacy

One of the biggest problems facing the delegates to the Constitutional Convention was the question of what would happen if a state law and a federal law conflicted. Which law would be followed? Who would decide? The second clause of Article VI answers those questions. When a federal law and a state law disagree, the federal law overrides the state law. The Constitution and other federal laws are the "supreme Law of the Land." This clause is often called the supremacy clause.

Article VII | Ratification

The Ratification of the Conventions of nine States, shall be sufficient for the Establishment of this Constitution between the States so ratifying the Same.

Done in Convention by the Unanimous Consent of the States present the Seventeenth Day of September in the Year of our Lord one thousand seven hundred and Eighty seven and of the Independence of the United States of America the Twelfth In witness whereof We have hereunto subscribed our Names,

George Washington—
President and deputy from Virginia

Delaware

George Read
Gunning Bedford Jr.
John Dickinson
Richard Bassett
Jacob Broom

Maryland

James McHenry
Daniel of
* St. Thomas Jenifer*
Daniel Carroll

Virginia

John Blair
James Madison Jr.

North Carolina

William Blount
Richard Dobbs Spaight
Hugh Williamson

South Carolina

John Rutledge
Charles Cotesworth
* Pinckney*
Charles Pinckney
Pierce Butler

Georgia

William Few
Abraham Baldwin

New Hampshire

John Langdon
Nicholas Gilman

Massachusetts

Nathaniel Gorham
Rufus King

Connecticut

William Samuel Johnson
Roger Sherman

New York

Alexander Hamilton

New Jersey

William Livingston
David Brearley
William Paterson
Jonathan Dayton

Pennsylvania

Benjamin Franklin
Thomas Mifflin
Robert Morris
George Clymer
Thomas FitzSimons
Jared Ingersoll
James Wilson
Gouverneur Morris

Attest:
William Jackson,
Secretary

Ratification

The Articles of Confederation called for all 13 states to approve any revision to the Articles. The Constitution required that 9 out of the 13 states would be needed to ratify the Constitution. The first state to ratify was Delaware, on December 7, 1787. Almost two-and-a-half years later, on May 29, 1790, Rhode Island became the last state to ratify the Constitution.

Vocabulary

[24] **quartered** housed

[25] **Warrants** written orders authorizing a person to make an arrest, a seizure, or a search

[26] **infamous** disgraceful

[27] **indictment** the act of charging with a crime

[28] **ascertained** found out

Rights of the Accused

The Fifth, Sixth, and Seventh Amendments describe the procedures that courts must follow when trying people accused of crimes.

Trials

The Sixth Amendment makes several guarantees, including a prompt trial and a trial by a jury chosen from the state and district in which the crime was committed.

Constitutional Amendments

Note: The first 10 amendments to the Constitution were ratified on December 15, 1791, and form what is known as the Bill of Rights.

Amendments 1–10. The Bill of Rights

Amendment I

Congress shall make no law respecting an establishment of religion, or prohibiting the free exercise thereof; or abridging the freedom of speech, or of the press; or the right of the people peaceably to assemble, and to petition the Government for a redress of grievances.

Amendment II

A well regulated Militia, being necessary to the security of a free State, the right of the people to keep and bear Arms, shall not be infringed.

Amendment III

No Soldier shall, in time of peace be **quartered**[24] in any house, without the consent of the Owner, nor in time of war, but in a manner to be prescribed by law.

Amendment IV

The right of the people to be secure in their persons, houses, papers, and effects, against unreasonable searches and seizures, shall not be violated, and no **Warrants**[25] shall issue, but upon probable cause, supported by Oath or affirmation, and particularly describing the place to be searched, and the persons or things to be seized.

Amendment V

No person shall be held to answer for a capital, or otherwise **infamous**[26] crime, unless on a presentment or **indictment**[27] of a Grand Jury, except in cases arising in the land or naval forces, or in the Militia, when in actual service in time of War or public danger; nor shall any person be subject for the same offence to be twice put in jeopardy of life or limb; nor shall be compelled in any criminal case to be a witness against himself, nor be deprived of life, liberty, or property, without due process of law; nor shall private property be taken for public use, without just compensation.

Amendment VI

In all criminal prosecutions, the accused shall enjoy the right to a speedy and public trial, by an impartial jury of the State and district wherein the crime shall have been committed, which district shall have been previously **ascertained**[28] by law, and to be informed of the nature and cause of the accusation; to be confronted with the witnesses against him; to have compulsory process for obtaining witnesses in his favor, and to have the Assistance of Counsel for his defence.

Amendment VII

In suits at common law, where the value in controversy shall exceed twenty dollars, the right of trial by jury shall be preserved, and no fact tried by a jury, shall be otherwise reexamined in any Court of the United States, than according to the rules of the common law.

Amendment VIII

Excessive bail shall not be required, nor excessive fines imposed, nor cruel and unusual punishments inflicted.

Amendment IX

The enumeration in the Constitution, of certain rights, shall not be construed to deny or disparage others retained by the people.

Amendment X

The powers not delegated to the United States by the Constitution, nor prohibited by it to the States, are reserved to the States respectively, or to the people.

Amendments 11–27

Amendment XI

Passed by Congress March 4, 1794. Ratified February 7, 1795.

The Judicial power of the United States shall not be **construed**[29] to extend to any suit in law or equity, commenced or prosecuted against one of the United States by Citizens of another State, or by Citizens or Subjects of any Foreign State.

Amendment XII

Passed by Congress December 9, 1803. Ratified June 15, 1804.

The Electors shall meet in their respective states and vote by ballot for President and Vice-President, one of whom, at least, shall not be an inhabitant of the same state with themselves; they shall name in their ballots the person voted for as President, and in distinct ballots the person voted for as Vice-President, and they shall make distinct lists of all persons voted for as President, and of all persons voted for as Vice-President, and of the number of votes for each, which lists they shall sign and certify, and transmit sealed to the seat of the government of the United States, directed to the President of the Senate;—the President of the Senate shall, in the presence of the Senate and House of Representatives, open all the certificates and the votes shall then be counted;—The person having the greatest number of votes for President, shall be the President, if such number be a majority of the whole number of Electors appointed; and if no person have such majority, then from the persons having the highest numbers not exceeding three on the list of those voted for as President, the House of Representatives shall choose immediately, by ballot, the President. But in choosing the

Vocabulary

[29] **construed** explained or interpreted

President and Vice President

The Twelfth Amendment changed the election procedure for president and vice president.

President, the votes shall be taken by states, the representation from each state having one vote; a quorum for this purpose shall consist of a member or members from two-thirds of the states, and a majority of all the states shall be necessary to a choice. ~~And if the House of Representatives shall not choose a President whenever the right of choice shall devolve upon them, before the fourth day of March next following, then the Vice-President shall act as President, as in case of the death or other constitutional disability of the President.~~ The person having the greatest number of votes as Vice-President, shall be the Vice-President, if such number be a majority of the whole number of Electors appointed, and if no person have a majority, then from the two highest numbers on the list, the Senate shall choose the Vice-President; a quorum for the purpose shall consist of two-thirds of the whole number of Senators, and a majority of the whole number shall be necessary to a choice. But no person constitutionally ineligible to the office of President shall be eligible to that of Vice-President of the United States.

Amendment XIII

Passed by Congress January 31, 1865. Ratified December 6, 1865.

1. Slavery Banned Neither slavery nor **involuntary servitude,**[30] except as a punishment for crime whereof the party shall have been duly convicted, shall exist within the United States, or any place subject to their jurisdiction.

2. Enforcement Congress shall have power to enforce this article by appropriate legislation.

Amendment XIV

Passed by Congress June 13, 1866. Ratified July 9, 1868.

1. Citizenship Defined All persons born or naturalized in the United States, and subject to the jurisdiction thereof, are citizens of the United States and of the State wherein they reside. No State shall make or enforce any law which shall abridge the privileges or immunities of citizens of the United States; nor shall any State deprive any person of life, liberty, or property, without due process of law; nor deny to any person within its jurisdiction the equal protection of the laws.

2. Voting Rights Representatives shall be apportioned among the several States according to their respective numbers, counting the whole number of persons in each State, ~~excluding Indians not taxed~~. But when the right to vote at any election for the choice of electors for President and Vice-President of the United States, Representatives in Congress, the Executive and Judicial officers of a State, or the members of the Legislature thereof, is denied to any of the ~~male~~ inhabitants of such State, ~~being twenty-one years of age~~, and citizens of the United States, or in any way abridged, except for participation in rebellion, or other crime, the basis of representation therein shall be reduced in the proportion which the number of such ~~male~~ citizens shall bear to the whole number of ~~male~~ citizens ~~twenty-one years of age~~ in such State.

Vocabulary

[30] **involuntary** servitude being forced to work against one's will

Abolishing Slavery

Although some slaves had been freed during the Civil War, slavery was not abolished until the Thirteenth Amendment took effect.

Protecting the Rights of Citizens

In 1833 the Supreme Court ruled that the Bill of Rights limited the federal government but not the state governments. This ruling was interpreted to mean that states were able to keep African Americans from becoming state citizens and keep the Bill of Rights from protecting them. The Fourteenth Amendment defines citizenship and prevents states from interfering in the rights of citizens of the United States.

3. Rebels Banned from Government No person shall be a Senator or Representative in Congress, or elector of President and Vice-President, or hold any office, civil or military, under the United States, or under any State, who, having previously taken an oath, as a member of Congress, or as an officer of the United States, or as a member of any State legislature, or as an executive or judicial officer of any State, to support the Constitution of the United States, shall have engaged in insurrection or rebellion against the same, or given aid or comfort to the enemies thereof. But Congress may by a vote of two-thirds of each House, remove such disability.

4. Payment of Debts The validity of the public debt of the United States, authorized by law, including debts incurred for payment of pensions and bounties for services in suppressing insurrection or rebellion, shall not be questioned. But neither the United States nor any State shall assume or pay any debt or obligation incurred in aid of insurrection or rebellion against the United States, ~~or any claim for the loss or emancipation of any slave~~; but all such debts, obligations and claims shall be held illegal and void.

5. Enforcement The Congress shall have the power to enforce, by appropriate legislation, the provisions of this article.

Amendment XV

Passed by Congress February 26, 1869. Ratified February 3, 1870.

1. Voting Rights The right of citizens of the United States to vote shall not be denied or abridged by the United States or by any State on account of race, color, or previous condition of servitude.

2. Enforcement The Congress shall have the power to enforce this article by appropriate legislation.

Amendment XVI

Passed by Congress July 2, 1909. Ratified February 3, 1913.

The Congress shall have power to lay and collect taxes on incomes, from whatever source derived, without apportionment among the several States, and without regard to any census or enumeration.

Amendment XVII

Passed by Congress May 13, 1912. Ratified April 8, 1913.

1. Senators Elected by Citizens The Senate of the United States shall be composed of two Senators from each State, elected by the people thereof, for six years; and each Senator shall have one vote. The electors in each State shall have the qualifications requisite for electors of the most numerous branch of the State legislatures.

2. Vacancies When vacancies happen in the representation of any State in the Senate, the executive authority of such State shall issue writs of election to fill such vacancies: *Provided*, That the legislature of any State may empower the executive thereof to make temporary appointments until the people fill the vacancies by election as the legislature may direct.

3. Future Elections ~~This amendment shall not be so construed as to affect the election or term of any Senator chosen before it becomes valid as part of the Constitution.~~

Amendment XVIII

Passed by Congress December 18, 1917. Ratified January 16, 1919. Repealed by Amendment XXI.

1. Liquor Banned ~~After one year from the ratification of this article the manufacture, sale, or transportation of intoxicating liquors within, the importation thereof into, or the exportation thereof from the United States and all territory subject to the jurisdiction thereof for beverage purposes is hereby prohibited.~~

2. Enforcement ~~The Congress and the several States shall have concurrent power to enforce this article by appropriate legislation.~~

3. Ratification ~~This article shall be inoperative unless it shall have been ratified as an amendment to the Constitution by the legislatures of the several States, as provided in the Constitution, within seven years from the date of the submission hereof to the States by the Congress.~~

Amendment XIX

Passed by Congress June 4, 1919. Ratified August 18, 1920.

1. Voting Rights The right of citizens of the United States to vote shall not be denied or abridged by the United States or by any State on account of sex.

2. Enforcement Congress shall have power to enforce this article by appropriate legislation.

Amendment XX

Passed by Congress March 2, 1932. Ratified January 23, 1933.

1. Presidential Terms The terms of the President and the Vice President shall end at noon on the 20th day of January, and the terms of Senators and Representatives at noon on the 3d day of January, of the years in which such terms would have ended if this article had not been ratified; and the terms of their successors shall then begin.

2. Meeting of Congress The Congress shall assemble at least once in every year, and such meeting shall begin at noon on the 3d day of January, unless they shall by law appoint a different day.

3. Succession of Vice President If, at the time fixed for the beginning of the term of the President, the President elect shall have died, the Vice President elect shall become President. If a President shall not have been chosen before the time fixed for the beginning of his term, or if the President elect

Prohibition

Although many people believed that the Eighteenth Amendment was good for the health and welfare of the American people, it was repealed 14 years later.

Women's Suffrage

Abigail Adams and others were disappointed that the Declaration of Independence and the Constitution did not specifically include women. It took many years and much campaigning before suffrage for women was finally achieved.

Taking Office

In the original Constitution, a newly elected president and Congress did not take office until March 4, which was four months after the November election. The officials who were leaving office were called lame ducks because they had little influence during those four months. The Twentieth Amendment changed the date that the new president and Congress take office. Members of Congress now take office during the first week of January, and the president takes office on January 20.

shall have failed to qualify, then the Vice President elect shall act as President until a President shall have qualified; and the Congress may by law provide for the case wherein neither a President elect nor a Vice President shall have qualified, declaring who shall then act as President, or the manner in which one who is to act shall be selected, and such person shall act accordingly until a President or Vice President shall have qualified.

4. Succession by Vote of Congress The Congress may by law provide for the case of the death of any of the persons from whom the House of Representatives may choose a President whenever the right of choice shall have devolved upon them, and for the case of the death of any of the persons from whom the Senate may choose a Vice President whenever the right of choice shall have devolved upon them.

5. Ratification Sections 1 and 2 shall take effect on the 15th day of October following the ratification of this article.

6. Ratification This article shall be inoperative unless it shall have been ratified as an amendment to the Constitution by the legislatures of three-fourths of the several States within seven years from the date of its submission.

Amendment XXI

Passed by Congress February 20, 1933. Ratified December 5, 1933.

1. 18th Amendment Repealed The eighteenth article of amendment to the Constitution of the United States is hereby repealed.

2. Liquor Allowed by Law The transportation or importation into any State, Territory, or Possession of the United States for delivery or use therein of intoxicating liquors, in violation of the laws thereof, is hereby prohibited.

3. Ratification This article shall be inoperative unless it shall have been ratified as an amendment to the Constitution by conventions in the several States, as provided in the Constitution, within seven years from the date of the submission hereof to the States by the Congress.

Amendment XXII

Passed by Congress March 21, 1947. Ratified February 27, 1951.

1. Term Limits No person shall be elected to the office of the President more than twice, and no person who has held the office of President, or acted as President, for more than two years of a term to which some other person was elected President shall be elected to the office of President more than once. But this Article shall not apply to any person holding the office of President when this Article was proposed by Congress, and shall not prevent any person who may be holding the office of President, or acting as President, during the term within which this Article becomes operative from holding the office of President or acting as President during the remainder of such term.

2. Ratification ~~This article shall be inoperative unless it shall have been ratified as an amendment to the Constitution by the legislatures of three-fourths of the several States within seven years from the date of its submission to the States by the Congress.~~

Amendment XXIII

Passed by Congress June 16, 1960. Ratified March 29, 1961.

1. District of Columbia Represented The District constituting the seat of Government of the United States shall appoint in such manner as Congress may direct:

A number of electors of President and Vice President equal to the whole number of Senators and Representatives in Congress to which the District would be entitled if it were a State, but in no event more than the least populous State; they shall be in addition to those appointed by the States, but they shall be considered, for the purposes of the election of President and Vice President, to be electors appointed by a State; and they shall meet in the District and perform such duties as provided by the twelfth article of amendment.

2. Enforcement The Congress shall have power to enforce this article by appropriate legislation.

Amendment XXIV

Passed by Congress August 27, 1962. Ratified January 23, 1964.

1. Voting Rights The right of citizens of the United States to vote in any primary or other election for President or Vice President, for electors for President or Vice President, or for Senator or Representative in Congress, shall not be denied or abridged by the United States or any State by reason of failure to pay poll tax or other tax.

2. Enforcement The Congress shall have power to enforce this article by appropriate legislation.

Amendment XXV

Passed by Congress July 6, 1965. Ratified February 10, 1967.

1. Sucession of Vice President In case of the removal of the President from office or of his death or resignation, the Vice President shall become President.

2. Vacancy of Vice President Whenever there is a vacancy in the office of the Vice President, the President shall nominate a Vice President who shall take office upon confirmation by a majority vote of both Houses of Congress.

3. Written Declaration Whenever the President transmits to the President pro tempore of the Senate and the Speaker of the House of Representatives his written declaration that he is unable to discharge the powers and duties of his office, and until he transmits to them a written declara-

---

Voting Rights

Until the ratification of the Twenty-third Amendment, the people of Washington, D.C., could not vote in presidential elections.

Presidential Disability

The illness of President Eisenhower in the 1950s and the assassination of President Kennedy in 1963 were the events behind the Twenty-fifth Amendment. The Constitution did not provide a clear-cut method for a vice president to take over for a disabled president or upon the death of a president. This amendment provides for filling the office of the vice president if a vacancy occurs, and it provides a way for the vice president—or someone else in the line of succession—to take over if the president is unable to perform the duties of that office.

tion to the contrary, such powers and duties shall be discharged by the Vice President as Acting President.

4. Removing the President Whenever the Vice President and a majority of either the principal officers of the executive departments or of such other body as Congress may by law provide, transmit to the President pro tempore of the Senate and the Speaker of the House of Representatives their written declaration that the President is unable to discharge the powers and duties of his office, the Vice President shall immediately assume the powers and duties of the office as Acting President.

Thereafter, when the President transmits to the President pro tempore of the Senate and the Speaker of the House of Representatives his written declaration that no inability exists, he shall resume the powers and duties of his office unless the Vice President and a majority of either the principal officers of the executive department or of such other body as Congress may by law provide, transmit within four days to the President pro tempore of the Senate and the Speaker of the House of Representatives their written declaration that the President is unable to discharge the powers and duties of his office. Thereupon Congress shall decide the issue, assembling within forty-eight hours for that purpose if not in session. If the Congress, within twenty-one days after receipt of the latter written declaration, or, if Congress is not in session, within twenty-one days after Congress is required to assemble, determines by two-thirds vote of both Houses that the President is unable to discharge the powers and duties of his office, the Vice President shall continue to discharge the same as Acting President; otherwise, the President shall resume the powers and duties of his office.

Amendment XXVI

Passed by Congress March 23, 1971. Ratified July 1, 1971.

1. Voting Rights The right of citizens of the United States, who are eighteen years of age or older, to vote shall not be denied or abridged by the United States or by any State on account of age.

2. Enforcement The Congress shall have power to enforce this article by appropriate legislation.

Amendment XXVII

Originally proposed September 25, 1789. Ratified May 7, 1992.

No law, varying the compensation for the services of the Senators and Representatives, shall take effect, until an election of representatives shall have intervened.

Expanded Suffrage

The Voting Rights Act of 1970 tried to set the voting age at 18. However, the Supreme Court ruled that the act set the voting age for national elections only, not for state or local elections. The Twenty-sixth Amendment gave 18-year-old citizens the right to vote in all elections.

ATLAS

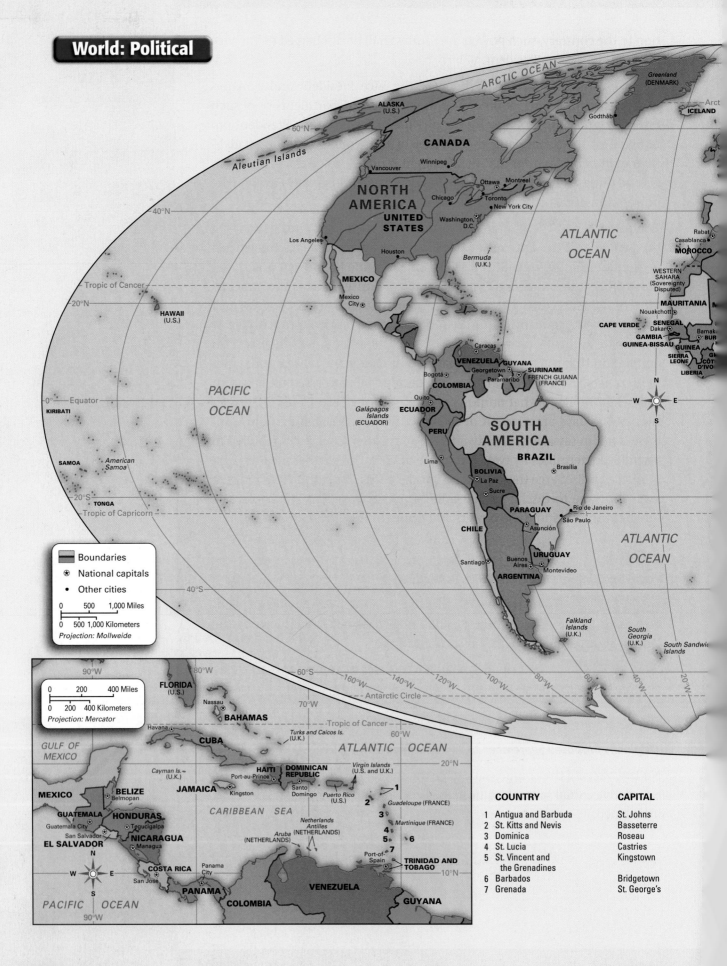

Boundaries
⊛ National capitals
• Other cities

0   500   1,000 Miles
0   500 1,000 Kilometers
Projection: Mollweide

0   200   400 Miles
0   200   400 Kilometers
Projection: Mercator

COUNTRY	CAPITAL
1 Antigua and Barbuda	St. Johns
2 St. Kitts and Nevis	Basseterre
3 Dominica	Roseau
4 St. Lucia	Castries
5 St. Vincent and the Grenadines	Kingstown
6 Barbados	Bridgetown
7 Grenada	St. George's

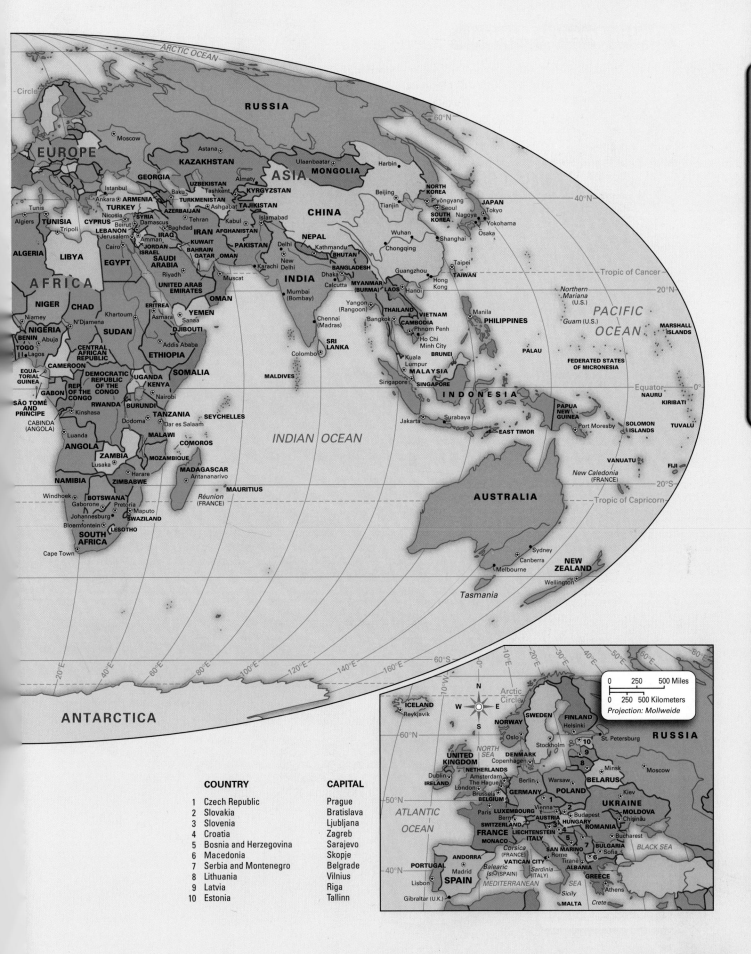

ARCTIC OCEAN

Circle

EUROPE

RUSSIA

Moscow

KAZAKHSTAN

ASIA

MONGOLIA

Astana

Ulaanbaatar

Harbin

GEORGIA

Almaty

Beijing

NORTH
KOREA

JAPAN

Istanbul

UZBEKISTAN

KYRGYZSTAN

Tianjin

P'yŏngyang

Tokyo

40°N

Ankara

ARMENIA

Baku

Tashkent

CHINA

Seoul

Nagoya

TURKEY

TURKMENISTAN

TAJIKISTAN

SOUTH
KOREA

Yokohama

Tunis

Nicosia

AZERBAIJAN

Ashgabat

Wuhan

Osaka

Algiers

TUNISIA

CYPRUS

SYRIA

Tehran

Kabul

Shanghai

Beirut

Damascus

Baghdad

IRAN

AFGHANISTAN

Islamabad

Chongqing

Tropic of Cancer

Tripoli

LEBANON

IRAQ

Delhi

NEPAL

20°N

ALGERIA

LIBYA

Jerusalem

Amman

JORDAN

KUWAIT

PAKISTAN

New
Delhi

Kathmandu

BHUTAN

Guangzhou

Taipei

Northern
Mariana
(U.S.)

PACIFIC
OCEAN

Cairo

ISRAEL

BAHRAIN

QATAR

Karachi

BANGLADESH

Hong
Kong

TAIWAN

EGYPT

SAUDI
ARABIA

OMAN

INDIA

Dhaka

Calcutta

MYANMAR
(BURMA)

LAOS

Hanoi

AFRICA

Riyadh

UNITED ARAB
EMIRATES

Mumbai
(Bombay)

Manila

Guam (U.S.)

MARSHALL
ISLANDS

NIGER

CHAD

ERITREA

YEMEN

OMAN

Chennai
(Madras)

Yangon
(Rangoon)

THAILAND

VIETNAM

PHILIPPINES

Khartoum

Asmara

Sanaa

Bangkok

CAMBODIA

PALAU

Niamey

N'Djamena

DJIBOUTI

SRI
LANKA

Phnom Penh

FEDERATED STATES
OF MICRONESIA

NIGERIA

SUDAN

Addis Ababa

Colombo

Ho Chi
Minh City

BRUNEI

BENIN

CENTRAL
AFRICAN
REPUBLIC

ETHIOPIA

SOMALIA

Kuala
Lumpur

MALAYSIA

TOGO

Abuja

MALDIVES

Lagos

CAMEROON

EQUA-
TORIAL
GUINEA

DEMOCRATIC
REPUBLIC
OF THE
CONGO

UGANDA

KENYA

Singapore

SINGAPORE

INDONESIA

Equator

NAURU

0°

KIRIBATI

GABON

REP.
OF THE
CONGO

RWANDA

BURUNDI

Nairobi

PAPUA
NEW
GUINEA

SOLOMON
ISLANDS

TUVALU

SÃO TOMÉ
AND
PRÍNCIPE

Kinshasa

TANZANIA

SEYCHELLES

Jakarta

Surabaya

Port Moresby

CABINDA
(ANGOLA)

Luanda

Dodoma

Dar es Salaam

EAST TIMOR

VANUATU

FIJI

ANGOLA

MALAWI

COMOROS

INDIAN OCEAN

New Caledonia
(FRANCE)

ZAMBIA

MOZAMBIQUE

Lusaka

MADAGASCAR

20°S

NAMIBIA

ZIMBABWE

Harare

Antananarivo

Réunion
(FRANCE)

MAURITIUS

AUSTRALIA

Tropic of Capricorn

Windhoek

BOTSWANA

Gaborone

Pretoria

SWAZILAND

Johannesburg

Maputo

SOUTH
AFRICA

Bloemfontein

LESOTHO

Sydney

Cape Town

Canberra

NEW
ZEALAND

Melbourne

Wellington

ANTARCTICA

Tasmania

20°E   40°E   60°E   80°E   100°E   120°E   140°E   160°E   60°S

	COUNTRY	CAPITAL
1	Czech Republic	Prague
2	Slovakia	Bratislava
3	Slovenia	Ljubljana
4	Croatia	Zagreb
5	Bosnia and Herzegovina	Sarajevo
6	Macedonia	Skopje
7	Serbia and Montenegro	Belgrade
8	Lithuania	Vilnius
9	Latvia	Riga
10	Estonia	Tallinn

10°E   20°E   30°E   40°E   50°E   60°E   70°E   80°E

0   250   500 Miles
0   250   500 Kilometers
Projection: Mollweide

ICELAND

Reykjavik

Arctic
Circle

SWEDEN

FINLAND

NORWAY

Helsinki

10

St. Petersburg

RUSSIA

60°N

NORTH
SEA

DENMARK

Oslo

Stockholm

9

UNITED
KINGDOM

Copenhagen

8

Minsk

Moscow

Dublin

NETHERLANDS

Berlin

Warsaw

BELARUS

IRELAND

Amsterdam

The Hague

London

Brussels

GERMANY

POLAND

1

UKRAINE

ATLANTIC
OCEAN

BELGIUM

Paris

LUXEMBOURG

Vienna

2

Budapest

Kiev

MOLDOVA

50°N

SWITZERLAND

Bern

AUSTRIA

HUNGARY

ROMANIA

Chişinău

MONACO

LIECHTENSTEIN

3

4

5

SAN MARINO

Bucharest

ANDORRA

Corsica
(FRANCE)

ITALY

7

BULGARIA

BLACK SEA

FRANCE

VATICAN CITY

Rome

Tirane

Sofia

PORTUGAL

Madrid

Balearic
Is. (SPAIN)

Sardinia
(ITALY)

ALBANIA

6

GREECE

40°N

Lisbon

SPAIN

MEDITERRANEAN

Sicily

Athens

Gibraltar (U.K.)

SEA

MALTA

Crete

North America: Physical

ASIA

ARCTIC OCEAN

+ North Pole

EUROPE

POLAR ICE PACK

Bering Strait

St. Lawrence Island

Bering Sea

Nunivak Island

Kodiak Island

Gulf of Alaska

BROOKS RANGE

Mt. McKinley 20,320 ft. (6,194 m)

ALASKA RANGE

YUKON PLATEAU

Alexander Archipelago

Queen Charlotte Islands

Vancouver Island

PACIFIC OCEAN

Cape Mendocino

COAST RANGES

CASCADE RANGE

Mount Rainier 14,410 ft. (4,392 m)

Columbia River

SIERRA NEVADA

CENTRAL VALLEY

GREAT BASIN

DEATH VALLEY

Mount Whitney 14,494 ft. (4,419 m)

COLORADO PLATEAU

Snake River

Great Salt Lake

ROCKY MOUNTAINS

GREAT PLAINS

Missouri River

BLACK HILLS

Platte River

Arkansas River

Red River

Guadalupe Island

BAJA CALIFORNIA

Gulf of California

SIERRA MADRE OCCIDENTAL

SIERRA MADRE ORIENTAL

Rio Grande

Brazos River

GULF COASTAL PLAIN

Gulf of Mexico

Popocatépetl 17,887 ft. (5,452 m)

YUCATÁN PENINSULA

SIERRA MADRE DEL SUR

Lake Nicaragua

CENTRAL AMERICA

ISTHMUS OF PANAMA

Beaufort Sea

Banks Island

Victoria Island

Great Bear Lake

Mackenzie River

Great Slave Lake

Lake Athabasca

Athabasca River

Saskatchewan River

Lake Winnipeg

Nelson River

Queen Elizabeth Islands

Ellesmere Island

Baffin Bay

Baffin Island

Southampton Island

Coats Island

Mansel Island

Hudson Bay

Hudson Strait

CANADIAN SHIELD

Greenland

Denmark Strait

Davis Strait

Labrador Sea

Cape Farewell

Newfoundland

Anticosti Island

Prince Edward Island

Gulf of St. Lawrence

Cape Breton Island

St. Lawrence River

INTERIOR PLAINS

Mississippi River

Lake Superior

L. Michigan

Lake Huron

Lake Erie

Lake Ontario

OZARK PLATEAU

Ohio River

Cumberland R.

Tennessee River

APPALACHIAN MOUNTAINS

PIEDMONT

ATLANTIC COASTAL PLAIN

Cape Cod

Long Island

Cape Hatteras

Bermuda

Cape Canaveral

FLORIDA PENINSULA

Florida Keys

Straits of Florida

Bahamas

Cuba

Greater Antilles

Jamaica

Hispaniola

Puerto Rico

Lesser Antilles

Caribbean Sea

Trinidad

ATLANTIC OCEAN

Tropic of Cancer

Equator

SOUTH AMERICA

Arctic Circle

North Pole

ELEVATION

Feet		Meters
13,120		4,000
6,560		2,000
1,640		500
656		200
(Sea level) 0		0 (Sea level)
Below sea level		Below sea level

Ice cap

0   300   600 Miles

0   300   600 Kilometers

Projection: Azimuthal Equal Area

N W E S

North America: Political

ARCTIC OCEAN

EUROPE

ASIA

North Pole

ATLAS

Boundaries

⊛ **National capitals**

• **Other cities**

0   300   600 Miles

0   300   600 Kilometers

Projection: Azimuthal Equal Area

0° Equator

South America: Physical

CENTRAL AMERICA

Caribbean Sea

Panama Canal

Gulf of Panama

Margarita Island
Tobago
Trinidad
Lake Maracaibo
Orinoco River Delta

LLANOS
Meta River
Orinoco River
Angel Falls
GUIANA HIGHLANDS
Devil's Island
Cape Orange

Malpelo Island

Mount Tolima
18,425 ft.
(5,616 m)

Magdalena River

Caquetá River

Japurá River

Río Negro

AMAZON

Amazon River Delta

ATLANTIC OCEAN

Equator 0°

Galápagos Islands

Gulf of Guayaquil

Mount Chimborazo
20,561 ft.
(6,267 m)

Marañón River

Amazon River

BASIN

Amazon River

Tapajós River

Tocantins River

Xingu River

A N D E S

Ucayali River

Juruá River

Purus

Madeira River

River

Mato Grosso Plateau

Araguaia River

BRAZILIAN HIGHLANDS

Parnaíba

Mount Huascarán
22,205 ft.
(6,768 m)

10°S

Ancohuma Peak
20,958 ft.
(6,388 m)

Mamoré

São Francisco River

PACIFIC OCEAN

Lake Titicaca

Beni River

Pilcomayo River

MATO GROSSO PLATEAU

BRAZILIAN PLATEAU

20°S

Lake Poopó

ATACAMA DESERT

CHACO

Paraguay River

Tropic of Capricorn

San Ambrosio Island

San Félix Island

A N D E S

Salado River

Paraná River

Uruguay River

30°S

Juan Fernández Islands

Mount Aconcagua
22,834 ft.
(6,960 m)

Salado River

PAMPAS

Río de la Plata

ATLANTIC OCEAN

Colorado River

Gulf of San Matías

PATAGONIA

Chiloé Island

Chonos Archipelago

Gulf of San Jorge

Cape Tres Puntas

40°S

Bahía Grande

Strait of Magellan

Falkland Islands

South Georgia Islands

Tierra del Fuego

Cape Horn

ELEVATION

Feet		Meters
13,120		4,000
6,560		2,000
1,640		500
656		200
(Sea level) 0		0 (Sea level)
Below sea level		Below sea level

0   250   500 Miles

0   250   500 Kilometers

Projection: Azimuthal Equal Area

South America: Political

CENTRAL
AMERICA

Caribbean Sea

Barranquilla
Cartagena
Caracas

VENEZUELA
Lake
Maracaibo

Orinoco River

Medellín

Bogotá

COLOMBIA
Cali

*Malpelo
Island*
(COLOMBIA)

Quito
ECUADOR
Guayaquil

*Galápagos
Islands
(ECUADOR)*

0° Equator

Georgetown
Paramaribo
GUYANA
Cayenne
SURINAME FRENCH
GUIANA
(FRANCE)

ATLANTIC
OCEAN

Río Negro

Amazon

Amazon River

Belém

Equator 0°

PERU

Marañón River

Ucayali River

Trujillo

Callao
Lima

Arequipa

Lake
Titicaca
La Paz
Lake
Poopó

BOLIVIA
Sucre

PACIFIC
OCEAN

BRAZIL

Recife

São Francisco River

Brasília

Salvador

Belo Horizonte

Paraguay River

PARAGUAY

Campinas
São Paulo

Rio de Janeiro
Curitiba

Tropic of
Capricorn

Asunción

Tropic of Capricorn

*San Ambrosio
Island
(CHILE)*

*San Félix Island
(CHILE)*

CHILE

*Paraná
River*

Uruguay River

Pôrto Alegre

Córdoba

*Juan Fernández
Islands
(CHILE)*

Valparaíso
Santiago

Rosario

URUGUAY

Buenos Aires
Montevideo

ATLANTIC
OCEAN

Río de la Plata

ARGENTINA

Boundaries
⊛ National capitals
• Other cities

0   250   500 Miles
0 250 500 Kilometers
Projection: Azimuthal Equal Area

Strait of
Magellan
Falkland
Islands (U.K.)

South Georgia
Island
(U.K.)

Tierra del
Fuego

Europe: Physical

ASIA

URAL MOUNTAINS

NORTHERN EUROPEAN PLAIN

Pechora River

Kama River

Volga River

Don River

Dnipro River

Caspian Sea

Mt. Elbrus 5,642 m. 18,510 ft.

CAUCASUS MTS.

CRIMEAN PENINSULA

Sea of Azov

Black Sea

SOUTHWEST ASIA

KOLA PENINSULA

White Sea

Barents Sea

Lake Onega

Lake Ladoga

Rybinsk Reservoir

Northern Dvina River

BALTIC PLAINS

Gulf of Finland

Gulf of Bothnia

Daugava River

Niemen River

Vistula River

Oder River

Dniester River

CARPATHIAN MTS.

TRANSYLVANIAN ALPS

BALKAN PENINSULA

Sea of Marmara

Aegean Sea

Rhodes

Crete

DINARIC ALPS

Adriatic Sea

APENNINES

North Cape

KJØLEN MOUNTAINS

BALTIC SEA

Baltic Sea

Lake Vänern

Lake Vättern

Elbe River

Danube River

ALPS

Mont Blanc 15,781 ft. 4,810 m.

Lake Geneva

Corsica

Sardinia

Tyrrhenian Sea

Sicily

Malta

Mediterranean Sea

ARCTIC OCEAN

Norwegian Sea

North Sea

Skagerrak

Kattegat

Shetland Islands

Orkney Islands

Faeroe Islands

Hebrides

BRITISH ISLES

PENNINES

Thames River

English Channel

Irish Sea

Rhine River

Seine River

Loire River

Garonne River

Bay of Biscay

PYRENEES

Cape Finisterre

IBERIAN PENINSULA

Douro River

Tagus River

Guadiana River

Guadalquivir River

Ebro River

Strait of Gibraltar

ATLANTIC OCEAN

AFRICA

Iceland

Arctic Circle

N E S W

70°N

60°N

50°N

40°N

30°N

70°E

60°E

50°E

40°E

30°E

20°E

10°E

0°

10°W

20°W

30°W

40°W

ELEVATION

Feet	Meters
13,120	4,000
6,560	2,000
1,640	500
656	200
(Sea level) 0	0 (Sea level)
Below sea level	Below sea level

Ice cap

0   150   300 Miles

0   150   300 Kilometers

Projection: Azimuthal Equal Area

Europe: Political

ASIA

MOUNTAINS

URAL

Ural River

RUSSIA

Nizhny Novgorod

Volga River

Caspian Sea

Don River

Moscow

SOUTHWEST ASIA

Black Sea

St. Petersburg

White Sea

Barents Sea

Dnipro River

Kiev

UKRAINE

MOLDOVA

Chişinău

Rhodes

Crete

FINLAND

Helsinki

Gulf of Finland

Tallinn

ESTONIA

LATVIA

Riga

LITHUANIA

Vilnius

RUSSIA

Minsk

BELARUS

Warsaw

ROMANIA

Bucharest

Danube River

BULGARIA

Sofia

Aegean Sea

Athens

MACEDONIA

Skopje

GREECE

ARCTIC OCEAN

North Cape

SWEDEN

Stockholm

Gulf of Bothnia

Baltic Sea

POLAND

Kraków

SLOVAKIA

Bratislava

HUNGARY

Budapest

Zagreb

CROATIA

SERBIA AND MONTENEGRO

Belgrade

BOSNIA AND HERZEGOVINA

Sarajevo

Tiranë

ALBANIA

Adriatic Sea

Sea

NORWAY

Oslo

Bergen

Göteborg

Copenhagen

DENMARK

Hamburg

Berlin

Dresden

Elbe River

GERMANY

Prague

CZECH REPUBLIC

Vienna

AUSTRIA

LIECHTENSTEIN

Vaduz

SLOVENIA

Ljubljana

Po River

Milan

ITALY

Rome

Naples

San Marino

SAN MARINO

MALTA

Valletta

Sicily

Mediterranean

North Sea

Amsterdam

THE NETHERLANDS

The Hague

Cologne

Bonn

Luxembourg

LUXEMBOURG

Danube River

Munich

SWITZERLAND

Bern

Lake Geneva

Rhine River

MONACO

Monaco

VATICAN CITY

Corsica (FRANCE)

Sardinia (ITALY)

AFRICA

ARCTIC CIRCLE

Faeroe Islands (DENMARK)

Shetland Islands

SCOTLAND

Edinburgh

UNITED KINGDOM

Belfast

Liverpool

ENGLAND

London

WALES

NORTHERN IRELAND

Dublin

IRELAND

British Isles

Channel Islands (U.K.)

English Channel

Thames R.

BELGIUM

Brussels

Paris

Seine River

FRANCE

Lyon

Rhône River

Marseille

PYRENEES

ANDORRA

Andorra la Vella

Barcelona

Balearic Islands (SPAIN)

ICELAND

Reykjavík

ATLANTIC OCEAN

Bay of Biscay

SPAIN

Madrid

Valencia

Seville

Gibraltar (U.K.)

Strait of Gibraltar

PORTUGAL

Lisbon

Tagus River

 Ebro River

N W E S

Boundaries

National capitals

Other cities

0 150 300 Miles

0 150 300 Kilometers

Projection: Azimuthal Equal Area

Asia: Physical

ELEVATION

Feet	Meters
13,120	4,000
6,560	2,000
1,640	500
656	200
0 (Sea level)	0 (Sea level)
Below sea level	Below sea level

Ice cap

0   250   500   750 Miles
0   250   500   750 Kilometers
Projection: Azimuthal Equal Area

PACIFIC OCEAN

AUSTRALIA

EUROPE

AFRICA

INDIAN OCEAN

North Pole

Arctic Circle

Tropic of Cancer

Equator

SIBERIA

Central Siberian Plateau
West Siberian Plain
Kolyma Mts.
Cherskiy Range
Verkhoyansk Range
Stanovoy Mountains
Yablonovy Range
Sayan Mountains
Altai Mountains
Mongolian Plateau
Greater Khingan Range
Gobi
Qin Ling
North China Plain
Tarim Basin
Taklimakan Desert
Kunlun Mountains
Tien Shan
Kazakh Uplands
Plateau of Tibet
Himalayas
Mount Everest 29,035 ft. (8,850 m)
Hindu Kush
Pamirs
Indo-Gangetic Plain
Thar Desert
Deccan Plateau
Eastern Ghats
Western Ghats
Ural Mountains
Turan Lowland
Ustyurt Plateau
Kara Kum
Kyzyl Kum
Great Salt Desert
Zagros Mts.
Anatolian Plateau
Caucasus Mts.
Mount Ararat 16,945 ft. (5,165 m)
Syrian Desert
An-Nafud
Rub' al-Khali
Sinai Peninsula

Kamchatka Peninsula
Central Range
Taymyr Peninsula
Sakhalin Island
Hokkaido
Honshu
Shikoku
Kyushu
Ryukyu Islands
Okinawa
Taiwan
Hainan
Borneo
Sumatra
Java
Bangka
Mentawai Islands
Nicobar Islands
Andaman Islands
Sri Lanka
Maldives
Lakshadweep Islands
Socotra Island
Cyprus
New Guinea
Maoke Mountains
Luzon
Mindanao
Mindoro
Philippines
Indochina Peninsula
Malay Peninsula
Chao Phraya River

Aleutian Islands
New Siberian Islands
Wrangel Island
Franz Josef Land
Novaya Zemlya
North Land
Severnaya Zemlya

Bering Sea
Sea of Okhotsk
Sea of Japan (East Sea)
Korea Strait
Yellow Sea
East China Sea
South China Sea
Luzon Strait
Celebes Sea
Banda Sea
Java Sea
Arafura Sea
Moluccas
Bay of Bengal
Andaman Sea
Arabian Sea
Gulf of Oman
Persian Gulf
Gulf of Thailand
Gulf of Tonkin
Caspian Sea
Black Sea
Bosporus
Sea of Azov
Mediterranean Sea
Red Sea
Gulf of Aden
Kara Sea
Barents Sea

Rivers:
Lena River
Amur River
Aldan River
Indigirka River
Lower Tunguska River
Yenisey River
Ob River
Irtysh River
Ishim River
Ural River
Volga River
Syr Darya
Amu Darya
Indus River
Ganges River
Sutlej
Godavari
Brahmaputra
Yangtze
Yellow River (Huang He)
Tigris
Euphrates
Mekong River
Angara River

Asia: Political

Boundaries
⊛ National capitals
• Other cities

0 250 500 750 Miles
0 250 500 750 Kilometers
Projection: Two-Point Equidistant

EUROPE

AFRICA

AUSTRALIA

EAST TIMOR

PACIFIC OCEAN

INDIAN OCEAN

RUSSIA

CHINA

MONGOLIA

KAZAKHSTAN

INDIA

JAPAN

NORTH KOREA

KOREA

UZBEKISTAN

TURKMENISTAN

KYRGYZSTAN

TAJIKISTAN

AFGHANISTAN

PAKISTAN

IRAN

IRAQ

SAUDI ARABIA

YEMEN

OMAN

UNITED ARAB EMIRATES

QATAR

BAHRAIN

KUWAIT

JORDAN

ISRAEL

LEBANON

SYRIA

CYPRUS

TURKEY

GEORGIA

ARMENIA

AZERBAIJAN

NEPAL

BHUTAN

BANGLADESH

MYANMAR (BURMA)

LAOS

THAILAND

VIETNAM

CAMBODIA

MALAYSIA

SINGAPORE

BRUNEI

INDONESIA

PHILIPPINES

TAIWAN

SRI LANKA

MALDIVES

North Pole

Arctic Circle

Aleutian Islands

Bering Sea

Sea of Okhotsk

Kuril Islands (RUSSIA)

Sakhalin Island

Lena River

Ob River

Irtysh River

Yenisey River

Angara River

Amur River

Ural River

Ural Mountains

Lake Baykal

Lake Balkhash

Caspian Sea

Black Sea

Mediterranean Sea

Red Sea

Gulf of Aden

Arabian Sea

Persian Gulf

Tigris River

Euphrates River

Indus River

Ganges River

Brahmaputra River

Nu River

Bay of Bengal

Andaman Islands (INDIA)

Nicobar Islands (INDIA)

Lakshadweep Islands (INDIA)

Andaman Sea

Gulf of Thailand

South China Sea

Java Sea

Celebes Sea

Arafura Sea

New Guinea

East China Sea

Yellow Sea

Ryukyu Islands (JAPAN)

Hainan (CHINA)

Socotra (YEMEN)

Huang He (Yellow River)

Chang (Yangtze) River

Great Wall of China

Mekong River

Equator

Tropic of Cancer

Moscow

Yekaterinburg

Chelyabinsk

Omsk

Novosibirsk

Astana

Irkutsk

Yakutsk

Vladivostok

Sapporo

Tokyo

Yokohama

Nagoya

Osaka

Kyoto

Hiroshima

Nagasaki

Seoul

P'yongyang

Pusan

Harbin

Changchun

Fushun

Dalian

Shenyang

Beijing

Nanjing

Shanghai

Wuhan

Xi'an

Chengdu

Chongqing

Guangzhou

Hong Kong

Macao

Taipei

Ulaanbaatar

Almaty

Bishkek

Tashkent

Ashgabat

Dushanbe

Mashhad

Tehran

Isfahan

Shiraz

Tabriz

Baku

Yerevan

T'bilisi

Ankara

Istanbul

Izmir

Nicosia

Beirut

Damascus

Aleppo

Mosul

Baghdad

Basra

Amman

Jerusalem

Tel Aviv

Kuwait City

Manama

Doha

Abu Dhabi

Masqat (Muscat)

Riyadh

Mecca

Jidda

Sanaa

Kabul

Islamabad

Lahore

Faisalabad

Karachi

New Delhi

Delhi

Jaipur

Ahmadabad

Bhopal

Nagpur

Mumbai (Bombay)

Hyderabad

Bangalore

Chennai (Madras)

Kolkata (Calcutta)

Kathmandu

Thimphu

Dhaka

Chittagong

Yangon (Rangoon)

Mandalay

Bangkok

Vientiane

Hanoi

Ho Chi Minh City

Phnom Penh

Kuala Lumpur

Singapore

Bandar Seri Begawan

Medan

Jakarta

Bandung

Semarang

Surabaya

Ujung Pandang

Manila

Colombo

Male

Africa: Physical

EUROPE

SOUTHWEST
ASIA

Azores

Madeira
Islands

Strait of
Gibraltar

Mediterranean Sea

Gulf of
Sidra

Suez Canal

Canary
Islands

ATLAS MOUNTAINS

Tropic of Cancer

Cape
Blanc

EL DJOUF

S   A   H   A   R   A

AHAGGAR
MOUNTAINS

AIR MTS.

TIBESTI
MOUNTAINS

LIBYAN DESERT

QATTARA
DEPRESSION

Lake
Nasser

NUBIAN
DESERT

Nile River

Red Sea

Persian Gulf

Cape Verde
Islands

Cape
Verde

S   A   H   E   L

Niger River

S   U   D   A   N

CHAD
BASIN

Lake
Chad

Gulf of Aden

FOUTA
DJALLON

Senegal R.

White Volta

Black Volta

Benue River

SUDAN
BASIN

Blue Nile

White Nile

ETHIOPIAN
HIGHLANDS

HORN OF AFRICA

SOMALI
PENINSULA

Cape
Palmas

Lake
Volta

Gulf of
Guinea

ADAMAWA
MTS.

Ubangi River

Congo River

Lake
Albert

Lake
Edward

Lake
Turkana

Mount Kenya
17,058 ft.
(5,199 m)

Cape
Lopez

CONGO
BASIN

Kasai River

Lake
Victoria

Lake
Kivu

SERENGETI
PLAIN

MASAI
STEPPE

Mount Kilimanjaro
19,340 ft.
(5,895 m)

INDIAN
OCEAN

Equator

Equator

Zanzibar

Ascension

Lake
Tanganyika

Lake Rukwa

Seychelles

ATLANTIC
OCEAN

Cuanza River

Lake
Mweru

Cape Delgado

Lake Malawi
(Nyasa)

Comoro
Islands

Zambezi River

Lake
Kariba

Victoria
Falls

Madagascar

Mozambique Channel

Mauritius

ELEVATION

Feet		Meters
13.120		4,000
6,560		2,000
1,640		500
656		200
(Sea level) 0		0 (Sea level)
Below sea level		Below sea level

0   250   500 Miles

0   250   500 Kilometers

Projection: Azimuthal Equal Area

Okavango
Delta

KALAHARI BASIN

NAMIB DESERT

KALAHARI
DESERT

Limpopo River

Réunion

Tropic of Capricorn

Tropic of
Capricorn

Orange River

Vaal River

GREAT
KARROO

DRAKENSBERG
MOUNTAINS

Cape of
Good Hope

Africa: Political

EUROPE

SOUTHWEST ASIA

Azores (PORTUGAL)

Madeira (PORTUGAL)

Strait of Gibraltar
Casablanca · Rabat
Algiers Tunis
TUNISIA
Tripoli
Mediterranean Sea

Alexandria
Giza · Cairo
Suez Canal

MOROCCO

Canary Islands (SPAIN)

El Aaiún
WESTERN SAHARA (Claimed by Morocco)

Tropic of Cancer

ALGERIA

LIBYA

EGYPT

Lake Nasser

Nile River

Red Sea

CAPE VERDE

Praia

MAURITANIA
Nouakchott

MALI

NIGER

CHAD

Khartoum

ERITREA
· Asmara

Gulf of Aden

SENEGAL
Dakar
GAMBIA
Banjul
Bissau
GUINEA-BISSAU

Niger River

Bamako
BURKINA FASO
Niamey
Ouagadougou

Lake Chad
N'Djamena

SUDAN

Blue Nile
White Nile

DJIBOUTI
Djibouti

Conakry
Freetown
SIERRA LEONE
Monrovia
LIBERIA

GUINEA
CÔTE D'IVOIRE
Yamoussoukro
GHANA
Abidjan Accra

BENIN
TOGO
Lomé
Porto-Novo

NIGERIA

· Abuja

Lagos

Gulf of Guinea
Malabo
EQUATORIAL GUINEA
Yaoundé

CAMEROON
Bangui

CENTRAL AFRICAN REPUBLIC

ETHIOPIA
· Addis Ababa

SOMALIA

· Mogadishu

SÃO TOMÉ AND PRÍNCIPE
São Tomé

REPUBLIC OF THE CONGO
Libreville
GABON

Congo River

Kisangani

UGANDA
Kampala

KENYA
· Nairobi

Equator 0°

DEMOCRATIC REPUBLIC OF THE CONGO

Brazzaville
CABINDA (ANGOLA)
Kinshasa

RWANDA
· Kigali
Bujumbura
BURUNDI

Lake Victoria

Mombasa
Pemba
Zanzibar
Dar es Salaam

Victoria

SEYCHELLES

ATLANTIC OCEAN

Luanda

TANZANIA
Dodoma

Lake Tanganyika

INDIAN OCEAN

St. Helena (U.K.)

ANGOLA

Lubumbashi

ZAMBIA
Lusaka

Lake Malawi (Nyasa)

COMOROS
· Moroni

MALAWI
· Lilongwe

Antananarivo

Zambezi River

Harare
ZIMBABWE
Bulawayo

MOZAMBIQUE

MADAGASCAR

MAURITIUS
Port Louis
Réunion (FRANCE)

NAMIBIA
Windhoek

BOTSWANA
Gaborone

Tropic of Capricorn

Pretoria
Maputo
Mbabane
SWAZILAND

Johannesburg
Bloemfontein
Maseru
LESOTHO

Orange River

SOUTH AFRICA

Cape Town

Legend

	Boundaries
⊛	National capitals
·	Other cities

0   250   500 Miles
0   250   500 Kilometers
Projection: Azimuthal Equal Area

N W S E

Gazetteer

A

Aegean Sea (ee-JEE-uhn) a sea east of Greece; the sea provided Greeks with a source of food and a means of trading with other peoples (p. 255)

Africa the second-largest continent (p. R36)

Akkad (A-kad) (33°N, 44°E) a city along the Euphrates River near modern Baghdad; started by Akkadian emperor Sargon in 2300s BC (p. 63)

Aksum (AHK-soom) an ancient state in southeast Nubia on the Red Sea, in what are now Ethiopia and Eritrea; through trade, Aksum became the most powerful state in the region (p. 131)

Alexandria (31°N, 30°E) a city in Egypt, named after Alexander the Great (p. 300)

Alps a mountain range extending across south-central Europe (p. R32)

Amazon River a river east of the Andes in South America; it flows through a rain forest and into the Atlantic Ocean (p. R30)

Americas the two continents of North America and South America (p. 429)

Andes Mountains a mountain range along the west coast of South America (p. R30)

Antarctica the ice-covered continent at the South Pole (p. R26–27)

Asia the world's largest continent, bounded by the Arctic, Pacific, and Indian oceans (p. R34)

Asia Minor a large peninsula in west Asia, between the Black Sea and the Mediterranean Sea, forming modern Turkey (p. 258)

Athens (38°N, 24°E) an ancient city and modern capital of Greece; the world's first democracy developed in Athens around 500 BC (p. 258)

Australia an island continent between the South Pacific and Indian oceans (p. R27)

B

Babylon (32°N, 45°E) an ancient city on the lower Euphrates River in modern central Iraq (p. 63)

Bering Strait a 55-mile-wide body of water between Alaska and Siberia; location of possible land bridge connecting Asia and the Americas during the Ice Ages (p. R28)

Bethlehem (BETH-li-hem) (32°N, 35°E) a town in Judea; traditionally regarded as the birthplace of Jesus (p. 385)

Black Sea a sea between southeast Europe and Asia, north of Asia Minor (p. R32)

Byzantine Empire the eastern part of the Roman Empire that developed non-Roman influences (p. 415)

C

Calakmul (kah-lahk-MOOL) an ancient Maya city; fought battles against its rival city, Tikal (p. 435)

Canaan (KAY-nuhn) a region in what is now Israel near the coast of the Mediterranean Sea; according to the Bible, Abraham settled in Canaan and his Hebrew descendants lived there for many years (p. 227)

Carthage (KAHR-thij) (37°N, 10°E) a key trade center built by the Phoenicians on the northern coast of Africa; it became one of the most powerful cities in the Mediterranean (p. 79)

Central America the part of North America between Mexico and South America; parts of the northern countries of Central America make up the area known as Mesoamerica (p. R28)

Chang Jiang (or Yangzi River) a river that cuts through central China, flowing from the mountains of Tibet to the Pacific Ocean (p. 183)

China a country located east of India and the Ganges River; a series of dynasties built China into a world power (p. 183)

Constantinople (KAHN-stant-uhn-oh-puhl) (42°N, 76°E) the capital of the Byzantine Empire, located in modern Turkey between the Black Sea and Mediterranean Sea (p. 415)

Crete an island in the Mediterranean Sea, south of Greece; a civilization formed there around 2000 BC (p. 255)

Damascus (34°N, 36°E) an ancient city and the modern capital of Syria; important in the spread of Christianity (p. 388)

Dead Sea a salty lake on the boundary between Israel and Jordan; 2,000-year-old scrolls discovered near there help scholars learn about the history of the Jews (p. 230)

Delhi (29°N, 77°E) historic city and capital of modern India; it was ruled by the Gupta dynasty (p. 170)

Delphi an ancient city in central Greece; Greeks traveled here to get advice from an oracle of Apollo (p. 270)

Egypt a country in northeast Africa and location of the mouth of the Nile River; ancient Egypt was famous for its temples, pyramids, art, and cultural achievements, such as an early writing system (p. R37)

Euphrates River a river that flows mainly through Iraq and empties into the Persian Gulf; silt from the Euphrates helped form the Fertile Crescent in Mesopotamia (p. 57)

Europe a continent of many peninsulas located between Asia and the Atlantic Ocean (p. R32)

Fertile Crescent a large arc of rich farmland between the Persian Gulf and the Mediterranean Sea (p. 57)

Gaul an ancient region in Western Europe, consisting mainly of parts of modern France and Belgium; the Frankish king, Clovis, built a kingdom in Gaul (p. 410)

Gaya (25°N, 85°E) a town in India; according to legend, Siddhartha Gautama found enlightenment in Gaya (p. 160)

Gibraltar, Strait of (ji-BRAHL-ter) a strait, or narrow sea passage, between Spain and Morocco, connecting the Mediterranean Sea and the Atlantic Ocean (p. R32)

Giza (30°N, 31°E) an Egyptian city and the site of large pyramids, including the Great Pyramid of Khufu (p. 98)

Gobi (GOH-bee) a desert covering much of northern China; the Gobi helped isolate China from its neighbors (p. R34)

Greece a country in southern Europe with mountains, rugged coastlines and scenic islands; the country is called the birthplace of democracy (p. R33)

Harappa (huh-RA-puh) a city that thrived between 2300 and 1700 BC in the Indus Valley, in what is now Pakistan (p. 147)

Himalayas a mountain range on the northern Indian border; they are the highest mountains in the world (p. R34)

Huang He (Yellow River) a river that stretches nearly 3,000 miles across China; it is sometimes called "China's Sorrow" (p. 183)

I

India a country and subcontinent in south Asia; India was home to one of the world's oldest civilizations (p. R35)

Indus Valley a river valley in modern Pakistan where one of the earliest civilizations began (p. 145)

GAZETTEER

Ionian Sea (eye-OH-nee-uhn) a sea west of Greece (p. 255)

Israel a country between the Mediterranean Sea and Jordan; it was the kingdom of the ancient Hebrews (p. 230)

Italy a country in southern Europe located on a peninsula in the Mediterranean; it was the center of the Roman Empire (p. R33)

Jerusalem (32°N, 35°E) a city established as the capital of Israel around 960–1000 BC (p. 230)

Judah (JOO-duh) one of the two kingdoms created when Israel was divided; the people in Judah came to be called Jews (p. 230)

Kerma (KAR-muh) a city on the Nile in the kingdom of Kush; it was captured by Egypt, forcing the Kushites to move their capital to Napata (p. 89)

Kish a city-state in Sumer that became powerful around 3500 BC (p. 63)

Kush the first great kingdom in Africa's interior; at times Kush ruled Egypt and at other times was ruled by Egypt (p. 123)

Macedonia a small kingdom located west of the Black Sea and north of the Aegean Sea; Macedonians conquered Greece in the 300s BC (p. 296)

Marathon an ancient city in Greece; it was the site of a battle in which the Greeks defeated the Persians (p. 290)

Mediterranean Sea a large sea surrounded by Europe, Africa, and Asia; it played a vital role in the development of civilizations and trade in the region (p. R32, R34)

Memphis (30°N, 31°E) an ancient Egyptian capital city at the southern tip of the Nile Delta; built around 3100 BC, it was the political and cultural center of Egypt for centuries (p. 89)

Meröe (MER-oh-wee) an ancient capital of Kush, located on the east bank of the Nile (p. 123)

Mesoamerica a region that includes the southern part of modern Mexico and part of northern Central America; the first permanent farming settlements in the Americas developed in Mesoamerica (p. 429)

Mesopotamia (mes-uh-puh-TAY-mee-uh) the region in southwest Asia between the Tigris and Euphrates rivers; it was the site of some of the world's earliest civilizations (p. 57)

Mohenjo Daro (mo-HEN-joh DAR-oh) (27°N, 68°E) an ancient city of the Harappan civilization, located in modern Pakistan (p. 147)

Mount Sinai according to the Bible, the mountain in Egypt where God gave Moses the stone tablets containing the Ten Commandments (p. 227)

Mycenae (my-SEE-nee) an ancient Greek city; the site of a strong fortress built by the Mycenaeans (p. 257)

Napata an ancient city on the Nile in Egypt; it was the capital of Kush in the 700s and 600s BC (p. 123)

Nile the longest river in the world; it flows from central Africa to the Mediterranean Sea and was vital to the development of civilizations in Egypt and Kush (p. R36)

Nineveh (37°N, 43°E) an ancient capital of Assyria, located on the Tigris River (p. 76)

North America a large continent in the northern and western hemispheres, bordered on the west by the Pacific Ocean and on the east by the Atlantic Ocean (p. R28)

Nubia a region in northeast Africa on the Nile, south of Egypt; the kingdom of Kush developed in Nubia (p. 123)

Palenque (pah-LENG-kay) (18°N, 92°W) an ancient Maya city in what is now southern Mexico (p. 435)

Persepolis (30°N, 53°E) the ancient capital of Persia, located in modern Iran (p. 287)

Persia an ancient empire in Southwest Asia in what is now Iran; it was one of the most powerful empires of the ancient world (p. 287)

Persian Gulf (PER-suhn) a body of water located between the Arabian Peninsula and the Zagros Mountains in Iran; the Tigris and Euphrates rivers empty into the gulf, (p. R34)

Phoenicia (fi-NI-shuh) an ancient country that was a strip of land at the western end of the Fertile Crescent, along the Mediterranean Sea; Phoenicians were some of the leading traders of the ancient world (p. 79)

Plateau of Tibet a high plateau in central Asia, mostly in Tibet and China (p. R34)

Pompeii (pom-PAY) (41°N, 14°E) an ancient city in the Roman Empire; the city was buried in a volcanic eruption in AD 79 (p. 361)

Q–S

Qinling Shandi (CHIN-LING shahn-DEE) a mountain range that extends east from the Plateau of Tibet; it separates northern and southern China (p. 183)

Rome (42°N, 13°E) a city in Italy near the Mediterranean Sea; it became the center of the Roman Empire, which controlled most of the lands around the Mediterranean (p. 325)

Silk Road an ancient trade route from China through Central Asia to the Mediterranean (p. 210)

South America a large continent in the southern and western hemispheres, bordered on the west by the Pacific Ocean and on the East by the Atlantic Ocean (p. R30)

Sparta (37°N, 22°E) an ancient city in Greece; its society was dominated by the military (p. 290)

Sumer (SOO-muhr) the region in southern Mesopotamia where the world's first civilization developed (p. 63)

T

Tanzania a country in East Africa; fossils from the earliest humans were discovered there (p. R37)

Thebes (38°N, 23°E) an ancient Greek city destroyed by Alexander (p. 89)

Tiber River a river that flows out of Italy's mountains; Rome was built on the Tiber (p. 325)

Tigris River a river that flows mainly through modern Iraq; silt from the Tigris and Euphrates formed the Fertile Crescent, where the world's first farming civilizations developed (p. 57)

Tikal (tee-KAHL) (17°N, 90°W) a major Maya city in modern Guatemala (p. 435)

Troy (40°N, 26°E) an ancient city in what is now Turkey; according to Greek legend and literature, it was the site of the Trojan War (p. 257)

Turkey a country occupying Asia Minor and a southeast portion of the Balkan Peninsula (p. R35)

U–Z

Ur a city in ancient Sumer, located on the Euphrates River near the Persian Gulf; it was one of the largest cities of ancient Mesopotamia (p. 63)

Uruk a city in ancient Sumer, located on the Euphrates River; Uruk and Ur fought for dominance around 3500–2500 BC (p. 63)

Xi'an (34°N, 109°E) a city in western China; Emperor Shi Huangdi built a capital city in Xianyang (now Xi'an) and it remained the capital for hundreds of years (p. R35)

Yucatán Peninsula a peninsula in southeast Mexico; many Maya cities were located on the Yucatán Peninsula (p. R28)

Ancient Civilizations

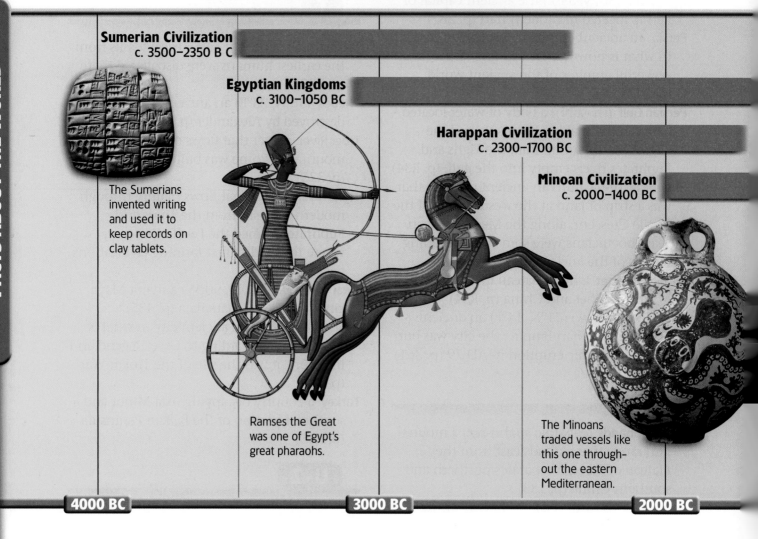

Sumerian Civilization
c. 3500–2350 B C

The Sumerians invented writing and used it to keep records on clay tablets.

Egyptian Kingdoms
c. 3100–1050 BC

Harappan Civilization
c. 2300–1700 BC

Minoan Civilization
c. 2000–1400 BC

Ramses the Great was one of Egypt's great pharaohs.

The Minoans traded vessels like this one throughout the eastern Mediterranean.

4000 BC   3000 BC   2000 BC

Important Dates

c. 4000–3000 BC The first cities are founded in Sumer.

c. 3500 BC The Sumerians invent writing.

c. 3500 BC Maize (corn) is domesticated in Mesoamerica.

c. 3200 BC The Sumerians invent the wheel.

c. 3100 BC Upper Egypt and Lower Egypt are united.

c. 2500 BC The Great Pyramid of Khufu is built in Egypt.

c. 2350 BC The first empire is created in Mesopotamia.

c. 1750 BC The earliest known set of written laws is issued by Hammurabi.

c. 1250 BC Hinduism begins to develop.

c. 1100 BC The Phoenicians create an alphabet.

c. 1050 BC Saul becomes the first King of Israel.

c. 500 BC Buddhism begins to develop.

c. 500 BC Athens becomes the world's first democracy.

c. 140 BC Confucianism becomes China's official government philosophy.

c. 100 BC The Silk Road connects China and Southwest Asia.

27 BC The Roman Empire begins.

c. AD 30 Christianity begins to develop.

c. AD 200 The Maya build large cities in Mesoamerica.

c. AD 320 The Gupta dynasty begins in India.

AD 476 The western Roman Empire falls.

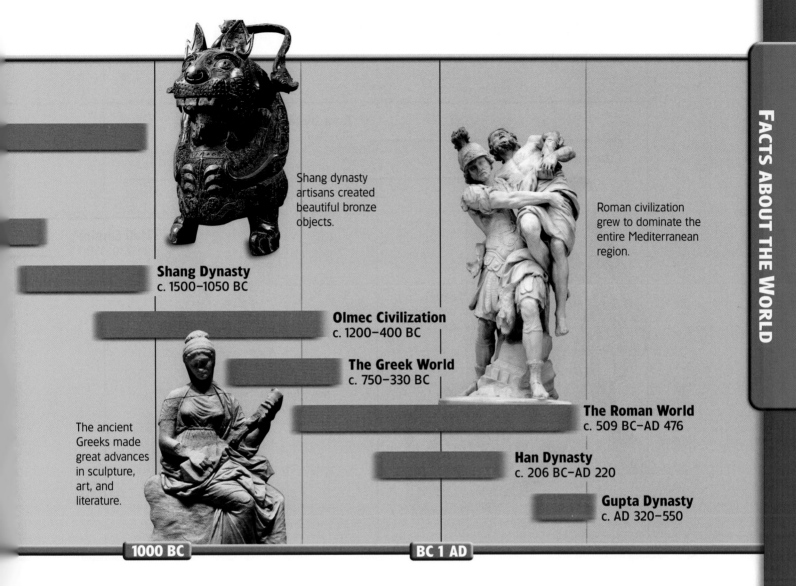

Shang dynasty artisans created beautiful bronze objects.

Shang Dynasty
c. 1500–1050 BC

Olmec Civilization
c. 1200–400 BC

The Greek World
c. 750–330 BC

Roman civilization grew to dominate the entire Mediterranean region.

The Roman World
c. 509 BC–AD 476

The ancient Greeks made great advances in sculpture, art, and literature.

Han Dynasty
c. 206 BC–AD 220

Gupta Dynasty
c. AD 320–550

1000 BC

BC 1 AD

Important People

Sargon (c. 2350 BC) was a king of Akkad, a land north of Sumer. He created a powerful army and used it to build the world's first empire.

Hammurabi (ruled c. 1792–1750 BC) founded the Babylonian Empire and issued the first known written code of laws.

Queen Hatshepsut (ruled c. 1503–1482 BC) was a ruler of Egypt who expanded trade routes.

Siddhartha Gautama (c. 563–483 BC) was an Indian prince who became known as the Buddha. His teachings became the foundation for Buddhism.

Confucius (c. 551–479 BC) was a Chinese philosopher and teacher. His teachings, known as Confucianism, became a major philosophy in China.

Alexander the Great (c. 356–323 BC) built one of the largest empires in the ancient world and spread Greek culture throughout his empire.

Pericles (c. 495–429 BC) was an Athenian orator and politician. During his 30-year rule, Athenian democracy reached its height.

Shi Huangdi (c. 259–210 BC), the first Qin emperor, united China for the first time and built what would become the Great Wall of China.

Augustus (c. 63 BC–AD 14) was Rome's first emperor. During his reign Rome entered the Pax Romana.

Jesus of Nazareth (c. AD 1–30) was one of the most influential people in history. His life and teachings were the basis for Christianity.

Medieval to Early Modern Times

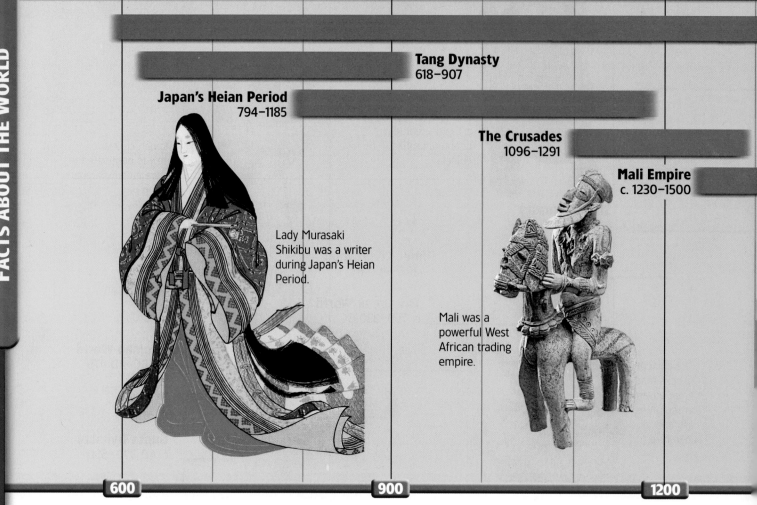

Tang Dynasty
618–907

Japan's Heian Period
794–1185

The Crusades
1096–1291

Mali Empire
c. 1230–1500

Lady Murasaki Shikibu was a writer during Japan's Heian Period.

Mali was a powerful West African trading empire.

600   900   1200

Important Dates

476 The western Roman Empire falls.

534 The Byzantine emperor Justinian creates a unified code of laws.

581 The Sui dynasty reunites China.

622 Muhammad leaves Mecca for Medina.

711 The Moors invade Spain.

800 Pope Leo III crowns Charlemagne Emperor of the Romans.

1066 William the Conqueror leads the Norman invasion of Britain.

1192 The first shogun takes power in Japan.

1215 A group of nobles forces King John to sign Magna Carta.

1324 Mansa Musa leaves Mali on a hajj to Mecca.

1347–1351 The Black Death strikes Europe.

1453 The Ottoman Turks capture Constantinople.

1492 Christopher Columbus sails to the Americas.

1517 Martin Luther posts his Ninety-Five Theses.

1521 Hernán Cortés conquers the Aztec Empire.

1533 Francisco Pizarro conquers the Inca Empire.

1545–1563 The Council of Trent meets to reform Catholic teachings.

1588 England defeats the Spanish Armada.

1633 Galileo is put on trial for promoting ideas that go against the Catholic Church.

1776 The American colonies declare independence from Great Britain.

1789 The French Revolution begins when a mob storms the Bastille in Paris.

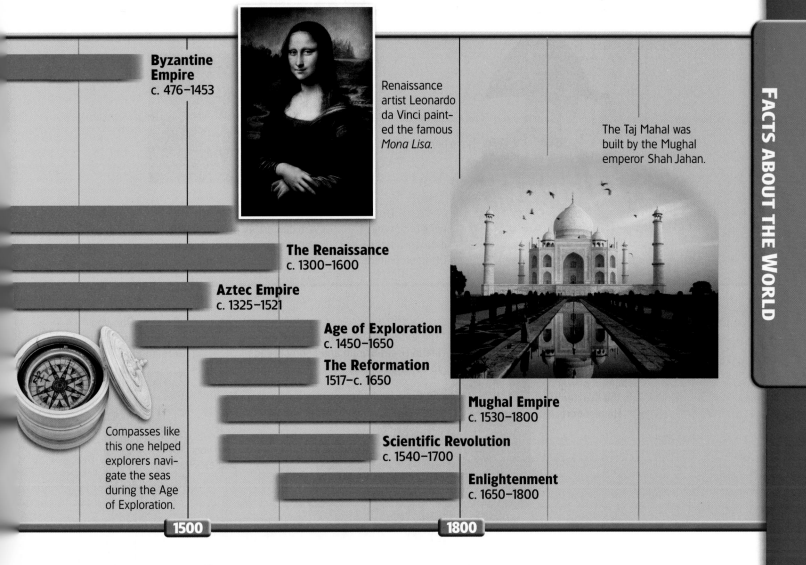

Byzantine Empire
c. 476–1453

Renaissance artist Leonardo da Vinci painted the famous *Mona Lisa.*

The Taj Mahal was built by the Mughal emperor Shah Jahan.

The Renaissance
c. 1300–1600

Aztec Empire
c. 1325–1521

Age of Exploration
c. 1450–1650

The Reformation
1517–c. 1650

Mughal Empire
c. 1530–1800

Scientific Revolution
c. 1540–1700

Enlightenment
c. 1650–1800

Compasses like this one helped explorers navigate the seas during the Age of Exploration.

1500

1800

Important People

Muhammad (c. 570–632) was the founder of Islam. He spread Islam's teachings to the people of Arabia. His teachings make up the Qur'an.

Charlemagne (742–814) was a Frankish king who ruled most of what is now France and Germany. He helped promote Christianity in western Europe.

Lady Murasaki Shikibu (c. 1000) was a court lady during Japan's Heian Period. She wrote *The Tale of Genji,* considered by some to be the world's first novel.

Kublai Khan (1215–1294) was a Mongol ruler who completed the conquest of China and founded the Yuan dynasty.

Mansa Musa (c. 1300) was the ruler of the Mali Empire at the height of its wealth and power. He helped spread Islam throughout West Africa.

Johann Gutenberg (c. 1390–1468) was a German inventor who invented a method of printing with moveable type.

Christopher Columbus (1451–1506) was an Italian navigator who sailed to the Americas for Spain searching for a route to Asia.

Leonardo da Vinci (1452–1519) painted the *Mona Lisa,* one of the world's most admired paintings.

Sir Isaac Newton (1642–1727) was one of the most influential scientists in history. He proposed a law of gravity to explain the movement of objects.

The Modern World

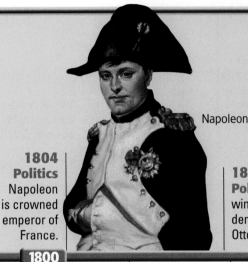

Napoleon

1804
Politics
Napoleon is crowned emperor of France.

1829
Politics Greece wins independence from the Ottoman Empire.

1850s–1890
Society and Culture
Artists portray ordinary people and events realistically during the Realism movement.

1800

1823
Politics
The Monroe Doctrine makes the United States the dominant power in the Western Hemisphere.

1830s
Science and Technology
The Industrial Revolution transforms life in Great Britain and soon spreads to other countries.

1875

1871
Politics Otto von Bismarck founds the German Empire.

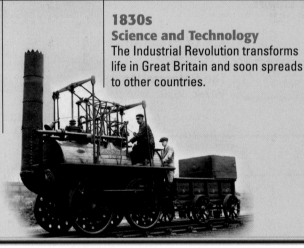

Otto von Bismarck

Events and People

Politics

1790s Toussaint-L' Ouverture successfully leads a rebellion of slaves against French rule in Haiti.

1811 Simon Bolívar helps Venezuela fight for its independence from Spain, influencing independence movements in Bolivia, Colombia, and Ecuador.

1837 Queen Victoria begins her 63-year reign in the United Kingdom.

1868 Tokugawa Keiki resigns as the last shogun of Japan.

1916 Jeanette Rankin becomes the first woman elected to the United States House of Representatives.

1933 Mohandas Gandhi begins a 21-day hunger strike as a non-violent protest against British rule in India.

1949 Mao Zedong transforms China into a Communist nation.

1994 Nelson Mandela is elected the first black president of South Africa after many years of struggling against apartheid.

Science and Technology

1856 Henry Bessemer develops a method for converting iron into steel.

1886 Josephine Cochran receives a patent for the first workable dishwasher.

1903 Orville and Wilbur Wright complete the first controlled aircraft flight.

Israeli flag

1948
Politics
The country
of Israel is
established .

1989
Politics Communist control
collapses in Bulgaria, Czechoslovakia,
East Germany, Hungary, Poland,
and Romania.

1950

2025

1939–1945
Politics World
War II is fought
in Europe, North
Africa, and Asia
between the Axis
powers and Allies.

1957
Science and Technology
The Soviet Union launches
the satellite Sputnik 1, beginning the space race.

1983
**Society and
Culture** The
Internet becomes
available to the
general public.

2001
Politics Terrorists attack the
World Trade Center in New York
City and the Pentagon in Washing-
ton, D.C. on September 11, 2001.

Sputnik 1

1905 Albert Einstein introduces the theory of
relativity.

1911 Marie Curie wins the Nobel Prize in chemistry
for discovering several radioactive elements
including radium.

1925 George Washington Carver publishes a book
on how to find industrial uses for agricultural
products.

1969 Neil Armstrong becomes the first person to
walk on the moon.

1996 Ian Wilmut clones a mammal, Dolly the
sheep.

Society and Culture

1824 Louis Braille introduces a reading system for
the blind.

1848 Karl Marx and Friedrich Engels introduce *The
Communist Manifesto.*

1880 Pyotr Ilyich Tchaikovsky pens the *1812 Over-
ture* to commemorate Russia's victory over
Napoleon in 1812.

1921 Pablo Picasso paints *The Three Musicians,* one
of the most renowned cubist works.

1937 Zora Neale Hurston writes *Their Eyes Were
Watching God.*

1997 J. K. Rowling publishes the first Harry Potter
book.

2004 Lance Armstrong wins a record 6th Tour de
France bicycle race.

Biographical Dictionary

A

Abraham Biblical figure, according to the Bible, God led Abraham to Canaan, and Abraham's descendants became the Jewish people. (p. 226)

Aeneas (i-NEE-uhs) (c. 2500s BC) Legendary Roman hero, the Romans traced their history back to Aeneas. Aeneas was a Trojan hero who left Troy after the Trojan War, eventually settling in Italy. (p. 326)

Aesop (EE-sahp) (before 400 BC) Ancient Greek storyteller, he was famous for his fables— short stories that teach important lessons about life. (p. 273)

Alexander the Great (c. 356–323 BC) Macedonian ruler, he was one of the greatest military commanders in history. The son of Philip II, Alexander conquered large areas of Asia and parts of Europe and Africa and spread Greek culture throughout his empire. (p. 300)

Antony, Marc (c. 82–30 BC) Roman general, he fought against Octavian after the death of Julius Caesar. Antony was allies with Cleopatra of Egypt, but was defeated by Octavian at the Battle of Actium in 31 BC. (p. 355)

Aristotle (ar-uh-STAH-tuhl) (384–322 BC) Greek philosopher, he was a student of Plato. Aristotle taught that people should live lives of moderation and use reason in their lives. (pp. 307, 309)

Asoka (uh-SOH-kuh) (ruled 270–232 BC) Ruler of the Mauryan Empire, he extended his control over most of India and promoted the spread of Buddhism. (pp. 163, 166)

Attila (AT-uhl-uh) (c. 406–453) Leader of the Huns, he led invasions of Constantinople, Greece, Gaul, and northern Italy and was greatly feared by the Romans. (p. 411)

Augustine of Hippo (AW-guhs-teen) (c. 300s–400s) Christian writer who taught that Christians should focus not on worldly goods but on God's plan for the world; his ideas helped shape Christian beliefs. (p. 394)

Augustus (aw-GUHS-tuhs) (63 BC–AD 14) First Roman emperor, he was originally named Octavian. He was the great-nephew of Julius Caesar and gained control of Rome after defeating Marc Antony in battle. As emperor, Augustus built many monuments and a new forum. (pp. 355, 357)

Augustus

B

Buddha (BOO-duh) (c. 563–483 BC) Founder of Buddhism, he was originally an Indian prince named Siddhartha Gautama. He founded the Buddhist religion after a long spiritual journey through India. (p. 157)

C

Caesar, Julius (JOOL-yuhs SEE-zuhr) (100–44 BC)
Roman general, he was one of the greatest
military leaders in history. Caesar conquered most of Gaul and was named
dictator for life, but was later murdered by
a group of senators. (p. 353)

Chandragupta II (kuhn-druh-GOOP-tuh) (300s–400s)
Gupta emperor, he ruled India during the
height of Gupta power. (p. 164)

Chandragupta Maurya (kuhn-druh-GOOP-tuh
mour-yuh) (late 300s BC) Mauryan ruler, he
founded the Mauryan Empire in northern
India. (p. 162)

Cicero (SIS-uh-roh) (106–43 BC) Roman orator
and philosopher, he tried to limit the power
of Rome's generals and give control of the
government back to the Senate. (p. 352)

Cincinnatus (sin-suh-NAT-uhs) (born c. 519) Roman
dictator, he was chosen by the Romans to
defend their lands from attack. Later, he
willingly gave up power and was considered an ideal leader by the Romans. (p. 329)

Cleopatra (69–30 BC) Egyptian queen, she
became a devoted ally of Julius Caesar and
Marc Antony. After Antony was defeated by
Octavian, she committed suicide. (p. 356)

Clovis (c. 466–511) King of the Franks, he was a
Christian leader who was one of the most
powerful rulers of the Germanic barbarians.
(p. 411)

Confucius (551–479 BC) Chinese philosopher, he
was the most influential teacher in Chinese
history. His teachings, called Confucianism,
focused on morality, family, society, and
government. (p. 191)

Constantine (KAHN-stuhn-teen) (c. 280–337)
Roman emperor, he was the first Roman
emperor to become a Christian. Constantine moved the empire's capital from Rome
to Constantinople and removed bans on
Christianity. (p. 395)

Cyrus the Great (SY-ruhs) (c. 585–529 BC) Persian
emperor, he created the Persian Empire by
conquering most of Southwest Asia. (p. 287)

D

Daniel Biblical figure, according to the Hebrew
Bible, he was a prophet who was thrown
into a lions' den after angering the king.
Daniel survived because of his faith in God.
(p. 235)

Darius I (da-RY-uhs) (550–486 BC) Persian emper-
or, he restored order to the Persian Empire
after a period of rebellion. Darius I built
roads and made other improvements to
Persian society. (p. 288)

David (c. 1000 BC) King of Israel, he defeated
the Philistines and established the capital
in Jerusalem as a governmental and religious center. (p. 229)

Diocletian (dy-uh-KLEE-shuhn) (c. 245–c. 316)
Roman emperor, he divided the Roman
Empire into eastern and western halves.
(p. 409)

Confucius

E

Euclid (YOO-kluhd) (c. 300 BC) Greek mathematician, he was one of the greatest mathematicians in history. Euclid is famous for his contributions to the field of geometry. (p. 308)

Ezana (AY-zah-nah) (c. 300s) Aksumite ruler, he destroyed Meroë and took over the kingdom of Kush around AD 350. (p. 131)

G

Galen (129–c. 199) Greek surgeon of the Roman Empire, he described heart valves and studied arteries and veins. (p. 366)

Gilgamesh (c. 3000 BC) King of Uruk, a city-state in Sumer, he became a legendary figure in Sumerian literature. (p. 63)

H

Hadrian (76–138) Roman emperor, he conquered most of Britain and built a huge wall across the northern part of the island to keep barbarian invaders from the north out of Roman territory. (p. 359)

Hammurabi (ruled c. 1792–1750 BC), Baylonian ruler, he was a brilliant military leader who brought all of Mesopotamia into the Babylonian Empire. Hammurabi is known for a unified code of 282 laws, the earliest known set of written laws, that was produced during his reign. (p. 75)

Hannibal (247–183 BC) Carthaginian general, he was one of the greatest generals of the ancient world. Hannibal invaded Italy during the Second Punic War but was eventually defeated by Scipio at the Battle of Zama. (p. 341)

Hatshepsut (ruled c. 1503–1482 BC) Egyptian queen, she worked to increase trade with places outside of Egypt and ordered many impressive monuments and temples built during her reign. (pp. 102, 103)

Hippocrates (hip-AHK-ruh-teez) (c. 460–c. 377 BC) Greek doctor, he is regarded as the father of medicine. Hippocrates tried to find out what caused diseases and is known today for his ideas on how doctors should conduct themselves. (p. 308)

Homer (800s–700s BC) Greek poet, he wrote the *Iliad* and the *Odyssey*, two famous Greek epic poems. They describe the deeds of heroes during and after the Trojan War. (p. 272)

Homer

Hypatia (hy-PAY-shuh) (c. 370–415) Greek mathematician and astronomer, she made important contributions to science. (p. 308)

Iceman (c. 3300 BC) Stone Age traveler, he was found in the Alps in 1991. Scientists have learned a great deal about Stone Age people from his clothing and tools. (p. 35)

Jesus of Nazareth (c. AD 1–30) Founder of Christianity, he taught about kindness and love for God. His teachings spread throughout the Roman Empire and the world. (p. 382)

John the Baptist (c. 1st Century AD) Biblical figure, according to the Bible, he was a prophet who announced that the Messiah was coming. (p. 383)

Justinian (juh-STIN-ee-uhn) (c. 483–565) Byzantine emperor, he reunited the Roman Empire, simplified Roman laws with Justinian's Code, and ordered Hagia Sophia built. (pp. 414, 419)

Khufu (KOO-foo) (ruled 2500s BC) Egyptian pharaoh, he ruled during Egypt's Old Kingdom and is known for the many monuments built to honor him. (p. 94)

Laozi (LOWD-zuh) (c. 500s or 400s BC) Chinese philospoher, he was the most famous Daoist teacher. Laozi is credited with writing *The Way and Its Power*, Daoism's basic text. (p. 192)

Marius, Gaius (GY-uhs MER-ee-uhs) (157–86 BC) Roman consul, he was a popular general who encouraged the unemployed poor to join the Roman army. (p. 342)

Menes (MEE-neez) (c. 3100 BC) Legendary Egyptian ruler, he unified the kingdoms of Upper and Lower Egypt and built the new capital city of Memphis. (p. 91)

Moses (c. 1200s BC) Biblical figure, according to the Bible, he led the Hebrew people out of Egypt and back to Canaan in the Exodus. During this journey, Moses received the Ten Commandments from God. (p. 227)

Naomi (nay-OH-mee) Bibilical figure, according to the Bible, she had a strong faith in God. (p. 231)

Ruth and Naomi

Nebuchadnezzar (neb-uh-kuhd-NEZ-uhr) (ruled 605–561 BC) Chaldean king, he rebuilt Babylon into a beautiful city, which featured the famed Hanging Gardens. (p. 77)

Noah (no-uh) Biblical figure, according to the Bible, God told Noah to build an ark, or great ship, to survive a great flood of the earth. (p. 238)

Ovid (ahv-uhd) (43 BC–AD 17) Roman poet and author, he was one of the greatest authors of the ancient world and wrote poems on Roman mythology. (p. 370)

P

Pacal (puh-KAHL) (603–683) Maya king of Palenque, he had a temple built in the city to record his achievements. (p. 437)

Paul (c. AD 10–67) One of the most important figures in the spread of Christianity, he worked to spread Jesus's teachings and wrote letters that explained key ideas of Christianity. (p. 387)

Pericles (PER-uh-kleez) (495–429 BC) Athenian leader, he encouraged the spread of democracy and led Athens when the city was at its height. (p. 266)

Philip II (ruled 359–336 BC) Macedonian king, he was a brilliant military leader who defeated the Greeks. Alexander the Great was his son. (p. 298)

Piankhi (PYANG-kee) (c. 751–716 BC) Ruler of Kush, he was one of Kush's most successful military leaders. His army captured all of Egypt. (p. 125)

Plato (PLAYT-oh) (428–389 BC) Greek philosopher, he was a student of Socrates. Plato started a school in Athens called the Academy and wrote *The Republic*, which describes an ideal society run by philosophers. (pp. 307, 309)

Pompey (106–48 BC) Roman general, he was an ally of Caesar but later the two went to war and Pompey was defeated in Egypt. (p. 353)

R

Ramses the Great (RAM-seez) (late 1300s and early 1200s BC) Egyptian pharaoh, he expanded the kingdom and built lasting temples at Karnak, Luxor, and Abu Simbel. Ramses the Great is often considered one of Egypt's greatest rulers. (pp. 103, 107)

Romulus and Remus (c. 753 BC) Legendary figures in Roman history, they built a city that eventually became Rome. (p. 327)

Ruth Biblical figure, according to the Bible, she left her family to care for her mother-in-law, Naomi. Ruth is an example of a model of devotion. (p. 231)

S

Sappho (SAF-oh) (c. 610–580 BC) Greek poet, she was one of the most famous lyric poets of Greece. (p. 273)

Sargon (c. 2300 BC) King of Akkad, a land north of Sumer, he built the world's first empire after defeating Sumer and northern Mesopotamia. (p. 63)

Shanakhdakheto (shah-nahk-dah-KEE-toh) (ruled 170–150 BC) Ruler of Kush, historians think she was the first woman to rule Kush. Her tomb is one of the largest pyramids in Meroë. (p. 129)

Shi Huangdi (SHEE hwahng-dee) (259–210 BC) Ruler of China, he united China for the first time. He built roads and canals and began the Great Wall of China. Shi Huangdi also imposed a standard system of laws, money, weights, and writing system in China. (pp. 194, 199)

Sima Qian (c. 145–190 BC) a Chinese historian, wrote a history of all the dynasties through the Han. His style became the model for later writings. (p. 204)

Socrates (SAHK-ruh-teez) (470–399 BC) Greek philosopher, his teaching style was based on asking questions. He wanted people to question their own beliefs. Socrates was arrested and condemned to death for challenging authority. (pp. 307, 309)

Solomon (SAHL-uh-muhn) (ruled c. 965–930 BC) King of Israel, he formed alliances with nearby kingdoms and built a temple to God in Jerusalem. (p. 229)

Spartacus (SPAHR-tuh-kuhs) (c. 73 BC) Former Roman gladiator, he led a slave revolt against Rome. (p. 343)

Sulla, Lucius Cornelius (LOO-shuhs kawr-NEEL-yuhs SUHL-uh) (138–78 BC) Roman consul, he battled Gaius Marius in a civil war. (p. 343)

Theodora (thee-uh-DOHR-uh) (c. 500–548) Wife of the Byzantine emperor Justinian, she was a smart and powerful woman who helped him rule effectively. (p. 419)

Thucydides (c. 400s BC) Greek historian, he was a former Athenian soldier who wrote a history of the Peloponnesian War based on his experiences. He tried to be impartial and study the causes and effects of war in hopes that future Greeks would not repeat their mistakes. (p. 306)

Tutankhamen (too-tang-KAHM-uhn) (c. 1300 BC) Egyptian pharaoh, he died while still a young king. The discovery of his tomb in 1922 has taught archaeologists much about Egyptian culture. (p. 113)

Xerxes I (ZUHRK-seez) (519–465 BC) Persian ruler, he tried to conquer Greece during the Persian Wars but was defeated. (p. 290)

Yohanan ben Zaccai (yoh-HAN-uhn ben ZAK-ay-y) (c. AD 70) Jewish teacher, he built a school near Jerusalem where he trained rabbis to carry on the Jewish religion after the Temple had been destroyed by the Romans. (p. 242)

Zealots (ZE-luhts) (AD 66–73) a group of Jews who rebelled against Roman rule (p. 240)

Justinian and Theodora

English and Spanish Glossary

MARK	AS IN	RESPELLING	EXAMPLE
a	alphabet	a	*AL-fuh-bet
ā	Asia	ay	AY-zhuh
ä	cart, top	ah	KAHRT, TAHP
e	let, ten	e	LET, TEN
ē	even, leaf	ee	EE-vuhn, LEEF
i	it, tip, British	i	IT, TIP, BRIT-ish
ī	site, buy, Ohio	y	SYT, BY, oh-HY-oh
	iris	eye	EYE-ris
k	card	k	KAHRD
ō	over, rainbow	oh	OH-vuhr, RAYN-boh
ù	book, wood	ooh	BOOHK, WOOHD
ò	all, orchid	aw	AWL, AWR-kid
òi	foil, coin	oy	FOYL, KOYN
aù	out	ow	OWT
ə	cup, butter	uh	KUHP, BUHT-uhr
ü	rule, food	oo	ROOL, FOOD
yü	few	yoo	FYOO
zh	vision	zh	VIZH-uhn

*A syllable printed in small capital letters receives heavier emphasis than the other syllable(s) in a word.

Phonetic Respelling and Pronunciation Guide

Many of the key terms in this textbook have been respelled to help you pronounce them. The letter combinations used in the respelling throughout the narrative are explained in the following phonetic respelling and pronunciation guide. The guide is adapted from *Merriam-Webster's Collegiate Dictionary, Eleventh Edition; Merriam-Webster's Biographical Dictionary;* and *Merriam-Webster's Geographical Dictionary.*

acropolis (uh-KRAH-puh-luhs) a high hill upon which a Greek fortress was built (p. 258)
acrópolis colina elevada sobre la que se construyó una fortaleza griega (pág. 258)

acupuncture (AK-yoo-punk-cher) the Chinese practice of inserting fine needles through the skin at specific points to cure disease or relieve pain (p. 205)
acupuntura práctica china que consiste en insertar pequeñas agujas en la piel en puntos específicos para curar enfermedades o aliviar el dolor (pág. 205)

afterlife life after death (p. 96)
la otra vida vida después de la muerte (pág. 96)

agriculture farming (p. 42)
agricultura cultivo de la tierra (pág. 42)

alliance an agreement to work together (p. 296)
alianza acuerdo de colaboración (pág. 296)

alloy a mixture of two or more metals (p. 170)
aleación mezcla de dos o más metales (pág. 170)

alphabet a set of letters that can be combined to form words (p. 79)
alfabeto conjunto de letras que pueden combinarse para formar palabras (pág. 79)

ancestor a relative who lived in the past (p. 28)
antepasado pariente que vivió hace muchos años (pág. 28)

Apostles (uh-PAHS-uhls) the 12 chosen disciples of Jesus who spread his teachings (p. 387)
apóstoles los 12 discípulos elegidos por Jesucristo que difundieron sus enseñanzas (pág. 387)

aqueduct a raised channel used to carry water (p. 367)

acueducto canal elevado que se utiliza para el transporte de agua (pág. 367)

archaeology (ar-kee-AH-luh-jee) the study of the past based on what people left behind (p. 7)

arqueología estudio del pasado a través de los objetos que dejaron las personas tras desaparecer (pág. 7)

architecture the science of building (p. 70)

arquitectura ciencia de la construcción (pág. 70)

aristocrat (uh-RIS-tuh-krat) a rich landowner or noble (p. 263)

aristócrata propietario de tierras o noble rico (pág. 263)

artifact an object created and used by humans (p. 10)

artefacto objeto creado y usado por los humanos (pág. 10)

astronomy the study of stars and planets (p. 171)

astronomía estudio de las estrellas y los planetas (pág. 171)

B

Bible the holy book of Judaism and Christianity. The Hebrew Bible is also part of the Christian Bible, where it is called the Old Testament. The Christian Bible includes the Old Testament and the New Testament. (p. 384)

Biblia libro sagrado del judaísmo y el cristianismo. La Biblia hebrea también forma parte de la Biblia cristiana, en donde se conoce como el Viejo Testamento. La Biblia cristiana incluye el Viejo Testamento y el Nuevo Testamento. (pág. 384)

bishops local leaders in the early Christian church (p. 393)

obispos líderes regionales en los comienzos de la iglesia cristiana (pág. 393)

Buddhism a religion based on the teachings of the Buddha that developed in India in the 500s BC (p. 158)

budismo religión basada en las enseñanzas de Buda, originada en la India en el siglo VI a. C. (pág. 158)

Byzantine Empire the society that developed in the eastern Roman Empire after the fall of the western Roman Empire (p. 416)

Imperio bizantino sociedad que surgió en el Imperio romano de oriente tras la caída del Imperio romano de occidente (pág. 416)

C

canal a human-made waterway (p. 58)

canal vía de agua hecha por el ser humano (pág. 58)

caste system the division of Indian society into groups based on rank, wealth, or occupation (p. 151)

sistema de castas división de la sociedad india en grupos basados en la clase social, el nivel económico o la profesión (pág. 151)

cataracts rapids along a river, such as those along the Nile in Egypt (p. 89)

rápidos fuertes corrientes a lo largo de un río, como las del Nilo en Egipto (pág. 89)

cavalry a group of soldiers who ride on horses (p. 288)

caballería grupo de soldados a caballo (pág. 288)

chariot a wheeled, horse-drawn cart used in battle (p. 76)

cuadriga carro tirado por caballos usado en las batallas (pág. 76)

checks and balances a system that balances the distribution of power in a government (p. 335)

pesos y contrapesos sistema creado para equilibrar la distribución del poder en un gobierno (pág. 335)

Christianity a religion based on the teachings of Jesus of Nazareth that developed in Judea at the beginning of the first century AD (p. 382)

cristianismo religión basada en las enseñanzas de Jesús de Nazaret que se desarrolló en Judea a comienzos del siglo I d. C. (pág. 382)

citizen a person who has the right to participate in government (p. 263)

ciudadano persona que tiene el derecho de participar en el gobierno (pág. 263)

city-state a political unit consisting of a city and its surrounding countryside (p. 62)

ciudad estado unidad política formada por una ciudad y los campos que la rodean (pág. 62)

civil law a legal system based on a written code of laws (p. 371)

derecho civil sistema jurídico basado en un código de leyes escritas (pág. 371)

classical an age marked by great achievements (p. 258)

clásica época marcada por grandes logros (pág. 258)

classical referring to the cultures of ancient Greece or Rome (p. 394)

clásica referente a las culturas de la Antigua Grecia y la Antigua Roma (pág. 394)

climate the average weather conditions in a certain area over a long period of time (p. 12)

clima condiciones del tiempo medias de una zona específica durante un largo período de tiempo (pág. 12)

Confucianism a philosophy based on the ideas of Confucius that focuses on morality, family order, social harmony, and government (p. 191)

confucianismo filosofía basada en las ideas de Confucio que se basa en la moralidad, el orden familiar, la armonía social y el gobierno (pág. 191)

consuls (KAHN-suhlz) the two most powerful officials in Rome (p. 333)

cónsules los dos funcionarios más poderosos en Roma (pág. 333)

corruption the decay of people's values (p. 412)

corrupción decadencia de los valores de las personas (pág. 412)

crucifixion (kroo-suh-FIK-shuhn) a type of execution in which a person was nailed to a cross (p. 385)

crucifixión tipo de ejecución en la que se clavaba a una persona en una cruz (pág. 385)

culture the knowledge, beliefs, customs, and values of a group of people (p. 7)

cultura el conocimiento, las creencias, las costumbres y los valores de un grupo de personas (pág. 7)

cuneiform (kyoo-NEE-uh-fohrm) the world's first system of writing; developed in Sumer (p. 67)

cuneiforme primer sistema de escritura del mundo; desarrollado en Sumeria (pág. 67)

currency money (p. 360)

moneda dinero (pág. 360)

D

Daoism (DOW-ih-zum) a philosophy that developed in China and stressed the belief that one should live in harmony with the Dao, the guiding force of all reality (p. 192)

taoismo filosofía que se desarrolló en China y que enfatizaba la creencia de que se debe vivir en armonía con el Tao, la fuerza que guía toda la realidad (pág. 192)

Dead Sea Scrolls writings about Jewish beliefs created about 2,000 years ago (p. 236)

manuscritos del mar Muerto escritos sobre las creencias judías, redactados hace unos 2,000 años (pág. 236)

delta a triangle-shaped area of land made from soil deposited by a river (p. 89)

delta zona de tierra de forma triangular creada a partir de los sedimentos que deposita un río (pág. 89)

democracy a type of government in which people rule themselves (p. 262)
democracia tipo de gobierno en el que el pueblo se gobierna a sí mismo (pág. 262)

Diaspora (dy-AS-pruh) the scattering of the Jews outside of Judah after the Babylonian Captivity (p. 230)
diáspora la dispersión de los judíos desde Judá tras el cautiverio en Babilonia (pág. 230)

dictator a ruler who has almost absolute power (p. 328)
dictador gobernante que tiene poder casi absoluto (pág. 328)

diffusion the spread of ideas from one culture to another (p. 211)
difusión traspaso de ideas de una cultura a otra (pág. 211)

disciples (di-SY-puhls) followers (p. 385)
discípulos seguidores (pág. 385)

division of labor an arrangement in which each worker specializes in a particular task or job (p. 58)
división del trabajo organización mediante la que cada trabajador se especializa en un trabajo o tarea en particular (pág. 58)

domestication the process of changing plants or animals to make them more useful to humans (p. 41)
domesticación proceso en el que se modifican los animales o las plantas para que sean más útiles para los humanos (pág. 41)

dynasty a series of rulers from the same family (p. 91)
dinastía serie de gobernantes pertenecientes a la misma familia (pág. 91)

E

ebony a dark, heavy wood (p. 124)
ébano madera oscura y pesada (pág. 124)

elite (AY-leet) people of wealth and power (p. 97)
élite personas ricas y poderosas (pág. 97)

empire land with different territories and peoples under a single rule (p. 63)
imperio zona que reúne varios territorios y pueblos bajo un mismo gobierno (pág. 63)

engineering the application of scientific knowledge for practical purposes (p. 98)
ingeniería aplicación del conocimiento científico para fines prácticos (pág. 98)

environment all the living and nonliving things that affect life in an area (p. 13)
medio ambiente todos los seres vivos y elementos inertes que afectan la vida de un área (pág. 13)

epics long poems that tell the stories of heroes (p. 68)
poemas épicos poemas largos que narran hazañas de héroes (pág. 68)

ethics moral values (p. 191)
ética valores morales (pág. 191)

Eucharist the central ceremony of the Christian church, honoring the last supper that Jesus shared with his Apostles before he died (p. 393)
Eucaristía ceremonia principal de la iglesia cristiana que conmemora la última cena que Jesús compartió con sus apóstoles antes de morir (pág. 393)

Exodus the journey of the Hebrews, led by Moses, from Egypt to Canaan after they were freed from slavery (p. 227)
Éxodo viaje de los hebreos, guiados por Moisés, desde Egipto hasta Canaán después de su liberación de la esclavitud (pág. 227)

exports items sent to other regions for trade (p. 128)
exportaciones productos enviados a otras regiones para el intercambio comercial (pág. 128)

fable a short story that teaches a lesson about life or gives advice on how to live (p. 273)

fábula relato breve que presenta una enseñanza u ofrece algún consejo sobre la vida (pág. 273)

fasting going without food for a period of time (p. 157)

ayunar dejar de comer durante un período de tiempo (pág. 157)

Fertile Crescent an area of rich farmland in Southwest Asia where the first civilizations began (p. 57)

Media Luna de las tierras fértiles zona de ricas tierras de cultivo situada en el sudoeste de Asia, en la que comenzaron las primeras civilizaciones (pág. 57)

forum a Roman public meeting place (p. 335)

foro lugar público de reuniones en Roma (pág. 335)

fossil a part or imprint of something that was once alive (p. 10)

fósil parte o huella de un ser vivo ya desaparecido (pág. 10)

geography the study of Earth's physical and cultural features (p. 12)

geografía estudio de las características físicas y culturales de la Tierra (pág. 12)

Great Wall a barrier made of walls across China's northern frontier (p. 197)

Gran Muralla barrera formada por muros situada a lo largo de la frontera norte de China (pág. 197)

Hammurabi's Code a set of 282 laws governing daily life in Babylon; the earliest known collection of written laws (p. 75)

Código de Hammurabi conjunto de 282 leyes que regían la vida cotidiana en Babilonia; la primera colección de leyes escritas conocida (pág. 75)

Hellenistic Greek-like; heavily influenced by Greek ideas (p. 301)

helenístico al estilo griego; muy influido por las ideas de la Grecia clásica (pág. 301)

hieroglyphics (hy-ruh-GLIH-fiks) the ancient Egyptian writing system that used picture symbols (p. 108)

jeroglíficos sistema de escritura del antiguo Egipto, en el cual se usaban símbolos ilustrados (pág. 108)

High Holy Days the two most sacred days of Jewish religious observance—Rosh Hashanah and Yom Kippur (p. 245)

Supremos Días Santos los dos días más sagrados de la práctica religiosa judía: Rosh Hashaná y Yom Kippur (pág. 245)

Hindu-Arabic numerals the number system we use today; it was created by Indian scholars during the Gupta dynasty (p. 170)

numerales indoarábigos sistema numérico que usamos hoy en día; fue creado por estudiosos de la India durante la dinastía Gupta (pág. 170)

Hinduism the main religion of India; it teaches that everything is part of a universal spirit called Brahman (p. 153)

hinduismo religión principal de la India; sus enseñanzas dicen que todo forma parte de un espíritu universal llamado Brahman (pág. 153)

ENGLISH AND SPANISH GLOSSARY

history the study of the past (p. 6)
  historia estudio del pasado (pág. 6)

hominid an early ancestor of humans (p. 28)
  homínido antepasado primitivo de los humanos (pág. 28)

hunter-gatherers people who hunt animals and gather wild plants, seeds, fruits, and nuts to survive (p. 33)
  cazadores y recolectores personas que cazan animales y recolectan plantas, semillas, frutas y nueces para sobrevivir (pág. 33)

ice ages long periods of freezing weather (p. 36)
  eras glaciales largos períodos de clima helado (pág. 36)

imports goods brought in from other regions (p. 128)
  importaciones bienes que se introducen en un país procedentes de otras regiones (pág. 128)

inoculation (i-nah-kyuh-LAY-shuhn) injecting a person with a small dose of a virus to help build up defenses to a disease (p. 170)
  inoculación acto de inyectar una pequeña dosis de un virus a una persona para ayudarla a crear defensas contra una enfermedad (pág. 170)

irrigation a way of supplying water to an area of land (p. 58)
  irrigación método para suministrar agua a un terreno (pág. 58)

ivory a white material made from elephant tusks (p. 124)
  marfil material de color blanco procedente de los colmillos de los elefantes (pág. 124)

jade a hard gemstone often used in jewelry (p. 185)
  jade piedra preciosa de gran dureza que se suele utilizar en joyería (pág. 185)

Jainism an Indian religion based on the teachings of Mahavira that teaches all life is sacred (p. 155)
  jainismo religión de la India basada en las enseñanzas de Mahavira, que proclama que toda forma de vida es sagrada (pág. 155)

Judaism (joo-dee-i-zuhm) the religion of the Hebrews (practiced by Jews today); it is the world's oldest monotheistic religion (p. 232)
  judaísmo religión de los hebreos (practicada por los judíos hoy en día); es la religión monoteísta más antigua del mundo (pág. 232)

karma in Buddhism and Hinduism, the effects that good or bad actions have on a person's soul (p. 154)
  karma en el budismo y el hinduismo, los efectos que las buenas o malas acciones producen en el alma de una persona (pág. 154)

land bridge a strip of land connecting two continents (p. 36)
  puente de tierra franja de tierra que conecta dos continentes (pág. 36)

landforms the natural features of the land's surface (p. 12)
  accidentes geográficos características naturales de la superficie terrestre (pág. 12)

ENGLISH AND SPANISH GLOSSARY

Latin the language of the Romans (p. 334)
latín idioma de los romanos (pág. 334)

Legalism the Chinese belief that people were bad by nature and needed to be controlled (p. 192)
legalismo creencia china de que las personas eran malas por naturaleza y debían ser controladas (pág. 192)

legion (LEE-juhn) a group of up to 6,000 Roman soldiers (p. 339)
legión grupo que podía incluir hasta 6,000 soldados romanos (pág. 339)

lord a person of high rank who owned land but owed loyalty to his king (p. 189)
señor feudal persona de alto nivel social que poseía tierras y debía lealtad al rey (pág. 189)

M

magistrate (MA-juh-strayt) an elected official in Rome (p. 333)
magistrado funcionario electo en Roma (pág. 333)

maize (MAYS) corn (p. 431)
maíz cereal conocido también como elote o choclo (pág. 431)

martyr a person who dies for his or her beliefs (p. 393)
mártir persona que muere por sus creencias (pág. 393)

meditation deep continued thought that focuses the mind on spiritual ideas (p. 157)
meditación reflexión profunda y continua, durante la cual la persona se concentra en ideas espirituales (pág. 157)

megalith a huge stone monument (p. 42)
megalito enorme monumento de piedra (pág. 42)

merchant a trader (p. 128)
mercader comerciante (pág. 128)

Mesoamerica a region that includes the southern part of what is now Mexico and parts of northern Central America (p. 428)
Mesoamérica región que incluye la zona sur del México actual y zonas del norte de Centroamérica (pág. 428)

Mesolithic Era the middle part of the Stone Age; marked by the creation of smaller and more complex tools (p. 38)
Mesolítico período central de la Edad de Piedra, caracterizado por la creación de herramientas más pequeñas y complejas (pág. 38)

Messiah (muh-SY-uh) in Judaism, a new leader that would appear among the Jews and restore the greatness of ancient Israel (p. 383)
Mesías en el judaísmo, nuevo líder que aparecería entre los judíos y restablecería la grandeza del antiguo Israel (pág. 383)

metallurgy (MET-uhl-uhr-jee) the science of working with metals (p. 170)
metalurgia ciencia de trabajar los metales (pág. 170)

Middle Kingdom the period of Egyptian history from about 2050 to 1750 BC and marked by order and stability (p. 102)
Reino Medio período de la historia de Egipto que abarca aproximadamente del 2050 al 1750 a. C. y que se caracterizó por el orden y la estabilidad (pág. 102)

migrate to move to a new place (p. 36)
migrar desplazarse a otro lugar (pág. 36)

missionary someone who works to spread religious beliefs (p. 160)
misionero alguien que trabaja para difundir sus creencias religiosas (pág. 160)

monarch (MAH-nark) a ruler of a kingdom or empire (p. 74)
monarca gobernante de un reino o imperio (pág. 74)

ENGLISH AND SPANISH GLOSSARY

monotheism the belief in only one God (p. 232)

monoteísmo creencia en un solo Dios (pág. 232)

monsoon a seasonal wind pattern that causes wet and dry seasons (p. 145)

monzón viento estacional cíclico que causa estaciones húmedas y secas (pág. 145)

mosaic a picture made with pieces of colored stone or glass (p. 417)

mosaico dibujo hecho con trozos de piedra o cristal de colores (pág. 417)

mummy a specially treated body wrapped in cloth for preservation (p. 96)

momia cadáver especialmente tratado y envuelto en tela para su conservación (pág. 96)

mythology stories about gods and heroes that try to explain how the world works (p. 269)

mitología relatos sobre dioses y héroes que tratan de explicar cómo funciona el mundo (pág. 269)

N

Neolithic Era the New Stone Age; when people learned to make fire and tools such as saws and drills (p. 41)

Neolítico Nueva Edad de Piedra; el ser humano aprendió a producir fuego y a fabricar herramientas como sierras y taladros manuales (pág. 41)

New Kingdom the period from about 1550 to 1050 BC in Egyptian history when Egypt reached the height of its power and glory (p. 102)

Reino Nuevo período de la historia egipcia que abarca aproximadamente desde el 1550 hasta el 1050 a. C., en el que Egipto alcanzó la cima de su poder y su gloria (pág. 102)

nirvana (nir-vah-nuh) in Buddhism, a state of perfect peace (p. 158)

nirvana en el budismo, estado de paz perfecta (pág. 158)

noble a rich and powerful person (p. 94)

noble persona rica y poderosa (pág. 94)

nonviolence the avoidance of violent actions (p. 155)

no violencia rechazo de las acciones violentas (pág. 155)

O

obelisk (AH-buh-lisk) a tall, pointed, four-sided pillar in ancient Egypt (p. 110)

obelisco pilar alto, de cuatro caras y acabado en punta, propio del antiguo Egipto (pág. 110)

observatory a building used to study astronomy (p. 442)

observatorio edificio usado para estudiar la astronomía (pág. 442)

obsidian a sharp, glasslike volcanic rock (p. 434)

obsidiana roca volcánica cortante y parecida al vidrio (pág. 434)

Old Kingdom the period from about 2700 to 2200 BC in Egyptian history that began shortly after Egypt was unified (p. 93)

Reino Antiguo período de la historia egipcia que abarca aproximadamente del 2700 hasta el 2200 a. C. y comenzó poco después de la unificación de Egipto (pág. 93)

oligarchy (AH-luh-gar-kee) a government in which only a few people have power (p. 263)

oligarquía gobierno en el que sólo unas pocas personas tienen el poder (pág. 263)

oracle a prediction by a wise person, or a person who makes a prediction (p. 186)

oráculo predicción de un sabio o de alguien que hace profecías (pág. 186)

ENGLISH AND SPANISH GLOSSARY

orator a public speaker (p. 352)
orador persona que habla en público (pág. 352)

P

Paleolithic Era (pay-lee-uh-LI-thik) the first part of the Stone Age; when people first used stone tools (p. 31)
Paleolítico primera parte de la Edad de Piedra; cuando el ser humano usó herramientas de piedra por primera vez (pág. 31)

papyrus (puh-PY-ruhs) a long-lasting, paper-like material made from reeds that the ancient Egyptians used to write on (p. 108)
papiro material duradero hecho de juncos, similar al papel, que los antiguos egipcios utilizaban para escribir (pág. 108)

Passover a holiday in which Jews remember the Exodus (p. 245)
Pascua judía festividad en la que los judíos recuerdan el Éxodo (pág. 245)

patricians (puh-TRI-shunz) the nobility in Roman society (p. 329)
patricios nobles de la sociedad romana (pág. 329)

Pax Romana Roman Peace; a period of general peace and prosperity in the Roman Empire that lasted from 27 BC to AD 180 (p. 361)
Pax Romana Paz Romana; período de paz y prosperidad generales en el Imperio romano que duró del 27 a. C. al 180 d. C. (pág. 361)

peasant a farmer with a small farm (p. 189)
campesino agricultor dueño de una pequeña granja (pág. 189)

Peloponnesian War a war between Athens and Sparta in the 400s BC (p. 297)
guerra del Peloponeso guerra entre Atenas y Esparta en el siglo V a. C. (pág. 297)

persecution (puhr-si-KYOO-shuhn) the punishment of a group because of its beliefs or differences (p. 393)
persecución castigo a un grupo debido a sus creencias o diferencias (pág. 393)

Persian Wars a series of wars between Persia and Greece in the 400s BC (p. 289)
guerras persas serie de guerras entre Persia y Grecia en el siglo V a. C. (pág. 289)

phalanx (FAY-langks) a group of Greek warriors who stood close together in a square formation (p. 299)
falange grupo de guerreros griegos que se mantenían unidos en formación compacta y cuadrada (pág. 299)

pharaoh (FEHR-oh) the title used by the rulers of Egypt (p. 91)
faraón título usado por los gobernantes de Egipto (pág. 91)

pictograph a picture symbol (p. 68)
pictograma símbolo ilustrado (pág. 68)

plebeians (pli-BEE-uhnz) the common people of ancient Rome (p. 329)
plebeyos gente común de la antigua Roma (pág. 329)

polis (PAH-luhs) the Greek word for a city-state (p. 258)
polis palabra griega para designar una ciudad estado (pág. 258)

polytheism the worship of many gods (p. 64)
politeísmo culto a varios dioses (pág. 64)

pope the bishop of Rome and the head of the Roman Catholic Church (p. 394)
Papa obispo de Roma y cabeza de la Iglesia católica romana (pág. 394)

Popol Vuh (poh-pohl VOO) a book containing Maya legends and history (p. 443)
Popol Vuh libro que contiene las leyendas y la historia de los mayas (pág. 443)

prehistory the time before there was writing (p. 28)
prehistoria período anterior a la existencia de la escritura (pág. 28)

priest a person who performs religious ceremonies (p. 65)

　sacerdote persona que lleva a cabo ceremonias religiosas (pág. 65)

primary source an account of an event by someone who took part in or witnessed the event (p. 10)

　fuente primaria relato de un hecho por parte de alguien que participó o presenció el hecho (pág. 10)

prophet someone who is said to receive messages from God to be taught to others (p. 235)

　profeta alguien del que se cree que recibe mensajes de Dios para transmitírselos a los demás (pág. 235)

provinces areas outside of Italy that the Romans controlled (p. 360)

　provincias zonas fuera de Italia que controlaban los romanos (pág. 360)

Punic Wars a series of wars between Rome and Carthage in the 200s and 100s BC (p. 339)

　guerras púnicas sucesión de guerras entre Roma y Cartago en los siglos III y II a. C. (pág. 339)

pyramid a huge triangular tomb built by the Egyptians and other peoples (p. 98)

　pirámide tumba triangular y gigantesca construida por los egipcios y otros pueblos (pág. 98)

Q, R

rabbi (RAB-y) a Jewish religious leader and teacher (p. 242)

　rabino líder y maestro religioso judío (pág. 242)

reason clear and ordered thinking (p. 307)

　razón pensamiento claro y ordenado (pág. 307)

region an area with one or more features that make it different from surrounding areas (p. 15)

　región zona con una o varias características que la diferencian de las zonas que la rodean (pág. 15)

reincarnation a Hindu and Buddhist belief that souls are born and reborn many times, each time into a new body (p. 153)

　reencarnación creencia hindú y budista de que las almas nacen y renacen muchas veces, siempre en un cuerpo nuevo (pág. 153)

republic a political system in which people elect leaders to govern them (p. 328)

　república sistema político en el que el pueblo elige a los líderes que lo gobernarán (pág. 328)

resources the materials found on Earth that people need and value (p. 16)

　recursos materiales de la Tierra que las personas necesitan y valoran (pág. 16)

Resurrection in Christianity, Jesus's rise from the dead (p. 385)

　Resurrección en el cristianismo, la vuelta a la vida de Jesús (pág. 385)

Roman Senate a council of wealthy and powerful citizens who advised Rome's leaders (p. 333)

　Senado romano consejo de ciudadanos ricos y poderosos que aconsejaba a los gobernantes de Roma (pág. 333)

Romance languages languages that developed from Latin, such as Italian, French, Spanish, Portuguese, and Romanian (p. 371)

　lenguas romances lenguas que surgieron del latín, como el italiano, el francés, el español, el portugués y el rumano (pág. 371)

ENGLISH AND SPANISH GLOSSARY

ENGLISH AND SPANISH GLOSSARY

Rosetta Stone a huge stone slab inscribed with hieroglyphics, Greek, and a later form of Egyptian that allowed historians to understand Egyptian writing (p. 109)
piedra Roseta gran losa de piedra en la que aparecen inscripciones en jeroglíficos, en griego y en una forma tardía del idioma egipcio que permitió a los historiadores descifrar la escritura egipcia (pág. 109)

rural a countryside area (p. 62)
rural zona del campo (pág. 62)

S

saint a person known and admired for his or her holiness (p. 388)
santo persona conocida y admirada por su santidad (pág. 388)

Sanskrit the most important language of ancient India (p. 149)
sánscrito el idioma más importante de la antigua India (pág. 149)

satire a style of writing that pokes fun at people or society (p. 370)
sátira estilo de escritura que hace burla de las personas o de la sociedad (pág. 370)

scribe a writer (p. 68)
escriba escritor (pág. 68)

secondary source information gathered by someone who did not take part in or witness an event (p. 10)
fuente secundaria información recopilada por alguien que no participó ni presenció un hecho (pág. 10)

seismograph a device that measures the strength of an earthquake (p. 204)
sismógrafo aparato que mide la fuerza de un terremoto (pág. 204)

silk a soft, light, and highly valued fabric developed in China (p. 209)
seda tejido suave, ligero y muy apreciado que se originó en China (pág. 209)

Silk Road a network of trade routes that stretched across Asia from China to the Mediterranean Sea (p. 209)
Ruta de la Seda red de rutas comerciales que se extendían a lo largo de Asia desde China hasta el mar Mediterráneo (pág. 209)

silt a mixture of fertile soil and tiny rocks that can make land ideal for farming (p. 57)
cieno mezcla de tierra fértil y piedrecitas que pueden crear un terreno ideal para el cultivo (pág. 57)

social hierarchy the division of society by rank or class (p. 65)
jerarquía social división de la sociedad en clases o niveles (pág. 65)

society a community of people who share a common culture (p. 33)
sociedad comunidad de personas que comparten la misma cultura (pág. 33)

sphinx (sfinks) an imaginary creature with a human head and the body of a lion that was often shown on Egyptian statues (p. 110)
esfinge criatura imaginaria con cabeza humana y cuerpo de león que aparecía representada a menudo en las estatuas egipcias (pág. 110)

subcontinent a large landmass that is smaller than a continent, such as India (p. 144)
subcontinente gran masa de tierra menor que un continente, como la India (pág. 144)

sundial a device that uses the position of shadows cast by the sun to tell the time of day (p. 204)
reloj de sol dispositivo que utiliza la posición de las sombras que proyecta el sol para indicar las horas del día (pág. 204)

surplus more of something than is needed (p. 58)
excedente cantidad que supera lo que se necesita (pág. 58)

synagogue (si-nuh-gawg) a Jewish house of worship (p. 234)
sinagoga lugar de culto judío (pág. 234)

Talmud (TAHL-moohd) a set of commentaries, stories, and folklore that explains Jewish law (p. 236)
Talmud conjunto de comentarios, relatos y folklore que explican la ley judía (pág. 236)

Ten Commandments in the Bible, a code of moral laws given to Moses by God (p. 228)
los Diez Mandamientos en la Biblia, código de leyes morales que Dios le entregó a Moisés (pág. 228)

tool an object that has been modified to help a person accomplish a task (p. 30)
herramienta objeto que ha sido modificado para ayudar a una persona a realizar una tarea (pág. 30)

Torah the most sacred text of Judaism (p. 234)
Torá el texto más sagrado del judaísmo (pág. 234)

trade network a system of people in different lands who trade goods back and forth (p. 128)
red comercial sistema de personas en diferentes lugares que comercian productos entre sí (pág. 128)

trade route a path followed by traders (p. 102)
ruta comercial itinerario seguido por los comerciantes (pág. 102)

tyrant an ancient Greek leader who held power through the use of force (p. 263)
tirano gobernante de la antigua Grecia que mantenía el poder mediante el uso de la fuerza (pág. 263)

urban a city area (p. 62)
urbano zona de ciudad (pág. 62)

vault a set of arches that supports the roof of a building (p. 367)
bóveda conjunto de arcos que sostienen el tejado de un edificio (pág. 367)

veto (VEE-toh) to reject or prohibit actions and laws of other government officials (p. 334)
vetar rechazar o prohibir acciones y leyes de otros funcionarios del gobierno (pág. 334)

villa a country home or estate (p. 362)
villa finca o casa de campo (pág. 362)

wheelbarrow a single-wheeled cart (p. 209)
carretilla carrito de una sola rueda (pág. 209)

X, Y, Z

Zealots (ZE-luhts) radical Jews who supported rebellion against the Romans (p. 240)
zelotes judíos radicales que apoyaron la rebelión contra los romanos (pág. 240)

ziggurat a pyramid-shaped temple in Sumer (p. 70)
zigurat templo sumerio en forma de pirámide (pág. 70)

ENGLISH AND SPANISH GLOSSARY

Index

KEY TO INDEX

c = chart	*m* = map
f = feature	*p* = photo

Abraham, 226, 232, 237; routes of, 227m
Abu Simbel, temple of, 107, 110
accord, 207
Achilles, 272
acropolis, 258
Actium, Battle of, 356
acupuncture, 205
Aegean Sea, 255
Aegeus (Greek king), 274
Aeneas, 326–27, 326f
Aeneid, The (Virgil), 326, 330–31, 370
Aeschylus, 306
Aesop, 273, 273f, 274
Africa: hominids in, 30, 37; northern, Roman control of, 341
afterlife, 96
agora, 258
agriculture, 42; in Americas, 431–33; in China, 184; in Egypt, 90–91f
ahimsa, 155
Ahmose (Egyptian king), 102
Ajanta, temple at, 167–68
Akkad (modern day Baghdad), 63; capture of, 64
Akkadians: rise of the empire of, 63–64; society of the, 63
Aksum, 131
Alexander the Great, 298–301; empire of, 300–301m; Greeks controlled by, 299–300; as ruler of the Persian Empire, 300
Alexandria, 242, 361
alliance, 296
alloys, 170
alphabet, 79
Alps, the, 324, 325p
Amazon River, 430
Americas, the: early civilization in, 433m; farming in, 431–33; geography of, 428–30, 429m;

hunter-gatherers in, 430; migration to, 430m
Amon-Re (Egyptian god), 95f, 96, 110f
Analects, the, 191–92f
Analysis Skills, H23; Analyzing Costs and Benefits, 278, 280; Analyzing Information, 33, 69, 154, 244, 271, 334, 386, 426–27, 448; Analyzing Points of View, 294, 432; Analyzing Primary Sources, 9, 15, 19, 38, 75, 114, 116, 192, 266, 306, 335, 355, 389, 443; Analyzing Visuals, 32, 42–43, 64–65, 94, 97, 99, 110–11, 112–13, 130, 146–47, 151, 171, 265, 269, 305, 336, 341, 361, 362, 364, 417, 437, 441; Cause and Effect, 120–21, 134, 246, 248; Chance, Error, and Oversight in History, 420, 422; Chronological Order, 26–27, 46; Continuity and Change in History, 396, 398; Fact and Opinion, 224–25, 248; Identifying Central Issues, 44, 46; Interpreting Maps, 29, 37, 41, 57, 61, 63, 76, 79, 80, 82, 89, 103, 105, 123, 125, 145, 149, 160, 163, 164, 183, 186, 189, 195, 201, 210, 213, 227, 230, 243, 255, 258, 261, 287, 290, 296, 301, 325, 328, 339, 342, 344, 359, 360, 365, 388, 394, 409, 410, 415, 429, 430, 433, 435; Reading and Using Time Lines, 229, 372, 374, 393, 413;
Analyzing Costs and Benefits, 278
ancestor(s): defined, 28; our early, discovery of, 28–29
Ancestors: In Search of Human Origins (Johanson), 28
Andes Mountains, 429f, 430; major civilization begins in, 432
Antony, Marc, 355
"Ants and the Grasshopper, The" (Aesop), 273
Anubis (Egyptian god), 96
Apedemek (Kushite god), 129
Apennines, the, 324–25
Aphrodite (goddess of love), 269

Apollo (god of the sun), 269
Apostles, 387
aqueduct, 367
archaeology, 7
arches, 367, 367p
architecture: of Greece, 304–5; of the Maya, 442; in Sumer, 70; supported by trade, 103
Ares (god of war), 269
aristocrats, 263
Aristophanes, 306
Aristotle, 307, 309f
art: of Buddhists, 167–68; Egyptian, 94–95, 112; Greek achievements in, 303–4; of Gupta, 165p, 167–68; of Han dynasty, 204–5f; of Harappans, 148p; Hindu, 167–68; in hunter-gatherer societies, 33–34; inspired by Greek myths, 274; of the Maya, 442; of Persian Wars, 289p; in Sumer, 70–71; supported by trade, 103
Artemis (goddess of the moon), 269
artifacts, 10, 11p
Aryan(s), 148–49; invasions by, 149m; language of, 149; social classes of, 150–51
Ashkenazim, the, 243f, 244
Asia Minor, 287, 359; trade with Egypt and, 103
Asoka (Mauryan king), 163, 166f
assemblies, 333–34
Assessing Primary and Secondary Sources, 114
Assyrian Empire, 76m
Assyrians, 76–77; Egypt invaded by, 126; and the fall of Israel, 230
astronomy, 171
Athens, 290. *See also* Greece; democracy and, 263, 264–67; early, 263; fighting between Sparta and, 296–97; government in, 262f–67; life in, 295f; women in, 264f, 295
atman, 153
Attila (the Hun), 411–12
Augustine of Hippo, 394
Augustus (Octavian)(emperor of Rome), 355, 356, 357f
Australopithecus, 30p

B

Babylon, 230; decline of, 75; rise of, 74–75; trade with Egypt and, 103
Babylonian captivity, 230
Babylonian Empire, 76m
Baghdad (ancient Akkad), 63, 74
barbarians, 408, 415
Bering Strait, 430
Bethlehem, 384
Bhagavad Gita, the, 169, 172–73f
Bible, 384, 386, 390–91; Gospels, 388, 393; New Testament, 384–85; Old Testament, 384
bishops, 393
Book of the Dead, The, 109
"Boy Who Cried Wolf, The" (Aesop), 273
Brahma (Hindu god), 153
Brahman, 152, 153
Brahmanism, 152
Brahmins, 150–51
Britain, 408
Brueghal, Pieter, 239f
Brutus, 355
Buddha, the, 157–59, 158p; defined, 157; Eightfold Path of, 159; Four Noble Truths of, 158; Hindu ideas challenged by, 159; statue of, in China, 211p; teachings of, 158
Buddhism, 156–61; branches of, 161; during the Han dynasty, 210–11; early spread of, 160–61, 159m
Burma, 160
Byzantine Empire, 414–19, 415m, 418f; Christianity and, 417; society of, 416–17
Byzantium, 414

C

cacao beans, 435
Caesar, Julius, 353; death of, 354f; views of 355
Calakmul, 437
California: maps of, 14–15m; San Francisco, 8p
Cambyses, 288
Canaan, 227
canals: defined, 58; in Mesopotamia, 58p

Canby, Thomas, 38f
Capitoline Hill, the, 337
Carter, Howard, 112f
Carthage, 78, 340 and Rome, 340–41f
caste system: defined, 151, 152; and Hinduism, 153–54
Catal Hüyük, Turkey, 42m, 42–43p
cataracts, 89, 123
cavalry, 288
cave paintings, 33–34, 34p
Chaldeans, 77, 230
Chance, Error, and Oversight in History, 420
chancellor, 207
Chandragupta I (Gupta emperor), 164
Chandragupta II (Gupta emperor), 164
Chang Jiang, 183–84
chariot(s), 76; race with, 362–63
Chávez, César, 154f, 154p
Chavín culture, 432
checks and balances, 334–35
Chichén Itzá, 442
China: Buddhism in, 161; development of farming, 184; dynasties, first, 185–87, 186m. Qin dynasty, 194–99, 195m; geography of, 182–85, 183m; Han acheivements, Han dynasty, 200–11, 201m; hominid migration to, 37 Warring States period, 190f;
Chinatown, San Francisco, 8p
Christianity, 237; in Byzantine Empire, 417; holidays of, 386f; origins of, 384–89; as religion, 382; spread of, to Rome, 392–95, 394m; time line, 392
Christmas, 386f
Christos, 385
Cicero, 352
Cincinnatus (Roman dictator), 328, 328f
circus, 371
citizens, 263
city-state(s): defined, 62; of Greece. *See* Greek city-states; of Kish, 63; of Sumer, 62–63; of Ur, 64–65f; of Uruk, 63
civilization, and irrigation, 58
civil law, 371
classical age, 258
Cleisthenes, 264

Cleopatra (queen of Egypt), 354, 356f
climate: defined, 12–13; of India, 145–46
clothing, of early people, 38
Clovis (Frankish king), 411
clues: from the past, 10p; using, 10–11
Coliseum, the, in Oakland, California, 368p
Colosseum, the, in Rome, 348–49p, 368–69p, 368f
Comparing and Contrasting Societies, 48
Confucianism, 191; main ideas of, 192
Confucius, 191f
Constantine (emperor of Rome), 395, 395f, 409
Constantinople, 409, 415m, 416f
Constitution of the Roman Republic, The (Polybius), 335
consuls, 333, 333c
Continuity and Change in History, 396
Corinth, 389
corruption, 412
Corsica, 341
counsel, 207
Crassus, 353
Crete, 271
Critical Thinking Skills: Analyzing, 198, 337, 426–27, 448; Categorizing, 11, 17, 79, 100, 106, 131, 149, 155, 165, 171, 205, 211, 275, 291, 383; Comparing and Contrasting, 92, 187, 245, 252–53, 267, 280, 297, 363, 371, 418; Drawing Conclusions, 54–55, 116, 413; Evaluating, 34; Explaining, 237; Finding Main Ideas, 54–55, 82, 193, 302, 309; Identifying Cause and Effect, 43, 71, 120–21, 126, 134; Sequencing, 26–27, 39, 46, 59, 66, 329, 356, 395; Summarizing, 113, 131, 161, 180–81, 216, 259, 308, 343;
crucifixion, 385
culture(s): defined, 7; in Kush, 129; shaped by geography, 16; trading, 256–57
cuneiform: defined, 67; use of symbols in, 68
currency, 360

cylinder seals, 70–71
Cyrus II (Cyrus the Great)(emperor of Persia), 286–87, 287f

Daniel, Book of, 235
Daoism, 192
Darius I (emperor of Persia), 286, 288, 288f, 289
Dark Age, the, 257
David (king of Israel), 229, 383
Davis, Kenneth C., 15f
Dead Sea Scrolls, 236–37, 236f
Death of Socrates, The (Plato), 306f
Deborah, 231
Delian League, 296
Delos, 296
Delphi, temple at, 251p
delta, 89
Demeter (goddess of agriculture), 269, 270
democracy: Athenian, 264–67; creation of, 264–66; defined, 262, 263f; differences between ancient and modern, 266, 267f; direct, 266–67; in action, 264f representative, 267
dharma, 154
Diaspora, the, 230, 243, 243f
dictators, 328
Diocletian, 409
Dionysus (god of celebration), 269
direct democracy, 266–67
disaster, natural, 260–61f
disciples, 385
division of labor, 58
Dixon, James, 38f
domestication, 41–42; early, 40–41m
Don't Know Much About Geography (Davis), 15f
Draco, 263
drama, 306
Drawing Conclusions, 86
dynasty, 91

early humans: hominids and, 30f; migration of, 36–39

Easter, 386f
economy, 59, 127–28, 131, 259, 263
education, views of, 294
Egypt, 161. *See also* Egyptian(s); ancient, 89m; daily life in, 104; development of civilization in, 90–91; early geography of, 88–89; farming in, 90–91p; great temples of, 110; Hellenistic, 302; historical periods of, 101; invaded by Assyrians, 126; kingdoms of, 90–91; Kush and, 122–26, 124, 125; pyramids and, 98–100; records from, 11p; religion in, 95–97, 95f; society in, 94–95, 94f, 104–6; time line, 89f; trade and, *See* Egyptian trade; women in, 106; writing of, 108–9, 109f
Egyptian(s). *See also* Egypt: art of, 94–95, 112; burial practices of, 97
Egyptian trade, 103m; with Asia Minor, 103; with Babylon, 103; with Greece, 103; with Nubia, 95; with Punt, 95, 103; with Syria, 95
Eightfold Path, 158–59f
embalming, 97
empire, 63–64
engineering, 98
Enki (Sumerian god), 64
Enlil (Sumerian god), 64
Epic of Gilgamesh, The, 72–73
epic poetry of Homer, the, 276
epics, 68
Eritrea, 131
Esther (Hebrew queen), 231
ethics, 191
Ethiopia, 131
Etruscans, 327
Eucharist, 393
Euclid, 307f, 308
Euphrates River, 60p, 74; as feature of Mesopotamia, 57; flooding of, 57; water levels in, 58
Evaluating Web-Based Information, 350
Exodus, the, 227–28
exports, 128
Ezana (Aksumite king), 131

fables, 273
farming: Chinese development of, 184; in early societies, 42f; in Egypt, 90–91p; during Han dynasty, 208; in Mesopotamia, 58
Fertile Crescent, 57m; civilizations developed in, 76; defined, 57; later people of, 74–79
Finding Main Ideas, 54
First Dynasty, the, 91–92, 93
flint, tools made of, 31
floodgates, 238
flooding: of Euphrates River, 57; floodgates and, 238; of Nile River, 89; of Tigris River, 57
fossil, 10
Franks, 410–11
French, as Romance language, 371
fresco, 370
fu, 204

Galen, 366
Gallic Wars, The (Caesar), 353f
Gandhi, Mohandas, 154f, 154p
Ganges River, 157
Gaugamela, 300
Gaul, 341, 353
Gauls, the, 338
Gautama, Siddhartha, 156–57, 157p
Gaya, 157
Geb (Egyptian god), 96
Geographies, The, 129
geography: of the Americas, 428–30, 429m; cultures shaped by, 16; defined, 12; of early China, 182–83; of early Egypt, 88–89; and the early Greeks, 254–59; and early India, 144–49; of early Kush, 122–23; history and, 16–17; human, 13; of Italy, 324–25; of Phoenicia, 78; physical, 12–13; and the rise of Rome, 324–29
Geography Skills, 29, 37, 41, 57, 61, 63, 76, 79, 80, 82, 89, 103, 105, 123, 125, 145, 149, 160,

163, 164, 183, 186, 189, 195,
201, 210, 213, 227, 230, 243,
255, 258, 261, 287, 290, 296,
301, 325, 328, 339, 342, 344,
359, 360, 365, 388, 394, 409,
410, 415, 429, 430, 433, 435
Germanic warriors, 408
Germany, 353
Gilgamesh, 63, 72–73
Giza, Egypt, pyramids of, 98–99f
gladiator, 362
Gobi, the, 182
gods, mythology and, 270
gold, 122, 124, 127–28
Gordium, 300
Gospels, 388, 393
Goths, the, 409–10, 411f
government: in Athens, 262–67;
of Rome, 332–35, 333c; of
Sparta, 294
Gracchus, Gaius, 342
Gracchus, Tiberius, 342
Great pyramid of Khufu, 98
Great Wall, 197, 198p
Greece, 254p, 255m. *See also*
Athens; Sparta; achievements
in the arts, 303–4; architecture
of, 304–5; city-states and. *See*
Greek city-states; conquered
by Macedonia, 298–99;
creation of drama, 306; early,
geography and, 254–59; and
Persia, 286–91; philosophers
in, 309f; second invasion of,
290–91; study of science, 308;
trade with Egypt and, 103;
trading cultures and, 256–57
Greeks- see Greek city-states
Greek city-states: colonies and,
258m; creation of, 258; life in,
258–59; trade in, 259
Greek gods, 269–70
Grove, David, 432
Gupta: art of, 165p, 167–68;
Hinduism promoted in, 164;
society of, 164–65; temples of,
167–68; women of, 164–65
Gupta dynasty, 164–65
Gupta Empire, 163m

Hades (god of the underworld),
269

Hadrian (emperor of Rome), 359,
382
Haggadah, the, 244f
Hagia Sophia, 418–19
Hammurabi, 74–75
Hammurabi's Code, 75f
Han dynasty, 200–211, 201m; art
of, 204–5f; belief of the Three
Bonds and, 203; farming
during, 208; inventions of,
204–5; manufacturing during,
208; religion of, 210–11; social
classes of, 202; time line, 200;
trade during, 209–10; women
of, 203–4, 203f
Hanging Gardens, 77
Hannibal, 340, 341f
Hanukkah, 244–45
Harappa, 147
Harappans, 146–48; art of, 148p;
society of, 148–49; writing
system developed by, 148
Hatshepsut (Egyptian queen), 102f,
103
Hebrews: early history of, 226–
31, 240–42; time line, 228–29;
women and, 231
Hellenistic, 301
Hellenistic Kingdoms, 302
helots, 294
Hephaestus (god of metalworking),
269, 270
Hera (queen of the gods), 269
Hercules, 271, 274
Hermes (messenger of the gods),
269
Herodotus, 289f
heroes, mythology and, 271
Hestia (goddess of the hearth), 269
Hebrew Bible, 235
Hebrew texts, 234f
hieroglyphics, 108–9
High Holy Days, 245
Himalayas, 144–45
Hindu(s). *See also* Hinduism:
bathing in Ganges River,
141p; beliefs of, 152, 153–54;
ideas challenged by Buddha
and, 159; temples of, 167–68,
168p
Hindu-Arabic numerals, 170
Hinduism, 150–55. *See also*
Hindu(s); caste system and,
153–54; gods and beliefs of,
152f; promotion of, in Gupta,
164; temples of, 167–68,
168p; women and, 154
Historical Problem and Solution,
400
Histories, The (Polybius), 9f
history: defined, 6–7; geography
and, 16–17; understanding
through, 8–9
History Begins at Sumer (Kramer),
68f
History Makers, 9
History of the Goths (Jordanes), 411f
History of Nations: India, 158
History of the Persian Wars (Herodotus), 289
Hittites, 76, 103
Homer, 272f, 274; epic poetry of,
276
hominid(s). *See also* humans:
defined, 28; early humans
and, 30; early sites and, 29m;
lands settled by, 37; migrations of, 36–39, 37m
Homo erectus, 30, 31p
Homo habilis, 30, 30p
Homo sapiens, 30, 31p
Hongshan, the, 185
Horus (Egyptian god), 95f, 96
Huang (Yellow River), China, 61p,
83, 184, 184p
human geography, 13
humans: early. *See* early humans;
first, 28–35
Huns, the, 165, 409–10, 411f
hunter-gatherers, 32p, 33–34; in
the Americas, 430; defined,
33; in Nile Valley, 90
Hydra, 271
Hyksos, 102

ice ages, 36
Iceman, the (Ötzi), 35f
Identifying Central Issues, 47
**Identifying Short- and Long-Term
Effects,** 246
Ides of March, 354, 354f
Iliad (Homer), 272, 276f
imports, 128
Inanna (Sumerian god), 64
India, 145m; achievements of,
167–71; climate of, 145–46;
early, geography and, 144–49;
hominid migration to, 37;

science of, 170–71; time line, 140–41; Ur trade with, 64
Indra (Hindu god), 152
Indus River, 145, 146, 148, 300
Indus Valley, 147m
Inner Mongolia, 195
inoculation, 170
Interpreting Culture Maps, 344
Interpreting Physical Maps, 83
Interpreting Time Lines, 372
Ionian Sea, 255
Iron Pillar, 170
iron plow, 209
irrigation: defined, 58; from Huang He (Yellow River), China, 61p; in Mesopotamia, 58
Isis (Egyptian god), 95f, 96
Islam, 237, 415
Israel: fall of, to the Assyrians, 230; kingdom of, 230, 230m
Israelites, 228, 229
Istanbul, Turkey, 259
Italy, 325m, 328m; geography of, 324–25
ivory, 124

jade, 185
Janism, 155
Janis, the, 155
Japan: Buddhism in, 161; Mongols' attempted invasion of, 17
Jason, 271
Jaxartes River (Syr Darya River today), 287
Jerusalem, 229
Jesus of Nazareth, 237, 382–83, 385f; followers of, 387; life and death of, 384–85; teachings of, 386–87
Jewish migration, 240, 242, 243m
Jewish revolt(s), 240–42; clash with Romans and, 240–42; 381; results of, 242
Jews, Conservative, 234
John, Gospel of, 388
Joseph, 385
Josephus, Flavius, 241f
Judah, kingdom of, 230, 230m
Judaism, 226, 232, 381, 383; beliefs, 232–37; in the

Americas, 237; Conservative Jews and, 234; development of Islam and, 237; in Europe, 237; over the Centuries, 240–45
Judea, 382, 383
Justinian (emperor of Rome), 414, 415, 419f
Justinian's Code, 415

ka, 96–97
Kalidasa, 169
karma, 152, 154
Karnak, temple of, 107, 110–11f
Kashta (Kushite king), 125
Kassites, 76
Kerma, 123, 124, 125
Khafre's pyramid, 98–99f
Khufu (Great pyramid of), 98
Khufu (Old Kingdom pharaoh), 94
Khyber Pass, 144
Kingdoms of Gold, Kingdoms of Jade (Fagan), 433f
King, Martin Luther, Jr., 154f, 154p
Kish, city-state of, 63
Korea, 161
kosher, 234
Kramer, Samuel Noah, 68f
Krishna, 172–73
Kshatriyas, 150–51
Kush, 102; ancient, 123m; culture in, 129; decline of, 131; development of Kushite society and, 122, 123; Egypt and, 122–26, 123m, 124, 125; iron industry in, 128; pyramids in, 119p; rulers of, 130f; trade network of, 128, 128f; women in, 129
Kushite dynasty, 126

Ladino, 244
land bridge, 36
landforms, 12–13
language(s): of the Aryans, 149; Greek influence on, 274, 274f; in hunter-gatherer societies, 33; Ladino as a, 243; Latin. See

Latin; of Mycenaeans, 257; Romance, 371; of Romans, 334, 370–71; Yiddish as, 243
Laozi (Daoist teacher), 192, 193f
Last Supper, the (da Vinci), 387p
Latin, 370–71; as language of the Romans, 334, 370–71; influence on other languages, 371; religious services performed in, 418; scientific naming systems, 371
Latins, 326–27
Law of the Twelve Tables, 335f
Leakey, Louis, 28
Leakey, Mary, 28, 29p
Leakey, Richard, 30
learning from maps, 14
Legalism, 192–93
legions, 339
Levite, 391
Life of Lycurgus (Plutarch), 293
literature: of ancient Greece, 272–73; Greek mythology and, 268–75
Literature in History, The Epic of Gilgamesh, 72; The Shiji, 206; the epic poetry of Homer, 276; The Aeneid, 330; The Popul Vuh, 444
Liu Bang (Chinese emperor), 200–201
Living Torah, The, 228f
location, studying, 14–15
lords, 189
Lower Egypt, 88–89, 91
Lucy, 28–29, 30
Luke, Gospel of, 388
Luxor, temple of, 107, 110
Lycurgus, 292, 294
lyric poetry, 273

Maccabees, the, 230, 244–45
Macedonia: Greece conquered by, 298–99; Hellenistic, 302
Macedonians, 266
magistrates, 333, 333c
Mahabharata, the, 169
Mahavira, 155
Mahayana, 161
maize, 431, 431p, 433
mammoth house, 39f
mammoths, 38

Manapii, the, 353

Mapping the Past, 18–19f

maps: defined, 14; learning from, 14; studying, 14–15

Maps, California: Climates, 14; California: Physical, 14; California: Population, 15; California: Roads, 15; Early Hominid Sites, 29; Early Human Migration, 37; Early Domestication, 40; Catal Hüyük, 42; The Fertile Crescent, 57; Sargon's Empire, c. 2330 BC, 63; Babylonian and Assyrian Empires, 76; Phoenicia, 79; Ancient Egypt, 89; Egyptian Trade, 103; Ancient Kush, 123; India: Physical, 145; Aryan Invasions, 149; Early Spread of Buddhism, 159; Gupta Empire, c. 400, 163; Mauryan Empire, c. 320–185 BC, 163; China: Physical, 183; Shang dynasty, c. 1500–1050 BC, 186; Zhou dynasty, c. 1050–400 BC, 189; Qin dynasty, c. 221–206 BC, 195; Han dynasty, c. 206 BC-AD 220, 201; The Silk Road, 210; Possible Routes of Abraham and Moses, 227; Kingdoms of Israel and Judah, c. 920 BC, 230; Jewish Migration After AD 70, 242; Greece: Physical, 255; Greek City-States and Colonies, c. 600 BC, 258; River Valley Civilizations, 260; The Persian Empire, 287; The Persian Wars, 290; The Peloponnesian War, c. 431–404 BC, 296; Alexander the Great's Empire, c. 323 BC, 300–01; Italy: Physical, 325; Italy, 500 BC, 328; The Roman Republic, 509–270 BC, 339; The Roman Republic, 270–100 BC, 342; Expansion of Rome, 100 BC–AD 117, 359; Roman Trade Routes, AD 200, 360; Paul's Journeys, 388; The Spread of Christianity, 300–400, 394; The Eastern and Western Empires, 409; Invasions of the Roman Empire, 340–500, 410; The Byzantine Empire, 1025, 415; The Americas: Physical, 429; Migration to the Americas, 430; Early Civilizations in the Americas, 433; Maya Civilization, 435

Atlas Maps: World: Political, R6; North America: Physical, R28; North America: Political, R29; South America: Physical, R30; South America: Political, R31; Europe: Physical, R32; Europe: Political, R33; Asia: Physical, R34; Asia: Political, R35; Africa: Physical, R36; Africa: Political, R37

Map Skills, Interpreting Culture Maps, 344; Interpreting Physical Maps, 83

Marathon, 290, 291m; battle of, 289, 290

Mare Nostrum, 359

Marius, Gaius, 342–43

Mark, Gospel of, 388

Marseille, France, 259

martyrs, 393

Mary, 384–85

Masada, 241

Matthew, Gospel of, 388

matzo, 245

Maurya, Chandragupta, 162

Mauryan Empire, 162–63, 163m

Maya, the, 434–42; achievements of, 441–42; architecture of, 425p, 442; art of, 442; civilization of, 434–35, 435m; decline of civilization of, 438; development of calendars, 442; king of, and his court, 440–41p; religion of, 441; science of, 442; society of, 439–40; study of astronomy, 442; trade and, 435, 440; writing of, 442

Maya classic age, 438

Maya society, 439–40

Medes, 286

meditation, 157

Mediterranean Sea, 255

Megaliths, 42–43

Memphis, Egypt, 91; ancient ruins near, 60p

Menes (Egyptian king), 91, 92f, 94

menorah, 245

merchants, 128

Meroë, 128, 131

Meroitic, 129

Mesoamerica, 428, 429m, 431

Mesolithic Era, 38

Mesopotamia, 226, 287, 359; civilization in, 62; controlling water in, 58; defined, 57; farming in, 58; growth of settlements in, 59; invasions of, 74–76; parts of, 57; settlements formed in, 57; Sumerians in, 62

Messiah, 383

metallurgy, 170

Mexico, artifacts from, 11p

Middle Kingdom, the, 101–2, 105

Middle Stone Age, 38–39

migrate, 36

migration(s): of hominids and early humans, 36–39, 37m; of the Jews, 242, 243m; to the Americas, 38, 430

Minoan Civilization, 257m; destruction of, 260–61f

Minoans, 256–57

Minotaur, 271

Miriam, 231

missionaries, 160

Mohenjo Daro, 146f

monarch, 74

Mongolia, Inner, 195

Mongols, 17

monotheism, 232

monsoon, 145–46

Mosaic law, 233–34

mosaics, 417

Moses, 227–28, 232, 233; Exodus and, 227; Golden Calf and, 233f; routes of, 227m; Ten Commandments and, 228

moska, 154

mummies, 97, and the afterlife, 96f

Muslims, 415

Mycenae, 257

Mycenaen civilization, 257m

Mycenaens, 256, 257, 257f

mythology: defined, 269; gods and, 270; heroes and, 271

N

Nalanda, 164

Nanna (Sumerian god), 64

Naomi, 231f

Napata, 125

Naples, Italy, 259

Natural History (Pliny the Elder), 362f

Nebuchadnezzar (Chaldean king), 77

INDEX

Nefertiti (queen of Egypt), 104f
Nekhen, 91
Neolithic Era: changes to societies in, 42; defined, 41; plants of, 41; religious ceremonies in, 42; tools of, 41
Neolithic Revolution, 41
neos, 41
New Kingdom, the, 102–6; trade in, 102–3
New Stone Age, 41
New Testament, 384, 385; Four Gospels of, 388, 393
Nile Delta, 89, 91, 103
Nile River, 88–92; floods of, 89; physical features of, 88–89
Nineveh, 77
nirvana, 158
Noah's ark, 238
nobles, 94
nonviolence, 154f
Note Cards for a Screenplay, 348
Nubia, 95, 122–23, 124; trade with Egypt and, 95

O

obelisk, 110
observatories, 442
obsidian: defined, 434; use as a tool, 33f
Octavian (Augustus)(emperor of Rome), 355, 356, 357f
Odysseus, 272
odyssey, 274
Odyssey (Homer), 272, 277f
Old Kingdom, the, 93–100; early pharaohs of, 93–94; life in, 93–94
Old Testament, 384
oligarchy, 262f, 263
Olmec, the, 431
Olympia, 271f
Olympic games, 271f
oracle: defined, 186; at Delphi, 270
orator, 352
Orthodox Church, 418
Orthodox Jews, 234
Osiris (Egyptian god), 95f, 96
Ottoman Turks, 415
Ötzi (the Iceman), 35f
Ovid, 370

Pacal (Maya king), 436, 437f
Pacific Ocean, 182, 430
Pakistan, 145–46
Palatine Hill, the, 337
Palenque, 436–37f
Paleolithic Era, 30
Palestine, 102
Panchatantra, the, 169
pantheons, 381
papacy, the, 394
papyrus, 108
Parable of the Good Samaritan, the, 391
Parthenon, the, 283p, 304–5f
Participating in Groups, 132
Participation Skills: Accepting Social Responsibility, 446, 448; Participating in Groups, 132, 134; Recognizing Personal Convictions and Bias, 20, 22
Passover, 244f, 245
patricians, 328, 332, 333
Paul of Tarsus, 387; journeys of, 388m; letter to the Romans, 389f
Pax Romana, the, 361
Pe, 91
peasants, 189
Peisistratus (ruler of Athens), 263
Peloponnesian War, the, 296–97, 296m, 306
people. See humans
Pericles, 266, 266f, 304f
Pericles' Funeral Oration, 266
persecution, 390, 393
Persia, Greece and, 286–91
Persian army, 287–88
Persian Empire, 286, 287m
Persians, the, 230, 415; society of, 288–89
Persian Wars, 289, 290m
Persuasion and Historical Issues, 450
Phaedo (Plato), 306f
phalanx, 299, 299p
pharaoh, 91
Philippi, 355; battle of, 356
Philistines, 229
Phillip II (king of Macedonia), 298–99
philosophers, 306
Phoenicia, 78–79m; expansion of trade, 78–79; geography of, 78

Phoenicians, 78–79, 339; development of alphabet and, 79
physical geography, 12–13
Piankhi (Kushite king), 125, 129
pictographs, 68
Pi-Ramesse, 107
pit houses, 38
Plataea, 291
Plateau of Tibet, 182
Plato, 294f, 307, 309f, 394
plebeians, 328, 332, 333
Pliny the Elder, 362
plow, 69
Plutarch, 293, 294f, 355f
Pnyx, 265f
Pohl, Mary, 432
polis, 258
Polybius, 9f, 335f
polytheism: defined, 64; Egyptian practice of, 95; Sumerian practice of, 64
Pompeii, 361f
Pompey, 353
pope, 394
Popol Vuh, the, 444
Portuguese, as Romance language, 371
Poseidon (god of the sea), 269
Practicing History: Selected Essays (Tuchman), 9f
Preamble, R6
prehistory, 28
priests, 65
primary sources, 10–11
Primary Sources, *The Histories, Book XXXVIII*, 9; History Makers, 9; What Geography Means, 15; *Ancestors: In Search of Human Origins*, 28; Views of Migration to the Americas, 38; *History Begins at Sumer*, 68; *The Epic of Gilgamesh*, 72; Hammurabi's Code, 75; *The Victory of Ramses over the Khita*, 107; *The Geographies*, 129; the *Rigveda*, 152; *The History of Nations: India*, 158; the *Panchatantra*, 169; the *Bhagavad Gita*, 172; the *Zhou Book of Songs*, 189; *The Analects*, 191; *The Living Torah*, 228; Psalms 23:1–3, 235; The Torah, 238; *The Wars of the Jews*, 241; Pericles' Funeral Oration, 266; "The Ants and the Grasshopper", 273; the epic poetry of

Homer, 276; *History of the Persian Wars*, 289; *Life of Lycurgus*, 293; Views of Education, 294; *The Death of Socrates*, 306; *The Aeneid*, 330; *Constitution of the Roman Republic*, 335; Law of the Twelve Tables, 335; *The Gallic Wars*, 353; Views of Caesar, 355; *Natural History*, 362; Paul's Letter to the Romans, 389; The Bible, 390; *History of the Goths*, 411; *The Story of the Building of the Church of Santa Sophia*, 418; Views of Writing, 432; *Kingdoms of Gold, Kingdoms of Jade*, 433; A Maya Carving, 443

princeps, 356
Prophets, 235
provinces, 360
Psalms 23:1–3, 235
Ptah (Egyptian god), 96
Punic Wars, the, 339–41
Punt, 95, 103
pyramid(s): building of, 98f, 99–100; defined, 98; of Egypt, 98–100; Great, of Khufu, 98; Khafre's, 98–99f; in Kush, 119p; significance of, 100
pyramid texts, 100

Qin dynasty, 194–98, 195m; achievements of, 196; fall of, 198; policies of, 196; time line, 194; trade and, 196; writing system of, 196
Qinling Shandi, 183
Quick Facts, Early Hominids, 30; Hammurabi's Code, 75; The Varnas, 151; Major Beliefs of Hinduism, 152; The Eightfold Path, 159; Zhou Society, 189; Main Ideas of Confucianism, 192; Emperor Shi Huangdi, 195; Government in Athens, 262; Democracy Then and Now, 267; Life in Sparta, 293; Life in Athens, 295; Legendary Founding of Rome, 326; Government of the Roman Republic, 333; Why Rome

Fell, 413; The Western Roman and Byzantine Empires, 418

rabbis, 242
raja, 148–49
Ramayana, the, 169
Ramses II (king of Egypt)(Ramses the Great), 103, 107f; temple of, 84–85p
Re (Egyptian god), 95f, 96
Reading Skills, Understanding Specialized Vocabulary, 3; Understanding Chronological Order, 26; Finding Main Ideas, 54; Drawing Conclusions, 86; Understanding Cause and Effect Structure, 120; Retelling, 142; Summarizing a Text, 180; Understanding Fact and Opinion; 224; Understanding Comparison-Contrast Structure, 284; Taking Notes with Outlines, 322; Evaluating Web-Based Information, 350; Understanding Through Questioning, 378; Understanding Stereotypes and Bias, 406; Understanding Texts by Setting a Purpose, 426
rebel, 438
Recognizing Personal Conviction and Bias, 20
Red Sea, 128
regions, 15
reincarnation, 152, 153
religion(s): Buddhism as. *See* Buddhism; Christianity as. *See* Christianity; Confucianism as, 191; Daoism as, 192; in Egypt, 95–97, 95f; as foundation of Sumerian society, 64–65; of the Han dynasty, 210–11; Hinduism as. *See* Hinduism; in hunter-gatherer societies, 33–34; Islam as, 237; Jainism as, 155; Judaism as. *See* Judaism; of Legalism, 192–93; of the Maya, 441; monotheism and, 232; Muslims and, 415; polytheism and. *See* polytheism; rituals of Vedic texts and,

152; in the Roman Empire, 380–83; services performed in Latin and, 418; Zoroastrianism as, 289
religious epics: *Mahabharata, the*, 169; *Ramayana, the*, 169, 169f
Remus, Romulus and, 327, 327f
representative democracy, 267
republic, 328
resources, 16
resurrection, 385
Retelling, 142
righteousness, 390
Rigveda, the, 152
River Valley civilizations, 60–61f, 260m
Roman(s): clash with Jews and, 381; engineering of, 367; science of, 366; writing of, 370
Roman aqueduct, 367f
Roman Arch, 367p
Roman Catholic Church, 377f
Romance languages, 371
Roman Empire, 242, 359m. *See also* Rome; expansion of, 358–59; fall of, 408–13; invasion of, 409–11, 410m; Jews conquered by, 230; language of, 370–71; religion and, 380–83; split of, 409m; time line, 412; trade in, 360, 360m; Western, 418f
Roman Forum, the, 320–21p, 335, 336–37, 336–37f
Romanian, as Romance language, 371
Roman Republic, 338–43, 333f, 342m; growth of, 338, 339
Roman Roads, 364–65f
Roman ruins, 405p
Roman Senate, 333
Rome. *See also* Roman Empire; architecture of, 368–69; art of, 369; battles Carthage, 340–41f; challenges within, 328–29; Colosseum in, 368–69f; early republic of, 328; fall of, 413f; fall of time line, 404; Forum in, 336–37; geography and rise of, 324–29; government and society of, 332–35, 333f, 329; law in, 335, 371; legacy of, 366–71; legendary origins of, 326–27f; from Republic to Empire, 352–56;

the sack of, 410–11; Senate of, 333; time line, 412; trade in, 339

Romulus: as first king of Rome, 327; Remus and, 327f

Rosetta Stone, the, 109

Rosh Hashanah, 245

Royal Road, the, 289

Rubicon River, 354

rural, 62

Russia, 418

Ruth, 231, 231f

S

Sabbath, 233

Sacred Texts, the Bhagavad Gita, 172; the Bible, 390; the Torah, 238

sage, 173

Saint Augustine of Hippo, 394

Saint Peter's Square, 376–77p

Salamis, 291m; battle of, 291; straits of, 291

salvation, 386

San Francisco, California, 8p

Sanskrit, 149, 169f

Santorini (formerly Thera), 260–61f

Sanxingdui, the, 184

Sappho, 274

Sargon I (Akkadian emperor), 63; empire of, 63m

Saul (king of Israel), 229

science: in Greece, 308; of India, 170–71; of the Maya, 442; in Sumer, 69

scribes, 68, 104

Sea Peoples, 103

secondary sources, 10–11

Second Dynasty, the, 92, 93

Second Temple, the, 230; the destruction of, 240–41f, 242; rededication of, 244

seder, 245

seismograph, 204

Sephardim, the, 242f, 244

Sermon on the Mount, the, 390

sewers, 69

Shabaka (Kushite king), 126

Shanakhdakheto (Kushite queen), 129f

Shang dynasty, 185–87, 186m; social order of, 185–87; writing of, 186, 187f

shelters, 38

shi, 204

Shi Huangdi (emperor of China), 199f; achievements of, 195f; defined, 194; guardians of tomb of, 196–97p; policies of, 195f

Shiji, the (Sima Qian), 206–7

Sicily, 341

silk, production of, 208–9f, 209

Silk Road, 210m, 212–13f; defined, 209; travel of, 209–10

silt: defined, 57; from Nile River, 89

Sima Qian, 204

Sinai, 228

Sinai Peninsula, 103

Siva (Hindu god), 153, 153p

social hierarchy, 65

Social Studies Skills, Recognizing Personal Conviction and Bias, 20; Identifying Central Issues, 47; Interpreting Physical Maps, 83; Assessing Primary and Secondary Sources, 114; Participating in Groups, 132; Interpreting Diagrams, 174; Conducting Internet Research, 214; Identifying Short- and Long-Term Effects, 246; Analyzing Costs and Benefits, 278; Interpreting Charts and Tables, 310; Interpreting Culture Maps, 344; Interpreting Time Lines, 372; Continuity and Change in History, 396; Chance, Error, and Oversight in History, 420

society: Akkadian, 63; Aryan, classes of, 150–51; Byzantine, 416–17; Confucianism and, 191; defined, 33; Egyptian, development of, 94–95; government of Rome and, 332–35; Gupta, 164–65; of the Han dynasty, 202; Harappan, 148–49; Hebrew, women in, 231; Kushite, development of, 122, 123; Maya roles in, 439–40; in Mesopotamia, 62; Persian, 288–89; Spartan, 292; of Zhou dynasty, 189

Socrates, 307, 309f

Socratic method, 307

Solomon (king of Israel), 229

Solon, 263

Sophocles, 306

Southwest Asia, 287

Spain, 341

Spanish, as Romance language, 371

Sparta. See also Greece: fighting between Athens and, 296–97; government of, 294; life in, 293f; soldier of, 293f; women in, 293–94

Spartacus, 343

Spartan society, 292

Spartans, the, 290

Speaking Skills (Focus on Speaking), Oral Presentation, 178; A Narrative Poem, 404

spear, invention of, 31

spear-thrower, 31

sphinx, 98f, 110

Sri Lanka, 160

Stone Age, 30–31

Stonehenge, 43

stone tools, 33f

Story of the Building of the Church of Santa Sophia, the, 418

studying location, 14

Study Skills: Conducting Internet Research, 214, 216, 350–51, 374; Interpreting Charts and Tables, 310, 312; Interpreting Diagrams, 174, 176; Interpreting Maps, 80, 82, 344, 346

stupas, 168

stylus, 67

subcontinent, 144

Sudras, 150–51

Suetonius, 355f

Sulla, Lucius, 343, 343f

Sumer: city-states of, 62–63; development of writing in, 67; early developments of, 69; priests in, 65; religion in, 64–66; rise of, 62–71; social order of, 65–66; women in, 66

Summarizing a Text, 180

sundial, 204–5

surplus, 58

sutras, 151

synagogue, 234

Syr Darya River (Jaxartes River in ancient Persia), 287

Syria, 102, 161; Hellenistic, 302; trade with Egypt and, 95

Taking Notes with Outlines, 322
Talmud, the, 235f, 236
Tanach, 235
Tanzania, 31
technologies: of the Mesolithic Era, 38; of the Middle Stone Age, 39
Tehenu, 103
Temple of Jupiter, the, 336f
temples: at Ajanta, 167–68; of Egypt, 110; of Gupta, 167–68; Maya, 425p
Ten Commandments, 228, 233, 237
Teotihauacan, Mexico, 18–19m
"The Ants and the Grasshopper," 273
Thebes, 103, 299, 300
Theodora, 415, 419f
Theodosius I (Roman emperor), 395
Thera (now Santorini), 260–61f
Theravada, 161
Thermopylae, 290
Theseus, 271
Third Dynasty, the, 93
Thoth (Egyptian god), 96
Thucydides, 306
Thutmose I (pharaoh of Egypt), 124
Tiber River, 325, 327
Tibet, 182–83
Tigris River: as feature of Mesopotamia, 57; flooding of, 57; water levels in, 58
Tikal, Guatemala, 437; Maya temple in, 425p
Time Lines, Periods of Egyptian History, 98; The Zhou Dynasty, 188; The Qin Dynasty, 194; The Han Dynasty, 200; Early Hebrew History, 228; Early Christianity, 392; Key Events in Roman History, 412
titanic, 274
tool(s): defined, 30–31; found in Tanzania, 31; made of flint, 31; of Mesolithic Era, 38–39; of Middle Stone Age, 38–39; of New Stone Age, 41; obsidian as, 33f; of Stone Age, 30–31
Torah, the, 234, 234f, 235, 238–39f

"Tortoise and the Hare, The" (Aesop), 273
Tower of Babel, The (Brueghal), 239
trade: architecture supported by, 103; art supported by, 103; in Greek city-states, 259; during Han dynasty, 209; Kush's trade network and, 128; the Maya and, 435, 440; network of the Olmec civilization and, 431; in the New Kingdom, 102–3; Phoenician expansion of, 78–79; protection of in the Aegean Sea, 296; and Qin dynasty, 196; in the Roman Empire, 339, 360; trading cultures and, 256–57
trade routes, 102
tribunes, 333c, 334
Trinity, the, 389
tripartite, 332
Trojan, 275p
Trojan War, 326
Troy, 326
tsunami, 260
Tuchman, Barbara W., 9f
Tutankhamen (King Tut)(Egyptian pharaoh), 112f, 113
tutor, 207
25th Dynasty, 126
tyranny, 263f
tyrant, 263
Tyre, 78

Unas (Old Kingdom pharaoh), 100
Understanding Cause and Effect Structure, 120
Understanding Chronological Order, 26
Understanding Comparison-Contrast Structure, 284
Understanding Fact and Opinion, 224
Understanding Specialized Vocabulary, 3
Understanding Stereotypes and Bias, 406
Understanding Texts by Setting a Purpose, 426
Understanding Through Questioning, 378
untouchables, 151

Upanishands, 152
Upper Egypt, 88–89, 91
Ur, 64–65m; city-state of, 63; India trade with, 64; royal tombs at, 71
urban, 62
Uruk, 63
Uta (Sumerian god), 64

Vaisyas, 150–51
Vandals, the, 411
Varnas, the, 151f
vault, 367, 369
Vedas, the, 148–49, 150, 152, 153
Vedic texts, 152
veto, 334, 371
Victory of Ramses over the Khita, the, 107
Vietnam, 195
Views of Caesar, 355
Views of Education, 294
Views of Migration to the Americas, 38
Views of Writing, 432
villas, 362
Virgil, 326, 330, 370
Vishnu (Hindu god), 153, 153p

Warring States, 190
Wars of the Jews, The (Josephus), 241f
Washington Monument, as an obelisk, 110f
Way and Its Power, The (Laozi), 192
wellsprings, 238
Western Wall, 223p, 243f
What Geography Means, 15
wheelbarrow, 209
wheels, development of, 69
White, Tim, 29
Why Things Happen, 218
women: in Athens, 264f, 295; in Egypt, 106; of Gupta, 164–65; in Han dynasty, 203–4, 203f; in Hebrew society, 231; Hinduism and, 154; in hunter-gatherer societies, 33;

INDEX

in Kushite society, 129; in Sparta, 293–94; in Sumerian society, 66

writing: in ancient Egypt, in China, 187; 108–9; development of, 68; first system of in the Americas, 431; Harappan development of, 148; invention of, 67; of laws, 335; of the Maya, 442; of the Olmec, 431; in the Qin dynasty, 196; Roman types of, 370; of Shang dynasty, 186, 187f; views of, 432

Writing Skills (Focus on Writing), A Job Description, 2; A Storyboard, 24; A Poster, 52; A Riddle, 84; A Fictional Narrative, 118; An Illustrated Poster, 140; A Web Site, 222; A Myth, 250; A Poem, 282; A Legend, 320; Note Cards for a Screenplay, 348; Magazine Article, 376; A Travel Brochure, 424

Writing Workshop, Comparing and Contrasting Societies, 48; A Description of a Historical Place, 136; Why Things Happen, 218; A Social Studies Report, 314; Historical Problem and Solution, 400; Persuasion and Historical Issues, 450

Wudi (emperor of China), 201

Xerxes I (Persian emperor), 290
Xia dynasty, 185

Yahweh, 232, 381
Yellow River (Huang He), China, 61p

Yiddish, 243
Ying Zheng (Qin king), 194
Yohanan ben Zaccai, 242
Yom Kippur, 245

Zama, 340f
Zealots, the, 240
Zeus (king of the gods), 269
Zhou Book of Songs, 189
Zhou dynasty, 188–93, 189m; decline of power, 190; society of, 189f; time line, 188
ziggurat, 70
Zoroastrianism, 289

INDEX

Credits and Acknowledgments

For permission to reproduce copyrighted material, grateful acknowledgment is made to the following sources:

Bantam Books, a division of Random House, Inc.: From *The Bhagavad-Gita,* translated by Barbara Stoler Miller. Copyright ©1986 by Barbara Stoler Miller.

Cesar E. Chavez Foundation: Quote from "Core Values of Cesar E. Chavez" from *Cesar E. Chavez Foundation* Web site; accessed September 24, 2004, at http://www.cesarechavezfoundation. org. Copyright © by The Cesar E. Chavez Foundation.

Columbia University Press: From *Records of the Grand Historian of China, Vol. II: The Age of Emperor Wu* by Burton Watson. Copyright ©1961 by Columbia University Press.

Benedict Fitzgerald for the Estate of Robert Fitzgerald: From *The Iliad* by Homer, translated by Robert Fitzgerald. Copyright ©1974 by Robert Fitzgerald. From *The Odyssey* by Homer, translated by Robert Fitzgerald. Copyright ©1961, 1963 by Robert Fitzgerald; copyright renewed ©1989 by Benedict R. C. Fitzgerald, on behalf of the Fitzgerald Children.

Penelope Fitzgerald for the Estate of Robert Fitzgerald: From *The Aeneid* by Virgil, translated by Robert Fitzgerald. Translation copyright ©1980, 1982, 1983 by Robert Fitzgerald.

Moznaim Publishing Corporation: Psalms 23:1–3 from *The Book of Tehillim,* edited by Rabbi Shmuel Yerushalmi, translated and adapted by Dr. Zvi Faier. Copyright ©1989 by Moznaim Publishing Corporation. From "The Ten Commandments;" "The Story of Noah;" "The Story of the Tower of Babel" from *The Living Torah,* edited by Rabbi Aryeh Kaplan. Copyright ©1981 by Moznaim Publishing Corporation.

RSV/NRSV: From Romans 12: 9–18; from Matthew 5:1–16; from "Luke 10:29-37 from the *New Revised Standard Version of the Bible.* Copyright ©1989 by the Division of Christian Education of the National Council of the Churches of Christ in the USA. All rights reserved.

Penguin Books Ltd.: From *The Epic of Gilgamesh,* translated by N. K. Sandars (Penguin Classics 1960, Third Edition 1972). Copyright ©1960, 1964, 1972 by N. K. Sandars.

John Porter: From *Polybius 6.11-18: The Constitution of the Roman Republic,* translated by John Porter. Copyright ©1995 by John Porter, University of Saskatchewan.

Princeton University Press.: From "Feudalism in China" by Derk Bodde from *Feudalism in History,* edited by Rushton Coulborn. Copyright ©1956 by Rushton Coulborn.

Simon & Schuster Adult Publishing Group: From *Popol Vuh* translated by Dennis Tedlock. Copyright ©1985, 1996 by Dennis Tedlock.

The University of Chicago Press: From *The Panchatantra,* translated from the Sanskrit by Arthur William Ryder. Copyright 1925 by the University of Chicago Press.

WGBH Educational Foundation: From "Women in Ancient Christianity: The New Discoveries" by Karen L. King from *From Jesus to Christ—The First Christians from Frontline/PBS* Web site accessed November 10, 2004, at http://www.pbs. org/wgbh/pages/frontline/shows/religion/first/ women.html. New content copyright ©1998 by PBS and WGBH/FRONTLINE.

Sources Cited:

From "The Pyramid of King Unas" from *Ancient Egypt: An illustrated reference to the myths, religions, pyramids and temples of the land of the pharaohs* by Lorna Oakes and Lucia Gahlin. Published by Barnes & Noble Books, New York, 2003.

From "Advice to Schoolboys" from *Wings of the Falcon, Life and Thought of Ancient Egypt,* translated and edited by Basil Joseph Kaster. Published by Henry Holt and Company, LLC., New York, 1968.

Illustrations and Photo Credits

Staff Credits

The people who contributed to *Holt California Social Studies: World History, Ancient Civilizations* are listed below. They represent editorial, design, intellectual property resources, production, emedia, and permissions.

Lissa B. Anderson, Melanie Baccus, Charles Becker, Jessica Bega, Ed Blake, Gillian Brody, Shirley Cantrell, Erin Cornett, Rose Degollado, Chase Edmond, Mescal Evler, Rhonda Fariss, Marsh Flournoy, Leanna Ford, Bob Fullilove, Matthew Gierhart, Janet Harrington, Rhonda Haynes, Rob Hrechko, Wilonda Ieans, Cathy Jenevein, Kadonna Knape, Cathy Kuhles, Debbie Lofland, Bob McClellan, Joe Melomo, Richard Metzger, Andrew Miles, Cynthia Munoz, Karl Pallmeyer, Chanda Pearmon, Jarred Prejean, Shelly Ramos, Désirée Reid, Curtis Riker, Marleis Roberts, Diana Rodriguez, Gene Rumann, Annette Saunders, Jenny Schaeffer, Kay Selke, Ken Shepardson, Michele Shukers, Chris Smith, Christine Stanford, Elaine Tate, Jeannie Taylor, Joni Wackwitz, Ken Whiteside